CONSTITUTIONAL LAW IN CONTEMPORARY AMERICA

Volume 1: Institutions, Politics, and Process

DAVID SCHULTZ
PROFESSOR OF POLITICAL SCIENCE
HAMLINE UNIVERSITY

JOHN R. VILE
DEAN AND PROFESSOR OF POLITICAL SCIENCE
MIDDLE TENNESSEE STATE UNIVERSITY

MICHELLE D. DEARDORFF
DEPARTMENT HEAD AND ADOLPH S. OCHS PROFESSOR OF GOVERNMENT
UNIVERSITY OF TENNESSEE AT CHATTANOOGA

444 Cedar Street, Suite 700
St. Paul, MN 55101
1-877-888-1330

Printed in the United States of America

ISBN: 978-1-68328-558-8

Preface

Volume I of *Constitutional Law in Contemporary America* introduces students to the key conflicts and debates surrounding institutions, politics, and processes addressed in the Constitution, focusing on the interrelationships among the presidency, Congress, and the Courts, and between the national government and the states. Collectively, the three of us have more than 85 years of teaching constitutional law to undergraduate, graduate, and law students at a variety of institutions. With this experience as a backdrop, we have designed this book to meet the needs of current political science students and professors. We realized that while every constitutional law class is organized differently, and that every professor emphasizes points or legal issues in a unique fashion, there are some key cases that all professors teach, that issues that were important to constitutional law twenty years ago have been replaced with new issues more relevant to contemporary America, and that textbooks need to be affordable so that they can be supplemented with other resources. With the help of West Academic Publishing, we have designed these two volumes to address these classroom needs.

In both volumes of Constitutional Law in Contemporary America, we have chosen Supreme Court cases that are most generally accepted as part of the constitutional canon and that illuminate the central concepts usually covered in constitutional law classes. In defining this canon, we have relied heavily upon a survey conducted by the Law and Politics section of the American Political Science Association. We have edited these cases carefully in order to highlight the primary political conflicts reflected within the Constitution and to include significant concurring and dissenting opinions. To help students gain a clearer understanding of the Constitution and to demonstrate how state and federal courts sometimes address issues differently in a federal system, we have included some cases that state courts have decided on the basis of state constitutional grounds. We have also included several lower federal court cases to demonstrate how Supreme Court decisions are implemented and challenged. Our focus here, as it is for most political scientists, is to use constitutional law as a means of explaining and describing American government. Although we think that students who use these volumes will learn legal thinking, we have not emphasized this as prominently as most law school texts, but have sought primarily to discuss both the law and the politics of the Constitution as a way of clarifying and imparting an understanding of American government and the political process.

While grounded firmly in the existing traditional canon of cases, this volume expands this canon to incorporate such topics by: exploring such topics as the post-9/11 ruling regarding the presidential war powers and the war on terror, emerging challenges in election law and political process cases and their impact on the right to vote, the manner in which the tension between state and federal constitutional law on sexual orientation and identity and same sex marriage is evolving, how issues of race and gender are moving beyond the Equal Protection Clause, and the new issues inherent in the conflict between eminent domain powers of government and the ownership of private property. As students read these cases and primary documents, they will be examining the boundaries of the three branches of the national government, federalism, and the relationship between the citizen and the political process, and they will see how property questions that dominated the Court through the first century of its history continue to be relevant today.

To help students understand the context in which cases are decided, we have begun each chapter with a timeline that notes relevant political developments, court decisions, and national events connected to the topic. The book also provides a topical introduction to each chapter and to each major area of law discussed within the chapter. We have provided contextual introductions to the cases, connected them to longer lines of precedent in the "Related Cases" feature, and provided questions that tie the case back to the larger issues of law and political science. We have also written a glossary containing terms with which students typically struggle and included a bibliography to enable students to continue their own learning through additional research. To meet our own interests, the flexible organization of the text ensures that professors can teach the cases and chapters in any order to achieve their own pedagogical objectives.

Many individuals and many institutions have come together to enable us to complete this book. David Schultz would like to thank Claude Teweles at Roxbury Publishing Company, the original publisher who signed this book and subsequently sold the book to Oxford University Press, which has in turn passed it on to West. In addition, Paul C. Barthlomew, whose original two volumes on constitutional law, which were published in 1978 and form the basis of part of our project, also deserves acknowledgment. David would also like to thank his many undergraduate constitutional law students over the years as well as his law students. Both groups have helped him focus his thoughts. Nate Hackman, his first constitutional law teacher at the State University of New York at Binghamton, remains a big influence on his thinking. Finally, he thanks his wife for her patience in talking about the law more than he should.

Michelle D. Deardorff is indebted to the colleagues with whom she has argued these constitutional issues over the years, most particularly Paul Folger of Heartland Community College, the late Isaiah Madison of Jackson State University, Jilda Aliotta of the University of Hartford, and Angela Kupenda of Mississippi College School of Law. She is appreciative of the late Augustus Jones, Jr., of Miami University who first introduced her to constitutional law and transitioned from being her professor to a valued co-author in her life. Stephen Hoffmann and Phil Loy of Taylor University must be thanked for feeding her enjoyment of political science and for encouraging her to pursue graduate school. Her parents, Earl and Fonda Donaldson, encouraged her curiosity and analytical skills by never rejecting her questions and letting her take risks—both intellectual and physical; she is very grateful for their continuing support. The wonderful political scientists who compose the American Political Science Association's Political Science Education organized section have transformed her pedagogy. Most significantly, she thanks the students at Millikin University, Jackson State University, and the University of Tennessee at Chattanooga whom it has been her honor and privilege to teach over the last twenty-five years. Their enduring excitement and engagement in these topics have made the classroom a "sacred place" to which it is always a pleasure to return. Finally, her husband, David Deardorff, has made her a better writer and a more thoughtful teacher; this has been the best collaboration of her life.

John R. Vile thanks his family members, especially his parents Ralph and Joanna, his wife Linda, and his daughters Virginia and Rebekah, for their continuing affection and support. He thanks his teachers at the College of William and Mary and the University of Virginia and NEH seminar directors at Princeton University and the University of Iowa who contributed to his own understanding of the Constitution; he will forever be indebted to Henry J. Abraham at Virginia, and Alpheus T. Mason and Walter Murphy of Princeton. He further appreciates his supervisors and colleagues, especially those at Middle Tennessee State University, who have facilitated his ongoing research, his students at McNeese State University, Middle Tennessee State University, and Vanderbilt University whose questions have sharpened his understanding of the Constitution, and his colleagues at the American Mock Trial Association for their continuing devotion to developing undergraduate thinking and advocacy skills. While adding his thanks to Claude Teweles, he further acknowledges the role of Kenneth Holland, now at Ball State University, and Mary Volcansek, at Texas Christian University, who first conceived of this project, and the many editors and publishers who, in helping him with other works, also contributed to constitutional knowledge.

All of us owe a great debt of gratitude to those colleagues and professionals at West Academic who have helped us improve this case law book in wonderful ways. Our executive editor, James Cahoy, has been a faithful supporter of this project, asking us the difficult questions regarding our purpose and intent and ensuring that we have a common voice when the three of us often had different visions that needed to be accommodated.

Heather Sieve and Laura Holle, the publication specialists, helped us keep to the necessary deadlines and bring this edition to print.

This book is very different from the one that was initially proposed many years ago. A large weight of these changes are born by the many helpful reviewers that read this text in its many iterations and communicated to us the ways in which this book could be enhanced and approved. To that end, we are very grateful to all the anonymous reviewers who offered their time and outstanding suggestions.

Last but not least, we offer our collective thanks to those who labored to create, ratify, amend, and interpret the U.S. Constitution. Because of their efforts, we continue to enjoy the "blessings of liberty," the appreciation and understanding of which we hope these volumes will further perpetuate.

David Schultz,
Professor,
Hamline University,
University of Minnesota School of Law

John R. Vile,
Professor of Political Science and Dean,
University Honors College,
Middle Tennessee State University

Michelle D. Deardorff,
Adolph S. Ochs Professor of Government and Department Head,
University of Tennessee at Chattanooga

March 20, 2017

Summary of Contents

Table of Contents

Table of Cases

The Constitution of the United States of America

Preamble

We the people of the United States, in order to form a more perfect union, establish justice, insure domestic tranquility, provide for the common defense, promote the general welfare, and secure the blessings of liberty to ourselves and our posterity, do ordain and establish this Constitution for the United States of America.

Article I

Section 1. All legislative powers herein granted shall be vested in a Congress of the United States, which shall consist of a Senate and House of Representatives.

Section 2. The House of Representatives shall be composed of members chosen every second year by the people of the several states, and the electors in each state shall have the qualifications requisite for electors of the most numerous branch of the state legislature.

No person shall be a Representative who shall not have attained to the age of twenty five years, and been seven years a citizen of the United States, and who shall not, when elected, be an inhabitant of that state in which he shall be chosen.

Representatives and direct taxes shall be apportioned among the several states which may be included within this union, according to their respective numbers, which shall be determined by adding to the whole number of free persons, including those bound to service for a term of years, and excluding Indians not taxed, three fifths of all other Persons. The actual Enumeration shall be made within three years after the first meeting of the Congress of the United States, and within every subsequent term of ten years, in such manner as they shall by law direct. The number of Representatives shall not exceed one for every thirty thousand, but each state shall have at least one Representative; and until such enumeration shall be made, the state of New Hampshire shall be entitled to chuse three, Massachusetts eight, Rhode Island and Providence Plantations one, Connecticut five, New York six, New Jersey four, Pennsylvania eight, Delaware one, Maryland six, Virginia ten, North Carolina five, South Carolina five, and Georgia three.

When vacancies happen in the Representation from any state, the executive authority thereof shall issue writs of election to fill such vacancies.

The House of Representatives shall choose their speaker and other officers; and shall have the sole power of impeachment.

Section 3. The Senate of the United States shall be composed of two Senators from each state, chosen by the legislature thereof, for six years; and each Senator shall have one vote.

Immediately after they shall be assembled in consequence of the first election, they shall be divided as equally as may be into three classes. The seats of the Senators of the first class shall be vacated at the expiration of the second year, of the second class at the expiration of the fourth year, and the third class at the expiration of the sixth year, so that one third may be chosen every second year; and if vacancies happen by resignation, or otherwise, during the recess of the legislature of any state, the executive thereof may make temporary appointments until the next meeting of the legislature, which shall then fill such vacancies.

No person shall be a Senator who shall not have attained to the age of thirty years, and been nine years a citizen of the United States and who shall not, when elected, be an inhabitant of that state for which he shall be chosen.

The Vice President of the United States shall be President of the Senate, but shall have no vote, unless they be equally divided.

The Senate shall choose their other officers, and also a President pro tempore, in the absence of the Vice President, or when he shall exercise the office of President of the United States.

The Senate shall have the sole power to try all impeachments. When sitting for that purpose, they shall be on oath or affirmation. When the President of the United States is tried, the Chief Justice shall preside: And no person shall be convicted without the concurrence of two thirds of the members present.

Judgment in cases of impeachment shall not extend further than to removal from office, and disqualification to hold and enjoy any office of honor, trust or profit under the United States: but the party convicted shall nevertheless be liable and subject to indictment, trial, judgment and punishment, according to law.

Section 4. The times, places and manner of holding elections for Senators and Representatives, shall be prescribed in each state by the legislature thereof; but the Congress may at any time by law make or alter such regulations, except as to the places of choosing Senators.

The Congress shall assemble at least once in every year, and such meeting shall be on the first Monday in December, unless they shall by law appoint a different day.

Section 5. Each House shall be the judge of the elections, returns and qualifications of its own members, and a majority of each shall constitute a quorum to do business; but a smaller number may adjourn from day to day, and may be authorized to compel the attendance of absent members, in such manner, and under such penalties as each House may provide.

Each House may determine the rules of its proceedings, punish its members for disorderly behavior, and, with the concurrence of two thirds, expel a member.

Each House shall keep a journal of its proceedings, and from time to time publish the same, excepting such parts as may in their judgment require secrecy; and the yeas and nays of the members of either House on any question shall, at the desire of one fifth of those present, be entered on the journal.

Neither House, during the session of Congress, shall, without the consent of the other, adjourn for more than three days, nor to any other place than that in which the two Houses shall be sitting.

Section 6. The Senators and Representatives shall receive a compensation for their services, to be ascertained by law, and paid out of the treasury of the United States. They shall in all cases, except treason, felony and breach of the peace, be privileged from arrest during their attendance at the session of their respective Houses, and in going to and returning from the same; and for any speech or debate in either House, they shall not be questioned in any other place.

No Senator or Representative shall, during the time for which he was elected, be appointed to any civil office under the authority of the United States, which shall have been created, or the emoluments whereof shall have been increased during such time: and no person holding any office under the United States, shall be a member of either House during his continuance in office.

Section 7. All bills for raising revenue shall originate in the House of Representatives; but the Senate may propose or concur with amendments as on other Bills.

Every bill which shall have passed the House of Representatives and the Senate, shall, before it become a law, be presented to the President of the United States; if he approve he shall sign it, but if not he shall return it, with his objections to that House in which it shall have originated, who shall enter the objections at large on their journal, and proceed to reconsider it. If after such reconsideration two thirds of that House shall agree to pass the bill, it shall be sent, together with the objections, to the other House, by which it shall likewise be reconsidered, and if approved by two thirds of that House, it shall become a law. But in all such cases the votes of both Houses shall be determined by yeas and nays, and the names of the persons voting for and against the bill shall be entered on the journal of each House respectively. If any bill shall not be returned by the President within ten days (Sundays excepted) after it shall have been presented to him, the same shall be a law, in like manner as if he had signed it, unless the Congress by their adjournment prevent its return, in which case it shall not be a law.

Every order, resolution, or vote to which the concurrence of the Senate and House of Representatives may be necessary (except on a question of adjournment) shall be presented to the President of the United States; and before the same shall take effect, shall be approved by him, or being disapproved by him, shall be repassed by two thirds of the Senate and House of Representatives, according to the rules and limitations prescribed in the case of a bill.

Section 8. The Congress shall have power to lay and collect taxes, duties, imposts and excises, to pay the debts and provide for the common defense and general welfare of the United States; but all duties, imposts and excises shall be uniform throughout the United States;

To borrow money on the credit of the United States;

To regulate commerce with foreign nations, and among the several states, and with the Indian tribes;

To establish a uniform rule of naturalization, and uniform laws on the subject of bankruptcies throughout the United States;

To coin money, regulate the value thereof, and of foreign coin, and fix the standard of weights and measures;

To provide for the punishment of counterfeiting the securities and current coin of the United States;

To establish post offices and post roads;

To promote the progress of science and useful arts, by securing for limited times to authors and inventors the exclusive right to their respective writings and discoveries;

To constitute tribunals inferior to the Supreme Court;

To define and punish piracies and felonies committed on the high seas, and offenses against the law of nations;

To declare war, grant letters of marque and reprisal, and make rules concerning captures on land and water;

To raise and support armies, but no appropriation of money to that use shall be for a longer term than two years;

To provide and maintain a navy;

To make rules for the government and regulation of the land and naval forces;

To provide for calling forth the militia to execute the laws of the union, suppress insurrections and repel invasions;

To provide for organizing, arming, and disciplining, the militia, and for governing such part of them as may be employed in the service of the United States, reserving to the states respectively, the appointment of the officers, and the authority of training the militia according to the discipline prescribed by Congress;

To exercise exclusive legislation in all cases whatsoever, over such District (not exceeding ten miles square) as may, by cession of particular states, and the acceptance of Congress, become the seat of the government of the United States, and to exercise like authority over all places purchased by the consent of the legislature of the state in which the same shall be, for the erection of forts, magazines, arsenals, dockyards, and other needful buildings;—And

To make all laws which shall be necessary and proper for carrying into execution the foregoing powers, and all other powers vested by this Constitution in the government of the United States, or in any department or officer thereof.

Section 9. The migration or importation of such persons as any of the states now existing shall think proper to admit, shall not be prohibited by the Congress prior to the year one thousand eight hundred and eight, but a tax or duty may be imposed on such importation, not exceeding ten dollars for each person.

The privilege of the writ of habeas corpus shall not be suspended, unless when in cases of rebellion or invasion the public safety may require it.

No bill of attainder or ex post facto Law shall be passed.

No capitation, or other direct, tax shall be laid, unless in proportion to the census or enumeration herein before directed to be taken.

No tax or duty shall be laid on articles exported from any state.

No preference shall be given by any regulation of commerce or revenue to the ports of one state over those of another: nor shall vessels bound to, or from, one state, be obliged to enter, clear or pay duties in another.

No money shall be drawn from the treasury, but in consequence of appropriations made by law; and a regular statement and account of receipts and expenditures of all public money shall be published from time to time.

No title of nobility shall be granted by the United States: and no person holding any office of profit or trust under them, shall, without the consent of the Congress, accept of any present, emolument, office, or title, of any kind whatever, from any king, prince, or foreign state.

Section 10. No state shall enter into any treaty, alliance, or confederation; grant letters of marque and reprisal; coin money; emit bills of credit; make anything but gold and silver coin a tender in payment of debts; pass any bill of attainder, ex post facto law, or law impairing the obligation of contracts, or grant any title of nobility.

No state shall, without the consent of the Congress, lay any imposts or duties on imports or exports, except what may be absolutely necessary for executing it's inspection laws: and the net produce of all duties and imposts, laid by any state on imports or exports, shall be for the use of the treasury of the United States; and all such laws shall be subject to the revision and control of the Congress.

No state shall, without the consent of Congress, lay any duty of tonnage, keep troops, or ships of war in time of peace, enter into any agreement or compact with another state, or with a foreign power, or engage in war, unless actually invaded, or in such imminent danger as will not admit of delay.

Article II

Section 1. The executive power shall be vested in a President of the United States of America. He shall hold his office during the term of four years, and, together with the Vice President, chosen for the same term, be elected, as follows:

Each state shall appoint, in such manner as the Legislature thereof may direct, a number of electors, equal to the whole number of Senators and Representatives to which the State may be entitled in the Congress: but no Senator or Representative, or person holding an office of trust or profit under the United States, shall be appointed an elector.

The electors shall meet in their respective states, and vote by ballot for two persons, of whom one at least shall not be an inhabitant of the same state with themselves. And they shall make a list of all the persons voted for, and of the number of votes for each; which list they shall sign and certify, and transmit sealed to the seat of the government of the United States, directed to the President of the Senate. The President of the Senate shall, in the presence of the Senate and House of Representatives, open all the certificates, and the votes shall then be counted. The person having the greatest number of votes shall be the President, if such number be a majority of the whole number of electors appointed; and if there be more than one who have such majority, and have an equal number of votes, then the House of Representatives shall immediately choose by ballot one of them for President; and if no person have a majority, then from the five highest on the list the said House shall in like manner choose the President. But in choosing the President, the votes shall be taken by States, the representation from each state having one vote; A quorum for this purpose shall consist of a member or members from two thirds of the states, and a majority of all the states shall be necessary to a choice. In every case, after the choice of the President, the person having the greatest number of votes of the electors shall be the Vice President. But if there should remain two or more who have equal votes, the Senate shall choose from them by ballot the Vice President.

The Congress may determine the time of choosing the electors, and the day on which they shall give their votes; which day shall be the same throughout the United States.

No person except a natural born citizen, or a citizen of the United States, at the time of the adoption of this Constitution, shall be eligible to the office of President; neither shall any person be eligible to that office who shall not have attained to the age of thirty five years, and been fourteen Years a resident within the United States.

In case of the removal of the President from office, or of his death, resignation, or inability to discharge the powers and duties of the said office, the same shall devolve on the Vice President, and the Congress may by law provide for the case of removal, death, resignation or inability, both of the President and Vice President, declaring what officer shall then act as President, and such officer shall act accordingly, until the disability be removed, or a President shall be elected.

The President shall, at stated times, receive for his services, a compensation, which shall neither be increased nor diminished during the period for which he shall have been elected, and he shall not receive within that period any other emolument from the United States, or any of them.

Before he enter on the execution of his office, he shall take the following oath or affirmation:—"I do solemnly swear (or affirm) that I will faithfully execute the office of President of the United States, and will to the best of my ability, preserve, protect and defend the Constitution of the United States."

Section 2. The President shall be commander in chief of the Army and Navy of the United States, and of the militia of the several states, when called into the actual service of the United States; he may require the opinion, in writing, of the principal officer in each of the executive departments, upon any subject relating to the duties of their respective offices, and he shall have power to grant reprieves and pardons for offenses against the United States, except in cases of impeachment.

He shall have power, by and with the advice and consent of the Senate, to make treaties, provided two thirds of the Senators present concur; and he shall nominate, and by and with the advice and consent of the Senate, shall appoint ambassadors, other public ministers and consuls, judges of the Supreme Court, and all other officers of the United States, whose appointments are not herein otherwise provided for, and which shall be established by law: but the Congress may by law vest the appointment of such inferior officers, as they think proper, in the President alone, in the courts of law, or in the heads of departments.

The President shall have power to fill up all vacancies that may happen during the recess of the Senate, by granting commissions which shall expire at the end of their next session.

Section 3. He shall from time to time give to the Congress information of the state of the union, and recommend to their consideration such measures as he shall judge necessary and expedient; he may, on extraordinary occasions, convene both Houses, or either of them, and in case of disagreement between them, with respect to the time of adjournment, he may adjourn them to such time as he shall think proper; he shall receive ambassadors and other public ministers; he shall take care that the laws be faithfully executed, and shall commission all the officers of the United States.

Section 4. The President, Vice President and all civil officers of the United States, shall be removed from office on impeachment for, and conviction of, treason, bribery, or other high crimes and misdemeanors.

Article III

Section 1. The judicial power of the United States, shall be vested in one Supreme Court, and in such inferior courts as the Congress may from time to time ordain and establish. The judges, both of the supreme and inferior courts, shall hold their offices during good behaviour, and shall, at stated times, receive for their services, a compensation, which shall not be diminished during their continuance in office.

Section 2. The judicial power shall extend to all cases, in law and equity, arising under this Constitution, the laws of the United States, and treaties made, or which shall be made, under their authority;—to all cases affecting ambassadors, other public ministers and consuls;—to all cases of admiralty and maritime jurisdiction;—to controversies to which the United States shall be a party;—to controversies between two or more states;—between a state and citizens of another state;—between citizens of different states;—between citizens of the same state claiming lands under grants of different states, and between a state, or the citizens thereof, and foreign states, citizens or subjects.

In all cases affecting ambassadors, other public ministers and consuls, and those in which a state shall be party, the Supreme Court shall have original jurisdiction. In all the other cases before mentioned, the Supreme Court shall have appellate jurisdiction, both as to law and fact, with such exceptions, and under such regulations as the Congress shall make.

The trial of all crimes, except in cases of impeachment, shall be by jury; and such trial shall be held in the state where the said crimes shall have been committed; but when not committed within any state, the trial shall be at such place or places as the Congress may by law have directed.

Section 3. Treason against the United States, shall consist only in levying war against them, or in adhering to their enemies, giving them aid and comfort. No person shall be convicted of treason unless on the testimony of two witnesses to the same overt act, or on confession in open court.

The Congress shall have power to declare the punishment of treason, but no attainder of treason shall work corruption of blood, or forfeiture except during the life of the person attainted.

Article IV

Section 1. Full faith and credit shall be given in each state to the public acts, records, and judicial proceedings of every other state. And the Congress may by general laws prescribe the manner in which such acts, records, and proceedings shall be proved, and the effect thereof.

Section 2. The citizens of each state shall be entitled to all privileges and immunities of citizens in the several states.

A person charged in any state with treason, felony, or other crime, who shall flee from justice, and be found in another state, shall on demand of the executive authority of the state from which he fled, be delivered up, to be removed to the state having jurisdiction of the crime.

No person held to service or labor in one state, under the laws thereof, escaping into another, shall, in consequence of any law or regulation therein, be discharged from such service or labor, but shall be delivered up on claim of the party to whom such service or labor may be due.

Section 3. New states may be admitted by the Congress into this union; but no new states shall be formed or erected within the jurisdiction of any other state; nor any state be formed by the junction of two or more states, or parts of states, without the consent of the legislatures of the states concerned as well as of the Congress.

The Congress shall have power to dispose of and make all needful rules and regulations respecting the territory or other property belonging to the United States; and nothing in this Constitution shall be so construed as to prejudice any claims of the United States, or of any particular state.

Section 4. The United States shall guarantee to every state in this union a republican form of government, and shall protect each of them against invasion; and on application of the legislature, or of the executive (when the legislature cannot be convened) against domestic violence.

Article V

The Congress, whenever two thirds of both houses shall deem it necessary, shall propose amendments to this Constitution, or, on the application of the legislatures of two thirds of the several states, shall call a convention for proposing amendments, which, in either case, shall be valid to all intents and purposes, as part of this Constitution, when ratified by the legislatures of three fourths of the several states, or by conventions in three fourths thereof, as the one or the other mode of ratification may be proposed by the Congress; provided that no amendment which may be made prior to the year one thousand eight hundred and eight shall in any manner affect the first and fourth clauses in the ninth section of the first article; and that no state, without its consent, shall be deprived of its equal suffrage in the Senate.

Article VI

All debts contracted and engagements entered into, before the adoption of this Constitution, shall be as valid against the United States under this Constitution, as under the Confederation.

This Constitution, and the laws of the United States which shall be made in pursuance thereof; and all treaties made, or which shall be made, under the authority of the United States, shall be the supreme law of the land; and the judges in every state shall be bound thereby, anything in the Constitution or laws of any State to the contrary notwithstanding.

The Senators and Representatives before mentioned, and the members of the several state legislatures, and all executive and judicial officers, both of the United States and of the several states, shall be bound by oath or affirmation, to support this Constitution; but no religious test shall ever be required as a qualification to any office or public trust under the United States.

Article VII

The ratification of the conventions of nine states, shall be sufficient for the establishment of this Constitution between the states so ratifying the same.

Done in convention by the unanimous consent of the states present the seventeenth day of September in the year of our Lord one thousand seven hundred and eighty seven and of the independence of the United States of America the twelfth. In witness whereof We have hereunto subscribed our Names,

G. Washington—Presidt. and deputy from Virginia

New Hampshire: John Langdon, Nicholas Gilman

Massachusetts: Nathaniel Gorham, Rufus King

Connecticut: Wm: Saml. Johnson, Roger Sherman

New York: Alexander Hamilton

New Jersey: Wil: Livingston, David Brearly, Wm. Paterson, Jona: Dayton

Pennsylvania: B. Franklin, Thomas Mifflin, Robt. Morris, Geo. Clymer, Thos. FitzSimons, Jared Ingersoll, James Wilson, Gouv Morris

Delaware: Geo: Read, Gunning Bedford jun, John Dickinson, Richard Bassett, Jaco: Broom

Maryland: James McHenry, Dan of St Thos. Jenifer, Danl Carroll

Virginia: John Blair--, James Madison Jr.

North Carolina: Wm. Blount, Richd. Dobbs Spaight, Hu Williamson

South Carolina: J. Rutledge, Charles Cotesworth Pinckney, Charles Pinckney, Pierce Butler

Georgia: William Few, Abr Baldwin

BILL OF RIGHTS

Amendment I

Congress shall make no law respecting an establishment of religion, or prohibiting the free exercise thereof; or abridging the freedom of speech, or of the press; or the right of the people peaceably to assemble, and to petition the Government for a redress of grievances.

Amendment II

A well regulated Militia, being necessary to the security of a free State, the right of the people to keep and bear Arms, shall not be infringed.

Amendment III

No Soldier shall, in time of peace be quartered in any house, without the consent of the Owner, nor in time of war, but in a manner to be prescribed by law.

Amendment IV

The right of the People to be secure in their persons, houses, papers, and effects, against unreasonable searches and seizures, shall not be violated, and no Warrants shall issue, but upon probable cause, supported by Oath or affirmation, and particularity describing the place to be searched, and the persons or things to be seized.

Amendment V

No person shall be held to answer for a capital, or otherwise infamous crime, unless on a presentment or indictment of a Grand Jury, except in cases arising in the land or naval forces, or in the Militia, when in actual service in time of War or public danger; nor shall any person be subject for the same offence to be twice put in jeopardy of life or limb; nor shall be compelled in any criminal case to be a witness against himself, nor be deprived of life, liberty, or property, without due process of law; nor shall private property be taken for public use, without just compensation.

Amendment VI

In all criminal prosecutions, the accused shall enjoy the right to a speedy and public trial, by an impartial jury of the State and district wherein the crime shall have been committed, which district shall have been previously ascertained by law, and to be informed of the nature and cause of the accusation; to be confronted with the witnesses against him; to have compulsory process for obtaining witnesses in his favor, and to have Assistance of Counsel for his defence.

Amendment VII

In Suits at common law, where the value in controversy shall exceed twenty dollars, the right of trial by jury shall be preserved, and no fact tried by a jury, shall be otherwise re-examined in any Court of the United States, than according to the rules of the common law.

Amendment VIII

Excessive bail shall not be required, nor excessive fines imposed, nor cruel and unusual punishments inflicted.

Amendment IX

The enumeration in the Constitution, of certain rights, shall not be construed to deny or disparage others retained by the people.

Amendment X

The powers not delegated to the United States by the Constitution, nor prohibited by it to the States, are reserved to the States respectively, or to the people.

OTHER AMENDMENTS TO THE CONSTITUTION

Amendment XI (Ratified in 1795)

The Judicial power of the United States shall not be construed to extend to any suit in law or equity, commenced or prosecuted against one of the United States by Citizens of another State, or by Citizens or Subjects of any Foreign State.

Amendment XII (Ratified in 1804)

The Electors shall meet in their respective states and vote by ballot for President and Vice-President, one of whom, at least, shall not be an inhabitant of the same state with themselves; they shall name in their ballots the person voted for as President, and in distinct ballots the person voted for as Vice-President, and they shall make distinct lists of all persons voted for as President, and of all persons voted for as Vice-President, and of the number of votes for each, which lists they shall sign and certify, and transmit sealed to the seat of the government of the United States, directed to the President of the Senate;—The President of the Senate shall, in the presence of the Senate and House of Representatives, open all the certificates and the votes shall then be counted;—The person having the greatest number of votes for President, shall be the President, if such number be a majority of the whole number of Electors appointed; and if no person have such majority, then from the persons having the highest numbers not exceeding three on the list of those voted for as President, the House of Representatives shall choose immediately, by ballot, the President. But in choosing the President, the votes shall be taken by states, the representation from each state having one vote; a quorum for this purpose shall consist of a member or members from two-thirds of the states, and a majority of all the states shall be necessary to a choice. And if the House of Representatives shall not choose a President whenever the right of choice shall devolve upon then, before the fourth day of March next following, then the Vice-President shall act as President, as in the case of the death or other constitutional disability of the President.—The person having the greatest number of votes as Vice-President, shall be the Vice-President, if such number be a majority of the whole number of Electors appointed, and if no person have a majority, then from the two highest numbers on the list, the Senate shall choose the Vice-President; a quorum for the purpose shall consist of two-thirds of the whole number of Senators, and a majority of the whole number shall be necessary to a choice. But no person constitutionally ineligible to the office of President shall be eligible to that of Vice-President of the United States.

Amendment XIII (Ratified in 1865)

Section 1. Neither slavery nor involuntary servitude, except as a punishment for crime whereof the party shall have been duly convicted, shall exist within the United States, or any place subject to their jurisdiction.

Section 2. Congress shall have power to enforce this article by appropriate legislation.

Amendment XIV (Ratified in 1868)

Section 1. All persons born or naturalized in the United States, and subject to the jurisdiction thereof, are citizens of the United States and of the State wherein they reside. No State shall make or enforce any law which shall abridge the privileges or immunities of citizens of the United States; nor shall any State deprive any person of life, liberty, or property, without due process of law; nor deny to any person within its jurisdiction the equal protection of the laws.

Section 2. Representatives shall be apportioned among the several States according to their respective numbers, counting the whole number of persons in each State, excluding Indians not taxed. But when the right to vote at any election for the choice of electors for President and Vice President of the United States, Representatives in Congress, the Executive and Judicial officers of a State, or the members of the Legislature thereof, is denied to any of the male inhabitants of such State, being twenty-one years of age, and citizens of the United States, or in any way abridged, except for participation in rebellion, or other crime, the basis of representation therein shall be reduced in the proportion which the number of such male citizens shall bear to the whole number of male citizens twenty-one years of age in such State.

Section 3. No person shall be a Senator or Representative in Congress, or elector of President and Vice President, or hold any office, civil or military, under the United States, or under any State, who, having previously taken an oath, as a member of Congress, or as an officer of the United States, or as a member of any State legislature, or as an executive or judicial officer of any State, to support the Constitution of the United States, shall have engaged in insurrection or rebellion against the same, or given aid or comfort to the enemies thereof. But Congress may by a vote of two-thirds of each House, remove such disability.

Section 4. The validity of the public debt of the United States, authorized by law, including debts incurred for payment of pensions and bounties for services in suppressing insurrection or rebellion, shall not be questioned. But neither the United States nor any State shall assume or pay any debt or obligation incurred in aid of insurrection or rebellion against the United States, or any claim for the loss or emancipation of any slave; but all such debts, obligations and claims shall be held illegal and void.

Section 5. The Congress shall have power to enforce, by appropriate legislation, the provisions of this article.

Amendment XV (Ratified in 1870)

Section 1. The right of citizens of the United States to vote shall not be denied or abridged by the United States or by any State on account of race, color, or previous condition of servitude.

Section 2. The Congress shall have power to enforce this article by appropriate legislation.

Amendment XVI (Ratified in 1913)

The Congress shall have power to lay and collect taxes on incomes, from whatever source derived, without apportionment among the several States, and without regard to any census or enumeration.

Amendment XVII (Ratified in 1913)

The Senate of the United States shall be composed of two Senators from each State, elected by the people thereof for six years; and each Senator shall have one vote. The electors in each State shall have the qualifications requisite for electors of the most numerous branch of the State legislatures.

When vacancies happen in the representation of any State in the Senate, the executive authority of such State shall issue writs of election to fill such vacancies: Provided, That the legislature of any State may empower the executive thereof to make temporary appointments until the people fill the vacancies by election as the legislature may direct.

This amendment shall not be so construed as to affect the election or term of any Senator chosen before it becomes valid as part of the Constitution.

Amendment XVIII (Ratified in 1919) (Repealed in 1933 by Amendment XXI)

Section 1. After one year from the ratification of this article the manufacture, sale, or transportation of intoxicating liquors within, the importation thereof into, or the exportation thereof from the United States and all territory subject to the jurisdiction thereof for beverage purposes is hereby prohibited.

Section 2. The Congress and the several States shall have concurrent power to enforce this article by appropriate legislation.

Section 3. This article shall be inoperative unless it shall have been ratified as an amendment to the Constitution by the legislatures of the several States as provided in the Constitution, within seven years from the date of the submission hereof to the States by the Congress.

Amendment XIX (Ratified in 1920)

The right of citizens of the United States to vote shall not be denied or abridged by the United States or by any State on account of sex.

Congress shall have power to enforce this article by appropriate legislation.

Amendment XX (Ratified in 1933)

Section 1. The terms of the President and Vice President shall end at noon on the 20th day of January, and the terms of Senators and Representatives at noon on the 3d day of January, of the years in which such terms would have ended if this article had not been ratified; and the terms of their successors shall then begin.

Section 2. The Congress shall assemble at least once in every year, and such meeting shall begin at noon on the 3d day of January, unless they shall by law appoint a different day.

Section 3. If, at the time fixed for the beginning of the term of the President, the President elect shall have died, the Vice President elect shall become President. If a President shall not have been chosen before the time fixed for the beginning of his term, or if the President elect shall have failed to qualify, then the Vice President elect shall act as President until a President shall have qualified; and the Congress may by law provide for the case wherein neither a President elect nor a Vice President elect shall have qualified, declaring who shall then act as President, or the manner in which one who is to act shall be selected, and such person shall act accordingly until a President or Vice President shall have qualified.

Section 4. The Congress may by law provide for the case of the death of any of the persons from whom the House of Representatives may choose a President whenever the right of choice shall have devolved upon them, and for the case of the death of any of the persons from whom the Senate may choose a Vice President whenever the right of choice shall have devolved upon them.

Section 5. Sections 1 and 2 shall take effect on the 15th day of October following the ratification of this article.

Section 6. This article shall be inoperative unless it shall have been ratified as an amendment to the Constitution by the legislatures of three-fourths of the several States within seven years from the date of its submission.

Amendment XXI (Ratified in 1933)

Section 1. The eighteenth article of amendment to the Constitution of the United States is hereby repealed.

Section 2. The transportation or importation into any State, Territory, or possession of the United States for delivery or use therein of intoxicating liquors, in violation of the laws thereof, is hereby prohibited.

Section 3. This article shall be inoperative unless it shall have been ratified as an amendment to the Constitution by conventions in the several States, as provided in the Constitution, within seven years from the date of the submission hereof to the States by the Congress.

Amendment XXII (Ratified in 1951)

Section 1. No person shall be elected to the office of the President more than twice, and no person who has held the office of President, or acted as President, for more than two years of a term to which some other person was elected President shall be elected to the office of the President more than once. But this Article shall not apply to any person holding the office of President when this Article was proposed by the Congress, and shall not prevent any person who may be holding the office of President, or acting as President, during the term within which this Article becomes operative from holding the office of President or acting as President during the remainder of such term.

Section 2. This Article shall be inoperative unless it shall have been ratified as an amendment to the Constitution by the legislatures of three-fourths of the several States within seven years from the date of its submission to the States by the Congress.

Amendment XXIII (Ratified in 1961)

Section 1. The District constituting the seat of Government of the United States shall appoint in such manner as the Congress may direct:

A number of electors of President and Vice President equal to the whole number of Senators and Representatives in Congress to which the District would be entitled if it were a State, but in no event more than the least populous State; they shall be in addition to those appointed by the States, but they shall be considered, for the purposes of the election of President and Vice President, to be electors appointed by a State; and they shall meet in the District and perform such duties as provided by the twelfth article of amendment.

Section 2. The Congress shall have power to enforce this article by appropriate legislation.

Amendment XXIV (Ratified in 1964)

Section 1. The right of citizens of the United States to vote in any primary or other election for President or Vice President, for electors for President or Vice President, or for Senator or Representative in Congress, shall not be denied or abridged by the United States or any State by reason of failure to pay any poll tax or other tax.

Section 2. The Congress shall have power to enforce this article by appropriate legislation.

Amendment XXV (Ratified in 1967)

Section 1. In case of the removal of the President from office or of his death or resignation, the Vice President shall become President.

Section 2. Whenever there is a vacancy in the office of the Vice President, the President shall nominate a Vice President who shall take office upon confirmation by a majority vote of both Houses of Congress.

Section 3. Whenever the President transmits to the President pro tempore of the Senate and the Speaker of the House of Representatives his written declaration that he is unable to discharge the powers and duties of his office, and until he transmits to them a written declaration to the contrary, such powers and duties shall be discharged by the Vice President as Acting President.

Section 4. Whenever the Vice president and a majority of either the principal officers of the executive departments or of such other body as Congress may by law provide, transmit to the President pro tempore of the Senate and the Speaker of the House of Representatives their written declaration that the President is unable to discharge the powers and duties of his office, the Vice President shall immediately assume the powers and duties of the office as Acting President.

Thereafter, when the President transmits to the President pro tempore of the Senate and the Speaker of the House of Representatives his written declaration that no inability exists, he shall resume the powers and duties of his office unless the Vice President and a majority of either the principal officers of the executive department or of such other body as Congress may by law provide, transmit within four days to the President pro tempore of the Senate and the Speaker of the House of Representatives their written declaration that the President is unable to discharge the powers and duties of his office. Thereupon Congress shall decide the issue, assembling within forty-eight hours for that purpose if not in session. If the Congress, within twenty-one days after receipt of the latter written declaration, or, if Congress is not in session, within twenty-one days after Congress is required to assemble, determines by two-thirds vote of both Houses that the President is unable to discharge the powers and duties of his office, the Vice President shall continue to discharge the same as Acting President; otherwise, the President shall resume the powers and duties of his office.

Amendment XXVI (Ratified in 1971)

Section 1. The right of citizens of the United States, who are eighteen years of age or older, to vote shall not be denied or abridged by the United States or by any State on account of age.

Section 2. The Congress shall have power to enforce this article by appropriate legislation.

Amendment XXVII (Ratified in 1992)

No law varying the compensation for the services of the Senators and Representatives shall take effect until an election of Representatives shall have intervened.

CONSTITUTIONAL LAW IN CONTEMPORARY AMERICA

Volume 1: Institutions, Politics, and Process

CHAPTER I

Foundation, Interpretation, and Amendment of the Constitution

---

Timeline: Interpretation and Amendment of the Constitution

1776 The Declaration of Independence includes concern over judicial independence as one of its accusations against the British.

1781 States ratify the Articles of Confederation proposed by the Second Continental Congress. It vests primary authority in individual states.

1786 The Annapolis Convention issues a call for a constitutional convention.

1787 The Constitutional Convention meets in Philadelphia.

1788 *Federalist Papers* are published, arguing that the judiciary will be "the least dangerous branch" of the new government.

1789 George Washington nominates John Jay as the first chief justice of the United States.

1789 Congress adopts the Judiciary Act, which outlines the federal court system with three tiers and six Supreme Court justices. Connecticut's Oliver Ellsworth, who had attended the Constitutional Convention, is a key author. Congress proposes the Bill of Rights.

1790 The Supreme Court holds its first session in the Royal Exchange Building in New York City.

1791 States ratify the first ten amendments to the Constitution, now collectively called the Bill of Rights.

1793 The Supreme Court decides in *Chisholm v. Georgia* that states can be sued without their consent.

1795 John Rutledge serves a recess appointment but is not confirmed as chief justice. States ratify the Eleventh Amendment, which overturns Supreme Court decision in *Chisholm v. Georgia.*

1796 Oliver Ellsworth is appointed and confirmed as chief justice.

1801 John Marshall is appointed and confirmed as chief justice. The outgoing Federalist Congress adopts a Judiciary Act cutting the number of justices from six to five and creating new judicial circuits.

1802 The incoming Democratic-Republican Congress adopts another Judiciary Act that repeals most provisions of the previous year and delays the Court's next term until February 1803.

1803 *Marbury v. Madison* invalidates a provision of a federal law.

1805 Justice Samuel Chase is tried but exonerated of impeachment charges before the U.S. Senate.

1821 *Cohens v. Virginia* reasserts the power of federal courts over states.

1825 Judge Gibson of Pennsylvania issues the decision in *Eakin v. Raub* questioning judicial review.

1836 John Marshall leaves the Court and is replaced by Roger Taney.

1849 The Supreme Court decides in *Luther v. Borden* that the issue of whether a state government is "republican" is a political question for the elected branches to answer.

1857 The *Dred Scott* decision declares a federal law (the Missouri Compromise) to be unconstitutional.

1866 The Judiciary Act fixes the size of the U.S. Supreme Court at nine justices.

1868 The Fourteenth Amendment overturns the *Dred Scott* decision by providing that all persons born or naturalized within the United States are citizens with rights.

1869 *Ex parte McCardle* accepts a congressional law that withdraws jurisdiction in a pending case.

1891 The Judiciary Act creates permanent federal courts of appeals—prior appellate courts had consisted of U.S. district judges and Supreme Court justices "riding circuit."

1911 *Muskrat v. United States* affirms that the Court will not issue advisory opinions.

1913 The Sixteenth Amendment reverses a Supreme Court decision that had invalidated the federal income tax.

1921 William Howard Taft, who had previously served as an associate justice, becomes the only ex-president ever to serve on the Supreme Court.

1923 *Massachusetts v. Mellon* and *Frothingham v. Mellon* reject federal taxpayer suits.

1925 A new Judiciary Act vests the Supreme Court with greater discretion over its caseload. It establishes the "rule of four" in establishing which cases the Court will hear.

Gitlow v. New York begins the process whereby the Court starts to apply provisions of the Bill of Rights to the states.

1935 The current Supreme Court building is completed.

1937 President Franklin Roosevelt proposes "packing" the federal court with new appointees. The Court reverses course on the constitutionality of a number of New Deal programs.

1939 *Coleman v. Miller* declares that most issues relative to the adoption of constitutional amendments are political questions.

1942 The *Carolene Product* footnote signals the Court's greater attention to the protection of civil rights and liberties and of democratic processes.

1953 President Dwight D. Eisenhower appoints Earl Warren as chief justice.

1954 Court issues historic desegregation decision in *Brown v. Board of Education.*

1958 *Cooper v. Aaron* asserts that state officials must obey federal court decisions. Congress rejects the Jenner-Butler bill, which was designed to limit federal appellate court jurisdiction.

1962 *Baker v. Carr* decides that the question of state legislative apportionment is a justiciable issue.

1967 Thurgood Marshall becomes the first African American to serve on the Supreme Court.

1968 *Flast v. Cohen* opens the door for some federal taxpayer suits in cases involving the establishment clause of the First Amendment.

1969 *Powell v. McCormack* decides that Congress is limited to deciding whether members meet age, citizenship, and residency requirements.

1974 The Court's decision in *United States v. Nixon* sets in motion forces that lead to the resignation of President Richard M. Nixon.

1984 *Chevron U.S.A., Inc. v. Natural Resources Defense Council, Inc.* issues a decision respecting administrative interpretations of federal laws.

1986 President Ronald Reagan elevates William H. Rehnquist as chief justice.

1989 Sandra Day O'Connor becomes the first woman to serve on the Supreme Court.

1992 *Lujan v. Defenders of Wildlife* rejects standing for individuals challenging the Endangered Species Act of 1973.

1995 *Missouri v. Jenkins* limits remediation in a school desegregation case.

2000 *Bush v. Gore* marks the first time the Court issues a decision that directly determines the outcome of a presidential election. The case also marks the first time that the Court releases oral arguments of a case on the same day that the case was argued.

2005 President George W. Bush nominates, and the U.S. Senate confirms, John Roberts as chief justice.

2012 Supreme Court upholds the Patient Protection and Affordable Care Act of 2010 in *National Federation of Independent Business v. Sebelius.*

2013 In *United States v. Windsor*, the Supreme Court rules that the Defense of Marriage Act is inconsistent with the equal liberty of persons protected by the Fifth Amendment.

2015 In *Obergefell v. Hodges*, the Supreme Court rules that states much issue marriage licenses to same-sex couples and accept such marriages from other states.

2016 President Barack Obama nominates Merrick Garland to replace Justice Antonin Scalia who died unexpectedly, but Senate Republicans delay in hopes that a Republican President will be able to make the appointment.

2017 Newly-elected President Donald Trump nominates Neal Gorsuch of the Tenth Circuit Court to the U.S. Supreme Court. U.S. Senate confirms Gorsuch by a vote of 54 to 45 after exercising the so called "nuclear option" and allowing a simple majority (rather than requiring 60 members) to end a filibuster.

THE ENGLISH BACKGROUND OF THE U.S. LEGAL SYSTEM

Fifty-five delegates met at the **Constitutional Convention** in Philadelphia in the summer of 1787 to draft the Constitution of the United States. The delegates from twelve of the existing thirteen states who assembled at this convention were chosen by state legislatures, each operating under its own constitution. These constitutions, in turn, replaced earlier charters from England and compacts, or agreements, that states had made to govern themselves.

Because it operated according to the principle that its legislative branch, the Parliament, was sovereign, the British mother country had no written constitution that was unchangeable by ordinary legislative means. It did, however, have a long history of attempting to restrain arbitrary power. This history was reflected in documents like the **Magna Carta** of 1215 and the English Bill of Rights of 1689. Individuals of English descent particularly associated the first of these documents with the principle of "no taxation without representation." In time, American colonists interpreted this principle to mean that the English Parliament could not tax them unless and until it first seated colonial representatives. As the British imposed taxes and trade restrictions on the colonies to pay for the expenses they had incurred in defending the colony in the French and Indian War (1754–63), the colonists remonstrated and petitioned the English King before ultimately calling two Continental Congresses.

Declaration of Independence:

We hold these truths to be self-evident, that all men are created equal, that they are endowed by their Creator with certain unalienable Rights, that among these are Life, Liberty and the pursuit of Happiness. That to secure these rights, Governments are instituted among Men, deriving their just powers from the consent of the governed.

THE DECLARATION OF INDEPENDENCE

In 1776, the second of these congresses decided to declare the colonists' independence from Britain. When the Second Continental Congress commissioned Thomas Jefferson to write the **Declaration of Independence** to explain why the colonists were cutting their ties to the mother country, he drew upon the British legal heritage and upon the **natural rights** philosophy of British **social contract** theorists, most notably John Locke. Jefferson declared that people were "created equal," that governments were designed to secure their rights of "life, liberty and the pursuit of happiness," and that legitimate government rested "on the consent of the governed" rather than on the divine right of kings or hereditary succession. The Declaration further affirmed the right of the people to alter or replace the government, by peaceful means when they were available and by revolutionary means when they were not.

THE ARTICLES OF CONFEDERATION

Recognizing that the colonies would need a superintending government if they wanted to avoid a **state of nature** where they might be at constant war with one another, the Second Continental Congress drafted a document known as the Articles of Confederation. It created a unicameral Congress, where each state was represented equally. Because the states were still jealous of their individual identities, the Articles continued to vest primary sovereignty, or power, in the states. Nine or more of the thirteen states needed to agree on most key legislative matters, and the Articles required them to act unanimously in amending the document.

Despite some signal accomplishments—most notably the victory in the Revolutionary War and the adoption of the Northwest Resolution of 1787 providing for the admission of further states—the Articles proved to be largely inadequate. Congress lacked key domestic powers, such as control over interstate commerce, and America's prestige was quickly deteriorating abroad. The requirement for unanimity blocked needed amendments.

Preamble, U.S. Constitution:

We the People of the United States, in Order to form a more perfect Union, establish Justice, insure domestic Tranquility, provide for the common defence, promote the general Welfare, and secure the Blessings of Liberty to ourselves and our Posterity, do ordain and establish this Constitution for the United States.

A NEW CONSTITUTION

In these circumstances, delegates from a meeting of five states who had discussed interstate navigation and commerce at Annapolis, Maryland, issued a call for a constitutional convention. Support for this convention was strengthened when in the winter of 1786–1787 the government under the Articles of Confederation responded lethargically to a taxpayer revolt in Massachusetts known as Shays' Rebellion. Although Congress had called the Convention to strengthen the **Articles of Confederation**, which the state legislatures had formally adopted in 1781, the Constitutional Convention of 1787 instead created an entirely new Constitution, which it hoped would establish "a more perfect Union."

The Document outlined the purposes of this document in its opening paragraph, known as the Preamble. A key purpose of the new Constitution, often particularly associated with the judiciary, was to "establish justice." Grievances against perceived judicial abuses had played a prominent part in events leading up to the Declaration of Independence from England.

The new constitution replaced the **unicameral** congress under the Articles of Confederation, where each state had a single vote, with a **bicameral** congress in which states were represented according to population in one house and equally in the other. While establishing a **federal system** that maintained existing states, the new Constitution further enlarged the powers of Congress at the expense of states, which had been largely sovereign under the Articles of Confederation. It then balanced congressional powers with powerful executive and judicial branches. The framers entrusted Congress with the powers to make the laws, the president with the power to enforce them, and the judiciary with the power to interpret them.

Article III, Sec. 1:

The judicial Power of the United States, shall be vested in one supreme Court, and in such inferior Courts as the Congress may from time to time ordain and establish.

The Organization and Operation of the Federal Judicial System

The Constitution outlines the powers of the three branches of government in its first three of seven main divisions, known as articles. Article I thus describes the legislative branch, Article II the executive branch, and Article III the judicial branch. Although this order arguably gives primacy to the legislative branch, casebooks commonly begin with the judicial branch because its written decisions, which constitute the bulk of these volumes, are critical to understanding the roles of the other two branches.

Article III's description of the judicial branch is far leaner than Article I's description of the legislative branch or Article II's description of the executive branch. Section 1 of Article III vests "[t]he judicial Power of the United States" in one Supreme Court and in such other courts as Congress shall create. This terse language left a good deal to the discretion of the other two branches, especially as regards the establishment and organization of lower federal courts.

The first Congress that met under the new Constitution consisted of a number of delegates who had attended the Constitutional Convention of 1787. It adopted a Judiciary Act that continues to serve as the basic outline for this system. The first reading in this chapter includes selections from this Act, which mirrored the hierarchical system that most states had already established and that continue today.

The Judiciary Act of 1789 and subsequent laws provide for federal cases to begin in **U.S. District Courts**, of which there are currently ninety-four. These courts are trial courts, or courts of **original jurisdiction**, where lawyers argue their cases and judges hear them for the first time. Each state has from one to four U.S. District Courts. On some occasions, laws provide for three-judge district courts, but more typically a single federal judge presides over each of these courts. Consistent with guarantees in the Sixth and Seventh Amendments to the U.S. Constitution, defendants before such courts have the right to jury trials.

U.S. District Courts, like the courts above them, have jurisdiction over (that is, the authority to hear) both civil and criminal cases. **Civil cases** involve suits by individual citizens, who have grievances against one another. **Plaintiffs** bring the suits, and **defendants** respond to them (losing parties who appeal cases become **appellants,** while winning parties against whom they file such appeals are **appellees**). Individuals might bring matters involving breaches of contracts, torts (wrongful actions that have caused damages), libel, etc., for which they generally seek monetary damages. Criminal cases involve charges that the government, as the **prosecution,** brings against **defendants** who it alleges have violated the law. Criminal conviction may result in fines, jail sentences, or, in extreme cases, even the death penalty.

A system of **U.S. Circuit Courts** (there are eleven numbered circuits, a D.C. circuit, and a specialized circuit) constitutes the next level. These are chiefly courts of **appellate jurisdiction.** They are so designated because they review judgments on appeal from the district courts. Either side in a civil case may file such appeals, but since the Fifth Amendment prohibits double jeopardy, only individuals who are convicted can file appeals in criminal cases. Judges of the courts of appeal usually meet in panels of three, although sometimes they meet ***en banc,*** or as a whole. Under the Judiciary Act of 1789, Supreme Court justices had to "ride circuit" and serve as judges on these courts in addition to their duties in the capital. Although justices nominally remain in charge of such circuits and sometimes oversee special appeals from them, the law no longer requires this onerous duty of circuit-riding that tested not only the endurance but also threatened the physical health of the early justices.

Individuals or entities who lose their cases in the circuit courts or in a state's highest court (usually, but not always, designated as a state supreme court) on matters involving the U.S. Constitution may in turn appeal to the **U.S. Supreme Court.** Like the Capitol Building and the White House, the Supreme Court is located in Washington, D.C. Although the Constitution does not specify the number of justices on this Court, Congress has set the number at nine since the Civil War.

The **chief justice** presides over the Supreme Court. Whereas the House of Representatives chooses its own speaker, the president appoints a new chief justice when the current chief leaves office. The **chief justice** is regarded as ***primus inter pares***, or first among equals. The chief oversees the administration of the federal courts and directs its secret discussion of cases in chambers. By tradition, if the chief votes with the majority on the case, the chief may either write the decision personally or choose the justice who will write the court's opinion; when the chief is in the minority, the ranking member of the majority exercises the same privilege.

In addition to a limited number of cases of original jurisdiction (cases that it hears for the first time) that the U.S. Constitution assigns to it, the Supreme Court accepts cases either from the U.S. Circuit Courts or, in cases involving federal jurisdiction, from the states' highest courts, through writs, or petitions, the most common of which is a **writ of certiorari**. In the past, the Court relied more heavily on **writs of appeal**, which the Court was technically required to hear, and on **writs of certification**, through which lower courts requested the Supreme Court to clarify an ambiguous provision of the law.

Congress has granted the Court discretion to decide which cases it will hear. It currently operates according to the **rule of four.** Under this rule, the Court will not listen to a case unless four or more members vote to do so. Of the thousands of petitions that the Court receives each year, it generally schedules oral arguments in less than seventy-five. When the Supreme Court accepts a case, it invites the parties to present oral arguments, the justices meet together in conference and vote in secret, opinions are written and reviewed, and the Court subsequently issues its decision.

Because the Court is not an elected branch, it is inappropriate for individuals to "lobby" the Court by arranging private meetings with justices and attempting to extract promises from them. Moreover, because they are not elected, individuals and organizations have no cause to give them campaign contributions. With the Court's permission, groups that are interested in cases may file ***amicus curiae***, or friend of the court, **briefs** in which they present arguments for the side they support. These briefs may provide background information about the effect of the general point of law—as on matters involving abortion or affirmative action—that the facts of an individual case or cases might not otherwise reveal.

Because it stands at the top of the federal judicial hierarchy, the U.S. Supreme Court is the most influential court in the land. Accordingly, almost all of the decisions in this and most other constitutional law casebooks are taken from its decisions. Most opinions will feature a **majority**, or plurality, opinion on behalf of the Court. Many will also feature **concurring** and **dissenting opinions**. Justices who write concurring opinions agree with the ruling in the case but not necessarily with the reasoning. Dissenters believe that the Court has ruled incorrectly and make their appeal to the larger audience who will read such decisions. When the Supreme Court justices tie—as when justices recuse themselves to avoid conflicts of interest or when there is a vacancy, decisions of the court from which the appeal came to the Court, remain in effect.

Article II, Sec. 2:

"He [the President] . . . shall nominate, and by and with the Advice and Consent of the Senate, shall appoint . . . Judges of the supreme Court. . . ."

Article III, Sec. 1:

The Judges, both of the supreme and inferior Courts, shall hold their Offices during good Behavior, and shall, at stated Times, receive for their Services a Compensation which shall not be diminished during their Continuance in Office.

The Appointment, Confirmation, and Tenure of Judges and Justices

The judiciary is the only one of the three branches of the national government whose members are appointed rather than elected. Advocates of the **Virginia** (large-state) **Plan** at the Constitutional Convention of 1787 had advocated legislative appointment of judges and justices, whereas advocates of the **New Jersey** (small-state) **Plan** had favored executive appointment. Ultimately, the Convention compromised by providing that the president would make such appointments, and the Senate would be responsible for deciding whether to give its "advice and consent"; by contrast, many states outline minimal qualifications but allow for the election of judges. In a well-known variant of this, often called the **Missouri Plan**, after its state of origination, governors appoint judges who are subsequently subject to electoral approval or disapproval.

Probably because federal judges are appointed rather than elected, the Constitution does not outline age, residency, and citizenship requirements for members of the judiciary as it does for Congress and the presidency. In modern times, it is practically inconceivable that these bodies would not at a minimum seek an individual with a law degree. Moreover, despite the absence of a constitutionally specified requirement to require them to do so, presidents have increasingly nominated individuals who have served in lower courts to the U.S. Supreme Court, where they are likely to have established a record by which the president might predict the kind of justices they would be.

Congress exercises far more scrutiny when deciding whether to confirm members of the judiciary than it does when confirming cabinet officers, and it typically extends greater scrutiny to nominees for the Supreme Court than to nominees for lower courts. Senators know that the Constitution specifies that judges and justices will serve "**during good behavior.**" This means that they will be in office until they die, retire, or, as specified in Article II, Section 4 of the Constitution, are impeached and convicted of "Treason, Bribery, or other high Crimes and Misdemeanors." Although a score of federal judges have been impeached and convicted, Congress has yet to remove a U.S. Supreme Court justice through this **impeachment** and conviction mechanism.

The Constitution intended for judges and justices to be independent. In addition to their terms, the Constitution prevented members of Congress from cutting judicial salaries in retaliation once they were in office. Article III does allow Congress to increase judicial salaries to enable judges who serve during long time periods to keep apace with inflation.

Because judges and justices will interpret and apply the Constitution and laws that are made under it, presidential candidates often describe the kinds of judicial appointments they will make. President Richard Nixon indicated that he would favor judges who favored law and order. In the election of 2008, Republican candidate John McCain stressed that he favored judges who would interpret the constitution strictly, whereas Democrat Barack Obama stressed the need for judges to be compassionate. Republican Presidential candidate Donald Trump took the unprecedented step of presenting a list of conservatives whom he would consider appointing even before receiving his party's nomination.

The Senate Judiciary Committee now televises its confirmation hearings, and special interest lobby groups increasingly weigh in to influence such votes. The hearings in the Reagan administration involving Robert Bork, a strong advocate of original intent whom the Senate ultimately rejected, took partisan controversy to a new level of bitterness; commentators still refer to the possibility that a judicial nominee will be "Borked." The bitter acrimony was repeated when George H. W. Bush nominated Clarence Thomas. Only the second African American ever nominated for such a post, Thomas was much more conservative than the African American justice, Thurgood Marshall, whom he was replacing. Critics challenged not only Thomas's ideology but aired allegations that he had engaged in sexual harassment. After classic "he said, she said" testimony from a former employee, Anita Hill, the Senate confirmed Thomas, and he serves on the Court today. When the Senate is controlled by members of an opposition party, its members have increasingly sought to delay nominations by an outgoing president that are made in presidential election years as Republicans Senators did in 2016 in refusing to hold hearings on President Obama's nomination of federal appeals judge Merrick Garland.

When they contemplate federal judicial appointments, presidents clearly have to consider the Senate's response. Presidents might purposely seek out individuals without a long paper trail that can be used against them, but presidents are just as likely to seek someone with a known judicial philosophy with which they agree.

Sometimes presidents sacrifice some perceived ideological compatibility in order to select individuals they think will have a greater chance of being confirmed.

The Federalist *Explains the Judicial Branch*

In understanding the judicial branch, it is helpful to appreciate what the American Founders intended for it to accomplish. The second reading in this chapter is an essay from *The Federalist*, an outstanding series of essays that Alexander Hamilton, James Madison, and John Jay authored under the pseudonym "Publius." Publius defended the proposed Constitution of 1787 against **Anti-Federalist** critics who had focused in part on fears that the new government had overly empowered the judiciary. In *Federalist* No. 78, Alexander Hamilton, who had served as a delegate to the Constitutional Convention from New York and was among the passionate advocates of a stronger national government, defended the exercise of judicial review and attempted to minimize its negative effects. He associated judicial power with constitutional supremacy rather than with judicial supremacy. He also attempted to defend both the process of appointing judges and justices and the lifetime tenure that most of them will have.

Article III, Sec. 2, para. 1:

The judicial Power shall extend to all Cases, in Law and Equity, arising under this Constitution, the Laws of the United States, and Treaties made, or which shall be made, under their authority; to all Cases affecting Ambassadors, other public Ministers and Consuls; to all Cases of admiralty and maritime Jurisdiction; to Controversies to which the United States shall be a Party; to Controversies between two or more states; between a State and Citizens of another State; between Citizens of different States between Citizens of the same State claiming Lands under Grants of different States, and between a State, or the Citizens thereof, and foreign States, Citizens or Subjects.

The Jurisdiction and Power of Federal Courts

Members of the legislative and executive branches typically campaign by committing themselves in advance to certain policies and programs. They may advocate stronger defense, better health care, better schools and highways, identify themselves as pro-life or pro-choice on abortion, or stick with more general themes like maintaining a healthy economy or advocating change. Politicians effectively act as policy entrepreneurs, hoping to identify and champion the issues or themes that will strike a responsive chord with their constituencies.

Although they ultimately wield tremendous powers, federal judges and justices do not run for office, and while they might be willing to share their general philosophies of decision making and constitutional interpretation with congressional committees, judicial nominees commonly refuse to answer questions about specific cases or issues that they think are likely to come before their courts. Such nominees recognize that members of the public expect them to uphold the law without fear or favor and that they will immediately lose credibility if they precommit themselves to one side or another.

In outlining "judicial power" in Article III, the U.S. Constitution continually refers to "cases" and "controversies." This language helps explain why judges must necessarily be more passive than members of the other branches of government. They must wait for controversies to reveal themselves in conflicts between individual litigants before they can either hear them or attempt to resolve them.

Drawing from English legal history, Article III extends the judicial power to a variety of cases in both "**law and equity**." The former cases are the more familiar controversies involving levying fines and punishments. By contrast, equity jurisdiction is wider, allowing courts to intervene to prevent impending harms. An individual bringing damages for a neighbor's tree that fell on his or her house would be bringing a case under "law," whereas an individual seeking an **injunction**, or judicial order, forbidding a neighbor from chopping down a tree without first securing protection for the residence would be bringing a case in "equity."

Between Judicial Activism and Judicial Restraint: Methods of Constitutional Interpretation

As discussed in this chapter, the Supreme Court exercises the power to interpret the laws and the Constitution. Differing approaches to interpreting the Constitution, like differing approaches to purely literary works or to holy books—the Bible, for example—can lead to different interpretations of these documents' meaning. Opponents of path-breaking judicial decisions often describe them as products of an "activist" court and call for judicial "restraint." The judges against whom the charges are made may see themselves as simply carrying out the job that they believe the Constitution has entrusted to them. Some jurists will distinguish between judicial "**interpretivism**," which largely focuses on the words and original meaning of the Constitution, while "**noninterpretivists**" will consider their mandate to be wider. In recent years, American judges have raised the question as to whether it is appropriate to look to foreign jurisdictions for ascertaining trends, as, for example, in matters related to capital punishment.

After more than two hundred years, the words of the Constitution are sometimes not only difficult to interpret in their own right but even more difficult to apply to contemporary situations. Different provisions might call for different approaches. No list of interpretive methods is likely to be exhaustive, or to serve equally for all provisions, but the following approaches are among the most common:

1. **Focus on the meaning of words**: Although every judge and justice pays considerable attention to the specific words of the Constitution, some consider this approach to be primary. Justice Hugo LaFayette Black was thus famous for observing that the words in the First Amendment providing that "Congress shall make no law" relative to speech meant precisely that.

2. **Original intent**: Often in combination with the focus on words, interpreters of the Constitution often seek to ascertain what words, phrases, and constitutional arrangements meant when they were originally proposed, ratified, and/or subsequently amended. Contemporary dictionaries and public statements of leading framers might prove useful, although they are often contradictory.

3. **Precedent**: Citing the legal doctrine of **stare decisis**, judges are especially likely to adhere to established precedents. Such adherence promotes stability in the law. Continuing adherence to a bad precedent, or series of precedents, can likewise perpetuate constitutional misunderstandings.

4. **Constitutional principles**: Judges often refer to principles that they believe are either stated, or implicit, within the Constitution. Examples include separation of church and state (a principle that observers often use to explain the establishment clause of the First Amendment), one person-one vote (used in legislative apportionment cases to require districts of approximately equal populations), separation of powers, federalism, etc. Of course, cases often involve conflicting principles among which judges and justices must choose. Judges sometimes liken their work to "balancing" various principles and considerations.

5. **Considerations of public policy**: Although legislators and executives are presumably the most likely to consider public policy implications of proposed legislation, judges often recognize that their decisions will have public policy consequences. They also recognize that they ultimately depend on the political branches for enforcement of their decisions.

6. **Living Constitution**: Often contrasted with original intent, advocates of a living constitution are likely to point to the difficulty of formally amending the Constitution and of the need for judicial interpretations that help keep the Constitution in touch with the times. In overturning more than fifty years of racial segregation in education, the Court observed in *Brown v. Board of Education* (1954) that education had a much larger role to play in society than it did at the time that the Court had approved the doctrine of "separate but equal."

This list is far from exhaustive, but students generally understand court decisions best when they understand the methods the judges applied to get to them. Students will want to pay particular attention to the method of interpretation when they do the "reasoning" section of their case briefs.

The Development of Judicial Review of National Legislation

Americans had brought a system of **common law** with them from England. Under this system, judges filled in gaps or interpreted ambiguous provisions of law while deciding cases. Cases in turn served as precedents that built upon one another. Under the British system of **parliamentary sovereignty**, the judicial role was fairly circumscribed by deference to the legislature.

The judiciary has arguably played a larger role in America, where it had once examined colonial laws to see that they were aligned with those of the motherland. Moreover, the new Constitution created a system embodying **separation of powers** and **checks and balances.** Separation of powers distributes powers among the three branches of government, each of which should adhere to the Constitution, but none of which can claim fully to embody the will of "We the People."

The framers of the Constitution fully expected that courts would interpret the laws. This is called **statutory interpretation.** When courts so interpret the laws, the law-making authority is free to adopt laws that state their intentions more clearly. In a 5–4 ruling in *Ledbetter v. Goodyear Tire and Rubber Co., Inc.* (550 U.S. 618, 2007), the Supreme Court rejected Lilly Ledbetter's sex discrimination claim under Title VII of the Civil Rights Act of 1964. She had filed a suit within 180 days of learning that the Goodyear Tire & Rubber Company was paying comparable male workers more than it paid her, but long after she was initially hired. The Court interpreted the law to require individuals to file suit within 180 days of the initial violation; Congress responded in early 2009 by passing the Lilly Ledbetter Fair Pay Restoration Act allowing employees to file claims within 180 days of their most recent paycheck.

Many Founders hoped, and some feared, that in addition to interpreting laws, courts would also exercise the power, now known as **judicial review**, to review the constitutionality of laws that arose in cases before them and strike down laws that they considered to be unconstitutional. Unless courts reverse themselves in such cases, lawmakers cannot override exercises of judicial review simply by adopting new laws. Instead, they must utilize the difficult power of constitutional amendment, as they did, for example, when adopting the Fourteenth Amendment to overturn the Supreme Court decision in *Dred Scott v. Sandford* (60 U.S. (19 How.) 393, 1857) declaring that blacks were not, and could not become, citizens of the United States. Consistent with common law antecedents, courts have established both the extent and the limitations of the power of judicial review through a process of case precedents, which are the subject of this chapter.

Also consistent with Hamilton's arguments in *Federalist* No. 78, Section 25 of the Judiciary Acts empowered the Supreme Court, when deciding on cases or controversies, to decide whether laws or actions that brought cases before them are constitutional or unconstitutional. Although the Court's power to review state laws for their conformity with the national Constitution is almost certainly essential to the perpetuation of a federal government, which attends to the interests of the entire nation, the power to review and invalidate national laws is more problematic because it pits the judgment of one unelected branch of government against that of one or both other branches that are more directly accountable to the people. Alexander Bickel, a prominent twentieth-century scholar, termed this the "countermajoritarian difficulty." *Marbury v. Madison* (5 U.S. (1 Cranch) 137, 1803), which is the first case in this and most other texts of this kind, represents Chief Justice John Marshall's attempt to establish and justify the exercise of such power.

Many of the Framers hoped that the Constitution might transcend partisan differences, but in George Washington's first term, controversies over the establishment of a national bank, federal assumption of state debts, and other matters eventually resulted in the establishment of the Federalist and the Democratic-Republican Parties. Under the administrations of George Washington and John Adams, the nation generally pursued policies favored by the Federalist Party, which Alexander Hamilton helped to found. It called for strong national authority that could further manufacturing and commercial interests and for broad interpretations of congressional powers. Members of the party, whose primary support was in the Northeast, were generally more sympathetic in foreign policy matters toward Great Britain.

By contrast, members of the Democratic-Republican Party, which Thomas Jefferson and James Madison founded, and which was especially strong in the South, were more wary of federal powers. They had opposed the establishment of a national bank, which they thought would aggrandize federal powers, and generally favored agrarian interests. In addition to arguing for "strict construction" of the federal constitution, they had vigorously opposed the Federalist-inspired Alien and Sedition Acts, the latter of which made it a crime to criticize members of the government. After the people elected Democratic-Republicans to power in Congress and the presidency in the elections of 1800, Federalists attempted to secure the government against revolutionary changes by creating new judicial posts to which they appointed fellow party members. A dispute over such an appointment led to the first "case or controversy" in *Marbury v. Madison*, which gave the Supreme Court the power to articulate and defend judicial review.

It is important to recognize that judicial review did not originate with *Marbury v. Madison*. Rather, this case represented the culmination of a series of precedents, some of which had originated a century before within Great Britain. State courts had repeatedly exercised the power of invalidating state statutes. North Carolina, Rhode Island, and New Jersey (*Holmes v. Walton,* 1780) are prime examples of this. Moreover, in *Hylton v. United States* (3 Dallas 171, 1796), the carriage tax case, the Supreme Court had assumed, but not exercised, the power to declare an act of Congress unconstitutional.

Justice Gibson Questions Judicial Review

Although the power to exercise judicial review may not have been altogether new, all Americans did not immediately embrace it. Even though Marshall had not issued the writ of mandamus commanding Democratic-Republican leaders to deliver Marbury's commission, they chafed under Marshall's chiding in *Marbury*, and even some judges maintained doubts. Twenty-two years after Marshall's historic decision in *Marbury*, a majority of Pennsylvania Supreme Court justices who heard the case of *Eakin v. Raub* (12 Sargeant & Rawle 330, Pa. 1825) asserted their own power of judicial review to invalidate a state law. By contrast, Justice John Gibson authored a powerful dissent in which he challenged almost every defense for judicial review that Marshall had mustered in *Marbury*. Although Gibson's dissent did not articulate the dominant thinking of his own court or that of the United States, scholars continue to examine his arguments and weigh them against those of Marshall. At a time when the Court was increasingly basing its decisions on the specific language of the Constitution, Justice John Bannister Gibson had the courage to point to the weaknesses of such textual defenses of judicial review as well as other problems.

Legislative Control of Judicial Jurisdiction

While the Constitution itself outlines most of the Supreme Court's jurisdiction, Article III vests the Court's appellate jurisdiction "with such Exceptions, and under such Regulations as the Congress shall make." From time to time, Congress has attempted to withdraw areas of appellate jurisdiction from the Court. On at least one occasion, the Court has concurred in this decision. In *Ex parte McCardle* (74 U.S. 506, 1869), it actually allowed Congress to withdraw jurisdiction over a case that it had already heard involving the military trial of a newspaper editor who had favored the South during the Civil War. Were such actions to become routine, they could well undermine judicial independence.

Judicial Review of State Legislation and Actions

Judicial review of congressional legislation generally receives considerably more attention than does judicial review of state legislative acts, and yet the latter power is arguably more essential to preserving the system of government that the Constitution of 1787 created than the former. The **supremacy clause** of Article VI of the Constitution makes the federal constitution and laws and treaties enacted under it the "supreme Law of the Land," and yet states accustomed to exercising their sovereignty under the Articles of Confederation did not relish giving it up under the new constitution and sometimes resisted federal measures with a vengeance.

In opposing the Alien and Sedition Acts of 1798, Thomas Jefferson and James Madison had anonymously authored the Virginia and Kentucky Resolutions, which suggested that states might "interpose" themselves against unconstitutional national legislation. However well intentioned, this seemed to open the door to what Hamilton had described as a hydra in government, where each state might become a law to itself. In *Cohens v. Virginia* (19 U.S. 264, 1821), the Court instead applied the logic of *Marbury v. Madison* and the supremacy clause to judicial invalidations of state laws.

Just as members of the other branches of government have sometimes found sanctuary within the doctrine of separation of powers to enforce their own views of the Constitution over those of the Court, so too, have states sometimes used the doctrine of states' rights to resist assertions of federal judicial power. Apart from controversies over slavery that were ultimately settled by force of arms, one of the most dramatic examples of state resistance to federal judicial decisions occurred in the aftermath of the Court's decision in *Brown v. Board of Education* (347 U.S. 483, 1954) declaring that racial discriminatory laws, which the Court had approved in *Plessy v. Ferguson* (163 U.S. 537, 1896), must come to an end. Although a majority of the American people probably supported this decision, it encountered much opposition in the South, where discriminatory Jim Crow laws had taken their strongest hold. Faced with a recalcitrant southern governor in *Cooper v. Aaron* (358 U.S. 1, 1958), the Supreme Court asserted its authority over state entities.

Advisory Opinions

The exercise of judicial review has raised many practical questions, including the power of the federal Supreme Court to issue **advisory opinions.** A number of the states provide for their supreme courts to do this. Briefly, an advisory opinion is an arrangement whereby the chief executive of the state or the legislature requests the court to issue an opinion as to the constitutionality of a pending piece of legislation. The determination is not binding on the court, the legislature, or the governor but furnishes some kind of professional advice to guide them. Delegates to the Constitutional Convention of 1787 had discussed establishing a Council of Revision, which would have granted members of the executive and judicial branches power to void laws that had not yet gone into its effect. Perhaps in part because the delegates decided to reject this mechanism, early in its history, the Supreme Court indicated that it would not issue such decisions to determine abstract constitutional issues.

Muskrat v. United States (219 U.S. 346, 1911) is the leading case (and it is still good law) on the point that the Court will not assume a theoretical case but only one where there is a valid case or controversy. The case is in entire accord with the principle of **delegated power** that determines the powers of all units of the federal government. The Supreme Court has only the jurisdiction delegated by the Constitution, and this includes only "cases and controversies." A hypothetical matter does not qualify. Thus, in any matter before the Court there must be actual litigants with concrete and specific interests involved. A suit may well be brought to test a statute, but the parties must raise conflicting legal claims. A collusive suit is one where there is no bona fide assertion of real and adequate legal claims.

In cases both before and since *Muskrat*, the Court has consistently held that "friendly" or collusive suits cannot be heard by the Court. Briefly, the object of a suit must be protection of asserted rights, and there must be adverse parties who have "**standing**" before the Court. The directness of the injury is one of the chief factors determining whether a person has the right to bring a suit. The right that a citizen has to have a government administered properly is not adequate. Neither is an action that invades the rights of another person without injuring the party who sues. Actions that are prematurely brought, that is, before the injury is actually impending in any immediate sense will not be entertained. As to the Court declaring a statute invalid because of its being contrary to the Constitution, the Court will pass on the constitutionality of a statute only if such a ruling is necessary to the disposition of a case that is properly before the Court.

A **declaratory judgment** is not to be confused with the advisory opinion involved in *Muskrat.* A declaratory judgment is the result of an actual case between contesting parties to determine actual rights and duties as between them. Further, a *declaratory* judgment is binding on the parties to the suit, thus emphasizing its distinction from the *advisory* opinion.

Taxpayer Suits

The rules of standing and justiciability that the Supreme Court has developed might be largely evaded if individuals with minute interests were able to bring their cases to the Court. In a number of cases, taxpayers have asserted their standing *as taxpayers* to challenge a law providing federal funds for child and maternity care.

This chapter includes two primary cases involving taxpayer suits. *Massachusetts v. Mellon* and *Frothingham v. Mellon* (262 US 447, 1923) demonstrate the Supreme Court's reluctance to grant standing to litigants whose only claim in challenging a federal appropriation was their status as taxpayers. *Flast v. Cohen* (392 U.S. 83, 1968) later opens the door for such suits in a limited number of cases involving challenges to federal legislation under the provision in the First Amendment prohibiting the establishment of religion.

State Standing

If there is some question regarding when individuals as taxpayers have standing to sue, there is also some controversy over when states have standing to sue on their own behalf or on behalf of their citizens. Especially in an era where the United States has become so partisan and divided, it has become more frequent for states controlled by one political party to challenge decisions by a presidency controlled by another. But to mount these challenges states still need to show standing and need to assert an injury. In *Massachusetts v. E.P.A.,* 549 U.S. 497 (2007) several organizations, local governments, and states sued the Environmental Protection Agency contending that they should have issued rules to address greenhouse gas emissions. The Supreme Court undertook a vigorous analysis of the potential injuries states would have to undertake to abate the costs of global warming. These costs, along with what the Supreme Court called the special status of states in the federal union, led it to grant standing. The holding here then laid the basis of states in *Texas v. United States*, 809 F.3d 134 (5th Cir. 2015), (included in chapter IV) suing to enjoin a presidential executive order entitled Deferred Action for

Parents of Americans and Lawful Permanent Residents (DAPA), which would have provided legal presence for illegal immigrants who were parents of citizens or lawful permanent residents, and to prevent expansion of program of Deferred Action for Childhood Arrivals (DACA). The Court of Appeals affirmed the standing of states to sue and then in *United States v. Texas*, ___ U.S. ___; 136 S.Ct. 2271 (2016), the Supreme Court deadlocked 4–4 and issued a per curiam decision that upheld a lower decision that issued an injunction to prevent enforcement of the executive order and as of the publication of this book had halted President Obama's effort to address immigration on his own.

Deference, Justiciability, and Standing

Executive agencies must often translate relatively broad congressional mandates into concrete rules. The case of *Chevron U.S.A., Inc. v. Natural Resources Defense Council, Inc.* (467 U.S. 837, 1984) demonstrates that courts are often fairly deferential to agency decisions. In *Chevron*, the Supreme Court upheld an interpretation of a law by the Environmental Protection Agency, which the Court believed the law permitted but did not specifically authorize. In so doing, it arguably deferred to the political branches.

Consistent with the Constitution's emphasis on "cases and controversies," American courts put great stress on the ideas of "**standing**" and "**justiciability**." The former prerequisite requires that parties to a suit are properly situated to raise the issues they bring there. The latter requires that courts be able to redress the grievances that have been raised. Many cases of standing and justiciability are relatively straightforward, but others are not. *Lujan v. Defenders of Wildlife* (504 U.S. 555, 1992) demonstrates that the Court will sometimes reject novel claims of standing. In *Lujan*, it specifically rejected the standing of some individuals who were attempting to challenge federal environmental legislation. In imposing limits on judicial review, rules of standing and justiciability mean that individuals may not always be able to utilize the courts to remedy real or perceived inequities and injustices.

The Political Questions Doctrine

Few judicial doctrines have been any more elusive than the "political questions" doctrine. This doctrine actually originated in *Marbury v. Madison* when Marshall observed that the Court would refuse to involve itself in "political questions," but *Marbury* demonstrated that the lines between political matters and nonpolitical questions are often unclear. In *Luther v. Borden* (48 U.S. 1, 1849), a case involving which of two rival state governments was "republican" and hence entitled to rule, Chief Justice Roger B. Taney cited the political questions doctrine to justify sticking with a decision on the matter that the president had already made under authority granted to him by Congress. Had both putative state governments elected representatives to Congress, it would have been up to Congress to determine which was republican and which it should therefore seat.

In 1939, the Court applied this doctrine in *Coleman v. Miller* (307 U.S. 433, 1939) to the constitutional amending process, which is outlined in Article V of the Constitution. Article V provides that Congress may propose amendments by two-thirds majorities of both houses of Congress or (in an unused mechanism) two-thirds of the state legislatures can petition Congress to call a special convention to propose amendments. For proposed amendments to become part of the law of the land, they must be ratified, at congressional specification, either by three-fourths of the state legislatures or by conventions called within three-fourths of the states. Article V does not set a time limit on the ratification of proposed amendments, does not specify whether states can ratify amendment that they have previously rejected or rescind ratifications of pending amendments, and does not spell out the rules by which state legislatures will ratify such amendments. In *Coleman*, the Court essentially decided that it would leave a host of such unanswered questions to the two elected, or "political," branches.

In reading *Coleman* it is important to recognize that the constitutional amending process serves as a potential check on the judiciary as well as the two elected branches. To date, at least four amendments have reversed Supreme Court decisions. The Eleventh Amendment overruled the decision in *Chisholm v. Georgia* (2 U.S. 49, 1793) that had extended judicial jurisdiction to suits that out-of-state citizens initiated against the states. The Fourteenth Amendment overturned the decision in *Dred Scott v. Sandford* (60 U.S. 393, 1857) which had declared that blacks were not, and could not be, U.S. citizens. The Sixteenth Amendment overruled the decision in *Pollock v. Farmers' Loan & Trust Co.* (158 U.S. 601, 1895), which had invalidated the national income tax, and the Twenty-sixth Amendment subsequently invalidated a decision in *Oregon v. Mitchell* (400 U.S. 112, 1971), which had limited the ability of Congress to extend the right to vote in state and local elections to individuals from eighteen to twenty-one years old.

In contrast to *Coleman v. Miller*, in *Baker v. Carr* (369 U.S. 186, 1962) the Court decided that it would no longer consider the question of state legislative apportionment to be a political question. In an exhaustive review of prior political questions cases, Justice William J. Brennan, Jr. declared that such cases involved review of the actions of coordinate political branches rather than the review of state matters. The six criteria that Brennan articulated largely continue to guide existing understandings of the subject.

In *Powell v. McCormack* (395 U.S. 486, 1968), the Court had to decide whether Congress could exclude a duly-elected member of the House of Representatives who met the age, citizenship, and residence requirements that the Constitution outlined. Its answer arguably later shaped the Senate's action in 2009 accepting the decision by Illinois Governor Rod Blagojevich, who was under indictment and would soon be impeached and removed from office for attempting to sell a Senate seat, to appoint Roland Burris to replace President-elect Barack Obama.

The Extent of Judicial Remedies

Few cases have been more earth-shaking, or required more follow-up decisions, than the Supreme Court's historic decision in *Brown v. Board of Education* (1954), which reversed decades of legalized de jure racial segregation in schools and in other institutions. As the reading from *Cooper v. Aaron* demonstrated, the Court was sometimes met not only with foot-dragging on the part of state and local officials but also with outright defiance. While leaving primary authority for implementing desegregation to local authorities, the Supreme Court maintained a role for federal courts in overseeing this process. The case of *Missouri v. Jenkins* (515 U.S. 70, 1995), which arose more than forty years after the original *Brown* decision, demonstrates both how long courts can continue to face issues that their prior decisions have generated and the limits that might constrain such enforcement. Critics of the lower courts were especially concerned about the manner in which these courts had mandated expenditures given the role that legislatures traditionally play on such matters. Although this case deals with desegregation, it raises issues similar to other cases in which courts have ordered massive changes in education, prison, or mental health facilities.

A Special Note on Briefing Cases and Preparing for Classes

Students of constitutional law can develop no more important skill than that of briefing a case. Like an outline, a brief is designed to highlight the essential elements of a case not only for present understanding but also for future reference and study. Although some professors may stress one or another element they want to emphasize (teachers of first-year classes in law school, for example, almost always emphasize lower court decisions that lead to cases), most agree on the essentials. A typical brief includes:

The Name and Date of the Case (*Note*: Individuals who are briefing cases for term papers will also want to include a citation here.)

Facts: A succinct statement of the parties and the conflict that has brought them together. It is often useful to include a record of what transpired in the lower courts here. In casebooks, essential information is often summarized in the head notes to the case, which this text sets apart in italics.

Issue: A question or set of questions, stated as questions, that the Court is attempting to answer in this case. In appellate cases, like most before the U.S. Supreme Court, students will seek to identify the legal principle or principles that, if not reversed, will govern other cases when the same issue arises.

Reasoning: An outline of the Court's central arguments. Briefs usually include the name of the justice who writes the majority opinion and the specific vote. This part of the brief often focuses on the method or methods of interpretation that justices utilize in coming to their decisions. These may include arguments from the language of the Constitution or the statute in question, arguments from the intent of those who wrote or ratified the Constitution; analysis of historical precedents, especially previous court decision; appeals to the "spirit" of the Constitution or to factors, like the nation's increasing diversity, that might call earlier understandings into question; etc.

Other Opinions: A brief outline of concurrences and dissents and a note of the justices who wrote them.

Special Notes: Although not obligatory for all cases, students can use these to indicate facts of special significance about the case and/or subsequent actions in later cases.

The best way in which students can typically gauge their understanding of cases prior to the first test is to read and brief cases prior to class and then compare the class discussion with what they have recorded. Professors of constitutional law will typically tailor their own questions to highlight the elements of a brief. They commonly begin by asking students to describe the facts and identify the central issue or issues before asking about the Court's reasoning. Students who read the chapter introductions, the head notes of a case, or consult a published brief or a brief written by another student might be able to "fake" sufficient knowledge for class discussion but will rarely get the same benefits as if they had read and outlined the cases for themselves. Many professors require students to turn in written briefs prior to class.

NOTE

Students interested in learning this format should consult John R. Vile, *Summaries of Leading Cases on the Constitution*, 16th ed. (Lanham, MD: Rowman & Littlefield, 2014).

SELECTIONS FROM THE JUDICIARY ACT OF 1789

1 Stat. 73

When the Congress of the United States assembled for its first session under the new Constitution in April of 1789, one of the first matters it acted upon was the implementation of Article III of the Constitution, which had left a great deal to the discretion of Congress in determining judicial organization and procedures. Oliver Ellsworth, a delegate from Connecticut who had participated in the Constitutional Convention of 1787, was particularly prominent in writing the Judiciary Act of 1789. Many provisions are still in force with only minor modifications. The act set the Supreme Court at six members and established two grades of inferior courts: circuit and district. The law provided for the removal of cases from state to federal courts of original jurisdiction, and for appeals through the hierarchy of federal courts, and from state courts of last resort to the Supreme Court of the United States.

CHAP. XX.—*An Act to establish the Judicial Courts of the United States.*

SECTION 1. *Be it enacted by the Senate and House of Representatives of the United States of America in Congress assembled*, That the supreme court of the United States shall consist of a chief justice and five associate justices, any four of whom shall be a quorum, and shall hold annually at the seat of government two sessions, the one commencing the first Monday of February, and the other the first Monday of August. That the associate justices shall have precedence according to the date of their commissions, or when the commissions of two or more of them bear date on the same day, according to their respective ages.

SEC. 2. *And be it further enacted*, That the United States shall be, and they hereby are divided into thirteen districts . . .

SEC. 3. *And be it further enacted*, That there be a court called a District Court, in each of the afore mentioned districts, to consist of one judge, who shall reside in the district for which he is appointed, and shall be called a District Judge . . .

SEC. 4. *And be it further enacted*, That the before mentioned districts, except those of Maine and Kentucky, shall be divided into three circuits, and be called the eastern, the middle, and the southern circuit . . . and that there shall be held annually in each district of said circuits, two courts, which shall be called Circuit Courts, and shall consist of any two justices of the Supreme Court, and the district judge of such districts, any two of whom shall constitute a quorum: *Provided*, That no district judge shall give a vote in any case of appeal or error from his own decision; but may assign the reasons of such his decision.

SEC. 13. *And be it further enacted*, That the Supreme Court shall have exclusive jurisdiction of all controversies of a civil nature, where a state is a party, except between a state and its citizens; and except also between a state and citizens of other states, or aliens, in which latter case it shall have original but not exclusive jurisdiction. And shall have exclusively all such jurisdiction of suits or proceedings against ambassadors, or other public ministers, or their domestics, or domestic servants, as a court of law can have or exercise consistently with the law of nations; and original, but not exclusive jurisdiction of all suits brought by ambassadors, or other public ministers, or in which a consul, or vice consul, shall be a party. And the trial of issues in fact in the Supreme Court, in all actions at law against citizens of the United States, shall be by jury. The Supreme Court shall also have appellate jurisdiction from the circuit courts and courts of the several states, in the cases herein after specially provided for; and shall have power to issue writs of prohibition to the district courts, when proceeding as courts of admiralty and maritime jurisdiction, and writs of *mandamus*, in cases warranted by the principles and usages of law, to any courts appointed, or persons holding office, under the authority of the United States.

SEC. 25. *And be it further enacted*, That a final judgment or decree in any suit, in the highest court of law or equity of a State in which a decision in the suit could be had, where is drawn in question the validity of a treaty or statute of, or an authority exercised under the United States, and the decision is against their validity; or where is drawn in question the validity of a statute of, or an authority exercised under any State, on the ground of their being repugnant to the constitution, treaties or laws of the United States, and the decision is in favour of such their validity, or where is drawn in question the construction of any clause of the constitution, or of a treaty, or statute of, or commission held under the United States, and the decision is against the title, right, privilege or exemption specially set up or claimed by either party, under such clause of the said Constitution, treaty, statute or commission, may be re-examined and reversed or affirmed in the Supreme Court of the United States upon a writ of error, the citation being signed by the chief justice, or judge or chancellor of the court rendering or passing the judgment or decree complained of, or by a justice of the Supreme Court of the United States, in the same manner and under the same regulations, and the writ shall have the same effect, as if the judgment or decree complained of had been rendered or passed in a circuit court, and the proceeding upon the reversal shall also be the same, except that the Supreme Court, instead of remanding the cause for a final decision as before provided, may at their discretion, if the cause shall have been once remanded before, proceed to a final decision of the same, and award execution. But no other error shall be assigned or regarded as a ground of reversal in any such case as aforesaid, than such as appears on the face of the record, and immediately respects the before mentioned questions of validity or construction of the said constitution, treaties, statutes, commissions, or authorities in dispute.

FOR DISCUSSION

The Constitution left open both the specific organization of lower courts and the question of how many judges should sit on the Supreme Court. Why do you think it did so? What would have been the advantages and disadvantages of settling these issues in the Constitution itself?

FEDERALIST NO. 78

Written during the U.S. Constitution's confirmation debates, this essay is Alexander Hamilton's classic defense of judicial review against Anti-Federalist critics who feared that it would elevate unelected judges over the people. Students will want to keep Hamilton's arguments in mind as they read *Marbury v. Madison* and subsequent cases that justify or exercise judicial review over legislation.

According to the plan of the convention, all judges who may be appointed by the United States are to hold their offices during good behavior; which is conformable to the most approved of the State constitutions and among the rest, to that of this State. Its propriety having been drawn into question by the adversaries of that plan, is no light symptom of the rage for objection, which disorders their imaginations and judgments. The standard of good behavior for the continuance in office of the judicial magistracy, is certainly one of the most valuable of the modern improvements in the practice of government. In a monarchy it is an excellent barrier to the despotism of the prince; in a republic it is a no less excellent barrier to the encroachments and oppressions of the representative body. And it is the best expedient which can be devised in any government, to secure a steady, upright, and impartial administration of the laws. Whoever attentively considers the different departments of power must perceive, that, in a government in which they are separated from each other, the judiciary, from the nature of its functions, will always be the least dangerous to the political rights of the Constitution; because it will be least in a capacity to annoy or injure them. The Executive not only dispenses the honors, but holds the sword of the community. The legislature not only commands the purse, but prescribes the rules by which the duties and rights of every citizen are to be regulated. The judiciary, on the contrary, has no influence over either the sword or the purse; no direction either of the strength or of the wealth of the society; and can take no active resolution whatever. It may truly be said to have neither FORCE nor WILL, but merely judgment; and must ultimately depend upon the aid of the executive arm even for the efficacy of its judgments.

This simple view of the matter suggests several important consequences. It proves incontestably, that the judiciary is beyond comparison the weakest of the three departments of power; that it can never attack with success either of the other two; and that all possible care is requisite to enable it to defend itself against their attacks. It equally proves, that though individual oppression may now and then proceed from the courts of justice, the general liberty of the people can never be endangered from that quarter; I mean so long as the judiciary remains truly distinct from both the legislature and the Executive. For I agree, that "there is no liberty, if the power of judging be not separated from the legislative and executive powers." And it proves, in the last place, that as liberty can have nothing to fear from the judiciary alone, but would have every thing to fear from its union with either of the other departments; that as all the effects of such a union must ensue from a dependence of the former on the latter, notwithstanding a nominal and apparent separation; that as, from the natural feebleness of the judiciary, it is in continual jeopardy of being overpowered, awed, or influenced by its co-ordinate branches; and that as nothing can contribute so much to its firmness and independence as permanency in office, this quality may therefore be justly regarded as an indispensable ingredient in its constitution, and, in a great measure, as the citadel of the public justice and the public security. The complete independence of the courts of justice is peculiarly essential in a limited Constitution. By a limited Constitution, I understand one which contains certain specified exceptions to the legislative authority; such, for instance, as that it shall pass no bills of attainder, no ex post facto laws, and the like. Limitations of this kind can be preserved in practice no other way than through the medium of courts of justice, whose duty it must be to declare all acts contrary to the manifest tenor of the Constitution void. Without this, all the reservations of particular rights or privileges would amount to nothing.

Some perplexity respecting the rights of the courts to pronounce legislative acts void, because contrary to the Constitution, has arisen from an imagination that the doctrine would imply a superiority of the judiciary to the legislative power. It is urged that the authority which can declare the acts of another void, must necessarily be superior to the one whose acts may be declared void. As this doctrine is of great importance in all the American constitutions, a brief discussion of the ground on which it rests cannot be unacceptable.

There is no position which depends on clearer principles, than that every act of a delegated authority, contrary to the tenor of the commission under which it is exercised, is void. No legislative act, therefore, contrary to the Constitution, can be valid. To deny this, would be to affirm, that the deputy is greater than his principal; that the servant is above his master; that the representatives of the people are superior to the people themselves; that men acting by virtue of powers, may do not only what their powers do not authorize, but what they forbid.

If it be said that the legislative body are themselves the constitutional judges of their own powers, and that the construction they put upon them is conclusive upon the other departments, it may be answered, that this cannot be the natural presumption, where it is not to be collected from any particular provisions in the Constitution. It is not otherwise to be supposed, that the Constitution could intend to enable the representatives of the people to substitute their will to that of their constituents. It is far more rational to suppose, that the courts were designed to be an intermediate body between the people and the legislature, in order, among other things, to keep the latter within the limits assigned to their authority. The interpretation of the laws is the proper and peculiar province of the courts. A constitution is, in fact, and must be regarded by the judges, as a fundamental law. It therefore belongs to them to ascertain its meaning, as well as the meaning of any particular act proceeding from the legislative body. If there should happen to be an irreconcilable variance between the two, that which has the superior obligation and validity ought, of course, to be preferred; or, in other words, the Constitution ought to be preferred to the statute, the intention of the people to the intention of their agents.

Nor does this conclusion by any means suppose a superiority of the judicial to the legislative power. It only supposes that the power of the people is superior to both; and that where the will of the legislature, declared in its statutes, stands in opposition to that of the people, declared in the Constitution, the judges ought to be governed by the latter rather than the former. They ought to regulate their decisions by the fundamental laws, rather than by those which are not fundamental. . . .

If, then, the courts of justice are to be considered as the bulwarks of a limited Constitution against legislative encroachments, this consideration will afford a strong argument for the permanent tenure of judicial offices, since nothing will contribute so much as this to that independent spirit in the judges which must be essential to the faithful performance of so arduous a duty.

This independence of the judges is equally requisite to guard the Constitution and the rights of individuals from the effects of those ill humors, which the arts of designing men, or the influence of particular conjunctures, sometimes disseminate among the people themselves, and which, though they speedily give place to better information, and more deliberate reflection, have a tendency, in the meantime, to occasion dangerous innovations in the government, and serious oppressions of the minor party in the community. Though I trust the friends of the proposed Constitution will never concur with its enemies, in questioning that fundamental principle of republican government, which admits the right of the people to alter or abolish the established Constitution, whenever they find it inconsistent with their happiness, yet it is not to be inferred from this principle, that the representatives of the people, whenever a momentary inclination happens to lay hold of a majority of their constituents, incompatible with the provisions in the existing Constitution, would, on that account, be justifiable in a violation of those provisions; or that the courts would be under a greater obligation to connive at infractions in this shape, than when they had proceeded wholly from the cabals of the representative body. Until the people have, by some solemn and authoritative act, annulled or changed the established form, it is binding upon themselves collectively, as well as individually; and no presumption, or even knowledge, of their sentiments, can warrant their representatives in a departure from it, prior to such an act. But it is easy to see, that it would require an uncommon portion of fortitude in the judges to do their duty as faithful guardians of the Constitution, where legislative invasions of it had been instigated by the major voice of the community.

But it is not with a view to infractions of the Constitution only, that the independence of the judges may be an essential safeguard against the effects of occasional ill humors in the society. These sometimes extend no farther than to the injury of the private rights of particular classes of citizens, by unjust and partial laws. Here also the firmness of the judicial magistracy is of vast importance in mitigating the severity and confining the operation of such laws. It not only serves to moderate the immediate mischiefs of those which may have been passed, but it operates as a check upon the legislative body in passing them; who, perceiving that obstacles to the success of iniquitous intention are to be expected from the scruples of the courts, are in a manner compelled, by the very motives of the injustice they meditate, to qualify their attempts. . . .

There is yet a further and a weightier reason for the permanency of the judicial offices, which is deducible from the nature of the qualifications they require. It has been frequently remarked, with great propriety, that a voluminous code of laws is one of the inconveniences necessarily connected with the advantages of a free government. To avoid an arbitrary discretion in the courts, it is indispensable that they should be bound down by strict rules and precedents, which serve to define and point out their duty in every particular case that comes before them; and it will readily be conceived from the variety of controversies which grow out of the folly and wickedness of mankind, that the records of those precedents must unavoidably swell to a very considerable bulk, and must demand long and laborious study to acquire a competent knowledge of them. Hence it is, that there can be but few men in the society who will have sufficient skill in the laws to qualify them for the stations of judges. And making the proper deductions for the ordinary depravity of human nature, the number must be still smaller of those who unite the requisite integrity with the requisite knowledge. These considerations apprise us, that the government can have no great option between fit character; and that a temporary duration in office, which would naturally discourage such characters from quitting a lucrative line of practice to accept a seat on the bench, would have a tendency to throw the administration of justice into hands less able, and less well qualified, to conduct it with utility and dignity. . . .

FOR DISCUSSION

Hamilton was arguably far more comfortable with the exercise of judicial review than was his primary co-author, James Madison. Whereas Hamilton often portrayed the judiciary as the primary interpreter of the Constitution,

Madison, and other Democratic-Republicans, tended to emphasize the equality of each of the branches. Do you think it is possible to square such an understanding with the exercise of judicial review of congressional legislation or executive actions?

Article III, Sec. 2, para. 2:

In all Cases affecting Ambassadors, other public Ministers and Consuls, and those in which a State shall be Party, the supreme Court shall have original Jurisdiction. In all the other Cases before mentioned, the supreme Court shall have appellate Jurisdiction, both as to Law and Fact, with such Exceptions, and under such Regulations as the Congress shall make.

MARBURY V. MADISON

1 Cr. 137, 2 L.Ed. 60 (1803)

Under provisions of the Judiciary Act of 1801, President Adams signed a commission for William Marbury to serve as a Justice of the Peace for Washington, D.C. John Marshall, serving both as secretary of state and as chief justice under Adams (by today's standards he would have to step aside, or **recuse**, himself in such situations), had sealed but not delivered Marbury's commission, which James Madison, Secretary of State under Jefferson, had refused to deliver. The Judiciary Act of 1789, Section 13, had empowered the Supreme Court to issue **writs of mandamus** "to any courts appointed or persons holding office, under the authority of the United States." Marbury filed suit with the Supreme Court, requesting it to issue a writ of mandamus to compel Madison to deliver the commission. As Federalists, the members of the Marshall Court were undoubtedly sympathetic to Marbury, but they recognized that President Jefferson might well call the Court's hand by defying any order that it issued demanding that Madison deliver Marbury's commission. The Court concentrated on establishing the more important power of judicial review rather than providing what it considered to be justice for Marbury.

Vote: Unanimous

CHIEF JUSTICE MARSHALL for the Court.

[Marshall divided the case into three questions.]

1st. Has the applicant a right to the commission he demands? [Marshall argued that the commission became official when it was signed and sealed.]

2dly. If he has a right, and that right has been violated, do the laws of his country afford him a remedy? [Marshall cited Section 13 of the Judiciary Act of 1789 as providing for the Court to issue a writ of mandamus.]

3dly. If they do afford him a remedy, is it a mandamus issuing from this court?

Whether it can issue from this court.

The act to establish the judicial courts of the United States authorizes the Supreme Court "to issue writs of mandamus in cases warranted by the principles and usages of law, to any courts appointed, or persons holding office, under the authority of the United States."

The Secretary of State, being a person holding an office under the authority of the United States, is precisely within the letter of the description, and if this court is not authorized to issue a writ of mandamus to such an officer, it must be because the law is unconstitutional, therefore absolutely incapable of conferring the authority, and assigning the duties which its words purport to confer and assign.

The Constitution vests the whole judicial power of the United States in one Supreme Court, and such inferior courts as Congress shall, from time to time, ordain and establish. This power is expressly extended to all cases arising under the laws of the United States. And, consequently, in some form, it may be exercised over the present case, because the right claimed is given by a law of the United States.

In the distribution of this power it is declared that "the Supreme Court shall have original jurisdiction in all cases affecting ambassadors, other public ministers and consuls, and those in which a state shall be a party. In all other cases, the Supreme Court shall have appellate jurisdiction."

It has been insisted, at the bar, that as the original grant of jurisdiction, to the supreme and inferior courts, is general, and the clause, assigning original jurisdiction to the Supreme Court, contains no negative or restrictive words, the power remains to the legislature to assign original jurisdiction to that court in other cases than those specified in the article which has been recited, provided those cases belong to the judicial power of the United States.

If intended to leave it in the discretion of the legislature to apportion the judicial power between the supreme and inferior courts according to the will of that body, it would certainly have been useless to have proceeded further than to have defined the judicial power, and the tribunals in which it should be vested. The subsequent part of the section is mere surplusage, is entirely without meaning, if such is to be the construction. If Congress remains at liberty to give this court . . . original jurisdiction, where the Constitution has declared it shall be appellate, the distribution of jurisdiction, made in the Constitution, is form without substance.

Affirmative words are often, in their operation, negative of other objects than those affirmed; in this case, a negative or exclusive sense must be given to them, or they have no operation at all.

It cannot be presumed that any clause in the Constitution is intended to be without effect; and, therefore, such a construction is inadmissible, unless the words require it. . . .

To enable this court, then, to issue a mandamus, it must be shown to be an exercise of appellate jurisdiction, or to be necessary to enable them to exercise appellate jurisdiction.

It has been stated at the bar that the appellate jurisdiction may be exercised in a variety of forms, and that if it be the will of the legislature that a mandamus should be used for that purpose that will must be obeyed. This is true, yet the jurisdiction must be appellate, not original.

It is the essential criterion of appellate jurisdiction, that it revises and corrects the proceedings in a cause already instituted, and does not create that cause. Although, therefore, a mandamus may be directed to courts, yet to issue such a writ to an officer for the delivery of a paper, is in effect the same as to sustain an original action for that paper, and, therefore, seems not to belong to appellate, but to original jurisdiction. Neither is it necessary, in such a case as this, to enable the court to exercise its appellate jurisdiction.

The authority, therefore, given to the Supreme Court, by the act establishing the judicial courts of the United States, to issue writs of mandamus to public officers, appears not to be warranted by the Constitution; and it becomes necessary to inquire whether a jurisdiction so conferred can be exercised.

The question, whether an act, repugnant to the Constitution, can become the law of the land, is a question deeply interesting to the United States; but, happily, not of an intricacy proportioned to its interest. It seems only necessary to recognize certain principles, supposed to have been long and well established, to decide it.

That the people have an original right to establish, for their future government, such principles, as, in their opinion, shall most conduce to their own happiness is the basis on which the whole American fabric has been erected. The exercise of this original right is a very great exertion; nor can it be, nor ought it to be, frequently repeated. The principles, therefore, so established, are deemed fundamental.

And as the authority from which they proceed is supreme, and can seldom act, they are designed to be permanent.

This original and supreme will organizes the government, and assigns to different departments their respective powers. A government may either stop here, or establish certain limits not to be transcended by those departments.

The government of the United States undertakes the latter. The powers of the legislature are defined and limited; and that those limits may not be mistaken, or forgotten, the Constitution is written. To what purpose are powers limited, and to what purpose is that limitation committed to writing, if these limits may, at any time, be passed by those intended to be restrained? The distinction between a government with limited and unlimited powers is abolished if those limits do not confine the persons on whom they are imposed, and if acts prohibited and acts allowed are of equal obligation. It is a proposition too plain to be contested, that the Constitution controls any legislative act repugnant to it, or that the legislature may alter the Constitution by an ordinary act.

Between these alternatives there is no middle ground. The Constitution is either a superior paramount law, unchangeable by ordinary means, or it is on a level with ordinary legislative acts, and, like other acts, is alterable when the legislature shall please to alter it.

If the former part of the alternative be true, then a legislative act contrary to the Constitution is not law; if the latter part be true, then written constitutions are absurd attempts, on the part of the people, to limit a power in its own nature illimitable.

Certainly all those who have framed written constitutions contemplate them as forming the fundamental and paramount law of the nation. Consequently, the theory of every such government must be that an act of the legislature repugnant to the constitution, is void.

This theory is essentially attached to a written constitution, and is, as a result, to be considered by this court as one of the fundamental principles of our society. It is not therefore to be lost sight of in the further consideration of this subject.

If an act of the legislature, repugnant to the Constitution, is void, . . . does it constitute a rule as operative as if it was a law? This would be to overthrow in fact what was established in theory, and would seem, at first view, an absurdity too gross to be insisted on. It shall, however, receive a more attentive consideration.

It is emphatically the province and duty of the judicial department to say what the law is. Those who apply the rule to particular cases, must of necessity expound and interpret that rule. If two laws conflict with each other, the courts must decide on the operation of each.

So if a law be in opposition to the Constitution—if both the law and the Constitution apply to a particular case, so that the court must either decide that case conformably to the law, disregarding the Constitution, or decide conformably to the Constitution, disregarding the law—the court must determine which of these conflicting rules governs the case. This is of the very essence of judicial duty.

If the courts are to regard the Constitution as superior to any ordinary act of the legislature, then the Constitution, and not such ordinary act, must govern the case to which they both apply.

Those, therefore, who controvert the principle that the Constitution is to be considered, in court, as a paramount law, are reduced to the necessity of maintaining that courts must close their eyes to the Constitution, and see only the law. . . .

From these, and many other selections which might be made, it is apparent that the framers of the Constitution contemplated this instrument as a rule for the government of the courts, as well as of the legislature.

Why otherwise does it direct the judges to take an oath to support it? This oath certainly applies in an especial manner to their conduct in their official character. How immoral to impose it on them, if they were to be used as the instruments, and the knowing instruments, for violating what they swear to support! . . .

It is also not entirely unworthy of observation that, in declaring what shall be the supreme law of the land, the Constitution itself is first mentioned; not the laws of the United States generally, but those only which shall be made in pursuance of the Constitution, have first rank.

Thus, the particular phraseology of the Constitution of the United States confirms and strengthens the principle, supposed to be essential to all written constitutions, that a law repugnant to the Constitution is void, and that courts, as well as other departments, are bound by that instrument.

The rule must be discharged.

FOR DISCUSSION

How do Marshall's arguments in *Marbury* compare to Hamilton's arguments in *Federalist* No. 78? Did Marshall succeed in establishing that courts should have the final word on the constitutionality of legislation, or did he merely establish that each branch should review the constitutionality of matters that come before it?

RELATED CASES

***Holmes v. Walton:* New Jersey (1780).**

(No written record of this opinion has been found. It is conjectured that it was delivered orally. American Historical Review, IV, 459.)

The Court ruled that a six-person jury in a criminal case was contrary to the New Jersey Constitution of 1776 and that the state statute authorizing such a jury was void. It appears that the state supreme court reversed the trial court's decision for other reasons also.

***Trevett v. Weeden:* Rhode Island (1786).**

The state supreme court of Rhode Island held void, under the property guarantees of the state constitution, a state statute requiring that paper money be accepted as legal tender and providing for trials without jury.

***Bayard v. Singleton:* 1 Martin 42: I N.C. 5 (1787).**

Declared void was an act of 1785 that confirmed the property titles of persons who had purchased land that had been confiscated from the Tories during the Revolution. The North Carolina Supreme Court held that "every citizen had undoubtedly a right to a decision of his property by trial by jury."

***Ware v. Hylton:* 3 Dall. 199 (1796).**

The Jay Treaty of Peace with England (1794) was held to void a statute of Virginia as to debts owed by American citizens to British subjects. This was a retroactive interpretation. The treaty had provided that there be no impediments on debts. There is no dual federalism in foreign relations.

Martin v. Hunter's Lessee: **1 Wheat. 304 (1816).**

The Constitution (in order to bring uniformity into our jurisprudence) extends the appellate jurisdiction of the Supreme Court to cases in state courts that involve the Constitution, laws, and treaties of the United States. Here a right based on Jay's Treaty of 1794 was upheld even though incompatible with Virginia law.

Dred Scott v. Sandford: **19 How. 393 (1857).**

Although blacks could be state citizens, they could not become citizens of the United States. The Missouri Compromise of 1820, which had attempted to outlaw slavery in certain territories of the United States, was an unconstitutional violation of the due process clause of the Fifth Amendment because it attempted to deprive slaveholders of their property in slaves simply because they sought to move to a particular area. As noncitizens, individuals of African descent did not have the right to bring suit in federal courts.

NOTE

The Fourteenth Amendment (1868) overturned this decision by declaring that all persons born or naturalized in the United States are citizens thereof.

EAKIN V. RAUB

12 Serg. & Rawle 330 (1825)

Federalist No. 78, the Judiciary Act of 1789, and *Marbury v. Madison* are impressive authorities, and yet the justifications for judicial review did not go unchallenged by those who recognized that such review could be utilized for partisan purposes and in opposition to democratically enacted policies. Although Chief Justice William Tilghman repeated commonplace arguments on behalf of judicial review in this Pennsylvania case involving the right of a state to pass legislation limiting the time during which individuals could eject others from their lands, Justice John Gibson's contrarian dissent, which focused on judicial review at the state, rather than at the national level, indicates that not everyone was persuaded by Marshall's arguments in *Marbury v. Madison* (5 U.S. (1 Cranch) 137, 1803). Although Gibson's opinion never had the force of law, and he would himself later capitulate as to the necessity for judicial review, scholars continue to ponder his arguments. Although they established no precedent, they continue to point to some of the difficulties that judicial review presents and thus affirm that democratic systems might find other alternatives by which to accomplish the objects that such review serves in the United States.

But it is said, that . . . the . . . act would be unconstitutional; and, instead of controverting this, I will avail myself of it to express an opinion which I have deliberately formed, on the abstract right of the judiciary to declare an unconstitutional act of the legislature void.

It seems to me there is a plain difference, hitherto unnoticed, between acts that are repugnant to the constitution of the particular state, and acts that are repugnant to the constitution of the *United States*; my opinion being, that the judiciary is bound to execute the former, but not the latter. I shall hereafter attempt to explain this difference, by pointing out the particular provisions in the constitution of the *United States* on which it depends. I am aware, that a right to declare all unconstitutional acts void, without distinction as to either constitution, is generally held as a professional dogma; but, I apprehend rather as a matter of faith than of reason. I admit that I once embraced the same doctrine, but without examination, and I shall therefore state the arguments that impelled me to abandon it, with great respect for those by whom it is still maintained. But I may premise, that it is not a little remarkable, that although the right in question has all along been claimed by the judiciary, no judge has ventured to discuss it, except Chief Justice Marshall, and if the argument of a jurist so distinguished for the strength of his ratiocinative powers to be found inconclusive, it may fairly be set down to the weakness of the position which he attempts to defend. . . .

The constitution of *Pennsylvania* contains no express grant of political powers to the judiciary. But, to establish a grant by implication, the constitution is said to be a law of superior obligation; and, consequently, that if it were to come into collision with an act of the legislature, the latter would have to give way. This is conceded. But it is a fallacy, to suppose that they can come into collision *before the judiciary*.

The constitution and the *right* of the legislature to pass the act, may be in collision. But is that a legitimate subject for judicial determination? If it be, the judiciary must be a peculiar organ, to revise the proceedings of the legislature, and to correct its mistakes; and in what part of the constitution are we to look for this proud pre-eminence? Viewing the matter in the opposite direction, what would be thought of an act of assembly in which it should be declared that the Supreme Court had, in a particular case, put a wrong construction on the constitution of the *United States*, and that the judgment should therefore be reversed? It would doubtless be thought a usurpation of judicial power. But it is by no means clear, that to declare a law void which has been enacted according to the forms prescribed in the constitution, is not a usurpation of legislative power. It is an act of sovereignty; and sovereignty and legislative power are said by Sir William *Blackstone* to be convertible terms. It is the business of the judiciary to interpret the laws, not scan the authority of the lawgiver; and without the latter, it cannot take cognizance of a collision between a law and the constitution. So that to affirm that the judiciary has a right to judge of the existence of such collision, is to take for granted the very thing to be proved. And, that a very cogent argument may be made in this way, I am not disposed to deny; for no conclusions are so strong as those that are drawn from the *petitio principii*.

But it has been said to be emphatically the business of the judiciary, to ascertain and pronounce what the law is; and that this necessarily involves a consideration of the constitution. It does so: but how far? If the judiciary will inquire into any thing beside the form of enactment, where shall it stop? There must be some point of limitation to such an inquiry; for no one will pretend, that a judge would be justifiable in calling for the election returns, or scrutinizing the qualifications of those who composed the legislature.

It is next supposed, that as the members of the legislature have no inherent right of legislation, but derive their authority from the people, no law can be valid where authority to pass it, is either simply not given or positively withheld. But it will not be pretended, that the legislature has not at least an equal right with the judiciary to put a construction on the constitution; nor that either of them is infallible; nor that either ought to be required to surrender its judgment to the other.

But suppose all to be of equal capacity in every respect, why should one exercise a controlling power over the rest? That the judiciary is of superior rank, has never been pretended, although it has been said to be co-ordinate. It is not easy, however, to comprehend how the power which gives law to all the rest, can be of no more than equal rank with one which receives it, and is answerable to the former for the observance of its statutes.

Every one knows how seldom men think exactly alike on ordinary subjects; and a government constructed on the principle of assent by all its parts, would be inadequate to the most simple operations. The notion of a complication of counter checks has been carried to an extent in theory, of which the framers of the constitution never dreamt. When the entire sovereignty was separated into its elementary parts, and distributed to the appropriate branches, all things incident to the exercise of its powers were committed to each branch exclusively. The negative which each part of the legislature may exercise, in regard to the acts of the other, was thought sufficient to prevent material infractions of the restraints which were put on the power of the whole; for, had it been intended to interpose the judiciary as an additional barrier, the matter would surely not have been left in doubt. The judges would not have been left to stand on the insecure and ever shifting ground of public opinion as to constructive powers: they would have been placed on the impregnable ground of an express grant.

But the judges are sworn to support the constitution, and are they not bound by it as the law of the land? In some respects they are. In the very few cases in which the judiciary, and not the legislature, is the immediate organ to execute its provisions, they are bound by it in preference to any act of assembly to the contrary. In such cases, the constitution is a rule to the courts. But what I have in view in this inquiry, is the supposed right of the judiciary, to interfere, in cases where the constitution is to be carried into effect through the instrumentality of the legislature, and where that organ must necessarily first decide on the constitutionality of its own act. The oath to support the constitution is not peculiar to the judges, but is taken indiscriminately by every officer of the government, and is designed rather as a test of the political principles of the man, than to bind the officer in the discharge of his duty: otherwise it were difficult to determine what operation it is to have in the case of a recorder of deeds, for instance, who, in the execution of his office, has nothing to do with the constitution. But granting it to relate to the official conduct of the judge, as well as every other officer, and not to his political principles, still it must be understood in reference to supporting the constitution, *only as far as that may be involved in his official duty*; and, consequently, if his official duty does not comprehend an inquiry into the authority of the legislature, neither does his oath.

But it has been said, that this construction would deprive the citizen of the advantages which are peculiar to a written constitution, by at once declaring the power of the legislature, in practice, to be illimitable. I ask, what are those advantages? The principles of a written constitution are more fixed and certain, and more apparent to the apprehension of the people, than principles which depend on tradition and the vague comprehension of the individuals who compose the nation, and who cannot all be expected to receive the same impressions or entertain the same notions on any given subject. But there is no magic or inherent power in parchment and ink, to command respect and protect principles from violation. In the business of government, a recurrence to first principles answers the end of an observation at sea with a view to correct the dead reckoning; and, for this purpose, a written constitution is an instrument of inestimable value. It is of inestimable value, also, in rendering its principles familiar to the mass of the people; for, after all, there is no effectual guard against legislative usurpation but public opinion, the force of which, in this country, is inconceivably great. Happily this is proved, by experience, to be a sufficient guard against palpable infractions. The constitution of this state has withstood the shocks of strong party excitement for thirty years, during which no act of the legislature has been declared unconstitutional, although the judiciary has constantly asserted a right to do so in clear cases. But it would be absurd to say, that this remarkable observance of the constitution has been produced, not by the responsibility of the legislature to the people, but by an apprehension of control by the judiciary. Once let public opinion be so corrupt as to sanction every misconstruction of the constitution and abuse of power which the temptation of the moment may dictate, and the party which may happen to be predominant, will laugh at the puny efforts of a dependent power to arrest it in its course.

For these reasons, I am of opinion that it rests with the people, in whom full and absolute sovereign power resides to correct abuses in legislation, by instructing their representatives to repeal the obnoxious act. What is wanting to plenary power in the government, is reserved by the people for their own immediate use; and to redress an infringement of their rights in this respect, would seem to be an accessory of the power thus reserved. It might, perhaps, have been better to vest the power in the judiciary; as it might be expected that its habits of deliberation, and the aid derived from the arguments of counsel, would more frequently lead to accurate conclusions. On the other hand, the judiciary is not infallible; and an error by it would admit of no remedy but a more distinct expression of the public will, through the extraordinary medium of a convention; whereas, an error by the legislature admits of a remedy by an exertion of the same will, in the ordinary exercise of the right of suffrage—a mode better calculated to attain the end, without popular excitement. It may be said, the people would probably not notice an error of their representatives. But they would as probably do so, as notice an error of the judiciary; and, beside, it is a *postulate* in the theory of our government, and the very basis of the superstructure, that the people are wise, virtuous, and competent to manage their own affairs: and if they are not so, in fact, still every question of this sort must be determined according to the principles of the constitution, as it came from the hands of its framers, and the existence of a defect which was not foreseen, would not justify those who administer the government, in applying a corrective in practice, which can be provided only by a convention. But in regard to an act of assembly, which is found to be in collision with the constitution, laws, or treaties of the *United States*, I take the duty of the judiciary to be exactly the reverse. By becoming parties to the federal constitution, the states have agreed to several limitations of their individual sovereignty, to enforce which, it was thought to be absolutely necessary to prevent them from giving effect to laws in violation of those limitations, through the instrumentality of their own judges. Accordingly, it is declared in the fifth [sic] article and second section of the federal constitution, that "This constitution, and the laws of the *United States* which shall be made in pursuance thereof, and all treaties made, or which shall be made, under the authority of the *United States*, shall be the *supreme* law of the land; and the *judges* in every *state* shall be BOUND thereby; any thing in the *laws* or *constitution* of any *state* to the contrary notwithstanding."

This is an express grant of a political power, and it is conclusive to show that no law of inferior obligation, as every state law must necessarily be, can be executed at the expense of the constitution, laws, or treaties of the *United States*.

FOR DISCUSSION

One of the reasons that scholars like *Eakin v. Raub* so well is that Gibson specifically addresses the issues that John Marshall raised on behalf of judicial review. How does Gibson address the issue that such review is a necessary aspect of separation of powers and a written constitution? If judges are not to use the Constitution to invalidate laws, what benefit, if any, does he think such a written constitution has? What does Gibson think about the argument based on the judicial oath? What is his solution to unconstitutional legislation?

Article III, Sec. 2, para. 2:

In all Cases affecting Ambassadors, other public Ministers and Consuls, and those in which a State shall be Party, the supreme Court shall have original Jurisdiction. In all the other Cases before mentioned, the supreme Court shall have appellate Jurisdiction, both as to Law and Fact, with such Exceptions, and under such Regulations as the Congress shall make.

EX PARTE MCCARDLE

7 Wallace 506, 19 L. Ed. 264 (1869)

Article III of the Constitution grants the Supreme Court appellate jurisdiction "with such exceptions, and under such regulations as the Congress shall make." McCardle, a newspaper editor in the South, was held in custody by military authorities for trial by a federal military commission as provided by Reconstruction legislation. Since he was a civilian, McCardle challenged the jurisdiction of the commission. While the case was yet undecided, but after completion of oral argument in the Supreme Court, Congress repealed the statute under which the Court was exercising appellate jurisdiction. In doing this, Congress overrode President Andrew Johnson's veto.

Congress feared that the Court would void the Reconstruction Acts. The Court had heard oral argument in the case in February 1868, repeal of the 1867 statute came in March 1868, and this decision was handed down in April 1869.

Vote: 9–0

CHIEF JUSTICE CHASE delivered the opinion.

. . . The first question necessarily is that of jurisdiction; for, if the Act of March, 1868, takes away the jurisdiction defined by the Act of February, 1867, it is useless, if not improper, to enter into any discussion of other questions.

It is quite true, as was argued by the counsel for the petitioner, that the appellate jurisdiction of this court is not derived from Acts of Congress. It is, strictly speaking, conferred by the Constitution. But it is conferred "with such exceptions and under such regulations as Congress shall make." . . .

The exception to appellate jurisdiction in the case before US, however, is not an inference from the affirmation of other appellate jurisdiction. It is made in terms. The provision of the Act of 1867, affirming the appellate jurisdiction of this Court in cases of habeas corpus, is expressly repealed. It is hardly possible to imagine a plainer instance of positive exception.

We are not at liberty to inquire into the motives of the Legislature. We can only examine into its power under the Constitution; and the power to make exceptions to the appellate jurisdiction of this court is given by express words. What, then, is the effect of the repealing Act upon the case before us? We cannot doubt as to this. Without jurisdiction the court cannot proceed at all in any cause. Jurisdiction is power to declare the law, and when it ceases to exist, the only function remaining to the Court is that of announcing the fact and dismissing the cause. And this is not less clear upon authority than upon principle. . . .

It is quite clear, therefore, that this court cannot proceed to pronounce judgment in this case, for it has no longer jurisdiction of the appeal; and judicial duty is not less fitly performed by declining ungranted jurisdiction than in exercising firmly that which the Constitution and the laws confer. . . .

The appeal of the petitioner in this case must be dismissed for want of jurisdiction.

RELATED CASES

***Turner v. Bank of North America*: 4 Dall. 8 (1799).**

Congress may deny to the lower federal courts a portion of the jurisdiction conferred by the Constitution. Here was involved an aspect of jurisdiction based on diversity of citizenship. Congress has freely exercised its power to distribute jurisdiction among the lower federal courts, for example, setting a requirement of over $10,000 for diversity of citizenship cases. Turner was a citizen of North Carolina, and the bank from Pennsylvania argued against the power of Congress in a case involving promissory notes.

***Ex parte Bollman*: 4 CT. 75 (1807).**

The federal courts are limited to their delegated jurisdiction. "The crime of treason should not be extended by construction to doubtful cases." The "laws of the United States" mentioned in Article III are federal statutes, not common law.

***United States v. Klein*: 80 U.S. 128 (1872).**

Congress may not alter judicial jurisdiction so as to control the results of a particular case, in this case by effectively seeking to annul a presidential pardon, which exempted an individual from having property seized by the government.

***Aetna Life Insurance Co. v. Haworth*: 300 U.S. 227 (1937).**

In this case the Court sustained the constitutionality of the Federal Declaratory Judgment Act of 1934. A justiciable controversy must be real and substantial, definite and concrete, touching legal relations of parties having adverse legal interests, this to guard against using the declaratory judgment as a means of obtaining an advisory opinion. Here the purpose was to determine the benefits of an insured person. As to the device, the Court noted that "Congress may create and improve as well as abolish and restrict."

***Maryland v. Baltimore Radio Show*: 338 U.S. 912 (1950).**

The Supreme Court refused certiorari in a case where the lower court had reversed the conviction of a broadcasting company of contempt for permitting the broadcast of prejudicial matter concerning a pending murder trial in which the victim was an eleven-year-old girl. Justice Frankfurter's opinion is notable for its explanation of why the Court denies petitions for certiorari.

FOR DISCUSSION

Many constitutional amendments (especially the first ten) have attempted to protect individual rights. Does the fact that these amendments were adopted *after* the provisions in Article III mean that they serve as exceptions to congressional control of appellate judicial jurisdiction? Could Congress adopt a law limiting the Court's jurisdiction over the freedom of speech and press, which the First Amendment guarantees?

COHENS V. VIRGINIA

19 U.S. 264, 5 L. Ed. 257 (1821)

Cohens v. Virginia tested judicial review of state legislation. Virginia had indicted the Cohens for selling lottery tickets in the state contrary to state law. The Cohens argued that the tickets they were selling had been authorized by Congress for Washington, D.C. Ultimately, the Supreme Court decided that the D.C. ordinance permitting the sale of tickets did not intend to authorize sales in states that opposed them, but the state of Virginia had defiantly questioned the Supreme Court's right even to intervene in this case. The Virginians observed that states had adopted the Eleventh Amendment, which prohibited suits against the states. The Marshall Court had to explain how this Amendment did not preclude the case at hand and show the potentially dire consequences that would emerge if each state were permitted to serve as a judge in its own case.

Vote: 6–0

CHIEF JUSTICE MARSHALL delivered the opinion of the Court.

This is a writ of error to a judgment rendered in the Court of Hustings for the borough of Norfolk, on an information for selling lottery tickets, contrary to an act of the Legislature of Virginia. In the State Court, the defendant claimed the protection of an act of Congress. . . .

In support of this motion, three points have been made, and argued with the ability which the importance of the question merits. These points are—

1st. That a State is a defendant.

2d. That no writ of error lies from this Court to a State Court.

3d. The third point has been presented in different forms by the gentlemen who have argued it. The counsel who opened the cause said, that the want of jurisdiction was shown by the subject matter of the case.

The counsel who followed him said, that jurisdiction was not given by the judiciary act. The Court has bestowed all its attention on the arguments of both gentlemen, and supposes that their tendency is to show that this Court has no jurisdiction of the case, or, in other words, has no right to review the judgment of the State Court, because neither the constitution nor any law of the United States has been violated by that judgment. . . .

1st. The first question to be considered is, whether the jurisdiction of this Court is excluded by the character of the parties, one of them being a State, and the other a citizen of that State?

The second section of the third article of the constitution defines the extent of the judicial power of the United States. Jurisdiction is given to the Courts of the Union in two classes of cases. In the first, their jurisdiction depends on the character of the cause, whoever may be the parties. This class comprehends "all cases in law and equity arising under this constitution, the laws of the United States, and treaties made, or which shall be made, under their authority." This clause extends the jurisdiction of the Court to all the cases described, without making in its terms any exception whatever, and without any regard to the condition of the party. If there be any exception, it is to be implied against the express words of the article.

In the second class, the jurisdiction depends entirely on the character of the parties. In this are comprehended "controversies between two or more States, between a State and citizens of another State," "and between a State and foreign States, citizens or subjects." If these be the parties, it is entirely unimportant what may be the subject of controversy. Be it what it may, these parties have a constitutional right to come into the Courts of the Union.

The counsel for the defendant in error have . . . laid down the general proposition, that a sovereign independent State is not suable, except by its own consent.

This general proposition will not be controverted. But its consent is not requisite in each particular case. It may be given in a general law. And if a State has surrendered any portion of its sovereignty, the question whether a liability to suit be a part of this portion, depends on the instrument by which the surrender is made. If, upon a just construction of that instrument, it shall appear that the State has submitted to be sued, then it has parted with this sovereign right of judging in every case on the justice of its own pretensions, and has entrusted that power to a tribunal in whose impartiality it confides.

The American States, as well as the American people, have believed a close and firm Union to be essential to their liberty and to their happiness. They have been taught by experience, that this Union cannot exist without a government for the whole; and they have been taught by the same experience that this government would be a mere shadow, that must disappoint all their hopes, unless invested with large portions of that sovereignty which belongs to independent States. Under the influence of this opinion, and thus instructed by experience, the American people, in the conventions of their respective States, adopted the present constitution.

If it could be doubted, whether from its nature, it were not supreme in all cases where it is empowered to act, that doubt would be removed by the declaration, that "this constitution, and the laws of the United States, which shall be made in pursuance thereof, and all treaties made, or which shall be made, under the authority of the United States, shall be the supreme law of the land; and the judges in every State shall be bound thereby; any thing in the constitution or laws of any State to the contrary notwithstanding."

This is the authoritative language of the American people; and, if gentlemen please, of the American States. It marks, with lines too strong to be mistaken, the characteristic distinction between the government of the Union, and those of the States. The general government, though limited as to its objects, is supreme with respect to those objects. This principle is a part of the constitution; and if there be any who deny its necessity, none can deny its authority.

To this supreme government ample powers are confided; and if it were possible to doubt the great purposes for which they were so confided, the people of the United States have declared, that they are given "in order to form a more perfect union, establish justice, ensure domestic tranquillity, provide for the common defence, promote the general welfare, and secure the blessings of liberty to themselves and their posterity." . . .

One of the express objects, then, for which the judicial department was established, is the decision of controversies between States, and between a State and individuals. The mere circumstance, that a State is a party, gives jurisdiction to the Court. How, then, can it be contended, that the very same instrument, in the very same section, should be so construed, as that this same circumstance should withdraw a case from the jurisdiction of the Court, where the constitution or laws of the United States are supposed to have been violated? The constitution gave to every person having a claim upon a State, a right to submit his case to the Court of the nation. However unimportant his claim might be, however little the community might be interested in its decision, the framers of our constitution thought it necessary for the purposes of justice, to provide a tribunal as superior to influence as possible, in which that claim might be decided. Can it be imagined, that the same persons considered a case involving the constitution of our country and the majesty of the laws, questions in which every American citizen must be deeply interested, as withdrawn from this tribunal, because a State is a party? . . .

The mischievous consequences of the construction contended for on the part of Virginia, are also entitled to great consideration. It would prostrate, it has been said, the government and its laws at the feet of every State in the Union. And would not this be its effect? What power of the government could be executed by its own means, in any State disposed to resist its execution by a course of legislation? The laws must be executed by individuals acting within the several States. If these individuals may be exposed to penalties, and if the Courts of the Union cannot correct the judgments by which these penalties may be enforced, the course of the government may be, at any time, arrested by the will of one of its members. Each member will possess a veto on the will of the whole. It is, then, the opinion of the Court, that the defendant who removes a judgment rendered against him by a State Court into this Court, for the purpose of re-examining the question, whether that judgment be in violation of the constitution or laws of the United States, does not commence or prosecute a suit against the State, whatever may be its opinion where the effect of the writ may be to restore the party to the possession of a thing which he demands.

But should we in this be mistaken, the error does not affect the case now before the Court. If this writ of error be a suit in the sense of the 11th amendment, it is not a suit commenced or prosecuted "by a citizen of another State, or by a citizen or subject of any foreign State." It is not then within the amendment, but is governed entirely by the constitution as originally framed, and we have already seen, that in its origin, in judicial power was extended to all cases arising under the constitution or laws of the United States, without respect to parties.

2d. The second objection to the jurisdiction of the Court is, that its appellate power cannot be exercised, in any case, over the judgment of a State Court.

This objection is sustained chiefly by arguments drawn from the supposed total separation of the judiciary of a State from that of the Union, and their entire independence of each other. The argument considers the federal judiciary as completely foreign to that of a State; and as being no more connected with it in any respect whatever, than the Court of a foreign State. If this hypothesis be just, the argument founded on it is equally so; but if the hypothesis be not supported by the constitution, the argument fails with it.

This hypothesis is not founded on any words in the constitution, which might seem to countenance it, but on the unreasonableness of giving a contrary construction to words which seem to require it; and on the incompatibility of the application of the appellate jurisdiction to the judgments of State Courts, with that constitutional relation which subsists between the government of the Union and the governments of those States which compose it.

Let this unreasonableness, this total incompatibility, be examined.

That the United States form, for many, and for most important purposes, a single nation, has not yet been denied. In war, we are one people. In making peace, we are one people. In all commercial regulations, we are one and the same people. In many other respects, the American people are one, and the government which is alone capable of controlling and managing their interests in all these respects, is the government of the Union. It is their government, and in that character they have no other. American has chosen to be, in many respects, and to many purposes, a nation; and for all these purposes, her government is complete; to all these objects, it is competent. The people have declared, that in the exercise of all powers given for these objects, it is supreme. It can, then, in effecting these objects, legitimately control all individuals or governments within the American territory. The constitution and laws of a State, so far as they are repugnant to the constitution and laws of the United States, are absolutely void. These States are constituent parts of the United States. They are members of one great empire—for some purposes sovereign, for some purposes subordinate.

In a government so constituted, is it unreasonable that the judicial power should be competent to give efficacy to the constitutional laws of the legislature? That department can decide on the validity of the constitution or law of a State, if it be repugnant to the constitution or to a law of the United States. Is it unreasonable that it should also be empowered to decide on the judgment of a State tribunal enforcing such unconstitutional law? Is it so very unreasonable as to furnish a justification for controlling the words of the constitution?

We think it is not. We think that in a government acknowledgedly supreme, with respect to objects of vital interest to the nation, there is nothing inconsistent with sound reason, nothing incompatible with the nature of government, in making all its departments supreme, so far as respects those objects, and so far as is necessary to their attainment. The exercise of the appellate power over those judgments of the State tribunals which may contravene the constitution or laws of the United States, is, we believe, essential to the attainment of those objects. . . .

3d. We come now to the third objection, which, though differently stated by the counsel, is substantially the same. One gentleman has said that the judiciary act does not give jurisdiction in the case. . . .

The whole merits of this case, then, consist in the construction of the constitution and the act of Congress. The jurisdiction of the Court, if acknowledged, goes no farther. This we are required to do without the exercise of jurisdiction.

The counsel for the State of Virginia have, in support of this motion, urged many arguments of great weight against the application of the act of Congress to such a case as this; but those arguments go to the construction of the constitution, or of the law, or of both; and seem, therefore, rather calculated to sustain their cause upon its merits, than to prove a failure of jurisdiction in the Court.

After having bestowed upon this question the most deliberate consideration of which we are capable, the Court is unanimously of opinion, that the objections to its jurisdiction are not sustained, and that the motion ought to be overruled.

Motion denied.

Article VI, para. 2:

This Constitution, and the Laws of the United States which shall be made in Pursuance thereof; and all Treaties made, or which shall be made, under the Authority of the United States, shall be the supreme Law of the Land; and the Judges in every State shall be bound thereby, any Thing in the Constitution or Laws of any State to the Contrary notwithstanding.

COOPER V. AARON

358 U.S. 1, 78 S. Ct. 1401, 3 L. Ed. 2d 5 (1985)

In the events leading up to this case, Arkansas Governor Orval Faubus, who found it politically expedient to play to racial hatred, had attempted to thwart the integration of Little Rock's Central High School. His opposition had been so intense that President Dwight D. Eisenhower, who disliked *Brown's* disruptive impact, had sent in the national guard to enforce the law and restore order. Faced with such disruption, the Little Rock School Board, which had been attempting to follow court orders, asked for an extension of time. This decision is one of the Court's clearest articulations of its authority, but it arguably rests for support on Eisenhower's forceful actions more than its own expansive rhetoric. Each of the justices listed their names at the top of the decision to show their solidarity, although Justice Frankfurter also wrote a concurring opinion, which is not included here.

Vote: 9–0

Opinion of the Court by CHIEF JUSTICE WARREN, and JUSTICES BLACK, FRANKFURTER, DOUGLAS, BURTON, CLARK, HARLAN, BRENNAN, WHITTAKER.

As this case reaches us it raises questions of the highest importance to the maintenance of our federal system of government. It necessarily involves a claim by the Governor and Legislature of a State that there is no duty on state officials to obey federal court orders resting on this Court's considered interpretation of the United States Constitution. Specifically it involves actions by the Governor and Legislature of Arkansas upon the premise that they are not bound by our holding in *Brown* v. *Board of Education*, 347 U.S. 483 (1954) . . . . We reject these contentions.

The following are the facts and circumstances so far as necessary to show how the legal questions are presented. [The Court reviews the *Brown* decision.]

On May 20, 1954, three days after the first *Brown* opinion, the Little Rock District School Board adopted, and on May 23, 1954, made public, a statement of policy entitled "Supreme Court Decision—Segregation in Public Schools." In this statement the Board recognized that "It is our responsibility to comply with Federal Constitutional Requirements and we intend to do so when the Supreme Court of the United States outlines the method to be followed."

On September 2, 1957, the day before these Negro students were to enter Central High, the school authorities were met with drastic opposing action on the part of the Governor of Arkansas who dispatched units of the Arkansas National Guard to the Central High School grounds and placed the school "off limits" to colored students. As found by the District Court in subsequent proceedings, the Governor's action had not been requested by the school authorities, and was entirely unheralded.

The next day, September 3, 1957, the Board petitioned the District Court for instructions, and the court, after a hearing, found that the Board's request of the Negro students to stay away from the high school had been made because of the stationing of the military guards by the state authorities. The court determined that this was not a reason for departing from the approved plan, and ordered the School Board and Superintendent to proceed with it.

On the morning of the next day, September 4, 1957, the Negro children attempted to enter the high school but, as the District Court later found, units of the Arkansas National Guard "acting pursuant to the Governor's order, stood shoulder to shoulder at the school grounds and thereby forcibly prevented the 9 Negro students . . . from entering," as they continued to do every school day during the following three weeks. That same day, September 4, 1957, the United States Attorney for the Eastern District of Arkansas was requested by the District Court to begin an immediate investigation in order to fix responsibility for the interference with the orderly implementation of the District Court's direction to carry out the desegregation program. Three days later, September 7, the District Court denied a petition of the School Board and the Superintendent of Schools for an order temporarily suspending continuance of the program.

Upon completion of the United States Attorney's investigation, he and the Attorney General of the United States, at the District Court's request, entered the proceedings and filed a petition on behalf of the United States, as *amicus curiae*, to enjoin the Governor of Arkansas and officers of the Arkansas National Guard from further attempts to prevent obedience to the court's order. After hearings on the petition, the District Court found that the School Board's plan had been obstructed by the Governor through the use of National Guard troops, and granted a preliminary injunction on September 20, 1957, enjoining the Governor and the officers of the Guard from preventing the attendance of Negro children at Central High School, and from otherwise obstructing or interfering with the orders of the court in connection with the plan. The National Guard was then withdrawn from the school.

The next school day was Monday, September 23, 1957. The Negro children entered the high school that morning under the protection of the Little Rock Police Department and members of the Arkansas State Police. But the officers caused the children to be removed from the school during the morning because they had difficulty controlling a large and demonstrating crowd which had gathered at the high school. On September 25, however, the President of the United States dispatched federal troops to Central High School and admission of the Negro students to the school was thereby effected. Regular army troops continued at the high school until November 27, 1957. They were then replaced by federalized National Guardsmen who remained throughout the balance of the school year. Eight of the Negro students remained in attendance at the school throughout the school year.

We come now to the aspect of the proceedings presently before us. On February 20, 1958, the School Board and the Superintendent of Schools filed a petition in the District Court seeking a postponement of their program for desegregation. Their position in essence was that because of extreme public hostility, which they stated had been engendered largely by the official attitudes and actions of the Governor and the Legislature, the maintenance of a sound educational program at Central High School, with the Negro students in attendance, would be impossible. The Board therefore proposed that the Negro students already admitted to the school be withdrawn and sent to segregated schools, and that all further steps to carry out the Board's desegregation program be postponed for a period later suggested by the Board to be two and one-half years.

[W]e have accepted without reservation the position of the School Board, the Superintendent of Schools, and their counsel that they displayed entire good faith in the conduct of these proceedings and in dealing with the unfortunate and distressing sequence of events which has been outlined. We likewise have accepted the findings of the District Court as to the conditions at Central High School during the 1957–1958 school year, and also the findings that the educational progress of all the students, white and colored, of that school has suffered and will continue to suffer if the conditions which prevailed last year are permitted to continue.

The significance of these findings, however, is to be considered in light of the fact, indisputably revealed by the record before us, that the conditions they depict are directly traceable to the actions of legislators and executive officials of the State of Arkansas, taken in their official capacities, which reflect their own determination to resist this Court's decision in the *Brown* case and which have brought about violent resistance to that decision in Arkansas. In its petition for certiorari filed in this Court, the School Board itself describes the situation in this language: "The legislative, executive, and judicial departments of the state government opposed the desegregation of Little Rock schools by enacting laws, calling out troops, making statements villifying federal law and federal courts, and failing to utilize state law enforcement agencies and judicial processes to maintain public peace."

One may well sympathize with the position of the Board in the face of the frustrating conditions which have confronted it, but, regardless of the Board's good faith, the actions of the other state agencies responsible for those conditions compel us to reject the Board's legal position. Had Central High School been under the direct management of the State itself, it could hardly be suggested that those immediately in charge of the school should be heard to assert their own good faith as a legal excuse for delay in implementing the constitutional rights of these respondents, when vindication of those rights was rendered difficult or impossible by the actions of other state officials. The situation here is in no different posture because the members of the School Board and the Superintendent of Schools are local officials; from the point of view of the Fourteenth Amendment, they stand in this litigation as the agents of the State.

The constitutional rights of respondents are not to be sacrificed or yielded to the violence and disorder which have followed upon the actions of the Governor and Legislature. . . .

What has been said, in the light of the facts developed, is enough to dispose of the case. However, we should answer the premise of the actions of the Governor and Legislature that they are not bound by our holding in the *Brown* case. It is necessary only to recall some basic constitutional propositions which are settled doctrine.

Article VI of the Constitution makes the Constitution the "supreme Law of the Land." In 1803, Chief Justice Marshall, speaking for a unanimous Court, referring to the Constitution as "the fundamental and paramount law of the nation," declared in the notable case of *Marbury* v. *Madison*, 1 Cranch 137, 177, that "It is emphatically the province and duty of the judicial department to say what the law is." This decision declared the basic principle that the federal judiciary is supreme in the exposition of the law of the Constitution, and that principle has ever since been respected by this Court and the Country as a permanent and indispensable feature of our constitutional system. It follows that the interpretation of the Fourteenth Amendment enunciated by this Court in the *Brown* case is the supreme law of the land, and Art. VI of the Constitution makes it of binding effect on the States "any Thing in the Constitution or Laws of any State to the Contrary notwithstanding." Every state legislator and executive and judicial officer is solemnly committed by oath taken pursuant to Art. VI, cl. 3, "to support this Constitution." Chief Justice Taney, speaking for a unanimous Court in 1859, said that this requirement reflected the framers' "anxiety to preserve it [the Constitution] in full force, in all its powers, and to guard against resistance to or evasion of its authority, on the part of a State . . . ." *Ableman* v. *Booth*, [62 U.S. 506 (1858), at] 524.

No state legislator or executive or judicial officer can war against the Constitution without violating his undertaking to support it. Chief Justice Marshall spoke for a unanimous Court in saying that: "If the legislatures of the several states may, at will, annul the judgments of the courts of the United States, and destroy the rights acquired under those judgments, the constitution itself becomes a solemn mockery. . . ." *United States* v. *Peters*, 5 Cranch 115, 136 (1809). A Governor who asserts a power to nullify a federal court order is similarly restrained. If he had such power, said Chief Justice Hughes, in 1932, also for a unanimous Court, "it is manifest that the fiat of a state Governor, and not the Constitution of the United States, would be the supreme law of the land; that the restrictions of the Federal Constitution upon the exercise of state power would be but impotent phrases. . . ." *Sterling* v. *Constantin*, 287 U.S. 378, 397–398 [(1932)].

It is, of course, quite true that the responsibility for public education is primarily the concern of the States, but it is equally true that such responsibilities, like all other state activity, must be exercised consistently with federal constitutional requirements as they apply to state action. The Constitution created a government dedicated to equal justice under law. The Fourteenth Amendment embodied and emphasized that ideal. State support of segregated schools through any arrangement, management, funds, or property cannot be squared with the Amendment's command that no State shall deny to any person within its jurisdiction the equal protection of the laws. The right of a student not to be segregated on racial grounds in schools so maintained is indeed so fundamental and pervasive that it is embraced in the concept of due process of law. *Bolling* v. *Sharpe*, 347 U.S. 497 (1954). The basic decision in *Brown* was unanimously reached by this Court only after the case had been briefed and twice argued and the issues had been given the most serious consideration. Since the first *Brown* opinion three new Justices have come to the Court. They are at one with the Justices still on the Court who participated in that basic decision as to its correctness, and that decision is now unanimously reaffirmed. The principles announced in that decision and the obedience of the States to them, according to the command of the Constitution, are indispensable for the protection of the freedoms guaranteed by our fundamental charter for all of us. Our constitutional ideal of equal justice under law is thus made a living truth.

FOR DISCUSSION

The cases involving civil rights arguably called for far greater judicial supervision of state actions than decisions in most other areas. Although it is difficult to sympathize with a racist governor seeking to thwart individual rights, some scholars are concerned that *Cooper v. Aaron* represents an overstated view of judicial authority. What exactly did the Court say about the relationship between its own decisions and the Constitution? Is the Court's gloss on the Constitution equivalent to the Constitution itself? Do you think the Court had a right to be more forceful in a case involving a state than if it had been proceeding against the actions of Congress or the President? Why or why not?

RELATED CASES

In part because the Supreme Court declared that the judiciary would exercise flexible equity remedies to enforce *Brown v. Board of Education*, courts have continued to deal with implementation of this decision. Prominent cases, some of which are included in Volume II of this book, include the following:

Swann v. Charlotte Mecklenburg Board of Education: **402 U.S. 1 (1970).**

Busing was a permissible tool to implement racial desegregation in cases of prior de jure (legally mandated) segregation.

Milliken v. Bradley: **418 U.S. 717 (1974).**

Busing remedies should be limited to districts that had actively participated in racial segregation, in this case excluding suburban areas around Detroit from busing that was designed to remedy segregation within the city.

United States v. Fordice: **505 U.S. 7178 (1992).**

The Court ruled that Mississippi had not yet met its duty to dismantle the system of racial segregation that continued to be manifest in state colleges and universities.

***Regents of the University of California v. Bakke:* 438 U.S. 265 (1978).**

J. Powell split the difference between four justices, led by J. Brennan, who would have accepted the use of race and of quotas, and four justices, led by J. Rehnquist, who would have struck down all uses of race in this case. Powell upheld the use of race (affirmative action) in admission to the Medical School at the University of California at Davis while ruling that the specific quotas that the college had adopted (sixteen out of one hundred seats of each entering class) were unconstitutional.

***Gratz v. Bollinger:* 123 S. Ct. 2411 (2003) and *Grutter v. Bollinger:* 123 S. Ct. 2235 (2003).**

The first decision struck down the admissions formula used by the undergraduate college at the University of Michigan, which automatically awarded twenty of a needed one hundred points required for admission as in violation of the equal protection clause of the Fourteenth Amendment. The second upheld the use of race considerations at the law school of the University of Michigan, which was apparently applied more flexibly.

See also *Missouri v. Jenkins* (1995), later in this chapter.

MUSKRAT V. UNITED STATES

219 U.S. 346, 31 S.Ct. 250, 55 L.Ed. 246 (1911)

Congress had by statute in 1907 authorized David Muskrat, a Native American Indian, to bring suit in the Court of Claims, with right of appeal to the Supreme Court, to test the constitutionality of acts of Congress that had changed the original allotments of Cherokee Indian lands. The new distribution reduced the amount of land and funds to which certain Indians were entitled. This action of Congress in vesting this jurisdiction in the Supreme Court was challenged as permitting the Court to judge an abstract question rather than an actual case or controversy.

Vote: No dissent — no jurisdiction

The opinion was delivered by JUSTICE DAY:

The first question in these cases, as in others, involves the jurisdiction of this court to entertain the proceeding, and that depends upon whether the jurisdiction conferred is within the power of Congress, having in view the limitations of the judicial power, as established by the Constitution of the United States. . . .

In the note to the report of the case in [*Hayburn's Case*, 2 Dall. 409 (1972), a federal pension case] it appeared that Chief Justice Jay, Mr. Justice Cushing, and District Judge Duane unanimously agreed:

> "That by the Constitution of the United States, the government thereof is divided into three distinct and independent branches, and that it is the duty of each to abstain from, and to oppose, encroachments on either.
>
> "That neither the legislative nor the executive branches can constitutionally assign to the judicial any duties but such as are properly judicial, and to be performed in a judicial manner. . . ."

As we have already seen, by the express terms of the Constitution, the exercise of the judicial power is limited to "cases" and "controversies." Beyond this it does not extend and, unless it is asserted in a case or controversy within the meaning of the Constitution, the power to exercise it is nowhere conferred.

What, then, does the Constitution mean in conferring this judicial power with the right to determine "cases" and "controversies." A "case" was defined by Mr. Chief Justice Marshall as early as the leading case of *Marbury v. Madison* (5 U.S. 137, 1803) . . . to be a suit instituted according to the regular course of judicial procedure. And what more, if anything, is meant in the use of the term "controversy"? That question was dealt with by Mr. Justice Field, at the circuit, in the case of *In re Pacific Railway Commission,* 32 Fed. 241. Of these terms that learned justice said:

> "The judicial article of the Constitution mentions cases and controversies. The term 'controversies,' if distinguishable at all from 'cases,' is so in that it is less comprehensive than the latter, and includes only suits of a civil nature. *Chisholm v. Georgia,* 2 Dall. 431 (1793). By cases and controversies are intended the claims of litigants brought before the courts for determination by such regular proceedings as are established by law or custom for the protection or enforcement of rights, or the prevention, redress, or punishment of wrongs. Whenever the claim of a party under the Constitution, laws, or treaties of the United States takes such a form that the judicial power is capable of acting upon it, then it has become a case. The term implies the existence of present or possible adverse parties, whose contentions are submitted to the court for adjudication."

The power being thus limited to require an application of the judicial power to cases and controversies, Is the act which undertook to authorize the present suits to determine the constitutional validity of certain legislation within the constitutional authority of the court? This inquiry in the case before us includes the broader question, When may this court, in the exercise of the judicial power, pass upon the constitutional validity of an act of Congress? That question has been settled from the early history of the court, the leading case on the subject being *Marbury v. Madison.*

In that case Chief Justice Marshall, who spoke for the court, was careful to point out that the right to declare an act of Congress unconstitutional could only be exercised when a proper case between opposing parties was submitted for judicial determination; that there was no general veto power in the court upon the legislation of Congress; and that the authority to declare an act unconstitutional sprang from the requirement that the court, in administering the law and pronouncing judgment between the parties to a case, and choosing between the requirements of the fundamental law established by the people and embodied in the Constitution and an act of the agents of the people, acting under authority of the Constitution, should enforce the Constitution as the supreme law of the land. The Chief Justice demonstrated, in a manner which has been regarded as settling the question, that with the choice thus given between a constitutional requirement and a conflicting statutory enactment, the plain duty of the court was to follow and enforce the Constitution as the supreme law established by the people. And the court recognized, in *Marbury v. Madison* and subsequent cases, that the exercise of this great power could only be invoked in cases which came regularly before the courts for determination, for, said the chief justice, in *Osborn v. Bank of the United States,* 9 Wheat. 738 (1824), speaking of the third article of the Constitution, conferring judicial power:

> "This clause enables the judicial department to receive jurisdiction to the full extent of the Constitution, laws, and treaties of the United States, when any question respecting them shall assume such a form that the judicial power is capable of acting on it. That power is capable of acting only when the subject is submitted to it by a party who asserts his rights in the form prescribed by law. It then becomes a case, and the Constitution declares that the judicial power shall extend to all cases arising under the Constitution, laws, and treaties of the United States. . . ."

It is therefore evident that there is neither more nor less in this procedure than an attempt to provide for a judicial determination, final in this court, of the constitutional validity of an act of Congress. Is such a determination within the judicial power conferred by the Constitution, as the same has been interpreted and defined in the authoritative decisions to which we have referred? We think it is not. That judicial power, as we have seen, is the right to determine actual controversies arising between adverse litigants, duly instituted in courts of proper jurisdiction. The right to declare a law unconstitutional arises because an act of Congress relied upon by one or the other of such parties in determining their rights is in conflict with the fundamental law. The exercise of this, the most important and delicate duty of this court, is not given to it as a body with revisory power over the action of Congress, but because the rights of the litigants in justiciable controversies require the court to choose between the fundamental law and a law purporting to be enacted within constitutional authority, but in fact beyond the power delegated to the legislative branch of the government. This attempt to obtain a judicial declaration of the validity of the act of Congress is not presented in a "case" or "controversy," to which, under the Constitution of the United States, the judicial power alone extends. It is true the United States is made a defendant to this action, but it has no interest adverse to the claimants. The object is not to assert a property right as against the government, or to demand compensation for alleged wrongs because of action upon its part. The whole purpose of the law is to determine the constitutional validity of this class of legislation, in a suit not arising between parties concerning a property right necessarily involved in the decision in question, but in a proceeding against the government in its sovereign capacity, and concerning which the only judgment required is to settle the doubtful character of the legislation in question. Such judgment will not conclude private parties, when actual litigation brings to the court the question of the constitutionality of such legislation. In a legal sense the judgment could not be executed, and amounts in fact to no more than an expression of opinion upon the validity of the acts in question. Confining the jurisdiction of this court within the limitations conferred by the Constitution, which the court has hitherto been careful to observe, and whose boundaries it has refused to transcend, we think the Congress, in the act of March 1, 1907, exceeded the limitations of legislative authority, so far as it required of this court action not judicial in its nature within the meaning of the Constitution.

. . . If such actions as are here attempted, to determine the validity of legislation, are sustained, the result will be that this court, instead of keeping within the limits of judicial power and deciding cases or controversies arising between opposing parties, as the Constitution intended it should, will be required to give opinions in the nature of advice concerning legislative action—a function never conferred upon it by the Constitution, and against the exercise of which this court has steadily set its face from the beginning. . . .

The judgments will be reversed and the cases remanded to the Court of Claims, with directions to dismiss the petitions for want of jurisdiction.

FOR DISCUSSION

In *Ashwander v. Tennessee Valley Authority*, 297 U.S. 288 (1936), in which the Court refused to invalidate a contract between the TVA and the Alabama Power Company, Justice Brandeis wrote a concurring opinion in which he set forth a series of maxims of judicial restraint. According to Brandeis: 1. "the Court will not pass upon the constitutionality of legislation in a friendly, non-adversary, proceeding"; 2. will not "anticipate a question of constitutional law in advance of the necessity of deciding it"; 3. will not "formulate a rule of constitutional law broader than is required by the precise facts to which it is to be applied"; 4. will "not pass upon a constitutional question" if there is an alternate ground on which to based its decision; 5. "will not pass upon the validity of a statute upon complaint of one who fails to show that he is injured by its operation"; 6. "will not pass upon the constitutionality of a statute at the instance of one who has availed himself of its benefits"; and 7. will, before voiding a law on constitutional grounds, "first ascertain whether a construction of the statute is fairly possible by which the question may be avoided."

In your judgment, should the Court seek to dodge constitutional questions when it can? What are the advantages of doing so? Disadvantages?

RELATED CASES

***United States v. Evans:* 213 U.S. 297 (1909).**

In order for there to be a case or controversy there must be opposing litigants. Where a verdict in favor of a defendant in a murder trial cannot be set aside on appeal, the acquittal of the defendant, in effect, removes one of the parties and the matter loses its character as a case. For the upper court to hear an appeal would be for the court to render an advisory opinion.

***Fairchild v. Hughes:* 258 U.S. 126 (1922).**

The general right of a citizen to have government administered according to law does not entitle a private citizen to bring suit in federal courts to determine whether a proposed statute or constitutional amendment will be valid if adopted. Here, the action was to enjoin Secretary of State Hughes from proclaiming the Nineteenth Amendment.

***Tileston v. Ullman:* 318 U.S. 44 (1943).**

Where appellant is claiming impairment of rights of third parties, he has no standing to litigate the constitutional question, and the Court need not consider whether there is a genuine case or controversy essential to the exercise of the jurisdiction of the Court. Here, suit was by a physician claiming rights for patients in Connecticut who wanted to use birth control.

***Doremus v. Board of Education:* 342 U.S. 429 (1952).**

A parent without children in school and a taxpayer without "direct and particular financial interest" has no standing to bring suit challenging the constitutionality of an act requiring Bible reading in school. The Court held this to be a fringe issue since there was no increase in the cost of education. In *Abington v. Schempp* (1963), the Court later did give standing to parents with students who alleged that Bible reading had interfered with their First Amendment rights.

***Poe v. Ullman:* 367 U.S. 497 (1961).**

The Connecticut law prohibiting the use of contraceptives has been on the state's books since 1879. The fact that Connecticut has not chosen to press the enforcement of this statute deprives these controversies of the immediacy that is an indispensable condition of constitutional adjudication.

In the landmark case, *Griswold v. Connecticut* (381 U.S. 479, 1965), in which the Court relied on a right to privacy, it later effectively bypassed both this case and *Tileston v. Ullman* (318 US 44, 1943) by accepting the standing of a doctor who was willing to break the law by actually prescribing such devices for her patients. Similarly, in *Roe v. Wade* (410 U.S. 113, 1973), which overturned most restrictions on abortion, it accepted standing of a woman who had already delivered her child on the basis that pregnancy was a condition that was capable of being repeated and would, because it lasted only nine months, otherwise be incapable of judicial review.

***Elk Grove Unified School District v. Newdow:* 542 U.S. 1 (2004).**

Newdow did not, as a noncustodial parent, have standing to challenge the words "under God" in the pledge of allegiance that was said in public schools.

Commonwealth of Massachusetts v. Mellon, Secretary of the Treasury, et al.; Frothingham v. Mellon, Secretary of the Treasury, et al.

262 U.S. 447, 43 S. Ct. 597, 67 L. Ed. 1078 (1923)

This case challenged the constitutionality of the Maternity Act of 1921, which appropriated federal monies to reduce maternal and infant mortality, as an invasion of state sovereignty and as a deprivation of property (through taxation) without due process of law. The plaintiff asserted standing as a federal taxpayer.

Vote: 9–0

Justice Sutherland delivered the opinion of the Court.

. . . The attack upon the statute in the *Frothingham* case is, generally, the same, but this plaintiff alleges in addition that she is a taxpayer of the United States; and her contention, though not clear, seems to be that the effect of the appropriations complained of will be to increase the burden of future taxation and thereby take her property without due process of law. The right of a taxpayer to enjoin the execution of a federal appropriation act, on the ground that it is invalid and will result in taxation for illegal purposes, has never been passed upon by this Court. In cases where it was presented, the question has either been allowed to pass *sub silentio* or the determination of it expressly withheld. *Millard v. Roberts,* 202 US 429 (1906); *Wilson v. Shaw*, 204 US 24 (1907); *Bradfield v. Roberts*, 175 US 291 (1899). The case last cited came here from the Court of Appeals of the District of Columbia, and that court sustained the right of the plaintiff to sue by treating the case as one directed against the District of Columbia, and therefore subject to the rule frequently stated by this Court, that resident taxpayers may sue to enjoin an illegal use of the moneys of a municipal corporation. The interest of a taxpayer of a municipality in the application of its moneys is direct and immediate and the remedy by injunction to prevent their misuse is not inappropriate. It is upheld by a large number of state cases and is the rule of this Court. Nevertheless, there are decisions to the contrary. The reasons which support the extension of the equitable remedy to a single taxpayer in such cases are based upon the peculiar relation of the corporate taxpayer to the corporation, which is not without some resemblance to that subsisting between stockholder and private corporation. But the relation of a taxpayer of the United States to the Federal Government is very different. His interest in the moneys of the Treasury—partly realized from taxation and partly from other sources—is shared with millions of others; is comparatively minute and indeterminable; and the effect upon future taxation, of any payment out of the funds, so remote, fluctuating and uncertain, that no basis is afforded for an appeal to the preventive powers of a court of equity.

The administration of any statute, likely to produce additional taxation to be imposed upon a vast number of taxpayers, the extent of whose several liability is indefinite and constantly changing, is essentially a matter of public and not of individual concern. If one taxpayer may champion and litigate such a cause, then every other taxpayer may do not same, not only in respect of the statute here under review but also in respect of every other appropriation act and statute whose administration requires the outlay of public money, and whose validity may be questioned. The bare suggestion of such a result, with its attendant inconveniences, goes far to sustain the conclusion which we have reached, that a suit of this character cannot be maintained. It is of much significance that no precedent sustaining the right to maintain suits like this has been called to our attention, although, since the formation of the government, as an examination of the acts of Congress will disclose, a large number of statutes appropriating or involving the expenditure of moneys for non-federal purposes have been enacted and carried into effect.

Standing = Personal Stake

The functions of government under our system are apportioned. To the legislative department has been committed the duty of making laws; to the executive the duty of executing them; and to the judiciary the duty of interpreting and applying them in cases properly brought before the courts. The general rule is that neither department may invade the province of the other and neither may control, direct or restrain the action of the other. We are not now speaking of the merely ministerial duties of officials. *Gaines v. Thompson*, 7 Wall. 347 (1869). We have no power per se to review and annul acts of Congress on the ground that they are unconstitutional. That question may be considered only when the justification for some direct injury suffered or threatened, presenting a justiciable issue, is made to rest upon such an act. Then the power exercised is that of ascertaining and declaring the law applicable to the controversy. It amounts to little more than the negative power to disregard an unconstitutional enactment, which otherwise would stand in the way of the enforcement of a legal right. The party who invokes the power must be able to show not only that the statute is invalid but that he has sustained or is immediately in danger of sustaining some direct injury as the result of its enforcement, and not merely that he suffers in some indefinite way in common with people generally. If a case for preventive relief be presented the court enjoins, in effect, not the execution of the statute, but the acts of the official, the statute notwithstanding. Here the parties plaintiff have no such case. Looking through forms of words to the substance of their complaint, it is merely that officials of the executive department of the government are executing and will execute an act of Congress asserted to be unconstitutional; and this we are asked to prevent. To do so would be not to decide a judicial controversy, but to assume a position of authority over the governmental acts of another and co-equal department, an authority which plainly we do not possess.

RELATED CASE

***Alabama Power Co. v. Ickes:* 302 U.S. 464 (1938).**

A taxpayer cannot question the expenditure of federal funds under the Public Works Administrator, Ickes, even though the use of the funds aided competition with the petitioner's business. The power company did not have an exclusive franchise. For a valid suit there must be a showing of actual injury or immediate danger of injury, and there must be the violation of a legal right.

FLAST V. COHEN

392 U.S. 83, 88 S. Ct. 1942, 20 L. Ed. 2d 947 (1968)

Relatively few questions in constitutional law are ever completely resolved. Despite relatively clear language in *Frothingham* rejecting taxpayer suits, the case that follows appears to open the door at least slightly to a limited number of such suits involving questions raised under the establishment clause of the First Amendment. In the process of clarifying *Frothingham*, Chief Justice Earl Warren outlines two nexuses, or connections, that taxpayers must show in challenging federal laws. The first section of this decision, omitted here, dealt with the appropriateness of the appeal from the three-judge district court.

Vote: 8–1

CHIEF JUSTICE WARREN delivered the opinion of the Court.

II.

Although the barrier *Frothingham* erected against federal taxpayer suits has never been breached, the decision has been the source of some confusion and the object of considerable criticism. The confusion has developed as commentators have tried to determine whether *Frothingham* establishes a constitutional bar to taxpayer suits or whether the Court was simply imposing a rule of self-restraint which was not constitutionally compelled. . . .

To the extent that *Frothingham* has been viewed as resting on policy considerations, it has been criticized as depending on assumptions not consistent with modern conditions. For example, some commentators have pointed out that a number of corporate taxpayers today have a federal tax liability running into hundreds of millions of dollars, and such taxpayers have a far greater monetary stake in the Federal Treasury than they do in any municipal treasury. To some degree, the fear expressed in *Frothingham* that allowing one taxpayer to sue would inundate the federal courts with countless similar suits has been mitigated by the ready availability of the devices of class actions and joinder under the Federal Rules of Civil Procedure, adopted subsequent to the decision in *Frothingham*. Whatever the merits of the current debate over *Frothingham*, its very existence suggests that we should undertake a fresh examination of the limitations upon standing to sue in a federal court and the application of those limitations to taxpayer suits.

III.

The jurisdiction of federal courts is defined and limited by Article III of the Constitution. In terms relevant to the question for decision in this case, the judicial power of federal courts is constitutionally restricted to "cases" and "controversies." As is so often the situation in constitutional adjudication, those two words have an iceberg quality, containing beneath their surface simplicity submerged complexities which go to the very heart of our constitutional form of government. Embodied in the words "cases" and "controversies" are two complementary but somewhat different limitations. In part those words limit the business of federal courts to questions presented in an adversary context and in a form historically viewed as capable of resolution through the judicial process. And in part those words define the role assigned to the judiciary in a tripartite allocation of power to assure that the federal courts will not intrude into areas committed to the other branches of government. Justiciability is the term of art employed to give expression to this dual limitation placed upon federal courts by the case-and-controversy doctrine.

Justiciability is itself a concept of uncertain meaning and scope. Its reach is illustrated by the various grounds upon which questions sought to be adjudicated in federal courts have been held not to be justiciable. Thus, no justiciable controversy is presented when the parties seek adjudication of only a political question, when the parties are asking for an advisory opinion, when the question sought to be adjudicated has been mooted by subsequent developments, and when there is no standing to maintain the action. Yet it remains true that "justiciability is . . . not a legal concept with a fixed content or susceptible of scientific verification. Its utilization is the resultant of many subtle pressures. . . ." *Poe* v. *Ullman*, 367 U.S. 497, 508 (1961).

Part of the difficulty in giving precise meaning and form to the concept of justiciability stems from the uncertain historical antecedents of the case-and-controversy doctrine. . . .

Additional uncertainty exists in the doctrine of justiciability because that doctrine has become a blend of constitutional requirements and policy considerations. . . .

It is in this context that the standing question presented by this case must be viewed and that the Government's argument on that question must be evaluated. As we understand it, the Government's position is that the constitutional scheme of separation of powers, and the deference owed by the federal judiciary to the other two branches of government within that scheme, present an absolute bar to taxpayer suits challenging the validity of federal spending programs. The Government views such suits as involving no more than the mere disagreement by the taxpayer "with the uses to which tax money is put." According to the Government, the resolution of such disagreements is committed to other branches of the Federal Government and not to the judiciary. Consequently, the Government contends that, under no circumstances, should standing be conferred on federal taxpayers to challenge a federal taxing or spending program. An analysis of the function served by standing limitations compels a rejection of the Government's position.

Standing is an aspect of justiciability and, as such, the problem of standing is surrounded by the same complexities and vagaries that inhere in justiciability. Standing has been called one of "the most amorphous [concepts] in the entire domain of public law." Some of the complexities peculiar to standing problems result because standing "serves, on occasion, as a shorthand expression for all the various elements of justicability." In addition, there are at work in the standing doctrine the many subtle pressures which tend to cause policy considerations to blend into constitutional limitations.

Despite the complexities and uncertainties, some meaningful form can be given to the jurisdictional limitations placed on federal court power by the concept of standing. The fundamental aspect of standing is that it focuses on the party seeking to get his complaint before a federal court and not on the issues he wishes to have adjudicated. The "gist of the question of standing" is whether the party seeking relief has "alleged such a personal stake in the outcome of the controversy as to assure that concrete adverseness which sharpens the presentation of issues upon which the court so largely depends for illumination of difficult constitutional questions." *Baker* v. *Carr,* 369 U.S. 186 (1962). In other words, when standing is placed in issue in a case, the question is whether the person whose standing is challenged is a proper party to request an adjudication of a particular issue and not whether the issue itself is justiciable. Thus, a party may have standing in a particular case, but the federal court may nevertheless decline to pass on the merits of the case because, for example, it presents a political question. A proper party is demanded so that federal courts will not be asked to decide "ill-defined controversies over constitutional issues," *United Public Workers* v. *Mitchell,* 330 U.S. 75 (1947), or a case which is of "a hypothetical or abstract character," *Aetna Life Insurance Co.* v. *Haworth,* 300 U.S. 227 (1937). So stated, the standing requirement is closely related to, although more general than, the rule that federal courts will not entertain friendly suits, *Chicago & Grand Trunk Ry. Co.* v. *Wellman,* 143 U.S. 339 (1892) or those which are feigned or collusive in nature, *United States* v. *Johnson,* 319 U.S. 302 (1943); *Lord* v. *Veazie,* 49 U.S. (8 How.) 251 (1850).

When the emphasis in the standing problem is placed on whether the person invoking a federal court's jurisdiction is a proper party to maintain the action, the weakness of the Government's argument in this case becomes apparent. The question whether a particular person is a proper party to maintain the action does not, by its own force, raise separation of powers problems related to improper judicial interference in areas committed to other branches of the Federal Government. Such problems arise, if at all, only from the substantive issues the individual seeks to have adjudicated. . . .

IV.

The various rules of standing applied by federal courts have not been developed in the abstract. Rather, they have been fashioned with specific reference to the status asserted by the party whose standing is challenged and to the type of question he wishes to have adjudicated. We have noted that, in deciding the question of standing, it is not relevant that the substantive issues in the litigation might be nonjusticiable. However, our decisions establish that, in ruling on standing, it is both appropriate and necessary to look to the substantive issues for another purpose, namely, to determine whether there is a logical nexus between the status asserted and the claim sought to be adjudicated. For example, standing requirements will vary in First Amendment religion cases depending upon whether the party raises an Establishment Clause claim or a claim under the Free Exercise Clause. See *McGowan* v. *Maryland,* 366 U.S. 420 (1961). Such inquiries into the nexus between the status asserted by the litigant and the claim he presents are essential to assure that he is a proper and appropriate party to invoke federal judicial power. Thus, our point of reference in this case is the standing of individuals who assert only the status of federal taxpayers and who challenge the constitutionality of a federal spending program. Whether such individuals have standing to maintain that form of action turns on whether they can demonstrate the necessary stake as taxpayers in the outcome of the litigation to satisfy Article III requirements.

The nexus demanded of federal taxpayers has two aspects to it. First, the taxpayer must establish a logical link between that status and the type of legislative enactment attacked. Thus, a taxpayer will be a proper party to allege the unconstitutionality only of exercises of congressional power under the taxing and spending clause of Art. I, § 8, of the Constitution. It will not be sufficient to allege an incidental expenditure of tax funds in the administration of an essentially regulatory statute. This requirement is consistent with the limitation imposed upon state-taxpayer standing in federal courts in *Doremus* v. *Board of Education*, 342 U.S. 429 (1952). Secondly, the taxpayer must establish a nexus between that status and the precise nature of the constitutional infringement alleged. Under this requirement, the taxpayer must show that the challenged enactment exceeds specific constitutional limitations imposed upon the exercise of the congressional taxing and spending power and not simply that the enactment is generally beyond the powers delegated to Congress by Art. I, § 8. When both nexuses are established, the litigant will have shown a taxpayer's stake in the outcome of the controversy and will be a proper and appropriate party to invoke a federal court's jurisdiction.

The taxpayer-appellants in this case have satisfied both nexuses to support their claim of standing under the test we announce today. Their constitutional challenge is made to an exercise by Congress of its power under Art. I, § 8, to spend for the general welfare, and the challenged program involves a substantial expenditure of federal tax funds. In addition, appellants have alleged that the challenged expenditures violate the Establishment and Free Exercise Clauses of the First Amendment. Our history vividly illustrates that one of the specific evils feared by those who drafted the Establishment Clause and fought for its adoption was that the taxing and spending power would be used to favor one religion over another or to support religion in general. . . .

The allegations of the taxpayer in *Frothingham v. Mellon,* 262 U.S. 447 (1923), were quite different from those made in this case, and the result in *Frothingham* is consistent with the test of taxpayer standing announced today. The taxpayer in *Frothingham* attacked a federal spending program and she, therefore, established the first nexus required. However, she lacked standing because her constitutional attack was not based on an allegation that Congress, in enacting the Maternity Act of 1921, had breached a specific limitation upon its taxing and spending power. The taxpayer in *Frothingham* alleged essentially that Congress, by enacting the challenged statute, had exceeded the general powers delegated to it by Art. I, § 8, and that Congress had thereby invaded the legislative province reserved to the States by the Tenth Amendment. . . .

We have noted that the Establishment Clause of the First Amendment does specifically limit the taxing and spending power conferred by Art. I, § 8. Whether the Constitution contains other specific limitations can be determined only in the context of future cases. However, whenever such specific limitations are found, we believe a taxpayer will have a clear stake as a taxpayer in assuring that they are not breached by Congress. Consequently, we hold that a taxpayer will have standing consistent with Article III to invoke federal judicial power when he alleges that congressional action under the taxing and spending clause is in derogation of those constitutional provisions which operate to restrict the exercise of the taxing and spending power. The taxpayer's allegation in such cases would be that his tax money is being extracted and spent in violation of specific constitutional protections against such abuses of legislative power. Such an injury is appropriate for judicial redress, and the taxpayer has established the necessary nexus between his status and the nature of the allegedly unconstitutional action to support his claim of standing to secure judicial review. Under such circumstances, we feel confident that the questions will be framed with the necessary specificity, that the issues will be contested with the necessary adverseness and that the litigation will be pursued with the necessary vigor to assure that the constitutional challenge will be made in a form traditionally thought to be capable of judicial resolution. We lack that confidence in cases such as *Frothingham* where a taxpayer seeks to employ a federal court as a forum in which to air his generalized grievances about the conduct of government or the allocation of power in the Federal System.

While we express no view at all on the merits of appellants' claims in this case, their complaint contains sufficient allegations under the criteria we have outlined to give them standing to invoke a federal court's jurisdiction for an adjudication on the merits.

Reversed.

JUSTICE STEWART, concurring.

I join the judgment and opinion of the Court, which I understand to hold only that a federal taxpayer has standing to assert that a specific expenditure of federal funds violates the Establishment Clause of the First Amendment. Because that clause plainly prohibits taxing and spending in aid of religion, every taxpayer can claim a personal constitutional right not to be taxed for the support of a religious institution. The present case is thus readily distinguishable from *Frothingham* v. *Mellon*, where the taxpayer did not rely on an explicit constitutional prohibition but instead questioned the scope of the powers delegated to the national legislature by Article I of the Constitution.

JUSTICE FORTAS, concurring.

I would confine the ruling in this case to the proposition that a taxpayer may maintain a suit to challenge the validity of a federal expenditure on the ground that the expenditure violates the Establishment Clause. As the Court's opinion recites, there is enough in the constitutional history of the Establishment Clause to support the thesis that this Clause includes a *specific* prohibition upon the use of the power to tax to support an establishment of religion. . . .

JUSTICE HARLAN, dissenting.

The problems presented by this case are narrow and relatively abstract, but the principles by which they must be resolved involve nothing less than the proper functioning of the federal courts, and so run to the roots of our constitutional system. The nub of my view is that the end result of *Frothingham* v. *Mellon*, was correct, even though, like others, I do not subscribe to all of its reasoning and premises. Although I therefore agree with certain of the conclusions reached today by the Court, I cannot accept the standing doctrine that it substitutes for *Frothingham*, for it seems to me that this new doctrine rests on premises that do not withstand analysis. Accordingly, I respectfully dissent. . . .

III.

It seems to me clear that public actions, whatever the constitutional provisions on which they are premised, may involve important hazards for the continued effectiveness of the federal judiciary. Although I believe such actions to be within the jurisdiction conferred upon the federal courts by Article III of the Constitution, there surely can be little doubt that they strain the judicial function and press to the limit judicial authority. There is every reason to fear that unrestricted public actions might well alter the allocation of authority among the three branches of the Federal Government. It is not, I submit, enough to say that the present members of the Court would not seize these opportunities for abuse, for such actions would, even without conscious abuse, go far toward the final transformation of this Court into the Council of Revision which, despite Madison's support, was rejected by the Constitutional Convention. I do not doubt that there must be "some effectual power in the government to restrain or correct the infractions" of the Constitution's several commands, but neither can I suppose that such power resides only in the federal courts. We must as judges recall that, as Mr. Justice Holmes wisely observed, the other branches of the Government "are ultimate guardians of the liberties and welfare of the people in quite as great a degree as the courts." *Missouri, Kansas & Texas R. Co.* v. *May*, 194 U.S. 267 (1904). The powers of the federal judiciary will be adequate for the great burdens placed upon them only if they are employed prudently, with recognition of the strengths as well as the hazards that go with our kind of representative government.

Presumably the Court recognizes at least certain of these hazards, else it would not have troubled to impose limitations upon the situations in which, and purposes for which, such suits may be brought. Nonetheless, the limitations adopted by the Court are, as I have endeavored to indicate, wholly untenable. This is the more unfortunate because there is available a resolution of this problem that entirely satisfies the demands of the principle of separation of powers. This Court has previously held that individual litigants have standing to represent the public interest, despite their lack of economic or other personal interests, if Congress has appropriately authorized such suits. I would adhere to that principle. Any hazards to the proper allocation of authority among the three branches of the Government would be substantially diminished if public actions had been pertinently authorized by Congress and the President. I appreciate that this Court does not ordinarily await the mandate of other branches of the Government, but it seems to me that the extraordinary character of public actions, and of the mischievous, if not dangerous, consequences they involve for the proper functioning of our constitutional system, and in particular of the federal courts, makes such judicial forbearance the part of wisdom. It must be emphasized that the implications of these questions of judicial policy are of fundamental significance for the other branches of the Federal Government. . . .

FOR DISCUSSION

The Court has been fairly strict in limiting federal taxpayer suits. What are the primary advantages and disadvantages of this approach? Has the Court provided adequate reasoning to suggest that the establishment clause of the First Amendment might warrant an exception to the general presumption against such suits?

RELATED CASES

Valley Forge Christian College v. Americans United for Separation of Church and State: **454 U.S. 464 (1982).**

The Court decided that members of Americans United for Separation of Church and State did not have adequate standing as taxpayers, or in any other capacity, to challenge a decision by the secretary of Health, Education, and Welfare to transfer surplus federal property (a former hospital facility) to Valley Forge Christian College. Members of Americans United had literally found out about the transaction through reading the newspaper.

Hein v. Freedom from Religion Foundation, Inc.: **551 U.S. 587 (2007).**

Relying on *Flast v. Cohen*, 392 U.S. 83 (1968), rejected a taxpayer suit brought by an organization opposed to White House offices designed to ensure that faith-based groups could compete for federal aid.

Arizona Christian School v. Winn: **563 U.S. 125 (2011).**

Distinguishing this case from *Flast v. Cohen*, the Court denied standing to Arizona taxpayers who sought to challenge a state law that provided tax credits for contributions to school tuition organizations (STOs), which provided scholarships to individuals attending private school. The majority emphasized that *Flast* created a narrow taxpayer challenge exception, and distinguished the government's use of tax credits, which relied on individual choice, from governmental expenditures, which relied on general tax revenues.

MASSACHUSETTS V. E.P.A.

549 U.S. 497, 127 S.Ct. 1438, 167 L.Ed.2d 248 (2007)

A variety of groups including local governments and individual states challenged a decision by the Environmental Protection Agency (EPA) which denied their petition for rulemaking to regulate greenhouse gas emissions from motor vehicles under the Clean Air Act. The Court of Appeals for the District of Columbia Circuit, dismissed or denied the petitions. Certiorari was granted and the Supreme Court reversed.

Vote: 5–4

JUSTICE STEVENS delivered the opinion of the Court.

A well-documented rise in global temperatures has coincided with a significant increase in the concentration of carbon dioxide in the atmosphere. Respected scientists believe the two trends are related. For when carbon dioxide is released into the atmosphere, it acts like the ceiling of a greenhouse, trapping solar energy and retarding the escape of reflected heat. It is therefore a species—the most important species—of a "greenhouse gas."

Calling global warming "the most pressing environmental challenge of our time," a group of States, local governments, and private organizations alleged in a petition for certiorari that the Environmental Protection Agency (EPA) has abdicated its responsibility under the Clean Air Act to regulate the emissions of four greenhouse gases, including carbon dioxide. Specifically, petitioners asked us to answer two questions concerning the meaning of § 202(a)(1) of the Act: whether EPA has the statutory authority to regulate greenhouse gas emissions from new motor vehicles; and if so, whether its stated reasons for refusing to do so are consistent with the statute.

In response, EPA, supported by 10 intervening States and six trade associations, correctly argued that we may not address those two questions unless at least one petitioner has standing to invoke our jurisdiction under Article III of the Constitution. Notwithstanding the serious character of that jurisdictional argument and the absence of any conflicting decisions construing § 202(a)(1), the unusual importance of the underlying issue persuaded us to grant the writ.

I

Section 202(a)(1) of the Clean Air Act provides:

> "The [EPA] Administrator shall by regulation prescribe (and from time to time revise) in accordance with the provisions of this section, standards applicable to the emission of any air pollutant from any class or classes of new motor vehicles or new motor vehicle engines, which in his judgment cause, or contribute to, air pollution which may reasonably be anticipated to endanger public health or welfare . . . ."

The Act defines "air pollutant" to include "any air pollution agent or combination of such agents, including any physical, chemical, biological, radioactive . . . substance or matter which is emitted into or otherwise enters the ambient air." § 7602(g). "Welfare" is also defined broadly: among other things, it includes "effects on . . . weather . . . and climate." § 7602(h).

When Congress enacted these provisions, the study of climate change was in its infancy. In 1959, shortly after the U.S. Weather Bureau began monitoring atmospheric carbon dioxide levels, an observatory in Mauna Loa, Hawaii, recorded a mean level of 316 parts per million. This was well above the highest carbon dioxide concentration—no more than 300 parts per million—revealed in the 420,000-year-old ice-core record. By the time Congress drafted § 202(a)(1) in 1970, carbon dioxide levels had reached 325 parts per million.

In the late 1970's, the Federal Government began devoting serious attention to the possibility that carbon dioxide emissions associated with human activity could provoke climate change. In 1978, Congress enacted the National Climate Program Act, 92 Stat. 601, which required the President to establish a program to "assist the Nation and the world to *508 understand and respond to natural and man-induced climate processes and their implications," President Carter, in turn, asked the National Research Council, the working arm of the National

Academy of Sciences, to investigate the subject. The Council's response was unequivocal: "If carbon dioxide continues to increase, the study group finds no reason to doubt that climate changes will result and no reason to believe that these changes will be negligible . . . . A wait-and-see policy may mean waiting until it is too late."

Congress next addressed the issue in 1987, when it enacted the Global Climate Protection Act, Title XI of Pub.L. 100–204, 101 Stat. 1407, note following 15 U.S.C. § 2901. Finding that "manmade pollution—the release of carbon dioxide, chlorofluorocarbons, methane, and other trace gases into the atmosphere—may be producing a long-term and substantial increase in the average temperature on Earth," Congress directed EPA to propose to Congress a "coordinated national policy on global climate change,", and ordered the Secretary of State to work "through the channels of multilateral diplomacy" and coordinate diplomatic efforts to combat global warming. Congress emphasized that "ongoing pollution and deforestation may be contributing now to an irreversible process" and that "[n]ecessary actions must be identified and implemented in time to protect the climate."

Meanwhile, the scientific understanding of climate change progressed. In 1990, the Intergovernmental Panel on Climate Change (IPCC), a multinational scientific body organized under the auspices of the United Nations, published its first comprehensive report on the topic. Drawing on expert opinions from across the globe, the IPCC concluded that "emissions resulting from human activities are substantially increasing the atmospheric concentrations of . . . greenhouse gases [which] will enhance the greenhouse effect, resulting on average in an additional warming of the Earth's surface."

Responding to the IPCC report, the United Nations convened the "Earth Summit" in 1992 in Rio de Janeiro. The first President Bush attended and signed the United Nations Framework Convention on Climate Change (UNFCCC), a nonbinding agreement among 154 nations to reduce atmospheric concentrations of carbon dioxide and other greenhouse gases for the purpose of "prevent[ing] dangerous anthropogenic [*i.e.,* human-induced] interference with the [Earth's] climate system." The Senate unanimously ratified the treaty.

Some five years later—after the IPCC issued a second comprehensive report in 1995 concluding that "[t]he balance of evidence suggests there is a discernible human influence on global climate"—the UNFCCC signatories met in Kyoto, Japan, and adopted a protocol that assigned mandatory targets for industrialized nations to reduce greenhouse gas emissions. Because those targets did not apply to developing and heavily polluting nations such as China and India, the Senate unanimously passed a resolution expressing its sense that the United States should not enter into the Kyoto Protocol. President Clinton did not submit the protocol to the Senate for ratification.

II

On October 20, 1999, a group of 19 private organizations filed a rulemaking petition asking EPA to regulate "greenhouse gas emissions from new motor vehicles under § 202 of the Clean Air Act." Petitioners maintained that 1998 was the "warmest year on record"; that carbon dioxide, methane, nitrous oxide, and hydrofluorocarbons are "heat trapping greenhouse gases"; that greenhouse gas emissions have significantly accelerated climate change; and that the IPCC's 1995 report warned that "carbon dioxide remains the most important contributor to [manmade] forcing of climate change." The petition further alleged that climate change will have serious adverse effects on human health and the environment. As to EPA's statutory authority, the petition observed that the Agency itself had already confirmed that it had the power to regulate carbon dioxide. In 1998, Jonathan Z. Cannon, then EPA's general counsel, prepared a legal opinion concluding that "CO_2 emissions are within the scope of EPA's authority to regulate," even as he recognized that EPA had so far declined to exercise that authority. Cannon's successor, Gary S. Guzy, reiterated that opinion before a congressional committee just two weeks before the rulemaking petition was filed.

Fifteen months after the petition's submission, EPA requested public comment on "all the issues raised in [the] petition," adding a "particular" request for comments on "any scientific, technical, legal, economic or other aspect of these issues that may be relevant to EPA's consideration of this petition." EPA received more than 50,000 comments over the next five months.

Before the close of the comment period, the White House sought "assistance in identifying the areas in the science of climate change where there are the greatest certainties and uncertainties" from the National Research Council, asking for a response "as soon as possible." The result was a 2001 report titled Climate Change Science: An Analysis of Some Key Questions (NRC Report), which, drawing heavily on the 1995 IPCC report, concluded that "[g]reenhouse gases are accumulating in Earth's atmosphere as a result of human activities, causing surface air temperatures and subsurface ocean temperatures to rise. Temperatures are, in fact, rising."

On September 8, 2003, EPA entered an order denying the rulemaking petition. 68 Fed.Reg. 52922. The Agency gave two reasons for its decision: (1) that contrary to the opinions of its former general counsels, the Clean Air Act does not authorize EPA to issue mandatory regulations to address global climate change, and (2) that even if the Agency had the authority to set greenhouse gas emission standards, it would be unwise to do so at this time.

In concluding that it lacked statutory authority over greenhouse gases, EPA observed that Congress "was well aware of the global climate change issue when it last comprehensively amended the [Clean Air Act] in 1990," yet it declined to adopt a proposed amendment establishing binding emissions limitations. Congress instead chose to authorize further investigation into climate change. EPA further reasoned that Congress' "specially tailored solutions to global atmospheric issues,"—in particular, its 1990 enactment of a comprehensive scheme to regulate pollutants that depleted the ozone layer,—counseled against reading the general authorization of § 202(a)(1) to confer regulatory authority over greenhouse gases.

EPA stated that it was "urged on in this view," by this Court's decision in *FDA v. Brown & Williamson Tobacco Corp.,* 529 U.S. 120, 120 S.Ct. 1291, 146 L.Ed.2d 121 (2000). In that case, relying on "tobacco['s] unique political history," *id.,* at 159, 120 S.Ct. 1291, we invalidated the Food and Drug Administration's reliance on its general authority to regulate drugs as a basis for asserting jurisdiction over an "industry constituting a significant portion of the American economy," *ibid.*

EPA reasoned that climate change had its own "political history": Congress designed the original Clean Air Act to address *local* air pollutants rather than a substance that "is fairly consistent in its concentration throughout the *world's* atmosphere," declined in 1990 to enact proposed amendments to force EPA to set carbon dioxide emission standards for motor vehicles, and addressed global climate change in other legislation, 68 Fed.Reg. 52927. Because of this political history, and because imposing emission limitations on greenhouse gases would have even greater economic and political repercussions than regulating tobacco, EPA was persuaded that it lacked the power to do so. In essence, EPA concluded that climate change was so important that unless Congress spoke with exacting specificity, it could not have meant the Agency to address it.

Having reached that conclusion, EPA believed it followed that greenhouse gases cannot be "air pollutants" within the meaning of the Act. The Agency bolstered this conclusion by explaining that if carbon dioxide were an air pollutant, the only feasible method of reducing tailpipe emissions would be to improve fuel economy. But because Congress has already created detailed mandatory fuel economy standards subject to Department of Transportation (DOT) administration, the Agency concluded that EPA regulation would either conflict with those standards or be superfluous.

Even assuming that it had authority over greenhouse gases, EPA explained in detail why it would refuse to exercise that authority. The Agency began by recognizing that the concentration of greenhouse gases has dramatically increased as a result of human activities, and acknowledged the attendant increase in global surface air temperatures. EPA nevertheless gave controlling importance to the NRC Report's statement that a causal link between the two " 'cannot be unequivocally established.' " Given that residual uncertainty, EPA concluded that regulating greenhouse gas emissions would be unwise.

The Agency furthermore characterized any EPA regulation of motor-vehicle emissions as a "piecemeal approach" to climate change, and stated that such regulation would conflict with the President's "comprehensive approach" to the problem, *ibid.* That approach involves additional support for technological innovation, the creation of nonregulatory programs to encourage voluntary private-sector reductions in greenhouse gas emissions, and further research on climate change—not actual regulation. According to EPA, unilateral EPA regulation of motor-vehicle greenhouse gas emissions might also hamper the President's ability to persuade key developing countries to reduce greenhouse gas emissions.

III

Petitioners, now joined by intervenor States and local governments, sought review of EPA's order in the United States Court of Appeals for the District of Columbia Circuit. Although each of the three judges on the panel wrote a separate opinion, two judges agreed "that the EPA Administrator properly exercised his discretion under § 202(a)(1) in denying the petition for rule making." The court therefore denied the petition for review.

IV

Article III of the Constitution limits federal-court jurisdiction to "Cases" and "Controversies." Those two words confine "the business of federal courts to questions presented in an adversary context and in a form historically viewed as capable of resolution through the judicial process." *Flast v. Cohen,* 392 U.S. 83, 95, 88 S.Ct. 1942, 20 L.Ed.2d 947 (1968). It is therefore familiar learning that no justiciable "controversy" exists when parties seek adjudication of a political question, *Luther v. Borden,* 7 How. 1, 12 L.Ed. 581 (1849), when they ask for an advisory opinion, *Hayburn's Case,* 2 Dall. 409, 1 L.Ed. 436 (1792), see also *Clinton v. Jones,* 520 U.S. 681, 700, n. 33, 117 S.Ct. 1636, 137 L.Ed.2d 945 (1997), or when the question sought to be adjudicated has been mooted by subsequent developments, *California v. San Pablo & Tulare R. Co.,* 149 U.S. 308, 13 S.Ct. 876, 37 L.Ed. 747 (1893). This case suffers from none of these defects.

The parties' dispute turns on the proper construction of a congressional statute, a question eminently suitable to resolution in federal court. Congress has moreover authorized this type of challenge to EPA action. That authorization is of critical importance to the standing inquiry: "Congress has the power to define injuries and articulate chains of causation that will give rise to a case or controversy where none existed before."

EPA maintains that because greenhouse gas emissions inflict widespread harm, the doctrine of standing presents an insuperable jurisdictional obstacle. We do not agree. At bottom, "the gist of the question of standing" is whether petitioners have "such a personal stake in the outcome of the controversy as to assure that concrete adverseness which sharpens the presentation of issues upon which the court so largely depends for illumination."

To ensure the proper adversarial presentation, *Lujan* holds that a litigant must demonstrate that it has suffered a concrete and particularized injury that is either actual or imminent, that the injury is fairly traceable to the defendant, and that it is likely that a favorable decision will redress that injury. However, a litigant to whom Congress has "accorded a procedural right to protect his concrete interests," "can assert that right without meeting all the normal standards for redressability and immediacy," When a litigant is vested with a procedural right, that litigant has standing if there is some possibility that the requested relief will prompt the injury-causing party to reconsider the decision that allegedly harmed the litigant.

Only one of the petitioners needs to have standing to permit us to consider the petition for review. We stress here, as did Judge Tatel below, the special position and interest of Massachusetts. It is of considerable relevance that the party seeking review here is a sovereign State and not, as it was in *Lujan,* a private individual.

Well before the creation of the modern administrative state, we recognized that States are not normal litigants for the purposes of invoking federal jurisdiction. As Justice Holmes explained in *Georgia v. Tennessee Copper Co.,* 206 U.S. 230, 237, 27 S.Ct. 618, 51 L.Ed. 1038 (1907), a case in which Georgia sought to protect its citizens from air pollution originating outside its borders:

> "The case has been argued largely as if it were one between two private parties; but it is not. The very elements that would be relied upon in a suit between fellow-citizens as a ground for equitable relief are wanting here. The State owns very little of the territory alleged to be affected, and the damage to it capable of estimate in money, possibly, at least, is small. This is a suit by a State for an injury to it in its capacity of *quasi*-sovereign. In that capacity the State has an interest independent of and behind the titles of its citizens, *519 in all the earth and air within its domain. It has the last word as to whether its mountains shall be stripped of their forests and its inhabitants shall breathe pure air."

Just as Georgia's independent interest "in all the earth and air within its domain" supported federal jurisdiction a century ago, so too does Massachusetts' well-founded desire to preserve its sovereign territory today. That Massachusetts does in fact own a great deal of the "territory alleged to be affected" only reinforces the conclusion that its stake in the outcome of this case is sufficiently concrete to warrant the exercise of federal judicial power.

When a State enters the Union, it surrenders certain sovereign prerogatives. Massachusetts cannot invade Rhode Island to force reductions in greenhouse gas emissions, it cannot negotiate an emissions treaty with China or India, and in some circumstances the exercise of its police powers to reduce in-state motor-vehicle emissions might well be pre-empted.

These sovereign prerogatives are now lodged in the Federal Government, and Congress has ordered EPA to protect Massachusetts (among others) by prescribing standards applicable to the "emission of any air pollutant from any class or classes of new motor vehicle engines, which in [the Administrator's] judgment cause, or contribute to, air pollution which may reasonably be anticipated to endanger public health or welfare." Congress has moreover recognized a concomitant procedural right to challenge the rejection of its rulemaking petition as arbitrary and capricious. Given that procedural right and Massachusetts' stake in protecting its quasi-sovereign interests, the Commonwealth is entitled to special solicitude in our standing analysis.

With that in mind, it is clear that petitioners' submissions as they pertain to Massachusetts have satisfied the most demanding standards of the adversarial process. EPA's steadfast refusal to regulate greenhouse gas emissions presents a risk of harm to Massachusetts that is both "actual" and "imminent." There is, moreover, a "substantial likelihood that the judicial relief requested" will prompt EPA to take steps to reduce that risk. *Duke Power Co. v. Carolina Environmental Study Group, Inc.,* 438 U.S. 59, 79, 98 S.Ct. 2620, 57 L.Ed.2d 595 (1978).

The Injury

The harms associated with climate change are serious and well recognized. Indeed, the NRC Report itself—which EPA regards as an "objective and independent assessment of the relevant science,"—identifies a number of environmental changes that have already inflicted significant harms, including "the global retreat of mountain glaciers, reduction in snow-cover extent, the earlier spring melting of ice on rivers and lakes, [and] the accelerated rate of rise of sea levels during the 20th century relative to the past few thousand years . . . ."

Petitioners allege that this only hints at the environmental damage yet to come. According to the climate scientist Michael MacCracken, "qualified scientific experts involved in climate change research" have reached a "strong consensus" that global warming threatens (among other things) a precipitate rise in sea levels by the end of the century, "severe and irreversible changes to natural ecosystems," a "significant reduction in water storage in winter snowpack in mountainous regions with direct and important economic consequences," *ibid.*, and an increase in the spread of disease, He also observes that rising ocean temperatures may contribute to the ferocity of hurricanes.

That these climate-change risks are "widely shared" does not minimize Massachusetts' interest in the outcome of this litigation. According to petitioners' unchallenged affidavits, global sea levels rose somewhere between 10 and 20 centimeters over the 20th century as a result of global warming. These rising seas have already begun to swallow Massachusetts' coastal land. Because the Commonwealth "owns a substantial portion of the state's coastal property," it has alleged a particularized injury in its capacity as a landowner. The severity of that injury will only increase over the course of the next century: If sea levels continue to rise as predicted, one Massachusetts official believes that a significant fraction of coastal property will be "either permanently lost through inundation or temporarily lost through periodic storm surge and flooding events." Remediation costs alone, petitioners allege, could run well into the hundreds of millions of dollars.

VIII

The judgment of the Court of Appeals is reversed, and the case is remanded for further proceedings consistent with this opinion.

It is so ordered.

CHIEF JUSTICE ROBERTS, with whom JUSTICE SCALIA, JUSTICE THOMAS, and JUSTICE ALITO join, dissenting.

Global warming may be a "crisis," even "the most pressing environmental problem of our time." Indeed, it may ultimately affect nearly everyone on the planet in some potentially adverse way, and it may be that governments have done too little to address it. It is not a problem, however, that has escaped the attention of policymakers in the Executive and Legislative Branches of our Government, who continue to consider regulatory, legislative, and treaty-based means of addressing global climate change.

Apparently dissatisfied with the pace of progress on this issue in the elected branches, petitioners have come to the courts claiming broad-ranging injury, and attempting to tie that injury to the Government's alleged failure to comply with a rather narrow statutory provision. I would reject these challenges as nonjusticiable. Such a conclusion involves no judgment on whether global warming exists, what causes it, or the extent of the problem. Nor does it render petitioners without recourse. This Court's standing jurisprudence simply recognizes that redress of grievances of the sort at issue here "is the function of Congress and the Chief Executive," not the federal courts. *Lujan v. Defenders of Wildlife,* 504 U.S. 555, 576, 112 S.Ct. 2130, 119 L.Ed.2d 351 (1992). I would vacate the judgment *536 below and remand for dismissal of the petitions for review.

I

Article III, § 2, of the Constitution limits the federal judicial power to the adjudication of "Cases" and "Controversies." "If a dispute is not a proper case or controversy, the courts have no business deciding it, or expounding the law in the course of doing so." *DaimlerChrysler Corp. v. Cuno,* 547 U.S. 332, 341, 126 S.Ct. 1854, 1860–1861, 164 L.Ed.2d 589 (2006). "Standing to sue is part of the common understanding of what it takes to make a justiciable case," *Steel Co. v. Citizens for Better Environment,* 523 U.S. 83, 102, 118 S.Ct. 1003, 140 L.Ed.2d 210 (1998), and has been described as "an essential and unchanging part of the case-or-controversy requirement of Article III," *Defenders of Wildlife, supra,* at 560, 112 S.Ct. 2130.

Our modern framework for addressing standing is familiar: "A plaintiff must allege personal injury fairly traceable to the defendant's allegedly unlawful conduct and likely to be redressed by the requested relief."

DaimlerChrysler, supra, at 342, 126 S.Ct., at 1861 (quoting *Allen v. Wright,* 468 U.S. 737, 751, 104 S.Ct. 3315, 82 L.Ed.2d 556 (1984); (internal quotation marks omitted)). Applying that standard here, petitioners bear the burden of alleging an injury that is fairly traceable to the Environmental Protection Agency's failure to promulgate new motor vehicle greenhouse gas emission standards, and that is likely to be redressed by the prospective issuance of such standards.

Before determining whether petitioners can meet this familiar test, however, the Court changes the rules. It asserts that "States are not normal litigants for the purposes of invoking federal jurisdiction," and that given "Massachusetts' stake in protecting its quasi-sovereign interests, the Commonwealth is entitled to *special solicitude* in our standing analysis."

FOR DISCUSSION

Should states be given special consideration when it comes to standing issues or representing their citizens? How are they different from ordinary taxpayers or citizens who can vote if they do not like a specific policy?

CHEVRON U.S.A., INC. V. NATURAL RESOURCES DEFENSE COUNCIL, INC.

467 U.S. 837, 104 S. Ct. 2778, 81 L. Ed. 2d 694 (1984)

This decision addresses an interpretation by the Environmental Protection Agency (EPA) of the Clean Air Act Amendments of 1977. Under its reading, a plant, normally subject to stringent requirements for alterations of existing facilities, could install or modify one piece of pollution equipment without meeting such requirements as long as it did not increase total pollution emissions. The Court had to decide whether this interpretation of the statute was reasonable.

Vote: 6–0 [JUSTICES MARSHALL, REHNQUIST, and O'CONNOR did not participate].

JUSTICE STEVENS delivered the opinion of the Court.

I

The EPA regulations containing the plantwide definition of the term stationary source were promulgated on October 14, 1981. 46 Fed.Reg. 50766. Respondents filed a timely petition for review in the United States Court of Appeals for the District of Columbia Circuit pursuant to 42 U.S. C. § 7607 (b)(1). The Court of Appeals set aside the regulations. *Natural Resources Defense Council, Inc. v. Gorsuch,* 222 U.S.App.D.C. 268, 685 F.2d 718 (1982). The court observed that the relevant part of the amended Clean Air Act "does not explicitly define what Congress envisioned as a 'stationary source, to which the permit program . . . should apply," and further stated that the precise issue was not "squarely addressed in the legislative history." In light of its conclusion that the legislative history bearing on the question was "at best contradictory," it reasoned that "the purposes of the nonattainment program should guide our decision here." Based on two of its precedents concerning the applicability of the bubble concept to certain Clean Air Act programs, the court stated that the bubble concept was "mandatory" in programs designed merely to maintain existing air quality, but held that it was "inappropriate" in programs enacted to improve air quality. Since the purpose of the permit program—its "*raison d'etre,*" in the court's view—was to improve air quality, the court held that the bubble concept was inapplicable in these cases under its prior precedents. It therefore set aside the regulations embodying the bubble concept as contrary to law. We granted certiorari to review that judgment, and we now reverse.

The basic legal error of the Court of Appeals was to adopt a static judicial definition of the term "stationary source" when it had decided that Congress itself had not commanded that definition. Respondents do not defend the legal reasoning of the Court of Appeals. Nevertheless, since this Court reviews judgments, not opinions, we must determine whether the Court of Appeals' legal error resulted in an erroneous judgment on the validity of the regulations.

II

When a court reviews an agency's construction of the statute which it administers, it is confronted with two questions. First, always, is the question whether Congress has directly spoken to the precise question at issue. If the intent of Congress is clear, that is the end of the matter; for the court, as well as the agency, must give effect to the unambiguously expressed intent of Congress. If, however, the court determines Congress has not directly addressed the precise question at issue, the court does not simply impose its own construction on the statute, as would be necessary in the absence of an administrative interpretation. Rather, if the statute is silent or ambiguous with respect to the specific issue, the question for the court is whether the agency's answer is based on a permissible construction of the statute.

The power of an administrative agency to administer a congressionally created . . . program necessarily requires the formulation of policy and the making of rules to fill any gap left, implicitly or explicitly, by Congress. *Morton v. Ruiz*, 415 U.S. 199 (1974).

If Congress has explicitly left a gap for the agency to fill, there is an express delegation of authority to the agency to elucidate a specific provision of the statute by regulation. Such legislative regulations are given controlling weight unless they are arbitrary, capricious, or manifestly contrary to the statute. Sometimes the legislative delegation to an agency on a particular question is implicit, rather than explicit. In such a case, a court may not substitute its own construction of a statutory provision for a reasonable interpretation made by the administrator of an agency.

We have long recognized that considerable weight should be accorded to an executive department's construction of a statutory scheme it is entrusted to administer, and the principle of deference to administrative interpretations has been consistently followed by this Court whenever decision as to the meaning or reach of a statute has involved reconciling conflicting policies, and a full understanding of the force of the statutory policy in the given situation has depended upon more than ordinary knowledge respecting the matters subjected to agency regulations. . . .

. . . If this choice represents a reasonable accommodation of conflicting policies that were committed to the agency's care by the statute, we should not disturb it unless it appears from the statute or its legislative history that the accommodation is not one that Congress would have sanctioned.

In light of these well-settled principles, it is clear that the Court of Appeals misconceived the nature of its role in reviewing the regulations at issue. Once it determined, after its own examination of the legislation, that Congress did not actually have an intent regarding the applicability of the bubble concept to the permit program, the question before it was not whether, in its view, the concept is "inappropriate" in the general context of a program designed to improve air quality, but whether the Administrator's view that it is appropriate in the context of this particular program is a reasonable one. Based on the examination of the legislation and its history which follows, we agree with the Court of Appeals that Congress did not have a specific intention on the applicability of the bubble concept in these cases, and conclude that the EPA's use of that concept here is a reasonable policy choice for the agency to make.

IV

The Clean Air Act Amendments of 1977 are a lengthy, detailed, technical, complex, and comprehensive response to a major social issue. A small portion of the statute expressly deals with nonattainment areas. The focal point of this controversy is one phrase in that portion of the Amendments. Basically, the statute required each State in a nonattainment area to prepare and obtain approval of a new SIP [plans] by July 1, 1979. In the interim, those States were required to comply with the EPA's interpretative Ruling of December 21, 1976. The deadline for attainment of the primary [National Ambient Air Quality Standards] (NAAQS's)] was extended until December 31, 1982, and in some cases until December 31, 1987, but the SIP's were required to contain a number of provisions designed to achieve the goals as expeditiously as possible.

V

The legislative history of the portion of the 1977 Amendments dealing with nonattainment areas does not contain any specific comment on the "bubble concept" or the question whether a plantwide definition of a stationary source is permissible under the permit program. It does, however, plainly disclose that in the permit program Congress sought to accommodate the conflict between the economic interest in permitting capital improvements to continue and the environmental interest in improving air quality. . . .

VI

In 1981, a new administration took office and initiated a "[g]overnment-wide reexamination of regulatory burdens and complexities." In the context of that review, the EPA reevaluated the various arguments that had been advanced in connection with the proper definition of the term "source" and concluded that the term should be given the same definition in both nonattainment areas and [Prevention of Significant Deterioration (PSD)] areas.

In explaining its conclusion, the EPA first noted that the definitional issue was not squarely addressed in either the statute or its legislative history, and therefore that the issue involved an agency "judgment as how to best carry out the Act." It then set forth several reasons for concluding that the plantwide definition was more appropriate. It pointed out that the dual definition "can act as a disincentive to new investment and modernization by discouraging modifications to existing facilities" and can actually retard progress in air pollution control by discouraging replacement of older, dirtier processes or pieces of equipment with new, cleaner ones. Moreover, the new definition would simplify EPA's rules by using the same definition of "source" for PSD, nonattainment new source review, and the construction moratorium. This reduces confusion and inconsistency. Finally, the agency explained that additional requirements that remained in place would accomplish the fundamental purposes of achieving attainment with NAAQS's as expeditiously as possible. These conclusions were expressed in a proposed rulemaking in August, 1981, that was formally promulgated in October.

VII

Statutory Language

We are not persuaded that parsing of general terms in the text of the statute will reveal an actual intent of Congress. We know full well that this language is not dispositive; the terms are overlapping, and the language is not precisely directed to the question of the applicability of a given term in the context of a larger operation. To the extent any congressional "intent" can be discerned from this language, it would appear that the listing of overlapping, illustrative terms was intended to enlarge, rather than to confine, the scope of the agency's power to regulate particular sources in order to effectuate the policies of the Act.

Legislative History

In addition, respondents argue that the legislative history and policies of the Act foreclose the plantwide definition, and that the EPA's interpretation is not entitled to deference, because it represents a sharp break with prior interpretations of the Act.

Based on our examination of the legislative history, we agree with the Court of Appeals that it is unilluminating. . . .

Our review of the EPA's varying interpretations of the word "source"—both before and after the 1977 Amendments—convinces us that the agency primarily responsible for administering this important legislation has consistently interpreted it flexibly—not in a sterile textual vacuum, but in the context of implementing policy decisions in a technical and complex arena. The fact that the agency has from time to time changed its interpretation of the term "source" does not, as respondents argue, lead us to conclude that no deference should be accorded the agency's interpretation of the statute. An initial agency interpretation is not instantly carved in stone. On the contrary, the agency, to engage in informed rulemaking, must consider varying interpretations and the wisdom of its policy on a continuing basis. Moreover, the fact that the agency has adopted different definitions in different contexts adds force to the argument that the definition itself is flexible, particularly since Congress has never indicated any disapproval of a flexible reading of the statute. . . .

Policy

Judges are not experts in the field, and are not part of either political branch of the Government. Courts must, in some cases, reconcile competing political interests, but not on the basis of the judges' personal policy preferences. In contrast, an agency to which Congress has delegated policymaking responsibilities may, within the limits of that delegation, properly rely upon the incumbent administration's views of wise policy to inform its judgments. While agencies are not directly accountable to the people, the Chief Executive is, and it is entirely appropriate for this political branch of the Government to make such policy choices—resolving the competing interests which Congress itself either inadvertently did not resolve, or intentionally left to be resolved by the agency charged with the administration of the statute in light of everyday realities.

When a challenge to an agency construction of a statutory provision, fairly conceptualized, really centers on the wisdom of the agency's policy, rather than whether it is a reasonable choice within a gap left open by Congress, the challenge must fail. In such a case, federal judges—who have no constituency—have a duty to respect legitimate policy choices made by those who do. The responsibilities for assessing the wisdom of such policy choices and resolving the struggle between competing views of the public interest are not judicial ones: "Our Constitution vests such responsibilities in the political branches." *TVA v. Hill,* 437 U.S. 153 (1978).

We hold that the EPA's definition of the term "source" is a permissible construction of the statute which seeks to accommodate progress in reducing air pollution with economic growth. The Regulations which the Administrator has adopted provide what the agency could allowably view as . . . [an] effective reconciliation of these twofold ends. . . . *United States v. Shimer,* 367 U.S. 374 (1961).

The judgment of the Court of Appeals is reversed.

LUJAN V. DEFENDERS OF WILDLIFE

504 U.S. 555, 112 S. Ct. 2130, 119 L. Ed. 2d 351 (1992)

The following case illustrates both the creativity that plaintiffs can sometimes employ in seeking standing and the fact that the Court is not always sympathetic to such claims.

Vote: 6–3

JUSTICE SCALIA delivered the opinion of the Court.

This case involves a challenge to a rule promulgated by the Secretary of the Interior interpreting § 7 of the Endangered Species Act of 1973 (ESA), 87 Stat. 892, as amended, 16 U.S. C. § 1536, in such fashion as to render it applicable only to actions within the United States or on the high seas. The preliminary issue, and the only one we reach, is whether respondents here, plaintiffs below, have standing to seek judicial review of the rule.

I

The ESA seeks to protect species of animals against threats to their continuing existence caused by man. See generally *TVA* v. *Hill*, [437 U.S. 153] (1978). The ESA instructs the Secretary of the Interior to promulgate by regulation a list of those species which are either endangered or threatened under enumerated criteria, and to define the critical habitat of these species. . . .

II

. . . Over the years, our cases have established that the irreducible constitutional minimum of standing contains three elements. First, the plaintiff must have suffered an "injury in fact"—an invasion of a legally protected interest which is (a) concrete and particularized, *Warth* v. *Seldin*, 422 U.S. 490 (1975); *Sierra Club* v. *Morton*, 405 U.S. 727 (1972); and (b) "actual or imminent, not 'conjectural' or 'hypothetical,'" *Whitmore* v. *Arkansas*, 495 U.S. 149 (1990). Second, there must be a causal connection between the injury and the conduct complained of—the injury has to be "fairly . . . trace[able] to the challenged action of the defendant, and not . . . the result [of] the independent action of some third party not before the court." *Simon* v. *Eastern Ky. Welfare Rights Organization*, 426 U.S. 26 (1976). Third, it must be "likely," as opposed to merely "speculative," that the injury will be "redressed by a favorable decision."

The party invoking federal jurisdiction bears the burden of establishing these elements. . . .

III

We think the Court of Appeals failed to apply the foregoing principles in denying the Secretary's motion for summary judgment. Respondents had not made the requisite demonstration of (at least) injury and redressability.

A

Respondents' claim to injury is that the lack of consultation with respect to certain funded activities abroad "increas[es] the rate of extinction of endangered and threatened species." Of course, the desire to use or observe an animal species, even for purely esthetic purposes, is undeniably a cognizable interest for purpose of standing. See, *e. g., Sierra Club* v. *Morton,* 405 U.S. 727 (1972). "But the 'injury in fact' test requires more than an injury to a cognizable interest. It requires that the party seeking review be himself among the injured." To survive the Secretary's summary judgment motion, respondents had to submit affidavits or other evidence showing, through specific facts, not only that listed species were in fact being threatened by funded activities abroad, but also that one or more of respondents' members would thereby be "directly" affected apart from their " 'special interest' in the subject."

With respect to this aspect of the case, the Court of Appeals focused on the affidavits of two Defenders' members—Joyce Kelly and Amy Skilbred. Ms. Kelly stated that she traveled to Egypt in 1986 and "observed the traditional habitat of the endangered nile crocodile there and intend[s] to do so again, and hope[s] to observe the crocodile directly," and that she "will suffer harm in fact as the result of [the] American . . . role . . . in overseeing the rehabilitation of the Aswan High Dam on the Nile . . . and [in] developing . . . Egypt's . . . Master Water Plan." Ms. Skilbred averred that she traveled to Sri Lanka in 1981 and "observed the habitat" of "endangered species such as the Asian elephant and the leopard" at what is now the site of the Mahaweli project funded by the Agency for International Development (AID), although she "was unable to see any of the endangered species"; "this development project," she continued, "will seriously reduce endangered, threatened, and endemic species habitat including areas that I visited . . . [, which] may severely shorten the future of these species"; that threat, she concluded, harmed her because she "intend[s] to return to Sri Lanka in the future and hope[s] to be more fortunate in spotting at least the endangered elephant and leopard." When Ms. Skilbred was asked at a subsequent deposition if and when she had any plans to return to Sri Lanka, she reiterated that "I intend to go back to Sri Lanka," but confessed that she had no current plans: "I don't know [when]. There is a civil war going on right now. I don't know. Not next year, I will say. In the future."

We shall assume for the sake of argument that these affidavits contain facts showing that certain agency-funded projects threaten listed species—though that is questionable. They plainly contain no facts, however, showing how damage to the species will produce "imminent" injury to Mses. Kelly and Skilbred. That the women "had visited" the areas of the projects before the projects commenced proves nothing. As we have said in a related context, " 'Past exposure to illegal conduct does not in itself show a present case or controversy regarding injunctive relief . . . if unaccompanied by any continuing, present adverse effects.' " *Los Angeles* v. *Lyons,* 461 U.S. 95, 102 (1983). And the affiants' profession of an "intent" to return to the places they had visited before—where they will presumably, this time, be deprived of the opportunity to observe animals of the endangered species—is simply not enough. Such "some day" intentions—without any description of concrete plans, or indeed even any specification of *when* the some day will be—do not support a finding of the "actual or imminent" injury that our cases require.

Besides relying upon the Kelly and Skilbred affidavits, respondents propose a series of novel standing theories. The first, inelegantly styled "ecosystem nexus," proposes that any person who uses *any part* of a "contiguous ecosystem" adversely affected by a funded activity has standing even if the activity is located a great distance away. This approach, as the Court of Appeals correctly observed, is inconsistent with our opinion in *Lujan* v. *National Wildlife Federation,* 497 U.S. 871 (1990), which held that a plaintiff claiming injury from environmental damage must use the area affected by the challenged activity and not an area roughly "in the vicinity" of it. . . .

Respondents' other theories are called, alas, the "animal nexus" approach, whereby anyone who has an interest in studying or seeing the endangered animals anywhere on the globe has standing; and the "vocational nexus" approach, under which anyone with a professional interest in such animals can sue. Under these theories, anyone who goes to see Asian elephants in the Bronx Zoo, and anyone who is a keeper of Asian elephants in the Bronx Zoo, has standing to sue because the Director of the Agency for International Development (AID) did not consult with the Secretary regarding the AID-funded project in Sri Lanka. This is beyond all reason. Standing is not "an ingenious academic exercise in the conceivable," *United States* v. *Students Challenging Regulatory Agency Procedures (SCRAP),* 412 U.S. 669 (1973), but as we have said requires, at the summary judgment stage, a factual showing of perceptible harm. . . .

It is clear that the person who observes or works with a particular animal threatened by a federal decision is facing perceptible harm, since the very subject of his interest will no longer exist. It is even plausible—though it goes to the outermost limit of plausibility—to think that a person who observes or works with animals of a particular species in the very area of the world where that species is threatened by a federal decision is facing such harm, since some animals that might have been the subject of his interest will no longer exist, see *Japan Whaling Assn.* v. *American Cetacean Society*, 478 U.S. 221 (1986). It goes beyond the limit, however, and into pure speculation and fantasy, to say that anyone who observes or works with an endangered species, anywhere in the world, is appreciably harmed by a single project affecting some portion of that species with which he has no more specific connection.

Besides failing to show injury, respondents failed to demonstrate redressability. Instead of attacking the separate decisions to fund particular projects allegedly causing them harm, respondents chose to challenge a more generalized level of Government action (rules regarding consultation), the invalidation of which would affect all overseas projects. This programmatic approach has obvious practical advantages, but also obvious difficulties insofar as proof of causation or redressability is concerned. As we have said in another context, "suits challenging, not specifically identifiable Government violations of law, but the particular programs agencies establish to carry out their legal obligations . . . [are], even when premised on allegations of several instances of violations of law, . . . rarely if ever appropriate for federal-court adjudication." *Allen* v. *Wright,* 468 U.S. 737, 759–760 (1984).

The most obvious problem in the present case is redressability. Since the agencies funding the projects were not parties to the case, the District Court could accord relief only against the Secretary: He could be ordered to revise his regulation to require consultation for foreign projects. But this would not remedy respondents' alleged injury unless the funding agencies were bound by the Secretary's regulation, which is very much an open question. . . .

A further impediment to redressability is the fact that the agencies generally supply only a fraction of the funding for a foreign project. AID, for example, has provided less than 10% of the funding for the Mahaweli project. Respondents have produced nothing to indicate that the projects they have named will either be suspended, or do less harm to listed species, if that fraction is eliminated. . . .

IV

We hold that respondents lack standing to bring this action and that the Court of Appeals erred in denying the summary judgment motion filed by the United States. The opinion of the Court of Appeals is hereby reversed, and the cause is remanded for proceedings consistent with this opinion.

It is so ordered.

JUSTICE STEVENS, concurring in the judgment.

Because I am not persuaded that Congress intended the consultation requirement in § 7(a)(2) of the Endangered Species Act of 1973 (ESA), to apply to activities in foreign countries, I concur in the judgment of reversal. I do not, however, agree with the Court's conclusion that respondents lack standing because the threatened injury to their interest in protecting the environment and studying endangered species is not "imminent." Nor do I agree with the plurality's additional conclusion that respondents' injury is not "redressable" in this litigation.

JUSTICE BLACKMUN, with whom Justice O'Connor joins, dissenting.

I part company with the Court in this case in two respects. First, I believe that respondents have raised genuine issues of fact—sufficient to survive summary judgment—both as to injury and as to redressability. Second, I question the Court's breadth of language in rejecting standing for "procedural" injuries. I fear the Court seeks to impose fresh limitations on the constitutional authority of Congress to allow citizen suits in the federal courts for injuries deemed "procedural" in nature. I dissent.

I

I think a reasonable finder of fact could conclude from the information in the affidavits and deposition testimony that either Kelly or Skilbred will soon return to the project sites, thereby satisfying the "actual or imminent" injury standard. The Court dismisses Kelly's and Skilbred's general statements that they intended to revisit the project sites as "simply not enough." But those statements did not stand alone. A reasonable finder of fact could conclude, based not only upon their statements of intent to return, but upon their past visits to the project sites, as well as their professional backgrounds, that it was likely that Kelly and Skilbred would make a return trip to the project areas. Contrary to the Court's contention that Kelly's and Skilbred's past visits "prove nothing," the fact of their past visits could demonstrate to a reasonable factfinder that Kelly and Skilbred have the requisite resources and personal interest in the preservation of the species endangered by the Aswan and Mahaweli projects to make good on their intention to return again. Cf. *Los Angeles* v. *Lyons*, 461 U.S. 95 (1983) ("Past wrongs were evidence bearing on whether there is a real and immediate threat of repeated injury"). Similarly, Kelly's and Skilbred's professional backgrounds in wildlife preservation, also make it likely—at least far more likely than for the average citizen—that they would choose to visit these areas of the world where species are vanishing. . . .

B

A plurality of the Court suggests that respondents have not demonstrated redressability: a likelihood that a court ruling in their favor would remedy their injury. . . .

Even if the action agencies supply only a fraction of the funding for a particular foreign project, it remains at least a question for the finder of fact whether threatened withdrawal of that fraction would affect foreign government conduct sufficiently to avoid harm to listed species.

The plurality states that "AID, for example, has provided less than 10% of the funding for the Mahaweli project." The plurality neglects to mention that this "fraction" amounts to $170 million, not so paltry a sum for a country of only 16 million people with a gross national product of less than $6 billion in 1986 when respondents filed the complaint in this action.

The plurality flatly states: "Respondents have produced nothing to indicate that the projects they have named will . . . do less harm to listed species, if that fraction is eliminated." As an initial matter, the relevant inquiry is not, as the plurality suggests, what will happen if AID or other agencies stop funding projects, but what will happen if AID or other agencies comply with the consultation requirement for projects abroad. Respondents filed suit to require consultation, not a termination of funding. Respondents have raised at least a genuine issue of fact that the projects harm endangered species and that the actions of AID and other United States agencies can mitigate that harm.

The plurality overlooks an Interior Department memorandum listing eight endangered or threatened species in the Mahaweli project area and recounting that "the Sri Lankan government has requested the assistance of AID in mitigating the negative impacts to the wildlife involved." Further, a letter from the Director of the Fish and Wildlife Service to AID states: "The Sri Lankan government lacks the necessary finances to undertake any long-term management programs to avoid the negative impacts to the wildlife. The donor nations and agencies that are financing the [Mahaweli project] will be the key as to how successfully the wildlife is preserved. If wildlife problems receive the same level of attention as the engineering project, then the negative impacts to the environment can be alleviated. This means that there has to be long-term funding in sufficient amounts to stem the negative impacts of this project."

I do not share the plurality's astonishing confidence that, on the record here, a factfinder could only conclude that AID was powerless to ensure the protection of listed species at the Mahaweli project.

As for the Aswan project, the record again rebuts the plurality's assumption that donor agencies are without any authority to protect listed species. Kelly asserted in her affidavit—and it has not been disputed—that the Bureau of Reclamation was "overseeing" the rehabilitation of the Aswan project.

I find myself unable to agree with the plurality's analysis of redressability, based as it is on its invitation of executive lawlessness, ignorance of principles of collateral estoppel, unfounded assumptions about causation, and erroneous conclusions about what the record does not say. In my view, respondents have satisfactorily shown a genuine issue of fact as to whether their injury would likely be redressed by a decision in their favor.

III

In conclusion, I cannot join the Court on what amounts to a slash-and-burn expedition through the law of environmental standing. In my view, "the very essence of civil liberty certainly consists in the right of every individual to claim the protection of the laws, whenever he receives an injury." *Marbury v. Madison*, 5 U.S. 137 (1803).

I dissent.

FOR DISCUSSION

Does the Court's decision completely close the door to litigants seeking to challenge the environmental law in question? Can you think of anyone who might have a more solid case of standing in this case?

RELATED CASES

Lujan appeared to represent a narrowing of prior cases dealing with standing. They include the following:

***United States v. Students Challenging Regulatory Agency Procedures:* 412 U.S. 669 (1973).**

The Court recognized broad standing for environmental groups.

***TVA v. Hill:* 437 U.S. 153 (1978).**

The Supreme Court interpreted the Endangered Species Act to halt construction of a dam that had nearly been completed in order to protect a small fish known as the snail darter.

Article IV, Sec. 4:

The United States shall guarantee to every State in this Union a Republican Form of Government, and shall protect each of them against Invasion; and on Application of the Legislature, or of the Executive (when the Legislature cannot be convened) against domestic Violence.

LUTHER V. BORDEN

7 How. 1, 12 L. Ed. 581 (1849)

The colonial charter that Rhode Island was continuing to use as its state constitution made no provision for formal constitutional change and severely limited suffrage. Under the leadership of Thomas W. Dorr, various mass meetings were held throughout the state, and a purported majority adopted a new constitution with liberalized voting provisions, under which. Dorr was elected governor. The existing charter government, however, did not recognize this new government. The state governor declared the attempt to form a new government to be an insurrection, or "rebellion," and he appealed to President Tyler for federal forces. Meanwhile, members of the state militia under Borden invaded the house of Luther, a Dorr adherent, who then sued for trespass. In order to legalize a suit in the federal courts on the basis of diversity of citizenship, Luther then moved to Massachusetts and challenged the legitimacy of the charter government as not being a lawful "republican form of government" guaranteed in Article IV, Section 4, of the Constitution, and accordingly designated the Guarantee Clause. Daniel Webster was counsel for Borden of the charter government. By the time the case reached the Supreme Court, another government was already in place.

Vote: 8–1

Opinion by CHIEF JUSTICE TANEY:

. . . The fourth section of the fourth article of the Constitution of the United States provides that the United States shall guarantee to every state in the Union a republican form of government, and shall protect each of them against invasion; and on the application of the legislature or of the executive (when the legislature cannot be convened) against domestic violence.

Under this article of the Constitution it rests with Congress to decide what government is the established one in a state. For as the United States guarantees to each state a republican government, Congress must necessarily decide what government is established in the state before it can determine whether it is republican or not. And when the Senators and Representatives of a state are admitted into the councils of the Union, the authority of the government under which they are appointed, as well as its republican character, is recognized by the proper constitutional authority. And its decision is binding on every other department of the government, and could not be questioned in a judicial tribunal. It is true that the contest in this case did not last long enough to bring the matter to this issue and, as no Senators or Representatives were elected under the authority of the government of which Mr. Dorr was the head, Congress was not called upon to decide the controversy. Yet the right to decide is placed there, and not in the courts.

So, too, as relates to the clause in the above-mentioned article of the Constitution, was provision made for cases of domestic violence. It rested with Congress, too, to determine upon the means proper to be adopted to fulfill this guarantee. They might, if they had deemed it most advisable to do so, have placed it in the power of a court to decide when the contingency had happened which required the federal government to interfere. But Congress thought otherwise—and no doubt wisely—and by the act of February 28, 1795 provided that, "in case of any insurrection in any state against the government thereof, it shall be lawful for the President of the United States, on application of the legislature of such state or of the executive (when the legislature cannot be convened) to call forth such number of militia of any other state or states, as may be applied for, as he may judge sufficient to suppress such insurrection."

By this act, the power of deciding whether the exigency had arisen upon which the government of the United States is bound to interfere, is given to the President. He is to act upon the application of the legislature or of the executive, and consequently he must determine what body of men constitute the legislature, and who is the governor, before he can act. The fact that both parties claim the right to the government cannot alter the case, for both cannot be entitled to it. If there is an armed conflict, like the one of which we are speaking, it is a case of domestic violence, and one of the parties must be in insurrection against the lawful government. And the President must, of necessity, decide which is the government, and which party is unlawfully arrayed against it, before he can perform the duty imposed upon him by the act of Congress.

After the President has acted and called out the militia, is a circuit court of the United States authorized to inquire whether his decision was right? Could the court, while the parties were actually contending in arms for the possession of the government, call witnesses before it and inquire which party represented a majority of the people? If it could, then it would become the duty of the court (provided it came to the conclusion that the President had decided incorrectly) to discharge those who were arrested or detained by the troops in the service of the United States or the government which the President was endeavoring to maintain. If the judicial power extends so far, the guarantee contained in the Constitution of the United States is a guarantee of anarchy, and not of order. Yet if this right does not reside in the courts when the conflict is raging, if the judicial power is, at that time, bound to follow the decision of the political, it must be equally bound when the contest is over. It cannot, when peace is restored, punish as offenses and crimes the acts which it before recognized, and was bound to recognize, as lawful.

It is true that in this case the militia were not called out by the President. But upon the application of the governor under the charter government, the President recognized him as the executive power of the state, and took measures to call out the militia to support his authority, if it should be found necessary for the general government to interfere. And it is admitted in the argument that it was the knowledge of this decision that put an end to the armed opposition to the charter government, and prevented any further efforts to establish by force the proposed constitution. The interference of the President, therefore, by announcing his determination, was as effectual as if the militia had been assembled under his orders. And it should be equally authoritative. For certainly no court of the United States, with a knowledge of this decision, would have been justified in recognizing the opposing party as the lawful government, or in treating as wrong-doers or insurgents the officers of the government which the President had recognized, and was prepared to support by an armed force. In the case of foreign nations, the government acknowledged by the President is always recognized in the courts of justice. And this principle has been applied by the act of Congress to the sovereign states of the Union.

It is said that this power in the President is dangerous to liberty, and may be abused. All power may be abused if placed in unworthy hands. But it would be difficult, we think, to point out any other hands in which this power would be more safe, and at the same time equally effectual. When citizens of the same state are in arms against each other, and the constituted authorities are unable to execute the laws, then the interposition of the United States must be prompt, or it is of little value. The ordinary course of proceedings in courts of justice would be utterly unfit for the crisis. And the elevated office of the President, chosen as he is by the people of the United States, and the high responsibility he could not fail to feel when acting in a case of so much moment, appear to furnish as strong safeguards against a willful abuse of power as human prudence and foresight might provide. At all events, it is conferred upon him by the Constitution and laws of the United States, and must, therefore, be respected and enforced in its judicial tribunals. . . .

Much of the argument on the part of the plaintiff turned upon political rights and political questions, upon which the court has been urged to express an opinion. We decline doing so. The high power has been conferred on this court of passing judgment upon the acts of the state sovereignties, and of the legislative and executive branches of the federal government, and of determining whether they are beyond the limits of power marked out for them respectively by the Constitution of the United States. This tribunal, therefore, should be the last to overstep the boundaries which limit its own jurisdiction. And while it should always be ready to meet any question confided to it by the Constitution, it is equally its duty not to pass beyond its appropriate sphere of action, and to take care not to involve itself in discussions which properly belong to other forums. No one, we believe, has ever doubted the proposition, that, according to the institutions of this country, the sovereignty in every state resides in the people of the state, and that they may alter and change their form of government at their own pleasure. But whether they have changed it or not by abolishing an old government, and establishing a new one in its place, is a question to be settled by the political power. And when that power has decided, the courts are bound to take notice of its decision, and to follow it.

The judgment of the circuit court must, therefore, be affirmed.

JUSTICE WOODBURY dissented.

He held that the use of martial law by the government operating under the old charter was violative of that charter or Constitution, as well as of the Constitution as an infringement on the power of Congress.

RELATED CASES

Martin v. Mott: **12 Wheat. 19 (1827).**

The president, under the act of 1795, was justified in calling out the militia. "The authority to decide whether the exigency has arisen, belongs exclusively to the President." This is a political matter and is not justiciable. The president is not judicially accountable for the use of the armed forces.

Ex parte Dorr: **3 How. 103 (1845).**

The Supreme Court held that it had no jurisdiction in a suit for a writ of *habeas corpus* by which an attempt was made to question the legality of the "Dorr" constitution and actions taken under it.

Pacific States Telephone and Telegraph Co. v. Oregon: **223 U.S. 118 (1912).**

Whether use of the initiative and referendum denies a state the essentials of a republican form of government is a point to be determined by the political units of the federal government and not by the judiciary. Congress had admitted the Senators and Representatives from Oregon.

Fergus v. Marks: **321 III. 510 (1926).**

A court cannot mandate a state legislature to redistrict the state for purposes of representation in the House of Representatives of the United States Congress.

Colegrove v. Green: **328 U.S. 549 (1946).**

The question of the legality of a state statute establishing congressional districts is a political matter and is not justiciable. *Note*: The Supreme Court later reversed this decision in *Baker v. Carr*, 369 U.S. 186 (1962).

Article V:

The Congress, whenever two thirds of both Houses shall deem it necessary, shall propose Amendments to this Constitution, or, on the Application of the Legislatures of two thirds of the several States, shall call a Convention for proposing Amendments, which, in either Case, shall be valid to all Intents and Purposes, as part of this Constitution, when ratified by the Legislatures of three fourths of the several States, or by Conventions in three fourths thereof, as the one or the other Mode of Ratification may be proposed by the Congress; Provided that no Amendment which may be made prior to the Year One thousand eight hundred and eight shall in any Manner affect the first and fourth Clauses in the Ninth Section of the first Article; and that no State, without its Consent, shall be deprived of its equal Suffrage in the Senate.

COLEMAN V. MILLER

307 U.S. 433, 59 S. Ct. 972, 83 L. Ed. 1385 (1939)

The state legislature of Kansas in 1925 rejected the ratification of the proposed Child Labor Amendment to the federal Constitution that Congress submitted to the states in June 1924. In January 1937 the Kansas Senate passed a resolution for the ratification of this proposed amendment. The passage resulted when the lieutenant governor, the presiding officer of the senate, cast his vote in favor of the resolution, which a majority vote of the Kansas House of Representatives later adopted. Three questions thus arose: (1) The right of the lieutenant governor to cast the deciding vote. (2) The continuing vitality of the proposed amendment so many years after its introduction by Congress. (3) The power of a state legislature to ratify after having previously rejected the proposed amendment. Coleman, a member of the Kansas Senate, represented the petitioning twenty senators, and Miller was the secretary of the Senate.

Vote: 7–2

CHIEF JUSTICE HUGHES delivered the opinion of the Court:

. . . In the light of this course of decisions, we find no departure from principle in recognizing in the instant case that at least the twenty senators whose votes, if their contention were sustained, would have been sufficient to defeat the resolution ratifying the proposed constitutional amendment, have an interest in the controversy which, treated by the state court as a basis for entertaining and deciding the federal questions, is sufficient to give the Court jurisdiction to review that decision.

First, the participation of the Lieutenant Governor.

Petitioners contend that, in the light of the powers and duties of the Lieutenant Governor and his relation to the Senate under the state constitution, as construed by the supreme court of the state, the Lieutenant Governor was not a part of the "legislature" so that under Article V of the Federal Constitution, he could be permitted to have a deciding vote on the ratification of the proposed amendment, when the Senate was equally divided.

Whether this contention presents a justiciable controversy, or a question which is political in its nature and hence not justiciable, is a question upon which the Court is equally divided and therefore the Court expresses no opinion upon that point.

Second and Third, the effect of the previous rejection of the amendment and of the lapse of time since its submission.

1. The state court adopted the view expressed by text-writers that a state legislature which has rejected an amendment proposed by the Congress may later ratify. The argument in support of that view is that Article Five says nothing of rejection but speaks only of ratification and provides that a proposed amendment shall be valid as part of the Constitution when ratified by three-fourths of the States; that the power to ratify is thus conferred upon the State by the Constitution and, as a ratifying power, persists despite a previous rejection. The opposing view proceeds on an assumption that if ratification by "Conventions" were prescribed by the Congress, a convention could not reject and, having adjourned *sine die,* be reassembled and ratify. It is also premised, in accordance with views expressed by text-writers, that ratification if once given cannot afterwards be rescinded and the amendment rejected, and it is urged that the same effect in the exhaustion of the State's power to act should be ascribed to rejection; that a State can act "but once, either by convention or through its legislature. . . ."

We think that in accordance with this historic precedent the question of the efficacy of ratifications by state legislatures, in the light of previous rejection or attempted withdrawal, should be regarded as a political question pertaining to the political departments, with the ultimate authority in the Congress in the exercise of its control over the promulgation of the adoption of the amendment.

The precise question as now raised is whether, when the legislature of the State, as we have found, has actually ratified the proposed amendment, the Court should restrain the state officers from certifying the ratification to the Secretary of State, because of an earlier rejection, and thus prevent the question from coming before the political departments. We find no basis in either Constitution or statute for such judicial action. Article Five, speaking solely of ratification, contains no provision as to rejection. Nor has the Congress enacted a statute relating to rejections.

The statute presupposes official notice to the Secretary of State when a state legislature had adopted a resolution of ratification. We see no warrant for judicial interference with the performance of that duty. . . .

2. The more serious question is whether the proposal by the Congress of the amendment has lost its vitality through lapse of time and hence it could not be ratified by the Kansas legislature in 1937. The argument of petitioners stresses the fact that nearly thirteen years elapsed between the proposal in 1924 and the ratification in question. It is said that when the amendment was proposed there was a definitely adverse popular sentiment and that at the end of 1925 there had been rejection by both houses of the legislatures of sixteen States and ratification by only four States, and that it was not until about 1933 that an aggressive campaign was started in favor of the amendment. In reply, it is urged that Congress did not fix a limit of time for ratification and that an unreasonably long time had not elapsed since the submission; that the conditions which gave rise to the amendment had not been eliminated; that the prevalence of child labor, the diversity of state laws and the disparity in their administration, with the resulting competitive inequalities, continued to exist. Reference is also made to the fact that a number of the States have treated the amendment as still pending and that in the proceedings of the national government there have been indications of the same view. It is said that there were fourteen ratifications in 1933, four in 1935, one in 1936 and three in 1937.

We have held that the Congress in proposing an amendment may fix a reasonable time for ratification. *Dillon v. Gloss*, 256 U.S. 368 (1921). There we sustained the action of the Congress in providing (in the proposed Eighteenth Amendment) that it should be inoperative unless ratified within seven years. No limitation of time for ratification is provided in the instant case either in the proposed amendment or in the resolution of submission. . . .

. . . But it does not follow that, whenever Congress has not exercised that power, the Court should take upon itself the responsibility of deciding what constitutes a reasonable time and determine accordingly the validity of ratifications. That question was not involved in *Dillon v. Gloss* and, in accordance with familiar principle, what was there said must be read in the light of the point decided. . . .

Our decision that the Congress has the power under Article Five to fix a reasonable limit of time for ratification in proposing an amendment proceeds upon the assumption that the question, what is a reasonable time, lies within the congressional province. If it be deemed that such a question is an open one when the limit has not been fixed in advance, we think that it should also be regarded as an open one for the consideration of the Congress when, in the presence of certified ratifications by three-fourths of the States, the time arrives for the promulgation of the adoption of the amendment. The decision by the Congress, in its control of the action of the Secretary of State, of the question whether the amendment has been adopted within a reasonable time would not be subject to review by the courts. . . .

For the reasons we have stated, which we think to be as compelling as those which underlay the cited decisions, we think that the Congress in controlling the promulgation of the adoption of a constitutional amendment has the final determination of the question—whether by lapse of time its proposal of the amendment has lost its vitality prior to the required ratifications. The state officials should not be restrained from certifying to the Secretary of State the adoption by the legislature of Kansas of the resolution of ratification.

As we find no reason for disturbing the decision of the Supreme Court of Kansas in denying the mandamus sought by petitioners, its judgment is affirmed but upon the grounds stated in this opinion.

Affirmed.

Concurring opinion by JUSTICE BLACK, in which JUSTICES ROBERTS, FRANKFURTER, and DOUGLAS joined:

The Constitution grants Congress exclusive power to control submission of constitutional amendments. Final determination by Congress that ratification by three-fourths of the States has taken place "is conclusive upon the courts." In the exercise of that power, Congress, of course, is governed by the Constitution. However, whether submission, intervening procedure or congressional determination of ratification conforms to the commands of the Constitution, call for decisions by a "political department" of questions of a type which this Court has frequently designated "political." And decision of a "political question" by the "political department" to which the Constitution has committed it "conclusively binds the judges, as well as all other officers, citizens, and subjects of . . . government." Proclamation under authority of Congress that an amendment has been ratified will carry with it a solemn assurance by the Congress that ratification has taken place as the Constitution commands. Upon this assurance a proclaimed amendment must be accepted as a part of the Constitution, leaving to the judiciary its traditional authority of interpretation. To the extent that the Court's opinion in the present case even impliedly assumes a power to make judicial interpretation of the exclusive constitutional authority of Congress over submission and ratification of amendments, we are unable to agree.

Opinion of JUSTICE FRANKFURTER.

It is the view of Mr. Justice Roberts, Mr. Justice Black, Mr. Justice Douglas and myself that the petitioners have no standing in this Court. . . . It was not for courts to meddle with matters that required no subtlety to be identified as political issues. And even as to the kinds of questions which were the staple of judicial business, it was not for courts to pass upon them as abstract, intellectual problems but only if a concrete, living contest between adversaries called for the arbitrament of law. . . .

JUSTICE BUTLER, joined by JUSTICE MCREYNOLDS, dissented:

. . . Upon the reasoning of our opinion in that case (*Dillon v. Gloss*), I would hold that more than a reasonable time had elapsed and that the judgment of the Kansas supreme court should be reversed.

The point, that the question—whether more than a reasonable time had elapsed—is not justiciable but one for Congress after attempted ratification by the requisite number of States, was not raised by the parties or by the United States appearing as *amicus curiae;* it was not suggested by us when ordering reargument. As the Court, in the Dillon case, did directly decide upon the reasonableness of the seven years fixed by the Congress, it ought not now, without hearing argument upon the point, hold itself to lack power to decide whether more than thirteen years between proposal by Congress and attempted ratification by Kansas is reasonable.

FOR DISCUSSION

Consistent with the Court's decision in *Coleman v. Miller*, Congress voted to certify the adoption of the Twenty-seventh Amendment in 1992, despite the fact that the requisite number of states had not ratified the amendment, which prohibited members of Congress from giving themselves pay raises until an intervening election, until more than two hundred years after it had first been proposed as part of the Bill of Rights. Although the precedent appeared to be in tension with the decision in *Dillon v. Gloss* providing that amendments should reflect a contemporary consensus of the states ratifying, states had continued to ratify the amendment over a long time period during which none attempted to rescind it. Although a lower court upheld such a rescission in *Idaho v. Freeman*, 529 F. Supp. 11078 (1981), the Supreme Court has yet to address the issue as to whether attempted rescissions are valid under Article V (the amending article) of the Constitution. If you were on the Court and faced this decision, how would you decide?

RELATED CASES

***Hollingsworth v. Virginia:* 3 Dall. 378 (1798).**

The requirement that acts of Congress must be submitted to the president applies only to ordinary legislation. A resolution proposing an amendment to the Constitution is not that sort of action. An amendment is effective on ratification. This case arose over the Eleventh Amendment.

***Hawke v. Smith:* 253 U.S. 221 (1920).**

A state cannot provide for ratification of a proposed amendment to the Constitution by direct popular vote. The Constitution specifies that ratification must be by state legislature or state convention and no other means can be used. The amendment function is derived from the Constitution, so the state here is really participating in a federal function. The "legislature" specified in the Constitution means a representative body, and the people of a state cannot change that unilaterally. Hawke was a taxpayer citizen of Ohio, and Smith was secretary of state of Ohio.

***National Prohibition Cases:* 253 U.S. 350 (1920).**

The two-thirds vote in each House of Congress required in proposing an amendment to the Constitution is a vote of two-thirds of the members present, assuming the presence of a quorum. The purpose of the Eighteenth Amendment was declared to be within the power to amend under Article V of the Constitution.

***Dillon v. Gloss:* 256 U.S. 368 (1921).**

Congress in proposing an amendment may fix a reasonable time for ratification. Seven years (as in the case of the Eighteenth) is a reasonable time. Presumably an amendment must be ratified within a reasonable time or it loses its validity. An amendment becomes effective when the last required state ratifies it.

***Leser v. Garnett:* 258 U.S. 130 (1922).**

Illegal irregularities in procedure in the process of ratification of the proposed Nineteenth Amendment did not affect the validity of the ratification by those states. The function of a state legislature in ratifying a proposed amendment is a federal function and transcends any limitation sought to be imposed by the people of a state. Leser was a voter of Maryland; Garnett represented the Board of Registry. Although the basic case was from Maryland, questions from other states were also involved. For example, the Court held invalid a provision of the Tennessee constitution that required an election of the state legislature before that body could vote on ratification. The Court also denied that the subject matter of an amendment might make the consent of all states necessary.

***United States v. Sprague:* 282 U.S. 716 (1931).**

Regardless of content of a proposed amendment, the choice of the mode of ratification (here the Eighteenth Amendment) lies in the sole discretion of Congress. New Jersey was the state involved here.

***Chandler v. Wise:* 307 U.S. 474 (1939).**

After the governor of a state has forwarded the certification of ratification to the secretary of state of the United States, there is no longer a controversy over the ratification (here the proposed Child Labor Amendment) that can be judicially determined. Governor "Happy" Chandler and Wise, a taxpayer of Kentucky, were the parties in this case.

BAKER V. CARR

369 U.S. 186, 82 S. Ct. 691, 7 L. Ed. 2d 663 (1962)

This civil action was brought to redress an alleged deprivation of federal constitutional rights. A 1901 statute of Tennessee had been the most recent apportionment of members of the state's general assembly, despite a state constitutional provision providing for decennial reapportionment. Because of the growth and redistribution of the state's population after 1901, voters from districts with larger populations challenged the existing apportionment as denying equal protection to voters under the Fourteenth Amendment as a debasement of their votes. The federal district court dismissed the case for lack of jurisdiction of the subject matter.

Vote: 6–2

JUSTICE BRENNAN delivered the opinion of the Court:

. . . In light of the District Court's treatment of the case, we hold today only (a) that the court possessed jurisdiction of the subject matter; (b) that a justiciable cause of action is stated upon which appellants would be entitled to appropriate relief; and (c) because appellees raise the issue before this Court, that the appellants have standing to challenge the Tennessee apportionment statutes. Beyond noting that we have no cause at this stage to doubt the District Court will be able to fashion relief if violations of constitutional rights are found, it is improper now to consider what remedy would be most appropriate if appellants prevail at the trial.

[*Jurisdiction of the Subject Matter.*] The District Court was uncertain whether our cases withholding federal judicial relief rested upon a lack of federal jurisdiction or upon the inappropriateness of the subject matter for judicial consideration—what we have designated "nonjusticiability." The distinction between the two grounds is significant. In the instance of nonjusticiability, consideration of the cause is not wholly and immediately foreclosed; rather, the Court's inquiry necessarily proceeds to the point of deciding whether the duty asserted can be judicially identified and its breach judicially determined, and whether protection for the right asserted can be judicially molded. In the instance of lack of jurisdiction the cause either does not "arise under" the Federal Constitution, laws or treaties (or fall within one of the other enumerated categories of Article Three, § 2), or is not a "case or controversy" within the meaning of that section; or the cause is not one described by any jurisdictional statute. Our conclusion . . . that this cause presents no nonjusticiable "political question" settles the only possible doubt that it is a case or controversy. Under the present heading of "Jurisdiction of the Subject Matter" we hold only that the matter set forth in the complaint does arise under the Constitution and is within 28 U.S.C. § 1343 (3). . . .

Article Three, § 2 of the Federal Constitution provides that "the judicial Power shall extend to all Cases, in Law and Equity, arising under this Constitution, the Laws of the United States, and Treaties made, or which shall be made, under their Authority. . . ." It is clear that the cause of action is one which "arises under" the Federal Constitution. The complaint alleges that the 1901 statute effects an apportionment that deprives the appellants of the equal protection of the laws in violation of the Fourteenth Amendment. . . .

Since the complaint plainly sets forth a case arising under the Constitution, the subject matter is within the federal judicial power defined in Article Three, § 2, and so within the power of Congress to assign to the jurisdiction of the District Courts. Congress has exercised that power in 28 U.S.C. § 1343(3). . . .

"The district Courts shall have original jurisdiction of any civil action authorized by law to be commenced by any person . . . to redress the deprivation, under color of any State law, statute, ordinance, regulation, custom or usage, of any right, privilege or immunity secured by the Constitution of the United States. . . ."

We hold that the District Court has jurisdiction of the subject matter of the federal constitutional claim asserted in the complaint.

[*Standing.*] A federal court cannot "pronounce any statute, either of a state or of the United States, void, because irreconcilable with the Constitution, except as it is called upon to adjudge the legal rights of litigants in actual controversies." *Liverpool, N. Y. & P. Steamship Co. v. Commissioners of Emigration*, 113 U.S. 33 (1885). Have the appellants alleged such a personal stake in the outcome of the controversy as to assure that concrete adverseness which sharpens the presentation of issues upon which the court so largely depends for illumination of difficult constitutional questions? This is the gist of the question of standing. It is, of course, a question of federal law.

The complaint was filed by residents of Davidson, Hamilton, Knox, Montgomery, and Shelby Counties. Each is a person allegedly qualified to vote for members of the General Assembly representing his county. These appellants sued "on their own behalf and on behalf of all qualified voters of their respective counties, and further, on behalf of all voters of the State of Tennessee who are similarly situated. . . ." The appellees are the Tennessee Secretary of State, Attorney General, Coordinator of Elections, and members of the State Board of Elections; the members of the State Board are sued in their own right and also as representatives of the County Election Commissioners whom they appoint.

We hold that the appellants do have standing to maintain this suit. Our decisions plainly support this conclusion. Many of the cases have assumed rather than articulated the premise in deciding the merits of similar claims. And *Colegrove v. Green,* 328 U.S. 549 (1946), squarely held that voters who allege facts showing disadvantage to themselves as individuals have standing to sue. A number of cases decided after *Colegrove* recognized the standing of the voters there involved to bring those actions. . . .

[*Justiciability.*] In holding that the subject matter of this suit was not justiciable, the District Court relied on *Colegrove v. Green* and subsequent *per curiam* cases. The court stated: "From a review of these decisions there can be no doubt that the federal rule . . . is that the federal courts . . . will not intervene in cases of this type to compel legislative reapportionment." We understand the District Court to have read the cited cases as compelling the conclusion that since the appellants sought to have a legislative apportionment held unconstitutional, their suit presented a "political question" and was therefore nonjusticiable. We hold that this challenge to an apportionment presents no nonjusticiable "political question." The cited cases do not hold the contrary.

[The Court proceeds to examine cases where the Court has analyzed the political questions doctrine. These include matters relative to foreign relations, dates and durations of hostilities, the validity of certain enactments, and the status of Indian tribes. The court summarizes it conclusions]:

> It is apparent that several formulations which vary slightly according to the settings in which the questions arise may describe a political question, although each has one or more elements which identify it as essentially a function of the separation of powers. Prominent on the surface of any case held to involve a political question is found a textually demonstrable constitutional commitment of the issue to a coordinate political department; or a lack of judicially discoverable and manageable standards for resolving it; or the impossibility of deciding without an initial policy determination of a kind clearly for nonjudicial discretion; or the impossibility of a court's undertaking independent resolution without expressing lack of the respect due coordinate branches of government; or an unusual need for unquestioning adherence to a political decision already made; or the potentiality of embarrassment from multifarious pronouncements by various departments on one question.

. . . The nonjusticiability of a political question is primarily a function of the separation of powers. Much confusion results from the capacity of the "political question" label to obscure the need for case-by-case inquiry. Deciding whether a matter has in any measure been committed by the Constitution to another branch of government, or whether the action of that branch exceeds whatever authority has been committed, is itself a delicate exercise in constitutional interpretation, and is a responsibility of this Court as ultimate interpreter of the Constitution. . . .

. . . The question here is the consistency of state action with the Federal Constitution. We have no question decided, or to be decided, by a political branch of government coequal with this Court. Nor do we risk embarrassment of our government abroad, or grave disturbance at home if we take issue with Tennessee as to the constitutionality of her action here challenged. Nor need the appellants, in order to succeed in this action, ask the Court to enter upon policy determinations for which judicially manageable standards are lacking. Judicial standards under the Equal Protection Clause are well developed and familiar, and it has been open to courts since the enactment of the Fourteenth Amendment to determine, if on the particular facts they must, that a discrimination reflects *no* policy, but simply arbitrary and capricious action.

We conclude that the complaint's allegations of a denial of equal protection present a justiciable constitutional cause of action upon which appellants are entitled to a trial and a decision. The right asserted is within the reach of judicial protection under the Fourteenth Amendment.

The judgment of the District Court is reversed and the cause is remanded for further proceedings consistent with this opinion.

Reversed and remanded.

JUSTICE DOUGLAS concurred:

There is no doubt that the federal courts have jurisdiction of controversies concerning voting rights. The Civil Rights Act gives them authority to redress the deprivation "under color of any state law" of any "right, privilege or immunity secured by the Constitution of the United States or by any Act of Congress providing for equal rights of citizens. . . ."

JUSTICE CLARK concurred:

. . . Although I find the Tennessee apportionment statute offends the Equal Protection Clause, I would not consider intervention by this Court into so delicate a field if there were any other relief available to the people of Tennessee. But the majority of the people of Tennessee have no "practical opportunities for exerting their political weight at the polls" to correct the existing "invidious discrimination." Tennessee has no initiative and referendum. I have searched diligently for other "practical opportunities" present under the law. I find none other than through the federal courts. The majority of the voters have been caught up in a legislative strait jacket. Tennessee has an "informed, civically militant electorate" and "an aroused popular conscience," but it does not sear "the conscience of the people's representatives." This is because the legislative policy has riveted the present seats in the Assembly to their respective constituencies, and by the votes of their incumbents a reapportionment of any kind is prevented. The people have been rebuffed at the hands of the Assembly; they have tried the constitutional convention route, but since the call must originate in the Assembly it, too, has been fruitless. They have tried Tennessee courts with the same result, and Governors have fought the tide only to flounder. It is said that there is recourse in Congress and perhaps that may be, but from a practical standpoint this is without substance. To date Congress has never undertaken such a task in any State. We therefore must conclude that the people of Tennessee are stymied and without judicial intervention will be saddled with the present discrimination in the affairs of their state government. . . .

. . . It is well for this Court to practice self-restraint and discipline in constitutional adjudication, but never in its history have those principles received sanction where the national rights of so many have been so clearly infringed for so long a time. National respect for the courts is more enhanced through the forthright enforcement of those rights rather than by rendering them nugatory through the interposition of subterfuges. In my view the ultimate decision today is in the greatest tradition of this Court.

JUSTICE FRANKFURTER, whom JUSTICE HARLAN joined, dissented:

The Court today reverses a uniform course of decision established by a dozen cases, including one by which the very claim now sustained was unanimously rejected only five years ago. The impressive body of rulings thus cast aside reflected the equally uniform course of our political history regarding the relationship between population and legislative representation—a wholly different matter from denial of the franchise to individuals because of race, color, religion or sex. Such a massive repudiation of the experience of our whole past in asserting destructively novel judicial power demands a detailed analysis of the role of this Court in our constitutional scheme. Disregard of inherent limits in the effective exercise of the Court's "judicial Power" not only presages the futility of judicial intervention in the essentially political conflict of forces by which the relation between population and representation has time out of mind been and now is determined. It may well impair the Court's position as the ultimate organ of "the supreme Law of the Land" in that vast range of legal problems, often strongly entangled in popular feeling, on which this Court must pronounce. The Court's authority—possessed neither of the purse nor the sword—ultimately rests on sustained public confidence in its moral sanction. Such feeling must be nourished by the Court's complete detachment, in fact and in appearance, from political entanglements and by abstention from injecting itself into the clash of political forces in political settlements. . . .

JUSTICE HARLAN gave a dissenting opinion, which JUSTICE FRANKFURTER joined:

. . . Once one cuts through the thicket of discussion devoted to "jurisdiction," "standing," "justiciability," and "political question," there emerges a straightforward issue which, in my view, is determinative of this case. Does the complaint disclose a violation of a federal constitutional right, in other words, a claim over which a United States District Court would have jurisdiction under 28 U.S.C. § 1343 (3) and 42 U.S.C. § 1983? The majority opinion does not actually discuss this basic question, but, as one concurring Justice observes, seems to decide it "*sub silentio.*" . . . However, in my opinion, appellants' allegations, accepting all of them as true, do not, parsed down or as a whole, show an infringement by Tennessee of any rights assured by the Fourteenth Amendment. Accordingly, I believe the complaint should have been dismissed for "failure to state a claim upon which relief can be granted."

It is at once essential to recognize this case for what it is. The issue here relates not to a method of state electoral apportionment by which seats in the *federal* House of Representatives are allocated, but solely to the right of a State to fix the basis of representation in its *own* legislature. Until it is first decided to what extent that right is limited by the Federal Constitution, and whether what Tennessee had done or failed to do in this instance runs afoul of any such limitation, we need not reach the issues of "justiciability" or "political question" or any of the other considerations which in such cases as *Colegrove v. Green*, 328 U.S. 549 (1946), led the Court to decline to adjudicate a challenge to a state apportionment affecting seats in the federal House of Representatives, in the absence of a controlling Act of Congress. . . .

I can find nothing in the Equal Protection Clause or elsewhere in the Federal Constitution which expressly or impliedly supports the view that state legislatures must be so structured as to reflect with approximate equality the voice of every voter. Not only is that proposition refuted by history, as shown by my Brother Frankfurter, but it strikes deep into the heart of our federal system. Its acceptance would require us to turn our backs on the regard which this Court has always shown for the judgment of state legislatures and courts on matters of basically local concern. . . .

FOR DISCUSSION

Examine the six criteria that Justice Brennan established for identifying political questions. Do they appear to capture past precedents? Do you think that Brennan was wise to separate questions involving federalism (the relation between the national government and the states) from questions of separation of powers involving the relations among the three branches of the national government? Do you think it mattered that litigants in *Baker v. Carr*, 369 U.S. 186 (1962), were evoking the equal protection clause of the Fourteenth Amendment rather than the Guarantee Clause in Article IV?:

Article I, Sec. 2, para. 2:

No Person shall be a Representative who shall not have attained to the Age of twenty five Years, and been seven Years a Citizen of the United States, and who shall not, when elected, be an Inhabitant of that State in which he shall be chosen.

Article I, Sec. 5, para. 1:

Each House shall be the Judge of the Elections, Returns and Qualification of its own Members . . .

Article I, Sec. 5, para. 2:

Each House may determine the Rules of its Proceedings, punish its Members for disorderly Behavior, and, with the Concurrence of two-thirds, expel a Member.

POWELL V. MCCORMACK

395 U.S. 486, 89 S. Ct. 1944, 23 L. ed. 491 (1969)

The basic facts of this case, which involved the attempted exclusion of a powerful and effective African American congressman known for a lavish lifestyle and for putting relatives on his congressional payroll from the U.S. House of Representatives, are described in the opening paragraph of the decision.

Vote: 7–1

CHIEF JUSTICE WARREN delivered the opinion of the Court.

In November 1966, petitioner Adam Clayton Powell, Jr., was duly elected from the 18th Congressional District of New York to serve in the United States House of Representatives for the 90th Congress. However, pursuant to a House resolution, he was not permitted to take his seat. Powell (and some of the voters of his district) then filed suit in Federal District Court, claiming that the House could exclude him only if it found he failed to meet the standing requirements of age, citizenship, and residence contained in Art. I, § 2, of the Constitution—requirements the House specifically found Powell met—and thus had excluded him unconstitutionally. The District Court dismissed petitioners' complaint "for want of jurisdiction of the subject matter." A panel of the Court of Appeals affirmed the dismissal, although on somewhat different grounds, each judge filing a separate opinion. We have determined that it was error to dismiss the complaint and that petitioner Powell is entitled to a declaratory judgment that he was unlawfully excluded from the 90th Congress.

I.

On February 10, 1967, the Select Committee issued another invitation to Powell. In the letter, the Select Committee informed Powell that its responsibility under the House Resolution extended to determining not only whether he met the standing qualifications of Art. I, § 2, but also to "inquir[ing] into the question of whether you should be punished or expelled pursuant to the powers granted . . . the House under Article I, Section 5, . . . of the Constitution. In other words, the Select Committee is of the opinion that at the conclusion of the present inquiry, it has authority to report back to the House recommendations with respect to . . . seating, expulsion or other punishment." Powell did not appear at the next hearing, held February 14, 1967. However, his attorneys were present, and they informed the Committee that Powell would not testify about matters other than his eligibility under the standing qualifications of Art. I, § 2. Powell's attorneys reasserted Powell's contention that the standing qualifications were the exclusive requirements for membership, and they further urged that punishment or expulsion was not possible until a member had been seated.

The Committee held one further hearing at which neither Powell nor his attorneys were present. Then, on February 23, 1967, the Committee issued its report, finding that Powell met the standing qualifications of Art. I, § 2. However, the Committee further reported that Powell had asserted an unwarranted privilege and immunity from the processes of the courts of New York; that he had wrongfully diverted House funds for the use of others and himself; and that he had made false reports on expenditures of foreign currency to the Committee on House Administration. The Committee recommended that Powell be sworn and seated as a member of the 90th Congress but that he be censured by the House, fined $40,000 and be deprived of his seniority.

The report was presented to the House on March 1, 1967, and the House debated the Select Committee's proposed resolution. At the conclusion of the debate, by a vote of 222 to 202 the House rejected a motion to bring the resolution to a vote. An amendment to the resolution was then offered; it called for the exclusion of Powell and a declaration that his seat was vacant. The Speaker ruled that a majority vote of the House would be sufficient to pass the resolution if it were so amended. After further debate, the amendment was adopted by a vote of 248 to 176. Then the House adopted by a vote of 307 to 116 House Resolution No. 278 in its amended form, thereby excluding Powell and directing that the Speaker notify the Governor of New York that the seat was vacant.

Powell and 13 voters of the 18th Congressional District of New York subsequently instituted this suit in the United States District Court for the District of Columbia. Five members of the House of Representatives were named as defendants individually and "as representatives of a class of citizens who are presently serving . . . as members of the House of Representatives." John W. McCormack was named in his official capacity as

Speaker, and the Clerk of the House of Representatives, the Sergeant at Arms and the Doorkeeper were named individually and in their official capacities. The complaint alleged that House Resolution No. 278 violated the Constitution, specifically Art. I, § 2, cl. 1, because the resolution was inconsistent with the mandate that the members of the House shall be elected by the people of each State, and Art. I, § 2, cl. 2, which, petitioners alleged, sets forth the exclusive qualifications for membership. The complaint further alleged that the Clerk of the House threatened to refuse to perform the service for Powell to which a duly elected Congressman is entitled, that the Sergeant at Arms refused to pay Powell his salary, and that the Doorkeeper threatened to deny Powell admission to the House chamber.

Petitioners asked that a three-judge court be convened. Further, they requested that the District Court grant a permanent injunction restraining respondents from executing the House Resolution, and enjoining the Speaker from refusing to administer the oath, the Clerk from refusing to perform the duties due a Representative, the Sergeant at Arms from refusing to pay Powell his salary, and the Doorkeeper from refusing to admit Powell to the Chamber. The complaint also requested a declaratory judgment that Powell's exclusion was unconstitutional.

The District Court granted respondents' motion to dismiss the complaint "for want of jurisdiction of the subject matter." The Court of Appeals for the District of Columbia Circuit affirmed on somewhat different grounds, with each judge of the panel filing a separate opinion. We granted certiorari. While the case was pending on our docket, the 90th Congress officially terminated and the 91st Congress was seated. In November 1968, Powell was again elected as the representative of the 18th Congressional District of New York and he was seated by the 91st Congress. The resolution seating Powell also fined him $25,000. Respondents then filed a suggestion of mootness. We postponed further consideration of this suggestion to a hearing on the merits.

Respondents press upon us a variety of arguments to support the court below; they will be considered in the following order. (1) Events occurring subsequent to the grant of certiorari have rendered this litigation moot. (2) The Speech or Debate Clause of the Constitution, Art. I, § 6, insulates respondents' action from judicial review. (3) The decision to exclude petitioner Powell is supported by the power granted to the House of Representatives to expel a member. (4) This Court lacks subject matter jurisdiction over petitioners' action. (5) Even if subject matter jurisdiction is present, this litigation is not justiciable either under the general criteria established by this Court or because a political question is involved.

II.

MOOTNESS.

After certiorari was granted, respondents filed a memorandum suggesting that two events which occurred subsequent to our grant of certiorari require that the case be dismissed as moot. On January 3, 1969, the House of Representatives of the 90th Congress officially terminated, and petitioner Powell was seated as a member of the 91st Congress. 115 Cong. Rec. H22 (daily ed., January 3, 1969). Respondents insist that the gravamen of petitioners' complaint was the failure of the 90th Congress to seat petitioner Powell and that, since the House of Representatives is not a continuing body and Powell has now been seated, his claims are moot. Petitioners counter that three issues remain unresolved and thus this litigation presents a "case or controversy" within the meaning of Art. III: (1) whether Powell was unconstitutionally deprived of his seniority by his exclusion from the 90th Congress; (2) whether the resolution of the 91st Congress imposing as "punishment" a $25,000 fine is a continuation of respondents' allegedly unconstitutional exclusion and (3) whether Powell is entitled to salary withheld after his exclusion from the 90th Congress. We conclude that Powell's claim for back salary remains viable even though he has been seated in the 91st Congress and thus find it unnecessary to determine whether the other issues have become moot. . . .

SPEECH OR DEBATE CLAUSE.

Respondents assert that the Speech or Debate Clause of the Constitution, Art. I, § 6, is an absolute bar to petitioners' action. . . .

The Speech or Debate Clause, adopted by the Constitutional Convention without debate or opposition, finds its roots in the conflict between Parliament and the Crown culminating in the Glorious Revolution of 1688 and the English Bill of Rights of 1689. Drawing upon this history, we concluded in *United States v. Johnson,* 383 US 169 (1966), that the purpose of this clause was "to prevent intimidation [of legislators] by the executive and accountability before a possibly hostile judiciary." Although the clause sprang from a fear of seditious libel actions instituted by the Crown to punish unfavorable speeches made in Parliament, we have held that it would be a "narrow view" to confine the protection of the Speech or Debate Clause to words spoken in debate. Committee reports, resolutions, and the act of voting are equally covered, as are "things generally done in a session of the House by one of its members in relation to the business before it." *Kilbourn v. Thompson*, 103 U.S. 168 (1880). Furthermore, the clause not only provides a defense on the merits but also protects a legislator from the burden of defending himself. *Dombrowski v. Eastland*; 387 US 82 (1967); see *Tenney v. Brandhove*, 341 US 367 (1951).

Our cases make it clear that the legislative immunity created by the Speech or Debate Clause performs an important function in representative government. It insures that legislators are free to represent the interests of their constituents without fear that they will be later called to task in the courts for that representation. Thus, in *Tenney* v. *Brandhove,* the Court quoted the writings of James Wilson as illuminating the reason for legislative immunity: "In order to enable and encourage a representative of the publick to discharge his publick trust with firmness and success, it is indispensably necessary, that he should enjoy the fullest liberty of speech, and that he should be protected from the resentment of every one, however powerful, to whom the exercise of that liberty may occasion offence."

Legislative immunity does not, of course, bar all judicial review of legislative acts. That issue was settled by implication as early as 1803, see *Marbury* v. *Madison*, 5 U.S. (1 Cranch) 137, and expressly in *Kilbourn* v. *Thompson*, the first of this Court's cases interpreting the reach of the Speech or Debate Clause. Challenged in *Kilbourn* was the constitutionality of a House Resolution ordering the arrest and imprisonment of a recalcitrant witness who had refused to respond to a subpoena issued by a House investigating committee. While holding that the Speech or Debate Clause barred Kilbourn's action for false imprisonment brought against several members of the House, the Court nevertheless reached the merits of Kilbourn's attack and decided that, since the House had no power to punish for contempt, Kilbourn's imprisonment pursuant to the resolution was unconstitutional. It therefore allowed Kilbourn to bring his false imprisonment action against Thompson, the House's Sergeant at Arms, who had executed the warrant for Kilbourn's arrest.

That House employees are acting pursuant to express orders of the House does not bar judicial review of the constitutionality of the underlying legislative decision. *Kilbourn* decisively settles this question, since the Sergeant at Arms was held liable for false imprisonment even though he did nothing more than execute the House Resolution that Kilbourn be arrested and imprisoned. . . .

IV.

EXCLUSION OR EXPULSION.

The resolution excluding petitioner Powell was adopted by a vote in excess of two-thirds of the 434 Members of Congress—307 to 116. Article I, § 5, grants the House authority to expel a member "with the Concurrence of two thirds." Respondents assert that the House may expel a member for any reason whatsoever and that, since a two-thirds vote was obtained, the procedure by which Powell was denied his seat in the 90th Congress should be regarded as an expulsion, not an exclusion. . . . Members of the House having expressed a belief that such strictures apply to its own power to expel, we will not assume that two-thirds of its members would have expelled Powell for his prior conduct had the Speaker announced that House Resolution No. 278 was for expulsion rather than exclusion. . . .

B. *Political Question Doctrine.*

1. Textually Demonstrable Constitutional Commitment.

. . . Respondents' first contention is that this case presents a political question because under Art. I, § 5, there has been a "textually demonstrable constitutional commitment" to the House of the "adjudicatory power" to determine Powell's qualifications. Thus it is argued that the House, and the House alone, has power to determine who is qualified to be a member.

In order to determine whether there has been a textual commitment to a co-ordinate department of the Government, we must interpret the Constitution. In other words, we must first determine what power the Constitution confers upon the House through Art. I, § 5, before we can determine to what extent, if any, the exercise of that power is subject to judicial review. Respondents maintain that the House has broad power under § 5, and, they argue, the House may determine which are the qualifications necessary for membership. On the other hand, petitioners allege that the Constitution provides that an elected representative may be denied his seat only if the House finds he does not meet one of the standing qualifications expressly prescribed by the Constitution.

If examination of § 5 disclosed that the Constitution gives the House judicially unreviewable power to set qualifications for membership and to judge whether prospective members meet those qualifications, further review of the House determination might well be barred by the political question doctrine. On the other hand, if the Constitution gives the House power to judge only whether elected members possess the three standing qualifications set forth in the Constitution, further consideration would be necessary to determine whether any of the other formulations of the political question doctrine are "inextricable from the case at bar." *Baker v. Carr*, 369 U.S. 186 (1962). In other words, whether there is a "textually demonstrable constitutional commitment of the issue to a coordinate political department" of government and what is the scope of such commitment are questions we must resolve for the first time in this case. For, as we pointed out in *Baker v. Carr,* "deciding whether a matter has in any measure been committed by the Constitution to another branch of government, or whether the action of that branch exceeds whatever authority has been committed, is itself a delicate exercise in constitutional interpretation, and is a responsibility of this Court as ultimate interpreter of the Constitution."

In order to determine the scope of any "textual commitment" under Art. I, § 5, we necessarily must determine the meaning of the phrase to "be the Judge of the Qualifications of its own Members." Petitioners argue that the records of the debates during the Constitutional Convention; available commentary from the post-Convention, pre-ratification period; and early congressional applications of Art. I, § 5, support their construction of the section. Respondents insist, however, that a careful examination of the pre-Convention practices of the English Parliament and American colonial assemblies demonstrates that by 1787, a legislature's power to judge the qualifications of its members was generally understood to encompass exclusion or expulsion on the ground that an individual's character or past conduct rendered him unfit to serve. When the Constitution and the debates over its adoption are thus viewed in historical perspective, argue respondents, it becomes clear that the "qualifications" expressly set forth in the Constitution were not meant to limit the long-recognized legislative power to exclude or expel at will, but merely to establish "standing incapacities," which could be altered only by a constitutional amendment. Our examination of the relevant historical materials leads us to the conclusion that petitioners are correct and that the Constitution leaves the House without authority to *exclude* any person, duly elected by his constituents, who meets all the requirements for membership expressly prescribed in the Constitution.

a. The Pre-Convention Precedents.

Even if these cases could be construed to support respondents' contention, their precedential value was nullified prior to the Constitutional Convention. By 1782, after a long struggle, the arbitrary exercise of the power to exclude was unequivocally repudiated by a House of Commons resolution which ended the most notorious English election dispute of the 18th century—the John Wilkes case. While serving as a member of Parliament in 1763, Wilkes published an attack on a recent peace treaty with France, calling it a product of bribery and condemning the Crown's ministers as " 'the tools of despotism and corruption.' " R. Postgate, *That Devil Wilkes* 53 (1929). Wilkes and others who were involved with the publication in which the attack appeared were arrested. Prior to Wilkes' trial, the House of Commons expelled him for publishing "a false, scandalous, and seditious libel." Wilkes then fled to France and was subsequently sentenced to exile. Wilkes returned to England in 1768, the same year in which the Parliament from which he had been expelled was dissolved. He was elected to the next Parliament, and he then surrendered himself to the Court of King's Bench. Wilkes was convicted of seditious libel and sentenced to 22 months' imprisonment. The new Parliament declared him ineligible for membership and ordered that he be "expelled this House." Although Wilkes was re-elected to fill the vacant seat three times, each time the same Parliament declared him ineligible and refused to seat him.

Wilkes was released from prison in 1770 and was again elected to Parliament in 1774. For the next several years, he unsuccessfully campaigned to have the resolutions expelling him and declaring him incapable of re-election expunged from the record. Finally, in 1782, the House of Commons voted to expunge them, resolving that the prior House actions were "subversive of the rights of the whole body of electors of this kingdom."

With the successful resolution of Wilkes' long and bitter struggle for the right of the British electorate to be represented by men of their own choice, it is evident that, on the eve of the Constitutional Convention, English precedent stood for the proposition that "the law of the land had regulated the qualifications of members to serve in parliament" and those qualifications were "not occasional but fixed.". . .

The resolution of the Wilkes case similarly undermined the precedential value of the earlier colonial exclusions, for the principles upon which they had been based were repudiated by the very body the colonial assemblies sought to imitate and whose precedents they generally followed. . . .

Wilkes' struggle and his ultimate victory had a significant impact in the American colonies. His advocacy of libertarian causes and his pursuit of the right to be seated in Parliament became a *cause celebre* for the colonists. "The cry of 'Wilkes and Liberty' echoed loudly across the Atlantic Ocean as wide publicity was given to every step of Wilkes's public career in the colonial press. . . . The reaction in America took on significant proportions. Colonials tended to identify their cause with that of Wilkes. They saw him as a popular hero and a martyr to the struggle for liberty. . . . They named towns, counties, and even children in his honour." It is within this historical context that we must examine the Convention debates in 1787, just five years after Wilkes' final victory.

b. Convention Debates.

Relying heavily on Charles Warren's analysis of the Convention debates, petitioners argue that the proceedings manifest the Framers' unequivocal intention to deny either branch of Congress the authority to add to or otherwise vary the membership qualifications expressly set forth in the Constitution. We do not completely agree, for the debates are subject to other interpretations. However, we have concluded that the records of the debates, viewed in the context of the bitter struggle for the right to freely choose representatives which had recently concluded in England and in light of the distinction the Framers made between the power to expel and the power to exclude, indicate that petitioners' ultimate conclusion is correct. [The Court proceeded to examine Convention debates.]

In view of what followed Madison's speech, it appears that on this critical day the Framers were facing and then rejecting the possibility that the legislature would have power to usurp the "indisputable right [of the people] to return whom they thought proper" to the legislature. Oliver Ellsworth, of Connecticut, noted that a legislative power to establish property qualifications was exceptional and "dangerous because it would be much more liable to abuse." Gouverneur Morris then moved to strike "with regard to property" from the Committee's proposal. His intention was "to leave the Legislature entirely at large." Hugh Williamson, of North Carolina, expressed concern that if a majority of the legislature should happen to be "composed of any particular description of men, of lawyers for example, . . . the future elections might be secured to their own body." Madison then referred to the British Parliament's assumption of the power to regulate the qualifications of both electors and the elected and noted that "the abuse they had made of it was a lesson worthy of our attention. They had made the changes in both cases subservient to their own views, or to the views of political or Religious parties." Shortly thereafter, the Convention rejected both Gouverneur Morris' motion and the Committee's proposal. Later the same day, the Convention adopted without debate the provision authorizing each House to be "the judge of the . . . qualifications of its own members."

One other decision made the same day is very important to determining the meaning of Art. I, § 5. When the delegates reached the Committee of Detail's proposal to empower each House to expel its members, Madison "observed that the right of expulsion . . . was too important to be exercised by a bare majority of a quorum: and in emergencies [one] faction might be dangerously abused." He therefore moved that "with the concurrence of two-thirds" be inserted. With the exception of one State, whose delegation was divided, the motion was unanimously approved without debate, although Gouverneur Morris noted his opposition. The importance of this decision cannot be over-emphasized. None of the parties to this suit disputes that prior to 1787 the legislative powers to judge qualifications and to expel were exercised by a majority vote. Indeed, without exception, the English and colonial antecedents to Art. I, § 5, cls. 1 and 2, support this conclusion. Thus, the Convention's decision to increase the vote required to expel, because that power was "too important to be exercised by a bare majority," while at the same time not similarly restricting the power to judge qualifications, is compelling evidence that they considered the latter already limited by the standing qualifications previously adopted.

. . . The debates at the state conventions also demonstrate the Framers' understanding that the qualifications for members of Congress had been fixed in the Constitution. . . .

c. Post-Ratification.

. . . There was no significant challenge to these principles for the next several decades. They came under heavy attack, however, "during the stress of civil war [but initially] the House of Representatives declined to exercise the power [to exclude], even under circumstances of great provocation." The abandonment of such restraint, however, was among the casualties of the general upheaval produced in war's wake. In 1868, the House voted for the first time in its history to exclude a member-elect. It refused to seat two duly elected representatives for giving aid and comfort to the Confederacy. "This change was produced by the North's bitter enmity toward those who failed to support the Union cause during the war, and was effected by the Radical Republican domination of Congress. It was a shift brought about by the naked urgency of power and was given little doctrinal support." Comment, Legislative Exclusion: Julian Bond and Adam Clayton Powell, 35 U. Chi. L. Rev. 151, 157 (1967). From that time until the present, congressional practice has been erratic; and on the few occasions when a member-elect was excluded although he met all the qualifications set forth in the Constitution, there were frequently vigorous dissents. . . .

d. Conclusion.

Had the intent of the Framers emerged from these materials with less clarity, we would nevertheless have been compelled to resolve any ambiguity in favor of a narrow construction of the scope of Congress' power to exclude members-elect. A fundamental principle of our representative democracy is, in Hamilton's words, "that the people should choose whom they please to govern them." 2 *Elliot's Debates* 257. As Madison pointed out at the Convention, this principle is undermined as much by limiting whom the people can select as by limiting the franchise itself. In apparent agreement with this basic philosophy, the Convention adopted his suggestion limiting the power to expel. To allow essentially that same power to be exercised under the guise of judging qualifications, would be to ignore Madison's warning, borne out in the Wilkes case and some of Congress' own post-Civil War exclusion cases, against "vesting an improper & dangerous power in the Legislature." 2 Farrand 249. Moreover, it would effectively nullify the Convention's decision to require a two-thirds vote for expulsion. Unquestionably, Congress has an interest in preserving its institutional integrity, but in most cases that interest can be sufficiently safeguarded by the exercise of its power to punish its members for disorderly behavior and, in extreme cases, to expel a member with the concurrence of two-thirds. In short, both the intention of the Framers, to the extent it can be determined, and an examination of the basic principles of our democratic system persuade us that the Constitution does not vest in the Congress a discretionary power to deny membership by a majority vote.

For these reasons, we have concluded that Art. I, § 5, is at most a "textually demonstrable commitment" to Congress to judge only the qualifications expressly set forth in the Constitution. Therefore, the "textual commitment" formulation of the political question doctrine does not bar federal courts from adjudicating petitioners' claims.

2. Other Considerations.

Respondents' alternate contention is that the case presents a political question because judicial resolution of petitioners' claim would produce a "potentially embarrassing confrontation between coordinate branches" of the Federal Government. But, as our interpretation of Art. I, § 5, discloses, a determination of petitioner Powell's right to sit would require no more than an interpretation of the Constitution. Such a determination falls within the traditional role accorded courts to interpret the law, and does not involve a "lack of the respect due [a] coordinate [branch] of government," nor does it involve an "initial policy determination of a kind clearly for nonjudicial discretion." *Baker* v. *Carr*. Our system of government requires that federal courts on occasion interpret the Constitution in a manner at variance with the construction given the document by another branch. The alleged conflict that such an adjudication may cause cannot justify the courts' avoiding their constitutional responsibility.

FOR DISCUSSION

The Court devoted a sizable portion of its decision to the events surrounding the British Parliament's attempt to exclude John Wilkes. Do you think this was relevant? Had the Senate responded to the decision by expelling Powell by a two-thirds vote, do you think that Powell could have won another favorable judgment from the Court? Might he have been able to do so if prominent members who voted for such a resolution had said they were doing it on the basis of race?

MISSOURI V. JENKINS

515 U.S. 70, 115 S. Ct. 2038, 132 L. Ed. 2d 63 (1995)

After eighteen years of litigation, Missouri challenged a U.S. district court order mandating salary increases for most employees and requiring further steps because student achievement levels were still "at or below national norms at many grade levels."

Vote: 5–4

CHIEF JUSTICE REHNQUIST delivered the opinion of the Court.

. . . This case has been before the same United States District Judge since 1977. *Missouri* v. *Jenkins,* 491 U.S. 274 (1989) *(Jenkins I).* In that year, the [Kansas City, Missouri School District (KCMSD)], the school board, and the children of two school board members brought suit against the State and other defendants. Plaintiffs alleged that the State, the surrounding suburban school districts (SSD's), and various federal agencies had caused and perpetuated a system of racial segregation in the schools of the Kansas City metropolitan area. . . .

After a trial that lasted 7 1/2 months, the District Court dismissed the case against the federal defendants and the SSD's, but determined that the State and the KCMSD were liable for an intradistrict violation, *i.e.,* they had operated a segregated school system within the KCMSD. The District Court determined that prior to 1954 "Missouri mandated segregated schools for black and white children." Furthermore, the KCMSD and the State had failed in their affirmative obligations to eliminate the vestiges of the State's dual school system within the KCMSD.

In June 1985, the District Court issued its first remedial order and established as its goal the "elimination of all vestiges of state imposed segregation." . . .

The District Court, pursuant to plans submitted by the KCMSD and the State, ordered a wide range of quality education programs for all students attending the KCMSD. First, the District Court ordered that the KCMSD be restored to an AAA classification, the highest classification awarded by the State Board of Education. Second, it ordered that the number of students per class be reduced so that the student-to-teacher ratio was below the level required for AAA standing. The District Court justified its reduction in class size as "an essential part of any plan to remedy the vestiges of segregation in the KCMSD. Reducing class size will serve to remedy the vestiges of past segregation by increasing individual attention and instruction, as well as increasing the potential for desegregative educational experiences for KCMSD students by maintaining and attracting non-minority enrollment."

The District Court also ordered programs to expand educational opportunities for all KCMSD students: full-day kindergarten; expanded summer school; before- and after-school tutoring; and an early childhood development program. Finally, the District Court implemented a state-funded "effective schools" program that consisted of substantial yearly cash grants to each of the schools within the KCMSD. Under the "effective schools" program, the State was required to fund programs at both the 25 racially identifiable schools as well as the 43 other schools within the KCMSD.

The KCMSD was awarded an AAA rating in the 1987–1988 school year, and there is no dispute that since that time it has " 'maintained and greatly exceeded AAA requirements.' " The total cost for these quality education programs has exceeded $220 million.

The District Court also set out to desegregate the KCMSD but believed that "to accomplish desegregation within the boundary lines of a school district whose enrollment remains 68.3% black is a difficult task." Because it had found no interdistrict violation, the District Court could not order mandatory interdistrict redistribution of students between the KCMSD and the surrounding SSD's. The District Court refused to order additional mandatory student reassignments because they would "increase the instability of the KCMSD and reduce the potential for desegregation." Relying on favorable precedent from the Eighth Circuit, the District Court determined that "achievement of AAA status, improvement of the quality of education being offered at the KCMSD schools, magnet schools, as well as other components of this desegregation plan can serve to maintain and hopefully attract non-minority student enrollment."

In November 1986, the District Court approved a comprehensive magnet school and capital improvements plan and held the State and the KCMSD jointly and severally liable for its funding. Under the District Court's plan, every senior high school, every middle school, and one-half of the elementary schools were converted into magnet schools. The District Court adopted the magnet-school program to "provide a greater educational opportunity to *all* KCMSD students," and because it believed "that the proposed magnet plan [was] so attractive that it would draw non-minority students from the private schools who have abandoned or avoided the KCMSD, and draw in additional non-minority students from the suburbs." The District Court felt that "the long-term benefit of all KCMSD students of a greater educational opportunity in an integrated environment is worthy of such an investment." Since its inception, the magnet school program has operated at a cost, including magnet transportation, in excess of $448 million. In April 1993, the District Court considered, but ultimately rejected, the plaintiffs' and the KCMSD's proposal seeking approval of a long-range magnet renewal program that included a 10-year budget of well over $500 million, funded by the State and the KCMSD on a joint-and-several basis.

In June 1985, the District Court ordered substantial capital improvements to combat the deterioration of the KCMSD's facilities. In formulating its capital-improvements plan, the District Court dismissed as "irrelevant" the "State's argument that the present condition of the facilities [was] not traceable to unlawful segregation." Instead, the District Court focused on its responsibility to "remedy the vestiges of segregation" and to "implement a desegregation plan which would maintain and attract non-minority enrollment." The initial phase of the capital improvements plan cost $37 million. . . .

In September 1987, the District Court adopted, for the most part, KCMSD's long-range capital improvements plan at a cost in excess of $ 187 million. The plan called for the renovation of approximately 55 schools, the closure of 18 facilities, and the construction of 17 new schools. The District Court rejected what it referred to as the " 'patch and repair' approach proposed by the State" because it "would not achieve suburban comparability or the visual attractiveness sought by the Court as it would result in floor coverings with unsightly sections of mismatched carpeting and tile, and individual walls possessing different shades of paint." The District Court reasoned that "if the KCMSD schools underwent the limited renovation proposed by the State, the schools would continue to be unattractive and substandard, and would certainly serve as a deterrent to parents considering enrolling their children in KCMSD schools." As of 1990, the District Court had ordered $260 million in capital improvements. Since then, the total cost of capital improvements ordered has soared to over $ 540 million.

As part of its desegregation plan, the District Court has ordered salary assistance to the KCMSD. In 1987, the District Court initially ordered salary assistance only for teachers within the KCMSD. Since that time, however, the District Court has ordered salary assistance to all but three of the approximately 5,000 KCMSD employees. The total cost of this component of the desegregation remedy since 1987 is over $200 million.

The District Court's desegregation plan has been described as the most ambitious and expensive remedial program in the history of school desegregation. The annual cost per pupil at the KCMSD far exceeds that of the neighboring SSD's or of any school district in Missouri. Nevertheless, the KCMSD, which has pursued a "friendly adversary" relationship with the plaintiffs, has continued to propose ever more expensive programs. As a result, the desegregation costs have escalated and now are approaching an annual cost of $200 million. These massive expenditures have financed "high schools in which every classroom will have air conditioning, an alarm system, and 15 microcomputers; a 2,000-square-foot planetarium; green houses and vivariums; a 25-acre farm with an air-conditioned meeting room for 104 people; a Model United Nations wired for language translation; broadcast capable radio and television studios with an editing and animation lab; a temperature controlled art gallery; movie editing and screening rooms; a 3,500-square-foot dust-free diesel mechanics room;

1,875-square-foot elementary school animal rooms for use in a zoo project; swimming pools; and numerous other facilities."

Not surprisingly, the cost of this remedial plan has "far exceeded KCMSD's budget, or for that matter, its authority to tax." The State, through the operation of joint-and-several liability, has borne the brunt of these costs. The District Court candidly has acknowledged that it has "allowed the District planners to dream" and "provided the mechanism for those dreams to be realized." In short, the District Court "has gone to great lengths to provide KCMSD with facilities and opportunities not available anywhere else in the country."

II

With this background, we turn to the present controversy. First, the State has challenged the District Court's requirement that it fund salary increases for KCMSD instructional and noninstructional staff. The State claimed that funding for salaries was beyond the scope of the District Court's remedial authority. Second, the State has challenged the District Court's order requiring it to continue to fund the remedial quality education programs for the 1992–1993 school year. The State contended that under *Freeman* v. *Pitts,* 503 U.S. 467 (1992), it had achieved partial unitary status with respect to the quality education programs already in place. As a result, the State argued that the District Court should have relieved it of responsibility for funding those programs.

The District Court rejected the State's arguments. . . .

The Court of Appeals for the Eighth Circuit affirmed. . . .

Because of the importance of the issues, we granted certiorari to consider the following: (1) whether the District Court exceeded its constitutional authority when it granted salary increases to virtually all instructional and noninstructional employees of the KCMSD, and (2) whether the District Court properly relied upon the fact that student achievement test scores had failed to rise to some unspecified level when it declined to find that the State had achieved partial unitary status as to the quality education programs.

III

. . . Instead of seeking to remove the racial identity of the various schools within the KCMSD, the District Court has set out on a program to create a school district that was equal to or superior to the surrounding SSD's. Its remedy has focused on "desegregative attractiveness," coupled with "suburban comparability." Examination of the District Court's reliance on "desegregative attractiveness" and "suburban comparability" is instructive for our ultimate resolution of the salary-order issue.

The purpose of desegregative attractiveness has been not only to remedy the systemwide reduction in student achievement, but also to attract nonminority students not presently enrolled in the KCMSD. This remedy has included an elaborate program of capital improvements, course enrichment, and extracurricular enhancement not simply in the formerly identifiable black schools, but in schools throughout the district. The District Court's remedial orders have converted every senior high school, every middle school, and one-half of the elementary schools in the KCMSD into "magnet" schools. The District Court's remedial order has all but made the KCMSD itself into a magnet district. . . . We previously have approved of intradistrict desegregation remedies involving magnet schools. . . .

The District Court's remedial plan in this case, however, is not designed solely to redistribute the students within the KCMSD in order to eliminate racially identifiable schools within the KCMSD. Instead, its purpose is to attract non-minority students from outside the KCMSD schools. But this interdistrict goal is beyond the scope of the intradistrict violation identified by the District Court. In effect, the District Court has devised a remedy to accomplish indirectly what it admittedly lacks the remedial authority to mandate directly: the interdistrict transfer of students. . . .

In *Freeman,* we stated that "the vestiges of segregation that are the concern of the law in a school case may be subtle and intangible but nonetheless they must be so real that they have a causal link to the *de jure* violation being remedied." The record here does not support the District Court's reliance on "white flight" as a justification for a permissible expansion of its intradistrict remedial authority through its pursuit of desegregative attractiveness. . . .

The District Court's pursuit of the goal of "desegregative attractiveness" results in so many imponderables and is so far removed from the task of eliminating the racial identifiability of the schools within the KCMSD that we believe it is beyond the admittedly broad discretion of the District Court. In this posture, we conclude that the District Court's order of salary increases, which was "grounded in remedying the vestiges of segregation by improving the desegregative attractiveness of the KCMSD," is simply too far removed from an acceptable implementation of a permissible means to remedy previous legally mandated segregation.

Similar considerations lead us to conclude that the District Court's order requiring the State to continue to fund the quality education programs because student achievement levels were still "at or below national norms at many grade levels" cannot be sustained. The State does not seek from this Court a declaration of partial unitary status with respect to the quality education programs. It challenges the requirement of indefinite funding of a quality education program until national norms are met, based on the assumption that while a mandate for significant educational improvement, both in teaching and in facilities, may have been justified originally, its indefinite extension is not.

On remand, the District Court must bear in mind that its end purpose is not only "to remedy the violation" to the extent practicable, but also "to restore state and local authorities to the control of a school system that is operating in compliance with the Constitution."

The judgment of the Court of Appeals is reversed.

It is so ordered.

JUSTICE THOMAS, concurring.

It never ceases to amaze me that the courts are so willing to assume that anything that is predominantly black must be inferior. Instead of focusing on remedying the harm done to those black schoolchildren injured by segregation, the District Court here sought to convert the Kansas City, Missouri, School District (KCMSD) into a "magnet district" that would reverse the "white flight" caused by desegregation. In this respect, I join the Court's decision concerning the two remedial issues presented for review. I write separately, however, to add a few thoughts with respect to the overall course of this litigation. In order to evaluate the scope of the remedy, we must understand the scope of the constitutional violation and the nature of the remedial powers of the federal courts.

Two threads in our jurisprudence have produced this unfortunate situation, in which a District Court has taken it upon itself to experiment with the education of the KCMSD's black youth. First, the court has read our cases to support the theory that black students suffer an unspecified psychological harm from segregation that retards their mental and educational development. This approach not only relies upon questionable social science research rather than constitutional principle, but it also rests on an assumption of black inferiority. Second, we have permitted the federal courts to exercise virtually unlimited equitable powers to remedy this alleged constitutional violation. The exercise of this authority has trampled upon principles of federalism and the separation of powers and has freed courts to pursue other agendas unrelated to the narrow purpose of precisely remedying a constitutional harm. . . .

JUSTICE GINSBURG, dissenting.

I join Justice Souter's illuminating dissent and emphasize a consideration key to this controversy.

The Court stresses that the present remedial programs have been in place for seven years. But compared to more than two centuries of firmly entrenched official discrimination, the experience with the desegregation remedies ordered by the District Court has been evanescent.

In 1724, Louis XV of France issued the Code Noir, the first slave code for the Colony of Louisiana, an area that included Missouri. When Missouri entered the Union in 1821, it entered as a slave State.

Before the Civil War, Missouri law prohibited the creation or maintenance of schools for educating blacks: "No person shall keep or teach any school for the instruction of negroes or mulattoes, in reading or writing, in this State."

Beginning in 1865, Missouri passed a series of laws requiring separate public schools for blacks. The Missouri Constitution first permitted, then required, separate schools.

After this Court announced its decision in *Brown v. Board of Education,* 347 U.S. 483 (1954), Missouri's Attorney General declared these provisions mandating segregated schools unenforceable. The statutes were repealed in 1957 and the constitutional provision was rescinded in 1976. Nonetheless, 30 years after *Brown,* the District Court found that "the inferior education indigenous of the state-compelled dual school system has lingering effects in the Kansas City, Missouri School District." The District Court concluded that "the State . . . cannot defend its failure to affirmatively act to eliminate the structure and effects of its past dual system on the basis of restrictive state law." Just ten years ago, in June 1985, the District Court issued its first remedial order.

Today, the Court declares illegitimate the goal of attracting nonminority students to the Kansas City, Missouri, School District, and thus stops the District Court's efforts to integrate a school district that was, in the 1984/1985 school year, sorely in need and 68.3% black. Given the deep, inglorious history of segregation in Missouri, to curtail desegregation at this time and in this manner is an action at once too swift and too soon.

FOR DISCUSSION

In this case, the Supreme Court ultimately limited the degree to which it would allow lower courts to go. Just as Alexander Hamilton observed in *Federalist* No. 78 that the Court would depend on the other branches of government to enforce its decisions, so too modern scholars observe that eager or belated attempts to implement judicial decisions can have a major impact. Public perceptions also play a role. Do you think the fact that an African American has now served two presidential terms may strengthen claims that future judicial decisions in this area are less necessary than they once were?

To what degree should the Court consider progress in race relations in determining which race-conscious policies are appropriate follow-ups to *Brown v. Board of Education*?

GLOSSARY

Advisory Opinions: Opinions, which U.S. courts refuse to issue, that advise what it would do in hypothetical situations.

Advice and Consent: Constitutional term for the Senate's role in deciding whether to accept or reject presidential nominations to the judiciary and other posts.

Amicus Curiae Briefs: "Friend of the Court" briefs filed by nonparties to a suit who want to have the Court consider their views on the matter.

Appellants: Losing parties who file appeals.

Appellate Jurisdiction: Jurisdiction that higher courts have to review judgments of lower trial courts. Courts generally limit appellate review to questions of law rather than determinations of facts.

Appellees: Winning parties against whom appeals are filed.

Articles of Confederation: The government for the thirteen states that preceded the U.S. Constitution. Ratified in 1781, the Articles remained in effect until 1789.

Cases and Controversies: Language used in Article III that courts have interpreted to avoid giving advisory opinions in cases where there are not litigants with concrete interests at stake.

Checks and Balances: A system of government in which various branches and levels of government are designed to prevent abuse of powers by the others.

Chief Justice of the United States: Designated by the U.S. Constitution to preside over the U.S. Supreme Court, the chief is generally considered to be *primus inter pares*, or first among equals. By tradition the chief either writes or assigns opinions when the chief is in the majority. The chief also presides over trials of presidential impeachments.

Civil Cases: Involve legal disputes between private individuals.

Common Law: The system of judge-made, or judge-discovered, law prominent in Great Britain that has been adapted to the system of most U.S. states. Louisiana uses a civil law system, based on French and Spanish codes.

Concurring Opinion: An opinion in which a judge or justice indicates agreement with a court's decision but adds further explanation, sometimes justifying a decision on alternate grounds.

Constitutional Convention of 1787: A convention of fifty-five delegates from twelve of the thirteen states (all but Rhode Island) that wrote the Constitution; sent to state conventions for ratification and became effective in 1789.

Declaration of Independence: A document, drafted largely by Thomas Jefferson for the Second Continental Congress, which proclaimed the reasons for American independence from Britain. The document articulated the natural rights doctrine that "all men are created equal" and that they are endowed with the rights of "life, liberty, and the pursuit of happiness."

Declaratory Judgment: A judgment of law (not to be confused with advisory opinions) that stems from an actual case and that is binding on the parties.

Defendants: Individuals responding either to civil cases filed against them or to government charges of criminal wrongdoing.

Delegated Powers: In order to justify exercises of powers, departments of government must be able trace them directly to enumerations of power within the Constitution. Most congressional powers are listed in Article I, Section 8. Delegated powers may form the basis of implied powers.

Dissenting Opinion: An opinion in which a judge or justice disagrees with the majority opinion and explains the judge's reasoning in hopes of persuading others that the opinion is wrong.

During Good Behavior: The constitutional provision that grants that judges and justices will serve until they die, retire, or are impeached, convicted, and removed from office.

En Banc: A meeting of all members of a court, typically a U.S. circuit court, whose members more typically serve on three-judge panels.

Federal System: Divides government between a national government and states. Such governments require a national constitution to delineate the boundaries and respective responsibilities of the two governments. In federal systems, both the national and state governments can act directly on the states.

Federalists: Individuals who supported ratification of the U.S. Constitution. They designated their opponents as Anti-Federalists. One of the first two political parties in the U.S. subsequently took this as its name.

Impeachment: A constitutional mechanism through which the House of Representatives may charge the president, judges, and other civil offices with "Treason, Bribery, or other High Crimes and Misdemeanors." Impeachment leads to a trial in the U.S. Senate, where it takes a two-thirds vote to convict and remove from office.

Interpretivism: A name sometimes given to jurists who believe that their task is limited to that of ascertaining and applying the original understanding of constitutional words. Noninterpretivists are more likely to supplement this understanding from extraconstitutional sources.

Judicial Activism and Judicial Restraint: Contrasting styles of judicial interpretation, the first stressing a broad judicial responsibility and the latter typically more deferential to judgments made by the two elected branches of government.

Judicial Review: A power not directly stated in the U.S. Constitution, but based both on constitutional principles and on long-standing precedents, by which courts determine whether laws brought before them in cases are consistent with the Constitution. Courts may exercise such review over both state and federal legislation.

Jurisdiction: The scope of a court's authority. Article III grants both original and appellate jurisdiction to the Supreme Court, with the latter being subject to "such Exceptions . . . as the Congress shall make."

Justiciability: Before a Court will deliver an opinion, the parties before it have to show that the controversy that brings them before the Court and/or the remedy that they seek is one that is appropriate for judges.

Law and Equity: Two divisions of English law, both of which the United States Constitution entrusted to review by the Supreme Court.

Magna Carta: A document signed by King John in England with his noblemen in England in 1215 and generally regarded as the origin of the British Parliament, and subsequent representative institutions, and of the idea of written constitutionalism.

Majority Opinion: An opinion that reflects a Supreme Court majority has the effect of operative law.

Missouri Plan: An arrangement adopted in some states whereby the governor appoints judges, who are later subject to a popular vote as to whether they should be retained or removed from office.

Mootness: Cases that have been effectively settled before they get to court are considered to be moot; courts refuse to hear such cases because they no longer present a live "case or controversy."

Natural Rights: Rights such as "life, liberty, and the pursuit of happiness" that the Declaration of Independence proclaimed belong to individuals by reason of their personhood. Just governments incorporate such natural rights into civil rights.

New Jersey Plan: A plan offered by small states at the Constitutional Convention of 1787 advocating equal state representation in a unicameral congress. This plan favored presidential appointment of federal judges.

Original Intent: A method of constitutional interpretation that emphasizes the intent of those who wrote, ratified, and/or amended the Constitution.

Original Jurisdiction: Cases that arrive before a court for their first hearing. The U.S. Supreme Court exercises relatively little original jurisdiction since most cases come to it on appeal.

Parliamentary Sovereignty: Under British law, the legislative body, or Parliament, is thought to be supreme. Americans rejected this notion as incompatible with natural rights and with a system of checks and balances.

Political Questions: Issues on which courts refuse to rule on the basis that they are matters for the two political, or elected, branches to handle.

Primus Inter Pares: First among equals. Often used to describe the role of the Chief Justice of the United States

Prosecution: Representative of the government in criminal cases.

Recusal: Judges are expected to step aside, or recuse, themselves in cases where they have a personal stake or interest.

Rule of Four: The Supreme Court will not accept review of a case unless four of the nine justices agree that they want to hear it. The rule points to the wide discretion that the Court has in setting its own docket.

Separation of Powers: A system that divides powers among various branches of government in order to prevent abuses by any of them. The U.S. Constitution divides the national government into legislative, executive, and judicial branches.

Social Contract: The idea that just governments are based on the consent of the governed. Social contract theorists, most notably Thomas Hobbes, John Locke, and Jean-Jacques Rousseau, argued that if individuals found themselves in a lawless state of nature, they would form a social contract to escape.

Standing: Before courts will accept a case, parties must establish that they have a proper interest in the case. This showing is called standing.

Stare Decisis: Let the precedent stand. Many court decisions are based on adherence to prior precedents.

State of Nature: A hypothetical prepolitical state in which laws would not be established, settled, known, or impartially enforced.

Statutory Interpretation: The power that courts exercise to determine the meaning of legislation.

Supremacy Clause: The provision in Article VI of the U.S. Constitution that affirms the supremacy of the Constitution over conflicting state or federal laws.

Unicameral Legislature: This type of legislature has one house or chamber.

U.S. Circuit Courts: Courts that sit midway between the ninety-four U.S. District Courts and the U.S. Supreme Court. There are currently eleven numbered circuits, a D.C. circuit, and a specialized circuit.

U.S. District Courts: Federal trial courts, of which there are currently ninety-four.

U.S. Supreme Court: The highest court in the federal system with power over both lower state and federal courts. Housed in Washington, D.C., the Court has eight associate justices and a chief justice.

Virginia Plan: The first plan introduced at the Constitutional Convention of 1787. It favored a bicameral Congress in which states would be represented according to population. It introduced the idea of separation of powers among the legislative, executive, and judicial branches. It called for legislative appointment of judges.

Writ of Appeal: A petition, which the Supreme Court used to be obligated to accept, under which litigants could request review of their cases by the Court.

Writ of Certification: A writ in which a lower court asked a higher court to clarify a matter of law.

Writ of Certiorari: The most common writ, or petition, by which cases come before the U.S. Supreme Court for appellate review.

Writ of Mandamus: A judicial order directed to an executive official ordering the official to produce or deliver a document.

SELECTED BIBLIOGRAPHY

Abraham, Henry J. 1998. *The Judicial Process: An Introductory Analysis of the Courts of the United States, England, and France*, 7th ed. New York: Oxford University Press.

Abraham, Henry J. 1999. *Justices, Presidents and Senators: A History of the U.S. Supreme Court Appointments from Washington to Clinton*, 3rd ed. Lanham, MD: Rowman & Littlefield Publishers, Inc.

Amar, Akhil Reed. 2005. *America's Constitution: A Biography*. New York: Random House.

Bickel, Alexander M. 1962. *The Least Dangerous Branch: The Supreme Court at the Bar of Politics*. New Haven, CT: Yale University Press.

Cooper, Phillip, and Howard Ball. 1966. *The United States Supreme Court: From the Inside Out*. Upper Saddle River, NJ: Prentice-Hall.

Farrand, Max. 1996. *The Records of the Federal Convention of 1787*, 4 vols. New Haven, CT: Yale University Press.

Hall, Kermit, ed. 2005. *The Oxford Companion to the Supreme Court of the United States,* 2nd ed. New York: Oxford University Press.

Hamburger, Philip. 2008. *Law and Judicial Duty*. Cambridge, MA: Harvard University Press.

Hamilton, Alexander, James Madison, and John Jay. 1961. *The Federalist Papers*, Clinton Rossiter, ed. New York: New American Library.

Lutz, Donald S. 1988. *The Origins of American Constitutionalis*m. Baton Rouge: Louisiana State University Press.

McCloskey, Robert G. 1994. *The American Supreme Court*, 2nd ed. Chicago: The University of Chicago Press.

O'Brien, David M. 2014. *Storm Center: The Supreme Court in American Politics*, 10th ed. New York: W.W. Norton.

Perry, Barbara A. 1999. *The Priestly Tribe: The Supreme Court's Image in the American Mind*. Westport, CT: Praeger.

Redish, Martin H. 1991. *The Federal Courts in the Political Order: Judicial Jurisdiction and American Political Theory*. Durham, NC: Carolina Academic Press.

Rehnquist, William H. 1987. *The Supreme Court: How It Was, How It Is*. New York: William Morrow & Company.

Slotnick, Elliott E., ed. 2005. *Judicial Politics: Readings from Judicature*, 3rd ed. Washington, DC: Congressional Quarterly Press.

Vile, John R. 2014. *Summaries of Leading Cases on the Constitution*, 16th ed. Lanham, MD: Rowman & Littlefield Publishers, Inc.

Vile, John R. 2015. *A Companion to the United States Constitution and Its Amendments*, 6th ed. Westport, CT: Praeger.

Vile, John R. 2016. *The Constitutional Convention of 1787: A Comprehensive Encyclopedia of America's Founding*, 2 vols., revised second ed. Clark, NJ: Talbot).

Wood, Gordon S. 1969. *The Creation of the American Republic: 1776–1787* Chapel Hill: The University of North Carolina Press.

CHAPTER II

Nature of the Federal Union

Timeline: Federalism

1781	Articles of Confederation ratified
1786	Shays' Rebellion
1787	Constitutional Convention meets to draft U.S. Constitution
1790	First National Bank of the United States chartered by Congress
1798	Alien and Sedition Acts
1798	Virginia and Kentucky Resolutions
1816	Second National Bank of the United States chartered
1819	In *McCulloch v. Maryland* the Supreme Court upholds the constitutionality of the National Bank of the United States and strikes down a state law that places a tax on the bank.
1821	*Cohens v. Virginia* reasserts the power of federal courts over the states.
1828	Election of Andrew Jackson as president.
1832	Andrew Jackson's veto of the rechartering of the National Bank
1920	In *Missouri v. Holland*, the Court upholds a federal treaty that regulates the migratory birds between Canada and the United States over state objections that it violated its power.
1938	Congress adopts the Fair Labor Standards Act.
1940	Congress adopts the Smith Act.
1941	In *Texas Railroad Commission v. Pullman* the Supreme Court rules that the federal courts should not decide a case while a state court is still adjudicating the issue.
1956	In *Pennsylvania v. Nelson* the Supreme Court rules that a state law seeking to punish espionage was preempted by federal law.
1958	*Cooper v. Aaron* asserts that state officials must obey federal court decisions.
1976	In *National League of Cities v. Usery* the Supreme Court rules that the Commerce clause did not give Congress the authority to enforce the Fair Labor Standards Act against the states.
1983	In *Michigan v. Long* the Supreme Court rules that it may not review state supreme court decisions if they are based on adequate and independent state grounds and there are no federal questions raised.

1983 In *Pacific Gas & Electric v. State Energy Resources* the Supreme Court rules that the state of California is not preempted by federal law regarding the licensing of nuclear power plants when it comes to determining the adequacy of nuclear waste disposal for a facility.

1985 In *Garcia v. San Antonio Metropolitan Transit Authority* the Supreme Court reverses its *Usery* opinion and rules that the Fair Labor Standards Act can be enforced against the states.

1986 In *Bowers v. Hardwick* the Supreme Court upholds a Georgia law against an adult homosexual couple making it illegal to engage in consensual sodomy.

1990 Congress adopts the Americans with Disabilities Act.

1995 In *U.S. Term Limits v. Thornton* the Supreme Court strikes down a state law imposing term limits upon members of its congressional delegation.

1996 Congress adopts the Defense of Marriage Act.

1996 In *Seminole Tribe of Florida v. Florida* the Supreme Court rules that the Eleventh Amendment bars an Indian tribe from suing a state in federal court.

1997 The Supreme Court rules in *City of Boerne v. Flores* that the federal Religious Freedom Restoration Act of 1993 as applied to state law was unconstitutional.

1998 In *Powell v. Georgia* the Georgia Supreme Court strikes down a state law making it illegal for adult homosexual couples to engage in consensual sodomy.

2000 In *Kimel v. Florida Board of Regents* the Supreme Court rules that the Age Discrimination in Employment Act of 1967 cannot be enforced by individuals against states.

2001 In *Board of Trustees of University of Alabama v. Garrett* the Supreme Court rules that the Eleventh Amendment bars the enforcement of the Americans with Disabilities Act against a state.

2003 In *Goodridge v. Commonwealth of Massachusetts* the Massachusetts Supreme Court declares that laws preventing same-sex couples from marrying violate the state constitution.

2003 The Supreme Court in *Lawrence v. Texas* reverses and overrules *Bowers v. Hardwick*.

2004 The Supreme Court upholds enforcement of the Americans with Disabilities Act as enforced against the states in *Tennessee v. Lane*.

2008 California voters passed a referendum, Proposition 8, which overturned a California State Supreme Court determination that same-sex marriages were constitutional and amended their constitution to prohibit them.

2013 In *Hollingsworth v. Perry* the US Supreme Court determined advocates for California's Proposition 8 did not have standing to appeal a district court decision countermanding the referendum.

2013 The Supreme Court finds in *United States v. Windsor* that § 3 of the federal Defense of Marriage Act is unconstitutional.

2015 In *Obergefell v. Hodges* the Supreme Court found the Due Process and Equal Protection Clauses guarantee same-sex couples a right to marry.

INTRODUCTION

The United States is composed of a union of equal states, albeit one with a national government that, according to Article VI of the Constitution, is supreme. This nation is a federal union, that is, a government in which the relations between the central and state governments, as well as the division of governmental powers between them, are set by a constitution that cannot be easily amended. Alteration of these powers is only possibly through a joint action of the central federal government and the local units, or, as we reference them, the states. Thus, neither the central nor the local units are entirely self-controlling—the hallmark of a federal relationship. Obviously, if the central government controlled itself, we would have a **unitary** system, while if each local unit, the state, remained a complete law unto itself, we would have a **confederation**. Where the relationship between the central government and the local units is one of **coordinate** exercise of the sovereign power, the result is a federal scheme. One of the benefits of a federal system is that the nation, as a whole, is shielded from tyranny and crisis. Like the principle of separation of powers, federalism ensures that different entities have sources of independent power that balances the authority of both.

A danger of the unitary system is that because all sovereign powers reside in the national government, if a crisis comes—for example, a tyrannical leader or fiscal emergency paralyzes the national government—there are no states or regional governments to assume decision-making authority. The entire nation would collapse. A confederacy represents the opposite threat to the security of the country; because **sovereignty** is localized in the individual states, the tendency is for the states to make independent decisions that may result in conflicting and splintering policies and values. One of the primary conflicts among the Founders in the crafting of the new Constitution was between those who believed a federal system would be the salvation of the new nation (Federalists) and those who feared the tyranny of the national government over the people as represented by the states (Anti-Federalists).

Federalist concerns over a unitary government reflected their experience as colonies with the English King George III. The colonies had no source of sovereign authority beyond what had been granted by the ruler, and the result had been tyranny culminating in the American Revolution. By contrast, a confederal system formulated under the **Articles of Confederation** demonstrated the inability of the national government to provide leadership amidst turmoil within the states during Shays' Rebellion. Under the Articles of Confederation the national government was unable to collect taxes or maintain a military force; consequently, when former Revolutionary War soldiers led by Daniel Shays rebelled because of the lack of pay from military service, high state taxes, and bankruptcies that resulted in a high number of bank foreclosures, the national government was helpless to intervene. The Federalist founders discovered life under both unitary and confederacy rule to be unsuccessful. After compromises with the Anti-Federalists to protect the sovereignty of the states and the rights of the individual citizens, a constitution was ratified that constructed a system of federalism.

This chapter will first examine the means by which the Constitution distributes powers between the states and national government, including the courts, and then explore the historical and judicial processes through which the federal government gained ascendancy over the states. The second portion of the chapter will explore contemporary manifestations of federalism, including the increasing importance of the Eleventh Amendment in defining state sovereignty and the current skirmishes among the states and the federal government regarding the constitutional protections surrounding sexual preference.

DISTRIBUTION OF FEDERAL POWER

One of the earliest conflicts surrounding the nascent Constitution was a careful determination of which powers belong to the national government and which powers remain with the state governments. While today the issue of federal supremacy seems settled, it was not at all clear in the early years of the Republic. As James McClellan notes in the third edition of *Liberty, Order, and Justice*,

> The Federalist Party, favoring an expansive or nationalistic interpretation, pointed to the Preamble of the Constitution as proof that sovereignty resided in "We the People," not "We the States." The several States, said Federalist leaders such as John Marshall, had surrendered their sovereignty to the

> national government. The Jeffersonian Republican-Democrats, favoring a narrow or States' Rights interpretation, argued that the Union was a compact of States, each of which had retained the essential attributes of sovereignty. The Preamble refers to the "People" rather than the "States," they countered, because at the time of the Federal Convention it would have been premature to speak for all of the States. (p. 491)

As the Virginia and Kentucky Resolutions demonstrated, states were concerned that the federal government would be able to pass laws with which states would not agree and to which they would not adhere. Virginia and Kentucky believed that they had retained the power to deny such an inappropriate exercise of national authority. After Congress, through the Alien and Sedition Acts of 1798, criminalized criticism of the national government, its leaders, and its policies while slashing immigration from targeted countries, states responded with their own interpretation of the Constitution. Just as the Anti-Federalists had feared, the federal government, in order to protect its own interests, was violating the right of the individual to criticize the government and preventing the states from protecting their own citizens. In the Virginia and Kentucky Resolutions, both states asserted their right to declare federal laws void within their state boundaries if the state perceived the law to conflict with the federal Constitution. It was not at all clear which branch of government or which level of authority had the right to determine the meaning and proper interpretation of the Constitution.

Some of the earliest Supreme Court decisions delineated specific issues that required clear federal guidance regarding the powers that could be safely retained by the states. The philosophical conflict between Founders, such as Thomas Jefferson and James Madison, who feared the excessive power of the national government, and those like Alexander Hamilton, John Adams, and John Marshall, who did not want the chaos of the Articles of Confederation to continue under the Constitution, would be illustrated through state legislation, judicial decision making, and federal elections.

The Necessary and Proper Clause

Article I, Sec. 8, para. 18:

The Congress shall have Power . . . To make all Laws which shall be necessary and proper for carrying into Execution the foregoing Powers, and all other Powers vested by this Constitution in the Government of the United States, or in any Department or Officer thereof.

Shortly after it started operation under the Constitution in the autumn of 1789, Congress directed Alexander Hamilton, as secretary of the treasury, to prepare a plan for the support of public credit. Under the Articles of Confederation, finance had been a very real problem, and the Congress was anxious to remedy the situation. In accordance with this directive, Hamilton made four recommendations to the legislature regarding public debt, excise taxes, a national bank, and manufacturing, including a protective tariff. In his third report, he recommended the establishment of a national bank; this proposal evoked great opposition. James Madison based his objection on the fact that the Constitutional Convention had rejected an explicit proposal granting Congress the power of incorporating a national bank. Further, in answer to the contention by Hamilton that the power to establish a bank could be based on the so-called "elastic clause" (Article I, Sec. 8, para. 18), which empowers Congress to do all that is necessary and proper to carry into operation their delegated powers, Madison held that Congress could use only means or methods that were indispensable for the execution of the delegated powers. Hamilton held that a bank was "necessary and proper" for the execution of the powers of taxation, borrowing, and regulation of the currency, and the elastic clause grants a similar explicit authority. He was, of course, interpreting "necessary" as convenient, or helpful, for implementation, not as indispensable.

President Washington signed the bill for the establishment of the bank that Congress adopted, and its legality was finally challenged in *McCulloch v. Maryland* (4 Wheaton 316, 1819). Chief Justice John Marshall's argument closely followed that of Hamilton's proposal in the First Congress. This analysis was simply that if the end to be served was within the bounds of the Constitution, then all means to reach that end were valid as long as the Constitution did not forbid such means. This was not to say that the end justified the means, since Hamilton was insisting that the means not be contrary to the Constitution. Madison had argued that the means being suggested, the incorporation of a bank, were unconstitutional. However, Marshall, in *McCulloch,* ignored this aspect of the argument. The decision in this case established the doctrine of **implied powers**. It was well recognized that under our federal system the central government was one of **delegated** and **limited** powers. But all constitutions require definition and interpretation, and the Madison-Hamilton conflict was itself only indicative of the long debate that was to continue through the following years between the liberal and strict constructionists. Here, and more importantly at the beginning of the country's history under the Constitution, the Hamiltonian point of view prevailed. Henceforth, Congress and the federal officials were to have not only the powers expressed in the Constitution but also those that could be reasonably deduced from those powers, those "necessary and proper," or rather, "convenient and helpful" to the execution of the expressed powers in the Constitution.

McCulloch v. Maryland is probably the best known and most significant of Marshall's decisions. *McCulloch* recognized the supremacy clause of the Constitution and proclaimed the doctrine of federal supremacy. Consequently, whenever federal and state governments are operating, each in its own independent and sovereign sphere of action, and the two collide, the state must give way even though the state may be operating within an area of power in which it could normally proceed.

Another matter determined by the Supreme Court, in this case, was the meaning of the so-called "elastic clause" of the Constitution. Henceforth, the powers that the federal government might exercise as necessary and proper to the carrying out of the powers delegated would be those that would be found convenient and helpful to reach a delegated end or purpose. This is the justification for the federal government's possession of implied powers—the authority that may be reasonably deduced as helpful in attaining the ends articulated in the expressed powers. The considerable criticism of the Court that followed the decision in *McCulloch v. Maryland* was chiefly directed to the fact that the act incorporating a bank had not been declared unconstitutional. There was no real criticism of the exercise of judicial review.

While the decision of the Supreme Court settled the constitutionality of the national bank, the appropriateness of the bank remained a contentious issue. President Andrew Jackson ended the continuing controversy by vetoing the rechartering of the bank near the end of his first term in office. For Jackson, the bank was contrary to the democratic nature of the United States and devastating to state sovereignty under federalism. The bank, in order to stabilize the national currency, required states to strengthen their own state notes in order to pay their debts. While this may have supported the national economy, it clearly limited the authority of the states because it allowed the national government to interfere in the regulation of the state's economy.

Even beyond the demise of the national bank, the impact of *McCulloch v. Maryland* is immense. By the early twentieth century, the combination of the explicit powers of the commerce clause and its implicit commerce powers under the Necessary and Proper Clause would allow Congress to justify an extensive exercise of substantive federal power, particularly in such areas as civil rights, labor rights, and the development of a national transportation infrastructure. In the cases of *Hammer v. Dagenhart* (247 U.S. 251, 1918) and *United States v. Darby Lumber Company* (312 U.S. 100, 1941), the Supreme Court accepts opposing points of view on the matter of substantive federal power under the implied power emerging from the commerce clause and involving specifically the power to control child labor. However, these decisions were over twenty years apart and would herald a new era in federal authority that could not be imagined in the time of *McCulloch*.

The Scope of the Treaty Power

One of the significant battles within federalism did not occur until the twentieth century and was waged over the power to make treaties with other countries. One of the immediate concerns with the Articles of Confederation was the ability of each state to make independent treaties with foreign nations. The United States Constitution had been careful to place the treaty-making powers within the scope of the federal government. But what happens when the treaty regulates a power within the constitutional authority of the states?

In 1913, Congress attempted to regulate the shooting of migratory birds; hunting has typically been centered within the authority of the states. The lower federal courts held that this was outside the bounds of Congressional power. (See *United States v. McCullagh,* 221 Fed. 288, 1915; *United States v. Shauver,* 214 Fed. 154, 1914.) The federal government then negotiated a treaty in 1916 with Great Britain by the terms of which closed seasons were established for the shooting of birds in the United States and Canada. Congress, in 1918, enacted a statute to implement the treaty. The resulting statute, the Migratory Bird Act, was challenged as an exercise of power which the Congress did not possess under the Constitution and which could not be vested in the Congress by the negotiation of a treaty.

The potential for Congress to leverage the implications of the *Missouri v. Holland* (252 U.S. 416, 1920) decision has never been realized. Under this decision a treaty need only be made under the authority of the United States; the subject matter of the treaty need be only in the general realm of matters properly the subject of an international arrangement. By contrast, a statute must be made in pursuance of the Constitution; there must be some specific basis for the action. Thus, within limits, the Constitution can be amended in practice by means of a treaty requiring or authorizing statutory implementation. By the terms of Article VI of the Constitution, a properly ratified treaty is part of the supreme law of the land, and no state law can prevail against a treaty. A federal statute and a treaty are equivalent in terms of legality, and the one that is later in point of time is the one to be enforced. However, even though a treaty in theory might effect a de facto amending of the Constitution, there appears to be limits in terms of its ability to alter basic rules of federalism. In *Medellín v. Texas,* 552 U.S. 491, 2008) (located on page 671 in chapter 8), the Supreme Court declared that the State of Texas did not have to follow an international agreement, or more specifically, an executive order and international court decision, requiring it to comply with the Vienna Convention. The *Medellín* decision for now seems to define some federalism outer limits to treaties.

In more recent years, presidents have circumvented the necessity of congressional approval for treaties by engaging in executive agreements with other nations. While such agreements are binding only during that president's administration, they hold the same power of treaties. Executive agreements have come to vastly outnumber the number of treaties since the 1940s. (Executive agreements are discussed in more detail in chapter 8 in the context of the Constitution and foreign affairs).

Federal Supersession

Article VI, para. 2:

This Constitution, and the Laws of the United States which shall be made in Pursuance thereof; and all Treaties made, or which shall be made, under the Authority of the United States, shall be the supreme Law of the Land; and the Judges in every State shall be bound thereby, any Thing in the Constitution or Laws of any State to the Contrary notwithstanding.

In any federal scheme of government there is bound to be an area of **concurrent powers**, that is, a field of governmental authority in which both the central government and the local units (here the states) may exercise power legitimately. Rooted in the Supremacy Clause (Article VI, para. 2 of the Constitution), **federal supersession** of preemption means that, within the exercise of concurrent powers, when federal and state statutes conflict, federal law must prevail over that of the state. Whenever an area of governmental power exists into which either or both federal and state governments may enter, and the nature of the power is such or the nature of the federal "occupancy" is such that there is no room for activity on the part of the states in that area of concurrent power, the state statutes must be sacrificed. Because of Article VI, federal statutes may preempt an area of regulation or supersede state statutes in that field.

One example of federal supersession is found in the power to punish the crime of sedition (or speaking against) against the central government. During the anticommunist Red Scare of the mid-1950s, most states had passed anti-sedition statutes in various forms; Pennsylvania's Sedition Act prohibited any conspiracy from overthrowing the government of the United States by force and violence. In the Cold War era, Congress was active also in the enactment of legislation prohibiting sedition, constructing such statutes as the Smith Act of 1940, the Internal Security Act of 1950, and the Communist Control Act of 1954. As a consequence, the Supreme Court was asked to determine in the case of *Pennsylvania v. Nelson* (350 U.S. 497, 1956) if the congressional activity superseded state prohibitions against sedition toward the federal government or if there was additional room for state legislation. If federal action preempted state action in issues of sedition, then the states would be left without power to govern in the arena. The supreme court of Pennsylvania held against the constitutionality of the Pennsylvania Sedition Act. In this opinion, the United States Supreme Court finds that the federal law, in particular the Smith Act, supersedes the Pennsylvania law. Because the Court determines that the federal law demonstrates intent to control all regulation of federal sedition, there is no space for state statutory guidance; the conflict with the dissenting opinion is not over the doctrine of federal supersession, but over the interpretation of the Smith Act as invoking supersedure. The resulting doctrine of the Supreme Court decision does not in any way affect the power of a state to guard itself against seditious activity, and Congress could elect to share the field of prosecution of offenses involving sedition against the federal government.

A similar question was revived surrounding the implications of the Supremacy Clause relative to the regulation of nuclear power plants in *Pacific Gas and Electric Co. v. State Energy Resources* (461 U.S. 190, 1983). In this case, a company challenged a 1976 California law, which required a state commission to control all new construction of nuclear plants in order to assure adequate storage and disposal of nuclear waste, as being preempted by the federal Atomic Energy Act of 1954. In this case, the Court found that the federal law was motivated to assuage and control safety concerns related to nuclear power, but that the state law was motivated by an economic interest. Consequently, the Court found no conflict between the two laws and upheld the California statute. This decision does make clear, however, that if the statutes were in conflict, the federal law would supercede the state law.

VIRGINIA AND KENTUCKY RESOLUTIONS OF 1798

President John Adams and the Federalist-controlled Congress passed the Alien and Sedition Acts in the spring of 1798. These statutes made criticizing the government a criminal act and severely limited immigration. Despite the fact that many people were punished under these laws, the Supreme Court did not determine the constitutionality of the Sedition Act until the 1964 Supreme Court decision of *New York Times v. Sullivan* (376 U.S. 254). Some citizens and leaders of state government found in the Alien and Sedition Acts the realization of their deepest fears regarding a federalist government. The national government was perceived as destroying the basic rights of citizenship under the guise of strong federal rule. The following resolutions were passed by Jeffersonian Republicans living in Virginia and Kentucky. James Madison drafted the Virginia Resolution and Thomas Jefferson the Kentucky Resolutions, but both did so secretly.

Virginia Resolution: 1798

1. RESOLVED, That the General Assembly of Virginia, doth unequivocably express a firm resolution to maintain and defend the Constitution of the United States, and the Constitution of this State, against every aggression either foreign or domestic, and that they will support the government of the United States in all measures warranted by the former.

2. That this assembly most solemnly declares a warm attachment to the Union of the States, to maintain which it pledges all its powers; and that for this end, it is their duty to watch over and oppose every infraction of those principles which constitute the only basis of that Union, because a faithful observance of them, can alone secure its existence and the public happiness.

3. That this Assembly doth explicitly and peremptorily declare, that it views the powers of the federal government, as resulting from the compact, to which the states are parties; as limited by the plain sense and intention of the instrument constituting the compact; as no further valid that they are authorized by the grants enumerated in that compact; and that in case of a deliberate, palpable, and dangerous exercise of other powers, not granted by the said compact, the states who are parties thereto, have the right, and are in duty bound, to interpose for arresting the progress of the evil, and for maintaining within their respective limits, the authorities, rights and liberties appertaining to them.

4. That the General Assembly doth also express its deep regret, that a spirit has in sundry instances, been manifested by the federal government, to enlarge its powers by forced constructions of the constitutional charter which defines them; and that implications have appeared of a design to expound certain general phrases (which having been copied from the very limited grant of power, in the former articles of confederation were the less liable to be misconstrued) so as to destroy the meaning and effect, of the particular enumeration which necessarily explains and limits the general phrases; and so as to consolidate the states by degrees, into one sovereignty, the obvious tendency and inevitable consequence of which would be, to transform the present republican system of the United States, into an absolute, or at best a mixed monarchy.

5. That the General Assembly doth particularly protest against the palpable and alarming infractions of the Constitution, in the two late cases of the "Alien and Sedition Acts" passed at the last session of Congress; the first of which exercises a power nowhere delegated to the federal government, and which by uniting legislative and judicial powers to those of executive, subverts the general principles of free government; as well as the particular organization, and positive provisions of the federal constitution; and the other of which acts, exercises in like manner, a power not delegated by the constitution, but on the contrary, expressly and positively forbidden by one of the amendments thereto; a power, which more than any other, ought to produce universal alarm, because it is levelled against that right of freely examining public characters and measures, and of free

communication among the people thereon, which has ever been justly deemed, the only effectual guardian of every other right.

6. That this state having by its Convention, which ratified the federal Constitution, expressly declared, that among other essential rights, "the Liberty of Conscience and of the Press cannot be cancelled, abridged, restrained, or modified by any authority of the United States," and from its extreme anxiety to guard these rights from every possible attack of sophistry or ambition, having with other states, recommended an amendment for that purpose, which amendment was, in due time, annexed to the Constitution; it would mark a reproachable inconsistency, and criminal degeneracy, if an indifference were now shewn, to the most palpable violation of one of the Rights, thus declared and secured; and to the establishment of a precedent which may be fatal to the other.

Agreed to by the Senate, December 24, 1798.

Kentucky Resolutions: 1798

1. *Resolved,* That the several States composing, the United States of America, are not united on the principle of unlimited submission to their general government; but that, by a compact under the style and title of a Constitution for the United States, and of amendments thereto, they constituted a general government for special purposes—delegated to that government certain definite powers, reserving, each State to itself, the residuary mass of right to their own self-government; and that whensoever the general government assumes undelegated powers, its acts are unauthoritative, void, and of no force: that to this compact each State acceded as a State, and is an integral part, its co-States forming, as to itself, the other party: that the government created by this compact was not made the exclusive or final judge of the extent of the powers delegated to itself; since that would have made its discretion, and not the Constitution, the measure of its powers; but that, as in all other cases of compact among powers having no common judge, each party has an equal right to judge for itself, as well of infractions as of the mode and measure of redress.

2. *Resolved,* That the Constitution of the United States, having delegated to Congress a power to punish treason, counterfeiting the securities and current coin of the United States, piracies, and felonies committed on the high seas, and offenses against the law of nations, and no other crimes, whatsoever; and it being true as a general principle, and one of the amendments to the Constitution having also declared, that "the powers not delegated to the United States by the Constitution, not prohibited by it to the States, are reserved to the States respectively, or to the people," therefore the act of Congress, passed on the 14th day of July, 1798, and intituled "An Act in addition to the act intituled An Act for the punishment of certain crimes against the United States," . . . (and all their other acts which assume to create, define, or punish crimes, other than those so enumerated in the Constitution,) are altogether void, and of no force; and that the power to create, define, and punish such other crimes is reserved, and, of right, appertains solely and exclusively to the respective States, each within its own territory.

3. *Resolved,* That it is true as a general principle, and is also expressly declared by one of the amendments to the Constitutions, that "the powers not delegated to the United States by the Constitution, or prohibited by it to the States, are reserved to the States respectively, or to the people"; and that no power over the freedom of religion, freedom of speech, or freedom of the press being delegated to the United States by the Constitution, nor prohibited by it to the States, all lawful powers respecting the same did of right remain, and were reserved to the States or the people: that thus was manifested their determination to retain to themselves the right of judging how far the licentiousness of speech and of the press may be abridged without lessening their useful freedom, and how far those abuses which cannot be separated from their use should be tolerated, rather than the use be destroyed. . . . And that in addition to this general principle and express declaration, another and more special provision has been made by one of the amendments to the Constitution, which expressly declares, that "Congress shall make no law respecting an establishment of religion, or prohibiting the free exercise thereof,

or abridging the freedom of speech or of the press": thereby guarding in the same sentence, and under the same words, the freedom of religion, of speech, and of the press: insomuch, that whatever violated either, throws down the sanctuary which covers the others, and that libels, falsehood, and defamation, equally with heresy and false religion, are withheld from the cognizance of federal tribunals. That, therefore, the act of Congress of the United States, passed on the 14th day of July, 1798, intituled "An Act in addition to the act intituled An Act for the punishment of certain crimes against the United States," which does abridge the freedom of the press, is not law, but is altogether void, and of no force.

4. *Resolved,* That alien friends are under the jurisdiction and protection of the laws of the State wherein they are: that no power over them has been delegated to the United States, nor prohibited to the individual States, distinct from their power over citizens. And it being true as a general principle, and one of the amendments to the Constitution having also declared, that "the powers not delegated to the United States by the Constitution, nor prohibited by it to the States, are reserved to the States respectively, or to the people," the act of the Congress of the United States, passed on the—day of July, 1798, intituled "An Act concerning aliens," which assumes powers over alien friends, not delegated by the Constitution, is not law, but is altogether void, and of no force.

November 10, 1798

FOR DISCUSSION

What would be the consequences for federalism if states possessed and exercised the authority claimed by Virginia and Kentucky in these resolutions? What do these resolutions say about the concerns of sovereign states in a federalist system?

MCCULLOCH V. MARYLAND

4 Wheaton 316, 4 L.Ed. 579 (1819)

By an act of Congress the National Bank of the United States was incorporated and a branch was established at Baltimore. Under Maryland law, any bank not chartered by the state was required to pay a tax on bank notes issued by the bank. The cashier of the Baltimore branch of the National Bank, James McCulloch, refused to pay this state tax. Maryland's suit to recover the payment raised two questions: (1) Has the Congress the power to incorporate a bank? (2) If so, may a state impose a tax on the activities of a branch of this bank located in that state?

Vote: 7–0

CHIEF JUSTICE MARSHALL delivered the opinion of the Court:

The first question made in the cause is—has Congress power to incorporate a bank?

The government of the Union, then (whatever may be the influence of this fact on the case), is emphatically and truly a government of the people. In form and in substance it emanates from them, its powers are granted by them, and are to be exercised directly on them, and for their benefit.

This government is acknowledged by all to be one of enumerated powers. The principle, that it can exercise only the powers granted to it, would seem too apparent to have required to be enforced by all those arguments which its enlightened friends, while it was depending before the people, found it necessary to urge. That principle is now universally admitted. But the question respecting the extent of the powers actually granted is perpetually arising, and will probably continue to arise, as long as our system shall exist.

In discussing these questions, the conflicting powers of the general and State governments must be brought into view, and the supremacy of their respective laws, when they are in opposition, must be settled.

If any one proposition could command the universal assent of mankind, we might expect it would be this: that the government of the Union, though limited in its powers, is supreme within its sphere of action. This would seem to result necessarily from its nature. It is the government of all; its powers are delegated by all; it represents all, and acts for all. Though any one State may be willing to control its operations, no State is willing to allow others to control them. The nation, on those subjects on which it can act, must necessarily bind its component parts. But this question is not left to mere reason: the people have, in express terms, decided it, by saying, "this Constitution, and the laws of the United States, which shall be made in pursuance thereof," "shall be the supreme law of the land," and by requiring that the members of the state legislatures, and the officers of the executive and judicial departments of the States, shall take the oath of fidelity to it.

The government of the United States, then, though limited in its powers, is supreme; and its laws, when made in pursuance of the Constitution, form the supreme law of the land, "anything in the Constitution or laws of any State to the contrary notwithstanding."

In considering this question, then, we must never forget, that it is a constitution we are expounding.

Although, among the enumerated powers of government, we do not find the word "bank," or "incorporation," we find the great powers to lay and collect taxes; to borrow money; to regulate commerce; to declare and conduct a war; and to raise and support armies and navies. The sword and the purse, all the external relations, and no inconsiderable portion of the industry of the nation, are entrusted to its government. It can never be pretended that these vast powers draw after them others of inferior importance, merely because they are inferior. Such an idea can never be advanced. But it may, with great reason, be contended, that a government, entrusted with such ample powers, on the due execution of which the happiness and prosperity of the nation so vitally depends, must also be entrusted with ample means for their execution. The power being given, it is the interest of the nation to facilitate its execution. It can never be their interest, and cannot be presumed to have been their intention, to clog and embarrass its execution by withholding the most appropriate means. . . .

It is not denied, that the powers given to the government imply the ordinary means of execution. That, for example, of raising revenue, and applying it to national purposes, is admitted to imply the power of conveying money from place to place, as the exigencies of the nation may require, and of employing the usual means of conveyance. But it is denied that the government has its choice of means; or, that it may employ the most convenient means, if, to employ them, it be necessary to erect a corporation.

The power of creating a corporation, though appertaining to sovereignty, is not, like the power of making war, or levying taxes, or of regulating commerce, a great substantive and independent power, which cannot be implied as incidental to other powers, or used as a means of executing them. It is never the end for which other powers are exercised, but a means by which other objects are accomplished. No city was ever built with the sole object of being incorporated, but is incorporated as affording the best means of being well governed. The power of creating a corporation is never used for its own sake, but for the purpose of effecting something else. No sufficient reason is, therefore, perceived, why it may not pass as incidental to those powers which are expressly given, if it be a direct mode of executing them.

But the Constitution of the United States has not left the right of Congress to employ the necessary means, for the execution of the powers conferred on the government, to general reasoning. To its enumeration of powers is added that of making "all laws which shall be necessary and proper, for carrying into execution the foregoing powers, and all other powers vested by this Constitution, in the government of the United States, or in any department thereof."

Is it true, that this is the sense in which the word "necessary" is always used? Does it always import an absolute physical necessity, so strong, that one thing, to which another may be termed necessary, cannot exist without that other? We think it does not. If reference be had to its use, in the common affairs of the world, or in approved authors, we find that it frequently imports no more than that one thing is convenient, or useful, or essential to another. To employ the means necessary to an end, is generally understood as employing any means calculated to produce the end, and not as being confined to those single means, without which the end would be entirely unattainable. Such is the character of human language, that no word conveys to the mind, in all situations, one single definite idea; and nothing is more common than to use words in a figurative sense. Almost all compositions contain words, which, taken in their rigorous sense, would convey a meaning different from that which is obviously intended. It is essential to just construction, that many words which import something excessive, should be understood in a more mitigated sense—in that sense which common usage justifies. The word "necessary" is of this description. It has not a fixed character peculiar to itself. It admits of all degrees of comparison; and is often connected with other words, which increase or diminish the impression the mind receives of the urgency it imports. A thing may be necessary, very necessary, absolutely or indispensably necessary. To no mind would the same idea be conveyed, by these several phrases. . . . This word, then, like others, is used in various senses; and, in its construction, the subject, the context, the intention of the person using them, are all to be taken into view.

We admit, as all must admit, that the powers of the government are limited, and that its limits are not to be transcended. But we think the sound construction of the Constitution must allow to the national legislature that discretion, with respect to the means by which the powers it confers are to be carried into execution, which will enable that body to perform the high duties assigned to it, in the manner most beneficial to the people. Let the end be legitimate, let it be within the scope of the Constitution, and all means which are appropriate, which are plainly adapted to that end, which are not prohibited, but consist with the letter and spirit of the Constitution, are constitutional.

If a corporation may be employed indiscriminately with other means to carry into execution the powers of the government, no particular reason can be assigned for excluding the use of a bank, if required for its fiscal operations. To use one, must be within the discretion of Congress, if it be an appropriate mode of executing the powers of government. That it is a convenient, a useful, and essential instrument of the prosecution of its fiscal operations, is not now a subject of controversy.

It being the opinion of the court that the act incorporating a bank is constitutional; and that the power of establishing a branch in the state of Maryland might be properly exercised by the bank itself, we proceed. . . .

The second question made in the cause is, "Whether the State of Maryland may, without violating the Constitution, tax that branch?"

That the power of taxation is one of vital importance; that it is retained by the States; that it is not abridged by the grant of a similar power to the government of the Union; that it is to be concurrently exercised by the two governments: are truths which have never been denied. But, such is the paramount character of the Constitution, that its capacity to withdraw any subject from the action of even this power, is admitted. The States are expressly forbidden to lay any duties on imports or exports, except what may be absolutely necessary for executing their inspection laws. If the obligation of this prohibition must be conceded—if it may restrain a State from the exercise of its taxing power on imports and exports; the same paramount character would seem to restrain, as it certainly may restrain, a State from such other exercise of this power, as is in its nature incompatible with, and repugnant to, the constitutional laws of the Union. A law, absolutely repugnant to another, as entirely repeals that other as if express terms of repeal were used.

This great principle is that the Constitution and the laws made in pursuance thereof are supreme; that they control the Constitution and laws of the respective States, and cannot be controlled by them. From this, which may be almost termed an axiom, other propositions are deduced as corollaries, on the truth or error of which, and on their application to this case, the cause has been supposed to depend. These are (1) That a power to create implies a power to preserve, (2) That a power to destroy, if wielded by a different hand, is hostile to, and incompatible with, these powers to create and preserve, (3) That where this repugnancy exists, that authority which is supreme must control, not yield to that over which it is supreme. . . .

[I] The power of Congress to create, and of course to continue, the bank was the subject of the preceding part of this opinion; and is no longer to be considered as questionable.

[II] That the power of taxing it by the States may be exercised so as to destroy it, is too obvious to be denied. But taxation is said to be an absolute power, which acknowledges no other limits than those expressly prescribed in the Constitution, and like sovereign power of every other description, is trusted to the discretion of those who use it.

The argument on the part of the State of Maryland, is, not that the States may directly resist a law of Congress, but that they may exercise their acknowledged powers upon it, and that the Constitution leaves them this right in the confidence that they will not abuse it.

That the power to tax involves the power to destroy; that the power to destroy may defeat and render useless the power to create; that there is a plain repugnance, in conferring on one government a power to control the constitutional measures of another, which other, with respect to those very measures, is declared to be supreme over that which exerts the control, are propositions not to be denied. But all inconsistencies are to be reconciled by the magic of the word "confidence." Taxation, it is said, does not necessarily and unavoidably destroy. To carry it to the excess of destruction would be an abuse, to presume which, would banish that confidence which is essential to all government.

If the States may tax one instrument, employed by the government in the execution of its powers, they may tax any and every other instrument. They may tax the mail; they may tax the mint; they may tax patent rights; they may tax the papers of the custom-house; they may tax judicial process; they may tax all the means employed by the government, to an excess which would defeat all the ends of government. This was not intended by the American people. They may not design to make their government dependent on the States.

It has also been insisted that, as the power of taxation in the General and State governments is acknowledged to be concurrent, every argument which would sustain the right of the general government to tax banks chartered by the States, will equally sustain the right of the States to tax banks chartered by the general government.

But the two cases are not on the same reason. The people of all the States have created the general government, and have conferred upon it the general power of taxation. The people of all the States, and the States themselves, are represented in Congress, and, by their representatives, exercise this power. When they tax the chartered institutions of the States, they tax their constituents, and these taxes must be uniform. But when a State taxes the operations of the government of the United States, it acts upon institutions created not by their own constituents, but by people over whom they can claim no control. It acts upon the measures of a government created by others as well as themselves. The difference is that which always exists, and always must exist, between the action of the whole on a part, and the action of a part on the whole—between the laws of a government declared to be supreme, and those of a government which, when in opposition to those laws, is not supreme. . . .

[III] The court has bestowed on this subject its most deliberate consideration. The result is a conviction that the States have no power, by taxation or otherwise, to retard, impede, burden, or in any manner control, the operations of the constitutional laws enacted by Congress to carry into execution the powers vested in the general government. This is, we think, the unavoidable consequence of that supremacy which the Constitution has declared.

We are unanimously of opinion, that the law passed by the legislature of Maryland, imposing a tax on the Bank of the United States, is unconstitutional and void. This opinion does not deprive the States of any resources which they originally possessed. It does not extend to a tax paid by the real property of the bank, in common with the other real property within the State, nor to a tax imposed on the interest which the citizens of Maryland may hold in this institution, in common with other property of the same description throughout the State. But this is a tax on the operation of an instrument employed by the government of the Union to carry its powers into execution. Such a tax must be unconstitutional. Judgment reversed.

FOR DISCUSSION

What are the consequences for federalism of having a broadly expansive necessary and proper clause as opposed to a narrowly construed one?

RELATED CASES

***Civil Rights Cases:* 109 U.S. 3 (1883).**

Only state action of a particular character is prohibited by the Fourteenth Amendment; individual or private transgression of individual rights is not the subject matter of the amendment. In this case, accommodations in a hotel, a theater, and a railroad ladies' car were denied to blacks, and the Court held these to be private actions.

***Hammer v. Dagenhart:* 247 U.S. 251 (1918).**

Power to control child labor is an aspect of the police power of the states. Congress cannot use the commerce power to exercise the power because it does not extend to the production of things that are intended for interstate trade. Moreover, goods in themselves not harmful cannot be excluded from interstate commerce.

***United States v. Darby Lumber Co.:* 312 U.S. 100 (1941).**

The power of Congress under the commerce clause is plenary to exclude any article from interstate commerce subject only to the specific prohibitions of the Constitution. Here the Federal Fair Labor Standards Act was upheld.

***Jones v. Alfred H. Mayer Co.:* 392 U.S. 409 (1968).**

The Civil Rights Act of 1866 enacted by Congress under its power to enforce the Thirteenth Amendment bars all racial discrimination, private as well as public, in the sale or rental of property. The statute does not include discrimination based on grounds of religion or national origin. Congress has the power to determine what are the badges and incidents of slavery. Among these are restraints on the same right to inherit, purchase, lease, sell, and convey property as is enjoyed by white citizens.

PRESIDENT JACKSON'S VETO MESSAGE REGARDING THE BANK OF THE UNITED STATES

July 10, 1832

Three years after his election in 1828, President Andrew Jackson helped end the debate over the legitimacy of Congress's creation of a national bank under the authority of the Commerce Clause by refusing to allow the rechartering of the Second National Bank of the United States. A populist, Jackson believed that the National Bank was "anti-democratic" in its orientation and destructive of the interests of the states.

To the Senate.

The bill "to modify and continue" the act entitled "An act to incorporate the subscribers to the Bank of the United States" was presented to me on the 4th July instant. Having considered it with that solemn regard to the principles of the Constitution which the day was calculated to inspire, and come to the conclusion that it ought not to become a law, I herewith return it to the Senate, in which it originated, with my objections.

It is maintained by the advocates of the bank that its constitutionality in all its features ought to be considered as settled by precedent and by the decision of the Supreme Court. To this conclusion I cannot assent. Mere precedent is a dangerous source of authority, and should not be regarded as deciding questions of constitutional power except where the acquiescence of the people and the States can be considered as well settled. So far from this being the case on this subject, an argument against the bank might be based on precedent. One Congress, in 1791, decided in favor of a bank; another, in 1811, decided against it. One Congress, in 1815, decided against a bank; another, in 1816, decided in its favor. Prior to the present Congress, therefore, the precedents drawn from that source were equal. If we resort to the States, the expressions of legislative, judicial, and executive opinions against the bank have been probably to those in its favor as 4 to 1. There is nothing in precedent, therefore, which, if its authority were admitted, ought to weigh in favor of the act before me.

If the opinion of the Supreme Court covered the whole ground of this act, it ought not to control the coordinate authorities of this Government. The Congress, the Executive, and the Court must each for itself be guided by its own opinion of the Constitution. Each public officer who takes an oath to support the Constitution swears that he will support it as he understands it, and not as it is understood by others. It is as much the duty of the House of Representatives, of the Senate, and of the President to decide upon the constitutionality of any bill or resolution which may be presented to them for passage or approval as it is of the supreme judges when it may be brought before them for judicial decision. The opinion of the judges has no more authority over Congress than the opinion of Congress has over the judges, and on that point the President is independent of both. The authority of the Supreme Court must not, therefore, be permitted to control the Congress or the Executive when acting in their legislative capacities, but to have only such influence as the force of their reasoning may deserve.

But in the case relied upon the Supreme Court have not decided that all the features of this corporation are compatible with the Constitution. It is true that the court have said that the law incorporating the bank is a constitutional exercise of power by Congress; but taking into view the whole opinion of the court and the reasoning by which they have come to that conclusion, I understand them to have decided that inasmuch as a bank is an appropriate means for carrying into effect the enumerated powers of the general government, therefore the law incorporating it is in accordance with that provision of the Constitution which declares that Congress shall have power "to make all laws which shall be necessary and proper for carrying those powers into execution." Having satisfied themselves that the word *"necessary"* in the Constitution means *"needful," "requisite," "essential," "conducive to,"* and that "a bank" is a convenient, a useful, and essential instrument in the prosecution of the Government's "fiscal operations," they conclude that to "use one must be within the discretion of Congress" and that "the act to incorporate the Bank of the United States is a law made in pursuance of the Constitution;" "but," say they, *"where the law is not prohibited and is really calculated to effect any of the objects intrusted to the Government, to undertake here to inquire into the degree of its necessity would be to pass the line which circumscribes the judicial department and to tread on legislative ground."*

The principle here affirmed is that the "degree of its necessity," involving all the details of a banking institution, is a question exclusively for legislative consideration. A bank is constitutional, but it is the province of the Legislature to determine whether this or that particular power, privilege, or exemption is "necessary and proper" to enable the bank to discharge its duties to the Government, and from their decision there is no appeal to the courts of justice. Under the decision of the Supreme Court, therefore, it is the exclusive province of Congress and the President to decide whether the particular features of this act are *necessary* and *proper* in order to enable the bank to perform conveniently and efficiently the public duties assigned to it as a fiscal agent, and therefore constitutional, or *unnecessary* and *improper*, and therefore unconstitutional.

Nor is our Government to be maintained or our Union preserved by invasions of the rights and powers of the several States. In thus attempting to make our General Government strong we make it weak. Its true strength consists in leaving individuals and States as much as possible to themselves—in making itself felt, not in its power, but in its beneficence; not in its control, but in its protection; not in binding the States more closely to the center, but leaving each to move unobstructed in its proper orbit.

Experience should teach us wisdom. Most of the difficulties our Government now encounters and most of the dangers which impend over our Union have sprung from an abandonment of the legitimate objects of Government by our national legislation, and the adoption of such principles as are embodied in this act. Many of our rich men have not been content with equal protection and equal benefits, but have besought us to make them richer by act of Congress. By attempting to gratify their desires we have in the results of our legislation arrayed section against section, interest against interest, and man against man, in a fearful commotion which threatens to shake the foundations of our Union. It is time to pause in our career to review our principles, and if possible revive that devoted patriotism and spirit of compromise which distinguished the sages of the Revolution and the fathers of our Union. If we can not at once, in justice to interests vested under improvident legislation, make our Government what it ought to be, we can at least take a stand against all new grants of monopolies and exclusive privileges, against any prostitution of our Government to the advancement of the few at the expense of the many, and in favor of compromise and gradual reform in our code of laws and system of political economy.

FOR DISCUSSION

Consider President Jackson's observations about the power of the Supreme Court and the legitimacy of *McCulloch v. Maryland*; what could be the consequences of such an attitude on the political legitimacy of the Supreme Court? Why might the Supreme Court be concerned? How does President Jackson construe federalism?

MISSOURI V. HOLLAND

252 U.S. 416, 40 S.Ct. 382, 64 L.Ed. 641 (1920)

The United States and Great Britain entered into a treaty agreement to protect migratory birds in the United States and Canada. The treaty included a provision that both countries would enact legislation to implement the purposes of the treaty. Congress enacted a statute forbidding the killing, capturing, or sale of the protected birds except in accordance with regulations established by the Secretary of Agriculture. Missouri challenged the Migratory Bird Act as an invasion of its state powers and sued to enjoin a federal game warden from enforcing the provisions of the statute and the regulations of the Secretary of Agriculture.

Vote: 7–2

JUSTICE HOLMES delivered the opinion of the Court:

Acts of Congress are the supreme law of the land only when made in pursuance of the Constitution, while treaties are declared to be so when made under the authority of the United States. It is open to question whether the authority of the United States means more than the formal acts prescribed to make the convention. We do not mean to imply that there are no qualifications to the treaty-making power; but they must be ascertained in a different way. It is obvious that there may be matters of the sharpest exigency for the national well-being that an act of Congress could not deal with, but that a treaty followed by such an act could, and it is not lightly to be assumed that, in matters requiring national action, "a power which must belong to and somewhere reside in every civilized government" is not to be found. . . . We are not yet discussing the particular case before us, but only are considering the validity of the test proposed. With regard to that, we may add that when we are dealing with words that also are a constituent act, like the Constitution of the United States, we must realize that they have called into life a being the development of which could not have been foreseen completely by the most gifted of its begetters. It was enough for them to realize or to hope that they had created an organism; it has taken a century and has cost their successors much sweat and blood to prove that they created a nation. The case before us must be considered in the light of our whole experience, and not merely in that of what was said a hundred years ago. The treaty in question does not contravene any prohibitory words to be found in the Constitution. The only question is whether it is forbidden by some invisible radiation from the general terms of the Tenth Amendment. We must consider what this country has become in deciding what that amendment has reserved.

The state, as we have intimated, founds its claim of exclusive authority upon an assertion of title to migratory birds—an assertion that is embodied in statute. No doubt it is true that, as between a state and its inhabitants, the state may regulate the killing and sale of such birds, but it does not follow that its authority is exclusive of paramount powers. To put the claim of the state upon title is to lean upon a slender reed. Wild birds are not in the possession of anyone; and possession is the beginning of ownership. The whole foundation of the state's rights is the presence within their jurisdiction of birds that yesterday had not arrived, tomorrow may be in another state, and in a week a thousand miles away. If we are to be accurate, we cannot put the case of the state upon higher ground than that the treaty deals with creatures that for the moment are within the state borders, that it must be carried out by officers of the United States within the same territory, and that, but for the treaty, the state would be free to regulate this subject itself. Here a national interest of very nearly the first magnitude is involved. It can be protected only by national action in concert with that of another power. The subject-matter is only transitory within the state, and has no permanent habitat therein. But for the treaty and the statute, there soon might be no birds for any powers to deal with. We see nothing in the Constitution that compels the government to sit by while a food supply is cut off and the protectors of our forests and our crops are destroyed. It is not sufficient to rely upon the states. The reliance is vain, and were it otherwise, the question is whether the United States is forbidden to act. We are of the opinion that the treaty and statute must be upheld.

Decree affirmed.

JUSTICES VAN DEVANTER and PITNEY dissented without a reported opinion.

FOR DISCUSSION

In a federal system, why would a national legislature have a broader scope of authority under a treaty than it might have under a statute? How does federalism apply to the regulation of issues under the independent control of a state at a particular moment in time (like birds), but that will eventually be under the control of multiple states?

RELATED CASES

Ware v. Hylton: **3 Dall. 199 (1796).**

A statute of Virginia cannot deny a British subject rights, such as concerned the payments of debts by Americans to British subjects established by the Jay Treaty between the United States and Britain. The Jay Treaty of 1794 was held to be retroactive and thus nullified the state law and action taken under it.

Chinese Exclusion Cases (Chae Chan Ping v. United States): **130 U.S. 581 (1889).**

A treaty and a federal statute are found to be on the same plane of legal equality; the most recent chronologically is to be enforced. Here, a Chinese national had left the United States possessing a certificate of re-entry under the terms of treaties between the United States and China; during his absence an act of Congress annulled the certificate and the Court held that this statute abrogated conflicting provisions of earlier treaties. The treaties were made in 1868 and 1880; the statute was enacted in 1888.

Cook v. United States: **288 U.S. 102 (1933).**

A treaty with Britain, providing for enforcement of prohibition laws off the coast of the United States for the "distance which can be traversed in one hour by the suspected vessel," was held to overrule a prior statute setting a flat twelve-mile limit as the distance of offshore enforcement. This is believed to be the only example of a treaty being held to repeal a statute.

PENNSYLVANIA V. NELSON

350 U.S. 497, 76 S.Ct. 477, 100 L.Ed. 640 (1956)

Steve Nelson, an admitted member of the Communist Party, had been convicted of violating the Pennsylvania Sedition Act. He challenged the validity of the state statute insofar as it proscribed sedition against the government of the United States, the offense with which he was charged. The federal government had previously regulated in this arena in 1940 through the Alien Registration Act, generally known as The Smith Act.

Vote: 6–3

CHIEF JUSTICE WARREN delivered the opinion of the Court:

In this case, we think that each of several tests of supersession is met.

First, "The scheme of federal regulation [is] so pervasive as to make reasonable the inference that Congress left no room for the States to supplement it. . . ." The Congress determined in 1940 that it was necessary for it to re-enter the field of antisubversive legislation, which had been abandoned by it in 1921. In that year, it enacted the Smith Act which proscribes advocacy of the overthrow of any government—federal, state or local—by force and violence and organization of and knowing membership in a group which so advocates. Conspiracy to commit any of these acts is punishable under the general criminal conspiracy provisions in 18 U.S.C. § 371.

We examine these Acts only to determine the congressional plan. Looking to all of them in the aggregate, the conclusion is inescapable that Congress has intended to occupy the field of sedition. Taken as a whole, they evince a congressional plan which makes it reasonable to determine that no room has been left for the States to supplement it. Therefore, a state sedition statute is superseded regardless of whether it purports to supplement the federal law.

Second, the federal statutes "touch a field in which the federal interest is so dominant that the federal system [must] be assumed to preclude enforcement of state laws on the same subject. . . ." Congress has devised an all-embracing program for resistance to the various forms of totalitarian aggression. It accordingly proscribed sedition against all government in the nation—national, state and local. Congress declared that these steps were taken "to provide for the common defense, to preserve the sovereignty of the United States as an independent nation, and to guarantee to each State a republican form of government. . . ." Congress having thus treated seditious conduct as a matter of vital national concern it is in no sense a local enforcement problem. As was said in the court below:

"Sedition against the United States is not a *local* offense. It is a crime against the *Nation.* As such, it should be prosecuted and punished in the Federal courts where this defendant has in fact been prosecuted and convicted and is now under sentence. It is not only important but vital that such prosecutions should be exclusively within the control of the Federal Government. . . ."

Third, enforcement of state sedition acts presents a serious danger of conflict with the administration of the federal program. Since 1939, in order to avoid a hampering of uniform enforcement of its program by sporadic local prosecutions, the Federal Government has urged local authorities not to intervene in such matters, but to turn over to the federal authorities immediately and unevaluated all information concerning subversive activities. The President made such a request on September 6, 1939, when he placed the Federal Bureau of Investigation in charge of investigation in this field.

Moreover, the Pennsylvania Statute presents a peculiar danger of interference with the federal program. For, as the court below observed:

> "Unlike the Smith Act, which can be administered only by federal officers acting in their official capacities, indictment for sedition under the Pennsylvania statute can be initiated upon an information made by a private individual. The opportunity thus present for the indulgence of personal spite and hatred or for furthering some selfish advantage or ambition need only be mentioned to be appreciated. Defense of the Nation by law, no less than by arms, should be a public and not a private undertaking. It is important that punitive sanctions for sedition *against the United States* be such as have been promulgated by the central governmental authority and administered under the supervision and review of that authority's judiciary. If that be done, sedition will be detected and punished, no less, wherever it may be found, and the right of the individual to speak freely and without fear, even in criticism of the government, will at the same time be protected."

In his brief, the Solicitor General states that forty-two States plus Alaska and Hawaii have statutes which in some form prohibit advocacy of the violent overthrow of established government. These statutes are entitled anti-sedition statutes, criminal anarchy laws, criminal syndicalist laws, etc. Although all of them are primarily directed against the overthrow of the United States Government, they are in no sense uniform. And our attention has not been called to any case where the prosecution has been successfully directed against an attempt to destroy state or local government. . . . Should the States be permitted to exercise a concurrent jurisdiction in this area, federal enforcement would encounter not only the difficulties mentioned by Mr. Justice Jackson, but the added conflict engendered by different criteria of substantive offenses.

Since we find that Congress has occupied the field to the exclusion of parallel state legislation, that the dominant interest of the Federal Government precludes state intervention, and that administration of state Acts would conflict with the operation of the federal plan, we are convinced that the decision of the Supreme Court of Pennsylvania is unassailable.

We are not unmindful of the risk of compounding punishments which would be created by finding concurrent state power. In our view of the case, we do not reach the question whether double or multiple punishment for the same overt acts directed against the United States has constitutional sanction. Without compelling indication to the contrary, we will not assume the Congress intended to permit the possibility of double punishment.

The judgment of the Supreme Court of Pennsylvania is affirmed.

Affirmed.

JUSTICE REED, with whom JUSTICES BURTON and MINTON joined, dissented.

Congress has not, in any of its statutes relating to sedition, specifically barred the exercise of state power to punish the same Acts under state law. And, we read the majority opinion to assume for this case that, absent federal legislation, there is no constitutional bar to punishment of sedition against the United States by both a State and the Nation. The majority limits to the federal courts the power to try charges of sedition against the Federal Government.

But the federal sedition laws are distinct statutes that punish willful advocacy of the use of force against "the government of the United States or the government of any State." These criminal laws proscribe certain local activity without creating any statutory or administrative regulation. There is, consequently, no question as to whether some general congressional regulatory scheme might be upset by a coinciding state plan. In these circumstances the conflict should be clear and direct before this Court reads a congressional intent to void state legislation into the federal sedition acts.

We cannot agree that the federal criminal sanctions against sedition directed at the United States are of such a pervasive character as to indicate an intention to void state action.

Finally, and this one point seems in and of itself decisive, there is an independent reason for reversing the Pennsylvania Supreme Court. The Smith Act appears in Title 18 of the United States Code, 18 U.S.C.A., which Title codifies the federal criminal laws. Section 3231 of that Title provides:

> "Nothing in this title shall be held to take away or impair the jurisdiction of the courts of the several States under the laws thereof."

FOR DISCUSSION

What might be the interest of a state in regulating sedition against the United States? How do the majority and dissenting opinions conflict in their assessment of the appropriateness of federal supersession in this case?

RELATED CASES

***Gilbert v. Minnesota:* 254 U.S. 325 (1920).**

The Federal Espionage Act of 1917 did not supersede a state statute forbidding interference with the war effort because the state act was an exercise of state police power and not of war power. The act was valid as long as there was no interference with federal activity.

***Testa v. Katt:* 330 U.S. 386 (1947).**

State courts are to enforce federal laws (here the Emergency Price Control Act) even though the federal law may be contrary to state policy. This is simply another example of federal supremacy.

***Hamm v. City of Rock Hill:* 379 U.S. 306 (1964).**

Convictions for conduct no longer unlawful must be suspended, if under direct review at the time. In this case, the Civil Rights Act of 1964 ran counter to state trespass statutes.

PACIFIC GAS & ELECTRIC CO. V. STATE ENERGY RESOURCES CONSERVATION AND DEVELOPMENT COMMISSION

461 U.S. 190, 103 S. Ct. 1713, 75 L. Ed. 2d 752 (1983)

In 1976, California passed several laws prohibiting the construction of nuclear plants unless the State Energy Resources Conservation and Development Commission determined that there were adequate storage facilities and means of disposing nuclear waste. These laws were challenged by energy companies who argued such regulations were preempted by the federal Atomic Energy Act of 1954.

Vote: 9–0

JUSTICE WHITE delivered the opinion of the Court.

The turning of swords into plowshares has symbolized the transformation of atomic power into a source of energy in American society. To facilitate this development the Federal Government relaxed its monopoly over fissionable materials and nuclear technology, and in its place, erected a complex scheme to promote the civilian development of nuclear energy, while seeking to safeguard the public and the environment from the unpredictable risks of a new technology. Early on, it was decided that the States would continue their traditional role in the regulation of electricity production. The interrelationship of federal and state authority in the nuclear energy field has not been simple; the federal regulatory structure has been frequently amended to optimize the partnership.

This case emerges from the intersection of the Federal Government's efforts to ensure that nuclear power is safe with the exercise of the historic state authority over the generation and sale of electricity. At issue is whether provisions in the 1976 amendments to California's Warren-Alquist Act, Cal. Pub. Res. Code Ann. §§ 25524.1(b) and 25524.2 (West 1977), which condition the construction of nuclear plants on findings by the State Energy Resources Conservation and Development Commission that adequate storage facilities and means of disposal are available for nuclear waste, are pre-empted by the Atomic Energy Act of 1954, 68 Stat. 919, as amended, 42 U.S.C. § 2011 et seq.

I

The California laws at issue here are responses to these concerns. In 1974, California adopted the Warren-Alquist State Energy Resources Conservation and Development Act, Cal. Pub. Res. Code Ann. §§ 25000–25986. The Act requires that a utility seeking to build in California any electric power generating plant, including a nuclear powerplant, must apply for certification to the State Energy Resources Conservation and Development Commission (Energy Commission). The Warren-Alquist Act was amended in 1976 to provide additional state regulation of new nuclear powerplant construction.

Two sections of these amendments are before us. Section 25524.1(b) provides that before additional nuclear plants may be built, the Energy Commission must determine on a case-by-case basis that there will be "adequate capacity" for storage of a plant's spent fuel rods "at the time such nuclear facility requires such . . . storage." In short, § 25524.1(b) addresses the interim storage of spent fuel.

Section 25524.2 deals with the long-term solution to nuclear wastes.

III

It is well established that within constitutional limits Congress may pre-empt state authority by so stating in express terms. Absent explicit pre-emptive language, Congress' intent to supersede state law altogether may be found from a " 'scheme of federal regulation . . . so pervasive as to make reasonable the inference that Congress left no room for the States to supplement it,' because 'the Act of Congress may touch a field in which the federal interest is so dominant that the federal system will be assumed to preclude enforcement of state laws on the same subject,' or because 'the object sought to be obtained by the federal law and the character of obligations imposed by it may reveal the same purpose.' " *Fidelity Federal Savings & Loan Assn. v. De la Cuesta*, 458 U.S. 141, 153 (1982), quoting *Rice v. Santa Fe Elevator Corp.*, 331 U.S. 218, 230 (1947). Even where Congress has not entirely displaced state regulation in a specific area, state law is pre-empted to the extent that it actually conflicts with federal law. Such a conflict arises when "compliance with both federal and state regulations is a physical impossibility," *Florida Lime & Avocado Growers, Inc. v. Paul*, 373 U.S. 132, 142–143 (1963), or where state law "stands as an obstacle to the accomplishment and execution of the full purposes and objectives of Congress." *Hines v. Davidowitz*, 312 U.S. 52, 67 (1941).

A

Even a brief perusal of the Atomic Energy Act reveals that, despite its comprehensiveness, it does not at any point expressly require the States to construct or authorize nuclear powerplants or prohibit the States from deciding, as an absolute or conditional matter, not to permit the construction of any further reactors. But as we view the issue, Congress, in passing the 1954 Act and in subsequently amending it, intended that the Federal Government should regulate the radiological safety aspects involved in the construction and operation of a nuclear plant, but that the States retain their traditional responsibility in the field of regulating electrical utilities for determining questions of need, reliability, cost, and other related state concerns.

Need for new power facilities, their economic feasibility, and rates and services, are areas that have been characteristically governed by the States.

[F]rom the passage of the Atomic Energy Act in 1954, through several revisions, and to the present day, Congress has preserved the dual regulation of nuclear-powered electricity generation: the Federal Government maintains complete control of the safety and "nuclear" aspects of energy generation; the States exercise their traditional authority over the need for additional generating capacity, the type of generating facilities to be licensed, land use, ratemaking, and the like.

The above is not particularly controversial. But deciding how § 25524.2 is to be construed and classified is a more difficult proposition. State safety regulation is not pre-empted only when it conflicts with federal law. Rather, the Federal Government has occupied the entire field of nuclear safety concerns, except the limited powers expressly ceded to the States. When the Federal Government completely occupies a given field or an identifiable portion of it, as it has done here, the test of pre-emption is whether "the matter on which the State asserts the right to act is in any way regulated by the Federal Act." *Rice v. Santa Fe Elevator Corp.*, 331 U.S., at 236. A state moratorium on nuclear construction grounded in safety concerns falls squarely within the prohibited field.

That being the case, it is necessary to determine whether there is a nonsafety rationale for § 25524.2. California has maintained, and the Court of Appeals agreed, that § 25524.2 was aimed at economic problems, not radiation hazards. The California Assembly Committee on Resources, Land Use, and Energy, which proposed a package of bills including § 25524.2, reported that the waste disposal problem was "largely economic or the result of poor planning, not safety related." Storage space was limited while more nuclear wastes were continuously produced. Without a permanent means of disposal, the nuclear waste problem could become critical, leading to unpredictably high costs to contain the problem or, worse, shutdowns in reactors.

Therefore, we accept California's avowed economic purpose as the rationale for enacting § 25524.2. Accordingly, the statute lies outside the occupied field of nuclear safety regulation.

B

It is contended that § 25524.2 conflicts with federal regulation of nuclear waste disposal, with the [Nuclear Regulatory Commission's (NRC)] decision that it is permissible to continue to license reactors, notwithstanding uncertainty surrounding the waste disposal problem, and with Congress' recent passage of legislation directed at that problem.

In its closing week, the 97th Congress passed the Nuclear Waste Policy Act of 1982, Pub. L. 97–425, 96 Stat. 2201, a complex bill providing for a multifaceted attack on the problem. [T]he bill authorizes repositories for disposal of high-level radioactive waste and spent nuclear fuel, provides for licensing and expansion of interim storage, authorizes research and development, and provides a scheme for financing. While the passage of this new legislation may convince state authorities that there is now a sufficient federal commitment to fuel storage and waste disposal that licensing of nuclear reactors may resume, and, indeed, this seems to be one of the purposes of the Act, it does not appear that Congress intended to make that decision for the States through this legislation. While we are correctly reluctant to draw inferences from the failure of Congress to act, it would, in this case, appear improper for us to give a reading to the Act that Congress considered and rejected. Moreover, it is certainly possible to interpret the Act as directed at solving the nuclear waste disposal problem for existing reactors without necessarily encouraging or requiring that future plant construction be undertaken.

C

Finally, it is strongly contended that § 25524.2 frustrates the Atomic Energy Act's purpose to develop the commercial use of nuclear power. It is well established that state law is pre-empted if it "stands as an obstacle to the accomplishment and execution of the full purposes and objectives of Congress." *Hines v. Davidowitz*, 312 U.S., at 67.

There is little doubt that a primary purpose of the Atomic Energy Act was, and continues to be, the promotion of nuclear power.

. . . [T]he promotion of nuclear power is not to be accomplished "at all costs." The elaborate licensing and safety provisions and the continued preservation of state regulation in traditional areas belie that. Moreover, Congress has allowed the States to determine—as a matter of economics—whether a nuclear plant vis-a-vis a fossil fuel plant should be built. The decision of California to exercise that authority does not, in itself, constitute a basis for pre-emption. Therefore, while the argument of petitioners and the United States has considerable force, the legal reality remains that Congress has left sufficient authority in the States to allow the development of nuclear power to be slowed or even stopped for economic reasons. Given this statutory scheme, it is for Congress to rethink the division of regulatory authority in light of its possible exercise by the States to undercut a federal objective. The courts should not assume the role which our system assigns to Congress.

The judgment of the Court of Appeals is Affirmed.

JUSTICE BLACKMUN, with whom JUSTICE STEVENS joins, concurring in part and concurring in the judgment.

I join the Court's opinion, except to the extent it suggests that a State may not prohibit the construction of nuclear powerplants if the State is motivated by concerns about the safety of such plants. Since the Court finds that California was not so motivated, this suggestion is unnecessary to the Court's holding. More important, I believe the Court's dictum is wrong in several respects.

The Court takes the position that a State's safety-motivated decision to prohibit construction of nuclear powerplants would be pre-empted for three distinct reasons. I cannot agree that a State's nuclear moratorium, even if motivated by safety concerns, would be pre-empted on any of these grounds.

I

First, Congress has occupied not the broad field of "nuclear safety concerns," but only the narrower area of how a nuclear plant should be constructed and operated to protect against radiation hazards. States traditionally have possessed the authority to choose which technologies to rely on in meeting their energy needs.

In short, there is an important distinction between the threshold determination whether to permit the construction of new nuclear plants and, if the decision is to permit construction, the subsequent determinations of how to construct and operate those plants. The threshold decision belongs to the State; the latter decisions are for the [Nuclear Regulatory Commission (NRC)].

II

The Court's second basis for suggesting that States may not prohibit the construction of nuclear plants on safety grounds is that such a prohibition would conflict with the NRC's judgment that construction of nuclear plants may safely proceed. The NRC has expressed its judgment that it is safe to proceed with construction and operation of nuclear plants, but neither the NRC nor Congress has mandated that States do so.

III

A state regulation also conflicts with federal law if it "stands as an obstacle to the accomplishment and execution of the full purposes and objectives of Congress." *Hines v. Davidowitz*, 312 U.S. 52, 67 (1941). The Court suggests that a safety-motivated state ban on nuclear plants would be pre-empted under this standard as well. But Congress has merely encouraged the development of nuclear technology so as to make another source of energy available to the States; Congress has not forced the States to accept this particular source. A ban on nuclear plant construction for safety reasons thus does not conflict with Congress' objectives or purposes.

In sum, Congress has not required States to "go nuclear," in whole or in part. The Atomic Energy Act's twin goals were to promote the development of a technology and to ensure the safety of that technology. Although that Act reserves to the NRC decisions about how to build and operate nuclear plants, the Court reads too much into the Act in suggesting that it also limits the States' traditional power to decide what types of electric power to utilize. Congress simply has made the nuclear option available, and a State may decline that option for any reason. Rather than rest on the elusive test of legislative motive, therefore, I would conclude that the decision whether to build nuclear plants remains with the States. In my view, a ban on construction of nuclear powerplants would be valid even if its authors were motivated by fear of a core meltdown or other nuclear catastrophe.

FOR DISCUSSION

What is the conflict between the majority and dissenting opinions regarding the potential scope of federal supersession of state laws? Is the majority arguing that the Supremacy Clause can be used to enforce congressional policy values like an insistence on the safeness of nuclear energy, and not just direct policy objectives? What might be the impact of this perspective on federalism?

RELATED CASES

American Insurance Association v. Garamendi: **539 U.S. 396 (2003).**

The Court found that a California law intended to help Californian Holocaust survivors benefit from unpaid German insurance claims conflicted with national foreign affairs policy and was thereby preempted. Dissenters objected that no federal text (law, treaty, or agreement) had delineated the federal position on the issue.

Gonzales v. Oregon: **546 U.S. 243 (2006).**

The Court determined that the federal Controlled Substance Act did not preempt state laws like Oregon's Death with Dignity Act, which authorized physicians under specific circumstances to prescribe fatal doses of controlled drugs for the terminally ill.

Levine v. Wyeth: **555 U.S. 555 (2009).**

The Supreme Court found that Federal Drug Administration approval regarding labeling of an approved drug does not preempt state requirements or shield from liability under state laws.

FEDERALISM

Tenth Amendment:

The powers not delegated to the United States by the Constitution, nor prohibited by it to the States, are reserved to the States respectively, or to the people.

After the signing of the Declaration of Independence, those engaged in creating a new government were most concerned by the possibility of a tyrannical central government that would destroy the liberties of the state. To avoid the potential abuses by a unitary government that provided all sovereign powers to an executive branch or federal authority, the first government of the United States was constructed as a confederacy, delineated in the Articles of Confederation. This governmental structure placed most of the governmental powers under the control of the states (e.g., power to coin money, enforce laws, make treaties, tax, and conduct commerce) and did not contain a national executive or judicial branch. In fact, Article II states: "Each state retains its sovereignty, freedom, and independence, and every power, jurisdiction, and right, which is not by this Confederation expressly delegated to the United States, in Congress assembled." The primary power that the Articles of Confederation granted to Congress was the power to wage war. Finally ratified in 1781, in less than ten years the limits of this approach became evident to many in the chaotic aftermath of the Revolutionary War. The nation had not paid its debt to other countries or to the veterans who had fought in the Revolutionary War, and local rebellions against increased taxation were threatening the states.

Many frightened state leaders deemed that a new system of government was necessary, and in 1787 they held a Constitutional Convention in Philadelphia. At this convention, one of the many concerns was the posited relationship between the state governments and the federal government. Where should sovereignty be located? Federalism, a structure of government that required shared sovereignty between the state authorities and the national government, appeared to provide a balance between the tyrannical threat posed by a unitary system and the threat of chaos that the confederal system had created. Federalism required that some governmental authority be explicitly placed under state control (e.g., most criminal law, intrastate commerce, and powers not granted to the national government) and other governmental authority be placed under national control (e.g., coining money, interstate commerce, foreign policy, the power to declare war, and control of the military). Most importantly, for the sustaining of federalism, other governmental responsibilities were seen as concurrent powers, placed under the shared authority of both state and federal governments, and were thus enumerated in the Constitution (e.g., such powers as conducting elections and taxation).

When James Madison in *Federalist 51* observed that "ambition must be made to counteract ambition," he was referring not only to the construction of separation of powers and checks and balances within the federal government, but also that between the national and state authorities. Federalism divides powers between the state and national authorities and limits both. Despite this clear distribution of powers, as technology develops, moral values transform, and governmental functions evolve, their meanings and parameters become less precise.

The judiciary, through its decisions, has helped determine what authority belongs to the state and municipal governments and when the federal government has the authority to intervene into the sovereignty typically exercised by the states. These interpretations can change in a fairly short period of time, in part because there is an inherent tension within federalism. On the one hand, citizens believe that the states are closer to them and therefore should have the flexibility to construct remedies for local problems that may have unique characteristics. This notion of the state as the "laboratory of democracy" recognizes that national problems may still require unique local solutions that the states are best situated to instigate. On the other hand, citizens should not possess different rights solely based on which state in which they reside. If the Constitution guarantees a fundamental right, that right should belong to all citizens regardless of their region or community. The judiciary is often forced to balance the right of the state to sovereignty with the right of a citizen (of both the state and the nation) to constitutional protection.

This tension is clearly demonstrated within a pair of cases that determined the capacity of the Fair Labor Standards Act of 1938 (FLSA) to provide the same labor protections to state and city employees that the laws had guaranteed to private employees throughout the country. The FLSA mandated that employers must pay a minimum wage and overtime to their employees; however, Congress initially excluded states and localities from the coverage of the Act. Congress amended the FLSA in 1974 to apply to all states and municipalities. The case of *National League of Cities v. Usery* (426 U.S. 833, 1976) was a closely decided ruling in which the Supreme Court found that the Commerce Clause (Article I, § 8, ¶ 3) did not allow Congress to enforce the overtime and minimum wage protections of the FLSA against the states and metropolitan governments in areas of traditional local government control (e.g., police and fire protection). Because the Commerce Clause is a concurrent power whereby the states exert power over intrastate commerce and the federal government has the explicit authority to regulation interstate commerce, foreign trade, and commerce with "the Indian tribes," its meaning is frequently contested.

In *National League of Cities*, states were given the authority to regulate employees engaged in traditional state and municipal activities—the federal government was not allowed to intervene in this relationship. Nine years later in *Garcia v. San Antonio Metropolitan Transit Authority* (469 U.S. 528, 1985), the Supreme Court attempted to reconcile several competing federal and state court decisions defining the scope of the states' authority. In *Garcia*, the city of San Antonio, Texas, claimed that its ownership and operation of a mass transit system was a traditional local government function and consequently exempt from the requirements of the FLSA. In its decision in this case, the Supreme Court decided to overturn their decision in *National League of Cities*, finding it inconsistent with the basic claims and principles of federalism. The decision in *Garcia* noted that while certain types of state activity are immune from any governmental regulation, the ruling in *National League of Cities* and other precedents (such as *Hodel v. Virginia Surface Mining and Reclamation Association*, 432 U.S. 264, 1981) had not provided clear guidance to Congress as to what was and was not permissible state regulations. Instead, the Court provided a larger test based on *E.E.O.C. v. Wyoming* (46 U.S. 226, 1983), which prohibits the Congress from regulating the states in a way that destroys state sovereignty or violates any constitutional prohibitions. This broader definition of state immunity allowed Congress to incorporate state and municipal employees under the provisions of the FLSA. These two cases, while complicated, clearly demonstrate the balancing of state and federal authorities by which the Supreme Court has attempted to define the scope and boundaries of the concurrent powers while preserving the protections inherent to federalism.

Qualifications Clauses

Article I, Sec. 2, para. 2 (which applies to the House of Representatives):

No Person shall be a Representative who shall not have attained to the Age of twenty five Years, and been seven Years a Citizen of the United States, and who shall not, when elected, be an Inhabitant of that State in which he shall be chosen.

Article I, Sec. 3, para. 3 (which applies to the Senate):

No Person shall be a Senator who shall not have attained to the Age of thirty Years, and been nine Years a Citizen of the United States, and who shall not, when elected, be an Inhabitant of that State for which he shall be chosen.

The representation provided in Congress is a clear microcosm of the federalist system. While elected officials in the House and Senate make federal law as part of the national government, they are elected by citizens of their state for the purpose of representing the interests of that state. In the case of *Powell v. McCormack* (395 U.S. 486, 1969), the Supreme Court determined that the Qualifications Clauses guarantee that Congress may determine the "Qualifications of its own Members" does not allow the House of Representatives or Senate to add additional qualifications beyond those articulated in Article I. According to *Powell*, a fundamental premise of representative democracy is that citizens have the right to choose their own elected officials.

This case gained increased relevance during the term limitation debates of the 1990s. In a state referendum in 1992, Arkansas passed Amendment 73, which amended the state constitution to restrict congressional representatives to only three terms and senators to two terms in office. In the case of *U.S. Term Limits v. Thornton* (514 U.S. 779, 1995), the Supreme Court considered whether such a state constitutional amendment would conflict with the Qualification Clauses of the Constitution by creating additional restrictions as to whom the voters could elect to serve in office. The Supreme Court agreed with the Arkansas Supreme Court in declaring such state term limitations for federal offices unconstitutional. While this has settled the question of federal term limitations, many states have amended their state constitutions to construct term limitations for state elected office. Of course, such internal limitations face no federal constitutional challenge.

Eleventh Amendment

Eleventh Amendment:

The Judicial power of the United States shall not be construed to extend to any suit in law or equity, commenced or prosecuted against one of the United States by Citizens of another State, or by Citizens or Subjects of any Foreign State.

In the case of *Chisholm v. Georgia* (2 U.S. (2 Dall.) 419, 1793), the state of Georgia purchased supplies from a private business in South Carolina. Although it received the purchased goods, Georgia did not pay the merchant. The Supreme Court was asked to determine if Georgia, as a sovereign state, was exempt from the authority of the federal courts. The Court determined that sovereignty was not retained by the state, but by the people of the state, and that Article III of the Constitution subjects the states to judicial authority. Consequently, states are subject to judicial review of the constitutionality and legality of their actions. The response to this decision from the states was immediate, and in 1795 the states ratified the Eleventh Amendment to the Constitution

The Eleventh Amendment to the Constitution guarantees **sovereign immunity** to the states, allowing them to protect their own sources of sovereignty through limiting their liability within the federal judicial process. While the text of the Eleventh Amendment only protects states from lawsuits from citizens of other states, Supreme Court decisions have extended this constitutional provision to legal challenges in federal court from citizens against their own state. Most recently, the Supreme Court has used the Eleventh Amendment to limit Congress's use of litigation as a means of regulating state behavior toward their own citizens under the Fourteenth Amendment's protection of due process and equal protection rights against state violation. For instance, Congress, in expanding the rights of citizens under the due process and equal protection clauses and such statutory protections as the Civil Rights Act of 1964, has allowed citizens to challenge state violations of these rights in federal court. Employees of states and municipalities have sued their employers in federal court for violation of labor law. The Supreme Court has recognized that Congress may legitimately **abrogate** states' immunity under the Eleventh Amendment, but only when Congress clearly communicates that it intends to and when it is acting pursuant to a legitimate grant of constitutional authority.

During the Rehnquist Court years, the Supreme Court became much more cautious about allowing federal regulation to circumvent what it understood to be arenas of state authority and autonomy. Some scholars have referred to this series of cases as being part of the "Rehnquist Revolution," which granted states greater autonomy against federal regulation in areas traditionally under state control. Critics noted that the national transition to a federal and international economy and greater societal mobility had eliminated many of the traditional distinctions between state and federal authority. These Supreme Court precedents have created a new understanding of how state interests are to be balanced against national concerns in our federalist system.

One of the first cases in this line of precedents emerged from the state of Florida and resulted from a conflict with one of the autonomous tribes residing within the state. In the 1996 case of *Seminole Tribe of Florida v. Florida* (517 U.S. 44), the Seminole Tribe sued the state of Florida under the provisions of a federal law—the Indian Gaming Regulatory Act of 1998. This law permits tribes to conduct gambling following agreements between the tribe and the state where the gaming activities are occurring. The Act requires states to negotiate with tribes and allows federal litigation to aid the tribes in enforcing these agreements. After the state of Florida refused to negotiate with the Seminole Tribe of Florida regarding a gambling agreement, the tribe cited the

Indian Gaming Regulatory Act and took the state to federal court. Florida claimed that both the Act and the lawsuit violated the premises of the Eleventh Amendment's guarantee of sovereign immunity. In this, and in subsequent cases, the Supreme Court wrestled with the question of when the federal government may lawfully **abrogate** the sovereign immunity of states by subjecting them to federal authority through litigation. The Court found that in order for the abrogation to be lawful, Congress must clearly indicate its intent to compromise state immunity within the legislation and Congress must have constitutional authority to do so in the area it is regulating. Although the regulation of Indian commerce is solely within the constitutional authority of the federal government, the Supreme Court found that the guarantee of the Eleventh Amendment was powerful enough to withstand this challenge. By putting new teeth into the Eleventh Amendment, *Seminole Tribe of Florida* challenged many of the federal laws protecting citizens of the latter part of the twentieth century.

The significance of *Seminole Tribe* would become clear when such seminal legislation as the Americans with Disabilities Act of 1990 (ADA) was challenged under the Eleventh Amendment. The ADA was designed to prevent covered employers, including states, from employment discrimination based on an employee's disability and requires employers to make reasonable accommodation for an employee unless the accommodation would be an undue hardship on the operation of the employer's business. In *Board of Trustees of the University of Alabama v. Garrett* (531 U.S. 356, 2001), the state of Alabama argued that the elements of the ADA that allowed employees to seek monetary damages from employers, without making an exception for states, exceeds congressional authority to abrogate state sovereignty under the Eleventh Amendment. In this case, the only portion of the ADA that was constitutionally challenged was the element regarding monetary damages from employees. The Court found that the guarantees of the Equal Protection Clause of the Fourteenth Amendment did not provide strong enough protections, nor was there a history of state discrimination to justify such a federal abrogation of state sovereignty.

In the case of *Kimel v. Florida Board of Regents* (528 U.S. 62, 2000), the same question was raised relative to the Age Discrimination in Employment Act of 1967 (ADEA). This Act prohibits employers, including states, from refusing to hire or from firing a person because an employee is over the age of forty. Several district courts had heard similar challenges and were divided in their response as to whether the ADEA was a legitimate abrogation of state sovereignty by the federal government. The Court found that this law had the same liability as the ADA—no clear constitutional provision and no evidence of historic state discrimination that the federal government was able to address. The Court did remind the litigants of the state laws prohibiting age discrimination; litigants could thus challenge discrimination by the states in many state courts under state laws. These laws would not fall under the Eleventh Amendment because remedies found within state laws allowing for damages from employers would grant the necessary state permission to file a lawsuit under the Eleventh Amendment.

Not all laws are found unconstitutional under the Eleventh Amendment. In two recent cases, the Supreme Court has found that the Congress could abrogate state sovereignty. In its opinion in *Nevada Department of Human Resources v. Hibbs* (538 U.S. 721, 2003), the Court questioned the legitimacy of the Family and Medical Leave Act of 1993 (FMLA), which allowed employees time off without pay in order to address family and medical emergencies. Like the ADEA and the ADA, the FMLA allowed for damages against an employer for violating the provisions of the law without making exceptions for state or municipal employees. The Court found this legislation different because it was intended to address gender discrimination in the workplace, although the law applies to both men and women. Because gender discrimination has been explicitly included in the Equal Protection Clause of the Fourteenth Amendment by Supreme Court precedent (e.g., *Reed v. Reed*, 404 U.S. 71, 1971) and has been clearly demonstrated as a historical problem within the states, the Congress had justification to abrogate under the remedial power of Section 5 of the Fourteenth Amendment. The 2004 case of *Tennessee v. Lane* (541 U.S. 509) also upheld congressional abrogation of another portion of the Americans with Disabilities Act of 1990. Title II of the Americans with Disabilities Act of 1990 prohibits public entities from excluding qualified individuals from benefits of services or participation in programs based on a disability and allows suits for damages. *Board of Trustees of University of Alabama v. Garrett* (2001) only found Title I remedies against states to be unlawful. Because Title II addressed access to general services—such as courts, voting booths, and other governmental services—as opposed to merely employment, the Court found that Congress has a specific constitutional interest in guaranteeing this protection to citizens.

Judicial Intervention

One question that might emerge from the Eleventh Amendment sovereign immunity cases is the right of the federal judiciary to intervene in matters of federalism. If the "referee" is a member of the federal courts, does this mean that the states cannot be adequately protected? When is it appropriate for these courts to make determination as to the federal constitutionality of state constitutions and state law? When should the state be responsible for protecting its own citizens? A search and seizure case emerging from the state of Michigan in 1983 argued that the federal courts do not need to intervene when the state laws are at stake. The Bill of Rights and other federal protections for citizens (e.g., statutory employment discrimination protections) are designed to create a "floor" of rights, these are the bare minimum guarantees that a state must provide. States, on the other hand, have the ability to construct their own ceilings, the maximum protections provided by the law. So it is possible that some states may provide greater protections for the criminally accused than others, but all states must at least provide the constitutional guarantees of the Fourth, Fifth, and Sixth Amendments that have been incorporated to the states through the Fourteenth Amendment.

In *Michigan v. Long* (463 U.S. 1032, 1983), the state appealed a basic search and seizure case to the federal courts when the Michigan Supreme Court overturned two lower state courts and denied the admission of drug evidence in a criminal trial, claiming that the justification for the search was invalid. The criminal defendant, David Long, claimed that the United States Supreme Court did not have the authority to decide a case based on Michigan law. He asserted that Michigan courts provide greater protection against searches and seizure under the Michigan state constitution than are granted under the Fourth Amendment. The Supreme Court disagreed, not with the premise of Long's claim but with its factual veracity, noting that the Supreme Court decision only cited the Michigan constitution twice and then relied upon federal Supreme Court precedents in rendering its verdict. Unless the state court clearly states that their decision rests on "an adequate and independent state ground," the federal courts do have jurisdiction to hear such a case.

Now consider, for instance, the case of *Railroad Commission of Texas v. Pullman Co.* (312 U.S. 496, 1941). At that time, many states still legally mandated the complete segregation of the races in public and private spheres. This regulation was justified by a particular interpretation of the Equal Protection Clause made in *Plessy v. Ferguson* (163 U.S. 537, 1896), which constitutionally accepted segregation as long as equivalent, but necessarily of equal quality, facilities were provided for all. The purpose of state segregation laws was to maintain the social, political, and economic power of whites. This state commitment to white superiority is illustrated by the usual exception to segregation requirements of personal servants or employees traveling with whites.

During the era of segregation, passenger trains in rural Texas usually only included one sleeping car. These smaller trains, unlike the larger ones with two or more sleepers, did not have a white Pullman conductor, but instead were controlled by a black Pullman porter. In response, the Texas Railroad Commission ruled that sleeping cars could only be operated in the state if there was a Pullman conductor on board. Consequently, a white railroad official was required to provide supervision on board; a black porter was not sufficient for the white customers in Texas. The Pullman Company and affected railroads challenged this regulation in federal courts as unauthorized by Texas law and a violation of the equal protection clause, the due process clause, and the commerce clause. The black Pullman porters were involved as plaintiffs, claiming racial discrimination under the Fourteenth Amendment, and the white Pullman conductors joined the litigation in favor of the Texas legislation. In this case, Justice Frankfurter argued that Texas law predominates and therefore the Court must decide if Texas law allows such discrimination. Because Texas law is at stake, the Court required that this case be remanded to state courts to determine if the decision of the Texas Railroad Commission was consistent with state law. The case is famous for a principle of judicial federalism. Federal courts will not act or intervene while state court proceedings are still actively addressing a legal issue. This doctrine, known as the **Pullman Abstention,** is one of several court rules of deference the Supreme Court has adopted to give deference to state courts.

The case of *Boerne v. Flores* (531 U.S. 507, 1997) raises a different question regarding the role of the judiciary. On its face, this case is a zoning dispute between a city council and a local Catholic parish, in which a local church challenged the zoning decision as violating the federal Religious Freedom Restoration Act of 1993 (RFRA). This law was Congress's attempt to challenge recent Supreme Court decisions, interpreting the First Amendment's Free Exercise Clause, including state protections of the free exercise of religion by its citizens. Congress relied upon its enforcement power under Section 5 of the Fourteenth Amendment to provide it the constitutional authority to pass this law. The Supreme Court found that Congress did not possess the power to define the meaning of the First Amendment's Free Exercise Clause and impose it on the state and federal government; the RFRA's application to state law was declared unconstitutional.

The case of *Boerne v. Flores* is constitutionally significant in several ways. First, as discussed in Volume II, this case is one of many detailing the evolution of the constitutional standard used by the Supreme Court in determining state violations of the Free Exercise Clause of the Constitution. In the case of *Employment Division, Department of Human Resources of Oregon v. Smith* (494 U.S. 872, 1990), the Court rebuked the historical standard originally stated in *Sherbert v. Verner* (374 U.S. 398, 1963), establishing a new test that provides more flexibility to state governments to pass neutral legislation that harms an individual's practice of his or her religion. Second, this case also is significant in the separation of powers battle between the Congress and the Supreme Court in terms of the appropriate constitutional standard. One response by Congress to the *Employment Division v. Smith* decision was the passage of the Religious Freedom Restoration Act of 1993; it was designed statutorily to force the Court to accept the constitutional standard articulated in *Sherbert* and rejected in *Smith*. The Court in *Boerne* rejects the authority of Congress to compel the judiciary to accept statutorily determined standards when exercising their duty of constitutional interpretation. Finally, this case has great significance in terms of federalism. Not only is this case significant in the recognition of state authority to regulate zoning, but many states responded to *Boerne* either by passing their own state RFRAs or by interpreting their state constitutions as requiring the *Sherbert* standard in interpreting the free exercise clause.

Sexual Orientation and Identity as an Issue of Federalism

While cases regarding individual rights are generally understood to be issues related to the Fourteenth Amendment and equal protection, such cases also demonstrate the shifting boundaries and conflicts within federalism. This discussion of federalism considers how our constitutional assessment of the validity of state regulation of private sexual behavior and state sanctioning of public choices has changed over time. In reading these cases, watch how the interest of the state in maintaining community interpretations of morality and societal values conflicts with the interest of the federal government in determining and protecting individual rights under the constitution. While the Supreme Court's understanding evolves along with the larger society, consider how the Court justifies these changes, how states respond, and what this means for the scope of federalism. In addition, once the federal courts began ruling on the question of same-sex marriage, changes in constitutional interpretation rapidly occurred.

Historically, the right to delineate and enforce appropriate sexual behavior was managed at the local or community level, where community standards were developed and replicated. As the 1986 case of *Bowers v.*

Hardwick (478 U.S. 186) demonstrates, state laws later provided uniformity of definitions of acceptable behavior. A Georgia law, passed in 1816, prohibited all sexual acts that were considered sodomy (oral and anal sex) regardless of the genders of the persons participating in the sexual activity; as written, the law applied to both heterosexual and homosexual couples. The private location of the activity or its consensual nature was irrelevant to the enforcement of the law. Despite the universal nature of the Georgia policy, the majority opinion in this case focused on whether there was a fundamental constitutional right for a homosexual person to engage in sexual acts characterized as "sodomy." The Court did note the evolution of social values regarding homosexual behavior: in 1961, all fifty states had criminalized sodomy; by 1986, only 25 states still had such laws. Justice White, writing for the Court, emphasized that this criminalization needed to be addressed by state legislatures.

> Against this background, to claim that a right to engage in such conduct is "deeply rooted in this Nation's history and tradition" or "implicit in the concept of ordered liberty" is, at best, facetious. Nor are we inclined to take a more expansive view of our authority to discover new fundamental rights imbedded in the Due Process Clause. The Court is most vulnerable and comes nearest to illegitimacy when it deals with judge-made constitutional law having little or no cognizable roots in the language or design of the Constitution. There should be, therefore, great resistance to expand the substantive reach of those Clauses, particularly if it requires redefining the category of rights deemed to be fundamental. Otherwise, the Judiciary necessarily takes to itself further authority to govern the country without express constitutional authority. The claimed right pressed on us today falls far short of overcoming this resistance.

Because the Court found there was no fundamental right "to commit homosexual sodomy," the Georgia rule was allowed to stand. The dissenters in this case challenged the Court's characterization, instead noting that the case was about the larger right to privacy in light of the broad sweep of the law and its potential for selective enforcement.

In 1998, the state of Georgia reevaluated its own statute. In *Powell v. The State* (270 Ga. 327), the same law was challenged as a violation of the right to privacy—not as a federally protected right, but as a value that had been guaranteed through the Georgia constitution and in Georgia case law. The majority noted that the 1905 state case of *Pavesich v. New England Life Ins. Co.* (122 Ga. 1990) was the first time a state supreme court had identified the right of privacy as a protected right, inherent within guarantees of due process of law. The Georgia Supreme Court noted that their decision to find the Georgia sodomy statute unconstitutional was not based on its own "personal notions of morality," but on the fact that the law infringes on both Georgia's and the United States' constitutional standards. "While many believe that acts of sodomy, even those involving consenting adults, are morally reprehensible, this repugnance alone does not create a compelling justification for state regulation of the activity." For the dissenting opinion, the mere fact that the law had been perceived as constitutional for ninety years called into question the new discovery that this statute was now unconstitutional. Where should these types of changes occur—through the judiciary or the legislature? At the federal level or within the states themselves?

The Supreme Court returned to consider the issue initially addressed in *Bowers v. Hardwick* in 2003 in the case of *Lawrence v. Texas* (539 U.S. 558). Unlike the Georgia statute, the Texas law prohibited sodomy only with an individual of the same gender; it specifically targeted homosexual sexual behavior. The law was not challenged, like *Bowers*, under the right to privacy, but as a violation of the Equal Protection Clause of both the federal and Texas state constitutions. Because the Texas statute allowed the same behavior to be legally engaged in by heterosexual couples, it fell under the scope of equal protection, which requires that similarly situated groups be treated similarly under the law unless there is a valid reason by the state to differentiate. The Court, under the federal Equal Protection Clause of the Fourteenth Amendment, has created a series of standards to evaluate the constitutionality of challenged statutes depending on who is targeted by the legislation. For instance, legislation that distinguishes on the basis of race is given the highest degree of scrutiny by the Court; legislation based on gender is given an intermediate degree of scrutiny; and legislation distinguishing between the drivers of commercial trucks and passenger cars is given the lowest level of scrutiny. The Court has determined that features such as a history of invidious discrimination (targeted, focused discrimination based on hatred of the group) and the immutability of the groups' characteristics help determine the degree of protection provided by the Constitution.

In one earlier case, *Romer v. Evans* (517 U.S. 620, 1996), the Court had considered a Colorado constitutional amendment that had prohibited municipalities from passing local ordinances prohibiting discrimination based on sexual orientation. In this case, the Court placed sexual orientation under the weakest standard of protection under the Equal Protection Clause and still found the amendment unconstitutional because it had no rational relationship to a legitimate governmental function. In *Lawrence*, the Court overturned *Bowers v. Hardwick* as incorrectly decided and on that ground decided that the Texas statute was similarly unconstitutional. However, the Court did not determine the constitutionality of the Texas statute on the basis of an equal protection violation. This left the law interestingly situated—it was clear that the right of privacy provides some protections against laws targeting sexual orientation, but it was not clear what type of protection the Equal Protection Clause provides for gays, lesbians, bisexuals, and transgendered persons. The law continued to evolve and develop, with the states often pushing for more expansive protections than those provided by the federal government.

One example of this phenomenon is found in the Massachusetts Supreme Court decision of *Goodridge v. Department of Public Health* (440 Mass. 309, 2003). In this case, several same-sex couples sued the Massachusetts Department of Public Health because it had denied them marriage licenses on the grounds that the state does not recognize same-sex marriages as legal. The majority opinion agreed that the Massachusetts law clearly defines marriage as being between only a man and a woman. The justices did not, however, believe that the state's rationale for such a definition met the rational basis test (lowest level of scrutiny) for either the Due Process or Equal Protection Clause. Consequently, the Court decided that the Massachusetts constitutional provisions of both individual liberty and equality require that "the protections, benefits, and obligations of civil marriage" be extended to opposite-sex couples. Vermont, New Hampshire, and Connecticut also passed state laws legitimizing same-sex civil unions, and several other states provided spousal benefits to gay couples in the absence of legal unions. In anticipation of potential changes in state law, more than half of the states passed amendments to their constitutions called "Defense of Marriage" amendments. These amendments limited the legal definition of marriage as lawful only between a man and a woman. Supporters pressured federal legislators to adopt a statute of the same nature.

In 1996, the federal government did just this. The Federal Defense of Marriage Act (DOMA) was initially passed in response to *Baehr v. Miike* (852 P.2d 44, 1993), a Hawaiian Supreme Court decision that found a Hawaiian statute limiting the definition of marriage to opposite-sex couples a violation of the Hawaiian constitution's Equal Protection Clause. Although the state amended its constitution in 1998 to grant the state legislature the power to limit marriage to opposite-sex couples, which it did, the Federal Defense of Marriage Act had already passed. The federal law was designed to prevent the Equal Protection Clause and the Due Process Clause of the Fourteenth Amendment from being interpreted as forcing the federal government to expand the definition of marriage to same-sex couples (Sec. 1). It was also intended to ensure that any interpretation of the Full Faith and Credit Clause (Article IV, Sec. I) of the Constitution did not require a state that does not allow same-sex marriage to recognize such a marriage legitimized by another state (Sec. 2). Subsequently, most state courts that extended the protection of marriage to same-sex couples relied upon their own state constitutions, not the federal Constitution. Over the next twenty years, the issue maintained its prominence as states wrestled with their own definitions of marriage in referendums, statehouses, and courthouses.

In the 2013 case of *United States v. Windsor* (570 US ___) the question was raised that if the regulating and recording of marriage is traditionally reserved to the states, on what grounds could the federal government assume the power to define the parameters of the definition of marriage. This decision allowed the Supreme Court to examine the constitutionality of the federal definition of marriage as limited to a male and female under the DOMA. While the Court found that the DOMA did allow states to define marriage as they desire, the federal definition controlled over 1,000 federal statutes and innumerable regulations. The President of the United States and the Justice department decided not to defend the constitutionality of this key part of the statute and the Supreme Court in *Windsor* found in the liberty interest of the Fifth Amendment that the Court found protections of equal protection of the laws for those in legally sanctioned same-sex marriages. The Court framed this as a federalism case, noting "[t]he federal statute is invalid, for no legitimate purpose overcomes the purpose and effect to disparage and to injure those whom the State, by its marriage laws, sought to protect in personhood and dignity."

The dissenting opinions challenge this characterization of the DOMA; Chief Justice Roberts, in particular, notes that this specific federalism argument should protect the diversity of state opinions on the matter of same-sex marriage, but he noted his fear that it would not. This concern arose in part around the debate in California that reached the Supreme Court at the same time. After the California Supreme Court found that the denial of same-sex couples the right to marry violated the California Constitution, the citizens passed Proposition 8. This state referendum allowed voters to amend the state constitution to preclude same-sex marriage. Between the Supreme Court decision and Proposition 8, the state recorded many marriages and then suspended them until appeals could be heard in the federal courts. The federal courts eventually determined that Proposition 8 was not valid and same-sex marriages were constitutionally required in the state.

Similar complexities arose in the Sixth Circuit of the federal court of appeals, where state DOMA legislation prevented same-sex marriages and several federal district court judges found such barriers to violate the Fourteenth Amendment. Claims from Michigan, Kentucky, Ohio, and Tennessee were consolidated and brought before the Supreme Court in *Obergefell v. Hodges* (576 US ___, 2015). In his majority decision, Justice Kennedy emphasized that "[a]fter years of litigation, legislation, referenda, and the discussions that attended these public acts, the States are now divided on the issue of same-sex marriage."

In fact, despite the appellate court's concern that the issue should remain in the state legislatures for the time being, the majority argued that "[l]eaving the current state of affairs in place would maintain and promote instability and uncertainty." It was this point that drew one of the strongest critiques from the dissenting opinions written by the multiple author combinations of Chief Justice Roberts and Justices Scalia, Thomas, and Alito. These opinions repeatedly reinforced the notion that the federal courts' intervention "usurped" the "constitutional right" of states and citizens to define the institution of marriage. Justice Kennedy and the majority, on the other hand, emphasized that both liberty and equality interests were inherent in the question of same-sex marriage and that understandings of both concepts—as well as the institution of marriage—had evolved over time.

While the constitutional and federal definition of marriage has been resolved, questions around sexuality and rights continue. Concerns regarding enforcement of these protections, the obligation of state and local employees to obey laws they believe challenge their religious understanding, and the First Amendment rights of religious institutions to define marriage for themselves continue. Questions of the rights afforded to the transgendered population and issues of sexual identity are currently being addressed under statutory law (e.g., Title VII of the Civil Rights Act of 1964 and in Title IX), but, like many contentious issues, will be constitutionally challenged.

Racial Discrimination and Federalism

While there are numerous examples of how the federal government has tried to regulate and prohibit social evils through legislation that frequently impinges on the power of the state to govern its own citizens, there is possibly no better evidence of this than the demise of legalized racial segregation. Throughout the nation, states (and the federal government) had controlled citizens racially since the founding of the republic. Slavery codes, **miscegenation laws**, racial covenants in housing, barriers to public education access, **disenfranchisement**, and criminal codes all regulated the economic and political activity of citizens on the basis of race. However, by the 1940s many of these state legal barriers had been dismantled in most of the country. One immense exception was the Jim Crow legal segregation requirements of the southern states. In part because of the organized legal activities of the National Association for the Advancement of Colored People (NAACP), the federal courts began slowly finding these state laws in violation of the Fourteenth Amendment's Equal Protection Clause. Although the issue of racial segregation's legal justification and subsequent demise will be explored much more fully in Volume II in the discussion of equal protection, it is an important issue relevant to federalism.

NATIONAL LEAGUE OF CITIES ET AL. V. USERY, SECRETARY OF LABOR

426 U.S. 833, 96 S. Ct. 2465, 49 L. Ed. 2d 245 (1976)

The Fair Labor Standards Act of 1938 (FLSA) [52 Stat. 1060, 29 U.S.C. § 201] required employers to pay a minimum wage and standardized overtime to their employees and explicitly excluded states and municipalities from the coverage of the FLSA. In 1974, Congress amended the Act to apply to the states and their political subdivisions. The petitioners claim that public employees of states and localities are beyond the scope of the congressional power to regulate the treatment of employees in the private sector under the Commerce Clause (Art. I, § 8, ¶ 3) and that the 1974 amendments were thereby unconstitutional.

Vote: 5–4

JUSTICE REHNQUIST delivered the opinion of the Court.

II

This Court has never doubted that there are limits upon the power of Congress to override state sovereignty, even when exercising its otherwise plenary powers to tax or to regulate commerce which are conferred by Art. I of the Constitution. . . .

One undoubted attribute of state sovereignty is the States' power to determine the wages which shall be paid to those whom they employ in order to carry out their governmental functions, what hours those persons will work, and what compensation will be provided where these employees may be called upon to work overtime. The question we must resolve here, then, is whether these determinations are "functions essential to separate and independent existence," quoting from *Lane County v. Oregon*, [7 Wall. 71 (1869)] at 76, so that Congress may not abrogate the States' otherwise plenary authority to make them.

In their complaint appellants advanced estimates of substantial costs which will be imposed upon them by the 1974 amendments.

Judged solely in terms of increased costs in dollars, these allegations show a significant impact on the functioning of the governmental bodies involved. The Metropolitan Government of Nashville and Davidson County, Tenn., for example, asserted that the Act will increase its costs of providing essential police and fire protection, without any increase in service or in current salary levels, by $938,000 per year. Cape Girardeau, Mo., estimated that its annual budget for fire protection may have to be increased by anywhere from $250,000 to $400,000 over the current figure of $350,000. The State of Arizona alleged that the annual additional expenditures which will be required if it is to continue to provide essential state services may total $2.5 million. The State of California, which must devote significant portions of its budget to fire-suppression endeavors, estimated that application of the Act to its employment practices will necessitate an increase in its budget of between $8 million and $16 million.

Increased costs are not, of course, the only adverse effects which compliance with the Act will visit upon state and local governments, and in turn upon the citizens who depend upon those governments. In its complaint in intervention, for example, California asserted that it could not comply with the overtime costs (approximately $750,000 per year) which the Act required to be paid to California Highway Patrol cadets during their academy training program. California reported that it had thus been forced to reduce its academy training program from 2,080 hours to only 960 hours, a compromise undoubtedly of substantial importance to those whose safety and welfare may depend upon the preparedness of the California Highway Patrol.

Quite apart from the substantial costs imposed upon the States and their political subdivisions, the Act displaces state policies regarding the manner in which they will structure delivery of those governmental services which their citizens require. The Act, speaking directly to the States qua States, requires that they shall pay all but an extremely limited minority of their employees the minimum wage rates currently chosen by Congress. It may well be that as a matter of economic policy it would be desirable that States, just as private employers, comply with these minimum wage requirements. But it cannot be gainsaid that the federal requirement directly supplants the considered policy choices of the States' elected officials and administrators as to how they wish to structure pay scales in state employment. The State might wish to employ persons with little or no training, or those who wish to work on a casual basis, or those who for some other reason do not possess minimum employment requirements, and pay them less than the federally prescribed minimum wage. It may wish to offer part-time or summer employment to teenagers at a figure less than the minimum wage, and if unable to do so may decline to offer such employment at all. But the Act would forbid such choices by the States. The only "discretion" left to them under the Act is either to attempt to increase their revenue to meet the additional financial burden imposed upon them by paying congressionally prescribed wages to their existing complement of employees, or to reduce that complement to a number which can be paid the federal minimum wage without increasing revenue.

The degree to which the [Fair Labor Standards Act (FLSA)] amendments would interfere with traditional aspects of state sovereignty can be seen even more clearly upon examining the overtime requirements of the Act. The general effect of these provisions is to require the States to pay their employees at premium rates whenever their work exceeds a specified number of hours in a given period. The asserted reason for these provisions is to provide a financial disincentive upon using employees beyond the work period deemed appropriate by Congress.

We do not doubt that this may be a salutary result, and that it has a sufficiently rational relationship to commerce to validate the application of the overtime provisions to private employers. But, like the minimum wage provisions, the vice of the Act as sought to be applied here is that it directly penalizes the States for choosing to hire governmental employees on terms different from those which Congress has sought to impose.

This congressionally imposed displacement of state decisions may substantially restructure traditional ways in which the local governments have arranged their affairs.

Our examination of the effect of the 1974 amendments, as sought to be extended to the States and their political subdivisions, satisfies us that both the minimum wage and the maximum hour provisions will impermissibly interfere with the integral governmental functions of these bodies. We . . . noted some disagreement between the parties regarding the precise effect the amendments will have in application. We do not believe particularized assessments of actual impact are crucial to resolution of the issue presented, however. For even if we accept [Congress's] assessments concerning the impact of the amendments, their application will nonetheless significantly alter or displace the States' abilities to structure employer-employee relationships in such areas as fire prevention, police protection, sanitation, public health, and parks and recreation. These activities are typical of those performed by state and local governments in discharging their dual functions of administering the public law and furnishing public services. Indeed, it is functions such as these which governments are created to provide, services such as these which the States have traditionally afforded their citizens. If Congress may withdraw from the States the authority to make those fundamental employment decisions upon which their systems for performance of these functions must rest, we think there would be little left of the States' "separate and independent existence." *Coyle* [*v. Oklahoma*], 221 U.S. [559 (1911)], at 580. Thus, even if appellants may have overestimated the effect which the Act will have upon their current levels and patterns of governmental activity, the dispositive factor is that Congress has attempted to exercise its Commerce Clause authority to prescribe minimum wages and maximum hours to be paid by the States in their capacities as sovereign governments. In so doing, Congress has sought to wield its power in a fashion that would impair the States' "ability to function effectively in a federal system," *Fry v. United States*, 421 U.S. 542 (1975)] at 547 n. 7. This exercise of congressional authority does not comport with the federal system of government embodied in the Constitution. We hold that insofar as the challenged amendments operate to directly displace the States' freedom to structure integral operations in areas of traditional governmental functions, they are not within the authority granted Congress by Art. I, § 8, cl. 3.

JUSTICE BLACKMUN concurring.

The Court's opinion and the dissents indicate the importance and significance of this litigation as it bears upon the relationship between the Federal Government and our States. Although I am not untroubled by certain possible implications of the Court's opinion—some of them suggested by the dissents—I do not read the opinion so despairingly as does my Brother Brennan. In my view, the result with respect to the statute under challenge here is necessarily correct. I may misinterpret the Court's opinion, but it seems to me that it adopts a balancing approach, and does not outlaw federal power in areas such as environmental protection, where the federal interest is demonstrably greater and where state facility compliance with imposed federal standards would be essential. With this understanding on my part of the Court's opinion, I join it.

JUSTICE BRENNAN, with whom JUSTICES WHITE and MARSHALL join, dissenting.

The Court concedes, as of course it must, that Congress enacted the 1974 amendments pursuant to its exclusive power under Art. I, § 8, cl. 3, of the Constitution "[t]o regulate Commerce... among the several States." It must therefore be surprising that my Brethren should choose this bicentennial year of our independence to repudiate principles governing judicial interpretation of our Constitution settled since the time of Mr. Chief Justice John Marshall, discarding his postulate that the Constitution contemplates that restraints upon exercise by Congress of its plenary commerce power lie in the political process and not in the judicial process.

My Brethren thus have today manufactured an abstraction without substance, founded neither in the words of the Constitution nor on precedent. An abstraction having such profoundly pernicious consequences is not made less so by characterizing the 1974 amendments as legislation directed against the "States qua States." Of course, regulations that this Court can say are not regulations of "commerce" cannot stand, *Santa Cruz Fruit Packing Co. v. NLRB*, 303 U.S. 453, 466 (1938), and in this sense "[t]he Court has ample power to prevent . . . 'the utter destruction of the State as a sovereign political entity.' " *Maryland v. Wirtz*, 392 U.S. 183, 196 (1968). But my Brethren make no claim that the 1974 amendments are not regulations of "commerce"; rather they overrule *Wirtz* in disagreement with historic principles that *United States v. California*, reaffirmed: "[W]hile the commerce power has limits, valid general regulations of commerce do not cease to be regulations of commerce because a State is involved. If a State is engaging in economic activities that are validly regulated by the Federal Government when engaged in by private persons, the State too may be forced to conform its activities to federal regulation." *Wirtz* at 196–197. Clearly, therefore, my Brethren are also repudiating the long line of our precedents holding that a judicial finding that Congress has not unreasonably regulated a subject matter of "commerce" brings to an end the judicial role.

Today's repudiation of this unbroken line of precedents that firmly reject my Brethren's ill-conceived abstraction can only be regarded as a transparent cover for invalidating a congressional judgment with which they disagree. The only analysis even remotely resembling that adopted today is found in a line of opinions dealing with the Commerce Clause and the Tenth Amendment that ultimately provoked a constitutional crisis for the Court in the 1930's. E.g., *Carter v. Carter Coal Co.*, 298 U.S. 238 (1936); *United States v. Butler*, 297 U.S. 1 (1936); *Hammer v. Dagenhart*, 247 U.S. 251 (1918). We tend to forget that the Court invalidated legislation during the Great Depression, not solely under the Due Process Clause, but also and primarily under the Commerce Clause and the Tenth Amendment.

Today's holding patently is in derogation of the sovereign power of the Nation to regulate interstate commerce. Can the States engage in businesses competing with the private sector and then come to the courts arguing that withdrawing the employees of those businesses from the private sector evades the power of the Federal Government to regulate commerce? No principle given meaningful content by my Brethren today precludes the States from doing just that.

It is unacceptable that the judicial process should be thought superior to the political process in this area. Under the Constitution the Judiciary has no role to play beyond finding that Congress has not made an unreasonable legislative judgment respecting what is "commerce." My Brother Blackmun suggests that controlling judicial supervision of the relationship between the States and our National Government by use of a balancing approach diminishes the ominous implications of today's decision. Such an approach, however, is a thinly veiled rationalization for judicial supervision of a policy judgment that our system of government reserves to Congress.

Judicial restraint in this area merely recognizes that the political branches of our Government are structured to protect the interests of the States, as well as the Nation as a whole, and that the States are fully able to protect their own interests in the premises. Congress is constituted of representatives in both the Senate and House elected from the States. Decisions upon the extent of federal intervention under the Commerce Clause into the affairs of the States are in that sense decisions of the States themselves. Judicial redistribution of powers granted the National Government by the terms of the Constitution violates the fundamental tenet of our federalism that the extent of federal intervention into the States' affairs in the exercise of delegated powers shall be determined by States' exercise of political power through their representatives in Congress. There is no reason whatever to suppose that in enacting the 1974 amendments Congress, even if it might extensively obliterate state sovereignty by fully exercising its plenary power respecting commerce, had any purpose to do so. Surely the presumption must be to the contrary.

We are left then with a catastrophic judicial body blow at Congress' power under the Commerce Clause. Even if Congress may nevertheless accomplish its objectives—for example, by conditioning grants of federal funds upon compliance with federal minimum wage and overtime standards—there is an ominous portent of disruption of our constitutional structure implicit in today's mischievous decision. I dissent.

JUSTICE STEVENS, dissenting.

The Court holds that the Federal Government may not interfere with a sovereign State's inherent right to pay a substandard wage to the janitor at the state capitol. The principle on which the holding rests is difficult to perceive.

The Federal Government may, I believe, require the State to act impartially when it hires or fires the janitor, to withhold taxes from his paycheck, to observe safety regulations when he is performing his job, to forbid him from burning too much soft coal in the capitol furnace, from dumping untreated refuse in an adjacent waterway, from overloading a state-owned garbage truck, or from driving either the truck or the Governor's limousine over 55 miles an hour. Even though these and many other activities of the capitol janitor are activities of the State qua State, I have no doubt that they are subject to federal regulation.

I agree that it is unwise for the Federal Government to exercise its power in the ways described in the Court's opinion. For the proposition that regulation of the minimum price of a commodity—even labor—will increase the quantity consumed is not one that I can readily understand. That concern, however, applies with even greater force to the private sector of the economy where the exclusion of the marginally employable does the greatest harm and, in all events, merely reflects my views on a policy issue which has been firmly resolved by the branches of government having power to decide such questions. As far as the complexities of adjusting police and fire departments to this sort of federal control are concerned, I presume that appropriate tailor-made regulations would soon solve their most pressing problems. After all, the interests adversely affected by this legislation are not without political power.

My disagreement with the wisdom of this legislation may not, of course, affect my judgment with respect to its validity. On this issue there is no dissent from the proposition that the Federal Government's power over the labor market is adequate to embrace these employees. Since I am unable to identify a limitation on that federal power that would not also invalidate federal regulation of state activities that I consider unquestionably permissible, I am persuaded that this statute is valid. Accordingly, with respect and a great deal of sympathy for the views expressed by the Court, I dissent from its constitutional holding.

FOR DISCUSSION

How is the Court attempting to balance the interests and obligations of both state and national governments, as Justice Blackmun's concurrence asserts? What is the concern of the dissenters in regard to such an exercise of the sovereign power of the federal government?

RELATED CASES

***U.S. v. Darby:* 312 U.S. 100 (1941).**

Court upheld the Fair Labor Standards Act of 1938 as a legitimate exercise of legislative power under the provisions of the Commerce Clause, Art. I, § 8, ¶ 3.

***Maryland v. Wirtz:* 392 U.S. 183 (1968).**

Upheld 1961 and 1966 Amendments to the Fair Labor Standards Act of 1938 that extended coverage to persons engaged in commerce and to employees of state hospitals, institutions, and schools.

***Fry v. United States:* 421 U.S. 542 (1975).**

Court found the Economic Stabilization Act of 1970 constitutionally froze the wages of state and local government authorities. Because it was an emergency measure designed to challenge severe inflation that threatened the national economy, the degree of intrusion on state sovereignty was acceptable.

GARCIA V. SAN ANTONIO METROPOLITAN TRANSIT AUTHORITY

469 U.S. 528, 105 S. Ct. 1005, 83 L. Ed. 2d 1016 (1985)

This case revisits *National League of Cities v. Usery* (426 U.S. 833, 1976), a closely decided case in which the Supreme Court found that the Commerce Clause did not allow Congress to enforce the overtime and minimum wage protections of the Fair Labor Standards Act (FLSA) against the states and metropolitan governments in areas of traditional local government control (e.g., police and fire protection). In this case, the Court attempts to reconcile competing federal and state court decisions. The question addressed is whether the municipal ownership and operation of a mass transit system is a traditional local governmental function and thereby exempt from the requirements of the FLSA.

Vote: 5–4

JUSTICE BLACKMUN delivered the opinion of the Court.

Although *National League of Cities* supplied some examples of traditional governmental functions, it did not offer a general explanation of how a "traditional" function is to be distinguished from a "nontraditional" one. Since then, federal and state courts have struggled with the task, thus imposed, of identifying a traditional function for purposes of state immunity under the Commerce Clause.

Our examination of this "function" standard applied in these and other cases over the last eight years now persuades us that the attempt to draw the boundaries of state regulatory immunity in terms of "traditional governmental function" is not only unworkable but is also inconsistent with established principles of federalism and, indeed, with those very federalism principles on which *National League of Cities* purported to rest. That case, accordingly, is overruled.

I

The history of public transportation in San Antonio, Tex., is characteristic of the history of local mass transit in the United States generally. Passenger transportation for hire within San Antonio originally was provided on a private basis by a local transportation company. In 1913, the Texas Legislature authorized the State's municipalities to regulate vehicles providing carriage for hire. Two years later, San Antonio enacted an ordinance setting forth franchising, insurance, and safety requirements for passenger vehicles operated for hire. The city continued to rely on such publicly regulated private mass transit until 1959, when it purchased the privately owned San Antonio Transit Company and replaced it with a public authority known as the San Antonio Transit System (SATS). SATS operated until 1978, when the city transferred its facilities and equipment to appellee San Antonio Metropolitan Transit Authority (SAMTA), a public mass-transit authority organized on a countywide basis. SAMTA currently is the major provider of transportation in the San Antonio metropolitan area; between 1978 and 1980 alone, its vehicles traveled over 26 million route miles and carried over 63 million passengers.

The present controversy concerns the extent to which SAMTA may be subjected to the minimum-wage and overtime requirements of the FLSA.

II

The prerequisites for governmental immunity under *National League of Cities* were summarized by this Court in *Hodel* [*v. Virginia Surface Mining and Reclamation Association,* 452 U.S.264, 276–277 (1981)]. Under that summary, four conditions must be satisfied before a state activity may be deemed immune from a particular federal regulation under the Commerce Clause. First, it is said that the federal statute at issue must regulate "the 'States as States.' " Second, the statute must "address matters that are indisputably '[attributes] of state sovereignty.' " Third, state compliance with the federal obligation must "directly impair [the States'] ability 'to structure integral operations in areas of traditional governmental functions.' " Finally, the relation of state and federal interests must not be such that "the nature of the federal interest . . . justifies state submission."

The controversy in the present cases has focused on the third *Hodel* requirement—that the challenged federal statute trench on "traditional governmental functions." The District Court voiced a common concern: "Despite the abundance of adjectives, identifying which particular state functions are immune remains difficult." Just how troublesome the task has been is revealed by the results reached in other federal cases. Thus, courts have held that regulating ambulance services, *Gold Cross Ambulance v. City of Kansas City*, 538 F.Supp. 956, 967–969 (WD Mo. 1982); licensing automobile drivers, *United States v. Best*, 573 F.2d 1095, 1102–1103 (CA9 1978); operating a municipal airport, *Amersbach v. City of Cleveland*, 598 F.2d 1033, 1037–1038 (CA6 1979); performing solid waste disposal, *Hybud Equipment Corp. v. City of Akron*, 654 F.2d 1187, 1196 (CA6 1981); and operating a highway authority, *Molina-Estrada v. Puerto Rico Highway Authority*, 680 F.2d 841, 845–846 (CA1 1982), are functions protected under *National League of Cities*. At the same time, courts have held that issuance of industrial development bonds, *Woods v. Homes and Structures of Pittsburg, Kansas, Inc.*, 489 F.Supp. 1270, 1296–1297 (Kan. 1980); regulation of intrastate natural gas sales, *Oklahoma ex rel. Derryberry v. FERC*, 494 F.Supp. 636, 657 (WD Okla. 1980); regulation of traffic on public roads, *Friends of the Earth v. Carey*, 552 F.2d 25, 38 (CA2); regulation of air transportation, *Hughes Air Corp. v. Public Utilities Comm'n of Cal.*, 644 F.2d 1334, 1340–1341 (CA9 1981); operation of a telephone system, *Puerto Rico Tel. Co. v. FCC*, 553 F.2d 694, 700–701 (CA1 1977); leasing and sale of natural gas, *Public Service Co. of N. C. v. FERC*, 587 F.2d 716, 721 (CA5); operation of a mental health facility, *Williams v. Eastside Mental Health Center, Inc.*, 669 F.2d 671, 680–681 (CA11); and provision of in-house domestic services for the aged and handicapped, *Bonnette v. California Health and Welfare Agency*, 704 F.2d 1465, 1472 (CA9 1983), are not entitled to immunity. We find it difficult, if not impossible, to identify an organizing principle that places each of the cases in the first group on one side of a line and each of the cases in the second group on the other side. The constitutional distinction between licensing drivers and regulating traffic, for example, or between operating a highway authority and operating a mental health facility, is elusive at best.

Thus far, this Court itself has made little headway in defining the scope of the governmental functions deemed protected under *National League of Cities*. In that case the Court set forth examples of protected and unprotected functions, but provided no explanation of how those examples were identified.

We therefore now reject, as unsound in principle and unworkable in practice, a rule of state immunity from federal regulation that turns on a judicial appraisal of whether a particular governmental function is "integral" or "traditional." Any such rule leads to inconsistent results at the same time that it disserves principles of democratic self-governance, and it breeds inconsistency precisely because it is divorced from those principles. If there are to be limits on the Federal Government's power to interfere with state functions—as undoubtedly there are—we must look elsewhere to find them. We accordingly return to the underlying issue that confronted this Court in *National League of Cities*—the manner in which the Constitution insulates States from the reach of Congress' power under the Commerce Clause.

III

The central theme of *National League of Cities* was that the States occupy a special position in our constitutional system and that the scope of Congress' authority under the Commerce Clause must reflect that position. Of course, the Commerce Clause by its specific language does not provide any special limitation on Congress' actions with respect to the States. It is equally true, however, that the text of the Constitution provides the beginning rather than the final answer to every inquiry into questions of federalism, for "[behind] the words of the constitutional provisions are postulates which limit and control." *Monaco v. Mississippi*, 292 U.S. 313, 322 (1934). *National League of Cities* reflected the general conviction that the Constitution precludes "the National

Government [from] [devouring] the essentials of state sovereignty." In order to be faithful to the underlying federal premises of the Constitution, courts must look for the "postulates which limit and control."

The States unquestionably do "[retain] a significant measure of sovereign authority." *EEOC v. Wyoming*, 460 U.S. [226], at 269, [1983] (Powell, J., dissenting). They do so, however, only to the extent that the Constitution has not divested them of their original powers and transferred those powers to the Federal Government.

As a result, to say that the Constitution assumes the continued role of the States is to say little about the nature of that role. Only recently, this Court recognized that the purpose of the constitutional immunity recognized in *National League of Cities* is not to preserve "a sacred province of state autonomy." *EEOC v. Wyoming*, 460 U.S. at 236. With rare exceptions, like the guarantee, in Article IV, § 3, of state territorial integrity, the Constitution does not carve out express elements of state sovereignty that Congress may not employ its delegated powers to displace.

The effectiveness of the federal political process in preserving the States' interests is apparent even today in the course of federal legislation. On the one hand, the States have been able to direct a substantial proportion of federal revenues into their own treasuries in the form of general and program-specific grants in aid. The federal role in assisting state and local governments is a longstanding one; Congress provided federal land grants to finance state governments from the beginning of the Republic, and direct cash grants were awarded as early as 1887 under the Hatch Act. In the past quarter century alone, federal grants to States and localities have grown from $7 billion to $96 billion. As a result, federal grants now account for about one-fifth of state and local government expenditures.

We realize that changes in the structure of the Federal Government have taken place since 1789, not the least of which has been the substitution of popular election of Senators by the adoption of the Seventeenth Amendment in 1913, and that these changes may work to alter the influence of the States in the federal political process. Nonetheless, against this background, we are convinced that the fundamental limitation that the constitutional scheme imposes on the Commerce Clause to protect the "States as States" is one of process rather than one of result. Any substantive restraint on the exercise of Commerce Clause powers must find its justification in the procedural nature of this basic limitation, and it must be tailored to compensate for possible failings in the national political process rather than to dictate a "sacred province of state autonomy." *EEOC v. Wyoming*, 460 U.S., at 236.

Insofar as the present cases are concerned, then, we need go no further than to state that we perceive nothing in the overtime and minimum-wage requirements of the FLSA, as applied to SAMTA, that is destructive of state sovereignty or violative of any constitutional provision. SAMTA faces nothing more than the same minimum-wage and overtime obligations that hundreds of thousands of other employers, public as well as private, have to meet.

In these cases, the status of public mass transit simply underscores the extent to which the structural protections of the Constitution insulate the States from federally imposed burdens. . . . In short, Congress has not simply placed a financial burden on the shoulders of States and localities that operate mass-transit systems, but has provided substantial countervailing financial assistance as well, assistance that may leave individual mass-transit systems better off than they would have been had Congress never intervened at all in the area. Congress' treatment of public mass transit reinforces our conviction that the national political process systematically protects States from the risk of having their functions in that area handicapped by Commerce Clause regulation.

IV

This analysis makes clear that Congress' action in affording SAMTA employees the protections of the wage and hour provisions of the FLSA contravened no affirmative limit on Congress' power under the Commerce Clause.

. . . [T]he Court in [*National League of Cities*] attempted to articulate affirmative limits on the Commerce Clause power in terms of core governmental functions and fundamental attributes of state sovereignty. But the model of democratic decisionmaking the Court there identified underestimated, in our view, the solicitude of the national political process for the continued vitality of the States. Attempts by other courts since then to draw guidance from this model have proved it both impracticable and doctrinally barren. In sum, in *National League of Cities* the Court tried to repair what did not need repair.

We do not lightly overrule recent precedent. We have not hesitated, however, when it has become apparent that a prior decision has departed from a proper understanding of congressional power under the Commerce Clause. Due respect for the reach of congressional power within the federal system mandates that we do so now.

National League of Cities v. Usery is overruled. The judgment of the District Court is reversed, and these cases are remanded to that court for further proceedings consistent with this opinion.

JUSTICE POWELL, with whom THE CHIEF JUSTICE, and JUSTICES REHNQUIST and O'CONNOR join, dissenting.

The Court today, in its 5–4 decision, overrules *National League of Cities v. Usery*, 426 U.S. 833 (1976), a case in which we held that Congress lacked authority to impose the requirements of the Fair Labor Standards Act on state and local governments. Because I believe this decision substantially alters the federal system embodied in the Constitution, I dissent.

I

There are, of course, numerous examples over the history of this Court in which prior decisions have been reconsidered and overruled. There have been few cases, however, in which the principle of *stare decisis* and the rationale of recent decisions were ignored as abruptly as we now witness. The reasoning of the Court in *National League of Cities*, and the principle applied there, have been reiterated consistently over the past eight years. Since its decision in 1976, *National League of Cities* has been cited and quoted in opinions joined by every Member of the present Court.

Whatever effect the Court's decision may have in weakening the application of *stare decisis*, it is likely to be less important than what the Court has done to the Constitution itself. A unique feature of the United States is the federal system of government guaranteed by the Constitution and implicit in the very name of our country. Despite some genuflecting in the Court's opinion to the concept of federalism, today's decision effectively reduces the Tenth Amendment to meaningless rhetoric when Congress acts pursuant to the Commerce Clause.

II

The Court apparently thinks that the States' success at obtaining federal funds for various projects and exemptions from the obligations of some federal statutes is indicative of the "effectiveness of the federal political process in preserving the States' interests. . . ." But such political success is not relevant to the question whether the political processes are the proper means of enforcing constitutional limitations. The fact that Congress generally does not transgress constitutional limits on its power to reach state activities does not make judicial review any less necessary to rectify the cases in which it does do so. The States' role in our system of government is a matter of constitutional law, not of legislative grace. "The powers not delegated to the United States by the

Constitution, nor prohibited by it to the States, are reserved to the States, respectively, or to the people." U.S. Const., Amdt. 10.

More troubling than the logical infirmities in the Court's reasoning is the result of its holding, i. e., that federal political officials, invoking the Commerce Clause, are the sole judges of the limits of their own power. This result is inconsistent with the fundamental principles of our constitutional system. At least since *Marbury v. Madison*, 1 Cranch 137, 177 (1803), it has been the settled province of the federal judiciary "to say what the law is" with respect to the constitutionality of Acts of Congress. In rejecting the role of the judiciary in protecting the States from federal overreaching, the Court's opinion offers no explanation for ignoring the teaching of the most famous case in our history. . . .

V

As I view the Court's decision today as rejecting the basic precepts of our federal system and limiting the constitutional role of judicial review, I dissent.

JUSTICE O'CONNOR, with whom JUSTICES POWELL and REHNQUIST join, dissenting.

The Court overrules *National League of Cities v. Usery*, 426 U.S. 833 (1976), on the grounds that it is not "faithful to the role of federalism in a democratic society." "The essence of our federal system," the Court concludes, "is that within the realm of authority left open to them under the Constitution, the States must be equally free to engage in any activity that their citizens choose for the common weal. . . ." *National League of Cities* is held to be inconsistent with this narrow view of federalism because it attempts to protect only those fundamental aspects of state sovereignty that are essential to the States' separate and independent existence, rather than protecting all state activities "equally."

Due to the emergence of an integrated and industrialized national economy, this Court has been required to examine and review a breathtaking expansion of the powers of Congress. In doing so the Court correctly perceived that the Framers of our Constitution intended Congress to have sufficient power to address national problems. But the Framers were not single-minded. The Constitution is animated by an array of intentions. Just as surely as the Framers envisioned a National Government capable of solving national problems, they also envisioned a republic whose vitality was assured by the diffusion of power not only among the branches of the Federal Government, but also between the Federal Government and the States. In the 18th century these intentions did not conflict because technology had not yet converted every local problem into a national one. A conflict has now emerged, and the Court today retreats rather than reconcile the Constitution's dual concerns for federalism and an effective commerce power.

Incidental to this expansion of the commerce power, Congress has been given an ability it lacked prior to the emergence of an integrated national economy. Because virtually every state activity, like virtually every activity of a private individual, arguably "affects" interstate commerce, Congress can now supplant the States from the significant sphere of activities envisioned for them by the Framers. It is in this context that recent changes in the workings of Congress, such as the direct election of Senators and the expanded influence of national interest groups become relevant. These changes may well have lessened the weight Congress gives to the legitimate interests of States as States. As a result, there is now a real risk that Congress will gradually erase the diffusion of power between State and Nation on which the Framers based their faith in the efficiency and vitality of our Republic.

It would be erroneous, however, to conclude that the Supreme Court was blind to the threat to federalism when it expanded the commerce power. The Court based the expansion on the authority of Congress, through the Necessary and Proper Clause, "to resort to all means for the exercise of a granted power which are appropriate and plainly adapted to the permitted end." *United States v. Darby*, [312 U.S. 100 (1941)], at 124. It is through this reasoning that an intrastate activity "affecting" interstate commerce can be reached through the commerce power.

It is worth recalling the cited passage in *McCulloch v. Maryland*, 4 Wheat. 316, 421 (1819), that lies at the source of the recent expansion of the commerce power. "Let the end be legitimate, let it be within the scope of the constitution," Chief Justice Marshall said, "and all means which are appropriate, which are plainly adapted to that end, which are not prohibited, but consist with the letter and spirit of the constitution, are constitutional." The spirit of the Tenth Amendment, of course, is that the States will retain their integrity in a system in which the laws of the United States are nevertheless supreme.

It is not enough that the "end be legitimate"; the means to that end chosen by Congress must not contravene the spirit of the Constitution. Thus many of this Court's decisions acknowledge that the means by which national power is exercised must take into account concerns for state autonomy.

This principle requires the Court to enforce affirmative limits on federal regulation of the States to complement the judicially crafted expansion of the interstate commerce power. *National League of Cities v. Usery* represented an attempt to define such limits. The Court today rejects *National League of Cities* and washes its hands of all efforts to protect the States. In the process, the Court opines that unwarranted federal encroachments on state authority are and will remain "horrible possibilities that never happen in the real world." There is ample reason to believe to the contrary.

The problems of federalism in an integrated national economy are capable of more responsible resolution than holding that the States as States retain no status apart from that which Congress chooses to let them retain. The proper resolution, I suggest, lies in weighing state autonomy as a factor in the balance when interpreting the means by which Congress can exercise its authority on the States as States. It is insufficient, in assessing the validity of congressional regulation of a State pursuant to the commerce power, to ask only whether the same regulation would be valid if enforced against a private party. That reasoning, embodied in the majority opinion, is inconsistent with the spirit of our Constitution. It remains relevant that a State is being regulated, as *National League of Cities* and every recent case have recognized.

Instead, the autonomy of a State is an essential component of federalism. If state autonomy is ignored in assessing the means by which Congress regulates matters affecting commerce, then federalism becomes irrelevant simply because the set of activities remaining beyond the reach of such a commerce power "may well be negligible."

It has been difficult for this Court to craft bright lines defining the scope of the state autonomy protected by *National League of Cities*. Such difficulty is to be expected whenever constitutional concerns as important as federalism and the effectiveness of the commerce power come into conflict. Regardless of the difficulty, it is and will remain the duty of this Court to reconcile these concerns in the final instance. That the Court shuns the task today by appealing to the "essence of federalism" can provide scant comfort to those who believe our federal system requires something more than a unitary, centralized government. I would not shirk the duty acknowledged by *National League of Cities* and its progeny, and I share Justice Rehnquist's belief that this Court will in time again assume its constitutional responsibility.

FOR DISCUSSION

What is the justification given by the majority for overturning a precedent of less than a decade? When should members of the Supreme Court choose to overrule themselves? Did this majority decision merely adapt the reasoning of the dissenters in *National League of Cities*, or were other factors relevant?

RELATED CASES

***EEOC v. Wyoming:* 460 U.S. 226 (1983).**

The Court held that the federal Age Discrimination in Employment Act of 1967 was applicable to situations in which the states were employers.

***Gregory v. Ashcroft:* 501 U.S. 452 (1991).**

The Supreme Court found that the constitutional requirement for mandatory retirement at age seventy for Missouri state judges did not violate the Age Discrimination in Employment Act of 1967 because the ADEA does not apply to state "policymaking appointees" such as state judges.

U.S. TERM LIMITS V. THORNTON

514 U.S. 779, 115 S. Ct. 1842, 131 L. Ed. 2d 881 (1995)

In November 1992, the citizens of Arkansas passed Amendment 73, which altered their state constitution to limit congressional representatives to three terms in office and senators to two terms. The Arkansas Supreme Court held that this amendment violated the federal Constitution by creating state qualifications for federal office in addition to those already articulated in the Qualifications Clauses of the Constitution (Article I, § 2, ¶ 2; Article I, § 3, ¶ 3).

Vote: 5–4

JUSTICE STEVENS delivered the opinion of the Court.

II

Twenty-six years ago, in *Powell v. McCormack*, 395 U.S. 486 (1969), we reviewed the history and text of the Qualifications Clauses in a case involving an attempted exclusion of a duly elected Member of Congress. The principal issue was whether the power granted to each House in Art. I, § 5, cl. 1, to judge the "Qualifications of its own Members" includes the power to impose qualifications other than those set forth in the text of the Constitution. In an opinion by Chief Justice Warren for eight Members of the Court, we held that it does not.

The Issue in Powell

In November 1966, Adam Clayton Powell, Jr. was elected from a District in New York to serve in the United States House of Representatives for the 90th Congress. Allegations that he had engaged in serious misconduct while serving as a committee chairman during the 89th Congress led to the appointment of a Select Committee to determine his eligibility to take his seat. That committee found that Powell met the age, citizenship, and residency requirements set forth in Art. I, § 2, cl. 2. The committee also found, however, that Powell had wrongfully diverted House funds for the use of others and himself and had made false reports on expenditures of foreign currency. Based on those findings, the House after debate adopted House Resolution 278, excluding Powell from membership in the House, and declared his seat vacant.

Powell and several voters of the district from which he had been elected filed suit seeking a declaratory judgment that the House Resolution was invalid because Art. I, § 2, cl. 2, sets forth the exclusive qualifications for House membership. We ultimately accepted that contention, concluding that the House of Representatives has no "authority to exclude any person, duly elected by his constituents, who meets all the requirements for membership expressly prescribed in the Constitution." In reaching that conclusion, we undertook a detailed historical review to determine the intent of the Framers. Though recognizing that the Constitutional Convention debates themselves were inconclusive, we determined that the "relevant historical materials" reveal that Congress has no power to alter the qualifications in the text of the Constitution.

Powell's *Reliance on Democratic Principles*

In *Powell*, of course, we did not rely solely on an analysis of the historical evidence, but instead complemented that analysis with "an examination of the basic principles of our democratic system." We noted that allowing Congress to impose additional qualifications would violate that "fundamental principle of our representative democracy . . . 'that the people should choose whom they please to govern them.' "

Our opinion made clear that this broad principle incorporated at least two fundamental ideas. First, we emphasized the egalitarian concept that the opportunity to be elected was open to all.

Second, we recognized the critical postulate that sovereignty is vested in the people, and that sovereignty confers on the people the right to choose freely their representatives to the National Government.

Powell thus establishes two important propositions: first, that the "relevant historical materials" compel the conclusion that, at least with respect to qualifications imposed by Congress, the Framers intended the qualifications listed in the Constitution to be exclusive; and second, that that conclusion is equally compelled by an understanding of the "fundamental principle of our representative democracy . . . 'that the people should choose whom they please to govern them.' "

III

Our reaffirmation of *Powell* does not necessarily resolve the specific questions presented in these cases. For petitioners argue that whatever the constitutionality of additional qualifications for membership imposed by Congress, the historical and textual materials discussed in *Powell* do not support the conclusion that the Constitution prohibits additional qualifications imposed by States. In the absence of such a constitutional prohibition, petitioners argue, the Tenth Amendment and the principle of reserved powers require that States be allowed to add such qualifications.

Before addressing these arguments, we find it appropriate to take note of the striking unanimity among the courts that have considered the issue. None of the overwhelming array of briefs submitted by the parties and *amici* has called to our attention even a single case in which a state court or federal court has approved of a State's addition of qualifications for a Member of Congress. To the contrary, an impressive number of courts have determined that States lack the authority to add qualifications.

Petitioners argue that the Constitution contains no express prohibition against state-added qualifications, and that Amendment 73 is therefore an appropriate exercise of a State's reserved power to place additional restrictions on the choices that its own voters may make. We disagree for two independent reasons. First, we conclude that the power to add qualifications is not within the "original powers" of the States, and thus is not reserved to the States by the Tenth Amendment. Second, even if States possessed some original power in this area, we conclude that the Framers intended the Constitution to be the exclusive source of qualifications for Members of Congress, and that the Framers thereby "divested" States of any power to add qualifications.

Source of the Power

Contrary to petitioners' assertions, the power to add qualifications is not part of the original powers of sovereignty that the Tenth Amendment reserved to the States. Petitioners' Tenth Amendment argument misconceives the nature of the right at issue because that Amendment could only "reserve" that which existed before.

In short, as the Framers recognized, electing representatives to the National Legislature was a new right, arising from the Constitution itself. The Tenth Amendment thus provides no basis for concluding that the States possess reserved power to add qualifications to those that are fixed in the Constitution. Instead, any state power to set the qualifications for membership in Congress must derive not from the reserved powers of state sovereignty, but rather from the delegated powers of national sovereignty. In the absence of any constitutional delegation to the States of power to add qualifications to those enumerated in the Constitution, such a power does not exist.

The Preclusion of State Power

Even if we believed that States possessed as part of their original powers some control over congressional qualifications, the text and structure of the Constitution, the relevant historical materials, and, most importantly, the "basic principles of our democratic system" all demonstrate that the Qualifications Clauses were intended to preclude the States from exercising any such power and to fix as exclusive the qualifications in the Constitution.

Democratic Principles

Permitting individual States to formulate diverse qualifications for their representatives would result in a patchwork of state qualifications, undermining the uniformity and the national character that the Framers envisioned and sought to ensure. Such a patchwork would also sever the direct link that the Framers found so critical between the National Government and the people of the United States.

V

The merits of term limits, or "rotation," have been the subject of debate since the formation of our Constitution, when the Framers unanimously rejected a proposal to add such limits to the Constitution. The cogent arguments on both sides of the question that were articulated during the process of ratification largely retain their force today. Over half the States have adopted measures that impose such limits on some offices either directly or indirectly, and the Nation as a whole, notably by constitutional amendment, has imposed a limit on the number of terms that the President may serve. Term limits, like any other qualification for office, unquestionably restrict the ability of voters to vote for whom they wish. On the other hand, such limits may provide for the infusion of fresh ideas and new perspectives, and may decrease the likelihood that representatives will lose touch with their constituents. It is not our province to resolve this longstanding debate.

We are, however, firmly convinced that allowing the several States to adopt term limits for congressional service would effect a fundamental change in the constitutional framework. Any such change must come not by legislation adopted either by Congress or by an individual State, but rather—as have other important changes in the electoral process—through the amendment procedures set forth in Article V. The Framers decided that the qualifications for service in the Congress of the United States be fixed in the Constitution and be uniform throughout the Nation. That decision reflects the Framers' understanding that Members of Congress are chosen by separate constituencies, but that they become, when elected, servants of the people of the United States. They are not merely delegates appointed by separate, sovereign States; they occupy offices that are integral and essential components of a single National Government. In the absence of a properly passed constitutional amendment, allowing individual States to craft their own qualifications for Congress would thus erode the structure envisioned by the Framers, a structure that was designed, in the words of the Preamble to our Constitution, to form a "more perfect Union."

The judgment is affirmed.

JUSTICE KENNEDY, concurring.

The majority and dissenting opinions demonstrate the intricacy of the question whether or not the Qualifications Clauses are exclusive. In my view, however, it is well settled that the whole people of the United States asserted their political identity and unity of purpose when they created the federal system. The dissent's course of reasoning suggesting otherwise might be construed to disparage the republican character of the National Government, and it seems appropriate to add these few remarks to explain why that course of argumentation runs counter to fundamental principles of federalism.

It is maintained by our dissenting colleagues that the State of Arkansas seeks nothing more than to grant its people surer control over the National Government, a control, it is said, that will be enhanced by the law at issue here. The arguments for term limitations (or ballot restrictions having the same effect) are not lacking in force; but the issue, as all of us must acknowledge, is not the efficacy of those measures but whether they have a legitimate source, given their origin in the enactments of a single State. There can be no doubt, if we are to respect the republican origins of the Nation and preserve its federal character, that there exists a federal right of citizenship, a relationship between the people of the Nation and their National Government, with which the States may not interfere. Because the Arkansas enactment intrudes upon this federal domain, it exceeds the boundaries of the Constitution.

JUSTICE THOMAS, with whom THE CHIEF JUSTICE, and JUSTICES O'CONNOR and SCALIA join, dissenting.

It is ironic that the Court bases today's decision on the right of the people to "choose whom they please to govern them." Under our Constitution, there is only one State whose people have the right to "choose whom they please" to represent Arkansas in Congress. The Court holds, however, that neither the elected legislature of that State nor the people themselves (acting by ballot initiative) may prescribe any qualifications for those representatives. The majority therefore defends the right of the people of Arkansas to "choose whom they please to govern them" by invalidating a provision that won nearly 60% of the votes cast in a direct election and that carried every congressional district in the State.

I dissent. Nothing in the Constitution deprives the people of each State of the power to prescribe eligibility requirements for the candidates who seek to represent them in Congress. The Constitution is simply silent on this question. And where the Constitution is silent, it raises no bar to action by the States or the people.

I

A

Our system of government rests on one overriding principle: All power stems from the consent of the people. To phrase the principle in this way, however, is to be imprecise about something important to the notion of "reserved" powers. The ultimate source of the Constitution's authority is the consent of the people of each individual State, not the consent of the undifferentiated people of the Nation as a whole.

When they adopted the Federal Constitution, of course, the people of each State surrendered some of their authority to the United States (and hence to entities accountable to the people of other States as well as to themselves). They affirmatively deprived their States of certain powers, see, e. g., Art. I, § 10, and they affirmatively conferred certain powers upon the Federal Government, see, e. g., Art. I, § 8. Because the people of the several States are the only true source of power, however, the Federal Government enjoys no authority beyond what the Constitution confers: The Federal Government's powers are limited and enumerated.

In each State, the remainder of the people's powers—"the powers not delegated to the United States by the Constitution, nor prohibited by it to the States," Amdt. 10—are either delegated to the state government or retained by the people. The Federal Constitution does not specify which of these two possibilities obtains; it is up to the various state constitutions to declare which powers the people of each State have delegated to their state government. As far as the Federal Constitution is concerned, then, the States can exercise all powers that the Constitution does not withhold from them. The Federal Government and the States thus face different default rules: Where the Constitution is silent about the exercise of a particular power—that is, where the Constitution does not speak either expressly or by necessary implication—the Federal Government lacks that power and the States enjoy it.

These basic principles are enshrined in the Tenth Amendment, which declares that all powers neither delegated to the Federal Government nor prohibited to the States "are reserved to the States respectively, or to the people." With this careful last phrase, the Amendment avoids taking any position on the division of power between the state governments and the people of the States: It is up to the people of each State to determine which "reserved" powers their state government may exercise. But the Amendment does make clear that powers reside at the state level except where the Constitution removes them from that level. All powers that the Constitution neither delegates to the Federal Government nor prohibits to the States are controlled by the people of each State.

. . . If we are to invalidate Arkansas' Amendment 73, we must point to something in the Federal Constitution that deprives the people of Arkansas of the power to enact such measures.

II

The majority settles on "the Qualifications Clauses" as the constitutional provisions that Amendment 73 violates. Because I do not read those provisions to impose any unstated prohibitions on the States, it is unnecessary for me to decide whether the majority is correct to identify Arkansas' ballot-access restriction with laws fixing true term limits or otherwise prescribing "qualifications" for congressional office. . . . [T]he Qualifications Clauses are merely straightforward recitations of the minimum eligibility requirements that the Framers thought it essential for every Member of Congress to meet. They restrict state power only in that they prevent the States from abolishing all eligibility requirements for membership in Congress.

III

It is radical enough for the majority to hold that the Constitution implicitly precludes the people of the States from prescribing any eligibility requirements for the congressional candidates who seek their votes. This holding, after all, does not stop with negating the term limits that many States have seen fit to impose on their Senators and Representatives. Today's decision also means that no State may disqualify congressional candidates whom a court has found to be mentally incompetent, who are currently in prison, or who have past vote-fraud convictions. Likewise, after today's decision, the people of each State must leave open the possibility that they will trust someone with their vote in Congress even though they do not trust him with a vote in the election for Congress.

FOR DISCUSSION

Why might term limitations for members of Congress "effect a fundamental change in the constitutional framework," as the majority claims? Do you agree with Justice Kennedy in his concurring opinion when he states: "There can be no doubt, if we are to respect the republican origins of the Nation and preserve its federal character, that there exists a federal right of citizenship, a relationship between the people of the Nation and their National Government, with which the States may not interfere?"

RELATED CASES

***Powell v. McCormack:* 395 U.S. 486 (1969).**

Determined the Qualification Clauses precluded the legislature from refusing to seat a duly elected member of the House of Representatives because the House had previously found evidence of ethics violation.

***Storer v. Brown:* 415 U.S. 724 (1974).**

Upheld provisions of the California Elections Code that regulated procedures by which candidates could be placed on the ballot in general elections against a challenge under the Qualifications Clause.

SEMINOLE TRIBE OF FLORIDA V. FLORIDA

517 U.S. 44, 116 S. Ct. 1114, 134 L. Ed. 2d 252 (1996)

The Indian Gaming Regulatory Act of 1988 [102 Stat. 2475, 25 U.S.C. § 2710(a)(1)(C)] allows an Indian tribe to conduct specific gaming activities pursuant to a valid agreement between the tribe and the state within which the gaming activities will occur. This Act requires states to negotiate with the tribes to form the agreement and allows a tribe to bring federal litigation against a state in case the subsequent agreement is breached. In September of 1991, the Seminole tribe of Florida sued the state for refusing to negotiate with the tribe regarding the inclusion of gaming activities in violation of the Indian Gaming Regulatory Act. The state sought to dismiss the complaint on the grounds that the litigation violates the sovereign immunity of the state protected under the Eleventh Amendment of the Constitution. The district court denied the State's motion, and the court of appeals reversed.

Vote: 5–4

CHIEF JUSTICE REHNQUIST delivered the opinion of the Court.

I

Petitioner sought our review of the Eleventh Circuit's decision, and we granted certiorari in order to consider two questions: (1) Does the Eleventh Amendment prevent Congress from authorizing suits by Indian tribes against States for prospective injunctive relief to enforce legislation enacted pursuant to the Indian Commerce Clause?; and (2) Does the doctrine of *Ex Parte Young* [208 U.S. 123 (1908)] permit suits against a State's Governor for prospective injunctive relief to enforce the good-faith bargaining requirement of the Act? We answer the first question in the affirmative, the second in the negative, and we therefore affirm the Eleventh Circuit's dismissal of petitioner's suit.

For over a century we have reaffirmed that federal jurisdiction over suits against unconsenting States "was not contemplated by the Constitution when establishing the judicial power of the United States." *Hans* [*v. Louisiana* 134 U.S. 1 (1890)] at 15.

Here, petitioner has sued the State of Florida and it is undisputed that Florida has not consented to the suit. Petitioner nevertheless contends that its suit is not barred by state sovereign immunity. First, it argues that Congress through the Act abrogated the States' sovereign immunity. Alternatively, petitioner maintains that its suit against the Governor may go forward under *Ex parte Young.* We consider each of those arguments in turn.

II

Petitioner argues that Congress through the Act abrogated the States' immunity from suit. In order to determine whether Congress has abrogated the States' sovereign immunity, we ask two questions: first, whether Congress has "unequivocally expressed its intent to abrogate the immunity," *Green v. Mansour*, 474 U.S. 64, 68 (1985); and second, whether Congress has acted "pursuant to a valid exercise of power."

A

Congress' intent to abrogate the States' immunity from suit must be obvious from "a clear legislative statement." *Blatchford* [*v. Natwe Village of Naotak* (501 U.S. 775 (1991)] at 786. This rule arises from a recognition of the important role played by the Eleventh Amendment and the broader principles that it reflects.

Here, we agree with the parties, with the Eleventh Circuit in the decision below and with virtually every other court that has confronted the question that Congress has in § 2710(d)(7) provided an "unmistakably clear" statement of its intent to abrogate. . . . In sum, we think that the numerous references to the "State" in the text of § 2710(d)(7)(B) make it indubitable that Congress intended through the Act to abrogate the States' sovereign immunity from suit.

B

. . . [O]ur inquiry into whether Congress has the power to abrogate unilaterally the States' immunity from suit is narrowly focused on one question: Was the Act in question passed pursuant to a constitutional provision granting Congress the power to abrogate? Previously, in conducting that inquiry, we have found authority to abrogate under only two provisions of the Constitution. In *Fitzpatrick* [*v. Bitzer*, 427 U.S. 445 (1976)], we recognized that the Fourteenth Amendment, by expanding federal power at the expense of state autonomy, had fundamentally altered the balance of state and federal power struck by the Constitution. We noted that § 1 of the Fourteenth Amendment contained prohibitions expressly directed at the States and that § 5 of the Amendment expressly provided that "The Congress shall have power to enforce, by appropriate legislation, the provisions of this article." We held that through the Fourteenth Amendment, federal power extended to intrude upon the province of the Eleventh Amendment and therefore that § 5 of the Fourteenth Amendment allowed Congress to abrogate the immunity from suit guaranteed by that Amendment.

In only one other case has congressional abrogation of the States' Eleventh Amendment immunity been upheld. In *Pennsylvania v. Union Gas Co.,* 491 U.S. 1 (1989), a plurality of the Court found that the Interstate Commerce Clause, Art. I, § 8, cl. 3, granted Congress the power to abrogate state sovereign immunity, stating that the power to regulate interstate commerce would be "incomplete without the authority to render States liable in damages." 491 U.S. at 19–20.

In arguing that Congress through the Act abrogated the States' sovereign immunity, petitioner does not challenge the Eleventh Circuit's conclusion that the Act was passed pursuant to neither the Fourteenth Amendment nor the Interstate Commerce Clause. Instead, accepting the lower court's conclusion that the Act was passed pursuant to Congress' power under the Indian Commerce Clause, petitioner now asks us to consider whether that Clause grants Congress the power to abrogate the States' sovereign immunity.

Following the rationale of the *Union Gas* plurality, our inquiry is limited to determining whether the Indian Commerce Clause, like the Interstate Commerce Clause, is a grant of authority to the Federal Government at the expense of the States. The answer to that question is obvious. If anything, the Indian Commerce Clause accomplishes a greater transfer of power from the States to the Federal Government than does the Interstate Commerce Clause. This is clear enough from the fact that the States still exercise some authority over interstate trade but have been divested of virtually all authority over Indian commerce and Indian tribes. Under the rationale of *Union Gas*, if the States' partial cession of authority over a particular area includes cession of the immunity from suit, then their virtually total cession of authority over a different area must also include cession of the immunity from suit. We agree with petitioner that the plurality opinion in *Union Gas* allows no principled distinction in favor of the States to be drawn between the Indian Commerce Clause and the Interstate Commerce Clause.

The Court in *Union Gas* reached a result without an expressed rationale agreed upon by a majority of the Court. . . . Since it was issued, *Union Gas* has created confusion among the lower courts that have sought to understand and apply the deeply fractured decision.

The plurality's rationale also deviated sharply from our established federalism jurisprudence and essentially eviscerated our decision in *Hans*. It was well established in 1989 when *Union Gas* was decided that the Eleventh Amendment stood for the constitutional principle that state sovereign immunity limited the federal courts' jurisdiction under Article III.

Never before the decision in *Union Gas* had we suggested that the bounds of Article III could be expanded by Congress operating pursuant to any constitutional provision other than the Fourteenth Amendment. . . . The plurality's citation of prior decisions for support was based upon what we believe to be a misreading of precedent. The plurality claimed support for its decision from a case holding the unremarkable, and completely unrelated, proposition that the States may waive their sovereign immunity.

In the five years since it was decided, *Union Gas* has proved to be a solitary departure from established law. Reconsidering the decision in *Union Gas*, we conclude that none of the policies underlying *stare decisis* require our continuing adherence to its holding. The decision has, since its issuance, been of questionable precedential value, largely because a majority of the Court expressly disagreed with the rationale of the plurality. The case involved the interpretation of the Constitution and therefore may be altered only by constitutional amendment or revision by this Court. Finally, both the result in *Union Gas* and the plurality's rationale depart from our established understanding of the Eleventh Amendment and undermine the accepted function of Article III. We feel bound to conclude that *Union Gas* was wrongly decided and that it should be, and now is, overruled.

The dissent, to the contrary, disregards our case law in favor of a theory cobbled together from law review articles and its own version of historical events. The dissent cites not a single decision since *Hans* (other than *Union Gas*) that supports its view of state sovereign immunity, instead relying upon the now-discredited decision in *Chisholm v. Georgia*, 2 U.S. 419 (1793). Its undocumented and highly speculative extralegal explanation of the decision in *Hans* is a disservice to the Court's traditional method of adjudication.

In putting forward a new theory of state sovereign immunity, the dissent develops its own vision of the political system created by the Framers, concluding with the statement that "the Framer's principal objectives in rejecting English theories of unitary sovereignty . . . would have been impeded if a new concept of sovereign immunity had taken its place in federal-question cases, and would have been substantially thwarted if that new immunity had been held untouchable by any congressional effort to abrogate it." This sweeping statement ignores the fact that the Nation survived for nearly two centuries without the question of the existence of such power ever being presented to this Court. And Congress itself waited nearly a century before even conferring federal-question jurisdiction on the lower federal courts.

In overruling *Union Gas* today, we reconfirm that the background principle of state sovereign immunity embodied in the Eleventh Amendment is not so ephemeral as to dissipate when the subject of the suit is an area, like the regulation of Indian commerce, that is under the exclusive control of the Federal Government.

IV

The Eleventh Amendment prohibits Congress from making the State of Florida capable of being sued in federal court. The narrow exception to the Eleventh Amendment provided by the *Ex parte Young* doctrine cannot be used to enforce § 2710(d)(3) because Congress enacted a remedial scheme, § 2710(d)(7), specifically designed for the enforcement of that right. The Eleventh Circuit's dismissal of petitioner's suit is hereby affirmed.

It is so ordered.

JUSTICE STEVENS, dissenting.

This case is about power—the power of the Congress of the United States to create a private federal cause of action against a State, or its Governor, for the violation of a federal right. In *Chisholm v. Georgia*, 2 U.S. 419 (1793), the entire Court—including Justice Iredell whose dissent provided the blueprint for the Eleventh Amendment—assumed that Congress had such power. In *Hans v. Louisiana*, 134 U.S. 1 (1890)—a case the Court purports to follow today—the Court again assumed that Congress had such power. In *Fitzpatrick v. Bitzer*, 427 U.S. 445 (1976), and [Justice Steven's concurrence in] *Pennsylvania v. Union Gas Co.*, 491 U.S. 1, 24 (1989), the Court squarely held that Congress has such power. In a series of cases beginning with *Atascadero State Hospital v. Scanlon*, 473 U.S. 234, 238–239 (1985), the Court formulated a special "clear statement rule" to determine whether specific Acts of Congress contained an effective exercise of that power. Nevertheless, in a sharp break with the past, today the Court holds that with the narrow and illogical exception of statutes enacted pursuant to the Enforcement Clause of the Fourteenth Amendment, Congress has no such power.

The importance of the majority's decision to overrule the Court's holding in *Pennsylvania v. Union Gas Co.* cannot be overstated. The majority's opinion does not simply preclude Congress from establishing the rather curious statutory scheme under which Indian tribes may seek the aid of a federal court to secure a State's good-faith negotiations over gaming regulations. Rather, it prevents Congress from providing a federal forum for a broad range of actions against States, from those sounding in copyright and patent law, to those concerning bankruptcy, environmental law, and the regulation of our vast national economy.

There may be room for debate over whether, in light of the Eleventh Amendment, Congress has the power to ensure that such a cause of action may be enforced in federal court by a citizen of another State or a foreign citizen. There can be no serious debate, however, over whether Congress has the power to ensure that such a cause of action may be brought by a citizen of the State being sued. Congress' authority in that regard is clear.

IV

Given the absence of precedent for the Court's dramatic application of the sovereign immunity doctrine today, it is nevertheless appropriate to identify the questionable heritage of the doctrine and to suggest that there are valid reasons for limiting, or even rejecting that doctrine altogether, rather than expanding it.

Except insofar as it has been incorporated into the text of the Eleventh Amendment, the doctrine is entirely the product of judge-made law. Three features of its English ancestry make it particularly unsuitable for incorporation into the law of this democratic Nation.

First, the assumption that it could be supported by a belief that "the King can do no wrong" has always been absurd; the bloody path trod by English monarchs both before and after they reached the throne demonstrated the fictional character of any such assumption.

Second, centuries ago the belief that the monarch served by divine right made it appropriate to assume that redress for wrongs committed by the sovereign should be the exclusive province of still higher authority. While such a justification for a rule that immunized the sovereign from suit in a secular tribunal might have been acceptable in a jurisdiction where a particular faith is endorsed by the government, it should give rise to skepticism concerning the legitimacy of comparable rules in a society where a constitutional wall separates the State from the Church.

Third, in a society where noble birth can justify preferential treatment, it might have been unseemly to allow a commoner to hale the monarch into court.

While I am persuaded that there is no justification for permanently enshrining the judge-made law of sovereign immunity, I recognize that federalism concerns—and even the interest in protecting the solvency of the States that was at work in *Chisholm* and *Hans*—may well justify a grant of immunity from federal litigation in certain classes of cases. Such a grant, however, should be the product of a reasoned decision by the policymaking branch of our Government. For this Court to conclude that timeworn shibboleths iterated and reiterated by judges should take precedence over the deliberations of the Congress of the United States is simply irresponsible.

JUSTICE SOUTER, with whom JUSTICES GINSBURG and BREYER join, dissenting.

In holding the State of Florida immune to suit under the Indian Gaming Regulatory Act, the Court today holds for the first time since the founding of the Republic that Congress has no authority to subject a State to the jurisdiction of a federal court at the behest of an individual asserting a federal right. Although the Court invokes the Eleventh Amendment as authority for this proposition, the only sense in which that amendment might be claimed as pertinent here was tolerantly phrased by Justice Stevens in his concurring opinion in *Pennsylvania v. Union Gas Co.,* 491 U.S. 1, 23 (1989). There, he explained how it has come about that we have two Eleventh Amendments, the one ratified in 1795, the other (so-called) invented by the Court nearly a century later in *Hans v. Louisiana*, 134 U.S. 1 (1890). Justice Stevens saw in that second Eleventh Amendment no bar to the exercise of congressional authority under the Commerce Clause in providing for suits on a federal question by individuals against a State, and I can only say that after my own canvass of the matter I believe he was entirely correct in that view, for reasons given below. His position, of course, was also the holding in *Union Gas*, which the Court now overrules and repudiates.

The fault I find with the majority today is not in its decision to reexamine *Union Gas*, for the Court in that case produced no majority for a single rationale supporting congressional authority. Instead, I part company from the Court because I am convinced that its decision is fundamentally mistaken, and for that reason I respectfully dissent.

I

A

The doctrine of sovereign immunity comprises two distinct rules, which are not always separately recognized. The one rule holds that the King or the Crown, as the font of law, is not bound by the law's provisions; the other provides that the King or Crown, as the font of justice, is not subject to suit in its own courts. The one rule limits the reach of substantive law; the other, the jurisdiction of the courts. We are concerned here only with the latter rule, which took its common-law form in the high Middle Ages.

B

The argument among the Framers and their friends about sovereign immunity in federal citizen-state diversity cases . . . was short lived and ended when this Court, in *Chisholm v. Georgia*, 2 U.S. 419 (1793), chose between the constitutional alternatives of abrogation and recognition of the immunity enjoyed at common law. The 4-to-1 majority adopted the reasonable (although not compelled) interpretation that the first of the two Citizen-State Diversity Clauses abrogated for purposes of federal jurisdiction any immunity the States might have enjoyed in their own courts, and Georgia was accordingly held subject to the judicial power in a common-law assumpsit action by a South Carolina citizen suing to collect a debt. The case also settled, by implication, any question there could possibly have been about recognizing state sovereign immunity in actions depending on the federal question (or "arising under") head of jurisdiction as well.

C

The Eleventh Amendment, of course, repudiated *Chisholm* and clearly divested federal courts of some jurisdiction as to cases against state parties[.]

The history and structure of the Eleventh Amendment convincingly show that it reaches only to suits subject to federal jurisdiction exclusively under the Citizen-State Diversity Clauses. In precisely tracking the language in Article III providing for citizen-state diversity jurisdiction, the text of the Amendment does, after all, suggest to common sense that only the Diversity Clauses are being addressed. If the Framers had meant the Amendment to bar federal-question suits as well, they could . . . have made their intentions clearer. . . .

We must therefore look elsewhere for the source of that immunity by which the Court says their suit is barred from a federal court.

II

The obvious place to look elsewhere, of course, is *Hans v. Louisiana*, 134 U.S. 1 (1890), and *Hans* was indeed a leap in the direction of today's holding, even though it does not take the Court all the way. The parties in *Hans* raised, and the Court in that case answered . . . whether the Constitution, without more, permits a State to plead sovereign immunity to bar the exercise of federal-question jurisdiction. Although the Court invoked a principle of sovereign immunity to cure what it took to be the Eleventh Amendment's anomaly of barring only those state suits brought by noncitizen plaintiffs, the *Hans* Court had no occasion to consider whether Congress could abrogate that background immunity by statute. Indeed (except in the special circumstance of Congress's power to enforce the Civil War Amendments), this question never came before our Court until *Union Gas*, and any intimations of an answer in prior cases were mere *dicta*. In *Union Gas* the Court held that the immunity recognized in *Hans* had no constitutional status and was subject to congressional abrogation. Today the Court overrules *Union Gas* and holds just the opposite. In deciding how to choose between these two positions, the place to begin is with *Hans's* holding that a principle of sovereign immunity derived from the common law insulates a State from federal-question jurisdiction at the suit of its own citizen. A critical examination of that case will show that it was wrongly decided, as virtually every recent commentator has concluded. It follows that the Court's further step today of constitutionalizing *Hans's* rule against abrogation by Congress compounds and immensely magnifies the century-old mistake of *Hans* itself and takes its place with other historic examples of textually untethered elevations of judicially derived rules to the status of inviolable constitutional law.

III

Three critical errors in *Hans* weigh against constitutionalizing its holding as the majority does today. The first we have already seen: the *Hans* Court misread the Eleventh Amendment. It also misunderstood the conditions under which common-law doctrines were received or rejected at the time of the founding, and it fundamentally mistook the very nature of sovereignty in the young Republic that was supposed to entail a State's immunity to federal-question jurisdiction in a federal court. While I would not, as a matter of *stare decisis*, overrule *Hans* today, an understanding of its failings on these points will show how the Court today simply compounds already serious error in taking *Hans* the further step of investing its rule with constitutional inviolability against the considered judgment of Congress to abrogate it.

Because neither text, precedent, nor history supports the majority's abdication of our responsibility to exercise the jurisdiction entrusted to us in Article III, I would reverse the judgment of the Court of Appeals.

FOR DISCUSSION

When should the federal government be able to abrogate the sovereignty of the states? Are there other means by which citizens of states can be protected from their state without appealing to the federal government?

RELATED CASES

***Hans v. Louisiana:* 134 U.S. 1 (1890).**

The Court determined that the states are sovereign units in the federal system and that sovereignty inherently contains the ability to not be sued by an individual without consent.

***United States v. Morrison:* 529 U.S. 598 (2000).**

Found sections of the Violence Against Women Act of 1994 unconstitutional, which allowed unauthorized lawsuits against the states for damages, without justification from Section 5 of the Fourteenth Amendment, in violation of the Eleventh Amendment.

BOARD OF TRUSTEES OF THE UNIVERSITY OF ALABAMA V. GARRETT

531 U.S. 356, 121 S. Ct. 955, 148 L. Ed. 2d 866 (2001)

Patricia Garrett was Director of Nursing for the University of Alabama's Birmingham Hospital. After a 1994 diagnosis and treatment for breast cancer, as well as a related medical leave, Garrett was transferred to the lower-paying position of nurse manager. Milton Ash was hired as a security officer for the Alabama Department of Youth Services. Upon his hiring he told the department of his chronic asthma and requested, based on medical advice, to have his duties modified to avoid carbon monoxide and cigarette smoke. A later diagnosis of sleep apnea led to a medical request to be transferred to a day shift. Neither request was granted; after Ash filed a discrimination claim with the Equal Employment Opportunity Commission (EEOC), he received lower performance evaluations. Both Ash and Garrett filed federal lawsuits seeking monetary damages from the State of Alabama under the provisions of the Americans with Disabilities Act of 1990 (ADA). The Act prevents covered employers from employment discrimination based on disability and requires such employers to make reasonable accommodation for an employee unless the accommodation would be an undue hardship on the operation of the employer's business. The state of Alabama claimed that the ADA exceeds congressional authority to abrogate the state's Eleventh Amendment immunity. The district court agreed with petitioners' (Garrett and Ash) position, but the Court of Appeals consolidated their cases and reversed it.

Vote: 5–4

CHIEF JUSTICE REHNQUIST delivered the opinion of the Court.

I

Although by its terms the [Eleventh] Amendment applies only to suits against a State by citizens of another State, our cases have extended the Amendment's applicability to suits by citizens against their own States. The ultimate guarantee of the Eleventh Amendment is that nonconsenting States may not be sued by private individuals in federal court.

We have recognized, however, that Congress may abrogate the States' Eleventh Amendment immunity when it both unequivocally intends to do so and "act[s] pursuant to a valid grant of constitutional authority." The question, then, is whether Congress acted within its constitutional authority by subjecting the States to suits in federal court for money damages under the ADA.

Congress may not, of course, base its abrogation of the States' Eleventh Amendment immunity upon the powers enumerated in Article I. In *Fitzpatrick* v. *Bitzer,* 427 U.S. 445 (1976), however, we held that "the Eleventh

Amendment, and the principle of state sovereignty which it embodies, are necessarily limited by the enforcement provisions of § 5 of the Fourteenth Amendment" at 456. As a result, we concluded, Congress may subject nonconsenting States to suit in federal court when it does so pursuant to a valid exercise of its § 5 power. Our cases have adhered to this proposition.

Section 1 of the Fourteenth Amendment provides, in relevant part:

> "No State shall make or enforce any law which shall abridge the privileges or immunities of citizens of the United States; nor shall any State deprive any person of life, liberty, or property, without due process of law; nor deny to any person within its jurisdiction the equal protection of the laws."

Section 5 of the Fourteenth Amendment grants Congress the power to enforce the substantive guarantees contained in § 1 by enacting "appropriate legislation." Congress is not limited to mere legislative repetition of this Court's constitutional jurisprudence. "Rather, Congress' power 'to enforce' the Amendment includes the authority both to remedy and to deter violation of rights guaranteed thereunder by prohibiting a somewhat broader swath of conduct, including that which is not itself forbidden by the Amendment's text." *Kimel* [v. *Board of Regents*, 528 U.S. 62 (2000)] at 81; *City of Boerne* [v. *Flores*, 521 U.S. 507 (1997)] at 536.

II

The first step in applying these now familiar principles is to identify with some precision the scope of the constitutional right at issue. Here, that inquiry requires us to examine the limitations § 1 of the Fourteenth Amendment places upon States' treatment of the disabled. As we did last Term in *Kimel*, we look to our prior decisions under the Equal Protection Clause dealing with this issue.

In *Cleburne* v. *Cleburne Living Center, Inc.*, 473 U.S. 432 (1985), we considered an equal protection challenge to a city ordinance requiring a special use permit for the operation of a group home for the mentally retarded. The specific question before us was whether the Court of Appeals had erred by holding that mental retardation qualified as a "quasi-suspect" classification under our equal protection jurisprudence. We answered that question in the affirmative, concluding instead that such legislation incurs only the minimum "rational-basis" review applicable to general social and economic legislation.

Under rational-basis review, where a group possesses "distinguishing characteristics relevant to interests the State has the authority to implement," a State's decision to act on the basis of those differences does not give rise to a constitutional violation. Moreover, the State need not articulate its reasoning at the moment a particular decision is made. Rather, the burden is upon the challenging party to negative "any reasonably conceivable state of facts that could provide a rational basis for the classification." *Heller* [v. *Doe*, 509 U.S. 312 (1993)], at 320 (quoting *FCC* v. *Beach Communications, Inc.*, 508 U.S. 307, 313 (1993)).

Justice Breyer suggests that *Cleburne* stands for the broad proposition that state decisionmaking reflecting "negative attitudes" or "fear" necessarily runs afoul of the Fourteenth Amendment. Although such biases may often accompany irrational (and therefore unconstitutional) discrimination, their presence alone does not a constitutional violation make.

Thus, the result of *Cleburne* is that States are not required by the Fourteenth Amendment to make special accommodations for the disabled, so long as their actions towards such individuals are rational. They could quite hard headedly—and perhaps hardheartedly—hold to job-qualification requirements which do not make allowance for the disabled. If special accommodations for the disabled are to be required, they have to come from positive law and not through the Equal Protection Clause.

III

Once we have determined the metes and bounds of the constitutional right in question, we examine whether Congress identified a history and pattern of unconstitutional employment discrimination by the States against the disabled. Just as § 1 of the Fourteenth Amendment applies only to actions committed "under color of state law," Congress' § 5 authority is appropriately exercised only in response to state transgressions. The legislative record of the ADA, however, simply fails to show that Congress did in fact identify a pattern of irrational state discrimination in employment against the disabled.

Congress made a general finding in the ADA that "historically, society has tended to isolate and segregate individuals with disabilities, and, despite some improvements, such forms of discrimination against individuals with disabilities continue to be a serious and pervasive social problem." 42 U.S.C. § 12101(a)(2). The record assembled by Congress includes many instances to support such a finding. But the great majority of these incidents do not deal with the activities of States.

Congressional enactment of the ADA represents its judgment that there should be a "comprehensive national mandate for the elimination of discrimination against individuals with disabilities." 42 U.S.C. § 12101(b)(1). Congress is the final authority as to desirable public policy, but in order to authorize private individuals to recover money damages against the States, there must be a pattern of discrimination by the States which violates the Fourteenth Amendment, and the remedy imposed by Congress must be congruent and proportional to the targeted violation. Those requirements are not met here, and to uphold the Act's application to the States would allow Congress to rewrite the Fourteenth Amendment law laid down by this Court in *Cleburne*. Section 5 does not so broadly enlarge congressional authority. The judgment of the Court of Appeals is therefore

Reversed.

JUSTICE KENNEDY, with whom JUSTICE O'CONNOR joins, concurring.

One of the undoubted achievements of statutes designed to assist those with impairments is that citizens have an incentive, flowing from a legal duty, to develop a better understanding, a more decent perspective, for accepting persons with impairments or disabilities into the larger society. The law works this way because the law can be a teacher. So I do not doubt that the Americans with Disabilities Act of 1990 will be a milestone on the path to a more decent, tolerant, progressive society.

It is a question of quite a different order, however, to say that the States in their official capacities, the States as governmental entities, must be held in violation of the Constitution on the assumption that they embody the misconceived or malicious perceptions of some of their citizens. It is a most serious charge to say a State has engaged in a pattern or practice designed to deny its citizens the equal protection of the laws, particularly where the accusation is based not on hostility but instead on the failure to act or the omission to remedy. States can, and do, stand apart from the citizenry. States act as neutral entities, ready to take instruction and to enact laws when their citizens so demand. The failure of a State to revise policies now seen as incorrect under a new understanding of proper policy does not always constitute the purposeful and intentional action required to make out a violation of the Equal Protection Clause.

For the reasons explained by the Court, an equal protection violation has not been shown with respect to the several States in this case. If the States had been transgressing the Fourteenth Amendment by their mistreatment or lack of concern for those with impairments, one would have expected to find in decisions of the courts of the States and also the courts of the United States extensive litigation and discussion of the constitutional violations. This confirming judicial documentation does not exist. That there is a new awareness, a new consciousness, a new commitment to better treatment of those disadvantaged by mental or physical impairments does not establish that an absence of state statutory correctives was a constitutional violation.

JUSTICE BREYER, with whom JUSTICES STEVENS, SOUTER and GINSBURG join, dissenting.

Reviewing the congressional record as if it were an administrative agency record, the Court holds the statutory provision before us, 42 U.S.C. § 12202, unconstitutional. The Court concludes that Congress assembled insufficient evidence of unconstitutional discrimination, that Congress improperly attempted to "re-write" the law we established in *Cleburne* v. *Cleburne Living Center, Inc.,* 473 U.S. 432 (1985), and that the law is not sufficiently tailored to address unconstitutional discrimination.

Section 5, however, grants Congress the "power to enforce, by appropriate legislation" the Fourteenth Amendment's equal protection guarantee. U.S. Const., Amdt. 14, § 5. As the Court recognizes, state discrimination in employment against persons with disabilities might "run afoul of the Equal Protection Clause" where there is no "rational relationship between the disparity of treatment and some legitimate governmental purpose." In my view, Congress reasonably could have concluded that the remedy before us constitutes an "appropriate" way to enforce this basic equal protection requirement. And that is all the Constitution requires.

I

The Court says that its primary problem with this statutory provision is one of legislative evidence. It says that "Congress assembled only . . . minimal evidence of unconstitutional state discrimination in employment." In fact, Congress compiled a vast legislative record documenting "massive, society-wide discrimination" against persons with disabilities. In addition to the information presented at 13 congressional hearings and its own prior experience gathered over 40 years during which it contemplated and enacted considerable similar legislation, Congress created a special task force to assess the need for comprehensive legislation. The task force hearings, Congress' own hearings, and an analysis of "census data, national polls, and other studies" led Congress to conclude that "people with disabilities, as a group, occupy an inferior status in our society, and are severely disadvantaged socially, vocationally, economically, and educationally." 42 U.S.C. § 12101(a)(6).

The powerful evidence of discriminatory treatment throughout society in general, including discrimination by private persons and local governments, implicates state governments as well, for state agencies form part of that same larger society.

There are roughly 300 examples of discrimination by state governments themselves in the legislative record. I fail to see how this evidence "fall[s] far short of even suggesting the pattern of unconstitutional discrimination on which § 5 legislation must be based."

The evidence in the legislative record bears out Congress' finding that the adverse treatment of persons with disabilities was often arbitrary or invidious in this sense, and thus unjustified.

Congress could have reasonably believed that these examples represented signs of a widespread problem of unconstitutional discrimination.

II

The Court's failure to find sufficient evidentiary support may well rest upon its decision to hold Congress to a strict, judicially created evidentiary standard, particularly in respect to lack of justification. Justice Kennedy's empirical conclusion—which rejects that of Congress—rests heavily upon his failure to find "extensive litigation and discussion of constitutional violations," in "*the courts* of the United States." . . . Imposing this special "burden" upon Congress, the Court fails to find in the legislative record sufficient indication that Congress has "negative[d]" the presumption that state action is rationally related to a legitimate objective.

The problem with the Court's approach is that neither the "burden of proof" that favors States nor any other rule of restraint applicable to *judges* applies to *Congress* when it exercises its § 5 power.

IV

The Court's harsh review of Congress' use of its § 5 power is reminiscent of the similar (now-discredited) limitation that it once imposed upon Congress' Commerce Clause power. I could understand the legal basis for such review were we judging a statute that discriminated against those of a particular race or gender, or a statute that threatened a basic constitutionally protected liberty such as free speech. The legislation before us, however, does not discriminate against anyone, nor does it pose any threat to basic liberty. And it is difficult to understand why the Court, which applies "minimum 'rational-basis' review" to statutes that *burden* persons with disabilities, subjects to far stricter scrutiny a statute that seeks to *help* those same individuals.

The Court, through its evidentiary demands, its non-deferential review, and its failure to distinguish between judicial and legislative constitutional competencies, improperly invades a power that the Constitution assigns to Congress. Its decision saps § 5 of independent force, effectively "confin[ing] the legislative power . . . to the insignificant role of abrogating only those state laws that the judicial branch [is] prepared to adjudge unconstitutional." Whether the Commerce Clause does or does not enable Congress to enact this provision, in my view, § 5 gives Congress the necessary authority.

For the reasons stated, I respectfully dissent.

FOR DISCUSSION

If congressional abrogation is limited as the majority defines it, what other options does Congress have to ensure that state employees are protected under the ADA?

RELATED CASE

***City of Cleburne v. Cleburne Living Center, Inc.:* 473 U.S. 432 (1985).**

The Supreme Court determined that the mentally disabled are not a suspect classification and therefore legislation that distinguishes them from the general population must only have a rational justification to be constitutional. The Court still found the legislation to be unconstitutional.

J. DANIEL KIMEL, JR. V. FLORIDA BOARD OF REGENTS

528 U.S. 62, 120 S. Ct. 631, 145 L. Ed. 2d 522 (2000)

The Age Discrimination in Employment Act of 1967 (ADEA) prohibits covered employers, including states, to refuse to hire or to fire persons as a function of their age, although there are several exceptions. The law covers only individuals over the age of forty. This case combines three plaintiff groups all seeking monetary damages from their state employers for alleged discrimination. In all three cases, the courts were asked whether the ADEA clearly demonstrates congressional intent to abrogate state's Eleventh Amendment immunity, and, if so, if the ADEA is an allowable exercise of congressional authority. The district courts were split in their conclusions; all of the cases were consolidated in the Eleventh Circuit Court of Appeals, which did not find a valid abrogation of state sovereign immunity.

Vote: 5–4

JUSTICE O'CONNOR delivered the opinion of the Court.

III

To determine whether a federal statute properly subjects States to suits by individuals, we apply a "simple but stringent test: 'Congress may abrogate the States' constitutionally secured immunity from suit in federal court only by making its intention unmistakably clear in the language of the statute.' " *Dellmuth v. Muth*, 491 U.S. 223, 228 (1989) (quoting *Atascadero State Hospital v. Scanlon*, 473 U.S. 234, 242 (1985)). We agree with petitioners that the ADEA satisfies that test. . . . Read as a whole, the plain language of these provisions clearly demonstrates Congress' intent to subject the States to suit for money damages at the hands of individual employees. . . .

IV

C

Our examination of the ADEA's legislative record confirms that Congress' 1974 extension of the Act to the States was an unwarranted response to a perhaps inconsequential problem. Congress never identified any pattern of age discrimination by the States, much less any discrimination whatsoever that rose to the level of constitutional violation. The evidence compiled by petitioners to demonstrate such attention by Congress to age discrimination by the States falls well short of the mark. That evidence consists almost entirely of isolated sentences clipped from floor debates and legislative reports. . . .

Petitioners place additional reliance on Congress' consideration of a 1966 report prepared by the State of California on age discrimination in its public agencies. Like the assorted sentences petitioners cobble together from a decade's worth of congressional reports and floor debates, the California study does not indicate that the State had engaged in any unconstitutional age discrimination. In fact, the report stated that the majority of the age limits uncovered in the state survey applied in the law enforcement and firefighting occupations. Those age limits were not only permitted under California law at the time, but are also currently permitted under the ADEA. Even if the California report had uncovered a pattern of unconstitutional age discrimination in the State's public agencies at the time, it nevertheless would have been insufficient to support Congress' 1974 extension of the ADEA to every State of the Union. The report simply does not constitute "evidence that [unconstitutional age discrimination] had become a problem of national import." *Florida Prepaid* [*v. College Savings Bank,* 527 U.S. 627], at 641 [1999].

Finally, the United States' argument that Congress found substantial age discrimination in the private sector is beside the point. Congress made no such findings with respect to the States. Although we also have doubts whether the findings Congress did make with respect to the private sector could be extrapolated to support a finding of unconstitutional age discrimination in the public sector, it is sufficient for these cases to note that Congress failed to identify a widespread pattern of age discrimination by the States.

A review of the ADEA's legislative record as a whole, then, reveals that Congress had virtually no reason to believe that state and local governments were unconstitutionally discriminating against their employees on the basis of age. Although that lack of support is not determinative of the § 5 inquiry, Congress' failure to uncover any significant pattern of unconstitutional discrimination here confirms that Congress had no reason to believe that broad prophylactic legislation was necessary in this field. In light of the indiscriminate scope of the Act's substantive requirements, and the lack of evidence of widespread and unconstitutional age discrimination by the States, we hold that the ADEA is not a valid exercise of Congress' power under § 5 of the Fourteenth Amendment. The ADEA's purported abrogation of the States' sovereign immunity is accordingly invalid.

D

Our decision today does not signal the end of the line for employees who find themselves subject to age discrimination at the hands of their state employers. We hold only that, in the ADEA, Congress did not validly abrogate the States' sovereign immunity to suits by private individuals. State employees are protected by state age discrimination statutes, and may recover money damages from their state employers, in almost every State of the Union. Those avenues of relief remain available today, just as they were before this decision.

Because the ADEA does not validly abrogate the States' sovereign immunity, however, the present suits must be dismissed. Accordingly, the judgment of the Court of Appeals is affirmed.

It is so ordered.

JUSTICE STEVENS, joined by JUSTICES SOUTER, GINSBURG, and BREYER, dissented in part and concurred in part.

JUSTICE THOMAS, joined by JUSTICE KENNEDY, concurred in part and dissented in part.

FOR DISCUSSION

What are benefits and liabilities of using state antidiscrimination laws as a remedy for employment discrimination? Using federal antidiscrimination laws? Does the change in the interpretation of the Eleventh Amendment to encompass citizens suing their own state enhance federalism or constrain it?

RELATED CASES

***E.E.O.C. v. Wyoming:* 460 U.S. 226 (1983).**

The Court found the ADEA to be a viable exercise of congressional power under the Commerce Clause.

***Nevada Department of Human Resources v. Hibbs:* 538 U.S. 721 (2003).**

The Family and Medical Leave Act of 1993, which allowed for litigation against public and private employers as a means of enforcement, was a valid exercise of Congress' Section 5 Enforcement powers in its abrogation of state sovereign immunity. This was allowed because a motivation for the law was to prevent gender discrimination, a phenomenon of which the Court had ample evidence.

TENNESSEE V. LANE

541 U.S. 509, 124 S. Ct. 1978, 158 L. Ed. 2d 820 (2004)

George Lane and Beverly Jones are paraplegics who depend on wheelchairs for their mobility. Lane was charged criminally and had to crawl up two flights of stairs to a courtroom for his hearing and was later jailed for failure to appear when he refused to crawl or be carried to the same inaccessible courtroom. Jones, a court reporter, alleged she has lost income because of the inaccessibility of many county courthouses. Both are suing the state of Tennessee for violating Title II of the Americans with Disabilities Act of 1990 (42 U.S.C. § 12131(2)), which prohibits public entities from excluding qualified individuals from benefits of services or participation in programs based on a disability. Tennessee challenged the lawsuit based on the Eleventh Amendment's provision of sovereign immunity. The district court denied the state of Tennessee's position and the state appealed. The United States government intervened to justify Title II abrogation of states immunity on the ground of the Enforcement Clause § 5 of the Fourteenth Amendment. The court of appeals ordered the case to be held until the Supreme Court's decision in *Board of Trustees v. Garrett* (531 U.S. 356, 2001). In *Garrett*, the Supreme Court determined that the Eleventh Amendment limited private suits for damages under Title I of the ADA, but left unanswered the question regarding Title II. After arguments, the appellate court affirmed the district court's denial of Tennessee's motion to dismiss the case.

Vote 5–4

JUSTICE STEVENS delivered the opinion of the Court.

III

The Eleventh Amendment renders the States immune from "any suit in law or equity, commenced or prosecuted . . . by Citizens of another State, or by Citizens or Subjects of any Foreign State." Even though the Amendment "by its terms . . . applies only to suits against a State by citizens of another State," our cases have repeatedly held that this immunity also applies to unconsented suits brought by a State's own citizens. *Garrett*, 531 U.S., at 363; *Kimel v. Florida Bd. of Regents*, 528 U.S. 62, 72–73 (2000). Our cases have also held that Congress may abrogate the State's Eleventh Amendment immunity. To determine whether it has done so in any given case, we "must resolve two predicate questions: first, whether Congress unequivocally expressed its intent to abrogate that immunity; and second, if it did, whether Congress acted pursuant to a valid grant of constitutional authority." [*Kimel*], at 73.

The first question is easily answered in this case. The Act specifically provides: "A State shall not be immune under the eleventh amendment to the Constitution of the United States from an action in Federal or State court of competent jurisdiction for a violation of this chapter." As in *Garrett*, no party disputes the adequacy of that expression of Congress' intent to abrogate the States' Eleventh Amendment immunity. The question, then, is whether Congress had the power to give effect to its intent.

In *Fitzpatrick v. Bitzer*, 427 U.S. 445 (1976), we held that Congress can abrogate a State's sovereign immunity when it does so pursuant to a valid exercise of its power under § 5 of the Fourteenth Amendment to enforce the substantive guarantees of that Amendment. When Congress seeks to remedy or prevent unconstitutional discrimination, § 5 authorizes it to enact prophylactic legislation proscribing practices that are discriminatory in effect, if not in intent, to carry out the basic objectives of the Equal Protection Clause.

Congress' § 5 power is not, however, unlimited. While Congress must have a wide berth in devising appropriate remedial and preventative measures for unconstitutional actions, those measures may not work a "substantive change in the governing law." [*City of*] *Boerne* [*v. Flores*], 521 U.S. [507 (1997)], at 519. In *Boerne*, we recognized that the line between remedial legislation and substantive redefinition is "not easy to discern," and that "Congress must have wide latitude in determining where it lies." Id., at 519–520. But we also confirmed that "the distinction exists and must be observed," and set forth a test for so observing it: Section 5 legislation is valid if it exhibits "a congruence and proportionality between the injury to be prevented or remedied and the means adopted to that end." Id., at 520.

Applying the *Boerne* test in *Garrett*, we concluded that Title I of the ADA was not a valid exercise of Congress' § 5 power to enforce the Fourteenth Amendment's prohibition on unconstitutional disability discrimination in public employment. . . . [W]e concluded Congress' exercise of its prophylactic § 5 power was unsupported by a relevant history and pattern of constitutional violations. Finally, we concluded that Title I's broad remedial scheme was insufficiently targeted to remedy or prevent unconstitutional discrimination in public employment. Taken together, the historical record and the broad sweep of the statute suggested that Title I's true aim was not so much to enforce the Fourteenth Amendment's prohibitions against disability discrimination in public employment as it was to "rewrite" this Court's Fourteenth Amendment jurisprudence.

In view of the significant differences between Titles I and II, however, *Garrett* left open the question whether Title II is a valid exercise of Congress' § 5 enforcement power. It is to that question that we now turn.

IV

The first step of the *Boerne* inquiry requires us to identify the constitutional right or rights that Congress sought to enforce when it enacted Title II.

Title II, like Title I, seeks to enforce [a] prohibition on irrational disability discrimination. But it also seeks to enforce a variety of other basic constitutional guarantees, infringements of which are subject to more searching judicial review. These rights include some, like the right of access to the courts at issue in this case, that are protected by the Due Process Clause of the Fourteenth Amendment. The Due Process Clause and the Confrontation Clause of the Sixth Amendment, as applied to the States via the Fourteenth Amendment, both guarantee to a criminal defendant such as respondent Lane the "right to be present at all stages of the trial where his absence might frustrate the fairness of the proceedings." *Faretta v. California*, 422 U.S. 806, 819, n. 15 (1975). The Due Process Clause also requires the States to afford certain civil litigants a "meaningful opportunity to be heard" by removing obstacles to their full participation in judicial proceedings. We have held that the Sixth Amendment guarantees to criminal defendants the right to trial by a jury composed of a fair cross section of the community, noting that the exclusion of "identifiable segments playing major roles in the community cannot be squared with the constitutional concept of jury trial." *Taylor v. Louisiana*, 419 U.S. 522, 530 (1975). And, finally, we have recognized that members of the public have a right of access to criminal proceedings secured by the First Amendment. *Press-Enterprise Co. v. Superior Court of Cal., County of Riverside*, 478 U.S. 1, 8–15 (1986).

While § 5 authorizes Congress to enact reasonably prophylactic remedial legislation, the appropriateness of the remedy depends on the gravity of the harm it seeks to prevent.

It is not difficult to perceive the harm that Title II is designed to address. Congress enacted Title II against a backdrop of pervasive unequal treatment in the administration of state services and programs, including systematic deprivations of fundamental rights. The historical experience that Title II reflects is also documented in this Court's cases, which have identified unconstitutional treatment of disabled persons by state agencies in a variety of settings, including unjustified commitment, e.g., *Jackson v. Indiana*, 406 U.S. 715 (1972); the abuse and neglect of persons committed to state mental health hospitals, *Youngberg v. Romeo*, 457 U.S. 307 (1982); and irrational discrimination in zoning decisions, *Cleburne v. Cleburne Living Center, Inc.*, 473 U.S. 432 (1985). The decisions of other courts, too, document a pattern of unequal treatment in the administration of a wide range of public services, programs, and activities, including the penal system, public education, and voting. Notably, these decisions also demonstrate a pattern of unconstitutional treatment in the administration of justice.

This pattern of disability discrimination persisted despite several federal and state legislative efforts to address it.

With respect to the particular services at issue in this case, Congress learned that many individuals, in many States across the country, were being excluded from courthouses and court proceedings by reason of their disabilities. A report before Congress showed that some 76% of public services and programs housed in state-owned buildings were inaccessible to and unusable by persons with disabilities, even taking into account the possibility that the services and programs might be restructured or relocated to other parts of the buildings.

The conclusion that Congress drew from this body of evidence is set forth in the text of the ADA itself: "[D]iscrimination against individuals with disabilities persists in such critical areas as . . . education, transportation, communication, recreation, institutionalization, health services, voting, and access to public services." This finding, together with the extensive record of disability discrimination that underlies it, makes clear beyond peradventure that inadequate provision of public services and access to public facilities was an appropriate subject for prophylactic legislation.

V

The only question that remains is whether Title II is an appropriate response to this history and pattern of unequal treatment. According to petitioner, the fact that Title II applies not only to public education and voting-booth access but also to seating at state-owned hockey rinks indicates that Title II is not appropriately tailored to serve its objectives. But nothing in our case law requires us to consider Title II, with its wide variety of applications, as an undifferentiated whole. Whatever might be said about Title II's other applications, the question presented in this case is not whether Congress can validly subject the States to private suits for money damages for failing to provide reasonable access to hockey rinks, or even to voting booths, but whether Congress had the power under § 5 to enforce the constitutional right of access to the courts. Because we find that Title II unquestionably is valid § 5 legislation as it applies to the class of cases implicating the accessibility of judicial services, we need go no further.

The remedy Congress chose is nevertheless a limited one. Recognizing that failure to accommodate persons with disabilities will often have the same practical effect as outright exclusion, Congress required the States to take reasonable measures to remove architectural and other barriers to accessibility. But Title II does not require States to employ any and all means to make judicial services accessible to persons with disabilities, and it does not require States to compromise their essential eligibility criteria for public programs. It requires only "reasonable modifications" that would not fundamentally alter the nature of the service provided, and only when the individual seeking modification is otherwise eligible for the service. And in no event is the entity required to undertake measures that would impose an undue financial or administrative burden, threaten historic preservation interests, or effect a fundamental alteration in the nature of the service.

. . . Title II's affirmative obligation to accommodate persons with disabilities in the administration of justice cannot be said to be "so out of proportion to a supposed remedial or preventive object that it cannot be understood as responsive to, or designed to prevent, unconstitutional behavior." *Boerne*, 521 U.S., at 532; *Kimel*, 528 U.S., at 86. It is, rather, a reasonable prophylactic measure, reasonably targeted to a legitimate end.

For these reasons, we conclude that Title II, as it applies to the class of cases implicating the fundamental right of access to the courts, constitutes a valid exercise of Congress' § 5 authority to enforce the guarantees of the Fourteenth Amendment. The judgment of the Court of Appeals is therefore affirmed.

It is so ordered.

JUSTICE SOUTER, with whom JUSTICE GINSBURG joins, concurring.

I join the Court's opinion subject to the same caveats about the Court's recent cases on the Eleventh Amendment and § 5 of the Fourteenth that I noted in *Nev. Dep't of Human Res. v. Hibbs*, 538 U.S. 721, 740 (2003) (Souter, J., concurring).

Although I concur in the Court's approach applying the congruence-and-proportionality criteria to Title II of the Americans with Disabilities Act of 1990 as a guarantee of access to courts and related rights, I note that if the Court engaged in a more expansive enquiry as The Chief Justice suggests, the evidence to be considered would underscore the appropriateness of action under § 5 to address the situation of disabled individuals before the courts, for that evidence would show that the judiciary itself has endorsed the basis for some of the very discrimination subject to congressional remedy under § 5. *Buck v. Bell*, 274 U.S. 200 (1927), was not grudging in sustaining the constitutionality of the once-pervasive practice of involuntarily sterilizing those with mental disabilities. Laws compelling sterilization were often accompanied by others indiscriminately requiring institutionalization, and prohibiting certain individuals with disabilities from marrying, from voting, from attending public schools, and even from appearing in public.

Many of these laws were enacted to implement the quondam science of eugenics, which peaked in the 1920's, yet the statutes and their judicial vindications sat on the books long after eugenics lapsed into discredit.

In sustaining the application of Title II today, the Court takes a welcome step away from the judiciary's prior endorsement of blunt instruments imposing legal handicaps.

JUSTICE GINSBURG, with whom JUSTICES SOUTER and BREYER join, concurring.

In *Olmstead v. L. C.,* 527 U.S. 581 (1999), this Court responded with fidelity to the ADA's accommodation theme when it held a State accountable for failing to provide community residential placements for people with disabilities. The State argued in *Olmstead* that it had acted impartially, for it provided no community placements for individuals without disabilities. Congress, the Court observed, advanced in the ADA "a more comprehensive view of the concept of discrimination," one that embraced failures to provide "reasonable accommodations," at 601. The Court today is similarly faithful to the Act's demand for reasonable accommodation to secure access and avoid exclusion.

Legislation calling upon all government actors to respect the dignity of individuals with disabilities is entirely compatible with our Constitution's commitment to federalism, properly conceived. It seems to me not conducive to a harmonious federal system to require Congress, before it exercises authority under § 5 of the Fourteenth Amendment, essentially to indict each State for disregarding the equal-citizenship stature of persons with disabilities. Members of Congress are understandably reluctant to condemn their own States as constitutional violators, complicit in maintaining the isolated and unequal status of persons with disabilities. I would not disarm a National Legislature for resisting an adversarial approach to lawmaking better suited to the courtroom.

CHIEF JUSTICE REHNQUIST, with whom JUSTICES KENNEDY and THOMAS join, dissenting.

In *Board of Trustees of Univ. of Ala. v. Garrett,* 531 U.S. 356 (2001), we held that Congress did not validly abrogate States' Eleventh Amendment immunity when it enacted Title I of the Americans with Disabilities Act of 1990 (ADA). Today, the Court concludes that Title II of that Act does validly abrogate that immunity, at least insofar "as it applies to the class of cases implicating the fundamental right of access to the courts." Because today's decision is irreconcilable with *Garrett* and the well-established principles it embodies, I dissent.

In this case, the task of identifying the scope of the relevant constitutional protection is more difficult because Title II purports to enforce a panoply of constitutional rights of disabled persons: not only the equal protection right against irrational discrimination, but also certain rights protected by the Due Process Clause. However, because the Court ultimately upholds Title II "as it applies to the class of cases implicating the fundamental right of access to the courts," the proper inquiry focuses on the scope of those due process rights. The Court cites four access-to-the-courts rights that Title II purportedly enforces[.]

But the majority identifies nothing in the legislative record that shows Congress was responding to widespread violations of the due process rights of disabled persons.

Rather than limiting its discussion of constitutional violations to the due process rights on which it ultimately relies, the majority sets out on a wide-ranging account of societal discrimination against the disabled. Some of this evidence would be relevant if the Court were considering the constitutionality of the statute as a whole; but the Court rejects that approach in favor of a narrower "as-applied" inquiry. We discounted much the same type of outdated, generalized evidence in *Garrett* as unsupportive of Title I's ban on employment discrimination. The evidence here is likewise irrelevant to Title II's purported enforcement of Due Process access-to-the-courts rights.

Even if it were proper to consider this broader category of evidence, much of it does not concern unconstitutional action by the States. The bulk of the Court's evidence concerns discrimination by nonstate governments, rather than the States themselves. Therefore, even outside the "access to the courts" context, the Court identifies few, if any, constitutional violations perpetrated by the States against disabled persons.

Indeed, there is nothing in the legislative record or statutory findings to indicate that disabled persons were systematically denied the right to be present at criminal trials, denied the meaningful opportunity to be heard in civil cases, unconstitutionally excluded from jury service, or denied the right to attend criminal trials.

Even if the anecdotal evidence and conclusory statements relied on by the majority could be properly considered, the mere existence of an architecturally "inaccessible" courthouse—i.e., one a disabled person cannot utilize without assistance—does not state a constitutional violation. A violation of due process occurs only when a person is actually denied the constitutional right to access a given judicial proceeding. We have never held that a person has a constitutional right to make his way into a courtroom without any external assistance. Indeed, the fact that the State may need to assist an individual to attend a hearing has no bearing on whether the individual successfully exercises his due process right to be present at the proceeding. Nor does an "inaccessible" courthouse violate the Equal Protection Clause, unless it is irrational for the State not to alter the courthouse to make it "accessible." But financial considerations almost always furnish a rational basis for a State to decline to make those alterations. Thus, evidence regarding inaccessible courthouses, because it is not evidence of constitutional violations, provides no basis to abrogate States' sovereign immunity.

I fear that the Court's adoption of an as-applied approach eliminates any incentive for Congress to craft § 5 legislation for the purpose of remedying or deterring actual constitutional violations. Congress can now simply rely on the courts to sort out which hypothetical applications of an undifferentiated statute, such as Title II, may be enforced against the States. All the while, States will be subjected to substantial litigation in a piecemeal attempt to vindicate their Eleventh Amendment rights. The majority's as-applied approach simply cannot be squared with either our recent precedent or the proper role of the Judiciary.

JUSTICE SCALIA, dissenting.

Section 5 of the Fourteenth Amendment provides that Congress "shall have power to enforce, by appropriate legislation, the provisions" of that Amendment—including, of course, the Amendment's Equal Protection and Due Process Clauses. In *Katzenbach v. Morgan*, 384 U.S. 641 (1966), we decided that Congress could, under this provision, forbid English literacy tests for Puerto Rican voters in New York State who met certain educational criteria. Though those tests were not themselves in violation of the Fourteenth Amendment, we held that § 5 authorizes prophylactic legislation—that is, "legislation that proscribes facially constitutional conduct," *Nev. Dep't of Human Res. v. Hibbs*, 538 U.S. 721, 728 (2003), when Congress determines such proscription is desirable "to make the amendments fully effective," *Morgan*, supra, at 648. We said that "the measure of what constitutes 'appropriate legislation' under § 5 of the Fourteenth Amendment" is the flexible "necessary and proper" standard of *McCulloch v. Maryland*, 17 U.S. 316 (1819).

I joined the Court's opinion in [*City of*] *Boerne* [*v. Flores*, 521 U.S. 507 (1997)] with some misgiving. I have generally rejected tests based on such malleable standards as "proportionality," because they have a way of turning into vehicles for the implementation of individual judges' policy preferences. Even so, I signed on to the "congruence and proportionality" test in *Boerne*, and adhered to it in later cases[.]

But these cases were soon followed by *Nevada Dept. of Human Resources v. Hibbs* [538 U.S. 721 (2003)], in which the Court held that the Family and Medical Leave Act of 1993, which required States to provide their employees up to 12 work weeks of unpaid leave (for various purposes) annually, was "congruent and proportional to its remedial object [of preventing sex discrimination], and can be understood as responsive to, or designed to prevent, unconstitutional behavior" 538 U.S., at 740. I joined Justice Kennedy's dissent, which established (conclusively, I thought) that Congress had identified no unconstitutional state action to which the statute could conceivably be a proportional response. And now we have today's decision, holding that Title II of the ADA is congruent and proportional to the remediation of constitutional violations, in the face of what seems to me a compelling demonstration of the opposite by the Chief Justice's dissent.

I yield to the lessons of experience. The "congruence and proportionality" standard, like all such flabby tests, is a standing invitation to judicial arbitrariness and policy-driven decisionmaking. Worse still, it casts this Court in the role of Congress's taskmaster. Under it, the courts (and ultimately this Court) must regularly check Congress's homework to make sure that it has identified sufficient constitutional violations to make its remedy congruent and proportional. As a general matter, we are ill advised to adopt or adhere to constitutional rules that bring us into constant conflict with a coequal branch of Government. And when conflict is unavoidable, we should not come to do battle with the United States Congress armed only with a test ("congruence and proportionality") that has no demonstrable basis in the text of the Constitution and cannot objectively be shown to have been met or failed.

I would replace "congruence and proportionality" with another test—one that provides a clear, enforceable limitation supported by the text of § 5. Nothing in § 5 allows Congress to go beyond the provisions of the Fourteenth Amendment to proscribe, prevent, or "remedy" conduct that does not itself violate any provision of the Fourteenth Amendment. So-called "prophylactic legislation" is reinforcement rather than enforcement.

Thus, principally for reasons of *stare decisis*, I shall henceforth apply the permissive *McCulloch* standard to congressional measures designed to remedy racial discrimination by the States. I would not, however, abandon the requirement that Congress may impose prophylactic § 5 legislation only upon those particular States in which there has been an identified history of relevant constitutional violations. I would also adhere to the requirement that the prophylactic remedy predicated upon such state violations must be directed against the States or state actors rather than the public at large. And I would not, of course, permit any congressional measures that violate other provisions of the Constitution. When those requirements have been met, however, I shall leave it to Congress, under constraints no tighter than those of the Necessary and Proper Clause, to decide what measures are appropriate under § 5 to prevent or remedy racial discrimination by the States.

Requiring access for disabled persons to all public buildings cannot remotely be considered a means of "enforcing" the Fourteenth Amendment. The considerations of long accepted practice and of policy that sanctioned such distortion of language where state racial discrimination is at issue do not apply in this field of social policy far removed from the principal object of the Civil War Amendments. It is past time to draw a line limiting the uncontrolled spread of a well-intentioned textual distortion. For these reasons, I respectfully dissent from the judgment of the Court.

JUSTICE THOMAS, dissenting.

I join The Chief Justice's dissent. I agree that Title II of the Americans with Disabilities Act of 1990 cannot be a congruent and proportional remedy to the States' alleged practice of denying disabled persons access to the courts. Not only did Congress fail to identify any evidence of such a practice when it enacted the ADA, Title II regulates far more than the provision of access to the courts.

FOR DISCUSSION

How does the Court distinguish between congressional authority to abrogate state sovereignty under Title I and Title II of the ADA? What does this say about the Court's conception of federalism? How does the dissent critique this vision?

RELATED CASES

***Popovich v. Cuyahoga County Court:* 276 F.3d 808 (CA6 2002).**

The Sixth Circuit Appellate Court interpreted *Board of Trustees v. Garrett* as enforcing state sovereign immunity based on equal protection, not on the basis of due process.

***United States v. Georgia:* 546 U.S. 151 (2006).**

The Supreme Court found that the state prisoners could make a valid federal claim against the state under the Americans with Disabilities Act of 1990. The Court limited this valid form of federal abrogation of the Eleventh Amendment to when an Eighth Amendment claim is made.

***Central Virginia Community College et al. v. Katz:* 546 U.S. 356 (2006).**

The Bankruptcy Clause of the Constitution (Article I, § 8) is a legitimate abrogation of the state sovereign immunity because the authority is granted in the enumerated powers of the Constitution granted to Congress and creates a national bankruptcy system.

MICHIGAN V. LONG

463 U.S. 1032, 103 S. Ct. 3469, 77 L. Ed. 2d 1201 (1983)

The facts of the case resemble a fairly typical search and seizure case, however, in hearing this case the Supreme Court was required on its own authority to decide a state case determined on an "adequate and independent state ground." David Long was arrested after a traffic stop resulted in a protective *Terry* search for weapons that revealed 75 pounds of marijuana. A *Terry* search, named after the *Terry v. Ohio* (392 U.S. 1, 1968) Supreme Court decision, allows a police officer to do a quick external "patdown" of a suspect's clothing if there is an articulable suspicion that the suspect might be dangerous. The circuit court denied Long's motion to suppress the marijuana, and he was convicted of possession. The Michigan Court of Appeals affirmed, but the Michigan Supreme Court reversed, finding that the justification for the search—the protection of the police and the public—was not supported by the facts. Hence, the drugs found resulted from an illegal search and therefore had to be suppressed. The Supreme Court granted certiorari to determine the extent of the police's authority to protect themselves with a so-called *Terry* search during a lawful investigatory stop of a vehicle. Prior to deciding the merits, however, the justices needed to resolve Long's contention that, as members of a federal court, they did not have the jurisdiction to decide the case.

Vote: 6–3

JUSTICE O'CONNOR delivered the opinion of the Court.

II

Before reaching the merits, we must consider Long's argument that we are without jurisdiction to decide this case because the decision below rests on an adequate and independent state ground. The court below referred twice to the State Constitution in its opinion, but otherwise relied exclusively on federal law. Long argues that the Michigan courts have provided greater protection from searches and seizures under the State Constitution than is afforded under the Fourth Amendment, and the references to the State Constitution therefore establish an adequate and independent ground for the decision below.

It is, of course, "incumbent upon this Court . . . to ascertain for itself . . . whether the asserted non-federal ground independently and adequately supports the judgment." *Abie State Bank v. Bryan*, 282 U.S. 765, 773 (1931).

Although we have announced a number of principles in order to help us determine whether various forms of references to state law constitute adequate and independent state grounds, we openly admit that we have thus far not developed a satisfying and consistent approach for resolving this vexing issue.

This ad hoc method of dealing with cases that involve possible adequate and independent state grounds is antithetical to the doctrinal consistency that is required when sensitive issues of federal-state relations are involved. Moreover, none of the various methods of disposition that we have employed thus far recommends itself as the preferred method that we should apply to the exclusion of others, and we therefore determine that it is appropriate to reexamine our treatment of this jurisdictional issue in order to achieve the consistency that is necessary.

Respect for the independence of state courts, as well as avoidance of rendering advisory opinions, have been the cornerstones of this Court's refusal to decide cases where there is an adequate and independent state ground. It is precisely because of this respect for state courts, and this desire to avoid advisory opinions, that we do not wish to continue to decide issues of state law that go beyond the opinion that we review, or to require state courts to reconsider cases to clarify the grounds of their decisions. Accordingly, when, as in this case, a state court decision fairly appears to rest primarily on federal law, or to be interwoven with the federal law, and when the adequacy and independence of any possible state law ground is not clear from the face of the opinion, we will accept as the most reasonable explanation that the state court decided the case the way it did because it believed that federal law required it to do so. If a state court chooses merely to rely on federal precedents as it would on the precedents of all other jurisdictions, then it need only make clear by a plain statement in its judgment or opinion that the federal cases are being used only for the purpose of guidance, and do not themselves compel the result that the court has reached. In this way, both justice and judicial administration will be greatly improved. If the state court decision indicates clearly and expressly that it is alternatively based on bona fide separate, adequate, and independent grounds, we, of course, will not undertake to review the decision.

Our review of the decision below under this framework leaves us unconvinced that it rests upon an independent state ground. Apart from its two citations to the State Constitution, the court below relied exclusively on its understanding of *Terry* and other federal cases. Not a single state case was cited to support the state court's holding that the search of the passenger compartment was unconstitutional. Indeed, the court declared that the search in this case was unconstitutional because "[the] Court of Appeals erroneously applied the principles of *Terry v. Ohio* [392 U.S. 1 (1968)] . . . to the search of the interior of the vehicle in this case." Even if we accept that the Michigan Constitution has been interpreted to provide independent protection for certain rights also secured under the Fourth Amendment, it fairly appears in this case that the Michigan Supreme Court rested its decision primarily on federal law.

Rather than dismissing the case, or requiring that the state court reconsider its decision on our behalf solely because of a mere possibility that an adequate and independent ground supports the judgment, we find that we have jurisdiction in the absence of a plain statement that the decision below rested on an adequate and independent state ground.

The court below held, and respondent Long contends, that Deputy Howell's entry into the vehicle cannot be justified under the principles set forth in *Terry* because "*Terry* authorized only a limited pat-down search of a person suspected of criminal activity" rather than a search of an area. Although *Terry* did involve the protective frisk of a person, we believe that the police action in this case is justified by the principles that we have already established in *Terry* and other cases.

Our past cases indicate . . . that protection of police and others can justify protective searches when police have a reasonable belief that the suspect poses a danger, that roadside encounters between police and suspects are especially hazardous, and that danger may arise from the possible presence of weapons in the area surrounding a suspect. These principles compel our conclusion that the search of the passenger compartment of an automobile, limited to those areas in which a weapon may be placed or hidden, is permissible if the police officer possesses a reasonable belief based on "specific and articulable facts which, taken together with the rational inferences from those facts, reasonably warrant" the officer in believing that the suspect is dangerous and the suspect may gain immediate control of weapons. If, while conducting a legitimate *Terry* search of the interior of the automobile, the officer should, as here, discover contraband other than weapons, he clearly cannot be required to ignore the contraband, and the Fourth Amendment does not require its suppression in such circumstances.

IV

The trial court and the Court of Appeals upheld the search of the trunk as a valid inventory search. . . . The Michigan Supreme Court did not address this holding, and instead suppressed the marihuana taken from the trunk as a fruit of the illegal search of the interior of the automobile. Our holding that the initial search was justified under *Terry* makes it necessary to determine whether the trunk search was permissible under the Fourth Amendment. However, we decline to address this question because it was not passed upon by the Michigan Supreme Court, whose decision we review in this case. We remand this issue to the court below, to enable it to determine whether the trunk search was permissible. . . .

JUSTICE BLACKMUN, concurring in part and concurring in the judgment.

While I am satisfied that the Court has jurisdiction in this particular case, I do not join the Court, in Part II of its opinion, in fashioning a new presumption of jurisdiction over cases coming here from state courts. Although I agree with the Court that uniformity in federal criminal law is desirable, I see little efficiency and an increased danger of advisory opinions in the Court's new approach.

JUSTICE BRENNAN, with whom JUSTICE MARSHALL joins, dissenting.

The Court today holds that "the protective search of the passenger compartment" of the automobile involved in this case "was reasonable under the principles articulated in *Terry* and other decisions of this Court." I disagree. *Terry v. Ohio*, 392 U.S. 1 (1968), does not support the Court's conclusion and the reliance on "other decisions" is patently misplaced. Plainly, the Court is simply continuing the process of distorting *Terry* beyond recognition and forcing it into service as an unlikely weapon against the Fourth Amendment's fundamental requirement that searches and seizures be based on probable cause. I, therefore, dissent.

Today's decision disregards the Court's warning in *Almeida-Sanchez* [*v. United States*, 413 U.S. 266 (1973)]: "The needs of law enforcement stand in constant tension with the Constitution's protections of the individual against certain exercises of official power. It is precisely the predictability of these pressures that counsels a resolute loyalty to constitutional safeguards." 413 U.S., at 273. Of course, police should not be exposed to unnecessary danger in the performance of their duties. But a search of a car and the containers within it based on nothing more than reasonable suspicion, even under the circumstances present here, cannot be sustained without doing violence to the requirements of the Fourth Amendment. There is no reason in this case why the officers could not have pursued less intrusive, but equally effective, means of insuring their safety. The Court takes a long step today toward "balancing" into oblivion the protections the Fourth Amendment affords. I dissent, for as Justice Jackson said in *Brinegar v. United States*, 338 U.S. 160 (1949):

> "[Fourth Amendment rights] are not mere second-class rights but belong in the catalog of indispensable freedoms. Among deprivations of rights, none is so effective in cowing a population, crushing the spirit of the individual and putting terror in every heart. Uncontrolled search and seizure is one of the first and most effective weapons in the arsenal of every arbitrary government." Id., at 180 (dissenting opinion).

JUSTICE STEVENS, dissenting.

The jurisprudential questions presented in this case are far more important than the question whether the Michigan police officer's search of respondent's car violated the Fourth Amendment. The case raises profoundly significant questions concerning the relationship between two sovereigns—the State of Michigan and the United States of America.

The Supreme Court of the State of Michigan expressly held "that the deputies' search of the vehicle was proscribed by the Fourth Amendment to the United States Constitution and art 1, § 11 of the Michigan Constitution." 413 Mich. 461, 472–473, 320 N. W. 2d 866, 870 (1982). The state law ground is clearly adequate to support the judgment, but the question whether it is independent of the Michigan Supreme Court's understanding of federal law is more difficult. Four possible ways of resolving that question present themselves: (1) asking the Michigan Supreme Court directly, (2) attempting to infer from all possible sources of state law what the Michigan Supreme Court meant, (3) presuming that adequate state grounds are independent unless it clearly appears otherwise, or (4) presuming that adequate state grounds are not independent unless it clearly appears otherwise. This Court has, on different occasions, employed each of the first three approaches; never until today has it even hinted at the fourth. In order to "achieve the consistency that is necessary," the Court today undertakes a reexamination of all the possibilities. It rejects the first approach as inefficient and unduly burdensome for state courts, and rejects the second approach as an inappropriate expenditure of our resources. Although I find both of those decisions defensible in themselves, I cannot accept the Court's decision to choose the fourth approach over the third—to presume that adequate state grounds are intended to be dependent on federal law unless the record plainly shows otherwise. I must therefore dissent.

The Court offers only one reason for asserting authority over cases such as the one presented today: "an important need for uniformity in federal law [that] goes unsatisfied when we fail to review an opinion that rests primarily upon federal grounds and where the independence of an alleged state ground is not apparent from the four corners of the opinion." Of course, the supposed need to "review an opinion" clashes directly with our oft-repeated reminder that "our power is to correct wrong judgments, not to revise opinions." *Herb v. Pitcairn*, 324 U.S. 117, 126 (1945). The clash is not merely one of form: the "need for uniformity in federal law" is truly an ungovernable engine. That same need is no less present when it is perfectly clear that a state ground is both independent and adequate. In fact, it is equally present if a state prosecutor announces that he believes a certain policy of nonenforcement is commanded by federal law. Yet we have never claimed jurisdiction to correct such errors, no matter how egregious they may be, and no matter how much they may thwart the desires of the state electorate. We do not sit to expound our understanding of the Constitution to interested listeners in the legal community; we sit to resolve disputes. If it is not apparent that our views would affect the outcome of a particular case, we cannot presume to interfere.

Finally, I am thoroughly baffled by the Court's suggestion that it must stretch its jurisdiction and reverse the judgment of the Michigan Supreme Court in order to show "[respect] for the independence of state courts." Would we show respect for the Republic of Finland by convening a special sitting for the sole purpose of declaring that its decision to release an American citizen was based upon a misunderstanding of American law?

I respectfully dissent.

FOR DISCUSSION

Why does Justice Blackmun worry that this approach by the Court will provide an "increased danger of advisory opinions"? Do you agree with the majority that this ruling will provide uniformity in federal criminal law greater than in the federal judiciary's absence in state determinations?

RELATED CASES

***Herb v. Pitcairn:* 324 U.S. 117 (1945).**

This decision established the principle that the Supreme Court does not review decisions of state courts that rest on independent and adequate state grounds.

***Oregon v. Kennedy:* 456 U.S. 667 (1982).**

Supreme Court refused to remand an issue to the state court for additional clarification because the case rested upon federal grounds. The Court notes that "[even] if the case admitted of more doubt as to whether federal and state grounds for decision were intermixed, the fact that the state court relied to the extent it did on federal ground requires us to reach the merits."

RAILROAD COMMISSION OF TEXAS V. PULLMAN CO.

312 U.S. 496, 61 S. Ct. 643, 85 L. Ed. 971 (1941)

In rural Texas, the passenger trains usually held one sleeping car. Such smaller trains, unlike the larger ones with two or more sleepers, did not have a Pullman conductor (who was white), but instead were in charge of a Pullman porter (who was black). In response, the Texas Railroad Commission ruled that "no sleeping car shall be operated on any line of railroad in the State of Texas . . . unless such cars are continuously in the charge of an employee . . . having the rank and position of Pullman conductor." The Pullman Company and affected railroads challenged this regulation in federal courts as unauthorized by Texas law and as a violation of the Equal Protection Clause, the Due Process Clause, and the Commerce Clause. Pullman porters intervened as plaintiffs, claiming racial discrimination under the Fourteenth Amendment, and Pullman conductors joined the litigation in support of the Texas legislation. A three-judge panel enjoined the statute's enforcement, and the case went to the Supreme Court.

Vote: 8–0

JUSTICE FRANKFURTER delivered the opinion of the Court.

The complaint of the Pullman porters undoubtedly tendered a substantial constitutional issue. It is more than substantial. It touches a sensitive area of social policy upon which the federal courts ought not to enter unless no alternative to its adjudication is open. Such constitutional adjudication plainly can be avoided if a definitive ruling on the state issue would terminate the controversy. It is therefore our duty to turn to a consideration of questions under Texas law.

The Commission found justification for its order in a Texas statute which we quote in the margin. It is common ground that if the order is within the Commission's authority its subject matter must be included in the Commission's power to prevent "unjust discrimination . . . and to prevent any and all other abuses" in the conduct of railroads. Whether arrangements pertaining to the staffs of Pullman cars are covered by the Texas concept of "discrimination" is far from clear. What practices of the railroads may be deemed to be "abuses" subject to the Commission's correction is equally doubtful. Reading the Texas statutes and the Texas decisions as outsiders without special competence in Texas law, we would have little confidence in our independent judgment regarding the application of that law to the present situation. The lower court did deny that the Texas statutes sustained the Commission's assertion of power. And this represents the view of an able and experienced circuit judge of the circuit which includes Texas and of two capable district judges trained in Texas law. Had we or they no choice in the matter but to decide what is the law of the state, we should hesitate long before rejecting their forecast of Texas law. But no matter how seasoned the judgment of the district court may be, it cannot escape being a forecast rather than a determination. The last word on the meaning of Article 6445 of the Texas Civil Statutes, and therefore the last word on the statutory authority of the Railroad Commission in this case, belongs neither to us nor to the district court but to the supreme court of Texas. In this situation a federal court of equity is asked to decide an issue by making a tentative answer which may be displaced tomorrow by a state adjudication. The reign of law is hardly promoted if an unnecessary ruling of a federal court is thus supplanted by a controlling decision of a state court. The resources of equity are equal to an adjustment that will avoid the waste of a tentative decision as well as the friction of a premature constitutional adjudication.

The history of equity jurisdiction is the history of regard for public consequences in employing the extraordinary remedy of the injunction. There have been as many and as variegated applications of this supple principle as the situations that have brought it into play.

Few public interests have a higher claim upon the discretion of a federal chancellor than the avoidance of needless friction with state policies, whether the policy relates to the enforcement of the criminal law; or the administration of a specialized scheme for liquidating embarrassed business enterprises; or the final authority of a state court to interpret doubtful regulatory laws of the state. These . . . reflect a doctrine of abstention appropriate to our federal system whereby the federal courts, "exercising a wise discretion", restrain their authority because of "scrupulous regard for the rightful independence of the state governments" and for the smooth working of the federal judiciary. This use of equitable powers is a contribution of the courts in furthering the harmonious relation between state and federal authority without the need of rigorous congressional restriction of those powers.

Regard for these important considerations of policy in the administration of federal equity jurisdiction is decisive here. If there was no warrant in state law for the Commission's assumption of authority there is an end of the litigation; the constitutional issue does not arise. The law of Texas appears to furnish easy and ample means for determining the Commission's authority. Article 6453 of the Texas Civil Statutes gives a review of such an order in the state courts. Or, if there are difficulties in the way of this procedure of which we have not been apprised, the issue of state law may be settled by appropriate action on the part of the State to enforce obedience to the order. In the absence of any showing that these obvious methods for securing a definitive ruling in the state courts cannot be pursued with full protection of the constitutional claim, the district court should exercise its wise discretion by staying its hands.

We therefore remand the cause to the district court, with directions to retain the bill pending a determination of proceedings, to be brought with reasonable promptness, in the state court in conformity with this opinion.

Reversed and remanded.

JUSTICE ROBERTS took no part in the consideration or decision of this case.

FOR DISCUSSION

Why was this state segregation law not perceived to fall under federal jurisdiction, but instead was regulated by the state? Why should federal courts defer to states while the latter are hearing a specific case or issue?

CITY OF BOERNE V. FLORES

521 U.S. 507, 117 S. Ct. 2157, 138 L. Ed. 2d 624 (1997)

St. Peter's Catholic Church needed to expand its building to meet the needs of its parishioners. Because it was housed in an historic building, the Boerne City Council denied it the right to change the building's structure. The archbishop challenged the local zoning decision as violative of the federal Religious Freedom Restoration Act of 1993 (RFRA). Congress had passed the RFRA to bolster the rights of individuals to exercise their religious faith when confronted with neutral state laws that indirectly infringed on some religious expressions. The district court found that in enacting the RFRA, Congress exceeded its enforcement power under § 5 of the Fourteenth Amendment; the Fifth Circuit Court of Appeals reversed and found RFRA to be constitutional.

Vote: 6–3

JUSTICE KENNEDY delivered the opinion of the Court.

The case calls into question the authority of Congress to enact RFRA. We conclude the statute exceeds Congress' power.

II

Congress enacted RFRA in direct response to the Court's decision in *Employment Div., Dept. of Human Resources of Ore[gon] v. Smith*, 494 U.S. 872 (1990). There we considered a Free Exercise Clause claim brought by members of the Native American Church who were denied unemployment benefits when they lost their jobs because they had used peyote. Their practice was to ingest peyote for sacramental purposes, and they challenged an Oregon statute of general applicability which made use of the drug criminal. In evaluating the claim, we declined to apply the balancing test set forth in *Sherbert v. Verner*, 374 U.S. 398 (1963), under which we would have asked whether Oregon's prohibition substantially burdened a religious practice and, if it did, whether the burden was justified by a compelling government interest.

The application of the *Sherbert* test, the *Smith* decision explained, would have produced an anomaly in the law, a constitutional right to ignore neutral laws of general applicability. The anomaly would have been accentuated, the Court reasoned, by the difficulty of determining whether a particular practice was central to an individual's religion.

The *Smith* decision acknowledged the Court had employed the *Sherbert* test in considering free exercise challenges to state unemployment compensation rules on three occasions where the balance had tipped in favor of the individual. Those cases, the Court explained, stand for "the proposition that where the State has in place a system of individual exemptions, it may not refuse to extend that system to cases of religious hardship without compelling reason." By contrast, where a general prohibition, such as Oregon's, is at issue, "the sounder approach, and the approach in accord with the vast majority of our precedents, is to hold the test inapplicable to [free exercise] challenges." *Smith* held that neutral, generally applicable laws may be applied to religious practices even when not supported by a compelling governmental interest.

Four Members of the Court disagreed. They argued the law placed a substantial burden on the Native American Church members so that it could be upheld only if the law served a compelling state interest and was narrowly tailored to achieve that end. Justice O'Connor concluded Oregon had satisfied the test, while Justice Blackmun, joined by Justice Brennan and Justice Marshall, could see no compelling interest justifying the law's application to the members.

These points of constitutional interpretation were debated by Members of Congress in hearings and floor debates. Many criticized the Court's reasoning, and this disagreement resulted in the passage of RFRA.

RFRA prohibits "government" from "substantially burdening" a person's exercise of religion even if the burden results from a rule of general applicability unless the government can demonstrate the burden "(1) is in furtherance of a compelling governmental interest; and (2) is the least restrictive means of furthering that compelling governmental interest." The Act's mandate applies to any "branch, department, agency, instrumentality, and official (or other person acting under color of law) of the United States," as well as to any "State, or . . . subdivision of a State." . . . RFRA "applies to all Federal and State law, and the implementation of that law, whether statutory or otherwise, and whether adopted before or after [RFRA's enactment]." In accordance with RFRA's usage of the term, we shall use "state law" to include local and municipal ordinances.

III

A

Under our Constitution, the Federal Government is one of enumerated powers. *McCulloch v. Maryland*, 17 U.S. 316, 4 Wheat. 316, 405 (1819). The judicial authority to determine the constitutionality of laws, in cases and controversies, is based on the premise that the "powers of the legislature are defined and limited; and that those limits may not be mistaken, or forgotten, the Constitution is written." *Marbury v. Madison*, 5 U.S. 137 (1803).

Congress relied on its Fourteenth Amendment enforcement power in enacting the most far reaching and substantial of RFRA's provisions, those which impose its requirements on the States.

The parties disagree over whether RFRA is a proper exercise of Congress' § 5 power "to enforce" by "appropriate legislation" the constitutional guarantee that no State shall deprive any person of "life, liberty, or property, without due process of law" nor deny any person "equal protection of the laws."

In defense of the Act respondent contends, with support from the United States as amicus, that RFRA is permissible enforcement legislation. Congress, it is said, is only protecting by legislation one of the liberties guaranteed by the Fourteenth Amendment's Due Process Clause, the free exercise of religion, beyond what is necessary under *Smith*.

All must acknowledge that § 5 is "a positive grant of legislative power" to Congress, *Katzenbach v. Morgan*, 384 U.S. 641, 651 (1966). In *Ex parte Virginia*, 100 U.S. 339, 345–346 (1880), we explained the scope of Congress' § 5 power in the following broad terms:

> "Whatever legislation is appropriate, that is, adapted to carry out the objects the amendments have in view, whatever tends to enforce submission to the prohibitions they contain, and to secure to all persons the enjoyment of perfect equality of civil rights and the equal protection of the laws against State denial or invasion, if not prohibited, is brought within the domain of congressional power."

Congress' power under § 5, however, extends only to "enforcing" the provisions of the Fourteenth Amendment. The Court has described this power as "remedial," *South Carolina v. Katzenbach* [383 U.S. 301 (1966)]. The design of the Amendment and the text of § 5 are inconsistent with the suggestion that Congress has the power to decree the substance of the Fourteenth Amendment's restrictions on the States. Legislation which alters the meaning of the Free Exercise Clause cannot be said to be enforcing the Clause. Congress does not enforce a constitutional right by changing what the right is. It has been given the power "to enforce," not the power to determine what constitutes a constitutional violation. Were it not so, what Congress would be enforcing would no longer be, in any meaningful sense, the "provisions of [the Fourteenth Amendment]."

2

The remedial and preventive nature of Congress' enforcement power, and the limitation inherent in the power, were confirmed in our earliest cases on the Fourteenth Amendment. In the *Civil Rights Cases*, 109 U.S. 3 (1883), the Court invalidated sections of the Civil Rights Act of 1875 which prescribed criminal penalties for denying to any person "the full enjoyment of" public accommodations and conveyances, on the grounds that it exceeded Congress' power by seeking to regulate private conduct. The Enforcement Clause, the Court said, did not authorize Congress to pass "general legislation upon the rights of the citizen, but corrective legislation; that is, such as may be necessary and proper for counteracting such laws as the States may adopt or enforce, and which, by the amendment, they are prohibited from making or enforcing. . . ." Id., at 13–14. The power to "legislate generally upon" life, liberty, and property, as opposed to the "power to provide modes of redress" against offensive state action, was "repugnant" to the Constitution. Although the specific holdings of these early cases might have been superseded or modified, their treatment of Congress' § 5 power as corrective or preventive, not definitional, has not been questioned.

If Congress could define its own powers by altering the Fourteenth Amendment's meaning, no longer would the Constitution be "superior paramount law, unchangeable by ordinary means." It would be "on a level with ordinary legislative acts, and, like other acts, . . . alterable when the legislature shall please to alter it." *Marbury v. Madison*, 1 Cranch at 177. Under this approach, it is difficult to conceive of a principle that would limit congressional power. Shifting legislative majorities could change the Constitution and effectively circumvent the difficult and detailed amendment process contained in Article V.

We now turn to consider whether RFRA can be considered enforcement legislation under § 5 of the Fourteenth Amendment.

B

Respondent contends that RFRA is a proper exercise of Congress' remedial or preventive power. The Act, it is said, is a reasonable means of protecting the free exercise of religion as defined by *Smith*. It prevents and remedies laws which are enacted with the unconstitutional object of targeting religious beliefs and practices. To avoid the difficulty of proving such violations, it is said, Congress can simply invalidate any law which imposes a substantial burden on a religious practice unless it is justified by a compelling interest and is the least restrictive means of accomplishing that interest. If Congress can prohibit laws with discriminatory effects in order to prevent racial discrimination in violation of the Equal Protection Clause, then it can do the same, respondent argues, to promote religious liberty.

While preventive rules are sometimes appropriate remedial measures, there must be a congruence between the means used and the ends to be achieved. The appropriateness of remedial measures must be considered in light of the evil presented. Strong measures appropriate to address one harm may be an unwarranted response to another, lesser one.

Regardless of the state of the legislative record, RFRA cannot be considered remedial, preventive legislation, if those terms are to have any meaning. RFRA is so out of proportion to a supposed remedial or preventive object that it cannot be understood as responsive to, or designed to prevent, unconstitutional behavior. It appears, instead, to attempt a substantive change in constitutional protections. Preventive measures prohibiting certain types of laws may be appropriate when there is reason to believe that many of the laws affected by the congressional enactment have a significant likelihood of being unconstitutional. Remedial legislation under § 5 "should be adapted to the mischief and wrong which the [Fourteenth] Amendment was intended to provide against." *Civil Rights Cases*, 109 U.S. at 13.

RFRA is not so confined. Sweeping coverage ensures its intrusion at every level of government, displacing laws and prohibiting official actions of almost every description and regardless of subject matter. RFRA's restrictions apply to every agency and official of the Federal, State, and local Governments. RFRA applies to all federal and state law, statutory or otherwise, whether adopted before or after its enactment. RFRA has no termination date or termination mechanism. Any law is subject to challenge at any time by any individual who alleges a substantial burden on his or her free exercise of religion.

The stringent test RFRA demands of state laws reflects a lack of proportionality or congruence between the means adopted and the legitimate end to be achieved. If an objector can show a substantial burden on his free exercise, the State must demonstrate a compelling governmental interest and show that the law is the least restrictive means of furthering its interest. Claims that a law substantially burdens someone's exercise of religion will often be difficult to contest. Requiring a State to demonstrate a compelling interest and show that it has adopted the least restrictive means of achieving that interest is the most demanding test known to constitutional law. Laws valid under *Smith* would fall under RFRA without regard to whether they had the object of stifling or punishing free exercise. We make these observations not to reargue the position of the majority in *Smith* but to illustrate the substantive alteration of its holding attempted by RFRA. Even assuming RFRA would be interpreted in effect to mandate some lesser test, say one equivalent to intermediate scrutiny, the statute nevertheless would require searching judicial scrutiny of state law with the attendant likelihood of invalidation. This is a considerable congressional intrusion into the States' traditional prerogatives and general authority to regulate for the health and welfare of their citizens.

The substantial costs RFRA exacts, both in practical terms of imposing a heavy litigation burden on the States and in terms of curtailing their traditional general regulatory power, far exceed any pattern or practice of unconstitutional conduct under the Free Exercise Clause as interpreted in *Smith*. Simply put, RFRA is not designed to identify and counteract state laws likely to be unconstitutional because of their treatment of religion. In most cases, the state laws to which RFRA applies are not ones which will have been motivated by religious bigotry. If a state law disproportionately burdened a particular class of religious observers, this circumstance might be evidence of an impermissible legislative motive. When the exercise of religion has been burdened in an incidental way by a law of general application, it does not follow that the persons affected have been burdened any more than other citizens, let alone burdened because of their religious beliefs. In addition, the Act imposes in every case a least restrictive means requirement—a requirement that was not used in the pre-*Smith* jurisprudence RFRA purported to codify—which also indicates that the legislation is broader than is appropriate if the goal is to prevent and remedy constitutional violations.

When Congress acts within its sphere of power and responsibilities, it has not just the right but the duty to make its own informed judgment on the meaning and force of the Constitution. Were it otherwise, we would not afford Congress the presumption of validity its enactments now enjoy.

Our national experience teaches that the Constitution is preserved best when each part of the government respects both the Constitution and the proper actions and determinations of the other branches. When the Court has interpreted the Constitution, it has acted within the province of the Judicial Branch, which embraces the duty to say what the law is. When the political branches of the Government act against the background of a judicial interpretation of the Constitution already issued, it must be understood that in later cases and controversies the Court will treat its precedents with the respect due them under settled principles, including *stare decisis*, and contrary expectations must be disappointed. RFRA was designed to control cases and controversies, such as the one before us; but as the provisions of the federal statute here invoked are beyond congressional authority, it is this Court's precedent, not RFRA, which must control.

* * *

It is for Congress in the first instance to "determine whether and what legislation is needed to secure the guarantees of the Fourteenth Amendment," and its conclusions are entitled to much deference. *Katzenbach v. Morgan*, 384 U.S. at 651. Congress' discretion is not unlimited, however, and the courts retain the power, as they have since *Marbury v. Madison* [5 U.S. 137 (1803)], to determine if Congress has exceeded its authority under the Constitution. Broad as the power of Congress is under the Enforcement Clause of the Fourteenth Amendment, RFRA contradicts vital principles necessary to maintain separation of powers and the federal balance. The judgment of the Court of Appeals sustaining the Act's constitutionality is reversed.

JUSTICE STEVENS, concurring.

In my opinion, the Religious Freedom Restoration Act of 1993 (RFRA) is a "law respecting an establishment of religion" that violates the First Amendment to the Constitution.

If the historic landmark on the hill in Boerne happened to be a museum or an art gallery owned by an atheist, it would not be eligible for an exemption from the city ordinances that forbid an enlargement of the structure. Because the landmark is owned by the Catholic Church, it is claimed that RFRA gives its owner a federal statutory entitlement to an exemption from a generally applicable, neutral civil law. Whether the Church would actually prevail under the statute or not, the statute has provided the Church with a legal weapon that no atheist or agnostic can obtain. This governmental preference for religion, as opposed to irreligion, is forbidden by the First Amendment. *Wallace v. Jaffree*, 472 U.S. 38, 52–55 (1985).

JUSTICE SCALIA, with whom JUSTICE STEVENS joins, concurring in part.

I write to respond briefly to the claim of Justice O'Connor's dissent that historical materials support a result contrary to the one reached in *Employment Div., Dept. of Human Resources of Ore. v. Smith*, 494 U.S. 872 (1990). We held in *Smith* that the Constitution's Free Exercise Clause "does not relieve an individual of the obligation to comply with a 'valid and neutral law of general applicability on the ground that the law proscribes (or prescribes) conduct that his religion prescribes (or proscribes).' " 494 U.S. at 879 (quoting *United States v. Lee*, 455 U.S. 252, 263, n.3 (1982) (Stevens, J., concurring)). The material that the dissent claims is at odds with *Smith* either has little to say about the issue or is in fact more consistent with *Smith* than with the dissent's interpretation of the Free Exercise Clause.

The dissent's approach has, of course, great popular attraction. Who can possibly be against the abstract proposition that government should not, even in its general, nondiscriminatory laws, place unreasonable burdens upon religious practice? Unfortunately, however, that abstract proposition must ultimately be reduced to concrete cases. The issue presented by *Smith* is, quite simply, whether the people, through their elected representatives, or rather this Court, shall control the outcome of those concrete cases. For example, shall it be the determination of this Court, or rather of the people, whether church construction will be exempt from zoning laws? The historical evidence put forward by the dissent does nothing to undermine the conclusion we reached in *Smith*: It shall be the people.

JUSTICE O'CONNOR, with whom JUSTICE BREYER joins except as to a portion of Part I, dissenting.

I dissent from the Court's disposition of this case. I agree with the Court that the issue before us is whether the Religious Freedom Restoration Act (RFRA) is a proper exercise of Congress' power to enforce § 5 of the Fourteenth Amendment. But as a yardstick for measuring the constitutionality of RFRA, the Court uses its holding in *Employment Div., Dept. of Human Resources of Ore. v. Smith*, 494 U.S. 872 (1990), the decision that prompted Congress to enact RFRA as a means of more rigorously enforcing the Free Exercise Clause. I remain of the view that *Smith* was wrongly decided, and I would use this case to reexamine the Court's holding there. Therefore, I would direct the parties to brief the question whether *Smith* represents the correct understanding of the Free Exercise Clause and set the case for reargument. If the Court were to correct the misinterpretation of the Free Exercise Clause set forth in *Smith*, it would simultaneously put our First Amendment jurisprudence back on course and allay the legitimate concerns of a majority in Congress who believed that *Smith* improperly restricted religious liberty. We would then be in a position to review RFRA in light of a proper interpretation of the Free Exercise Clause.

III

The Religion Clauses of the Constitution represent a profound commitment to religious liberty. Our Nation's Founders conceived of a Republic receptive to voluntary religious expression, not of a secular society in which religious expression is tolerated only when it does not conflict with a generally applicable law. . . . [T]he Free Exercise Clause is properly understood as an affirmative guarantee of the right to participate in religious activities without impermissible governmental interference, even where a believer's conduct is in tension with a law of general application. Certainly, it is in no way anomalous to accord heightened protection to a right identified in the text of the First Amendment. Given the centrality of freedom of speech and religion to the American concept of personal liberty, it is altogether reasonable to conclude that both should be treated with the highest degree of respect.

Although it may provide a bright line, the rule the Court declared in *Smith* does not faithfully serve the purpose of the Constitution. Accordingly, I believe that it is essential for the Court to reconsider its holding in *Smith*—and to do so in this very case. I would therefore direct the parties to brief this issue and set the case for reargument.

I respectfully dissent from the Court's disposition of this case.

JUSTICE SOUTER, dissenting.

To decide whether the Fourteenth Amendment gives Congress sufficient power to enact the Religious Freedom Restoration Act, the Court measures the legislation against the free-exercise standard of *Employment Div., Dept. of Human Resources of Ore. v. Smith*, 494 U.S. 872 (1990). For the reasons stated in my opinion in *Church of Lukumi Babalu Aye, Inc. v. Hialeah*, 508 U.S. 520, 564–577 (1993) (opinion concurring in part and concurring in judgment), I have serious doubts about the precedential value of the *Smith* rule and its entitlement to adherence. These doubts are intensified today by the historical arguments going to the original understanding of the Free Exercise Clause presented in Justice O'Connor's opinion, which raises very substantial issues about the soundness of the *Smith* rule. But without briefing and argument on the merits of that rule (which this Court has never had in any case, including *Smith* itself), I am not now prepared to join Justice O'Connor in rejecting it or the majority in assuming it to be correct. In order to provide full adversarial consideration, this case should be set down for reargument permitting plenary reexamination of the issue. Since the Court declines to follow that course, our free-exercise law remains marked by an "intolerable tension," *Lukumi*, 508 U.S. at 574, and the constitutionality of the Act of Congress to enforce the free-exercise right cannot now be soundly decided. I would therefore dismiss the writ of certiorari as improvidently granted, and I accordingly dissent from the Court's disposition of this case.

JUSTICE BREYER, also wrote a separate dissent.

FOR DISCUSSION

How does this case help clarify the evolving relations between the state and federal government under the rubric of federalism? Does the justices' relative endorsement of the *Smith* test seem to influence their interpretations of the constitutionality of RFRA?

RELATED CASE

***Gonzales v. O Centro Espirita Beneficiente Uniao Do Vegetal:* 546 U.S. 418 (2006).**

Unanimous decision that the RFRA allows the federal courts to make an individualized determination on whether the religious use of drugs should be excluded from federal drug statutory enforcement when there is no compelling government interest for the drug's inclusion.

Bowers, Attorney General of Georgia v. Hardwick

478 U.S. 186, 106 S. Ct. 2841, 92 L. Ed. 2d 140 (1986)

Michael Hardwick was charged with violating the Georgia law that prohibited sexual acts classified as sodomy. He was found by a police officer committing such an act in the bedroom of his home. The district attorney declined to bring the charges to the grand jury. In response, Hardwick challenged the Georgia law in federal court as unconstitutional in that it criminalized consensual sodomy. He claimed that the Georgia law, as currently administered, placed him in "imminent danger of arrest." The district court granted a motion to dismiss for failure to submit a claim and the Supreme Court summarily affirmed. The Court of Appeals for the Eleventh Circuit reversed, finding the Georgia statute violated Hardwick's fundamental rights. The court found that his sexual activities were private and intimate activities that the Ninth Amendment and the Due Process Clause of the Fourteenth Amendment prohibited it from regulating. The case was remanded for trial. The Supreme Court accepted the attorney general's petition to determine if the sodomy statute violated Hardwick's fundamental rights. In that case, for the Georgia statute to withstand constitutional challenge, the state would have to demonstrate that the law was supported by a compelling state interest and was narrowly tailored.

Vote: 5–4

Justice White delivered the opinion of the Court.

This case does not require a judgment on whether laws against sodomy between consenting adults in general, or between homosexuals in particular, are wise or desirable. It raises no question about the right or propriety of state legislative decisions to repeal their laws that criminalize homosexual sodomy, or of state-court decisions invalidating those laws on state constitutional grounds. The issue presented is whether the Federal Constitution confers a fundamental right upon homosexuals to engage in sodomy and hence invalidates the laws of the many States that still make such conduct illegal and have done so for a very long time. The case also calls for some judgment about the limits of the Court's role in carrying out its constitutional mandate.

We first register our disagreement with the Court of Appeals and with respondent that the Court's prior cases have construed the Constitution to confer a right of privacy that extends to homosexual sodomy and for all intents and purposes have decided this case. The reach of this line of cases was sketched in *Carey v. Population Services International*, 431 U.S. 678, 685 (1977). *Pierce v. Society of Sisters*, 268 U.S. 510 (1925), and *Meyer v. Nebraska*, 262 U.S. 390 (1923), were described as dealing with child rearing and education; *Prince v. Massachusetts*, 321 U.S. 158 (1944), with family relationships; *Skinner v. Oklahoma ex rel. Williamson*, 316 U.S. 535 (1942), with procreation; *Loving v. Virginia*, 388 U.S. 1 (1967), with marriage; *Griswold v. Connecticut*, [381 U.S. 479 (1965)], and *Eisenstadt v. Baird*, [405 U.S. 438 (1972)], with contraception; and *Roe v. Wade*, 410 U.S. 113 (1973), with abortion. The latter three cases were interpreted as construing the Due Process Clause of the Fourteenth Amendment to confer a fundamental individual right to decide whether or not to beget or bear a child.

Accepting the decisions in these cases and the above description of them, we think it evident that none of the rights announced in those cases bears any resemblance to the claimed constitutional right of homosexuals to engage in acts of sodomy that is asserted in this case. No connection between family, marriage, or procreation on the one hand and homosexual activity on the other has been demonstrated, either by the Court of Appeals or by respondent. Precedent aside, however, respondent would have us announce, as the Court of Appeals did, a fundamental right to engage in homosexual sodomy. This we are quite unwilling to do. It is true that despite the language of the Due Process Clauses of the Fifth and Fourteenth Amendments, which appears to focus only on the processes by which life, liberty, or property is taken, the cases are legion in which those Clauses have been interpreted to have substantive content, subsuming rights that to a great extent are immune from federal or state regulation or proscription. Among such cases are those recognizing rights that have little or no textual support in the constitutional language. *Meyer*, *Prince*, and *Pierce* fall in this category, as do the privacy cases from *Griswold* to *Carey*.

Striving to assure itself and the public that announcing rights not readily identifiable in the Constitution's text involves much more than the imposition of the Justices' own choice of values on the States and the Federal Government, the Court has sought to identify the nature of the rights qualifying for heightened judicial protection. In *Palko v. Connecticut*, 302 U.S. 319, 325, 326 (1937), it was said that this category includes those fundamental liberties that are "implicit in the concept of ordered liberty," such that "neither liberty nor justice would exist if [they] were sacrificed." A different description of fundamental liberties appeared in *Moore v. East Cleveland*, 431 U.S. 494, 503 (1977), where they are characterized as those liberties that are "deeply rooted in this Nation's history and tradition."

It is obvious to us that neither of these formulations would extend a fundamental right to homosexuals to engage in acts of consensual sodomy. Proscriptions against that conduct have ancient roots. Sodomy was a criminal offense at common law and was forbidden by the laws of the original 13 States when they ratified the Bill of Rights. In 1868, when the Fourteenth Amendment was ratified, all but 5 of the 37 States in the Union had criminal sodomy laws. In fact, until 1961, all 50 States outlawed sodomy, and today, 24 States and the District of Columbia continue to provide criminal penalties for sodomy performed in private and between consenting adults. Against this background, to claim that a right to engage in such conduct is "deeply rooted in this Nation's history and tradition" or "implicit in the concept of ordered liberty" is, at best, facetious.

Nor are we inclined to take a more expansive view of our authority to discover new fundamental rights imbedded in the Due Process Clause. The Court is most vulnerable and comes nearest to illegitimacy when it deals with judge-made constitutional law having little or no cognizable roots in the language or design of the Constitution. There should be, therefore, great resistance to expand the substantive reach of those Clauses, particularly if it requires redefining the category of rights deemed to be fundamental. Otherwise, the Judiciary necessarily takes to itself further authority to govern the country without express constitutional authority. The claimed right pressed on us today falls far short of overcoming this resistance.

Respondent, however, asserts that the result should be different where the homosexual conduct occurs in the privacy of the home. He relies on *Stanley v. Georgia*, 394 U.S. 557[, 565] (1969), where the Court held that the First Amendment prevents conviction for possessing and reading obscene material in the privacy of one's home: "If the First Amendment means anything, it means that a State has no business telling a man, sitting alone in his house, what books he may read or what films he may watch."

Stanley did protect conduct that would not have been protected outside the home, and it partially prevented the enforcement of state obscenity laws; but the decision was firmly grounded in the First Amendment. The right pressed upon us here has no similar support in the text of the Constitution, and it does not qualify for recognition under the prevailing principles for construing the Fourteenth Amendment. Its limits are also difficult to discern.

Even if the conduct at issue here is not a fundamental right, respondent asserts that there must be a rational basis for the law and that there is none in this case other than the presumed belief of a majority of the electorate in Georgia that homosexual sodomy is immoral and unacceptable. This is said to be an inadequate rationale to support the law. The law, however, is constantly based on notions of morality, and if all laws representing essentially moral choices are to be invalidated under the Due Process Clause, the courts will be very busy indeed. Even respondent makes no such claim, but insists that majority sentiments about the morality of homosexuality should be declared inadequate. We do not agree, and are unpersuaded that the sodomy laws of some 25 States should be invalidated on this basis.

CHIEF JUSTICE BURGER, concurring.

I join the Court's opinion, but I write separately to underscore my view that in constitutional terms there is no such thing as a fundamental right to commit homosexual sodomy.

As the Court notes, the proscriptions against sodomy have very "ancient roots." Decisions of individuals relating to homosexual conduct have been subject to state intervention throughout the history of Western civilization. Condemnation of those practices is firmly rooted in Judeo-Christian moral and ethical standards. In 1816 the Georgia Legislature passed the statute at issue here, and that statute has been continuously in force in one form or another since that time. To hold that the act of homosexual sodomy is somehow protected as a fundamental right would be to cast aside millennia of moral teaching.

This is essentially not a question of personal "preferences" but rather of the legislative authority of the State. I find nothing in the Constitution depriving a State of the power to enact the statute challenged here.

JUSTICE POWELL, concurring.

I join the opinion of the Court. I agree with the Court that there is no fundamental right—i.e., no substantive right under the Due Process Clause—such as that claimed by respondent Hardwick, and found to exist by the Court of Appeals. This is not to suggest, however, that respondent may not be protected by the Eighth Amendment of the Constitution. The Georgia statute at issue in this case, authorizes a court to imprison a person for up to 20 years for a single private, consensual act of sodomy. In my view, a prison sentence for such conduct—certainly a sentence of long duration—would create a serious Eighth Amendment issue.

In this case, however, respondent has not been tried, much less convicted and sentenced. Moreover, respondent has not raised the Eighth Amendment issue below. For these reasons this constitutional argument is not before us.

JUSTICE BLACKMUN, with whom JUSTICES BRENNAN, MARSHALL, and STEVENS join, dissenting.

This case is no more about "a fundamental right to engage in homosexual sodomy," as the Court purports to declare, than *Stanley v. Georgia*, 394 U.S. 557 (1969), was about a fundamental right to watch obscene movies, or *Katz v. United States*, 389 U.S. 347 (1967), was about a fundamental right to place interstate bets from a telephone booth. Rather, this case is about "the most comprehensive of rights and the right most valued by civilized men," namely, "the right to be let alone." *Olmstead v. United States*, 277 U.S. 438, 478 (1928) (Brandeis, J., dissenting).

I believe we must analyze respondent Hardwick's claim in the light of the values that underlie the constitutional right to privacy. If that right means anything, it means that, before Georgia can prosecute its citizens for making choices about the most intimate aspects of their lives, it must do more than assert that the choice they have made is an "abominable crime not fit to be named among Christians." *Herring v. State*, 119 Ga. 709, 721 (1904).

I

First, the Court's almost obsessive focus on homosexual activity is particularly hard to justify in light of the broad language Georgia has used. Unlike the Court, the Georgia Legislature has not proceeded on the assumption that homosexuals are so different from other citizens that their lives may be controlled in a way that would not be tolerated if it limited the choices of those other citizens. Rather, Georgia has provided that "[a] person commits the offense of sodomy when he performs or submits to any sexual act involving the sex organs of one person and the mouth or anus of another." The sex or status of the persons who engage in the act is irrelevant as a matter of state law. In fact, to the extent I can discern a legislative purpose for Georgia's 1968 enactment of § 16–6–2, that purpose seems to have been to broaden the coverage of the law to reach heterosexual as well as homosexual activity. I therefore see no basis for the Court's decision to treat this case as an "as applied" challenge to § 16–6–2, or for Georgia's attempt, both in its brief and at oral argument, to defend § 16–6–2 solely on the grounds that it prohibits homosexual activity. Michael Hardwick's standing may rest in significant part on Georgia's apparent willingness to enforce against homosexuals a law it seems not to have any desire to enforce against heterosexuals. But his claim that § 16–6–2 involves an unconstitutional intrusion into his privacy and his right of intimate association does not depend in any way on his sexual orientation.

Second, I disagree with the Court's refusal to consider whether § 16–6–2 runs afoul of the Eighth or Ninth Amendments or the Equal Protection Clause of the Fourteenth Amendment. Respondent's complaint expressly invoked the Ninth Amendment, and he relied heavily before this Court on *Griswold v. Connecticut*, 381 U.S. 479, 484 (1965), which identifies that Amendment as one of the specific constitutional provisions giving "life and substance" to our understanding of privacy. More importantly, the procedural posture of the case requires that we affirm the Court of Appeals' judgment if there is any ground on which respondent may be entitled to relief.

III

First, petitioner asserts that the acts made criminal by the statute may have serious adverse consequences for "the general public health and welfare," such as spreading communicable diseases or fostering other criminal activity. Inasmuch as this case was dismissed by the District Court on the pleadings, it is not surprising that the record before us is barren of any evidence to support petitioner's claim.

The core of petitioner's defense of § 16–6–2, however, is that respondent and others who engage in the conduct prohibited by § 16–6–2 interfere with Georgia's exercise of the "right of the Nation and of the States to maintain a decent society," *Paris Adult Theatre I v. Slaton*, 413 U.S.[49], at 59–60 [(1973)], quoting *Jacobellis v. Ohio*, 378 U.S. 184, 199 (1964) (Warren, C. J., dissenting). Essentially, petitioner argues, and the Court agrees, that the fact that the acts described in § 16–6–2 "for hundreds of years, if not thousands, have been uniformly condemned as immoral" is a sufficient reason to permit a State to ban them today.

I cannot agree that either the length of time a majority has held its convictions or the passions with which it defends them can withdraw legislation from this Court's scrutiny. It is precisely because the issue raised by this case touches the heart of what makes individuals what they are that we should be especially sensitive to the rights of those whose choices upset the majority.

The assertion that "traditional Judeo-Christian values proscribe" the conduct involved cannot provide an adequate justification for § 16–6–2. That certain, but by no means all, religious groups condemn the behavior at issue gives the State no license to impose their judgments on the entire citizenry. The legitimacy of secular legislation depends instead on whether the State can advance some justification for its law beyond its conformity to religious doctrine.

Certainly, some private behavior can affect the fabric of society as a whole. Petitioner and the Court fail to see the difference between laws that protect public sensibilities and those that enforce private morality. Statutes banning public sexual activity are entirely consistent with protecting the individual's liberty interest in decisions concerning sexual relations: the same recognition that those decisions are intensely private which justifies protecting them from governmental interference can justify protecting individuals from unwilling exposure to the sexual activities of others. But the mere fact that intimate behavior may be punished when it takes place in public cannot dictate how States can regulate intimate behavior that occurs in intimate places.

This case involves no real interference with the rights of others, for the mere knowledge that other individuals do not adhere to one's value system cannot be a legally cognizable interest, let alone an interest that can justify invading the houses, hearts, and minds of citizens who choose to live their lives differently.

IV

It took but three years for the Court to see the error in its analysis in *Minersville School District v. Gobitis*, 310 U.S. 586 (1940), and to recognize that the threat to national cohesion posed by a refusal to salute the flag was vastly outweighed by the threat to those same values posed by compelling such a salute. I can only hope that here, too, the Court soon will reconsider its analysis and conclude that depriving individuals of the right to choose for themselves how to conduct their intimate relationships poses a far greater threat to the values most deeply rooted in our Nation's history than tolerance of nonconformity could ever do. Because I think the Court today betrays those values, I dissent.

JUSTICE STEVENS, with whom JUSTICES BRENNAN and MARSHALL join, dissenting.

Like the statute that is challenged in this case, the rationale of the Court's opinion applies equally to the prohibited conduct regardless of whether the parties who engage in it are married or unmarried, or are of the same or different sexes. Sodomy was condemned as an odious and sinful type of behavior during the formative period of the common law. That condemnation was equally damning for heterosexual and homosexual sodomy. Moreover, it provided no special exemption for married couples. The license to cohabit and to produce legitimate offspring simply did not include any permission to engage in sexual conduct that was considered a "crime against nature."

The history of the Georgia statute before us clearly reveals this traditional prohibition of heterosexual, as well as homosexual, sodomy. Indeed, at one point in the 20th century, Georgia's law was construed to permit certain sexual conduct between homosexual women even though such conduct was prohibited between heterosexuals. The history of the statutes cited by the majority as proof for the proposition that sodomy is not constitutionally protected, and similarly reveals a prohibition on heterosexual, as well as homosexual, sodomy.

Because the Georgia statute expresses the traditional view that sodomy is an immoral kind of conduct regardless of the identity of the persons who engage in it, I believe that a proper analysis of its constitutionality requires consideration of two questions: First, may a State totally prohibit the described conduct by means of a neutral law applying without exception to all persons subject to its jurisdiction? If not, may the State save the statute by announcing that it will only enforce the law against homosexuals? The two questions merit separate discussion.

I

Our prior cases make two propositions abundantly clear. First, the fact that the governing majority in a State has traditionally viewed a particular practice as immoral is not a sufficient reason for upholding a law prohibiting the practice; neither history nor tradition could save a law prohibiting miscegenation from constitutional attack. Second, individual decisions by married persons, concerning the intimacies of their physical relationship, even when not intended to produce offspring, are a form of "liberty" protected by the Due Process Clause of the Fourteenth Amendment.

II

If the Georgia statute cannot be enforced as it is written—if the conduct it seeks to prohibit is a protected form of liberty for the vast majority of Georgia's citizens—the State must assume the burden of justifying a selective application of its law. Either the persons to whom Georgia seeks to apply its statute do not have the same interest in "liberty" that others have, or there must be a reason why the State may be permitted to apply a generally applicable law to certain persons that it does not apply to others.

The first possibility is plainly unacceptable. Although the meaning of the principle that "all men are created equal" is not always clear, it surely must mean that every free citizen has the same interest in "liberty" that the members of the majority share. From the standpoint of the individual, the homosexual and the heterosexual have the same interest in deciding how he will live his own life, and, more narrowly, how he will conduct himself in his personal and voluntary associations with his companions. State intrusion into the private conduct of either is equally burdensome.

The second possibility is similarly unacceptable. A policy of selective application must be supported by a neutral and legitimate interest—something more substantial than a habitual dislike for, or ignorance about, the disfavored group. Neither the State nor the Court has identified any such interest in this case. The Court has posited as a justification for the Georgia statute "the presumed belief of a majority of the electorate in Georgia that homosexual sodomy is immoral and unacceptable." But the Georgia electorate has expressed no such belief—instead, its representatives enacted a law that presumably reflects the belief that all sodomy is immoral and unacceptable. Unless the Court is prepared to conclude that such a law is constitutional, it may not rely on the work product of the Georgia Legislature to support its holding. For the Georgia statute does not single out homosexuals as a separate class meriting special disfavored treatment.

III

The Court orders the dismissal of respondent's complaint even though the State's statute prohibits all sodomy; even though that prohibition is concededly unconstitutional with respect to heterosexuals; and even though the State's post hoc explanations for selective application are belied by the State's own actions. At the very least, I think it clear at this early stage of the litigation that respondent has alleged a constitutional claim sufficient to withstand a motion to dismiss.

I respectfully dissent.

FOR DISCUSSION

When should a federal court be willing to enforce new constitutional substantive rights that result in state laws being found unconstitutional? Consider the impact of such cases as *Brown v. Board of Education* (1954), *Mapp v. Ohio* (1961), *Gideon v. Wainwright* (1963), and *Reed v. Reed* (1971).

RELATED CASES

***Boy Scouts of America v. Dale:* 530 U.S. 640 (2000).**

After the state of New Jersey amended its discrimination laws to protect sexual orientation, the Boy Scouts revoked a local leader's adult membership based on his homosexuality. Relying on the rights of association developed under the First Amendment, the Court upheld the right of the Boy Scouts of America to control their membership as a private organization.

***Romer v. Evans:* 517 U.S. 620 (1996).**

The Court struck down a Colorado constitutional amendment that explicitly prevented municipalities from enacting regulations prohibiting discrimination based on sexual preference or homosexuality. The Court relied on the Equal Protection Clause.

Powell v. State

270 Ga. 327, 510 S.E.2d 18, 98 Fulton County D. Rep. 4177 (1998)

Anthony San Juan Powell was charged with the rape of and aggravated sodomy with his wife's seventeen-year-old niece. The jury acquitted Powell of the rape charges but found him guilty of violating the Georgia antisodomy law. The jury believed he had not forced the niece to behave against her will but that testimony demonstrated he had engaged in illicit consensual sodomy. Powell appealed to the Georgia Supreme Court, arguing that the Georgia law is an unconstitutional violation of the right to privacy.

Vote 6–1

Chief Justice Benham wrote the majority opinion.

The right of privacy has a long and distinguished history in Georgia. In 1905, this Court expressly recognized that Georgia citizens have a "liberty of privacy" guaranteed by the Georgia constitutional provision which declares that no person shall be deprived of liberty except by due process of law. *Pavesich v. New England Life Ins. Co.*, 122 Ga. 190, 197 (1905). The *Pavesich* decision constituted the first time any court of last resort in this country recognized the right of privacy, making this Court a pioneer in the realm of the right of privacy. Since that time, the Georgia courts have developed a rich appellate jurisprudence in the right of privacy which recognizes the right of privacy as a fundamental constitutional right. . . .

In *Pavesich*, the Court found the right of privacy to be "ancient law," with "its foundation in the instincts of nature[,]" derived from "the Roman's conception of justice" and natural law, making it immutable and absolute. Stated succinctly, the Court ringingly endorsed the "right 'to be let alone' so long as [one] was not interfering with the rights of other individuals or of the public."

In the ensuing years since *Pavesich* was decided and Georgia's right of privacy recognized, the Georgia appellate courts have expounded on the right of privacy, describing it as protection for the individual from unnecessary public scrutiny (*Athens Observer v. Anderson*, 245 Ga. 63 (1980)); as the right of the individual "to be free from . . . the publicizing of one's private affairs with which the public has no legitimate concern" (*Gouldman-Taber Pontiac v. Zerbst*, 213 Ga. [682,] 683 [(1957)]); "the right to define one's circle of intimacy" (*Macon-Bibb County Water & Auth. v. Reynolds*, 165 Ga. App. 348, 350 (1983)); and the right "to be free of unwarranted interference by the public about matters [with] which the public is not necessarily concerned, or to be protected from any wrongful intrusion into an individual's private life which would outrage . . . a person of ordinary sensibilities." *Georgia Power Co. v. Busbin*, 149 Ga. App. 274 (1979). This Court has determined that a citizen's right of privacy is strong enough to withstand a variety of attempts by the State to intrude in the citizen's life. It is clear from the right of privacy appellate jurisprudence which emanates from *Pavesich* that the "right to be let alone" guaranteed by the Georgia Constitution is far more extensive than the right of privacy protected by the U.S. Constitution, which protects only those matters "deeply rooted in this Nation's history and tradition" or which are "implicit in the concept of ordered liberty. . . ." *Bowers v. Hardwick*, 478 U.S. 186, 191–192 (1986).

Today, we are faced with whether the constitutional right of privacy screens from governmental interference a non-commercial sexual act that occurs without force in a private home between persons legally capable of consenting to the act. We cannot think of any other activity that reasonable persons would rank as more private and more deserving of protection from governmental interference than unforced, private, adult sexual activity. We conclude that such activity is at the heart of the Georgia Constitution's protection of the right of privacy.

Having determined that appellant's behavior falls within the area protected by the right of privacy, we next examine whether the government's infringement upon that right is constitutionally sanctioned. As judicial consideration of the right to privacy has developed, this Court has concluded that the right of privacy is a fundamental right and that a government-imposed limitation on the right to privacy will pass constitutional muster if the limitation is shown to serve a compelling state interest and to be narrowly tailored to effectuate only that compelling interest. Implicit in our decisions curtailing the assertion of a right to privacy in sexual assault cases involving sexual activity taking place in public, performed with those legally incapable of giving consent, performed in exchange for money, or performed with force and against the will of a participant, is the determination that the State has a role in shielding the public from inadvertent exposure to the intimacies of others, in protecting minors and others legally incapable of consent from sexual abuse, and in preventing people from being forced to submit to sex acts against their will. In light of the existence of these statutes, the sodomy statute's *raison d' etre* can only be to regulate the private sexual conduct of consenting adults, something which Georgians' right of privacy puts beyond the bounds of government regulation.

Citing *Christensen* [*v. State*] 266 Ga. 474 [(1996)], the State reminds us that the plurality decision therein held that the proscription against sodomy was a valid exercise of the State's police power in furtherance of the public's moral welfare, and that the Georgia Constitution did not deny the General Assembly the right to prohibit such conduct. "Police power" is the governing authority's ability to legislate for the protection of the citizens' lives, health, and property, and to preserve good order and public morals. . . . [T]he legislation must serve a public purpose and the means adopted to achieve the purpose must be reasonably necessary for the accomplishment of the purpose and not unduly oppressive upon the persons regulated. Thus, the suggestion that O.C.G.A. § 16–6–2 is a valid exercise of the police power requires us to consider whether it benefits the public generally without unduly oppressing the individual. Since, as determined earlier, the only possible purpose for the statute is to regulate the private conduct of consenting adults, the public gains no benefit, and the individual is unduly oppressed by the invasion of the right to privacy. Consequently, we must conclude that the legislation exceeds the permissible bounds of the police power.

The State also maintains that the furtherance of "social morality," giving "due regard to the collective will of the citizens of Georgia," is a constitutional basis for legislative control of the non-commercial, unforced, private sexual activity of those legally capable of consenting to such activity. "Social morality legislation," like any legislative enactment, is subject to the scrutiny of the judicial branch under our tripartite system of "checks and balances."

In undertaking the judiciary's constitutional duty, it is not the prerogative of members of the judiciary to base decisions on their personal notions of morality. Indeed, if we were called upon to pass upon the propriety of the conduct herein involved, we would not condone it. Rather, the judiciary is charged with the task of examining a legislative enactment when it is alleged to impinge upon the freedoms and guarantees contained in the Georgia Bill of Rights and the U.S. Constitution, and scrutinizing the law, the interests it promotes, and the means by which it seeks to achieve those interests, to ensure that the law meets constitutional standards. While many believe that acts of sodomy, even those involving consenting adults, are morally reprehensible, this repugnance alone does not create a compelling justification for state regulation of the activity.

We conclude that O.C.G.A. § 16–6–2, insofar as it criminalizes the performance of private, unforced, non-commercial acts of sexual intimacy between persons legally able to consent, "manifestly infringes upon a constitutional provision" (*Miller v. State*, 266 Ga. 850 [(1996]) which guarantees to the citizens of Georgia the right of privacy. Appellant was convicted for performing an unforced act of sexual intimacy with one legally capable of consenting thereto in the privacy of his home. Accordingly, appellant's conviction for such behavior must be reversed.

JUSTICE SEARS, concurring.

In broad terms, the dissent urges that once the legislature criminalizes any activity, courts are forbidden from passing on the "wisdom" of such laws. Otherwise, the dissent foretells that "anarchy" will reign. In making these statements, the dissent mischaracterizes the majority opinion. In this opinion, this Court in no way usurps the legislative function of promulgating social policy. Rather, in an inspired opinion, a majority of this Court today has fulfilled its constitutional responsibility within the American tripartite system of checks and balances. As well stated in the majority opinion, merely because the legislature has enacted a law which may impact upon the public's moral choices, courts are not "bound to simply acquiesce." It is the duty of this Court, and all courts, to ensure that, absent a compelling state interest, legislative acts do not impinge upon the inalienable rights guaranteed by our State Constitution. The dissent would default on its constitutional duty to protect these rights, and would defer instead to what it believes to be the moral choice of a majority. Yet, it is the very definition of a constitutional right that it cannot be made wholly subject to the will of the majority. Otherwise, the principles that serve as bedrock for our Federal and State Bill of Rights will be reduced to mere rhetoric.

Today, a majority of this Court fulfills its duties with a clearheaded and courageous decision. I fully concur with it.

JUSTICE CARLEY, dissenting.

The issue in this case is not whether private and consensual acts of sodomy should be legal or illegal in Georgia, because that question has already been resolved by the General Assembly. Therefore, the only issue presented for decision is whether the General Assembly has the constitutional authority to prohibit such conduct. It is my opinion that there is no state constitutional impediment to the General Assembly's enactment of O.C.G.A. § 16–6–2 (a) and that, by holding otherwise, the Court has exceeded the limits of its judicial authority and usurped the legislative power "to enact laws to promote the public health, safety, morals, and welfare of its citizens." *Christensen v. State*, 266 Ga. 474, 476 (1996). Therefore, the only perceptible unconstitutionality in this case is that which is evidenced by the majority's determination, acting as social engineers rather than as jurists, to elevate their notion of individual "liberty" over the collective wisdom of the people's elected representatives that a proscription on sodomy, consensual or otherwise, is "in furtherance of the moral welfare of the public." *Christensen v. State*, at 476. Therefore, I respectfully, but vigorously, dissent to the holding that O.C.G.A. § 16–6–2 (a) is unconstitutional.

The premise of the majority is that the right of privacy guaranteed by the Georgia Constitution grants to the citizens of this state the right to engage in private consensual sodomy. Unlike the constitutions of some other states, the Georgia Constitution contains no express recognition of a right to privacy. That right stems entirely from this Court's holding in *Pavesich v. New England Life Ins. Co.*, 122 Ga. 190 (1905).

Although, as the majority notes, the right of privacy has a long history in Georgia dating from *Pavesich*, until today this Court has never cited that right as authority for the incongruous proposition that a citizen is at liberty to commit an act which has constituted criminal conduct throughout the even longer history of Georgia as a state and, indeed, throughout the entire history of English common law. In its haste to confer upon Powell a constitutionally protected right to engage in private consensual acts of sodomy, the majority simply seizes upon Pavesich's general recognition of the guarantee of "liberty" afforded to Georgia citizens under the *state* constitution, while choosing to ignore completely *Pavesich's* equally important recognition of the principle that Georgia citizens also have the responsibility to comply with this state's criminal law. Thus, unlike the majority, I believe that *Pavesich* is clear-cut authority for the proposition that a violation of the criminal law of this state can never be justified as an element of the "liberty" guaranteed by the Due Process Clause of this state's constitution. In my opinion, freedom to violate the criminal law is simply anarchy and, thus, the antithesis of an ordered constitutional system.

The only factor which has changed since *Pavesich* was decided is the composition of this Court.

Legislatures alone determine the wisdom of laws, and courts, despite their belief that the law is unwise, nevertheless are bound by the Constitution to confine their considerations of such laws to their constitutionality alone. Courts possess neither the facilities, the experience, nor the wisdom of legislators to qualify them to pass upon the wisdom of laws. According to the majority, O.C.G.A. § 16–6–2 (a) is unconstitutional for the entirely erroneous reason that, by ratifying the Constitution of Georgia, this state's voters implicitly guaranteed the right of its citizens to commit an act which its legislators nevertheless have expressly determined should continue to be prohibited. Retaining the long-standing proscription on sodomy may or may not be good public policy, but it is a public policy determination which, as a matter of constitutional law, only the General Assembly can make. Thus, in *Christensen v. State*, we held that "the right to determine what is harmful to health and morals or what is criminal to the public welfare belongs to the people through their elected representatives." 266 Ga. at 477. Unfortunately, as of today, that is no longer the law of this state. By holding that the constitutional guarantee of "liberty" precludes the General Assembly from enacting an express ban on the commission of consensual private acts of sodomy, the Court has usurped the legislative authority of the General Assembly to establish the public policy of this state.

Because the majority's discovery of a constitutional right to engage in sodomy notwithstanding this legislative ban is based upon a serious misinterpretation of the Constitution of Georgia and is completely contrary to the constitutional principle of separation of powers, I dissent.

FOR DISCUSSION

The dissent claims that the law criminalizing sodomy, the *Pavesich* precedent, and the constitutional guarantee of due process have all been in effect for over ninety years. For him, the only thing that has changed is the change in the personnel of the Court. Is this a fair critique of this decision? Why or why not?

RELATED CASES

***Commonwealth of Kentucky v. Jeffrey Wasson:* S.Ct of Kentucky, 842 S.W. 2d 487 (1992).**

A Kentucky law criminalizing homosexual sodomy was found unconstitutional under the Kentucky constitution because the state constitution offered greater privacy protections than that of the federal Constitution, as interpreted by *Bowers v. Hardwick* (1986).

***Gryczan v. Montana:* 942 P.2d 112 (1997).**

The Montana Supreme Court, based on the state's own constitutional protections, found its criminalization of sodomy unconstitutional.

LAWRENCE V. TEXAS

539 U.S. 558, 123 S. Ct. 2472, 156 L. Ed. 2d 508 (2003)

Upon entering an apartment on a weapons disturbance complaint, two Harris County police officers observed John Geddes Lawrence and Tyrone Garner engaged in a sexual act. The men were arrested on the charge of "deviate sexual intercourse," or sodomy with an individual of the same sex. The petitioner challenged the Texas statute as a violation of the Equal Protection Clause of the Fourteenth Amendment and of a similar provision in the Texas constitution. The criminal court rejected these claims and fined the petitioners $200.00 each plus court costs. The Texas Court of Appeals (14th District) rejected the challenge and affirmed the decision.

Vote: 6–3

JUSTICE KENNEDY delivered the opinion of the Court.

I

We granted certiorari to consider three questions:

"1. Whether Petitioners' criminal convictions under the Texas "Homosexual Conduct" law—which criminalizes sexual intimacy by same-sex couples, but not identical behavior by different-sex couples—violate the Fourteenth Amendment guarantee of equal protection of laws?

"2. Whether Petitioners' criminal convictions for adult consensual sexual intimacy in the home violate their vital interests in liberty and privacy protected by the Due Process Clause of the Fourteenth Amendment?

"3. Whether *Bowers v. Hardwick*, 478 U.S. 186 (1986), should be overruled?"

II

We conclude the case should be resolved by determining whether the petitioners were free as adults to engage in the private conduct in the exercise of their liberty under the Due Process Clause of the Fourteenth Amendment to the Constitution. For this inquiry we deem it necessary to reconsider the Court's holding in *Bowers*.

The facts in *Bowers* had some similarities to the instant case. A police officer, whose right to enter seems not to have been in question, observed Hardwick, in his own bedroom, engaging in intimate sexual conduct with another adult male. The conduct was in violation of a Georgia statute making it a criminal offense to engage in sodomy. One difference between the two cases is that the Georgia statute prohibited the conduct whether or not the participants were of the same sex, while the Texas statute, as we have seen, applies only to participants of the same sex. Hardwick was not prosecuted, but he brought an action in federal court to declare the state statute invalid. He alleged he was a practicing homosexual and that the criminal prohibition violated rights guaranteed to him by the Constitution. The Court, in an opinion by Justice White, sustained the Georgia law. Chief Justice Burger and Justice Powell joined the opinion of the Court and filed separate, concurring opinions. Four Justices dissented.

The Court began its substantive discussion in *Bowers* as follows: "The issue presented is whether the Federal Constitution confers a fundamental right upon homosexuals to engage in sodomy and hence invalidates the laws of the many States that still make such conduct illegal and have done so for a very long time." Id., at 190. That statement, we now conclude, discloses the Court's own failure to appreciate the extent of the liberty at stake. To say that the issue in *Bowers* was simply the right to engage in certain sexual conduct demeans the claim the individual put forward, just as it would demean a married couple were it to be said marriage is simply about the right to have sexual intercourse. The laws involved in *Bowers* and here are, to be sure, statutes that purport to do no more than prohibit a particular sexual act. Their penalties and purposes, though, have more far-reaching consequences, touching upon the most private human conduct, sexual behavior, and in the most private of places, the home. The statutes do seek to control a personal relationship that, whether or not entitled to formal recognition in the law, is within the liberty of persons to choose without being punished as criminals.

Having misapprehended the claim of liberty there presented to it, and thus stating the claim to be whether there is a fundamental right to engage in consensual sodomy, the *Bowers* Court said: "Proscriptions against that conduct have ancient roots." Id., at 192. In academic writings, and in many of the scholarly amicus briefs filed to assist the Court in this case, there are fundamental criticisms of the historical premises relied upon by the majority and concurring opinions in *Bowers*. We need not enter this debate in the attempt to reach a definitive historical judgment, but the following considerations counsel against adopting the definitive conclusions upon which *Bowers* placed such reliance.

At the outset it should be noted that there is no longstanding history in this country of laws directed at homosexual conduct as a distinct matter.

Laws prohibiting sodomy do not seem to have been enforced against consenting adults acting in private. Instead of targeting relations between consenting adults in private, 19th-century sodomy prosecutions typically involved relations between men and minor girls or minor boys, relations between adults involving force, relations between adults implicating disparity in status, or relations between men and animals.

It was not until the 1970's that any State singled out same-sex relations for criminal prosecution, and only nine States have done so. Post-*Bowers* even some of these States did not adhere to the policy of suppressing homosexual conduct. Over the course of the last decades, States with same-sex prohibitions have moved toward abolishing them.

Of even more importance, almost five years before *Bowers* was decided the European Court of Human Rights considered a case with parallels to *Bowers* and to today's case. An adult male resident in Northern Ireland alleged he was a practicing homosexual who desired to engage in consensual homosexual conduct. The laws of Northern Ireland forbade him that right. He alleged that he had been questioned, his home had been searched, and he feared criminal prosecution. The court held that the laws proscribing the conduct were invalid under the European Convention on Human Rights. *Dudgeon v. United Kingdom*, 45 Eur. Ct. H. R. (1981) P 52. Authoritative in all countries that are members of the Council of Europe (21 nations then, 45 nations now), the decision is at odds with the premise in *Bowers* that the claim put forward was insubstantial in our Western civilization.

In our own constitutional system the deficiencies in *Bowers* became even more apparent in the years following its announcement. The 25 States with laws prohibiting the relevant conduct referenced in the *Bowers* decision are reduced now to 13, of which 4 enforce their laws only against homosexual conduct. In those States where sodomy is still proscribed, whether for same-sex or heterosexual conduct, there is a pattern of nonenforcement with respect to consenting adults acting in private.

Two principal cases decided after *Bowers* cast its holding into even more doubt. In *Planned Parenthood of Southeastern Pa. v. Casey*, 505 U.S. 833 (1992), the Court reaffirmed the substantive force of the liberty protected by the Due Process Clause. The *Casey* decision again confirmed that our laws and tradition afford constitutional protection to personal decisions relating to marriage, procreation, contraception, family relationships, child rearing, and education.

The second post-*Bowers* case of principal relevance is *Romer v. Evans*, 517 U.S. 620 (1996). There the Court struck down class-based legislation directed at homosexuals as a violation of the Equal Protection Clause. We concluded that the provision was "born of animosity toward the class of persons affected" and further that it had no rational relation to a legitimate governmental purpose.

Equality of treatment and the due process right to demand respect for conduct protected by the substantive guarantee of liberty are linked in important respects, and a decision on the latter point advances both interests. If protected conduct is made criminal and the law which does so remains unexamined for its substantive validity, its stigma might remain even if it were not enforceable as drawn for equal protection reasons. When homosexual conduct is made criminal by the law of the State, that declaration in and of itself is an invitation to subject homosexual persons to discrimination both in the public and in the private spheres. The central holding of *Bowers* has been brought in question by this case, and it should be addressed. Its continuance as precedent demeans the lives of homosexual persons.

The foundations of *Bowers* have sustained serious erosion from our recent decisions in *Casey* and *Romer*.

To the extent *Bowers* relied on values we share with a wider civilization, it should be noted that the reasoning and holding in *Bowers* have been rejected elsewhere. The European Court of Human Rights has followed not *Bowers* but its own decision in *Dudgeon v. United Kingdom*.

Other nations, too, have taken action consistent with an affirmation of the protected right of homosexual adults to engage in intimate, consensual conduct.

The doctrine of *stare decisis* is essential to the respect accorded to the judgments of the Court and to the stability of the law. It is not, however, an inexorable command. The holding in *Bowers*, however, has not induced detrimental reliance comparable to some instances where recognized individual rights are involved. Indeed, there has been no individual or societal reliance on *Bowers* of the sort that could counsel against overturning its holding once there are compelling reasons to do so. *Bowers* itself causes uncertainty, for the precedents before and after its issuance contradict its central holding.

Bowers was not correct when it was decided, and it is not correct today. It ought not to remain binding precedent. *Bowers v. Hardwick* should be and now is overruled.

Had those who drew and ratified the Due Process Clauses of the Fifth Amendment or the Fourteenth Amendment known the components of liberty in its manifold possibilities, they might have been more specific. They did not presume to have this insight. They knew times can blind us to certain truths and later generations can see that laws once thought necessary and proper in fact serve only to oppress. As the Constitution endures, persons in every generation can invoke its principles in their own search for greater freedom.

The judgment of the Court of Appeals for the Texas Fourteenth District is reversed, and the case is remanded for further proceedings not inconsistent with this opinion.

JUSTICE O'CONNOR, concurring in the judgment.

The Court today overrules *Bowers v. Hardwick*, 478 U.S. 186 (1986). I joined *Bowers*, and do not join the Court in overruling it. Nevertheless, I agree with the Court that Texas' statute banning same-sex sodomy is unconstitutional. Rather than relying on the substantive component of the Fourteenth Amendment's Due Process Clause, as the Court does, I base my conclusion on the Fourteenth Amendment's Equal Protection Clause.

The Equal Protection Clause of the Fourteenth Amendment "is essentially a direction that all persons similarly situated should be treated alike." *Cleburne v. Cleburne Living Center, Inc.*, 473 U.S. 432, 439 (1985); see also *Plyler v. Doe*, 457 U.S. 202, 216 (1982). Under our rational basis standard of review, "legislation is presumed to be valid and will be sustained if the classification drawn by the statute is rationally related to a legitimate state interest." *Cleburne v. Cleburne Living Center*, at 440.

We have consistently held, however, that some objectives, such as "a bare . . . desire to harm a politically unpopular group," are not legitimate state interests. When a law exhibits such a desire to harm a politically unpopular group, we have applied a more searching form of rational basis review to strike down such laws under the Equal Protection Clause.

We have been most likely to apply rational basis review to hold a law unconstitutional under the Equal Protection Clause where, as here, the challenged legislation inhibits personal relationships.

The statute at issue here makes sodomy a crime only if a person "engages in deviate sexual intercourse with another individual of the same sex." Sodomy between opposite-sex partners, however, is not a crime in Texas. That is, Texas treats the same conduct differently based solely on the participants. Those harmed by this law are people who have a same-sex sexual orientation and thus are more likely to engage in behavior prohibited by § 21.06.

The Texas statute makes homosexuals unequal in the eyes of the law by making particular conduct—and only that conduct—subject to criminal sanction. It appears that prosecutions under Texas' sodomy law are rare. This case shows, however, that prosecutions under § 21.06 do occur. And while the penalty imposed on petitioners in this case was relatively minor, the consequences of conviction are not. As the Court notes, petitioners' convictions, if upheld, would disqualify them from or restrict their ability to engage in a variety of professions, including medicine, athletic training, and interior design. Indeed, were petitioners to move to one of four States, their convictions would require them to register as sex offenders to local law enforcement.

Texas attempts to justify its law, and the effects of the law, by arguing that the statute satisfies rational basis review because it furthers the legitimate governmental interest of the promotion of morality. In *Bowers*, we held that a state law criminalizing sodomy as applied to homosexual couples did not violate substantive due process. We rejected the argument that no rational basis existed to justify the law, pointing to the government's interest in promoting morality. The only question in front of the Court in *Bowers* was whether the substantive component of the Due Process Clause protected a right to engage in homosexual sodomy. *Bowers* did not hold that moral disapproval of a group is a rational basis under the Equal Protection Clause to criminalize homosexual sodomy when heterosexual sodomy is not punished.

Texas argues, however, that the sodomy law does not discriminate against homosexual persons. Instead, the State maintains that the law discriminates only against homosexual conduct. While it is true that the law applies only to conduct, the conduct targeted by this law is conduct that is closely correlated with being homosexual.

A State can of course assign certain consequences to a violation of its criminal law. But the State cannot single out one identifiable class of citizens for punishment that does not apply to everyone else, with moral disapproval as the only asserted state interest for the law.

That this law as applied to private, consensual conduct is unconstitutional under the Equal Protection Clause does not mean that other laws distinguishing between heterosexuals and homosexuals would similarly fail under rational basis review. Texas cannot assert any legitimate state interest here, such as national security or preserving the traditional institution of marriage. Unlike the moral disapproval of same-sex relations—the asserted state interest in this case—other reasons exist to promote the institution of marriage beyond mere moral disapproval of an excluded group.

A law branding one class of persons as criminal solely based on the State's moral disapproval of that class and the conduct associated with that class runs contrary to the values of the Constitution and the Equal Protection Clause, under any standard of review. I therefore concur in the Court's judgment that Texas' sodomy law banning "deviate sexual intercourse" between consenting adults of the same sex, but not between consenting adults of different sexes, is unconstitutional.

JUSTICE SCALIA, with whom the CHIEF JUSTICE and JUSTICE THOMAS join, dissenting.

"Liberty finds no refuge in a jurisprudence of doubt." *Planned Parenthood of Southeastern Pa. v. Casey*, 505 U.S. 833, 844 (1992). That was the Court's sententious response, barely more than a decade ago, to those seeking to overrule *Roe v. Wade*, 410 U.S. 113 (1973). The Court's response today, to those who have engaged in a 17-year crusade to overrule *Bowers v. Hardwick*, 478 U.S. 186 (1986), is very different. The need for stability and certainty presents no barrier.

I

I begin with the Court's surprising readiness to reconsider a decision rendered a mere 17 years ago in *Bowers v. Hardwick*. I do not myself believe in rigid adherence to *stare decisis* in constitutional cases; but I do believe that we should be consistent rather than manipulative in invoking the doctrine.

Today, however, the widespread opposition to *Bowers*, a decision resolving an issue as "intensely divisive" as the issue in *Roe*, is offered as a reason in favor of overruling it. Gone, too, is any "enquiry" (of the sort conducted in *Casey*) into whether the decision sought to be overruled has "proven 'unworkable,' " *Casey*, supra, at 855.

Today's approach to *stare decisis* invites us to overrule an erroneously decided precedent (including an "intensely divisive" decision) if: (1) its foundations have been "eroded" by subsequent decisions; (2) it has been subject to "substantial and continuing" criticism; and (3) it has not induced "individual or societal reliance" that counsels against overturning. The problem is that *Roe* itself—which today's majority surely has no disposition to overrule—satisfies these conditions to at least the same degree as *Bowers*.

II

Having decided that it need not adhere to *stare decisis*, the Court still must establish that *Bowers* was wrongly decided and that the Texas statute, as applied to petitioners, is unconstitutional.

Texas Penal Code Ann. § 21.06(a) (2003) undoubtedly imposes constraints on liberty. So do laws prohibiting prostitution, recreational use of heroin, and, for that matter, working more than 60 hours per week in a bakery. But there is no right to "liberty" under the Due Process Clause, though today's opinion repeatedly makes that claim. The Fourteenth Amendment expressly allows States to deprive their citizens of "liberty," so long as "due process of law" is provided: "No state shall . . . deprive any person of life, liberty, or property, without due process of law."

IV

I turn now to the ground on which the Court squarely rests its holding: the contention that there is no rational basis for the law here under attack. This proposition is so out of accord with our jurisprudence—indeed, with the jurisprudence of any society we know—that it requires little discussion.

The Texas statute undeniably seeks to further the belief of its citizens that certain forms of sexual behavior are "immoral and unacceptable," *Bowers* at 196—the same interest furthered by criminal laws against fornication, bigamy, adultery, adult incest, bestiality, and obscenity. *Bowers* held that this was a legitimate state interest. The Court today reaches the opposite conclusion. This effectively decrees the end of all morals legislation. If, as the Court asserts, the promotion of majoritarian sexual morality is not even a legitimate state interest, none of the above-mentioned laws can survive rational-basis review.

V

Finally, I turn to petitioners' equal-protection challenge, which no Member of the Court save Justice O'Connor embraces: On its face § 21.06(a) applies equally to all persons. Men and women, heterosexuals and homosexuals, are all subject to its prohibition of deviate sexual intercourse with someone of the same sex. To be sure, § 21.06 does distinguish between the sexes insofar as concerns the partner with whom the sexual acts are performed: men can violate the law only with other men, and women only with other women. But this cannot itself be a denial of equal protection, since it is precisely the same distinction regarding partner that is drawn in state laws prohibiting marriage with someone of the same sex while permitting marriage with someone of the opposite sex.

Today's opinion is the product of a Court, which is the product of a law-profession culture, that has largely signed on to the so-called homosexual agenda, by which I mean the agenda promoted by some homosexual activists directed at eliminating the moral opprobrium that has traditionally attached to homosexual conduct. I noted in an earlier opinion the fact that the American Association of Law Schools (to which any reputable law school must seek to belong) excludes from membership any school that refuses to ban from its job-interview facilities a law firm (no matter how small) that does not wish to hire as a prospective partner a person who openly engages in homosexual conduct.

One of the most revealing statements in today's opinion is the Court's grim warning that the criminalization of homosexual conduct is "an invitation to subject homosexual persons to discrimination both in the public and in the private spheres." It is clear from this that the Court has taken sides in the culture war, departing from its role of assuring, as neutral observer, that the democratic rules of engagement are observed. Many Americans do not want persons who openly engage in homosexual conduct as partners in their business, as scoutmasters for their children, as teachers in their children's schools, or as boarders in their home. They view this as protecting themselves and their families from a lifestyle that they believe to be immoral and destructive. The Court views it as "discrimination" which it is the function of our judgments to deter. So imbued is the Court with the law profession's anti-anti-homosexual culture, that it is seemingly unaware that the attitudes of that culture are not obviously "mainstream"; that in most States what the Court calls "discrimination" against those who engage in homosexual acts is perfectly legal; that proposals to ban such "discrimination" under Title VII have repeatedly been rejected by Congress; that in some cases such "discrimination" is mandated by federal statute; and that in some cases such "discrimination" is a constitutional right.

Let me be clear that I have nothing against homosexuals, or any other group, promoting their agenda through normal democratic means. Social perceptions of sexual and other morality change over time, and every group has the right to persuade its fellow citizens that its view of such matters is the best. That homosexuals have achieved some success in that enterprise is attested to by the fact that Texas is one of the few remaining States that criminalize private, consensual homosexual acts. But persuading one's fellow citizens is one thing, and imposing one's views in absence of democratic majority will is something else.

The matters appropriate for this Court's resolution are only three: Texas's prohibition of sodomy neither infringes a "fundamental right" (which the Court does not dispute), nor is unsupported by a rational relation to what the Constitution considers a legitimate state interest, nor denies the equal protection of the laws. I dissent.

JUSTICE THOMAS, dissenting.

I join Justice Scalia's dissenting opinion. I write separately to note that the law before the Court today "is . . . uncommonly silly." *Griswold v. Connecticut*, 381 U.S. 479, 527 (1965) (Stewart, J., dissenting). If I were a member of the Texas Legislature, I would vote to repeal it. Punishing someone for expressing his sexual preference through noncommercial consensual conduct with another adult does not appear to be a worthy way to expend valuable law enforcement resources.

Notwithstanding this, I recognize that as a member of this Court I am not empowered to help petitioners and others similarly situated. My duty, rather, is to "decide cases 'agreeably to the Constitution and laws of the United States.' " And, just like Justice Stewart, I "can find [neither in the Bill of Rights nor any other part of the Constitution a] general right of privacy," or as the Court terms it today, the "liberty of the person both in its spatial and more transcendent dimensions."

FOR DISCUSSION

What is the significance of the protection against same-sex discrimination being placed within the Due Process Clause as opposed to the Equal Protection Clause? How do you respond to Justice Thomas's claim that while it is an "uncommonly silly" law, it needs to be addressed by the Texas legislature and not the federal Supreme Court?

RELATED CASE

Rumsfeld v. Forum for Academic and Institutional Rights: **547 U.S. 47 (2006).**

Law schools that refuse access to military recruiters due to conflict between the military's "don't ask, don't tell" policy and the law schools' antidiscrimination policy regarding sexual orientation are still subject to the penalties of the Solomon Amendment. This policy denies federal funding to institutions that do not allow military recruiters access to students.

GOODRIDGE V. DEPARTMENT OF PUBLIC HEALTH

440 Mass. 309, 798 N.E.2d 941 (2003)

Seven same-sex couples representing five Massachusetts counties attempted to obtain marriage licenses from their city or town clerk office. In every case, the clerk refused to accept their application or denied a marriage license on the legal ground that Massachusetts does not recognize same-sex marriage. The plaintiffs filed a lawsuit in the Massachusetts Superior Court against the Department of Public Health on the grounds that excluding same-sex couples from access to marriage licenses "and the legal and social status of civil marriage, as well as the protections, benefits and obligations of marriage, violates Massachusetts law." A superior court judge ruled in favor of the Department of Public Health based on the clear wording of the marriage statute. The plaintiffs appealed to the Massachusetts Supreme Court.

Vote: 4–3

CHIEF JUSTICE MARSHALL delivered the majority opinion.

II

Although the plaintiffs refer in passing to "the marriage statutes," they focus, quite properly, on G.L. c. 207, the marriage licensing statute, which controls entry into civil marriage.

General Laws c. 207 is both a gatekeeping and a public records statute. It sets minimum qualifications for obtaining a marriage license and directs city and town clerks, the registrar, and the department to keep and maintain certain "vital records" of civil marriages.

In short, for all the joy and solemnity that normally attend a marriage, G.L. c. 207, governing entrance to marriage, is a licensing law. The plaintiffs argue that because nothing in that licensing law specifically prohibits marriages between persons of the same sex, we may interpret the statute to permit "qualified same sex couples" to obtain marriage licenses, thereby avoiding the question whether the law is constitutional. This claim lacks merit.

Far from being ambiguous, the undefined word "marriage," as used in G.L. c. 207, confirms the General Court's intent to hew to the term's common-law and quotidian meaning concerning the genders of the marriage partners.

We conclude, as did the judge, that G.L. c. 207 may not be construed to permit same-sex couples to marry.

III

A

The larger question is whether, as the [Department of Public Health] claims, government action that bars same-sex couples from civil marriage constitutes a legitimate exercise of the State's authority to regulate conduct, or whether, as the plaintiffs claim, this categorical marriage exclusion violates the Massachusetts Constitution. We have recognized the long-standing statutory understanding, derived from the common law, that "marriage" means the lawful union of a woman and a man. But that history cannot and does not foreclose the constitutional question.

The plaintiffs' claim that the marriage restriction violates the Massachusetts Constitution can be analyzed in two ways. Does it offend the Constitution's guarantees of equality before the law? Or do the liberty and due process provisions of the Massachusetts Constitution secure the plaintiffs' right to marry their chosen partner? In matters implicating marriage, family life, and the upbringing of children, the two constitutional concepts frequently overlap, as they do here. Much of what we say concerning one standard applies to the other.

We begin by considering the nature of civil marriage itself. Simply put, the government creates civil marriage. In Massachusetts, civil marriage is, and since pre-Colonial days has been, precisely what its name implies: a wholly secular institution. No religious ceremony has ever been required to validate a Massachusetts marriage.

Civil marriage is created and regulated through exercise of the police power. "Police power" (now more commonly termed the State's regulatory authority) is an old-fashioned term for the Commonwealth's lawmaking authority, as bounded by the liberty and equality guarantees of the Massachusetts Constitution and its express delegation of power from the people to their government. In broad terms, it is the Legislature's power to enact rules to regulate conduct, to the extent that such laws are "necessary to secure the health, safety, good order, comfort, or general welfare of the community." *Opinion of the Justices,* 341 Mass. 760, 785 (1960).

Because it fulfils yearnings for security, safe haven, and connection that express our common humanity, civil marriage is an esteemed institution, and the decision whether and whom to marry is among life's momentous acts of self-definition.

Tangible as well as intangible benefits flow from marriage. The marriage license grants valuable property rights to those who meet the entry requirements, and who agree to what might otherwise be a burdensome degree of government regulation of their activities.

The benefits accessible only by way of a marriage license are enormous, touching nearly every aspect of life and death. The department states that "hundreds of statutes" are related to marriage and to marital benefits. With no attempt to be comprehensive, we note that some of the statutory benefits conferred by the Legislature on those who enter into civil marriage include, as to property: joint Massachusetts income tax filing; . . . automatic rights to inherit the property of a deceased spouse who does not leave a will; the rights of elective share and of dower (which allow surviving spouses certain property rights where the decedent spouse has not made adequate provision for the survivor in a will); entitlement to wages owed to a deceased employee; eligibility to continue certain businesses of a deceased spouse; the right to share the medical policy of one's spouse; thirty-nine week continuation of health coverage for the spouse of a person who is laid off or dies; . . . the equitable division of marital property on divorce; temporary and permanent alimony rights; the right to separate support on separation of the parties that does not result in divorce; and the right to bring claims for wrongful death and loss of consortium, and for funeral and burial expenses and punitive damages resulting from tort actions.

Other statutory benefits of a personal nature available only to married individuals include qualification for bereavement or medical leave to care for individuals related by blood or marriage; an automatic "family member" preference to make medical decisions for an incompetent or disabled spouse who does not have a contrary health care proxy; the application of predictable rules of child custody, visitation, support, and removal out-of-State when married parents divorce; priority rights to administer the estate of a deceased spouse who dies without a will, and requirement that surviving spouse must consent to the appointment of any other person as administrator; and the right to interment in the lot or tomb owned by one's deceased spouse.

Because civil marriage is central to the lives of individuals and the welfare of the community, our laws assiduously protect the individual's right to marry against undue government incursion.

Unquestionably, the regulatory power of the Commonwealth over civil marriage is broad, as is the Commonwealth's discretion to award public benefits. Individuals who have the choice to marry each other and nevertheless choose not to may properly be denied the legal benefits of marriage. But that same logic cannot hold for a qualified individual who would marry if she or he only could.

B

For decades, indeed centuries, in much of this country (including Massachusetts) no lawful marriage was possible between white and black Americans. That long history availed not when the Supreme Court of California held in 1948 that a legislative prohibition against interracial marriage violated the due process and equality guarantees of the Fourteenth Amendment, *Perez v. Sharp,* 32 Cal.2d 711, 728 (1948), or when, nineteen years later, the United States Supreme Court also held that a statutory bar to interracial marriage violated the Fourteenth Amendment, *Loving v. Virginia,* 388 U.S. 1 (1967). As both *Perez* and *Loving* make clear, the right to marry means little if it does not include the right to marry the person of one's choice, subject to appropriate government restrictions in the interests of public health, safety, and welfare. In this case, as in *Perez* and *Loving,* a statute deprives individuals of access to an institution of fundamental legal, personal, and social significance—the institution of marriage—because of a single trait: skin color in *Perez* and *Loving,* sexual orientation here. As it did in *Perez* and *Loving,* history must yield to a more fully developed understanding of the invidious quality of the discrimination.

The Massachusetts Constitution protects matters of personal liberty against government incursion as zealously, and often more so, than does the Federal Constitution, even where both Constitutions employ essentially the same language.

The individual liberty and equality safeguards of the Massachusetts Constitution protect both "freedom from" unwarranted government intrusion into protected spheres of life and "freedom to" partake in benefits created by the State for the common good. Both freedoms are involved here. Whether and whom to marry, how to express sexual intimacy, and whether and how to establish a family—these are among the most basic of every individual's liberty and due process rights. And central to personal freedom and security is the assurance that the laws will apply equally to persons in similar situations. The liberty interest in choosing whether and whom to marry would be hollow if the Commonwealth could, without sufficient justification, foreclose an individual from freely choosing the person with whom to share an exclusive commitment in the unique institution of civil marriage.

The plaintiffs challenge the marriage statute on both equal protection and due process grounds. With respect to each such claim, we must first determine the appropriate standard of review. Where a statute implicates a fundamental right or uses a suspect classification, we employ "strict judicial scrutiny." *Lowell v. Kowalski,* 380 Mass. 663, 666 (1980). For all other statutes, we employ the " 'rational basis' test." *English v. New England Med. Ctr.,* 405 Mass. 423, 428 (1989). For due process claims, rational basis analysis requires that statutes "bear[ ] a real and substantial relation to the public health, safety, morals, or some other phase of the general welfare." *Coffee-Rich, Inc. v. Commissioner of Pub. Health,* 348 Mass. 763, 778 (2002), quoting *Sperry & Hutchinson Co. v. Director of the Div. on the Necessaries of Life,* 307 Mass. 408, 418 (1940). For equal protection challenges, the rational basis test requires that "an impartial lawmaker could logically believe that the classification would serve a legitimate public purpose that transcends the harm to the members of the disadvantaged class." *English v. New England Med. Ctr., supra* at 429, quoting *Cleburne v. Cleburne Living Ctr., Inc.,* 473 U.S. 432, 452 (1985) (Stevens, J., concurring).

The department argues that no fundamental right or "suspect" class is at issue here, and rational basis is the appropriate standard of review. For the reasons we explain below, we conclude that the marriage ban does not meet the rational basis test for either due process or equal protection. Because the statute does not survive rational basis review, we do not consider the plaintiffs' arguments that this case merits strict judicial scrutiny.

The department posits three legislative rationales for prohibiting same-sex couples from marrying: (1) providing a "favorable setting for procreation"; (2) ensuring the optimal setting for child rearing, which the department defines as "a two-parent family with one parent of each sex"; and (3) preserving scarce State and private financial resources. We consider each in turn.

Our laws of civil marriage do not privilege procreative heterosexual intercourse between married people above every other form of adult intimacy and every other means of creating a family. General Laws c. 207 contains no requirement that the applicants for a marriage license attest to their ability or intention to conceive children by coitus. Fertility is not a condition of marriage, nor is it grounds for divorce.

The "marriage is procreation" argument singles out the one unbridgeable difference between same-sex and opposite-sex couples, and transforms that difference into the essence of legal marriage.

The department's first stated rationale, equating marriage with unassisted heterosexual procreation, shades imperceptibly into its second: that confining marriage to opposite-sex couples ensures that children are raised in the "optimal" setting. Protecting the welfare of children is a paramount State policy. The "best interests of the child" standard does not turn on a parent's sexual orientation or marital status.

The third rationale advanced by the department is that limiting marriage to opposite-sex couples furthers the Legislature's interest in conserving scarce State and private financial resources.

An absolute statutory ban on same-sex marriage bears no rational relationship to the goal of economy. First, the department's conclusory generalization—that same-sex couples are less financially dependent on each other than opposite-sex couples—ignores that many same-sex couples, such as many of the plaintiffs in this case, have children and other dependents (here, aged parents) in their care. The department does not contend, nor could it, that these dependents are less needy or deserving than the dependents of married couples. Second, Massachusetts marriage laws do not condition receipt of public and private financial benefits to married individuals on a demonstration of financial dependence on each other; the benefits are available to married couples regardless of whether they mingle their finances or actually depend on each other for support.

The department suggests additional rationales for prohibiting same-sex couples from marrying, which are developed by some amici. It argues that broadening civil marriage to include same-sex couples will trivialize or destroy the institution of marriage as it has historically been fashioned. Certainly our decision today marks a significant change in the definition of marriage as it has been inherited from the common law, and understood by many societies for centuries. But it does not disturb the fundamental value of marriage in our society.

Recognizing the right of an individual to marry a person of the same sex will not diminish the validity or dignity of opposite-sex marriage, any more than recognizing the right of an individual to marry a person of a different race devalues the marriage of a person who marries someone of her own race. If anything, extending civil marriage to same-sex couples reinforces the importance of marriage to individuals and communities. That same-sex couples are willing to embrace marriage's solemn obligations of exclusivity, mutual support, and commitment to one another is a testament to the enduring place of marriage in our laws and in the human spirit.

It has been argued that, due to the State's strong interest in the institution of marriage as a stabilizing social structure, only the Legislature can control and define its boundaries. Accordingly, our elected representatives legitimately may choose to exclude same-sex couples from civil marriage in order to assure all citizens of the Commonwealth that (1) the benefits of our marriage laws are available explicitly to create and support a family setting that is, in the Legislature's view, optimal for child rearing, and (2) the State does not endorse gay and lesbian parenthood as the equivalent of being raised by one's married biological parents. These arguments miss the point. The Massachusetts Constitution requires that legislation meet certain criteria and not extend beyond certain limits. It is the function of courts to determine whether these criteria are met and whether these limits are exceeded. In most instances, these limits are defined by whether a rational basis exists to conclude that legislation will bring about a rational result. The Legislature in the first instance, and the courts in the last instance, must ascertain whether such a rational basis exists. To label the court's role as usurping that of the Legislature, is to misunderstand the nature and purpose of judicial review. We owe great deference to the Legislature to decide social and policy issues, but it is the traditional and settled role of courts to decide constitutional issues.

We also reject the argument suggested by the department, and elaborated by some amici, that expanding the institution of civil marriage in Massachusetts to include same-sex couples will lead to interstate conflict. We would not presume to dictate how another State should respond to today's decision. But neither should considerations of comity prevent us from according Massachusetts residents the full measure of protection available under the Massachusetts Constitution. The genius of our Federal system is that each State's Constitution has vitality specific to its own traditions, and that, subject to the minimum requirements of the Fourteenth Amendment, each State is free to address difficult issues of individual liberty in the manner its own Constitution demands.

The marriage ban works a deep and scarring hardship on a very real segment of the community for no rational reason. The absence of any reasonable relationship between, on the one hand, an absolute disqualification of same-sex couples who wish to enter into civil marriage and, on the other, protection of public health, safety, or general welfare, suggests that the marriage restriction is rooted in persistent prejudices against persons who are (or who are believed to be) homosexual. Limiting the protections, benefits, and obligations of civil marriage to opposite-sex couples violates the basic premises of individual liberty and equality under law protected by the Massachusetts Constitution.

JUSTICE GREANEY delivered a concurring opinion.

I agree with the result reached by the court, the remedy ordered, and much of the reasoning in the court's opinion. In my view, however, the case is more directly resolved using traditional equal protection analysis.

Analysis begins with the indisputable premise that the deprivation suffered by the plaintiffs is no mere legal inconvenience. The right to marry is not a privilege conferred by the State, but a fundamental right that is protected against unwarranted State interference. This right is essentially vitiated if one is denied the right to marry a person of one's choice.

Because our marriage statutes intend, and state, the ordinary understanding that marriage under our law consists only of a union between a man and a woman, they create a statutory classification based on the sex of the two people who wish to marry. That the classification is sex based is self-evident. The marriage statutes prohibit some applicants, such as the plaintiffs, from obtaining a marriage license, and that prohibition is based solely on the applicants' gender. As a factual matter, an individual's choice of marital partner is constrained because of his or her own sex. Stated in particular terms, Hillary Goodridge cannot marry Julie Goodridge because she (Hillary) is a woman. Likewise, Gary Chalmers cannot marry Richard Linnell because he (Gary) is a man. Only their gender prevents Hillary and Gary from marrying their chosen partners under the present law.

A classification may be gender based whether or not the challenged government action apportions benefits or burdens uniformly along gender lines. This is so because constitutional protections extend to individuals and not to categories of people. Thus, when an individual desires to marry, but cannot marry his or her chosen partner because of the traditional opposite-sex restriction, a violation of art. 1 has occurred. I find it disingenuous, at best, to suggest that such an individual's right to marry has not been burdened at all, because he or she remains free to choose another partner, who is of the opposite sex.

JUSTICE SPINA delivered a dissenting opinion, with which JUSTICES SOSMAN and CORDY join.

What is at stake in this case is not the unequal treatment of individuals or whether individual rights have been impermissibly burdened, but the power of the Legislature to effectuate social change without interference from the courts, pursuant to art. 30 of the Massachusetts Declaration of Rights. The power to regulate marriage lies with the Legislature, not with the judiciary. Today, the court has transformed its role as protector of individual rights into the role of creator of rights, and I respectfully dissent.

1. *Equal protection.* Although the court did not address the plaintiffs' gender discrimination claim, G.L. c. 207 does not unconstitutionally discriminate on the basis of gender. It creates no distinction between the sexes, but applies to men and women in precisely the same way. It does not create any disadvantage identified with gender as both men and women are similarly limited to marrying a person of the opposite sex.

Similarly, the marriage statutes do not discriminate on the basis of sexual orientation. As the court correctly recognizes, constitutional protections are extended to individuals, not couples. The marriage statutes do not disqualify individuals on the basis of sexual orientation from entering into marriage. All individuals, with certain exceptions not relevant here, are free to marry. Whether an individual chooses not to marry because of sexual orientation or any other reason should be of no concern to the court.

Unlike the *Loving* [*v. Virginia*, 388 U.S. 1 (1967)] and [*Perez v.*] *Sharp* [32 Cal. 2d 711 (1948)] cases, the Massachusetts Legislature has erected no barrier to marriage that intentionally discriminates against anyone. Within the institution of marriage, anyone is free to marry, with certain exceptions that are not challenged. In the absence of any discriminatory purpose, the State's marriage statutes do not violate principles of equal protection. This court should not have invoked even the most deferential standard of review within equal protection analysis because no individual was denied access to the institution of marriage.

2. *Due process.* The marriage statutes do not impermissibly burden a right protected by our constitutional guarantee of due process implicit in art. 10 of our Declaration of Rights. There is no restriction on the right of any plaintiff to enter into marriage. Each is free to marry a willing person of the opposite sex.

Substantive due process protects individual rights against unwarranted government intrusion. The court states, as we have said on many occasions, that the Massachusetts Declaration of Rights may protect a right in ways that exceed the protection afforded by the Federal Constitution. However, today the court does not fashion a remedy that affords greater protection of a right. Instead, using the rubric of due process it has redefined marriage.

Although this court did not state that same-sex marriage is a fundamental right worthy of strict scrutiny protection, it nonetheless deemed it a constitutionally protected right by applying rational basis review. Before applying any level of constitutional analysis there must be a recognized right at stake. In this Commonwealth and in this country, the roots of the institution of marriage are deeply set in history as a civil union between a single man and a single woman. There is no basis for the court to recognize same-sex marriage as a constitutionally protected right.

The court has extruded a new right from principles of substantive due process, and in doing so it has distorted the meaning and purpose of due process. The purpose of substantive due process is to protect existing rights, not to create new rights. Its aim is to thwart government intrusion, not invite it. The court asserts that the Massachusetts Declaration of Rights serves to guard against government intrusion into each individual's sphere of privacy. Similarly, the Supreme Court has called for increased due process protection when individual privacy and intimacy are threatened by unnecessary government imposition. These cases . . . focus on the threat to privacy when government seeks to regulate the most intimate activity behind bedroom doors. The statute in question does not seek to regulate intimate activity within an intimate relationship, but merely gives formal recognition to a particular marriage. The State has respected the private lives of the plaintiffs, and has done nothing to intrude in the relationships that each of the plaintiff couples enjoy. Ironically, by extending the marriage laws to same-sex couples the court has turned substantive due process on its head and used it to interject government into the plaintiffs' lives.

JUSTICE SOSMAN, wrote a dissenting opinion with whom JUSTICES SPINA and CORDY join.

As a matter of social history, today's opinion may represent a great turning point that many will hail as a tremendous step toward a more just society. As a matter of constitutional jurisprudence, however, the case stands as an aberration. To reach the result it does, the court has tortured the rational basis test beyond recognition. I fully appreciate the strength of the temptation to find this particular law unconstitutional—there is much to be said for the argument that excluding gay and lesbian couples from the benefits of civil marriage is cruelly unfair and hopelessly outdated; the inability to marry has a profound impact on the personal lives of committed gay and lesbian couples (and their children) to whom we are personally close (our friends, neighbors, family members, classmates, and co-workers); and our resolution of this issue takes place under the intense glare of national and international publicity. Speaking metaphorically, these factors have combined to turn the case before us into a "perfect storm" of a constitutional question. In my view, however, such factors make it all the more imperative that we adhere precisely and scrupulously to the established guideposts of our constitutional jurisprudence, a jurisprudence that makes the rational basis test an extremely deferential one that focuses on the rationality, not the persuasiveness, of the potential justifications for the classifications in the legislative scheme. I trust that, once this particular "storm" clears, we will return to the rational basis test as it has always been understood and applied. Applying that deferential test in the manner it is customarily applied, the exclusion of gay and lesbian couples from the institution of civil marriage passes constitutional muster. I respectfully dissent.

JUSTICE CORDY, wrote a dissenting opinion with whom JUSTICES SPINA and SOSMAN join.

The court's opinion concludes that the Department of Public Health has failed to identify any "constitutionally adequate reason" for limiting civil marriage to opposite-sex unions, and that there is no "reasonable relationship" between a disqualification of same-sex couples who wish to enter into a civil marriage and the protection of public health, safety, or general welfare. Consequently, it holds that the marriage statute cannot withstand scrutiny under the Massachusetts Constitution. Because I find these conclusions to be unsupportable in light of the nature of the rights and regulations at issue, the presumption of constitutional validity and significant deference afforded to legislative enactments, and the "undesirability of the judiciary substituting its notions of correct policy for that of a popularly elected Legislature" responsible for making such policy, *Zayre Corp.* v. *Attorney Gen.*, 372 Mass. 423, 433 (1977), I respectfully dissent. Although it may be desirable for many reasons to extend to same-sex couples the benefits and burdens of civil marriage (and the plaintiffs have made a powerfully reasoned case for that extension), that decision must be made by the Legislature, not the court.

The Massachusetts marriage statute does not impair the exercise of a recognized fundamental right, or discriminate on the basis of sex in violation of the equal rights amendment to the Massachusetts Constitution. Consequently, it is subject to review only to determine whether it satisfies the rational basis test. Because a conceivable rational basis exists upon which the Legislature could conclude that the marriage statute furthers the legitimate State purpose of ensuring, promoting, and supporting an optimal social structure for the bearing and raising of children, it is a valid exercise of the State's police power.

A. *Limiting marriage to the union of one man and one woman does not impair the exercise of a fundamental right.* Although public attitudes toward marriage in general and same-sex marriage in particular have changed and are still evolving, "the asserted contemporary concept of marriage and societal interests for which [plaintiffs] contend" are "manifestly [less] deeply founded" than the "historic institution" of marriage. *Matter of the Estate of Cooper,* 187 A.D.2d 128, 133–134 (N.Y.1993). Indeed, it is not readily apparent to what extent contemporary values have embraced the concept of same-sex marriage. No State Legislature has enacted laws permitting same-sex marriages; and a large majority of States, as well as the United States Congress, have affirmatively prohibited the recognition of such marriages for any purpose.

Given this history and the current state of public opinion, as reflected in the actions of the people's elected representatives, it cannot be said that a right to same-sex marriage is so rooted in the traditions and collective conscience of our people that failure to recognize it would violate the fundamental principles of liberty and justice that lie at the base of all our civil and political institutions. In such circumstances, the law with respect to same-sex marriages must be left to develop through legislative processes, subject to the constraints of rationality, lest the court be viewed as using the liberty and due process clauses as vehicles merely to enforce its own views regarding better social policies, a role that the strongly worded separation of powers principles in art. 30 of the Declaration of Rights of our Constitution forbids, and for which the court is particularly ill suited.

B. *The marriage statute, in limiting marriage to heterosexual couples, does not constitute discrimination on the basis of sex in violation of the Equal Rights Amendment [(ERA)] to the Massachusetts Constitution.* The central purpose of the ERA was to eradicate discrimination against women and in favor of men or vice versa. Consistent with this purpose, we have construed the ERA to prohibit laws that advantage one sex at the expense of the other, but not laws that treat men and women equally. The Massachusetts marriage statute does not subject men to different treatment from women; each is equally prohibited from precisely the same conduct.

C. *The marriage statute satisfies the rational basis standard.* The burden of demonstrating that a statute does not satisfy the rational basis standard rests on the plaintiffs. It is a weighty one.

In analyzing whether a statute satisfies the rational basis standard, we look to the nature of the classification embodied in the enactment, then to whether the statute serves a legitimate State purpose, and finally to whether the classification is reasonably related to the furtherance of that purpose.

1. *Classification.* The nature of the classification at issue is readily apparent. Opposite-sex couples can obtain a license and same-sex couples cannot. The classification is not drawn between men and women or between heterosexuals and homosexuals, any of whom can obtain a license to marry a member of the opposite sex; rather, it is drawn between same-sex couples and opposite-sex couples.

2. *State purpose.* The court's opinion concedes that the civil marriage statute serves legitimate State purposes. . . .

It is difficult to imagine a State purpose more important and legitimate than ensuring, promoting, and supporting an optimal social structure within which to bear and raise children. At the very least, the marriage statute continues to serve this important State purpose.

3. *Rational relationship.* The question we must turn to next is whether the statute, construed as limiting marriage to couples of the opposite sex, remains a rational way to further that purpose. Stated differently, we ask whether a conceivable rational basis exists on which the Legislature could conclude that continuing to limit the institution of civil marriage to members of the opposite sex furthers the legitimate purpose of ensuring, promoting, and supporting an optimal social structure for the bearing and raising of children.

There is no question that many same-sex couples are capable of being good parents, and should be (and are) permitted to be so. The policy question that a legislator must resolve is a different one, and turns on an assessment of whether the marriage structure proposed by the plaintiffs will, over time, if endorsed and supported by the State, prove to be as stable and successful a model as the one that has formed a cornerstone of our society since colonial times, or prove to be less than optimal, and result in consequences, perhaps now unforeseen, adverse to the State's legitimate interest in promoting and supporting the best possible social structure in which children should be born and raised. Given the critical importance of civil marriage as an organizing and stabilizing institution of society, it is eminently rational for the Legislature to postpone making fundamental changes to it until such time as there is unanimous scientific evidence, or popular consensus, or both, that such changes can safely be made.

D. *Conclusion.* While "the Massachusetts Constitution protects matters of personal liberty against government intrusion at least as zealously, and often more so than does the Federal Constitution," this case is not about government intrusions into matters of personal liberty. It is not about the rights of same-sex couples to choose to live together, or to be intimate with each other, or to adopt and raise children together. It is about whether the State must endorse and support their choices by changing the institution of civil marriage to make its benefits, obligations, and responsibilities applicable to them. While the courageous efforts of many have resulted in increased dignity, rights, and respect for gay and lesbian members of our community, the issue presented here is a profound one, deeply rooted in social policy, that must, for now, be the subject of legislative not judicial action.

FOR DISCUSSION

How does the state of Massachusetts reflect a different understanding of the protections under the Equal Protection Clause for matters of sexual orientation than under the federal decision of *Lawrence v. Texas*?

RELATED CASE

***Baehr v. Miike*: 852 P.2d 44 (1993).**
The Hawaiian Supreme Court determined that a state statute limiting the definition of marriage to opposite-sex couples violaged of the Hawaiian constitution's Equal Protection Clause. In 1998, the state amended its constitution to grant the state legislature the power to limit marriage to opposite-sex couples, which it subsequently did.

FEDERAL DEFENSE OF MARRIAGE ACT

110 Stat. 2419 (1996)

This act attempted to ensure that the Equal Protection Clause and the Due Process Clause of the Fourteenth Amendment would not be interpreted as forcing the federal government to expand the definition of marriage to same-sex couples (§ 1). It was also designed to lay a foundation to prevent an interpretation of the Full Faith and Credit Clause (Article IV, § I) of the Constitution to require a state that does not recognize same-sex marriage from recognizing such a marriage legitimized by another state (§ 2).

Section 1.

In determining the meaning of any Act of Congress, or of any ruling, regulation, or interpretation of the various administrative bureaus and agencies of the United States, the word "marriage" means only a legal union between one man and one woman as husband and wife, and the word "spouse" refers only to a person of the opposite sex who is a husband or a wife. Pub. L. 104–199, sec 1, 100 Stat. 2419 (Sep. 21, 1996) codified at 1 U.S.C. § 7 (1997).

Section 2.

No State, territory, or possession of the United States, or Indian tribe, shall be required to give effect to any public act, record, or judicial proceeding of any other State, territory, possession or tribe, respecting a relationship between persons of the same sex that is treated as a marriage under the laws of such other state, territory, possession or tribe, or a right or claim arising from such relationship. Pub. L. 104–199 sec. 2, 100 Stat. 2419 (Sep. 21, 1996) codified at 28 U.S.C. § 1738C (1997).

FOR DISCUSSION

The regulation and recording of marriage is traditionally reserved to the state. On what grounds would the federal government assume the power to define the parameters of the marriage requirement?

UNITED STATES V. WINDSOR

570 U.S. ___, 133 S.Ct. 2675, 186 L.Ed.2d 808 (2013)

Edith Windsor and Thea Spyer were legally married in Ontario, Canada in 2007, subsequently returning to their home in New York City. After Spyer's death in 2009, her estate was left to Windsor, but when she tried to claim the spousal exemption to the estate tax, she was federally prohibited. The Defense of Marriage Act explicitly excluded a same-sex partner under the definition of "spouse" when used in federal law. This statutory prohibition left Windsor with over a $360,000 tax bill. She paid the tax and filed a lawsuit challenging the constitutionality of this provision. Both federal district court and the court of appeals found this portion of the statute to be unconstitutional, ordering the United States to pay Windsor a refund.

Vote: 5–4

JUSTICE KENNEDY delivered the majority opinion.

I

In 1996, as some States were beginning to consider the concept of same-sex marriage, see, *e.g.*, *Baehr* v. *Lewin*, 74 Haw. 530, 852 P. 2d 44 (1993), and before any State had acted to permit it, Congress enacted the Defense of Marriage Act (DOMA), 110 Stat. 2419. DOMA contains two operative sections: Section 2, which has not been challenged here, allows States to refuse to recognize same-sex marriages performed under the laws of other States. Section 3 is at issue here. It amends the Dictionary Act in Title 1, § 7, of the United States Code to provide a federal definition of "marriage" and "spouse."

The definitional provision does not by its terms forbid States from enacting laws permitting same-sex marriages or civil unions or providing state benefits to residents in that status. The enactment's comprehensive definition of marriage for purposes of all federal statutes and other regulations or directives covered by its terms, however, does control over 1,000 federal laws in which marital or spousal status is addressed as a matter of federal law.

While the tax refund suit was pending, the Attorney General of the United States notified the Speaker of the House of Representatives that the Department of Justice would no longer defend the constitutionality of DOMA's § 3. Noting that "the Department has previously defended DOMA against . . . challenges involving legally married same-sex couples," the Attorney General informed Congress that "the President has concluded that given a number of factors, including a documented history of discrimination, classifications based on sexual orientation should be subject to a heightened standard of scrutiny."

Although "the President . . . instructed the Department not to defend the statute in *Windsor*," he also decided "that Section 3 will continue to be enforced by the Executive Branch" and that the United States had an "interest in providing Congress a full and fair opportunity to participate in the litigation of those cases." The stated rationale for this dual-track procedure (determination of unconstitutionality coupled with ongoing enforcement) was to "recogniz[e] the judiciary as the final arbiter of the constitutional claims raised."

In response to the notice from the Attorney General, the Bipartisan Legal Advisory Group (BLAG) of the House of Representatives voted to intervene in the litigation to defend the constitutionality of § 3 of DOMA. The Department of Justice did not oppose limited intervention by BLAG.

In granting certiorari on the question of the constitutionality of § 3 of DOMA, the Court requested argument on two additional questions: whether the United States' agreement with Windsor's legal position precludes further review and whether BLAG has standing to appeal the case.

III

When at first Windsor and Spyer longed to marry, neither New York nor any other State granted them that right. After waiting some years, in 2007 they traveled to Ontario to be married there. It seems fair to conclude that, until recent years, many citizens had not even considered the possibility that two persons of the same sex might aspire to occupy the same status and dignity as that of a man and woman in lawful marriage. For marriage between a man and a woman no doubt had been thought of by most people as essential to the very definition of that term and to its role and function throughout the history of civilization. That belief, for many who long have held it, became even more urgent, more cherished when challenged. For others, however, came the beginnings of a new perspective, a new insight. Accordingly some States concluded that same-sex marriage ought to be given recognition and validity in the law for those same-sex couples who wish to define themselves by their commitment to each other. The limitation of lawful marriage to heterosexual couples, which for centuries had been deemed both necessary and fundamental, came to be seen in New York and certain other States as an unjust exclusion.

Slowly at first and then in rapid course, the laws of New York came to acknowledge the urgency of this issue for same-sex couples who wanted to affirm their commitment to one another before their children, their family, their friends, and their community. And so New York recognized same-sex marriages performed elsewhere; and then it later amended its own marriage laws to permit same- sex marriage. New York, in common with, as of this writing, 11 other States and the District of Columbia, decided that same-sex couples should have the right to marry and so live with pride in themselves and their union and in a status of equality with all other married persons. After a statewide deliberative process that enabled its citizens to discuss and weigh arguments for and against same-sex marriage, New York acted to enlarge the definition of marriage to correct what its citizens and elected representatives perceived to be an injustice that they had not earlier known or understood.

Against this background of lawful same-sex marriage in some States, the design, purpose, and effect of DOMA should be considered as the beginning point in deciding whether it is valid under the Constitution. By history and tradition the definition and regulation of marriage . . . has been treated as being within the authority and realm of the separate States. Yet it is further established that Congress, in enacting discrete statutes, can make determinations that bear on marital rights and privileges.

[P]recedents involving congressional statutes which affect marriages and family status . . . illustrate this point. In addressing the interaction of state domestic relations and federal immigration law Congress determined that marriages "entered into for the purpose of procuring an alien's admission [to the United States] as an immigrant" will not qualify the noncitizen for that status, even if the noncitizen's marriage is valid and proper for state-law purposes. And in establishing income-based criteria for Social Security benefits, Congress decided that although state law would determine in general who qualifies as an applicant's spouse, common-law marriages also should be recognized, regardless of any particular State's view on these relationships.

Though these discrete examples establish the constitutionality of limited federal laws that regulate the meaning of marriage in order to further federal policy, DOMA has a far greater reach; for it enacts a directive applicable to over 1,000 federal statutes and the whole realm of federal regulations. And its operation is directed to a class of persons that the laws of New York, and of 11 other States, have sought to protect. See *Goodridge* v. *Department of Public Health*, 440 Mass. 309, 798 N. E. 2d 941 (2003).

In order to assess the validity of that intervention it is necessary to discuss the extent of the state power and authority over marriage as a matter of history and tradition. State laws defining and regulating marriage, of course, must respect the constitutional rights of persons; but, subject to those guarantees, "regulation of domestic relations" is "an area that has long been regarded as a virtually exclusive province of the States." *Sosna v. Iowa*, 419 U.S. 393, 403 (1975).

The recognition of civil marriages is central to state domestic relations law applicable to its residents and citizens. The definition of marriage is the foundation of the State's broader authority to regulate the subject of domestic relations with respect to the "[p]rotection of offspring, property interests, and the enforcement of marital responsibilities." *Williams v. North Carolina*, 317 U.S. 287, 298 (1942). "[T]he states, at the time of the adoption of the Constitution, possessed full power over the subject of marriage and divorce... [and] the Constitution delegated no authority to the Government of the United States on the subject of marriage and divorce." *Haddock v. Haddock*, 201 U.S. 562, 575 (1906).

Consistent with this allocation of authority, the Federal Government, through our history, has deferred to state-law policy decisions with respect to domestic relations. In order to respect this principle, the federal courts, as a general rule, do not adjudicate issues of marital status even when there might otherwise be a basis for federal jurisdiction.

The significance of state responsibilities for the definition and regulation of marriage dates to the Nation's beginning; for "when the Constitution was adopted the common understanding was that the domestic relations of husband and wife and parent and child were matters reserved to the States." *Ohio ex rel. Popovici v. Angler*, 280 U.S. 379–384 (1930). Marriage laws vary in some respects from State to State. For example, the required minimum age is 16 in Vermont, but only 13 in New Hampshire. Likewise the permissible degree of consanguinity can vary (most States permit first cousins to marry, but a handful—such as Iowa and Washington—prohibit the practice). But these rules are in every event consistent within each State.

Against this background DOMA rejects the long-established precept that the incidents, benefits, and obligations of marriage are uniform for all married couples within each State, though they may vary, subject to constitutional guarantees, from one State to the next. Despite these considerations, it is unnecessary to decide whether this federal intrusion on state power is a violation of the Constitution because it disrupts the federal balance. The State's power in defining the marital relation is of central relevance in this case quite apart from principles of federalism. Here the State's decision to give this class of persons the right to marry conferred upon them a dignity and status of immense import. When the State used its historic and essential authority to define the marital relation in this way, its role and its power in making the decision enhanced the recognition, dignity, and protection of the class in their own community. DOMA, because of its reach and extent, departs from this history and tradition of reliance on state law to define marriage.

The Federal Government uses this state-defined class for the opposite purpose—to impose restrictions and disabilities. That result requires this Court now to address whether the resulting injury and indignity is a deprivation of an essential part of the liberty protected by the Fifth Amendment. What the State of New York treats as alike the federal law deems unlike by a law designed to injure the same class the State seeks to protect. In acting first to recognize and then to allow same-sex marriages, New York was responding "to the initiative of those who [sought] a voice in shaping the destiny of their own times." These actions were without doubt a proper exercise of its sovereign authority within our federal system, all in the way that the Framers of the Constitution intended. The dynamics of state government in the federal system are to allow the formation of consensus respecting the way the members of a discrete community treat each other in their daily contact and constant interaction with each other.

The States' interest in defining and regulating the marital relation, subject to constitutional guarantees, stems from the understanding that marriage is more than a routine classification for purposes of certain statutory benefits. Private, consensual sexual intimacy between two adult persons of the same sex may not be punished by the State, and it can form "but one element in a personal bond that is more enduring." *Lawrence* v. *Texas*, 539 U.S. 558, 567 (2003). By its recognition of the validity of same-sex marriages performed in other jurisdictions and then by authorizing same-sex unions and same-sex marriages, New York sought to give further protection and dignity to that bond. *Bond v. U.S.*, 564 U.S. [211] (2011). For same-sex couples who wished to be married, the State acted to give their lawful conduct a lawful status. This status is a far-reaching legal acknowledgment of the intimate relationship between two people, a relationship deemed by the State worthy of dignity in the community equal with all other marriages. It reflects both the community's considered perspective on the historical roots of the institution of marriage and its evolving understanding of the meaning of equality.

IV

DOMA seeks to injure the very class New York seeks to protect. By doing so it violates basic due process and equal protection principles applicable to the Federal Government. The Constitution's guarantee of equality "must at the very least mean that a bare congressional desire to harm a politically unpopular group cannot" justify disparate treatment of that group. In determining whether a law is motived by an improper animus or purpose, " '[d]iscriminations of an unusual character' " especially require careful consideration. DOMA cannot survive under these principles. The responsibility of the States for the regulation of domestic relations is an important indicator of the substantial societal impact the State's classifications have in the daily lives and customs of its people. DOMA's unusual deviation from the usual tradition of recognizing and accepting state definitions of marriage here operates to deprive same-sex couples of the benefits and responsibilities that come with the federal recognition of their marriages. This is strong evidence of a law having the purpose and effect of disapproval of that class. The avowed purpose and practical effect of the law here in question are to impose a disadvantage, a separate status, and so a stigma upon all who enter into same-sex marriages made lawful by the unquestioned authority of the States.

The history of DOMA's enactment and its own text demonstrate that interference with the equal dignity of same-sex marriages, a dignity conferred by the States in the exercise of their sovereign power, was more than an incidental effect of the federal statute. It was its essence. The House Report announced its conclusion that "it is both appropriate and necessary for Congress to do what it can to defend the institution of traditional heterosexual marriage. . . . H. R. 3396 is appropriately entitled the 'Defense of Marriage Act.' The effort to redefine 'marriage' to extend to homosexual couples is a truly radical proposal that would fundamentally alter the institution of marriage." The House concluded that DOMA expresses "both moral disapproval of homosexuality, and a moral conviction that heterosexuality better comports with traditional (especially Judeo-Christian) morality." The stated purpose of the law was to promote an "interest in protecting the traditional moral teachings reflected in heterosexual-only marriage laws." Were there any doubt of this far-reaching purpose, the title of the Act confirms it: The Defense of Marriage.

DOMA's operation in practice confirms this purpose. When New York adopted a law to permit same-sex marriage, it sought to eliminate inequality; but DOMA frustrates that objective through a system-wide enactment with no identified connection to any particular area of federal law. DOMA writes inequality into the entire United States Code. The particular case at hand concerns the estate tax, but DOMA is more than a simple determination of what should or should not be allowed as an estate tax refund. Among the over 1,000 statutes and numerous federal regulations that DOMA controls are laws pertaining to Social Security, housing, taxes, criminal sanctions, copyright, and veterans' benefits.

DOMA's principal effect is to identify a subset of state-sanctioned marriages and make them unequal. The principal purpose is to impose inequality, not for other reasons like governmental efficiency. Responsibilities, as well as rights, enhance the dignity and integrity of the person. And DOMA contrives to deprive some couples married under the laws of their State, but not other couples, of both rights and responsibilities. By creating two contradictory marriage regimes within the same State, DOMA forces same-sex couples to live as married for the purpose of state law but unmarried for the purpose of federal law, thus diminishing the stability and predictability of basic personal relations the State has found it proper to acknowledge and protect. By this dynamic DOMA undermines both the public and private significance of state- sanctioned same-sex marriages; for it tells those couples, and all the world, that their otherwise valid marriages are unworthy of federal recognition. This places same-sex couples in an unstable position of being in a second-tier marriage. The differentiation demeans the couple, whose moral and sexual choices the Constitution protects, see *Lawrence*, 539 U.S. 558, and whose relationship the State has sought to dignify. And it humiliates tens of thousands of children now being raised by same-sex couples. The law in question makes it even more difficult for the children to understand the integrity and closeness of their own family and its concord with other families in their community and in their daily lives.

* * *

The power the Constitution grants it also restrains. And though Congress has great authority to design laws to fit its own conception of sound national policy, it cannot deny the liberty protected by the Due Process Clause of the Fifth Amendment.

What has been explained to this point should more than suffice to establish that the principal purpose and the necessary effect of this law are to demean those persons who are in a lawful same-sex marriage. This requires the Court to hold, as it now does, that DOMA is unconstitutional as a deprivation of the liberty of the person protected by the Fifth Amendment of the Constitution.

The liberty protected by the Fifth Amendment's Due Process Clause contains within it the prohibition against denying to any person the equal protection of the laws. While the Fifth Amendment itself withdraws from Government the power to degrade or demean in the way this law does, the equal protection guarantee of the Fourteenth Amendment makes that Fifth Amendment right all the more specific and all the better understood and preserved.

The class to which DOMA directs its restrictions and restraints are those persons who are joined in same-sex marriages made lawful by the State. DOMA singles out a class of persons deemed by a State entitled to recognition and protection to enhance their own liberty. It imposes a disability on the class by refusing to acknowledge a status the State finds to be dignified and proper. DOMA instructs all federal officials, and indeed all persons with whom same-sex couples interact, including their own children, that their marriage is less worthy than the marriages of others. The federal statute is invalid, for no legitimate purpose overcomes the purpose and effect to disparage and to injure those whom the State, by its marriage laws, sought to protect in personhood and dignity. By seeking to displace this protection and treating those persons as living in marriages less respected than others, the federal statute is in violation of the Fifth Amendment. This opinion and its holding are confined to those lawful marriages.

The judgment of the Court of Appeals for the Second Circuit is affirmed.

It is so ordered.

CHIEF JUSTICE ROBERTS, dissenting.

On the merits of the constitutional dispute the Court decides to decide, I . . . agree with Justice Scalia that Congress acted constitutionally in passing the Defense of Marriage Act (DOMA). Interests in uniformity and stability amply justified Congress's decision to retain the definition of marriage that, at that point, had been adopted by every State in our Nation, and every nation in the world.

The majority sees a more sinister motive, pointing out that the Federal Government has generally (though not uniformly) deferred to state definitions of marriage in the past. That is true, of course, but none of those prior state-by-state variations had involved differences over something—as the majority puts it—"thought of by most people as essential to the very definition of [marriage] and to its role and function throughout the history of civilization." That the Federal Government treated this fundamental question differently than it treated variations over consanguinity or minimum age is hardly surprising—and hardly enough to support a conclusion that the "principal purpose," of the 342 Representatives and 85 Senators who voted for it, and the President who signed it, was a bare desire to harm. Nor do the snippets of legislative history and the banal title of the Act to which the majority points suffice to make such a showing. At least without some more convincing evidence that the Act's principal purpose was to codify malice, and that it furthered *no* legitimate government interests, I would not tar the political branches with the brush of bigotry.

But while I disagree with the result to which the majority's analysis leads it in this case, I think it more important to point out that its analysis leads no further. The Court does not have before it, and the logic of its opinion does not decide, the distinct question whether the States, in the exercise of their "historic and essential authority to define the marital relation," may continue to utilize the traditional definition of marriage.

The majority goes out of its way to make this explicit in the penultimate sentence of its opinion. It states that "[t]his opinion and its holding are confined to those lawful marriages,"—referring to same-sex marriages that a State has already recognized as a result of the local "community's considered perspective on the historical roots of the institution of marriage and its evolving understanding of the meaning of equality." Justice Scalia believes this is a " 'bald, unreasoned disclaime[r].' " In my view, though, the disclaimer is a logical and necessary consequence of the argument the majority has chosen to adopt. The dominant theme of the majority opinion is that the Federal Government's intrusion into an area "central to state domestic relations law applicable to its residents and citizens" is sufficiently "unusual" to set off alarm bells. I think the majority goes off course, as I have said, but it is undeniable that its judgment is based on federalism.

The majority extensively chronicles DOMA's departure from the normal allocation of responsibility between State and Federal Governments, emphasizing that DOMA "rejects the long-established precept that the incidents, benefits, and obligations of marriage are uniform for all married couples within each State." But there is no such departure when one State adopts or keeps a definition of marriage that differs from that of its neighbor, for it is entirely expected that state definitions would "vary, subject to constitutional guarantees, from one State to the next." Thus, while "[t]he State's power in defining the marital relation is of central relevance" to the majority's decision to strike down DOMA here, that power will come into play on the other side of the board in future cases about the constitutionality of state marriage definitions. So too will the concerns for state diversity and sovereignty that weigh against DOMA's constitutionality in this case.

We may in the future have to resolve challenges to state marriage definitions affecting same-sex couples. That issue, however, is not before us in this case. . . . I write only to highlight the limits of the majority's holding and reasoning today, lest its opinion be taken to resolve not only a question that I believe is not properly before us—DOMA's constitutionality—but also a question that all agree, and the Court explicitly acknowledges, is not at issue.

JUSTICE SCALIA, with whom JUSTICE THOMAS joins, and with whom THE CHIEF JUSTICE joins as to Part I, dissenting.

This case is about power in several respects. It is about the power of our people to govern themselves, and the power of this Court to pronounce the law. Today's opinion aggrandizes the latter, with the predictable consequence of diminishing the former. We have no power to decide this case. And even if we did, we have no power under the Constitution to invalidate this democratically adopted legislation. The Court's errors on both points spring forth from the same diseased root: an exalted conception of the role of this institution in America.

I A

The Court is eager—*hungry*—to tell everyone its view of the legal question at the heart of this case. Standing in the way is an obstacle, a technicality of little interest to anyone but the people of We the People, who created it as a barrier against judges' intrusion into their lives. They gave judges, in Article III, only the "judicial Power," a power to decide not abstract questions but real, concrete "Cases" and "Controversies." Yet the plaintiff and the Government agree entirely on what should happen in this lawsuit. They agree that the court below got it right; and they agreed in the court below that the court below that one got it right as well. What, then, are we *doing* here?

The answer lies at the heart of the jurisdictional portion of today's opinion, where a single sentence lays bare the majority's vision of our role. The Court says that we have the power to decide this case because if we did not, then our "primary role in determining the constitutionality of a law" (at least one that "has inflicted real injury on a plaintiff") would "become only secondary to the President's." But wait, the reader wonders—Windsor won below, and so *cured* her injury, and the President was glad to see it. True, says the majority, but judicial review must march on regardless, lest we "undermine the clear dictate of the separation-of-powers principle that when an Act of Congress is alleged to conflict with the Constitution, it is emphatically the province and duty of the judicial department to say what the law is."

That is jaw-dropping. It is an assertion of judicial supremacy over the people's Representatives in Congress and the Executive. It envisions a Supreme Court standing (or rather enthroned) at the apex of government, empowered to decide all constitutional questions, always and everywhere "primary" in its role.

Our authority begins and ends with the need to adjudge the rights of an injured party who stands before us seeking redress.

That is completely absent here. Windsor's injury was cured by the judgment in her favor. And while, in ordinary circumstances, the United States is injured by a directive to pay a tax refund, this suit is far from ordinary. Whatever injury the United States has suffered will surely not be redressed by the action that it, as a litigant, asks us to take. The final sentence of the Solicitor General's brief on the merits reads: "For the foregoing reasons, the judgment of the court of appeals *should be affirmed*." That will not cure the Government's injury, but carve it into stone. One could spend many fruitless afternoons ransacking our library for any other petitioner's brief seeking an affirmance of the judgment against it. What the petitioner United States asks us to do in the case before us is exactly what the respondent Windsor asks us to do: not to provide relief from the judgment below but to say that that judgment was correct. And the same was true in the Court of Appeals: Neither party sought to undo the judgment for Windsor, and so that court should have dismissed the appeal (just as we should dismiss) for lack of jurisdiction. Since both parties agreed with the judgment of the District Court for the Southern District of New York, the suit should have ended there. The further proceedings have been a contrivance, having no object in mind except to elevate a District Court judgment that has no precedential effect in other courts, to one that has precedential effect throughout the Second Circuit, and then (in this Court) precedential effect throughout the United States.

II

For the reasons above, I think that this Court has, and the Court of Appeals had, no power to decide this suit. We should vacate the decision below and remand to the Court of Appeals for the Second Circuit, with instructions to dismiss the appeal. Given that the majority has volunteered its view of the merits, however, I proceed to discuss that as well.

A

There are many remarkable things about the majority's merits holding. The first is how rootless and shifting its justifications are. For example, the opinion starts with seven full pages about the traditional power of States to define domestic relations—initially fooling many readers, I am sure, into thinking that this is a federalism opinion. But we are eventually told that "it is unnecessary to decide whether this federal intrusion on state power is a violation of the Constitution," and that "[t]he State's power in defining the marital relation is of central relevance in this case quite apart from principles of federalism" because "the State's decision to give this class of persons the right to marry conferred upon them a dignity and status of immense import." But no one questions the power of the States to define marriage (with the concomitant conferral of dignity and status), so what is the point of devoting seven pages to describing how long and well established that power is? Even after the opinion has formally disclaimed reliance upon principles of federalism, mentions of "the usual tradition of recognizing and accepting state definitions of marriage" continue. What to make of this? The opinion never explains. My guess is that the majority, while reluctant to suggest that defining the meaning of "marriage" in federal statutes is unsupported by any of the Federal Government's enumerated powers, nonetheless needs some rhetorical basis to support its pretense that today's prohibition of laws excluding same-sex marriage is confined to the Federal Government (leaving the second, state-law shoe to be dropped later, maybe next Term). But I am only guessing.

Equally perplexing are the opinion's references to "the Constitution's guarantee of equality." Near the end of the opinion, we are told that although the "equal protection guarantee of the Fourteenth Amendment makes [the] Fifth Amendment [due process] right all the more specific and all the better understood and preserved"—what can *that* mean?—"the Fifth Amendment itself withdraws from Government the power to degrade or demean in the way this law does." The only possible interpretation of this statement is that the Equal Protection Clause, even the Equal Protection Clause as incorporated in the Due Process Clause, is not the basis for today's holding. But the portion of the majority opinion that explains why DOMA is unconstitutional (Part IV) begins by citing . . . equal-protection cases. And those three cases are the *only* authorities that the Court cites in Part IV about the Constitution's meaning, except for its citation of *Lawrence* v. *Texas*, 539 U.S. 558 (2003) (not an equal-protection case) to support its passing assertion that the Constitution protects the "moral and sexual choices" of same-sex couples.

Moreover, if this is meant to be an equal-protection opinion, it is a confusing one. The opinion does not resolve and indeed does not even mention what had been the central question in this litigation: whether, under the Equal Protection Clause, laws restricting marriage to a man and a woman are reviewed for more than mere rationality. That is the issue that divided the parties and the court below. In accord with my previously expressed skepticism about the Court's "tiers of scrutiny" approach, I would review this classification only for its rationality. As nearly as I can tell, the Court agrees with that; its opinion does not apply strict scrutiny, and its central propositions are taken from rational-basis cases like *Moreno*. But the Court certainly does not *apply* anything that resembles that deferential framework.

The majority opinion need not get into the strict-vs-rational-basis scrutiny question, and need not justify its holding under either, because it says that DOMA is unconstitutional as "a deprivation of the liberty of the person protected by the Fifth Amendment of the Constitution," that it violates "basic due process" principles, and that it inflicts an "injury and indignity" of a kind that denies "an essential part of the liberty protected by the Fifth Amendment." The majority never utters the dread words "substantive due process," perhaps sensing the disrepute into which that doctrine has fallen, but that is what those statements mean. Yet the opinion does not argue that same-sex marriage is "deeply rooted in this Nation's history and tradition," a claim that would of course be quite absurd. So would the further suggestion (also necessary, under our substantive-due-process precedents) that a world in which DOMA exists is one bereft of " 'ordered liberty.' "

Some might conclude that this loaf could have used a while longer in the oven. But that would be wrong; it is already overcooked. The most expert care in preparation cannot redeem a bad recipe. The sum of all the Court's nonspecific hand-waving is that this law is invalid (maybe on equal-protection grounds, maybe on substantive-due-process grounds, and perhaps with some amorphous federalism component playing a role) because it is motivated by a " 'bare . . . desire to harm' " couples in same-sex marriages. It is this proposition with which I will therefore engage.

B

As I have observed before, the Constitution does not forbid the government to enforce traditional moral and sexual norms. I will not swell the U.S. Reports with restatements of that point. It is enough to say that the Constitution neither requires nor forbids our society to approve of same-sex marriage, much as it neither requires nor forbids us to approve of no-fault divorce, polygamy, or the consumption of alcohol.

However, even setting aside traditional moral disapproval of same-sex marriage (or indeed same-sex sex), there are many perfectly valid—indeed, downright boring—justifying rationales for this legislation. Their existence ought to be the end of this case. For they give the lie to the Court's conclusion that only those with hateful hearts could have voted "aye" on this Act. And more importantly, they serve to make the contents of the legislators' hearts quite irrelevant: "It is a familiar principle of constitutional law that this Court will not strike down an otherwise constitutional statute on the basis of an alleged illicit legislative motive." *United States* v. *O'Brien*, 391 U.S. 367, 383 (1968). Or at least it *was* a familiar principle. By holding to the contrary, the majority has declared open season on any law that (in the opinion of the law's opponents and any panel of like-minded federal judges) can be characterized as mean-spirited.

The majority concludes that the only motive for this Act was the "bare . . . desire to harm a politically unpopular group." Bear in mind that the object of this condemnation is not the legislature of some once-Confederate Southern state (familiar objects of the Court's scorn, but our respected coordinate branches, the Congress and Presidency of the United States. Laying such a charge against them should require the most extraordinary evidence, and I would have thought that every attempt would be made to indulge a more anodyne explanation for the statute. The majority does the opposite—affirmatively concealing from the reader the arguments that exist in justification. It makes only a passing mention of the "arguments put forward" by the Act's defenders, and does not even trouble to paraphrase or describe them. I imagine that this is because it is harder to maintain the illusion of the Act's supporters as unhinged members of a wild-eyed lynch mob when one first describes their views as *they* see them.

* * *

By formally declaring anyone opposed to same-sex marriage an enemy of human decency, the majority arms well every challenger to a state law restricting marriage to its traditional definition. Henceforth those challengers will lead with this Court's declaration that there is "no legitimate purpose" served by such a law, and will claim that the traditional definition has "the purpose and effect to disparage and to injure" the "personhood and dignity" of same-sex couples. The majority's limiting assurance will be meaningless in the face of language like that, as the majority well knows. That is why the language is there. The result will be a judicial distortion of our society's debate over marriage—a debate that can seem in need of our clumsy "help" only to a member of this institution.

As to that debate: Few public controversies touch an institution so central to the lives of so many, and few inspire such attendant passion by good people on all sides. Few public controversies will ever demonstrate so vividly the beauty of what our Framers gave us, a gift the Court pawns today to buy its stolen moment in the spotlight: a system of government that permits us to rule *ourselves*. Since DOMA's passage, citizens on all sides of the question have seen victories and they have seen defeats. There have been plebiscites, legislation, persuasion, and loud voices—in other words, democracy. Victories in one place are offset by victories in other places for others. Even in a *single State*, the question has come out differently on different occasions.

In the majority's telling, this story is black-and-white: Hate your neighbor or come along with us. The truth is more complicated. It is hard to admit that one's political opponents are not monsters, especially in a struggle like this one, and the challenge in the end proves more than today's Court can handle. Too bad. A reminder that disagreement over something so fundamental as marriage can still be politically legitimate would have been a fit task for what in earlier times was called the judicial temperament. We might have covered ourselves with honor today, by promising all sides of this debate that it was theirs to settle and that we would respect their resolution. We might have let the People decide.

But that the majority will not do. Some will rejoice in today's decision, and some will despair at it; that is the nature of a controversy that matters so much to so many. But the Court has cheated both sides, robbing the winners of an honest victory, and the losers of the peace that comes from a fair defeat. We owed both of them better. I dissent.

JUSTICE ALITO, with whom JUSTICE THOMAS joins as to Parts II and III, dissenting.

Our Nation is engaged in a heated debate about same- sex marriage. That debate is, at bottom, about the nature of the institution of marriage. Respondent Edith Windsor, supported by the United States, asks this Court to intervene in that debate, and although she couches her argument in different terms, what she seeks is a holding that enshrines in the Constitution a particular understanding of marriage under which the sex of the partners makes no difference. The Constitution, however, does not dictate that choice. It leaves the choice to the people, acting through their elected representatives at both the federal and state levels. I would therefore hold that Congress did not violate Windsor's constitutional rights by enacting § 3 of the Defense of Marriage Act (DOMA), which defines the meaning of marriage under federal statutes that either confer upon married persons certain federal benefits or impose upon them certain federal obligations.

II

Windsor and the United States argue that § 3 of DOMA violates the equal protection principles that the Court has found in the Fifth Amendment's Due Process Clause. The Court rests its holding on related arguments.

Same-sex marriage presents a highly emotional and important question of public policy—but not a difficult question of constitutional law. The Constitution does not guarantee the right to enter into a same-sex marriage. Indeed, no provision of the Constitution speaks to the issue.

The Court has sometimes found the Due Process Clauses to have a substantive component that guarantees liberties beyond the absence of physical restraint. And the Court's holding that "DOMA is unconstitutional as a deprivation of the liberty of the person protected by the Fifth Amendment of the Constitution," suggests that substantive due process may partially underlie the Court's decision today. But it is well established that any "substantive" component to the Due Process Clause protects only "those fundamental rights and liberties which are, objectively, 'deeply rooted in this Nation's history and tradition,' " as well as " 'implicit in the concept of ordered liberty,' such that 'neither liberty nor justice would exist if they were sacrificed.' "

It is beyond dispute that the right to same-sex marriage is not deeply rooted in this Nation's history and tradition. In this country, no State permitted same-sex marriage until the Massachusetts Supreme Judicial Court held in 2003 that limiting marriage to opposite-sex couples violated the State Constitution. Nor is the right to same-sex marriage deeply rooted in the traditions of other nations. No country allowed same-sex couples to marry until the Netherlands did so in 2000.

What Windsor and the United States seek, therefore, is not the protection of a deeply rooted right but the recognition of a very new right, and they seek this innovation not from a legislative body elected by the people, but from unelected judges. Faced with such a request, judges have cause for both caution and humility.

The family is an ancient and universal human institution. Family structure reflects the characteristics of a civilization, and changes in family structure and in the popular understanding of marriage and the family can have profound effects. Past changes in the understanding of marriage—for example, the gradual ascendance of the idea that romantic love is a prerequisite to marriage—have had far-reaching consequences. But the process by which such consequences come about is complex, involving the interaction of numerous factors, and tends to occur over an extended period of time.

We can expect something similar to take place if same-sex marriage becomes widely accepted. The long-term consequences of this change are not now known and are unlikely to be ascertainable for some time to come. There are those who think that allowing same-sex marriage will seriously undermine the institution of marriage. Others think that recognition of same-sex marriage will fortify a now-shaky institution.

At present, no one—including social scientists, philosophers, and historians—can predict with any certainty what the long-term ramifications of widespread acceptance of same-sex marriage will be. And judges are certainly not equipped to make such an assessment. The Members of this Court have the authority and the responsibility to interpret and apply the Constitution. Thus, if the Constitution contained a provision guaranteeing the right to marry a person of the same sex, it would be our duty to enforce that right. But the Constitution simply does not speak to the issue of same-sex marriage. In our system of government, ultimate sovereignty rests with the people, and the people have the right to control their own destiny. Any change on a question so fundamental should be made by the people through their elected officials.

III

Perhaps because they cannot show that same-sex marriage is a fundamental right under our Constitution, Windsor and the United States couch their arguments in equal protection terms. They argue that § 3 of DOMA discriminates on the basis of sexual orientation, that classifications based on sexual orientation should trigger a form of "heightened" scrutiny, and that § 3 cannot survive such scrutiny. They further maintain that the governmental interests that § 3 purports to serve are not sufficiently important and that it has not been adequately shown that § 3 serves those interests very well. The Court's holding, too, seems to rest on "the equal protection guarantee of the Fourteenth Amendment"—although the Court is careful not to adopt most of Windsor's and the United States' argument.

In my view, the approach that Windsor and the United States advocate is misguided. Our equal protection framework, upon which Windsor and the United States rely, is a judicial construct that provides a useful mechanism for analyzing a certain universe of equal protection cases. But that framework is ill suited for use in evaluating the constitutionality of laws based on the traditional understanding of marriage, which fundamentally turn on what marriage is.

JUSTICE ALITO, dissenting.

III.

Underlying our equal protection jurisprudence is the central notion that "[a] classification 'must be reasonable, not arbitrary, and must rest upon some ground of difference having a fair and substantial relation to the object of the legislation, so that all persons similarly circumstanced shall be treated alike.' " *Reed v. Reed*, 404 U.S. 71, 76 (1971). The modern tiers of scrutiny—on which Windsor and the United States rely so heavily—are a heuristic to help judges determine when classifications have that "fair and substantial relation to the object of the legislation," *Reed*, at 76.

In asking the Court to determine that § 3 of DOMA is subject to and violates heightened scrutiny, Windsor and the United States thus ask us to rule that the presence of two members of the opposite sex is as rationally related to marriage as white skin is to voting or a Y-chromosome is to the ability to administer an estate. That is a striking request and one that unelected judges should pause before granting. Acceptance of the argument would cast all those who cling to traditional beliefs about the nature of marriage in the role of bigots or superstitious fools.

By asking the Court to strike down DOMA as not satisfying some form of heightened scrutiny, Windsor and the United States are really seeking to have the Court resolve a debate between two competing views of marriage.

The first and older view, which I will call the "traditional" or "conjugal" view, sees marriage as an intrinsically opposite-sex institution. [The Bipartisan Legal Advisory Group of the House of Representatives (BLAG)] notes that virtually every culture, including many not influenced by the Abrahamic religions, has limited marriage to people of the opposite sex. And BLAG attempts to explain this phenomenon by arguing that the institution of marriage was created for the purpose of channeling heterosexual intercourse into a structure that supports child rearing.

Others explain the basis for the institution in more philosophical terms. They argue that marriage is essentially the solemnizing of a comprehensive, exclusive, permanent union that is intrinsically ordered to producing new life, even if it does not always do so. While modern cultural changes have weakened the link between marriage and procreation in the popular mind, there is no doubt that, throughout human history and across many cultures, marriage has been viewed as an exclusively opposite-sex institution and as one inextricably linked to procreation and biological kinship.

The other, newer view is what I will call the "consent-based" vision of marriage, a vision that primarily defines marriage as the solemnization of mutual commitment—marked by strong emotional attachment and sexual attraction—between two persons. At least as it applies to heterosexual couples, this view of marriage now plays a very prominent role in the popular understanding of the institution. Indeed, our popular culture is infused with this understanding of marriage. Proponents of same-sex marriage argue that because gender differentiation is not relevant to this vision, the exclusion of same-sex couples from the institution of marriage is rank discrimination. The Constitution does not codify either of these views of marriage (although I suspect it would have been hard at the time of the adoption of the Constitution or the Fifth Amendment to find Americans who did not take the traditional view for granted). The silence of the Constitution on this question should be enough to end the matter as far as the judiciary is concerned. Yet, Windsor and the United States implicitly ask us to endorse the consent-based view of marriage and to reject the traditional view, thereby arrogating to ourselves the power to decide a question that philosophers, historians, social scientists, and theologians are better qualified to explore. Because our constitutional order assigns the resolution of questions of this nature to the people, I would not presume to enshrine either vision of marriage in our constitutional jurisprudence.

Legislatures, however, have little choice but to decide between the two views. We have long made clear that neither the political branches of the Federal Government nor state governments are required to be neutral between competing visions of the good, provided that the vision of the good that they adopt is not countermanded by the Constitution. Accordingly, both Congress and the States are entitled to enact laws recognizing either of the two understandings of marriage. And given the size of government and the degree to which it now regulates daily life, it seems unlikely that either Congress or the States could maintain complete neutrality even if they tried assiduously to do so.

Rather than fully embracing the arguments made by Windsor and the United States, the Court strikes down § 3 of [The Defense of Marriage Act (DOMA)] as a classification not properly supported by its objectives. The Court reaches this conclusion in part because it believes that § 3 encroaches upon the States' sovereign prerogative to define marriage. Indeed, the Court's ultimate conclusion is that DOMA falls afoul of the Fifth Amendment because it "singles out a class of persons deemed *by a State* entitled to recognition and protection to enhance their own liberty" and "imposes a disability on the class by refusing to acknowledge a status *the State finds* to be dignified and proper."

To the extent that the Court takes the position that the question of same-sex marriage should be resolved primarily at the state level, I wholeheartedly agree. I hope that the Court will ultimately permit the people of each State to decide this question for themselves. Unless the Court is willing to allow this to occur, the whiffs of federalism in the today's opinion of the Court will soon be scattered to the wind.

In any event, § 3 of DOMA, in my view, does not encroach on the prerogatives of the States, assuming of course that the many federal statutes affected by DOMA have not already done so. Section 3 does not prevent any State from recognizing same-sex marriage or from extending to same-sex couples any right, privilege, benefit, or obligation stemming from state law. All that § 3 does is to define a class of persons to whom federal law extends certain special benefits and upon whom federal law imposes certain special burdens. In these provisions, Congress used marital status as a way of defining this class—in part, I assume, because it viewed marriage as a valuable institution to be fostered and in part because it viewed married couples as comprising a unique type of economic unit that merits special regulatory treatment. Assuming that Congress has the power under the Constitution to enact the laws affected by § 3, Congress has the power to define the category of persons to whom those laws apply.

FOR DISCUSSION

The opinions articulate different understandings of the role of the court in addressing conflicts between states, federal legislatures, and the executive. What are these interpretations? Did § 3 of DOMA impinge on the authority of the state to regulate marriage? Why or why not?

RELATED CASES

***Hollingsworth v. Perry:* 133 S.Ct. 2652, 570 U.S. ___ (2013).**

The US Supreme Court determined advocates for California's Proposition 8, which overturned a State Supreme Court decision allowing for same sex marriage, did not have standing to appeal a district court decision countermanding the referendum as violating the Equal Protection Clause of the Constitution.

OBERGEFELL V. HODGES, DIRECTOR, OHIO DEPARTMENT OF HEALTH

576 U.S. ___, 135 S.Ct. 2584, 192 L. Ed. 2d 609 (2015)

Fourteen same-sex couples and two men whose partners were deceased challenged state laws in Michigan, Kentucky, Ohio, and Tennessee that prohibited same-sex marriages. They brought a Fourteenth Amendment claim against their state officials responsible for enforcing these state laws. The petitioners argued that the federal constitution was violated when states denied them the right to marry or refused to recognize their marriage when lawfully performed in another state. Each of the federal district courts ruled in favor of the petitioners. Upon the four states' appeal, the Sixth Circuit consolidated these cases and reversed the lower courts in *DeBoer v. Synder*, 772 F.3d 388 (2014).

Vote: 5–4

JUSTICE KENNEDY delivered the opinion of the Court.

The Constitution promises liberty to all within its reach, a liberty that includes certain specific rights that allow persons, within a lawful realm, to define and express their identity. The petitioners in these cases seek to find that liberty by marrying someone of the same sex and having their marriages deemed lawful on the same terms and conditions as marriages between persons of the opposite sex.

I

These cases come from Michigan, Kentucky, Ohio, and Tennessee. States that define marriage as a union between one man and one woman.

This Court granted review, limited to two questions. The first, presented by the cases from Michigan and Kentucky, is whether the Fourteenth Amendment requires a State to license a marriage between two people of the same sex. The second, presented by the cases from Ohio, Tennessee, and, again, Kentucky, is whether the Fourteenth Amendment requires a State to recognize a same-sex marriage licensed and performed in a State which does grant that right.

II

Before addressing the principles and precedents that govern these cases, it is appropriate to note the history of the subject now before the Court.

A

From their beginning to their most recent page, the annals of human history reveal the transcendent importance of marriage. The lifelong union of a man and a woman always has promised nobility and dignity to all persons, without regard to their station in life. Marriage is sacred to those who live by their religions and offers unique fulfillment to those who find meaning in the secular realm. Its dynamic allows two people to find a life that could not be found alone, for a marriage becomes greater than just the two persons. Rising from the most basic human needs, marriage is essential to our most profound hopes and aspirations.

The centrality of marriage to the human condition makes it unsurprising that the institution has existed for millennia and across civilizations

That history is the beginning of these cases. The respondents say it should be the end as well. To them, it would demean a timeless institution if the concept and lawful status of marriage were extended to two persons of the same sex. Marriage, in their view, is by its nature a gender-differentiated union of man and woman. This view long has been held—and continues to be held—in good faith by reasonable and sincere people here and throughout the world.

The petitioners acknowledge this history but contend that these cases cannot end there. Were their intent to demean the revered idea and reality of marriage, the petitioners' claims would be of a different order. But that is neither their purpose nor their submission. To the contrary, it is the enduring importance of marriage that underlies the petitioners' contentions. This, they say, is their whole point. Far from seeking to devalue marriage, the petitioners seek it for themselves because of their respect—and need—for its privileges and responsibilities. And their immutable nature dictates that same-sex marriage is their only real path to this profound commitment.

Recounting the circumstances of three of these cases illustrates the urgency of the petitioners' cause from their perspective. Petitioner James Obergefell, a plaintiff in the Ohio case, met John Arthur over two decades ago. They fell in love and started a life together, establishing a lasting, committed relation. In 2011, however, Arthur was diagnosed with amyotrophic lateral sclerosis, or ALS. This debilitating disease is progressive, with no known cure. Two years ago, Obergefell and Arthur decided to commit to one another, resolving to marry before Arthur died. To fulfill their mutual promise, they traveled from Ohio to Maryland, where same-sex marriage was legal. It was difficult for Arthur to move, and so the couple was wed inside a medical transport plane as it remained on the tarmac in Baltimore. Three months later, Arthur died. Ohio law does not permit Obergefell to be listed as the surviving spouse on Arthur's death certificate. By statute, they must remain strangers even in death, a state-imposed separation Obergefell deems "hurtful for the rest of time." He brought suit to be shown as the surviving spouse on Arthur's death certificate.

April DeBoer and Jayne Rowse are co-plaintiffs in the case from Michigan. They celebrated a commitment ceremony to honor their permanent relation in 2007. They both work as nurses, DeBoer in a neonatal unit and Rowse in an emergency unit. In 2009, DeBoer and Rowse fostered and then adopted a baby boy. Later that same year, they welcomed another son into their family. The new baby, born prematurely and abandoned by his biological mother, required around-the-clock care. The next year, a baby girl with special needs joined their family. Michigan, however, permits only opposite-sex married couples or single individuals to adopt, so each child can have only one woman as his or her legal parent. If an emergency were to arise, schools and hospitals may treat the three children as if they had only one parent. And, were tragedy to befall either DeBoer or Rowse, the other would have no legal rights over the children she had not been permitted to adopt. This couple seeks relief from the continuing uncertainty their unmarried status creates in their lives.

Army Reserve Sergeant First Class Ijpe DeKoe and his partner Thomas Kostura, co-plaintiffs in the Tennessee case, fell in love. In 2011, DeKoe received orders to deploy to Afghanistan. Before leaving, he and Kostura married in New York. A week later, DeKoe began his deployment, which lasted for almost a year. When he returned, the two settled in Tennessee, where DeKoe works full-time for the Army Reserve. Their lawful marriage is stripped from them whenever they reside in Tennessee, returning and disappearing as they travel across state lines. DeKoe, who served this Nation to preserve the freedom the Constitution protects, must endure a substantial burden.

B

The ancient origins of marriage confirm its centrality, but it has not stood in isolation from developments in law and society. The history of marriage is one of both continuity and change. That institution—even as confined to opposite-sex relations—has evolved over time.

Under the centuries-old doctrine of coverture, a married man and woman were treated by the State as a single, male-dominated legal entity. As women gained legal, political, and property rights, and as society began to understand that women have their own equal dignity, the law of coverture was abandoned. These and other developments in the institution of marriage over the past centuries were not mere superficial changes. Rather, they worked deep transformations in its structure, affecting aspects of marriage long viewed by many as essential.

This dynamic can be seen in the Nation's experiences with the rights of gays and lesbians. Until the mid-20th century, same-sex intimacy long had been condemned as immoral by the state itself in most Western nations, a belief often embodied in the criminal law. For this reason, among others, many persons did not deem homosexuals to have dignity in their own distinct identity. A truthful declaration by same-sex couples of what was in their hearts had to remain unspoken. Even when a greater awareness of the humanity and integrity of homosexual persons came in the period after World War II, the argument that gays and lesbians had a just claim to dignity was in conflict with both law and widespread social conventions. Same-sex intimacy remained a crime in many States. Gays and lesbians were prohibited from most government employment, barred from military service, excluded under immigration laws, targeted by police, and burdened in their rights to associate.

In the late 20th century, following substantial cultural and political developments, same-sex couples began to lead more open and public lives and to establish families. This development was followed by a quite extensive discussion of the issue in both governmental and private sectors and by a shift in public attitudes toward greater tolerance. As a result, questions about the rights of gays and lesbians soon reached the courts, where the issue could be discussed in the formal discourse of the law.

This Court first gave detailed consideration to the legal status of homosexuals in *Bowers* v. *Hardwick*, 478 U.S. 186 (1986). There it upheld the constitutionality of a Georgia law deemed to criminalize certain homosexual acts. Ten years later, in *Romer* v. *Evans*, 517 U.S. 620 (1996), the Court invalidated an amendment to Colorado's Constitution that sought to foreclose any branch or political subdivision of the State from protecting persons against discrimination based on sexual orientation. Then, in 2003, the Court overruled *Bowers*, holding that laws making same-sex intimacy a crime "demea[n] the lives of homosexual persons." *Lawrence* v. *Texas*, 539 U.S. 558, 575.

Against this background, the legal question of same-sex marriage arose. In 1993, the Hawaii Supreme Court held Hawaii's law restricting marriage to opposite-sex couples constituted a classification on the basis of sex and was therefore subject to strict scrutiny under the Hawaii Constitution. *Baehr* v. *Lewin*, 74 Haw. 530, 852 P. 2d 44. Although this decision did not mandate that same-sex marriage be allowed, some States were concerned by its implications and reaffirmed in their laws that marriage is defined as a union between opposite-sex partners. So too in 1996, Congress passed the Defense of Marriage Act (DOMA), 110 Stat. 2419, defining marriage for all federal-law purposes as "only a legal union between one man and one woman as husband and wife."

The new and widespread discussion of the subject led other States to a different conclusion. In 2003, the Supreme Judicial Court of Massachusetts held the State's Constitution guaranteed same-sex couples the right to marry. See *Goodridge* v. *Department of Public Health*, 440 Mass. 309, 798 N. E. 2d 941 (2003). After that ruling, some additional States granted marriage rights to same- sex couples, either through judicial or legislative processes. Two Terms ago, in *United States* v. *Windsor*, 570 U.S. ___ (2013), this Court invalidated DOMA to the extent it barred the Federal Government from treating same-sex marriages as valid even when they were lawful in the State where they were licensed. DOMA, the Court held, impermissibly disparaged those same-sex couples "who wanted to affirm their commitment to one another before their children, their family, their friends, and their community."

Numerous cases about same-sex marriage have reached the United States Courts of Appeals in recent years. In accordance with the judicial duty to base their decisions on principled reasons and neutral discussions, without scornful or disparaging commentary, courts have written a substantial body of law considering all sides of these issues. That case law helps to explain and formulate the underlying principles this Court now must consider. With the exception of the opinion here under review and one other, the Courts of Appeals have held that excluding same-sex couples from marriage violates the Constitution. There also have been many thoughtful

District Court decisions addressing same-sex marriage—and most of them, too, have concluded same-sex couples must be allowed to marry. In addition the highest courts of many States have contributed to this ongoing dialogue in decisions interpreting their own State Constitutions.

After years of litigation, legislation, referenda, and the discussions that attended these public acts, the States are now divided on the issue of same-sex marriage.

III

Under the Due Process Clause of the Fourteenth Amendment, no State shall "deprive any person of life, liberty, or property, without due process of law." The fundamental liberties protected by this Clause include most of the rights enumerated in the Bill of Rights. In addition these liberties extend to certain personal choices central to individual dignity and autonomy, including intimate choices that define personal identity and beliefs.

The nature of injustice is that we may not always see it in our own times. The generations that wrote and ratified the Bill of Rights and the Fourteenth Amendment did not presume to know the extent of freedom in all of its dimensions, and so they entrusted to future generations a charter protecting the right of all persons to enjoy liberty as we learn its meaning. When new insight reveals discord between the Constitution's central protections and a received legal stricture, a claim to liberty must be addressed. Applying these established tenets, the Court has long held the right to marry is protected by the Constitution. In *Loving* v. *Virginia*, 388 U.S. 1, 12 (1967), which invalidated bans on interracial unions, a unanimous Court held marriage is "one of the vital personal rights essential to the orderly pursuit of happiness by free men." The Court reaffirmed that holding in *Zablocki* v. *Redhail*, 434 U.S. 374, 384 (1978), which held the right to marry was burdened by a law prohibiting fathers who were behind on child support from marrying. The Court again applied this principle in *Turner* v. *Safley*, 482 U.S. 78, 95 (1987), which held the right to marry was abridged by regulations limiting the privilege of prison inmates to marry. Over time and in other contexts, the Court has reiterated that the right to marry is fundamental under the Due Process Clause.

It cannot be denied that this Court's cases describing the right to marry presumed a relationship involving opposite-sex partners. The Court, like many institutions, has made assumptions defined by the world and time of which it is a part.

This analysis compels the conclusion that same-sex couples may exercise the right to marry. The four principles and traditions to be discussed demonstrate that the reasons marriage is fundamental under the Constitution apply with equal force to same-sex couples.

A first premise of the Court's relevant precedents is that the right to personal choice regarding marriage is inherent in the concept of individual autonomy. This abiding connection between marriage and liberty is why *Loving* invalidated interracial marriage bans under the Due Process Clause. Like choices concerning contraception, family relationships, procreation, and childrearing, all of which are protected by the Constitution, decisions concerning marriage are among the most intimate that an individual can make.

The nature of marriage is that, through its enduring bond, two persons together can find other freedoms, such as expression, intimacy, and spirituality. This is true for all persons, whatever their sexual orientation. There is dignity in the bond between two men or two women who seek to marry and in their autonomy to make such profound choices.

A second principle in this Court's jurisprudence is that the right to marry is fundamental because it supports a two-person union unlike any other in its importance to the committed individuals. This point was central to *Griswold* v. *Connecticut* [381 U.S. 479 (1965)], which held the Constitution protects the right of married couples to use contraception. Suggesting that marriage is a right "older than the Bill of Rights," *Griswold* described marriage this way:

> "Marriage is a coming together for better or for worse, hopefully enduring, and intimate to the degree of being sacred. It is an association that promotes a way of life, not causes; a harmony in living, not political faiths; a bilateral loyalty, not commercial or social projects. Yet it is an association for as noble a purpose as any involved in our prior decisions." [381 U.S., at 486.]

Marriage responds to the universal fear that a lonely person might call out only to find no one there. It offers the hope of companionship and understanding and assurance that while both still live there will be someone to care for the other.

As this Court held in *Lawrence [v. Texas,* 539 U.S. 558 (2003)], same-sex couples have the same right as opposite-sex couples to enjoy intimate association. *Lawrence* invalidated laws that made same-sex intimacy a criminal act. And it acknowledged that "[w]hen sexuality finds overt expression in intimate conduct with another person, the conduct can be but one element in a personal bond that is more enduring." 539 U.S., at 567. But while *Lawrence* confirmed a dimension of freedom that allows individuals to engage in intimate association without criminal liability, it does not follow that freedom stops there. Outlaw to outcast may be a step forward, but it does not achieve the full promise of liberty.

A third basis for protecting the right to marry is that it safeguards children and families and thus draws meaning from related rights of childrearing, procreation, and education. Under the laws of the several States, some of marriage's protections for children and families are material. But marriage also confers more profound benefits.

As all parties agree, many same-sex couples provide loving and nurturing homes to their children, whether biological or adopted. And hundreds of thousands of children are presently being raised by such couples. Most States have allowed gays and lesbians to adopt, either as individuals or as couples, and many adopted and foster children have same-sex parents. This provides powerful confirmation from the law itself that gays and lesbians can create loving, supportive families.

Excluding same-sex couples from marriage thus conflicts with a central premise of the right to marry. Without the recognition, stability, and predictability marriage offers, their children suffer the stigma of knowing their families are somehow lesser. They also suffer the significant material costs of being raised by unmarried parents, relegated through no fault of their own to a more difficult and uncertain family life. The marriage laws at issue here thus harm and humiliate the children of same-sex couples.

That is not to say the right to marry is less meaningful for those who do not or cannot have children. An ability, desire, or promise to procreate is not and has not been a prerequisite for a valid marriage in any State. In light of precedent protecting the right of a married couple not to procreate, it cannot be said the Court or the States have conditioned the right to marry on the capacity or commitment to procreate.

Fourth and finally, this Court's cases and the Nation's traditions make clear that marriage is a keystone of our social order. This idea has been reiterated even as the institution has evolved in substantial ways over time, superseding rules related to parental consent, gender, and race once thought by many to be essential. Marriage remains a building block of our national community. For that reason, just as a couple vows to support each other, so does society pledge to support the couple, offering symbolic recognition and material benefits to protect and nourish the union. Indeed, while the States are in general free to vary the benefits they confer on all married couples, they have throughout our history made marriage the basis for an expanding list of governmental rights, benefits, and responsibilities. These aspects of marital status include: taxation; inheritance and property rights; rules of intestate succession; spousal privilege in the law of evidence; hospital access; medical decision-making authority; adoption rights; the rights and benefits of survivors; birth and death certificates; professional ethics rules; campaign finance restrictions; workers' compensation benefits; health insurance; and child custody, support, and visitation rules. Valid marriage under state law is also a significant status for over a thousand provisions of federal law. The States have contributed to the fundamental character of the marriage right by placing that institution at the center of so many facets of the legal and social order.

There is no difference between same- and opposite-sex couples with respect to this principle. Yet by virtue of their exclusion from that institution, same-sex couples are denied the constellation of benefits that the States have linked to marriage. This harm results in more than just material burdens. Same-sex couples are consigned to an instability many opposite-sex couples would deem intolerable in their own lives. As the State itself makes marriage all the more precious by the significance it attaches to it, exclusion from that status has the effect of teaching that gays and lesbians are unequal in important respects. It demeans gays and lesbians for the State to lock them out of a central institution of the Nation's society. Same-sex couples, too, may aspire to the transcendent purposes of marriage and seek fulfillment in its highest meaning.

The limitation of marriage to opposite-sex couples may long have seemed natural and just, but its inconsistency with the central meaning of the fundamental right to marry is now manifest. With that knowledge must come the recognition that laws excluding same-sex couples from the marriage right impose stigma and injury of the kind prohibited by our basic charter.

Objecting that this does not reflect an appropriate framing of the issue, the respondents refer to *Washington* v. *Glucksberg*, 521 U.S. 702, 721 (1997), which called for a " 'careful description' " of fundamental rights. They assert the petitioners do not seek to exercise the right to marry but rather a new and nonexistent "right to same-sex marriage." *Glucksberg* did insist that liberty under the Due Process Clause must be defined in a most circumscribed manner, with central reference to specific historical practices. Yet while that approach may have been appropriate for the asserted right there involved (physician-assisted suicide), it is inconsistent with the approach this Court has used in discussing other fundamental rights, including marriage and intimacy. *Loving* did not ask about a "right to inter-racial marriage"; *Turner* did not ask about a "right of inmates to marry"; and *Zablocki* did not ask about a "right of fathers with unpaid child support duties to marry." Rather, each case inquired about the right to marry in its comprehensive sense, asking if there was a sufficient justification for excluding the relevant class from the right.

That principle applies here. If rights were defined by who exercised them in the past, then received practices could serve as their own continued justification and new groups could not invoke rights once denied. This Court has rejected that approach, both with respect to the right to marry and the rights of gays and lesbians. Under the Constitution, same-sex couples seek in marriage the same legal treatment as opposite-sex couples, and it would disparage their choices and diminish their personhood to deny them this right.

The right of same-sex couples to marry that is part of the liberty promised by the Fourteenth Amendment is derived, too, from that Amendment's guarantee of the equal protection of the laws. The Due Process Clause and the Equal Protection Clause are connected in a profound way, though they set forth independent principles. Rights implicit in liberty and rights secured by equal protection may rest on different precepts and are not always co-extensive, yet in some instances each may be instructive as to the meaning and reach of the other. In any particular case one Clause may be thought to capture the essence of the right in a more accurate and comprehensive way, even as the two Clauses may converge in the identification and definition of the right. This interrelation of the two principles furthers our understanding of what freedom is and must become.

Each concept—liberty and equal protection—leads to a stronger understanding of the other. Indeed, in interpreting the Equal Protection Clause, the Court has recognized that new insights and societal understandings can reveal unjustified inequality within our most fundamental institutions that once passed unnoticed and unchallenged.

Other cases confirm this relation between liberty and equality. In *Lawrence* the Court acknowledged the interlocking nature of these constitutional safeguards in the context of the legal treatment of gays and lesbians.

Although *Lawrence* elaborated its holding under the Due Process Clause, it acknowledged, and sought to remedy, the continuing inequality that resulted from laws making intimacy in the lives of gays and lesbians a crime against the State. *Lawrence* therefore drew upon principles of liberty and equality to define and protect the rights of gays and lesbians, holding the State "cannot demean their existence or control their destiny by making their private sexual conduct a crime." *Id.*, at 578.

This dynamic also applies to same-sex marriage. It is now clear that the challenged laws burden the liberty of same-sex couples, and it must be further acknowledged that they abridge central precepts of equality. Here the marriage laws enforced by the respondents are in essence unequal: same-sex couples are denied all the benefits afforded to opposite-sex couples and are barred from exercising a fundamental right. Especially against a long history of disapproval of their relationships, this denial to same-sex couples of the right to marry works a grave and continuing harm. The imposition of this disability on gays and lesbians serves to disrespect and subordinate them. And the Equal Protection Clause, like the Due Process Clause, prohibits this unjustified infringement of the fundamental right to marry.

These considerations lead to the conclusion that the right to marry is a fundamental right inherent in the liberty of the person, and under the Due Process and Equal Protection Clauses of the Fourteenth Amendment couples of the same-sex may not be deprived of that right and that liberty. The Court now holds that same-sex couples may exercise the fundamental right to marry. No longer may this liberty be denied to them. . . .[T]he State laws challenged by Petitioners in these cases are now held invalid to the extent they exclude same-sex couples from civil marriage on the same terms and conditions as opposite-sex couples.

IV

There may be an initial inclination in these cases to proceed with caution—to await further legislation, litigation, and debate. The respondents warn there has been insufficient democratic discourse before deciding an issue so basic as the definition of marriage. In its ruling on the cases now before this Court, the majority opinion for the Court of Appeals made a cogent argument that it would be appropriate for the respondents' States to await further public discussion and political measures before licensing same-sex marriages.

Yet there has been far more deliberation than this argument acknowledges. There have been referenda, legislative debates, and grassroots campaigns, as well as countless studies, papers, books, and other popular and scholarly writings. There has been extensive litigation in state and federal courts. Judicial opinions addressing the issue have been informed by the contentions of parties and counsel, which, in turn, reflect the more general, societal discussion of same-sex marriage and its meaning that has occurred over the past decades. As more than 100 *amici* make clear in their filings, many of the central institutions in American life—state and local governments, the military, large and small businesses, labor unions, religious organizations, law enforcement, civic groups, professional organizations, and universities—have devoted substantial attention to the question. This has led to an enhanced understanding of the issue—an understanding reflected in the arguments now presented for resolution as a matter of constitutional law.

Of course, the Constitution contemplates that democracy is the appropriate process for change, so long as that process does not abridge fundamental rights.

The dynamic of our constitutional system is that individuals need not await legislative action before asserting a fundamental right. The Nation's courts are open to injured individuals who come to them to vindicate their own direct, personal stake in our basic charter. An individual can invoke a right to constitutional protection when he or she is harmed, even if the broader public disagrees and even if the legislature refuses to act. The issue before the Court here is the legal question whether the Constitution protects the right of same- sex couples to marry.

This is not the first time the Court has been asked to adopt a cautious approach to recognizing and protecting fundamental rights. In *Bowers* [*v. Hardwick,* 478 U.S. 186 (1986)], a bare majority upheld a law criminalizing same-sex intimacy. That approach might have been viewed as a cautious endorsement of the democratic process, which had only just begun to consider the rights of gays and lesbians. Yet, in effect, *Bowers* upheld state action that denied gays and lesbians a fundamental right and caused them pain and humiliation. As evidenced by the dissents in that case, the facts and principles necessary to a correct holding were known to the *Bowers* Court. That is why *Lawrence* held *Bowers* was "not correct when it was decided." 539 U.S., at 578. Although *Bowers* was eventually repudiated in *Lawrence*, men and women were harmed in the interim, and the substantial effects of these injuries no doubt lingered long after *Bowers* was overruled. Dignitary wounds cannot always be healed with the stroke of a pen.

A ruling against same-sex couples would have the same effect—and, like *Bowers*, would be unjustified under the Fourteenth Amendment. The petitioners' stories make clear the urgency of the issue they present to the Court. James Obergefell now asks whether Ohio can erase his marriage to John Arthur for all time. April DeBoer and Jayne Rowse now ask whether Michigan may continue to deny them the certainty and stability all mothers desire to protect their children, and for them and their children the childhood years will pass all too soon. Ijpe DeKoe and Thomas Kostura now ask whether Tennessee can deny to one who has served this Nation the basic dignity of recognizing his New York marriage. Properly presented with the petitioners' cases, the Court has a duty to address these claims and answer these questions.

Indeed, faced with a disagreement among the Courts of Appeals—a disagreement that caused impermissible geographic variation in the meaning of federal law—the Court granted review to determine whether same-sex couples may exercise the right to marry. Were the Court to uphold the challenged laws as constitutional, it would teach the Nation that these laws are in accord with our society's most basic compact. Were the Court to stay its hand to allow slower, case-by-case determination of the required availability of specific public benefits to same-sex couples, it still would deny gays and lesbians many rights and responsibilities intertwined with marriage.

The respondents also argue allowing same-sex couples to wed will harm marriage as an institution by leading to fewer opposite-sex marriages. This may occur, the respondents contend, because licensing same-sex marriage severs the connection between natural procreation and marriage. That argument, however, rests on a counterintuitive view of opposite-sex couple's decisionmaking processes regarding marriage and parenthood. Decisions about whether to marry and raise children are based on many personal, romantic, and practical considerations; and it is unrealistic to conclude that an opposite-sex couple would choose not to marry simply because same-sex couples may do so. The respondents have not shown a foundation for the conclusion that allowing same-sex marriage will cause the harmful outcomes they describe. Indeed, with respect to this asserted basis for excluding same-sex couples from the right to marry, it is appropriate to observe these cases involve only the rights of two consenting adults whose marriages would pose no risk of harm to themselves or third parties.

Finally, it must be emphasized that religions, and those who adhere to religious doctrines, may continue to advocate with utmost, sincere conviction that, by divine precepts, same-sex marriage should not be condoned. The First Amendment ensures that religious organizations and persons are given proper protection as they seek to teach the principles that are so fulfilling and so central to their lives and faiths, and to their own deep aspirations to continue the family structure they have long revered. The same is true of those who oppose same-sex marriage for other reasons. In turn, those who believe allowing same-sex marriage is proper or indeed essential, whether as a matter of religious conviction or secular belief, may engage those who disagree with their view in an open and searching debate. The Constitution, however, does not permit the State to bar same-sex couples from marriage on the same terms as accorded to couples of the opposite sex.

V

These cases also present the question whether the Constitution requires States to recognize same-sex marriages validly performed out of State. As made clear by the case of Obergefell and Arthur, and by that of DeKoe and Kostura, the recognition bans inflict substantial and continuing harm on same-sex couples.

Leaving the current state of affairs in place would maintain and promote instability and uncertainty. For some couples, even an ordinary drive into a neighboring State to visit family or friends risks causing severe hardship in the event of a spouse's hospitalization while across state lines. In light of the fact that many States already allow same-sex marriage—and hundreds of thousands of these marriages already have occurred—the disruption caused by the recognition bans is significant and ever-growing.

As counsel for the respondents acknowledged at argument, if States are required by the Constitution to issue marriage licenses to same-sex couples, the justifications for refusing to recognize those marriages performed elsewhere are undermined. The Court, in this decision, holds same-sex couples may exercise the fundamental right to marry in all States. It follows that the Court also must hold—and it now does hold—that there is no lawful basis for a State to refuse to recognize a lawful same-sex marriage performed in another State on the ground of its same-sex character.

* * *

No union is more profound than marriage, for it embodies the highest ideals of love, fidelity, devotion, sacrifice, and family. In forming a marital union, two people become something greater than once they were. As some of the petitioners in these cases demonstrate, marriage embodies a love that may endure even past death. It would misunderstand these men and women to say they disrespect the idea of marriage. Their plea is that they do respect it, respect it so deeply that they seek to find its fulfillment for themselves. Their hope is not to be condemned to live in loneliness, excluded from one of civilization's oldest institutions. They ask for equal dignity in the eyes of the law. The Constitution grants them that right.

The judgment of the Court of Appeals for the Sixth Circuit is reversed.
It is so ordered.

CHIEF JUSTICE ROBERTS, with whom JUSTICES SCALIA and THOMAS join, dissenting.

Petitioners make strong arguments rooted in social policy and considerations of fairness. They contend that same-sex couples should be allowed to affirm their love and commitment through marriage, just like opposite-sex couples. That position has undeniable appeal; over the past six years, voters and legislators in eleven States and the District of Columbia have revised their laws to allow marriage between two people of the same sex.

But this Court is not a legislature. Whether same-sex marriage is a good idea should be of no concern to us. Under the Constitution, judges have power to say what the law is, not what it should be.

Although the policy arguments for extending marriage to same-sex couples may be compelling, the legal arguments for requiring such an extension are not. The fundamental right to marry does not include a right to make a State change its definition of marriage. And a State's decision to maintain the meaning of marriage that has persisted in every culture throughout human history can hardly be called irrational. In short, our Constitution does not enact any one theory of marriage. The people of a State are free to expand marriage to include same-sex couples, or to retain the historic definition.

Today, however, the Court takes the extraordinary step of ordering every State to license and recognize same-sex marriage. Many people will rejoice at this decision, and I begrudge none their celebration. But for those who believe in a government of laws, not of men, the majority's approach is deeply disheartening.

Supporters of same-sex marriage have achieved considerable success persuading their fellow citizens—through the democratic process—to adopt their view. That ends today. Five lawyers have closed the debate and enacted their own vision of marriage as a matter of constitutional law. Stealing this issue from the people will for many cast a cloud over same-sex marriage, making a dramatic social change that much more difficult to accept.

The majority's decision is an act of will, not legal judgment. The right it announces has no basis in the Constitution or this Court's precedent. The majority expressly disclaims judicial "caution" and omits even a pretense of humility, openly relying on its desire to remake society according to its own "new insight" into the "nature of injustice." As a result, the Court invalidates the marriage laws of more than half the States and orders the transformation of a social institution that has formed the basis of human society for millennia, for the Kalahari Bushmen and the Han Chinese, the Carthaginians and the Aztecs. Just who do we think we are?

It can be tempting for judges to confuse our own preferences with the requirements of the law. But as this Court has been reminded throughout our history, the Constitution "is made for people of fundamentally differing views." *Lochner* v. *New York*, 198 U.S. 45, 76 (1905) (Holmes, J., dissenting). Accordingly, "courts are not concerned with the wisdom or policy of legislation." *Id.*, at 69 (Harlan, J., dissenting). The majority today neglects that restrained conception of the judicial role. It seizes for itself a question the Constitution leaves to the people, at a time when the people are engaged in a vibrant debate on that question. And it answers that question based not on neutral principles of constitutional law, but on its own "understanding of what freedom is and must become." I have no choice but to dissent.

Understand well what this dissent is about: It is not about whether, in my judgment, the institution of marriage should be changed to include same-sex couples. It is instead about whether, in our democratic republic, that decision should rest with the people acting through their elected representatives, or with five lawyers who happen to hold commissions authorizing them to resolve legal disputes according to law. The Constitution leaves no doubt about the answer.

IV

The Court's accumulation of power does not occur in a vacuum. It comes at the expense of the people. And they know it. Here and abroad, people are in the midst of a serious and thoughtful public debate on the issue of same-sex marriage. They see voters carefully considering same-sex marriage, casting ballots in favor or opposed, and sometimes changing their minds. They see political leaders similarly reexamining their positions, and either reversing course or explaining adherence to old convictions confirmed anew. They see governments and businesses modifying policies and practices with respect to same-sex couples, and participating actively in the civic discourse. They see countries overseas democratically accepting profound social change, or declining to do so. This deliberative process is making people take seriously questions that they may not have even regarded as questions before. When decisions are reached through democratic means, some people will inevitably be disappointed with the results. But those whose views do not prevail at least know that they have had their say, and accordingly are—in the tradition of our political culture—reconciled to the result of a fair and honest debate. In addition, they can gear up to raise the issue later, hoping to persuade enough on the winning side to think again.

But today the Court puts a stop to all that. By deciding this question under the Constitution, the Court removes it from the realm of democratic decision. There will be consequences to shutting down the political process on an issue of such profound public significance. Closing debate tends to close minds. People denied a voice are less likely to accept the ruling of a court on an issue that does not seem to be the sort of thing courts usually decide. Indeed, however heartened the proponents of same-sex marriage might be on this day, it is worth acknowledging what they have lost, and lost forever: the opportunity to win the true acceptance that comes from persuading their fellow citizens of the justice of their cause. And they lose this just when the winds of change were freshening at their backs.

Federal courts are blunt instruments when it comes to creating rights. They have constitutional power only to resolve concrete cases or controversies; they do not have the flexibility of legislatures to address concerns of parties not before the court or to anticipate problems that may arise from the exercise of a new right. Today's decision, for example, creates serious questions about religious liberty. Many good and decent people oppose same-sex marriage as a tenet of faith, and their freedom to exercise religion is—unlike the right imagined by the majority—actually spelled out in the Constitution.

Respect for sincere religious conviction has led voters and legislators in every State that has adopted same-sex marriage democratically to include accommodations for religious practice. The majority's decision imposing same-sex marriage cannot, of course, create any such accommodations. The majority graciously suggests that religious believers may continue to "advocate" and "teach" their views of marriage. The First Amendment guarantees, however, the freedom to "*exercise*" religion. Ominously, that is not a word the majority uses.

Hard questions arise when people of faith exercise religion in ways that may be seen to conflict with the new right to same-sex marriage—when, for example, a religious college provides married student housing only to opposite-sex married couples, or a religious adoption agency declines to place children with same-sex married couples. Indeed, the Solicitor General candidly acknowledged that the tax exemptions of some religious institutions would be in question if they opposed same-sex marriage. There is little doubt that these and similar questions will soon be before this Court. Unfortunately, people of faith can take no comfort in the treatment they receive from the majority today.

Perhaps the most discouraging aspect of today's decision is the extent to which the majority feels compelled to sully those on the other side of the debate. The majority offers a cursory assurance that it does not intend to disparage people who, as a matter of conscience, cannot accept same- sex marriage. That disclaimer is hard to square with the very next sentence, in which the majority explains that "the necessary consequence" of laws codifying the traditional definition of marriage is to "demea[n] or stigmatiz[e]" same-sex couples. The majority reiterates such characterizations over and over. By the majority's account, Americans who did nothing more than follow the understanding of marriage that has existed for our entire history—in particular, the tens of millions of people who voted to reaffirm their States' enduring definition of marriage—have acted to "lock . . . out," "disparage," "disrespect and subordinate," and inflict "[d]ignitary wounds" upon their gay and lesbian neighbors. These apparent assaults on the character of fairminded people will have an effect, in society and in court. Moreover, they are entirely gratuitous. It is one thing for the majority to conclude that the Constitution protects a right to same-sex marriage; it is something else to portray everyone who does not share the majority's "better informed understanding" as bigoted.

In the face of all this, a much different view of the Court's role is possible. That view is more modest and restrained. It is more skeptical that the legal abilities of judges also reflect insight into moral and philosophical issues. It is more sensitive to the fact that judges are unelected and unaccountable, and that the legitimacy of their power depends on confining it to the exercise of legal judgment. It is more attuned to the lessons of history, and what it has meant for the country and Court when Justices have exceeded their proper bounds. And it is less pretentious than to suppose that while people around the world have viewed an institution in a particular way for thousands of years, the present generation and the pre- sent Court are the ones chosen to burst the bonds of that history and tradition.

* * *

If you are among the many Americans—of whatever sexual orientation—who favor expanding same-sex marriage, by all means celebrate today's decision. Celebrate the achievement of a desired goal. Celebrate the opportunity for a new expression of commitment to a partner. Celebrate the availability of new benefits. But do not celebrate the Constitution. It had nothing to do with it. I respectfully dissent.

JUSTICE SCALIA, with whom JUSTICE THOMAS joins, dissenting.

I join The Chief Justice's opinion in full. I write separately to call attention to this Court's threat to American democracy.

The substance of today's decree is not of immense personal importance to me. The law can recognize as marriage whatever sexual attachments and living arrangements it wishes, and can accord them favorable civil consequences, from tax treatment to rights of inheritance. Those civil consequences—and the public approval that conferring the name of marriage evidences—can perhaps have adverse social effects, but no more adverse than the effects of many other controversial laws. So it is not of special importance to me what the law says about marriage. It is of overwhelming importance, however, who it is that rules me. Today's decree says that my Ruler, and the Ruler of 320 million Americans coast-to-coast, is a majority of the nine lawyers on the Supreme Court. The opinion in these cases is the furthest extension in fact—and the furthest extension one can even imagine—of the Court's claimed power to create "liberties" that the Constitution and its Amendments neglect to mention. This practice of constitutional revision by an unelected committee of nine, always accompanied (as it is today) by extravagant praise of liberty, robs the People of the most important liberty they asserted in the Declaration of Independence and won in the Revolution of 1776: the freedom to govern themselves.

I

Until the courts put a stop to it, public debate over same-sex marriage displayed American democracy at its best. Individuals on both sides of the issue passionately, but respectfully, attempted to persuade their fellow citizens to accept their views. Americans considered the arguments and put the question to a vote. The electorates of 11 States, either directly or through their representatives, chose to expand the traditional definition of marriage. Many more decided not to. Win or lose, advocates for both sides continued pressing their cases, secure in the knowledge that an electoral loss can be negated by a later electoral win. That is exactly how our system of government is supposed to work.

But the Court ends this debate, in an opinion lacking even a thin veneer of law. Buried beneath the mummeries and straining-to-be-memorable passages of the opinion is a candid and startling assertion: No matter *what* it was the People ratified, the Fourteenth Amendment protects those rights that the Judiciary, in its "reasoned judgment," thinks the Fourteenth Amendment ought to protect. That is so because "[t]he generations that wrote and ratified the Bill of Rights and the Fourteenth Amendment did not presume to know the extent of freedom in all of its dimensions . . . ." One would think that sentence would continue: ". . . and therefore they provided for a means by which the People could amend the Constitution," or perhaps ". . . and therefore they left the creation of additional liberties, such as the freedom to marry someone of the same sex, to the People, through the never-ending process of legislation." But no. What logically follows, in the majority's judge-empowering estimation, is: "and so they entrusted to future generations a charter protecting the right of all persons to enjoy liberty as we learn its meaning." The "we," needless to say, is the nine of us. "History and tradition guide and discipline [our] inquiry but do not set its outer boundaries." Thus, rather than focusing on *the People's* understanding of "liberty"—at the time of ratification or even today—the majority focuses on four "principles and traditions" that, *in the majority's view*, prohibit States from defining marriage as an institution consisting of one man and one woman.

This is a naked judicial claim to legislative—indeed, *super*-legislative—power; a claim fundamentally at odds with our system of government. Except as limited by a constitutional prohibition agreed to by the People, the States are free to adopt whatever laws they like, even those that offend the esteemed Justices' "reasoned judgment." A system of government that makes the People subordinate to a committee of nine unelected lawyers does not deserve to be called a democracy.

II

But what really astounds is the hubris reflected in today's judicial Putsch. The five Justices who compose today's majority are entirely comfortable concluding that every State violated the Constitution for all of the 135 years between the Fourteenth Amendment's ratification and Massachusetts' permitting of same-sex marriages in 2003. *Goodridge* v. *Department of Public Health*, 440 Mass. 309, 798 N. E.2d 941 (2003). They have discovered in the Fourteenth Amendment a "fundamental right" overlooked by every person alive at the time of ratification, and almost everyone else in the time since. They see what lesser legal minds—minds like Thomas Cooley, John Marshall Harlan, Oliver Wendell Holmes, Jr., Learned Hand, Louis Brandeis, William Howard Taft, Benjamin Cardozo, Hugo Black, Felix Frankfurter, Robert Jackson, and Henry Friendly—could not. They are certain that the People ratified the Fourteenth Amendment to bestow on them the power to remove questions from the democratic process when that is called for by their "reasoned judgment."

The opinion is couched in a style that is as pretentious as its content is egotistic. It is one thing for separate concurring or dissenting opinions to contain extravagances, even silly extravagances, of thought and expression; it is something else for the official opinion of the Court to do so. Of course the opinion's showy profundities are often profoundly incoherent. "The nature of marriage is that, through its enduring bond, two persons together can find other freedoms, such as expression, intimacy, and spirituality." (Really? Who ever thought that intimacy and spirituality [whatever that means] were freedoms? And if intimacy is, one would think Freedom of Intimacy is abridged rather than expanded by marriage. Ask the nearest hippie. Expression, sure enough, *is* a freedom, but anyone in a long-lasting marriage will attest that that happy state constricts, rather than expands, what one can prudently say.) Rights, we are told, can "rise . . . from a better informed understanding of how constitutional imperatives define a liberty that remains urgent in our own era." (Huh? How can a better informed understanding of how constitutional imperatives [whatever that means] define [whatever that means] an urgent liberty [never mind], give birth to a right?) And we are told that, "[i]n any particular case," either the Equal Protection or Due Process Clause "may be thought to capture the essence of [a] right in a more accurate and comprehensive way," than the other, "even as the two Clauses may converge in the identification and definition of the right." (What say? What possible "essence" does substantive due process "capture" in an "accurate and comprehensive way"? It stands for nothing whatever, except those freedoms and entitlements that this Court *really* likes. And the Equal Protection Clause, as employed today, identifies nothing except a difference in treatment that this Court *really* dislikes. Hardly a distillation of essence. If the opinion is correct that the two clauses "converge in the identification and definition of [a] right," that is only because the majority's likes and dislikes are predictably compatible.) I could go on. The world does not expect logic and precision in poetry or inspirational pop- philosophy; it demands them in the law. The stuff contained in today's opinion has to diminish this Court's reputation for clear thinking and sober analysis.

* * *

Hubris is sometimes defined as o'erweening pride; and pride, we know, goeth before a fall. The Judiciary is the "least dangerous" of the federal branches because it has "neither Force nor Will, but merely judgment; and must ultimately depend upon the aid of the executive arm" and the States, "even for the efficacy of its judgments." *The Federalist* No. 78, pp. 522, 523 (J. Cooke ed. 1961) (A. Hamilton). With each decision of ours that takes from the People a question properly left to them—with each decision that is unabashedly based not on law, but on the "reasoned judgment" of a bare majority of this Court—we move one step closer to being reminded of our impotence.

JUSTICE THOMAS, with whom JUSTICE SCALIA joins, dissenting.

The Court's decision today is at odds not only with the Constitution, but with the principles upon which our Nation was built. Since well before 1787, liberty has been understood as freedom from government action, not entitlement to government benefits. The Framers created our Constitution to preserve that understanding of liberty. Yet the majority invokes our Constitution in the name of a "liberty" that the Framers would not have recognized, to the detriment of the liberty they sought to protect. Along the way, it rejects the idea—captured in our Declaration of Independence—that human dignity is innate and suggests instead that it comes from the Government. This distortion of our Constitution not only ignores the text, it inverts the relationship between the individual and the state in our Republic. I cannot agree with it.

II B

Whether we define "liberty" as locomotion or freedom from governmental action more broadly, petitioners have in no way been deprived of it.

Petitioners cannot claim, under the most plausible definition of "liberty," that they have been imprisoned or physically restrained by the States for participating in same-sex relationships. To the contrary, they have been able to cohabitate and raise their children in peace. They have been able to hold civil marriage ceremonies in States that recognize same-sex marriages and private religious ceremonies in all States. They have been able to travel freely around the country, making their homes where they please. Far from being incarcerated or physically restrained, petitioners have been left alone to order their lives as they see fit.

Nor, under the broader definition, can they claim that the States have restricted their ability to go about their daily lives as they would be able to absent governmental restrictions. Petitioners do not ask this Court to order the States to stop restricting their ability to enter same-sex relationships, to engage in intimate behavior, to make vows to their partners in public ceremonies, to engage in religious wedding ceremonies, to hold themselves out as married, or to raise children. The States have imposed no such restrictions. Nor have the States prevented petitioners from approximating a number of incidents of marriage through private legal means, such as wills, trusts, and powers of attorney.

Instead, the States have refused to grant them governmental entitlements. Petitioners claim that as a matter of "liberty," they are entitled to access privileges and benefits that exist solely *because of* the government. They want, for example, to receive the State's *imprimatur* on their marriages—on state issued marriage licenses, death certificates, or other official forms. And they want to receive various monetary benefits, including reduced inheritance taxes upon the death of a spouse, compensation if a spouse dies as a result of a work-related injury, or loss of consortium damages in tort suits. But receiving governmental recognition and benefits has nothing to do with any understanding of "liberty" that the Framers would have recognized.

JUSTICE ALITO, with whom JUSTICES SCALIA and THOMAS join, dissenting.

Until the federal courts intervened, the American people were engaged in a debate about whether their States should recognize same-sex marriage. The question in these cases, however, is not what States *should* do about same-sex marriage but whether the Constitution answers that question for them. It does not. The Constitution leaves that question to be decided by the people of each State.

III

Today's decision usurps the constitutional right of the people to decide whether to keep or alter the traditional understanding of marriage. The decision will also have other important consequences.

It will be used to vilify Americans who are unwilling to assent to the new orthodoxy. In the course of its opinion, the majority compares traditional marriage laws to laws that denied equal treatment for African-Americans and women. The implications of this analogy will be exploited by those who are determined to stamp out every vestige of dissent.

Perhaps recognizing how its reasoning may be used, the majority attempts, toward the end of its opinion, to reassure those who oppose same-sex marriage that their rights of conscience will be protected. We will soon see whether this proves to be true. I assume that those who cling to old beliefs will be able to whisper their thoughts in the recesses of their homes, but if they repeat those views in public, they will risk being labeled as bigots and treated as such by governments, employers, and schools.

The system of federalism established by our Constitution provides a way for people with different beliefs to live together in a single nation. If the issue of same-sex marriage had been left to the people of the States, it is likely that some States would recognize same-sex marriage and others would not. It is also possible that some States would tie recognition to protection for conscience rights. The majority today makes that impossible. By imposing its own views on the entire country, the majority facilitates the marginalization of the many Americans who have traditional ideas. Recalling the harsh treatment of gays and lesbians in the past, some may think that turn-about is fair play. But if that sentiment prevails, the Nation will experience bitter and lasting wounds.

Today's decision will also have a fundamental effect on this Court and its ability to uphold the rule of law. If a bare majority of Justices can invent a new right and impose that right on the rest of the country, the only real limit on what future majorities will be able to do is their own sense of what those with political power and cultural influence are willing to tolerate. Even enthusiastic supporters of same-sex marriage should worry about the scope of the power that today's majority claims.

Today's decision shows that decades of attempts to restrain this Court's abuse of its authority have failed. A lesson that some will take from today's decision is that preaching about the proper method of interpreting the Constitution or the virtues of judicial self-restraint and humility cannot compete with the temptation to achieve what is viewed as a noble end by any practicable means. I do not doubt that my colleagues in the majority sincerely see in the Constitution a vision of liberty that happens to coincide with their own. But this sincerity is cause for concern, not comfort. What it evidences is the deep and perhaps irremediable corruption of our legal culture's conception of constitutional interpretation.

Most Americans—understandably—will cheer or lament today's decision because of their views on the issue of same-sex marriage. But all Americans, whatever their thinking on that issue, should worry about what the majority's claim of power portends.

FOR DISCUSSION

It may be surprising to some readers to see that the majority opinion focuses on the expanding understanding of the Fourteenth Amendment to encompass same-sex marriage and the dissenting opinions to focus on the appropriate role of the Court in interpreting the Constitution. How do you attempt to reconcile these two positions? Is it possible? As Justice Scalia suggests in *U.S. v. Windsor* (2013), was this decision inevitable after *Windsor*?

GLOSSARY

Abrogate: To legitimately cancel or revoke the power of another sovereign entity.

Adequate and Independent State Grounds: A doctrine developed by the Supreme Court in *Michigan v. Long* stating that federal courts may not review decisions of state courts if there are no federal questions present and a state court makes a clear statement that it is making its decision solely on state law.

Articles of Confederation: The first formal governing document of the United States of America. This governmental system placed most power and authority in the hands of the individual states, with limited sovereignty granted to the federal government.

Concurrent Powers: Enumerated authority granted in the Constitution shared by both the states and the federal government simultaneously. Two examples of concurrent powers are the power to tax and the power to regulate elections. However, when state and federal law conflict, federal law, as specified in the U.S. Constitution's supremacy clause, prevails.

Confederate Government: A form of government in which most authority is secured by the state government; the federal government serves mostly as a loose coalition of states. The Articles of Confederation was a confederate form of government.

Disenfranchisement: Laws designed to prohibit individuals from voting. In the United States, typical grounds of state disenfranchisement have been gender, race, lack of personal property, age, and a felony conviction.

Federal Government: The national government structure that exists independently from the states and possesses sovereign powers and authority.

Federal Supersession: The understanding, based on the Supremacy Clause of the Constitution, Article VI, that when the legitimate exercise of both state and federal sovereignty conflicts, the federal statute or decision will replace the state statute or decision.

Federalism: A structure of government that requires shared sovereignty between the local segments (e.g., states, provinces) and the federal government. Typically, both levels of government have independent sources of sovereignty and exercise concurrent powers. This form of government can serve as a means of checks and balances against tyranny by any individual element of governance.

Miscegenation Laws: State statutes designed to prohibit people of different races (typically decided between "white" and "nonwhite") from marrying and reproducing.

Pullman Abstention: A doctrine developed by the Supreme Court requiring federal courts to abstain from deciding a case or issue while a state court is actively addressing the matter.

Sovereign: A person or entity to whom authority to rule has been legitimately granted.

Sovereign Immunity: This legal doctrine, found in the Eleventh Amendment, allows a state to protect its independence by prohibiting it from being sued without the state's consent.

Sovereignty: The legitimate granting or exercising of authority to govern or rule in an independent fashion.

Unitary Government: A form of government in which all sovereignty is placed in the hands of a single entity, person, or level of government. There is no shared sovereignty with the states.

SELECTED BIBLIOGRAPHY

Conlan, Timothy J. 1998. *From New Federalism to Devolution: Twenty-Five Years of Intergovernmental Reform.* Washington, DC: Brookings Institution Press.

Dangerfield, George. 1965. *The Awakening of American Nationalism, 1815–1828.* New York: Harper & Row Publishers.

Derthick, Martha. 2001. *Keeping the Compound Republic: Essays on American Federalism.* Washington, DC: Brookings Institution Press.

Diamond, Martin. 1959. "Democracy and the Federalist: A Reconsideration of the Framers' Intent." *American Political Science Review*, Vol. 53, No. 1 (March), pp. 52–68.

Elazar, Daniel J. 1987. *Federalism as Grand Design: Political Philosophers and the Federal Principle.* Lanham, MD: University Press of America.

Elazar, Daniel J. 1997. "Contrasting Unitary and Federal Systems." *International Political Science Review*, Vol. 18, No.3, pp. 327–251.

Gerston, Larry N. 2007. *American Federalism: A Concise Introduction*. Armonk, N.Y.: M.E. Sharpe.

Hall, Kermit L. 1989. *The Magic Mirror: Law in American History*. New York: Oxford University Press.

McClellan, James. 2000. *Liberty, Order, and Justice: An Introduction to the Constitutional Principles of American Government*. Indianapolis, IN: Liberty Fund.

McConnell, Michael W. 1987. "Federalism: Evaluating the Founders' Design." *University of Chicago Law Review*, Vol. 54, p. 1484.

Purcell, Jr., Edward A. 2014. *Originalism, Federalism, and the American Constitutional Enterprise: A Historical Inquiry*. New Haven, CT: Yale University Press.

Robertson, David B. 2012. *Federalism and the Making of America*. New York: Routledge.

Smelser, Marshall. 1968. *The Democratic Republic, 1801–1815*. New York: Harper & Row Publishers.

Tushnet, Mark. 1985. "Federalism and the Traditions of American Political Theory." *Georgia Law Review*, Vol. 19, p. 981.

Walker, David. 2000. *The Rebirth of Federalism: Slouching toward Washington*, 2d ed. New York: Chatham House Publishers.

White, G. Edward. 1991. *The Marshall Court & Cultural Change, 1815–1833*. New York: Oxford University Press.

Yarbrough, Tinsley E. 2000. *The Rehnquist Court and the Constitution*. New York: Oxford University Press.

CHAPTER III

Legislative Powers over Commerce, Taxing, and Spending

Timeline: Legislative Powers

1215 The Magna Carta helps create a foundation for representative government that will later be reflected in the creation of the British Parliament.

1619 Virginia creates a House of Burgesses.

1765 The Stamp Act Congress meets to protest British taxes.

1774 The First Continental Congress meets in response to British Coercive Acts.

1775 The Second Continental Congress meets after fighting begins between British and Americans.

1776 The Declaration of Independence condemns King George III, in part for his treatment of colonial legislatures.

1781 The states adopt the Articles of Confederation, which affirms the existing unicameral legislature in which each state has an equal vote.

1787 The Constitutional Convention proposes a bicameral Congress in which states are represented in the House of Representatives according to population and in the Senate equally.

1789 The first Congress meets under the new government. It decides that the president's power to appoint includes the power to dismiss cabinet officers.

1791 Congress follows the recommendation of secretary of the treasury, Alexander Hamilton, and establishes a national bank despite the lack of an explicit constitutional provision giving it the power to do so.

1801 The House of Representatives has to resolve the presidential election after a tie between two Democratic-Republicans, Thomas Jefferson and Aaron Burr.

1803 In *Marbury v. Madison*, the U.S. Supreme Court for the first time voids provisions of a federal law.

1824 In *Gibbons v. Ogden*, the Supreme Court rules that a federal piloting law took precedent over a state's attempt to regulate interstate commerce.

1825 The House of Representatives resolves a deadlocked presidential election when one of the three main candidates, Speaker of the House Henry Clay, throws his support to John Quincy Adams, who then captured more votes than Andrew Jackson.

1857 *Dred Scott v. Sandford* represents only the second time that the Supreme Court declares a federal law (in this case the Missouri Compromise) to be unconstitutional.

1858 Abraham Lincoln and Stephen Douglas engage in debates as they campaign for an Illinois Senate seat.

1860–61 A number of southern states secede, and the nation faces four years of civil war.

1865 The Thirteenth Amendment, abolishing involuntary servitude, grants specific enforcement power to Congress.

1868 The Fourteenth Amendment, granting rights to newly freed slaves, also grants enforcement powers to Congress.

The Senate impeachment trial of President Andrew Johnson falls a single vote short of the two-thirds majority needed to convict him.

1887 Congress establishes the Interstate Commerce Commission as the first independent regulatory commission.

1895 *Pollock v. Farmers' Loan & Trust Co.* strikes down a federal income tax.

1903 In *Champion v. Ames*, the Supreme Court upholds a federal prohibition of the interstate transportation of lottery tickets.

1913 The Sixteenth Amendment overturns *Pollock v. Farmers' Loan & Trust Co.* and legitimizes federal income tax.

The Seventeenth Amendment provides that U.S. Senators will be popularly elected rather than, as previously, being appointed by state legislatures.

1918 *Hammer v. Dagenhart* strikes down a federal law that attempts to regulate child labor under the Commerce Clause.

1919 The Eighteenth Amendment launches an ultimately unsuccessful attempt at granting Congress the power to abolish the sale of alcohol.

1922 *Bailey v. Drexel Furniture* strikes down a congressional attempt to regulate child labor through taxation.

1932 President Franklin D. Roosevelt is elected with the promise of expanded federal authority to be enacted as part of his New Deal.

1935 *United States v. Schechter Poultry Corporation* strikes down the National Industrial Recovery Act.

1936 *United States v. Butler* rules that provisions of the Agricultural Adjustment Act improperly encroach upon state police powers.

1937 President Franklin D. Roosevelt threatens to "pack" the Supreme Court.

NLRB v. Jones & Laughlin Steel Corp. upholds key provisions of the National Labor Relations Act.

Steward *Machine Co. v. Davis* upholds the Social Security payroll tax.

1941 *United States v. Darby* upholds provision of the Fair Labor Standards Act of 1938 against claims that it violates the Tenth Amendment.

1942 *Wickard v. Filburn* rules that even wheat grown for "home" consumption affects interstate commerce enough to grant Congress power over the subject.

1964 *Heart of Atlanta Motel v. United States* uses the interstate Commerce Clause to uphold the Civil Rights Act of 1964.

1987 *South Dakota v. Dole* affirms the right of Congress to condition funds on state adherence to federal guidelines.

1992 *United States v. Lopez* strikes down a provision of the Gun-Free School Zones Act of 1990 as exceeding federal commerce powers.

The Twenty-seventh Amendment (originally proposed as part of the Bill of Rights) limits the timing of congressionally mandated pay raises for its members.

2000 *United States v. Morrison* strikes down provision of the Violence Against Women Act of 1994 as exceeding federal commerce powers.

2005 *Granholm v. Heald* strikes down state laws with differential impact on the sales of wine to in-state versus out-of-state residents.

Gonzalez v. Raich strikes down California law permitting the use of medical marijuana contrary to federal laws.

2012 *National Federation of Independent Business v. Sebelius* upholds the constitutionality of the Patient Protection and Affordable Care Act of 2010 under authority on the congressional power to tax and spend.

Article I, Sec. 1:

All legislative Powers herein granted shall be vested in a Congress of the United States, which shall consist of a Senate and House of Representatives.

INTRODUCTION

The first of the seven articles of the Constitution deals with the legislative branch, which is at the heart of American representative government. The English legislature, the Parliament, was so important that the British (but not the colonists, at least not in regard to taxation) regarded it as sovereign. Congress was effectively the only branch under the preceding government under the Articles of Confederation. The Constitutional Convention of 1787 debated this branch first and devoted the most debates to it. As a consequence, Article I is the longest article within the Constitution.

In contrast to the **unicameral** Congress under the Articles, in which each state was equally represented, but similar, at least in this respect, to the British Parliament, the Constitution created a **bicameral** legislature composed of a House of Representatives and a Senate. States were represented according to population (originally counting each slave as three-fifths of a person) in apportioning the House. The people directly elected its members for two-year renewable terms. As a result of the **Great**, or **Connecticut, Compromise**, which Article V specifies cannot be changed without the states' consent, each state received two senators, who served six-year terms. Although senators were originally selected by state legislatures, the Seventeenth Amendment (1913) subsequently mandated that the people would directly elect their senators. Unlike its counterpart in Britain, the House of Lords, Senate seats have never been hereditary.

The Constitution establishes minimal age, residency, and citizenship qualifications for members of Congress, with the requirements for members of the Senate being somewhat greater than those for members of the House. The decision in *Powell v. McCormack* (395 U.S. 486, 1969) (see Chapter I) indicates that the qualifications for members of Congress are exclusive.

Congress's primary job is to make laws. In so doing, it is often the first branch to consider the constitutionality of such proposals. Congress is a policy-determining body, a political unit that typically originates the legal phase of policy formation, but it has its own responsibility to introduce legislation that it believes to be compatible with the Constitution. Allied with Congress's law-making authority is the need to "educate" the citizenry on some issue. Congress is the great forum of debate on issues and the "complaint department" of the federal government to which citizens may go for a redress of grievances as well as the branch that conducts investigations into matters of public concern to enlighten not only its members but also the general public. Congress further exercises some general supervisory power in connection with the administrative branch. This is particularly true in areas where the Congress has set general policies and permitted an exercise of executive discretion within limiting standards.

INCREASED POWERS UNDER THE CURRENT CONSTITUTION

The Congress under the Articles of Confederation had very limited powers. It did not, for example, have the power to control interstate commerce. States could coin their own money, and Congress had to appeal to the states both in raising money and military forces. Moreover, at least nine state delegations within Congress had to agree on most key matters.

By contrast, Article I, Sec. 8 of the new Constitution vested Congress with a wide range of powers. These **enumerated powers** included a host of powers related to appropriating and spending money that are generally connected to "**the power of the purse**" as well as power over foreign affairs, which Congress shares with the president (see Chapter IV). In contrast to the Congress under the Articles of Confederation, the Constitution vests Congress with the power to tax individual citizens rather than simply requisitioning the states for money—a power that the Sixteenth Amendment reinforced by legitimating the national income tax. In addition to the powers that the Constitution specifically delegates to Congress, Congress also exercises **implied powers**, as illustrated by the decision in *McCulloch v. Maryland* (17 U.S. 316, 1819) legitimating the National Bank. The power to conduct investigations is an example of an important power that the Supreme Court has recognized as being a necessary concomitant to effective law making; the knowledge that such investigations unearth is often essential to formulating wise laws.

Federal Commerce Powers

Of all of the powers that the Constitution grants to Congress, none has had such intensive and extensive use as has its power over commerce among the states, with foreign nations, and with the Indian tribes. One of the difficulties under the Articles of Confederation was the inability of the central government to control interstate commerce and the virtual anarchy resulting from the efforts of the states to do so; internal tariffs pitted states against one another and disrupted trade among them. The Commerce Clause was designed to open American markets so that the large nation would effectively become a single free-trade zone.

The Court's first decision on the subject was in *Gibbons v. Ogden* (22 U.S. 1, 1824). The state of New York had granted a monopoly to steamship operators Robert R. Livingston and his partner, Robert Fulton, to navigate state waters. Gibbons, who was operating under a federal coastal license, challenged this monopoly. In what is sometimes called the "Emancipation Proclamation" of interstate commerce, Chief Justice John Marshall asserted the supremacy of federal law over conflicting state grants. This was one of Marshall's most popular decisions, since it struck at monopolies, which people generally associated both with special privilege and with increased prices.

An outstanding feature of *Gibbons* was Marshall's broad definition of commerce. Not only did he define commerce to include all commercial intercourse, but he spoke of federal jurisdiction as extending to commerce that "concerns" or "affects" more than one state. A casual review of recent decisions will reveal how very much this is the law today. Something that does not cross a state line may well *affect* other states.

Although this decision remains decisive in rejecting state laws that directly interfere with congressional laws relative to commerce, Chapter II's discussion of federalism demonstrates that the Court continues to examine the residual powers states could exercise in the absence of congressional legislation. In upholding state regulations of navigation in the port of Philadelphia, the Supreme Court established in *Cooley v. Board of Wardens* (53 U.S. 299, 1851) that some areas of commerce require a single uniform national rule and others permit state variation. The Court has essentially reserved for itself the determination in individual cases as to which category of commerce applies. In *Cooley*, the Court was able to rely on a congressional law that effectively left state navigation laws in place, but it must often decide such cases with far less explicit legislative authorization. Students will find examples of such cases in Chapter II's discussion of federalism and in Chapter V's discussion of state powers.

The Development of Two Rival Lines of Precedent

When the Framers drafted the U.S. Constitution, the economy was far less complex and interconnected than it is today, and most people did not expect the national government to do as much. One can look in vain through Article I to find explicit authorization for Congress to regulate banking, manufacturing, environmental issues, agriculture, education, or a host of other activities. Indeed, from time to time members of Congress propose amendments specifically granting the body such powers.

As the nation industrialized, Congress depended increasingly on the commerce power to regulate such matters that were not specifically entrusted to it by the Constitution. From the period that roughly began at the time of *United States v. E. C. Knight* (156 U.S. 1, 1895) and continued to 1937, the Court established two major rival lines of precedent. One line of precedents, fully consistent with *Gibbons*, upheld congressional regulations. Perhaps consistent with the moral concerns that dominated the Victorian era, the Court was particularly partial to cases in which Congress attempted to deal with issues of morality.

Champion v. Ames (188 U.S. 321, 1903), which this chapter includes, presents one such example. The Supreme Court upheld a law designed to limit the interstate transportation of lottery tickets. In other cases, the Court allowed both Congress and the states to regulate matters like prostitution and alcohol, which, like gambling, were widely regarded as moral evils.

The Supreme Court also upheld laws that it thought were designed to prevent fraud or protect public health. In *McCray v. United States* (195 U.S. 27, 1904), for example, the Court allowed Congress to tax oleomargarine colored to look like butter on the basis that this helped prevent fraud. It also upheld laws designed to prevent the transportation of impure food and drugs or diseased livestock.

At times, the Court focused on a metaphor to uphold federal powers. Most notably in *Swift & Co. v. United States* (196 U.S. 375, 1905), the Court upheld an injunction against a combination of meatpackers in the stockyards on the basis that they were in the "current" or "flow" of commerce. It reaffirmed this decision in *Stafford v. Wallace* (258 U.S. 495, 1922), where it classified such establishments as being in the very "throat" of commerce. The Court had used a similar rationale when it permitted regulation of grain elevators in *Munn v. Illinois* (94 U.S. 113, 1877) on the basis that such elevators, which were essential to the storage and transportation of grain, were in the very "gateway" of commerce.

Another line of precedents, however, was less to either state or congressional attempts to regulate the economy. Highly sympathetic to ***laissez-faire* economics**, the Court majority often struck down congressional exercises of power over more purely economic matters. It typically argued that such regulation improperly attempted to regulate matters that were local rather than national; that such regulation involved manufacturing, mining, or production rather than subsequent commerce; that such regulation interfered with "liberty of contract" as embodied in the due process clause of the Fourteenth Amendment; that such regulation involved "indirect," rather than "direct," influences on commerce; that such regulation was improper because it involved goods that were harmless as opposed to those that were harmful; and the like. Hence, in *United States v. E. C. Knight* (156 U.S. 1, 1895), the Court struck down the application of the Sherman Antitrust Act, which the government was attempting to use to prevent the purchase of sugar refineries. The Court thought both that this was an unconstitutional attempt to regulate the manufacture, or production, of sugar as well as that it was an attempt to regulate a matter (monopolies) that the Constitution reserved to the states.

Hammer v. Dagenhart (247 U.S. 251, 1918) is a prime example of this attitude. Confronted with a law that limited the transportation of goods that had been produced by child labor, the Court drew upon earlier decisions, largely devoted to the regulation of moral evils, to distinguish the transportation of goods that were inherently harmful from those that were not. This was, of course, a completely extraconstitutional distinction, but it enabled the Court to uphold regulations it favored and strike down those that it did not. The distinction is not unlike that where the Court in *Lochner v. New York* (198 U.S. 45, 1905) struck down regulations on the number of hours that mostly male bakers could work while upholding regulations of the hours that women could work in factories and laundries in *Muller v. Oregon* (208 U.S. 412, 1908). These issues will be examined in more depth in Chapter V.

The New Deal

Amid apparent prosperity, the stock market crashed in 1929, leading to a period of deep and prolonged economic depression. This crisis was a major contributor to the election of Franklin D. Roosevelt in 1932. In addition to exuding an air of optimism, Roosevelt proposed a host of new governmental programs, which he popularized as the New Deal.

Schechter Poultry Corp. v. United States (295 U.S. 495, 1935) is typical of the Court's initial response to such legislation. Faced with a complex code of industrial regulations that Congress had established in the National Industrial Recovery Act, the Court, in examining the application of this law to the poultry industry, decided both that the law represented an excessive delegation of legislative powers to the president and that the law was beyond congressional commerce powers because the chickens in question had come to their final destination and were thus no longer in commerce. Rather than attributing the unanimity of the Court to the possibility that the law had been badly drawn (many contemporary decisions were narrow 5–4 verdicts), Roosevelt decided that he had to strike back.

Biding his time until after his reelection in 1936, Roosevelt announced a calculated plan to add justices (up to fifteen) for each justice over the age of seventy who did not retire. It took little time for Roosevelt's opponents, and for the country as a whole, to recognize that Roosevelt was attempting to "pack" the Court with more sympathetic justices rather than to alleviate its workload, but his proposal certainly encouraged soul-searching on the part of the justices who were concerned about maintaining the Court's authority. Popular wisdom has it that Justice Owen Roberts shortly thereafter switched his vote and that the Court executed the "switch-in-time-that-saved-nine." Contemporary scholars point out that a shift in judicial thinking had begun even before Roosevelt's plan.

In any event, the Court demonstrated its greater acceptance of economic regulations in *West Coast Hotel v. Parrish* (300 U.S. 379) and in *N.L.R.B. v. Jones & Laughlin Steel Corp.* (301 U.S. 1), both decided in 1937. In the first case, the Court upheld a Washington State minimum wage law against charges that it violated substantive due process. In the second, the Court largely dismissed its earlier distinctions between manufacturing and commerce, direct and indirect, and local and national regulations in upholding the constitutional of the National Labor Relations Act. The Court began a period during which it was almost completely deferential to congressional economic regulations, although it soon began giving stricter scrutiny to matters involving other matters related to civil rights and civil liberties.

MODERN APPLICATIONS OF THE COMMERCE CLAUSE

Once the Commerce Clause had been held to empower Congress to regulate the conditions of the production of goods, the next step to wage and hour and child labor legislation under this same power was relatively easy. In *United States v. Darby Lumber Co.* (312 U.S. 100, 1941), the Court endorsed the general proposition that Congress may deny the use of the facilities of interstate commerce to persons who would use those facilities to do harm.

Darby is additionally noteworthy because it not only overruled *Hammer v. Dagenhart* but also questioned the doctrine of "dual federalism." This is the doctrine that the states and the federal government constituted two mutually exclusive systems of government. Dual sovereignty called for federal-state equality rather than federal supremacy in fields covered by federally delegated powers. Under this doctrine no power delegated to the federal government could be interpreted so as to involve an infringement on any reserved powers of the states. This notion had its roots in Taney's, and even Madison's, time and had been revived from time to time by the Court, most notably in *Hammer v. Dagenhart*, and even in some post-Reagan decisions.

Darby marks a return of "the judicial pendulum" to the Marshall point of view that commerce is to be regarded as an organic whole. The Court has specifically disavowed any power on the part of the Court to look into the motives and purpose of a regulation of interstate commerce.

Wickard v. Filburn (317 U.S. 111, 1942) is a classic example of the Court's post-1937 general deferential posture toward congressional regulations of commerce. In this milestone case, a unanimous Court allowed Congress to regulate the growing of wheat even for home consumption. It reasoned that, while one farmer's impact on interstate commerce was relatively minimal, the collective impact of farmers growing for home consumption hung over the market and clearly affected such commerce.

With expansive decisions like *Wickard*, the Commerce Clause became Congress's typical justification of last resort. On occasion, its decision was influenced by other factors. One good example is the landmark Civil Rights Act of 1964, in which Congress sought to outlaw racial segregation in places of public accommodation. As is detailed in volume's two's discussion of equal protection and civil rights, in the *Civil Rights Cases* of 1883 (109 U.S. 3) the Court examined the Civil Rights Act of 1875, which Congress had enacted toward the end of the reconstruction (1865–1877) of the South. Like the Civil Rights Act of 1964, the law had sought to eliminate racial discrimination in places of public accommodation. In the *Civil Rights Cases*, the Court had decided that the Fourteenth Amendment, which had sought to include newly freed slaves among the recipients of American rights, prohibited only discriminatory state action; it had no force in regulating private conduct. With such a precedent, Congress justified the Civil Rights Act of 1964 through its power to control interstate commerce. Significantly, Congress held hearings in which witnesses testified to the negative impact that racial segregation was having on such commerce by deterring those who faced discriminatory treatment and making such travel far less commodious than it would otherwise have been.

As follow-up cases suggested, courts almost always upheld congressional exercises under the Commerce Clause as long as such powers did not contradict a specific constitutional guarantee. Courts continue to give wide berth to such regulations, but in recent years it has given greater scrutiny to federal laws that appeared to conflict with state powers. As Chapter II shows, in *National League of Cities v. Usery* (426 U.S. 833, 1976), the Court struck down an expansion of the Fair Labor Standards Act that attempted to apply maximum hours and minimum wage legislation to state employees. Over time, the Court found that its distinction between traditional state functions and nontraditional functions was tenuous, and in *Garcia v. San Antonio Metropolitan Transit Authority* (469 U.S. 528, 1985), it thus overruled *Usery* and decided that states could work through their representation within Congress and the Electoral College to protect their own interests.

The Court remained sensitive, however, to the idea that there might be exercises of congressional power that even the Commerce Clause might not justify. In *United States v. Lopez* (514 U.S. 549, 1995), the Court thus struck down the Gun-Free School Zones Act of 1990. Congress had asserted, without offering the kind of proof that it had in enacting the Civil Rights Act of 1964, that the presence of guns in school might adversely affect education and hence commerce, but it had not limited the scope of the law to guns that had actually been purchased or carried in interstate commerce. Chief Justice Rehnquist expressed concern that if the Court were to permit such legislation in a matter of criminal law traditionally exercised by the states (and most states already had laws regulating guns in schools), there would be little that Congress could not do. He thought that Congress should only be able to regulate matters involving channels of interstate commerce (roads, canals, air spaces, and the like), instrumentalities of such commerce (trains, ships, and planes), or, more ambiguously, matters having a substantial affect upon such commerce.

Members of Congress speculated about the breadth of this decision: Was the Court simply punishing Congress for failing to demonstrate a connection between legislation and commerce, or would it subject congressional findings to further review? In drafting the 1994 Violence Against Women Act, which allowed women to file civil suits in federal courts against alleged attackers, Congress held hearings attempting to provide the economic links between such violence and commerce that it had failed to establish in *United States v. Lopez*. In *United States v. Morrison* (529 U.S. 598, 2000), however, the Supreme Court rejected this evidence and repeated concerns about federal intervention in matters that it thought the Constitution had reserved to the states.

Two other cases in this chapter help round out this picture. The decision in *Granholm v. Heald* (544 U.S. 460, 2005) demonstrates that the Court continues to decide when the federal grant over interstate commerce interferes with state regulation. The case, which involved laws in Michigan and California that make it easier for in-state wineries to sell alcohol than for out-of-state wineries, has additional import because it also examines whether the Twenty-first Amendment, which repealed national alcoholic prohibition, was also designed to increase state powers over this commodity.

Gonzales v. Raich (545 U.S. 1, 2005) adds yet another wrinkle to the debate by examining the degree to which federal criminal laws involving marijuana and other illegal drugs precludes state attempts to allow the use of such drugs for medical treatment. In what might be regarded as a mirror image of the *Lopez* case, the Court suggested that, in this area, federal regulation was paramount. Finally, in *National Federation of Independent Business v. Sebelius* (567 U.S. ___, 2012) (see below) the Supreme Court ruled that the Patent Protection and Affordability Act (Obamacare) went beyond the power Congress had under the Commerce Clause, even though it did uphold it under its power to tax and spend. The *Sebelius* opinion seems to define some outer boundary to Congressional commerce power, suggesting that the federal power in this area is not unlimited.

Taxation and Spending Powers

Article I, Sec. 8:

The Congress shall have Power To lay and collect Taxes, Duties, Imposts and Excises, to pay the Debts and provide for the common Defence and general Welfare of the United States; but all Duties, Imposts and Excises shall be uniform throughout the United States.

Article I, Sec. 9:

No Capitation or other direct, Tax shall be laid, unless in Proportion to the Census or Enumeration herein before directed to be taken

No Tax or Duty shall be laid on Articles exported from any State.

The Constitution vests Congress with what is called "the **power of the purse**." The power to tax is hedged about by the most minimal requirements, not all of which have been particularly clear.

Article I, Sec. 9, which limits congressional powers, requires capitation or "direct taxes" to be laid "in Proportion to the Census or Enumeration herein before directed to be taken," but the Constitution does not define what a "direct" tax is. An early decision in *Hylton v. United States* (3 Dallas 171; 1 L. Ed. 556, 1796) upholding a tax on carriages suggested that it was not a capitation tax, and in *Springer v. United States* (102 U.S. 586, 1881), the Court further upheld an income tax. In *Pollock v. Farmers' Loan & Trust Co.* (157 U.S. 429, 1895), however, the Court heeded appeals by opponents of socialism and populism to invalidate a later income tax in a decision that the Sixteenth Amendment eventually repudiated.

As a result of this and subsequent decisions, it has been determined that a **direct tax** is one the burden of which is borne by the person upon whom it is levied by the taxing authority. The courts have agreed that there are only three specific kinds of direct taxes: income taxes, poll taxes, and property taxes. Of these, the first has been made exempt from apportionment by the Sixteenth Amendment, the second has never been used by the federal government, and only five times has the federal government used the property tax, most recently in 1861.

In authorizing Congress to enact taxes in Article I, Sec. 8, the Constitution provides that "all Duties, Imposts and Excises shall be uniform throughout the United States." In a provision that was particularly important to southern agricultural states, it also prohibited the taxation of exports. Otherwise, the central constitutional limitation on taxes in Article I, Sec. 8 is that such taxes provide for "the general Welfare of the United States."

This has not prevented the Court from occasionally imposing other limitations. In *Bailey v. Drexel Furniture* (259 U.S. 20, 1922), for example, the Court distinguished a tax designed to raise money from a tax used as a penalty in striking down tax legislation that would have sought to circumvent the Court's earlier ruling in *Hammer v. Dagenhart* (1918) by taxing goods produced by child labor. Similarly, in *United States v. Butler* (297 U.S. 1, 1936), the Court invalidated an agricultural tax not because it exceeded constitutional authorization per se but because the Court thought that it represented the exercise of powers reserved to the states by the Tenth Amendment. Significantly, however, in its first interpretation of the general welfare clause in Article I, Sec. 8 of the Constitution, the Court ruled that Congress can tax and spend the money derived for any purpose that falls within the total area of "the general welfare." Although the Court overruled the tax at issue, it has never held that the mere expenditure of funds (apart from regulation) violates the "general welfare" provision. In other words, unless there is some attempt to use money derived from a specific tax to bring about some regulatory result outside the realm of federal power, the Court will take the judgment of Congress that the expenditure is in the interests of the general welfare and not coercive.

In addition to the cases above, cases involving intergovernmental tax immunities date at least as far back to the Court's decision in *McCulloch v. Maryland* (17 U.S. 316, 1819) disallowing Maryland's tax on the national bank. The Court no longer considers it improper, as it once did, for the federal government to tax the salaries of a state worker or vice versa (assuming they are taxed at the same rate as everyone else), but it continues to assure that one government does not gain power over the other by attempting to tax it directly.

Steward Machine Company v. Davis (301 U.S. 548, 1937) is something of a counterpart to cases from the same year that recognized federal power over interstate commerce. In allowing Congress to levy taxes for the Social Security system, the Court allowed for the continuing growth of the federal government.

South Dakota v. Dole (483 U.S. 203, 1987) raised another provocative issue, namely, the degree to which the national government can use its power to appropriate or fail to appropriate monies as leverage against states. In this case, the Court had to consider the degree to which the national government could condition state highway funds on state compliance with a minimum drinking age that the national government approved. Note that this case, like *Granholm v. Heald* (2005), interprets state powers under the Twenty-first Amendment, which repealed national alcoholic prohibition.

National Federation of Independent Business v. Sebelius (567 U.S. ___, 2012) rounds out this chapter in a case that examines the constitutionality of one of the most far-reaching pieces of legislation in recent times. The Patient Protection and Affordable Care Act of 2010 was designed to meet a variety of problems including the high number of U.S. citizens without health care. To this end, the act sought to use congressional powers under the commerce and the taxing and spending clauses to get all Americans to buy health insurance or face a penalty. Chief Justice John Roberts wrote a long opinion, joined by equally long concurring and dissenting opinions, in which he sided with four other justices in denying that Congress had the power under the commerce either to pass this legislation or to force states to expand their existing Medicaid programs but then joining four other justices to uphold the former provision under the taxing power.

Congressional spending is the counterpart to congressional taxation. The discussion on the First Amendment in the companion volume to this one examines a number of other cases in which the Court has allowed Congress to condition its expenditures on certain behaviors. Thus, in *Rust v. Sullivan* (500 U.S. 173, 1971), the Court allowed Congress to restrict information that family planners could give about abortion. Similarly, in *National Endowment of the Arts v. Finley* (524 U.S. 569, 1998), it allowed the National Endowment to consider public sensibilities in determining which artists it would fund.

Other Congressional Powers

In addition to the powers that Congress gained through the Sixteenth Amendment, it has also increased power through a number of enforcement clauses appended to various amendments. The most important of these is found within Sec. 5 of the Fourteenth Amendment. In a number of decisions, most of which will be outlined in the second volume of this casebook, the Supreme Court has ruled that this clause has given Congress the power to make rules that the courts could not make on their own. In *Katzenbach v. Morgan* (384 U.S. 641, 1966), for example, the Court upheld congressionally imposed limits on state literacy tests under Sec. 5 that it had previously ruled did not violate the Equal Protection Clause per se. Still, the Enforcement Clause does not give Congress a blank check. In *City of Boerne v. Flores* (521 U.S. 507, 1997), the Court emphasized that the power to *enforce* the Fourteenth Amendment did not include the power to *change* it.

GIBBONS V. OGDEN

9 Wheat. 1, 6 L.Ed. 23 (1824)

This was the first case to go to the Court under the Commerce Clause. The New York legislature had given Robert R. Livingston and his partner, Robert Fulton, exclusive rights to navigate the waters of the state. Other states from New Hampshire to Georgia passed retaliatory acts granting exclusive franchises. Livingston and Fulton licensed Ogden to operate between New York and Elizabethtown, New Jersey. Meanwhile, Gibbons had secured a license from the federal government under the Coasting Act of Congress and was operating ships between New York and Elizabethtown. Ogden brought suit for an injunction to restrain the activities of Gibbons. This was granted by the state court under Chancellor James Kent, and Gibbons, who was represented by none other than Daniel Webster, appealed to the Supreme Court of the United States. In the process of defining commerce and the degree of control that Congress exercised over it, the Court also addressed the corresponding power of the states over commercial matters.

Vote: 7–0

CHIEF JUSTICE MARSHALL delivered the opinion of the Court:

. . . The words are: "Congress shall have power to regulate commerce with foreign nations, and among the several States, and with the Indian tribes." The subject to be regulated is commerce; and our Constitution being, as was aptly said at the Bar, one of enumeration, and not of definition, to ascertain the extent of the power, it becomes necessary to settle the meaning of the word. The counsel for the appellee would limit it to traffic, to buying and selling, or the interchange of commodities, and do not admit that it comprehends navigation. This would restrict a general term, applicable to many objects, to one of its significations. . . . Commerce, undoubtedly, is traffic, but it is something more—it is intercourse. It describes the commercial intercourse between nations, and parts of nations, in all its branches, and is regulated by prescribing rules for carrying on that intercourse. The mind can scarcely conceive a system for regulating commerce between nations which shall exclude all laws concerning navigation, which shall be silent on the admission of the vessels of the one nation into the ports of the other, and be confined to prescribing rules for the conduct of individuals, in the actual employment of buying and selling, or of barter.

If commerce does not include navigation, the government of the Union has no direct power over that subject, and can make no law prescribing what shall constitute American vessels, or requiring that they shall be navigated by American seamen. Yet this power has been exercised from the commencement of the government, has been exercised with the consent of all, and has been understood by all to be a commercial regulation. All America understands, and has uniformly understood, the word "commerce" to comprehend navigation. It was so understood, and must have been so understood, when the Constitution was framed. The power over commerce, including navigation, was one of the primary objects for which the people of America adopted their government, and must have been contemplated in forming it. The convention must have used the word in that sense, because all have understood it in that sense; and the attempt to restrict it comes too late. . . .

The word used in the Constitution, then, comprehends, and has been always understood to comprehend, navigation within its meaning; and a power to regulate navigation is as expressly granted as if that term had been added to the word "commerce."

To what commerce does this power extend? The Constitution informs us, to commerce "with foreign nations, and among the several States, and with the Indian tribes." It has, we believe, been universally admitted that these words comprehend every species of commercial intercourse between the United States and foreign nations. No sort of trade can be carried on between this country and any other to which this power does not extend. It has been truly said that commerce, as the word is used in the Constitution, is a unit, every part of which is indicated by the term. If this be the admitted meaning of the word, in its application to foreign nations, it must carry the same meaning through the sentence, and remain a unit, unless there be some plain intelligible cause which alters it.

The subject to which the power is next applied is to commerce "among the several States." The word "among" means intermingled with. A thing which is among others is intermingled with them. Commerce among the States cannot stop at the external boundary-line of each State, but may be introduced into the interior.

It is not intended to say that these words comprehend that commerce which is completely internal, which is carried on between man and man in a State, or between different parts of the same State, and which does not extend to or affect other States. Such a power would be inconvenient and is certainly unnecessary.

Comprehensive as the word "among" is, it may very properly be restricted to that commerce which concerns more States than one. . . . The completely internal commerce of a State, then, may be considered as reserved for the State itself.

But, in regulating commerce with foreign nations, the power of Congress does not stop at the jurisdictional lines of the several States. It would be a very useless power if it could not pass those lines. The commerce of the United States with foreign nations is that of the whole United States. Every district has a right to participate in it. The deep streams which penetrate our country in every direction pass through the interior of almost every State in the Union, and furnish the means of exercising this right. If Congress has the power to regulate it, that power must be exercised whenever the subject exists. If it exists within the States, if a foreign voyage may commence or terminate at a port within a State, then the power of Congress may be exercised within a state.

This principle is, if possible, still more clear when applied to commerce "among the several States." They either join each other, in which case they are separated by a mathematical line, or they are remote from each other, in which case other States lie between them. What is commerce "among" them; and how is it to be conducted? Can a trading expedition between two adjoining States commence and terminate outside of each? And if the trading intercourse be between two States remote from each other, must it not commence in one, terminate in the other, and probably pass through a third? Commerce among the States must, of necessity, be commerce with the States. In the regulation of trade with the Indian tribes, the action of the law, especially when the Constitution was made, was chiefly within a State. The power of Congress, then, whatever it may be, must be exercised within the territorial jurisdiction of the several states. . . .

We are now arrived at the inquiry—What is this power?

It is the power to regulate; that is, to prescribe the rule by which commerce is to be governed. This power, like all others vested in Congress, is complete in itself, may be exercised to its utmost extent, and acknowledges no limitations other than are prescribed in the Constitution. These are expressed in plain terms, and do not affect the questions which arise in this case, or which have been discussed at the Bar. . . .

The power of Congress, then, comprehends navigation within the limits of every State in the Union, so far as that navigation may be, in any manner, connected with "commerce with foreign nations, or among the several States, or with the Indian tribes." It may, of consequence, pass the jurisdictional line of New York, and act upon the very waters to which the prohibition now under consideration applies.

But it has been urged with great earnestness that, although the power of Congress to regulate commerce with foreign nations, and among the several States, be coextensive with the subject itself, and have no other limits than are prescribed in the Constitution, yet the States may severally exercise the same power within their respective jurisdictions. In support of this argument, it is said that they possessed it as an inseparable attribute of sovereignty before the formation of the Constitution, and still retain it, except so far as they have surrendered it by that instrument; that this principle results from the nature of the government, and is secured by the Tenth

Amendment; that an affirmative grant of power is not exclusive, unless in its own nature it be such that the continued exercise of it by the former possessor is inconsistent with the grant, and that this is not of that description. . . .

Since, however, in exercising the power of regulating their own purely internal affairs, whether of trading or police, the States may sometimes enact laws, the validity of which depends on their interfering with, and being contrary to, an act of Congress passed in pursuance of the Constitution, the court will enter upon the inquiry whether the laws of New York, as expounded by the highest tribunal of that State, have, in their application to this case, come into collision with an act of Congress, and deprived a citizen of a right to which that act entitles him. Should this collision exist, it will be immaterial whether those laws were passed in virtue of a concurrent power "to regulate commerce with foreign nations and among the several States," or, in virtue of a power to regulate their domestic trade and police. In one case and the other, the acts of New York must yield to the law of Congress, and the decision sustaining the privilege they confer, against a right given by a law of the Union must be erroneous. . . .

JUSTICE JOHNSON concurred. [He held that federal control of commerce was exclusive.]

FOR DISCUSSION

Article I does not define commerce in general or interstate commerce in particular. What definition does Marshall provide? What other definitions does he offer? Do you think he was correct in thinking that Congress intended to exempt ships from state regulation by issuing them a federal license?

RELATED CASES

***The License Cases:* 5 Howard 504 (1847).**

A state may prohibit the sale of liquor or provide for licensing of the sale of liquor in that state even though the liquor came through foreign or interstate commerce. Since Congress had not regulated the matter, the state regulation was valid. A state's police power is the power to govern persons and things. These cases came from New Hampshire, Massachusetts, and Rhode Island.

***The Passenger Cases* (*Smith v. Turner; Norris v. Boston*)*:* 7 How. 283 (1849).**

States (here New York and Massachusetts) cannot impose a head tax on passengers on ships from foreign or other state ports. The funds derived were to be used to give physical examinations to the passengers and to pay hospitalization for those found in need of it. These laws were held to be contrary to the grant over commerce to the Congress even though Congress had not seen fit to exercise this particular facet of the power. The state laws were a direct regulation of interstate commerce. The Court here used the *dormant power theory* under which, even though a granted power has not been used by Congress, the states are prevented from using it. *Cooley* indicates that the Court does not always apply this doctrine.

***Wabash, St. L. & P. Railway Co. v. Illinois* (*Wabash Case*)*:* 118 U.S. 557 (1886).**

Interstate railroad rates cannot be controlled by state action since these rates must be uniform and subject to general rules and principles by federal authority under the Commerce Clause of the Constitution. A state cannot regulate rates within that state for transportation that is a part of a total interstate journey. This would burden commerce. The specific commerce here was from New York to Illinois. This decision is said to have influenced enactment of the Interstate Commerce Act of 1887.

CHAMPION V. AMES

188 U.S. 321, 23 S. Ct. 321, 47 L. Ed. 492 (1903)

This case belongs to the line of precedents described in the introduction to this chapter, where the Court upheld congressional exercises of power under the Commerce Clause in large part because they involved the regulation of what it considered to be a moral evil, in this case gambling.

Vote: 5–4

JUSTICE HARLAN delivered the opinion of the Court.

The appellant insists that the carrying of lottery tickets from one State to another State by an express company engaged in carrying freight and packages from State to State, although such tickets may be contained in a box or package, does not constitute, and cannot by any act of Congress be legally made to constitute, commerce among the States within the meaning of the clause of the Constitution of the United States providing that Congress shall have power " "to regulate commerce with foreign nations, and among the several States, and with the Indian tribes;" consequently, that Congress cannot make it an offence to cause such tickets to be carried from one State to another. . . .

[Harlan extensively examines past cases defining the commerce power.]

This reference to prior adjudications could be extended if it were necessary to do so. The cases cited, however, sufficiently indicate the grounds upon which this court has proceeded when determining the meaning and scope of the commerce clause. They show that commerce among the States embraces navigation, intercourse, communication, traffic, the transit of persons, and the transmission of messages by telegraph. They also show that the power to regulate commerce among the several States is vested in Congress as absolutely as it would be in a single government, having in its constitution the same restrictions on the exercise of the power as are found in the Constitution of the United States; that such power is plenary, complete in itself, and may be exerted by Congress to its utmost extent, subject only to such limitations as the Constitution imposes upon the exercise of the powers granted by it; and that in determining the character of the regulations to be adopted Congress has a large discretion which is not to be controlled by the courts, simply because, in their opinion, such regulations may not be the best or most effective that could be employed.

We come then to inquire whether there is any solid foundation upon which to rest the contention that Congress may not regulate the carrying of lottery tickets from one State to another, at least by corporations or companies whose business it is, for hire, to carry tangible property from one State to another.

It was said in argument that lottery tickets are not of any real or substantial value in themselves, and therefore are not subjects of commerce. If that were conceded to be the only legal test as to what are to be deemed subjects of the commerce that may be regulated by Congress, we cannot accept as accurate the broad statement that such tickets are of no value. Upon their face they showed that the lottery company offered a large capital prize, to be paid to the holder of the ticket winning the prize at the drawing advertised to be held at Asuncion, Paraguay. Money was placed on deposit in different banks in the United States to be applied by the agents representing the lottery company to the prompt payment of prizes. These tickets were the subject of traffic; they could have been sold; and the holder was assured that the company would pay to him the amount of the prize drawn. That the holder might not have been able to enforce his claim in the courts of any country making the drawing of lotteries illegal, and forbidding the circulation of lottery tickets, did not change the fact that the tickets issued by the foreign company represented so much money payable to the person holding them and who might draw the prizes affixed to them. Even if a holder did not draw a prize, the tickets, before the drawing, had a money value in the market among those who chose to sell or buy lottery tickets. In short, a lottery ticket is a subject of traffic, and is so designated in the act of 1895. That fact is not without significance in view of what this court has said. That act, counsel for the accused well remarks, was intended to supplement the provisions of prior acts excluding lottery tickets from the mails and prohibiting the importation of lottery matter from abroad, and to prohibit the causing lottery tickets to be carried, and lottery tickets and lottery advertisements to be transferred, from one State to another by any means or method.

We are of opinion that lottery tickets are subjects of traffic and therefore are subjects of commerce, and the regulation of the carriage of such tickets from State to State, at least by independent carriers, is a regulation of commerce among the several States.

But it is said that the statute in question does not regulate the carrying of lottery tickets from State to State, but by punishing those who cause them to be so carried Congress in effect prohibits such carrying; that in respect of the carrying from one State to another of articles or things that are, in fact, or according to usage in business, the subjects of commerce, the authority given Congress was not to prohibit, but only to regulate. This view was earnestly pressed at the bar by learned counsel, and must be examined.

It is to be remarked that the Constitution does not define what is to be deemed a legitimate regulation of interstate commerce. In *Gibbons v. Ogden*, 22 U.S. 1 (1824), it was said that the power to regulate such commerce is the power to prescribe the rule by which it is to be governed. But this general observation leaves it to be determined, when the question comes before the court, whether Congress in prescribing a particular rule has exceeded its power under the Constitution. While our Government must be acknowledged by all to be one of enumerated powers (*McCulloch v. Maryland,* 17 U.S. 316 (Wheat.) (1819)), the Constitution does not attempt to set forth all the means by which such powers may be carried into execution. It leaves to Congress a large discretion as to the means that may be employed in executing a given power. "The sound construction of the Constitution," this court has said, "must allow to the national legislature that discretion, with respect to the means by which the powers it confers are to be carried into execution, which will enable that body to perform the high duties assigned to it, in the manner most beneficial to the people. Let the end be legitimate, let it be within the scope of the Constitution, and all means which are appropriate, which are plainly adapted to that end, which are not prohibited, but consistent with the letter and spirit of the Constitution, are constitutional."

We have said that the carrying from State to State of lottery tickets constitutes interstate commerce, and that the regulation of such commerce is within the power of Congress under the Constitution. Are we prepared to say that a provision which is, in effect, a prohibition of the carriage of such articles from State to State is not a fit or appropriate mode for the regulation of that particular kind of commerce? If lottery traffic, carried on through interstate commerce, is a matter of which Congress may take cognizance and over which its power may be exerted, can it be possible that it must tolerate the traffic, and simply regulate the manner in which it may be carried on? Or may not Congress, for the protection of the people of all the States, and under the power to regulate interstate commerce, devise such means, within the scope of the Constitution, and not prohibited by it, as will drive that traffic out of commerce among the States?

In determining whether regulation may not under some circumstances properly take the form or have the effect of prohibition, the nature of the interstate traffic which it was sought by the act of May 2, 1895, to suppress cannot be overlooked. When enacting that statute Congress no doubt shared the views upon the subject of lotteries heretofore expressed by this court. In *Phalen v. Virginia*, 49 U.S. 163 (1850), after observing that the suppression of nuisances injurious to public health or morality is among the most important duties of Government, this court said: "Experience has shown that the common forms of gambling are comparatively innocuous when placed in contrast with the widespread pestilence of lotteries. The former are confined to a few persons and places, but the latter infests the whole community; it enters every dwelling; it reaches every class; it preys upon the hard earnings of the poor; it plunders the ignorant and simple." In other cases we have adjudged that authority given by legislative enactment to carry on a lottery, although based upon a consideration in money, was not protected by the contract clause of the Constitution; this, for the reason that no State may bargain away its power to protect the public morals, nor excuse its failure to perform a public duty by saying that it had agreed, by legislative enactment, not to do so. *Stone v. Mississippi*, 101 US 814 (1880), *Douglas v. Kentucky*, 168 U.S. 488 (1897).

If a State, when considering legislation for the suppression of lotteries within its own limits, may properly take into view the evils that inhere in the raising of money, in that mode, why may not Congress, invested with the Power to regulate commerce among the several States, provide that such commerce shall not be polluted by the carrying of lottery tickets from one State to another? In this connection it must not be forgotten that the power of Congress to regulate commerce among the States is plenary, is complete in itself, and is subject to no limitations except such as may be found in the Constitution. What provision in that instrument can be regarded as limiting the exercise of the power granted? What clause can be cited which, in any degree, countenances the suggestion that one may, of right, carry or cause to be carried from one State to another that which will harm the public morals? We cannot think of any clause of that instrument that could possibly be invoked by those who assert their right to send lottery tickets from State to State except the one providing that no person shall be deprived of his liberty without due process of law. We have said that the liberty protected by the Constitution embraces the right to be free in the enjoyment of one's faculties; "to be free to use them in all lawful ways; to live and work where he will; to earn his livelihood by any lawful calling; to pursue any livelihood or avocation, and for that purpose to enter into all contracts that may be proper." *Allgeyer v. Louisiana,* 165 U.S. 578 (1897). But surely it will not be said to be a part of any one's liberty, as recognized by the supreme law of the land, that he shall be allowed to introduce into commerce among the States an element that will be confessedly injurious to the public morals.

If it be said that the act of 1895 is inconsistent with the Tenth Amendment, reserving to the States respectively or to the people the powers not delegated to the United States, the answer is that the power to regulate commerce among the States has been expressly delegated to Congress.

Besides, Congress, by that act, does not assume to interfere with traffic or commerce in lottery tickets carried on exclusively within the limits of any State, but has in view only commerce of that kind among the several States. It has not assumed to interfere with the completely internal affairs of any State, and has only legislated in respect of a matter which concerns the people of the United States. As a State may, for the purpose of guarding the morals of its own people, forbid all sales of lottery tickets within its limits, so Congress, for the purpose of guarding the people of the United States against the "widespread pestilence of lotteries" and to protect the commerce which concerns all the States, may prohibit the carrying of lottery tickets from one State to another. In legislating upon the subject of the traffic in lottery tickets, as carried on through interstate commerce, Congress only supplemented the action of those States—perhaps all of them—which, for the protection of the public morals, prohibit the drawing of lotteries, as well as the sale or circulation of lottery tickets, within their respective limits. It said, in effect, that it would not permit the declared policy of the States, which sought to protect their people against the mischiefs of the lottery business, to be overthrown or disregarded by the agency of interstate commerce. We should hesitate long before adjudging that an evil of such appalling character, carried on through interstate commerce, cannot be met and crushed by the only power competent to that end. We say competent to that end, because Congress alone has the power to occupy, by legislation, the whole field of interstate commerce. What was said by this court upon a former occasion may well be here repeated: "The Framers of the Constitution never intended that the legislative power of the Nation should find itself incapable of disposing of a subject matter specifically committed to its charge." *In re Rahrer,* 140 U.S. 545 (1891). If the carrying of lottery tickets from one State to another be interstate commerce, and if Congress is of the opinion that an effective regulation for the suppression of lotteries, carried on through such commerce, is to make it a criminal offence to cause lottery tickets to be carried from one State to another, we know of no authority in the courts to hold that the means thus devised are not appropriate and necessary to protect the country at large against a species of interstate commerce which, although in general use and somewhat favored in both national and state legislation in the early history of the country, has grown into disrepute and has become offensive to the entire people of the Nation. It is a kind of traffic which no one can be entitled to pursue as of right.

That regulation may sometimes appropriately assume the form of prohibition is also illustrated by the case of diseased cattle, transported from one State to another. Such cattle may have, notwithstanding their condition, a value in money for some purposes, and yet it cannot be doubted that Congress, under its power to regulate commerce, may either provide for their being inspected before transportation begins, or, in its discretion, may prohibit their being transported from one State to another. Indeed, by the act of May 29, 1884, c. 60, Congress has provided: "That no railroad company within the United States, or the owners or masters of any steam or sailing or other vessel or boat, shall receive for transportation or transport, from one State or Territory to another, or from any State into the District of Columbia, or from the District into any State, any live stock affected with any contagious, infectious, or communicable disease, and especially the disease known as pleuro-pneumonia; nor shall any person, company, or corporation deliver for such transportation to any railroad company, or master or owner of any boat or vessel, any live stock, knowing them to be affected with any contagious, infectious, or communicable disease; nor shall any person, company, or corporation drive on foot or transport in private conveyance from one State or Territory to another, or from any State into the District of Columbia, or from the District into any State, any live stock, knowing them to be affected with any contagious, infectious, or communicable disease, and especially the disease known as pleuro-pneumonia." *Reid v. State of Colorado,* 187 U.S. 137 (1902).

The act of July 2, 1890, known as the Sherman Anti-Trust Act, and which is based upon the power of Congress to regulate commerce among the States, is an illustration of the proposition that regulation may take the form of prohibition. The object of that act was to protect trade and commerce against unlawful restraints and monopolies. To accomplish that object Congress declared certain contracts to be illegal. That act, in effect, prohibited the doing of certain things, and its prohibitory clauses have been sustained in several cases as valid under the power of Congress to regulate interstate commerce. . . .

[Harlan cites other examples where regulation of commerce involved prohibition of certain items.]

It is said, however, that if, in order to suppress lotteries carried on through interstate commerce, Congress may exclude lottery tickets from such commerce, that principle leads necessarily to the conclusion that Congress may arbitrarily exclude from commerce among the States any article, commodity or thing, of whatever kind or nature, or however useful or valuable, which it may choose, no matter with what motive, to declare shall not be carried from one State to another. It will be time enough to consider the constitutionality of such legislation when we must do so. The present case does not require the court to declare the full extent of the power that Congress may exercise in the regulation of commerce among the States. We may, however, repeat, in this connection, what the court has heretofore said, that the power of Congress to regulate commerce among the States, although plenary, cannot be deemed arbitrary, since it is subject to such limitations or restrictions as are prescribed by the Constitution. This power, therefore, may not be exercised so as to infringe rights secured or protected by that instrument. It would not be difficult to imagine legislation that would be justly liable to such an objection as that stated, and be hostile to the objects for the accomplishment of which Congress was invested with the general power to regulate commerce among the several States. But, as often said, the possible abuse of a power is not an argument against its existence. There is probably no governmental power that may not be exerted to the injury of the public. If what is done by Congress is manifestly in excess of the powers granted to it, then upon the courts will rest the duty of adjudging that its action is neither legal nor binding upon the people. But if what Congress does is within the limits of its power, and is simply unwise or injurious, the remedy is that suggested by Chief Justice Marshall in *Gibbons v. Ogden* [22 U.S. 1 (1824)], when he said: "The wisdom and the discretion of Congress, their identity with the people, and the influence which their constituents possess at elections, are, in this, as in many other instances, as that, for example, of declaring war, the sole restraints on which they have relied, to secure them from its abuse. They are the restraints on which the people must often rely solely, in all representative governments."

The whole subject is too important, and the questions suggested by its consideration are too difficult of solution, to justify any attempt to lay down a rule for determining in advance the validity of every statute that may be enacted under the commerce clause. We decide nothing more in the present case than that lottery tickets are subjects of traffic among those who choose to sell or buy them; that the carriage of such tickets by independent carriers from one State to another is therefore interstate commerce; that under its power to regulate commerce among the several States Congress—subject to the limitations imposed by the Constitution upon the exercise of the powers granted—has plenary authority over such commerce, and may prohibit the carriage of such tickets from State to State; and that legislation to that end, and of that character, is not inconsistent with any limitation or restriction imposed upon the exercise of the powers granted to Congress.

The judgment is

Affirmed.

CHIEF JUSTICE FULLER, with whom concur JUSTICES BREWER, SHIRAS and PECKHAM, dissenting.

The power of the State to impose restraints and burdens on persons and property in conservation and promotion of the public health, good order and prosperity is a power originally and always belonging to the States, not surrendered by them to the General Government nor directly restrained by the Constitution of the United States, and essentially exclusive, and the suppression of lotteries as a harmful business falls within this power, commonly called of police. *Douglas v. Kentucky,* [168 U.S. 488 (1897)].

It is urged, however, that because Congress is empowered to regulate commerce between the several States, it, therefore, may suppress lotteries by prohibiting the carriage of lottery matter. Congress may indeed make all laws necessary and proper for carrying the powers granted to it into execution, and doubtless an act prohibiting the carriage of lottery matter would be necessary and proper to the execution of a power to suppress lotteries; but that power belongs to the States and not to Congress. To hold that Congress has general police power would be to hold that it may accomplish objects not entrusted to the General Government, and to defeat the operation of the Tenth Amendment, declaring that: "The powers not delegated to the United States by the Constitution, nor prohibited by it to the States, are reserved to the States respectively, or to the people." . . .

FOR DISCUSSION

Today almost every state has a form of legalized gambling. What do you think would happen if the national government tried to occupy this field for itself? Could Congress use its power over interstate commerce to drive state lotteries and casinos out of business?

RELATED CASES

***United States v. E. C. Knight Co.:* 156 U.S. 1 (1895).**

The Sherman Anti-Trust Act did not apply to a monopoly in the manufacture of sugar since the Sherman Act is based on the commerce power, and manufacturing is not a part of commerce but is antecedent to commerce and is a matter for the states to police.

***Swift & Co. v. United States:* 196 U.S. 375 (1905).**

A unanimous Court held that the Sherman Anti-Trust Act could be applied to the Beef Trust. Justice Oliver Wendell Holmes argued that beef was in the "stream of commerce" and thus subject to federal jurisdiction.

***The Shreveport Case* [*Houston, E. & W. Texas Ry. Co. v. United States:* 234 U.S. 342 (1914)].**

In a 7–2 vote, with Justices Hughes, Lurton, and Pitnesy dissenting without opinion, the Court upheld the power of the Interstate Commerce Commission to raise intrastate railroad rates within Texas to those that the railroad was charging on interstate routes between Texas and Louisiana.

***Stafford v. Wallace:* 258 U.S. 495 (1922).**

The Court again applied the "stream of commerce" rationale to uphold the Packers and Stockyards Act of 1921.

HAMMER V. DAGENHART

247 U.S. 251, 38 S. Ct. 529, 62 L. Ed. 1101 (1918)

Whereas *Champion v. Ames* (168 U.S. 488, 1897), represents one of the cases in the line of precedents under which the Supreme Court interpreted congressional powers under the Commerce Clause broadly, this decision represents a decision where it narrowed them. Rather than overruling prior expansive precedents, the Court chose to distinguish them. The case was brought by a father of two sons, ages fourteen and sixteen, who wanted them to be able to work in a North Carolina cotton mill contrary to a national child labor law that Congress sought to enforce under its commerce powers. Judicial concerns about congressional interference in state affairs make this case worthy of consideration in relation to the chapters relative to federalism and the exercise of state powers.

Vote: 5–4

JUSTICE DAY delivered the opinion of the court.

The attack upon the act rests upon three propositions: First: It is not a regulation of interstate and foreign commerce; Second: It contravenes the Tenth Amendment to the Constitution; Third: It conflicts with the Fifth Amendment to the Constitution.

The controlling question for decision is: Is it within the authority of Congress in regulating commerce among the States to prohibit the transportation in interstate commerce of manufactured goods, the product of a factory in which, within thirty days prior to their removal therefrom, children under the age of fourteen have been employed or permitted to work, or children between the ages of fourteen and sixteen years have been employed or permitted to work more than eight hours in any day, or more than six days in any week, or after the hour of seven o'clock P.M. or before the hour of 6 o'clock A.M.?

The power essential to the passage of this act, the Government contends, is found in the commerce clause of the Constitution which authorizes Congress to regulate commerce with foreign nations and among the States.

In *Gibbons v. Ogden*, 22 U.S. 1 (1824), Chief Justice Marshall, speaking for this court, and defining the extent and nature of the commerce power, said, "It is the power to regulate; that is, to prescribe the rule by which commerce is to be governed." In other words, the power is one to control the means by which commerce is carried on, which is directly the contrary of the assumed right to forbid commerce from moving and thus destroy it as to particular commodities. But it is insisted that adjudged cases in this court establish the doctrine that the power to regulate given to Congress incidentally includes the authority to prohibit the movement of ordinary commodities and therefore that the subject is not open for discussion. The cases demonstrate the contrary. They rest upon the character of the particular subjects dealt with and the fact that the scope of governmental authority, state or national, possessed over them is such that the authority to prohibit is as to them but the exertion of the power to regulate.

The first of these cases is *Champion v. Ames*, 188 U.S. 321 (1903), the so-called *Lottery Case*, in which it was held that Congress might pass a law having the effect to keep the channels of commerce free from use in the transportation of tickets used in the promotion of lottery schemes. In *Hipolite Egg Co.* v. *United States*, 220 U.S. 45 (1911), this court sustained the power of Congress to pass the Pure Food and Drug Act which prohibited the introduction into the States by means of interstate commerce of impure foods and drugs. In *Hoke* v. *United States*, 227 U.S. 308 (1913), this court sustained the constitutionality of the so-called "White Slave Traffic Act" whereby the transportation of a woman in interstate commerce for the purpose of prostitution was forbidden. In that case we said, having reference to the authority of Congress, under the regulatory power, to protect the channels of interstate commerce: "If the facility of interstate transportation can be taken away from the demoralization of lotteries, the debasement of obscene literature, the contagion of diseased cattle or persons, the impurity of food and drugs, the like facility can be taken away from the systematic enticement to and the enslavement in prostitution and debauchery of women, and, more insistently, of girls."

In *Caminetti* v. *United States*, 242 U.S. 470 (1917), we held that Congress might prohibit the transportation of women in interstate commerce for the purposes of debauchery and kindred purposes. In *Clark Distilling Co.* v. *Western Maryland Ry. Co.*, 242 U.S. 311 (1917), the power of Congress over the transportation of intoxicating liquors was sustained. In the course of the opinion it was said: "The power conferred is to regulate, and the very terms of the grant would seem to repel the contention that only prohibition of movement in interstate commerce was embraced. And the cogency of this is manifest since if the doctrine were applied to those manifold and important subjects of interstate commerce as to which Congress from the beginning has regulated, not prohibited, the existence of government under the Constitution would be no longer possible." And, concluding the discussion which sustained the authority of the Government to prohibit the transportation of liquor in interstate commerce, the court said: ". . . the exceptional nature of the subject here regulated is the basis upon which the exceptional power exerted must rest and affords no ground for any fear that such power may be constitutionally extended to things which it may not, consistently with the guarantees of the Constitution, embrace."

In each of these instances the use of interstate transportation was necessary to the accomplishment of harmful results. In other words, although the power over interstate transportation was to regulate, that could only be accomplished by prohibiting the use of the facilities of interstate commerce to effect the evil intended.

This element is wanting in the present case. The thing intended to be accomplished by this statute is the denial of the facilities of interstate commerce to those manufacturers in the States who employ children within the prohibited ages. The act in its effect does not regulate transportation among the States, but aims to standardize the ages at which children may be employed in mining and manufacturing within the States. The goods shipped are of themselves harmless. The act permits them to be freely shipped after thirty days from the time of their removal from the factory. When offered for shipment, and before transportation begins, the labor of their production is over, and the mere fact that they were intended for interstate commerce transportation does not make their production subject to federal control under the commerce power.

Commerce "consists of intercourse and traffic . . . and includes the transportation of persons and property, as well as the purchase, sale and exchange of commodities." The making of goods and the mining of coal are not commerce, nor does the fact that these things are to be afterwards shipped or used in interstate commerce, make their production a part thereof.

Over interstate transportation, or its incidents, the regulatory power of Congress is ample, but the production of articles, intended for interstate commerce, is a matter of local regulation.

When the commerce begins is determined, not by the character of the commodity, nor by the intention of the owner to transfer it to another state for sale, nor by his preparation of it for transportation, but by its actual delivery to a common carrier for transportation, or the actual commencement of its transfer to another state. If it were otherwise, all manufacture intended for interstate shipment would be brought under federal control to the practical exclusion of the authority of the States, a result certainly not contemplated by the framers of the Constitution when they vested in Congress the authority to regulate commerce among the States.

It is further contended that the authority of Congress may be exerted to control interstate commerce in the shipment of child-made goods because of the effect of the circulation of such goods in other States where the evil of this class of labor has been recognized by local legislation, and the right to thus employ child labor has been more rigorously restrained than in the State of production. In other words, that the unfair competition, thus engendered, may be controlled by closing the channels of interstate commerce to manufacturers in those States where the local laws do not meet what Congress deems to be the more just standard of other States.

There is no power vested in Congress to require the States to exercise their police power so as to prevent possible unfair competition. Many causes may cooperate to give one State, by reason of local laws or conditions, an economic advantage over others. The Commerce Clause was not intended to give to Congress a general authority to equalize such conditions. In some of the States laws have been passed fixing minimum wages for women, in others the local law regulates the hours of labor of women in various employments. Business done in such States may be at an economic disadvantage when compared with States which have no such regulations; surely, this fact does not give Congress the power to deny transportation in interstate commerce to those who carry on business where the hours of labor and the rate of compensation for women have not been fixed by a standard in use in other States and approved by Congress.

The grant of power to Congress over the subject of interstate commerce was to enable it to regulate such commerce, and not to give it authority to control the States in their exercise of the police power over local trade and manufacture.

The grant of authority over a purely federal matter was not intended to destroy the local power always existing and carefully reserved to the States in the Tenth Amendment to the Constitution.

Police regulations relating to the internal trade and affairs of the States have been uniformly recognized as within such control. "This," said this court in *United States* v. *Dewitt*, 76 U.S. 41 (1869), "has been so frequently declared by this court, results so obviously from the terms of the Constitution, and has been so fully explained and supported on former occasions, that we think it unnecessary to enter again upon the discussion."

That there should be limitations upon the right to employ children in mines and factories in the interest of their own and the public welfare, all will admit. That such employment is generally deemed to require regulation is shown by the fact that the brief of counsel states that every State in the Union has a law upon the subject, limiting the right to thus employ children. In North Carolina, the State wherein is located the factory in which the employment was had in the present case, no child under twelve years of age is permitted to work.

It may be desirable that such laws be uniform, but our Federal Government is one of enumerated powers; "this principle," declared Chief Justice Marshall in *McCulloch* v. *Maryland*, [17 U.S. 316 (1819),] "is universally admitted."

A statute must be judged by its natural and reasonable effect. *Collins* v. *New Hampshire*, 171 U.S. 30 (1898). The control by Congress over interstate commerce cannot authorize the exercise of authority not entrusted to it by the Constitution. The maintenance of the authority of the States over matters purely local is as essential to the preservation of our institutions as is the conservation of the supremacy of the federal power in all matters entrusted to the Nation by the Federal Constitution.

In interpreting the Constitution it must never be forgotten that the Nation is made up of States to which are entrusted the powers of local government. And to them and to the people the powers not expressly delegated to the National Government are reserved. The power of the States to regulate their purely internal affairs by such laws as seem wise to the local authority is inherent and has never been surrendered to the general government. To sustain this statute would not be in our judgment a recognition of the lawful exertion of congressional authority over interstate commerce, but would sanction an invasion by the federal power of the control of a matter purely local in its character, and over which no authority has been delegated to Congress in conferring the power to regulate commerce among the States.

We have neither authority nor disposition to question the motives of Congress in enacting this legislation. The purposes intended must be attained consistently with constitutional limitations and not by an invasion of the powers of the States. This court has no more important function than that which devolves upon it the obligation to preserve inviolate the constitutional limitations upon the exercise of authority, federal and state, to the end that each may continue to discharge, harmoniously with the other, the duties entrusted to it by the Constitution.

In our view the necessary effect of this act is, by means of a prohibition against the movement in interstate commerce of ordinary commercial commodities, to regulate the hours of labor of children in factories and mines within the States, a purely state authority. Thus the act in a twofold sense is repugnant to the Constitution. It not only transcends the authority delegated to Congress over commerce but also exerts a power as to a purely local matter to which the federal authority does not extend. The far reaching result of upholding the act cannot be more plainly indicated than by pointing out that if Congress can thus regulate matters entrusted to local authority by prohibition of the movement of commodities in interstate commerce, all freedom of commerce will be at an end, and the power of the States over local matters may be eliminated, and thus our system of government be practically destroyed.

For these reasons we hold that this law exceeds the constitutional authority of Congress. It follows that the decree of the District Court must be

Affirmed.

JUSTICE HOLMES, dissenting.

The single question in this case is whether Congress has power to prohibit the shipment in interstate or foreign commerce of any product of a cotton mill situated in the United States, in which within thirty days before the removal of the product children under fourteen have been employed, or children between fourteen and sixteen have been employed more than eight hours in a day, or more than six days in any week, or between seven in the evening and six in the morning. The objection urged against the power is that the States have exclusive control over their methods of production and that Congress cannot meddle with them, and taking the proposition in the sense of direct intermeddling I agree to it and suppose that no one denies it. But if an act is within the powers specifically conferred upon Congress, it seems to me that it is not made any less constitutional because of the indirect effects that it may have, however obvious it may be that it will have those effects, and that we are not at liberty upon such grounds to hold it void.

The first step in my argument is to make plain what no one is likely to dispute—that the statute in question is within the power expressly given to Congress if considered only as to its immediate effects and that if invalid it is so only upon some collateral ground. The statute confines itself to prohibiting the carriage of certain goods in interstate or foreign commerce. Congress is given power to regulate such commerce in unqualified terms. It would not be argued today that the power to regulate does not include the power to prohibit. Regulation means the prohibition of something, and when interstate commerce is the matter to be regulated I cannot doubt that the regulation may prohibit any part of such commerce that Congress sees fit to forbid. At all events it is established by the *Lottery Case* and others that have followed it that a law is not beyond the regulative power of Congress merely because it prohibits certain transportation out and out. *Champion v. Ames.* So I repeat that this statute in its immediate operation is clearly within the Congress's constitutional power.

The question then is narrowed to whether the exercise of its otherwise constitutional power by Congress can be pronounced unconstitutional because of its possible reaction upon the conduct of the States in a matter upon which I have admitted that they are free from direct control. I should have thought that that matter had been disposed of so fully as to leave no room for doubt. I should have thought that most conspicuous decisions of this Court had made it clear that the power to regulate commerce and other constitutional powers could not be cut down or qualified by the fact that it might interfere with the carrying out of the domestic policy of any State.

[Holmes proceeded to examine regulations of goods that the Court had previously upheld under the Commerce Clause.] . . .

The notion that prohibition is any less prohibition when applied to things now thought evil I do not understand. But if there is any matter upon which civilized countries have agreed—far more unanimously than they have with regard to intoxicants and some other matters over which this country is now emotionally aroused—it is the evil of premature and excessive child labor. I should have thought that if we were to introduce our own moral conceptions where in my opinion they do not belong, this was preeminently a case for upholding the exercise of all its powers by the United States.

But I had thought that the propriety of the exercise of a power admitted to exist in some cases was for the consideration of Congress alone and that this Court always had disavowed the right to intrude its judgment upon questions of policy or morals. It is not for this Court to pronounce when prohibition is necessary to regulation if it ever may be necessary—to say that it is permissible as against strong drink but not as against the product of ruined lives.

The act does not meddle with anything belonging to the States. They may regulate their internal affairs and their domestic commerce as they like. But when they seek to send their products across the state line they are no longer within their rights. If there were no Constitution and no Congress their power to cross the line would depend upon their neighbors. Under the Constitution such commerce belongs not to the States but to Congress to regulate. It may carry out its views of public policy whatever indirect effect they may have upon the activities of the States. Instead of being encountered by a prohibitive tariff at her boundaries the State encounters the public policy of the United States which it is for Congress to express. The public policy of the United States is shaped with a view to the benefit of the nation as a whole. If, as has been the case within the memory of men still living, a State should take a different view of the propriety of sustaining a lottery from that which generally prevails, I cannot believe that the fact would require a different decision from that reached in *Champion v. Ames.* Yet in that case it would be said with quite as much force as in this that Congress was attempting to intermeddle with the State's domestic affairs. The national welfare as understood by Congress may require a different attitude within its sphere from that of some self-seeking State. It seems to me entirely constitutional for Congress to enforce its understanding by all the means at its command.

FOR DISCUSSION

Justice Holmes's dissent in this case is widely known. What were his central arguments? Is child labor a state or a national issue? Can you think of other areas where states might be tempted to "race for the bottom" or enact minimal regulations in hope of attracting businesses or industries from other states? Should states be allowed to compete against one another or does this defeat the purpose of the Commerce Clause?

RELATED CASE

***Adair v. United States:* 208 U.S. 161 (1908).**

The Court held that a federal statute of 1898 forbidding "yellow dog contracts" (agreements by employees not to join unions) in the business of carriers engaged in interstate commerce was void as a violation of the company's and employees' contractual rights under the Due Process Clause of the Fifth Amendment. The statute here was the Erdman Act of 1898, Sec. 10. The Court held that there was no connection between commerce and union membership, and the statute impaired freedom of contract.

A.L.A. SCHECHTER POULTRY CORP. V. UNITED STATES

295 U.S. 495, 55 S.Ct. 837, 79 L.Ed. 1570 (1935)

The National Industrial Recovery Act (NIRA), which was a New Deal measure, authorized industries to set up codes of fair competition that, after authorization by executive orders, would provide for both civil and criminal penalties. In this case, the president had authorized a "Live Poultry Code" for that industry. Schechter, a poultry dealer in New York City, was found guilty of disregarding the code on eighteen counts, a number of which could be considered to be relatively petty. The National Recovery Administration (NRA) was the enforcement agency under NIRA.

Vote: 9–0

CHIEF JUSTICE HUGHES delivered the opinion of the Court.

. . . The "Live Poultry Code" was promulgated under § 3 of the National Industrial Recovery Act. That section . . . authorizes the President to approve "codes of fair competition." . . .

The "Live Poultry Code" was approved by the President on April 13, 1934. . . . The Code is established as "a code for fair competition for the live poultry industry of the metropolitan area in and about the City of New York. . . ."

The Code fixes the number of hours for workdays. It provides that no employee, with certain exceptions, shall be permitted to work in excess of forty (40) hours in anyone week, and that no employee, save as stated, "shall be paid in any pay period less than at the rate of fifty (50) cents per hour." The article containing "general labor provisions" prohibits the employment of any person under sixteen years of age, and declares that employees shall have the right of "collective bargaining" and freedom of choice with respect to labor organizations, in the terms of § 7(a) of the Act. The minimum number of employees who shall be employed by slaughterhouse operators is fixed, the numbers being graduated according to the average volume of weekly sales. . . . The seventh article, containing "trade practice provisions," prohibits various practices which are said to constitute "unfair methods of competition. . . ."

The President approved the Code by an executive order. . . . [The first question was: Was the law justified in the light of the grave national crisis. The answer was that such action was precluded by the Tenth Amendment.]

Second. The question of the delegation of legislative power. . . . The Constitution provides that "all legislative powers herein granted shall be vested in a Congress of the United States, which shall consist of a Senate and House of Representatives." Article One, § 1. And the Congress is authorized "to make all laws which shall be necessary and proper for carrying into execution" its general power. Article One, § 8, paragraph 18. The Congress is not permitted to abdicate or to transfer to others the essential legislative functions with which it is thus vested. We have repeatedly recognized the necessity of adapting legislation to complex conditions involving a host of details with which the national Legislature cannot deal directly. We pointed out in the Panama Company case that the Constitution has never been regarded as denying to Congress the necessary resources of flexibility and practicality, which will enable it to perform its function in laying down policies and establishing standards, while leaving to selected instrumentalities the making of subordinate rules within prescribed limits and the determination of facts to which the policy as declared by the Legislature is to apply. But we said that the constant recognition of the necessity and validity of such provisions, and the wide range of administrative authority which has been developed by means of them, cannot be allowed to obscure the limitations of the authority to delegate, if our constitutional system is to be maintained. . . .

Accordingly, we turn to the Recovery Act to ascertain what limits have been set to the exercise of the President's discretion. *First,* the President, as a condition of approval, is required to find that the trade or industrial associations or groups which propose a code "impose no inequitable restrictions on admission to membership" and are "truly representative." That condition, however, relates only to the status of the initiators of the new laws and not to the permissible scope of such laws. *Second,* the President is required to find that the code is not "designed to promote monopolies or to eliminate or oppress small enterprises and will not operate to discriminate against them." And to this is added a proviso that the code "shall not permit monopolies or monopolistic practices." But these restrictions leave virtually untouched the field of policy envisaged by § 1, and in that wide field of legislative possibilities the proponents of a code, refraining from monopolistic designs, may roam at will and the President may approve or disapprove their proposals as he may see fit. . . .

To summarize and conclude upon this point: § 3 of the Recovery Act is without precedent. It supplies no standards for any trade, industry or activity. It does not undertake to prescribe rules of conduct to be applied to particular states of fact determined by appropriate administrative procedure. Instead of prescribing rules of conduct, it authorizes the making of codes to prescribe them. For that legislative undertaking, § 3 sets up no standards, aside from the statement of the general aims of rehabilitation, correction and expansion described in § 1. In view of the scope of that broad declaration, and of the nature of the few restrictions that are imposed, the discretion of the President in approving or prescribing codes, and in enacting laws for the government of trade and industry throughout the country, is virtually unfettered. We think that the code-making authority thus conferred is an unconstitutional delegation of legislative power.

Third. The question of the application of the provisions of the Live Poultry Code to intrastate transactions. . . . But under § 3(f) penalties are confined to violations of a code provision "in any transaction in or affecting interstate or foreign commerce." This aspect of the case presents the question whether the particular provisions of the Live Poultry Code, which the defendants were convicted for violating and for having conspired to violate, were within the regulating powers of Congress. These provisions relate to the hours and wages of those employed by defendants in their slaughterhouses in Brooklyn and to the sales there made to retail dealers and butchers.

(1) Were these transactions "*in*" interstate commerce? Much is made of the fact that almost all [96 percent] the poultry coming to New York is sent there from other states. But the code provisions as here applied do not concern the transportation of the poultry from other states to New York, or the transactions of the commission men or others to whom it is consigned, or the sales made by such consignees to defendants. When defendants had made their purchases, whether at the West Washington Market in New York City or at the railroad terminals serving the city, or elsewhere, the poultry was trucked to their slaughterhouses in Brooklyn for local disposition. The interstate transactions in relation to that poultry then ended. Defendants held the poultry at their slaughterhouse markets for slaughter and local sale to retail dealers and butchers, who in turn sold directly to consumers. Neither the slaughtering nor the sales by defendants were transactions in interstate commerce. . . .

The undisputed facts thus afford no warrant for the argument that the poultry handled by defendants at their slaughterhouse markets was in "*current*" or "*flow*" of interstate commerce and was thus subject to congressional regulation. The mere fact that there may be a constant flow of commodities into a state does not mean that the flow continues after the property has arrived and has become commingled with the mass of property within the state and is there held solely for local disposition and use. So far as the poultry herein questioned is concerned, the flow in interstate commerce had ceased. The poultry had come to a permanent rest within the state. It was not held, used or sold by defendants in relation to any further transaction in interstate commerce and was not destined for transportation to other states. Hence, decisions which deal with a stream of interstate commerce—where goods come to rest within a state temporarily and are later to go forward in interstate commerce—and with the regulations of transactions involved in that practical continuity of movement, are not applicable here. . . .

(2) Did the defendant's transactions directly "*affect*" interstate commerce so as to be subject to federal regulation? The power of Congress extends not only to the regulation of transactions which are part of interstate commerce, but to the protection of that commerce from injury. It matters not that the injury may be due to the conduct of those engaged in intrastate operations. Thus, Congress may protect the safety of those employed in interstate transportation "no matter what may be the source of the dangers which threaten it. . . ."

. . . Defendants have been convicted, not upon direct charges of injury to interstate commerce or of interference with persons engaged in that commerce, but of violations of certain provisions of the Live Poultry Code and of conspiracy to commit these violations. Interstate commerce is brought in only upon the charge that violations of these provisions—as to hours and wages of employees and local sales—"*affected*" interstate commerce.

In determining how far the federal government may go in controlling intrastate transactions upon the ground that they "affect" interstate commerce, there is a necessary and well-established distinction between direct and indirect effects. The precise line can be drawn only as individual cases arise, but the distinction is clear in principle. . . . If the commerce clause were construed to reach all enterprises and transactions which could be said to have an indirect effect upon interstate commerce, the federal authority would embrace practically all the activities of the people and the authority of the state over its domestic concerns would exist only by sufferance of the federal government. Indeed, on such a theory, even the development of the state's commercial facilities would be subject to federal control. . . .

. . . Otherwise, as we have said, there would be virtually no limit to the federal power, and for all practical purposes we should have a completely centralized government. We must consider the provisions here in question in the light of this distinction. . . .

We are of the opinion that the attempt through the provisions of the code to fix the hours and wages of employees of defendants in their intrastate business was not a valid exercise of federal power.

The other violations for which defendants were convicted related to the making of local sales. Ten counts, for violation of the provision as to "straight killing," were for permitting customers to make "selections of individual chickens taken from particular coops and half coops." Whether or not this practice is good or bad for the local trade, its effect, if any, upon interstate commerce was only indirect. The same may be said of violations of the Code by intrastate transactions consisting of the sale "of an unfit chicken" and of sales which were not in accord with the ordinances of the City of New York. The requirement of reports as to prices and volumes of defendants' sales was incident to the effort to control their intrastate business.

In view of these conclusions, we find it unnecessary to discuss other questions which have been raised as to the validity of certain provisions of the Code under the due process clause of the Fifth Amendment.

On both the grounds we have discussed, the attempted delegation of legislative power and the attempted regulation of intrastate transactions which affect interstate commerce only indirectly, we hold the code provisions here in question to be invalid. . . .

Judgment reversed.

JUSTICE CARDOZO concurred:

. . . This is delegation running riot. No such plenitude of power is susceptible of transfer. . . .

But there is another objection, far-reaching and incurable, aside from any defect of unlawful delegation.

If this code had been adopted by Congress itself, and not by the President on the advice of an industrial association, it would even then be void unless authority to adopt it is included in the grant of power "to regulate commerce with foreign nations and among the several states." . . .

I find no authority in that grant for the regulation of wages and hours of labor in the intrastate transactions that make up the defendants' business. . . .

. . . Wages and the hours of labor are essential features of the plan, its very bone and sinew. There is no opportunity in such circumstances for the severance of the infected parts in the hope of saving the remainder. A code collapses utterly with bone and sinew gone.

I am authorized to state that Mr. Justice Stone joins in this opinion.

FOR DISCUSSION

This case is one of only a few decisions in which the Court has struck down a law for improper delegation of legislative power. What specific dangers does the Court fear? Does such delegation contradict the doctrine of separation of powers?

RELATED CASE

***Carter v. Carter Coal Co.:* 298 U.S. 238 (1936).**

The Court held the Guffy Coal Act, which created local boards that set minimum coal prices, to be an improper delegation of legislative power to members of the coal industry, private persons. *Schechter* and this decision helped prompt Franklin D. Roosevelt's "Court-packing plan," in which he proposed adding one justice (up to 15) for every justice over the age of 70.

NATIONAL LABOR RELATIONS BOARD V. JONES AND LAUGHLIN STEEL CO.

301 U.S. 1, 57 S.Ct. 615, 81 L.Ed. 893 (1937)

The National Labor Relations Board (NLRB) brought suit against the Jones and Laughlin Steel Corp. for violating the National Labor Relations Act (Wagner Act) of 1935 by engaging in unfair labor practices. These were specifically that the corporation was discriminating against members of the union with regard to hiring and tenure of employment and was coercing and intimidating its employees in order to interfere with their self-organization. In line with this, certain employees had been discharged. The corporation refused to follow the directives of the NLRB. The Act was challenged as an improper use of interstate commerce power.

Vote: 5–4

CHIEF JUSTICE HUGHES delivered the opinion of the Court.

. . . It is a familiar principle that acts which directly burden or obstruct interstate or foreign commerce, or its free flow, are within the reach of the congressional power. Acts having that affect are not rendered immune because they grow out of labor disputes. . . . It is the effect upon commerce, not the source of the inquiry, which is the criterion. . . . Whether or not particular action does affect commerce in such a close and intimate fashion as to be subject to federal control, and hence to lie within the authority conferred upon the Board, is left by the statute to be determined as individual cases arise. We are thus to inquire whether in the instant case the constitutional boundary has been passed.

. . . The congressional authority to protect interstate commerce from burdens and obstructions is not limited to transactions which can be deemed to be an essential part of a "flow" of interstate or foreign commerce. Burdens and obstructions may be due to injurious action springing from other sources. The fundamental principle is that the power to regulate commerce is the power to enact "all appropriate legislation" for "its protection and advancement" . . .; to adopt measures "to promote its growth and insure its safety" . . .; "to foster, protect, control and restrain." . . . That power is plenary and may be exerted to protect interstate commerce "no matter what the source of the dangers which threaten it."

. . . Although activities may be intrastate in character when separately considered, if they have such a close and substantial relation to interstate commerce that their control is essential or appropriate to protect that commerce from burdens, and obstructions, Congress cannot be denied the power to exercise that control. . . . Undoubtedly the scope of this power must be considered in the light of our dual system of government and may not be extended so as to embrace effects upon interstate commerce so indirect and remote that to embrace them, in view of our complex society, would effectually obliterate the distinction between what is national and what is local and create a completely centralized government. The question is necessarily one of degree. . . .

The close and intimate effect which brings the subject within the reach of federal power may be due to activities in relation to productive industry although the industry when separately viewed is local. This has been abundantly illustrated in the application of the Federal Anti-Trust Act. . . .

. . . Giving full weight to respondent's contention with respect to a break in the complete continuity of the "stream of commerce" by reason of respondent's manufacturing operations, the fact remains that the stoppage of those operations by industrial strife would have a most serious effect upon interstate commerce. In view of respondent's far-flung activities, it is idle to say that the effect would be indirect or remote. It is obvious that it would be immediate and might be catastrophic. We are asked to shut our eyes to the plainest facts of our national life and to deal with the question of direct and indirect effects in an intellectual vacuum. Because there may be but indirect and remote effects upon interstate commerce in connection with a host of local enterprises throughout the country, it does not follow that other industrial activities do not have such a close and intimate relation to interstate commerce as to make the presence of industrial strife a matter of the most urgent national concern. When industries organize themselves on a national scale, making their relation to interstate commerce the dominant factor in their activities, how can it be maintained that their industrial labor relations constitute a forbidden field into which Congress may not enter when it is necessary to protect interstate commerce from the paralyzing consequences of industrial war? We have often said that interstate commerce itself is a practical conception. It is equally true that interference with that commerce must be appraised by a judgment that does not ignore actual experience.

Experience has abundantly demonstrated that the recognition of the right of employees to self-organization and to have representatives of their own choosing for the purpose of collective bargaining is often an essential condition of industrial peace. Refusal to confer and negotiate has been one of the most prolific causes of strife. This is such an outstanding fact in the history of labor disturbances that it is a proper subject of judicial notice and requires no citation of instances. . . .

. . . Respondent asserts its right to conduct its business in an orderly manner without being subjected to arbitrary restraints. What we have said points to the fallacy in the argument. Employees have their correlative right to organize for the purpose of securing the redress of grievances and to promote agreements with employers relating to rate of pay and conditions of work. . . . Restraint for the purpose of preventing an unjust interference with that right cannot be considered arbitrary or capricious. . . .

The Act does not compel agreements between employers and employees. It does not compel any agreement whatever. It does not prevent the employer "from refusing to make a collective contract and hiring individuals on whatever terms" the employer "may by unilateral action determine." The Act expressly provides in Section 9 (a) that any individual employee or a group of employees shall have the right at any time to present grievances to their employer. The theory of the Act is that free opportunity for negotiation with accredited representatives of employees is likely to promote industrial peace and may bring about the adjustments and agreements which the Act in itself does not attempt to compel. . . . The Act does not interfere with the normal exercise of the right of the employer to select its employees or to discharge them. The employer may not, under cover of that right, intimidate or coerce its employees with respect to their self-organization and representation, and, on the other hand, the Board is not entitled to make its authority a pretext for interference with the right of discharge when that right is exercised for other reasons than such intimidation and coercion. The true purpose is the subject of investigation with full opportunity to show the facts. It would seem that when employers freely recognize the right of their employees to their own organizations and their unrestricted right of representation there will be much less occasion for controversy in respect to the free and appropriate exercise of the right of selection and discharge.

The Act has been criticized as one-sided in its application; that it subjects the employer to supervision and restraint and leaves untouched the abuses for which employees may be responsible. That it fails to provide a more comprehensive plan—with better assurances of fairness to both sides and with increased chances of success in bringing about, if not compelling, equitable solutions of industrial disputes affecting interstate commerce. But we are dealing with the power of Congress, not with a particular policy, or with the extent to which policy should go. We have frequently said that the legislative authority, exerted within its proper field, need not embrace all the evils within its reach. The Constitution does not forbid "cautious advance, step by step," in dealing with the evils which are exhibited in activities within the range of legislative power. . . . The question in such cases is whether the legislature, in what it does prescribe, has gone beyond constitutional limits.

The procedural provisions of the Act are assailed. But these provisions, as we construe them, do not offend against the constitutional requirements governing the creation and action of administrative bodies. . . .

Respondent complains that the Board not only ordered reinstatement but directed the payment of wages for the time lost by the discharge, less amounts earned by the employee during that period. . . . It is argued that the requirement is equivalent to a money judgment and hence contravenes the Seventh Amendment with respect to trial by jury. The Seventh Amendment provides that "In suits at common law, where the value in controversy shall exceed twenty dollars, the right of trial by jury shall be preserved." . . .

The instant case is not a suit at common law or in the nature of such a suit. The proceeding is one unknown to the common law. It is a statutory proceeding. Reinstatement of the employee and payment for time lost are requirements imposed for violation of the statute and are remedies appropriate to its enforcement. The contention under the Seventh Amendment is without merit.

Our conclusion is that the order of the Board was within its competency and that the Act is valid as here applied. . . .

Reversed.

JUSTICE MCREYNOLDS dissented with the concurrence of JUSTICES VAN DEVANTER, SUTHERLAND, and BUTLER.

The Court as we think departs from well-established principles followed in *A.L.A. Schechter Poultry Corp. v. United States,* [295 U.S. 495 (1935)], and *Carter v. Carter Coal Co.*[, 298 U.S. 238 (1936)]. Upon the authority of those decisions . . . the power of Congress under the commerce clause does not extend to relations between employers and their employees engaged in manufacture, and therefore the act conferred upon the National Labor Relations Board no authority in respect of matters covered by the questioned orders. . . . No decision or judicial opinion to the contrary has been cited, and we find none. Every consideration brought forward to uphold the Act before us was applicable to support the Acts held unconstitutional in causes decided within two years. And the lower courts rightly deemed them controlling. . . .

Any effect on interstate commerce by the discharge of employees shown here would be indirect and remote in the highest degree, as consideration of the facts will show. In No. 419 [*Jones & Laughlin*] ten men out of ten thousand were discharged; in the other cases only a few. The immediate effect in the factory may be to create discontent among all those employed and a strike may follow, which, in turn, may result in reducing production, which ultimately may reduce the volume of goods moving in interstate commerce. By this chain of indirect and progressively remote events we finally reach the evil with which it is said the legislation under consideration undertakes to deal. A more remote and indirect interference with interstate commerce or a more definite invasion of the powers reserved to the states is difficult, if not impossible, to imagine.

The Constitution still recognizes the existence of States with indestructible powers; the Tenth Amendment was supposed to put them beyond controversy. . . .

FOR DISCUSSION

This case, along with *West Coast Hotel v. Parrish*, is understood to represent a significant change in judicial philosophy. How, if at all, does the Court seek to reconcile this case with earlier precedents? Is the Court convincing?

RELATED CASE

***West Coast Hotel v. Parrish*, 300 U.S. 379 (1937).**

The Court upheld a Washington State minimum wage law against charges that it violated freedom of contract and substantive due process, thus granting states similar regulatory power to that which it had upheld on the part of Congress.

UNITED STATES V. F. W. DARBY LUMBER CO.

312 U.S. 100, 61 S.Ct. 451, 85 L.Ed. 609 (1941)

The Darby Company was engaged in the state of Georgia in the business of acquiring raw materials, which were then manufactured into finished lumber with the intention of shipping this product in interstate commerce to customers outside the state. The company was charged on numerous counts with employing workmen in the production of the goods so shipped at less than the prescribed minimum wage or more than the prescribed maximum hours without payment to them of any wage for overtime, as well as not keeping proper records, all of which violated the Fair Labor Standards Act of 1938. The statute also prohibited the shipment in interstate commerce of products where child labor had been used during the previous thirty days. The Act was challenged as not being a proper exercise of power under the Commerce Clause.

Vote: 9–0

JUSTICE STONE delivered the opinion of the Court.

. . . While manufacture is not of itself interstate commerce, the shipment of manufactured goods interstate is such commerce and the prohibition of such shipment by Congress is indubitably a regulation of the commerce. The power to regulate commerce is the power "to prescribe the rule by which commerce is governed." *Gibbons v. Ogden*, 22 U.S. 1 (1824). It extends not only to those regulations which aid, foster and protect the commerce, but embraces those which prohibit it. . . . It is conceded that the power of Congress to prohibit transportation in interstate commerce includes noxious articles, Lottery Case (*Champion v. Ames,* 188 U.S. 321 (1903)); stolen articles, *Brooks v. United States,* 337 U.S. 49 (1949); kidnapped persons, *Gooch v. United States,* 297 U.S. 124 (1936), and articles such as intoxicating liquor or convict made goods, traffic in which is forbidden or restricted by the laws of the state of destination. *Kentucky Whip & Collar Co. v. Illinois Central Railway Co.*, 299 U.S. 334 (1937), but instead, under the guise of a regulation of interstate commerce, it undertakes to regulate wages and hours within the state contrary to the policy of the state which has elected to leave them unregulated.

The power of Congress over interstate commerce "is complete in itself, may be exercised to its utmost extent, and acknowledges no limitations other than are prescribed in the Constitution." *Gibbons v. Ogden*[, 22 U.S. 1 (1824)]. That power can neither be enlarged nor diminished by the exercise or nonexercise of state power. . . . Congress, following its own conception of public policy concerning the restrictions which may appropriately be imposed on interstate commerce, is free to exclude from the commerce articles whose use in the states for which they are destined it may conceive to be injurious to the public health, morals or welfare, even though the state has not sought to regulate their use. . . .

Such regulation is not a forbidden invasion of state power merely because either its motive or its consequence is to restrict the use of articles of commerce within the states of destination and is not prohibited unless by other constitutional provisions. It is no objection to the assertion of the power to regulate interstate commerce that its exercise is attended by the same incidents which attend the exercise of the police power of the states. . . .

The motive and purpose of the present regulation are plainly to make effective the Congressional conception of public policy that interstate commerce should not be made the instrument of competition in the distribution of goods produced under substandard labor conditions, which competition is injurious to the commerce and to the states from and to which the commerce flows. The motive and purpose of a regulation of interstate commerce are matters for the legislative judgment upon the exercise of which the Constitution places no restriction and over which the courts are given no control. . . .

In the more than a century which has elapsed since the decision of *Gibbons v. Ogden,* these principles of constitutional interpretation have been so long and repeatedly recognized by this Court as applicable to the commerce clause, that there would be little occasion for repeating them now were it not for the decision of this Court twenty-two years ago in *Hammer v. Dagenhart*[, 247 U.S. 251 (1918)]. In that case it was held by a bare majority of the Court over the powerful and now classic dissent of Mr. Justice Holmes setting forth the fundamental issues involved, the Congress was without power to exclude the products of child labor from interstate commerce. The reasoning and conclusion of the Court's opinion there cannot be reconciled with the conclusion which we have reached, that the power of Congress under the commerce clause is plenary to exclude any article from interstate commerce subject only to the specific prohibitions of the Constitution. *Hammer v. Dagenhart* has not been followed. The distinction on which the decision was rested that congressional power to prohibit interstate commerce is limited to articles which in themselves have some harmful or deleterious property—a distinction which was novel when made or unsupported by any provision of the Constitution—has long since been abandoned. . . . The thesis of the opinion that the motive of the prohibition or its effect to control in some measure the use or production within the states of the article thus excluded from the commerce can operate to deprive the regulation of its constitutional authority has long since ceased to have force. . . . And finally we have declared "The authority of the federal government over interstate commerce does not differ in extent or character from that retained by the states over intrastate commerce." *United States v. Rock Royal Co-operative,* 307 U.S. 533 (1939).

The conclusion is inescapable that *Hammer v. Dagenhart* was a departure from the principles which have prevailed in the interpretation of the commerce clause both before and since the decision and that such vitality, as a precedent, as it then had has long since been exhausted. It should be and now is overruled. . . .

There remains the question whether such restriction on the production of goods for commerce is a permissible exercise of the commerce power. The power of Congress over interstate commerce is not confined to the regulation of commerce among the states. It extends to those activities intrastate which so affect interstate commerce or the exercise of the power of Congress over it as to make regulation of them appropriate means to the attainment of a legitimate end, the exercise of the granted power of Congress to regulate interstate commerce. . . .

Our conclusion is unaffected by the Tenth Amendment which provides: "The powers not delegated to the United States by the Constitution nor prohibited by it to the states are reserved to the states respectively or to the people." The amendment states but a truism that all is retained which has not been surrendered. There is nothing in the history of its adoption to suggest that it was more than declaratory of the relationship between the national and state governments as it had been established by the Constitution before the amendment or that its purpose was other than to allay fears that the new national government might seek to exercise powers not granted, and that the states might not be able to exercise fully their reserved powers. . . .

From the beginning and for many years the amendment has been construed as not depriving the national government of authority to resort to all means for the exercise of a granted power which are appropriate and plainly adapted to the permitted end. . . . Whatever doubts may have arisen of the soundness of that conclusion they have been put at rest by the decisions under the Sherman Act and the National Labor Relations Act which we have cited. . . .

Validity of the requirement of records of wages and hours. . . . These requirements are incidental to those for the prescribed wages and hours, and hence validity of the former turns on validity of the latter. Since, as we have held, Congress may require production for interstate commerce to conform to those conditions, it may require the employer, as a means of enforcing the valid law, to keep a record showing whether he has in fact complied with it. The requirement for records even of the intrastate transaction is an appropriate means to the legitimate end. . . .

Validity of the wage and hour provisions under the Fifth Amendment. Both provisions are minimum wage requirements compelling the payment of a minimum standard wage with a prescribed increased wage for overtime. . . . Since our decision in *West [Coast] Hotel Co. v. Parrish,* it is no longer open to question that the fixing of a minimum wage is within the legislative power and that the bare fact of its exercise is not a denial of due process under the Fifth more than under the Fourteenth Amendment. Nor is it any longer open to question that it is within the legislative power to fix maximum hours. . . . Similarly the statute is not objectionable because applied alike to both men and women. . . .

The Act is sufficiently definite to meet constitutional demands. One who employs persons, without conforming to the prescribed wage and hour conditions, to work on goods which he ships or expects to ship across state lines, is warned that he may be subject to the criminal penalties of the Act. No more is required. . . .

Reversed.

FOR DISCUSSION

How does J. Stone deal with objections to this case based on the Tenth Amendment (powers reserved to the states)? What does Stone mean when he calls the amendment a truism? Are there any other constitutional provisions that might be so labeled?

WICKARD V. FILBURN

317 U.S. 111, 63 S.Ct. 82, 87 L.Ed. 122 (1942)

In this case Filburn a small dairy farmer, was allotted 11.1 acres under the Agricultural Adjustment Act to plant wheat, but sowed 23 acres, planning to use the excess for private consumption on the farm. Wickard resisted paying the penalty that the law required. The unanimity of the Court demonstrates that its composition had changed significantly since its decisions recognizing broad congressional powers in 1937.

Vote: 9–0

JUSTICE JACKSON delivered the opinion of the Court.

The general scheme of the Agricultural Adjustment Act of 1938 as related to wheat is to control the volume moving in interstate and foreign commerce in order to avoid surpluses and shortages and the consequent abnormally low or high wheat prices and obstructions to commerce. Within prescribed limits and by prescribed standards the Secretary of Agriculture is directed to ascertain and proclaim each year a national acreage allotment for the next crop of wheat, which is then apportioned to the states and their counties, and is eventually broken up into allotments for individual farms. Loans and payments to wheat farmers are authorized in stated circumstances. . . .

On May 19, 1941, the Secretary of Agriculture made a radio address to the wheat farmers of the United States in which he advocated approval of the quotas and called attention to the pendency of the amendment of May 26, 1941, which had at the time been sent by Congress to the White House, and pointed out its provision for an increase in the loans on wheat to 85 per cent of parity. He made no mention of the fact that it also increased the penalty from 15 cents a bushel to one-half of the parity loan rate of about 98 cents, but stated that "Because of the uncertain world situation, we deliberately planted several million extra acres of wheat. . . . Farmers should not be penalized because they have provided insurance against shortages of food."

Pursuant to the Act, the referendum of wheat growers was held on May 31, 1941. According to the required published statement of the Secretary of Agriculture, 81 per cent of those voting favored the marketing quota, with 19 per cent opposed. . . .

I

[This section of the decision deals with the validity of the referendum.]

II

It is urged that under the Commerce Clause of the Constitution, Article I, § 8, clause 3, Congress does not possess the power it has in this instance sought to exercise. The question would merit little consideration since our decision in *United States* v. *Darby*[, 312 U.S. 100 (1941),] sustaining the federal power to regulate production of goods for commerce, except for the fact that this Act extends federal regulation to production not intended in any part for commerce but wholly for consumption on the farm. The Act includes a definition of "market" and its derivatives, so that as related to wheat, in addition to its conventional meaning, it also means to dispose of "by feeding (in any form) to poultry or livestock which, or the products of which, are sold, bartered, or exchanged, or to be so disposed of." Hence, marketing quotas not only embrace all that may be sold without penalty but also what may be consumed on the premises. Wheat produced on excess acreage is designated as "available for marketing" as so defined, and the penalty is imposed thereon. Penalties do not depend upon whether any part of the wheat, either within or without the quota, is sold or intended to be sold. The sum of this is that the Federal Government fixes a quota including all that the farmer may harvest for sale or for his own farm needs, and declares that wheat produced on excess acreage may neither be disposed of nor used except upon payment of the penalty, or except it is stored as required by the Act or delivered to the Secretary of Agriculture.

Appellee says that this is a regulation of production and consumption of wheat. Such activities are, he urges, beyond the reach of Congressional power under the Commerce Clause, since they are local in character, and their effects upon interstate commerce are at most "indirect." In answer the Government argues that the statute regulates neither production nor consumption, but only marketing; and, in the alternative, that if the Act does go beyond the regulation of marketing it is sustainable as a "necessary and proper" implementation of the power of Congress over interstate commerce.

The Government's concern lest the Act be held to be a regulation of production or consumption, rather than of marketing, is attributable to a few dicta and decisions of this Court which might be understood to lay it down that activities such as "production," "manufacturing," and "mining" are strictly "local" and, except in special circumstances which are not present here, cannot be regulated under the commerce power because their effects upon interstate commerce are, as matter of law, only "indirect." Even today, when this power has been held to have great latitude, there is no decision of this Court that such activities may be regulated where no part of the product is intended for interstate commerce or intermingled with the subjects thereof. We believe that a review of the course of decision under the Commerce Clause will make plain, however, that questions of the power of Congress are not to be decided by reference to any formula which would give controlling force to nomenclature such as "production" and "indirect" and foreclose consideration of the actual effects of the activity in question upon interstate commerce. . . .

[The Court reviews the history of such precedents.]

Whether the subject of the regulation in question was "production," "consumption," or "marketing" is, therefore, not material for purposes of deciding the question of federal power before us. That an activity is of local character may help in a doubtful case to determine whether Congress intended to reach it. The same consideration might help in determining whether in the absence of Congressional action it would be permissible for the state to exert its power on the subject matter, even though in so doing it to some degree affected interstate commerce. But even if appellee's activity be local and though it may not be regarded as commerce, it may still, whatever its nature, be reached by Congress if it exerts a substantial economic effect on interstate commerce, and this irrespective of whether such effect is what might at some earlier time have been defined as "direct" or "indirect."

The parties have stipulated a summary of the economics of the wheat industry. Commerce among the states in wheat is large and important. Although wheat is raised in every state but one, production in most states is not equal to consumption. Sixteen states on average have had a surplus of wheat above their own requirements for feed, seed, and food. Thirty-two states and the District of Columbia, where production has been below consumption, have looked to these surplus-producing states for their supply as well as for wheat for export and carry-over.

The wheat industry has been a problem industry for some years. Largely as a result of increased foreign production and import restrictions, annual exports of wheat and flour from the United States during the ten-year period ending in 1940 averaged less than 10 per cent of total production, while during the 1920's they averaged more than 25 per cent. The decline in the export trade has left a large surplus in production which, in connection with an abnormally large supply of wheat and other grains in recent years, caused congestion in a number of markets; tied up railroad cars; and caused elevators in some instances to turn away grains, and railroads to institute embargoes to prevent further congestion. . . . [The Court continues to review the economics of wheat production.]

The effect of consumption of home-grown wheat on interstate commerce is due to the fact that it constitutes the most variable factor in the disappearance of the wheat crop. Consumption on the farm where grown appears to vary in an amount greater than 20 per cent of average production. The total amount of wheat consumed as food varies but relatively little, and use as seed is relatively constant.

The maintenance by government regulation of a price for wheat undoubtedly can be accomplished as effectively by sustaining or increasing the demand as by limiting the supply. The effect of the statute before us is to restrict the amount which may be produced for market and the extent as well to which one may forestall resort to the market by producing to meet his own needs. That appellee's own contribution to the demand for wheat may be trivial by itself is not enough to remove him from the scope of federal regulation where, as here, his contribution, taken together with that of many others similarly situated, is far from trivial.

It is well established by decisions of this Court that the power to regulate commerce includes the power to regulate the prices at which commodities in that commerce are dealt in and practices affecting such prices. One of the primary purposes of the Act in question was to increase the market price of wheat, and to that end to limit the volume thereof that could affect the market. It can hardly be denied that a factor of such volume and variability as home-consumed wheat would have a substantial influence on price and market conditions. This may arise because being in marketable condition such wheat overhangs the market and, if induced by rising prices, tends to flow into the market and check price increases. But if we assume that it is never marketed, it supplies a need of the man who grew it which would otherwise be reflected by purchases in the open market. Home-grown wheat in this sense competes with wheat in commerce. The stimulation of commerce is a use of the regulatory function quite as definitely as prohibitions or restrictions thereon. This record leaves us in no doubt that Congress may properly have considered that wheat consumed on the farm where grown, if wholly outside the scheme of regulation, would have a substantial effect in defeating and obstructing its purpose to stimulate trade therein at increased prices.

It is said, however, that this Act, forcing some farmers into the market to buy what they could provide for themselves, is an unfair promotion of the markets and prices of specializing wheat growers. It is of the essence of regulation that it lays a restraining hand on the self-interest of the regulated and that advantages from the regulation commonly fall to others. The conflicts of economic interest between the regulated and those who advantage by it are wisely left under our system to resolution by the Congress under its more flexible and responsible legislative process. Such conflicts rarely lend themselves to judicial determination. And with the wisdom, workability, or fairness, of the plan of regulation we have nothing to do. . . .

FOR DISCUSSION

Has this decision effectively eliminated the distinction between matters that are local and those that are national? If it has, is this development positive or negative?

HEART OF ATLANTA MOTEL, INC. V. UNITED STATES

379 U.S. 241, 85 S.Ct. 348, 13 L.Ed. 2d 258 (1964)

Appellant, the owner of a large motel in Atlanta, Georgia, which restricted its clientele to white persons, three-fourths of whom were transient interstate travelers, sued for declaratory relief and to enjoin enforcement of the Civil Rights Act of 1964, contending that the prohibition of racial discrimination in places of public accommodation affecting commerce exceeded Congress's powers under the Commerce Clause and violated other parts of the Constitution. The motel in question was located close to an interstate highway and advertised in out-of-state venues. A three-judge District Court upheld the constitutionality of Title II, §§ 201 (a), (b) (1), and (c) (1), and on appellees' counterclaim permanently enjoined appellant from refusing to accommodate African American guests for racial reasons.

Vote: 9–0

JUSTICE CLARK delivered the opinion of the Court.

. . . The sole question posed is, therefore, the constitutionality of the Civil Rights Act of 1964 as applied to these facts. The legislative history of the Act indicates that Congress based the Act on § 5 and the Equal Protection Clause of the Fourteenth Amendment as well as its power to regulate interstate commerce under Article I, § 8, clause 3 of the Constitution. . . . Thus the power of Congress to promote interstate commerce also includes the power to regulate the local incidents thereof, including local activities in both the States of origin and destination, which might have a substantial and harmful effect upon that commerce. One need only examine the evidence which we have discussed above to see that Congress may—as it has—prohibit racial discrimination by motels serving travelers, however "local" their operations may appear. [Congress had conducted hearings that racial discrimination was affecting both the quality and quantity of interstate travel on the part of African Americans.]

Nor does the Act deprive appellant of liberty or property under the Fifth Amendment. The commerce power invoked here by the Congress is a specific and plenary one authorized by the Constitution itself. The only questions are: (1) whether Congress had a rational basis for finding that racial discrimination by motels affected commerce, and (2) if it had such a basis, whether the means it selected to eliminate that evil are reasonable and appropriate. If they are, appellant has no "right" to select its guests as it sees fit, free from governmental regulation.

There is nothing novel about such legislation. Thirty-two States now have it on their books either by statute or executive order and many cities provide such regulation. Some of these Acts go back fourscore years. It has been repeatedly held by this Court that such laws do not violate the Due Process Clause of the Fourteenth Amendment. Perhaps the first such holding was in the *Civil Rights Cases*, 109 U.S. 3 (1883), themselves, where Mr. Justice Bradley for the Court inferentially found that innkeepers, "by the laws of all the States, so far as we are aware, are bound, to the extent of their facilities, to furnish proper accommodation to all unobjectionable persons who in good faith apply for them." . . .

It is doubtful if in the long run appellant will suffer economic loss as a result of the Act. Experience is to the contrary where discrimination is completely obliterated as to all public accommodations. But whether this be true or not is of no consequence since this Court has specifically held that the fact that a "member of the class which is regulated may suffer economic losses not shared by others . . . has never been a barrier" to such legislation.

We, therefore, conclude that the action of the Congress in the adoption of the Act as applied here to a motel which concededly serves interstate travelers is within the power granted it by the Commerce Clause of the Constitution, as interpreted by this Court for 140 years. It may be argued that Congress could have pursued other methods to eliminate the obstructions it found in interstate commerce caused by racial discrimination. But this is a matter of policy that rests entirely with the Congress not with the courts. How obstructions in commerce may be removed—what means are to be employed—is within the sound and exclusive discretion of the Congress. It is subject only to one caveat—that the means chosen by it must be reasonably adapted to the end permitted by the Constitution. We cannot say that its choice here was not so adapted. The Constitution requires no more.

Affirmed.

JUSTICE BLACK concurred

. . . Because the Civil Rights Act of 1964 as applied here is wholly valid under the Commerce Clause and the Necessary and Proper Clause, there is no need to consider whether this Act is also constitutionally supportable under section 5 of the Fourteenth Amendment which grants Congress "power to enforce, by appropriate legislation, the provisions of this article."

JUSTICE DOUGLAS concurred.

Though I join the Court's opinion, I am somewhat reluctant here, as I was in *Edwards v. California,* 314 U.S. 160 (1941), to rest solely on the Commerce Clause. My reluctance is not due to any conviction that Congress lacks power to regulate commerce in the interests of human rights. It is rather my belief that the right of people to be free of state action that discriminates against them because of race, like the "right of persons to move freely from State to State," "occupies a more protected position in our constitutional system than does the movement of cattle, fruit, steel and coal across state lines."

I repeat what I said earlier, that our decision should be based on the Fourteenth Amendment, thereby putting an end to all obstructionist strategies and allowing every person—whatever his race, creed, or color—to patronize all places of public accommodation without discrimination whether he travels interstate or intrastate.

FOR DISCUSSION

Congress chose to justify this law under its commerce powers for fear that the Fourteenth Amendment limited its power to regulate private conduct rather than state action. Given the Court's broad conception of federal power under the Commerce Clause, is it realistic to continue its distinction between state action and private action under the Fourteenth Amendment?

RELATED CASES

***Katzenbach v. McClung:* 379 U.S. 294 (1964).**

Congress acted within its power to protect and foster commerce in extending coverage of the Civil Rights Act of 1964 to restaurants serving food a substantial portion of which has moved in interstate commerce, since it had ample basis to conclude that racial discrimination by such restaurants burdened interstate commerce. This was a family-owned restaurant, not a chain.

***Daniel v. Paul:* 395 U.S. 298 (1969).**

A private recreational facility that is chiefly engaged in the selling of food that has moved in interstate commerce to be consumed on the premises by persons some of whom are from out of the state is subject to the public accommodations provisions of the Civil Rights Act of 1964. Also, the facility's "sources of entertainment" are from outside the state. The latter consisted chiefly of paddleboats and a jukebox.

UNITED STATES V. LOPEZ

514 U.S. 549, 115 S.Ct. 1624, 131 L.Ed. 2d 626 (1995)

This case involves the constitutionality of the Gun-Free School Zones Act of 1990 in which Congress made it a federal offense "for any individual knowingly to possess a firearm at a place that the individual knows, or has reasonable cause to believe, is a school zone." Most states already had similar legislation on the subject, but members of Congress were definitely concerned about well-publicized acts of school violence, often involving multiple victims. The U.S. 5th Circuit Court of Appeals had overturned the conviction of a twelfth grader on the basis that the law exceeded congressional powers under the Commerce Clause.

Vote: 5–4

CHIEF JUSTICE REHNQUIST delivered the opinion of the Court.

We start with first principles. The Constitution creates a Federal Government of enumerated powers. See Art. I, § 8. As James Madison wrote, "the powers delegated by the proposed Constitution to the federal government are few and defined. Those which are to remain in the State governments are numerous and indefinite." *The Federalist* No. 45, pp. 292–293 (C. Rossiter ed. 1961). This constitutionally mandated division of authority "was adopted by the Framers to ensure protection of our fundamental liberties." *Gregory* v. *Ashcroft,* 501 U.S. 452 (1991). "Just as the separation and independence of the coordinate branches of the Federal Government serve to prevent the accumulation of excessive power in any one branch, a healthy balance of power between the States and the Federal Government will reduce the risk of tyranny and abuse from either front."

The Constitution delegates to Congress the power "to regulate Commerce with foreign Nations, and among the several States, and with the Indian Tribes." Art. I, § 8, cl. 3. The Court, through Chief Justice Marshall, first defined the nature of Congress' commerce power in *Gibbons v. Ogden,* 22 U.S. 1 (1824): "Commerce, undoubtedly, is traffic, but it is something more: it is intercourse. It describes the commercial intercourse between nations, and parts of nations, in all its branches, and is regulated by prescribing rules for carrying on that intercourse."

The commerce power "is the power to regulate; that is, to prescribe the rule by which commerce is to be governed. This power, like all others vested in Congress, is complete in itself, may be exercised to its utmost extent, and acknowledges no limitations, other than are prescribed in the Constitution." The *Gibbons* Court, however, acknowledged that limitations on the commerce power are inherent in the very language of the Commerce Clause. "It is not intended to say that these words comprehend that commerce which is completely internal, which is carried on between man and man in a State, or between different parts of the same State, and which does not extend to or affect other States. Such a power would be inconvenient, and is certainly unnecessary.

Comprehensive as the word 'among' is, it may very properly be restricted to that commerce which concerns more States than one. . . . The enumeration presupposes something not enumerated; and that something, if we regard the language, or the subject of the sentence, must be the exclusively internal commerce of a State."

For nearly a century thereafter, the Court's Commerce Clause decisions dealt but rarely with the extent of Congress' power, and almost entirely with the Commerce Clause as a limit on state legislation that discriminated against interstate commerce. [Rehnquist cites some of these cases up to, and including, *Wickard v. Filburn,* 317 U.S. 111 (1942).]

[National Labor Relations Board v.] Jones & Laughlin Steel, 301 U.S. 1 (1937), *U.S. v. Darby Lumber Co.,* 312 U.S. 100 (1941), and *Wickard* ushered in an era of Commerce Clause jurisprudence that greatly expanded the previously defined authority of Congress under that Clause. In part, this was a recognition of the great changes that had occurred in the way business was carried on in this country. Enterprises that had once been local or at most regional in nature had become national in scope. But the doctrinal change also reflected a view that earlier Commerce Clause cases artificially had constrained the authority of Congress to regulate interstate commerce.

But even these modern-era precedents which have expanded congressional power under the Commerce Clause confirm that this power is subject to outer limits. In *Jones & Laughlin Steel,* the Court warned that the scope of the interstate commerce power "must be considered in the light of our dual system of government and may not be extended so as to embrace effects upon interstate commerce so indirect and remote that to embrace them, in view of our complex society, would effectually obliterate the distinction between what is national and what is local and create a completely centralized government." (Congress may regulate intrastate activity that has a "substantial effect" on interstate commerce); *Wickard* (Congress may regulate activity that "exerts a substantial economic effect on interstate commerce"). Since that time, the Court has heeded that warning and undertaken to decide whether a rational basis existed for concluding that a regulated activity sufficiently affected interstate commerce. [Rehnquist cites and analyzes a number of these cases.]

Consistent with this structure, we have identified three broad categories of activity that Congress may regulate under its commerce power. . . . First, Congress may regulate the use of the channels of interstate commerce. . . . Second, Congress is empowered to regulate and protect the instrumentalities of interstate commerce, or persons or things in interstate commerce, even though the threat may come only from intrastate activities. . . . Finally, Congress' commerce authority includes the power to regulate those activities having a substantial relation to interstate commerce . . .

Within this final category, admittedly, our case law has not been clear whether an activity must "affect" or "substantially affect" interstate commerce in order to be within Congress' power to regulate it under the Commerce Clause. . . . We conclude, consistent with the great weight of our case law, that the proper test requires an analysis of whether the regulated activity "substantially affects" interstate commerce.

We now turn to consider the power of Congress, in the light of this framework, to enact § 922(q). The first two categories of authority may be quickly disposed of: § 922(q) is not a regulation of the use of the channels of interstate commerce, nor is it an attempt to prohibit the interstate transportation of a commodity through the channels of commerce; nor can § 922(q) be justified as a regulation by which Congress has sought to protect an instrumentality of interstate commerce or a thing in interstate commerce. Thus, if § 922(q) is to be sustained, it must be under the third category as a regulation of an activity that substantially affects interstate commerce.

First, we have upheld a wide variety of congressional Acts regulating intrastate economic activity where we have concluded that the activity substantially affected interstate commerce. Examples include the regulation of intrastate coal mining; *Hodel v. Virginia Surface Mining & Reclamation Assn.,* 452 U.S. 264 (1981), intrastate extortionate credit transactions, *Perez v. United States,* 402 U.S. 146 (1971), restaurants utilizing substantial interstate supplies, *Katzenbach v. McClung,* 379 U.S. 294 (1964), inns and hotels catering to interstate guests, *Heart of Atlanta Motel, Inc. v. United States,* 379 U.S. 241 (1964), and production and consumption of homegrown wheat, *Wickard v. Filburn*[, 317 U.S. 111] (1942). These examples are by no means exhaustive, but the pattern is clear. Where economic activity substantially affects interstate commerce, legislation regulating that activity will be sustained.

Even *Wickard,* which is perhaps the most far reaching example of Commerce Clause authority over intrastate activity, involved economic activity in a way that the possession of a gun in a school zone does not. [Rehnquist analyzes that case.]

Section 922(q) is a criminal statute that by its terms has nothing to do with "commerce" or any sort of economic enterprise, however broadly one might define those terms. Section 922(q) is not an essential part of a larger regulation of economic activity, in which the regulatory scheme could be undercut unless the intrastate activity were regulated. It cannot, therefore, be sustained under our cases upholding regulations of activities that arise out of or are connected with a commercial transaction, which viewed in the aggregate, substantially affects interstate commerce.

Second, § 922(q) contains no jurisdictional element which would ensure, through case-by-case inquiry, that the firearm possession in question affects interstate commerce. . . .

Although as part of our independent evaluation of constitutionality under the Commerce Clause we of course consider legislative findings, and indeed even congressional committee findings, regarding effect on interstate commerce, see, *e. g., Preseault* v. *ICC,* 494 U.S. 1 (1990), the Government concedes that "neither the statute nor its legislative history contain[s] express congressional findings regarding the effects upon interstate commerce of gun possession in a school zone." We agree with the Government that Congress normally is not required to make formal findings as to the substantial burdens that an activity has on interstate commerce. . . . But to the extent that congressional findings would enable us to evaluate the legislative judgment that the activity in question substantially affected interstate commerce, even though no such substantial effect was visible to the naked eye, they are lacking here.

The Government argues that Congress has accumulated institutional expertise regarding the regulation of firearms through previous enactments. . . . We agree, however, with the Fifth Circuit that importation of previous findings to justify § 922(q) is especially inappropriate here because the "prior federal enactments or Congressional findings [do not] speak to the subject matter of section 922(q) or its relationship to interstate commerce. Indeed, section 922(q) plows thoroughly new ground and represents a sharp break with the long-standing pattern of federal firearms legislation."

The Government's essential contention, *in fine,* is that we may determine here that § 922(q) is valid because possession of a firearm in a local school zone does indeed substantially affect interstate commerce. The Government argues that possession of a firearm in a school zone may result in violent crime and that violent crime can be expected to affect the functioning of the national economy in two ways. First, the costs of violent crime are substantial, and, through the mechanism of insurance, those costs are spread throughout the population. . . . Second, violent crime reduces the willingness of individuals to travel to areas within the country that are perceived to be unsafe. The Government also argues that the presence of guns in schools poses a substantial threat to the educational process by threatening the learning environment. A handicapped educational process, in turn, will result in a less productive citizenry. That, in turn, would have an adverse effect on the Nation's economic well-being. As a result, the Government argues that Congress could rationally have concluded that § 922(q) substantially affects interstate commerce.

We pause to consider the implications of the Government's arguments. The Government admits, under its "costs of crime" reasoning, that Congress could regulate not only all violent crime, but all activities that might lead to violent crime, regardless of how tenuously they relate to interstate commerce. Similarly, under the Government's "national productivity" reasoning, Congress could regulate any activity that it found was related to the economic productivity of individual citizens: family law (including marriage, divorce, and child custody), for example. Under the theories that the Government presents in support of § 922(q), it is difficult to perceive any limitation on federal power, even in areas such as criminal law enforcement or education where States historically have been sovereign. Thus, if we were to accept the Government's arguments, we are hard pressed to posit any activity by an individual that Congress is without power to regulate.

[Rehnquist proceeds to answer the dissent of Justice Breyer and to provide his own analysis of past precedents.]

These are not precise formulations, and in the nature of things they cannot be. But we think they point the way to a correct decision of this case. The possession of a gun in a local school zone is in no sense an economic activity that might, through repetition elsewhere, substantially affect any sort of interstate commerce. Respondent was a local student at a local school; there is no indication that he had recently moved in interstate commerce, and there is no requirement that his possession of the firearm have any concrete tie to interstate commerce.

To uphold the Government's contentions here, we would have to pile inference upon inference in a manner that would bid fair to convert congressional authority under the Commerce Clause to a general police power of the sort retained by the States. Admittedly, some of our prior cases have taken long steps down that road, giving great deference to congressional action. The broad language in these opinions has suggested the possibility of additional expansion, but we decline here to proceed any further. To do so would require us to conclude that the Constitution's enumeration of powers does not presuppose something not enumerated, cf. *Gibbons* v. *Ogden,* and that there never will be a distinction between what is truly national and what is truly local, cf. *Jones & Laughlin Steel.* This we are unwilling to do.

For the foregoing reasons the judgment of the Court of Appeals is

Affirmed.

JUSTICE KENNEDY, with whom JUSTICE O'CONNOR joins, concurring.

The history of the judicial struggle to interpret the Commerce Clause during the transition from the economic system the Founders knew to the single, national market still emergent in our own era counsels great restraint before the Court determines that the Clause is insufficient to support an exercise of the national power. That history gives me some pause about today's decision, but I join the Court's opinion with these observations on what I conceive to be its necessary though limited holding.

[Kennedy conducts a survey of commerce clause cases.]

The history of our Commerce Clause decisions contains at least two lessons of relevance to this case. The first, as stated at the outset, is the imprecision of content-based boundaries used without more to define the limits of the Commerce Clause. The second, related to the first but of even greater consequence, is that the Court as an institution and the legal system as a whole have an immense stake in the stability of our Commerce Clause jurisprudence as it has evolved to this point. *Stare decisis* operates with great force in counseling us not to call in question the essential principles now in place respecting the congressional power to regulate transactions of a commercial nature. That fundamental restraint on our power forecloses us from reverting to an understanding of commerce that would serve only an 18th-century economy, dependent then upon production and trading practices that had changed but little over the preceding centuries; it also mandates against returning to the time when congressional authority to regulate undoubted commercial activities was limited by a judicial determination that those matters had an insufficient connection to an interstate system. Congress can regulate in the commercial sphere on the assumption that we have a single market and a unified purpose to build a stable national economy.

In referring to the whole subject of the federal and state balance, we said this just three Terms ago: "This framework has been sufficiently flexible over the past two centuries to allow for enormous changes in the nature of government. The Federal Government undertakes activities today that would have been unimaginable to the Framers in two senses: first, because the Framers would not have conceived that any government would conduct such activities; and second, because the Framers would not have believed that the Federal Government, rather than the States, would assume such responsibilities. Yet the powers conferred upon the Federal Government by the Constitution were phrased in language broad enough to allow for the expansion of the Federal Government's role." . . .

It does not follow, however, that in every instance the Court lacks the authority and responsibility to review congressional attempts to alter the federal balance. This case requires us to consider our place in the design of the Government and to appreciate the significance of federalism in the whole structure of the Constitution.

[Kennedy proceeds to argue that the judiciary has an important role to play in maintaining federalism.]

JUSTICE THOMAS, concurring.

The Court today properly concludes that the Commerce Clause does not grant Congress the authority to prohibit gun possession within 1,000 feet of a school, as it attempted to do in the Gun-Free School Zones Act of 1990. Although I join the majority, I write separately to observe that our case law has drifted far from the original understanding of the Commerce Clause. In a future case, we ought to temper our Commerce Clause jurisprudence in a manner that both makes sense of our more recent case law and is more faithful to the original understanding of that Clause.

We have said that Congress may regulate not only "Commerce . . . among the several States," U.S. Const., Art. I, § 8, cl. 3, but also anything that has a "substantial effect" on such commerce. This test, if taken to its logical extreme, would give Congress a "police power" over all aspects of American life. Unfortunately, we have never come to grips with this implication of our substantial effects formula. [Thomas cites a number of these cases.]

While the principal dissent concedes that there are limits to federal power, the sweeping nature of our current test enables the dissent to argue that Congress can regulate gun possession. But it seems to me that the power to regulate "commerce" can by no means encompass authority over mere gun possession, any more than it empowers the Federal Government to regulate marriage, littering, or cruelty to animals, throughout the 50 States. Our Constitution quite properly leaves such matters to the individual States, notwithstanding these activities' effects on interstate commerce. Any interpretation of the Commerce Clause that even suggests that Congress could regulate such matters is in need of reexamination.

In an appropriate case, I believe that we must further reconsider our "substantial effects" test with an eye toward constructing a standard that reflects the text and history of the Commerce Clause without totally rejecting our more recent Commerce Clause jurisprudence.

. . .

JUSTICE STEVENS, dissenting.

The welfare of our future "Commerce with foreign Nations, and among the several States," U.S. Const., Art. I, § 8, cl. 3, is vitally dependent on the character of the education of our children. I therefore agree entirely with Justice Breyer's explanation of why Congress has ample power to prohibit the possession of firearms in or near schools—just as it may protect the school environment from harms posed by controlled substances such as asbestos or alcohol. I also agree with Justice Souter's exposition of the radical character of the Court's holding and its kinship with the discredited, pre-Depression version of substantive due process. . . . I believe, however, that the Court's extraordinary decision merits this additional comment.

JUSTICE SOUTER, dissenting.

It was not ever thus, however, as even a brief overview of Commerce Clause history during the past century reminds us. The modern respect for the competence and primacy of Congress in matters affecting commerce developed only after one of this Court's most chastening experiences, when it perforce repudiated an earlier and untenably expansive conception of judicial review in derogation of congressional commerce power. A look at history's sequence will serve to show how today's decision tugs the Court off course, leading it to suggest opportunities for further developments that would be at odds with the rule of restraint to which the Court still wisely states adherence.

I

Notwithstanding the Court's recognition of a broad commerce power in *Gibbons* v. *Ogden*, [22 U.S. 1 (1824),] Congress saw few occasions to exercise that power prior to Reconstruction, see generally 2 C. Warren, *The Supreme Court in United States History* 729–739 (rev. ed. 1935), and it was really the passage of the Interstate Commerce Act of 1887 that opened a new age of congressional reliance on the Commerce Clause for authority to exercise general police powers at the national level. [Souter engages in an extensive review of these cases.]

II

There is today, however, a backward glance at both the old pitfalls, as the Court treats deference under the rationality rule as subject to gradation according to the commercial or noncommercial nature of the immediate subject of the challenged regulation. The distinction between what is patently commercial and what is not looks much like the old distinction between what directly affects commerce and what touches it only indirectly. And the act of calibrating the level of deference by drawing a line between what is patently commercial and what is less purely so will probably resemble the process of deciding how much interference with contractual freedom was fatal. Thus, it seems fair to ask whether the step taken by the Court today does anything but portend a return to the untenable jurisprudence from which the Court extricated itself almost 60 years ago. The answer is not reassuring. To be sure, the occasion for today's decision reflects the century's end, not its beginning. But if it seems anomalous that the Congress of the United States has taken to regulating school yards, the Act in question is still probably no more remarkable than state regulation of bake shops 90 years ago. In any event, there is no reason to hope that the Court's qualification of rational basis review will be any more successful than the efforts at substantive economic review made by our predecessors as the century began. Taking the Court's opinion on its own terms, Justice Breyer has explained both the hopeless porosity of "commercial" character as a ground of Commerce Clause distinction in America's highly connected economy, and the inconsistency of this categorization with our rational basis precedents from the last 50 years.

Further glosses on rationality review, moreover, may be in the offing. Although this case turns on commercial character, the Court gestures toward two other considerations that it might sometime entertain in applying rational basis scrutiny (apart from a statutory obligation to supply independent proof of a jurisdictional element): does the congressional statute deal with subjects of traditional state regulation, and does the statute contain explicit factual findings supporting the otherwise implicit determination that the regulated activity substantially affects interstate commerce? Once again, any appeal these considerations may have depends on ignoring the painful lesson learned in 1937, for neither of the Court's suggestions would square with rational basis scrutiny.

JUSTICE BREYER, with whom JUSTICES STEVENS, SOUTER, and GINSBURG join, dissenting.

The issue in this case is whether the Commerce Clause authorizes Congress to enact a statute that makes it a crime to possess a gun in, or near, a school. In my view, the statute falls well within the scope of the commerce power as this Court has understood that power over the last half century.

I

In reaching this conclusion, I apply three basic principles of Commerce Clause interpretation. First, the power to "regulate Commerce . . . among the several States," encompasses the power to regulate local activities insofar as they significantly affect interstate commerce. . . .

Second, in determining whether a local activity will likely have a significant effect upon interstate commerce, a court must consider, not the effect of an individual act (a single instance of gun possession), but rather the cumulative effect of all similar instances (*i.e.*, the effect of all guns possessed in or near schools). See, *e.g., Wickard [v. Filburn*, 317 U.S. 111 (1942)]. As this Court put the matter almost 50 years ago: "It is enough that the individual activity when multiplied into a general practice . . . contains a threat to the interstate economy that requires preventative regulation." . . .

Third, the Constitution requires us to judge the connection between a regulated activity and interstate commerce, not directly, but at one remove. Courts must give Congress a degree of leeway in determining the existence of a significant factual connection between the regulated activity and interstate commerce—both because the Constitution delegates the commerce power directly to Congress and because the determination requires an empirical judgment of a kind that a legislature is more likely than a court to make with accuracy. The traditional words "rational basis" capture this leeway. See *Hodel [v. Virginia Surface Mining & Reclamation Assn., Inc.*, 452 U.S. 264 (1981)]. Thus, the specific question before us, as the Court recognizes, is not whether the "regulated activity sufficiently affected interstate commerce," but, rather, whether Congress could have had "*a rational basis*" for so concluding.

I recognize that we must judge this matter independently. "Simply because Congress may conclude that a particular activity substantially affects interstate commerce does not necessarily make it so." *Hodel.* And, I also recognize that Congress did not write specific "interstate commerce" findings into the law under which Lopez was convicted. Nonetheless, as I have already noted, the matter that we review independently (*i.e.*, whether there is a "rational basis") already has considerable leeway built into it. And, the absence of findings, at most, deprives a statute of the benefit of some *extra* leeway. . . .

II

Applying these principles to the case at hand, we must ask whether Congress could have had a *rational basis* for finding a significant (or substantial) connection between gun-related school violence and interstate commerce. Or, to put the question in the language of the *explicit* finding that Congress made when it amended this law in 1994: Could Congress rationally have found that "violent crime in school zones," through its effect on the "quality of education," significantly (or substantially) affects "interstate" or "foreign commerce"? As long as one views the commerce connection, not as a "technical legal conception," but as "a practical one," *Swift & Co.* v. *United States*, the answer to this question must be yes. Numerous reports and studies—generated both inside and outside government—make clear that Congress could reasonably have found the empirical connection that its law, implicitly or explicitly, asserts.

For one thing, reports, hearings, and other readily available literature make clear that the problem of guns in and around schools is widespread and extremely serious. [Breyer cites evidence of this.]

Having found that guns in schools significantly undermine the quality of education in our Nation's classrooms, Congress could also have found, given the effect of education upon interstate and foreign commerce, that gun-related violence in and around schools is a commercial, as well as a human, problem. Education, although far more than a matter of economics, has long been inextricably intertwined with the Nation's economy. When this Nation began, most workers received their education in the workplace, typically (like Benjamin Franklin) as apprentices. As late as the 1920's, many workers still received general education directly from their employers—from large corporations, such as General Electric, Ford, and Goodyear, which created schools within their firms to help both the worker and the firm. (Throughout most of the 19th century fewer than one percent of all Americans received secondary education through attending a high school.) As public school enrollment grew in the early 20th century, the need for industry to teach basic educational skills diminished. But, the direct economic link between basic education and industrial productivity remained. Scholars estimate that nearly a quarter of America's economic growth in the early years of this century is traceable directly to increased schooling; that investment in "human capital" (through spending on education) exceeded investment in "physical capital" by a ratio of almost two to one; and that the economic returns to this investment in education exceeded the returns to conventional capital investment.

In recent years the link between secondary education and business has strengthened, becoming both more direct and more important. . . .

Increasing global competition also has made primary and secondary education economically more important. . . .

Finally, there is evidence that, today more than ever, many firms base their location decisions upon the presence, or absence, of a work force with a basic education. . . .

To hold this statute constitutional is not to "obliterate" the "distinction between what is national and what is local"; nor is it to hold that the Commerce Clause permits the Federal Government to "regulate any activity that it found was related to the economic productivity of individual citizens," to regulate "marriage, divorce, and child custody," or to regulate any and all aspects of education. First, this statute is aimed at curbing a particularly acute threat to the educational process—the possession (and use) of life-threatening firearms in, or near, the classroom. The empirical evidence that I have discussed above unmistakably documents the special way in which guns and education are incompatible. This Court has previously recognized the singularly disruptive potential on interstate commerce that acts of violence may have. Second, the immediacy of the connection between education and the national economic well-being is documented by scholars and accepted by society at large in a way and to a degree that may not hold true for other social institutions. It must surely be the rare case, then, that a statute strikes at conduct that (when considered in the abstract) seems so removed from commerce, but which (practically speaking) has so significant an impact upon commerce.

In sum, a holding that the particular statute before us falls within the commerce power would not expand the scope of that Clause. Rather, it simply would apply pre-existing law to changing economic circumstances. See *Heart of Atlanta Motel, Inc.* v. *United States* [,379 U.S. 241] (1964). It would recognize that, in today's economic world, gun-related violence near the classroom makes a significant difference to our economic, as well as our social, well-being. In accordance with well-accepted precedent, such a holding would permit Congress "to act in terms of economic . . . realities," would interpret the commerce power as "an affirmative power commensurate with the national needs," and would acknowledge that the "commerce clause does not operate so as to render the nation powerless to defend itself against economic forces that Congress decrees inimical or destructive of the national economy." . . .

III

The majority's holding—that § 922 falls outside the scope of the Commerce Clause—creates three serious legal problems. First, the majority's holding runs contrary to modern Supreme Court cases that have upheld congressional actions despite connections to interstate or foreign commerce that are less significant than the effect of school violence. [Breyer analyzes a number of these cases.]

The second legal problem the Court creates comes from its apparent belief that it can reconcile its holding with earlier cases by making a critical distinction between "commercial" and noncommercial "transaction[s]." That is to say, the Court believes the Constitution would distinguish between two local activities, each of which has an identical effect upon interstate commerce, if one, but not the other, is "commercial" in nature. As a general matter, this approach fails to heed this Court's earlier warning not to turn "questions of the power of Congress" upon "formula[s]" that would give "controlling force to nomenclature such as 'production' and 'indirect' and foreclose consideration of the actual effects of the activity in question upon interstate commerce."

The third legal problem created by the Court's holding is that it threatens legal uncertainty in an area of law that, until this case, seemed reasonably well settled. Congress has enacted many statutes (more than 100 sections of the United States Code), including criminal statutes (at least 25 sections), that use the words "affecting commerce" to define their scope. Do these, or similar, statutes regulate noncommercial activities? If so, would that alter the meaning of "affecting commerce" in a jurisdictional element? More importantly, in the absence of a jurisdictional element, are the courts nevertheless to take *Wickard* (and later similar cases) as inapplicable, and to judge the effect of a single noncommercial activity on interstate commerce without considering similar instances of the forbidden conduct? However these questions are eventually resolved, the legal uncertainty now created will restrict Congress' ability to enact criminal laws aimed at criminal behavior that, considered problem by problem rather than instance by instance, seriously threatens the economic, as well as social, well-being of Americans.

IV

In sum, to find this legislation within the scope of the Commerce Clause would permit "Congress . . . to act in terms of economic . . . realities." *North American Co.* v. *SEC*, 327 U.S. 686 (1946). It would interpret the Clause as this Court has traditionally interpreted it, with the exception of one wrong turn subsequently corrected. Upholding this legislation would do no more than simply recognize that Congress had a "rational basis" for finding a significant connection between guns in or near schools and (through their effect on education) the interstate and foreign commerce they threaten. For these reasons, I would reverse the judgment of the Court of Appeals. Respectfully, I dissent.

FOR DISCUSSION

What three areas of regulation does Chief Justice Rehnquist identify under the Commerce Clause? To what degree do these areas (especially the last) recapitulate distinctions that the Court had attempted to maintain in the time period prior to 1937? Can you think of a fair and consistent measure that the Court might employ to measure a "substantial effect" on commerce, or will this necessarily vary from case to case? Do you think the Court adequately established such an effect in *Wickard v. Filburn*?

UNITED STATES V. MORRISON

529 U.S. 598, 120 S. Ct. 1740, 146 L. Ed. 2d 658 Together with No. 99–29, *Brzonkala v. Morrison et al.*, also on certiorari to the same court.(2000)

This dramatic case examines the constitutionality of the Violence Against Women Act of 1994, which provided a federal civil remedy for victims of gender-motivated violence. In adopting the law, Congress had taken greater care than it had in *United States v. Lopez* (1995) to document a link between the violence it was attempting to punish and economic harm to the nation. Still, a U.S. circuit court had ruled that the law exceeded federal powers.

Vote: 5–4

CHIEF JUSTICE REHNQUIST delivered the opinion of the Court.

I

Petitioner Christy Brzonkala enrolled at Virginia Polytechnic Institute (Virginia Tech) in the fall of 1994. In September of that year, Brzonkala met respondents Antonio Morrison and James Crawford, who were both students at Virginia Tech and members of its varsity football team. Brzonkala alleges that, within 30 minutes of meeting Morrison and Crawford, they assaulted and repeatedly raped her. After the attack, Morrison allegedly told Brzonkala, "You better not have any . . . diseases." In the months following the rape, Morrison also allegedly announced in the dormitory's dining room that he "liked" to get girls drunk and. . . ." The omitted portions, quoted verbatim in the briefs on file with this Court, consist of boasting, debased remarks about what Morrison would do to women, vulgar remarks that cannot fail to shock and offend.

Brzonkala alleges that this attack caused her to become severely emotionally disturbed and depressed. She sought assistance from a university psychiatrist, who prescribed antidepressant medication. Shortly after the rape Brzonkala stopped attending classes and withdrew from the university.

In early 1995, Brzonkala filed a complaint against respondents under Virginia Tech's Sexual Assault Policy. During the school-conducted hearing on her complaint, Morrison admitted having sexual contact with her despite the fact that she had twice told him "no." After the hearing, Virginia Tech's Judicial Committee found insufficient evidence to punish Crawford, but found Morrison guilty of sexual assault and sentenced him to immediate suspension for two semesters.

Virginia Tech's dean of students upheld the judicial committee's sentence. However, in July 1995, Virginia Tech informed Brzonkala that Morrison intended to initiate a court challenge to his conviction under the Sexual Assault Policy. University officials told her that a second hearing would be necessary to remedy the school's error in prosecuting her complaint under that policy, which had not been widely circulated to students. The university therefore conducted a second hearing under its Abusive Conduct Policy, which was in force prior to the dissemination of the Sexual Assault Policy. Following this second hearing the Judicial Committee again found Morrison guilty and sentenced him to an identical 2-semester suspension. This time, however, the description of Morrison's offense was, without explanation, changed from "sexual assault" to "using abusive language."

Morrison appealed his second conviction through the university's administrative system. On August 21, 1995, Virginia Tech's senior vice president and provost set aside Morrison's punishment. She concluded that it was " 'excessive when compared with other cases where there has been a finding of violation of the Abusive Conduct Policy.' " Virginia Tech did not inform Brzonkala of this decision. After learning from a newspaper that Morrison would be returning to Virginia Tech for the fall 1995 semester, she dropped out of the university.

In December 1995, Brzonkala sued Morrison, Crawford, and Virginia Tech in the United States District Court for the Western District of Virginia. Her complaint alleged that Morrison's and Crawford's attack violated § 13981 and that Virginia Tech's handling of her complaint violated Title IX of the Education Amendments of 1972. Morrison and Crawford moved to dismiss this complaint on the grounds that it failed to state a claim and that § 13981's civil remedy is unconstitutional. The United States, petitioner in No. 99–5, intervened to defend § 13981's constitutionality.

The District Court dismissed Brzonkala's Title IX claims against Virginia Tech for failure to state a claim upon which relief can be granted. It then held that Brzonkala's complaint stated a claim against Morrison and Crawford under § 13981, but dismissed the complaint because it concluded that Congress lacked authority to enact the section under either the Commerce Clause or § 5 of the Fourteenth Amendment.

A divided panel of the Court of Appeals reversed the District Court, reinstating Brzonkala's § 13981 claim and her Title IX hostile environment claim. The full Court of Appeals vacated the panel's opinion and reheard the case en banc. The en banc court then issued an opinion affirming the District Court's conclusion that Brzonkala stated a claim under § 13981 because her complaint alleged a crime of violence and the allegations of Morrison's crude and derogatory statements regarding his treatment of women sufficiently indicated that his crime was motivated by gender animus. Nevertheless, the court by a divided vote affirmed the District Court's conclusion that Congress lacked constitutional authority to enact § 13981's civil remedy. Because the Court of Appeals invalidated a federal statute on constitutional grounds, we granted certiorari.

Section 13981 was part of the Violence Against Women Act of 1994. It states that "persons within the United States shall have the right to be free from crimes of violence motivated by gender." To enforce that right, subsection (c) declares: "A person (including a person who acts under color of any statute, ordinance, regulation, custom, or usage of any State) who commits a crime of violence motivated by gender and thus deprives another of the right declared in subsection (b) of this section shall be liable to the party injured, in an action for the recovery of compensatory and punitive damages, injunctive and declaratory relief, and such other relief as a court may deem appropriate."

Section 13981 defines a "crime" of violence motivated by "gender" as "a crime of violence committed because of gender or on the basis of gender, and due, at least in part, to an animus based on the victim's gender." It also provides that the term "crime of violence" includes any "(A) . . . act or series of acts that would constitute a felony against the person or that would constitute a felony against property if the conduct presents a serious risk of physical injury to another, and that would come within the meaning of State or Federal offenses described in section 16 of Title 18, whether or not those acts have actually resulted in criminal charges, prosecution, or conviction and whether or not those acts were committed in the special maritime, territorial, or prison jurisdiction of the United States; and "(B) includes an act or series of acts that would constitute a felony described in subparagraph (A) but for the relationship between the person who takes such action and the individual against whom such action is taken."

Further clarifying the broad scope of § 13981's civil remedy, subsection (e)(2) states that "nothing" in this section requires a prior criminal complaint, prosecution, or conviction to establish the elements of a cause of action under subsection (c) of this section." And subsection (e)(3) provides a § 13981 litigant with a choice of forums: Federal and state courts "shall have concurrent jurisdiction" over complaints brought under the section.

Although the foregoing language of § 13981 covers a wide swath of criminal conduct, Congress placed some limitations on the section's federal civil remedy. Subsection (e)(1) states that "nothing" in this section entitles a person to a cause of action under subsection (c) of this section for random acts of violence unrelated to gender or for acts that cannot be demonstrated, by a preponderance of the evidence, to be motivated by gender." Subsection (e)(4) further states that § 13981 shall not be construed "to confer on the courts of the

United States jurisdiction over any State law claim seeking the establishment of a divorce, alimony, equitable distribution of marital property, or child custody decree."

Every law enacted by Congress must be based on one or more of its powers enumerated in the Constitution. "The powers of the legislature are defined and limited; and that those limits may not be mistaken or forgotten, the constitution is written." *Marbury* v. *Madison*, 5 U.S. (1 Cranch) 137 (1803). Congress explicitly identified the sources of federal authority on which it relied in enacting § 13981. It said that a "federal civil rights cause of action" is established "pursuant" to the affirmative power of Congress . . . under section 5 of the Fourteenth Amendment to the Constitution, as well as under section 8 of Article I of the Constitution." We address Congress' authority to enact this remedy under each of these constitutional provisions in turn.

II

Due respect for the decisions of a coordinate branch of Government demands that we invalidate a congressional enactment only upon a plain showing that Congress has exceeded its constitutional bounds. With this presumption of constitutionality in mind, we turn to the question whether § 13981 falls within Congress' power under Article I, § 8, of the Constitution. Brzonkala and the United States rely upon the third clause of the Article, which gives Congress power "to regulate Commerce with foreign Nations, and among the several States, and with the Indian Tribes."

As we discussed at length in *United States v. Lopez*, 514 U.S. 549 (1995), our interpretation of the Commerce Clause has changed as our Nation has developed. . . . We need not repeat that detailed review of the Commerce Clause's history here; it suffices to say that, in the years since *NLRB v. Jones & Laughlin Steel Corp.*, 301 U.S. 1 (1937), Congress has had considerably greater latitude in regulating conduct and transactions under the Commerce Clause than our previous case law permitted. . . .

Lopez emphasized, however, that even under our modern, expansive interpretation of the Commerce Clause, Congress' regulatory authority is not without effective bounds. "Even [our] modern-era precedents which have expanded congressional power under the Commerce Clause confirm that this power is subject to outer limits. In *Jones & Laughlin Steel*, the Court warned that the scope of the interstate commerce power 'must be considered in the light of our dual system of government and may not be extended so as to embrace effects upon interstate commerce so indirect and remote that to embrace them, in view of our complex society, would effectually obliterate the distinction between what is national and what is local and create a completely centralized government.' "

As we observed in *Lopez*, modern Commerce Clause jurisprudence has "identified three broad categories of activity that Congress may regulate under its commerce power." . . . "First, Congress may regulate the use of the channels of interstate commerce." . . . "Second, Congress is empowered to regulate and protect the instrumentalities of interstate commerce, or persons or things in interstate commerce, even though the threat may come only from intrastate activities." . . . "Finally, Congress' commerce authority includes the power to regulate those activities having a substantial relation to interstate commerce, . . . *i.e.*, those activities that substantially affect interstate commerce." . . .

Petitioners do not contend that these cases fall within either of the first two of these categories of Commerce Clause regulation. They seek to sustain § 13981 as a regulation of activity that substantially affects interstate commerce. Given § 13981's focus on gender-motivated violence wherever it occurs (rather than violence directed at the instrumentalities of interstate commerce, interstate markets, or things or persons in interstate commerce), we agree that this is the proper inquiry.

Since *Lopez* most recently canvassed and clarified our case law governing this third category of Commerce Clause regulation, it provides the proper framework for conducting the required analysis of § 13981. In *Lopez*, we held that the Gun-Free School Zones Act of 1990, which made it a federal crime to knowingly possess a firearm in a school zone, exceeded Congress' authority under the Commerce Clause. Several significant considerations contributed to our decision.

First, we observed that § 922(q) was "a criminal statute that by its terms has nothing to do with 'commerce' or any sort of economic enterprise, however broadly one might define those terms." . . . .

The second consideration that we found important in analyzing § 922(q) was that the statute contained "no express jurisdictional element which might limit its reach to a discrete set of firearm possessions that additionally have an explicit connection with or effect on interstate commerce." Such a jurisdictional element may establish that the enactment is in pursuance of Congress' regulation of interstate commerce.

Third, we noted that neither § 922(q) " 'nor its legislative history contains express congressional findings regarding the effects upon interstate commerce of gun possession in a school zone.' " . . . .

Finally, our decision in *Lopez* rested in part on the fact that the link between gun possession and a substantial effect on interstate commerce was attenuated. The United States argued that the possession of guns may lead to violent crime, and that violent crime "can be expected to affect the functioning of the national economy in two ways. First, the costs of violent crime are substantial, and, through the mechanism of insurance, those costs are spread throughout the population. Second, violent crime reduces the willingness of individuals to travel to areas within the country that are perceived to be unsafe." The Government also argued that the presence of guns at schools poses a threat to the educational process, which in turn threatens to produce a less efficient and productive workforce, which will negatively affect national productivity and thus interstate commerce.

We rejected these "costs of crime" and "national productivity" arguments because they would permit Congress to "regulate not only all violent crime, but all activities that might lead to violent crime, regardless of how tenuously they relate to interstate commerce." We noted that, under this but-for reasoning: "Congress could regulate any activity that it found was related to the economic productivity of individual citizens: family law (including marriage, divorce, and child custody), for example. Under these theories . . ., it is difficult to perceive any limitation on federal power, even in areas such as criminal law enforcement or education where States historically have been sovereign. Thus, if we were to accept the Government's arguments, we are hard pressed to posit any activity by an individual that Congress is without power to regulate."

With these principles underlying our Commerce Clause jurisprudence as reference points, the proper resolution of the present cases is clear. Gender-motivated crimes of violence are not, in any sense of the phrase, economic activity. While we need not adopt a categorical rule against aggregating the effects of any noneconomic activity in order to decide these cases, thus far in our Nation's history our cases have upheld Commerce Clause regulation of intrastate activity only where that activity is economic in nature.

Like the Gun-Free School Zones Act at issue in *Lopez*, § 13981 contains no jurisdictional element establishing that the federal cause of action is in pursuance of Congress' power to regulate interstate commerce. Although *Lopez* makes clear that such a jurisdictional element would lend support to the argument that § 13981is sufficiently tied to interstate commerce, Congress elected to cast § 13981's remedy over a wider, and more purely intrastate, body of violent crime.

In contrast with the lack of congressional findings that we faced in *Lopez*, § 13981 *is* supported by numerous findings regarding the serious impact that gender-motivated violence has on victims and their families. . . . But the existence of congressional findings is not sufficient, by itself, to sustain the constitutionality of Commerce Clause legislation. As we stated in *Lopez*, " 'Simply because Congress may conclude that a particular activity substantially affects interstate commerce does not necessarily make it so.' " Rather, " 'whether particular operations affect interstate commerce sufficiently to come under the constitutional power of Congress to regulate them is ultimately a judicial rather than a legislative question, and can be settled finally only by this Court.' "

In these cases, Congress' findings are substantially weakened by the fact that they rely so heavily on a method of reasoning that we have already rejected as unworkable if we are to maintain the Constitution's enumeration of powers. Congress found that gender-motivated violence affects interstate commerce "by deterring potential victims from traveling interstate, from engaging in employment in interstate business, and from transacting with business, and in places involved in interstate commerce; . . . by diminishing national productivity, increasing medical and other costs, and decreasing the supply of and the demand for interstate products."

Given these findings and petitioners' arguments, the concern that we expressed in *Lopez* that Congress might use the Commerce Clause to completely obliterate the Constitution's distinction between national and local authority seems well founded. The reasoning that petitioners advance seeks to follow the but-for causal chain from the initial occurrence of violent crime (the suppression of which has always been the prime object of the States' police power) to every attenuated effect upon interstate commerce. If accepted, petitioners' reasoning would allow Congress to regulate any crime as long as the nationwide, aggregated impact of that crime has substantial effects on employment, production, transit, or consumption. Indeed, if Congress may regulate gender-motivated violence, it would be able to regulate murder or any other type of violence since gender-motivated violence, as a subset of all violent crime, is certain to have lesser economic impacts than the larger class of which it is a part.

Petitioners' reasoning, moreover, will not limit Congress to regulating violence but may, as we suggested in *Lopez*, be applied equally as well to family law and other areas of traditional state regulation since the aggregate effect of marriage, divorce, and childrearing on the national economy is undoubtedly significant. Congress may have recognized this specter when it expressly precluded § 13981 from being used in the family law context. Under our written Constitution, however, the limitation of congressional authority is not solely a matter of legislative grace. . . .

We accordingly reject the argument that Congress may regulate noneconomic, violent criminal conduct based solely on that conduct's aggregate effect on interstate commerce. The Constitution requires a distinction between what is truly national and what is truly local. In recognizing this fact we preserve one of the few principles that has been consistent since the Clause was adopted. The regulation and punishment of intrastate violence that is not directed at the instrumentalities, channels, or goods involved in interstate commerce has always been the province of the States. . . . Indeed, we can think of no better example of the police power, which the Founders denied the National Government and reposed in the States, than the suppression of violent crime and vindication of its victims. . . .

III

[Rehnquist rejects the idea that Congress had authority to adopt legislation under its enforcement power in Section 5 of the Fourteenth Amendment.]

IV

Petitioner Brzonkala's complaint alleges that she was the victim of a brutal assault. But Congress' effort in § 13981 to provide a federal civil remedy can be sustained neither under the Commerce Clause nor under § 5 of the Fourteenth Amendment. If the allegations here are true, no civilized system of justice could fail to provide her a remedy for the conduct of respondent Morrison. But under our federal system that remedy must be provided by the Commonwealth of Virginia, and not by the United States. The judgment of the Court of Appeals is

Affirmed.

JUSTICE THOMAS, concurring.

The majority opinion correctly applies our decision in *United States* v. *Lopez*, 514 U.S. 549 (1995), and I join it in full. I write separately only to express my view that the very notion of a "substantial effects" test under the Commerce Clause is inconsistent with the original understanding of Congress' powers and with this Court's early Commerce Clause cases. By continuing to apply this rootless and malleable standard, however circumscribed, the Court has encouraged the Federal Government to persist in its view that the Commerce Clause has virtually no limits. Until this Court replaces its existing Commerce Clause jurisprudence with a standard more consistent with the original understanding, we will continue to see Congress appropriating state police powers under the guise of regulating commerce.

JUSTICE SOUTER, with whom JUSTICES STEVENS, GINSBURG, and BREYER join, dissenting.

The Court says both that it leaves Commerce Clause precedent undisturbed and that the Civil Rights Remedy of the Violence Against Women Act of 1994 . . . exceeds Congress's power under that Clause. I find the claims irreconcilable and respectfully dissent.

I

Our cases, which remain at least nominally undisturbed, stand for the following propositions. Congress has the power to legislate with regard to activity that, in the aggregate, has a substantial effect on interstate commerce. . . . The fact of such a substantial effect is not an issue for the courts in the first instance, but for the Congress, whose institutional capacity for gathering evidence and taking testimony far exceeds ours. By passing legislation, Congress indicates its conclusion, whether explicitly or not, that facts support its exercise of the commerce power. The business of the courts is to review the congressional assessment, not for soundness but simply for the rationality of concluding that a jurisdictional basis exists in fact. Any explicit findings that Congress chooses to make, though not dispositive of the question of rationality, may advance judicial review by identifying factual authority on which Congress relied. Applying those propositions in these cases can lead to only one conclusion.

One obvious difference from *United States* v. *Lopez* . . . is the mountain of data assembled by Congress, here showing the effects of violence against women on interstate commerce. Passage of the Act in 1994 was preceded by four years of hearings, which included testimony from physicians and law professors; from survivors of rape and domestic violence; and from representatives of state law enforcement and private business. The record includes reports on gender bias from task forces in 21 States, and we have the benefit of specific factual findings in the eight separate Reports issued by Congress and its committees over the long course leading to enactment. . . .

With respect to domestic violence, Congress received evidence for the following findings: [Souter proceeds to quote extensively from these findings.]

Congress thereby explicitly stated the predicate for the exercise of its Commerce Clause power. Is its conclusion irrational in view of the data amassed? True, the methodology of particular studies may be challenged, and some of the figures arrived at may be disputed. But the sufficiency of the evidence before Congress to provide a rational basis for the finding cannot seriously be questioned. . . .

Indeed, the legislative record here is far more voluminous than the record compiled by Congress and found sufficient in two prior cases upholding Title II of the Civil Rights Act of 1964 against Commerce Clause challenges. . . .

II

[This section is devoted to a comprehensive review of judicial precedents.]

III

All of this convinces me that today's ebb of the commerce power rests on error, and at the same time leads me to doubt that the majority's view will prove to be enduring law. . . .

JUSTICE BREYER, with whom JUSTICE STEVENS joins, and with whom JUSTICES SOUTER and GINSBURG join as to Part I-A, dissenting.

No one denies the importance of the Constitution's federalist principles. Its state/federal division of authority protects liberty—both by restricting the burdens that government can impose from a distance and by facilitating citizen participation in government that is closer to home. The question is how the judiciary can best implement that original federalist understanding where the Commerce Clause is at issue.

I

The majority holds that the federal commerce power does not extend to such "noneconomic" activities as "noneconomic, violent criminal conduct" that significantly affects interstate commerce only if we "aggregate" the interstate "effects" of individual instances. Justice Souter explains why history, precedent, and legal logic militate against the majority's approach. I agree and join his opinion. I add that the majority's holding illustrates the difficulty of finding a workable judicial Commerce Clause touchstone—a set of comprehensible interpretive rules that courts might use to impose some meaningful limit, but not too great a limit, upon the scope of the legislative authority that the Commerce Clause delegates to Congress. . . .

FOR DISCUSSION

How, if at all, do you think this decision differs from cases prior to 1937 such as *Lochner v. New York* (198 U.S. 45, 1905) in which the Supreme Court counterposed its own judgment about the anticipated effects of a law against those of either Congress or the state legislatures?

GRANHOLM V. HEALD

544 U.S. 460, 125 S. Ct. 1885, 161 L. Ed. 2d 796 (2005)

The Supreme Court must often balance congressional powers over interstate commerce against state police powers. This case provides a further complication, when defenders of Michigan and New York regulations of wineries, which limited out-of-state mail order sales, cite the Twenty-first Amendment, which, in repealing national alcoholic prohibition (established by the Eighteenth Amendment), continued to give states broad authority over the subject.

Vote: 5–4

JUSTICE KENNEDY delivered the opinion of the Court.

These consolidated cases present challenges to state laws regulating the sale of wine from out-of-state wineries to consumers in Michigan and New York. The details and mechanics of the two regulatory schemes differ, but the object and effect of the laws are the same: to allow in-state wineries to sell wine directly to consumers in that State but to prohibit out-of-state wineries from doing so, or, at the least, to make direct sales impractical from an economic standpoint. It is evident that the object and design of the Michigan and New York statutes is to grant in-state wineries a competitive advantage over wineries located beyond the States' borders.

We hold that the laws in both States discriminate against interstate commerce in violation of the Commerce Clause, Art. I, § 8, cl. 3, and that the discrimination is neither authorized nor permitted by the Twenty-first Amendment. Accordingly, we affirm the judgment of the Court of Appeals for the Sixth Circuit, which invalidated the Michigan laws; and we reverse the judgment of the Court of Appeals for the Second Circuit, which upheld the New York laws.

I

Like many other States, Michigan and New York regulate the sale and importation of alcoholic beverages, including wine, through a three-tier distribution system. Separate licenses are required for producers, wholesalers, and retailers. . . . The three-tier scheme is preserved by a complex set of overlapping state and federal regulations. For example, both state and federal laws limit vertical integration between tiers. . . . We have held previously that States can mandate a three-tier distribution scheme in the exercise of their authority under the Twenty-first Amendment. . . . As relevant to today's cases, though, the three-tier system is, in broad terms and with refinements to be discussed, mandated by Michigan and New York only for sales from out-of-state wineries. In-state wineries, by contrast, can obtain a license for direct sales to consumers. The differential treatment between in-state and out-of-state wineries constitutes explicit discrimination against interstate commerce.

This discrimination substantially limits the direct sale of wine to consumers, an otherwise emerging and significant business. [Kennedy assesses the economic impact of such regulations.]

The wine producers in the cases before us are small wineries that rely on direct consumer sales as an important part of their businesses. Domaine Alfred, one of the plaintiffs in the Michigan suit, is a small winery located in San Luis Obispo, California. It produces 3,000 cases of wine per year. Domaine Alfred has received requests for its wine from Michigan consumers but cannot fill the orders because of the State's direct-shipment ban. Even if the winery could find a Michigan wholesaler to distribute its wine, the wholesaler's markup would render shipment through the three-tier system economically infeasible.

Similarly, Juanita Swedenburg and David Lucas, two of the plaintiffs in the New York suit, operate small wineries in Virginia (the Swedenburg Estate Vineyard) and California (the Lucas Winery). Some of their customers are tourists, from other States, who purchase wine while visiting the wineries. If these customers wish to obtain Swedenburg or Lucas wines after they return home, they will be unable to do so if they reside in a State with restrictive direct-shipment laws. For example, Swedenburg and Lucas are unable to fill orders from New York, the Nation's second-largest wine market, because of the limits that State imposes on direct wine shipments.

A

We first address the background of the suit challenging the Michigan direct-shipment law. Most alcoholic beverages in Michigan are distributed through the State's three-tier system. Producers or distillers of alcoholic beverages, whether located in state or out of state, generally may sell only to licensed in-state wholesalers. . . . Wholesalers, in turn, may sell only to in-state retailers. . . . Licensed retailers are the final link in the chain, selling alcoholic beverages to consumers at retail locations and, subject to certain restrictions, through home delivery. . . .

Under Michigan law, wine producers, as a general matter, must distribute their wine through wholesalers. There is, however, an exception for Michigan's approximately 40 in-state wineries, which are eligible for "wine maker" licenses that allow direct shipment to in-state consumers. . . . The cost of the license varies with the size of the winery. For a small winery, the license is $25. . . . Out-of-state wineries can apply for a $300 "outside seller of wine" license, but this license only allows them to sell to in-state wholesalers. . . .

Some Michigan residents brought suit against various state officials in the United States District Court for the Eastern District of Michigan. Domaine Alfred, the San Luis Obispo winery, joined in the suit. The plaintiffs contended that Michigan's direct-shipment laws discriminated against interstate commerce in violation of the Commerce Clause. The trade association Michigan Beer & Wine Wholesalers intervened as a defendant. Both the State and the wholesalers argued that the ban on direct shipment from out-of-state wineries is a valid exercise of Michigan's power under § 2 of the Twenty-first Amendment.

On cross-motions for summary judgment the District Court sustained the Michigan scheme. The Court of Appeals for the Sixth Circuit reversed. Relying on *Bacchus Imports, Ltd.* v. *Dias,* 468 U.S. 263 (1984), the court rejected the argument that the Twenty-first Amendment immunizes all state liquor laws from the strictures of the Commerce Clause, and held the Michigan scheme was unconstitutional because the defendants failed to demonstrate the State could not meet its proffered policy objectives through nondiscriminatory means.

B

[Here Kennedy reviews New York's licensing system.]

C

We consolidated these cases and granted certiorari on the following question: " 'Does a State's regulatory scheme that permits in-state wineries directly to ship alcohol to consumers but restricts the ability of out-of-state wineries to do so violate the dormant Commerce Clause in light of § 2 of the Twenty-first Amendment?' " . . .

II

A

Time and again this Court has held that, in all but the narrowest circumstances, state laws violate the Commerce Clause if they mandate "differential treatment of in-state and out-of-state economic interests that benefits the former and burdens the latter." . . .

Laws of the type at issue in the instant cases contradict these principles. They deprive citizens of their right to have access to the markets of other States on equal terms. The perceived necessity for reciprocal sale privileges risks generating the trade rivalries and animosities, the alliances and exclusivity, that the Constitution and, in particular, the Commerce Clause were designed to avoid. State laws that protect local wineries have led to the enactment of statutes under which some States condition the right of out-of-state wineries to make direct wine sales to in-state consumers on a reciprocal right in the shipping State. California, for example, passed a reciprocity law in 1986, retreating from the State's previous regime that allowed unfettered direct shipments from out-of-state wineries. Prior to 1986, all but three States prohibited direct-shipments of wine. The obvious aim of the California statute was to open the interstate direct-shipping market for the State's many wineries. The current patchwork of laws—with some States banning direct shipments altogether, others doing so only for out-of-state wines, and still others requiring reciprocity—is essentially the product of an ongoing, low-level trade war. Allowing States to discriminate against out-of-state wine "invite[s] a multiplication of preferential trade areas destructive of the very purpose of the Commerce Clause." . . .

B

The discriminatory character of the Michigan system is obvious. Michigan allows in-state wineries to ship directly to consumers, subject only to a licensing requirement. Out-of-state wineries, whether licensed or not, face a complete ban on direct shipment. The differential treatment requires all out-of-state wine, but not all in-state wine, to pass through an in-state wholesaler and retailer before reaching consumers. These two extra layers of overhead increase the cost of out-of-state wines to Michigan consumers. The cost differential, and in some cases the inability to secure a wholesaler for small shipments, can effectively bar small wineries from the Michigan market.

The New York regulatory scheme differs from Michigan's in that it does not ban direct shipments altogether. Out-of-state wineries are instead required to establish a distribution operation in New York in order to gain the privilege of direct shipment. This, though, is just an indirect way of subjecting out-of-state wineries, but not local ones, to the three-tier system. New York and those allied with its interests defend the scheme by arguing that an out-of-state winery has the same access to the State's consumers as in-state wineries: All wine must be sold through a licensee fully accountable to New York; it just so happens that in order to become a licensee, a winery must have a physical presence in the State. There is some confusion over the precise steps out-of-state wineries must take to gain access to the New York market, in part because no winery has run the State's regulatory gauntlet. New York's argument, in any event, is unconvincing. . . .

We have no difficulty concluding that New York, like Michigan, discriminates against interstate commerce through its direct-shipping laws.

III

State laws that discriminate against interstate commerce face "a virtually *per se* rule of invalidity." *Philadelphia v. New Jersey*, 437 U.S. 617 (1978). The Michigan and New York laws by their own terms violate this proscription. The two States, however, contend their statutes are saved by § 2 of the Twenty-first Amendment, which provides: "The transportation or importation into any State, Territory, or possession of the United States for delivery or use therein of intoxicating liquors, in violation of the laws thereof, is hereby prohibited."

The States' position is inconsistent with our precedents and with the Twenty-first Amendment's history. Section 2 does not allow States to regulate the direct shipment of wine on terms that discriminate in favor of in-state producers.

A

[Kennedy reviews the events leading up to the adoption of the Eighteenth Amendment, providing for national alcoholic prohibition.]

B

The ratification of the Eighteenth Amendment in 1919 provided a brief respite from the legal battles over the validity of state liquor regulations. With the ratification of the Twenty-first Amendment 14 years later, however, nationwide Prohibition came to an end. Section 1 of the Twenty-first Amendment repealed the Eighteenth Amendment. Section 2 of the Twenty-first Amendment is at issue here.

Michigan and New York say the provision grants to the States the authority to discriminate against out-of-state goods. The history we have recited does not support this position. To the contrary, it provides strong support for the view that § 2 restored to the States the powers they had under the Wilson and Webb-Kenyon Acts. "The wording of § 2 of the Twenty-first Amendment closely follows the Webb-Kenyon and Wilson Acts, expressing the framers' clear intention of constitutionalizing the Commerce Clause framework established under those statutes." *Craig v. Boren,* 429 U.S. 190 (1976).

The aim of the Twenty-first Amendment was to allow States to maintain an effective and uniform system for controlling liquor by regulating its transportation, importation, and use. The Amendment did not give States the authority to pass nonuniform laws in order to discriminate against out-of-state goods, a privilege they had not enjoyed at any earlier time.

[Kennedy examines precedents in this area.]

Our more recent cases, furthermore, confirm that the Twenty-first Amendment does not supersede other provisions of the Constitution and, in particular, does not displace the rule that States may not give a discriminatory preference to their own producers. . . .

IV

[Kennedy argues that state regulations are not needed either to deter underage drinking or to prevent tax evasion.]

V

States have broad power to regulate liquor under § 2 of the Twenty-first Amendment. This power, however, does not allow States to ban, or severely limit, the direct shipment of out-of-state wine while simultaneously authorizing direct shipment by in-state producers. If a State chooses to allow direct shipment of wine, it must do so on evenhanded terms. Without demonstrating the need for discrimination, New York and Michigan have enacted regulations that disadvantage out-of-state wine producers. Under our Commerce Clause jurisprudence, these regulations cannot stand.

JUSTICE STEVENS, with whom JUSTICE O'CONNOR joins, dissenting.

Congress' power to regulate commerce among the States includes the power to authorize the States to place burdens on interstate commerce. . . . Absent such congressional approval, a state law may violate the unwritten rules described as the "dormant Commerce Clause" either by imposing an undue burden on both out-of-state and local producers engaged in interstate activities or by treating out-of-state producers less favorably than their local competitors. . . . A state law totally prohibiting the sale of an ordinary article of commerce might impose an even more serious burden on interstate commerce. If Congress may nevertheless authorize the States to enact such laws, surely the people may do so through the process of amending our Constitution.

The New York and Michigan laws challenged in these cases would be patently invalid under well settled dormant Commerce Clause principles if they regulated sales of an ordinary article of commerce rather than wine. But ever since the adoption of the Eighteenth Amendment and the Twenty-first Amendment, our Constitution has placed commerce in alcoholic beverages in a special category. Section 2 of the Twenty-first Amendment expressly provides that "[t]he transportation or importation into any State, Territory, or possession of the United States for delivery or use therein of intoxicating liquors, in violation of the laws thereof, is hereby prohibited."

Today many Americans, particularly those members of the younger generations who make policy decisions, regard alcohol as an ordinary article of commerce, subject to substantially the same market and legal controls as other consumer products. That was definitely not the view of the generations that made policy in 1919 when the Eighteenth Amendment was ratified or in 1933 when it was repealed by the Twenty-first Amendment. On the contrary, the moral condemnation of the use of alcohol as a beverage represented not merely the convictions of our religious leaders, but the views of a sufficiently large majority of the population to warrant the rare exercise of the power to amend the Constitution on two occasions. The Eighteenth Amendment entirely prohibited commerce in "intoxicating liquors" for beverage purposes throughout the United States and the territories subject to its jurisdiction. While § 1 of the Twenty-first Amendment repealed the nationwide prohibition, § 2 gave the States the option to maintain equally comprehensive prohibitions in their respective jurisdictions. . . .

JUSTICE THOMAS, with whom THE CHIEF JUSTICE, JUSTICE STEVENS and JUSTICE O'CONNOR join, dissenting.

[This opinion chiefly focused on arguments from the Twenty-first Amendment.]

FOR DISCUSSION

Does this decision indicate that all state regulation of interstate winery sales are illegal, or only those that are different from intrastate regulations? If this decision were to result in a discernable increase in juvenile access to wine, do you think the Court might be willing to reconsider its decision?

GONZALEZ V. RAICH

545 U.S. 1, 125 S. Ct. 2195, 162 L. Ed. 2d 1 (2005)

The federal government has long been involved in a "war" on illegal drugs. This case involves another clash between congressional powers under the Commerce Clause and state police powers—in this case, relative to medical uses of marijuana.

Vote: 6–3

JUSTICE STEVENS delivered the opinion of the Court.

California is one of at least nine States that authorize the use of marijuana for medicinal purposes. The question presented in this case is whether the power vested in Congress by Article I, § 8, of the Constitution "[t]o make all Laws which shall be necessary and proper for carrying into Execution" its authority to "regulate Commerce with foreign Nations, and among the several States" includes the power to prohibit the local cultivation and use of marijuana in compliance with California law.

I

California has been a pioneer in the regulation of marijuana. In 1913, California was one of the first States to prohibit the sale and possession of marijuana, and at the end of the century, California became the first State to authorize limited use of the drug for medicinal purposes. In 1996, California voters passed Proposition 215, now codified as the Compassionate Use Act of 1996. The proposition was designed to ensure that "seriously ill" residents of the State have access to marijuana for medical purposes, and to encourage Federal and State Governments to take steps towards ensuring the safe and affordable distribution of the drug to patients in need. The Act creates an exemption from criminal prosecution for physicians, as well as for patients and primary caregivers who possess or cultivate marijuana for medicinal purposes with the recommendation or approval of a physician. A "primary caregiver" is a person who has consistently assumed responsibility for the housing, health, or safety of the patient.

Respondents Angel Raich and Diane Monson are California residents who suffer from a variety of serious medical conditions and have sought to avail themselves of medical marijuana pursuant to the terms of the Compassionate Use Act. They are being treated by licensed, board-certified family practitioners, who have concluded, after prescribing a host of conventional medicines to treat respondents' conditions and to alleviate their associated symptoms, that marijuana is the only drug available that provides effective treatment. Both women have been using marijuana as a medication for several years pursuant to their doctors' recommendation, and both rely heavily on cannabis to function on a daily basis. Indeed, Raich's physician believes that forgoing cannabis treatments would certainly cause Raich excruciating pain and could very well prove fatal.

Respondent Monson cultivates her own marijuana, and ingests the drug in a variety of ways including smoking and using a vaporizer. Respondent Raich, by contrast, is unable to cultivate her own, and thus relies on two caregivers, litigating as "John Does," to provide her with locally grown marijuana at no charge. These caregivers also process the cannabis into hashish or keif, and Raich herself processes some of the marijuana into oils, balms, and foods for consumption.

On August 15, 2002, county deputy sheriffs and agents from the federal Drug Enforcement Administration (DEA) came to Monson's home. After a thorough investigation, the county officials concluded that her use of marijuana was entirely lawful as a matter of California law. Nevertheless, after a 3-hour standoff, the federal agents seized and destroyed all six of her cannabis plants.

Respondents thereafter brought this action against the Attorney General of the United States and the head of the DEA seeking injunctive and declaratory relief prohibiting the enforcement of the federal Controlled Substances Act (CSA), to the extent it prevents them from possessing, obtaining, or manufacturing cannabis for their personal medical use. In their complaint and supporting affidavits, Raich and Monson described the severity of their afflictions, their repeatedly futile attempts to obtain relief with conventional medications, and the opinions of their doctors concerning their need to use marijuana. Respondents claimed that enforcing the CSA against them would violate the Commerce Clause, the Due Process Clause of the Fifth Amendment, the Ninth and Tenth Amendments of the Constitution, and the doctrine of medical necessity.

The District Court denied respondents' motion for a preliminary injunction. . . . Although the court found that the federal enforcement interests "wane[d]" when compared to the harm that California residents would suffer if denied access to medically necessary marijuana, it concluded that respondents could not demonstrate a likelihood of success on the merits of their legal claims.

A divided panel of the Court of Appeals for the Ninth Circuit reversed and ordered the District Court to enter a preliminary injunction. . . . The court found that respondents had "demonstrated a strong likelihood of success on their claim that, as applied to them, the CSA is an unconstitutional exercise of Congress' Commerce Clause authority." The Court of Appeals distinguished prior Circuit cases upholding the CSA in the face of Commerce Clause challenges by focusing on what it deemed to be the "*separate and distinct class of activities*" at issue in this case: "the intrastate, noncommercial cultivation and possession of cannabis for personal medical purposes as recommended by a patient's physician pursuant to valid California state law." The court found the latter class of activities "different in kind from drug trafficking" because interposing a physician's recommendation raises different health and safety concerns, and because "this limited use is clearly distinct from the broader illicit drug market—as well as any broader commercial market for medicinal marijuana—insofar as the medicinal marijuana at issue in this case is not intended for, nor does it enter, the stream of commerce."

The majority placed heavy reliance on our decisions in *United States v. Lopez,* 514 U.S. 549 (1995), and *United States v. Morrison,* 529 U.S. 598 (2000), as interpreted by recent Circuit precedent, to hold that this separate class of purely local activities was beyond the reach of federal power. In contrast, the dissenting judge concluded that the CSA, as applied to respondents, was clearly valid under *Lopez* and *Morrison;* moreover, he thought it "simply impossible to distinguish the relevant conduct surrounding the cultivation and use of the marijuana crop at issue in this case from the cultivation and use of the wheat crop that affected interstate commerce in *Wickard* v. *Filburn,* 317 U.S. 111 (1942)." . . .

The obvious importance of the case prompted our grant of certiorari. The case is made difficult by respondents' strong arguments that they will suffer irreparable harm because, despite a congressional finding to the contrary, marijuana does have valid therapeutic purposes. The question before us, however, is not whether it is wise to enforce the statute in these circumstances; rather, it is whether Congress' power to regulate interstate markets for medicinal substances encompasses the portions of those markets that are supplied with drugs produced and consumed locally. Well-settled law controls our answer. The CSA is a valid exercise of federal power, even as applied to the troubling facts of this case. We accordingly vacate the judgment of the Court of Appeals.

II

[Stevens reviews the history of drug laws in the U.S.]

III

Respondents in this case do not dispute that passage of the CSA, as part of the Comprehensive Drug Abuse Prevention and Control Act, was well within Congress' commerce power. Nor do they contend that any provision or section of the CSA amounts to an unconstitutional exercise of congressional authority. Rather, respondents' challenge is actually quite limited; they argue that the CSA's categorical prohibition of the manufacture and possession of marijuana as applied to the intrastate manufacture and possession of marijuana for medical purposes pursuant to California law exceeds Congress' authority under the Commerce Clause.

In assessing the validity of congressional regulation, none of our Commerce Clause cases can be viewed in isolation. As charted in considerable detail in *United States* v. *Lopez*, our understanding of the reach of the Commerce Clause, as well as Congress' assertion of authority thereunder, has evolved over time. The Commerce Clause emerged as the Framers' response to the central problem giving rise to the Constitution itself: the absence of any federal commerce power under the Articles of Confederation. For the first century of our history, the primary use of the Clause was to preclude the kind of discriminatory state legislation that had once been permissible. Then, in response to rapid industrial development and an increasingly interdependent national economy, Congress "ushered in a new era of federal regulation under the commerce power," beginning with the enactment of the Interstate Commerce Act in 1887, 24 Stat. 379, and the Sherman Antitrust Act in 1890, as amended.

Cases decided during that "new era," which now spans more than a century, have identified three general categories of regulation in which Congress is authorized to engage under its commerce power. First, Congress can regulate the channels of interstate commerce. *Perez v. United States,* 402 U.S. 146 (1971). Second, Congress has authority to regulate and protect the instrumentalities of interstate commerce, and persons or things in interstate commerce. Third, Congress has the power to regulate activities that substantially affect interstate commerce. Only the third category is implicated in the case at hand. . . .

The similarities between this case and *Wickard* are striking. Like the farmer in *Wickard*, respondents are cultivating, for home consumption, a fungible commodity for which there is an established, albeit illegal, interstate market. Just as the Agricultural Adjustment Act was designed "to control the volume [of wheat] moving in interstate and foreign commerce in order to avoid surpluses . . ." and consequently control the market price, a primary purpose of the CSA is to control the supply and demand of controlled substances in both lawful and unlawful drug markets. In *Wickard*, we had no difficulty concluding that Congress had a rational basis for believing that, when viewed in the aggregate, leaving home-consumed wheat outside the regulatory scheme would have a substantial influence on price and market conditions. Here too, Congress had a rational basis for concluding that leaving home-consumed marijuana outside federal control would similarly affect price and market conditions.

More concretely, one concern prompting inclusion of wheat grown for home consumption in the 1938 Act was that rising market prices could draw such wheat into the interstate market, resulting in lower market prices. The parallel concern making it appropriate to include marijuana grown for home consumption in the CSA is the likelihood that the high demand in the interstate market will draw such marijuana into that market. While the diversion of homegrown wheat tended to frustrate the federal interest in stabilizing prices by regulating the volume of commercial transactions in the interstate market, the diversion of homegrown marijuana tends to frustrate the federal interest in eliminating commercial transactions in the interstate market in their entirety. In both cases, the regulation is squarely within Congress' commerce power because production of the commodity meant for home consumption, be it wheat or marijuana, has a substantial effect on supply and demand in the national market for that commodity. . . .

IV

To support their contrary submission, respondents rely heavily on two of our more recent Commerce Clause cases. In their myopic focus, they overlook the larger context of modern-era Commerce Clause jurisprudence preserved by those cases. Moreover, even in the narrow prism of respondents' creation, they read those cases far too broadly.

Those two cases, of course, are *Lopez* and [*United States v. Morrison*, 529 U.S. 598 (2000)]. As an initial matter, the statutory challenges at issue in those cases were markedly different from the challenge respondents pursue in the case at hand. Here, respondents ask us to excise individual applications of a concededly valid statutory scheme. In contrast, in both *Lopez* and *Morrison*, the parties asserted that a particular statute or provision fell outside Congress' commerce power in its entirety. This distinction is pivotal for we have often reiterated that "[w]here the class of activities is regulated and that class is within the reach of federal power, the courts have no power 'to excise, as trivial, individual instances' of the class." . . . .

Unlike those at issue in *Lopez* and *Morrison*, the activities regulated by the CSA are quintessentially economic. "Economics" refers to "the production, distribution, and consumption of commodities." *Webster's Third New International Dictionary* 720 (1966). The CSA is a statute that regulates the production, distribution, and consumption of commodities for which there is an established, and lucrative, interstate market. Prohibiting the intrastate possession or manufacture of an article of commerce is a rational (and commonly utilized) means of regulating commerce in that product. Such prohibitions include specific decisions requiring that a drug be withdrawn from the market as a result of the failure to comply with regulatory requirements as well as decisions excluding Schedule I drugs entirely from the market. Because the CSA is a statute that directly regulates economic, commercial activity, our opinion in *Morrison* casts no doubt on its constitutionality. . . .

First, the fact that marijuana is used "for personal medical purposes on the advice of a physician" cannot itself serve as a distinguishing factor. The CSA designates marijuana as contraband for *any* purpose; in fact, by characterizing marijuana as a Schedule I drug, Congress expressly found that the drug has no acceptable medical uses. Moreover, the CSA is a comprehensive regulatory regime specifically designed to regulate which controlled substances can be utilized for medicinal purposes, and in what manner. Indeed, most of the substances classified in the CSA "have a useful and legitimate medical purpose." . . .

Second, limiting the activity to marijuana possession and cultivation "in accordance with state law" cannot serve to place respondents' activities beyond congressional reach. The Supremacy Clause unambiguously provides that if there is any conflict between federal and state law, federal law shall prevail. It is beyond peradventure that federal power over commerce is " 'superior to that of the States to provide for the welfare or necessities of their inhabitants,' " however legitimate or dire those necessities may be.

Respondents acknowledge this proposition, but nonetheless contend that their activities were not "an essential part of a larger regulatory scheme" because they had been "isolated by the State of California, and [are] policed by the State of California," and thus remain "entirely separated from the market." The dissenters fall prey to similar reasoning. The notion that California law has surgically excised a discrete activity that is hermetically sealed off from the larger interstate marijuana market is a dubious proposition, and, more importantly, one that Congress could have rationally rejected. . . .

JUSTICE SCALIA, concurring in the judgment.

I agree with the Court's holding that the Controlled Substances Act (CSA) may validly be applied to respondents' cultivation, distribution, and possession of marijuana for personal, medicinal use. I write separately because my understanding of the doctrinal foundation on which that holding rests is, if not inconsistent with that of the Court, at least more nuanced.

Since *Perez* v. *United States* [22 U.S. 579] (1971), our cases have mechanically recited that the Commerce Clause permits congressional regulation of three categories: (1) the channels of interstate commerce; (2) the instrumentalities of interstate commerce, and persons or things in interstate commerce; and (3) activities that "substantially affect" interstate commerce. . . . The first two categories are self-evident, since they are the ingredients of interstate commerce itself. See *Gibbons* v. *Ogden* [22 U.S. 1] (1824). The third category, however, is different in kind, and its recitation without explanation is misleading and incomplete.

It is *misleading* because, unlike the channels, instrumentalities, and agents of interstate commerce, activities that substantially affect interstate commerce are not themselves part of interstate commerce, and thus the power to regulate them cannot come from the Commerce Clause alone. Rather, as this Court has acknowledged since at least *United States v. Coombs,* 37 U.S. 72 (1838), Congress's regulatory authority over intrastate activities that are not themselves part of interstate commerce (including activities that have a substantial effect on interstate commerce) derives from the Necessary and Proper Clause. And the category of "activities that substantially affect interstate commerce," *Lopez,* is *incomplete* because the authority to enact laws necessary and proper for the regulation of interstate commerce is not limited to laws governing intrastate activities that substantially affect interstate commerce. Where necessary to make a regulation of interstate commerce effective, Congress may regulate even those intrastate activities that do not themselves substantially affect interstate commerce. . . .

JUSTICE O'CONNOR with whom the CHIEF JUSTICE and JUSTICE THOMAS join as to all but Part III, dissenting.

We enforce the "outer limits" of Congress' Commerce Clause authority not for their own sake, but to protect historic spheres of state sovereignty from excessive federal encroachment and thereby to maintain the distribution of power fundamental to our federalist system of government. *United States* v. *Lopez* (1995); *NLRB* v. *Jones & Laughlin Steel Corp.* (1937). One of federalism's chief virtues, of course, is that it promotes innovation by allowing for the possibility that "a single courageous State may, if its citizens choose, serve as a laboratory; and try novel social and economic experiments without risk to the rest of the country." *New State Ice Co.* v. *Liebmann*, 285 U.S. 262 (1932).

This case exemplifies the role of States as laboratories. The States' core police powers have always included authority to define criminal law and to protect the health, safety, and welfare of their citizens. . . . Exercising those powers, California (by ballot initiative and then by legislative codification) has come to its own conclusion about the difficult and sensitive question of whether marijuana should be available to relieve severe pain and suffering. Today the Court sanctions an application of the federal Controlled Substances Act that extinguishes that experiment, without any proof that the personal cultivation, possession, and use of marijuana for medicinal purposes, if economic activity in the first place, has a substantial effect on interstate commerce and is therefore an appropriate subject of federal regulation. In so doing, the Court announces a rule that gives Congress a perverse incentive to legislate broadly pursuant to the Commerce Clause—nestling questionable assertions of its authority into comprehensive regulatory schemes—rather than with precision. That rule and the result it produces in this case are irreconcilable with our decisions in *Lopez,* and *United States v. Morrison* (2000). Accordingly I dissent.

I

[O'Connor examines the decisions in *U.S. v. Lopez* and *U.S. v. Morrison.*]

II

A

What is the relevant conduct subject to Commerce Clause analysis in this case? The Court takes its cues from Congress, applying the above considerations to the activity regulated by the Controlled Substances Act (CSA) in general. The Court's decision rests on two facts about the CSA: (1) Congress chose to enact a single statute providing a comprehensive prohibition on the production, distribution, and possession of all controlled substances, and (2) Congress did not distinguish between various forms of intrastate noncommercial cultivation, possession, and use of marijuana. Today's decision suggests that the federal regulation of local activity is immune to Commerce Clause challenge because Congress chose to act with an ambitious, all-encompassing statute, rather than piecemeal. In my view, allowing Congress to set the terms of the constitutional debate in this way, *i.e.*, by packaging regulation of local activity in broader schemes, is tantamount to removing meaningful limits on the Commerce Clause.

B

Having thus defined the relevant conduct, we must determine whether, under our precedents, the conduct is economic and, in the aggregate, substantially affects interstate commerce. Even if intrastate cultivation and possession of marijuana for one's own medicinal use can properly be characterized as economic, and I question whether it can, it has not been shown that such activity substantially affects interstate commerce. Similarly, it is neither self-evident nor demonstrated that regulating such activity is necessary to the interstate drug control scheme.

The Court's definition of economic activity is breathtaking. It defines as economic any activity involving the production, distribution, and consumption of commodities. And it appears to reason that when an interstate market for a commodity exists, regulating the intrastate manufacture or possession of that commodity is constitutional either because that intrastate activity is itself economic, or because regulating it is a rational part of regulating its market. Putting to one side the problem endemic to the Court's opinion—the shift in focus from the activity at issue in this case to the entirety of what the CSA regulates, see *Lopez*, ("depending on the level of generality, any activity can be looked upon as commercial")—the Court's definition of economic activity for purposes of Commerce Clause jurisprudence threatens to sweep all of productive human activity into federal regulatory reach.

The Court uses a dictionary definition of economics to skirt the real problem of drawing a meaningful line between "what is national and what is local," *Jones & Laughlin Steel.* It will not do to say that Congress may regulate noncommercial activity simply because it may have an effect on the demand for commercial goods, or because the noncommercial endeavor can, in some sense, substitute for commercial activity. Most commercial goods or services have some sort of privately producible analogue. Home care substitutes for daycare. Charades games substitute for movie tickets. Backyard or windowsill gardening substitutes for going to the supermarket. To draw the line wherever private activity affects the demand for market goods is to draw no line at all, and to declare everything economic. We have already rejected the result that would follow—a federal police power. . . .

There is simply no evidence that homegrown medicinal marijuana users constitute, in the aggregate, a sizable enough class to have a discernable, let alone substantial, impact on the national illicit drug market—or otherwise to threaten the CSA regime. Explicit evidence is helpful when substantial effect is not "visible to the naked eye." See *Lopez*. And here, in part because common sense suggests that medical marijuana users may be limited in number and that California's Compassionate Use Act and similar state legislation may well isolate activities relating to medicinal marijuana from the illicit market, the effect of those activities on interstate drug traffic is not self-evidently substantial.

In this regard, again, this case is readily distinguishable from *Wickard.* To decide whether the Secretary could regulate local wheat farming, the Court looked to "the actual effects of the activity in question upon interstate commerce." Critically, the Court was able to consider "actual effects" because the parties had "stipulated a summary of the economics of the wheat industry." After reviewing in detail the picture of the industry provided in that summary, the Court explained that consumption of homegrown wheat was the most variable factor in the size of the national wheat crop, and that on-site consumption could have the effect of varying the amount of wheat sent to market by as much as 20 percent. With real numbers at hand, the *Wickard* Court could easily conclude that "a factor of such volume and variability as home-consumed wheat would have a substantial influence on price and market conditions" nationwide.

The Court recognizes that "the record in the *Wickard* case itself established the causal connection between the production for local use and the national market" and argues that "we have before us findings by Congress *to the same effect.*" The Court refers to a series of declarations in the introduction to the CSA saying that (1) local distribution and possession of controlled substances causes "swelling" in interstate traffic; (2) local production and distribution cannot be distinguished from interstate production and distribution; (3) federal control over intrastate incidents "is essential to effective control" over interstate drug trafficking. These bare declarations cannot be compared to the record before the Court in *Wickard.*

They amount to nothing more than a legislative insistence that the regulation of controlled substances must be absolute. They are asserted without any supporting evidence—descriptive, statistical, or otherwise. "[S]imply because Congress may conclude a particular activity substantially affects interstate commerce does not necessarily make it so." . . .

III

We would do well to recall how James Madison, the father of the Constitution, described our system of joint sovereignty to the people of New York: "The powers delegated by the proposed constitution to the federal government are few and defined. Those which are to remain in the State governments are numerous and indefinite. . . . The powers reserved to the several States will extend to all the objects which, in the ordinary course of affairs, concern the lives, liberties, and properties of the people, and the internal order, improvement, and prosperity of the State." *The Federalist* No. 45.

Relying on Congress' abstract assertions, the Court has endorsed making it a federal crime to grow small amounts of marijuana in one's own home for one's own medicinal use. This overreaching stifles an express choice by some States, concerned for the lives and liberties of their people, to regulate medical marijuana differently. If I were a California citizen, I would not have voted for the medical marijuana ballot initiative; if I were a California legislator I would not have supported the Compassionate Use Act. But whatever the wisdom of California's experiment with medical marijuana, the federalism principles that have driven our Commerce Clause cases require that room for experiment be protected in this case. For these reasons I dissent.

JUSTICE THOMAS, dissenting.

Respondents Diane Monson and Angel Raich use marijuana that has never been bought or sold, that has never crossed state lines, and that has had no demonstrable effect on the national market for marijuana. If Congress can regulate this under the Commerce Clause, then it can regulate virtually anything—and the Federal Government is no longer one of limited and enumerated powers.

I

Respondents' local cultivation and consumption of marijuana is not "Commerce . . . among the several States." By holding that Congress may regulate activity that is neither interstate nor commerce under the Interstate Commerce Clause, the Court abandons any attempt to enforce the Constitution's limits on federal power. The majority supports this conclusion by invoking, without explanation, the Necessary and Proper Clause. Regulating respondents' conduct, however, is not "necessary and proper for carrying into Execution" Congress' restrictions on the interstate drug trade. Thus, neither the Commerce Clause nor the Necessary and Proper Clause grants Congress the power to regulate respondents' conduct.

FOR DISCUSSION

By this point in the chapter, it should be clear that exercises of congressional powers under the commerce clause must often be balanced against powers that are reserved to the states. Conservatives often favor states rights and strict laws against drug use, whereas liberals more often favor state powers and more liberal drug laws. How did the justices resolve the issue in the case above? Which value dominated?

BAILEY V. DREXEL FURNITURE CO. (THE CHILD LABOR TAX CASE)

259 U.S. 20, 42 S.Ct. 449, 66 L.Ed. 817 (1922)

In 1919 Congress passed the Child Labor Tax Law. This required employers of children under the age of fourteen to pay a tax of 10 percent of their net profits. Here Drexel Furniture Co. had employed a boy under the statutory age of fourteen, and Bailey, Collector of Internal Revenue, collected the tax, the company paying under protest. The company challenged the act as an invasion of state powers rather than a proper exercise of federal taxing power.

Vote: 8–1

CHIEF JUSTICE TAFT delivered the opinion of the Court.

. . . The amount is not to be proportioned in any degree to the extent or frequency of the departures, but is to be paid by the employer in full measure whether he employs five hundred children for a year, or employs only one for a day. Moreover, if he does not know the child is within the named age limit, he is not to pay; that is to say, it is only where he knowingly departs from the prescribed course that payment is to be exacted. *Scienter* [*mens rea* or guilty knowledge that makes the person liable for their action] is associated with penalties, not with taxes. The employer's factory is to be subject to inspection at any time not only by the taxing officers of the Treasury, the Department normally charged with the collection of taxes, but also by the Secretary of Labor and his subordinates, whose normal function is the advancement and protection of the welfare of the workers. In the light of these features of the act, a court must be blind not to see that the so-called tax is imposed to stop the employment of children within the age limits prescribed. Its prohibitory and regulatory effect and purpose are palpable. All others can see and understand this. How can we properly shut our minds to it?

It is the high duty and function of this Court in cases regularly brought to its bar to decline to recognize or enforce seeming laws of Congress, dealing with subjects not intrusted to Congress, but left or committed by the supreme law of the land to the control of the States. We cannot avoid the duty even though it require us to refuse to give effect to legislation designed to promote the highest good. The good sought in unconstitutional legislation is an insidious feature because it leads citizens and legislators of good purpose to promote it without thought of the serious breach it will make in the ark of our covenant or the harm which will come from breaking down recognized standards. In the maintenance of local self-government, on the one hand, and the national power, on the other, our country has been able to endure and prosper for near a century and a half.

Out of a proper respect for the acts of a coordinate branch of the Government, this Court has gone far to sustain taxing acts as such, even though there has been ground for suspecting, from the weight of the tax, it was intended to destroy its subject. But in the act before us, the presumption of validity cannot prevail, because the proof of the contrary is found on the very face of its provisions. Grant the validity of this law, and all that Congress would need to do hereafter, in seeking to take over to its control anyone of the great number of subjects of public interest, jurisdiction of which the States have never parted with, and which are reserved to them by the Tenth Amendment, would be to enact a detailed measure of complete regulation of the subject and enforce it by a so-called tax upon departures from it. To give such magic to the word "tax" would be to break down all constitutional limitation of the powers of Congress and completely wipe out the sovereignty of the States.

The difference between a tax and a penalty is sometimes difficult to define, and yet the consequences of the distinction in the required method of their collection often are important. Where the sovereign enacting the law has power to impose both tax and penalty, the difference between revenue production and mere regulation may be immaterial; but not so when one sovereign can impose a tax only, and the power of regulation rests in another. Taxes are occasionally imposed in the discretion of the legislature on proper subjects with the primary motive of obtaining revenue from them, and with the incidental motive of discouraging them by making their continuance onerous. They do not lose their character as taxes because of the incidental motive. But there comes a time in the extension of the penalizing features of the so-called tax when it loses its character as such and becomes a mere penalty, with the characteristics of regulation and punishment. Such is the case in the law before us. Although Congress does not invalidate the contract of employment, or expressly declare that the employment within the mentioned ages is illegal, it does exhibit its intent practically to achieve the latter result by adopting the criteria of wrongdoing and imposing its principal consequence on those who transgress its standard.

The case before us cannot be distinguished from that of *Hammer v. Dagenhart.* Justice Clarke's dissenting opinion is not reported.

FOR DISCUSSION

In this case the Court attempts to distinguish a tax that is used to raise money from one that is designed to penalize individuals for behavior that the government seeks to discourage. Is this distinction viable? Is it advisable for the Court to be examining congressional motives of tax legislation? If the Court had permitted the tax in this case, would it also have had to overrule *Hammer v. Dagenhart*?

UNITED STATES V. BUTLER (FIRST AAA CASE)

297 U.S. 1, 56 S.Ct. 312, 80 L.Ed. 477 (1936)

Butler was one of the receivers for the Hoosac Mills Corporation, defendant in a suit for processing and floor stock taxes under the Agricultural Adjustment Act of 1933. These taxes were levied and earmarked for the payment of crop reduction benefits on cotton. The processing tax was levied on the first domestic processing of a commodity, while the floor tax was on stocks on land and was to be equivalent to the processing tax had it been in effect earlier. The attempted regulation of agricultural production through the use of the taxing power was challenged.

Vote: 6–3

JUSTICE ROBERTS delivered the opinion of the Court.

. . . The tax can only be sustained by ignoring the avowed purpose and operation of the act, and holding it a measure merely laying an excise upon processors to raise revenue for the support of government. Beyond cavil the sole object of the legislation is to restore the purchasing power of agricultural products to a parity with that prevailing in an earlier day; to take money from the processor and bestow it upon farmers who will reduce their acreage for the accomplishment of the proposed end, and, meanwhile, to aid these farmers during the period required to bring the prices of their crops to the desired level.

The tax plays an indispensable part in the plan of regulation. As stated by the Agricultural Adjustment Administrator, it is "The heart of the law"; a means of "accomplishing one or both of two things intended to help farmers attain parity prices and purchasing power." A tax automatically goes into effect for a commodity when the Secretary of Agriculture determines that rental or benefit payments are to be made for reduction of production of that commodity. The tax is to cease when rental or benefit payments cease. The rate is fixed with the purpose of bringing about crop-reduction and price-raising. It is to equal the difference between the "current average farm price" and "fair exchange value." It may be altered to such amount as will prevent accumulation of surplus stocks. If the Secretary finds the policy of the act will not be promoted by the levy of the tax for a given commodity, he may exempt it. (Section Two.) The whole revenue from the levy is appropriated in aid of crop control; none of it is made available for general governmental use. . . .

The statute not only avows an aim foreign to the procurement of revenue for the support of government, but by its operation shows the exaction laid upon processors to be the necessary means for the intended control of agricultural production. . . .

It is inaccurate and misleading to speak of the exaction from processors prescribed by the challenged act as a tax, or to say that as a tax it is subject to no infirmity. A tax, in the general understanding of the term, and as used in the Constitution, signifies an exaction for the support of the Government. The word has never been thought to connote the expropriation of money from one group for the benefit of another. . . .

We conclude that the act is one regulating agricultural production; that the tax is a mere incident of such regulation; and that the respondents have standing to challenge the legality of the exaction. . . .

The clause thought to authorize the legislation, the first, confers upon the Congress power "to lay and collect Taxes, Duties, Imports and Excises, to pay the Debts and provide for the common Defence and general Welfare of the United States. . . ." It is not contended that this provision grants power to regulate agricultural production upon the theory that such legislation would promote the general welfare. The Government concedes that the phrase "to provide for the general welfare" qualifies the power "to lay and collect taxes." The view that the clause grants power to provide for the general welfare, independently of the taxing power, has never been authoritatively accepted. Mr. Justice Story points out that, if it were adopted, "it is obvious that under color of the generality of the words, to 'provide for the common defence and general welfare,' the government of the United States is, in reality, a government of general and unlimited powers, notwithstanding the subsequent enumeration of specific powers." The true construction undoubtedly is that the only thing granted is the power to tax for the purpose of providing funds for payment of the nation's debts and making provision for the general welfare.

Nevertheless, the Government asserts that warrant is found in this clause for the adoption of the Agricultural Adjustment Act. The argument is that Congress may appropriate and authorize the spending of moneys for the "general welfare"; that the phrase should be liberally construed to cover anything conducive to national welfare; that the decision as to what will promote such welfare rests with Congress alone, and the courts may not review its determination; and, finally, that the appropriation under attack was in fact for the general welfare of the United States. . . .

We are not now required to ascertain the scope of the phrase "general welfare of the United States" or to determine whether an appropriation in and of agriculture falls within it. Wholly apart from that question, another principle embedded in our Constitution prohibits the enforcement of the Agricultural Adjustment Act. The act invades the reserved rights of the states. It is a statutory plan to regulate and control agricultural production, a matter beyond the powers delegated to the federal government. The tax, the appropriation of the funds raised, and the direction for their disbursement, are but parts of the plan. They are but means to an unconstitutional end. . . .

Congress has no power to enforce its commands on the farmer to the ends sought by the Agricultural Adjustment Act. It must follow that it may not indirectly accomplish those ends by taxing and spending to purchase compliance. The Constitution and the entire plan of our government is negative as to any such use of the power to tax and to spend as the act undertakes to authorize. It does not help to declare that local conditions throughout the nation have created a situation of national concern; for this is but to say that whenever there is a widespread similarity of local conditions, Congress may ignore constitutional limitations upon its own powers and usurp those reserved to the states. If, in lieu of compulsory regulation of subjects within the states' reserved jurisdiction, which is prohibited, the Congress could invoke the taxing and spending power as a means to accomplish the same end, Clause 1 of Section 8 of Article One would become the instrument for total subversion of the governmental powers reserved to the individual states. . . .

Until recently no suggestion of the existence of any such power in the federal government has been advanced. The expressions of the framers of the Constitution, the decisions of this court interpreting that instrument and the writings of great commentators will be searched in vain for any suggestion that there exists in the clause under discussion or elsewhere in the Constitution, the authority whereby every provision and every fair implication from that instrument may be subverted, the independence of the individual states obliterated, and the United States converted into a central government exercising uncontrolled police power in every state of the Union, superseding all local control or regulation of the affairs or concerns of the states. . . .

The judgment is affirmed.

JUSTICE STONE dissented with the concurrence of JUSTICES BRANDEIS and CARDOZO.

I think the judgment should be reversed. . . . [The] pivot on which the decision of the Court is made to turn . . . is that a levy unquestionably within the taxing power of Congress may be treated as invalid because it is a step in a plan to regulate agricultural production and is thus a forbidden infringement of state power. The levy is not any the less an exercise of taxing power because it is intended to defray an expenditure for the general welfare rather than for some other support of government. Nor is the levy and collection of the tax pointed to as affecting the regulation. While all federal taxes inevitably have some influence on the internal economy of the states, it is not contended that the levy of a processing tax upon manufacturers using agricultural products as raw materials has any perceptible regulatory effect upon either their production or manufacture. The tax is unlike the penalties which were held invalid . . . because they were themselves the instruments of regulation by virtue of their coercive effect on matters left to the control of the States. Here regulation, if any there be, is accomplished not by the tax, but by the method by which its proceeds are expended, and would equally be accomplished by any like use of public funds, regardless of their source. . . .

Such a limitation is contradictory and destructive of the power to appropriate for the public welfare, and is incapable of practical application. The spending power of Congress is in addition to the legislative power and not subordinate to it. This independent grant of the power of the purse, and its very nature, involving in its exercise the duty to insure expenditure within the granted power, presuppose freedom of selection among diverse ends and aims, and the capacity to impose such conditions as will render the choice effective. It is a contradiction in terms to say that there is power to spend for the national welfare, while rejecting any power to impose conditions reasonably adapted to the attainment of the end which alone would justify the expenditure. . . .

That the governmental power of the purse is a great one is not now for the first time announced. Every student of the history of government and economics is aware of its magnitude and of its existence in every civilized government. Both were well understood by the framers of the Constitution when they sanctioned the grant of the spending power to the federal government, and both were recognized by Hamilton and Story, whose views of the spending power as standing on a parity with the other powers specifically granted, have hitherto been generally accepted. . . . The power to tax and spend is not without constitutional restraints. . . . One restriction is that the purpose must be truly national. Another is that it may not be used to coerce action left to state control. Another is the conscience and patriotism of Congress and the Executive. . . .

STEWARD MACHINE CO. V. DAVIS (THE SOCIAL SECURITY ACT CASE)

301 U.S. 548, 57 S.Ct. 883, 81 L.Ed. 1279 (1937)

This was a suit against the Commissioner of Internal Revenue for recovery of a tax paid by the company in compliance with the terms of the Social Security Act. The funds collected from the payroll tax are used to assist the states in the carrying out of their unemployment compensation laws but are not earmarked in any way. The company challenged the constitutionality of the tax.

Vote: 5–4

JUSTICE CARDOZO delivered the opinion of the Court.

. . . The assault on the statute proceeds on an extended front. Its assailants take the ground that the tax is not an excise; that it is not uniform throughout the United States as excises are required to be; that its exceptions are so many and arbitrary as to violate the Fifth Amendment; that its purpose was not revenue, but an unlawful invasion of the reserved powers of the states; and that the states in submitting to it have yielded to coercion and have abandoned governmental functions which they are not permitted to surrender. . . .

In the presence of this urgent need for some remedial expedient, the question is to be answered whether the expedient adopted has overleapt the bounds of power. The assailants of the statute say that its dominant end and aim is to drive the state legislatures under the whip of economic pressure into the enactment of unemployment compensation laws at the bidding of the central government. Supporters of the statute say that its operation is not constraint, but the creation of a larger freedom, the states and the nation joining in a cooperative endeavor to avert a common evil. . . .

. . . Duplicated taxes, or burdens that approach them, are recognized hardships that government, state or national, may properly avoid. . . . If Congress believed that the general welfare would better be promoted by relief through local units than by the system then in vogue, the cooperating localities ought not in all fairness to pay a second time.

Who then is coerced through the operation of this statute? Not the taxpayer. He pays in fulfillment of the mandate of the local legislature. Not the state. Even now she does not offer a suggestion that in passing the unemployment laws she was affected by duress. . . . For all that appears she is satisfied with her choice, and would be sorely disappointed if it were now to be annulled. The difficulty with the petitioner's contention is that it confuses motive with coercion. "Every tax is in some measure regulatory. To some extent it interposes an economic impediment to the activity taxed as compared with others not taxed." . . . In like manner every rebate from a tax when conditioned upon conduct is in some measure a temptation. But to hold that motive or temptation is equivalent to coercion is to plunge the law in endless difficulties. The outcome of such a doctrine is the acceptance of a philosophical determinism by which choice becomes impossible. Till now the law has been guided by a robust common sense which assumes the freedom of the will as a working hypothesis in the solution of its problems. The wisdom of the hypothesis has illustration in this case. Nothing in the case suggests the exertion of a power akin to undue influence, if we assume that such a concept can ever be applied with fitness to the relations between state and nation. Even on that assumption the location of the point at which pressure turns into compulsion, and ceases to be inducement, would be a question of degree—at times, perhaps, of fact. The point had not been reached when Alabama made her choice. We cannot say that she was acting, not of her unfettered will, but under strain of a persuasion equivalent to undue influence, when she chose to have relief administered under laws of her own making, by agents of her own selection, instead of under federal laws, administered by federal officers, with all the ensuing evils at least to many minds, of federal patronage and power. There would be a strange irony, indeed, if her choice were now to be annulled on the basis of an assumed duress in the enactment of a statute which her courts have accepted as a true expression of her will. . . . We think the choice must stand.

In ruling as we do, we leave many questions open. We do not say that a tax is valid, when imposed by act of Congress, if it is laid upon the condition that a state may escape its operation through the adoption of a statute unrelated in subject matter to activities fairly within the scope of national policy and power. No such question is before us. In the tender of this credit Congress does not intrude upon fields foreign to its function. The purpose of its intervention, as we have shown, is to safeguard its own treasury and as an incident to that protection to place the states upon a footing of equal opportunity. Drains upon its own resources are to be checked; obstructions to the freedom of the states are to be leveled. It is one thing to impose a tax dependent upon the conduct of the taxpayers, or of the state in which they live, where the conduct to be stimulated or discouraged is unrelated to the fiscal need subserved by the tax in its normal operation, or to any other end legitimately national. . . . It is quite another thing to say that a tax will be abated upon the doing of an act that will satisfy the fiscal need, the tax and the alternative being approximate equivalents. In such circumstances, if in no others, inducement or persuasion does not go beyond the bounds of power. We do not fix the outermost line. Enough for present purposes that wherever the line may be, this statute is within it. Definition more precise must abide the wisdom of the future.

JUSTICE SUTHERLAND dissented in part, with the concurrence of JUSTICE VAN DEVANTER.

With most of what is said in the opinion just handed down, I concur. . . .

But the question with which I have difficulty is whether the administrative provisions of the act invade the governmental administrative powers of the several states reserved by the Tenth Amendment. A state may enter into contracts; but a state cannot, by contract or statute, surrender the execution, or a share in the execution, of any of its governmental powers either to a sister state or to the federal government, any more than the federal government can surrender the control of any of its governmental powers to a foreign nation. . . . Here, the state must deposit the proceeds of its taxation in the federal treasury, upon terms which make the deposit suspiciously like a forced loan to be repaid only in accordance with restrictions imposed by federal law. . . .

. . . The threat implicit in the present encroachment upon the administrative functions of the states is that greater encroachments, and encroachments upon other functions, will follow. . . .

JUSTICE MCREYNOLDS dissented:

. . . No defense is offered for the legislation under review upon the basis of emergency. The hypothesis is that hereafter it will continuously benefit unemployed members of a class. Forever, so far as we can see, the states are expected to function under federal direction concerning an internal matter. By the sanction of this adventure, the door is open for progressive inauguration of others of like kind under which it can hardly be expected that the states will retain genuine independence of action. And without independent states a Federal Union as contemplated by the Constitution becomes impossible. . . .

JUSTICE BUTLER dissented.

. . . I am also of the opinion that, in principle, and as applied to bring about and to gain control over state unemployment compensation, the statutory scheme is repugnant to the Tenth Amendment: . . .

. . . Obviously the Act creates the peril of federal tax not to raise revenue but to persuade. Of course, each state was free to reject any measure so proposed. But, if it failed to adopt a plan acceptable to federal authority, the full burden of the federal tax would be exacted. And, as federal demands similarly conditioned may be increased from time to time as Congress shall determine, possible federal pressure in that field is without limit. Already at least forty-three states, yielding to the inducement resulting immediately from the application of the federal tax and credit device, have provided for unemployment compensation in form to merit approval of the Social Security Board. Presumably the remaining states will comply whenever convenient for their legislatures to pass the necessary laws.

The terms of the measure make it clear that the tax and credit device was intended to enable federal officers virtually to control the exertion of powers of the state in a field in which they alone have jurisdiction and from which the United States is by the Constitution excluded.

I am of opinion that the judgment of the Circuit Court of Appeals should be reversed.

RELATED CASES

***Carmichael v. Southern Coal and Coke Co.:* 301 U.S. 495 (1937).**

Here Alabama's Unemployment Compensation Act was held valid even though not all employees were covered by the Act. "When public evils ensue from individual misfortunes or needs, the legislature may strike at the evil at its source. If the purpose is legitimate because public, it will be defeated because the execution of it involves payments to individuals." A tax is not an assessment of benefits.

***Helvering v. Davis:* 301 U.S. 619 (1937).**

Use of tax money to maintain the Social Security system of old-age benefits is within the limits of the "general welfare." The determination of what is within these limits is up to the discretion of Congress "unless the choice is clearly wrong, a display of arbitrary power, not an exercise of judgment." This case was decided the same day as Steward and with heavy reliance on Steward.

SOUTH DAKOTA V. DOLE

483 U.S. 203, 107 S. Ct. 2793, 97 L. Ed. 2d 171 (1987)

At a time when Congress has numerous grant-in-aid programs to funnel money to the states, Congress gains substantial power through its ability to condition federal spending on state adherence to certain conditions. This case tests the limits of this authority while also examining state powers to regulate alcohol under the Twenty-first Amendment.

Vote: 7–1

CHIEF JUSTICE REHNQUIST delivered the opinion of the Court.

Petitioner South Dakota permits persons 19 years of age or older to purchase beer containing up to 3.2% alcohol. In 1984 Congress enacted 23 U. S. C. § 158 (1982 ed., Supp. III), which directs the Secretary of Transportation to withhold a percentage of federal highway funds otherwise allocable from States "in which the purchase or public possession . . . of any alcoholic beverage by a person who is less than twenty-one years of age is lawful." The State sued in United States District Court seeking a declaratory judgment that § 158 violates the constitutional limitations on congressional exercise of the spending power and violates the Twenty-first Amendment to the United States Constitution. The District Court rejected the State's claims, and the Court of Appeals for the Eighth Circuit affirmed.

In this Court, the parties direct most of their efforts to defining the proper scope of the Twenty-first Amendment. Relying on our statement in *California Retail Liquor Dealers Assn.* v. *Midcal Aluminum, Inc.*, 445 U.S. 97 (1980) that the "Twenty-first Amendment grants the States virtually complete control over whether to permit importation or sale of liquor and how to structure the liquor distribution system," South Dakota asserts that the setting of minimum drinking ages is clearly within the "core powers" reserved to the States under § 2 of the Amendment. Section 158, petitioner claims, usurps that core power. The Secretary in response asserts that the Twenty-first Amendment is simply not implicated by § 158; the plain language of § 2 confirms the States' broad power to impose restrictions on the sale and distribution of alcoholic beverages but does not confer on them any power to *permit* sales that Congress seeks to *prohibit.* That Amendment, under this reasoning, would not prevent Congress from affirmatively enacting a national minimum drinking age more restrictive than that provided by the various state laws; and it would follow *a fortiori* that the indirect inducement involved here is compatible with the Twenty-first Amendment.

These arguments present questions of the meaning of the Twenty-first Amendment, the bounds of which have escaped precise definition. *Bacchus Imports, Ltd. v. Dias*, 468 U.S. 263 (1984); *Craig v. Boren*, 429 U.S. 190 (1976). Despite the extended treatment of the question by the parties, however, we need not decide in this case whether that Amendment would prohibit an attempt by Congress to legislate directly a national minimum drinking age. Here, Congress has acted indirectly under its spending power to encourage uniformity in the States' drinking ages. As we explain below, we find this legislative effort within constitutional bounds even if Congress may not regulate drinking ages directly.

The Constitution empowers Congress to "lay and collect Taxes, Duties, Imposts, and Excises, to pay the Debts and provide for the common Defence and general Welfare of the United States." Art. I, § 8, cl. 1. Incident to this power, Congress may attach conditions on the receipt of federal funds, and has repeatedly employed the power "to further broad policy objectives by conditioning receipt of federal moneys upon compliance by the recipient with federal statutory and administrative directives." . . . The breadth of this power was made clear in *United States v. Butler*, 297 U.S. 1 (1936), where the Court, resolving a longstanding debate over the scope of the Spending Clause, determined that "the power of Congress to authorize expenditure of public moneys for public purposes is not limited by the direct grants of legislative power found in the Constitution." Thus, objectives not thought to be within Article I's "enumerated legislative fields" may nevertheless be attained through the use of the spending power and the conditional grant of federal funds.

The spending power is of course not unlimited, *Pennhurst State School and Hospital v. Halderman*, 451 U.S. 1, 17 (1981), but is instead subject to several general restrictions articulated in our cases. The first of these limitations is derived from the language of the Constitution itself: the exercise of the spending power must be in pursuit of "the general welfare." See *Helvering v. Davis*, 301 U.S. 619 (1937); *United States v. Butler.* In considering whether a particular expenditure is intended to serve general public purposes, courts should defer substantially to the judgment of Congress. Second, we have required that if Congress desires to condition the States' receipt of federal funds, it "must do so unambiguously . . ., enabl[ing] the States to exercise their choice knowingly, cognizant of the consequences of their participation." *Pennhurst State School and Hospital* v. *Halderman*. Third, our cases have suggested (without significant elaboration) that conditions on federal grants might be illegitimate if they are unrelated "to the federal interest in particular national projects or programs." *Massachusetts* v. *United States*, 435 U.S. 444, 461 (1978). . . . Finally, we have noted that other constitutional provisions may provide an independent bar to the conditional grant of federal funds. . . .

South Dakota does not seriously claim that § 158 is inconsistent with any of the first three restrictions mentioned above. We can readily conclude that the provision is designed to serve the general welfare, especially in light of the fact that "the concept of welfare or the opposite is shaped by Congress. . . ." *Helvering* v. *Davis*. Congress found that the differing drinking ages in the States created particular incentives for young persons to combine their desire to drink with their ability to drive, and that this interstate problem required a national solution. The means it chose to address this dangerous situation were reasonably calculated to advance the general welfare. The conditions upon which States receive the funds, moreover, could not be more clearly stated by Congress. And the State itself, rather than challenging the germaneness of the condition to federal purposes, admits that it "has never contended that the congressional action was . . . unrelated to a national concern in the absence of the Twenty-first Amendment." Indeed, the condition imposed by Congress is directly related to one of the main purposes for which highway funds are expended—safe interstate travel. This goal of the interstate highway system had been frustrated by varying drinking ages among the States. A Presidential commission appointed to study alcohol-related accidents and fatalities on the Nation's highways concluded that the lack of uniformity in the States' drinking ages created "an incentive to drink and drive" because "young persons commut[e] to border States where the drinking age is lower." By enacting § 158, Congress conditioned the receipt of federal funds in a way reasonably calculated to address this particular impediment to a purpose for which the funds are expended.

The remaining question about the validity of § 158—and the basic point of disagreement between the parties—is whether the Twenty-first Amendment constitutes an "independent constitutional bar" to the conditional grant of federal funds. Petitioner, relying on its view that the Twenty-first Amendment prohibits *direct* regulation of drinking ages by Congress, asserts that "Congress may not use the spending power to regulate that which it is prohibited from regulating directly under the Twenty-first Amendment." But our cases show that this "independent constitutional bar" limitation on the spending power is not of the kind petitioner suggests. *United States v. Butler,* for example, established that the constitutional limitations on Congress when exercising its spending power are less exacting than those on its authority to regulate directly.

We have also held that a perceived Tenth Amendment limitation on congressional regulation of state affairs did not concomitantly limit the range of conditions legitimately placed on federal grants. In *Oklahoma v. Civil Service Comm'n*, 330 U.S. 127 (1947), the Court considered the validity of the Hatch Act insofar as it was applied to political activities of state officials whose employment was financed in whole or in part with federal funds. The State contended that an order under this provision to withhold certain federal funds unless a state official was removed invaded its sovereignty in violation of the Tenth Amendment. Though finding that "the United States is not concerned with, and has no power to regulate, local political activities as such of state officials," the Court nevertheless held that the Federal Government "does have power to fix the terms upon which its money allotments to states shall be disbursed." The Court found no violation of the State's sovereignty because the State could, and did, adopt "the 'simple expedient' of not yielding to what she urges is federal coercion. The offer of benefits to a state by the United States dependent upon cooperation by the state with federal plans, assumedly for the general welfare, is not unusual." . . .

These cases establish that the "independent constitutional bar" limitation on the spending power is not, as petitioner suggests, a prohibition on the indirect achievement of objectives which Congress is not empowered to achieve directly. Instead, we think that the language in our earlier opinions stands for the unexceptionable proposition that the power may not be used to induce the States to engage in activities that would themselves be unconstitutional. Thus, for example, a grant of federal funds conditioned on invidiously discriminatory state action or the infliction of cruel and unusual punishment would be an illegitimate exercise of the Congress' broad spending power. But no such claim can be or is made here. Were South Dakota to succumb to the blandishments offered by Congress and raise its drinking age to 21, the State's action in so doing would not violate the constitutional rights of anyone.

Our decisions have recognized that in some circumstances the financial inducement offered by Congress might be so coercive as to pass the point at which "pressure turns into compulsion." *Steward Machine Co. v. Davis*, 301 U.S. 548 (1937). Here, however, Congress has directed only that a State desiring to establish a minimum drinking age lower than 21 lose a relatively small percentage of certain federal highway funds. Petitioner contends that the coercive nature of this program is evident from the degree of success it has achieved. We cannot conclude, however, that a conditional grant of federal money of this sort is unconstitutional simply by reason of its success in achieving the congressional objective.

When we consider, for a moment, that all South Dakota would lose if she adheres to her chosen course as to a suitable minimum drinking age is 5% of the funds otherwise obtainable under specified highway grant programs, the argument as to coercion is shown to be more rhetoric than fact. As we said a half century ago in *Steward Machine Co.* v. *Davis*: "Every rebate from a tax when conditioned upon conduct is in some measure a temptation. But to hold that motive or temptation is equivalent to coercion is to plunge the law in endless difficulties. The outcome of such a doctrine is the acceptance of a philosophical determinism by which choice becomes impossible. Till now the law has been guided by a robust common sense which assumes the freedom of the will as a working hypothesis in the solution of its problems."

Here Congress has offered relatively mild encouragement to the States to enact higher minimum drinking ages than they would otherwise choose. But the enactment of such laws remains the prerogative of the States not merely in theory but in fact. Even if Congress might lack the power to impose a national minimum drinking age directly, we conclude that encouragement to state action found in § 158 is a valid use of the spending power. Accordingly, the judgment of the Court of Appeals is *Affirmed.*

JUSTICE BRENNAN, dissenting.

I agree with Justice O'Connor that regulation of the minimum age of purchasers of liquor falls squarely within the ambit of those powers reserved to the States by the Twenty-first Amendment. Since States possess this constitutional power, Congress cannot condition a federal grant in a manner that abridges this right. The Amendment, itself, strikes the proper balance between federal and state authority. I therefore dissent.

JUSTICE O'CONNOR, dissenting.

The Court today upholds the National Minimum Drinking Age Amendment, 23 U. S. C. § 158 (1982 ed., Supp. III), as a valid exercise of the spending power conferred by Article I, § 8. But § 158 is not a condition on spending reasonably related to the expenditure of federal funds and cannot be justified on that ground. Rather, it is an attempt to regulate the sale of liquor, an attempt that lies outside Congress' power to regulate commerce because it falls within the ambit of § 2 of the Twenty-first Amendment.

My disagreement with the Court is relatively narrow on the spending power issue: it is a disagreement about the application of a principle rather than a disagreement on the principle itself. I agree with the Court that Congress may attach conditions on the receipt of federal funds to further "the federal interest in particular national projects or programs." . . . I also subscribe to the established proposition that the reach of the spending power "is not limited by the direct grants of legislative power found in the Constitution." *United States v. Butler*, 297 U.S. 1 (1936). Finally, I agree that there are four separate types of limitations on the spending power: the expenditure must be for the general welfare, *Helvering v. Davis,* 301 U.S. 619 (1937), the conditions imposed must be unambiguous, *Pennhurst State School and Hospital v. Halderman*, 451 U.S. 1, 17 (1981), they must be reasonably related to the purpose of the expenditure, *Massachusetts* v. *United States,* 435 U.S. 444 at 461 (1978), and the legislation may not violate any independent constitutional prohibition, *Lawrence County v. Lead-Deadwood School Dist.*, 469 U.S. 256 (1985). Insofar as two of those limitations are concerned, the Court is clearly correct that § 158 is wholly unobjectionable. Establishment of a national minimum drinking age certainly fits within the broad concept of the general welfare and the statute is entirely unambiguous. I am also willing to assume, *arguendo*, that the Twenty-first Amendment does not constitute an "independent constitutional bar" to a spending condition.

But the Court's application of the requirement that the condition imposed be reasonably related to the purpose for which the funds are expended is cursory and unconvincing. We have repeatedly said that Congress may condition grants under the spending power only in ways reasonably related to the purpose of the federal program. . . . In my view, establishment of a minimum drinking age of 21 is not sufficiently related to interstate highway construction to justify so conditioning funds appropriated for that purpose.

In support of its contrary conclusion, the Court relies on a supposed concession by counsel for South Dakota that the State "has never contended that the congressional action was . . . unrelated to a national concern in the absence of the Twenty-first Amendment." In the absence of the Twenty-first Amendment, however, there is a strong argument that the Congress might regulate the conditions under which liquor is sold under the commerce power, just as it regulates the sale of many other commodities that are in or affect interstate commerce. The fact that the Twenty-first Amendment is crucial to the State's argument does not, therefore, amount to a concession that the condition imposed by § 158 is reasonably related to highway construction. The Court also relies on a portion of the argument transcript in support of its claim that South Dakota conceded the reasonable relationship point. But counsel's statements there are at best ambiguous. Counsel essentially said no more than that he was not prepared to argue the reasonable relationship question discussed at length in the Brief for the National Conference of State Legislatures et al. as *Amici Curiae.*

Aside from these "concessions" by counsel, the Court asserts the reasonableness of the relationship between the supposed purpose of the expenditure—"safe interstate travel"—and the drinking age condition. The Court reasons that Congress wishes that the roads it builds may be used safely, that drunken drivers threaten highway safety, and that young people are more likely to drive while under the influence of alcohol under existing law than would be the case if there were a uniform national drinking age of 21. It hardly needs saying, however, that if the purpose of § 158 is to deter drunken driving, it is far too over- and under-inclusive. It is over-inclusive because it stops teenagers from drinking even when they are not about to drive on interstate highways. It is under-inclusive because teenagers pose only a small part of the drunken driving problem in this Nation. . . .

When Congress appropriates money to build a highway, it is entitled to insist that the highway be a safe one. But it is not entitled to insist as a condition of the use of highway funds that the State impose or change regulations in other areas of the State's social and economic life because of an attenuated or tangential relationship to highway use or safety. Indeed, if the rule were otherwise, the Congress could effectively regulate almost any area of a State's social, political, or economic life on the theory that use of the interstate transportation system is somehow enhanced. If, for example, the United States were to condition highway moneys upon moving the state capital, I suppose it might argue that interstate transportation is facilitated by locating local governments in places easily accessible to interstate highways—or, conversely, that highways might become overburdened if they had to carry traffic to and from the state capital. In my mind, such a relationship is hardly more attenuated than the one which the Court finds supports § 158.

There is a clear place at which the Court can draw the line between permissible and impermissible conditions on federal grants. It is the line identified in the Brief for the National Conference of State Legislatures et al. as *Amici Curiae*: "Congress has the power to *spend* for the general welfare, it has the power to *legislate* only for delegated purposes. . . .

"The appropriate inquiry, then, is whether the spending requirement or prohibition is a condition on a grant or whether it is regulation. The difference turns on whether the requirement specifies in some way how the money should be spent, so that Congress' intent in making the grant will be effectuated. Congress has no power under the Spending Clause to impose requirements on a grant that go beyond specifying how the money should be spent. A requirement that is not such a specification is not a condition, but a regulation, which is valid only if it falls within one of Congress' delegated regulatory powers."

This approach harks back to *United States v. Butler* (1936), the last case in which this Court struck down an Act of Congress as beyond the authority granted by the Spending Clause. There the Court wrote that "there is an obvious difference between a statute stating the conditions upon which moneys shall be expended and one effective only upon assumption of a contractual obligation to submit to a regulation which otherwise could not be enforced." The *Butler* Court saw the Agricultural Adjustment Act for what it was—an exercise of regulatory, not spending, power. The error in *Butler* was not the Court's conclusion that the Act was essentially regulatory, but rather its crabbed view of the extent of Congress' regulatory power under the Commerce Clause. The Agricultural Adjustment Act was regulatory but it was regulation that today would likely be considered within Congress' commerce power. . . .

While *Butler*'s authority is questionable insofar as it assumes that Congress has no regulatory power over farm production, its discussion of the spending power and its description of both the power's breadth and its limitations remain sound. The Court's decision in *Butler* also properly recognizes the gravity of the task of appropriately limiting the spending power. If the spending power is to be limited only by Congress' notion of the general welfare, the reality, given the vast financial resources of the Federal Government, is that the Spending Clause gives "power to the Congress to tear down the barriers, to invade the states' jurisdiction, and to become a parliament of the whole people, subject to no restrictions save such as are self-imposed." This, of course, as *Butler* held, was not the Framers' plan and it is not the meaning of the Spending Clause.

Our later cases are consistent with the notion that, under the spending power, the Congress may only condition grants in ways that can fairly be said to be related to the expenditure of federal funds. For example, in *Oklahoma* v. *CSC*, 330 U.S. 127 (1947), the Court upheld application of the Hatch Act to a member of the Oklahoma State Highway Commission who was employed in connection with an activity financed in part by loans and grants from a federal agency. This condition is appropriately viewed as a condition relating to how federal moneys were to be expended. Other conditions that have been upheld by the Court may be viewed as independently justified under some regulatory power of the Congress. Thus, in *Fullilove* v. *Klutznick*, 448 U.S. 448 (1980), the Court upheld a condition on federal grants that 10% of the money be "set aside" for contracts with minority business enterprises. But the Court found that the condition could be justified as a valid regulation under the commerce power and § 5 of the Fourteenth Amendment. . . .

This case, however, falls into neither class. As discussed above, a condition that a State will raise its drinking age to 21 cannot fairly be said to be reasonably related to the expenditure of funds for highway construction. The only possible connection, highway safety, has nothing to do with how the funds Congress has appropriated are expended. Rather than a condition determining how federal highway money shall be expended, it is a regulation determining who shall be able to drink liquor. As such it is not justified by the spending power. . . .

FOR DISCUSSION

What limitations in the national government's power to condition its expenditures on certain state behaviors does this case acknowledge? Should states continue to exercise some autonomy? Do you think these limitations are sufficient to protect this autonomy? According to this opinion, is it possible for Congress to make an offer that the states cannot refuse? Does the limitation imposed need to be related at all to the money being provided? For example, could Congress require states, as a condition for receiving federal transportation funding, to enact laws outlawing the use of medical marijuana?

NATIONAL FEDERATION OF INDEPENDENT BUSINESS V. SEBELIUS

567 U.S. 519, 132 S.Ct. 2566, 183 L.Ed.2d 450 (2012)

This milestone case considered the constitutionality of the Patient Protection and Affordable Care Act of 2010, which was often designated as Obamacare because of President Obama's role in its passage. The individual mandate provision of this law required individuals without health insurance either to purchase such insurance or face a penalty. The law also threatened to cut off Medicaid funds to states that refused to extend coverage to all above the poverty line. Congress sought to justify the law under the interstate commerce clause and its power to tax and spend. Chief Justice John Roberts wrote the majority opinion in which Justices Scalia, Kennedy, Thomas, and Alito joined his views denying congressional authority under the commerce clause. He also joined in invalidating the threat to cut off funding to states who refused to expand Medicare. But he joined Justices Ginsburg, Breyer, Sotomayor, and Kagan who justified the law under the taxing and spending clause. By focusing on both major constitutional provisions, this case is a particularly appropriate capstone for this chapter. The case also raises important questions about both judicial review and federalism.

Vote: 5–4

CHIEF JUSTICE ROBERTS delivered the opinion of the Court:

In our federal system, the National Government possesses only limited powers; the States and the people retain the remainder. Nearly two centuries ago, Chief Justice Marshall observed that "the question respecting the extent of the powers actually granted" to the Federal Government "is perpetually arising, and will probably continue to arise, as long as our system shall exist." *McCulloch* v. *Maryland*, 4 Wheat. 316, 405 (1819). In this case we must again determine whether the Constitution grants Congress powers it now asserts, but which many States and individuals believe it does not possess. Resolving this controversy requires us to examine both the limits of the Government's power, and our own limited role in policing those boundaries.

The Federal Government "is acknowledged by all to be one of enumerated powers." That is, rather than granting general authority to perform all the conceivable functions of government, the Constitution lists, or enumerates, the Federal Government's powers. Congress may, for example, "coin Money," "establish Post Offices," and "raise and support Armies." Art. I, § 8, cls. 5, 7, 12. The enumeration of powers is also a limitation of powers, because "[t]he enumeration presupposes something not enumerated." *Gibbons* v. *Ogden*, 9 Wheat. 1, 195 (1824). The Constitution's express conferral of some powers makes clear that it does not grant others. And the Federal Government "can exercise only the powers granted to it." *McCulloch*, *supra*, at 405.

Today, the restrictions on government power foremost in many Americans' minds are likely to be affirmative prohibitions, such as contained in the Bill of Rights. These affirmative prohibitions come into play, however, only where the Government possesses authority to act in the first place. If no enumerated power authorizes Congress to pass a certain law, that law may not be enacted, even if it would not violate any of the express prohibitions in the Bill of Rights or elsewhere in the Constitution. . . .

The same does not apply to the States, because the Constitution is not the source of their power. The Constitution may restrict state governments—as it does, for example, by forbidding them to deny any person the equal protection of the laws. But where such prohibitions do not apply, state governments do not need constitutional authorization to act. The States thus can and do perform many of the vital functions of modern government—punishing street crime, running public schools, and zoning property for development, to name but a few—even though the Constitution's text does not authorize any government to do so. Our cases refer to this general power of governing, possessed by the States but not by the Federal Government, as the "police power." See, *e.g., United States* v. *Morrison*, 529 U.S. 598, 618–619 (2000). . . .

This case concerns two powers that the Constitution does grant the Federal Government, but which must be read carefully to avoid creating a general federal authority akin to the police power. The Constitution authorizes Congress to "regulate Commerce with foreign Nations, and among the several States, and with the Indian Tribes." Art. I, § 8, cl. 3. Our precedents read that to mean that Congress may regulate "the channels of interstate commerce," "persons or things in interstate commerce," and "those activities that substantially affect interstate commerce." *Morrison, supra*, at 609. The power over activities that substantially affect interstate commerce can be expansive. That power has been held to authorize federal regulation of such seemingly local matters as a farmer's decision to grow wheat for himself and his livestock, and a loan shark's extortionate collections from a neighborhood butcher shop. See *Wickard* v. *Filburn*, 317 U.S. 111 (1942); *Perez* v. *United States*, 402 U.S. 146 (1971).

Congress may also "lay and collect Taxes, Duties, Imposts and Excises, to pay the Debts and provide for the common Defence and general Welfare of the United States." U. S. Const., Art. I, § 8, cl. 1. Put simply, Congress may tax and spend. This grant gives the Federal Government considerable influence even in areas where it cannot directly regulate. The Federal Government may enact a tax on an activity that it cannot authorize, forbid, or otherwise control. See, *e.g., License Tax Cases*, 5 Wall. 462 (1867). And in exercising its spending power, Congress may offer funds to the States, and may condition those offers on compliance with specified conditions. See, *e.g., College Savings Bank* v. *Florida Prepaid Postsecondary Ed. Expense Bd.*, 527 U.S. 666 (1999). These offers may well induce the States to adopt policies that the Federal Government itself could not impose. See, *e.g., South Dakota* v. *Dole*, 483 U.S. 203 (1987) (conditioning federal highway funds on States raising their drinking age to 21).

The reach of the Federal Government's enumerated powers is broader still because the Constitution authorizes Congress to "make all Laws which shall be necessary and proper for carrying into Execution the foregoing Powers." Art. I, § 8, cl. 18. We have long read this provision to give Congress great latitude in exercising its powers: "Let the end be legitimate, let it be within the scope of the constitution, and all means which are appropriate, which are plainly adapted to that end, which are not prohibited, but consist with the letter and spirit of the constitution, are constitutional." *McCulloch*, 4 Wheat., at 421.

Our permissive reading of these powers is explained in part by a general reticence to invalidate the acts of the Nation's elected leaders. "Proper respect for a co-ordinate branch of the government" requires that we strike down an Act of Congress only if "the lack of constitutional authority to pass [the] act in question is clearly demonstrated." *United States* v. *Harris*, 106 U.S. 629, 635 (1883). Members of this Court are vested with the authority to interpret the law; we possess neither the expertise nor the prerogative to make policy judgments. Those decisions are entrusted to our Nation's elected leaders, who can be thrown out of office if the people disagree with them. It is not our job to protect the people from the consequences of their political choices.

Our deference in matters of policy cannot, however, become abdication in matters of law. "The powers of the legislature are defined and limited; and that those limits may not be mistaken, or forgotten, the constitution is written." *Marbury* v. *Madison*, 1 Cranch 137, 176 (1803). Our respect for Congress's policy judgments thus can never extend so far as to disavow restraints on federal power that the Constitution carefully constructed. "The peculiar circumstances of the moment may render a measure more or less wise, but cannot render it more or less constitutional." Chief Justice John Marshall, A Friend of the Constitution No. V, Alexandria Gazette, July 5, 1819, in John Marshall's Defense of *McCulloch v. Maryland* 190–191 (G. Gunther ed. 1969). And there can be no question that it is the responsibility of this Court to enforce the limits on federal power by striking down acts of Congress that transgress those limits.

The questions before us must be considered against the background of these basic principles.

In 2010, Congress enacted the Patient Protection and Affordable Care Act, 124 Stat. 119. The Act aims to increase the number of Americans covered by health insurance and decrease the cost of health care. The Act's 10 titles stretch over 900 pages and contain hundreds of provisions. This case concerns constitutional challenges to two key provisions, commonly referred to as the individual mandate and the Medicaid expansion.

The individual mandate requires most Americans to maintain "minimum essential" health insurance coverage. . . .

The second provision of the Affordable Care Act directly challenged here is the Medicaid expansion. Enacted in 1965, Medicaid offers federal funding to States to assist pregnant women, children, needy families, the blind, the elderly, and the disabled in obtaining medical care. In order to receive that funding, States must comply with federal criteria governing matters such as who receives care and what services are provided at what cost. By 1982 every State had chosen to participate in Medicaid. Federal funds received through the Medicaid program have become a substantial part of state budgets, now constituting over 10 percent of most States' total revenue.

The Affordable Care Act expands the scope of the Medicaid program and increases the number of individuals the States must cover. For example, the Act requires state programs to provide Medicaid coverage to adults with incomes up to 133 percent of the federal poverty level, whereas many States now cover adults with children only if their income is considerably lower, and do not cover childless adults at all. The Act increases federal funding to cover the States' costs in expanding Medicaid coverage, although States will bear a portion of the costs on their own. If a State does not comply with the Act's new coverage requirements, it may lose not only the federal funding for those requirements, but all of its federal Medicaid funds.

Along with their challenge to the individual mandate, the state plaintiffs in the Eleventh Circuit argued that the Medicaid expansion exceeds Congress's constitutional powers. . . .

II

Before turning to the merits, we need to be sure we have the authority to do so. The Anti-Injunction Act provides that "no suit for the purpose of restraining the assessment or collection of any tax shall be maintained in any court by any person, whether or not such person is the person against whom such tax was assessed." This statute protects the Government's ability to collect a consistent stream of revenue, by barring litigation to enjoin or otherwise obstruct the collection of taxes. Because of the Anti-Injunction Act, taxes can ordinarily be challenged only after they are paid, by suing for a refund. See *Enochs v. Williams Packing & Nav. Co.*, 370 U.S. 1 (1962).

The penalty for not complying with the Affordable Care Act's individual mandate first becomes enforceable in 2014. The present challenge to the mandate thus seeks to restrain the penalty's future collection. *Amicus* contends that the Internal Revenue Code treats the penalty as a tax, and that the Anti-Injunction Act therefore bars this suit.

The text of the pertinent statutes suggests otherwise. The Anti-Injunction Act applies to suits "for the purpose of restraining the assessment or collection of any *tax*." Congress, however, chose to describe the "[s]hared responsibility payment" imposed on those who forgo health insurance not as a "tax," but as a "penalty." There is no immediate reason to think that a statute applying to "any tax" would apply to a "penalty."

Congress's decision to label this exaction a "penalty" rather than a "tax" is significant because the Affordable Care Act describes many other exactions it creates as "taxes." Where Congress uses certain language in one part of a statute and different language in another, it is generally presumed that Congress acts intentionally. See *Russello* v. *United States*, 464 U.S. 16 (1983).

Amicus argues that even though Congress did not label the shared responsibility payment a tax, we should treat it as such under the Anti-Injunction Act because it functions like a tax. It is true that Congress cannot change whether an exaction is a tax or a penalty for *constitutional* purposes simply by describing it as one or the other. Congress may not, for example, expand its power under the Taxing Clause, or escape the Double Jeopardy Clause's constraint on criminal sanctions, by labeling a severe financial punishment a "tax." See *Bailey* v. *Drexel Furniture Co.*, 259 U.S. 20 (1922); *Department of Revenue of Mont.* v. *Kurth Ranch*, 511 U.S. 767 (1994). . . .

The Affordable Care Act does not require that the penalty for failing to comply with the individual mandate be treated as a tax for purposes of the Anti-Injunction Act. The Anti-Injunction Act therefore does not apply to this suit, and we may proceed to the merits.

III

The Government advances two theories for the proposition that Congress had constitutional authority to enact the individual mandate. First, the Government argues that Congress had the power to enact the mandate under the Commerce Clause. Under that theory, Congress may order individuals to buy health insurance because the failure to do so affects interstate commerce, and could undercut the Affordable Care Act's other reforms. Second, the Government argues that if the commerce power does not support the mandate, we should nonetheless uphold it as an exercise of Congress's power to tax. According to the Government, even if Congress lacks the power to direct individuals to buy insurance, the only effect of the individual mandate is to raise taxes on those who do not do so, and thus the law may be upheld as a tax.

A

The Government's first argument is that the individual mandate is a valid exercise of Congress's power under the Commerce Clause and the Necessary and Proper Clause. According to the Government, the health care market is characterized by a significant cost-shifting problem. Everyone will eventually need health care at a time and to an extent they cannot predict, but if they do not have insurance, they often will not be able to pay for it. Because state and federal laws nonetheless require hospitals to provide a certain degree of care to individuals without regard to their ability to pay, hospitals end up receiving compensation for only a portion of the services they provide. To recoup the losses, hospitals pass on the cost to insurers through higher rates, and insurers, in turn, pass on the cost to policy holders in the form of higher premiums. Congress estimated that the cost of uncompensated care raises family health insurance premiums, on average, by over $1,000 per year. In the Affordable Care Act, Congress addressed the problem of those who cannot obtain insurance coverage because of preexisting conditions or other health issues. It did so through the Act's "guaranteed-issue" and "community-rating" provisions. These provisions together prohibit insurance companies from denying coverage to those with such conditions or charging unhealthy individuals higher premiums than healthy individuals.

The guaranteed-issue and community-rating reforms do not, however, address the issue of healthy individuals who choose not to purchase insurance to cover potential health care needs. In fact, the reforms sharply exacerbate that problem, by providing an incentive for individuals to delay purchasing health insurance until they become sick, relying on the promise of guaranteed and affordable coverage.

The reforms also threaten to impose massive new costs on insurers, who are required to accept unhealthy individuals but prohibited from charging them rates necessary to pay for their coverage. This will lead insurers to significantly increase premiums on everyone. See Brief for America's Health Insurance Plans et al. as *Amici Curiae* in No. 11– 393 etc. 8–9.

The individual mandate was Congress's solution to these problems. By requiring that individuals purchase health insurance, the mandate prevents cost-shifting by those who would otherwise go without it. In addition, the mandate forces into the insurance risk pool more healthy individuals, whose premiums on average will be higher than their health care expenses. This allows insurers to subsidize the costs of covering the unhealthy individuals the reforms require them to accept. The Government claims that Congress has power under the Commerce and Necessary and Proper Clauses to enact this solution.

1

The Government contends that the individual mandate is within Congress's power because the failure to purchase insurance "has a substantial and deleterious effect on interstate commerce" by creating the cost-shifting problem. The path of our Commerce Clause decisions has not always run smooth, see *United States* v. *Lopez*, 514 U.S. 549 (1995), but it is now well established that Congress has broad authority under the Clause. We have recognized, for example, that "[t]he power of Congress over interstate commerce is not confined to the regulation of commerce among the states," but extends to activities that "have a substantial effect on interstate commerce." *United States* v. *Darby*, 312 U.S. 100, 118–119 (1941). Congress's power, moreover, is not limited to regulation of an activity that by itself substantially affects interstate commerce, but also extends to activities that do so only when aggregated with similar activities of others. See *Wickard*, 317 U.S., at 127–128.

Given its expansive scope, it is no surprise that Congress has employed the commerce power in a wide variety of ways to address the pressing needs of the time. But Congress has never attempted to rely on that power to compel individuals not engaged in commerce to purchase an unwanted product. Legislative novelty is not necessarily fatal; there is a first time for everything. But sometimes "the most telling indication of [a] severe constitutional problem . . . is the lack of historical precedent" for Congress's action. *Free Enterprise Fund* v. *Public Company Accounting Oversight Bd.*, 561 U.S. ___ (2010). At the very least, we should "pause to consider the implications of the Government's arguments" when confronted with such new conceptions of federal power. *Lopez*, *supra*, at 564.

The Constitution grants Congress the power to "*regulate* Commerce." Art. I, § 8, cl. 3 (emphasis added). The power to *regulate* commerce presupposes the existence of commercial activity to be regulated. If the power to "regulate" something included the power to create it, many of the provisions in the Constitution would be superfluous.

The individual mandate, however, does not regulate existing commercial activity. It instead compels individuals to *become* active in commerce by purchasing a product, on the ground that their failure to do so affects interstate commerce. Construing the Commerce Clause to permit Congress to regulate individuals precisely *because* they are doing nothing would open a new and potentially vast do- main to congressional authority. Every day individuals do not do an infinite number of things. In some cases they decide not to do something; in others they simply fail to do it. Allowing Congress to justify federal regulation by pointing to the effect of inaction on commerce would bring countless decisions an individual could *potentially* make within the scope of federal regulation, and—under the Government's theory—empower Congress to make those decisions for him. . . .

Wickard has long been regarded as "perhaps the most far reaching example of Commerce Clause authority over intrastate activity," *Lopez*, 514 U.S., at 560, but the Government's theory in this case would go much further. Under *Wickard* it is within Congress's power to regulate the market for wheat by supporting its price. But price can be supported by increasing demand as well as by decreasing supply. The aggregated decisions of some consumers not to purchase wheat have a substantial effect on the price of wheat, just as decisions not to purchase health insurance have on the price of insurance. Congress can therefore command that those not buying wheat do so, just as it argues here that it may command that those not buying health insurance do so. The farmer in *Wickard* was at least actively engaged in the production of wheat, and the Government could regulate that activity because of its effect on commerce. The Government's theory here would effectively override that limitation, by establishing that individuals may be regulated under the Commerce Clause whenever enough of them are not doing something the Government would have them do.

Indeed, the Government's logic would justify a mandatory purchase to solve almost any problem. . . .

People, for reasons of their own, often fail to do things that would be good for them or good for society. Those failures—joined with the similar failures of others—can readily have a substantial effect on interstate commerce. Under the Government's logic, that authorizes Congress to use its commerce power to compel citizens to act as the Government would have them act. . . .

To an economist, perhaps, there is no difference between activity and inactivity; both have measurable economic effects on commerce. But the distinction between doing something and doing nothing would not have been lost on the Framers, who were "practical statesmen," not metaphysical philosophers. *Industrial Union Dept., AFL-CIO* v. *American Petroleum Institute*, 448 U.S. 607, 673 (1980) (Rehnquist, J., concurring in judgment). As we have explained, "the framers of the Constitution were not mere visionaries, toying with speculations or theories, but practical men, dealing with the facts of political life as they understood them, putting into form the government they were creating, and prescribing in language clear and intelligible the powers that government was to take." *South Carolina* v. *United States*, 199 U.S. 437, 449 (1905). The Framers gave Congress the power to *regulate* commerce, not to *compel* it, and for over 200 years both our decisions and Congress's actions have reflected this understanding. There is no reason to depart from that understanding now.

Everyone will likely participate in the markets for food, clothing, transportation, shelter, or energy; that does not authorize Congress to direct them to purchase particular products in those or other markets today. The Commerce Clause is not a general license to regulate an individual from cradle to grave, simply because he will predictably engage in particular transactions. Any police power to regulate individuals as such, as opposed to their activities, remains vested in the States.

The Government argues that the individual mandate can be sustained as a sort of exception to this rule, because health insurance is a unique product. According to the Government, upholding the individual mandate would not justify mandatory purchases of items such as cars or broccoli because, as the Government puts it, "[h]ealth insurance is not purchased for its own sake like a car or broccoli; it is a means of financing health-care consumption and covering universal risks." But cars and broccoli are no more purchased for their "own sake" than health insurance. They are purchased to cover the need for transportation and food. . . .

2

The Government next contends that Congress has the power under the Necessary and Proper Clause to enact the individual mandate because the mandate is an "integral part of a comprehensive scheme of economic regulation"—the guaranteed-issue and community-rating insurance reforms. Under this argument, it is not necessary to consider the effect that an individual's inactivity may have on interstate commerce; it is enough that Congress regulate commercial activity in a way that requires regulation of inactivity to be effective. . . .

Applying these principles, the individual mandate cannot be sustained under the Necessary and Proper Clause as an essential component of the insurance reforms. Each of our prior cases upholding laws under that Clause involved exercises of authority derivative of, and in service to, a granted power. For example, we have upheld provisions permitting continued confinement of those *already in federal custody* when they could not be safely released, *Comstock*, *supra*; criminalizing bribes involving organizations *receiving federal funds*, *Sabri v. United*

States, 541 U.S. 600 (2004); and tolling state statutes of limitations while cases are *pending in federal court*, *Jinks v. Richland County*, 538 U.S. 456 (2003). The individual mandate, by contrast, vests Congress with the extraordinary ability to create the necessary predicate to the exercise of an enumerated power.

B

That is not the end of the matter. Because the Commerce Clause does not support the individual mandate, it is necessary to turn to the Government's second argument: that the mandate may be upheld as within Congress's enumerated power to "lay and collect Taxes." Art. I, § 8, cl. 1.

The Government's tax power argument asks us to view the statute differently than we did in considering its commerce power theory. In making its Commerce Clause argument, the Government defended the mandate as a regulation requiring individuals to purchase health insurance. The Government does not claim that the taxing power allows Congress to issue such a command. Instead, the Government asks us to read the mandate not as ordering individuals to buy insurance, but rather as imposing a tax on those who do not buy that product. . . .

The most straightforward reading of the mandate is that it commands individuals to purchase insurance. . . .

C

The exaction the Affordable Care Act imposes on those without health insurance looks like a tax in many respects. The "[s]hared responsibility payment," as the statute entitles it, is paid into the Treasury by "taxpayer[s]" when they file their tax returns. It does not apply to individuals who do not pay federal income taxes because their household income is less than the filing threshold in the Internal Revenue Code. For taxpayers who do owe the payment, its amount is determined by such familiar factors as taxable income, number of dependents, and joint filing status. The requirement to pay is found in the Internal Revenue Code and enforced by the IRS, which—as we previously explained—must assess and collect it "in the same manner as taxes." This process yields the essential feature of any tax: it produces at least some revenue for the Government. *United States* v. *Kahriger*, 345 U.S. 22 (1953). Indeed, the payment is expected to raise about $4 billion per year by 2017. Congressional Budget Office, Payments of Penalties for Being Uninsured Under the Patient Pro- tection and Affordable Care Act (Apr. 30, 2010), in Selected CBO Publications Related to Health Care Legislation, 2009–2010, p. 71 (rev. 2010).

It is of course true that the Act describes the payment as a "penalty," not a "tax." But while that label is fatal to the application of the Anti-Injunction Act, it does not determine whether the payment may be viewed as an exercise of Congress's taxing power. It is up to Congress whether to apply the Anti-Injunction Act to any particular statute, so it makes sense to be guided by Congress's choice of label on that question. That choice does not, however, control whether an exaction is within Congress's constitutional power to tax. . . .

The same analysis here suggests that the shared responsibility payment may for constitutional purposes be considered a tax, not a penalty: First, for most Americans the amount due will be far less than the price of insurance, and, by statute, it can never be more. It may often be a reasonable financial decision to make the payment rather than purchase insurance, unlike the "prohibitory" financial punishment in [*Bailey v.*] *Drexel Furniture Co.*, 259 U.S. 20 (1922). Second, the individual mandate contains no scienter requirement. Third, the payment is collected solely by the IRS through the normal means of taxation—except that the Service is *not* allowed to use those means most suggestive of a punitive sanction, such as criminal prosecution. The reasons the Court in *Drexel Furniture* held that what was called a "tax" there was a penalty support the conclusion that what is called a "penalty" here may be viewed as a tax.

None of this is to say that the payment is not intended to affect individual conduct. Although the payment will raise considerable revenue, it is plainly designed to expand health insurance coverage. But taxes that seek to influence conduct are nothing new. Some of our earliest federal taxes sought to deter the purchase of imported manufactured goods in order to foster the growth of domestic industry. . . .

A tax on going without health insurance does not fall within any recognized category of direct tax. It is not a capitation. Capitations are taxes paid by every person, "without regard to property, profession, or *any other circumstance*." *Hylton*, *supra*, at 175 (opinion of Chase, J.) (emphasis altered). The whole point of the shared responsibility payment is that it is triggered by specific circumstances—earning a certain amount of income but not obtaining health insurance. The payment is also plainly not a tax on the ownership of land or personal property. The shared responsibility payment is thus not a direct tax that must be apportioned among the several States.

There may, however, be a more fundamental objection to a tax on those who lack health insurance. Even if only a tax, the payment under § 5000A(b) remains a burden that the Federal Government imposes for an omission, not an act. If it is troubling to interpret the Commerce Clause as authorizing Congress to regulate those who abstain from commerce, perhaps it should be similarly troubling to permit Congress to impose a tax for not doing something.

Three considerations allay this concern. First, and most importantly, it is abundantly clear the Constitution does not guarantee that individuals may avoid taxation through inactivity. A capitation, after all, is a tax that everyone must pay simply for existing, and capitations are expressly contemplated by the Constitution. . . .

Second, Congress's ability to use its taxing power to influence conduct is not without limits. A few of our cases policed these limits aggressively, invalidating punitive exactions obviously designed to regulate behavior otherwise regarded at the time as beyond federal authority. . . .

Third, although the breadth of Congress's power to tax is greater than its power to regulate commerce, the taxing power does not give Congress the same degree of control over individual behavior. . . .

IV A

The States also contend that the Medicaid expansion exceeds Congress's authority under the Spending Clause. They claim that Congress is coercing the States to adopt the changes it wants by threatening to withhold all of a State's Medicaid grants, unless the State accepts the new expanded funding and complies with the conditions that come with it. This, they argue, violates the basic principle that the "Federal Government may not compel the States to enact or administer a federal regulatory program." *New York [v. United States*, 505 U.S. 144], at 188 (1992)]. . . .

Permitting the Federal Government to force the States to implement a federal program would threaten the political accountability key to our federal system. "[W]here the Federal Government directs the States to regulate, it may be state officials who will bear the brunt of public disapproval, while the federal officials who devised the regulatory program may remain insulated from the electoral ramifications of their decision." *Id.,* at 169. Spending Clause programs do not pose this danger when a State has a legitimate choice whether to accept the federal conditions in exchange for federal funds. In such a situation, state officials can fairly be held politically accountable for choosing to accept or refuse the federal offer. But when the State has no choice, the Federal Government can achieve its objectives without accountability, just as in *New York* and *Printz*. Indeed, this danger is heightened when Congress acts under the Spending Clause, because Congress can use that power to implement federal policy it could not impose directly under its enumerated powers. . . .

The States, however, argue that the Medicaid expansion is far from the typical case. They object that Congress has "crossed the line distinguishing encouragement from coercion," *New York*, *supra*, at 175, in the way it has structured the funding: Instead of simply refusing to grant the new funds to States that will not accept the new conditions, Congress has also threatened to withhold those States' existing Medicaid funds. The States claim that this threat serves no purpose other than to force unwilling States to sign up for the dramatic expansion in health care coverage effected by the Act.

Given the nature of the threat and the programs at issue here, we must agree. We have upheld Congress's authority to condition the receipt of funds on the States' complying with restrictions on the use of those funds, because that is the means by which Congress ensures that the funds are spent according to its view of the "general Welfare." Conditions that do not here govern the use of the funds, however, cannot be justified on that basis. When, for example, such conditions take the form of threats to terminate other significant independent grants, the conditions are properly viewed as a means of pressuring the States to accept policy changes. . . .

In this case, the financial "inducement" Congress has chosen is much more than "relatively mild encouragement"—it is a gun to the head. . . .

B

Nothing in our opinion precludes Congress from offering funds under the Affordable Care Act to expand the availability of health care, and requiring that States accepting such funds comply with the conditions on their use. What Congress is not free to do is to penalize States that choose not to participate in that new program by taking away their existing Medicaid funding. Section 1396c gives the Secretary of Health and Human Services the authority to do just that. It allows her to withhold *all* "further [Medicaid] payments . . . to the State" if she determines that the State is out of compliance with any Medicaid requirement, including those contained in the expansion. In light of the Court's holding, the Secretary cannot apply § 1396c to withdraw existing Medicaid funds for failure to comply with the requirements set out in the expansion. . . .

JUSTICE GINSBURG delivered a concurring opinion.

. . . The Framers understood that the "general Interests of the Union" would change over time, in ways they could not anticipate. Accordingly, they recognized that the Constitution was of necessity a "great outlin[e]," not a detailed blueprint, see *McCulloch* v. *Maryland*, 4 Wheat. 316, 407 (1819), and that its provisions included broad concepts, to be "explained by the context or by the facts of the case," Letter from James Madison to N. P. Trist (Dec. 1831), in 9 Writings of James Madison 471, 475 (G. Hunt ed. 1910). "Nothing . . . can be more fallacious," Alexander Hamilton emphasized, "than to infer the extent of any power, proper to be lodged in the national government, from . . . its immediate necessities. There ought to be a CAPACITY to provide for future contingencies[,] as they may happen; and as these are illimitable in their nature, it is impossible safely to limit that capacity." *Federalist* No. 34, pp. 205, 206 (John Harvard Library ed. 2009).

B

Until today, this Court's pragmatic approach to judging whether Congress validly exercised its commerce power was guided by two familiar principles. First, Congress has the power to regulate economic activities "that substantially affect Interstate commerce." *Gonzales* v. *Raich*, 545 U.S. 1, 17 (2005). This capacious power extends even to local activities that, viewed in the aggregate, have a substantial impact on interstate commerce.

Second, we owe a large measure of respect to Congress when it frames and enacts economic and social legislation. See *Raich*, 545 U. S., at 17. See also *Pension Benefit Guaranty Corporation* v. *R. A. Gray & Co.*, 467 U.S. 717, 729 (1984) ("[S]trong deference [is] accorded legislation in the field of national economic policy."); *Hodel* v. *Indiana*, 452 U.S. 314, 326 (1981) ("This [C]ourt will certainly not substitute its judgment for that of Congress unless the relation of the subject to interstate commerce and its effect upon it are clearly non-existent." (internal quotation marks omitted)). When appraising such legislation, we ask only (1) whether Congress had a "rational basis" for concluding that the regulated activity substantially affects interstate commerce, and (2) whether there is a "reasonable connection between the regulatory means selected and the asserted ends." *Id.,* at 323–324. . . .

C

Straightforward application of these principles would require the Court to hold that the minimum coverage provision is proper Commerce Clause legislation. Beyond dispute, Congress had a rational basis for concluding that the uninsured, as a class, substantially affect interstate commerce. . .

The minimum coverage provision, furthermore, bears a "reasonable connection" to Congress' goal of protecting the health-care market from the disruption caused by individuals who fail to obtain insurance. By requiring those who do not carry insurance to pay a toll, the minimum coverage provision gives individuals a strong incentive to insure. This incentive, Congress had good reason to believe, would reduce the number of uninsured and, correspondingly, mitigate the adverse impact the uninsured have on the national healthcare market. . .

III A

For the reasons explained above, the minimum coverage provision is valid Commerce Clause legislation. When viewed as a component of the entire ACA, the provision's constitutionality becomes even plainer.

The Necessary and Proper Clause "empowers Congress to enact laws in effectuation of its [commerce] powe[r] that are not within its authority to enact in isolation." *Raich,* 545 U.S., at 39 (SCALIA, J., concurring in judgment). Hence, "[a] complex regulatory program . . . can survive a Commerce Clause challenge without a showing that every single facet of the program is independently and directly related to a valid congressional goal." [*Hodel v.*] *Indiana,* 452 U.S. [314 (1981)], at 329, n. 17. "It is enough that the challenged provisions are an integral part of the regulatory program and that the regulatory scheme when considered as a whole satisfies this test." *Ibid.* . . .

V

Medicaid, as amended by the ACA, however, is not two spending programs; it is a single program with a constant aim—to enable poor persons to receive basic health care when they need it. Given past expansions, plus express statutory warning that Congress may change the requirements participating States must meet, there can be no tenable claim that the ACA fails for lack of notice. Moreover, States have no entitlement to receive any Medicaid funds; they enjoy only the opportunity to accept funds on Congress' terms. Future Congresses are not bound by their predecessors' dispositions; they have authority to spend federal revenue as they see fit. The Federal Government, therefore, is not, as the Chief Justice charges, threatening States with the loss of "existing" funds from one spending program in order to induce them to opt into another program. Congress is simply requiring States to do what States have long been required to do to receive Medicaid funding: comply with the conditions Congress prescribes for participation.

JUSTICES SCALIA, KENNEDY, THOMAS, and ALITO, dissenting.

The case is easy and straightforward, however, in another respect. What is absolutely clear, affirmed by the text of the 1789 Constitution, by the Tenth Amendment ratified in 1791, and by innumerable cases of ours in the 220 years since, is that there are structural limits upon federal power—upon what it can prescribe with respect to private conduct, and upon what it can impose upon the sovereign States. Whatever may be the conceptual limits upon the Commerce Clause and upon the power to tax and spend, they cannot be such as will enable the Federal Government to regulate all private conduct and to com pel the States to function as administrators of federal programs. . . .

The Act before us here exceeds federal power both in mandating the purchase of health insurance and in denying nonconsenting States all Medicaid funding. These parts of the Act are central to its design and operation, and all the Act's other provisions would not have been enacted without them. In our view it must follow that the entire statute is inoperative.

II

The Taxing Power

As far as § 5000A is concerned, we would stop there. Congress has attempted to regulate beyond the scope of its Commerce Clause authority, and § 5000A is therefore invalid. The Government contends, however, as expressed in the caption to Part II of its brief, that "THE MINIMUM COVERAGE PROVISION IS INDEPENDENTLY AUTHORIZED BY CONGRESS'S TAXING POWER." The phrase "independently authorized" suggests the existence of a creature never hitherto seen in the United States Reports: A penalty for constitutional purposes that is *also* a tax for constitutional purposes. In all our cases the two are mutually exclusive. The provision challenged under the Constitution is either a penalty or else a tax. Of course in many cases what was a regulatory mandate enforced by a penalty *could have been* imposed as a tax upon permissible action; or what was imposed as a tax upon permissible action *could have been* a regulatory mandate enforced by a penalty. But we know of no case, and the Government cites none, in which the imposition was, for constitutional purposes, both. The two are mutually exclusive. Thus, what the Government's caption should have read was "ALTERNATIVELY, THE MINIMUM COVERAGE PROVISION IS NOT A MANDATE-WITH-PENALTY BUT A TAX." It is important to bear this in mind in evaluating the tax argument of the Government and of those who support it: The issue is not whether Congress had the *power* to frame the minimum-coverage provision as a tax, but whether it *did* so. . . .

Our cases establish a clear line between a tax and a penalty: " '[A] tax is an enforced contribution to provide for the support of government; a penalty . . . is an exaction imposed by statute as punishment for an unlawful act.' " *United States* v. *Reorganized CF&I Fabricators of Utah, Inc.*, 518 U.S. 213, 224 (1996) (quoting *United States* v. *La Franca*, 282 U.S. 568, 572 (1931)). In a few cases, this Court has held that a "tax" imposed upon private conduct was so onerous as to be in effect a penalty. But we have never held—*never*—that a penalty imposed for violation of the law was so trivial as to be in effect a tax. We have never held that *any* exaction imposed for violation of the law is an exercise of Congress' taxing power—even when the statute *calls* it a tax, much less when (as here) the statute repeatedly calls it a penalty. When an act "adopt[s] the criteria of wrongdoing" and then imposes a monetary penalty as the "principal consequence on those who transgress its standard," it creates a regulatory penalty, not a tax. *Child Labor Tax Case*, 259 U.S. 20, 38 (1922).

JUSTICE THOMAS, dissenting.

I dissent for the reasons stated in our joint opinion, but I write separately to say a word about the Commerce Clause. The joint dissent and the Chief Justice correctly apply our precedents to conclude that the Individual Mandate is beyond the power granted to Congress under the Commerce Clause and the Necessary and Proper Clause. Under those precedents, Congress may regulate "economic activity [that] substantially affects interstate commerce." *United States* v. *Lopez*, 514 U. S. 549, 560 (1995). I adhere to my view that "the very notion of a 'substantial effects' test under the Commerce Clause is inconsistent with the original understanding of Congress' powers and with this Court's early Commerce Clause cases. . .

FOR DISCUSSION

This case was one of the most anticipated and closely watched of the last decade. Do you think the justices were at all affected by the consequences that might have ensued had the Court struck down such a consequential piece of legislation? Does it make sense for the majority to classify the same law as a penalty in one section and as a tax in another? Do you think the Court majority was correct in distinguishing between regulating commercial activity and attempting to regulate commercial inactivity? Do you think the majority was correct in deciding that the national government was attempting to exercise undue coercion on the states to expand their Medicaid programs? Do you think the decision is consistent with the decision in *South Dakota v. Dole* (483 U.S. 203, 1987) in Chapter II? Do you think the overall effect of the case will be to expand or restrict the range of congressional powers? Why?

NOTE

In *House of Representatives v. Burwell*, Judge Rosemary M. Collyer, issuing a decision on behalf of the U.S. District Court for the District of Columbia, decided on May 12, 2016 that although the Affordable Care Act both authorized and appropriated money for continuing tax credits to make health care more affordable for individuals, the same legislation authorized, but did not appropriate, monies for reimbursements to insurers who reduced deductibles, co-payments, and other forms of cost-sharing for their customers. The court therefore enjoined further reimbursements, which President Obama had authorized, until a valid appropriation was in place, although it stayed this injunction pending appeal.

The court's distinction between authorization and appropriation further emphasized the complexities of the congressional power to tax and spend.

GLOSSARY

Bicameral Legislature: Legislature, like the British Parliament or the U.S. Congress, that has two houses. A unicameral legislature has a single house.

Connecticut Compromise: Also sometimes called the Great Compromise, this is the agreement that was reached at the Constitutional Convention under which states would be represented, as the Virginia Plan had proposed, in the House of Representatives according to state population and, as the New Jersey Plan had proposed, equally in the U.S. Senate.

Direct Tax: Not defined in the U.S. Constitution but required to be assessed proportionally.

Enumerated Powers: Powers specifically listed in the Constitution. The Congress lists most congressional powers in Article I, Sec. 8.

Implied Powers: Powers not specifically listed in the Constitution, but derived from powers that are. In *McCulloch v. Maryland* (1819), Chief Justice John Marshall decided that the power of Congress to establish a national bank was such a power.

Income Tax: Legitimized by the Sixteenth Amendment to the U.S. Constitution after the Supreme Court declared such taxes to be unconstitutional. This tax is currently the federal government's largest source of income.

Injunction: A legal order prohibiting a certain action.

Laissez-faire Economics: An economic policy largely derived from the writings of the Scottish philosopher, Adam Smith, that favors relatively little government interference in the marketplace, which it believes will function through the "invisible hand" of supply and demand.

New Deal: The spending and regulatory policies pursued by President Franklin D. Roosevelt, which were designed to help the nation emerge from the Great Depression. Court invalidation of many of these programs led Roosevelt to propose his Court-packing plan.

Power of the Purse: A name given to the powers of Congress to appropriate, spend, and borrow money. The American Framers contrasted with the president's power of the sword and the Court's power of judgment.

Supremacy Clause: A provision in Article VI of the Constitution that declares the U.S. Constitution and laws and treaties made under it to be the supreme law of the land.

Switch-in-Time-That-Saved-Nine: A play on the phrase, "a stitch in time saves nine." It is used to describe the apparent switch in 1937 by Justice Owen Roberts away from opinions that were largely critical of New Deal programs to those that generally accepted their constitutionality.

SELECTED BIBLIOGRAPHY

Barber, Sotorious. 1975. *The Constitution and the Delegation of Congressional Power.* Chicago: The University of Chicago Press.

Bittker, Boris I. 1999. *Bittker on the Regulation of Interstate and Foreign Commerce.* Gaithersburg, PA: Aspen Law & Business.

Devins, Neil, and Keith E. Whittington, eds. 2005. *Congress and the Constitution.* Durham, NC: Duke University Press.

Diamond, Robert A. 1976. *Powers of Congress.* Washington, DC: Congressional Quarterly, Inc.

Fisher, Louis. 1987. *The Politics of Shared Powers: Congress and the Executive*, 2nd ed. Washington, DC: Congressional Quarterly Press.

Fisher, Louis. 2008. *The Supreme Court and Congress: Rival Interpretations.* Washington, DC: Congressional Quarterly Press.

Frankfurter, Felix. 1937. *The Commerce Clause under Marshall, Taney and Waite.* Chapel Hill: University of North Carolina Press.

Pyle, Christopher H., and Richard M. Pious. 1984. *The President, Congress, and the Constitution: Power and Legitimacy in American Politics.* New York: The Free Press.

Schmidhauser, John R., and Larry L. Berg. 1972. *The Supreme Court and Congress: Conflict and Interaction, 1945–1968.* New York: The Free Press.

CHAPTER IV

Congress and the President

Timeline: Congress and the President

1788	George Washington selected as the first president of the United States
1792	Washington issues the first presidential veto, contending that a bill by Congress setting the size of the House of Representatives is unconstitutional.
1800	Congress selects Thomas Jefferson over Aaron Burr to be president of the United States after the Electoral College produces a deadlock in picking the president.
1803	Thomas Jefferson authorizes the purchase of the Louisiana Territory from France without congressional approval after originally arguing he needed a constitutional amendment to act.
1845	The first congressional override of a presidential veto occurs when President John Tyler's veto of an appropriation bill is overridden.
1866	The Supreme Court upholds in *Ex Parte Garland* the authority of the president to pardon an individual for activity undertaken in support of the Confederacy during the Civil War.
1922	Uncovering of the Teapot Dome Scandal by the *Wall Street Journal.*
1927	In *McGrain v. Daugherty* the Supreme Court upholds the authority of Congress to subpoena a member of the executive department to question him about the Teapot Dome scandal and then to hold him in contempt and order him arrested for her failure to appear to testify.
1932	Franklin Roosevelt is elected president.
1933	Start of the New Deal.
1935	The Supreme Court in *A.L.A. Schechter Poultry v. United States* declares unconstitutional portions of the National Industrial Recovery Act giving the president authority to establish codes of conduct for industrial production.
1957	In *Watkins v. United States* the Supreme Court rules that Congress could not question a person about his political activities with the Communist Party and then find him in contempt because of his refusal to answer questions not relevant to their investigation.
1959	The Supreme Court rules in *Barenblatt v. United States* that Congress had the authority to hold a person in contempt for his refusal to answer questions about his political activity with the Communist Party.
1968	Richard Nixon is elected president.
1971	Publishing of the Pentagon Papers by the *New York Times.*

1972 Burglary and wiretapping of the Democratic National Headquarters at the Watergate office complex.

1972 In *Gravel v. United States* the Supreme Court rules that the Speech and Debate Clause of the Constitution precluded Congress from issuing a subpoena to a member of the House of Representatives who read the entire Pentagon Papers into the *Congressional Record.*

1974 Nixon resigns; Gerald Ford becomes president.

1974 In *United States v. Nixon* the Supreme Court rules that executive privilege did not protect the president from having to turn over subpoenaed records to a federal judge as part of an investigation into criminal activity surrounding Watergate and the office of the presidency.

1974 President Ford pardons former President Nixon.

1975 In *Murphy v. Ford*, a Michigan federal district court upholds the authority of President Ford to issue a pardon to former president Richard Nixon.

1983 In *Immigration and Naturalization Services v. Chadha* the Supreme Court declares unconstitutional a one-house veto under the Immigration and Nationality Act of an executive department decision regarding deportation of an individual.

1986 In *Bowsher v. Synar* the Supreme Court declares unconstitutional provisions of the Balanced Budget and Emergency Deficit Control Act of 1985 on the grounds that it violated separation of powers of the Constitution.

1988 In *Morrison v. Olson* the Supreme Court upholds provisions in the Ethics in Government Act of 1978 that allow for a federal judge to appoint a special prosecutor to investigate alleged illegal activities in the executive department.

1989 The Supreme Court in *Mistretta v. United States* upholds the constitutionality of federal sentencing guidelines.

1992 Bill Clinton is elected president.

1997 The Supreme Court rules in *Clinton v. Jones* that a sexual harassment civil suit against President Clinton arising out of actions allegedly committed while he was governor of Arkansas could proceed while he served as president of the United States.

1997 In *In re Grand Jury Subpoena Duces Tecum*, the 8th Circuit ruled that the White House should be required to turn over the records of conversations between First Lady Hillary Clinton and the White House counsel to a special prosecutor investigating the Clintons regarding possible criminal activity.

1998 In *Clinton v. City of New York* the Supreme Court strikes down a federal law giving the president a line-item veto.

INTRODUCTION

In *Federalist Paper 51*, James Madison argued that the necessity to distribute the powers needed for governance into different branches of government was a guarantee against tyranny.

> Ambition must be made to counteract ambition. The interest of the man must be connected with the constitutional rights of the place. It may be a reflection on human nature, that such devices should be necessary to control the abuses of government. But what is government itself, but the greatest of all reflections on human nature? If men were angels, no government would be necessary. If angels were to govern men, neither external nor internal controls on government would be necessary. In framing a government which is to be administered by men over men, the great difficulty lies in this:

> you must first enable the government to control the governed; and in the next place oblige it to control itself.

Through the concept of **separation of powers** as embodied in the Constitution, the Founders ensured that there would be constant struggles between the branches over power exercised and power contained. In this chapter we will consider three primary manifestations of the battles between the executive and legislative branches. Initially we will consider the lawful and unlawful delegation of power from one branch to another entity. In most cases this has been the legislative branch creating a regulatory agency or a commission to create specialized rules and then ensure their implementation. Second, we look at the conflict between the Congress and the president over the appointment and the removal of officers—while this power is shared, the constitutional guidelines are not clear. Finally we examine the more recent creation of presidential signing statements, through which an executive attempts to direct the future judicial interpretation and executive implementation of a newly passed law.

SEPARATION OF POWERS

Within the U.S. Constitution, the three federal branches of government are granted explicit **enumerated** powers that are directly provided to each discrete segment (executive, judicial, and legislative). In addition, both the state and federal levels of government are also provided **explicit powers**. The purpose of this distribution of powers, according to *Federalist Paper 51* and James Madison, is to ensure that "ambition counteracts ambition" and that one element of the government cannot tyrannize or destroy the other elements. By ensuring that each branch has the ability to limit the other branches through the exercise of **checks and balances,** the Founders believed the government might be less efficient but also less likely to be susceptible to abuse and corruption. Over time, the explicit powers have been expanded by practice or judicial interpretation to include the **implied powers** of each branch, or the authority that results from the exercise of the explicit powers. One of the continuous functions of the Supreme Court is to assess the constitutional implications when the delegated and implicit powers conflict with each other.

It is conventional wisdom that the legislative branch "makes law," the executive branch "enforces law," and the judicial branch "interprets law." The study of the behavior and choices of these three branches quickly reveals that in actuality each does all three. While the first three articles of the Constitution provide the branches' enumerated powers, all of them have pushed to expand their explicit powers in response to new world events, technological advances, and domestic crises. As the judiciary interprets the Constitution and statutory and regulatory law, it is also enforcing prior decision making through the use of precedent, and in making decisions regarding the meaning of law, new law is created. The same is true for the executive and the legislative branches; when presidents issue an executive order, they are making law, and when they provide a signing statement upon endorsing a bill so that it becomes law, they are interpreting the law. Congress frequently provides clear responsibilities and obligations to regulatory agencies and organizations; in so doing they are enforcing the very law they have written. At times they have written bills (such as the Civil Rights Act of 1991 or the Religious Freedom and Restoration Act of 1993) that deliberately describe how previously passed legislation should be understood or how the Constitution should be interpreted. So the barriers between the branches may be more permeable than initially explained by the language of the Constitution. If this is the case, how are the distinctions between the branches maintained?

In the following selection of Supreme Court cases, we will see the battles between the legislative and executive branches over the distribution of powers manifest in several ways: the delegation of legislative power to regulatory and administrative agencies, the appointment and removal of executive officers, and the presidential use of a signing statement to influence the enforcement of new law. In each of these instances, examine how the struggle for authority both limits efficiency and ideally prevents tyranny. Does the separation of powers in these examples meet the objectives of the Founders as articulated in *Federalist Paper 51*? What is the role the Court is playing in the negotiation of these conflicts? Do these conflicts move to resolution or simply evolve in their manifestations? Did the Framers want a pure separation of powers or a sharing of powers? Finally, how far can the Court be in deciding on its own powers?

Delegation of Legislative Power

A consequence of the doctrine of separation of powers is that once a branch of government is delegated specific authority, that branch cannot **delegate** that power in turn to another. Subdelegation is prohibited. However, over the years there have been very few instances of the Supreme Court declaring acts of legislative bodies void on these grounds.

There is no bright line distinguishing constitutional and unconstitutional delegation of legislative authority, but in general Congress must at least set a general policy or standard to guide the president or another administrative officer who has been granted legislative authority. Then within the limits of this standard, this "floor and ceiling," the executive may use his discretion. This is lawful "delegation." For example, in the case of *J.W. Hampton, Jr. Co. v. United States* (276 U.S. 394, 1928), the Court found that the president had the right to make adjustments to a tariff as long as he stays within the rate fixed by Congress. On the other hand, in the case of *Clinton v. City of New York* (524 U.S. 417, 1988), the Court found that the Line Item Veto Act of 1996, through which Congress had allowed the president to strike down specific elements of a bill while signing the remainder into law, was unconstitutional. The Court found that Congress had unlawfully given one of its delegated powers to another branch, in this case, the authority granted to Congress in the Presentment Clause of Article I, Sec. 7, para. 2.

The cases that follow wrestle with the constitutional limits of congressional delegation of their lawmaking and regulatory authority to both a New Deal enforcement agency, *Schechter Poultry v. United States* (295 U.S. 495, 1935), better known as the "sick chicken" case, and to the Immigration and Naturalization Services in *INS v. Chadha* (462 U.S. 919, 1983). In the case of *Schechter Poultry,* Congress allowed the president through the National Industrial Recovery Act to create codes regulating working hours, age and number of employees, and minimum wages in the poultry industry. The case was challenged as an unlawful delegation of Congress's lawmaking powers to the executive branch and the Supreme Court agreed. The problem the Court found was that the law passed by Congress did not establish the rules or guidelines, but allowed the president to make the regulations, and in so doing the legislature unlawfully delegated their power.

Two years later in *National Labor Relations Board v. Jones & Laughlin Steel Corporation,* (301 U.S. 1, 1937), the Court held as an incidental part of its decision that there was no delegation of power as regards the activities of the NLRB. "The procedural provisions of the act are assailed. But these provisions, as we construe them, do not offend against the constitutional requirements governing the creation and action of administrative bodies" (301 U.S. 1 at 46–47). The Court has indicated that a valid statute should have (1) a definition of the subject of delegation (a policy), (2) standards set, (3) procedure established, with delegation only to an official agency, (4) certain conditions set, including the finding of facts and circumstances, and (5) penal sanctions established. There must be adequate and proper standards to guide administrative officers in carrying out the will of Congress (the standard is to let the officer know just what the will of Congress is), and the limited discretion that is granted must not be given to any private person or persons, but only to public officials.

The case of *Immigration and Naturalization Service v. Chadha,* (462 U.S. 919, 1983), raises different questions on the same theme. In this case, the Immigration and Nationality Act provided the executive branch the power to regulate and decide immigration and naturalization decisions and appeals; however, the law also allows one house of Congress to invalidate such decisions by a simple resolution. The constitutionality of this legislative veto was challenged. Although the Court found that legislative vetoes violate the design of the separation of powers doctrine, since the decision in 1983 post-*INS v. Chadha,* Congress has created over four hundred new legislative vetoes. These legislative acts require the executive to obtain approval for certain decisions from congressional committees and also provide these committees with veto authority over executive determinations. After *Chadha*, Congress attempted to create a formula resembling a legislative veto that does not violate the Court's guidelines regarding the separation of power or to amend the Constitution to protect legislative vetoes. While the Congress was unsuccessful in this effort, it has maintained the use of committee suspensions in the arena of appropriations, with the acquiescence of the executive branch. One reason the executive branch has accepted these conditions (see, for instance, the War Powers Act of 1973) is that it gives them more delegated decision-making authority than they would have absent a legislative veto. However, the constitutionality of all of these conditions and legislative vetoes remains unclear.

More recently, the Court has wrestled with the constitutionality of legislatively mandated sentencing guidelines under the auspices of separation of powers. Because a legislatively created commission designed the sentencing guidelines that federal courts were directed to use, it was challenged as an unlawful delegation of legislative authority (*Mistretta v. United States*, 488 U.S. 361, 1989). Historically, Congress had allowed federal judges complete autonomy in determining the consequences for violating federal law. By the 1980s and the federal engagement in the "war on drugs," however, the wide disparities in federal sentencing gained public attention and disapproval. Through the Sentencing Reform Act of 1984, the legislature created the Sentencing Commission and gave it the authority to make guidelines binding on the courts, with a few exceptions for judicial independence. Although the Court allowed the constitutionality of the mandatory Sentencing Guidelines in *Mistretta*, by 2005 the justices were rethinking their conclusions.

In the split-opinion decision in *United States v. Booker* (543 U.S. 220, 2005), the Court reviewed two cases in which the lower federal court judge awarded a sentence beyond that determined by the sentencing guidelines, arguing that they relied upon additional facts of which the jury had been unaware in their decision making. In Justice Stevens's majority decision, the Court stated that if a judge could render a decision based on information absent from jury consideration, the defendant would be denied his Sixth Amendment right to a jury trial. In Justice Breyer's majority opinion, he notes that the decision to add the jury presentation element to the Sentencing Act radically changed the law that Congress had passed. To make the new constitutional requirement regarding juries and sentencing compatible with the Sentencing Reform Act of 1984, the Court found that the statutory provisions that made the Sentencing Guidelines mandatory were invalid. As a consequence of *U.S. v. Booker*, the Sentencing Guidelines are no longer mandatory for federal judges, but simply advisory. Justice Breyer recognizes that determination challenges the intent and purpose of Congress in passing the Sentencing Reform Act and notes the following: "Ours, of course, is not the last word: The ball now lies in Congress' court. The National Legislature is equipped to devise and install, long term, the sentencing system, compatible with the Constitution, that Congress judges best for the federal system of justice" (543 U.S. 265).

This is how the challenge of separation of powers continues and evolves. Congress now has the opportunity to revise the Sentencing Act or continue with the law in its modified *Booker* form. Whatever their decision, the separation of powers between the branches will continue its evolution, and so will the Court's decisions in this area of law.

A.L.A. Schechter Poultry Corp. v. United States

295 U.S. 495, 55 S. Ct. 837, 79 L. Ed. 1570 (1935)

Under the National Industrial Recovery Act (NIRA), an executive order of the president established the "Live Poultry Code." The NIRA provided for the establishment of codes that would establish certain standards for various industries, and these codes were to be enforced by both civil and criminal action. The National Recovery

Administration (NRA) was the enforcement agency under NIRA. The A.L.A. Schechter Poultry Corp., a poultry dealer in New York City, was found guilty of disregarding the code on eighteen counts. Schechter challenged the legitimacy of the Act in that the Code had been adopted pursuant to an unconstitutional delegation of congressional authority.

Vote: 9–0

CHIEF JUSTICE HUGHES delivered the opinion of the Court:

The "Live Poultry Code" was promulgated under § 3 of the National Industrial Recovery Act. That section . . . authorizes the President to approve "codes of fair competition."

The "Live Poultry Code" was approved by the President on April 13, 1934. The Code is established as "a code for fair competition for the live poultry industry of the metropolitan area in and about the City of New York."

The Code fixes the number of hours for workdays. It provides that no employee, with certain exceptions, shall be permitted to work in excess of forty (40) hours in any one week, and that no employee, save as stated, "shall be paid in any pay period less than at the rate of fifty (50) cents per hour." The article containing "general labor provisions" prohibits the employment of any person under sixteen years of age, and declares that employees shall have the right of "collective bargaining" and freedom of choice with respect to labor organizations, in the terms of § 7(a) of the Act. The minimum number of employees who shall be employed by slaughterhouse operators is fixed, the numbers being graduated according to the average volume of weekly sales. The seventh article, containing "trade practice provisions," prohibits various practices which are said to constitute "unfair methods of competition."

The President approved the Code by an executive order. . . . [The first question was if the law was justified in the light of the grave national crisis. The answer was that the Tenth Amendment precluded such action.]

Second. The question of the delegation of legislative power. The Constitution provides that "all legislative powers herein granted shall be vested in a Congress of the United States, which shall consist of a Senate and House of Representatives." Article One, § 1. And the Congress is authorized "to make all laws which shall be necessary and proper for carrying into execution" its general power. Article One, § 8, paragraph 18. The Congress is not permitted to abdicate or to transfer to others the essential legislative functions with which it is thus vested. We have repeatedly recognized the necessity of adapting legislation to complex conditions involving a host of details with which the national Legislature cannot deal directly. . . . [T]he Constitution has never been regarded as denying to Congress the necessary resources of flexibility and practicality, which will enable it to perform its function in laying down policies and establishing standards, while leaving to selected instrumentalities the making of subordinate rules within prescribed limits and the determination of facts to which the policy as declared by the Legislature is to apply. But we said that the constant recognition of the necessity and validity of such provisions, and the wide range of administrative authority which has been developed by means of them, cannot be allowed to obscure the limitations of the authority to delegate, if our constitutional system is to be maintained.

Accordingly, we turn to the Recovery Act to ascertain what limits have been set to the exercise of the President's discretion. *First,* the President, as a condition of approval, is required to find that the trade or industrial associations or groups which propose a code "impose no inequitable restrictions on admission to membership" and are "truly representative." That condition, however, relates only to the status of the initiators of the new laws and not to the permissible scope of such laws. *Second,* the President is required to find that the code is not "designed to promote monopolies or to eliminate or oppress small enterprises and will not operate to discriminate against them." And to this is added a proviso that the code "shall not permit monopolies or monopolistic practices." But these restrictions leave virtually untouched the field of policy envisaged by section one, and in that wide field of legislative possibilities the proponents of a code, refraining from monopolistic designs, may roam at will and the President may approve or disapprove their proposals as he may see fit.

To summarize and conclude upon this point: Section 3 of the Recovery Act is without precedent. It supplies no standards for any trade, industry or activity. It does not undertake to prescribe rules of conduct to be applied to particular states of fact determined by appropriate administrative procedure. Instead of prescribing rules of conduct, it authorizes the making of codes to prescribe them. For that legislative undertaking, § 3 sets up no standards, aside from the statement of the general aims of rehabilitation, correction and expansion described in section one. In view of the scope of that broad declaration, and of the nature of the few restrictions that are imposed, the discretion of the President in approving or prescribing codes, and thus enacting laws for the government of trade and industry throughout the country, is virtually unfettered. We think that the code-making authority thus conferred is an unconstitutional delegation of legislative power.

Third. The question of the application of the provisions of the Live Poultry Code to intrastate transactions. . . . But under § 3(f), penalties are confined to violations of a code provision "in any transaction in or affecting interstate or foreign commerce." This aspect of the case presents the question whether the particular provisions of the Live Poultry Code, which the defendants were convicted for violating and for having conspired to violate, were within the regulating powers of Congress.

These provisions relate to the hours and wages of those employed by defendants in their slaughterhouses in Brooklyn and to the sales there made to retail dealers and butchers.

(1) Were these transactions "*in*" interstate commerce? Much is made of the fact that almost all [96 percent] the poultry coming to New York is sent there from other states. But the code provisions as here applied do not concern the transportation of the poultry from other states to New York, or the transactions of the commission men or others to whom it is consigned, or the sales made by such consignees to defendants. When defendants had made their purchases, whether at the West Washington Market in New York City or at the railroad terminals serving the city, or elsewhere, the poultry was trucked to their slaughterhouses in Brooklyn for local disposition. The interstate transactions in relation to that poultry then ended. Defendants held the poultry at their slaughterhouse markets for slaughter and local sale to retail dealers and butchers, who in turn sold directly to consumers. Neither the slaughtering nor the sales by defendants were transactions in interstate commerce.

The undisputed facts thus afford no warrant for the argument that the poultry handled by defendants at their slaughterhouse markets was in a "*current*" or "*flow*" of interstate commerce and was thus subject to congressional regulation. The mere fact that there may be a constant flow of commodities into a state does not mean that the flow continues after the property has arrived and has become commingled with the mass of property within the state and is there held solely for local disposition and use. So far as the poultry herein questioned is concerned, the flow in interstate commerce had ceased. The poultry had come to a permanent rest within the state. It was not held, used or sold by defendants in relation to any further transaction in interstate commerce and was not destined for transportation to other states. Hence, decisions which deal with a stream of interstate commerce—where goods come to rest within a state temporarily and are later to go forward in interstate commerce—and with the regulations of transactions involved in that practical continuity of movement, are not applicable here. . . .

(2) Did the defendant's transactions directly "*affect*" interstate commerce so as to be subject to federal regulation? The power of Congress extends not only to the regulation of transactions which are part of interstate commerce, but to the protection of that commerce from injury. It matters not that the injury may be due to the conduct of those engaged in intrastate operations. Thus, Congress may protect the safety of those employed in interstate transportation "no matter what may be the source of the dangers which threaten it. . . ."

. . . Defendants have been convicted, not upon direct charges of injury to interstate commerce or of interference with persons engaged in that commerce, but of violations of certain provisions of the Live Poultry Code and of conspiracy to commit these violations. Interstate commerce is brought in only upon the charge that violations of these provisions—as to hours and wages of employees and local sales—"*affected*" interstate commerce.

In determining how far the federal government may go in controlling intrastate transactions upon the ground that they "affect" interstate commerce, there is a necessary and well-established distinction between direct and indirect effects. The precise line can be drawn only as individual cases arise, but the distinction is clear in principle. If the commerce clause were construed to reach all enterprises and transactions which could be said to have an indirect effect upon interstate commerce, the federal authority would embrace practically all the activities of the people, and the authority of the state over its domestic concerns would exist only by sufferance of the federal government. Indeed, on such a theory, even the development of the state's commercial facilities would be subject to federal control.

Otherwise, as we have said, there would be virtually no limit to the federal power, and for all practical purposes we should have a completely centralized government. We must consider the provisions here in question in the light of this distinction.

We are of the opinion that the attempt through the provisions of the code to fix the hours and wages of employees of defendants in their intrastate business was not a valid exercise of federal power.

The other violations for which defendants were convicted related to the making of local sales. Ten counts, for violation of the provision as to "straight killing," were for permitting customers to make "selections of individual chickens taken from particular coops and half coops." Whether or not this practice is good or bad for the local trade, its effect, if any, upon interstate commerce was only indirect. The same may be said of violations of the Code by intrastate transactions consisting of the sale "of an unfit chicken" and of sales which were not in accord with the ordinances of the City of New York. The requirement of reports as to prices and volumes of defendants' sales was incident to the effort to control their intrastate business.

In view of these conclusions, we find it unnecessary to discuss other questions which have been raised as to the validity of certain provisions of the Code under the due process clause of the Fifth Amendment.

On both the grounds we have discussed, the attempted delegation of legislative power and the attempted regulation of intrastate transactions which affect interstate commerce only indirectly, we hold the code provisions here in question to be invalid. . . .

Judgment reversed.

JUSTICE CARDOZO concurred.

This is delegation running riot. No such plenitude of power is susceptible of transfer.

But there is another objection, far-reaching and incurable, aside from any defect of unlawful delegation.

If this code had been adopted by Congress itself, and not by the President on the advice of an industrial association, it would even then be void unless authority to adopt it is included in the grant of power "to regulate commerce with foreign nations and among the several states."

I find no authority in that grant for the regulation of wages and hours of labor in the intrastate transactions that make up the defendants' business.

Wages and the hours of labor are essential features of the plan, its very bone and sinew. There is no opportunity in such circumstances for the severance of the infected parts in the hope of saving the remainder. A code collapses utterly with bone and sinew gone.

I am authorized to state that Mr. Justice Stone joins in this opinion.

FOR DISCUSSION

Why does the Court believe that controlling the delegation of authority by the legislature also protects the integrity of federalism? Should the nature of the national emergency as understood by the executive and legislative branches in implementing the New Deal affect the Supreme Court's interpretation of the delegation of powers?

RELATED CASES

***Carter v. Carter Coal Co.:* 298 U.S. 238 (1936).**

Congress was not able indirectly to regulate the mining and distribution of coal under the Commerce Clause through delegation. The Guffy Coal Act was held to be an improper delegation of legislative power, not to government officials, but to members of the coal industry, who were private persons.

***Panama Refining Company v. Ryan:* 293 U.S. 388 (1935).**

This decision struck down part of the New Deal's National Industrial Recovery Act of 1933 because it delegated to the executive branch the authority to exclude oil produced beyond the state regulations from interstate commerce. The Court found that inadequate guidelines were provided to control presidential decision making. Dissenting Justice Cardozo found this was the distinct element from the precedents of *Schecter* and *Carter*.

***Chevron U.S.A. v. Natural Resources Defense Council:* 467 U.S. 837 (1984).**

This case evaluated an amendment to the Clean Air Act of 1977 that allowed the president to deregulate air pollution control standards previously established by Congress. The decision of the Court indicated that the judiciary should defer to the executive and regulatory agencies' interpretations of vague legislative mandates.

Article I, Sec. 7, para. 2:

Every Bill which shall have passed the House of Representatives and the Senate, shall, before it become a Law, be presented to the President of the United States; If he approve he shall sign it, but if not he shall return it, with his Objections to that House in which it shall have originated, who shall enter the Objections at large on their Journal, and proceed to reconsider it. If after such Reconsideration two thirds of that House shall agree to pass the Bill, it shall be sent, together with the Objections, to the other House, by which it shall likewise be reconsidered, and if approved by two thirds of that House, it shall become a Law.

IMMIGRATION AND NATURALIZATION SERVICE V. CHADHA

462 U.S. 919, 103 S. Ct. 2764, 77 L. Ed. 2d 317 (1983)

Chadha was an East Indian born in Kenya who held a British passport. He was lawfully admitted to the United States in 1966 on a nonimmigrant student visa that expired on June 30, 1972. After numerous hearings, his status was adjusted to permanent resident alien, absent any Congressional action. The House of Representatives ordered him deported under the legislative branch veto provision § 244(c)(d) of the Immigration and

Nationality Act, 66 Stat. 216, as amended, 8 U.S.C. § 1254(c)(d). The law authorizes one house of Congress, by a resolution, to invalidate the decision of the executive branch, based on the authority delegated by Congress to the attorney general, to allow a deportable alien to remain in the United States. Chadha challenged the constitutionality of the legislative veto; the immigration judge and Board of Immigration Appeals found that they were powerless to declare an act of Congress unconstitutional. The Court of Appeals for the Ninth Circuit found that the House did not have the congressional authority to order Chadha's deportation.

Vote: 7–2

CHIEF JUSTICE BURGER delivered the opinion of the Court.

III A

We turn . . . to the question whether action of one House of Congress under § 244(c)(2) violates strictures of the Constitution. We begin, of course, with the presumption that the challenged statute is valid.

By the same token, the fact that a given law or procedure is efficient, convenient, and useful in facilitating functions of government, standing alone, will not save it if it is contrary to the Constitution. Convenience and efficiency are not the primary objectives—or the hallmarks—of democratic government and our inquiry is sharpened rather than blunted by the fact that congressional veto provisions are appearing with increasing frequency in statutes which delegate authority to executive and independent agencies[.]

Justice White undertakes to make a case for the proposition that the one-House veto is a useful "political invention," and we need not challenge that assertion. We can even concede this utilitarian argument although the long-range political wisdom of this "invention" is arguable. But policy arguments supporting even useful "political inventions" are subject to the demands of the Constitution which defines powers and, with respect to this subject, sets out just how those powers are to be exercised. Explicit and unambiguous provisions of the Constitution prescribe and define the respective functions of the Congress and of the Executive in the legislative process.

[The] provisions of Art. I are integral parts of the constitutional design for the separation of powers. We have recently noted that "[the] principle of separation of powers was not simply an abstract generalization in the minds of the Framers: it was woven into the document that they drafted in Philadelphia in the summer of 1787." *Buckley v. Valeo*, 424 U.S., at 124. Just as we relied on the textual provision of Art. II, § 2, cl. 2, to vindicate the principle of separation of powers in *Buckley*, we see that the purposes underlying the Presentment Clauses, Art. I, § 7, cls. 2, 3, and the bicameral requirement of Art. I, § 1, and § 7, cl. 2, guide our resolution of the important question presented in these cases. The very structure of the Articles delegating and separating powers under Arts. I, II, and III exemplifies the concept of separation of powers. . . .

B

The Presentment Clauses

The records of the Constitutional Convention reveal that the requirement that all legislation be presented to the President before becoming law was uniformly accepted by the Framers. Presentment to the President and the Presidential veto were considered so imperative that the draftsmen took special pains to assure that these requirements could not be circumvented.

The decision to provide the President with a limited and qualified power to nullify proposed legislation by veto was based on the profound conviction of the Framers that the powers conferred on Congress were the powers to be most carefully circumscribed. It is beyond doubt that lawmaking was a power to be shared by both Houses and the President.

The President's role in the lawmaking process also reflects the Framers' careful efforts to check whatever propensity a particular Congress might have to enact oppressive, improvident, or ill-considered measures.

C

Bicameralism

The bicameral requirement of Art. I, §§ 1, 7, was of scarcely less concern to the Framers than was the Presidential veto, and indeed the two concepts are interdependent. By providing that no law could take effect without the concurrence of the prescribed majority of the Members of both Houses, the Framers reemphasized their belief, already remarked upon in connection with the Presentment Clauses, that legislation should not be enacted unless it has been carefully and fully considered by the Nation's elected officials.

We see therefore that the Framers were acutely conscious that the bicameral requirement and the Presentment Clauses would serve essential constitutional functions. The President's participation in the legislative process was to protect the Executive Branch from Congress and to protect the whole people from improvident laws. The division of the Congress into two distinctive bodies assures that the legislative power would be exercised only after opportunity for full study and debate in separate settings. The President's unilateral veto power, in turn, was limited by the power of two-thirds of both Houses of Congress to overrule a veto, thereby precluding final arbitrary action of one person. It emerges clearly that the prescription for legislative action in Art. I, §§ 1, 7, represents the Framers' decision that the legislative power of the Federal Government be exercised in accord with a single, finely wrought and exhaustively considered, procedure.

IV

The Constitution sought to divide the delegated powers of the new Federal Government into three defined categories, Legislative, Executive, and Judicial, to assure, as nearly as possible, that each branch of government would confine itself to its assigned responsibility. The hydraulic pressure inherent within each of the separate Branches to exceed the outer limits of its power, even to accomplish desirable objectives, must be resisted.

Although not "hermetically" sealed from one another, *Buckley v. Valeo*, 424 U.S., at 121, the powers delegated to the three Branches are functionally identifiable. When any Branch acts, it is presumptively exercising the power the Constitution has delegated to it. When the Executive acts, he presumptively acts in an executive or administrative capacity as defined in Art. II. And when, as here, one House of Congress purports to act, it is presumptively acting within its assigned sphere.

Beginning with this presumption, we must nevertheless establish that the challenged action under § 244(c)(2) is of the kind to which the procedural requirements of Art. I, § 7, apply. Not every action taken by either House is subject to the bicameralism and presentment requirements of Art. I. Whether actions taken by either House are, in law and fact, an exercise of legislative power depends not on their form but upon "whether they contain matter which is properly to be regarded as legislative in its character and effect." S. Rep. No. 1335, 54th Cong., 2d Sess., 8 (1897).

Examination of the action taken here by one House pursuant to § 244(c)(2) reveals that it was essentially legislative in purpose and effect. In purporting to exercise power defined in Art. I, § 8, cl. 4, to "establish an uniform Rule of Naturalization," the House took action that had the purpose and effect of altering the legal rights, duties, and relations of persons, including the Attorney General, Executive Branch officials and Chadha, all outside the Legislative Branch.

The legislative character of the one-House veto in these cases is confirmed by the character of the congressional action it supplants. Neither the House of Representatives nor the Senate contends that, absent the veto provision in § 244(c)(2), either of them, or both of them acting together, could effectively require the Attorney General to deport an alien once the Attorney General, in the exercise of legislatively delegated authority, had determined the alien should remain in the United States. Without the challenged provision in § 244(c)(2), this could have been achieved, if at all, only by legislation requiring deportation. Similarly, a veto by one House of Congress under § 244(c)(2) cannot be justified as an attempt at amending the standards set out in § 244(a)(1), or as a repeal of § 244 as applied to Chadha. Amendment and repeal of statutes, no less than enactment, must conform with Art. I.

Finally, we see that, when the Framers intended to authorize either House of Congress to act alone and outside of its prescribed bicameral legislative role, they narrowly and precisely defined the procedure for such action. There are four provisions in the Constitution, explicit and unambiguous, by which one House may act alone with the unreviewable force of law, not subject to the President's veto:

(a) The House of Representatives alone was given the power to initiate impeachments. Art. I, § 2, cl. 5;

(b) The Senate alone was given the power to conduct trials following impeachment on charges initiated by the House and to convict following trial. Art. I, § 3, cl. 6;

(c) The Senate alone was given final unreviewable power to approve or to disapprove Presidential appointments. Art. II, § 2, cl. 2;

(d) The Senate alone was given unreviewable power to ratify treaties negotiated by the President. Art. II, § 2, cl. 2.

Clearly, when the Draftsmen sought to confer special powers on one House, independent of the other House, or of the President, they did so in explicit, unambiguous terms.

Since it is clear that the action by the House under § 244(c)(2) was not within any of the express constitutional exceptions authorizing one House to act alone, and equally clear that it was an exercise of legislative power, that action was subject to the standards prescribed in Art. I. The bicameral requirement, the Presentment Clauses, the President's veto, and Congress' power to override a veto were intended to erect enduring checks on each Branch and to protect the people from the improvident exercise of power by mandating certain prescribed steps. To preserve those checks, and maintain the separation of powers, the carefully defined limits on the power of each Branch must not be eroded. To accomplish what has been attempted by one House of Congress in this case requires action in conformity with the express procedures of the Constitution's prescription for legislative action: passage by a majority of both Houses and presentment to the President.

The choices we discern as having been made in the Constitutional Convention impose burdens on governmental processes that often seem clumsy, inefficient, even unworkable, but those hard choices were consciously made by men who had lived under a form of government that permitted arbitrary governmental acts to go unchecked. There is no support in the Constitution or decisions of this Court for the proposition that the cumbersomeness and delays often encountered in complying with explicit constitutional standards may be avoided, either by the Congress or by the President. With all the obvious flaws of delay, untidiness, and potential for abuse, we have not yet found a better way to preserve freedom than by making the exercise of power subject to the carefully crafted restraints spelled out in the Constitution.

V

We hold that the congressional veto provision in § 244(c)(2) is severable from the Act and that it is unconstitutional. Accordingly, the judgment of the Court of Appeals is

Affirmed.

JUSTICE POWELL, concurring.

The Court's decision, based on the Presentment Clauses, Art. I, § 7, cls. 2 and 3, apparently will invalidate every use of the legislative veto. The breadth of this holding gives one pause. Congress has included the veto in literally hundreds of statutes, dating back to the 1930's. Congress clearly views this procedure as essential to controlling the delegation of power to administrative agencies. One reasonably may disagree with Congress' assessment of the veto's utility, but the respect due its judgment as a coordinate branch of Government cautions that our holding should be no more extensive than necessary to decide these cases. In my view, the cases may be decided on a narrower ground. When Congress finds that a particular person does not satisfy the statutory criteria for permanent residence in this country, it has assumed a judicial function in violation of the principle of separation of powers. Accordingly, I concur only in the judgment.

JUSTICE WHITE, dissenting.

Today the Court not only invalidates § 244(c)(2) of the Immigration and Nationality Act, but also sounds the death knell for nearly 200 other statutory provisions in which Congress has reserved a "legislative veto." For this reason, the Court's decision is of surpassing importance. And it is for this reason that the Court would have been well advised to decide the cases, if possible, on the narrower grounds of separation of powers, leaving for full consideration the constitutionality of other congressional review statutes operating on such varied matters as war powers and agency rulemaking, some of which concern the independent regulatory agencies.

The prominence of the legislative veto mechanism in our contemporary political system and its importance to Congress can hardly be overstated. It has become a central means by which Congress secures the accountability of executive and independent agencies. Without the legislative veto, Congress is faced with a Hobson's choice: either to refrain from delegating the necessary authority, leaving itself with a hopeless task of writing laws with the requisite specificity to cover endless special circumstances across the entire policy landscape, or in the alternative, to abdicate its law-making function to the Executive Branch and independent agencies. To choose the former leaves major national problems unresolved; to opt for the latter risks unaccountable policymaking by those not elected to fill that role. Accordingly, over the past five decades, the legislative veto has been placed in nearly 200 statutes. The device is known in every field of governmental concern: reorganization, budgets, foreign affairs, war powers, and regulation of trade, safety, energy, the environment, and the economy.

V

I regret that I am in disagreement with my colleagues on the fundamental questions that these cases present. But even more I regret the destructive scope of the Court's holding. It reflects a profoundly different conception of the Constitution than that held by the courts which sanctioned the modern administrative state. Today's decision strikes down in one fell swoop provisions in more laws enacted by Congress than the Court has cumulatively invalidated in its history. I fear it will now be more difficult to "[insure] that the fundamental policy decisions in our society will be made not by an appointed official but by the body immediately responsible to the people," *Arizona v. California*, 373 U.S. 546, 626 (1963) (Harlan, J., dissenting in part). I must dissent.

JUSTICE REHNQUIST, with whom Justice White joins, dissenting.

The Court finds that the legislative history of § 244 shows that Congress intended § 244(c)(2) to be severable because Congress wanted to relieve itself of the burden of private bills. But the history elucidated by the Court shows that Congress was unwilling to give the Executive Branch permission to suspend deportation on its own. Over the years, Congress consistently rejected requests from the Executive for complete discretion in this area. Congress always insisted on retaining ultimate control, whether by concurrent resolution, as in the 1948 Act, or by one-House veto, as in the present Act. Congress has never indicated that it would be willing to permit suspensions of deportation unless it could retain some sort of veto.

It is doubtless true that Congress has the power to provide for suspensions of deportation without a one-House veto. But the Court has failed to identify any evidence that Congress intended to exercise that power. On the contrary, Congress' continued insistence on retaining control of the suspension process indicates that it has never been disposed to give the Executive Branch a free hand. By severing § 244(c)(2) the Court has " 'confounded' " Congress' " 'intention' " to permit suspensions of deportation " 'with their power to carry that intention into effect.' " *Davis*, supra, at 484, quoting *State ex rel. McNeal v. Dombaugh*, 20 Ohio St. 167, 174 (1870).

Because I do not believe that § 244(c)(2) is severable, I would reverse the judgment of the Court of Appeals.

FOR DISCUSSION

How does the decision regarding the constitutionality of the legislative veto reflect the concerns of the delegation of powers seen in the *Schechter* case? Compare the *Schechter* and *Chadha* cases—in what way does *Chadha* demonstrate the realities of the separation of powers in a more complex administrative state?

RELATED CASES

***Field v. Clark:* 143 U.S. 649 (1892).**

This decision sustained the constitutionality of the Tariff Act of 1890, which required the president to suspend or cancel tariff provisions when he found that three legislative provisions had been met. The Court found that the mandated suspensions were not exercises of legislative power and therefore did not violate separation of powers.

***Bowsher v. Synar:* 478 U.S. 714 (1986).**

The Court held the Balanced Budget and Emergency Deficit Control Act of 1985 unconstitutional on the grounds that Congress had controlled executive action through a means reminiscent of a legislative veto. By ensuring that they had removal authority over the implementer of the Budget Act, the comptroller general, the legislature violated the separation of powers requirement of *Chadha*.

***Washington Airports Authority v. Noise Abatement Citizens:* 501 U.S. 252 (1991).**

Congress allowed the transfer of control of two national airports from the federal government to the Metropolitan Washington Airports Authority. A condition of the transfer was the creation of a review board filled by nine members of Congress and granted a veto power over the Airports Authority. The Court found this violated the principle of separation of powers by granting an illegitimate legislative veto to Congress.

MISTRETTA V. UNITED STATES

488 U.S. 361, 109 S. Ct. 647, 102 L. Ed. 2d 714 (1989)

Petitioner John Mistretta was indicted on three counts related to a cocaine sale. Mistretta challenged the promulgated federal sentencing guidelines as unconstitutional because the U.S. Sentencing Commission, created by the Sentencing Reform Act of 1984, violates the doctrine of separation of powers. Mistretta claimed that Congress delegated excessive authority to the Sentencing Commission in the structuring of the sentencing guidelines. The District Court rejected these claims, and the case was appealed to the Supreme Court.

Vote: 8–1

JUSTICE BLACKMUN delivered the opinion of the Court.

Historically, federal sentencing—the function of determining the scope and extent of punishment—never has been thought to be assigned by the Constitution to the exclusive jurisdiction of any one of the three branches of Government. Congress, of course, has the power to fix the sentence for a federal crime, *United States v. Wiltberger*, 5 Wheat. 76 (1820), and the scope of judicial discretion with respect to a sentence is subject to congressional control. *Ex parte United States*, 242 U.S. 27 (1916). Congress delegated almost unfettered discretion to the sentencing judge to determine what the sentence should be within the customarily wide range so selected.

Serious disparities in sentences, however, were common. In 1958, Congress authorized the creation of judicial sentencing institutes and joint councils, see 28 U.S. C. § 334, to formulate standards and criteria for sentencing.

Congress had wrestled with the problem for more than a decade when, in 1984, it enacted the sweeping reforms that are at issue here.

The Act, as adopted, revises the old sentencing process in several ways:

1. It rejects imprisonment as a means of promoting rehabilitation, and it states that punishment should serve retributive, educational, deterrent, and incapacitative goals.

2. It consolidates the power that had been exercised by the sentencing judge and the Parole Commission to decide what punishment an offender should suffer.

3. It makes all sentences basically determinate. A prisoner is to be released at the completion of his sentence reduced only by any credit earned by good behavior while in custody.

4. It makes the Sentencing Commission's guidelines binding on the courts, although it preserves for the judge the discretion to depart from the guideline applicable to a particular case if the judge finds an aggravating or mitigating factor present that the Commission did not adequately consider when formulating guidelines.

5. It authorizes limited appellate review of the sentence.

III
Delegation of Power

Petitioner argues that in delegating the power to promulgate sentencing guidelines for every federal criminal offense to an independent Sentencing Commission, Congress has granted the Commission excessive legislative discretion in violation of the constitutionally based nondelegation doctrine. We do not agree.

The nondelegation doctrine is rooted in the principle of separation of powers that underlies our tripartite system of Government. We also have recognized, however, that the separation-of-powers principle, and the nondelegation doctrine in particular, do not prevent Congress from obtaining the assistance of its coordinate Branches. In a passage now enshrined in our jurisprudence, Chief Justice Taft, writing for the Court, explained our approach to such cooperative ventures: "In determining what [Congress] may do in seeking assistance from another branch, the extent and character of that assistance must be fixed according to common sense and the inherent necessities of the government co-ordination." *J. W. Hampton, Jr., & Co. v. United States*, 276 U.S. 394, 406 (1928). So long as Congress "shall lay down by legislative act an intelligible principle to which the person or body authorized to [exercise the delegated authority] is directed to conform, such legislative action is not a forbidden delegation of legislative power." Id., at 409.

Applying this "intelligible principle" test to congressional delegations, our jurisprudence has been driven by a practical understanding that in our increasingly complex society, replete with ever changing and more technical problems, Congress simply cannot do its job absent an ability to delegate power under broad general directives.

In light of our approval of these broad delegations, we harbor no doubt that Congress' delegation of authority to the Sentencing Commission is sufficiently specific and detailed to meet constitutional requirements.

In addition, Congress prescribed the specific tool—the guidelines system—for the Commission to use in regulating sentencing.

[A]lthough Congress granted the Commission substantial discretion in formulating guidelines, in actuality it legislated a full hierarchy of punishment—from near maximum imprisonment, to substantial imprisonment, to some imprisonment, to alternatives—and stipulated the most important offense and offender characteristics to place defendants within these categories.

We cannot dispute petitioner's contention that the Commission enjoys significant discretion in formulating guidelines. The Commission does have discretionary authority to determine the relative severity of federal crimes and to assess the relative weight of the offender characteristics that Congress listed for the Commission to consider. The Commission also has significant discretion to determine which crimes have been punished too leniently, and which too severely. Congress has called upon the Commission to exercise its judgment about which types of crimes and which types of criminals are to be considered similar for the purposes of sentencing.

Developing proportionate penalties for hundreds of different crimes by a virtually limitless array of offenders is precisely the sort of intricate, labor-intensive task for which delegation to an expert body is especially appropriate. Although Congress has delegated significant discretion to the Commission to draw judgments from its analysis of existing sentencing practice and alternative sentencing models, "Congress is not confined to that method of executing its policy which involves the least possible delegation of discretion to administrative officers." *Yakus v. United States*, 321 U.S. 414, at 425–426 (1944).

IV

Separation of Powers

Having determined that Congress has set forth sufficient standards for the exercise of the Commission's delegated authority, we turn to Mistretta's claim that the Act violates the constitutional principle of separation of powers.

This Court consistently has given voice to, and has reaffirmed, the central judgment of the Framers of the Constitution that, within our political scheme, the separation of governmental powers into three coordinate Branches is essential to the preservation of liberty.

In a passage now commonplace in our cases, Justice Jackson summarized the pragmatic, flexible view of differentiated governmental power to which we are heir:

> "While the Constitution diffuses power the better to secure liberty, it also contemplates that practice will integrate the dispersed powers into a workable government. It enjoins upon its branches separateness but interdependence, autonomy but reciprocity." *Youngstown Sheet & Tube Co. v. Sawyer*, 343 U.S. 579, 635 (1952) (concurring opinion).

In adopting this flexible understanding of separation of powers, we simply have recognized Madison's teaching that the greatest security against tyranny—the accumulation of excessive authority in a single Branch—lies not in a hermetic division among the Branches, but in a carefully crafted system of checked and balanced power within each Branch.

[W]e have not hesitated to strike down provisions of law that either accrete to a single Branch powers more appropriately diffused among separate Branches or that undermine the authority and independence of one or another coordinate Branch.

In *Nixon v. Administrator of General Services* 433 U.S. 425 (1977), upholding, against a separation-of-powers challenge, legislation providing for the General Services Administration to control Presidential papers after resignation, we described our separation-of-powers inquiry as focusing "on the extent to which [a provision of law] prevents the Executive Branch from accomplishing its constitutionally assigned functions." (citing *United States v. Nixon*, 418 U.S., at 711–712). In cases specifically involving the Judicial Branch, we have expressed our vigilance against two dangers: first, that the Judicial Branch neither be assigned nor allowed "tasks that are more properly accomplished by [other] branches," *Morrison v. Olson*, 487 U.S., at 680–681, and, second, that no provision of law "impermissibly threatens the institutional integrity of the Judicial Branch." *Commodity Futures Trading Comm'n v. Schor*, 478 U.S., at 851.

Mistretta argues that the Act suffers from each of these constitutional infirmities. He argues that Congress, in constituting the Commission as it did, effected an unconstitutional accumulation of power within the Judicial Branch while at the same time undermining the Judiciary's independence and integrity. Specifically, petitioner claims that in delegating to an independent agency within the Judicial Branch the power to promulgate sentencing guidelines, Congress unconstitutionally has required the Branch, and individual Article III judges, to exercise not only their judicial authority, but legislative authority—the making of sentencing policy—as well. Such rulemaking authority, petitioner contends, may be exercised by Congress, or delegated by Congress to the Executive, but may not be delegated to or exercised by the Judiciary.

Although the unique composition and responsibilities of the Sentencing Commission give rise to serious concerns about a disruption of the appropriate balance of governmental power among the coordinate Branches, we conclude, upon close inspection, that petitioner's fears for the fundamental structural protections of the Constitution prove, at least in this case, to be "more smoke than fire," and do not compel us to invalidate Congress' considered scheme for resolving the seemingly intractable dilemma of excessive disparity in criminal sentencing.

A

Location of the Commission

The Sentencing Commission unquestionably is a peculiar institution within the framework of our Government. Although placed by the Act in the Judicial Branch, it is not a court and does not exercise judicial power. Rather, the Commission is an "independent" body comprised of seven voting members including at least three federal judges, entrusted by Congress with the primary task of promulgating sentencing guidelines. [W]e observe that Congress' decision to create an independent rulemaking body to promulgate sentencing guidelines and to locate that body within the Judicial Branch is not unconstitutional unless Congress has vested in the Commission powers that are more appropriately performed by the other Branches or that undermine the integrity of the Judiciary.

[S]ince substantive judgment in the field of sentencing has been and remains appropriate to the Judicial Branch, and the methodology of rulemaking has been and remains appropriate to that Branch, Congress' considered decision to combine these functions in an independent Sentencing Commission and to locate that Commission within the Judicial Branch does not violate the principle of separation of powers.

C

Presidential Control

The Act empowers the President to appoint all seven members of the Commission with the advice and consent of the Senate. The Act further provides that the President shall make his choice of judicial appointees to the Commission after considering a list of six judges recommended by the Judicial Conference of the United States. The Act also grants the President authority to remove members of the Commission, although "only for neglect of duty or malfeasance in office or for other good cause shown."

Mistretta argues that this power of Presidential appointment and removal prevents the Judicial Branch from performing its constitutionally assigned functions. Although we agree with petitioner that the independence of the Judicial Branch must be "jealously guarded" against outside interference, and that, as Madison admonished at the founding, "neither of [the Branches] ought to possess directly or indirectly, an overruling influence over the others in the administration of their respective powers," *The Federalist No. 48*, p. 332 (J. Cooke ed. 1961), we do not believe that the President's appointment and removal powers over the Commission afford him influence over the functions of the Judicial Branch or undue sway over its members.

[S]ince the President has no power to affect the tenure or compensation of Article III judges, even if the Act authorized him to remove judges from the Commission at will, he would have no power to coerce the judges in the exercise of their judicial duties. In any case, Congress did not grant the President unfettered authority to remove Commission members. Instead, precisely to ensure that they would not be subject to coercion even in the exercise of their nonjudicial duties, Congress insulated the members from Presidential removal except for good cause. Under these circumstances, we see no risk that the President's limited removal power will compromise the impartiality of Article III judges serving on the Commission and, consequently, no risk that the Act's removal provision will prevent the Judicial Branch from performing its constitutionally assigned function of fairly adjudicating cases and controversies

V

We conclude that in creating the Sentencing Commission—an unusual hybrid in structure and authority—Congress neither delegated excessive legislative power nor upset the constitutionally mandated balance of powers among the coordinate Branches. The Constitution's structural protections do not prohibit Congress from delegating to an expert body located within the Judicial Branch the intricate task of formulating sentencing guidelines consistent with such significant statutory direction as is present here. Nor does our system of checked and balanced authority prohibit Congress from calling upon the accumulated wisdom and experience of the Judicial Branch in creating policy on a matter uniquely within the ken of judges. Accordingly, we hold that the Act is constitutional.

JUSTICE SCALIA, dissenting.

While the products of the Sentencing Commission's labors have been given the modest name "Guidelines," they have the force and effect of laws, prescribing the sentences criminal defendants are to receive. A judge who disregards them will be reversed. I dissent from today's decision because I can find no place within our constitutional system for an agency created by Congress to exercise no governmental power other than the making of laws.

II

Precisely because the scope of delegation is largely uncontrollable by the courts, we must be particularly rigorous in preserving the Constitution's structural restrictions that deter excessive delegation. The major one, it seems to me, is that the power to make law cannot be exercised by anyone other than Congress, except in conjunction with the lawful exercise of executive or judicial power.

The delegation of lawmaking authority to the Commission is, in short, unsupported by any legitimating theory to explain why it is not a delegation of legislative power. To disregard structural legitimacy is wrong in itself—but since structure has purpose, the disregard also has adverse practical consequences.

By reason of today's decision, I anticipate that Congress will find delegation of its lawmaking powers much more attractive in the future. If rulemaking can be entirely unrelated to the exercise of judicial or executive powers, I foresee all manner of "expert" bodies, insulated from the political process, to which Congress will delegate various portions of its lawmaking responsibility. This is an undemocratic precedent that we set—not because of the scope of the delegated power, but because its recipient is not one of the three Branches of Government. The only governmental power the Commission possesses is the power to make law; and it is not the Congress.

III

Today's decision may aptly be described as the *Humphrey's Executor* [*v. United States,* 295 U.S. 602 (1935)] of the Judicial Branch, and I think we will live to regret it. Henceforth there may be agencies "within the Judicial Branch" (whatever that means), exercising governmental powers, that are neither courts nor controlled by courts, nor even controlled by judges. If an "independent agency" such as this can be given the power to fix sentences previously exercised by district courts, I must assume that a similar agency can be given the powers to adopt rules of procedure and rules of evidence previously exercised by this Court. The bases for distinction would be thin indeed.

Today's decision follows the regrettable tendency of our recent separation-of-powers jurisprudence, to treat the Constitution as though it were no more than a generalized prescription that the functions of the Branches should not be commingled too much—how much is too much to be determined, case-by-case, by this Court. The Constitution is not that. Rather, as its name suggests, it is a prescribed structure, a framework, for the conduct of government.

I think the Court errs, in other words, not so much because it mistakes the degree of commingling, but because it fails to recognize that this case is not about commingling, but about the creation of a new Branch altogether, a sort of junior varsity Congress. It may well be that in some circumstances such a Branch would be desirable; perhaps the agency before us here will prove to be so. But there are many desirable dispositions that do not accord with the constitutional structure we live under. And in the long run the improvisation of a constitutional structure on the basis of currently perceived utility will be disastrous.

FOR DISCUSSION

The primary conflict between the majority's opinion and Scalia's dissent is over the characterization of the Commission's function: Why is this distinction key? Consider the following related cases: Was Scalia's concern realized or not? What does the 2005 ruling in *U.S. v. Booker* mean for our understanding of the separation of powers?

RELATED CASES

***Rust v. Sullivan:* 500 U.S. 173 (1991).**

This decision upheld a presidential regulation forbidding federal funding of organizations that fostered family planning, despite twenty years of prior federal funding. The Court found that ambiguous statutory interpretation requires courts to defer to the executive's interpretation of law, even to the extent of reversing a previous interpretation of the legislation.

***Clinton v. City of New York:* 524 U.S. 417 (1998).**

The Court determined that the Line Item Veto Act of 1996 allowed the president to void specific provisions of appropriation bills presented to him for approval. The Court found the law illegally violated the Presentment Clause of the Constitution and was an unlawful delegation of congressional authority.

Presidential Executive Orders

Article I, Section 7 of the Constitution describes the process for how a bill becomes a law. The process requires both houses of Congress to pass legislation with identical language and for it to be signed by the president. In the alternative, Congress by two-thirds majorities in both Houses can override a presidential veto to make something a law, and in some cases bills the president has not signed but not vetoed and returned to Congress may also become a law (if the president refuses to return a bill adopted in the last 10 days of a session, the president has exercised what is known as a pocket veto). Once a bill becomes a law it is legally binding, enforceable by the executive branch.

Yet the congressional route is not the only way law is created. Orders by the courts become binding and enforceable as law by the courts. In some circumstances, orders issued by the President of the United States too carry the force of law. These **executive orders** have been issued by presidents since the time George Washington became president, and over time they have been used by almost every president, often either with support or controversy.

The legal or constitutional basis for executive orders has several sources. The first is in Article II, Section I, Clause 1,which vests in the president the executive power, and Article II, Section 3, which requires that presidents "take care that the laws be faithfully executed." While lacking precise definition, the executive power gives presidents broad enforcement authority to use their discretion to determine how to enforce the law or to otherwise manage the resources and staff of the executive department. Second, executive orders have a legal basis in power delegated by Congress to the president or executive department agencies. Congress may delegate to the Environmental Protection Agency, for example, authority to make determinations about what constitutes clean air or water under the Clean Water Act of 1972 or Clean Air Act of 1973. This delegation power is subject to the constitutional limits described in the separation of powers cases discussed earlier.

Third, since the adoption of the Administrative Procedures Act (APA) in 1946, there is a complex process and structure for how administrative agencies and members of the executive branch can make rules and have them become legally binding. In chapter one, the case of *Chevron, U.S.A. v. Natural Resources Defense Council*, described many of the issues surrounding judicial recognition of and deference to administrative agency determinations of what laws mean. Taken together, these constitutional clauses, specific congressional delegation, and the rule making process of the APA form the legal basis of presidential executive orders.

With the exception of President William Henry Harrison who died barely a month after being sworn into office, every president has issued executive orders. George Washington issued the first one, directing officers of the Articles of Confederation government to compose a report for his administration on the status or state of affairs of America. Other famous orders included Thomas Jefferson ordering the Louisiana Purchase, James Knox Polk ordering the annexation of Texas, Abraham Lincoln's Emancipation Proclamation, Franklin Roosevelt ordering the internment of Japanese-Americans during World War II, and John Kennedy creating the Peace Corps. The numbering of executive orders began in 1907, and not until the Federal Registration Act of 1936 was there a formal process for recording executive orders. Prior to 1936 and 1907 executive orders were issued less formally.

From 1789 to the end of the Obama presidency there have been nearly 14,000 executive orders. Franklin Roosevelt holds the record with 3,721 orders, with second place going to Woodrow Wilson at 1,803, and third place to Calvin Coolidge with 1,203. Among recent presidents, Bill Clinton issued 364, George Bush 291, and Barack Obama 276. The American Presidency Project at http://www.presidency.ucsb.edu/data/orders.php maintains a list of all executive orders.

In the last several years, partisan and political gridlock between Congress and the president has led the latter into using executive orders as a way of addressing issues or creating rules of laws in the absence of explicit congressional action. The Obama Administration through the EPA issued rules regulating carbon emissions. Yet in *Murray Energy Company v. Environmental Protection Agency*, ___ U.S., ___; 136 S.Ct. 999; 194 L.Ed.2d 18 (2016) in a suit brought by more than two dozen states and several utility company, the Supreme Court in a 5–3 vote issued a stay on the rules pending review by the Court of Appeals. In *United States v. Texas*, ___ U.S. ___; 136 S.Ct. 2271 (2016), the Supreme Court deadlocked 4–4 and issued a per curiam decision that upheld a lower decision that issued an injunction to prevent enforcement of an executive order or program entitled Deferred Action for Parents of Americans and Lawful Permanent Residents (DAPA), which would provide legal presence for illegal immigrants who were parents of citizens or lawful permanent residents. This decision effectively ended President Obama's effort to use an executive order to effect immigration reform. The lower court decision is provided in this book.

While many criticize executive orders as a way to circumvent Congress and the separation of powers process, there is no question that these orders are a major part of federal executive power that is unlikely to disappear in the future.

TEXAS V. UNITED STATES

809 F.3d 134 (2015)

States and state officials sought an injunction against the Department of Homeland Security (DHS) to prevent enforcement of an executive order or program entitled Deferred Action for Parents of Americans and Lawful Permanent Residents (DAPA), which would provide legal presence for illegal immigrants who were parents of citizens or lawful permanent residents, and prevent expansion of program of Deferred Action for Childhood Arrivals (DACA). The District Court granted a preliminary injunction, and the Fifth Circuit Court of Appeals upheld the injunction, contending that the states were likely to win in their argument that the order violated the Administrative Procedures Act. The United States appealed to the Supreme Court, which deadlocked 4–4 after Justice Scalia's death. This meant that the Court of Appeals decision, which appears below was affirmed.

Vote: 2–1

JERRY E. SMITH, CIRCUIT JUDGE.

The United States appeals a preliminary injunction, pending trial, forbidding implementation of the Deferred Action for Parents of Americans and Lawful Permanent Residents program ("DAPA"). Twenty-six states (the "states") challenged DAPA under the Administrative Procedure Act ("APA") and the Take Care Clause of the Constitution; in an impressive and thorough Memorandum Opinion and Order issued February 16, 2015, the district court enjoined the program on the ground that the states are likely to succeed on their claim that DAPA is subject to the APA's procedural requirements.

I.

A.

In June 2012, the Department of Homeland Security ("DHS") implemented the Deferred Action for Childhood Arrivals program ("DACA"). In the DACA Memo to agency heads, the DHS Secretary "set[ ] forth how, in the exercise of . . . prosecutorial discretion, [DHS] should enforce the Nation's immigration laws against certain young people" and listed five "criteria [that] should be satisfied before an individual is considered for an exercise of prosecutorial discretion." The Secretary further instructed that "[n]o individual should receive deferred action . . . unless they [*sic*] first pass a background check and requests for relief . . . are to be decided on a case by case basis." Although stating that "[f]or individuals who are granted deferred action . . ., [U.S. Citizenship and Immigration Services ('USCIS')] shall accept applications to determine whether these individuals qualify for work authorization," the DACA Memo purported to "confer[ ] no substantive right, immigration status or pathway to citizenship." At least 1.2 million persons qualify for DACA, and approximately 636,000 applications were approved through 2014.

In November 2014, by what is termed the "DAPA Memo," DHS expanded DACA by making millions more persons eligible for the program and extending "[t]he period for which DACA and the accompanying employment authorization is granted . . . to three-year increments, rather than the current two-year increments." The Secretary also "direct[ed] USCIS to establish a process, similar to DACA," known as DAPA, which applies to "individuals who . . . have, [as of November 20, 2014], a son or daughter who is a U.S. citizen or lawful permanent resident" and meet five additional criteria. The Secretary stated that, although "[d]eferred action does not confer any form of legal status in this country, much less citizenship [,] it [does] mean[ ] that, for a specified period of time, an individual is permitted to be *lawfully present* in the United States." Of the approximately 11.3 million illegal aliens in the United States, 4.3 million would be eligible for lawful presence pursuant to DAPA.

"Lawful presence" is not an enforceable right to remain in the United States and can be revoked at any time, but that classification nevertheless has significant legal consequences. Unlawfully present aliens are generally not eligible to receive federal public benefits, or state and local public benefits unless the state otherwise provides. But as the government admits in its opening brief, persons granted lawful presence pursuant to DAPA are no longer "bar[red] . . . from receiving social security retirement benefits, social security disability benefits, or health insurance under Part A of the Medicare program." That follows from § 1611(b)(2)–(3), which provides that the exclusion of benefits in § 1611(a) "shall not apply to any benefit[s] payable under title[s] II [and XVIII] of the Social Security Act . . . to an alien who is *lawfully present* in the United States as determined by the Attorney General. . . ." (emphasis added). A lawfully present alien is still required to satisfy independent qualification criteria before receiving those benefits, but the grant of lawful presence removes the categorical bar and thereby makes otherwise ineligible persons eligible to qualify.

"Each person who applies for deferred action pursuant to the [DAPA] criteria . . . shall also be eligible to apply for work authorization for the [renewable three-year] period of deferred action." The United States concedes that "[a]n alien with work authorization may obtain a Social Security Number," "accrue quarters of covered employment," and "correct wage records to add prior covered employment within approximately three years of the year in which the wages were earned or in limited circumstances thereafter." The district court determined—and the government does not dispute—"that DAPA recipients would be eligible for earned income tax credits once they received a Social Security number."

As for state benefits, although "[a] State may provide that an alien who is *not lawfully present* in the United States is eligible for any State or local public benefit for which such alien would otherwise be ineligible under subsection (a)," § 1621(d), Texas has chosen not to issue driver's licenses to unlawfully present aliens. Texas maintains that documentation confirming lawful presence pursuant to DAPA would allow otherwise ineligible aliens to become eligible for state-subsidized driver's licenses. Likewise, certain unemployment compensation "[b]enefits are not payable based on services performed by an alien unless the alien . . . was *lawfully present* for purposes of performing the services. . . ." Texas contends that DAPA recipients would also become eligible for unemployment insurance.

B.

The states sued to prevent DAPA's implementation on three grounds. First, they asserted that DAPA violated the procedural requirements of the APA as a substantive rule that did not undergo the requisite notice-and-comment rulemaking. Second, the states claimed that DHS lacked the authority to implement the program even if it followed the correct rulemaking process, such that DAPA was substantively unlawful under the APA. Third, the states urged that DAPA was an abrogation of the President's constitutional duty to "take Care that the Laws be faithfully executed." U.S. Const. art. II, § 3.

The district court held that Texas has standing. It concluded that the state would suffer a financial injury by having to issue driver's licenses to DAPA beneficiaries at a loss. Alternatively, the court relied on a new theory it called "abdication standing": Texas had standing because the United States has exclusive authority over immigration but has refused to act in that area. The court also considered but ultimately did not accept the notions that Texas could sue as *parens patriae* on behalf of citizens facing economic competition from DAPA beneficiaries and that the state had standing based on the losses it suffers generally from illegal immigration.

The court temporarily enjoined DAPA's implementation after determining that Texas had shown a substantial likelihood of success on its claim that the program must undergo notice and comment. Despite full briefing, the court did not rule on the "Plaintiffs' likelihood of success on their *substantive* APA claim or their constitutional claims under the Take Care Clause/separation of powers doctrine." On appeal, the United States maintains that the states do not have standing or a right to judicial review and, alternatively, that DAPA is exempt from the notice-and-comment requirements. The government also contends that the injunction, including its nationwide scope, is improper as a matter of law.

III.

The government claims the states lack standing to challenge DAPA. As we will analyze, however, their standing is plain, based on the driver's-license rationale, so we need not address the other possible grounds for standing.

As the parties invoking federal jurisdiction, the states have the burden of establishing standing. They must show an injury that is "concrete, particularized, and actual or imminent; fairly traceable to the challenged action; and redressable by a favorable ruling." "When a litigant is vested with a procedural right, that litigant has standing if there is some possibility that the requested relief will prompt the injury-causing party to reconsider the decision that allegedly harmed the litigant." *Massachusetts v. EPA,* 549 U.S. 497, 518 (2007).

A.

We begin by considering whether the states are entitled to "special solicitude" in our standing inquiry under *Massachusetts v. EPA*. They are.

The Court held that Massachusetts had standing to contest the EPA's decision not to regulate greenhouse-gas emissions from new motor vehicles, which allegedly contributed to a rise in sea levels and a loss of the state's coastal land. "It is of considerable relevance that the party seeking review here is a sovereign State and not . . . a private individual" because "States are not normal litigants for the purposes of invoking federal jurisdiction."

The Court identified two additional considerations that entitled Massachusetts "to special solicitude in [the Court's] standing analysis." First, the Clean Air Act created a procedural right to challenge the EPA's decision.

The parties' dispute turns on the proper construction of a congressional statute, a question eminently suitable to resolution in federal court. Congress has moreover authorized this type of challenge to EPA action. That authorization is of critical importance to the standing inquiry: "Congress has the power to define injuries and articulate chains of causation that will give rise to a case or controversy where none existed before." "In exercising this power, however, Congress must at the very least identify the injury it seeks to vindicate and relate the injury to the class of persons entitled to bring suit." We will not, therefore, "entertain citizen suits to vindicate the public's nonconcrete interest in the proper administration of the laws."

Second, the EPA's decision affected Massachusetts's "quasi-sovereign" interest in its territory. When a State enters the Union, it surrenders certain sovereign prerogatives. Massachusetts cannot invade Rhode Island to force reductions in greenhouse gas emissions, it cannot negotiate an emissions treaty with China or India, and in some circumstances the exercise of its police powers to reduce in-state motor-vehicle emissions might well be pre-empted.

These sovereign prerogatives are now lodged in the Federal Government, and Congress has ordered EPA to protect Massachusetts (among others) by prescribing standards applicable to the "emission of any air pollutant from any class or classes of new motor vehicle engines, which in [the Administrator's] judgment cause, or contribute to, air pollution which may reasonably be anticipated to endanger public health or welfare."

Like Massachusetts, the instant plaintiffs—the states—"are not normal litigants for the purposes of invoking federal jurisdiction," and the same two additional factors are present. First, "[t]he parties' dispute turns on the proper construction of a congressional statute," the APA, which authorizes challenges to "final agency action for which there is no other adequate remedy in a court." Similarly, the disagreement in *Massachusetts v. EPA* concerned the interpretation of the Clean Air Act, which provides for judicial review of "final action taken[ ] by the Administrator." Further, as we will explain, the states are within the zone of interests of the Immigration and Nationality Act ("INA"); they are not asking us to "entertain citizen suits to vindicate the public's nonconcrete interest in the proper administration of the laws."

In enacting the APA, Congress intended for those "suffering legal wrong because of agency action" to have judicial recourse, and the states fall well within that definition. The Clean Air Act's review provision is more specific than the APA's, but the latter is easily adequate to justify "special solicitude" here. The procedural right to challenge EPA decisions created by the Clean Air Act provided important support to Massachusetts because the challenge Massachusetts sought to bring—a challenge to an agency's decision *not to act*—is traditionally the type for which it is most difficult to establish standing and a justiciable issue. Texas, by contrast, challenges DHS's affirmative decision to set guidelines for granting lawful presence to a broad class of illegal aliens. Because the states here challenge DHS's decision to act, rather than its decision to remain inactive, a procedural right similar to that created by the Clean Air Act is not necessary to support standing.

As we will show, DAPA would have a major effect on the states' fiscs, causing millions of dollars of losses in Texas alone, and at least in Texas, the causal chain is especially direct: DAPA would enable beneficiaries to apply for driver's licenses, and many would do so, resulting in Texas's injury.

Second, DAPA affects the states' "quasi-sovereign" interests by imposing substantial pressure on them to change their laws, which provide for issuing driver's licenses to some aliens and subsidizing those licenses. "[S]tates have a sovereign interest in 'the power to create and enforce a legal code.' " Pursuant to that interest, states may have standing based on (1) federal assertions of authority to regulate matters they believe they control, (2) federal preemption of state law, and (3) federal interference with the enforcement of state law, at least where "the state statute at issue regulate[s] behavior or provide[s] for the administration of a state program" and does not "simply purport [ ] to immunize [state] citizens from federal law." Those intrusions are analogous to pressure to change state law.

Moreover, these plaintiff states' interests are like Massachusetts's in ways that implicate the same sovereignty concerns. When the states joined the union, they surrendered some of their sovereign prerogatives over immigration. They cannot establish their own classifications of aliens, just as "Massachusetts cannot invade Rhode Island to force reductions in greenhouse gas emissions [and] cannot negotiate an emissions treaty with China or India." The states may not be able to discriminate against subsets of aliens in their driver's license programs without running afoul of preemption or the Equal Protection Clause; similarly, "in some circumstances[, Massachusetts's] exercise of its police powers to reduce in-state motor-vehicle emissions might well be pre-empted. Both these plaintiff states and Massachusetts now rely on the federal government to protect their interests. These parallels confirm that DAPA affects the states' "quasi-sovereign" interests.

C.

Texas has satisfied the second standing requirement by establishing that its injury is "fairly traceable" to DAPA. It is undisputed that DAPA would enable beneficiaries to apply for driver's licenses, and there is little doubt that many would do so because driving is a practical necessity in most of the state.

1.

The Secretary has broad discretion to "decide whether it makes sense to pursue removal at all" and urges that deferred action—a grant of "lawful presence" and subsequent eligibility for otherwise unavailable benefits—is a presumptively unreviewable exercise of prosecutorial discretion. "The general exception to reviewability provided by § 701(a)(2) for action 'committed to agency discretion' remains a narrow one, but within that exception are included agency refusals to institute investigative or enforcement proceedings, unless Congress has indicated otherwise." Where, however, "an agency *does* act to enforce, that action itself provides a focus for judicial review, inasmuch as the agency must have exercised its power in some manner. The action at least can be reviewed to determine whether the agency exceeded its statutory powers."

Part of DAPA involves the Secretary's decision—at least temporarily—not to enforce the immigration laws as to a class of what he deems to be low-priority illegal aliens. But importantly, the states have not challenged the priority levels he has established, and neither the preliminary injunction nor compliance with the APA requires the Secretary to remove any alien or to alter his enforcement priorities.

Deferred action, however, is much more than nonenforcement: It would affirmatively confer "lawful presence" and associated benefits on a class of unlawfully present aliens. Though revocable, that change in designation would trigger (as we have already explained) eligibility for federal benefits—for example, under title II and XVIII of the Social Security Act—and state benefits—for example, driver's licenses and unemployment insurance—that would not otherwise be available to illegal aliens.

The United States maintains that DAPA is presumptively unreviewable prosecutorial discretion because " 'lawful presence' is not a status and is not something that the alien can legally enforce; the agency can alter or revoke it at any time." The government further contends that "[e]very decision under [DAPA] to defer enforcement action against an alien necessarily entails allowing the individual to be lawfully present. . . . Deferred action under DAPA and 'lawful presence' during that limited period are thus two sides of the same coin."

Revocability, however, is not the touchstone for whether agency is action is reviewable. Likewise, to be reviewable agency action, DAPA need not directly confer public benefits—removing a categorical bar on receipt of those benefits and thereby making a class of persons newly eligible for them "provides a focus for judicial review."

2.

"The mere fact that a statute grants broad discretion to an agency does not render the agency's decisions completely unreviewable under the 'committed to agency discretion by law' exception unless the statutory scheme, taken together with other relevant materials, provides absolutely no guidance as to how that discretion is to be exercised." In *Perales v. Casillas*, 903 F. 3d 1043 (5th Cir. 1990), we held that the INS's decision *not* to grant pre-hearing voluntary departures and work authorizations to a group of aliens was committed to agency discretion because "[t]here are no statutory standards for the court to apply. . . . There is nothing in the [INA] expressly providing for the grant of employment authorization or pre-hearing voluntary departure to [the plaintiff class of aliens]." Although we stated that "the agency's decision to grant voluntary departure and work authorization has been committed to agency discretion by law," that case involved a challenge to the *denial* of voluntary departure and work authorization.

Under those facts, *Perales* faithfully applied *Chaney*'s presumption against judicial review of agency inaction "because there are no meaningful standards against which to judge the agency's exercise of discretion." But where there is affirmative agency action—as with DAPA's issuance of lawful presence and employment authorization—and in light of the INA's intricate regulatory scheme for changing immigration classifications and issuing employment authorization, "[t]he action at least can be reviewed to determine whether the agency exceeded its statutory powers."

The United States asserts that 8 C.F.R. § 274a.12(c)(14), rather than DAPA, makes aliens granted deferred action eligible for work authorizations. But if DAPA's deferred-action program must be subjected to notice-and-comment, then work authorizations may not be validly issued pursuant to that subsection until that process has been completed and aliens have been "granted deferred action."

Moreover, the government's limitless reading of that subsection—allowing for the issuance of employment authorizations to any class of illegal aliens whom DHS declines to remove—is beyond the scope of what the INA can reasonably be interpreted to authorize, as we will explain. And even assuming, *arguendo,* that the government does have that power, Texas is also injured by the grant of lawful presence itself, which makes DAPA recipients newly eligible for state-subsidized driver's licenses. As an affirmative agency action with meaningful standards against which to judge it, DAPA is not an unreviewable "agency action . . . committed to agency discretion by law."

The district court did not err and most assuredly did not abuse its discretion. The order granting the preliminary injunction is AFFIRMED.

Appointment and Removal Powers

Under separation of powers, the legislative and executive branches often **share powers** in the appointment of officials (e.g., federal judges, key bureaucratic positions) and deciding when these officials are removed from office (*Bowsher v. Synar,* 428 U.S. 714, 1986). This issue can become even more complex when the officers being appointed are designed to provide oversight of the legislative and executive branches (*Morrison v. Olson,* 487 U.S. 654, 1988). The tension between the two may be exacerbated when the limits of each branch's authority is not clear.

Often the Constitution is vague as to the extent of the powers granted to each of the branches; this can occur for many reasons. The government is much more complex today than it was in 1789; the consequences of powers awarded and powers denied may not be clear until those powers are implemented; and, the implications of judicial precedents or new constitutional amendments may not become clear until years later. As a result, when the Constitution is not precise in the delegation of powers, the consequence may be additional conflict between the branches.

Although the Appointments Clause delegates to the executive the power of appointing officers of the government, the president must exercise this power in conjunction with the Senate. The Clause also allows Congress to give the president sole authority over the appointment of inferior officers, or Congress may bypass the executive and place this appointment power of inferior officers elsewhere. The extent of the power of the executive to appoint officials is based on whether the appointee is perceived to be an "inferior" official or not. The lack of clarity over the distinction between an "officer of the United States" and an "inferior officer" has led to much litigation and several Supreme Court precedents. Unlike the appointments power, the Constitution is silent on the removal of appointed officials outside of the provisions for impeachment. The cases that follow illustrate how the Court attempted to create clear guidelines for the executive and legislative sharing of both the appointment authority and the removal powers.

In the case of *Bowsher v. Synar* (478 U.S. 714, 1986), the Court examined a clear challenge between the legislative and executive branches within the context of the Balanced Budget and Emergency Deficit Control Act of 1985. This law was designed to force the federal budget to be annually balanced as an attempt to bring the national deficit, which was rapidly climbing, under control. One of the primary points of contention in the Act was that Congress had assigned the comptroller general specific functions and enforcement authorities, but had also reserved for the legislature the ability to remove the official from office under certain circumstances. The constitutional challenge focused upon the fact that the enforcement power belongs to the executive branch and the Act, through reserving the power of removing an executive official for the legislature, was violating separation of powers. By placing the power of removal in the legislature, the Act made the comptroller general subservient to Congress; the Court ruled that the position therefore could not have any executive powers, such as the enforcement of federal statutes. While the Balanced Budget Act stood as constitutional, the power of the comptroller general was drastically limited through this decision.

The potential for the removal power to be used in order to advance partisan goals of one branch over the other is a continuous challenge to the barriers of separation of powers. This is of particular concern when the contested offices are designed to investigate or provide oversight of the branches, as in the case of *Morrison v. Olson* (487 U.S. 654, 1988). As a result of the abuses of the Nixon administration, in 1978 the legislature passed the Ethics in Government Act, which allowed for the appointment of an independent counsel to investigate officials for criminal violations. According to the Act, the attorney general (executive branch) recommends the need for an investigation to a special judicial division (created by this piece of legislation), who appoints the independent counsel and defines the jurisdictional scope of the officer. *Morrison v. Olson* is a challenge to the constitutionality of the process because it bypasses the president's authority to appoint officials under Article II. The Court found no conflict with separation of powers; the president has the authority to appoint principal officials, but Congress has the constitutional authority to determine which branch has the authority to appoint inferior officials. By finding the independent counsel to be an inferior officer under the Constitution, the Court was able both to uphold the significance of separation of powers and allow the executive branch to be held accountable for potential ethics violations.

As you read these cases, pay specific attention to how the Supreme Court defines the boundaries of separation of powers and how they interpret the Constitution. Look at the use of prior precedents to clarify the understanding of the Appointments Clause and Article II of the Constitution, and consider how the Court lays the foundation for future conflicts surrounding separation of powers.

Normally presidential appointments require Senate confirmation. But what if the Senate is in recess and unable to confirm a needed appointment? Article II, Section 2 allows for the President to make recess appointments to fill vacancies on a temporary basis. The original idea of recess appointments addressed the issue of a part-time Senate or one which was adjourned and it would take time for Senators to reconvene due to the slow travel time it would take to get to the capital. But recess appointments have also been used to fill

Article II, Sec. 2 (Appointments Clause):

He shall have Power, by and with the Advice and Consent of the Senate, to make Treaties, provided two thirds of the Senators present concur; and he shall nominate, and by and with the Advice and Consent of the Senate, shall appoint Ambassadors, other public Ministers and Consuls, Judges of the supreme Court, and all other Officers of the United States, whose Appointments are not herein otherwise provided for, and which shall be established by Law: but the Congress may by Law vest the Appointment of such inferior Officers, as they think proper, in the President alone, in the Courts of Law, or in the Heads of Departments.

The President shall have power to fill up all vacancies that may happen during the recess of the Senate, by granting commissions which shall expire at the end of their next session.

vacancies when the President and the Senate have disagreements over whom the former wishes to appoint. Justices William Brennan, Earl Warren, and Potter Stewart were originally recess appointments to the Supreme Court by President Eisenhower. All were later confirmed by the Senate. President Ronald Reagan made 240 recess appointments, Bill Clinton 139, George W. Bush 171, and Barack Obama made 32.

But what exactly does it mean for the Senate to be in recess? This is the subject of *National Labor Relations Board v. Noel Canning*, 573 U.S. ___; 134 S.Ct. 2550 (2014). Here a company challenged the validity of a National Labor Relations Board decision, asserting that several of President Obama's recess appointments were not valid because the Senate was not actually in recess. The Court agreed. The decision took the Court back to the Constitutional Framers seeking to understand what they thought a recess was, how long temporally the Senate must be unavailable for it to qualify as a recess, and how many Senate members must be available to meet or not regarding what type of business. In the end, the Court concluded that significant deference must be given to the Senate in defining and determining whether it was in session, and since it considered itself to be in continuing session, Obama's appointments without Senate confirmation were invalid.

The *Noel Canning* decision provided significant clarification as to when the president may use recess appointments. But to critics it also allowed the Senate to use some tricks to claim it was in session and to take away the ability of a president to fill appointments when the Senate does not want to act. As new technologies become available and which potentially change how the Senate meets, one may again see the Court revisit this issue.

BOWSHER V. SYNAR

478 U.S. 714, 106 S. Ct. 3181, 92 L. Ed. 2d 583 (1986)

Congress enacted the Balanced Budget and Emergency Deficit Control Act of 1985 to eliminate the federal deficit by setting a maximum deficit spending level that would be reduced to zero over a multiyear period. The plaintiffs challenged the constitutionality of the Act because they believed that the Act violated the separation of powers because in it Congress assigned to the comptroller general of the United States legislative functions. The District Court agreed.

Vote: 7–2

CHIEF JUSTICE BURGER delivered the opinion of the Court.

The question presented by these appeals is whether the assignment by Congress to the Comptroller General of the United States of certain functions under the Balanced Budget and Emergency Deficit Control Act of 1985 violates the doctrine of separation of powers.

III

Even a cursory examination of the Constitution reveals the influence of Montesquieu's thesis that checks and balances were the foundation of a structure of government that would protect liberty. The Framers provided a vigorous Legislative Branch and a separate and wholly independent Executive Branch, with each branch responsible ultimately to the people. The Framers also provided for a Judicial Branch equally independent with "[the] judicial Power . . . [extending] to all Cases, in Law and Equity, arising under this Constitution, and the Laws of the United States." Art. III, § 2.

That this system of division and separation of powers produces conflicts, confusion, and discordance at times is inherent, but it was deliberately so structured to assure full, vigorous, and open debate on the great issues affecting the people and to provide avenues for the operation of checks on the exercise of governmental power.

The Constitution does not contemplate an active role for Congress in the supervision of officers charged with the execution of the laws it enacts.

This Court first directly addressed this issue in *Myers v. United States*, 272 U.S. 52 (1925). At issue in *Myers* was a statute providing that certain postmasters could be removed only "by and with the advice and consent of the Senate." The President removed one such Postmaster without Senate approval, and a lawsuit ensued. Chief Justice Taft, writing for the Court, declared the statute unconstitutional on the ground that for Congress to "draw to itself, or to either branch of it, the power to remove or the right to participate in the exercise of that power . . . would be . . . to infringe the constitutional principle of the separation of governmental powers." Id., at 161.

A decade later, in *Humphrey's Executor v. United States*, 295 U.S. 602 (1935), relied upon heavily by appellants, a Federal Trade Commissioner who had been removed by the President sought backpay. *Humphrey's Executor* involved an issue not presented either in the *Myers* case or in this case—i. e., the power of Congress to limit the President's powers of removal of a Federal Trade Commissioner. The Court distinguished *Myers*, reaffirming its holding that congressional participation in the removal of executive officers is unconstitutional.

In light of these precedents, we conclude that Congress cannot reserve for itself the power of removal of an officer charged with the execution of the laws except by impeachment. The structure of the Constitution does not permit Congress to execute the laws; it follows that Congress cannot grant to an officer under its control what it does not possess.

Our decision in *INS v. Chadha*, 462 U.S. 919 (1983), supports this conclusion. In *Chadha*, we struck down a one-House "legislative veto" provision by which each House of Congress retained the power to reverse a decision Congress had expressly authorized the Attorney General to make[.]

To permit an officer controlled by Congress to execute the laws would be, in essence, to permit a congressional veto. Congress could simply remove, or threaten to remove, an officer for executing the laws in any fashion found to be unsatisfactory to Congress. This kind of congressional control over the execution of the laws, *Chadha* makes clear, is constitutionally impermissible.

The dangers of congressional usurpation of Executive Branch functions have long been recognized. "[The] debates of the Constitutional Convention, and the Federalist Papers, are replete with expressions of fear that the Legislative Branch of the National Government will aggrandize itself at the expense of the other two branches." *Buckley v. Valeo*, 424 U.S. 1, 129 (1976). Indeed, we also have observed only recently that "[the] hydraulic pressure inherent within each of the separate Branches to exceed the outer limits of its power, even to accomplish desirable objectives, must be resisted." *Chadha* at 951. With these principles in mind, we turn to consideration of whether the Comptroller General is controlled by Congress.

IV

The critical factor lies in the provisions of the statute defining the Comptroller General's office relating to removability. Although the Comptroller General is nominated by the President from a list of three individuals recommended by the Speaker of the House of Representatives and the President pro tempore of the Senate and confirmed by the Senate, he is removable only at the initiative of Congress.

It is clear that Congress has consistently viewed the Comptroller General as an officer of the Legislative Branch.

Against this background, we see no escape from the conclusion that, because Congress has retained removal authority over the Comptroller General, he may not be entrusted with executive powers. The remaining question is whether the Comptroller General has been assigned such powers in the Balanced Budget and Emergency Deficit Control Act of 1985.

V

The primary responsibility of the Comptroller General under the instant Act is the preparation of a "report." This report must contain detailed estimates of projected federal revenues and expenditures. The report must also specify the reductions, if any, necessary to reduce the deficit to the target for the appropriate fiscal year.

[W]e view these functions as plainly entailing execution of the law in constitutional terms. Interpreting a law enacted by Congress to implement the legislative mandate is the very essence of "execution" of the law. Under § 251, the Comptroller General must exercise judgment concerning facts that affect the application of the Act. He must also interpret the provisions of the Act to determine precisely what budgetary calculations are required. Decisions of that kind are typically made by officers charged with executing a statute.

The executive nature of the Comptroller General's functions under the Act is revealed in § 252(a)(3) which gives the Comptroller General the ultimate authority to determine the budget cuts to be made. Indeed, the Comptroller General commands the President himself to carry out, without the slightest variation (with exceptions not relevant to the constitutional issues presented), the directive of the Comptroller General as to the budget reductions[.]

VII

No one can doubt that Congress and the President are confronted with fiscal and economic problems of unprecedented magnitude, but "the fact that a given law or procedure is efficient, convenient, and useful in facilitating functions of government, standing alone, will not save it if it is contrary to the Constitution. Convenience and efficiency are not the primary objectives—or the hallmarks—of democratic government. . . ." *Chadha*, supra, at 944.

We conclude that the District Court correctly held that the powers vested in the Comptroller General under § 251 violate the command of the Constitution that the Congress play no direct role in the execution of the laws. Accordingly, the judgment and order of the District Court are affirmed.

JUSTICE STEVENS, with whom JUSTICE MARSHALL joins, concurring in the judgment.

When this Court is asked to invalidate a statutory provision that has been approved by both Houses of the Congress and signed by the President, particularly an Act of Congress that confronts a deeply vexing national problem, it should only do so for the most compelling constitutional reasons. I agree with the Court that the "Gramm-Rudman-Hollings" Act contains a constitutional infirmity so severe that the flawed provision may not stand. I disagree with the Court, however, on the reasons why the Constitution prohibits the Comptroller General from exercising the powers assigned to him by § 251(b) and § 251(c)(2) of the Act. It is not the dormant, carefully circumscribed congressional removal power that represents the primary constitutional evil. Nor do I agree with the conclusion of both the majority and the dissent that the analysis depends on a labeling of the functions assigned to the Comptroller General as "executive powers." Rather, I am convinced that the Comptroller General must be characterized as an agent of Congress because of his longstanding statutory responsibilities; that the powers assigned to him under the Gramm-Rudman-Hollings Act require him to make policy that will bind the Nation; and that, when Congress, or a component or an agent of Congress, seeks to make policy that will bind the Nation, it must follow the procedures mandated by Article I of the Constitution—through passage by both Houses and presentment to the President. In short, Congress may not exercise its fundamental power to formulate national policy by delegating that power to one of its two Houses, to a legislative committee, or to an individual agent of the Congress such as the Speaker of the House of Representatives, the Sergeant at Arms of the Senate, or the Director of the Congressional Budget Office. *INS v. Chadha*, 462 U.S. 919 (1983). That principle, I believe, is applicable to the Comptroller General.

JUSTICE WHITE, dissenting.

The Court, acting in the name of separation of powers, takes upon itself to strike down the Gramm-Rudman-Hollings Act, one of the most novel and far-reaching legislative responses to a national crisis since the New Deal. The basis of the Court's action is a solitary provision of another statute that was passed over 60 years ago and has lain dormant since that time. I cannot concur in the Court's action. Like the Court, I will not purport to speak to the wisdom of the policies incorporated in the legislation the Court invalidates; that is a matter for the Congress and the Executive, both of which expressed their assent to the statute barely half a year ago. I will, however, address the wisdom of the Court's willingness to interpose its distressingly formalistic view of separation of powers as a bar to the attainment of governmental objectives through the means chosen by the Congress and the President in the legislative process established by the Constitution. Twice in the past four years I have expressed my view that the Court's recent efforts to police the separation of powers have rested on untenable constitutional propositions leading to regrettable results. Today's result is even more misguided. [T]he Court's decision rests on a feature of the legislative scheme that is of minimal practical significance and that presents no substantial threat to the basic scheme of separation of powers. In attaching dispositive significance to what should be regarded as a triviality, the Court neglects what has in the past been recognized as a fundamental principle governing consideration of disputes over separation of powers:

> "The actual art of governing under our Constitution does not and cannot conform to judicial definitions of the power of any of its branches based on isolated clauses or even single Articles torn from context. While the Constitution diffuses power the better to secure liberty, it also contemplates that practice will integrate the dispersed powers into a workable government." *Youngstown Sheet & Tube Co. v. Sawyer*, 343 U.S. 579, 635 (1952) (Jackson, J. concurring).

II

The Act vesting budget-cutting authority in the Comptroller General represents Congress' judgment that the delegation of such authority to counteract ever-mounting deficits is "necessary and proper" to the exercise of the powers granted the Federal Government by the Constitution; and the President's approval of the statute signifies his unwillingness to reject the choice made by Congress. Under such circumstances, the role of this

Court should be limited to determining whether the Act so alters the balance of authority among the branches of government as to pose a genuine threat to the basic division between the lawmaking power and the power to execute the law. Because I see no such threat, I cannot join the Court in striking down the Act.

JUSTICE BLACKMUN, dissenting.

The Court may be correct when it says that Congress cannot constitutionally exercise removal authority over an official vested with the budget-reduction powers that § 251 of the Balanced Budget and Emergency Deficit Control Act of 1985 gives to the Comptroller General. This, however, is not because "the removal powers over the Comptroller General's office dictate that he will be subservient to Congress[;]" I agree with Justice White that any such claim is unrealistic. Furthermore, I think it is clear under *Humphrey's Executor v. United States*, 295 U.S. 602 (1935), that "executive" powers of the kind delegated to the Comptroller General under the Deficit Control Act need not be exercised by an officer who serves at the President's pleasure; Congress certainly could prescribe the standards and procedures for removing the Comptroller General. But it seems to me that an attempt by Congress to participate directly in the removal of an executive officer—other than through the constitutionally prescribed procedure of impeachment—might well violate the principle of separation of powers by assuming for Congress part of the President's constitutional responsibility to carry out the laws.

In my view, however, that important and difficult question need not be decided in this litigation, because no matter how it is resolved the plaintiffs, now appellees, are not entitled to the relief they have requested. Appellees have not sought invalidation of the 1921 provision that authorizes Congress to remove the Comptroller General by joint resolution; indeed, it is far from clear they would have standing to request such a judgment. The only relief sought in this case is nullification of the automatic budget-reduction provisions of the Deficit Control Act, and that relief should not be awarded even if the Court is correct that those provisions are constitutionally incompatible with Congress' authority to remove the Comptroller General by joint resolution. Any incompatibility, I feel, should be cured by refusing to allow congressional removal—if it ever is attempted—and not by striking down the central provisions of the Deficit Control Act. However wise or foolish it may be, that statute unquestionably ranks among the most important federal enactments of the past several decades. I cannot see the sense of invalidating legislation of this magnitude in order to preserve a cumbersome, 65-year-old removal power that has never been exercised and appears to have been all but forgotten until this litigation.

II

I do not claim that the 1921 removal provision is a piece of statutory deadwood utterly without contemporary significance. But it comes close. Rarely if ever invoked even for symbolic purposes, the removal provision certainly pales in importance beside the legislative scheme the Court strikes down today—an extraordinarily far-reaching response to a deficit problem of unprecedented proportions. Because I believe that the constitutional defect found by the Court cannot justify the remedy it has imposed, I respectfully dissent.

FOR DISCUSSION

In this case, how did the Court connect this struggle over the appointment and removal powers to the larger concerns of maintaining and balancing separation of powers?

RELATED CASES

***Parsons v. United States:* 167 U.S. 324 (1897).**

A U.S. Attorney from the state of Alabama was removed by a succeeding president before the end of the attorney's four-year term. The Court found that when Congress directly stipulates the conditions for removal of an appointed inferior officer from office, presidential removal power is limited.

***Myers v. United States:* 272 U.S. 52 (1926).**

An 1876 Act of Congress provided that first, second, and third class postmasters are appointed and may be removed by the president with the advice and consent of the Senate. The Court ruled that by denying the president unrestricted power of removal of an official with purely "executive functions," Congress had unconstitutionally encroached upon the executive authority of the president.

***Humphrey's Executor v. United States:* 295 U.S. 602 (1935).**

The president cannot remove a member of the Federal Trade Commission for reasons of policy disagreement. Presidents have the power to remove a "purely executive" official at their discretion; however, officials with "quasi-legislative and quasi-judicial" functions may only be removed on the grounds articulated by Congress.

***Weiner v. United States:* 357 U.S. 349 (1958).**

Applying the precedent of *Humphrey's Executor v. United States*, the Court found that the president did not have the unlimited authority to remove an appointed member of the War Crimes Commission.

MORRISON V. OLSON

487 U.S. 654, 108 S. Ct. 2597, 101 L. Ed. 2d 569 (1988)

Title VI of the Ethics in Government Act of 1978 allows an independent counsel to be appointed to investigate and, if appropriate, prosecute high-ranking officials for federal criminal violations. The attorney general reports the necessity of an independent counsel to a judicial special division created by the Act; the special division then appoints an independent counsel and defines the scope of the prosecutorial jurisdiction. Appellant Morrison was appointed as independent counsel to investigate appellee Olson regarding the suppression of documents related to the enforcement of Environmental Protection Agency regulations. Olson challenged the legitimacy of the independent counsel provision of the Act.

Vote: 7–1 (Justice Kennedy did not participate)

CHIEF JUSTICE REHNQUIST delivered the opinion of the Court.

This case presents us with a challenge to the independent counsel provisions of the Ethics in Government Act of 1978. We hold today that these provisions of the Act do not violate the Appointments Clause of the Constitution, Art. II, § 2, cl. 2, or the limitations of Article III, nor do they impermissibly interfere with the President's authority under Article II in violation of the constitutional principle of separation of powers.

III

As we stated in *Buckley v. Valeo*, 424 U.S. 1, 132 (1976): "Principal officers are selected by the President with the advice and consent of the Senate. Inferior officers Congress may allow to be appointed by the President alone, by the heads of departments, or by the Judiciary." The initial question is, accordingly, whether appellant is an "inferior" or a "principal" officer. If she is the latter, as the Court of Appeals concluded, then the Act is in violation of the Appointments Clause.

We need not attempt here to decide exactly where the line falls between the two types of officers, because in our view appellant clearly falls on the "inferior officer" side of that line.

First, appellant is subject to removal by a higher Executive Branch official. Although appellant may not be "subordinate" to the Attorney General (and the President) insofar as she possesses a degree of independent discretion to exercise the powers delegated to her under the Act, the fact that she can be removed by the Attorney General indicates that she is to some degree "inferior" in rank and authority. Second, appellant is empowered by the Act to perform only certain, limited duties. An independent counsel's role is restricted primarily to investigation and, if appropriate, prosecution for certain federal crimes.

Third, appellant's office is limited in jurisdiction. Not only is the Act itself restricted in applicability to certain federal officials suspected of certain serious federal crimes, but an independent counsel can only act within the scope of the jurisdiction that has been granted by the Special Division pursuant to a request by the Attorney General. Finally, appellant's office is limited in tenure. There is concededly no time limit on the appointment of a particular counsel. Nonetheless, the office of independent counsel is "temporary" in the sense that an independent counsel is appointed essentially to accomplish a single task, and when that task is over the office is terminated, either by the counsel herself or by action of the Special Division.

This does not, however, end our inquiry under the Appointments Clause. Appellees argue that even if appellant is an "inferior" officer, the Clause does not empower Congress to place the power to appoint such an officer outside the Executive Branch. They contend that the Clause does not contemplate congressional authorization of "interbranch appointments," in which an officer of one branch is appointed by officers of another branch. The relevant language of the Appointments Clause is worth repeating. It reads: ". . . but the Congress may by Law vest the Appointment of such inferior Officers, as they think proper, in the President alone, in the courts of Law, or in the Heads of Departments." On its face, the language of this "excepting clause" admits of no limitation on interbranch appointments. Indeed, the inclusion of "as they think proper" seems clearly to give Congress significant discretion to determine whether it is "proper" to vest the appointment of, for example, executive officials in the "courts of Law." We recognized as much in one of our few decisions in this area, *Ex parte Siebold* [100 U.S. 371 (1880)].

[T]here is very little, if any, express discussion of the propriety of interbranch appointments in our decisions, and we see no reason now to depart from the holding of *Siebold* that such appointments are not proscribed by the excepting clause.

We do not mean to say that Congress' power to provide for interbranch appointments of "inferior officers" is unlimited. In addition to separation-of-powers concerns, which would arise if such provisions for appointment had the potential to impair the constitutional functions assigned to one of the branches, *Siebold* itself suggested that Congress' decision to vest the appointment power in the courts would be improper if there was some "incongruity" between the functions normally performed by the courts and the performance of their duty to appoint. In the light of the Act's provision making the judges of the Special Division ineligible to participate in any matters relating to an independent counsel they have appointed, we do not think that appointment of the independent counsel by the court runs afoul of the constitutional limitation on "incongruous" interbranch appointments.

IV

Appellees next contend that the powers vested in the Special Division by the Act conflict with Article III of the Constitution. We have long recognized that by the express provision of Article III, the judicial power of the United States is limited to "Cases" and "Controversies." The purpose of this limitation is to help ensure the independence of the Judicial Branch and to prevent the Judiciary from encroaching into areas reserved for the other branches.

Most importantly, the Act vests in the Special Division the power to choose who will serve as independent counsel and the power to define his or her jurisdiction. Clearly, once it is accepted that the Appointments Clause gives Congress the power to vest the appointment of officials such as the independent counsel in the "courts of Law," there can be no Article III objection to the Special Division's exercise of that power, as the power itself derives from the Appointments Clause, a source of authority for judicial action that is independent of Article III. Appellees contend, however, that the Division's Appointments Clause powers do not encompass the power to define the independent counsel's jurisdiction. We disagree. In our view, Congress' power under the Clause to vest the "Appointment" of inferior officers in the courts may, in certain circumstances, allow Congress to give the courts some discretion in defining the nature and scope of the appointed official's authority. This said, we do not think that Congress may give the Division unlimited discretion to determine the independent counsel's jurisdiction.

The Act simply does not give the Division the power to "supervise" the independent counsel in the exercise of his or her investigative or prosecutorial authority. And, the functions that the Special Division is empowered to perform are not inherently "Executive"; indeed, they are directly analogous to functions that federal judges perform in other contexts, such as deciding whether to allow disclosure of matters occurring before a grand jury, deciding to extend a grand jury investigation, or awarding attorney's fees.

We think both the special court and its judges are sufficiently isolated by these statutory provisions from the review of the activities of the independent counsel so as to avoid any taint of the independence of the Judiciary such as would render the Act invalid under Article III.

V

We now turn to consider whether the Act is invalid under the constitutional principle of separation of powers. Two related issues must be addressed: The first is whether the provision of the Act restricting the Attorney General's power to remove the independent counsel to only those instances in which he can show "good cause," taken by itself, impermissibly interferes with the President's exercise of his constitutionally appointed functions. The second is whether, taken as a whole, the Act violates the separation of powers by reducing the President's ability to control the prosecutorial powers wielded by the independent counsel.

A

We held in *Bowsher* [*v. Synar*, 478 U.S. 714, 730 (1986)] that "Congress cannot reserve for itself the power of removal of an officer charged with the execution of the laws except by impeachment." Id., at 726. A primary antecedent for this ruling was our 1926 decision in *Myers v. United States*, 272 U.S. 52. Myers had considered the propriety of a federal statute by which certain postmasters of the United States could be removed by the President only "by and with the advice and consent of the Senate." There too, Congress' attempt to involve itself in the removal of an executive official was found to be sufficient grounds to render the statute invalid.

Unlike both *Bowsher* and *Myers*, this case does not involve an attempt by Congress itself to gain a role in the removal of executive officials other than its established powers of impeachment and conviction. The Act instead puts the removal power squarely in the hands of the Executive Branch[.] In our view, the removal provisions of the Act make this case more analogous to *Humphrey's Executor v. United States*, 295 U.S. 602 (1935), and *Wiener v. United States*, 357 U.S. 349 (1958), than to *Myers* or *Bowsher*.

In *Humphrey's Executor*, the issue was whether a statute restricting the President's power to remove the Commissioners of the Federal Trade Commission (FTC) only for "inefficiency, neglect of duty, or malfeasance in office" was consistent with the Constitution. We stated that whether Congress can "condition the [President's power of removal] by fixing a definite term and precluding a removal except for cause, will depend upon the character of the office." In *Humphrey's Executor*, we found it "plain" that the Constitution did not give the President "illimitable power of removal" over the officers of independent agencies.

Similarly, in *Wiener* we considered whether the President had unfettered discretion to remove a member of the War Claims Commission, which had been established by Congress in the War Claims Act of 1948, 62 Stat. 1240. The Commission's function was to receive and adjudicate certain claims for compensation from those who had suffered personal injury or property damage at the hands of the enemy during World War II. As in *Humphrey's Executor*, however, the Commissioners were entrusted by Congress with adjudicatory powers that were to be exercised free from executive control. Accordingly, we rejected the President's attempt to remove a Commissioner "merely because he wanted his own appointees on [the] Commission," stating that "no such power is given to the President directly by the Constitution, and none is impliedly conferred upon him by statute." [357 U.S., at 356].

Appellees contend that *Humphrey's Executor* and *Wiener* are distinguishable from this case because they did not involve officials who performed a "core executive function." They argue that our decision in *Humphrey's Executor* rests on a distinction between "purely executive" officials and officials who exercise "quasi-legislative" and "quasi-judicial" powers. In their view, when a "purely executive" official is involved, the governing precedent is *Myers*, not *Humphrey's Executor*. And, under *Myers*, the President must have absolute discretion to discharge "purely" executive officials at will.

We undoubtedly did rely on the terms "quasi-legislative" and "quasi-judicial" to distinguish the officials involved in *Humphrey's Executor* and *Wiener* from those in *Myers*, but our present considered view is that the determination of whether the Constitution allows Congress to impose a "good cause"-type restriction on the President's power to remove an official cannot be made to turn on whether or not that official is classified as "purely executive." The analysis contained in our removal cases is designed not to define rigid categories of those officials who may or may not be removed at will by the President, but to ensure that Congress does not interfere with the President's exercise of the "executive power" and his constitutionally appointed duty to "take care that the laws be faithfully executed" under Article II. At the other end of the spectrum from *Myers*, the characterization of the agencies in *Humphrey's Executor* and *Wiener* as "quasi-legislative" or "quasi-judicial" in large part reflected our judgment that it was not essential to the President's proper execution of his Article II powers that these agencies be headed up by individuals who were removable at will. But the real question is whether the removal restrictions are of such a nature that they impede the President's ability to perform his constitutional duty, and the functions of the officials in question must be analyzed in that light.

Considering for the moment the "good cause" removal provision in isolation from the other parts of the Act at issue in this case, we cannot say that the imposition of a "good cause" standard for removal by itself unduly trammels on executive authority. [T]he independent counsel is an inferior officer under the Appointments Clause, with limited jurisdiction and tenure and lacking policymaking or significant administrative authority. Although the counsel exercises no small amount of discretion and judgment in deciding how to carry out his or her duties under the Act, we simply do not see how the President's need to control the exercise of that discretion is so central to the functioning of the Executive Branch as to require as a matter of constitutional law that the counsel be terminable at will by the President.

We do not think that this limitation as it presently stands sufficiently deprives the President of control over the independent counsel to interfere impermissibly with his constitutional obligation to ensure the faithful execution of the laws.

B

The final question to be addressed is whether the Act, taken as a whole, violates the principle of separation of powers by unduly interfering with the role of the Executive Branch. Time and again we have reaffirmed the importance in our constitutional scheme of the separation of governmental powers into the three coordinate branches. As we stated in *Buckley v. Valeo*, 424 U.S. 1 (1976), the system of separated powers and checks and balances established in the Constitution was regarded by the Framers as "a self-executing safeguard against the encroachment or aggrandizement of one branch at the expense of the other." We have not hesitated to invalidate provisions of law which violate this principle. On the other hand, we have never held that the Constitution requires that the three branches of Government "operate with absolute independence." *United States v. Nixon*, 418 U.S., at 707[.]

We observe first that this case does not involve an attempt by Congress to increase its own powers at the expense of the Executive Branch. Indeed, with the exception of the power of impeachment—which applies to all officers of the United States—Congress retained for itself no powers of control or supervision over an independent counsel. The Act does empower certain Members of Congress to request the Attorney General to apply for the appointment of an independent counsel, but the Attorney General has no duty to comply with the request, although he must respond within a certain time limit. Other than that, Congress' role under the Act is limited to receiving reports or other information and oversight of the independent counsel's activities, functions that we have recognized generally as being incidental to the legislative function of Congress.

Similarly, we do not think that the Act works any judicial usurpation of properly executive functions. As should be apparent from our discussion of the Appointments Clause above, the power to appoint inferior officers such as independent counsel is not in itself an "executive" function in the constitutional sense, at least when Congress has exercised its power to vest the appointment of an inferior office in the "courts of Law." In addition, once the court has appointed a counsel and defined his or her jurisdiction, it has no power to supervise or control the activities of the counsel.

Finally, we do not think that the Act "impermissibly undermine[s]" the powers of the Executive Branch, or "disrupts the proper balance between the coordinate branches [by] prevent[ing] the Executive Branch from accomplishing its constitutionally assigned functions," *Nixon v. Administrator of General Services*, 433 US 425 (1977). It is undeniable that the Act reduces the amount of control or supervision that the Attorney General and, through him, the President exercises over the investigation and prosecution of a certain class of alleged criminal activity. Nonetheless, the Act does give the Attorney General several means of supervising or controlling the prosecutorial powers that may be wielded by an independent counsel. Most importantly, the Attorney General retains the power to remove the counsel for "good cause," a power that we have already concluded provides the Executive with substantial ability to ensure that the laws are "faithfully executed" by an independent counsel. Notwithstanding the fact that the counsel is to some degree "independent" and free from executive supervision to a greater extent than other federal prosecutors, in our view these features of the Act give the Executive Branch sufficient control over the independent counsel to ensure that the President is able to perform his constitutionally assigned duties.

VI

In sum, we conclude today that it does not violate the Appointments Clause for Congress to vest the appointment of independent counsel in the Special Division; that the powers exercised by the Special Division under the Act do not violate Article III; and that the Act does not violate the separation-of-powers principle by impermissibly interfering with the functions of the Executive Branch. The decision of the Court of Appeals is therefore

Reversed.

JUSTICE SCALIA, dissenting.

It is the proud boast of our democracy that we have "a government of laws and not of men."

The Framers of the Federal Constitution similarly viewed the principle of separation of powers as the absolutely central guarantee of a just Government.

That is what this suit is about. Power. The allocation of power among Congress, the President, and the courts in such fashion as to preserve the equilibrium the Constitution sought to establish—so that "a gradual concentration of the several powers in the same department," *Federalist No. 51*, p. 321 (J. Madison), can effectively be resisted. Frequently an issue of this sort will come before the Court clad, so to speak, in sheep's clothing: the potential of the asserted principle to effect important change in the equilibrium of power is not immediately evident, and must be discerned by a careful and perceptive analysis. But this wolf comes as a wolf.

II

The Court devotes most of its attention to such relatively technical details as the Appointments Clause and the removal power, addressing briefly and only at the end of its opinion the separation of powers. As my prologue suggests, I think that has it backwards.

[T]he decision of the Court of Appeals invalidating the present statute must be upheld on fundamental separation-of-powers principles if the following two questions are answered affirmatively: (1) Is the conduct of a criminal prosecution (and of an investigation to decide whether to prosecute) the exercise of purely executive power? (2) Does the statute deprive the President of the United States of exclusive control over the exercise of that power? Surprising to say, the Court appears to concede an affirmative answer to both questions, but seeks to avoid the inevitable conclusion that since the statute vests some purely executive power in a person who is not the President of the United States it is void.

[T]his statute does deprive the President of substantial control over the prosecutory functions performed by the independent counsel, and it does substantially affect the balance of powers. That the Court could possibly conclude otherwise demonstrates both the wisdom of our former constitutional system, in which the degree of reduced control and political impairment were irrelevant, since all purely executive power had to be in the President; and the folly of the new system of standardless judicial allocation of powers we adopt today.

III

Because appellant (who all parties and the Court agree is an officer of the United States, was not appointed by the President with the advice and consent of the Senate, but rather by the Special Division of the United States Court of Appeals, her appointment is constitutional only if (1) she is an "inferior" officer within the meaning of the above Clause, and (2) Congress may vest her appointment in a court of law.

The independent counsel is not even subordinate to the President. The Court essentially admits as much, noting that "appellant may not be 'subordinate' to the Attorney General (and the President) insofar as she possesses a degree of independent discretion to exercise the powers delegated to her under the Act." In fact, there is no doubt about it.

Because appellant is not subordinate to another officer, she is not an "inferior" officer and her appointment other than by the President with the advice and consent of the Senate is unconstitutional.

V

By its shortsighted action today, I fear the Court has permanently encumbered the Republic with an institution that will do it great harm.

Worse than what it has done, however, is the manner in which it has done it. A government of laws means a government of rules. Today's decision on the basic issue of fragmentation of executive power is ungoverned by rule, and hence ungoverned by law. It extends into the very heart of our most significant constitutional function the "totality of the circumstances" mode of analysis that this Court has in recent years become fond of. Taking all things into account, we conclude that the power taken away from the President here is not really too much. The next time executive power is assigned to someone other than the President we may conclude, taking all things into account, that it is too much. That opinion, like this one, will not be confined by any rule. [I]t fails to explain why it is not true that—as the text of the Constitution seems to require, as the Founders seemed to expect, and as our past cases have uniformly assumed—all purely executive power must be under the control of the President.

FOR DISCUSSION

Do you perceive the train of precedent surrounding the shared power appointment/removal as reflecting a consistent understanding of separation of powers? What seems to be the prevailing challenge to the Court's decision in *Morrison*? Does this decision prevent the president from adequately exercising constitutional authority?

RELATED CASES

***United States v. Ferreira:* 54 U.S. (13 How.) 40 (1851).**

When Congress creates a new office to which a person is to be appointed, Congress may not identify the person to be named to the office. Such an action would be a violation of separation of powers.

***Buckley v. Valeo:* 424 U.S. 1 (1976).**

Within the 1979 amendments to the Federal Election Campaign Act, Congress created the Federal Election Commission, to which the legislature was able to appoint some of its members. The Court found that the Appointments Clause requires than any appointee who has "significant authority pursuant to the laws of the United States" is an "officer of the United States" and must therefore be appointed by the president with the advice and consent of the Senate.

***Weiss v. United States:* 510 U.S. 163 (1994).**

.Many court martial trials are heard before a military judge temporarily assigned by the Judge Advocate General. The Court determined that such temporary appointments to military courts under the Uniform Code of Military Justice do not violate the Appointments Clause.

NATIONAL LABOR RELATIONS BOARD V. NOEL CANNING

573 U.S. __, 134 S.Ct. 2550, 189 L.Ed.2d 538 (2014)

Employer challenged an order by the National Labor Relations Board (NLRB), claiming that the Board lacked a lacked a quorum because President's recess appointments for three positions in five-member Board were invalid. The Court of Appeals invalidated the order and the Supreme Court affirmed.

Vote: 9–0

JUSTICE BREYER delivered the opinion for the Court.

Ordinarily the President must obtain "the Advice and Consent of the Senate" before appointing an "Office[r] of the United States." U.S. Const., Art. II, § 2, cl. 2. But the Recess Appointments Clause creates an exception. It gives the President alone the power "to fill up all Vacancies that may happen during the Recess of the Senate, by granting Commissions which shall expire at the End of their next Session." Art. II, § 2, cl. 3. We here consider three questions about the application of this Clause.

The first concerns the scope of the words "recess of the Senate." Does that phrase refer only to an inter-session recess (*i.e.,* a break between formal sessions of Congress), or does it also include an intra-session recess, such as a summer recess in the midst of a session? We conclude that the Clause applies to both kinds of recess.

The second question concerns the scope of the words "vacancies that may happen." Does that phrase refer only to vacancies that first come into existence during a recess, or does it also include vacancies that arise prior to a recess but continue to exist during the recess? We conclude that the Clause applies to both kinds of vacancy.

The third question concerns calculation of the length of a "recess." The President made the appointments here at issue on January 4, 2012. At that time the Senate was in recess pursuant to a December 17, 2011, resolution providing for a series of brief recesses punctuated by "*pro forma* session[s]," with "no business . . . transacted," every Tuesday and Friday through January 20, 2012. S. J., 112th Cong., 1st Sess., 923 (2011) (hereinafter 2011 S. J.). In calculating the length of a recess are we to ignore the *pro forma* sessions, thereby treating the series of brief recesses as a single, month-long recess? We conclude that we cannot ignore these *pro forma* sessions.

Our answer to the third question means that, when the appointments before us took place, the Senate was in the midst of a 3-day recess. Three days is too short a time to bring a recess within the scope of the Clause. Thus we conclude that the President lacked the power to make the recess appointments here at issue.

I

The case before us arises out of a labor dispute. The National Labor Relations Board (NLRB) found that a Pepsi-Cola distributor, Noel Canning, had unlawfully refused to reduce to writing and execute a collective-bargaining agreement with a labor union. The Board ordered the distributor to execute the agreement and to make employees whole for any losses.

The Pepsi-Cola distributor subsequently asked the Court of Appeals for the District of Columbia Circuit to set the Board's order aside. It claimed that three of the five Board members had been invalidly appointed, leaving the Board without the three lawfully appointed members necessary for it to act.

The three members in question were Sharon Block, Richard Griffin, and Terence Flynn. In 2011 the President had nominated each of them to the Board. As of January 2012, Flynn's nomination had been pending in the Senate awaiting confirmation for approximately a year. The nominations of each of the other two had been pending for a few weeks. On January 4, 2012, the President, invoking the Recess Appointments Clause, appointed all three to the Board.

The distributor argued that the Recess Appointments Clause did not authorize those appointments. It pointed out that on December 17, 2011, the Senate, by unanimous consent, had adopted a resolution providing that it would take a series of brief recesses beginning the following day. Pursuant to that resolution, the Senate held *pro forma* sessions every Tuesday and Friday until it returned for ordinary business on January 23, 2012. The President's January 4 appointments were made between the January 3 and January 6 *pro forma* sessions. In the distributor's view, each *pro forma* session terminated the immediately preceding recess. Accordingly, the appointments were made during a 3-day adjournment, which is not long enough to trigger the Recess Appointments Clause.

We granted the Solicitor General's petition for certiorari. We asked the parties to address not only the Court of Appeals' interpretation of the Clause but also the distributor's initial argument, namely, "[w]hether the President's recess-appointment power may be exercised when the Senate is convening every three days in *pro forma* sessions."

II

Before turning to the specific questions presented, we shall mention two background considerations that we find relevant to all three. First, *the Recess Appointments Clause sets forth a subsidiary, not a primary, method for appointing officers of the United States.* The immediately preceding Clause—Article II, Section 2, Clause 2—provides the primary method of appointment. It says that the President "shall nominate, *and by and with the Advice and Consent of the Senate,* shall appoint Ambassadors, other public Ministers and Consuls, Judges of the supreme Court, and all other Officers of the United States" (emphasis added).

The *Federalist Papers* make clear that the Founders intended this method of appointment, requiring Senate approval, to be the norm (at least for principal officers). Alexander Hamilton wrote that the Constitution vests the power of *nomination* in the President alone because "one man of discernment is better fitted to analise and estimate the peculiar qualities adapted to particular offices, than a body of men of equal, or perhaps even of superior discernment." The *Federalist* No. 76, p. 510 (J. Cooke ed. 1961). At the same time, the need to secure Senate approval provides "an excellent check upon a spirit of favoritism in the President, and would tend greatly to preventing the appointment of unfit characters from State prejudice, from family connection, from personal attachment, or from a view to popularity." Hamilton further explained that the "ordinary power of appointment is confided to the President and Senate *jointly,* and can therefore only be exercised during the session of the Senate; but as it would have been improper to oblige this body to be continually in session for the appointment of officers; and as vacancies might happen *in their recess,* which it might be necessary for the public service to fill without delay, the succeeding clause is evidently intended to authorise the President *singly* to make temporary appointments."

Thus the Recess Appointments Clause reflects the tension between, on the one hand, the President's continuous need for "the assistance of subordinates," *Myers v. United States,* and, on the other, the Senate's practice, particularly during the Republic's early years, of meeting for a single brief session each year, see Art. I, § 4, cl. 2; Amdt. 20, § 2 (requiring the Senate to "assemble" only "once in every year"); 3 J. Story, *Commentaries on the Constitution of the United States* § 1551, p. 410 (1833) (it would be "burthensome to the senate, and expensive to the public" to require the Senate to be "perpetually in session"). We seek to interpret the Clause as granting the President the power to make appointments during a recess but not offering the President the authority routinely to avoid the need for Senate confirmation.

Second, *in interpreting the Clause, we put significant weight upon historical practice.* For one thing, the interpretive questions before us concern the allocation of power between two elected branches of Government. Long ago Chief Justice Marshall wrote that

> "a doubtful question, one on which human reason may pause, and the human judgment be suspended, in the decision of which the great principles of liberty are not concerned, but the respective powers of those who are equally the representatives of the people, are to be adjusted; if not put at rest by the practice of the government, ought to receive a considerable impression from that practice." *McCulloch v. Maryland,* 4 Wheat. 316, 401, 4 L.Ed. 579 (1819).

And we later confirmed that "[l]ong settled and established practice is a consideration of great weight in a proper interpretation of constitutional provisions" regulating the relationship between Congress and the President. *The Pocket Veto Case,* 279 U.S. 655, 689 (1929).

There is a great deal of history to consider here. Presidents have made recess appointments since the beginning of the Republic. Their frequency suggests that the Senate and President have recognized that recess appointments can be both necessary and appropriate in certain circumstances. We have not previously interpreted the Clause, and, when doing so for the first time in more than 200 years, we must hesitate to upset the compromises and working arrangements that the elected branches of Government themselves have reached.

III

The first question concerns the scope of the phrase "*the recess* of the Senate." Art. II, § 2, cl. 3 (emphasis added). The Constitution provides for congressional elections every two years. And the 2-year life of each elected Congress typically consists of two formal 1-year sessions, each separated from the next by an "inter-session recess." Congressional Research Service, H. Hogue, Recess Appointments: Frequently Asked Questions 2 (2013). The Senate or the House of Representatives announces an inter-session recess by approving a resolution stating that it will "adjourn *sine die,*" *i.e.,* without specifying a date to return (in which case Congress will reconvene when the next formal session is scheduled to begin).

The Senate and the House also take breaks in the midst of a session. The Senate or the House announces any such "intra-session recess" by adopting a resolution stating that it will "adjourn" to a fixed date, a few days or weeks or even months later. All agree that the phrase "the recess of the Senate" covers inter-session recesses. The question is whether it includes intra-session recesses as well.

In our view, the phrase "the recess" includes an intra-session recess of substantial length. Its words taken literally can refer to both types of recess. Founding-era dictionaries define the word "recess," much as we do today, simply as "a period of cessation from usual work." 13 *The Oxford English Dictionary* 322–323 (2d ed. 1989). The Founders themselves used the word to refer to intra-session, as well as to inter-session, breaks.

Since 1929, and particularly since the end of World War II, Congress has shortened its inter-session breaks as it has taken longer and more frequent intra-session breaks; Presidents have correspondingly made more intra-session recess appointments. Indeed, if we include military appointments, Presidents have made thousands of intra-session recess appointments. President Franklin Roosevelt, for example, commissioned Dwight Eisenhower as a permanent Major General during an intra-session recess; President Truman made Dean Acheson Under Secretary of State; and President George H.W. Bush reappointed Alan Greenspan as Chairman of the Federal Reserve Board. Justice Scalia does not dispute any of these facts.

Not surprisingly, the publicly available opinions of Presidential legal advisers that we have found are nearly unanimous in determining that the Clause authorizes these appointments.

What about the Senate? Since Presidents began making intra-session recess appointments, individual Senators have taken differing views about the proper definition of "the recess." But neither the Senate considered as a body nor its committees, despite opportunities to express opposition to the practice of intra-session recess appointments, has done so. Rather, to the extent that the Senate or a Senate committee has expressed a view, that view has favored a functional definition of "recess," and a functional definition encompasses intra-session recesses.

IV

The second question concerns the scope of the phrase "vacancies *that may happen* during the recess of the Senate." Art. II, § 2, cl. 3 (emphasis added). All agree that the phrase applies to vacancies that initially occur during a recess. But does it also apply to vacancies that initially occur before a recess and continue to exist during the recess? In our view the phrase applies to both kinds of vacancy.

Common sense also suggests that many recess appointees filled vacancies that arose before the recess began. We have compared the list of *intra*-session recess appointments in the Solicitor General's brief with the chart of congressional recesses. Where a specific date of appointment can be ascertained, more than half of those intra-session appointments were made within two weeks of the beginning of a recess. That short window strongly suggests that many of the vacancies initially arose prior to the recess. Thus, it is not surprising that the Congressional Research Service, after examining the vacancy dates associated with a random sample of 24 inter-session recess appointments since 1981, concluded that "[i]n most of the 24 cases, the preponderance of evidence indicated that the vacancy arose prior to the recess during which the appointment was made." Further, with research assistance from the Supreme Court Library, we have examined a random sample of the recess appointments made by our two most recent Presidents, and have found that almost all of those appointments filled pre-recess vacancies: Of a sample of 21 recess appointments, 18 filled pre-recess vacancies and only 1 filled a vacancy that arose during the recess in which he was appointed. The precise date on which 2 of the vacancies arose could not be determined. Taken together, we think it is a fair inference that a large proportion of the recess appointments in the history of the Nation have filled pre-existing vacancies.

The upshot is that the President has consistently and frequently interpreted the Recess Appointments Clause to apply to vacancies that initially occur before, but continue to exist during, a recess of the Senate. The Senate as a body has not countered this practice for nearly three-quarters of a century, perhaps longer. See A. Amar, *The Unwritten Constitution* 576–577, n. 16 (2012) (for nearly 200 years "the overwhelming mass of actual practice" supports the President's interpretation). The tradition is long enough to entitle the practice "to great regard in determining the true construction" of the constitutional provision. And we are reluctant to upset this traditional practice where doing so would seriously shrink the authority that Presidents have believed existed and have exercised for so long.

In light of some linguistic ambiguity, the basic purpose of the Clause, and the historical practice we have described, we conclude that the phrase "all vacancies" includes vacancies that come into existence while the Senate is in session.

V

The third question concerns the calculation of the length of the Senate's "recess." On December 17, 2011, the Senate by unanimous consent adopted a resolution to convene "*pro forma* session[s]" only, with "no business . . . transacted," on every Tuesday and Friday from December 20, 2011, through January 20, 2012. 2011 S.J. 923. At the end of each *pro forma* session, the Senate would "adjourn until" the following *pro forma* session. During that period, the Senate convened and adjourned as agreed. It held *pro forma* sessions on December 20, 23, 27, and 30, and on January 3, 6, 10, 13, 17, and 20; and at the end of each *pro forma* session, it adjourned until the time and date of the next.

The President made the recess appointments before us on January 4, 2012, in between the January 3 and the January 6 *pro forma* sessions. We must determine the significance of these sessions—that is, whether, for purposes of the Clause, we should treat them as periods when the Senate was in session or as periods when it was in recess. If the former, the period between January 3 and January 6 was a 3-day recess, which is too short to trigger the President's recess-appointment power. If the latter, however, then the 3-day period was part of a much longer recess during which the President did have the power to make recess appointments, see *ibid.*

The Solicitor General argues that we must treat the *pro forma* sessions as periods of recess. He says that these "sessions" were sessions in name only because the Senate was in recess as a *functional* matter. The Senate, he contends, remained in a single, unbroken recess from January 3, when the second session of the 112th

Congress began by operation of the Twentieth Amendment, until January 23, when the Senate reconvened to do regular business.

In our view, however, the *pro forma* sessions count as sessions, not as periods of recess. We hold that, for purposes of the Recess Appointments Clause, the Senate is in session when it says it is, provided that, under its own rules, it retains the capacity to transact Senate business. The Senate met that standard here.

The standard we apply is consistent with the Constitution's broad delegation of authority to the Senate to determine how and when to conduct its business. The Constitution explicitly empowers the Senate to "determine the Rules of its Proceedings." Art. I, § 5, cl. 2. And we have held that "all matters of method are open to the determination" of the Senate, as long as there is "a reasonable relation between the mode or method of proceeding established by the rule and the result which is sought to be attained" and the rule does not "ignore constitutional restraints or violate fundamental rights."

Applying this standard, we find that the *pro forma* sessions were sessions for purposes of the Clause. First, the Senate said it was in session. The *Journal of the Senate* and the *Congressional Record* indicate that the Senate convened for a series of twice-weekly "sessions" from December 20 through January 20. 2011 S.J. 923–924; 158 Cong. Rec. S1–S11. (The *Journal of the Senate* for 2012 has not yet been published.) And these reports of the Senate "must be assumed to speak the truth."

Second, the Senate's rules make clear that during its *pro forma* sessions, despite its resolution that it would conduct no business, the Senate retained the power to conduct business. During any *pro forma* session, the Senate could have conducted business simply by passing a unanimous consent agreement. Given our answer to the last question before us, we conclude that the Recess Appointments Clause does not give the President the constitutional authority to make the appointments here at issue.

Because the Court of Appeals reached the same ultimate conclusion (though for reasons we reject), its judgment is affirmed.

FOR DISCUSSION

Why did the Supreme Court give so much deference to the Senate to determine when it was in session? Is that deference always warranted?

PRESIDENTIAL SIGNING STATEMENTS

Another example of the challenges mediated through the paradigm of separation of powers is seen in the executive's use of **signing statements** to influence the implementation of laws without ever engaging in a direct conflict with Congress. These statements, issued at the time when the president signs a bill, have been around since the early days of the presidency. But it was Attorney General Ed Meese, during the Reagan presidency, who advocated using signing statements as a way of interjecting the intent or understanding of the president regarding the meaning of a particular law. The goal was for this interpretation of the law to guide its judicial construction in court. When judges and justices interpret legislation, a frequent strategy of both interpreting and legitimizing the interpretation is to appeal to the original understanding of the law when initially passed. In addition, some members of the Supreme Court and lower courts will look to the legislative intent of Congress when reading statutes. However, so far the Court has assigned no interpretative value to presidential signing statements. These statements have been seldom used, but President George W. Bush used them during his presidency from 2001 to 2008 as a major tool to defend executive power.

During his first five years in office, President Bush used these signing statements to claim authority to disobey or ignore the law in more than 750 situations. In an earlier statistical analysis of these signing statements, Phillip Cooper found that of the 505 signing statements, 82 involved the authority to supervise a unitary executive, 77 the exclusivity of presidential power in foreign affairs, 48 the presidential power to classify national security information and withhold information, and 37 commander-in-chief issues.[1] The signing statements clumped around foreign policy and defense issues. Among the more prominent signing statements was one indicating that the president did not have to comply with the McCain Amendment, which barred U.S. officials from using torture and cruel and inhuman treatment against prisoners. For example, in his signing statement for the McCain Amendment, Bush asserted:

> The executive branch shall construe Title X in Division A of the Act, relating to detainees, in a manner consistent with the constitutional authority of the President to supervise the unitary executive branch and as Commander in Chief and consistent with the constitutional limitations on the judicial power, which will assist in achieving the shared objective of the Congress and the President, evidenced in Title X, of protecting the American people from further terrorist attacks. Further, in light of the principles enunciated by the Supreme Court of the United States in 2001 in *Alexander v. Sandoval*, and noting that the text and structure of Title X do not create a private right of action to enforce Title X, the executive branch shall construe Title X not to create a private right of action. Finally, given the decision of the Congress reflected in subsections 1005(e) and 1005(h) that the amendments made to section 2241 of title 28, United States Code, shall apply to past, present, and future actions, including applications for writs of habeas corpus, described in that section, and noting that section 1005 does not confer any constitutional right upon an alien detained abroad as an enemy combatant, the executive branch shall construe section 1005 to preclude the Federal courts from exercising subject matter jurisdiction over any existing or future action, including applications for writs of habeas corpus, described in section 1005.[2]

President Bush's employment of signing statements was controversial. In 2009 President Barack Obama ordered a Justice Department review of signing statements, causing federal agencies not to rely upon them without approval. Yet despite this order and the controversy surrounding them, President Obama early in his administration continued to issue these statements.

While signing statements became popular tools of assertions of presidential authority, their constitutional value and treatment by the Supreme Court is limited. According to Neil Kinkopf, in Court decisions dating back to John Marshall: "[A] President's interpretation of his own authority was not entitled to deference and was to be given no weight in construing a statute."[3] Moreover, so far the Supreme Court has referred to signing statements only in five cases, three of which refer to constitutional issues. These three cases are *United States v. Lopez* (514 U.S. 549, 1995), *Bowsher v. Synar* (478 U.S. 714, 1986), and *I.N.S. v. Chadha* (462 U.S. 919, 1983). In these and other decisions where statutory interpretation of laws is at issue, the Supreme Court has generally ignored or not relied upon the signing statements as the basis of their decisions. At best, they are noted or referenced. None of this should come as a surprise in that ever since *Marbury v. Madison* the Court has stated: "It is emphatically the duty of the Judicial Department to say what the law is."

---

1 Phillip J. Cooper, "George W. Bush, Edgar Allen Poe, and the Use and Abuse of Presidential Signing Statements," 35 *PRES. STUDIES Q.* 515, 516–520 (2005).

2 "President's statement on signing of H.R. 2863, the Department of Defense, Emergency Supplemental Appropriations to Address Hurricanes in the Gulf of Mexico, and Pandemic Influenza Act, 2006.

3 Neil Kinkopf, "The Statutory Commander in Chief," 81 *INDIANA L. J.* 1169, 1190–1191 (citing *Talbot v. Seeman*, 5 U.S. 1 Cranch 1, 10 (1801) and *Murray v. Schooner Charming Betsy*, 6 U.S. (2 Cranch) 64, 118 (1804)).

The tension between branches' authority under separation of powers has its intentional origination in the Constitution. While branches continuously struggle to delegate and retain power, the Court will endeavor to mediate. Although the issues under contention change, the conflict will not abate and it should not, for this conflict helps prevent tyranny by one branch dominating and destroying the others.

CONGRESSIONAL INVESTIGATORY POWER

Intelligent decisions require adequate and accurate information. This is as true of legislative bodies as it is of individuals. Since the legislative branch has been given the power and the duty of making decisions on statutes, the courts have held that the Congress and state legislatures may make use of the means of investigations or inquiries as a means of gathering the information necessary to do their jobs. This authority is referred to as **the investigatory power.** The scope of this investigatory power is rather broad. In *McGrain v. Daugherty* (273 U.S. 135, 1927) the Supreme Court had its first opportunity to rule on the scope of the investigatory power. While noting that no express clause of the Constitution conferred or delineated this investigatory power, the Court nonetheless affirmed it in this case by declaring that: "We are of opinion that the power of inquiry—with process to enforce it—is an essential and appropriate auxiliary to the legislative function."

Indeed, the courts have been so concerned about this that they have become indulgent to the extent of permitting the legislatures to use the basic judicial power of contempt by way of a sanction in connection with investigations, and they have held that such use is not a violation of the doctrine of separation of powers. This is essentially what the Court affirmed in *McGrain* in 1927. The courts, of course, enforce such contempt citations. Eventually the investigatory power was expressly mentioned in the Legislative Reorganization Act of 1946.

Congress has actively used the power of investigation during its entire history, beginning during the Washington's presidency. The exercise of this power loomed larger and larger during the nineteenth century, until the congressional investigation has now become the most spectacular feature of congressional life. The security or communist "scare" of the post–World War II period served to accelerate the prominence of the investigatory role of Congress. Beginning first with the House Un-American Activities Committee (HUAC) before World War II and then in the 1950s in a Senate subcommittee, notoriously led by Wisconsin Senator Joseph McCarthy, Congress used its investigatory power to gather information about alleged communist infiltration into the State Department and to track down communist activity in American society, including in the motion picture industry. These hearings, especially the ones presided over by Senator McCarthy, often subpoenaed witnesses, accused them of being communists, and then asked them to name names of other communist sympathizers. These hearings, or witch hunts as some described them, often also included witnesses "taking the Fifth," or refusing to testify, claiming a right against self-incrimination. Such refusals to testify only heightened suspicion that the witnesses had something to hide.

Eventually the Court was called upon to examine the authority of Congress to conduct these types of hearings. In *Watkins v. United States* (354 U.S. 178, 1957) the Court narrowed the boundaries for these investigations, indicating that Congress could not engage in hearings simply for the sake of exposing individuals. The hearings had to have a purpose, and they were required to respect the First Amendment rights of witnesses. In *Watkins* the Court had seemingly clipped the wings of Congress, but threats by the latter to retaliate against the judiciary and efforts to overturn the decision paid off merely two years later. In *Barenblatt v. United States* (360 U.S. 109, 1959) the Court appeared to back down from *Watkins*. Here, in looking at the alleged communist activity of a student at the University of Michigan, a divided Court affirmed the broad investigatory power it had affirmed in *McGrain*, and it also ruled that the investigation struck an appropriate balance between this authority and the First Amendment rights of the witness. It is not clear that Congress was doing anything differently than before—it simply looked like the Court had blinked.

As noted, for some time the assumption had been made that the Court had given Congress a virtual "blank check" in *McGrain* in the area of investigations. *Watkins* served to remind all concerned that all investigations must be concerned at least with the ultimate possibility of legislation. Indeed, a witness might demand a determination of the legislative relationship and pertinency of each question asked in a probe. Thus, there is now a rule against vagueness in legislative investigations. This does not mean that investigations must be confined to the area of proposed or impending legislation. There is only the requirement that an investigation be concerned with matters on which Congress might legislate, and questions asked of witnesses must bear some pertinency to such potential legislation, that is, to the end purpose of the investigation. There can be no exposure of private wrongdoing just for the sake of such exposure. Cases since *Watkins* have emphasized that the purpose of an investigation (by which the pertinency of questions will be judged) is to be indicated in some way by the legislative body involved.

In *Barenblatt* the Court introduced a new concept—that of the "balancing test." This means that when both individual and governmental interests and rights are at stake, a balance must be struck so as to give priority to whichever appears to be more necessary.

Whether or not the Court legitimately found distinctions between the hearings at issue in *Watkins* and *Barenblatt*, the strength and sting of the House Un-American Activities Committee waned in the 1960s. Vietnam War protestors examined by the committee, such as Jerry Rubin and Abbie Hoffman in 1967, often mocked the HUAC or dressed up in costume. Clearly the terror associated with appearing before the committee had faded.

However, investigations surrounding the Vietnam War led to new issues, such as the scope of immunity given to members of Congress to comment upon testimony and leak information to the media. This immunity grows out of the **Speech and Debate Clause** of the Constitution. The Pentagon Papers were classified materials documenting America's involvement in the Vietnam War. Senator Gravel of Alaska had obtained these papers and sought to publicize them by reading them into the *Congressional Record* and getting them privately published. The Supreme Court ruled in *Gravel v. United States* (408 U.S. 606, 1972) that reading the papers into the Record was protected by the Speech and Debate Clause, but that private publication was not. As you read the *Gravel* opinion, ask yourself why the clause protects one type of activity but not the other? How broadly should the Speech and Debate Clause be read? Should the power be read as adjacent to the investigatory powers? What are the remedies for its abuse?

McGrain v. Daugherty

273 U.S. 135, 47 S. Ct. 319, 71 L. Ed. 580 (1927)

In the famous Teapot Dome investigation of the scandals of the Harding administration, the Senate subpoenaed Mally S. Daugherty, a brother of the attorney general under President Harding. When Daugherty refused to appear before the committee, the Senate ordered his arrest. McGrain, deputy sergeant-at-arms, made the arrest in Ohio. Daugherty then made application to a federal district court for a writ of habeas corpus. After a hearing, the district court discharged Daugherty from custody on the ground that the Senate had exceeded its constitutional powers.

Vote: 8–0

Justice Van Devanter delivered the opinion of the Court.

. . . The Constitution provides for a Congress consisting of a Senate and House of Representatives and invests it with "all legislative powers" granted to the United States, and with power "to make all laws which shall be necessary and proper" for carrying into execution these powers and "all other powers" vested by the Constitution in the United States or in any department or officer thereof. Article One, sections 1, 8. . . . But there is no provision expressly investing either house with power to make investigations and exact testimony to the end that it may exercise its legislative function advisedly and effectively. So the question arises whether this power is so far incidental to the legislative function as to be implied.

In actual legislative practice power to secure needed information by such means has long been treated as an attribute of the power to legislate. It was so regarded in the British Parliament and in the colonial legislatures before the American Revolution; and a like view has prevailed and been carried into effect in both houses of Congress and in most of the state legislatures.

. . . While these cases are not decisive of the question we are considering, they definitely settle two propositions which we recognize as entirely sound and having a bearing on its solution: One, that the two houses of Congress, in their separate relations, possess not only such powers as are expressly granted to them by the Constitution, but such auxiliary powers as are necessary and appropriate to make the express powers effective; and, the other, that neither house is invested with "general" power to inquire into private affairs and compel disclosures, but only with such limited power of inquiry as is shown to exist when the rule of constitutional interpretation just stated is rightly applied. . . .

With this review of the legislative practice, congressional enactments and court decisions, we proceed to a statement of our conclusions on the question.

We are of opinion that the power of inquiry—with process to enforce it—is an essential and appropriate auxiliary to the legislative function. It was so regarded and employed in American legislatures before the Constitution was framed and ratified. Both houses of Congress took this view of it early in their history—the House of Representatives with the approving votes of Mr. Madison and other members whose service in the convention which framed the Constitution gives special significance to their action—and both houses have employed the power accordingly up to the present time. The acts of 1798 and 1857, judged by their comprehensive terms, were intended to recognize the existence of this power in both houses and to enable them to employ it "more effectually" than before. So, when their practice in the matter is appraised according to the circumstances in which it was begun and to those in which it has been continued, it falls nothing short of a practical construction, long continued, of the constitutional provisions respecting their powers, and therefore should be taken as fixing the meaning of those provisions, if otherwise doubtful.

We are further of opinion that the provisions are not of doubtful meaning, but, as was held by this court in the cases we have reviewed, are intended to be effectively exercised, and therefore to carry with them such auxiliary powers as are necessary and appropriate to that end. While the power to exact information in aid of the legislative function was not involved in those cases, the rule of interpretation applied there is applicable here. A legislative body cannot legislate wisely or effectively in the absence of information respecting the conditions which the legislation is intended to affect or change; and where the legislative body does not itself possess the requisite information—which not infrequently is true—recourse must be had to others who do possess it. Experience has taught that mere requests for such information often are unavailing, and also that information which is volunteered is not always accurate or complete; so some means of compulsion are essential to obtain what is needed. . . .

It is quite true that the resolution directing the investigation does not in terms avow that it is intended to be in aid of legislation; but it does show that the subject to be investigated was the administration of the Department of Justice—whether its functions were being properly discharged or were being neglected or misdirected, and particularly whether the Attorney General and his assistants were performing or neglecting their duties in respect of the institution and prosecution of proceedings to punish crimes and enforce appropriate remedies against the wrongdoers—specific instances of alleged neglect being cited. Plainly the subject was one on which legislation could be had and would be materially aided by the information which the investigation was calculated to elicit. This becomes manifest when it is reflected that the functions of the Department of Justice, the powers and duties of the Attorney General and the duties of his assistants, are all subject to regulation by congressional legislation, and that the department is maintained and its activities are carried on under such appropriations as in the judgment of Congress are needed from year to year.

The only legitimate object the Senate could have in ordering the investigation was to aid in legislating; and we think the subject-matter was such that the presumption should be indulged that this was the real object. An express avowal of the object would have been better; but in view of the particular subject-matter was not indispensable.

We conclude that the investigation was ordered for a legitimate object; that the witness wrongfully refused to appear and testify before the committee and was lawfully attached; that the Senate is entitled to have him give testimony pertinent to the inquiry, either at its bar or before the committee; and that the district court erred in discharging him from custody under the attachment. . . .

JUSTICE STONE did not participate in the case.

FOR DISCUSSION

Where in the Constitution is Congress's investigatory power located? Should it have contempt powers for those who refuse to comply? What if it used this power to harass someone—is there a limit on what it can do?

RELATED CASES

Anderson v. Dunn: **6 Wheat. 204 (1821).**

The House of Representatives has the power to punish a person other than a member for contempt of its authority as a means to the execution of its powers. Imprisonment resulting from such contempt conviction cannot extend beyond the session of Congress in which it occurs. Anderson had attempted to bribe a member of the House and then brought civil suit against Dunn, sergeant-at-arms of the House, for assault upon his arrest.

Kilbourn v. Thompson: **103 U.S. 168 (1881).**

Neither house of Congress possesses a general power of inquiry into the private affairs of citizens. Such inquiry must relate to matters over which the particular house has jurisdiction and the power to legislate. Punishment for contempt must be only in connection with such an inquiry. Kilbourn was a witness in an investigation of Jay Cooke and Co. Thompson was sergeant-at-arms of the House.

In re Chapman: **166 U.S. 661 (1897).**

An injury related to the integrity and fidelity of senators in the discharge of their duties is a matter of proper senatorial investigation. Chapman, a broker, had made charges that senators were speculating in stocks affected by a tariff bill then under consideration. He was called as a witness, refused to answer questions, and then was ordered to answer.

Marshall v. Gordon: **243 U.S. 521 (1917).**

An act that is not calculated to affect the House in its proceedings or in the exercise of its functions cannot be punished as contempt. Here a defamatory and insulting letter had been written to a newspaper by a person not a member of the House.

WATKINS V. UNITED STATES

354 U.S. 178, 77 S. Ct. 1173, I L. Ed. 2d 1273 (1957)

In this case John T. Watkins, a Farm Equipment Workers Union organizer, appeared as a witness before a subcommittee of the House Un-American Activities Committee in answer to a subpoena. Watkins agreed to answer questions relating to his own Communist Party activities as well as questions concerning persons known to him to be current members of the Party. However, he refused to testify concerning persons who, to the best of his knowledge, were no longer members. Such questions he held not to be relevant to the work of the committee. He was then indicted, tried in a federal district court, and convicted of contempt of Congress.

Vote: 6–1

CHIEF JUSTICE WARREN delivered the opinion of the Court.

We start with several premises on which there is general agreement. The power of the Congress to conduct investigations is inherent in the legislative process. That power is broad. It encompasses inquiries concerning the administration of existing laws as well as proposed or possibly needed statutes. It includes surveys of defects in our social, economic or political system for the purpose of enabling the Congress to remedy them. It comprehends probes into departments of the Federal Government to expose corruption, inefficiency or waste. But broad as is this power of inquiry, it is not unlimited. There is no general authority to expose the private affairs of individuals without justification in terms of the functions of the Congress. This was freely conceded by the Solicitor General in his argument of this case. Nor is the Congress a law enforcement or trial agency. These are functions of the executive and judicial departments of government. No inquiry is an end in itself; it must be related to and in furtherance of a legitimate task of the Congress. Investigations conducted solely for the personal aggrandizement of the investigators or to "punish" those investigated are indefensible.

It is unquestionably the duty of all citizens to cooperate with the Congress in its efforts to obtain the facts needed for intelligent legislative action. It is their unremitting obligation to respond to subpoenas, to respect the dignity of the Congress and its committees and to testify fully with respect to matters within the province of proper investigation. This, of course, assumes that the constitutional rights of witnesses will be respected by the Congress as they are in a court of justice. The Bill of Rights is applicable to investigations as to all forms of governmental action. Witnesses cannot be compelled to give evidence against themselves. They cannot be subjected to unreasonable search and seizure. Nor can the First Amendment freedoms of speech, press, religion, or political belief and association be abridged. . . .

A far more difficult task evolved from the claim by witnesses that the committees' interrogations were infringements upon the freedoms of the First Amendment. Clearly, an investigation is subject to the command that the Congress shall make no law abridging freedom of speech or press or assembly. While it is true that there is no statute to be reviewed, and that an investigation is not a law, nevertheless an investigation is part of law-making. It is justified solely as an adjunct to the legislative process. The First Amendment may be invoked against infringement of the protected freedoms by law or by law-making.

Abuses of the investigative process may imperceptibly lead to abridgment of protected freedoms. The mere summoning of a witness and compelling him to testify, against his will, about his beliefs, expressions or association, is a measure of governmental interference. And when those forced revelations concern matters that are unorthodox, unpopular, or even hateful to the general public, the reaction in the life of the witness may be disastrous. This effect is even more harsh when it is past beliefs, expressions or associations that are disclosed and judged by current standards rather than those contemporary with the matters exposed. Nor does the witness alone suffer the consequences. Those who are identified by witnesses and thereby placed in the same glare of publicity are equally subject to public stigma, scorn and obloquy. Beyond that there is the more subtle and immeasurable effect upon those who tend to adhere to the most orthodox and uncontroversial views and associations in order to avoid a similar fate at some future time. That this impact is partly the result of non-governmental activity by private persons cannot relieve the investigators of their responsibility for initiating the reaction. . . . Accommodation of the congressional need for particular information with the individual and personal interest in privacy is an arduous and delicate task for any court. We do not underestimate the difficulties that would attend such an undertaking. It is manifest that despite the adverse effects which follow upon compelled disclosure of private matters, not all such inquiries are barred. . . . The critical element is the existence of, and the weight to be ascribed to, the interest of the Congress in demanding disclosures from an unwilling witness. We cannot simply assume, however, that every congressional investigation is justified by a public need that overbalances any private rights affected. To do so would be to abdicate the responsibility placed by the Constitution upon the judiciary to insure that the Congress does not unjustifiably encroach upon an individual's right to privacy nor abridge his liberty of speech, press, religion or assembly. . . .

We have no doubt that there is no congressional power to expose for the sake of exposure. The public is, of course, entitled to be informed concerning the workings of its government. That cannot be inflated into a general power to expose where the predominant result can only be an invasion of the private rights of individuals. But a solution to our problem is not to be found in testing the motives of committee members for this purpose. Such is not our function. Their motives alone would not vitiate an investigation which had been instituted by a House of Congress if that assembly's legislative purpose is being served.

. . . The theory of a committee inquiry is that the committee members are serving as the representatives of the parent assembly in collecting information for a legislative purpose. Their function is to act as the eyes and ears of the Congress in obtaining facts upon which the full legislature can act. . . .

An essential premise in this situation is that the House or Senate shall have instructed the committee members on what they are to do with the power delegated to them. It is the responsibility of the Congress, in the first instance, to insure that compulsory process is used only in furtherance of a legislative purpose. That requires that the instructions to an investigating committee spell out that group's jurisdiction and purpose with sufficient particularity. Those instructions are embodied in the authorizing resolution. That document is the committee's charter. Broadly drafted and loosely worded, however, such resolutions can leave tremendous latitude to the discretion of the investigators. The more vague the committee's charter is, the greater becomes the possibility that the committee's specific actions are not in conformity with the will of the parent House of Congress.

The authorizing resolution of the Un-American Activities Committee was adopted in 1938 when a select committee, under the chairmanship of Representative Dies, was created. Several years later, the Committee was made a standing organ of the House with the same mandate. It defines the Committee's authority as follows:

The Committee on Un-American Activities, as a whole or by subcommittee, is authorized to make from time to time investigations of (i) the extent, character, and objects of un-American propaganda activities in the United States, (ii) the diffusion within the United States of subversive and un-American propaganda that is instigated from foreign countries or of a domestic origin and attacks the principle of the form of government as guaranteed by our Constitution, and (iii) all other questions in relation thereto that would aid Congress in any necessary remedial legislation.

It would be difficult to imagine a less explicit authorizing resolution. Who can define the meaning of "un-American"? What is that single, solitary "principle of the form of government as guaranteed by our Constitution"? There is no need to dwell upon the language, however. At one time, perhaps, the resolution might have been read narrowly to confine the Committee to the subject of propaganda. The events that have transpired in the fifteen years before the interrogation of petitioner make such a construction impossible at this date.

The members of the Committee have clearly demonstrated that they did not feel themselves restricted in any way to propaganda in the narrow sense of the word. Unquestionably the committee conceived of its task in the grand view of its name. Un-American activities were its target, no matter how or where manifested. Notwithstanding the broad purview of the Committee's experience, the House of Representatives repeatedly approved its continuation. . . .

Combining the language of the resolution with the construction it has been given, it is evident that the preliminary control of the Committee exercised by the House of Representatives is slight or non-existent. . . .

The problem attains proportion when viewed from the standpoint of the witness who appears before a congressional committee. He must decide at the time the questions are propounded whether or not to answer. As the Court said in *Sinclair v. United States,* 279 U.S. 263, the witness acts at his peril. He is ". . . bound rightly to construe the statute." An erroneous determination on his part, even if made in the utmost good faith, does not exculpate him if the court should later rule that the questions were pertinent to the question under inquiry.

It is obvious that a person compelled to make this choice is entitled to have knowledge of the subject to which the interrogation is deemed pertinent. That knowledge must be available with the same degree of explicitness and clarity that the Due Process Clause requires in the expression of any element of a criminal offense. The "vice of vagueness" must be avoided here as in all other crimes. There are several sources that can outline the "question under inquiry" in such a way that the rules against vagueness are satisfied. The authorizing resolution, the remarks of the chairman or members of the committee, or even the nature of the proceedings themselves might sometimes make the topic clear. This case demonstrates however, that these sources often leave the matter in grave doubt.

The first possibility is that the authorizing resolution itself will so clearly declare the "question under inquiry" that a witness can understand the pertinency of questions asked him. The Government does not contend that the authorizing resolution of the Un-American Activities Committee could serve such a purpose. Its confusing breadth is amply illustrated by the innumerable and diverse questions into which the Committee has inquired under this charter since 1938. If the "question under inquiry" were stated with such sweeping and uncertain scope, we doubt that it would withstand an attack on the ground of vagueness. . . .

No aid is given as to the "question under inquiry" in the action of the full Committee that authorized the creation of the Subcommittee before which petitioner appeared. The Committee adopted a formal resolution giving the Chairman the power to appoint subcommittees ". . . for the purpose of performing any and all acts which the Committee as a whole is authorized to do." In effect, this was a device to enable the investigations to proceed with a quorum of one or two members and sheds no light on the relevancy of the questions asked of petitioner.

The Government believes that the topic of inquiry before the subcommittee concerned Communist infiltration in labor. In his introductory remarks, the Chairman made reference to a bill, then pending before the Committee, which would have penalized labor unions controlled or dominated by persons who were, or had been, members of a "Communist-action" organization, as defined in the Internal Security Act of 1950. The Subcommittee, it is intended, might have been endeavoring to determine the extent of such a problem. . . .

Having exhausted the several possible indicia of the "question under inquiry," we remain unenlightened as to the subject to which the questions asked petitioner were pertinent. Certainly, if the point is that obscure after trial and appeal, it was not adequately revealed to petitioner when he had to decide at his peril whether or not to answer. Fundamental fairness demands that no witness be compelled to make such a determination with so little guidance. Unless the subject matter has been made to appear with undisputable clarity, it is the duty of the investigative body, upon objection of the witness on grounds of pertinency, to state for the record the subject under inquiry at that time and the manner in which the propounded questions are pertinent thereto. To be meaningful, the explanation must describe what the topic under inquiry is and the connective reasoning whereby the precise questions asked relate to it.

The statement of the Committee Chairman in this case, in response to petitioner's protest, was woefully inadequate to convey sufficient information as to the pertinency of the questions to the subject under inquiry. Petitioner was thus not accorded a fair opportunity to determine whether he was within his rights in refusing to answer, and his conviction is necessarily invalid under the Due Process Clause of the Fifth Amendment.*

. . . The conclusions we have reached in this case will not prevent the Congress, through its committees, from obtaining any information it needs for the proper fulfillment of its role in our scheme of government. The legislature is free to determine the kinds of data that should be collected. It is only those investigations that are conducted by use of compulsory process that give rise to a need to protect the rights of individuals against illegal encroachment. That protection can be readily achieved through procedures which prevent the separation of power from responsibility and which provide the constitutional requisites of fairness for witnesses. A measure of added care on the part of the House and the Senate in authorizing the use of compulsory process and by their committees in exercising that power would suffice. That is a small price to pay if it serves to uphold the principles of limited, constitutional government without constricting the power of the Congress to inform itself.

The judgment of the Court of Appeals is reversed, and the case is remanded to the District Court with instructions to dismiss the indictment. It is so ordered.

JUSTICES BURTON and WHITTAKER took no part in the consideration or decision of this case.

JUSTICE FRANKFURTER concurred:

. . . To turn to the immediate problem before us, the scope of inquiry that a committee is authorized to pursue must be defined with sufficiently unambiguous clarity to safeguard a witness from the hazards of vagueness in the enforcement of the criminal process against which the Due Process Clause protects. The questions must be put with relevance and definiteness sufficient to enable the witness to know whether this refusal to answer may lead to conviction for criminal contempt and to enable both the trial and the appellate courts readily to determine whether the particular circumstances justify a finding of guilt. . . .

JUSTICE CLARK dissented:

As I see it the chief fault in the majority opinion is its mischievous curbing of the informing function of the Congress. While I am not versed in its procedures, my experience in the executive branch of the Government leads me to believe that the requirements laid down in the opinion for the operation of the committee system of inquiry are both unnecessary and unworkable. . . .

I think the Committee here was acting entirely within its scope and that the purpose of its inquiry was set out with "undisputable clarity." In the first place, the authorizing language of the Reorganization Act must be read as a whole, not dissected. It authorized investigation into subversive activity, its extent, character, objects, and diffusion. While the language must have been more explicit than using such words as "un-American," or phrases like "principle of the form of government," still these are fairly well understood terms. We must construe them to give them meaning if we can. . . .

The Court condemns the long-established and long-recognized committee system of inquiry of the House because it raises serious questions concerning the protection it affords to constitutional rights. It concludes that compelling a witness to reveal his "beliefs, expressions or associations" impinges upon First Amendment rights. The system of inquiry, it says, must "insure that the Congress does not unjustifiably encroach upon an

---

* A witness by his refusal to answer exposes himself to criminal prosecution for contempt and so is entitled to know the pertinency of questions. Unrestrained inquiries challenge the First Amendment right not to speak.

individual's right to privacy nor abridge his liberty of speech, press, religion or assembly." In effect the Court honors Watkins' claim of a "right to silence" which brings all inquiries, as we know, to a "dead end." I do not see how any First Amendment rights were endangered here. There is nothing in the First Amendment that provides the guarantees Watkins claims. That Amendment was designed to prevent attempts by law to curtail freedom of speech. . . . It forbids Congress from making any law "abridging the freedom of speech, or of the press." It guarantees Watkins' right to join any organization and make any speech that does not have an intent to incite to crime. . . . But Watkins was asked if he knew named individuals and whether they were Communists. He refused to answer on the ground that his rights were being abridged. What he was actually seeking to do was to protect his former associates, not himself, from embarrassment. He had already admitted his own involvement. He sought to vindicate the rights, if any, of his associates. It is settled that one cannot invoke the constitutional rights of another. . . .

We should afford to Congress the presumption that it takes every precaution possible to avoid unnecessary damage to reputations. Some committees have codes of procedure, and others use the executive hearing technique to this end. The record in this case shows no conduct on the part of the Un-American Activities Committee that justifies condemnation. That there may have been such occasions is not for us to consider here. Nor should we permit its past transgressions, if any, to lead to the rigid restraint of all congressional committees. To carry on its heavy responsibility the compulsion of truth that does not incriminate is not only necessary to the Congress but is permitted within the limits of the Constitution.

FOR DISCUSSION

How broad is the investigatory power after *Watkins*? What limits does the Court impose on this power?

RELATED CASES

***United States v. Rumely:* 345 U.S. 41 (1953).**

Because the House resolution authorizing the investigation did not include the attempted inquiry, a witness refusing to answer could not be held in contempt. By adopting a particular construction of "lobbying," the Court avoided a constitutional issue under the First Amendment, that is, "Representations made directly to Congress, its members, or its committees." Such lobbying did not prevent influencing the community at large. The Court's decision in *Rumely* illustrates a principle of construing statutes in such a manner as to avoid constitutional issues. Rumely was secretary of the Committee for Constitutional Government.

***Sweezy v. New Hampshire:* 354 U.S. 234 (1957).**

A state legislature in authorizing an investigation must specify the information desired. Freedom of speech and press cannot be infringed upon in the course of an investigation. Here the legislature had constituted the state's attorney general as a one-man investigating committee of subversive activities. Sweezy was a faculty member at the University of New Hampshire.

***Scull v. Virginia:* 359 U.S. 344 (1959).**

Held that questions asked by an investigating committee of the Virginia legislature were not pertinent to the purpose of the inquiry as defined in the legislative resolution setting up the committee. The inquiry was regarding activities aiding in the desegregation of schools.

Barenblatt v. United States

360 U.S. 109, 79 S. Ct. 1081, 3 L. Ed. 2d 1115 (1959)

Barenblatt, a graduate student and teaching fellow at the University of Michigan, was convicted of contempt for refusal to answer questions concerning his membership in the Communist Party in testimony before a subcommittee of the House Un-American Activities Committee.

Vote: 5–4

JUSTICE HARLAN delivered the opinion of the Court.

Once more the Court is required to resolve the conflicting constitutional claims of congressional power and of an individual's right to resist its exercise. The congressional power in question concerns the internal process of Congress in moving within its legislative domain; it involves the utilization of its committees to secure "testimony needed to enable it efficiently to exercise a legislative function belonging to it under the Constitution." *McGrain v. Daugherty,* 273 U.S. 135, 160 (1927). The power of inquiry has been employed by Congress throughout our history, over the whole range of the national interests concerning which Congress might legislate or decide upon due investigation not to legislate; it has similarly been utilized in determining what to appropriate from the national purse, or whether to appropriate. The scope of the power of inquiry, in short, is as penetrating and far-reaching as the potential power to enact and appropriate under the Constitution.

Broad as it is, the power is not, however, without limitations. Since Congress may only investigate into those areas in which it may potentially legislate or appropriate, it cannot inquire into matters which are within the exclusive province of one of the other branches of Government

. . . When academic teaching-freedom and its corollary learning-freedom, so essential to the well-being of the Nation, are claimed, this Court will always be on the alert against intrusion by Congress into this constitutionally protected domain. But this does not mean that the Congress is precluded from interrogating a witness merely because he is a teacher. An educational institution is not a constitutional sanctuary from inquiry into matters that may otherwise be within the constitutional legislative domain merely for the reason that inquiry is made of someone within its walls. . . .

In this framework of the Committee's history we must conclude that its legislative authority to conduct the inquiry presently under consideration is unassailable, and that independently of whatever bearing the broad scope of Rule XI may have on the issue of "pertinency" in a given investigation into Communist activities, as in *Watkins v. United States,* 354 U.S. 178 (1957), the Rule cannot be said to be constitutionally infirm on the score of vagueness. The constitutional permissibility of that authority otherwise is a matter to be discussed later. . . .

The precise constitutional issue confronting us is whether the Subcommittee's inquiry into petitioner's past or present membership in the Communist Party transgressed the provisions of the First Amendment, which of course reach and limit congressional investigations. . . .

The Court's past cases establish sure guides to decision. Undeniably, the First Amendment in some circumstances protects an individual from being compelled to disclose his associational relationships. However, the protections of the First Amendment, unlike a proper claim of the privilege against self-incrimination under the Fifth Amendment, do not afford a witness the right to resist inquiry in all circumstances. Where First Amendment rights are asserted to bar governmental interrogation resolution of the issue always involves a balancing by the courts of the competing private and public interest at stake in the particular circumstances shown. . . .

Nor can we accept the further contention that this investigation should not be deemed to have been in furtherance of a legislative purpose because the true objective of the Committee and of the Congress was purely "exposure." So long as Congress acts in pursuance of its constitutional power, the judiciary lacks authority to intervene on the basis of the motives which spurred the exercise of that power. . . .

We conclude that the balance between the individual and the governmental interests here at stake must be struck in favor of the latter, and that therefore the provisions of the First Amendment have not been offended.

We hold that petitioner's conviction for contempt of Congress discloses no infirmity, and that the judgment of the Court of Appeals must be affirmed.

Affirmed.

JUSTICE BLACK, with whom CHIEF JUSTICE WARREN, and JUSTICE DOUGLAS join, dissented.

. . . Measured by the foregoing standards, Rule XI cannot support any conviction for refusal to testify. In substance it authorizes the Committee to compel witnesses to give evidence about all "un-American propaganda," whether instigated in this country or abroad. The word "propaganda" seems to mean anything that people say, write, think or associate together about. The term "un-American" is equally vague.

. . . Such a balance, however, mistakes the factors to be weighed. In the first place, it completely leaves out the real interest in Barenblatt's silence, the interest of the people as a whole in being able to join organizations, advocate causes and make political "mistakes" without later being subjected to governmental penalties for having dared to think for themselves. It is this right, the right to err politically, which keeps us strong as a Nation. For no number of laws against communism can have as much effect as the personal conviction which comes from having heard its arguments and rejected them, or from having once accepted its tenets and later recognized their worthlessness. . . . Thus if communism is to be made a crime, and Communists are to be subjected to "pains and penalties," I would still hold this conviction bad, for the crime of communism, like all others, can be punished only by court and jury after a trial with all judicial safeguards. . . . Ultimately all the questions in this case really boil down to one—whether we as a people will try fearfully and futilely to preserve Democracy by adopting totalitarian methods, or whether in accordance with our traditions and our Constitution we will have the confidence and courage to be free.

I would reverse this conviction.

JUSTICE BRENNAN dissented.

I would reverse this conviction. It is sufficient that I state my complete agreement with my Brother Black that no purpose for the investigation of Barenblatt is revealed by the record except exposure purely for the sake of exposure. This is not a purpose to which Barenblatt's rights under the First Amendment can validly be subordinated. . . .

FOR DISCUSSION

What had changed from *Watkins* to *Barenblatt*? What was the balance struck in the latter that did not exist in the former? Since *Barenblatt,* what practical limits on the investigatory power exist?

GRAVEL V. UNITED STATES

408 U.S. 606, 92 S. Ct. 2614, 33 L. Ed. 2d 583 (1972)

Senator Mike Gravel of Alaska placed the entire Pentagon Papers into the public record after reading excerpts of it into the *Congressional Record*. He also arranged with Beacon Press to have the Pentagon Papers privately published. He and one of his congressional aides were then subpoenaed by a grand jury regarding possible violations of federal law. They sought to fight the subpoenas.

JUSTICE WHITE wrote the opinion of the Court, which was announced by JUSTICE BLACKMUN.

These cases arise out of the investigation by a federal grand jury into possible criminal conduct with respect to the release and publication of a classified Defense Department study entitled History of the United States Decision-Making Process on Viet Nam Policy. This document, popularly known as the Pentagon Papers, bore a Defense security classification of Top Secret-Sensitive. The crimes being investigated included the retention of public property or records with intent to convert (18 U.S.C. § 641), the gathering and transmitting of national defense information (18 U.S.C. § 793), the concealment or removal of public records or documents (18 U.S.C. § 2071), and conspiracy to commit such offenses and to defraud the United States (18 U.S.C. § 371).

Among the witnesses subpoenaed were Leonard S. Rodberg, an assistant to Senator Mike Gravel of Alaska and a resident fellow at the Institute of Policy Studies, and Howard Webber, Director of M.I.T. Press. Senator Gravel, as intervenor, filed motions to quash the subpoenas and to require the Government to specify the particular questions to be addressed to Rodberg. He asserted that requiring these witnesses to appear and testify would violate his privilege under the Speech or Debate Clause of the United States Constitution, Art. I, § 6, cl. 1.

It appeared that on the night of June 29, 1971, Senator Gravel, as Chairman of the Subcommittee on Buildings and Grounds of the Senate Public Works Committee, convened a meeting of the subcommittee and there read extensively from a copy of the Pentagon Papers. He then placed the entire 47 volumes of the study in the public record. Rodberg had been added to the Senator's staff earlier in the day and assisted Gravel in preparing for and conducting the hearing. Some weeks later there were press reports that Gravel had arranged for the papers to be published by Beacon Press and that members of Gravel's staff had talked with Webber as editor of M.I.T. Press.

The District Court overruled the motions to quash and to specify questions but entered an order proscribing certain categories of questions. The Government's contention that for purposes of applying the Speech or Debate Clause the courts were free to inquire into the regularity of the subcommittee meeting was rejected. Because the Clause protected all legislative acts, it was held to shield from inquiry anything the Senator did at the subcommittee meeting and "certain acts done in preparation therefor." The Senator's privilege also prohibited "inquiry into things done by Dr. Rodberg as the Senator's agent or assistant which would have been legislative acts, and therefore privileged, if performed by the Senator personally." The trial court, however, held the private publication of the documents was not privileged by the Speech or Debate Clause.

The Court of Appeals affirmed the denial of the motions to quash but modified the protective order to reflect its own views of the scope of the congressional privilege. Agreeing that Senator and aide were one for the purposes of the Speech or Debate Clause and that the Clause foreclosed inquiry of both Senator and aide with respect to legislative acts, the Court of Appeals also viewed the privilege as barring direct inquiry of the Senator or his aide, but not of third parties, as to the sources of the Senator's information used in performing legislative duties. Although it did not consider private publication by the Senator or Beacon Press to be protected by the Constitution, the Court of Appeals apparently held that neither Senator nor aide could be questioned about it because of a common-law privilege akin to the judicially created immunity of executive officers from liability for libel contained in a news release issued in the course of their normal duties. This privilege, fashioned by the Court of Appeals, would not protect third parties from similar inquiries before the grand jury.

I

Because the claim is that a Member's aide shares the Member's constitutional privilege, we consider first whether and to what extent Senator Gravel himself is exempt from process or inquiry by a grand jury investigating the commission of a crime. Our frame of reference is Art. I, § 6, cl. 1, of the Constitution:

> The Senators and Representatives shall receive a Compensation for their Services, to be ascertained by Law, and paid out of the Treasury of the United States. They shall in all Cases, except Treason, Felony and Breach of the Peace, be privileged from Arrest during their Attendance at the Session of their respective Houses, and in going to and returning from the same; and for any Speech or Debate in either House, they shall not be questioned in any other Place.

The last sentence of the Clause provides Members of Congress with two distinct privileges. Except in cases of "Treason, Felony and Breach of the Peace," the Clause shields Members from arrest while attending or traveling to and from a session of their House. History reveals, and prior cases so hold, that this part of the Clause exempts Members from arrest in civil cases only.

When the Constitution was adopted, arrests in civil suits were still common in America. It is only to such arrests that the provision applies. . . . Since . . . the term treason, felony, and breach of the peace, as used in the constitutional provision relied upon, excepts from the operation of the privilege all criminal offenses, the conclusion results that the claim of privilege of exemption from arrest and sentence was without merit. . . .

Nor does freedom from arrest confer immunity on a Member from service of process as a defendant in civil matters, or as a witness in a criminal case.

The constitution gives to every man, charged with an offence, the benefit of compulsory process, to secure the attendance of his witnesses. I do not know of any privilege to exempt members of congress from the service, or the obligations, of a subpoena, in such cases.

It is, therefore, sufficiently plain that the constitutional freedom from arrest does not exempt Members of Congress from the operation of the ordinary criminal laws, even though imprisonment may prevent or interfere with the performance of their duties as Members. Indeed, implicit in the narrow scope of the privilege of freedom from arrest is, as Jefferson noted, the judgment that legislators ought not to stand above the law they create but ought generally to the bound by it as are ordinary persons.

In recognition, no doubt, of the force of this part of § 6, Senator Gravel disavows any assertion of general immunity from the criminal law. But he points out that the last portion of § 6 affords Members of Congress another vital privilege—they may not be questioned in any other place for any speech or debate in either House. The claim is not that while one part of § 6 generally permits prosecutions for treason, felony, and breach of the peace, another part nevertheless broadly forbids them. Rather, his insistence is that the Speech or Debate Clause at the very least protects him from criminal or civil liability and from questioning elsewhere than in the Senate, with respect to the events occurring at the subcommittee hearing at which the Pentagon Papers were introduced into the public record. To us this claim is incontrovertible. The Speech or Debate Clause was designed to assure a co-equal branch of the government wide freedom of speech, debate, and deliberation without intimidation or threats from the Executive Branch. It thus protects Members against prosecutions that directly impinge upon or threaten the legislative process. We have no doubt that Senator Gravel may not be made to answer—either in terms of questions or in terms of defending himself from prosecution—for the events that occurred at the subcommittee meeting. Our decision is made easier by the fact that the United States appears to have abandoned whatever position it took to the contrary in the lower courts.

Even so, the United States strongly urges that because the Speech or Debate Clause confers a privilege only upon "Senators and Representatives," Rodberg himself has no valid claim to constitutional immunity from grand jury inquiry. In our view, both courts below correctly rejected this position. We agree with the Court of Appeals that for the purpose of construing the privilege a Member and his aide are to be "treated as one," or, as the District Court put it: the "Speech or Debate Clause prohibits inquiry into things done by Dr. Rodberg as the Senator's agent or assistant which would have been legislative acts, and therefore privileged, if performed by the Senator personally." Both courts recognized what the Senate of the United States urgently presses here: that it is literally impossible, in view of the complexities of the modern legislative process, with Congress almost constantly in session and matters of legislative concern constantly proliferating, for Members of Congress to perform their legislative tasks without the help of aides and assistants; that the day-to-day work of such aides is so critical to the Members' performance that they must be treated as the latter's alter egos; and that if they are not so recognized, the central role of the Speech or Debate Clause—to prevent intimidation of legislators by the Executive and accountability before a possibly hostile judiciary—will inevitably be diminished and frustrated.

The Court has already embraced similar views in *Barr v. Matteo* (360 U.S. 564, 1959), where, in immunizing the Acting Director of the Office of Rent Stabilization from liability for an alleged libel contained in a press release, the Court held that the executive privilege recognized in prior cases could not be restricted to those of cabinet rank. As stated by Mr. Justice Harlan, the privilege is not a badge or emolument of exalted office, but an expression of a policy designed to aid in the effective functioning of government. The complexities and magnitude of governmental activity have become so great that there must of necessity be a delegation and redelegation of authority as to many functions, and we cannot say that these functions become less important simply because they are exercised by officers of lower rank in the executive hierarchy.

It is true that the Clause itself mentions only "Senators and Representatives," but prior cases have plainly not taken a literalistic approach in applying the privilege. The Clause also speaks only of "Speech or Debate," but the Court's consistent approach has been that to confine the protection of the Speech or Debate Clause to words spoken in debate would be an unacceptably narrow view. Committee reports, resolutions, and the act of voting are equally covered; "[i]n short, . . . things generally done in a session of the House by one of its members in relation to the business before it." Rather than giving the clause a cramped construction, the Court has sought to implement its fundamental purpose of freeing the legislator from executive and judicial oversight that realistically threatens to control his conduct as a legislator. We have little doubt that we are neither exceeding our judicial powers nor mistakenly construing the Constitution by holding that the Speech or Debate Clause applies not only to a Member but also to his aides insofar as the conduct of the latter would be a protected legislative act if performed by the Member himself.

Nor can we agree with the United States that our conclusion is foreclosed by *Kilbourn v. Thompson* (103 U.S. 168, 1880), where the speech or debate privilege was held unavailable to certain House and committee employees. Those cases do not hold that persons other than Members of Congress are beyond the protection of the Clause when they perform or aid in the performance of legislative acts. In *Kilbourn*, the Speech or Debate Clause protected House Members who had adopted a resolution authorizing Kilbourn's arrest; that act was clearly legislative in nature. But the resolution was subject to judicial review insofar as its execution impinged on a citizen's rights as it did there. That the House could with impunity order an unconstitutional arrest afforded no protection for those who made the arrest. The Court quoted with approval from *Stockdale v. Hansard* (1839): "So if the speaker by authority of the House order an illegal act, though that authority shall exempt him from question, his order shall no more justify the person who executed it than King Charles's warrant for levying ship-money could justify his revenue officer." The Speech or Debate Clause could not be construed to immunize an illegal arrest even though directed by an immune legislative act. The Court was careful to point out that the Members themselves were not implicated in the actual arrest, and, significantly enough, reserved the question whether there might be circumstances in which "there may . . . be things done, in the one House or the other, of an extraordinary character, for which the members who take part in the act may be held legally responsible."

None of this, as we see it, involves distinguishing between a Senator and his personal aides with respect to legislative immunity. In *Kilbourn*-type situations, both aide and Member should be immune with respect to committee and House action leading to the illegal resolution. So, too, in *Dombrowski v. Eastland* (387 U.S. 82, 1967), as in this litigation, senatorial aides should enjoy immunity for helping a Member conduct committee hearings. On the other hand, no prior case has held that Members of Congress would be immune if they executed an invalid resolution by themselves carrying out an illegal arrest, or if, in order to secure information for a hearing, themselves seized the property or invaded the privacy of a citizen. Neither they nor their aides should be immune from liability or questioning in such circumstances. Such acts are no more essential to legislating than the conduct held unprotected in *United States v. Johnson* (383 U.S. 169, 1966).

The United States fears the abuses that history reveals have occurred when legislators are invested with the power to relieve others from the operation of otherwise valid civil and criminal laws. But these abuses, it seems to us, are for the most part obviated if the privilege applicable to the aide is viewed, as it must be, as the privilege of the Senator, and invocable only by the Senator or by the aide on the Senator's behalf, and if in all events the privilege available to the aide is confined to those services that would be immune legislative conduct if performed by the Senator himself. This view places beyond the Speech or Debate Clause a variety of services characteristically performed by aides for Members of Congress, even though within the scope of their employment. It likewise provides no protection for criminal conduct threatening the security of the person or property of others, whether performed at the direction of the Senator in preparation for or in execution of a legislative act or done without his knowledge or direction. Neither does it immunize Senator or aide from testifying at trials or grand jury proceedings involving third-party crimes where the questions do not require testimony about or impugn a legislative act. Thus our refusal to distinguish between Senator and aide in applying the Speech or Debate Clause does not mean that Rodberg is for all purposes exempt from grand jury questioning.

II

We are convinced also that the Court of Appeals correctly determined that Senator Gravel's alleged arrangement with Beacon Press to publish the Pentagon Papers was not protected speech or debate within the meaning of Art. I, § 6, cl. 1, of the Constitution.

Historically, the English legislative privilege was not viewed as protecting republication of an otherwise immune libel on the floor of the House. *Stockdale v. Hansard* recognized that "(f)or speeches made in Parliament by a member to the prejudice of any other person, or hazardous to the public peace, that member enjoys complete impunity." But it was clearly stated that, "if the calumnious or inflammatory speeches should be reported and published, the law will attach responsibility on the publisher." This was accepted in *Kilbourn v. Thompson* as a "sound statement of the legal effect of the Bill of Rights and of the parliamentary law of England" and as a reasonable basis for inferring "that the framers of the Constitution meant the same thing by the use of language borrowed from that source."

But the Clause has not been extended beyond the legislative sphere. That Senators generally perform certain acts in their official capacity as Senators does not necessarily make all such acts legislative in nature. Members of Congress are constantly in touch with the Executive Branch of the Government and with administrative agencies—they may cajole, and exhort with respect to the administration of a federal statute—but such conduct, though generally done, is not protected legislative activity. *United States v. Johnson* decided at least this much. "No argument is made, nor do we think that it could be successfully contended, that the Speech or Debate Clause reaches conduct, such as was involved in the attempt to influence the Department of Justice, that is in no wise related to the due functioning of the legislative process."

Legislative acts are not all-encompassing. The heart of the Clause is speech or debate in either House. Insofar as the Clause is construed to reach other matters, they must be an integral part of the deliberative and communicative processes by which Members participate in committee and House proceedings with respect to the consideration and passage or rejection of proposed legislation or with respect to other matters which the Constitution places within the jurisdiction of either House. As the Court of Appeals put it, the courts have extended the privilege to matters beyond pure speech or debate in either House, but "only when necessary to prevent indirect impairment of such deliberations."

Here, private publication by Senator Gravel through the cooperation of Beacon Press was in no way essential to the deliberations of the Senate; nor does questioning as to private publication threaten the integrity or independence of the Senate by impermissibly exposing its deliberations to executive influence. The Senator had conducted his hearings; the record and any report that was forthcoming were available both to his committee and the Senate. Insofar as we are advised, neither Congress nor the full committee ordered or authorized the publication. We cannot but conclude that the Senator's arrangements with Beacon Press were not part and parcel of the legislative process.

The judgment of the Court of Appeals is vacated and the cases are remanded to that court for further proceedings consistent with this opinion.

So ordered.

Judgment of Court of Appeals vacated and cases remanded.

JUSTICE DOUGLAS, dissenting.

I would construe the Speech or Debate Clause to insulate Senator Gravel and his aides from inquiry concerning the Pentagon Papers, and Beacon Press from inquiry concerning publication of them, for that publication was but another way of informing the public as to what had gone on in the privacy of the Executive Branch concerning the conception and pursuit of the so-called "war" in Vietnam. Alternatively, I would hold that Beacon Press is protected by the First Amendment from prosecution or investigations for publishing or undertaking to publish the Pentagon Papers.

FOR DISCUSSION

Could a member of Congress read anything into the record and not face prosecution? Does this decision give members of Congress the power to libel and slander others?

EXECUTIVE PRIVILEGE

The constitutional concept of separation of powers raised numerous new questions about presidential power. In addition to implicating the issue of the scope of presidential war powers, there were also questions about the ability of the chief executive to impound or refuse to spend money allocated by Congress and issues regarding the ability of the other branches of government to secure information from the president. All of these issues came to a head during the presidency of Richard Nixon.

Allegations that President Nixon had ordered the burglary and wiretapping of Democratic National Headquarters in 1972 in the Washington, D.C., Watergate office complex led to a series of congressional investigations that sought to secure answers to questions about not only this criminal act, but also a host of other alleged illegal activities undertaken by the Nixon administration. These hearings reached a peak during the spring and summer of 1974 as the House and Senate Judiciary Committees separately subpoenaed members of the Nixon administration as witnesses. During one of the hearings it was revealed that Nixon had recorded many of the Oval Office conversations. While Congress was holding hearings, the special prosecutor appointed to investigate the Nixon administration—Leon Jaworski (who had replaced Archibald Cox, the first special prosecutor, whom Nixon had fired in the October 1973 "Saturday Night Massacre")—sought to subpoena these tapes. Nixon refused to produce them, citing **executive privilege**. The idea of executive privilege, rooted in separation of powers, seemed to assert that there were certain executive department conversations and information insulated from forced disclosure to Congress or the courts. In effect, the president and the executive branch enjoyed some inherent authority protecting it from the other branches of the government. *United States v. Nixon*, 418 U.S. 683 (1974), tested this privilege and authority. Here the Court ruled that while such a privilege existed and was rooted in the concept of separation of powers, it needed to give way to the demands of a criminal investigation by a grand jury.

United States v. Nixon was a watershed case in American constitutional law and history. In purely historical terms, the decision forced the president to turn over the tapes, the contents of which, along with the House Judiciary Committee's votes on several articles of impeachment, led to the eventual resignation of President Nixon in August 1974. Constitutionally, the decision broke down an important wall of separation of powers. While the Court conceded that executive privilege did exist, in *Nixon* it ruled that its claims must give way to the needs of the criminal justice system. Left unclear was the scope of this privilege. Did it protect the vice president, the first lady, or other officials in the executive branch? In addition, did it extend to civil lawsuits and investigations? These were some of the questions examined during the presidency of Bill Clinton during the 1990s.

Clinton shares an ignoble honor with Andrew Johnson—they were the only two presidents impeached by the House of Representatives. Both were acquitted by the Senate. Clinton was faced with numerous accusations of illegal behavior he had allegedly engaged in while governor of Arkansas. One claim, made by Paula Jones, an Arkansas state employee, was that Governor Clinton had sexually harassed her. Jones sought to sue him for civil damages. The question, however, was whether a sitting president could be subject to such a lawsuit. In effect, does the principle of separation of powers grant the president at least a temporary immunity from civil suits while he or she is still in office? Clinton maintained that a civil suit unrelated to his activities as president would place a burden on the presidency, distracting him from important functions. More important, such a suit would place him under the scrutiny of the judiciary—the core of the separation of powers claim. The Court in *Clinton v. Jones*, 520 U.S. 681 (1997), rejected the president's arguments, contending instead that: "[i]t is settled law that the separation-of-powers doctrine does not bar every exercise of jurisdiction over the President of the United States. . . . If the Judiciary may severely burden the Executive Branch by reviewing the legality of the President's official conduct, and if it may direct appropriate process to the President himself, it must follow that the federal courts have power to determine the legality of his unofficial conduct. The burden on the President's time and energy that is a mere byproduct of such review surely cannot be considered as onerous as the direct burden imposed by judicial review and the occasional invalidation of his official actions."

If *United States v. Nixon* was a defining moment for the Nixon presidency, the *Jones* case had a similar impact on the Clinton presidency. Once it was clear that the sexual harassment civil suit could proceed, and contrary to the claims made by the Court, the suit proved time consuming for President Clinton.

A second investigation involving President Clinton included his wife, Hillary Rodham Clinton. Allegations had been made that the Clintons and their business partners in the Whitewater Development Corporation had engaged in illegally activity in Arkansas while Bill Clinton was still governor. Kenneth Starr was originally appointed special prosecutor to look into the Whitewater matter. As part of that investigation, Starr sought White House records and communications that might shed light on this matter. The records included communications involving White House counsel and Hillary Clinton. The argument was raised by the White House that executive privilege protected these records and conversations, but The Eighth Circuit Court of Appeals in *In re Grand Jury Subpoena Duces Tecum*, 112 F. 3d 910 (8th Cir. 1997), ruled otherwise. While initially executive privilege was raised in the case by the Clintons, the case hung on issues of attorney-client privilege and attorney work product. Both of these concepts are privileges meant to protect the privacy of communications between clients and their attorneys. The Court rejected these two claims raised by the Clintons.

The Eighth Circuit opinion, while nominally a case about lawyer-client privilege, demonstrated how weak the executive privilege claim had become. Like the 1974 *Nixon* case, which forced the surrender of taped conversations, this decision required the president and his legal counsel to turn over information that would be damaging. Almost in a replay of 1974, the House Judiciary Committee and then eventually the entire House of Representatives voted to impeach the president for obstruction of justice, among other charges. A trial was held in the Senate and presided over by then Chief Justice William Rehnquist. The Senate failed to amass the two-thirds vote necessary to convict and oust Bill Clinton from office.

UNITED STATES V. NIXON

418 U.S. 683, 94 S. Ct. 3090, 41 L. Ed. 2d 1039 (1974)

As a result of a break-in at the headquarters of the Democratic National Committee at the Watergate complex in Washington, D.C., in 1972, the investigation and subsequent trial of a number of persons brought out the fact that President Nixon had taped an indefinite number of conversations in the Oval Office of the White House. Realizing the potential of an examination of the tapes, Special Prosecutor Leon Jaworski had a subpoena duces tecum issued to President Nixon. This ordered the surrender of certain of the tapes and papers to federal District Judge John J. Sirica for his judgment as to what portions of the tapes were irrelevant and inadmissible. The president's claim was that these materials were immune from subpoena under the theory of executive privilege.

Vote: 8–0

CHIEF JUSTICE BURGER delivered the opinion of the Court.

This litigation presents for review the denial of a motion, filed in the District Court on behalf of the President of the United States, in the case of United States v. Mitchell et al., to quash a third-party ***subpoena duces tecum*** issued by the United States District Court for the District of Columbia, pursuant to Fed. Rule Crim. Proc. 17(c). The subpoena directed the President to produce certain tape recordings and documents relating to his conversations with aides and advisers. The court rejected the President's claims of absolute executive privilege, of lack of jurisdiction, and of failure to satisfy the requirements of Rule 17(c). The President appealed to the Court of Appeals. We granted both the United States' petition for certiorari before judgment and also the President's cross-petition for certiorari before judgment because of the public importance of the issues presented and the need for their prompt resolution.

On March 1, 1974, a grand jury of the United States District Court for the District of Columbia returned an indictment charging seven named individuals with various offenses, including conspiracy to defraud the United States and to obstruct justice. Although he was not designated as such in the indictment, the grand jury named the President, among others, as an unindicted coconspirator. On April 18, 1974, upon motion of the Special Prosecutor, . . . a subpoena duces tecum was issued pursuant to Rule 17(c) to the President by the United States District Court and made returnable on May 2, 1974. This subpoena required the production, in advance of the September 9 trial date, of certain tapes, memoranda, papers, transcripts or other writings relating to certain precisely identified meetings between the President and others. The Special Prosecutor was able to fix the time, place, and persons present at these discussions because the White House daily logs and appointment records had been delivered to him. On April 30, the President publicly released edited transcripts of 43 conversations; portions of 20 conversations subject to subpoena in the present case were included. On May 1, 1974, the President's counsel filed a "special appearance" and a motion to quash the subpoena under Rule 17(c). This motion was accompanied by a formal claim of privilege. At a subsequent hearing, further motions to expunge the grand jury's action naming the President as an unindicted coconspirator and for protective orders against the disclosure of that information were filed or raised orally by counsel for the President.

On May 20, 1974, the District Court denied the motion to quash and the motions to expunge and for protective orders. It further ordered "the President or any subordinate officer, official, or employee with custody or control of the documents or objects subpoenaed" to deliver to the District Court, on or before May 31, 1974, the originals of all subpoenaed items, as well as an index and analysis of those items, together with tape copies of those portions of the subpoenaed recordings for which transcripts had been released to the public by the President on April 30. The District Court rejected jurisdictional challenges based on a contention that the dispute was nonjusticiable because it was between the Special Prosecutor and the Chief Executive and hence "intra-executive" in character; it also rejected the contention that the Judiciary was without authority to review an assertion of executive privilege by the President. The court's rejection of the first challenge was based on the authority and powers vested in the Special Prosecutor by the regulation promulgated by the Attorney General; the court concluded that a justiciable controversy was presented. The second challenge was held to be foreclosed by the decision in *Nixon v. Sirica* (487 F.2d 700, 1973).

The District Court held that the judiciary, not the President, was the final arbiter of a claim of executive privilege. The court concluded that under the circumstances of this case the presumptive privilege was overcome by the Special Prosecutor's prima facie "demonstration of need sufficiently compelling to warrant judicial examination in chambers. . . ." The court held, finally, that the Special Prosecutor had satisfied the requirements of Rule 17(c). The District Court stayed its order pending appellate review on condition that review was sought before 4 p.m., May 24. The court further provided that matters filed under seal remain under seal when transmitted as part of the record.

On May 24, 1974, the President filed a timely notice of appeal from the District Court order, and the certified record from the District Court was docketed in the United States Court of Appeals for the District of Columbia Circuit. On the same day, the President also filed a petition for writ of mandamus in the Court of Appeals seeking review of the District Court order.

Later on May 24, the Special Prosecutor also filed, in this Court, a petition for a writ of certiorari before judgment. On May 31, the petition was granted with an expedited briefing schedule. On June 6, the President filed, under seal, a cross-petition for writ of certiorari before judgment. This cross-petition was granted June 15, 1974, and the case was set for argument on July 8, 1974.

II

Justiciability

In the District Court, the President's counsel argued that the court lacked jurisdiction to issue the subpoena because the matter was an intra-branch dispute between a subordinate and superior officer of the Executive Branch and hence not subject to judicial resolution. That argument has been renewed in this Court with emphasis on the contention that the dispute does not present a "case" or "controversy" which can be adjudicated in the federal courts. The President's counsel argues that the federal courts should not intrude into areas committed to the other branches of Government. He views the present dispute as essentially a "jurisdictional" dispute within the Executive Branch which he analogizes to a dispute between two congressional committees. Since the Executive Branch has exclusive authority and absolute discretion to decide whether to prosecute a case, it is contended that a President's decision is final in determining what evidence is to be used in a given criminal case. Although his counsel concedes that the President has delegated certain specific powers to the Special Prosecutor, he has not "waived nor delegated to the Special Prosecutor the President's duty to claim privilege as to all materials . . . which fall within the President's inherent authority to refuse to disclose to any executive officer." The Special Prosecutor's demand for the items therefore presents, in the view of the President's counsel, a political question under *Baker v. Carr* (369 U.S. 186, 1962), since it involves a "textually demonstrable" grant of power under Art. II.

The mere assertion of a claim of an "intra-branch dispute," without more, has never operated to defeat federal jurisdiction; justiciability does not depend on such a surface inquiry. In *United States v. ICC* (337 U.S. 426, 1949), the Court observed, "courts must look behind names that symbolize the parties to determine whether a justiciable case or controversy is presented."

Our starting point is the nature of the proceeding for which the evidence is sought—here a pending criminal prosecution. It is a judicial proceeding in a federal court alleging violation of federal laws and is brought in the name of the United States as sovereign. Under the authority of Art. II, § 2, Congress has vested in the Attorney General the power to conduct the criminal litigation of the United States Government. It has also vested in him the power to appoint subordinate officers to assist him in the discharge of his duties. Acting pursuant to those statutes, the Attorney General has delegated the authority to represent the United States in these particular matters to a Special Prosecutor with unique authority and tenure. The regulation gives the Special Prosecutor explicit power to contest the invocation of executive privilege in the process of seeking evidence deemed relevant to the performance of these specially delegated duties.

So long as this regulation is extant it has the force of law. In *United States ex rel. Accardi v. Shaughnessy* (347 US 260, 1954), regulations of the Attorney General delegated certain of his discretionary powers to the Board of Immigration Appeals and required that Board to exercise its own discretion on appeals in deportation cases. The Court held that so long as the Attorney General's regulations remained operative, he denied himself the authority to exercise the discretion delegated to the Board even though the original authority was his and he could reassert it by amending the regulations.

Here, as in *Accardi*, it is theoretically possible for the Attorney General to amend or revoke the regulation defining the Special Prosecutor's authority. But he has not done so. So long as this regulation remains in force the Executive Branch is bound by it, and indeed the United States as the sovereign composed of the three branches is bound to respect and to enforce it. Moreover, the delegation of authority to the Special Prosecutor in this case is not an ordinary delegation by the Attorney General to a subordinate officer: with the authorization of the President, the Acting Attorney General provided in the regulation that the Special Prosecutor was not to be removed without the "consensus" of eight designated leaders of Congress.

The demands of and the resistance to the subpoena present an obvious controversy in the ordinary sense, but that alone is not sufficient to meet constitutional standards. In the constitutional sense, controversy means more than disagreement and conflict; rather it means the kind of controversy courts traditionally resolve. Here at issue is the production or nonproduction of specified evidence deemed by the Special Prosecutor to be relevant and admissible in a pending criminal case. It is sought by one official of the Executive Branch within the scope of his express authority; it is resisted by the Chief Executive on the ground of his duty to preserve the confidentiality of the communications of the President. Whatever the correct answer on the merits, these issues are "of a type which are traditionally justiciable." The independent Special Prosecutor with his asserted need for the subpoenaed material in the underlying criminal prosecution is opposed by the President with his steadfast assertion of privilege against disclosure of the material. This setting assures there is "that concrete adverseness which sharpens the presentation of issues upon which the court so largely depends for illumination of difficult constitutional questions." Moreover, since the matter is one arising in the regular course of a federal criminal prosecution, it is within the traditional scope of Art. III power.

IV

The Claim of Privilege

A

Having determined that the requirements of Rule 17(c) were satisfied, we turn to the claim that the subpoena should be quashed because it demands "confidential conversations between a President and his close advisors that it would be inconsistent with the public interest to produce." The first contention is a broad claim that the separation of powers doctrine precludes judicial review of a President's claim of privilege. The second contention is that if he does not prevail on the claim of absolute privilege, the court should hold as a matter of constitutional law that the privilege prevails over the subpoena duces tecum.

In the performance of assigned constitutional duties each branch of the Government must initially interpret the Constitution, and the interpretation of its powers by any branch is due great respect from the others. The President's counsel, as we have noted, reads the Constitution as providing an absolute privilege of confidentiality for all Presidential communications. Many decisions of this Court, however, have unequivocally reaffirmed the holding of *Marbury v. Madison* that "[i]t is emphatically the province and duty of the judicial department to say what the law is."

No holding of the Court has defined the scope of judicial power specifically relating to the enforcement of a subpoena for confidential Presidential communications for use in a criminal prosecution, but other exercises of power by the Executive Branch and the Legislative Branch have been found invalid as in conflict with the Constitution. In a series of cases, the Court interpreted the explicit immunity conferred by express provisions of the Constitution on Members of the House and Senate by the Speech or Debate Clause, U.S. Const. Art. I, § 6. Since this Court has consistently exercised the power to construe and delineate claims arising under express powers, it must follow that the Court has authority to interpret claims with respect to powers alleged to derive from enumerated powers.

Our system of government "requires that federal courts on occasion interpret the Constitution in a manner at variance with the construction given the document by another branch."

B

In support of his claim of absolute privilege, the President's counsel urges two grounds, one of which is common to all governments and one of which is peculiar to our system of separation of powers. The first ground is the valid need for protection of communications between high Government officials and those who advise and assist them in the performance of their manifold duties; the importance of this confidentiality is too plain to require further discussion. Human experience teaches that those who expect public dissemination of their remarks may well temper candor with a concern for appearances and for their own interests to the detriment of the decisionmaking process. Whatever the nature of the privilege of confidentiality of Presidential communications in the exercise of Art. II powers, the privilege can be said to derive from the supremacy of each branch within its own assigned area of constitutional duties. Certain powers and privileges flow from the nature of enumerated powers; the protection of the confidentiality of Presidential communications has similar constitutional underpinnings.

The second ground asserted by the President's counsel in support of the claim of absolute privilege rests on the doctrine of separation of powers. Here it is argued that the independence of the Executive Branch within its own sphere insulates a President from a judicial subpoena in an ongoing criminal prosecution, and thereby protects confidential Presidential communications.

However, neither the doctrine of separation of powers, nor the need for confidentiality of high-level communications, without more, can sustain an absolute, unqualified Presidential privilege of immunity from judicial process under all circumstances. The President's need for complete candor and objectivity from advisers calls for great deference from the courts. However, when the privilege depends solely on the broad, undifferentiated claim of public interest in the confidentiality of such conversations, a confrontation with other values arises. Absent a claim of need to protect military, diplomatic, or sensitive national security secrets, we find it difficult to accept the argument that even the very important interest in confidentiality of Presidential communications is significantly diminished by production of such material for in camera inspection with all the protection that a district court will be obliged to provide.

The impediment that an absolute, unqualified privilege would place in the way of the primary constitutional duty of the Judicial Branch to do justice in criminal prosecutions would plainly conflict with the function of the courts under Art. III. In designing the structure of our Government and dividing and allocating the sovereign power among three co-equal branches, the Framers of the Constitution sought to provide a comprehensive system, but the separate powers were not intended to operate with absolute independence. "While the Constitution diffuses power the better to secure liberty, it also contemplates that practice will integrate the dispersed powers into a workable government. It enjoins upon its branches separateness but interdependence, autonomy but reciprocity."

To read the Art. II powers of the President as providing an absolute privilege as against a subpoena essential to enforcement of criminal statutes on no more than a generalized claim of the public interest in confidentiality of nonmilitary and nondiplomatic discussions would upset the constitutional balance of "a workable government" and gravely impair the role of the courts under Art. III.

C

Since we conclude that the legitimate needs of the judicial process may outweigh Presidential privilege, it is necessary to resolve those competing interests in a manner that preserves the essential functions of each branch. The right and indeed the duty to resolve that question does not free the Judiciary from according high respect to the representations made on behalf of the President.

The expectation of a President to the confidentiality of his conversations and correspondence, like the claim of confidentiality of judicial deliberations, for example, has all the values to which we accord deference for the privacy of all citizens and, added to those values, is the necessity for protection of the public interest in candid, objective, and even blunt or harsh opinions in Presidential decision-making. A President and those who assist him must be free to explore alternatives in the process of shaping policies and making decisions and to do so in a way many would be unwilling to express except privately. These are the considerations justifying a presumptive privilege for Presidential communications. The privilege is fundamental to the operation of Government and inextricably rooted in the separation of powers under the Constitution. In *Nixon v. Sirica*, the Court of Appeals held that such Presidential communications are "presumptively privileged," and this position is accepted by both parties in the present litigation.

We agree with Mr. Chief Justice Marshall's observation, therefore, that "[i]n no case of this kind would a court be required to proceed against the president as against an ordinary individual."

But this presumptive privilege must be considered in light of our historic commitment to the rule of law. This is nowhere more profoundly manifest than in our view that "the twofold aim (of criminal justice) is that guilt shall not escape or innocence suffer." We have elected to employ an adversary system of criminal justice in which the parties contest all issues before a court of law. The need to develop all relevant facts in the adversary system is both fundamental and comprehensive. The ends of criminal justice would be defeated if judgments were to be founded on a partial or speculative presentation of the facts. The very integrity of the judicial system and public confidence in the system depend on full disclosure of all the facts, within the framework of the rules of evidence. To ensure that justice is done, it is imperative to the function of courts that compulsory process be available for the production of evidence needed either by the prosecution or by the defense.

In this case the President challenges a subpoena served on him as a third party requiring the production of materials for use in a criminal prosecution; he does so on the claim that he has a privilege against disclosure of confidential communications. He does not place his claim of privilege on the ground they are military or diplomatic secrets. As to these areas of Art. II duties the courts have traditionally shown the utmost deference to Presidential responsibilities. In *C. & S. Air Lines v. Waterman S.S. Corp.* (333 US 103, 1948), dealing with Presidential authority involving foreign policy considerations, the Court said:

> "The President, both as Commander-in-Chief and as the Nation's organ for foreign affairs, has available intelligence services whose reports are not and ought not to be published to the world. It would be intolerable that courts, without the relevant information, should review and perhaps nullify actions of the Executive taken on information properly held secret."

In *United States v. Reynolds* (345 U.S. 1, 1953), dealing with a claimant's demand for evidence in a Tort Claims Act case against the Government, the Court said:

> "It may be possible to satisfy the court, from all the circumstances of the case, that there is a reasonable danger that compulsion of the evidence will expose military matters which, in the interest of national security, should not be divulged. When this is the case, the occasion for the privilege is appropriate, and the court should not jeopardize the security which the privilege is meant to protect by insisting upon an examination of the evidence, even by the judge alone, in chambers."

No case of the Court, however, has extended this high degree of deference to a President's generalized interest in confidentiality. Nowhere in the Constitution, as we have noted earlier, is there any explicit reference to a privilege of confidentiality, yet to the extent this interest relates to the effective discharge of a President's powers, it is constitutionally based.

In this case we must weigh the importance of the general privilege of confidentiality of Presidential communications in performance of the President's responsibilities against the inroads of such a privilege on the fair administration of criminal justice. The interest in preserving confidentiality is weighty indeed and entitled to great respect. However, we cannot conclude that advisers will be moved to temper the candor of their remarks by the infrequent occasions of disclosure because of the possibility that such conversations will be called for in the context of a criminal prosecution.

We conclude that when the ground for asserting privilege as to subpoenaed materials sought for use in a criminal trial is based only on the generalized interest in confidentiality, it cannot prevail over the fundamental demands of due process of law in the fair administration of criminal justice. The generalized assertion of privilege must yield to the demonstrated, specific need for evidence in a pending criminal trial.

Affirmed.

JUSTICE REHNQUIST took no part in the consideration or decision of these cases.

FOR DISCUSSION

Does executive privilege exist? Did the Court not recognize it in this case? If so, why did it reject the claims of this privilege and order the president to turn over the tapes? Would the Court have reached the same result if this were a civil and not a criminal matter?

CLINTON V. JONES

520 U.S. 681, 117 S. Ct. 1636, 137 L. Ed. 2d 945 (1997)

Paula Jones was a state employee when Bill Clinton was governor of Arkansas. She alleged that he had sexually harassed her while he was governor, and she sought to sue him while he was president. Clinton challenged the suit, claiming it could not proceed while he was president.

Vote: 9–0

JUSTICE STEVENS delivered the opinion of the Court.

This case raises a constitutional and a prudential question concerning the Office of the President of the United States. Respondent, a private citizen, seeks to recover damages from the current occupant of that office based on actions allegedly taken before his term began. The President submits that in all but the most exceptional cases the Constitution requires federal courts to defer such litigation until his term ends and that, in any event, respect for the office warrants such a stay. Despite the force of the arguments supporting the President's submissions, we conclude that they must be rejected.

I

Petitioner, William Jefferson Clinton, was elected to the Presidency in 1992, and re-elected in 1996. His term of office expires on January 20, 2001. In 1991 he was the Governor of the State of Arkansas. Respondent, Paula Corbin Jones, is a resident of California. In 1991 she lived in Arkansas, and was an employee of the Arkansas Industrial Development Commission.

On May 6, 1994, she commenced this action in the United States District Court for the Eastern District of Arkansas by filing a complaint naming petitioner and Danny Ferguson, a former Arkansas State Police officer, as defendants. The complaint alleges two federal claims, and two state-law claims over which the federal court has jurisdiction because of the diverse citizenship of the parties. As the case comes to us, we are required to assume the truth of the detailed—but as yet untested—factual allegations in the complaint.

Those allegations principally describe events that are said to have occurred on the afternoon of May 8, 1991, during an official conference held at the Excelsior Hotel in Little Rock, Arkansas. The Governor delivered a speech at the conference; respondent—working as a state employee—staffed the registration desk. She alleges that Ferguson persuaded her to leave her desk and to visit the Governor in a business suite at the hotel, where he made "abhorrent" sexual advances that she vehemently rejected. She further claims that her superiors at work subsequently dealt with her in a hostile and rude manner, and changed her duties to punish her for rejecting those advances. Finally, she alleges that after petitioner was elected President, Ferguson defamed her by making a statement to a reporter that implied she had accepted petitioner's alleged overtures, and that various persons authorized to speak for the President publicly branded her a liar by denying that the incident had occurred.

Respondent seeks actual damages of $75,000 and punitive damages of $100,000. Her complaint contains four counts. The first charges that petitioner, acting under color of state law, deprived her of rights protected by the Constitution, in violation of Rev. Stat. § 1979, 42 U.S.C. § 1983. The second charges that petitioner and Ferguson engaged in a conspiracy to violate her federal rights, also actionable under federal law. See Rev. Stat. § 1980, 42 U.S.C. § 1985. The third is a state common law claim for intentional infliction of emotional distress, grounded primarily on the incident at the hotel. The fourth count, also based on state law, is for defamation, embracing both the comments allegedly made to the press by Ferguson and the statements of petitioner's agents. Inasmuch as the legal sufficiency of the claims has not yet been challenged, we assume, without deciding, that each of the four counts states a cause of action as a matter of law. With the exception of the last charge, which arguably may involve conduct within the outer perimeter of the President's official responsibilities, it is perfectly clear that the alleged misconduct of petitioner was unrelated to any of his official duties as President of the United States and, indeed, occurred before he was elected to that office.

II

In response to the complaint, petitioner promptly advised the District Court that he intended to file a motion to dismiss on grounds of Presidential immunity, and requested the court to defer all other pleadings and motions until after the immunity issue was resolved. Relying on our cases holding that immunity questions should be decided at the earliest possible stage of the litigation, our recognition of the " 'singular importance of the President's duties,' " and the fact that the question did not require any analysis of the allegations of the complaint, the court granted the request. Petitioner thereupon filed a motion "to dismiss . . . without prejudice and to toll any statutes of limitation [that may be applicable] until he is no longer President, at which time the plaintiff may refile the instant suit." Extensive submissions were made to the District Court by the parties and the Department of Justice.

The District Judge denied the motion to dismiss on immunity grounds and ruled that discovery in the case could go forward, but ordered any trial stayed until the end of petitioner's Presidency. Although she recognized that a "thin majority" in *Nixon v. Fitzgerald* (457 U.S. 731, 1982) had held that "the President has absolute immunity from civil damage actions arising out of the execution of official duties of office," she was not convinced that "a President has absolute immunity from civil causes of action arising prior to assuming the office." She was, however, persuaded by some of the reasoning in our opinion in *Fitzgerald* that deferring the trial if one were required would be appropriate. Relying in part on the fact that respondent had failed to bring her complaint until two days before the 3-year period of limitations expired, she concluded that the public interest in avoiding litigation that might hamper the President in conducting the duties of his office outweighed any demonstrated need for an immediate trial.

III

The President, represented by private counsel, filed a petition for certiorari. The Acting Solicitor General, representing the United States, supported the petition, arguing that the decision of the Court of Appeals was "fundamentally mistaken" and created "serious risks for the institution of the Presidency." In her brief in opposition to certiorari, respondent argued that this "one-of-a-kind case is singularly inappropriate" for the exercise of our certiorari jurisdiction because it did not create any conflict among the Courts of Appeals, it "does not pose any conceivable threat to the functioning of the Executive Branch," and there is no precedent supporting the President's position.

While our decision to grant the petition expressed no judgment concerning the merits of the case, it does reflect our appraisal of its importance. The representations made on behalf of the Executive Branch as to the potential impact of the precedent established by the Court of Appeals merit our respectful and deliberate consideration.

It is true that we have often stressed the importance of avoiding the premature adjudication of constitutional questions. That doctrine of avoidance, however, is applicable to the entire Federal Judiciary, not just to this Court, and comes into play after the court has acquired jurisdiction of a case. It does not dictate a discretionary denial of every certiorari petition raising a novel constitutional question. It does, however, make it appropriate to identify two important constitutional issues not encompassed within the questions presented by the petition for certiorari that we need not address today.

First, because the claim of immunity is asserted in a federal court and relies heavily on the doctrine of separation of powers that restrains each of the three branches of the Federal Government from encroaching on the domain of the other two, it is not necessary to consider or decide whether a comparable claim might succeed in a state tribunal. If this case were being heard in a state forum, instead of advancing a separation-of-powers argument, petitioner would presumably rely on federalism and comity concerns, as well as the interest in protecting federal officials from possible local prejudice that underlies the authority to remove certain cases brought against federal officers from a state to a federal court. Whether those concerns would present a more compelling case for immunity is a question that is not before us.

Second, our decision rejecting the immunity claim and allowing the case to proceed does not require us to confront the question whether a court may compel the attendance of the President at any specific time or place. We assume that the testimony of the President, both for discovery and for use at trial, may be taken at the White House at a time that will accommodate his busy schedule, and that, if a trial is held, there would be no necessity for the President to attend in person, though he could elect to do so.

IV

Petitioner's principal submission—that "in all but the most exceptional cases," the Constitution affords the President temporary immunity from civil damages litigation arising out of events that occurred before he took office—cannot be sustained on the basis of precedent.

Only three sitting Presidents have been defendants in civil litigation involving their actions prior to taking office. Complaints against Theodore Roosevelt and Harry Truman had been dismissed before they took office; the dismissals were affirmed after their respective inaugurations. Two companion cases arising out of an automobile accident were filed against John F. Kennedy in 1960 during the Presidential campaign. After taking office, he unsuccessfully argued that his status as Commander in Chief gave him a right to a stay under the Soldiers' and Sailors' Civil Relief Act of 1940. The motion for a stay was denied by the District Court, and the matter was settled out of court. Thus, none of those cases sheds any light on the constitutional issue before us.

The principal rationale for affording certain public servants immunity from suits for money damages arising out of their official acts is inapplicable to unofficial conduct. In cases involving prosecutors, legislators, and judges we have repeatedly explained that the immunity serves the public interest in enabling such officials to perform their designated functions effectively without fear that a particular decision may give rise to personal liability.

As public servants, the prosecutor and the judge represent the interest of society as a whole. The conduct of their official duties may adversely affect a wide variety of different individuals, each of whom may be a potential source of future controversy. The societal interest in providing such public officials with the maximum ability to deal fearlessly and impartially with the public at large has long been recognized as an acceptable justification for official immunity. The point of immunity for such officials is to forestall an atmosphere of intimidation that would conflict with their resolve to perform their designated functions in a principled fashion.

That rationale provided the principal basis for our holding that a former President of the United States was "entitled to absolute immunity from damages liability predicated on his official acts." Our central concern was to avoid rendering the President "unduly cautious in the discharge of his official duties."

This reasoning provides no support for an immunity for *unofficial* conduct. As we explained in *Fitzgerald,* "the sphere of protected action must be related closely to the immunity's justifying purposes." Because of the President's broad responsibilities, we recognized in that case an immunity from damages claims arising out of official acts extending to the "outer perimeter of his authority." But we have never suggested that the President, or any other official, has an immunity that extends beyond the scope of any action taken in an official capacity.

Moreover, when defining the scope of an immunity for acts clearly taken *within* an official capacity, we have applied a functional approach. "Frequently our decisions have held that an official's absolute immunity should extend only to acts in performance of particular functions of his office." Hence, for example, a judge's absolute immunity does not extend to actions performed in a purely administrative capacity. As our opinions have made clear, immunities are grounded in "the nature of the function performed, not the identity of the actor who performed it."

Petitioner's effort to construct an immunity from suit for unofficial acts grounded purely in the identity of his office is unsupported by precedent.

V

We are also unpersuaded by the evidence from the historical record to which petitioner has called our attention. He points to a comment by Thomas Jefferson protesting the **subpoena *duces tecum*** Chief Justice Marshall directed to him in the Burr trial, a statement in the diaries kept by Senator William Maclay of the first Senate debates, in which then-Vice President John Adams and Senator Oliver Ellsworth are recorded as having said that "the President personally [is] not . . . subject to any process whatever," lest it be "put . . . in the power of a common Justice to exercise any Authority over him and Stop the Whole Machine of Government," and to a quotation from Justice Story's. None of these sources sheds much light on the question at hand.

VI

Petitioner's strongest argument supporting his immunity claim is based on the text and structure of the Constitution. He does not contend that the occupant of the Office of the President is "above the law," in the sense that his conduct is entirely immune from judicial scrutiny. The President argues merely for a postponement of the judicial proceedings that will determine whether he violated any law. His argument is grounded in the character of the office that was created by Article II of the Constitution, and relies on separation-of-powers principles that have structured our constitutional arrangement since the founding.

As a starting premise, petitioner contends that he occupies a unique office with powers and responsibilities so vast and important that the public interest demands that he devote his undivided time and attention to his public duties. He submits that—given the nature of the office—the doctrine of separation of powers places limits on the authority of the Federal Judiciary to interfere with the Executive Branch that would be transgressed by allowing this action to proceed.

We have no dispute with the initial premise of the argument. Former Presidents, from George Washington to George Bush, have consistently endorsed petitioner's characterization of the office. After serving his term, Lyndon Johnson observed: "Of all the 1,886 nights I was President, there were not many when I got to sleep before 1 or 2 a.m., and there were few mornings when I didn't wake up by 6 or 6:30." In 1967, the Twenty-fifth Amendment to the Constitution was adopted to ensure continuity in the performance of the powers and duties of the office; one of the sponsors of that Amendment stressed the importance of providing that "at all times" there be a President "who has complete control and will be able to perform" those duties. As Justice Jackson has pointed out, the Presidency concentrates executive authority "in a single head in whose choice the whole Nation has a part, making him the focus of public hopes and expectations. In drama, magnitude and finality his decisions so far overshadow any others that almost alone he fills the public eye and ear." We have, in short, long recognized the "unique position in the constitutional scheme" that this office occupies. Thus, while we suspect that even in our modern era there remains some truth to Chief Justice Marshall's suggestion that the duties of the Presidency are not entirely "unremitting," we accept the initial premise of the Executive's argument.

It does not follow, however, that separation-of-powers principles would be violated by allowing this action to proceed. The doctrine of separation of powers is concerned with the allocation of official power among the three coequal branches of our Government. The Framers "built into the tripartite Federal Government . . . a self-executing safeguard against the encroachment or aggrandizement of one branch at the expense of the other." Thus, for example, the Congress may not exercise the judicial power to revise final judgments, or the executive power to manage an airport. Similarly, the President may not exercise the legislative power to authorize the seizure of private property for public use. And, the judicial power to decide cases and controversies does not include the provision of purely advisory opinions to the Executive, or permit the federal courts to resolve non justiciable questions.

Of course the lines between the powers of the three branches are not always neatly defined. But in this case there is no suggestion that the Federal Judiciary is being asked to perform any function that might in some way be described as "executive." Respondent is merely asking the courts to exercise their core Article III jurisdiction to decide cases and controversies. Whatever the outcome of this case, there is no possibility that the decision will curtail the scope of the official powers of the Executive Branch. The litigation of questions that relate entirely to the unofficial conduct of the individual who happens to be the President poses no perceptible risk of misallocation of either judicial power or executive power.

Rather than arguing that the decision of the case will produce either an aggrandizement of judicial power or a narrowing of executive power, petitioner contends that—as a byproduct of an otherwise traditional exercise of judicial power—burdens will be placed on the President that will hamper the performance of his official duties. We have recognized that "[e]ven when a branch does not arrogate power to itself . . . the separation-of-powers doctrine requires that a branch not impair another in the performance of its constitutional duties." As a factual matter, petitioner contends that this particular case—as well as the potential additional litigation that an affirmance of the Court of Appeals judgment might spawn—may impose an unacceptable burden on the President's time and energy, and thereby impair the effective performance of his office.

Petitioner's predictive judgment finds little support in either history or the relatively narrow compass of the issues raised in this particular case. As we have already noted, in the more than 200-year history of the Republic, only three sitting Presidents have been subjected to suits for their private actions. If the past is any indicator, it seems unlikely that a deluge of such litigation will ever engulf the Presidency. As for the case at hand, if properly managed by the District Court, it appears to us highly unlikely to occupy any substantial amount of petitioner's time.

Of greater significance, petitioner errs by presuming that interactions between the Judicial Branch and the Executive, even quite burdensome interactions, necessarily rise to the level of constitutionally forbidden impairment of the Executive's ability to perform its constitutionally mandated functions. "[O]ur . . . system imposes upon the Branches a degree of overlapping responsibility, a duty of interdependence as well as independence the absence of which 'would preclude the establishment of a Nation capable of governing itself effectively.' " As Madison explained, separation of powers does not mean that the branches "ought to have no *partial agency* in, or no *controul* over the acts of each other." The fact that a federal court's exercise of its traditional Article III jurisdiction may significantly burden the time and attention of the Chief Executive is not sufficient to establish a violation of the Constitution. Two long-settled propositions, first announced by Chief Justice Marshall, support that conclusion.

First, we have long held that when the President takes official action, the Court has the authority to determine whether he has acted within the law. Perhaps the most dramatic example of such a case is our holding that President Truman exceeded his constitutional authority when he issued an order directing the Secretary of

Commerce to take possession of and operate most of the Nation's steel mills in order to avert a national catastrophe. Despite the serious impact of that decision on the ability of the Executive Branch to accomplish its assigned mission, and the substantial time that the President must necessarily have devoted to the matter as a result of judicial involvement, we exercised our Article III jurisdiction to decide whether his official conduct conformed to the law. Our holding was an application of the principle established in *Marbury v. Madison* (5 U.S. (1 Cranch) 137, 1803) that "[i]t is emphatically the province and duty of the judicial department to say what the law is."

Second, it is also settled that the President is subject to judicial process in appropriate circumstances. Although Thomas Jefferson apparently thought otherwise, Chief Justice Marshall, when presiding in the treason trial of Aaron Burr, ruled that a subpoena *duces tecum* could be directed to the President. We unequivocally and emphatically endorsed Marshall's position when we held that President Nixon was obligated to comply with a subpoena commanding him to produce certain tape recordings of his conversations with his aides. As we explained, "neither the doctrine of separation of powers, nor the need for confidentiality of high-level communications, without more, can sustain an absolute, unqualified Presidential privilege of immunity from judicial process under all circumstances."

Sitting Presidents have responded to court orders to provide testimony and other information with sufficient frequency that such interactions between the Judicial and Executive Branches can scarcely be thought a novelty. President Monroe responded to written interrogatories, President Nixon—as noted above—produced tapes in response to a subpoena *duces tecum*. President Ford complied with an order to give a deposition in a criminal trial, and President Clinton has twice given videotaped testimony in criminal proceedings. Moreover, sitting Presidents have also voluntarily complied with judicial requests for testimony. President Grant gave a lengthy deposition in a criminal case under such circumstances.

In sum, "[i]t is settled law that the separation-of-powers doctrine does not bar every exercise of jurisdiction over the President of the United States." If the Judiciary may severely burden the Executive Branch by reviewing the legality of the President's official conduct, and if it may direct appropriate process to the President himself, it must follow that the federal courts have power to determine the legality of his unofficial conduct. The burden on the President's time and energy that is a mere byproduct of such review surely cannot be considered as onerous as the direct burden imposed by judicial review and the occasional invalidation of his official actions. We therefore hold that the doctrine of separation of powers does not require federal courts to stay all private actions against the President until he leaves office.

FOR DISCUSSION

How might a civil suit against the president hurt the presidency? Is the damage legal, constitutional, or simply political? Is there any explicit text in the Constitution that supports the president's claims in this case? In light of the impeachment of President Clinton, do you think this case was decided correctly or that the arguments about civil suits damaging the presidency have more or less merit?

IN RE GRAND JURY SUBPOENA DUCES TECUM

112 F. 3d 910 (8th Cir. 1997)

Kenneth Starr was appointed special prosecutor to investigate alleged illegal financial dealings involving the Clintons when Bill Clinton was governor of Arkansas. Starr sought to obtain documents from the White House regarding possible conversations about this matter that involved first lady Hillary Clinton. The president sought to quash the subpoena for these records.

BOWMAN, CIRCUIT JUDGE.

The Office of Independent Counsel (OIC) appeals from an order of the District Court denying the OIC's motion to compel the production of documents subpoenaed by a federal grand jury. We reverse and remand.

I.

The task assigned to Independent Counsel Kenneth W. Starr is to investigate and prosecute matters "relating in any way to James B. McDougal's, President William Jefferson Clinton's, or Mrs. Hillary Rodham Clinton's relationships with Madison Guaranty Savings & Loan Association, Whitewater Development Corporation, or Capital Management Services, Inc." *In re Madison Guar. Sav. & Loan Ass'n,* Div. No. 94–1, Order at 1–2 (D.C.Cir.Sp.Div. Aug. 5, 1994). Mr. Starr also is charged with the duty of pursuing evidence of other violations of the law developed during and connected with or arising out of his primary investigation, known generally as "Whitewater."

On June 21, 1996, as part of its investigation, the OIC directed to the White House a grand jury subpoena that required production of "[a]ll documents created during meetings attended by any attorney from the Office of Counsel to the President and Hillary Rodham Clinton (regardless whether any other person was present)" pertaining to several Whitewater-related subjects. The White House identified nine sets of notes responsive to the subpoena but refused to produce them, citing executive privilege, attorney-client privilege, and the attorney work product doctrine.

On August 19, 1996, the OIC filed a motion before the District Court to compel production of two of the nine sets of documents identified by the White House. The first set of documents comprises notes taken by Associate Counsel to the President Miriam Nemetz on July 11, 1995, at a meeting attended by Mrs. Clinton, Special Counsel to the President Jane Sherburne, and Mrs. Clinton's personal attorney, David Kendall. The subject of this meeting was Mrs. Clinton's activities following the death of Deputy Counsel to the President Vincent W. Foster, Jr. The documents in the second collection are notes taken by Ms. Sherburne on January 26, 1996, during meetings attended by Mrs. Clinton, Mr. Kendall, Nicole Seligman (a partner of Mr. Kendall's), and, at times, John Quinn, Counsel to the President. These meetings, which took place during breaks in and immediately after Mrs. Clinton's testimony before a federal grand jury in Washington, D.C., concerned primarily the discovery of certain billing records from the Rose Law Firm in the residence area of the White House.

The White House abandoned its claim of executive privilege before the District Court, relying solely on the attorney-client privilege and the work product doctrine. Mrs. Clinton also entered a personal appearance through counsel in the District Court and asserted her personal attorney-client privilege. The District Court found it unnecessary to reach the broadest question presented by the OIC, whether a federal governmental entity may assert the attorney-client privilege or the work product doctrine in response to a subpoena by a federal grand jury. Instead, the court concluded that because Mrs. Clinton and the White House had a "genuine and reasonable (whether or not mistaken)" belief that the conversations at issue were privileged, the attorney-client privilege applied. In addition, the court held that the work product doctrine prevented disclosure of the notes to the grand jury.

The OIC appealed, and we granted expedited review. Mrs. Clinton moved to intervene formally, and we granted her motion. The case was submitted following oral arguments in a closed session. The District Court did not find it necessary to examine the disputed materials in camera, and neither do we.

At the request of the White House, and in order to preserve the secrecy of the grand jury's proceedings, we filed our opinion under seal on April 9, 1997, intending to publish a redacted opinion shortly thereafter.

Since we filed our opinion, however, press reports have related some of the substance of our decision. Believing that these disclosures have portrayed the White House in an unfairly negative light, the White House and Mrs. Clinton moved this Court to publish its opinion and to unseal the briefs and appendices filed in this Court, and the OIC joined in the motion. The motion is granted. Accordingly, this opinion, as amended, together with Judge Kopf's dissent, is released for publication, and the briefs and appendices are ordered unsealed.

III.

We will address first the issue that the District Court found it unnecessary to decide: whether an entity of the federal government may use the attorney-client privilege to avoid complying with a subpoena by a federal grand jury. Before we confront the merits of this question, however, we believe it is important to identify what is not at issue in this case. The OIC does not seek to invade the attorney-client relationship existing between Mrs. Clinton, in her personal capacity, and Mr. Kendall, her personal lawyer. The privilege set up by the White House is strictly a governmental privilege, with the White House (or the Office of the President, alternatively) as client and Ms. Sherburne and Ms. Nemetz as attorneys. Accordingly, the White House is the real party in interest in this case, although Mrs. Clinton presents arguments similar to those of the White House in her capacity as an intervenor.

The discussion that follows can be summed up rather simply. We need not decide whether a governmental attorney-client privilege exists in other contexts, for it is enough to conclude that even if it does, the White House may not use the privilege to withhold potentially relevant information from a federal grand jury.

A.

"[T]he privilege of a witness, person, government, State, or political subdivision thereof [is] governed by the principles of the common law as they may be interpreted by the courts of the United States in the light of reason and experience." We must therefore apply the federal common law of attorney-client privilege to the situation presented by this case.

The OIC and the White House have taken strikingly different rhetorical approaches to the question presented here. The OIC argues that recognizing an attorney-client privilege in these circumstances would be tantamount to establishing a new privilege, which courts ordinarily undertake with great reluctance. The White House, in contrast, argues that the attorney-client privilege is already the best-established of the common-law privileges and that, furthermore, it is an absolute privilege. The White House is correct, of course, in its assertion that the attorney-client privilege is the oldest known to the common law. But the lengthy roots of the privilege do not necessarily mean that it must apply in this dispute within the federal government, especially because the privilege has not previously been so applied. Nor does the White House advance its case significantly by arguing that the attorney-client privilege is absolute, in the sense that it cannot be overcome by a showing of need. This argument merely begs the true question, whether a governmental attorney-client privilege exists at all in the context of a federal criminal investigation.

We address this question by beginning with Proposed Federal Rule of Evidence 503, which we have described as "a useful starting place" for an examination of the federal common law of attorney-client privilege The commentary makes it clear that "[t]he definition of 'client' includes governmental bodies." But neither the proposed rule nor the commentary has anything to say about the particular situation before us in this case; they represent only the broad proposition that a governmental body may be a client for purposes of the attorney-client privilege.

Lacking persuasive direction in the case law, we turn to general principles.

> "For more than three centuries it has now been recognized as a fundamental maxim that the public (in the words sanctioned by Lord Hardwicke) has a right to every man's evidence. When we

come to examine the various claims of exemption, we start with the primary assumption that there is a general duty to give what testimony one is capable of giving, and that any exemptions which may exist are distinctly exceptional, being so many derogations from a positive general rule."

Privileges, as exceptions to the general rule, "are not lightly created nor expansively construed, for they are in derogation of the search for truth." It is appropriate to recognize a privilege " 'only to the very limited extent that permitting a refusal to testify or excluding relevant evidence has a public good transcending the normally predominant principle of utilizing all rational means for ascertaining truth.' "

The White House does not dispute that a grand jury has broad investigatory powers. As the Supreme Court has recognized, the principle that the public is entitled to "every man's evidence" is "particularly applicable to grand jury proceedings." "[O]ur historic commitment to the rule of law," and particularly to the twin goals of criminal justice " 'that guilt shall not escape or innocence suffer,' " are strong factors weighing against the applicability of a privilege.

In essence, the parties' arguments center on two cases, neither of which is directly analogous to this case, but each of which has relevance to our decision: In *United States v. Nixon* (418 U.S. 683, 1974), a special prosecutor directed a **subpoena *duces tecum*** to President Nixon, seeking tapes and other materials for use in the criminal trial of seven defendants, including former White House officials. The President refused to comply with the subpoena, claiming executive privilege. After concluding that the special prosecutor had made the showing required by Federal Rule of Criminal Procedure 17(c) for a trial subpoena, the Supreme Court considered the President's claim of privilege. The Court recognized that the need for confidential presidential communication "can be said to derive from the supremacy of each branch within its own assigned area of constitutional duties," and that the privilege for presidential communications "is fundamental to the operation of Government and inextricably rooted in the separation of powers under the Constitution." Despite the strong constitutional foundations of the privilege, however, the Court concluded that it had to give way to the special prosecutor's subpoena:

> A President's acknowledged need for confidentiality in the communications of his office is general in nature, whereas the constitutional need for production of relevant evidence in a criminal proceeding is specific and central to the fair adjudication of a particular criminal case in the administration of justice. Without access to specific facts a criminal prosecution may be totally frustrated. The President's broad interest in confidentiality of communications will not be vitiated by disclosure of a limited number of conversations preliminarily shown to have some bearing on the pending criminal cases.

The OIC argues that under the logic of *Nixon,* the White House's claim of privilege must give way here, for if the governmental attorney-client privilege exists at all, it is certainly not constitutionally based. It is true, as the White House responds, that the President did not assert an attorney-client privilege in *Nixon,* and so the case is not directly controlling. We agree with the OIC, however, that *Nixon* is indicative of the general principle that the government's need for confidentiality may be subordinated to the needs of the government's own criminal justice processes.

We also find it significant that executive branch employees, including attorneys, are under a statutory duty to report criminal wrongdoing by other employees to the Attorney General. Even more importantly, however, the general duty of public service calls upon government employees and agencies to favor disclosure over concealment. The difference between the public interest and the private interest is perhaps, by itself, reason enough to find *Upjohn* unpersuasive in this case. The importance of the public interest in questions of disclosure versus privilege is not unique to this case, for it was a key reason the Supreme Court rejected the concept of work product immunity for accountants:

> By certifying the public reports that collectively depict a corporation's financial status, the independent auditor assumes a *public* responsibility transcending any employment relationship with the client. The independent public accountant performing this special function owes ultimate allegiance to the corporation's creditors and stockholders, as well as to the investing public. This "public watchdog" function demands that the accountant maintain total independence from the client at all times and requires complete fidelity to the public trust. To insulate from disclosure a certified public accountant's interpretations of the client's financial statements would be to ignore the significance of the accountant's role as a disinterested analyst charged with public obligations.

The public responsibilities of the White House are, of course, far greater than those of a private accountant performing a service with public implications. We believe the strong public interest in honest government and in exposing wrongdoing by public officials would be ill-served by recognition of a governmental attorney-client privilege applicable in criminal proceedings inquiring into the actions of public officials. We also believe that to allow any part of the federal government to use its in-house attorneys as a shield against the production of information relevant to a federal criminal investigation would represent a gross misuse of public assets

We recognize the White House's concern that "[a]n uncertain privilege, or one which purports to be certain but results in widely varying applications by the courts, is little better than no privilege at all." *Upjohn* [*Co. v. U.S.*], 449 U.S. 383 (1981) at 393. Our first response is that the White House assumes that the attorney-client privilege is more predictable ex ante than it actually is. A client discussing an issue with a lawyer cannot know, for example, whether a bankruptcy trustee will later waive the privilege or whether the lawyer's assistance will later become an issue in a proceeding, *see* Restatement § 130(1), or whether the lawyer and client will later become involved in a dispute, *see* Restatement § 133, any of which may result in disclosure of the conversation. Even so, we believe our holding in this case does not make the duties of government attorneys significantly more difficult. Assuming arguendo that there is a governmental attorney-client privilege in other circumstances, confidentiality will suffer only in those situations that a grand jury might later see fit to investigate. Because agencies and entities of the government are not themselves subject to criminal liability, a government attorney is free to discuss anything with a government official—except for potential criminal wrongdoing by that official—without fearing later revelation of the conversation. An official who fears he or she may have violated the criminal law and wishes to speak with an attorney in confidence should speak with a private attorney, not a government attorney.

Nor do we foresee any likely effect of our decision on the ability of a government lawyer to advise an official who is contemplating a future course of conduct. If the attorney explains the law accurately and the official follows that advice, no harm can come from later disclosure of the advice, which would be unlikely anyway. Like the *Nixon* Court, "we cannot conclude that advisers will be moved to temper the candor of their remarks by the infrequent occasions of disclosure because of the possibility that such conversations will be called for in the context of a criminal prosecution." [*U.S. v.*] *Nixon,* 418 U.S. [683 (1974)] at 712. The White House's "chilling effect" argument is no more persuasive in this case than it was in *Nixon.*

D.

For the reasons stated, we conclude that the White House may not use the attorney-client privilege to avoid complying with the subpoena issued in this case by a federal grand jury calling for the notes in question of Ms. Nemetz and Ms. Sherburne.

IV.

The District Court held that the work product doctrine also applied in this case to protect the White House attorneys' notes from disclosure. We disagree.

VI.

To sum up, we hold that neither the attorney-client privilege nor the attorney work product doctrine is available to the White House in the circumstances of this case. Accordingly, the order of the District Court is reversed, and the case is remanded for the entry of an order granting the OIC's motion to compel.

FOR DISCUSSION

What remains of executive privilege after this case? Moreover, given the dicta in the case, can the president make any claims of privilege or secrecy against any investigations about potential criminal activity that might involve him or the White House? Does it matter who is doing the investigation?

VETO POWER

Article I, Sec. 7 of the Constitution grants the president the veto power. This is the power to refuse to approve bills passed by Congress. Congress, however, may, with a two-thirds vote of each body, repass the legislation over the veto, at which time it will become law.

Unlike at the state level, where almost every governor has some ability to veto a portion of some types of bills, when presidents veto a bill they must veto the entire bill. The ability on the part of governors to veto parts of bills is referred to as a line-item veto. Governors and supporters of executive power endorse line-item vetoes as a way of giving the former the ability to check what is perceived as excessive and wasteful spending by state legislatures. At the state level, governors can line-item veto spending bills but generally are more limited in their ability to do the same for policy bills. Even though studies of the line-item veto reveal that it saves very little money—about 1% compared to what the state legislature originally allocated—many argue that the threat of this type of veto forces legislators to be more fiscally responsible.

For many years presidents called for a constitutional amendment giving them the same line-item authority as governors. In 1996, Congress enacted a statutory-based line-item veto because of the inability to muster the votes necessary for a constitutional amendment.

CLINTON V. CITY OF NEW YORK

524 U.S. 417, 118 S. Ct. 2091, 141 L. Ed. 2d 393 (1998)

Congress enacted a law giving the president line-item veto authority, and it was challenged as unconstitutional by several members of Congress.

Vote: 6–3

JUSTICE STEVENS delivered the opinion of the Court.

The Line Item Veto Act (Act) was enacted in April 1996 and became effective on January 1, 1997. The following day, six Members of Congress who had voted against the Act brought suit in the District Court for the District of Columbia challenging its constitutionality. On April 10, 1997, the District Court entered an order holding that the Act is unconstitutional. In obedience to the statutory direction to allow a direct, expedited appeal to this Court, see §§ 692(b)-(c), we promptly noted probable jurisdiction and expedited review. We determined, however, that the Members of Congress did not have standing to sue because they had not "alleged a sufficiently concrete injury to have established Article III standing," thus, "[i]n . . . light of [the] overriding and time-honored concern about keeping the Judiciary's power within its proper constitutional sphere," we remanded the case to the District Court with instructions to dismiss the complaint for lack of jurisdiction.

Less than two months after our decision in that case, the President exercised his authority to cancel one provision in the Balanced Budget Act of 1997, Pub. L. 105–33, 111 Stat. 251, 515, and two provisions in the Taxpayer Relief Act of 1997, Pub. L. 105–34, 111 Stat. 788, 895–896, 990–993. Appellees, claiming that they had been injured by two of those cancellations, filed these cases in the District Court. That Court again held the statute invalid, and we again expedited our review. We now hold that these appellees have standing to challenge the constitutionality of the Act and, reaching the merits, we agree that the cancellation procedures set forth in the Act violate the Presentment Clause, Art. I, § 7, cl. 2, of the Constitution.

IV

The Line Item Veto Act gives the President the power to "cancel in whole" three types of provisions that have been signed into law: "(1) any dollar amount of discretionary budget authority; (2) any item of new direct spending; or (3) any limited tax benefit." It is undisputed that the New York case involves an "item of new direct spending" and that the Snake River case involves a "limited tax benefit" as those terms are defined in the Act. It is also undisputed that each of those provisions had been signed into law pursuant to Article I, § 7, of the Constitution before it was canceled.

The Act requires the President to adhere to precise procedures whenever he exercises his cancellation authority. In identifying items for cancellation he must consider the legislative history, the purposes, and other relevant information about the items. He must determine, with respect to each cancellation, that it will "(i) reduce the Federal budget deficit; (ii) not impair any essential Government functions; and (iii) not harm the national interest." Moreover, he must transmit a special message to Congress notifying it of each cancellation within five calendar days (excluding Sundays) after the enactment of the canceled provision. It is undisputed that the President meticulously followed these procedures in these cases.

A cancellation takes effect upon receipt by Congress of the special message from the President. If, however, a "disapproval bill" pertaining to a special message is enacted into law, the cancellations set forth in that message become "null and void." The Act sets forth a detailed expedited procedure for the consideration of a "disapproval bill," but no such bill was passed for either of the cancellations involved in these cases. A majority vote of both Houses is sufficient to enact a disapproval bill. The Act does not grant the President the authority to cancel a disapproval bill, but he does, of course, retain his constitutional authority to veto such a bill.

The effect of a cancellation is plainly stated in § 691e, which defines the principal terms used in the Act. With respect to both an item of new direct spending and a limited tax benefit, the cancellation prevents the item "from having legal force or effect." Thus, under the plain text of the statute, the two actions of the President that are challenged in these cases prevented one section of the Balanced Budget Act of 1997 and one section of the Taxpayer Relief Act of 1997 "from having legal force or effect." The remaining provisions of those statutes, with the exception of the second canceled item in the latter, continue to have the same force and effect as they had when signed into law.

In both legal and practical effect, the President has amended two Acts of Congress by repealing a portion of each. "[R]epeal of statutes, no less than enactment, must conform with Art. I." There is no provision in the Constitution that authorizes the President to enact, to amend, or to repeal statutes. Both Article I and Article II assign responsibilities to the President that directly relate to the lawmaking process, but neither addresses the issue presented by these cases. The President "shall from time to time give to the Congress Information on the State of the Union, and recommend to their Consideration such Measures as he shall judge necessary and expedient. . . ." Thus, he may initiate and influence legislative proposals. Moreover, after a bill has passed both Houses of Congress, but "before it become[s] a Law," it must be presented to the President. If he approves it, "he shall sign it, but if not he shall return it, with his Objections to that House in which it shall have originated, who shall enter the Objections at large on their Journal, and proceed to reconsider it." His "return" of a bill, which is usually described as a "veto," is subject to being overridden by a two-thirds vote in each House.

There are important differences between the President's "return" of a bill pursuant to Article I, § 7, and the exercise of the President's cancellation authority pursuant to the Line Item Veto Act. The constitutional return takes place *before* the bill becomes law; the statutory cancellation occurs *after* the bill becomes law. The constitutional return is of the entire bill; the statutory cancellation is of only a part. Although the Constitution expressly authorizes the President to play a role in the process of enacting statutes, it is silent on the subject of unilateral Presidential action that either repeals or amends parts of duly enacted statutes.

There are powerful reasons for construing constitutional silence on this profoundly important issue as equivalent to an express prohibition. The procedures governing the enactment of statutes set forth in the text of Article I were the product of the great debates and compromises that produced the Constitution itself. Familiar historical materials provide abundant support for the conclusion that the power to enact statutes may only "be exercised in accord with a single, finely wrought and exhaustively considered, procedure." Our first President understood the text of the Presentment Clause as requiring that he either "approve all the parts of a Bill, or reject it in toto." What has emerged in these cases from the President's exercise of his statutory cancellation powers, however, are truncated versions of two bills that passed both Houses of Congress. They are not the product of the "finely wrought" procedure that the Framers designed.

The judgment of the District Court is affirmed.

It is so ordered.

JUSTICE KENNEDY, concurring.

Separation of powers was designed to implement a fundamental insight: Concentration of power in the hands of a single branch is a threat to liberty. *The Federalist* states the axiom in these explicit terms: "The accumulation of all powers, legislative, executive, and judiciary, in the same hands . . . may justly be pronounced the very definition of tyranny." *The Federalist No. 47*, p. 301 (C. Rossiter ed. 1961). So convinced were the Framers that liberty of the person inheres in structure that at first they did not consider a Bill of Rights necessary. *The Federalist No. 84*, pp. 513, 515. It was at Madison's insistence that the First Congress enacted the Bill of Rights. It would be a grave mistake, however, to think a Bill of Rights in Madison's scheme then or in sound constitutional theory now renders separation of powers of lesser importance.

In recent years, perhaps, we have come to think of liberty as defined by that word in the Fifth and Fourteenth Amendments and as illuminated by the other provisions of the Bill of Rights. The conception of liberty embraced by the Framers was not so confined. They used the principles of separation of powers and federalism to secure liberty in the fundamental political sense of the term, quite in addition to the idea of freedom from intrusive governmental acts. The idea and the promise were that when the people delegate some degree of control to a remote central authority, one branch of government ought not possess the power to shape their destiny without a sufficient check from the other two. In this vision, liberty demands limits on the ability of any one branch to influence basic political decisions. Quoting Montesquieu, the *Federalist Papers* made the point in the following manner:

> " 'When the legislative and executive powers are united in the same person or body,' says he, 'there can be no liberty, because apprehensions may arise lest *the same* monarch or senate should *enact* tyrannical laws to *execute* them in a tyrannical manner.' Again: 'Were the power of judging joined with the legislative, the life and liberty of the subject would be exposed to arbitrary control, for *the judge* would then be *the legislator*. Were it joined to the executive power, *the judge* might behave with all the violence of *an oppressor*.' "

Separation of powers helps to ensure the ability of each branch to be vigorous in asserting its proper authority. In this respect the device operates on a horizontal axis to secure a proper balance of legislative, executive, and judicial authority. Separation of powers operates on a vertical axis as well, between each branch and the citizens in whose interest powers must be exercised. The citizen has a vital interest in the regularity of the exercise of governmental power. If this point was not clear before *Chadha,* it should have been so afterwards. Though *Chadha* involved the deportation of a person, while the case before us involves the expenditure of money or the grant of a tax exemption, this circumstance does not mean that the vertical operation of the separation of powers is irrelevant here. By increasing the power of the President beyond what the Framers envisioned, the statute compromises the political liberty of our citizens, liberty which the separation of powers seeks to secure.

The Constitution is not bereft of controls over improvident spending. Federalism is one safeguard, for political accountability is easier to enforce within the States than nationwide. The other principal mechanism, of course, is control of the political branches by an informed and responsible electorate. Whether or not federalism and control by the electorate are adequate for the problem at hand, they are two of the structures the Framers designed for the problem the statute strives to confront. The Framers of the Constitution could not command statesmanship. They could simply provide structures from which it might emerge. The fact that these mechanisms, plus the proper functioning of the separation of powers itself, are not employed, or that they prove insufficient, cannot validate an otherwise unconstitutional device. With these observations, I join the opinion of the Court.

JUSTICE SCALIA, with whom JUSTICE O'CONNOR joins, and with whom JUSTICE BREYER joins as to Part III, concurring in part and dissenting in part.

III

The Presentment Clause requires, in relevant part, that "[e]very Bill which shall have passed the House of Representatives and the Senate, shall, before it become a Law, be presented to the President of the United States; If he approve he shall sign it, but if not he shall return it." U.S. Const., Art. I, § 7, cl. 2. There is no question that enactment of the Balanced Budget Act complied with these requirements: the House and Senate passed the bill, and the President signed it into law. It was only *after* the requirements of the Presentment Clause had been satisfied that the President exercised his authority under the Line Item Veto Act to cancel the spending item. Thus, the Court's problem with the Act is not that it authorizes the President to veto parts of a bill and sign others into law, but rather that it authorizes him to "cancel"—prevent from "having legal force or effect"—certain parts of duly enacted statutes.

Article I, § 7, of the Constitution obviously prevents the President from canceling a law that Congress has not authorized him to cancel. Such action cannot possibly be considered part of his execution of the law, and if it is legislative action, as the Court observes, " 'repeal of statutes, no less than enactment, must conform with Art. I.' " But that is not this case. It was certainly arguable, as an original matter, that Art. I, § 7, also prevents the President from canceling a law which itself *authorizes* the President to cancel it. But as the Court acknowledges, that argument has long since been made and rejected.

As much as the Court goes on about Art. I, § 7, therefore, that provision does not demand the result the Court reaches. It no more categorically prohibits the Executive *reduction* of congressional dispositions in the course of implementing statutes that authorize such reduction, than it categorically prohibits the Executive *augmentation* of congressional dispositions in the course of implementing statutes that authorize such augmentation—generally known as substantive rulemaking. There are, to be sure, limits upon the former just as there are limits upon the latter—and I am prepared to acknowledge that the limits upon the former may be much more severe. Those limits are established, however, not by some categorical prohibition of Art. I, § 7, which our cases conclusively disprove, but by what has come to be known as the doctrine of unconstitutional delegation of legislative authority: When authorized Executive reduction or augmentation is allowed to go too far, it usurps the nondelegable function of Congress and violates the separation of powers.

IV

I would hold that the President's cancellation of § 4722(c) of the Balanced Budget Act of 1977 as an item of direct spending does not violate the Constitution.

For the foregoing reasons, I respectfully dissent.

BUDGETARY AND SPENDING AUTHORITY

Clinton v. City of New York (524 U.S. 417, 1998) highlighted some of the issues surrounding control of federal budget and spending. Article I of the Constitution describes the budgetary authority of Congress, including the requirement in Section 7 that all revenue bills shall originate in the House of Representatives. Until the 1920s, there was no federal budget, and it was not until the Budget and Accounting Act of 1921 that a presidential or federal budget was mandated. The Act created, among other things, the Office of Management and Budget as an executive department agency under the president to prepare and monitor the budget.

Beginning in the late 1960s and early 1970s, concern over federal spending and deficits prompted Congress and the president to take a variety of steps to reduce the budget. Some of these actions led to disagreements between the two branches.

In *Train v. City of New York* (420 U.S. 35, 1975), Congress, over President Nixon's veto, passed the Federal Water Pollution Control Act Amendments of 1972, which provide a comprehensive program for controlling and abating water pollution. President Nixon ordered the director of the Environmental Protection Agency not to spend all of the money allotted by Congress for the Act, contending that the president had the authority to spend less than what was budgeted. On statutory grounds the Supreme Court rejected that assertion, leaving unanswered the constitutional issue of whether the president had the authority to impound unalloted funds.

President Nixon fought with Congress on several occasions regarding the authority of the former to impound congressionally authorized funds. *Train* was one of first cases to test presidential impoundment authority. In 1974 Congress passed the Congressional Budget and Impoundment Control Act to prohibit presidential impoundments. The Act also created the Congressional Budget Office, a legislative office with functions parallel to the Office of Management and Budget.

In 1985 Congress passed another law—the Balanced Budget and Emergency Deficit Act—better known as the Gramm-Rudman-Hollings Act. It directed the comptroller general to make mandatory across-the-board cuts in the federal budget if Congress and the president did not agree upon spending targets. The constitutionality of that act was addressed in *Bowsher v. Synar* (478 U.S. 714, 1986).

Clinton v. City of New York thus followed other efforts in Congress and in the courts to address budgetary issues for the federal government. Other proposals have included calls to enact the Balanced Budget Amendment, with introductions in Congress in multiple years (e.g., 1982, 1997, and 2005) and with different language. The most recent (2005) version stated, in part:

> *Section 1.* Total outlays for any fiscal year shall not exceed total receipts for that fiscal year, unless three-fifths of the whole number of each House of Congress shall provide by law for a specific excess of outlays over receipts by a rollcall vote.

Section 2. The limit on the debt of the United States held by the public shall not be increased, unless three-fifths of the whole number of each House shall provide by law for such an increase by a rollcall vote.

Section 3. Prior to each fiscal year, the President shall transmit to the Congress a proposed budget for the United States Government for that fiscal year in which total outlays do not exceed total receipts.

Section 4. No bill to increase revenue shall become law unless approved by a majority of the whole number of each House by a rollcall vote.

Section 5. The Congress may waive the provisions of this article for any fiscal year in which a declaration of war is in effect. The provisions of this article may be waived for any fiscal year in which the United States is engaged in military conflict which causes an imminent and serious military threat to national security and is so declared by a joint resolution, adopted by a majority of the whole number of each House, which becomes law.

PRESIDENTIAL PARDONING POWER

Article II, Sec. 2:

The President . . . shall have Power to Grant Reprieves and Pardons for Offenses against the United States, except in Cases of Impeachment.

The Constitution grants the President of the United States broad power to issue **pardons**. A pardon results in a grant or exemption from a punishment. In the case of a prison sentence, it may mean the commuting of remaining time unserved, or it may mean exemption from paying any unpaid fine. Pardons also restore any civil rights, such as voting privileges, lost as a result of a conviction. The scope of presidential pardoning power was addressed by the Court in *Ex parte Garland* (71 U.S. 333, 1866).

EX PARTE GARLAND

71 U.S. 333, 18 L. Ed. 366, 4 Wall. 333 (1867)

In 1862 Congress passed an act that prescribed an oath to be taken by every person elected or appointed to any federal office except the presidency. A later amendment to the statute, the Federal Test Act of 1865, provided that no one should be admitted to the federal bar without having taken the oath. The oath in question affirmed that the person had never voluntarily borne arms against the United States since acquiring citizenship, or given aid, counsel, or encouragement to those engaged in such activities, or in any way aided or supported any government within the United States hostile thereto.

In this case, A. H. Garland, an attorney, had served in the legislature of Arkansas and in the Confederate Congress. He had received from the president a full pardon for his participation, direct or implied, in the Rebellion of 1861 and in 1885 became attorney general under President Cleveland. Here he was seeking readmission to practice before the Supreme Court and challenged the 1862 statute as being a bill of attainder, as being ex post facto in its operation, as an infringement on the judicial power, and as an infringement on the president's power of pardon.

Vote: 5–4

JUSTICE FIELD delivered the opinion of the court.

On the second of July, 1862, Congress passed an act prescribing an oath to be taken by every person elected or appointed to any office of honor or profit under the government of the United States, either in the civil, military, or naval departments of the public service, except the President, before entering upon the duties of his office, and before being entitled to its salary, or other emoluments. On the 24th of January, 1865, Congress, by a supplementary act, extended its provisions so as to embrace attorneys and counsellors of the courts of the United States. This latter act provides that after its passage no person shall be admitted as an attorney and counsellor to the bar of the Supreme Court, and, after the fourth of March, 1865, to the bar of any Circuit or District Court of the United States, or of the Court of Claims, or be allowed to appear and be heard by virtue of any previous admission, or any special power of attorney, unless he shall have first taken and subscribed the oath prescribed by the act of July 2d, 1862. It also provides that the oath shall be preserved among the files of the court; and if any person take it falsely he shall be guilty of perjury, and, upon conviction, shall be subject to the pains and penalties of that offence.

At the December Term, 1860, the petitioner was admitted as an attorney and counsellor of this court, and took and subscribed the oath then required. By the second rule, as it then existed, it was only requisite to the admission of attorneys and counsellors of this court that they should have been such officers for the three previous years in the highest courts of the States to which they respectively belonged, and that their private and professional character should appear to be fair.

In March, 1865, this rule was changed by the addition of a clause requiring the administration of the oath, in conformity with the act of Congress.

In May, 1861, the State of Arkansas, of which the petitioner was a citizen, passed an ordinance of secession, which purported to withdraw the State from the Union, and afterwards, in the same year, by another ordinance, attached herself to the so-called Confederate States, and by act of the congress of that confederacy was received as one of its members.

The petitioner followed the State, and was one of her representatives—first in the lower house, and afterwards in the senate, of the congress of that confederacy, and was a member of the senate at the time of the surrender of the Confederate forces to the armies of the United States.

In July, 1865, he received from the President of the United States a full pardon for all offences committed by his participation, direct or implied, in the Rebellion. He now produces his pardon, and asks permission to continue to practise as an attorney and counsellor of the court without taking the oath required by the act of January 24th, 1865, and the rule of the court, which he is unable to take, by reason of the offices he held under the Confederate government. . . .

. . . The Constitution provides that the President "shall have power to grant reprieves and pardons for offences against the United States, except in cases of impeachment."

The power thus conferred is unlimited, with the exception stated. It extends to every offence known to the law, and may be exercised at any time after its commission, either before legal proceedings are taken, or during their pendency, or after conviction and judgment. This power of the President is not subject to legislative control. Congress can neither limit the effect of his pardon, nor exclude from its exercise any class of offenders. The benign prerogative of mercy reposed in him cannot be fettered by any legislative restrictions.

Such being the case, the inquiry arises as to the effect and operation of a pardon, and on this point all the authorities concur. A pardon reaches both the punishment prescribed for the offence and the guilt of the offender; and when the pardon is full, it releases the punishment and blots out of existence the guilt, so that in the eye of the law the offender is as innocent as if he had never committed the offence. If granted before conviction, it prevents any of the penalties and disabilities consequent upon conviction from attaching; if granted after conviction, it removes the penalties and disabilities and restores him to all his civil rights; it makes him, as it were, a new man, and gives him a new credit and capacity.

There is only this limitation to its operation: it does not restore offices forfeited or property or interests vested in others in consequence of the conviction and judgment.

The pardon produced by the petitioner is a full pardon "for all offences by him committed, arising from participation, direct or implied, in the Rebellion," and is subject to certain conditions which have been complied with. The effect of this pardon is to relieve the petitioner from all penalties and disabilities attached to the offence of treason, committed by his participation in the Rebellion. So far as that offence is concerned, he is thus placed beyond the reach of punishment of any kind. But to exclude him, by reason of that offence, from continuing in the enjoyment of a previously acquired right, is to enforce a punishment for that offence notwithstanding the pardon. If such exclusion can be effected by the exaction of an expurgatory oath covering the offence, the pardon may be avoided, and that accomplished indirectly which cannot be reached by direct legislation. It is not within the constitutional power of Congress thus to inflict punishment beyond the reach of executive clemency. From the petitioner, therefore, the oath required by the act of January 24th, 1865, could not be exacted, even if that act were not subject to any other objection than the one thus stated.

It follows, from the views expressed, that the prayer of the petitioner must be granted.

FOR DISCUSSION

Can the president pardon individuals before they are convicted of a crime or face penalties? What if they were facing impeachment but had not been convicted? Can a president pardon himself or herself?

MURPHY V. FORD

390 F. Supp. 1372 (1975)

Consumer advocate Ralph Nader and others challenged the constitutionality of President Gerald Ford's pardon of former President Richard Nixon.

CHIEF JUDGE FOX delivered the opinion of the Court.

The plaintiff, F. Gregory Murphy, is an attorney residing in Marquette, Michigan. The defendant is Gerald R. Ford, President of the United States

The plaintiff seeks a declaratory judgment that the unconditional pardon of Richard M. Nixon by President Ford on September 8, 1974, is void and of no effect. The plaintiff contends, among other things, that the pardon could not be validly granted to a person who had never been indicted or convicted and who had therefore never been formally charged with an offense against the United States. The plaintiff also alleges that the pardoning of Mr. Nixon creates a system of unequal enforcement of the laws and has substantially increased the likelihood of non-compliance with the criminal justice system.

The court observes that the Pardoning Power is in the same section of the Constitution which makes the President Commander-in-Chief of the armed forces.

Article II, Section 2, of the United States Constitution provides, "The President . . . shall have Power to grant Reprieves and Pardons for Offenses against the Unied States, except in Cases of Impeachment."

In granting a pardon to Mr. Nixon, President Ford was not presuming to end the impeachment proceeding then pending in Congress. That was exclusively a Congressional affair. The impeachment exception to the Pardoning Power does not apply here.

The main issue is, did President Ford have the constitutional power to pardon former President Nixon for the latter's offenses against the United States?

In *The Federalist No. 74*, written in 1788 in support of the proposed Constitution, Alexander Hamilton explained why the Founding Fathers gave the President a discretionary power to pardon: "The principal argument for reposing the power of pardoning . . . (in) the Chief Magistrate," Hamilton wrote, "is this: in seasons of insurrection or rebellion, there are often critical moments, when a well-timed offer of pardon to the insurgents or rebels may restore the tranquility of the commonwealth; and which, if suffered to pass unimproved, it may never be possible afterwards to recall."

Few would today deny that the period from the break-in at the Watergate in June 1972, until the resignation of President Nixon in August 1974, was a "season of insurrection or rebellion" by many actually in the Government. Since the end of 1970, various top officials of the Nixon Administration at times during this period deliberately and flagrantly violated the civil liberties of individual citizens and engaged in criminal violations of the campaign laws in order to preserve and expand their own and Nixon's personal power beyond constitutional limitations. When many illegal activities were threatened with exposure, some Nixon Administration officials formed and executed a criminal conspiracy to obstruct justice. Evidence now available suggests a strong probability that the Nixon Administration was conducting a covert assault on American liberty and an insurrection and rebellion against constitutional government itself, an insurrection and rebellion which might have succeeded but for timely intervention by a courageous free press, an enlightened Congress, and a diligent Judiciary dedicated to preserving the rule of law.

Certainly the summer and early fall of 1974 were a period of popular discontent, as the full extent of the Nixon Administration's misdeeds became known, and public trust in government virtually collapsed. After Mr. Nixon's resignation in August, the public clamor over the whole Watergate episode did not immediately subside; attention continued to focus on Mr. Nixon and his fate. When Mr. Ford became President, the executive branch was foundering in the wreckage of Watergate, and the country was in the grips of an apparently uncontrollable inflationary spiral and an energy crisis of unprecedented proportions.

Under these circumstances, President Ford concluded that the public interest required positive steps to end the divisions caused by Watergate and to shift the focus of attention from the immediate problem of Mr. Nixon to the hard social and economic problems which were of more lasting significance.

By pardoning Richard Nixon, who many believed was the leader of a conspiratorial insurrection and rebellion against American liberty and constitutional government, President Ford was taking steps, in the words of Alexander Hamilton in the Federalist, to "restore the tranquillity of the commonwealth" by a "well-timed offer of pardon" to the putative rebel leader. President Ford's pardon of Richard M. Nixon was thus within the letter and the spirit of the Presidential Pardoning Power granted by the Constitution. It was prudent public policy judgment.

The fact that Mr. Nixon had been neither indicted nor convicted of an offense against the United States does not affect the validity of the pardon. In that case the Supreme Court considered the nature of the President's Pardoning Power, and the effect of a Presidential pardon. Mr. Justice Field, speaking for the court, said that the Pardoning Power is "unlimited," except in cases of impeachment. "[The Power] extends to every offense known to the law, and may be exercised at any time after its commission, either before legal proceedings are taken, or during their pendency, or after conviction and judgment. . . . The benign prerogative of mercy reposed in (the President) cannot be fettered by any legislative restrictions.

"Such being the case, the inquiry arises as to the effect and operation of a pardon, and on this point all the authorities concur. A pardon reaches both the punishment prescribed for the offense and the guilt of the offender; and when the pardon is full, it releases the punishment and blots out of existence the guilt, . . . If granted before conviction, it prevents any of the penalties and disabilities consequent from conviction from attaching. . . .

"There is only this limitation to its operation: it does not restore offices forfeited, or property or interests vested in others in consequence of the conviction and judgment."

However, ". . . as the very essence of a pardon is forgiveness or remission of penalty, a pardon implies it does not obliterate the fact of the commission of the crime and the conviction thereof; it does not wash out the moral stain; as has been tersely said; it involves forgiveness and not forgetfulness."

For the above-stated reasons, plaintiff's motion to add the special prosecutor as a party defendant is denied.

NOTE

President Ford's pardon of Richard Nixon was controversial, and some say it was the reason why Gerald Ford eventually lost a very close presidential race to Jimmy Carter in 1976. Since this pardon, other presidents have used their powers to pardon for political reasons. In 1981, President Ronald Reagan pardoned two FBI agents convicted for authorizing illegal searches of property of antiwar protestors in 1973. In 1992, President George Bush pardoned former defense secretary Caspar Weinberger and other individuals associated with the Iran-Contra Affair during the Reagan administration; and in 2001, President Bill Clinton pardoned Patty Hearst, a kidnapped heiress turned member of the Symbionese Liberation Army, and Marc Rich, who had been indicted on charges of making illegal oil deals and tax evasion. The latter pardon was considered controversial because Rich's wife was a significant political donor to Clinton campaigns. George W. Bush issued very few pardons and in the last year of his presidency Barack Obama through July 2016 issued 348 pardons to individuals, many convicted for non-violent drug offenses.

FOR DISCUSSION

Is the presidential pardoning power unlimited? Should it be?

GLOSSARY

Checks and Balances: These are the powers granted to branches and different levels of government (local, state, and federal) in order to prevent a single branch or level from obtaining so much authority as to be tyrannical or destructive of other elements of government.

Delegated Authority: When a branch of government gives a part of its own power to another branch of government to exercise—for example, if the legislative branch allowed the executive to make a formal declaration of war. The constitutional authority to declare war belongs to the Congress; if this power were granted by Congress to the executive branch, the judiciary may find it a legitimate or illegitimate delegation of authority.

Enumerated Powers: Authority that is explicitly listed within the original articles of the Constitution and granted to the three branches of government.

Executive Privilege: A power of the president and the executive branch rooted in separation of powers. It is the authority to withhold some information from the other branches of government. In *U.S. v. Nixon* the Court said executive privilege was not absolute and had to give way to the needs of a criminal investigation.

Explicit Powers: This term is used to refer to the enumerated powers—the rights and specific authority assigned to each branch of government within the Constitution.

Implied Powers: Authority that the branches of government have assumed over time and through its exercise, despite an absence of constitutional recognition. A classic example of implied powers is the authority the president has assumed during times of national emergency, such as war.

Pardon Powers: The constitutional authority of the president to issue pardons to individuals convicted or crimes or even to those who have not yet been convicted.

Per Curiam: An unsigned decision of the Supreme Court of the United States. The decision is not listed under the name of a specific justice, but reflects the Court in its entirety.

Separation of Powers: The assigning of distinct powers to each of the three major branches of the national government.

Shared Powers: Authority granted to multiple branches of government simultaneously.

Signing Statement: Statement issued by the president at the time he or she signs legislation. Such a statement expresses what the president thinks the legislation means.

Speech and Debate Clause: This refers to Article I, Sec. 6 of the Constitution, which states that members of Congress shall be "privileged from Arrest during their Attendance at the Session of their respective Houses, and in going to and returning from the same; and for any Speech or Debate in either House, they shall not be questioned in any other Place." This clause appears to protect members of Congress from having to face legal reprisal for statements they make in their official capacity.

Subpoena *Duces Tecum*: This term references a formal legal process in which a witness summoned before a court must produce explicitly identified documents, papers, or other tangible forms of evidence.

SELECTED BIBLIOGRAPHY

Baum, Lawrence. 2016. *The Supreme Court*, 12th ed. Washington, DC: Congressional Quarterly Press.

Campbell, Tom. 2004. *Separation of Powers in Practice*. Palo Alto, CA: Stanford University Press.

Canon, Bradley, and Charles Johnson. 1999. *Judicial Policies: Implementation and Impact,* 2nd ed. Washington, DC: Congressional Quarterly Press.

Cheney, Timothy D. 1998. *Who Makes The Law: The Supreme Court, Congress, The States, And Society*. Upper Saddle River, NJ: Prentice Hall.

Epstein, Lee, Jeffrey Segal, Harold Spaeth, and Thomas Walker. 2015. *The Supreme Court Compendium*, 6th ed. Washington, DC: Congressional Quarterly Press.

Fallon, Jr., Richard H. 2004. *The Dynamic Constitution: An Introduction to American Constitutional Law*. Cambridge, UK: Cambridge University Press.

Fisher, Louis. 1998. *The Politics of Shared Power: Congress and the Executive*, 4th ed. College Station, TX: Texas A&M University Press.

Fisher, Louis. 2014. *Constitutional Conflicts Between Congress and the President*, 6th ed. Laurence, KA: University Press of Kansas.

Fisher, Louis. 2014. *The Law of the Executive Branch: Presidential Power.* New York: Oxford.

Ivers, Gregg, and Kevin T. McGuire. 2004. *Creating Constitutional Change: Clashes over Power and Liberty in the Supreme Court.* Charlottesville, VA: University of Virginia Press.

Van Geel, T. R. 2004. *Understanding Supreme Court Opinions,* 4th ed. New York: Longman.

Whittington, Keith E. 1999. *Constitutional Construction: Divided Powers and Constitutional Meaning.* Cambridge, MA: Harvard University Press.

CHAPTER V

Property Rights and Substantive Due Process

Timeline: Property Rights and Substantive Due Process

1690 John Locke publishes his *Second Treatise of Government*, which puts great emphasis on property rights.

1776 U.S. Revolutionary War begins, in large part to protest "taxation without representation."

1781 The Articles of Confederation is adopted. It grants Congress no power to coin money or control interstate commerce.

1786 Shays' Rebellion in Massachusetts strikes fear into many property owners.

1787 Constitutional Convention proposes a constitution denying states the right to abridge freedom of contracts.

1791 Ratification of the Fifth Amendment prohibits deprivation of "life, liberty, or property, without due process of law" and prohibits the taking of property for public use without "just compensation."

1798 The Supreme Court decides in *Calder v. Bull* that the constitutional provision relative to ex post facto laws is limited to criminal law.

1800 John Marshall becomes Chief Justice of the United States Supreme Court.

1810 *Fletcher v. Peck* decides that a state cannot revoke a land sale, even if members who voted for the act were bribed.

1819 In *Dartmouth College v. Woodward*, the Court affirms that a charter issued to college trustees by the English king is a contract protected by the Constitution.

1820 Congress agrees to the Missouri Compromise which admitted Missouri as a state but prohibited slavery in the remainder of the Louisiana Purchase north of the 36th parallel.

1823 In *Corfield v. Coryell*, Justice Washington, sitting as a circuit court judge, describes several economic rights protected by the Article IV Privileges and Immunities Clause.

1836 Roger Taney becomes Chief Justice of the U.S. Supreme Court.

1854 Congress passes the Stephen Douglas sponsored Kansas-Nebraska Act which repeals the Missouri Compromise and allows Kansas and Nebraska to decide whether to be free or slave states.

1857 The Supreme Court lays the groundwork for substantive due process in *Dred Scott v. Sandford* which strikes down the Kansas-Nebraska Act.

1860 Abraham Lincoln is elected president.

1865 Civil War ends and Reconstruction begins.

1866 Civil Rights Act of 1866 is enacted.

1868 The Fourteenth Amendment, which limits the states, includes a due process clause similar to that in the Fifth Amendment.

1873 In the *Slaughterhouse Cases* the Supreme Court rules that the Privileges or Immunities Clause of the Fourteenth Amendment does not prevent a state from regulating the operation of slaughterhouses.

1877 In *Munn v. Illinois* the Supreme Court upholds a state law regulating the rates charged by grain elevators operators.

1887 In *Mugler v. Kansas* the Supreme Court upholds a state law banning the brewing of beer and declares it will subject economic regulation to more than a rational basis test.

1897 The Supreme Court in *Allgeyer v. State of Louisiana* holds that liberty of contract is protected by the Due Process Clause of the Fourteenth Amendment.

1905 In *Lochner v. New York*, the Supreme Court invalidates a New York law regulating the hours of bakers.

1908 Louis Brandeis offers brief in *Muller v. Oregon* to urge the Supreme Court to uphold an Oregon law regulating the number of hours women can work.

1908 In *Muller v. Oregon* the Supreme Court unanimously upholds the Oregon law.

1923 The Supreme Court in *Adkins v. Children's Hospital* declares unconstitutional a congressional law mandating minimum wages for women and children working in the District of Columbia.

1929 A stock market collapse leads to the Great Depression.

1932 Franklin D. Roosevelt is elected president and proposes a series of New Deal programs that call for expanded governmental intervention in the economy.

1933 Congress adopts the Glass-Steagall Act creating two types of banks, commercial and investment, with the former barred from investing in Wall Street securities.

1934 In *Nebbia v. New York* the Supreme Court upholds a state law regulating the minimum price for which milk can be sold.

1937 Roosevelt proposes his "Court-packing" plan.

1937 In *West Coast Hotel Co. v. Parrish*, the Supreme Court upholds a state minimum wage law.

1938 In *United States v. Carolene Products* the Supreme Court declares that it will subject economic regulation to a rational basis test.

1963 In *Ferguson v. Skrupa* the Supreme Court declares an end to the doctrine of economic due process.

1977 The Supreme Court limits state abridgement of its own contractual obligation in *United States Trust Company of New York v. New Jersey*.

1978 In *Allied v. Spannuus* the Court recognizes limits on a state's power to regulate pension funds from firms that have left the state.

1996 In *BMW of North America, Inc. v. Gore* the Supreme Court rules that the Fourteenth Amendment Due Process Clause limits the amount of punitive damages that can be awarded in a case.

1999 Congress repeals the Glass-Steagall Act.

2005 In *Lingle v. Chevron U.S.A. Inc.* the Supreme Court reaffirms its decision in *Ferguson v. Skrupa* that economic due process is over.

2008 The federal government adopts a major bailout of the nation's banks.

2016 Senator Bernie Sanders runs for the Democratic nomination proclaiming himself to be a Democratic Socialist but loses to Hillary Clinton. Billionaire Donald Trump captures the Republican nomination.

INTRODUCTION

Charles Beard's *An Economic Interpretation of the Constitution of the United States* (1913) famously argued that the Framers who wrote the Constitution were antidemocratic elitists who did so to protect their property interests, which were being hurt by the government under the Articles of Confederation. While many scholars have taken exception to the Beard thesis, his arguments underscored the importance that the Constitution attached to property rights.

The importance attached to property rights has its roots in various political theories. In outlining his social compact theory of government, the English philosopher John Locke (1632–1704), who significantly influenced the American Founders, emphasized that men who found themselves in a prepolitical **state of nature,** where law was not established, settled, or known, would seek to create a civil society that would protect their lives, liberties, and estates. These three concepts he referred to as property. "Property" was a general political term referring to all the personal and political rights of individuals, with ownership of one's body and talents premised upon the natural freedom of individuals. Property was a natural right. These natural rights are not lost to the state, but instead for Locke: "The Supream Power cannot take from any Man any part of his Property without his own consent. For the preservation of Property being the end of Government, and that for which Men enter into Society, it necessarily supposes and requires, that the People should have Property. . . ." The importance that the American colonists placed on the principle of "**no taxation without representation**" during the Revolutionary War was one strong indication of their commitment to the importance of property rights both as an end in itself and as a way of giving citizens the means to secure life and liberty.

Republican political theory, which included British writers such as James Harrington (1611–1677), also held property to be of central importance in its views of government. Harrington's *Oceana* describes the political institutions necessary to maintain a republican form of government. He argues in that work for the need to achieve a balance of power in a commonwealth between the king, the nobility, and the people if tyranny is to be avoided and a limited republican form of government is to be sustained. Crucial to that balance of power, or the "doctrine of balance," in Harrington's words, was the equal distribution of property among the above three groups.

Finally, Sir William Blackstone (1723–1780), in his *Commentaries on the Laws of England*, was an often overlooked yet important influence on early American views of property. Blackstone's views were more legalistic and conventional than either Locke's or Harrington's, yet at times it appears that the jurist's views were similar to those of Locke. For example, in volume two of the *Commentaries* Blackstone states: "There is nothing which so generally strikes the imagination and engages the affections of mankind, as the right of property; or the sole and despotic dominion which one man claims and exercises over the external things of the world, in total exclusion of the right of any other individual in the universe."

Blackstone's views on property, as well as those of Locke and Harrington (or of republican theory in general) significantly influenced the constitutional Framers. For example, James Madison wrote in *Federalist* No. 10 that unequal divisions of property are one of the chief sources of quarrel in society. Madison described property broadly to include even one's opinions and beliefs. He argued that property as well as personal rights are an "essential object of the laws" necessary to the promotion of free government. Alexander Hamilton stated that the preservation of private property was essential to liberty and republican government. Thomas Jefferson depicted property as a "natural right of mankind" and linked ownership to public virtue and republican government. John Adams described a proper balance of property in society as important to maintaining republican government and connected property ownership to moral worth. Thomas Paine felt that the state was instituted to protect the natural right of property, and Daniel Webster would later link property to virtue, freedom, and power. Numerous Anti-Federalists described a society as free when it protected property rights or equalized property distributions. For example, Samuel Bryan, in his *Letters of Centinel*, argued that a "republican, or free government, can only exist where the body of the people are virtuous, and where property is pretty equally divided."

These various political theories invoked to justify property rights influenced the Framers when drafting the Constitution. As noted above, while Beard's argument in his *Economic Interpretation of the Constitution* that the Constitution was an economic document prepared by elites who wanted to protect property interests that had been damaged or hurt under the Articles of Confederation has been extensively criticized, those who wrote the Constitution certainly included slaveholders who were conscious of the demands by some that the values of the Declaration of Independence and the freedoms discussed under the Constitution were in conflict with the institution of slavery. Slaves could be considered either as persons or property, and slaveholders tended to emphasize the latter. Much of the debate and disagreement at the Constitutional Convention centered on fights over slavery, with the thee-fifths compromise, the limits on the ban on slave importation for twenty years, limits on the ability of states to regulate interstate commerce (and prevent slave trade) and perhaps even the concept of federalism (as a way to protect the les populous slave states from being out-voted by the free states) as examples. The point here is that one should think about the constitutional battles over property rights in light of slavery in America.

Given the importance ascribed to property rights among the Founders, it is not a surprise that a similar concern was articulated in the law and in constitutional decisions and Supreme Court opinions. At various times in United States history the Supreme Court has invoked different clauses of the Constitution to protect property rights. During the Marshall and, to a lesser extent, the Taney Courts, the Contract Clause was used in cases such as *Trustees of Dartmouth College v. Woodward* (17 U.S. (4 Wheat.) 518, 1819), to protect these rights. In the nineteenth and early twentieth centuries, the Due Process Clause of the Fourteenth Amendment, in cases such as *Lochner v. New York* (198 U.S. 45, 1905), was also used to restrict government interference with economic rights. The use of these two clauses to defend property rights preceded both the employment of the Commerce Clause in cases such as *Hammer v. Dagenhart* (247 U.S. 251, 1918) and the Fifth Amendment Takings Clause in cases such as *First English Evangelical Lutheran Church of Glendale v. County of Los Angeles* (482 U.S. 304, 1987). While Chapter III examined the treatment of property rights and economic regulation via the Commerce clause by the Supreme Court and Chapter VI will do that in the context of eminent domain under the Fifth Amendment, this chapter looks to the constitutional limits imposed upon states and the national government under the ex post facto laws and Contract Clause and the Fourteenth Amendment to protect property and economic rights.

EX POST FACTO LAWS

Article I, Sec. 9:

No Bill of Attainder or ex post facto Law shall be passed.

Article I, Sec. 10:

No State shall . . . pass . . . any Bill of Attainder [or] ex post facto Law. . . .

Both Article I, Sec. 9, which limits the powers of Congress, and Article I, Sec. 10, which limits the powers of the states, prohibit the imposition of **bills of attainder**, or **ex post facto laws**. The former related to arbitrary legislative punishments that the English Parliament had imposed on specific individuals without benefit of trial. *Ex post facto* is a Latin term for something done after the fact; Americans borrowed the term from English **common law**, which helps illuminate its meaning. In struggling to protect property rights, the pre-Marshall Court had to consider whether it might use these clauses for that purpose.

Calder v. Bull (3 U.S. 386, 1798) was the most important early case on the subject. Faced with a decision by the Connecticut state legislature that allowed for a new hearing on a probate matter that had already been decided in state courts, the U.S. Supreme Court had to decide whether the legislative action was barred either by general principles of justice or by the ex post facto clause. Although the justices disagreed on the method of constitutional interpretation, they agreed that the ex post facto provision was designed to deal with matters of criminal, rather than civil, law. If the Court were to protect the rights of private property, it would have to seek another means of so doing.

The Clause Protecting the Obligation of Contract

Although the Constitutional Convention of 1787 chiefly addressed weaknesses, or perceived weaknesses, in the government under the Articles of Confederation, it also directed some attention (most notably in Article I, Sec. 10) to perceived legislative abuses by state legislatures, one of James Madison's primary concerns. The Framers adopted the **Contract Clause** to keep the states from passing legislation relieving debtors of their obligations.

The absence of a similar stated restriction on the powers of Congress might indicate that the Founding Fathers assumed that the economics of the country would be basically in the hands of the states. Alternatively, and consistent with the theory of factions that James Madison developed in *Federalist* No. 10, the Framers might have anticipated that because Congress represented a significantly larger territory, with considerably more factions in which it would be notably more difficult for any single class to dominate, such restraints would not be as essential at the national level.

The Court under Chief Justice John Marshall (1801–1835) frequently used the Contract Clause to uphold property rights. In *Fletcher v. Peck* (10 U.S. 87, 1810), Marshall decided that the Contract Clause prevented a state from rescinding a land grant, even though there was substantial evidence that most members of the legislature had accepted bribes. In *Trustees of Dartmouth College v. Woodward* (17 U.S. (4 Wheat.) 518, 1819), facing a Democratic-Republican state legislature determined to rewrite the charter of a college, the Court had to decide whether a charter granted by the English Crown even before the United States was a country was a contract. Not only did the Court so rule, but it also decided that the state legislature's attempt to interfere with this charter violated the contract clause.

When Chief Justice Marshall left the Court, Andrew Jackson was president. Whereas Marshall had emphasized property rights, Jackson emphasized popular sovereignty. Chief Justice Roger Taney, whom Jackson had nominated to replace Marshall, reflected this new emphasis, which influenced the Court's interpretation of the Contract Clause. In the case of *Charles River Bridge v. Warren Bridge* (36 U.S. 420, 1837), the Court had to decide whether state authorization of the construction of a new bridge violated the implicit rights of the neighboring toll bridge, which had in turn replaced an exclusive ferry service. Over the dissent of Justice Joseph Story, a holdover from the Marshall Court, Taney announced that while he was willing to uphold the letter of contracts, he was not willing to enforce implicit restrictions. Absent a specific provision stating that the right of the first bridge was exclusive, the shareholders of that company would have to take their lumps. Taney's decision was in large part based on his perception that overly restrictive interpretations of the Contract clause would stifle the progress of new technologies. Taney's decision cautioned investors that they would need to protect themselves when they entered into contracts rather than seek remedial judicial actions.

In the years after *Charles River Bridge*, the Court found other ways of protecting private property, most notably through the idea of substantive due process. When the national government responded to the Great Depression of 1929 with a variety of New Deal programs, there was yet another unsuccessful attempt to revive the contract clause in *Home Building and Loan Assoc. v. Blaisdell* (290 U.S. 398, 1934). At issue was the Minnesota Mortgage Moratorium Act, which lengthened the time period during which individuals could pay off their loans. Over loud dissents by the "Four Horsemen" (conservative justices who largely opposed New Deal policies), the majority decided that the Minnesota law was not the kind of class action legislation that the Framers had attempted to prevent but a reasonable accommodation to economic exigencies.

United States Trust Corp. of New York v. New Jersey (431 U.S. 1, 1977), however, indicated that the contract clause was not completely moribund. In this case, the Court ruled that a state had ignored its responsibilities under the Contract Clause when it sought to renege on an agreement it had accepted.

Moreover in *Allied v. Spannaus* (438 U.S. 234, 1978), the Court ruled that the Contract Clause provided some boundaries on state modifications of private contracts, even when such modifications were designed with the public good in mind. In this case, the Court limited the effect of Minnesota's Private Pension Benefits Protection Act on businesses that were leaving the state. The Contract Clause was designed to protect private industries against at least some retroactive state impositions of economic regulations.

CALDER V. BULL

3 U.S. 386, 1 L. Ed. 648, 3 Dall. 386 (1798)

Although the Marshall Court was intent on protecting property rights, it was not initially clear whether it would rely on general principles or upon specific constitutional provisions, and, if the latter, which ones. This case is significant both for limiting the scope of the ex post facto clause to criminal prosecutions (rather than civil suits) and for the exchange between Justices Samuel Chase and James Iredell over appropriate methods of constitutional interpretation. At issue was the constitutionality of a decision by the Connecticut state legislature allowing for a new hearing in a probate case that would otherwise have been barred by statute.

Vote: 4–0

JUSTICE CHASE delivered the opinion of the Court.

Whether the Legislature of any of the States can revise and correct by law, a decision of any of its Courts of Justice, although not prohibited by the Constitution of the State, is a question of very great importance, and not necessary now to be determined; because the resolution or law in question does not go so far. I cannot subscribe to the omnipotence of a State Legislature, or that it is absolute and without controul; although its authority should not be expressly restrained by the Constitution, or fundamental law, of the State. The people of the United States erected their Constitutions, or forms of government, to establish justice, to promote the general welfare, to secure the blessings of liberty; and to protect their persons and property from violence. The purposes for which men enter into society will determine the nature and terms of the social compact; and as they are the foundation of the legislative power, they will decide what are the proper objects of it: The nature, and ends of legislative power will limit the exercise of it. This fundamental principle flows from the very nature of our free Republican governments, that no man should be compelled to do what the laws do not require; nor to refrain from acts which the laws permit. There are acts which the Federal, or State, Legislature cannot do, without exceeding their authority. There are certain vital principles in our free Republicans governments, which will determine and over-rule an apparent and flagrant abuse of legislative power; as to authorize manifest injustice by positive law; or to take away that security for personal liberty, or private property, for the protection whereof the government was established. An act of the Legislature (for I cannot call it a law) contrary to the great first principles of the social compact, cannot be considered a rightful exercise of legislative authority. The obligation of a law in governments established on express compact, and on republican principles, must be determined by the nature of the power, on which it is founded. A few instances will suffice to explain what I mean. A law that punished a citizen for an innocent action, or, in other words, for an act, which, when done, was in violation of no existing law; a law that destroys, or impairs, the lawful private contracts of citizens; a law that makes a man a Judge in his own cause; or a law that takes property from A. and gives it to B. It is against all reason and justice, for a people to entrust a Legislature with such powers; and, therefore, it cannot be presumed that they have done it. The genius, the nature, and the spirit, of our State Governments, amount to a prohibition of such acts of legislation; and the general principles of law and reason forbid them. The Legislature may enjoin, permit, forbid, and punish; they may declare new crimes; and establish rules of conduct for all its citizens in future cases; they may command what is right, and prohibit what is wrong; but they cannot change innocence into guilt; or punish innocence as a crime; or violate the right of an antecedent lawful private contract; or the right of private property. To maintain that our Federal, or State, Legislature possesses such powers, if they had not been expressly restrained; would, in my opinion, be a political heresy, altogether inadmissible in our free republican governments.

All the restrictions contained in the Constitution of the United States on the power of the State Legislatures, were provided in favour of the authority of the Federal Government. The prohibition against their making any ex post facto laws was introduced for greater caution, and very probably arose from the knowledge, that the Parliament of Great Britain claimed and exercised a power to pass such laws, under the denomination of bills of attainder, or bills of pains and penalties; the first inflicting capital, and the other less, punishment. These acts were legislative judgments; and an exercise of judicial power. Sometimes they respected the crime, by declaring acts to be treason, which were not treason, when committed; at other times, they violated the rules of evidence (to supply a deficiency of legal proof) by admitting one witness, when the existing law required two; by receiving evidence without oath; or the oath of the wife against the husband; or other testimony, which the courts of justice would not admit at other times they inflicted punishments, where the party was not, by law, liable to any punishment; and in other cases, they inflicted greater punishment, than the law annexed to the offence. . . .

The Constitution of the United States, article 1, section 9, prohibits the Legislature of the United States from passing any ex post facto law; and, in section 10, lays several restrictions on the authority of the Legislatures of the several states; and, among them, "that no state shall pass any ex post facto law."

It may be remembered, that the legislatures of several of the states, to wit, Massachusetts, Pennsylvania, Delaware, Maryland, and North and South Carolina, are expressly prohibited, by their state Constitutions, from passing any ex post facto law.

I shall endeavour to show what law is to be considered an ex post facto law, within the words and meaning of the prohibition in the Federal Constitution. The prohibition, "that no state shall pass any ex post facto law," necessarily requires some explanation; for, naked and without explanation, it is unintelligible, and means nothing. Literally, it is only that a law shall not be passed concerning, and after the fact, or thing done, or action committed. I would ask, what fact; of what nature, or kind; and by whom done? That Charles 1st. king of England, was beheaded; that Oliver Cromwell was Protector of England; that Louis 16th, late King of France, was guillotined; are all facts, that have happened; but it would be nonsense to suppose, that the States were prohibited from making any law after either of these events, and with reference thereto. The prohibition, in the letter, is not to pass any law concerning, and after the fact; but the plain and obvious meaning and intention of the prohibition is this; that the Legislatures of the several states, shall not pass laws, after a fact done by a subject, or citizen, which shall have relation to such fact, and shall punish him for having done it. The prohibition considered in this light, is an additional bulwark in favour of the personal security of the subject, to protect his person from punishment by legislative acts, having a retrospective operation. I do not think it was inserted to secure the citizen in his private rights, of either property, or contracts. The prohibitions not to make any thing but gold and silver coin a tender in payment of debts, and not to pass any law impairing the obligation of contracts, were inserted to secure private rights; but the restriction not to pass any ex post facto law, was to secure the person of the subject from injury, or punishment, in consequence of such law. . . .

I will state what laws I consider ex post facto laws, within the words and the intent of the prohibition. 1st. Every law that makes an action done before the passing of the law, and which was innocent when done, criminal; and punishes such action. 2d. Every law that aggravates a crime, or makes it greater than it was, when committed. 3d. Every law that changes the punishment, and inflicts a greater punishment, than the law annexed to the crime, when committed. 4th. Every law that alters the legal rules of evidence, and receives less, or different, testimony, than the law required at the time of the commission of the offence, in order to convict the offender. All these, and similar laws, are manifestly unjust and oppressive. In my opinion, the true distinction is between ex post facto laws, and retrospective laws. Every ex post facto law must necessarily be retrospective; but every retrospective law is not an ex post facto law: The former, only, are prohibited. Every law that takes away, or impairs, rights vested, agreeably to existing laws, is retrospective, and is generally unjust, and may be oppressive; and it is a good general rule, that a law should have no retrospect: but there are cases in which laws may justly, and for the benefit of the community, and also of individuals, relate to a time antecedent to their commencement; as statutes of oblivion, or of pardon. They are certainly retrospective, and literally both concerning, and after, the facts committed. But I do not consider any law ex post facto, within the prohibition, that mollifies the rigor of the criminal law; but only those that create, or aggravate, the crime; or encrease the punishment, or change the rules of evidence, for the purpose of conviction. Every law that is to have an operation before the making thereof, as to commence at an antecedent time; or to save time from the statute of limitations; or to excuse acts which were unlawful, and before committed, and the like; is retrospective. But such laws may be proper or necessary, as the case may be. There is a great and apparent difference between making an unlawful act lawful; and the making an innocent action criminal, and punishing it as a crime. . . .

[Chase further examines other documents that discuss ex post facto laws.]

If the term ex post facto law is to be construed to include and to prohibit the enacting any law after a fact, it will greatly restrict the power of the federal and state legislatures; and the consequences of such a construction may not be foreseen. . . .

It seems to me, that the right of property, in its origin, could only arise from compact express, or implied, and I think it the better opinion, that the right, as well as the mode, or manner, of acquiring property, and of alienating or transferring, inheriting, or transmitting it, is conferred by society; it is regulated by civil institutions, and is always subject to the rules prescribed by positive law. When I say that a right is vested in a citizen, I mean, that he has the power to do certain actions; or to possess certain things, according to the law of the land.

If any one has a right to property such right is a perfect and exclusive right; but no one can have such right before he has acquired a better right to the property, than any other person in the world: a right, therefore, only to recover property cannot be called a perfect and exclusive right. I cannot agree, that a right to property vested in Calder and wife, in consequence of the decree disapproving of the will of Morrison, the Grandson. If the will was valid, Mrs. Calder could have no rights, as heiress of Morrison, the physician; but if the will was set aside, she had an undoubted title.

The resolution (or law) alone had no manner of effect on any right whatever vested in Calder and wife. The Resolution (or law) combined with the new hearing, and the decision, in virtue of it, took away their right to recover the property in question. But when combined they took away no right of property vested in Calder and wife; because the decree against the will did not vest or transfer any property to them.

I am under a necessity to give a construction, or explanation of the words "ex post facto laws," because they have not any certain meaning attached to them. But I will not go farther than I feel myself bound to do; and if I ever exercise the jurisdiction I will not decide any law to be void, but in a very clear case.

JUSTICE IREDELL concurred with the opinion.

Though I concur in the general result of the opinions, which have been delivered, I cannot entirely adopt the reasons that are assigned upon the occasion.

From the best information to be collected, relative to the Constitution of Connecticut, it appears, that the Legislature of that State has been in the uniform, uninterrupted, habit of exercising a general superintending power over its courts of law, by granting new trials. . . .

But, let us, for a moment, suppose, that the resolution, granting a new trial, was a legislative act, it will by no means follow, that it is an act affected by the constitutional prohibition, that "no State shall pass any ex post facto law." I will endeavour to state the general principles, which influence me on this point, succinctly and clearly, though I have not had an opportunity to reduce my opinion to writing.

If, then, a government, composed of Legislative, Executive and Judicial departments, were established, by a Constitution, which imposed no limits on the legislative power, the consequence would inevitably be, that whatever the legislative power chose to enact, would be lawfully enacted, and the judicial power could never interpose to pronounce it void. It is true, that some speculative jurists have held, that a legislative act against natural justice must, in itself, be void; but I cannot think that, under such a government, any Court of Justice would possess a power to declare it so. Sir William Blackstone, having put the strong case of an act of Parliament, which should authorize a man to try his own cause, explicitly adds, that even in that case, "there is no court that has power to defeat the intent of the Legislature, when couched in such evident and express words, as leave no doubt whether it was the intent of the Legislature, or no."

In order, therefore, to guard against so great an evil, it has been the policy of all the American states, which have, individually, framed their state constitutions since the revolution, and of the people of the United States, when they framed the Federal Constitution, to define with precision the objects of the legislative power, and to restrain its exercise within marked and settled boundaries. If any act of Congress, or of the Legislature of a state, violates those constitutional provisions, it is unquestionably void; though, I admit, that as the authority to declare it void is of a delicate and awful nature, the Court will never resort to that authority, but in a clear and urgent case. If, on the other hand, the Legislature of the Union, or the Legislature of any member of the Union, shall pass a law, within the general scope of their constitutional power, the Court cannot pronounce it to be void, merely because it is, in their judgment, contrary to the principles of natural justice. The ideas of natural justice are regulated by no fixed standard: the ablest and the purest men have differed upon the subject; and all that the Court could properly say, in such an event, would be, that the Legislature (possessed of an equal right of opinion) had passed an act which, in the opinion of the judges, was inconsistent with the abstract principles of natural justice. There are then but two lights, in which the subject can be viewed: 1st. If the Legislature pursue the authority delegated to them, their acts are valid. 2d. If they transgress the boundaries of that authority, their acts are invalid. In the former case, they exercise the discretion vested in them by the people, to whom alone they are responsible for the faithful discharge of their trust: but in the latter case, they violate a fundamental law, which must be our guide, whenever we are called upon as judges to determine the validity of a legislative act.

Still, however, in the present instance, the act or resolution of the Legislature of Connecticut, cannot be regarded as an ex post facto law; for, the true construction of the prohibition extends to criminal, not to civil, cases. . . .

FOR DISCUSSION

Compare the approaches to constitutional interpretation that Justices Chase and Iredell advanced in this case. What are the respective advantages and disadvantages of allowing judges to apply general principles when interpreting the Constitution? How do these different interpretive techniques affect the protections afforded to property rights?

Article I, Sec. 10:

No State shall . . . pass any . . . Law impairing the Obligation of Contracts. . . .

TRUSTEES OF DARTMOUTH COLLEGE V. WOODWARD

4 Wheat. 518, 4 L.Ed. 629 (1819)

Dartmouth College was chartered by the English Crown in 1769. The state legislature of New Hampshire in 1816 attempted by statute a complete reorganization of the government of the College, including changing the name to Dartmouth University. Woodward, secretary-treasurer of the college, had joined the new university movement and retained the seal, records, and other articles of the college. The trustees of the old college brought an action in the state court against Woodward for the recovery of this property. The state court decided against the college trustees.

Vote: 5–1

CHIEF JUSTICE MARSHALL delivered the opinion of the Court.

. . . The points for consideration are, 1. Is this contract protected by the Constitution of the United States? 2. Is it impaired by the acts under which the defendant holds? . . .

A corporation is an artificial being, invisible, intangible, and existing only in contemplation of law. Being the mere creature of law, it possesses only those properties which the charter of its creation confers upon it, either expressly or as incidental to its very existence. These are such as are supposed best calculated to effect the object for which it was created. Among the most important are immortality, and, if the expression may be allowed, individuality; properties, by which a perpetual succession of many persons are considered as the same, and may act as a single individual. They enable a corporation to manage its own affairs, and to hold property without the perplexing intricacies, the hazardous and endless necessity, of perpetual conveyances for the purpose of transmitting it from hand to hand. It is chiefly for the purpose of clothing bodies of men in succession with these qualities and capacities that corporations were invented and are in use. By these means, a perpetual succession of individuals are capable of acting for the promotion of the particular object, like one immortal being. . . .

. . . They [the donors] are represented by the corporation. The corporation is the assignee of their rights, stands in their place, and distributes their bounty, as they would themselves have distributed it had they been immortal. So, with respect to the students who are to derive learning from this source, the corporation is a trustee for them also. Their potential rights, which, taken distributively, are imperceptible, amount collectively to a most important interest. These are, in the aggregate, to be exercised, asserted, and protected by the corporation. . . .

This is plainly a contract to which the donors, the trustees, and the crown (to whose rights and obligations New Hampshire succeeds) were the original parties. It is a contract made on a valuable consideration. It is a contract for the security and disposition of property. It is a contract on the faith of which real and personal estate has been conveyed to the corporation. It is then a contract within the letter of the Constitution, and within its spirit also, unless the fact that the property is invested by the donors in trustees for the promotion of religion and education, for the benefit of persons who are perpetually changing, though the objects remain the same, shall create a particular exception, taking this case out of the prohibition contained in the Constitution.

It is more than possible that the preservation of rights of this description was not particularly in the view of the framers of the Constitution when the clause under consideration was introduced into that instrument. It is probable that interferences of more frequent recurrence, to which the temptation was stronger and of which the mischief was more extensive, constituted the great motive for imposing this restriction on the state legislatures. But although a particular and a rare case may not in itself be of sufficient magnitude to induce a rule, yet it must be governed by the rule, when established, unless some plain and strong reason for excluding it can be given. It is not enough to say that this particular case was not in the mind of the convention when the article was framed, nor of the American people when it was adopted. It is necessary to go farther, and to say that, had this particular case been suggested, the language would have been so varied as to exclude it, or it would have been made a special exception. The case, being within the words of the rule, must be within its operation likewise, unless there be something in the literal construction so obviously absurd, or mischievous, or repugnant to the general spirit of the instrument as to justify those who expound the Constitution in making it an exception. . . .

The opinion of the Court, after mature deliberation, is that this is a contract, the obligation of which cannot be impaired without violating the Constitution of the United States. This opinion appears to us to be equally supported by reason and by the former decisions of this court.

2. We next proceed to the inquiry whether its obligation has been impaired by those acts of the Legislature of New Hampshire to which the special verdict refers. . . .

On the effect of this law two opinions cannot be entertained. Between acting directly and acting through the agency of trustees and overseers no essential difference is perceived. The whole power of governing the college is transferred from trustees appointed according to the will of the founder, expressed in the charter, to the executive of New Hampshire. The management and application of the funds of this eleemosynary institution, which are placed by the donors in the hands of trustees named in the charter, and empowered to perpetuate themselves, are placed by this act under the control of the government of the state. The will of the state is substituted for the will of the donors in every essential operation of the college. This is not an immaterial change.

The founders of the college contracted, not merely for the perpetual application of the funds which they gave to the objects for which those funds were given, they contracted also to secure that application by the constitution of the corporation. They contracted for a system which should, as far as human foresight can provide, retain forever the government of the literary institution they had formed, in the hands of persons approved by themselves. This system is totally changed. The charter of 1769 exists no longer. It is reorganized, and reorganized in such a manner as to convert a literary institution, moulded according to the will of its founders and placed under the control of private literary men, into a machine entirely subservient to the will of government. This may be for the advantage of this college in particular, and may be for the advantage of literature in general; but it is not according to the will of the donors, and is subversive of that contract on the faith of which their property was given. . . .

Judgment reversed.

JUSTICE STORY concurred.

. . . When a private eleemosynary corporation is thus created by the charter of the crown, it is subject to no other control on the part of the crown, than what is expressly or implicitly reserved by the charter itself. Unless a power be reserved for this purpose, the crown cannot, in virtue of its prerogative, without the consent of the corporation, alter or amend the charter, or divest the corporation of any of its franchises, or add to them, or add to, or diminish, the number of the trustees, or remove any of the members, or change, or control the administration of the charity, or compel the corporation to receive a new charter. This is the uniform language of the authorities, and forms one of the most stubborn, and well settled doctrines of the common law. . . .

JUSTICE WASHINGTON also concurred with the same holding as Justice Story.

JUSTICE DUVALL dissented without an opinion.

FOR DISCUSSION

Does the logic of this case suggest that once a contract has been made a state can never modify it? Or that once a property right has been given it can never be altered? Can you think of situations when contracts and property rights should be allowed to be impaired or modified by a state?

RELATED CASES

Fletcher v. Peck: 6 Cr. 87 (1810)

In a 4–1 decision, the Court held that Georgia's sale of land in much of what is today Mississippi and Alabama constituted a contract that was protected by the Constitution from revocation, even after revelations that the sale resulted from bribery and corruption. The Court was especially concerned about the effect that a contrary decision might have on the rights of innocent third parties who had subsequently purchased the land.

New Jersey v. Wilson: 7 Cr. 164 (1812)

A state may contract away a portion of its taxing power, and when this privilege is attached by the state to land and the state does not withdraw the privilege at the time of sale, the purchaser succeeds to this privilege. Otherwise there would be impairment of the obligation of contract.

Sturges v. Crowninshield: 4 Wheat. 122 (1819)

State bankruptcy laws cannot be made to apply to contracts previously made since this would, in effect, be a law impairing the obligation of contract.

Ogden v. Saunders: **12 Wheat. 213 (1827)**

A state bankruptcy law may be applied to contracts made subsequent to the enactment of the statute without violation of the constitutional prohibition of impairment of the obligation of contract.

CHARLES RIVER BRIDGE V. WARREN BRIDGE

36 U.S. 420, 9 L. Ed. 773 (1837)

This classic decision highlights a difference in emphasis between the Court under Chief Justice John Marshall (who was appointed by John Adams and remained on the Court until 1835) and Roger Taney (who was appointed by Andrew Johnson and arrived at the Court in 1836). Marshall elevated property rights generally, and the Contract Clause in particular, to the status of **vested rights**, whereas Taney provided greater flexibility for governmental regulations consistent with the Jacksonian notion of **popular sovereignty**. Proprietors of the Charles River Bridge, which collected tolls, were suing the proprietors of a nearby bridge that threatened to destroy its toll business. Proprietors of the Charles River Bridge argued that the contract they had received from the state of Massachusetts to build a toll bridge implicitly included a monopoly that Harvard College had previously exercised through its operation of a ferry, and for which the Charles River Bridge had paid.

Vote: 5–2

CHIEF JUSTICE TANEY delivered the opinion of the Court.

. . . In 1828, the legislature of Massachusetts incorporated a company by the name of "The Proprietors of the Warren Bridge," for the purpose of erecting another bridge over Charles river. This bridge is only sixteen rods, at its commencement [a rod is about 5.5 yards], on the Charlestown side, from the commencement of the bridge of the plaintiffs; and they are about fifty rods apart at their termination on the Boston side. The travellers who pass over either bridge, proceed from Charlestown square, which receives the travel of many great public roads leading from the country; and the passengers and travellers who go to and from Boston, used to pass over the Charles River Bridge, from and through this square, before the erection of the Warren Bridge.

The Warren Bridge, by the terms of its charter, was to be surrendered to the state, as soon as the expenses of the proprietors in building and supporting it should be reimbursed; but this period was not, in any event, to exceed six years from the time the company commenced receiving toll.

When the original bill in this case was filed, the Warren Bridge had not been built; and the bill was filed after the passage of the law, in order to obtain an injunction to prevent its erection, and for general relief. The bill, among other things, charged as a ground for relief, that the act for the erection of the Warren Bridge impaired the obligation of the contract between the commonwealth and the proprietors of the Charles River Bridge; and was therefore repugnant to the constitution of the United States. . . .

A good deal of evidence has been offered to show the nature and extent of the ferry right granted to the college; and also to show the rights claimed by the proprietors of the bridge at different times, by virtue of their charter; and the opinions entertained by committees of the legislature, and others, upon that subject. But as these circumstances do not affect the judgment of this Court, it is unnecessary to recapitulate them.

The plaintiffs in error insist, mainly, upon two grounds: 1st. That by virtue of the grant of 1650, Harvard college was entitled, in perpetuity, to the right of keeping a ferry between Charlestown and Boston; that this right was exclusive; and that the legislature had not the power to establish another ferry on the same line of travel, because it would infringe the rights of the college; and that these rights, upon the erection of the bridge in the place of the ferry, under the charter of 1785, were transferred to, and became vested in "the proprietors of the Charles River Bridge;" and that under, and by virtue of this transfer of the ferry right, the rights of the bridge company were as exclusive in that line of travel, as the rights of the ferry. 2d. That independently of the ferry right, the acts of the legislature of Massachusetts of 1785, and 1792, by their true construction, necessarily implied that the legislature would not authorize another bridge, and especially a free one, by the side of this, and placed in the same line of travel, whereby the franchise granted to the "proprietors of the Charles River Bridge" should be rendered of no value; and the plaintiffs in error contend, that the grant of the ferry to the college, and of the charter to the proprietors of the bridge, are both contracts on the part of the state; and that the law authorizing the erection of the Warren Bridge in 1828, impairs the obligation of one or both of these contracts. . . .

The nature and extent of the ferry right granted to Harvard college, in 1650, must depend upon the laws of Massachusetts; and the character and extent of this right has been elaborately discussed at the bar. But in the view which the Court take of the case before them, it is not necessary to express any opinion on these questions. For assuming that the grant to Harvard college, and the charter to the Bridge company, were both contracts, and that the ferry right was as extensive and exclusive as the plaintiffs contend for; still they cannot enlarge the privileges granted to the bridge, unless it can be shown, that the rights of Harvard college in this ferry- have, by assignment, or in some other way, been transferred to the proprietors of the Charles River Bridge, and still remain in existence, vested in them, to the same extent with that in which they were held and enjoyed by the college before the bridge was built. . . .

Neither can the extent of the pre-existing ferry right, whatever it may have been, have any influence upon the construction of the written charter for the bridge. It does not, by any means, follow, that because the legislative power in Massachusetts, in 1650, may have granted to a justly favoured seminary of learning, the exclusive right of ferry between Boston and Charlestown, they would, in 1785, give the same extensive privilege to another corporation, who were about to erect a bridge in the same place. The fact that such a right was granted to the college, cannot by any sound rule of construction, be used to extend the privileges of the Bridge company beyond what the words of the charter naturally and legally import. Increased population, longer in legislation, the different character of the corporations which owned the ferry from that which owned the bridge, might well have induced a change in the policy of the state in this respect; and as the franchise of the ferry, and that of the bridge, are different in their nature, and were each established by separate grants, which have no words to connect the privileges of the one with the privileges of the other; there is no rule of legal interpretation, which would authorize the Court to associate these grants together, and to infer that any privilege was intended to be given to the Bridge company, merely because it had been conferred on the ferry. The charter to the bridge is a written instrument which must speak for itself, and be interpreted by its own terms.

This brings us to the act of the legislature of Massachusetts, of 1785, by which the plaintiffs were incorporated by the name of "The Proprietors of the Charles River Bridge;" and it is here, and in the law of 1792, prolonging their charter, that we must look for the extent and nature of the franchise conferred upon the plaintiffs.

Much has been said in the argument of the principles of construction by which this law is to be expounded, and what undertakings, on the part of the state, may be implied. The Court think there can be no serious difficulty on that head. It is the grant of certain franchises by the public to a private corporation, and in a matter where the public interest is concerned. The rule of construction in such cases is well settled, both in England, and by the decisions of our own tribunals. In 2 Barn. & Adol. 793, in the case of the *Proprietors of the Stourbridge Canal v. Wheely* and others, the court says, "the canal having been made under an act of parliament, the rights of the plaintiffs are derived entirely from that act. This, like many other cases, is a bargain between a company of adventurers and the public, the terms of which are expressed in the statute; and the rule of construction in all such cases, is now fully established to be this; that any ambiguity in the terms of the contract, must operate against the adventurers, and in favour of the public, and the plaintiffs can claim nothing that is not clearly given them by the act." And the doctrine thus laid down is abundantly sustained by the authorities referred to in this decision. . . .

Borrowing, as we have done, our system of jurisprudence from the English law; and having adopted, in every other case, civil and criminal, its rules for the construction of statutes; is there any thing in our local situation, or in the nature of our political institutions, which should lead us to depart from the principle where corporations are concerned? Are we to apply to acts of incorporation, a rule of construction differing from that of the English law, and, by implication, make the terms of a charter in one of the states, more unfavourable to the public, than upon an act of parliament, framed in the same words, would be sanctioned in an English court? Can any good reason be assigned for excepting this particular class of cases from the operation of the general principle; and for introducing a new and adverse rule of construction in favour of corporations, while we adopt and adhere to the rules of construction known to the English common law, in every other case, without exception? We think not; and it would present a singular spectacle, if, while the courts in England are restraining, within the strictest limits, the spirit of monopoly, and exclusive privileges in nature of monopolies, and confining corporations to the privileges plainly given to them in their charter; the courts of this country should be found enlarging these privileges by implication; and construing a statute more unfavourably to the public, and to the rights of the community, than would be done in a like case in an English court of justice.

[Taney proceeds to examine cases that support this principle.]

Adopting the rule of construction above stated as the settled one, we proceed to apply it to the charter of 1785, to the proprietors of the Charles River Bridge. This act of incorporation is in the usual form, and the privileges such as are commonly given to corporations of that kind. It confers on them the ordinary faculties of a corporation, for the purpose of building the bridge; and establishes certain rates of toll, which the company are authorized to take. This is the whole grant. There is no exclusive privilege given to them over the waters of Charles river, above or below their bridge. No right to erect another bridge themselves, nor to prevent other persons from erecting one. No engagement from the state, that another shall not be erected; and no undertaking not to sanction competition, nor to make improvements that may diminish the amount of its income. Upon all these subjects the charter is silent; and nothing is said in it about a line of travel, so much insisted on in the argument, in which they are to have exclusive privileges. No words are used, from which an intention to grant any of these rights can be inferred. If the plaintiff is entitled to them, it must be implied, simply, from the nature of the grant; and cannot be inferred from the words by which the grant is made.

The relative position of the Warren Bridge has already been described. It does not interrupt the passage over the Charles River Bridge, nor make the way to it or from it less convenient. None of the faculties or franchises granted to that corporation, have been revoked by the legislature; and its right to take the tolls granted by the charter remains unaltered. In short, all the franchises and rights of property enumerated in the charter, and there mentioned to have been granted to it, remain unimpaired. But its income is destroyed by the Warren Bridge; which, being free, draws off the passengers and property which would have gone over it, and renders their franchise of no value. This is the gist of the complaint. For it is not pretended, that the erection of the Warren Bridge would have done them any injury, or in any degree affected their right of property; if it had not diminished the amount of their tolls. In order then to entitle themselves to relief, it is necessary to show, that the legislature contracted not to do the act of which they complain, and that they impaired, or in other words, violated that contract by the erection of the Warren Bridge.

The inquiry then is, does the charter contain such a contract on the part of the state? Is there any such stipulation to be found in that instrument? It must be admitted on all hands, that there is none—no words that even relate to another bridge, or to the diminution of their tolls, or to the line of travel. If a contract on that subject can be gathered from the charter, it must be by implication; and cannot be found in the words used. Can such an agreement be implied? The rule of construction before stated is an answer to the question. In charters of this description, no rights are taken from the public, or given to the corporation, beyond those which the words of the charter, by their natural and proper construction, purport to convey. There are no words which import such a contract as the plaintiffs in error contend for, and none can be implied; and the same answer must be given to them that was given by this Court to the Providence Bank. The whole community are interested in this inquiry, and they have a right to require that the power of promoting their comfort and convenience, and of advancing the public prosperity, by providing safe, convenient, and cheap ways for the transportation of produce, and the purposes of travel, shall not be construed to have been surrendered or diminished by the state; unless it shall appear by plain words, that it was intended to be done.

Indeed, the practice and usage of almost every state in the Union, old enough to have commenced the work of internal improvement, is opposed to the doctrine contended for on the part of the plaintiffs in error. Turnpike roads have been made in succession, on the same line of travel; the later ones interfering materially with the profits of the first. These corporations have, in some instances, been utterly ruined by the introduction of newer and better modes of transportation, and travelling. In some cases, rail roads have rendered the turnpike roads on the same line of travel so entirely useless, that the franchise of the turnpike corporation is not worth preserving. Yet in none of these cases have the corporations supposed that their privileges were invaded, or any contract violated on the part of the state. . . .

And what would be the fruits of this doctrine of implied contracts on the part of the states, and of property in a line of travel by a corporation, if it should now be sanctioned by this Court? To what results would it lead us? If it is to be found in the charter to this bridge, the same process of reasoning must discover it, in the various acts which have been passed, within the last forty years, for turnpike companies. And what is to be the extent of the privileges of exclusion on the different sides of the road? The counsel who have so ably argued this case, have not attempted to define it by any certain boundaries. How far must the new improvement be distant from the old one? How near may you approach without invading its rights in the privileged line? If this Court should establish the principles now contended for, what is to become of the numerous rail roads established on the same line of travel with turnpike companies; and which have rendered the franchises of the turnpike corporations of no value? Let it once be understood that such charters carry with them these implied contracts, and give this unknown and undefined property in a line of travelling; and you will soon find the old turnpike corporations awakening from their sleep, and calling upon this Court to put down the improvements which have taken their place. The millions of property which have been invested in rail roads and canals, upon lines of travel which had been before occupied by turnpike corporations, will be put in jeopardy. We shall be thrown back to the improvements of the last century, and obliged to stand still, until the claims of the old turnpike corporations shall be satisfied; and they shall consent to permit these states to avail themselves of the lights of modern science, and to partake of the benefit of those improvements which are now adding to the wealth and prosperity, and the convenience and comfort, of every other part of the civilized world. Nor is this all. This Court will find itself compelled to fix, by some arbitrary rule, the width of this new kind of property in a line of travel; for if such a right of property exists, we have no lights to guide us in marking out its extent, unless, indeed, we resort to the old feudal grants, and to the exclusive rights of ferries, by prescription, between towns; and are prepared to decide that when a turnpike road from one town to another, had been made, no rail road or canal, between these two points, could afterwards be established. This Court are not prepared to sanction principles which must lead to such results.

JUSTICE STORY, dissenting. [Separate dissents by Justices McLean and Thompson have been omitted.]

Such is the substance of the charter of incorporation, which the Court is called upon to construe. But, before we can properly enter upon the consideration of this subject, a preliminary inquiry is presented as to the proper rules of interpretation applicable to the charter. Is the charter to receive a strict or a liberal construction?

Are any implications to be made, beyond the express terms? And if so, to what extent are they justifiable by the principles of law? No one doubts, that the charter is a contract, and a grant; and that it is to receive such a construction as belong to contracts and grants, as contradistinguished from mere laws. But the argument has been pressed here, with unwonted earnestness; and it seems to have had an irresistible influence elsewhere; that this charter is to be construed as a royal grant, and that such grants are always construed with a stern and parsimonious strictness. . . .

It is a well known rule in the construction of private grants, if the meaning of the words be doubtful, to construe them most strongly against the grantor. But it is said that an opposite rule prevails, in cases of grants by the king; for, where there is any doubt, the construction is made most favourably for the king, and against the grantee. The rule is not disputed. But it is a rule of very limited application. To what cases does it apply? To such cases only, where there is a real doubt, where the grant admits of two interpretations, one of which is more extensive, and the other more restricted; so that a choice is fairly open, and either may be adopted without any violation of the apparent objects of the grant. If the king's grant admits of two interpretations, one of which will make it utterly void and worthless, and the other will give it a reasonable effect, then the latter is to prevail: for the reason (says the common law), "that it will be more for the benefit of the subject, and the honour of the king, which is to be more regarded than his profit." Com. Dig. Grant, G. 12. And in every case, the rule is made to bend to the real justice and integrity of the case. No strained or extravagant construction is to be made in favour of the king. And, if the intention of the grant is obvious, a fair and liberal interpretation of its terms is enforced. . . .

The present, however, is not the case of a royal grant, but of a legislative grant, by a public statute. The rules of the common law in relation to royal grants have, therefore, in reality, nothing to do with the case. We are to give this act of incorporation a rational and fair construction, according to the general rules which govern in all cases of the exposition of public statutes. We are to ascertain the legislative intent; and that once ascertained, it is our duty to give it a full and liberal operation. . . .

I admit, that where the terms of a grant are to impose burdens upon the public, or to create a restraint injurious to the public interest, there is sound reason for interpreting the terms, if ambiguous, in favour of the public. But at the same time, I insist, that there is not the slightest reason for saying, even in such a case, that the grant is not to be construed favourably to the grantee, so as to secure him in the enjoyment of what is actually granted.

Upon the whole, my judgment is, that the act of the legislature of Massachusetts granting the charter of Warren Bridge, is an act impairing the obligation of the prior contract and grant to the proprietors of Charles River Bridge; and, by the constitution of the United States, it is, therefore, utterly void. I am for reversing the decree of the state court, (dismissing the bill) and for remanding the cause to the state court for further proceedings, as to law and justice shall appertain.

FOR DISCUSSION

Does this holding in this case overturn or modify *Trustees of Dartmouth College v. Woodward*? What can states now do that they could not do under Marshall's opinion in *Woodward*?

What were Taney's chief arguments for deciding that the Court would not read implicit limits into contracts issued by the states? If you were advising a client who was considering entering into such a contract with the state after this decision, how might the decision alter the advice you would give? How might the arguments in *Woodward* be useful in arguments to defend slavery or the slave trade?

RELATED CASES

***Piqua Branch of the State Bank v. Knoop:* 16 How. 369 (1853)**

When a state exempts certain property from taxation and substitutes an agreement for a specific type of levy or tax, the contract is binding, and the rights vested under it must be recognized.

***Stone v. Mississippi:* 101 U.S. 814 (1880)**

Writing for a unanimous Court (8–0), Chief Justice Waite upheld the right of a state to outlaw a lottery enterprise that it had previously approved. Waite emphasized that a state could not bargain away its power (known as the police power) over public health and morals.

***Manigault v. Springs:* 199 U.S. 473 (1905)**

"It is the settled law of this court that the interdiction of statutes impairing the obligation of contracts does not prevent the State from exercising such powers as are vested in it for the promotion of the common weal, or are necessary for the general good of the public, though contracts previously entered into between individuals may thereby be affected."

***Larson v. South Dakota:* 278 U.S. 429 (1929)**

An exclusive grant by a municipality, under legislative authority, of a ferry franchise to an individual does not prevent the legislature from subsequently granting the right to another to build a bridge near the ferry. A public grant is to be strictly construed.

NOTE

The net result of these cases is that legislative grants of charters to all kinds of private corporations are contracts, and grants of public franchises are to be strictly construed, that is, there is to be no "mind reading" of the legislature; only what is clearly granted has been granted. After *Charles River Bridge*, individuals seeking privileges from the government could continue to protect their interests, but they had to do so by specifically identifying such interests within the contracts that they signed.

HOME BUILDING AND LOAN ASSN. V. BLAISDELL

290 U.S. 398, 54 S.Ct. 231, 78 L.Ed. 413 (1934)

The Home Building and Loan Association held a mortgage on Blaisdell's land. By reason of default, the mortgage was foreclosed. The Supreme Court of Minnesota held the action of foreclosure invalid because of the 1933 Minnesota Mortgage Moratorium Law, which provided that when any person was unable to pay or retire a mortgage at the date of redemption, he could, by petitioning a court, be granted a moratorium from a foreclosure sale. The Home Building and Loan Association appealed to the Supreme Court of the United States on the basis that the statute was contrary to the Contract Clause of the Constitution as well as contrary to the Due Process and Equal Protection Clauses of the Fourteenth Amendment.

Vote: 5–4

CHIEF JUSTICE HUGHES delivered the opinion of the Court.

. . . In determining whether the provision for this temporary and conditional relief exceeds the power of the state by reason of the clause in the Federal Constitution prohibiting impairment of the obligations of contracts, we must consider the relation of emergency to constitutional power, the historical setting of the contract clause, the development of the jurisprudence of this Court in the construction of that clause, and the principles of construction which we may consider to be established.

Emergency does not create power. Emergency does not increase granted power or remove or diminish the restrictions imposed upon power granted or reserved. The Constitution was adopted in a period of grave emergency. Its grants of power to the Federal Government and its limitations of the power of the states were determined in the light of emergency and they are not altered by emergency. What power was thus granted and what limitations were thus imposed are questions which have always been, and always will be, the subject of close examination under our constitutional system.

While emergency does not create power, emergency may furnish the occasion for the exercise of power. "Although an emergency may not call into life a power which has never lived, nevertheless emergency may afford a reason for the exertion of a living power already enjoyed." *Wilson v. New,* 243 U. S. 332 (1917). The constitutional question presented in the light of an emergency is whether the power possessed embraces the particular exercise of it in response to particular conditions. Thus, the war power of the Federal Government is not created by the emergency of war, but it is a power given to meet that emergency. It is a power to wage war successfully, and thus it permits the harnessing of the entire energies of the people in a supreme effort to preserve the nation. But even the war power does not remove constitutional limitations safeguarding essential liberties. When the provisions of the Constitution, in grant or restriction, are specific, so particularized as not to admit of construction, no question is presented. Thus, emergency would not permit a state to have more than two Senators in the Congress, or permit the election of a President by a general popular vote without regard to the number of electors to which the states are respectively entitled, or permit the states to "coin money" or "to make anything but gold and silver coin a tender in payment of debts." But where constitutional grants and limitations of power are set forth in general clauses, which afford a broad outline, the process of construction is essential to fill in the details. That is true of the contract clause. . . .

Not only is the constitutional provision qualified by the measure of control which the state retains over remedial processes, but the state also continues to possess authority to safeguard the vital interests of its people. It does not matter that legislation appropriate to that end "has the result of modifying or abrogating contracts already in effect." . . . Not only are existing laws read into contracts in order to fix obligations as between the parties, but the reservation of essential attributes of sovereign power is also read into contracts as a postulate of the legal order. The policy of protecting contracts against impairment presupposes the maintenance of a government by virtue of which contractual relations are worthwhile—a government which retains adequate authority to secure the peace and good order of society. This principle of harmonizing the constitutional prohibition with the necessary residuum of state power has had progressive recognition in the decisions of this Court.

. . . The reservation of state power appropriate to such extraordinary conditions may be deemed to be as much a part of all contracts, as is the reservation of state power to protect the public interest in the other situations to which we have referred. And if state power exists to give temporary relief from the enforcement of contracts in the presence of disasters due to physical causes such as fire, flood or earthquake, that power cannot be said to be non-existent when the urgent public need demanding such relief is produced by other and economic causes. . . .

It is no answer to say that this public need was not apprehended a century ago, or to insist that what the provision of the Constitution meant to the vision of that day it must mean to the vision of our time. If by the statement that what the Constitution meant at the time of its adoption it means today, it is intended to say that the great clauses of the Constitution must be confined to the interpretation which the framers, with the conditions and outlook of their time, would have placed upon them, the statement carries its own refutation.

It was to guard against such a narrow conception that Chief Justice Marshall uttered the memorable warning: "We must never forget, that it is a constitution we are expounding."

Applying the criteria established by our decisions we conclude:

1. An emergency existed in Minnesota which furnished a proper occasion for the exercise of the reserved power of the state to protect the vital interests of the community.

2. The legislation was addressed to a legitimate end, that is, the legislation was not for the mere advantage of particular individuals but for the protection of a basic interest of society.

3. In view of the nature of the contracts in question—mortgages of unquestionable validity—the relief afforded and justified by the emergency, in order not to contravene the constitutional provision, could only be of a character appropriate to that emergency and could be granted only upon reasonable conditions.

4. The conditions upon which the period of redemption is extended do not appear to be unreasonable. . . .

As already noted, the integrity of the mortgage indebtedness is not impaired; interest continues to run; the validity of the sale and the right of a mortgagee-purchaser to title or to obtain a deficiency judgment, if the mortgagor fails to redeem within the extended period, are maintained; and the conditions of redemption, if redemption there be, stand as they were under the prior law. The mortgagor during the extended period is not ousted from possession, but he must pay the rental value of the premises as ascertained in judicial proceedings and this amount is applied to the carrying of the property and to interest upon the indebtedness. . . .

. . . If it be determined, as it must be, that the contract clause is not an absolute and utterly unqualified restriction of the state's protective power, this legislation is clearly so reasonable as to be within the legislative competency.

5. The legislation is temporary in operation. It is limited to the exigency which called it forth. While the postponement of the period of redemption from the foreclosure sale is to May 1, 1935, that period may be reduced by the order of the court under the statute, in case of a change in circumstances, and the operation of the statute itself could not validly outlast the emergency or be so extended as virtually to destroy the contracts.

We are of the opinion that the Minnesota statute as here applied does not violate the contract clause of the Federal Constitution. Whether the legislation is wise or unwise as a matter of policy is a question with which we are not concerned. What has been said on that point is also applicable to the contention presented under the due process clause. . . .

Nor do we think that the statute denies to the appellant the equal protection of the laws. The classification which the statute makes cannot be said to be an arbitrary one. . . .

Judgment affirmed.

JUSTICE SUTHERLAND dissented, joined by JUSTICES VAN DEVANTER, MCREYNOLDS, and BUTLER.

. . . The whole aim of construction, as applied to a provision of the Constitution, is to discover the meaning, to ascertain and give effect to the intent, of its framers and the people who adopted it. . . . The necessities which gave rise to the provision, the controversies which preceded, as well as the conflicts of opinion which were settled by its adoption, are matters to be considered to enable us to arrive at a correct result. . . . The history of the times, the state of things existing when the provision was framed and adopted, should be looked to in order to ascertain the mischief and the remedy. . . . As nearly as possible we should place ourselves in the condition of those who framed and adopted it. . . . And if the meaning be at all doubtful the doubt should be resolved, wherever reasonably possible to do so, in a way to forward the evident purpose with which the provision was adopted. . . .

An application of these principles to the question under review removes any doubt, if otherwise there would be any, that the contract impairment clause denies to the several states the power to mitigate hard consequences resulting to debtors from financial or economic exigencies by an impairment of the obligation of contracts of indebtedness. A candid consideration of the history and circumstances which led up to and accompanied the framing and adoption of this clause will demonstrate conclusively that it was framed and adopted with the specific and studied purpose of preventing legislation designed to relieve debtors *especially* in time of financial distress. Indeed, it is not probable that any other purpose was definitely in the minds of those who composed the framers' convention or the ratifying state conventions which followed, although the restriction has been given a wider application upon principles clearly stated by Chief Justice Marshall in the *Trustees of Dartmouth College v. Woodward*, 17 U.S. 518 (1819), case. . . .

The defense of the Minnesota law is made upon grounds which were discountenanced by the makers of the Constitution and have many times been rejected by this court. That defense should not now succeed, because it constitutes an effort to overthrow the constitutional provision by an appeal to facts and circumstances identical with those which brought it into existence. With due regard for the processes of logical thinking, it legitimately cannot be urged that conditions which produced the rule may now be invoked to destroy it. . . .

The Minnesota statute either impairs the obligation of contracts or it does not. If it does not, the occasion to which it relates becomes immaterial, since, then the passage of the statute is the exercise of a normal, unrestricted, state power and requires no special occasion to render it effective. If it does, the emergency no more furnishes a proper occasion for its exercise than if the emergency were nonexistent.

We come back, then, directly, to the question of impairment. As to that, the conclusion reached by the court here seems to be that the relief afforded by the statute does not contravene the constitutional provision because it is of a character appropriate to the emergency and allowed upon what are said to be reasonable conditions. . . .

A statute which materially delays enforcement of the mortgagee's contractual right of ownership and possession does not modify the remedy merely; it destroys, for the period of delay, *all* remedy so far as the enforcement of that right is concerned. The phrase, "obligation of a contract," in the constitutional sense imports a legal duty to perform the specified obligation of that contract, not to substitute and perform, against the will of one of the parties, a different, albeit equally valuable, obligation. And a state, under the contract impairment clause, has no more power to accomplish such a substitution than has one of the parties to the contract against the will of the other. It cannot do so either by acting directly upon the contract, or by bringing about the result under the guise of a statute in form acting only upon the remedy. If it could, the efficacy of the constitutional restriction would, in large measure, be made to disappear. . . .

NOTE

Although it was decided three years prior to the Supreme Court's so-called "switch-in-time-that-saves-nine," *Blaisdell* represented a similar 5–4 split to the post-1936 Court and recognized a relatively expansive right for states to provide for economic disasters. In *Blaisdell* the Court observed that every contract is deemed to have been made subject to a proper exercise of the police power of the state. This power is paramount to any rights that might be claimed by individuals under contracts between themselves. This is sometimes referred to as the "doctrine of paramount power." In 2007, both the president and Congress took a number of steps designed to allow individuals who had taken out subprime loans with balloon payments to renegotiate these loans after numerous foreclosures resulted in falling real estate prices and seemed to be leading to a general economic recession. In 2008, Congress subsequently authorized massive federal bailouts of banks, many of which had foreclosed on homes that no longer maintained their original value.

RELATED CASES

***Worthen Co. v. Kavanaugh:* 295 U.S. 56 (1935)**

Statutes that so diminish the remedies of holders of bonds of a municipal improvement district with regard to mortgage security for the bonds that the holders are left for some time with no power to enforce the obligation to pay either installments of principal or coupons on the bonds violate the contract clause of the Constitution.

***East New York Savings Bank v. Hahn:* 326 U.S. 230 (1945)**

In sustaining New York's mortgage moratorium, the Court noted that **state police power** is a "paramount power" and is so important to the very existence of the state that the power cannot be contracted away. The state police power is an implied condition of every contract and is superior to any rights of individuals under a contract.

UNITED STATES TRUST COMPANY OF NEW YORK V. NEW JERSEY

431 U.S. 1, 97 S.Ct. 1505, 52 L.Ed. 2d 92 (1977)

This case involved a challenge to attempts on the part of the states of New York and New Jersey to repeal a covenant through which they had limited subsidies by the joint Port Authority of the two states for rail passenger transportation from revenues and reserves. Lower courts had upheld the repeal, which remains of contemporary interest during a time of continuing concern about energy shortages, global warming, and American dependence upon foreign energy sources.

Vote: 4–3, two justices not participating.

JUSTICE BLACKMUN delivered the opinion of the Court.

I. Background

New Jersey had previously prevented outright repeal of the 1962 covenant, but its attitude changed with the election of a new Governor in 1973. In early 1974, when bills were pending in the two States' legislatures to repeal the covenant retroactively, a national energy crisis was developing. On November 27, 1973, Congress had enacted the Emergency Petroleum Allocation Act. In that Act Congress found that the hardships caused by the oil shortage "jeopardize the normal flow of commerce and constitute a national energy crisis which is a threat to the public health, safety, and welfare." This time, proposals for retroactive repeal of the 1962 covenant were passed by the legislature and signed by the Governor of each State.

On April 10, 1975, the Port Authority announced an increase in its basic bridge and tunnel tolls designed to raise an estimated $40 million annually. This went into effect May 5 and was, it was said, "[t]o increase [the Port Authority's] ability to finance vital mass transit improvements."

II

At the time the Constitution was adopted, and for nearly a century thereafter, the Contract Clause was one of the few express limitations on state power. The many decisions of this Court involving the Contract Clause are evidence of its important place in our constitutional jurisprudence. Over the last century, however, the Fourteenth Amendment has assumed a far larger place in constitutional adjudication concerning the States. We feel that the present role of the Contract Clause is largely illuminated by two of this Court's decisions. In each, legislation was sustained despite a claim that it had impaired the obligations of contracts.

Home Building & Loan Assn. v. Blaisdell, 290 U.S. 398 (1934), is regarded as the leading case in the modern era of Contract Clause interpretation. At issue was the Minnesota Mortgage Moratorium Law, enacted in 1933, during the depth of the Depression and when that State was under severe economic stress, and appeared to have no effective alternative. The statute was a temporary measure that allowed judicial extension of the time for redemption; a mortgagor who remained in possession during the extension period was required to pay a reasonable income or rental value to the mortgagee. A closely divided Court, in an opinion by Mr. Chief Justice Hughes, observed that "emergency may furnish the occasion for the exercise of power" and that the "constitutional question presented in the light of an emergency is whether the power possessed embraces the particular exercise of it in response to particular conditions." It noted that the debates in the Constitutional Convention were of little aid in the construction of the Contract Clause, but that the general purpose of the Clause was clear: to encourage trade and credit by promoting confidence in the stability of contractual obligations. Nevertheless, a State "continues to possess authority to safeguard the vital interests of its people. . . . This principle of harmonizing the constitutional prohibition with the necessary residuum of state power has had progressive recognition in the decisions of this Court." The great clauses of the Constitution are to be considered in the light of our whole experience, and not merely as they would be interpreted by its Framers in the conditions and with the outlook of their time.

This Court's most recent Contract Clause decision is *El Paso v. Simmons*, 379 U.S. 497 (1965). That case concerned a 1941 Texas statute that limited to a 5-year period the reinstatement rights of an interest-defaulting purchaser of land from the State. For many years prior to the enactment of that statute, such a defaulting purchaser, under Texas law, could have reinstated his claim to the land upon written request and payment of delinquent interest, unless rights of third parties had intervened. This Court held that "it is not every modification of a contractual promise that impairs the obligation of contract under federal law." It observed that the State "has the 'sovereign right . . . to protect the . . . general welfare of the people' " and " 'we must respect the "wide discretion on the part of the legislature in determining what is and what is not necessary.' " The Court recognized that "the power of a State to modify or affect the obligation of contract is not without limit," but held that "the objects of the Texas statute make abundantly clear that it impairs no protected right under the Contract Clause."

Both of these cases eschewed a rigid application of the Contract Clause to invalidate state legislation. Yet neither indicated that the Contract Clause was without meaning in modern constitutional jurisprudence, or that its limitation on state power was illusory. Whether or not the protection of contract rights comports with current views of wise public policy, the Contract Clause remains a part of our written Constitution. We therefore must attempt to apply that constitutional provision to the instant case with due respect for its purpose and the prior decisions of this Court.

III

We first examine appellant's general claim that repeal of the 1962 covenant impaired the obligation of the States' contract with the bondholders. It long has been established that the Contract Clause limits the power of the States to modify their own contracts as well as to regulate those between private parties. *Fletcher v. Peck*, 6 Cranch 87 (1810); *Dartmouth College v. Woodward*, 4 Wheat. 518 (1819). Yet the Contract Clause does not prohibit the States from repealing or amending statutes generally, or from enacting legislation with retroactive effects. Thus, as a preliminary matter, appellant's claim requires a determination that the repeal has the effect of impairing a contractual obligation.

In this case the obligation was itself created by a statute, the 1962 legislative covenant. It is unnecessary, however, to dwell on the criteria for determining whether state legislation gives rise to a contractual obligation. The trial court found, and appellees do not deny, that the 1962 covenant constituted a contract between the two States and the holders of the Consolidated Bonds issued between 1962 and the 1973 prospective repeal. The intent to make a contract is clear from the statutory language. . . .

Having thus established that the repeal impaired a contractual obligation of the States, we turn to the question whether that impairment violated the Contract Clause.

IV

Although the Contract Clause appears literally to proscribe "any" impairment, this Court observed in *Blaisdell* that "the prohibition is not an absolute one and is not to be read with literal exactness like a mathematical formula." Thus, a finding that there has been a technical impairment is merely a preliminary step in resolving the more difficult question whether that impairment is permitted under the Constitution. In the instant case, as in *Blaisdell*, we must attempt to reconcile the strictures of the Contract Clause with the "essential attributes of sovereign power," necessarily reserved by the States to safeguard the welfare of their citizens.

The trial court concluded that repeal of the 1962 covenant was a valid exercise of New Jersey's police power because repeal served important public interests in mass transportation, energy conservation, and environmental protection. Yet the Contract Clause limits otherwise legitimate exercises of state legislative authority, and the existence of an important public interest is not always sufficient to overcome that limitation. "Undoubtedly, whatever is reserved of state power must be consistent with the fair intent of the constitutional limitation of that power." *Blaisdell.* Moreover, the scope of the State's reserved power depends on the nature of the contractual relationship with which the challenged law conflicts.

The States must possess broad power to adopt general regulatory measures without being concerned that private contracts will be impaired, or even destroyed, as a result. Otherwise, one would be able to obtain immunity from state regulation by making private contractual arrangements. This principle is summarized in Mr. Justice Holmes' well-known dictum: "One whose rights, such as they are, are subject to state restriction, cannot remove them from the power of the State by making a contract about them." *Hudson Water Co. v. McCarter*, 209 U.S. 349 (1908).

Yet private contracts are not subject to unlimited modification under the police power. The Court in *Blaisdell* recognized that laws intended to regulate existing contractual relationships must serve a legitimate public purpose. A State could not "adopt as its policy the repudiation of debts or the destruction of contracts or the denial of means to enforce them." Legislation adjusting the rights and responsibilities of contracting parties must be upon reasonable conditions and of a character appropriate to the public purpose justifying its adoption. As is customary in reviewing economic and social regulation, however, courts properly defer to legislative judgment as to the necessity and reasonableness of a particular measure.

When a State impairs the obligation of its own contract, the reserved-powers doctrine has a different basis. The initial inquiry concerns the ability of the State to enter into an agreement that limits its power to act in the future. As early as *Fletcher v. Peck*, the Court considered the argument that "one legislature cannot abridge the powers of a succeeding legislature." It is often stated that "the legislature cannot bargain away the police power of a State." *Stone v. Mississippi,* 101 U.S. 814 (1880). This doctrine requires a determination of the State's power to create irrevocable contract rights in the first place, rather than an inquiry into the purpose or reasonableness of the subsequent impairment. In short, the Contract Clause does not require a State to adhere to a contract that surrenders an essential attribute of its sovereignty.

In deciding whether a State's contract was invalid *ab initio* [from the beginning] under the reserved-powers doctrine, earlier decisions relied on distinctions among the various powers of the State. Thus, the police power and the power of eminent domain were among those that could not be "contracted away," but the State could bind itself in the future exercise of the taxing and spending powers. Such formalistic distinctions perhaps cannot be dispositive, but they contain an important element of truth. Whatever the propriety of a State's binding itself to a future course of conduct in other contexts, the power to enter into effective financial contracts cannot be questioned. Any financial obligation could be regarded in theory as a relinquishment of the State's spending power, since money spent to repay debts is not available for other purposes. Similarly, the taxing power may have to be exercised if debts are to be repaid. Notwithstanding these effects, the Court has regularly held that the States are bound by their debt contracts.

The instant case involves a financial obligation and thus as a threshold matter may not be said automatically to fall within the reserved powers that cannot be contracted away. Not every security provision, however, is necessarily financial. For example, a revenue bond might be secured by the State's promise to continue operating the facility in question; yet such a promise surely could not validly be construed to bind the State never to close the facility for health or safety reasons. The security provision at issue here, however, is different: The States promised that revenues and reserves securing the bonds would not be depleted by the Port Authority's operation of deficit-producing passenger railroads beyond the level of "permitted deficits." Such a promise is purely financial and thus not necessarily a compromise of the State's reserved powers.

V

Mass transportation, energy conservation, and environmental protection are goals that are important and of legitimate public concern. Appellees contend that these goals are so important that any harm to bondholders from repeal of the 1962 covenant is greatly outweighed by the public benefit. We do not accept this invitation to engage in a utilitarian comparison of public benefit and private loss. Contrary to Mr. Justice Black's fear, expressed in sole dissent in *El Paso v. Simmons*, the Court has not "balanced away" the limitation on state action imposed by the Contract Clause. Thus a State cannot refuse to meet its legitimate financial obligations simply because it would prefer to spend the money to promote the public good rather than the private welfare of its creditors. We can only sustain the repeal of the 1962 covenant if that impairment was both reasonable and necessary to serve the admittedly important purposes claimed by the State.

The more specific justification offered for the repeal of the 1962 covenant was the States' plan for encouraging users of private automobiles to shift to public transportation. The States intended to discourage private automobile use by raising bridge and tunnel tolls and to use the extra revenue from those tolls to subsidize improved commuter railroad service. Appellees contend that repeal of the 1962 covenant was necessary to implement this plan because the new mass transit facilities could not possibly be self-supporting and the covenant's "permitted deficits" level had already been exceeded. We reject this justification because the repeal was neither necessary to achievement of the plan nor reasonable in light of the circumstances.

The determination of necessity can be considered on two levels. First, it cannot be said that total repeal of the covenant was essential; a less drastic modification would have permitted the contemplated plan without entirely removing the covenant's limitations on the use of Port Authority revenues and reserves to subsidize commuter railroads. Second, without modifying the covenant at all, the States could have adopted alternative means of achieving their twin goals of discouraging automobile use and improving mass transit. Appellees contend, however, that choosing among these alternatives is a matter for legislative discretion. But a State is not completely free to consider impairing the obligations of its own contracts on a par with other policy alternatives. Similarly, a State is not free to impose a drastic impairment when an evident and more moderate course would serve its purposes equally well. In *El Paso v. Simmons*, the imposition of a five-year statute of limitations on what was previously a perpetual right of redemption was regarded by this Court as "quite clearly necessary" to achieve the State's vital interest in the orderly administration of its school lands program. In the instant case the State has failed to demonstrate that repeal of the 1962 covenant was similarly necessary.

We also cannot conclude that repeal of the covenant was reasonable in light of the surrounding circumstances. In this regard a comparison with *El Paso v. Simmons* again is instructive. There a 19th century statute had effects that were unforeseen and unintended by the legislature when originally adopted. As a result speculators were placed in a position to obtain windfall benefits. The Court held that adoption of a statute of limitation was a reasonable means to "restrict a party to those gains reasonably to be expected from the contract" when it was adopted.

By contrast, in the instant case the need for mass transportation in the New York metropolitan area was not a new development, and the likelihood that publicly owned commuter railroads would produce substantial deficits was well known. As early as 1922, over a half century ago, there were pressures to involve the Port Authority in mass transit. It was with full knowledge of these concerns that the 1962 covenant was adopted. Indeed, the covenant was specifically intended to protect the pledged revenues and reserves against the possibility that such concerns would lead the Port Authority into greater involvement in deficit mass transit.

During the 12-year period between adoption of the covenant and its repeal, public perception of the importance of mass transit undoubtedly grew because of increased general concern with environmental protection and energy conservation. But these concerns were not unknown in 1962, and the subsequent changes were of degree and not of kind. We cannot say that these changes caused the covenant to have a substantially different impact in 1974 than when it was adopted in 1962. And we cannot conclude that the repeal was reasonable in the light of changed circumstances.

We therefore hold that the Contract Clause of the United States Constitution prohibits the retroactive repeal of the 1962 covenant. The judgment of the Supreme Court of New Jersey is reversed.

JUSTICE BRENNAN, with whom JUSTICES WHITE and MARSHALL join, dissenting.

Decisions of this Court for at least a century have construed the Contract Clause largely to be powerless in binding a State to contracts limiting the authority of successor legislatures to enact laws in furtherance of the health, safety, and similar collective interests of the polity. In short, those decisions established the principle that lawful exercises of a State's police powers stand paramount to private rights held under contract. Today's decision, in invalidating the New Jersey Legislature's 1974 repeal of its predecessor's 1962 covenant, rejects this previous understanding and remolds the Contract Clause into a potent instrument for overseeing important policy determinations of the state legislature. At the same time, by creating a constitutional safe haven for property rights embodied in a contract, the decision substantially distorts modern constitutional jurisprudence governing regulation of private economic interests. I might understand, though I could not accept, this revival of the Contract Clause were it in accordance with some coherent and constructive view of public policy. But elevation of the Clause to the status of regulator of the municipal bond market at the heavy price of frustration of sound legislative policymaking is as demonstrably unwise as it is unnecessary. The justification for today's decision, therefore, remains a mystery to me, and I respectfully dissent. . . .

FOR DISCUSSION

This decision is often analyzed with respect to liberal and conservative views. Historically, what are the reasons that American conservatives are more likely to hail the majority opinion than American liberals?

ALLIED V. SPANNAUS

438 U.S. 234, 98 S. Ct. 2716, 57 L. Ed. 2d 727 (1978)

This case, which considered whether a Minnesota law designed to provide pension benefits for individuals whose firms left the state violated the Contract Clause, provides a good transition to the rest of the chapter because it shows how concerns about the Contract Clause are sometimes entwined with concerns over whether legislation offends the Due Process Clause or other clauses that protect property rights.

Vote: 5–3

JUSTICE STEWART delivered the opinion of the Court.

The issue in this case is whether the application of Minnesota's Private Pension Benefits Protection Act to the appellant violates the Contract Clause of the United States Constitution.

I

In 1974 appellant Allied Structural Steel Co. (company), a corporation with its principal place of business in Illinois, maintained an office in Minnesota with 30 employees. Under the company's general pension plan, adopted in 1963 and qualified as a single-employer plan under § 401 of the Internal Revenue Code, salaried employees were covered as follows: At age 65 an employee was entitled to retire and receive a monthly pension generally computed by multiplying 1% of his average monthly earnings by the total number of his years of employment with the company. Thus, an employee aged 65 or more could retire without satisfying any particular length-of-service requirement, but the size of his pension would reflect the length of his service with the company. . . .

The company was the sole contributor to the pension trust fund, and each year it made contributions to the fund based on actuarial predictions of eventual payout needs. Although those contributions once made were irrevocable, in the sense that they remained part of the pension trust fund, the plan neither required the company to make specific contributions nor imposed any sanction on it for failing to contribute adequately to the fund.

The company not only retained a virtually unrestricted right to amend the plan in whole or in part, but was also free to terminate the plan and distribute the trust assets at any time and for any reason. In the event of a termination, the assets of the fund were to go, first, to meet the plan's obligation to those employees already retired and receiving pensions; second, to those eligible for retirement; and finally, if any balance remained, to the other employees covered under the plan whose pension rights had not yet vested. Employees within each of these categories were assured payment only to the extent of the pension assets.

On April 9, 1974, Minnesota enacted the law here in question, the Private Pension Benefits Protection Act. Under the Act, a private employer of 100 employees or more—at least one of whom was a Minnesota resident—who provided pension benefits under a plan meeting the qualifications of § 401 of the Internal Revenue Code, was subject to a "pension funding charge" if he either terminated the plan or closed a Minnesota office. . . .

During the summer of 1974 the company began closing its Minnesota office. On July 31, it discharged 11 of its 30 Minnesota employees, and the following month it notified the Minnesota Commissioner of Labor and Industry, as required by the Act, that it was terminating an office in the State. At least nine of the discharged employees did not have any vested pension rights under the company's plan, but had worked for the company for 10 years or more and thus qualified as pension obligees of the company under the law that Minnesota had enacted a few months earlier. On August 18, the State notified the company that it owed a pension funding charge of approximately $185,000 under the provisions of the Private Pension Benefits Protection Act.

The company brought suit in a Federal District Court asking for injunctive and declaratory relief. It claimed that the Act unconstitutionally impaired its contractual obligations to its employees under its pension agreement. The three-judge court upheld the constitutional validity of the Act as applied to the company, and an appeal was brought to this Court. We noted probable jurisdiction.

II

A

There can be no question of the impact of the Minnesota Private Pension Benefits Protection Act upon the company's contractual relationships with its employees. The Act substantially altered those relationships by superimposing pension obligations upon the company conspicuously beyond those that it had voluntarily agreed to undertake. But it does not inexorably follow that the Act, as applied to the company, violates the Contract Clause of the Constitution.

The language of the Contract Clause appears unambiguously absolute: "No State shall . . . pass any . . . Law impairing the Obligation of Contracts." The Clause is not, however, the Draconian provision that its words might seem to imply. As the Court has recognized, "literalism in the construction of the contract clause . . . would make it destructive of the public interest by depriving the State of its prerogative of self-protection." *W. B. Worthen Co. v. Thomas*, 292 U.S. 426 (1934).

Although it was perhaps the strongest single constitutional check on state legislation during our early years as a Nation, the Contract Clause receded into comparative desuetude with the adoption of the Fourteenth Amendment, and particularly with the development of the large body of jurisprudence under the Due Process Clause of that Amendment in modern constitutional history. Nonetheless, the Contract Clause remains part of the Constitution. It is not a dead letter. And its basic contours are brought into focus by several of this Court's 20th-century decisions.

First of all, it is to be accepted as a commonplace that the Contract Clause does not operate to obliterate the police power of the States. "It is the settled law of this court that the interdiction of statutes impairing the obligation of contracts does not prevent the State from exercising such powers as are vested in it for the promotion of the common weal, or are necessary for the general good of the public, though contracts previously entered into between individuals may thereby be affected. This power, which in its various ramifications is known as the police power, is an exercise of the sovereign right of the Government to protect the lives, health, morals, comfort and general welfare of the people, and is paramount to any rights under contracts between individuals." *Manigault v. Springs*, 199 U.S. 473 (1905). As Mr. Justice Holmes succinctly put the matter in his opinion for the Court in *Hudson Water Co. v. McCarter*, 209 U.S. 349 (1908): "One whose rights, such as they are, are subject to state restriction, cannot remove them from the power of the State by making a contract about them. The contract will carry with it the infirmity of the subject matter."

B

If the Contract Clause is to retain any meaning at all, however, it must be understood to impose *some* limits upon the power of a State to abridge existing contractual relationships, even in the exercise of its otherwise legitimate police power. The existence and nature of those limits were clearly indicated in a series of cases in this Court arising from the efforts of the States to deal with the unprecedented emergencies brought on by the severe economic depression of the early 1930's.

[Justice Stewart reviews key cases.]

The most recent Contract Clause case in this Court was *United States Trust Co. v. New Jersey*, 431 U.S. 1 (1977). In that case the Court again recognized that although the absolute language of the Clause must leave room for "the 'essential attributes of sovereign power,' . . . necessarily reserved by the States to safeguard the welfare of their citizens," that power has limits when its exercise effects substantial modifications of private contracts. Despite the customary deference courts give to state laws directed to social and economic problems, "[legislation] adjusting the rights and responsibilities of contracting parties must be upon reasonable conditions and of a character appropriate to the public purpose justifying its adoption." Evaluating with particular scrutiny a modification of a contract to which the State itself was a party, the Court in that case held that legislative alteration of the rights and remedies of Port Authority bondholders violated the Contract Clause because the legislation was neither necessary nor reasonable.

III

In applying these principles to the present case, the first inquiry must be whether the state law has, in fact, operated as a substantial impairment of a contractual relationship. The severity of the impairment measures the height of the hurdle the state legislation must clear. Minimal alteration of contractual obligations may end the inquiry at its first stage. Severe impairment, on the other hand, will push the inquiry to a careful examination of the nature and purpose of the state legislation.

The severity of an impairment of contractual obligations can be measured by the factors that reflect the high value the Framers placed on the protection of private contracts. Contracts enable individuals to order their personal and business affairs according to their particular needs and interests. Once arranged, those rights and obligations are binding under the law, and the parties are entitled to rely on them.

Here, the company's contracts of employment with its employees included as a fringe benefit or additional form of compensation, the pension plan. The company's maximum obligation was to set aside each year an amount based on the plan's requirements for vesting. The plan satisfied the current federal income tax code and was subject to no other legislative requirements. And, of course, the company was free to amend or terminate the pension plan at any time. The company thus had no reason to anticipate that its employees' pension rights could become vested except in accordance with the terms of the plan. It relied heavily, and reasonably, on this legitimate contractual expectation in calculating its annual contributions to the pension fund.

The effect of Minnesota's Private Pension Benefits Protection Act on this contractual obligation was severe. The company was required in 1974 to have made its contributions throughout the pre-1974 life of its plan as if employees' pension rights had vested after 10 years, instead of vesting in accord with the terms of the plan. Thus a basic term of the pension contract—one on which the company had relied for 10 years—was substantially modified. The result was that, although the company's past contributions were adequate when made, they were not adequate when computed under the 10-year statutory vesting requirement. The Act thus forced a current recalculation of the past 10 years' contributions based on the new, unanticipated 10-year vesting requirement.

Not only did the state law thus retroactively modify the compensation that the company had agreed to pay its employees from 1963 to 1974, but also it did so by changing the company's obligations in an area where the element of reliance was vital—the funding of a pension plan. As the Court has recently recognized: "These [pension] plans, like other forms of insurance, depend on the accumulation of large sums to cover contingencies. The amounts set aside are determined by a painstaking assessment of the insurer's likely liability. Risks that the insurer foresees will be included in the calculation of liability, and the rates or contributions charged will reflect that calculation. The occurrence of major unforeseen contingencies, however, jeopardizes the insurer's solvency and, ultimately, the insureds' benefits. Drastic changes in the legal rules governing pension and insurance funds, like other unforeseen events, can have this effect." *Los Angeles Dept. of Water & Power v. Manhart*, 435 U.S. 702 (1978).

Moreover, the retroactive state-imposed vesting requirement was applied only to those employers who terminated their pension plans or who, like the company, closed their Minnesota offices. The company was thus forced to make all the retroactive changes in its contractual obligations at one time. By simply proceeding to close its office in Minnesota, a move that had been planned before the passage of the Act, the company was assessed an immediate pension funding charge of approximately $185,000.

Thus, the statute in question here nullifies express terms of the company's contractual obligations and imposes a completely unexpected liability in potentially disabling amounts. There is not even any provision for gradual applicability or grace periods. Yet there is no showing in the record before us that this severe disruption of contractual expectations was necessary to meet an important general social problem. The presumption favoring "legislative judgment as to the necessity and reasonableness of a particular measure," *United States Trust Co.*, simply cannot stand in this case.

The only indication of legislative intent in the record before us is to be found in a statement in the District Court's opinion: "It seems clear that the problem of plant closure and pension plan termination was brought to the attention of the Minnesota legislature when the Minneapolis-Moline Division of White Motor Corporation closed one of its Minnesota plants and attempted to terminate its pension plan."

But whether or not the legislation was aimed largely at a single employer, it clearly has an extremely narrow focus. It applies only to private employers who have at least 100 employees, at least one of whom works in Minnesota, and who have established voluntary private pension plans, qualified under § 401 of the Internal Revenue Code. And it applies only when such an employer closes his Minnesota office or terminates his pension plan. Thus, this law can hardly be characterized, like the law at issue in the [*Home Building & Loan Assn. v.*] *Blaisdell*[, 290 U.S. 398 (1934)] case, as one enacted to protect a broad societal interest rather than a narrow class.

Moreover, in at least one other important respect the Act does not resemble the mortgage moratorium legislation whose constitutionality was upheld in the *Blaisdell* case. This legislation, imposing a sudden, totally unanticipated, and substantial retroactive obligation upon the company to its employees, was not enacted to deal with a situation remotely approaching the broad and desperate emergency economic conditions of the early 1930's—conditions of which the Court in *Blaisdell* took judicial notice.

Entering a field it had never before sought to regulate, the Minnesota Legislature grossly distorted the company's existing contractual relationships with its employees by superimposing retroactive obligations upon the company substantially beyond the terms of its employment contracts. And that burden was imposed upon the company only because it closed its office in the State.

This Minnesota law simply does not possess the attributes of those state laws that in the past have survived challenge under the Contract Clause of the Constitution. The law was not even purportedly enacted to deal with a broad, generalized economic or social problem. It did not operate in an area already subject to state regulation at the time the company's contractual obligations were originally undertaken, but invaded an area never before subject to regulation by the State. It did not effect simply a temporary alteration of the contractual relationships of those within its coverage, but worked a severe, permanent, and immediate change in those relationships—irrevocably and retroactively. And its narrow aim was leveled, not at every Minnesota employer, not even at every Minnesota employer who left the State, but only at those who had in the past been sufficiently enlightened as voluntarily to agree to establish pension plans for their employees.

"Not Blaisdell's case, but Worthen's (*W. B. Worthen Co. v. Thomas*) supplies the applicable rule" here. It is not necessary to hold that the Minnesota law impaired the obligation of the company's employment contracts "without moderation or reason or in a spirit of oppression." But we do hold that if the Contract Clause means anything at all, it means that Minnesota could not constitutionally do what it tried to do to the company in this case.

The judgment of the District Court is reversed.

It is so ordered.

JUSTICE BRENNAN, with whom JUSTICES WHITE and MARSHALL join, dissenting.

In cases involving state legislation affecting private contracts, this Court's decisions over the past half century, consistently with both the constitutional text and its original understanding, have interpreted the Contract Clause as prohibiting state legislative Acts which, "[with] studied indifference to the interests of the [contracting party] or to his appropriate protection," effectively diminished or nullified the obligation due him under the terms of a contract. *W. B. Worthen Co. v. Kavanaugh*, 295 U.S. 56 (1935). But the Contract Clause has not, during this period, been applied to state legislation that, while creating new duties, in nowise diminished the efficacy of any contractual obligation owed the constitutional claimant. The constitutionality of such legislation has, rather, been determined solely by reference to other provisions of the Constitution, *e. g.*, the Due Process Clause, insofar as they operate to protect existing economic values.

Today's decision greatly expands the reach of the Clause. The Minnesota Private Pension Benefits Protection Act (Act) does not abrogate or dilute any obligation due a party to a private contract; rather, like all positive social legislation, the Act imposes new, additional obligations on a particular class of persons. In my view, any constitutional infirmity in the law must therefore derive, not from the Contract Clause, but from the Due Process Clause of the Fourteenth Amendment. I perceive nothing in the Act that works a denial of due process and therefore I dissent.

I

I begin with an assessment of the operation and effect of the Minnesota statute. Although the Court disclaims knowledge of the purposes of the law, both the terms of the Act and the opinion of the State Supreme Court disclose that it was designed to remedy a serious social problem arising from the operation of private pension plans. . . .

II

The primary question in this case is whether the Contract Clause is violated by state legislation enacted to protect employees covered by a pension plan by requiring an employer to make outlays—which, although not in this case, will largely be offset against future savings—to provide terminated employees with the equivalent of benefits reasonably to be expected under the plan. The Act does not relieve either the employer or his employees of any existing contract obligation. Rather, the Act simply creates an additional, supplemental duty of the employer, no different in kind from myriad duties created by a wide variety of legislative measures which defeat settled expectations but which have nonetheless been sustained by this Court. For this reason, the Minnesota Act, in my view, does not implicate the Contract Clause in any way. The basic fallacy of today's decision is its mistaken view that the Contract Clause protects all contract-based expectations, including that of an employer that his obligations to his employees will not be legislatively enlarged beyond those explicitly provided in his pension plan.

A

Historically, it is crystal clear that the Contract Clause was not intended to embody a broad constitutional policy of protecting all reliance interests grounded in private contracts. It was made part of the Constitution to remedy a particular social evil—the state legislative practice of enacting laws to relieve individuals of their obligations under certain contracts—and thus was intended to prohibit States from adopting "as [their] policy the repudiation of debts or the destruction of contracts or the denial of means to enforce them," *Blaisdell.* But the Framers never contemplated that the Clause would limit the legislative power of States to enact laws creating duties that might burden some individuals in order to benefit others.

B

The terms of the Contract Clause negate any basis for its interpretation as protecting all contract-based expectations from unjustifiable interference. It applies, as confirmed by consistent judicial interpretations, only to *state legislative* Acts. See generally *Tidal Oil Co. v. Flanagan*, 263 U.S. 444 (1924). Its inapplicability to impairments by state judicial acts or by national legislation belies interpretation of the Clause as intended broadly to make all contract expectations inviolable. Rather, the only possible interpretation of its terms, especially in view of its history, is as a limited prohibition directed at a particular, narrow social evil, likely to occur only through state legislative action. This evil is identified with admirable precision: "[Laws] *impairing* the Obligation of Contracts." It is nothing less than an abuse of the English language to interpret, as does the Court, the term "impairing" as including laws which create new duties. While such laws may be conceptualized as "enlarging" the obligation of a contract when they add to the burdens that had previously been imposed by a private agreement, such laws cannot be prohibited by the Clause because they do not dilute or nullify a duty a person had previously obligated himself to perform. . . .

C

The Court seems to attempt to justify its distortion of the meaning of the Contract Clause on the ground that imposing new duties on one party to a contract can upset his contract-based expectations as much as can laws that effectively relieve the other party of any duty to perform. But it is no more anomalous to give effect to the term "impairment" and deny a claimant protection under the Contract Clause when new duties are created than it is to give effect to the Clause's inapplicability to acts of the National Government and deny a Contract Clause remedy when an Act of Congress denies a creditor the ability to enforce a contract right to payment. Both results are simply consequences of the fact that the Clause does not protect all contract-based expectations.

More fundamentally, the Court's distortion of the meaning of the Contract Clause creates anomalies of its own and threatens to undermine the jurisprudence of property rights developed over the last 40 years. The Contract Clause, of course, is but one of several clauses in the Constitution that protect existing economic values from governmental interference. The Fifth Amendment's command that "private property [shall not] be taken for public use, without just compensation" is such a clause. A second is the Due Process Clause, which during the heyday of substantive due process, see *Lochner v. New York*, 198 U.S. 45 (1905), largely supplanted the Contract Clause in importance and operated as a potent limitation on government's ability to interfere with economic expectations. Decisions over the past 50 years have developed a coherent, unified interpretation of all the constitutional provisions that may protect economic expectations and these decisions have recognized a broad latitude in States to effect even severe interference with existing economic values when reasonably necessary to promote the general welfare. . . . At the same time the prohibition of the Contract Clause, consistently with its wording and historic purposes, has been limited in application to state laws that diluted, with utter indifference to the legitimate interests of the beneficiary of a contract duty, the existing contract obligation. . . .

Today's conversion of the Contract Clause into a limitation on the power of States to enact laws that impose duties additional to obligations assumed under private contracts must inevitably produce results difficult to square with any rational conception of a constitutional order. Under the Court's opinion, any law that may be characterized as "superimposing" new obligations on those provided for by contract is to be regarded as creating "sudden, substantial, and unanticipated burdens" and then to be subjected to the most exacting scrutiny. The validity of such a law will turn upon whether judges see it as a law that deals with a generalized social problem, whether it is temporary (as few will be) or permanent, whether it operates in an area previously subject to regulation, and, finally, whether its duties apply to a broad class of persons. The necessary consequence of the extreme malleability of these rather vague criteria is to vest judges with broad subjective discretion to protect property interests that happen to appeal to them.

To permit this level of scrutiny of laws that interfere with contract-based expectations is an anomaly. There is nothing sacrosanct about expectations rooted in contract that justify according them a constitutional immunity denied other property rights. Laws that interfere with settled expectations created by state property law (and which impose severe economic burdens) are uniformly held constitutional where reasonably related to the promotion of the general welfare. *Hadacheck* v. *Sebastian*, 239 U.S. 394 (1915) is illustrative. There a property owner had established on a particular parcel of land a perfectly lawful business of a brickyard, and, in reliance on the existing law, continued to operate that business for a number of years. However, a local ordinance was passed prohibiting the operation of brickyards in the particular locale and diminishing the value of the claimant's parcel and thus of his investment by nearly 90%. Notwithstanding the effect of the ordinance on the value of the investment, the ordinance was sustained against a taking claim. . . .

III

But my view that the Contract Clause has no applicability whatsoever to the Minnesota Act does not end the inquiry in this case. The Due Process Clause of the Fourteenth Amendment limits a State's power to enact such laws and I therefore address that related challenge to the Act's validity. I think that any claim based on due process has no merit. . . .

FOR DISCUSSION

The U.S. economic system is generally described as capitalistic, but in 2008 and 2009 Congress adopted legislation bailing out banks and other financial institutions. How, if at all, are these actions likely to affect future adjudication?

THE RISE OF SUBSTANTIVE DUE PROCESS

The Court has had to decide what property deserved constitutional protection. Specifically, what types of things or ownership rights are protected by the Constitution and what is the extent of that protection? In claiming that property is protected by the Constitution, one has hardly stated anything. Instead, one needs to ask what clause of the Constitution protects property, and what is the degree of the property that is afforded? Are all forms of state or federal regulation barred, or are there some situations in which some types of regulation is permitted? These are the basic issues that are examined in this section's cases.

While early court decisions such as *Dartmouth College v. Woodward* (17 U.S. 518, 1819) employed the Contract Clause to protect property rights, and cases such as *Corfield v. Coryell* (6 Fed. Cas. 546, Pa., 1823) invoked the Privileges and Immunities Clause of Article IV, Sec. 2 of the Constitution to protect economic rights, the adoption of the Fourteenth Amendment ushered in a new era of jurisprudence referred to as the "**Lochner Era.**" This period, from the early 1870s until the New Deal, was named after a 1905 Supreme Court case, *Lochner v. New York* (198 U.S. 45, 1905). During this period scholars point to the Supreme Court's use of the Privileges or Immunities or Due Process Clause of the Fourteenth Amendment to strike down a host of legislation that would regulate property rights, working conditions, and wages. Especially in its interpretations of the Due Process Clause, the Court read it not just as having a procedural component prescribing how the government may do certain things, but also a substantive limit on certain forms of economic activities. Using **substantive due process**, the Court fashioned doctrines such as **economic due process** or **liberty of contract** to limit government regulation. In doing so, the Court took upon itself the authority to apply stricter scrutiny or a more intense examination to economic legislation than it gave to laws aimed at protecting or restricting the rights of individuals. For some, the irony of the Court's jurisprudence during this era was that while the Fourteenth

Amendment was a Civil War era protection to further the rights of the freed slaves, it was instead invoked to protect corporations, property, and limit business regulation at the same time that cases such as *Plessy v. Ferguson* (163 U.S. 537, 1896) upheld discriminatory laws against African Americans. Given these decisions, it may not be a surprise that Charles Beard concluded that the Constitution was a pro-property rights document.

This section examines the rise and fall of substantive or economic due process primarily during the *Lochner* era. It concentrates on the development and eventual abandonment of these doctrines over a nearly 100-year period. Today many critics would say that the Court offers little protection to property rights, leaving them since the New Deal vulnerable to government regulation.

Fourteenth Amendment, Sec. 1:

All persons born or naturalized in the United States, and subject to the jurisdiction thereof, are citizens of the United States and of the State wherein they reside. No State shall make or enforce any law which shall abridge the privileges or immunities of citizens of the United States; nor shall any State deprive any person of life, liberty, or property, without due process of law; nor deny to any person within its jurisdiction the equal protection of the laws.

Both Article IV and the Fourteenth Amendment refer to "privileges and immunities" or "privileges or immunities." Exactly what the Privileges or Immunities Clause of the Fourteenth Amendment means has never been clear, even in the few Court decisions pertaining to it. In *Crandall v. Nevada* (6 Wallace 35, 1868), which was decided before the Fourteenth Amendment became effective, the Court held that the state tax in question there violated the implied guarantees of the original Constitution. In regard to the Fourteenth Amendment, generally the Court has consistently held to the point that the prohibitions in the amendment apply only to states and that an individual as an individual cannot violate any of its provisions. However, one critical case decided by Supreme Court Justice Bushrod Washington (George Washington's nephew) while riding as a circuit judge sought to clarify what Article IV meant. This was in *Corfield v. Coryell* (6 Fed. Cas. 546, (E.D. Pa. 1823)).

Corfield dicta suggested that Article IV protected economic rights. This claim influenced justices when they were called upon in the next case to interpret the Privileges or Immunities Clause of the Fourteenth Amendment. This first occurred in *The Slaughterhouse Cases* in 1873.

The Slaughterhouse Cases (83 U.S. 36, 1873) were decided only five years after the adoption of the Fourteenth Amendment and were the first interpretation of that amendment. At this time "due process" still basically meant procedure. Substantive due process, by which the "what" of governmental activity as well as the "how" can be questioned, came later, although in *Dred Scott v. Sandford* (60 U.S. 393, 1857) and *Hepburn v. Griswold* (75 U.S. 603, 1870) the Court had alluded to substantive due process.

In *The Slaughterhouse Cases* the Court distinguished sharply between the privileges and immunities of state citizenship and of federal citizenship, noting that only the latter were protected from transgression by the states in the Fourteenth Amendment. As to the former, the Court noted that these would be determined as cases arose. In fact, the Court (except once) has never held a state statute to conflict with the Privileges or Immunities Clause of the Fourteenth Amendment. In general, the test of such a privilege is that it be derived from federal law (including, of course, the Constitution) and be the property only of citizens. In this latter respect this provision differs from most of the guarantees of the Constitution which are enjoyed by "persons," citizens and noncitizens alike.

Munn v. Illinois (94 U.S. 113, 1877) was the first Fourteenth Amendment case in which the entire court—both majority and minority—were concerned with due process. Here the Court was concerned with the regulatory power of the state and the ability to set rates for grain storage. While upholding the regulation, the Court began to articulate some limits on the power to regulate property, seeking to show that some activities are public and therefore subject to government regulation, while also noting that some entities or activities are purely private and therefore beyond the scope of regulation. If there are in fact some activities that are private, such as those involving economic transactions, then the question becomes how the judiciary should examine government efforts to regulate them. The Court began to answer that question in *Mugler v. Kansas* (123 U.S. 623, 1887).

One should pay particular note to *Mugler*'s dicta: "While every possible presumption is to be indulged in favor of the validity of a statute, the courts must obey the constitution rather than the law-making department of government, and must, upon their own responsibility, determine whether, in any particular case, these limits have been passed." This statement is often cited as one of the first instances of the Court invoking for itself the right to second-guess the wisdom of the substance of economic legislation. This language, as well as the entire analysis of the case, seemed to reserve for the Court the prerogative to give economic legislation a more demanding look, or **heightened scrutiny,** than normally offered. In comparison to the deferential reading of "necessary and proper" offered by Justice Marshall in *McCulloch v. Maryland* (17 U.S. 316, 1819), the Court here was less willing to offer an expansive reading of the Constitution. Instead, the document through the Fourteenth Amendment placed a limit on what the government could do, and the Supreme Court would use it authority to police that limit.

In *Allgeyer v. State of Louisiana* (165 U.S. 578, 1897) the Court explicated upon its notion of substantive due process, beginning to invoke the term "liberty of contract" as a constitutional concept that appeared to protect private economic activity from state regulation. The idea of liberty of contract, perhaps indebted to the Social Darwinist or laissez-faire doctrines of the nineteenth century, assumed that work relations or the terms of conditions of employment between employers and employees were the product of free and equal negotiations and therefore should not be second-guessed by the government via the imposition of a minimum wage or other labor law restrictions. In *Allgeyer* the concept of liberty of contract was embedded in the Fourteenth Amendment. This doctrine was more famously invoked a few years later in *Lochner v. New York.*

Lochner v. New York may be the high point of the substantive due process era. Here the Court declared unconstitutional a state law that sought to regulate workplace conditions in bakeries. Justice Holmes's dissent in *Lochner* may be the most famous in Supreme Court history, earning him the nickname the Great Dissenter. Because of his criticism of the majority opinion for its adoption of an economic **laissez-faire** philosophy that underscored substantive due process and liberty of contract and because of his writing style, later criticisms of this era of jurisprudence referred to *Lochner* or used the term "Lochnerizing" to attack Court opinions limiting government economic regulation.

While during the *Lochner* era the Court appeared hostile to many types of workplace regulation, its paternalism showed when it came to women. Before he became a Supreme Court Justice, Louis Brandeis was a famous Progressive Era attorney who triumphed many causes. One that would make him famous was his legal brief in the 1908 case *Muller v. Oregon* (208 U.S. 412). In seeking to argue in favor of a state law regulating the working conditions of women, his brief was short on law—merely a few sentences, as noted below. It was accompanied by more than one hundred pages of empirical data regarding the intolerable working conditions women faced. After the *Muller* decision, in which the Court upheld state law, the phrase "Brandeis brief" came to refer to legal arguments stressing social and economic and not simply legal facts and arguments. Today, many of the amicus curiae briefs submitted to the Court are full of facts that groups hope the justices will consider when rendering a decision. Despite *Muller*, the logic of *Lochner* lived on. *Adkins v. Children's Hospital* (261 U.S.

525, 1923) represents a strange blending of liberty of contract, paternalism, and feminism used to strike down laws aimed at protecting women. The passage of the Nineteenth Amendment suggested that women could now protect themselves at work and did not need the paternalism of *Muller* or state legislatures to help them.

By the Depression, which started in 1929, the Court had begun to respond to changing economic conditions—or perhaps political pressures or a change in justices—and it became more sympathetic to economic regulation. In *Nebbia v. New York* (291 U.S. 502, 1934) the Court appeared to retreat from its views in *Munn v. Illinois* (94 U.S. 113, 1877). The Court dropped the concept of "**affected with a public interest**" as the basis for its decisions on government regulation cases and held that such regulations depend for their reasonableness upon all of the relevant facts. This marked a departure, and, in a sense, the opinion can be regarded as the beginning of the "New Deal era" from the point of view of the judiciary. It involved state rather than federal statutory enactment, but the basic philosophy is that of the New Deal, as McReynolds's dissent indicates.

The New Deal and the End of *Lochner Era*

As described in Chapter III the New Deal was the high water mark and end of many legal doctrines. The same was true with economic due process and liberty of contract. Both doctrines were assaulted in the *West Coast Hotel Co. v. Parrish* (300 U.S. 379, 1937) and *United States v. Carolene Products Company* (304 U.S. 144, 1938) decisions.

West Coast Hotel was the case that involved Justice Roberts's famous "switch in time that saved nine" position. The decision came after President Franklin Roosevelt's Court-packing plan and has been credited by some with undermining the Roosevelt scheme. The statute here had no "value of services" standard contrary to the New York statute of *Morehead v. People of State of New York ex rel. Tipaldo* (298 U.S. 587, 1936), so the decision of the Court in *West Coast Hotel* definitely overruled *Adkins*. It should be noted that *Carolene Products* contains perhaps the most famous footnote in American law. In *Carolene Products* note four the Court abandoned (along with its analysis in *West Coast Hotel*) its strict scrutiny in favor of economic rights. The old dual standard of heightened scrutiny for economic but not personal rights is rejected, with the footnote suggesting a reversal. Specifically, *Carolene Products* sets the Court up for a New Deal jurisprudence that emphasized other noneconomic Bill of Rights protections (see Volume II, Chapter I of this text).

But did that mean that the Court would no longer invoke substantive due process for economic rights, or that the doctrine was dead? Its economic death did not come in *Carolene Products* or *West Coast Hotel*, but later in a case also reminiscent of *Muller* because it involved economic regulation of working conditions affecting women. Here the Court effectively reverses *Adkins* and appears to bury liberty of contract and substantive due process as theories. However, it is not until *Ferguson v. Skrupa* (372 U.S. 726) in 1963 that the Court officially buries these doctrines. While Chapter VI details more fully the efforts to use the Fifth Amendment Takings Clause to protect economic and property rights, *Lingle v. Chevron U.S.A. Inc.* (544 U.S. 528, 2005) is an example of how efforts to use it with a substantive due process emphasis have generally been dismissed by the Court.

Does the Due Process Clause have any substantive teeth to it when it comes to economic rights? Defendants who faced what they thought were extraordinarily high **punitive damages** claims in jury verdicts hoped that would be the case. In *BMW of North America, Inc. v. Gore* (517 U.S. 559, 1996), the Supreme Court agreed, breathing at least minimal life into the substantive Due Process Clause of the Fourteenth Amendment. Yet *BMW* was not the only instance in which the Supreme Court effectively used due process to invalidate or lower punitive damages. In *Exxon Shipping v. Baker* (554 U.S. ___, 2008) the Supreme Court lowered the punitive damages arising out of the 1989 crash of the oil tanker *Exxon Valdez* off the coast of Alaska, which resulted in the spilling of more than 11 million gallons of oil into the water and onto the shore. The crash was the result of the negligent behavior of the ship's captain, who apparently had been drinking. The Court reduced the punitive damages against ExxonMobil from $2.5 billion to $500 million. In so ruling the Court held that the proper ratio of punitive to compensatory damages was nearly one-to-one. While the decision in this case was based upon a special maritime law, many Court observers believe the decision signals the Court's continued insistence on using some form of substantive due process to reign in what it believes to be excessive punitive damages. If this is correct, despite the language of *Lingle*, economic due process appears to live on in some form.

Concurring in *Lynch v. Household Finance Corporation* (405 U.S. 538, 1972), Justice Stewart commented upon the apparent dual standard the Court had imposed on property and individual rights that characterized the *Lochner* and New Deal eras.

> [T]he federal courts have been particularly bedeviled by "mixed" cases in which both personal and property rights are implicated, and the line between has been difficult to draw with any consistency or principled objectivity. . . . Such difficulties indicate that the dichotomy between personal liberties and property rights is a false one. Property does not have rights. People have rights. . . . In fact, a fundamental interdependence exists between the personal right to liberty and the personal right to property. Neither could have meaning without the other. That rights in property are basic civil rights has long been recognized.

The *Lochner* era and its jurisprudence of economic due process is over, yet many believe that protection of property rights remains an important cornerstone of personal liberty that should not be overlooked.

CORFIELD V. CORYELL

6 F.Cas. 546 (1823)

This decision from a federal circuit court decided that a New Jersey law that prohibited non-residents from gathering oysters did not violate either the Privileges and Immunities Clause in Article IV or congressional regulation of interstate commerce.

CIRCUIT JUSTICE BUSHROD WASHINGTON delivered the opinion of the court.

. . . The next question is, whether this act infringes that section of the constitution which declares that "the citizens of each state shall be entitled to all the privileges and immunities of citizens in the several states"? The inquiry is, what are the privileges and immunities of citizens in the several states? We feel no hesitation in confining these expressions to those privileges and immunities which are, in their nature, fundamental; which belong, of right, to the citizens of all free governments; and which have, at all times, been enjoyed by the citizens of the several states which compose this Union, from the time of their becoming free, independent, and sovereign. What these fundamental principles are, it would perhaps be more tedious than difficult to enumerate. They may, however, be all comprehended under the following general heads: Protection by the government; the enjoyment of life and liberty, with the right to acquire and possess property of every kind, and to pursue and obtain happiness and safety; subject nevertheless to such restraints as the government may justly prescribe for the general good of the whole. The right of a citizen of one state to pass through, or to reside in any other state, for purposes of trade, agriculture, professional pursuits, or otherwise; to claim the benefit of the writ of habeas corpus; to institute and maintain actions of any kind in the courts of the state; to take, hold and dispose of property, either real or personal; and an exemption from higher taxes or impositions than are paid by the other citizens of the state; may be mentioned as some of the particular privileges and immunities of citizens, which are clearly embraced by the general description of privileges deemed to be fundamental: to which may be added, the elective franchise, as regulated and established by the laws or constitution of the state in which it is to be exercised. These, and many others which might be mentioned, are, strictly speaking, privileges and immunities, and the enjoyment of them by the citizens of each state, in every other state, was manifestly calculated (to use the expressions of the preamble of the corresponding provision in the old articles of confederation) "the better to secure and perpetuate mutual friendship and intercourse among the people of the different states of the Union."

FOR DISCUSSION

What economic rights do you think are protected by the Constitution? Do you agree with Justice Washington's list?

SLAUGHTERHOUSE CASES

16 Wall. 36, 21 L.Ed. 394 (1873)

The first cases brought to the Supreme Court under the Fourteenth Amendment were these. They arose under a Louisiana statute of 1869 regulating the business of slaughtering livestock in New Orleans. The obviously corrupt legislature of the Reconstruction period had granted a monopoly to the facilities of one corporation. Other butchers were to have access to these facilities on payment of a reasonable fee, but the net result was that more than a thousand other persons and companies were prevented from continuing in the business.

Vote: 5–4

JUSTICE MILLER delivered the opinion of the Court.

The plaintiffs in error accepting this issue, allege that the statute is a violation of the Constitution of the United States in these several particulars:—

That it creates an involuntary servitude forbidden by the thirteenth article of amendment;

That it abridges the privileges and immunities of citizens of the United States;

That it denies to the plaintiffs the equal protection of the laws; and,

That it deprives them of their property without due process of law; contrary to the provisions of the first section of the fourteenth article of amendment. . . .

The next observation is more important in view of the arguments of counsel in the present case. It is, that the distinction between citizenship of the United States and citizenship of a State is clearly recognized and established. Not only may a man be a citizen of the United States without being a citizen of a State, but an important element is necessary to convert the former into the latter. He must reside within the State to make him a citizen of it, but it is only necessary that he should be born or naturalized in the United States to be a citizen of the Union.

It is quite clear, then, that there is a citizenship of the United States, and a citizenship of a State, which are distinct from each other, and which depend upon different characteristics or circumstances in the individual.

We think this distinction and its explicit recognition in this amendment of great weight in this argument, because the next paragraph of this same section, which is the one mainly relied on by the plaintiffs in error, speaks only of privileges and immunities of citizens of the United States, and does not speak of those of citizens of the several States. The argument, however, in favor of the plaintiffs rests wholly on the assumption that the citizenship is the same, and the privileges and immunities guaranteed by the clause are the same.

The language is, "No State shall make or enforce any law which shall abridge the privileges or immunities of citizens of the United States." It is a little remarkable, if this clause was intended as a protection to the citizen of a State against the legislative power of his own State, that the word citizen of the State should be left out when it is so carefully used, and used in contradistinction to citizens of the United States, in the very sentence which preceded it. It is too clear for argument that the change in phraseology was adopted understandingly and with a purpose.

Of the privileges and immunities of the citizen of the United States, and of the privileges and immunities of the citizen of the State, and what they respectively are, we will presently consider; but we wish to state here that it is only the former which are placed by this clause under the protection of the Federal Constitution, and that the latter, whatever they may be, are not intended to have any additional protection by this paragraph of the amendment.

If, then, there is a difference between the privileges and immunities belonging to a citizen of the United States as such, and those belonging to the citizen of the State as such, the latter must rest for their security and protection where they have heretofore rested; for they are not embraced by this paragraph of the amendment.

Having shown that the privileges and immunities relied on in the argument are those which belong to citizens of the States as such, and that they are left to the State governments for security and protection, and not by this article placed under the special care of the Federal government, we may hold ourselves excused from defining the privileges and immunities of citizens of the United States which no State can abridge, until some case involving those privileges may make it necessary to do so.

But lest it should be said that no such privileges and immunities are to be found if those we have been considering are excluded, we venture to suggest some which owe their existence to the Federal Government, its national character, its Constitution, or its laws.

One of these is well described in the case of *Crandall v. Nevada,* 73 U.S. 35 (1867). It is said to be the right of the citizen of this great country, protected by implied guarantees of its Constitution, "to come to the seat of government to assert any claim he may have upon that government, to transact any business he may have with it, to seek its protection, to share its offices, to engage in administering its functions. He has the right of free access to its seaports, through which all operations of foreign commerce are conducted, to the sub-treasuries, land offices, and courts of justice in the several states."

Another privilege of a citizen of the United States is to demand the care and protection of the Federal government over his life, liberty, and property when on the high seas or within the jurisdiction of a foreign government. Of this there can be no doubt, nor that the right depends upon his character as a citizen of the United States. The right to peaceably assemble and petition for redress of grievances, the privilege of the writ of habeas corpus, are rights of the citizen guaranteed by the Federal Constitution. The right to use the navigable waters of the United States, however they may penetrate the territory of the several States, all rights secured to our citizens by treaties with foreign nations, are dependent upon citizenship of the United States, and not citizenship of a State. One of these privileges is conferred by the very article under consideration. It is that a citizen of the United States can, of his own volition, become a citizen of any State of the Union by a bona fide residence therein, with the same rights as other citizens of that State. To these may be added the rights secured by the thirteenth and fifteenth articles of amendment, and by the other clause of the fourteenth, next to be considered. . . .

The argument has not been much pressed in these cases that the defendant's charter deprives the plaintiffs of their property without due process of law, or that it denies to them the equal protection of the law. The first of these paragraphs has been in the Constitution since the adoption of the fifth amendment, as a restraint upon the federal power. It is also to be found in some form of expression in the constitutions of nearly all of the States, as a restraint upon the power of the States. This law, then, has practically been the same as it now is during the existence of the government, except so far as the present amendment may place the restraining power over the States in this matter in the hands of the Federal government.

We are not without judicial interpretation, therefore, both State and national, of the meaning of this clause. And it is sufficient to say that under no construction of that provision that we have ever seen, or any that we deem admissible, can the restraint imposed by the State of Louisiana upon the exercise of their trade by the butchers of New Orleans be held to be a deprivation of property within the meaning of that provision.

"Nor shall any State deny to any person within its jurisdiction the equal protection of the laws."

In the light of the history of these amendments, and the pervading purpose of them, which we have already discussed, it is not difficult to give a meaning to this clause. The existence of laws in the States where the newly emancipated Negroes resided, which discriminated with gross injustice and hardship against them as a class, was the evil to be remedied by this clause, and by it such laws are forbidden.

If, however, the States did not conform their laws to its requirements, then by the fifth section of the article of amendment Congress was authorized to enforce it by suitable legislation. We doubt very much whether any action of a State not directed by way of discrimination against the Negroes as a class, or on account of their race, will ever be held to come within the purview of this provision. It is so clearly a provision for that race and that emergency, that a strong case would be necessary for its application to any other. But as it is a State that is to be dealt with, and not alone the validity of its laws, we may safely leave that matter until Congress shall have exercised its power, or some case of State oppression, by denial of equal justice in its courts, shall have claimed a decision at our hands. We find no such case in the one before us, and do not deem it necessary to go over the argument again, as it may have relation to this particular clause of the amendment.

Judgment affirmed.

JUSTICE FIELD dissented, with the concurrence of CHIEF JUSTICE CHASE, and JUSTICES SWAYNE and BRADLEY:

What, then, are the privileges and immunities which are secured against abridgement by State legislation?

The terms, privileges and immunities, are not new in the amendment; they were in the Constitution before the amendment was adopted. They are found in the second section of the fourth article, which declares that "the citizens of each State shall be entitled to all privileges and immunities of citizens in the several States," and they have been the subject of frequent consideration in judicial decisions. In *Corfield v. Coryell*, 6 Fed. Cas. 546, Pa. (1823), Mr. Justice Washington said he had "no hesitation in confining these expressions to those privileges and immunities which were, in their nature, fundamental; which belong of right to citizens of all free governments, and which have at all times been enjoyed by the citizens of the several States which compose the Union, from the time of their becoming free, independent, and sovereign;" and, in considering what those fundamental privileges were, he said that perhaps it would be more tedious than difficult to enumerate them, but that they might be "all comprehended under the following general heads; protection by the government; the enjoyment of life and liberty, with the right to acquire and possess property of every kind, and to pursue and obtain happiness and safety, subject, nevertheless to such restraints as the government may justly prescribe for the general good of the whole." This appears to me to be a sound construction of the clause in question. The privileges and immunities designated are those *which of right belong to the citizens of all free governments.* Clearly among these must be placed the right to pursue a lawful employment in a lawful manner, without other restraint than such as equally affects all persons. In the discussions in Congress upon the passage of the Civil Rights Act repeated reference was made to this language of Mr. Justice Washington. It was cited by Senator Trumbull with the observation that it enumerated the very rights belonging to a citizen of the United States set forth in the first section of the act, and with the statement that all persons born in the United States being declared by the act citizens of the United States, would thenceforth be entitled to the rights of citizens, and that these were the great fundamental rights set forth in the act; and that they were set forth "as appertaining to every freeman."

This equality of right, with exemption from all disparaging and partial enactments, in the lawful pursuits of life, throughout the whole country, is the distinguishing privilege of citizens of the United States. To them, everywhere, all pursuits, all professions, all avocations are open without other restrictions than such as are imposed equally upon all others of the same age, sex, and condition. The State may prescribe such regulations for every pursuit and calling of life as will promote the public health, secure the good order and advance the general prosperity of society, but when once prescribed, the pursuit or calling must be free to be followed by every citizen who is within the conditions designated, and will conform to the regulations. This is the fundamental idea upon which our institutions rest, and unless adhered to in the legislation of the country our government will be a republic only in name. The Fourteenth Amendment, in my judgment, makes it essential to the validity of the legislation of every State that this equality of right should be respected. How widely this equality has been departed from, how entirely rejected and trampled upon by the act of Louisiana, I have already shown. And it is to be a matter of profound regret that its validity is recognized by a majority of this court, for by it the right of free labor, one of the most sacred and imprescriptible rights of man, is violated. That only is a free government, in the American sense of the term, under which the inalienable right of every citizen to pursue his happiness is unrestrained, except by just, equal, and impartial laws.

JUSTICES SWAYNE and BRADLEY also filed separate dissenting opinions.

FOR DISCUSSION

Did the majority effectively read the Privileges or Immunities Clause from the Fourteen Amendment? Note how the *Corfield* dicta find their way into the dissent. Are you persuaded by the claims that the Fourteenth Amendment protects those economic rights referred to by Justice Washington?

RELATED CASES

Crandall v. Nevada: **6 Wall. 35 (1868)**

A state cannot impose a tax on persons leaving the state by any common carrier to be collected by the carrier since this would transgress the rights of United States citizens to move freely about the country.

Colgate v. Harvey: **296 U.S. 404 (1935)**

A state income tax law that levies higher rates on money loaned outside the state than that loaned within the state denies equal protection of the laws and abridges the privilege of United States citizenship to carry on business across state lines.

Hague v. CIO: **307 U.S. 496 (1939)**

Municipal ordinances forbidding the distribution of printed matter and the holding of public meetings in streets and other public places without permits are a deprivation of rights under the Constitution. A concurring opinion held that the Privileges or Immunities Clause had been violated.

Madden v. Kentucky: **309 U.S. 83 (1940)**

An annual state *ad valorem* tax on bank deposits outside a state at a rate five times that imposed on bank deposits within a state is not invalid in the absence of the most explicit demonstration that the classification "is a hostile and offensive discrimination against particular persons and classes." This decision overruled *Colgate v. Harvey.*

MUNN V. ILLINOIS

94 U.S. 113, 24 L.Ed. 77 (1877)

The state of Illinois brought suit against Ira Y. Munn and others, grain warehousemen in Chicago, for transacting business without a state license contrary to a state statute setting maximum charges for the storage of grain in warehouses. The statute was challenged as violating the provisions of the Constitution vesting in Congress the power to regulate both foreign and interstate commerce and the Due Process Clause of the Fourteenth Amendment.

Vote: 7–2

CHIEF JUSTICE WAITE delivered the opinion of the Court:

When one becomes a member of society, he necessarily parts with some rights or privileges which, as an individual not affected by his relations to others, he might retain. "A body politic," as aptly defined in the preamble of the constitution of Massachusetts, "is a social compact by which the whole people covenants with each citizen, and each citizen with the whole people, that all shall be governed by certain laws for the common good." This does not confer power upon the whole people to control rights which are purely and exclusively private, *Thorpe v. R. & B. Railroad Co.,* 27 Vt. 140; but it does authorize the establishment of laws requiring each citizen to so conduct himself, and so use his own property, as not unnecessarily to injure another. This is the very essence of government, and has found expression in the maxim, *sic utere tuo ut alienum non laedas* [use your property in a manner that will not injure the property of another]. From this source came the police powers, which "are nothing more or less than the powers of government inherent in every sovereignty, that is to say, the power to govern men and things." Under these powers the government regulates the conduct of its citizens one towards another, and the manner in which each shall use his own property, when such regulation becomes necessary for the public good. In their exercise it has been customary in England from time immemorial, and in this country from its first colonization, to regulate ferries, common carriers, hackmen, bakers, millers, wharfingers, innkeepers, etc., and in so doing to fix a maximum of charge to be made for services rendered, accommodations furnished, and articles sold. To this day, statutes are to be found in many of the states upon some or all these subjects; and we think it has never yet been successfully contended that such legislation came within any of the constitutional prohibitions against interference with private property.

From this it is apparent that, down to the time of the adoption of the Fourteenth Amendment, it was not supposed that statutes regulating the use, or even the price of the use, of private property necessarily deprived an owner of his property without due process of law. Under some circumstances they may, but not under all. The amendment does not change the law in this particular: it simply prevents the states from doing that which will operate as such a deprivation.

Property does become clothed with a public interest when used in a manner to make it of public consequence, and affect the community at large. When, therefore, one devotes his property to a use in which the public has an interest, he, in effect, grants to the public an interest in that use, and must submit to be controlled by the public for the common good, to the extent of the interest he has thus created. He may withdraw his grant by discontinuing the use; but, so long as he maintains the use, he must submit to the control.

But we need not go further. Enough has already been said to show that, when private property is devoted to a public use, it is subject to public regulation. It remains only to ascertain whether the warehouses of these plaintiffs in error, and the business which is carried on there, come within the operation of this principle.

Undoubtedly, in mere private contracts, relating to matters in which the public has no interest, what is reasonable must be ascertained judicially. But this is because the legislature has no control over such a contract. So, too, in matters which do affect the public interest, as to which legislative control may be exercised, if there are no statutory regulations upon the subject, the courts must determine what is reasonable. The controlling fact is the power to regulate at all. If that exists, the right to establish the maximum of charge, as one of the means of regulation, is implied. In fact, the common-law rule, which requires the charge to be reasonable, is itself a regulation as to price. Without it the owner could make his rates at will, and compel the public to yield to his terms, or forgo the use.

But a mere common-law regulation of trade or business may be changed by statute. A person has no property, no vested interest, in any rule of the common law. That is only one of the forms of municipal law, and is no more sacred than any other. Rights of property which have been created by the common law cannot be taken away without due process; but the law itself, as a rule of conduct, may be changed at the will, or even at the whim, of the legislature, unless prevented by constitutional limitations. Indeed, the great office of statutes is to remedy defects in the common law as they are developed, and to adapt it to the changes of time and circumstances. To limit the rate of charge for services rendered in a public employment, or for the use of property in which the public has an interest, is only changing a regulation which existed before. It established no new principle in the law, but only gives a new effect to an old one.

We know that this is a power which may be abused; but that is no argument against its existence. For protection against abuses by legislatures the people must resort to the polls, not to the courts.

We conclude, therefore, that the statute in question is not repugnant to the Constitution of the United States, and that there is no error in the judgment.

Judgment affirmed.

JUSTICE FIELD dissented, with the concurrence of JUSTICE STRONG.

I am compelled to dissent from the decision of the court in this case and from the reasons upon which that decision is founded. The principle upon which the opinion of the majority proceeds is, in my judgment, subversive of the rights of private property, heretofore believed to be protected by constitutional guarantees against legislative interference, and is in conflict with the authorities cited in its support.

There is nothing in the character of the business of the defendants as warehousemen which called for the interference complained of in this case. Their buildings are not nuisances; their occupation of receiving and storing grain infringes upon no rights of others, disturbs no neighborhood, infects not the air, and in no respect prevents others from using and enjoying their property as to them may seem best. The legislation in question is nothing less than a bold assertion of absolute power by the State to control at its discretion the property and business of the citizen, and fix the compensation he shall receive. The will of the legislature is made the condition upon which the owner shall receive the fruits of his property and the just reward of his labor, industry, and enterprise.

It requires no comment to point out the radical differences between the cases of public mills and interest on money, and that of the warehouses in Chicago. No prerogative or privilege of the crown to establish warehouses was ever asserted at the common law. The business of a warehouseman was, at common law, a private business, and is so in its nature. It has no special privileges connected with it, nor did the law ever extend to it any greater protection than it extended to all other private business. No reason can be assigned to justify legislation interfering with the legitimate profits of that business, that would not equally justify an intermeddling with the business of every man in the community, so soon, at least, as his business became generally useful.

I am of the opinion that the judgment of the Supreme Court of Illinois should be reversed.

FOR DISCUSSION

What does it mean for property to become clothed with a public interest? Is there a clear constitutional line that distinguishes public from private property to provide a constitutional guideline for how to decide what can be regulated? Do the majority and dissents agree on this?

RELATED CASES

***Davidson v. New Orleans:* 96 U.S. 97 (1878)**

The determination of the intent and application of the Due Process Clause of the Fourteenth Amendment is to be "by the gradual process of judicial inclusion and exclusion, as the cases presented for decision shall require." Here the Court upheld a special assessment by the city for the drainage of swamplands.

***Chicago, Milwaukee & St. Paul R. Co. v. Minnesota:* 134 U.S. 418 (1890)**

A railroad company must be permitted to have the question of rates established by a state commissioner subject to judicial investigation or it amounts to lack of due process of law.

***Smyth v. Ames:* 169 U.S. 466 (1898)**

Courts may not only review the reasonableness of rates established by a state commission but must also consider the matter of a fair return on the proper value of the property involved.

***Willcox v. Consolidated Gas Co.:* 212 U.S. 19 (1909)**

Where the element of business risk was reduced to a minimum, as in the case of a gas company, a return of 6 percent was reasonable.

MUGLER V. KANSAS

123 U.S. 623, 8 S.Ct. 273, 31 L.Ed. 205 (1887)

Mugler was engaged in the business of brewing beer in violation of a state constitutional amendment and law prohibiting this activity. He challenged it as a violation of his Fourteenth Amendment substantive due process rights.

Vote: 8–1

JUSTICE HARLAN delivered the opinion of the court.

The general question in each case is whether the foregoing statutes of Kansas are in conflict with that clause of the fourteenth amendment, which provides that "no state shall make or enforce any law which shall abridge the privileges or immunities of citizens of the United States; nor shall any state deprive any person of life, liberty, or property without due process of law." That legislation by a state prohibiting the manufacture within her limits of intoxicating liquors, to be there sold or bartered for general use as a beverage, does not necessarily infringe any right, privilege, or immunity secured by the constitution of the United States, is made clear by the decisions of this court, rendered before and since the adoption of the fourteenth amendment; to some of which, in view of questions to be presently considered, it will be well to refer.

In the *License Cases,* 46 US 504 (1847), the question was whether certain statutes of Massachusetts, Rhode Island, and New Hampshire, relating to the sale of spirituous liquors, were repugnant to the constitution of the

United States. In determining that question, it became necessary to inquire whether there was any conflict between the exercise by congress of its power to regulate commerce with foreign countries, or among the several states, and the exercise by a state of what are called police powers. Although the members of the court did not fully agree as to the grounds upon which the decision should be placed, they were unanimous in holding that the statutes then under examination were not inconsistent with the constitution of the United States, or with any act of congress. Chief Justice Taney said: "If any state deems the retail and internal traffic in ardent spirits injurious to its citizens, and calculated to produce idleness, vice, or debauchery, I see nothing in the constitution of the United States to prevent it from regulating and restraining the traffic, or from prohibiting it altogether, if it thinks proper." Mr. Justice McLean, among other things, said: "A state regulates its domestic commerce, contracts, the transmission of estates, real and personal, and acts upon internal matters which relate to its moral and political welfare. Over these subjects the federal government has no power. . . . The acknowledged police power of a state extends often to the destruction of property. A nuisance may be abated. Everything prejudicial to the health or morals of a city may be removed." Mr. Justice Woodbury observed: "How can they [the states] be sovereign within their respective spheres, without power to regulate all their internal commerce, as well as police, and direct how, when, and where it shall be conducted in articles intimately connected either with public morals or public safety or public prosperity?" Mr. Justice Grier, in still more empathic language, said: "The true question presented by these cases, and one which I am not disposed to evade, is whether the states have a right to prohibit the sale and consumption of an article of commerce which they believe to be pernicious in its effects, and the cause of disease, pauperism, and crime. . . . Without attempting to define what are the peculiar subjects or limits of this power, it may safely be affirmed that every law for the restraint or punishment of crime, for the preservation of the public peace, health, and morals must come within this category. . . . It is not necessary, for the sake of justifying the state legislation now under consideration, to array the appalling statistics of misery, pauperism, and crime which have their origin in the use or abuse of ardent spirits. The police power, which is exclusively in the states, is alone competent to the correction of these great evils, and all measures of restraint or prohibition necessary to effect the purpose are within the scope of that authority."

It is, however, contended that, although the state may prohibit the manufacture of intoxicating liquors for sale or barter within her limits, for general use as a beverage, "no convention or legislature has the right, under our form of government, to prohibit any citizen from manufacturing for his own use, or for export or storage, any article of food or drink not endangering or affecting the rights of others." The argument made in support of the first branch of this proposition, briefly stated, is that, in the implied compact between the state and the citizen, certain rights are reserved by the latter, which are guarantied by the constitutional provision protecting persons against being deprived of life, liberty, or property, without due process of law, and with which the state cannot interfere; that among those rights is that of manufacturing for one's use either food or drink; and that while, according to the doctrines of the commune, the state may control the tastes, appetites, habits, dress, food, and drink of the people, our system of government, based upon the individuality and intelligence of the citizen, does not claim to control him, except as to his conduct to others, leaving him the sole judge as to all that only affects himself. It will be observed that the proposition, and the argument made in support of it, equally concede that the right to manufacture drink for one's personal use is subject to the condition that such manufacture does not endanger or affect the rights of others. If such manufacture does prejudicially affect the rights and interests of the community, it follows, from the very premises stated, that society has the power to protect itself, by legislation, against the injurious consequences of that business. As was said in *Munn* v. *Illinois*, [94 U.S. 113 (1877),] while power does not exist with the whole people to control rights that are purely and exclusively private, government may require "each citizen to so conduct himself, and so use his own property, as not unnecessarily to injure another." But by whom, or by what authority, is it to be determined whether the manufacture of particular articles of drink, either for general use or for the personal use of the maker, will injuriously affect the public? Power to determine such questions, so as to bind all, must exist somewhere; else society will be at the mercy of the few, who, regarding only their own appetites or passions, may be willing to imperil the peace and security of the many, provided only they are permitted to do as they please. Under our system that power is lodged with the legislative branch of the government. It belongs to that department to exert what are known as the police powers of the state, and to determine, primarily, what measures are appropriate or needful for the protection of the public morals, the public health, or the public safety.

It does not at all follow that every statute enacted ostensibly for the promotion of these ends is to be accepted as a legitimate exertion of the police powers of the state. There are, of necessity, limits beyond which legislation cannot rightfully go. While every possible presumption is to be indulged in favor of the validity of a statute, the courts must obey the constitution rather than the law-making department of government, and must, upon their own responsibility, determine whether, in any particular case, these limits have been passed. "To what purpose," it was said in *Marbury* v. *Madison*, 5 U.S. 137 (1803), "are powers limited, and to what purpose is that limitation committed to writing, if these limits may, at any time, be passed by those intended to be restrained? The distinction between a government with limited and unlimited powers is abolished, if those limits do not confine the persons on whom they are imposed, and if acts prohibited and acts allowed are of equal obligation." The courts are not bound by mere forms, nor are they to be misled by mere pretenses. They are at liberty, indeed, are under a solemn duty, to look at the substance of things, whenever they enter upon the inquiry whether the legislature has transcended the limits of its authority. If, therefore, a statute purporting to have been enacted to protect the public health, the public morals, or the public safety, has no real or substantial relation to those objects, or is a palpable invasion of rights secured by the fundamental law, it is the duty of the courts to so adjudge, and thereby give effect to the constitution.

Keeping in view these principles, as governing the relations of the judicial and legislative departments of government with each other, it is difficult to perceive any ground for the judiciary to declare that the prohibition by Kansas of the manufacture or sale, within her limits, of intoxicating liquors for general use there as a beverage, is not fairly adapted to the end of protecting the community against the evils which confessedly result from the excessive use of ardent spirits. There is no justification for holding that the state, under the guise merely of police regulations, is here aiming to deprive the citizen of his constitutional rights; for we cannot shut out of view the fact, within the knowledge of all, that the public health, the public morals, and the public safety, may be endangered by the general use of intoxicating drinks; nor the fact established by statistics accessible to every one, that the idleness, disorder, pauperism, and crime existing in the country, are, in some degree at least, traceable to this evil. If, therefore, a state deems the absolute prohibition of the manufacture and sale within her limits, of intoxicating liquors, for other than medical, scientific, and mechanical purposes, to be necessary to the peace and security of society, the courts cannot, without usurping legislative functions, override the will of the people as thus expressed by their chosen representatives. They have nothing to do with the mere policy of legislation. Indeed, it is a fundamental principle in our institutions, indispensable to the preservation of public liberty, that one of the separate departments of government shall not usurp powers committed by the constitution to another department. And so, if, in the judgment of the legislature, the manufacture of intoxicating liquors for the maker's own use, as a beverage, would tend to cripple, if it did not defeat, the efforts to guard the community against the evils attending the excessive use of such liquors, it is not for the courts, upon their views as to what is best and safest for the community, to disregard the legislative determination of that question. So far from such a regulation having no relation to the general end sought to be accomplished, the entire scheme of prohibition, as embodied in the constitution and laws of Kansas, might fail, if the right of each citizen to manufacture intoxicating liquors for his own use as a beverage were recognized. Such a right does not inhere in citizenship. Nor can it be said that government interferes with or impairs any one's constitutional rights of liberty or of property, when it determines that the manufacture and sale of intoxicating drinks, for general or individual use, as a beverage, are, or may become, hurtful to society, and constitute, therefore, a business in which no one may lawfully engage. Those rights are best secured, in our government, by the observance, upon the part of all, of such regulations as are established by competent authority to promote the common good. No one may rightfully do that which the law-making power, upon reasonable grounds, declares to be prejudicial to the general welfare.

JUSTICE FIELD wrote a dissenting opinion.

I concur in the judgment rendered by this court in the first two cases,—those coming from the supreme court of Kansas. I dissent from the judgment in the last case, the one coming from the circuit court of the United States. I agree to so much of the opinion as asserts that there is nothing in the constitution or laws of the United States affecting the validity of the act of Kansas prohibiting the sale of intoxicating liquors manufactured in the state, except for the purposes mentioned. But I am not prepared to say that the state can prohibit the manufacture of such liquors within its limits if they are intended for exportation, or forbid their sale within its limits, under proper regulations for the protection of the health and morals of the people, if congress has authorized their importation, though the act of Kansas is broad enough to include both such manufacture and sale. The right to import an article of merchandise, recognized as such by the commercial world, whether the right be given by act of congress or by treaty with a foreign country, would seem necessarily to carry the right to sell the article when imported.

If one state can forbid the sale within its limits of an imported article, so may all the states, each selecting a different article. There would then be little uniformity of regulations with respect to articles of foreign commerce imported into different states, and the same may be also said of regulations with respect to articles of interstate commerce. And we know it was one of the objects of the formation of the federal constitution to secure uniformity of commercial regulations against discriminating state legislation. The construction of the commercial clause of the constitution, upon which the *License Cases* were decided, appears to me to have been substantially abandoned in later decisions. I make this reservation that I may not hereafter be deemed concluded by a general concurrence in the opinion of the majority.

It is plain that great wrong will often be done to manufacturers of liquors if legislation like that embodied in this thirteenth section can be upheld. The supreme court of Kansas admits that the legislature of the state, in destroying the values of such kinds of property, may have gone to the utmost verge of constitutional authority. In my opinion it has passed beyond that verge, and crossed the line which separates regulation from confiscation.

FOR DISCUSSION

The majority suggests that there are limits to government and regulation beyond which it may not go. What limits are there, and who should be the judge of this? Should the judiciary make this decision, or should Congress or state legislatures make this call? If the Court is to make this decision and apply the Constitution to regulating economic activity, what type of test should it use, and how carefully should it scrutinize acts passed by elected bodies?

ALLGEYER V. STATE OF LOUISIANA

165 U.S. 578, 17 S.Ct. 427, 41 L.Ed. 832 (1897)

The state of Louisiana enacted a law preventing out-of-state insurance corporations from doing business within its borders unless licensed to do so. An individual who had contracted with an unlicensed out-of-state business for insurance challenged the law as a violation of liberty of contract under the Fourteenth Amendment.

Vote: 9–0

JUSTICE PECKHAM delivered the opinion for the Court.

There is no doubt of the power of the state to prohibit foreign insurance companies from doing business within its limits. The state can impose such conditions as it pleases upon the doing of any business by those companies within its borders, and unless the conditions be complied with the prohibition may be absolute.

A conditional prohibition in regard to foreign insurance companies doing business within the state of Louisiana is to be found in article 236 of the constitution of that state, which reads as follows: "No foreign corporation shall do any business in this state without having one or more known places of business and an authorized agent or agents in the state upon whom process may be served."

It is not claimed in this suit that the Atlantic Mutual Insurance Company has violated this provision of the constitution by doing business within the state.

"The question presented is the simple proposition whether under the act a party while in the state can insure property in Louisiana in a foreign insurance company, which has not complied with the laws of the state, under an open policy,-the special contract of insurance and the open policy being contracts made and entered into beyond the limits of the state."

"We are not dealing with the contract. If it be legal in New York, it is valid elsewhere. We are concerned only with the fact of its having been entered into by a citizen of Louisiana while within her limits affecting property within her territorial limits. It is the act of the party, and not the contract, which we are to consider. The defendants who made the contract did so while they were in the state, and it had reference to property located within the state. Such a contract is in violation of the laws of the state, and the defendants who made it were within the jurisdiction of the state, and must be necessarily subject to its penalties, unless there is some inhibition in the federal or state constitution, or that it violates, one of those inalienable rights elating to persons and property that are inherent, although not expressed, in the organic law. It does not forbid the carrying on by the insurance company of its legalized business within the state. It is a means of preventing its doing so without subscribing to certain conditions which are recognized as legitimate and proper. It does not destroy the constitutional right of the citizens of New York to do business within the state of Louisiana or of the citizens of Louisiana from insuring property. It says to the citizens of New York engaged in insurance business that they must, like its own citizens, pay a license and have an authorized agent in the state as prerequisite to their doing said business within its state, and says to its own citizens: You shall not make a contract while in the state with any foreign insurance company which has not complied with the laws. You shall not in this manner contravene the public policy of the state in aiding and assisting in the violation of the laws of the state. The sovereignty of the state would be a mockery if it had not the power to compel its citizens to respect its laws."

"There is in the statute an apparent interference with the liberty of defendants in restricting their rights to place insurance on property of their own whenever and in what company they desired, but in exercising this liberty they would interfere with the policy of the state that forbids insurance companies which have not complied with the laws of the state from doing business within its limits. Individual liberty of action must give way to the greater right of the collective people in the assertion of well-defined policy, designed and intended for the general welfare."

Upon the question as to the place where the contract was made, Mr. Justice White, speaking for the court, said: "It is claimed, however, that, irrespective of this [commerce] clause, the conviction here was illegal—first, because the statute is by its terms invalid, in that it undertakes to forbid the procurement of a contract outside of the state; and, secondly, because the evidence shows that the contract was in fact entered into without the territory of California. The language of the Statute is not fairly open to this construction. It punishes 'every person who in this state procures or agrees to procure for a resident of this state any insurance,' etc. The words 'who in this state' cannot be read out of the law in order to nullify it under the constitution."

In the case before us the contract was made beyond the territory of the state of Louisiana, and the only thing that the facts show was done within that state was the mailing of a letter of notification, as above mentioned, which was done after the principal contract had been made.

The distinction between a contract made within and that made without the state is again referred to by Mr. Justice White in the same case, as follows: "It is said that the right of a citizen to contract for insurance for himself is guarantied by the fourteenth amendment, and that, therefore, he cannot be deprived by the state of the capacity to so contract through an agent. The fourteenth amendment, however, does not guaranty the citizen the right to make within his state, either directly or indirectly, a contract, the making whereof is constitutionally forbidden by the state. The proposition that, because a citizen might make such a contract for himself beyond the confines of his state, therefore he might authorize an agent to violate in his behalf the laws of his state, within her own limits, involves a clear non sequitur, and ignores the vital distinction between acts done within and acts done beyond a state's jurisdiction."

We have, then, a contract which it is conceded was made outside and beyond the limits of the jurisdiction of the state of Louisiana, being made and to be performed within the state of New York, where the premiums were to be paid, and losses, if any, adjusted. The letter of notification did not constitute a contract made or entered into within the state of Louisiana. It was but the performance of an act rendered necessary by the provisions of the contract already made between the parties outside of the state. It was a mere notification that the contract already in existence would attach to that particular property. In any event, the contract was made in New York, outside of the jurisdiction of Louisiana, even though the policy was not to attach to the particular property until the notification was sent.

It is natural that the state court should have remarked that there is in this "statute an apparent interference with the liberty of defendants in restricting their rights to place insurance on property of their own whenever and in what company they desired." Such interference is not only apparent, but it is real, and we do not think that it is justified for the purpose of upholding what the state says is its policy with regard to foreign insurance companies which had not complied with the laws of the state for doing business within its limits. In this case the company did no business within the state, and the contracts were not therein made.

The supreme court of Louisiana says that the act of writing within that state the letter of notification was an act therein done to effect an insurance on property then in the state, in a marine insurance company which had not complied with its laws, and such act was therefore prohibited by the statute. As so construed, we think the statute is a violation of the fourteenth amendment of the federal constitution, in that it deprives the defendants of their liberty without due process of law. The statute which forbids such act does not become due process of law, because it is inconsistent with the provisions of the constitution of the Union. The "liberty" mentioned in that amendment means, not only the right of the citizen to be free from the mere physical restraint of his person, as by incarceration, but the term is deemed to embrace the right of the citizen to be free in the enjoyment of all his faculties; to be free to use them in all lawful ways; to live and work where he will; to earn his livelihood by any lawful calling; to pursue any livelihood or avocation; and for that purpose to enter into all contracts which may be proper, necessary, and essential to his carrying out to a successful conclusion the purposes above mentioned.

It was said by Mr. Justice Bradley, in *Butchers' Union Slaughterhouse Co. v. Crescent City Live-Stock Landing Co.*, 111 U.S. 746 (1884), in the course of his concurring opinion in that case, that "the right to follow any of the common occupations of life is an inalienable right. It was formulated as such under the phrase 'pursuit of happiness' in the Declaration of Independence, which commenced with the fundamental proposition that 'all men are created equal; that they are endowed by their Creator with certain inalienable rights; that among these are life, liberty, and the pursuit of happiness.' This right is a large ingredient in the civil liberty of the citizen." Again, the learned justice said: "I hold that the liberty of pursuit—the right to follow any of the ordinary callings of life—is one of the privileges of a citizen of the United States." And again: "But if it does not abridge the privileges and immunities of a citizen of the United States to prohibit him from pursuing his chosen calling, and giving to others the exclusive right of pursuing it, it certainly does deprive him (to a certain extent) of his liberty; for it takes from him the freedom of adopting and following the pursuit which he prefers, which, as already intimated, is a material part of the liberty of the citizen." It is true that these remarks were made in regard to questions of monopoly, but they well describe the rights which are covered by the word "liberty," as contained in the fourteenth amendment.

Has not a citizen of a state, under the provisions of the federal constitution above mentioned, a right to contract outside of the state for insurance on his property—a right of which state legislation cannot deprive him? We are not alluding to acts done within the state by an insurance company or its agents doing business therein, which are in violation of the state statutes. Such acts come within the principle of [*Hooper v. California*, 155 U.S. 648 (1895)], and would be controlled by it. When we speak of the liberty to contract for insurance or to do an act to effectuate such a contract already existing, we refer to and have in mind the facts of this case, where the contract was made outside the state, and as such was a valid and proper contract. The act done within the limits of the state, under the circumstances of this case and for the purpose therein mentioned, we hold a proper act—one which the defendants were at liberty to perform, and which the state legislature had no right to prevent, at least with reference to the federal constitution. To deprive the citizen of such a right as herein described without due process of law is illegal. Such a statute as this in question is not due process of law, because it prohibits an act which under the federal constitution the defendants had a right to perform. This does not interfere in any way with the acknowledged right of the state to enact such legislation in the legitimate exercise of its police or other powers as to it may seem proper. In the exercise of such right, however, care must be taken not to infringe upon those other rights of the citizen which are protected by the federal constitution.

In the privilege of pursuing an ordinary calling or trade, and of acquiring, holding, and selling property, must be embraced the right to make all proper contracts in relation thereto; and although it may be conceded that this right to contract in relation to persons or property or to do business within the jurisdiction of the state may be regulated, and sometimes prohibited, when the contracts or business conflict with the policy of the state as contained in its statutes, yet the power does not and cannot extend to prohibiting a citizen from making contracts of the nature involved in this case outside of the limits and jurisdiction of the state, and which are also to be performed outside of such jurisdiction; nor can the state legally prohibit its citizens from doing such an act as writing this letter of notification, even though the property which is the subject of the insurance may at the time when such insurance attaches be within the limits of the state. The mere fact that a citizen may be within the limits of a particular state does not prevent his making a contract outside its limits while he himself remains within it. The contract in this case was thus made. It was a valid contract, made outside of the state, to be performed outside of the state, although the subject was property temporarily within the state. As the contract was valid in the place where made and where it was to be performed, the party to the contract, upon whom is devolved the right or duty to send the notification in order that the insurance provided for by the contract may attach to the property specified in the shipment mentioned in the notice, must have the liberty to do that act and to give that notification within the limits of the state, any prohibition of the state statute to the contrary notwithstanding. The giving of the notice is a mere collateral matter. It is not the contract itself, but is an act performed pursuant to a valid contract, which the state had no right or jurisdiction to prevent its citizen from making outside the limits of the state.

In such a case as the facts here present, the policy of the state in forbidding insurance companies which had not complied with the laws of the state from doing business within its limits cannot be so carried out as to prevent the citizen from writing such a letter of notification as was written by the plaintiffs in error in the state of Louisiana, when it is written pursuant to a valid contract made outside the state, and with reference to a company which is not doing business within its limits.

For these reasons we think the statute in question was a violation of the federal constitution, and afforded no justification for the judgment awarded by that court against the plaintiffs in error. That judgment must therefore be reversed, and the case remanded to the supreme court of Louisiana for further proceedings not inconsistent with this opinion.

FOR DISCUSSION

Do you think the Court is correct in effectively asserting that employees and employers have entered into a contract for employment that is the product of free and equal negotiations? Should the government ever second-guess or regulate workplace conditions among adults?

LOCHNER V. NEW YORK

198 U.S. 45, 25 S.Ct. 539, 49 L.Ed. 937 (1905)

The state of New York enacted a law prescribing the maximum working hours for individuals in the baking industry. The law was challenged as a violation of the Fourteenth Amendment.

Vote: 5–4

JUSTICE PECKHAM delivered the opinion of the Court.

The indictment, it will be seen, charges that the plaintiff in error violated the 110th section of article 8, chapter 415, of the Laws of 1897, known as the labor law of the state of New York, in that he wrongfully and unlawfully required and permitted an employee working for him to work more than sixty hours in one week. There is nothing in any of the opinions delivered in this case, either in the supreme court or the court of appeals of the state, which construes the section, in using the word "required," as referring to any physical force being used to obtain the labor of an employee. It is assumed that the word means nothing more than the requirement arising from voluntary contract for such labor in excess of the number of hours specified in the statute. There is no pretense in any of the opinions that the statute was intended to meet a case of involuntary labor in any form. All the opinions assume that there is no real distinction, so far as this question is concerned, between the words "required" and " 'permitted." The mandate of the statute, that "no employee shall be required or permitted to work," is the substantial equivalent of an enactment that "no employee shall contract or agree to work," more than ten hours per day; and, as there is no provision for special emergencies, the statute is mandatory in all cases. It is not an act merely fixing the number of hours which shall constitute a legal day's work, but an absolute prohibition upon the employer permitting, under any circumstances, more than ten hours' work to be done in his establishment. The employee may desire to earn the extra money which would arise from his working more than the prescribed time, but this statute forbids the employer from permitting the employee to earn it.

The statute necessarily interferes with the right of contract between the employer and employees, concerning the number of hours in which the latter may labor in the bakery of the employer. The general right to make a contract in relation to his business is part of the liberty of the individual protected by the 14th Amendment of the Federal Constitution. Under that provision no state can deprive any person of life, liberty, or property without due process of law. The right to purchase or to sell labor is part of the liberty protected by this amendment, unless there are circumstances which exclude the right. There are, however, certain powers, existing in the sovereignty of each state in the Union, somewhat vaguely termed police powers, the exact description and limitation of which have not been attempted by the courts. Those powers, broadly stated, and without, at present, any attempt at a more specific limitation, relate to the safety, health, morals, and general welfare of the public. Both property and liberty are held on such reasonable conditions as may be imposed by the governing power of the state in the exercise of those powers, and with such conditions the 14th Amendment was not designed to interfere.

The state, therefore, has power to prevent the individual from making certain kinds of contracts, and in regard to them the Federal Constitution offers no protection. If the contract be one which the state, in the legitimate exercise of its police power, has the right to prohibit, it is not prevented from prohibiting it by the 14th Amendment. Contracts in violation of a statute, either of the Federal or state government, or a contract to let one's property for immoral purposes, or to do any other unlawful act, could obtain no protection from the Federal Constitution, as coming under the liberty of person or of free contract. Therefore, when the state, by its legislature, in the assumed exercise of its police powers, has passed an act which seriously limits the right to labor or the right of contract in regard to their means of livelihood between persons who are *sui juris* (both employer and employee), it becomes of great importance to determine which shall prevail—the right of the individual to labor for such time as he may choose, or the right of the state to prevent the individual from laboring, or from entering into any contract to labor, beyond a certain time prescribed by the state.

The question whether this act is valid as a labor law, pure and simple, may be dismissed in a few words. There is no reasonable ground for interfering with the liberty of person or the right of free contract, by determining the hours of labor, in the occupation of a baker. There is no contention that bakers as a class are not equal in intelligence and capacity to men in other trades or manual occupations, or that they are not able to assert their rights and care for themselves without the protecting arm of the state, interfering with their independence of judgment and of action. They are in no sense wards of the state. Viewed in the light of a purely labor law, with no reference whatever to the question of health, we think that a law like the one before us involves neither the safety, the morals, nor the welfare, of the public, and that the interest of the public is not in the slightest degree affected by such an act. The law must be upheld, if at all, as a law pertaining to the health of the individual engaged in the occupation of a baker. It does not affect any other portion of the public than those who are engaged in that occupation. Clean and wholesome bread does not depend upon whether the baker works but ten hours per day or only sixty hours a week. The limitation of the hours of labor does not come within the police power on that ground.

It is a question of which of two powers or rights shall prevail—the power of the state to legislate or the right of the individual to liberty of person and freedom of contract. The mere assertion that the subject relates, though but in a remote degree, to the public health, does not necessarily render the enactment valid. The act must have a more direct relation, as a means to an end, and the end itself must be appropriate and legitimate, before an act can be held to be valid which interferes with the general right of an individual to be free in his person and in his power to contract in relation to his own labor.

We think the limit of the police power has been reached and passed in this case. There is, in our judgment, no reasonable foundation for holding this to be necessary or appropriate as a health law to safeguard the public health, or the health of the individuals who are following the trade of a baker.

Some occupations are more healthy than others, but we think there are none which might not come under the power of the legislature to supervise and control the hours of working therein, if the mere fact that the occupation is not absolutely and perfectly healthy is to confer that right upon the legislative department of the government. It might be safely affirmed that almost all occupations more or less affect the health. There must be more than the mere fact of the possible existence of some small amount of unhealthiness to warrant legislative interference with liberty. It is unfortunately true that labor, even in any department, may possibly carry with it the seeds of unhealthiness. But are we all, on that account, at the mercy of legislative majorities? A printer, a tinsmith, a locksmith, a carpenter, a cabinetmaker, a dry goods clerk, a bank's, a lawyer's, or a physician's clerk, or a clerk in almost any kind of business, would all come under the power of the legislature, on this assumption. No trade, no occupation, no mode of earning one's living, could escape this all-pervading power, and the acts of the legislature in limiting the hours of labor in all employments would be valid, although such limitation might seriously cripple the ability of the laborer to support himself and his family

It is impossible for us to shut our eyes to the fact that many of the laws of this character, while passed under what is claimed to be the police power for the purpose of protecting the public health or welfare, are, in reality, passed from other motives. We are justified in saying so when, from the character of the law and the subject upon which it legislates, it is apparent that the public health or welfare bears but the most remote relation to the law. The purpose of a statute must be determined from the natural and legal effect of the language employed; and whether it is or is not repugnant to the Constitution of the United States must be determined from the natural effect of such statutes when put into operation, and not from their proclaimed purpose.

It is manifest to us that the limitation of the hours of labor as provided for in this section of the statute under which the indictment was found, and the plaintiff in error convicted, has no such direct relation to, and no such substantial effect upon, the health of the employee, as to justify us in regarding the section as really a health law. It seems to us that the real object and purpose were simply to regulate the hours of labor between the master and his employees (all being men, *Sui juris*), in a private business, not dangerous in any degree to morals, or in any real and substantial degree to the health of the employees. Under such circumstances the freedom of master and employee to contract with each other in relation to their employment, and in defining the same, cannot be prohibited or interfered with, without violating the Federal Constitution.

The judgment of the Court of Appeals of New York, as well as that of the Supreme Court and of the County Court of Oneida County, must be reversed and the case remanded to the County Court for further proceedings not inconsistent with this opinion.

Reversed.

JUSTICE HOLMES dissenting:

I regret sincerely that I am unable to agree with the judgment in this case, and that I think it my duty to express my dissent.

This case is decided upon an economic theory which a large part of the country does not entertain. If it were a question whether I agreed with that theory, I should desire to study it further and long before making up my mind. But I do not conceive that to be my duty, because I strongly believe that my agreement or disagreement has nothing to do with the right of a majority to embody their opinions in law. It is settled by various decisions of this court that state constitutions and state laws may regulate life in many ways which we as legislators might think as injudicious, or if you like as tyrannical, as this, and which, equally with this, interfere with the liberty to contract. Sunday laws and usury laws are ancient examples. A more modern one is the prohibition of lotteries. The liberty of the citizen to do as he likes so long as he does not interfere with the liberty of others to do the same, which has been a shibboleth for some well-known writers, is interfered with by school laws, by the Post Office, by every state or municipal institution which takes his money for purposes thought desirable, whether he likes it or not. The 14th Amendment does not enact Mr. Herbert Spencer's *Social Statics*. The other day we sustained the Massachusetts vaccination law. Two years ago we upheld the prohibition of sales of stock on margins, or for future delivery, in the Constitution of California. The decision sustaining an eight-hour law for miners is still recent. Some of these laws embody convictions or prejudices which judges are likely to share. Some may not. But a Constitution is not intended to embody a particular economic theory, whether of paternalism and the organic relation of the citizen to the state or of *laissez faire.* It is made for people of fundamentally differing views, and the accident of our finding certain opinions natural and familiar, or novel, and even shocking, ought not to conclude our judgment upon the question whether statutes embodying them conflict with the Constitution of the United States.

General propositions do not decide concrete cases. The decision will depend on a judgment or intuition more subtle than any articulate major premise. But I think that the proposition just stated, if it is accepted, will carry us far toward the end. Every opinion tends to become a law. I think that the word "liberty," in the 14th Amendment, is perverted when it is held to prevent the natural outcome of a dominant opinion, unless it can be said that a rational and fair man necessarily would admit that the statute proposed would infringe fundamental principles as they have been understood by the traditions of our people and our law. It does not need research to show that no such sweeping condemnation can be passed upon the statute before us. A reasonable man might think it a proper measure on the score of health. Men whom I certainly could not pronounce unreasonable would uphold it as a first installment of a general regulation of the hours of work. Whether in the latter aspect it would be open to the charge of inequality I think it unnecessary to discuss.

JUSTICE HARLAN, with whom JUSTICES WHITE and DAY concurred, dissenting.

While this court has not attempted to mark the precise boundaries of what is called the police power of the state, the existence of the power has been uniformly recognized, equally by the Federal and State courts.

All the cases agree that this power extends at least to the protection of the lives, the health, and the safety of the public against the injurious exercise by any citizen of his own rights.

Speaking generally, the state, in the exercise of its powers, may not unduly interfere with the right of the citizen to enter into contracts that may be necessary and essential in the enjoyment of the inherent rights belonging to everyone, among which rights is the right "to be free in the enjoyment of all his faculties, to be free to use them in all lawful ways, to live and work where he will, to earn his livelihood by any lawful calling, to pursue any livelihood or avocation." This was declared in *Allgeyer* v. *Louisiana,* 165 US 578 (1897). But in the same case it was conceded that the right to contract in relation to persons and property, or to do business, within a state, may be "regulated, and sometimes prohibited, when the contracts or business conflict with the policy of the state as contained in its statutes."

'This right of contract, however, is itself subject to certain limitations which the state may lawfully impose in the exercise of its police powers. While this power is inherent in all governments, it has doubtless been greatly expanded in its application during the past century, owing to an enormous increase in the number of occupations which are dangerous, or so far detrimental, to the health of employees as to demand special precautions for their well-being and protection, or the safety of adjacent property. While this court has held . . . that the police power cannot be put forward as an excuse for oppressive and unjust legislation, it may be lawfully resorted to for the purpose of preserving the public health, safety, or morals, or the abatement of public nuisances; and a large discretion "is necessarily vested in the legislature to determine, not only what the interests of the public required, but what measures are necessary for the protection of such interests."

I take it to be firmly established that what is called the liberty of contract may, within certain limits, be subjected to regulations designed and calculated to promote the general welfare, or to guard the public health, the public morals, or the public safety. "The liberty secured by the Constitution of the United States to every person within its jurisdiction does not import," this court has recently said, "an absolute right in each person to be at all times and in all circumstances wholly freed from restraint. There are manifold restraints to which every person is necessarily subject for the common good." *Jacobson v. Massachusetts*, 97 U.S. 11 (1905).

Granting, then, that there is a liberty of contract which cannot be violated even under the sanction of direct legislative enactment, but assuming, as according to settled law we may assume, that such liberty of contract is subject to such regulations as the state may reasonably prescribe for the common good and the well-being of society, what are the conditions under which the judiciary may declare such regulations to be in excess of legislative authority and void? Upon this point there is no room for dispute; for the rule is universal that a legislative enactment, Federal or state, is never to be disregarded or held invalid unless it be, beyond question, plainly and palpably in excess of legislative power. In *Jacobson* v. *Massachusetts* . . . we said that the power of the courts to review legislative action in respect of a matter affecting the general welfare exists *only* "when that which the legislature has done comes within the rule that, if a statute purporting to have been enacted to protect the public health, the public morals, or the public safety has no real or substantial relation to those objects, or is, beyond all question, a plain, palpable invasion of rights secured by the fundamental law," citing *Mugler* v. *Kansas*, 123 U.S. 623 (1887). If there be doubt as to the validity of the statute, that doubt must therefore be resolved in favor of its validity, and the courts must keep their hands off, leaving the legislature to meet the responsibility for unwise legislation. If the end which the legislature seeks to accomplish be one to which its power extends, and if the means employed to that end, although not the wisest or best, are yet not plainly and palpably unauthorized by law, then the court cannot interfere. In other words, when the validity of a statute is questioned, the burden of proof, so to speak, is upon those who assert it to be unconstitutional.

Let these principles be applied to the present case. By the statute in question it is provided that "no employee shall be required, or permitted, to work in a biscuit, bread, or cake bakery, or confectionery establishment, more than sixty hours in any one week, or more than ten hours in any one day, unless for the purpose of making a shorter work day on the last day of the week; nor more hours in any one week than will make an average of ten hours per day for the number of days during such week in which such employee shall work."

It is plain that this statute was enacted in order to protect the physical well-being of those who work in bakery and confectionery establishments. It may be that the statute had its origin, in part, in the belief that employers and employees in such establishments were not upon an equal footing, and that the necessities of the latter often compelled them to submit to such exactions as unduly taxed their strength. Be this as it may, the statute must be taken as expressing the belief of the people of New York that, as a general rule, and in the case of the average man, labor in excess of sixty hours during a week in such establishments may endanger the health of those who thus labor. Whether or not this be wise legislation it is not the province of the court to inquire. Under our systems of government the courts are not concerned with the wisdom or policy of legislation. So that, in determining the question of power to interfere with liberty of contract, the court may inquire whether the means devised by the state are germane to an end which may be lawfully accomplished and have a real or substantial relation to the protection of health, as involved in the daily work of the persons, male and female, engaged in bakery and confectionery establishments. But when this inquiry is entered upon I find it impossible, in view of common experience, to say that there is here no real or substantial relation between the means employed by the state and the end sought to be accomplished by its legislation. Nor can I say that the statute has no appropriate or direct connection with that protection to health which each state owes to her citizens; or that it is not promotive of the health of the employees in question; or that the regulation prescribed by the state is utterly unreasonable and extravagant or wholly arbitrary. Still less can I say that the statute is, beyond question, a plain, palpable invasion of rights secured by the fundamental law. Therefore I submit that this court will transcend its functions if it assumes to annul the statute of New York. It must be remembered that this statute does not apply to all kinds of business. It applies only to work in bakery and confectionery establishments, in which, as all know, the air constantly breathed by workmen is not as pure and healthful as that to be found in some other establishments or out of doors.

When this court had before it the question of the constitutionality of a statute of Kansas making it a criminal offense for a contractor for public work to permit or require his employees to perform labor upon such work in excess of eight hours each day, it was contended that the statute was in derogation of the liberty both of employees and employer. It was further contended that the Kansas statute was mischievous in its tendencies. This court, while disposing of the question only as it affected public work, held that the Kansas statute was not void under the 14th Amendment. But it took occasion to say what may well be here repeated: "The responsibility therefor rests upon legislators, not upon the courts. No evils arising from such legislation could be more far reaching than those that might come to our system of government if the judiciary, abandoning the sphere assigned to it by the fundamental law, should enter the domain of legislation, and upon grounds merely of justice or reason or wisdom annul statutes that had received the sanction of the people's representatives. We are reminded by counsel that it is the solemn duty of the courts in cases before them to guard the constitutional rights of the citizen against merely arbitrary power. That is unquestionably true. But it is equally true—indeed, the public interests imperatively demand—that legislative enactments should be recognized and enforced by the courts as embodying the will of the people, unless they are plainly and palpably beyond all question in violation of the fundamental law of the Constitution."

The judgment, in my opinion, should be affirmed.

FOR DISCUSSION

The dissents accuse the majority of rejecting the New York legislature's opinion about the wisdom of economic legislation and substituting their own opinions. Do you think this is a fair assessment of the majority opinion? Is this substitution of judicial opinion about legislation the core of what judicial review is? Is this what substantive due process is? Is this what judicial activism or legislating from the bench is?

MULLER V. OREGON

208 U.S. 412, 28 S.Ct. 324, 52 L.Ed. 551 (1908)

The state of Oregon enacted a law limiting the number of hours per week women could work. The law was justified as necessary to protect their health. The law was challenged as a violation of the Fourteenth Amendment.

Vote: 9–0

JUSTICE BREWER delivered the opinion of the Court:

On February 19, 1903, the legislature of the state of Oregon passed an act, the first section of which is in these words:

> "Sec. 1. That no female (shall) be employed in any mechanical establishment, or factory, or laundry in this state more than ten hours during any one day. The hours of work may be so arranged as to permit the employment of females at any time so that they shall not work more than ten hours during the twenty-four hours of any one day."

Sec. 3 made a violation of the provisions of the prior sections a misdemeanor subject to a fine of not less than $10 nor more than $25. On September 18, 1905, an information was filed in the circuit court of the state for the county of Multnomah, charging that the defendant "on the 4th day of September, A.D. 1905, in the county of Multnomah and state of Oregon, then and there being the owner of a laundry, known as the Grand Laundry, in the city of Portland, and the employer of females therein, did then and there unlawfully permit and suffer one Joe Haselbock, he, the said Joe Haselbock, then and there being an overseer, superintendent, and agent of said Curt Muller, in the said Grand Laundry, to require a female, to wit, one Mrs. E. Gotcher, to work more than ten hours in said laundry on said 4th day of September, A. D. 1905, contrary to the statutes in such cases made and provided, and against the peace and dignity of the state of Oregon."

A trial resulted in a verdict against the defendant, who was sentenced to pay a fine of $10. The supreme court of the state affirmed the conviction, whereupon the case was brought here on writ of error.

The single question is the constitutionality of the statute under which the defendant was convicted, so far as it affects the work of a female in a laundry. That it does not conflict with any provisions of the state Constitution is settled by the decision of the supreme court of the state. The contentions of the defendant, now plaintiff in error, are thus stated in his brief:

(1) Because the statute attempts to prevent persons *sui juris* from making their own contracts, and thus violates the provisions of the 14th Amendment, as follows:

No state shall make or enforce any law which shall abridge the privileges or immunities of citizens of the United States; nor shall any state deprive any person of life, liberty, or property, without due process of law; nor deny to any person within its jurisdiction the equal protection of the laws.

(2) Because the statute does not apply equally to all persons similarly situated, and is class legislation.

(3) The statute is not a valid exercise of the police power. The kinds of work prescribed are not unlawful, nor are they declared to be immoral or dangerous to the public health; nor can such a law be sustained on the ground that it is designed to protect women on account of their sex. There is no necessary or reasonable connection between the limitation prescribed by the act and the public health, safety, or welfare.

It is the law of Oregon that women, whether married or single, have equal contractual and personal rights with men. . . . It thus appears that, putting to one side the elective franchise, in the matter of personal and contractual rights they stand on the same plane as the other sex. Their rights in these respects can no more be infringed than the equal rights of their brothers. We held in *Lochner v. New York* [,198 US 45 (1905),] that a law providing that no laborer shall be required or permitted to work in bakeries more than sixty hours in a week or ten hours in a day was not as to men a legitimate exercise of the police power of the state, but an unreasonable, unnecessary, and arbitrary interference with the right and liberty of the individual to contract in relation to his labor, and as such was in conflict with, and void under, the Federal Constitution. That decision is invoked by plaintiff in error as decisive of the question before us. But this assumes that the difference between the sexes does not justify a different rule respecting a restriction of the hours of labor.

It is undoubtedly true, as more than once declared by this court, that the general right to contract in relation to one's business is part of the liberty of the individual, protected by the 14th Amendment to the Federal Constitution; yet it is equally well settled that this liberty is not absolute and extending to all contracts, and that a state may, without conflicting with the provisions of the 14th Amendment, restrict in many respects the individual's power of contract.

That woman's physical structure and the performance of maternal functions place her at a disadvantage in the struggle for subsistence is obvious. This is especially true when the burdens of motherhood are upon her. Even when they are not, by abundant testimony of the medical fraternity, continuance for a long time on her feet at work, repeating this from day to day, tends to injurious effects upon the body, and, as healthy mothers are essential to vigorous offspring, the physical well-being of woman becomes an object of public interest and care in order to preserve the strength and vigor of the race.

Still again, history discloses the fact that woman has always been dependent upon man. He established his control at the outset by superior physical strength, and this control in various forms, with diminishing intensity, has continued to the present. As minors, though not to the same extent, she has been looked upon in the courts as needing especial care that her rights may be preserved. Education was long denied her, and while now the doors of the schoolroom are opened and her opportunities for acquiring knowledge are great, yet even with that and the consequent increase of capacity for business affairs it is still true that in the struggle for subsistence she is not an equal competitor with her brother. Though limitations upon personal and contractual rights may be removed by legislation, there is that in her disposition and habits of life which will operate against a full assertion of those rights. She will still be where some legislation to protect her seems necessary to secure a real equality of right. Doubtless there are individual exceptions, and there are many respects in which she has an advantage over him; but looking at it from the viewpoint of the effort to maintain an independent position in life, she is not upon an equality. Differentiated by these matters from the other sex, she is properly placed in a class by herself, and legislation designed for her protection may be sustained, even when like legislation is not necessary for men, and could not be sustained. It is impossible to close one's eyes to the fact that she still looks to her brother and depends upon him. Even though all restrictions on political, personal, and contractual rights were taken away, and she stood, so far as statutes are concerned, upon an absolutely equal plane with him, it would still be true that she is so constituted that she will rest upon and look to him for protection; that her physical structure and a proper discharge of her maternal functions—having in view not merely her own health, but the well-being of the race—justify legislation to protect her from the greed as well as the passion of man. The limitations which this statute places upon her contractual powers, upon her right to agree with her employer as to the time she shall labor, are not imposed solely for her benefit, but also largely for the benefit of all. Many words cannot make this plainer. The two sexes differ in structure of body, in the functions to be performed by each, in the amount of physical strength, in the capacity for long continued labor, particularly when done standing, the influence of vigorous health upon the future well-being of the race, the self-reliance which enables one to assert full rights, and in the capacity to maintain the struggle for subsistence. This difference justifies a difference in legislation, and upholds that which is designed to compensate for some of the burdens which rest upon her.

We have not referred in this discussion to the denial of the elective franchise in the state of Oregon, for while that may disclose a lack of political equality in all things with her brother, that is not of itself decisive. The reason runs deeper, and rests in the inherent difference between the two sexes, and in the different functions in life which they perform.

For these reasons, and without questioning in any respect the decision in *Lochner v. New York*, we are of the opinion that it cannot be adjudged that the act in question is in conflict with the Federal Constitution, so far as it respects the work of a female in a laundry, and the judgment of the Supreme Court of Oregon is affirmed.

FOR DISCUSSION

How do you distinguish the holding in *Muller* from that of *Lochner?* Is there a persuasive reason for distinguishing the two and rejecting a state law in one instance but upholding it in another?

ADKINS V. CHILDREN'S HOSPITAL OF THE DISTRICT OF COLUMBIA

261 U.S. 525, 43 S.Ct. 394, 67 L.Ed. 785 (1923)

The Alabama constitution provided that each county receive one state representative. This mandate resulted in some districts having more than forty times the voters as others. This apportionment schema was challenged under the Fourteenth Amendment.

Congress passed a minimum wage for women and children working in the District of Columbia. The law was challenged as a violation of the Fifth Amendment Takings Clause.

Vote: 5–3 (Justice Brandeis not voting)

JUSTICE SUTHERLAND delivered the opinion of the Court.

The question presented for determination by these appeals is the constitutionality of the Act of September 19, 1918, providing for the fixing of minimum wages for women and children in the District of Columbia. 40 Stat. 960, c. 174.

We come then, at once, to the substantive question involved.

The judicial duty of passing upon the constitutionality of an act of Congress is one of great gravity and delicacy. The statute here in question has successfully borne the scrutiny of the legislative branch of the government, which, by enacting it, has affirmed its validity, and that determination must be given great weight. This court, by an unbroken line of decisions from Chief Justice Marshall to the present day, has steadily adhered to the rule that every possible presumption is in favor of the validity of an act of Congress until overcome beyond rational doubt. But, if by clear and indubitable demonstration a statute be opposed to the Constitution, we have no choice but to say so. The Constitution, by its own terms, is the supreme law of the land, emanating from the people, the repository of ultimate sovereignty under our form of government. A congressional statute, on the other hand, is the act of an agency of this sovereign authority, and if it conflict with the Constitution must fall; for that which is not supreme must yield to that which is. To hold it invalid (if it be invalid) is a plain exercise of the judicial power—that power vested in courts to enable them to administer justice according to law. From the authority to ascertain and determine the law in a given case, there necessarily results, in case of conflict, the duty to declare and enforce the rule of the supreme law and reject that of an inferior act of legislation which, transcending the Constitution, is of no effect and binding on no one. This is not the exercise of a substantive power to review and nullify acts of Congress, for no such substantive power exists. It is simply a necessary concomitant of the power to hear and dispose of a case or controversy properly before the court, to the determination of which must be brought the test and measure of the law.

The statute now under consideration is attacked upon the ground that it authorizes an unconstitutional interference with the freedom of contract included within the guaranties of the due process clause of the Fifth Amendment. That the right to contract about one's affairs is a part of the liberty of the individual protected by this clause is settled by the decisions of this court and is no longer open to question. Within this liberty are contracts of employment of labor. In making such contracts, generally speaking, the parties have an equal right to obtain from each other the best terms they can as the result of private bargaining.

In *Adair v. United States*, 208 U.S. 161 (1908), Mr. Justice Harlan speaking for the court said:

> The right of a person to sell his labor upon such terms as he deems proper is, in its essence, the same as the right of the purchaser of labor to prescribe the conditions upon which he will accept such labor from the person offering to sell. . . . In all such particulars the employer and the employee have

equality of right, and any legislation that disturbs that equality is an arbitrary interference with the liberty of contract which no government can legally justify in a free land.

In *Coppage v. Kansas*, 236 U.S. 1 (1915), this court, speaking through Mr. Justice Pitney, said:

Included in the right of personal liberty and the right of private property—partaking of the nature of each—is the right to make contracts for the acquisition of property. Chief among such contracts is that of personal employment, by which labor and other services are exchanged for money or other forms of property. If this right be struck down or arbitrarily interfered with, there is a substantial impairment of liberty in the long-established constitutional sense. The right is as essential to the laborer as to the capitalist, to the poor as to the rich; for the vast majority of persons have no other honest way to begin to acquire property, save by working for money.

An interference with this liberty so serious as that now under consideration, and so disturbing of equality of right must be deemed to be arbitrary, unless it be supportable as a reasonable exercise of the police power of the state.

There is, of course, no such thing as absolute freedom of contract. It is subject to a great variety of restraints. But freedom of contract is, nevertheless, the general rule and restraint the exception, and the exercise of legislative authority to abridge it can be justified only by the existence of exceptional circumstances. Whether these circumstances exist in the present case constitutes the question to be answered. It will be helpful to this end to review some of the decisions where the interference has been upheld and consider the grounds upon which they rest.

(1) *Those dealing with statutes fixing rates and charges to be exacted by businesses impressed with a public interest.* There are many cases, but it is sufficient to cite Munn v. Illinois. The power here rests upon the ground that, where property is devoted to a public use, the owner thereby in effect grants to the public an interest in the use which may be controlled by the public for the common good to the extent of the interest thus created. It is upon this theory that these statutes have been upheld, and, it may be noted in passing, so upheld, even in respect of their incidental and injurious or destructive effect upon preexisting contracts.

(2) *Statutes relating to contracts for the performance of public work.* These cases sustain such statutes as depending, not upon the right to condition private contracts, but upon the right of the government to prescribe the conditions upon which it will permit work of a public character to be done for it, or, in the case of a state, for its municipalities. We may therefore, in like manner, dismiss these decisions from consideration as inapplicable.

(3) *Statutes prescribing the character, methods, and time for payment of wages.* Under this head may be included [those] sustaining a state statute requiring coal to be measured for payment of miners' wages before screening; sustaining a Tennessee statute requiring the redemption in cash of store orders issued in payment of wages; upholding a statute regulating the time within which wages shall be paid to employees in certain specified industries; and other cases sustaining statutes of like import and effect. In none of the statutes thus sustained was the liberty of employer or employee to fix the amount of wages the one was willing to pay and the other willing to receive interfered with. Their tendency and purpose was to prevent unfair, and perhaps fraudulent, methods in the payment of wages, and in no sense can they be said to be, or to furnish a precedent for, wagefixing statutes.

(4) *Statutes fixing hours of labor.* It is upon this class that the greatest emphasis is laid in argument, and therefore, and because such cases approach most nearly the line of principle applicable to the statute here involved, we shall consider them more at length In some instances the statute limited the hours of labor for men in certain occupations, and in others it was confined in its application to women. No statute has thus far been brought to the attention of this court which by its terms, applied to all occupations.

That this constituted the basis of the decision is emphasized by the subsequent decision in *Lochner v. New York* [198 US 45 (1905),] reviewing a state statute which restricted the employment of all persons in bakeries to 10 hours in any one day. The court referred to *Holden v. Hardy*, 169 U.S. 366 (1898), and, declaring it to be inapplicable, held the statute unconstitutional as an unreasonable, unnecessary and arbitrary interference with the liberty of contract and therefore void under the Constitution.

Mr. Justice Peckham, speaking for the court, said:

> It must, of course, be conceded that there is a limit to the valid exercise of the police power by the state. There is no dispute concerning this general proposition. Otherwise the Fourteenth Amendment would have no efficacy and the legislatures of the states would have unbounded power, and it would be enough to say that any piece of legislation was enacted to conserve the morals, the health or the safety of the people; such legislation would be valid, no matter how absolutely without foundation the claim might be. The claim of the police power would be a mere pretext—become another and delusive name for the supreme sovereignty of the state to be exercised free from constitutional restraint.

And again:

> It is a question of which of two powers or rights shall prevail—the power of the state to legislate or the right of the individual to liberty of person and freedom of contract. The mere assertion that the subject relates, though but in a remote degree, to the public health does not necessarily render the enactment valid. The act must have a more direct relation, as a means to an end, and the end itself must be appropriate and legitimate, before an act can be held to be valid which interferes with the general right of an individual to be free in his person and in his power to contract in relation to his own labor.

In addition to the cases cited above, there are decisions of this court dealing with laws especially relating to hours of labor for women: *Muller v. Oregon*, 208 U.S. 412 (1908); *Riley v. Massachusetts*, 232 US 671 (1914); *Miller v. Wilson*, 236 US 373 (1915); *Bosley v. McLaughlin*, 236 US 385 (1915).

In the *Muller* Case the validity of an Oregon statute, forbidding the employment of any female in certain industries more than 10 hours during any one day was upheld. The decision proceeded upon the theory that the difference between the sexes may justify a different rule respecting hours of labor in the case of women than in the case of men. It is pointed out that these consist in differences of physical structure, especially in respect of the maternal functions, and also in the fact that historically woman has always been dependent upon man, who has established his control by superior physical strength. The Cases of *Riley*, *Miller*, and *Bosley* follow in this respect the *Muller* Case. But the ancient inequality of the sexes, otherwise than physical, as suggested in the *Muller* Case has continued "with diminishing intensity." In view of the great—not to say revolutionary—changes which have taken place since that utterance, in the contractual, political, and civil status of women, culminating in the Nineteenth Amendment, it is not unreasonable to say that these differences have now come almost, if not quite, to the vanishing point. In this aspect of the matter, while the physical differences must be recognized in appropriate cases, and legislation fixing hours or conditions of work may properly take them into account, we cannot accept the doctrine that women of mature age, *sui juris* [having legal competence], require or may be subjected to restrictions upon their liberty of contract which could not lawfully be imposed in the case of men under similar circumstances. To do so would be to ignore all the implications to be drawn from the present day trend of legislation, as well as that of common thought and usage, by which woman is accorded emancipation from the old doctrine that she must be given special protection or be subjected to special restraint in her contractual and civil relationships. In passing, it may be noted that the instant statute applies in the case of a woman employer contracting with a woman employee as it does when the former is a man.

The essential characteristics of the statute now under consideration, which differentiate it from the laws fixing hours of labor, will be made to appear as we proceed. It is sufficient now to point out that the latter, as well as the statutes mentioned under paragraph (3), deal with incidents of the employment having no necessary effect upon the heart of the contract; that is, the amount of wages to be paid and received. A law forbidding work to continue beyond a given number of hours leaves the parties free to contract about wages and thereby equalize whatever additional burdens may be imposed upon the employer as a result of the restrictions as to hours, by an adjustment in respect of the amount of wages. Enough has been said to show that the authority to fix hours of labor cannot be exercised except in respect of those occupations where work of long continued duration is detrimental to health. This court has been careful in every case where the question has been raised, to place its decision upon this limited authority of the Legislature to regulate hours of labor and to disclaim any purpose to uphold the legislation as fixing wages, thus recognizing an essential difference between the two. It seems plain that these decisions afford no real support for any form of law establishing minimum wages.

If now, in the light furnished by the foregoing exceptions to the general rule forbidding legislative interference with freedom of contract, we examine and analyze the statute in question, we shall see that it differs from them in every material respect. It is not a law dealing with any business charged with a public interest or with public work, or to meet and tide over a temporary emergency. It has nothing to do with the character, methods or periods of wage payments. It does not prescribe hours of labor or conditions under which labor is to be done. It is not for the protection of persons under legal disability or for the prevention of fraud. It is simply and exclusively a price-fixing law, confined to adult women (for we are not now considering the provisions relating to minors), who are legally as capable of contracting for themselves as men. It forbids two parties having lawful capacity—under penalties as to the employer—to freely contract with one another in respect of the price for which one shall render service to the other in a purely private employment where both are willing, perhaps anxious, to agree, even though the consequence may be to oblige one to surrender a desirable engagement and the other to dispense with the services of a desirable employee. The price fixed by the board need have no relation to the capacity or earning power of the employee, the number of hours which may happen to constitute the day's work, the character of the place where the work is to be done, or the circumstances or surroundings of the employment, and, while it has no other basis to support its validity than the assumed necessities of the employee, it takes no account of any independent resources she may have. It is based wholly on the opinions of the members of the board and their advisers—perhaps an average of their opinions, if they do not precisely agree—as to what will be necessary to provide a living for a woman, keep her in health and preserve her morals. It applies to any and every occupation in the District, without regard to its nature or the character of the work.

The standard furnished by the statute for the guidance of the board is so vague as to be impossible of practical application with any reasonable degree of accuracy. . . .

The feature of this statute which, perhaps more than any other, puts upon it the stamp of invalidity, is that it exacts from the employer an arbitrary payment for a purpose and upon a basis having no causal connection with his business, or the contract or the work the employee engages to do. The declared basis, as already pointed out, is not the value of the service rendered, but the extraneous circumstance that the employee needs to get a prescribed sum of money to insure her subsistence, health, and morals. The ethical right of every worker, man or woman, to a living wage may be conceded. One of the declared and important purposes of trade organizations is to secure it. And with that principle and with every legitimate effort to realize it in fact, no one can quarrel; but the fallacy of the proposed method of attaining it is that it assumes that every employer is bound at all events to furnish it. The moral requirement implicit in every contract of employment, viz., that the amount to be paid and the service to be rendered shall bear to each other some relation of just equivalence, is completely ignored. The necessities of the employee are alone considered, and these arise outside of the employment, are the same when there is no employment, and as great in one occupation as in another. Certainly the employer, by paying a fair equivalent for the service rendered, though not sufficient to support the employee, has neither caused nor contributed to her poverty. On the contrary, to the extent of what he pays, he has relieved it. In principle, there can be no difference between the case of selling labor and the case of selling goods. If one goes to the butcher, the baker, or grocer to buy food, he is morally entitled to obtain the worth of his money; but he is not entitled to more. If what he gets is worth what he pays, he is not justified in demanding more, simply because he needs more; and the shopkeeper, having dealt fairly and honestly in that transaction, is not concerned in any peculiar sense with the question of his customer's necessities. Should a statute undertake to vest in a commission power to determine the quantity of food necessary for individual support, and require the shopkeeper, if he sell to the individual at all, to furnish that quantify at not more than a fixed maximum, it would undoubtedly fall before the constitutional test. The fallacy of any argument in support of the validity of such a statute would be quickly exposed. The argument in support of that now being considered is equally fallacious, though the weakness of it may not be so plain. A statute requiring an employer to pay in money, to pay at prescribed and regular intervals, to pay the value of the services rendered, even to pay with fair relation to the extent of the benefit obtained from the service, would be understandable. But a statute which prescribes payment without regard to any of these things, and solely with relation to circumstances apart from the contract of employment, the business affected by it, and the work done under it, is so clearly the product of a naked, arbitrary exercise of power that it cannot be allowed to stand under the Constitution of the United States.

The liberty of the individual to do as he pleases, even in innocent matters, is not absolute. It must frequently yield to the common good, and the line beyond which the power of interference may not be pressed is neither definite nor unalterable, but may be made to move, within limits not well defined, with changing need and circumstance. Any attempt to fix a rigid boundary would be unwise as well as futile. But, nevertheless, there are limits to the power, and, when these have been passed, it becomes the plain duty of the courts in the proper exercise of their authority to so declare. To sustain the individual freedom of action contemplated by the Constitution is not to strike down the common good, but to exalt it; for surely the good of society as a whole cannot be better served than by the preservation against arbitrary restraint of the liberties of its constituent members.

Affirmed.

JUSTICE BRANDEIS took no part in the consideration or decision of these cases.

CHIEF JUSTICE TAFT, dissenting.

I regret much to differ from the court in these cases.

The boundary of the police power beyond which its exercise becomes an invasion of the guaranty of liberty under the Fifth and Fourteenth Amendments to the Constitution is not easy to mark. Our court has been laboriously engaged in pricking out a line in successive cases. We must be careful, it seems to me, to follow that line as well as we can, and not to depart from it by suggesting a distinction that is formal rather than real.

Legislatures in limiting freedom of contract between employee and employer by a minimum wage proceed on the assumption that employees, in the class receiving least pay, are not upon a full level of equality of choice with their employer and in their necessitous circumstances are prone to accept pretty much anything that is offered. They are peculiarly subject to the overreaching of the harsh and greedy employer. The evils of the sweating system and of the long hours and low wages which are characteristic of it are well known. Now, I agree that it is a disputable question in the field of political economy how far a statutory requirement of maximum hours or minimum wages may be a useful remedy for these evils, and whether it may not make the case of the oppressed employee worse than it was before. But it is not the function of this court to hold congressional acts invalid simply because they are passed to carry out economic views which the court believes to be unwise or unsound.

Legislatures which adopt a requirement of maximum hours or minimum wages may be presumed to believe that when sweating employers are prevented from paying unduly low wages by positive law they will continue their business, abating that part of their profits, which were wrung from the necessities of their employees, and will concede the better terms required by the law, and that while in individual cases, hardship may result, the restriction will inure to the benefit of the general class of employees in whose interest the law is passed, and so to that of the community at large.

The right of the Legislature under the Fifth and Fourteenth Amendments to limit the hours of employment on the score of the health of the employee, it seems to me, has been firmly established. As to that, one would think, the line had been pricked out so that it has become a well formulated rule.

JUSTICE HOLMES, dissenting.

The question in this case is the broad one, Whether Congress can establish minimum rates of wages for women in the District of Columbia with due provision for special circumstances, or whether we must say that Congress had no power to meddle with the matter at all. To me, notwithstanding the deference due to the prevailing judgment of the Court, the power of Congress seems absolutely free from doubt. The end, to remove conditions leading to ill health, immorality and the deterioration of the race, no one would deny to be within the scope of constitutional legislation. The means are means that have the approval of Congress, of many States, and of those governments from which we have learned our greatest lessons. When so many intelligent persons, who have studied the matter more than any of us can, have thought that the means are effective and are worth the price it seems to me impossible to deny that the belief reasonably may be held by reasonable men. If the law encountered no other objection than that the means bore no relation to the end or that they cost too much I do not suppose that anyone would venture to say that it was bad. I agree, of course, that a law answering the foregoing requirements might be invalidated by specific provisions of the Constitution. For instance it might take private property without just compensation. But in the present instance the only objection that can be urged is found within the vague contours of the Fifth Amendment, prohibiting the depriving any person of liberty or property without due process of law.

I confess that I do not understand the principle on which the power to fix a minimum for the wages of women can be denied by those who admit the power to fix a maximum for their hours of work. I fully assent to the proposition that here as elsewhere the distinctions of the law are distinctions of degree, but I perceive no difference in the kind or degree of interference with liberty, the only matter with which we have any concern, between the one case and the other. The bargain is equally affected whichever half you regulate. *Muller v. Oregon*, I take it, is as good law today as it was in 1908. It will need more than the Nineteenth Amendment to convince me that there are no differences between men and women, or that legislation cannot take those differences into account. I should not hesitate to take them into account if I thought it necessary to sustain this Act.

This statute does not compel anybody to pay anything. It simply forbids employment at rates below those fixed as the minimum requirement of health and right living. It is safe to assume that women will not be employed at even the lowest wages allowed unless they earn them, or unless the employer's business can sustain the burden. In short the law in its character and operation is like hundreds of so-called police laws that have been upheld. I see no greater objection to using a Board to apply the standard fixed by the Act than there is to the other commissions with which we have become familiar or than there is to the requirement of a license in other cases. The fact that the statute warrants classification, which like all classifications may bear hard upon some individuals, or in exceptional cases, notwithstanding the power given to the Board to issue a special license, is no greater infirmity than is incident to all law. But the ground on which the law is held to fail is fundamental and therefore it is unnecessary to consider matters of detail.

The criterion of constitutionality is not whether we believe the law to be for the public good. We certainly cannot be prepared to deny that a reasonable man reasonably might have that belief in view of the legislation of

Great Britain, Victoria and a number of the States of this Union. The belief is fortified by a very remarkable collection of documents submitted on behalf of the appellants, material here, I conceive, only as showing that the belief reasonably may be held. In Australia the power to fix a minimum for wages in the case of industrial disputes extending beyond the limits of any one State was given to a Court, and its President wrote a most interesting account of its operation. If a legislature should adopt what he thinks the doctrine of modern economists of all schools, that "freedom of contract is a misnomer as applied to a contract between an employer and an ordinary individual employee," I could not pronounce an opinion with which I agree impossible to be entertained by reasonable men. If the same legislature should accept his further opinion that industrial peace was best attained by the device of a Court having the above powers, I should not feel myself able to contradict it, or to deny that the end justified restrictive legislation quite as adequately as beliefs concerning Sunday or exploded theories about usury. I should have my doubts, as I have them about this statute—but they would be whether the bill that has to be paid for every gain, although hidden as interstitial detriments, was not greater than the gain was worth: a matter that it is not for me to decide.

I am of opinion that the statute is valid and that the decree should be reversed.

FOR DISCUSSION

Is *Adkins* more consistent with *Lochner* than *Muller*? Is there a way to reconcile the three cases? All three involved regulation of workplace conditions, with two of them also addressing laws that affected women in the workplace

NEBBIA V. NEW YORK

291 U.S. 502, 54 S.Ct. 505, 78 L.Ed. 940 (1934)

Nebbia, the proprietor of a grocery store in Rochester, New York, was found guilty of violation of an order issued by the New York State Milk Control Board. This order had set the selling price of milk, and Nebbia had sold milk below this stipulated price. He appealed his conviction on the grounds that both the state statute and the order of the board issued under it were contrary to the Equal Protection and Due Process Clauses of the Fourteenth Amendment.

Vote: 5–4

JUSTICE ROBERTS delivered the opinion of the Court:

We think the contention that the discrimination deprives the appellant of equal protection is not well founded. For aught that appears, the appellant purchased his supply of milk from a farmer as do distributors, or could have procured it from a farmer if he so desired. There is therefore no showing that the order placed him at a disadvantage, or in fact affected him adversely, and this alone is fatal to the claim of denial of equal protection. But if it were shown that the appellant is compelled to buy from a distributor, the difference in the retail price he is required to charge his customers, from that prescribed for sales by distributors is not on its face arbitrary or unreasonable, for there are obvious distinctions between the two sorts of merchants which may well justify a difference of treatment, if the legislature possesses the power to control the prices to be charged for fluid milk.

The more serious question is whether, in the light of the conditions disclosed, the enforcement of section 312 (e) denied the appellant the due process secured to him by the Fourteenth Amendment.

Under our form of government the use of property and the making of contracts are normally matters of private and not of public concern. The general rule is that both shall be free of governmental interference. But neither property rights nor contract rights are absolute; for government cannot exist if the citizen may at will use his property to the detriment of his fellows, or exercise his freedom of contract to work them harm. Equally fundamental with the private right is that of the public to regulate it in the common interest.

The Fifth Amendment, in the field of federal activity, and the Fourteenth, as respects state action, do not prohibit governmental regulation for the public welfare. They merely condition the exertion of the admitted power, by securing that the end shall be accomplished by methods consistent with due process. And the guaranty of due process, as has often been held, demands only that the law shall not be unreasonable, arbitrary, or capricious, and that the means selected shall have a real and substantial relation to the object sought to be attained. It results that a regulation valid for one sort of business, or in given circumstances, may be invalid for another sort, or for the same business under other circumstances, because the reasonableness of each regulation depends upon the relevant facts.

We may as well say at once that the dairy industry is not, in the accepted sense of the phrase, a public utility. We think the appellant is also right in asserting that there is in this case no suggestion of any monopoly or monopolistic practice. It goes without saying that those engaged in the business are in no way dependent upon public grants or franchises for the privilege of conducting their activities. But if, as must be conceded, the industry is subject to regulation in the public interest, what constitutional principle bars the state from correcting existing maladjustments by legislation touching prices? We think there is no such principle. The due process clause makes no mention of sales or of prices any more than it speaks of business or contracts or buildings or other incidents of property. The thought seems nevertheless to have persisted that there is something peculiarly sacrosanct above the price one may charge for what he makes or sells, and that, however able to regulate other elements of manufacture or trade, with incidental effect upon price, the state is incapable of directly controlling the price itself. This view was negatived many years ago. *Munn v. Illinois,* 94 U.S. 113 (1877).

It is clear that there is no closed class or category of businesses affected with a public interest, and the function of courts in the application of the Fifth and Fourteenth Amendments is to determine in each case whether circumstances vindicate the challenged regulation as a reasonable exertion of governmental authority or condemn it as arbitrary or discriminatory. The phrase "affected with a public interest" can, in the nature of things, mean no more than that an industry, for adequate reason, is subject to control for the public good. In several of the decisions of this court wherein the expressions "affected with a public interest," and "clothed with a public use," have been brought forward as the criteria of the validity of price control, it has been admitted that they are not susceptible of definition and form an unsatisfactory test of the constitutionality of legislation directed at business practices or prices. These decisions must rest, finally, upon the basis that the requirements of due process were not met because the laws were found arbitrary in their operation and effect. But there can be no doubt that upon proper occasion and by appropriate measure the state may regulate a business in any of its aspects, including the prices to be charged for the products or commodities it sells.

So far as the requirement of due process is concerned, and in the absence of other constitutional restriction, a state is free to adopt whatever economic policy may reasonably be deemed to promote public welfare, and to enforce that policy by legislation adapted to its purpose. The courts are without authority either to declare such policy, or when it is declared by the legislative arm, to override it. If the laws passed are seen to have a reasonable relation to a proper legislative purpose, and are neither arbitrary nor discriminatory, the requirements of due process are satisfied, and judicial determination to that effect renders a court *functus officio* [having performed its function].

The Constitution does not secure to anyone liberty to conduct his business in such fashion as to inflict injury upon the public at large, or upon any substantial group of the people. Price control, like any other form of regulation, is unconstitutional only if arbitrary, discriminatory, or demonstrably irrelevant to the policy the legislature is free to adopt, and hence an unnecessary and unwarranted interference with individual liberty.

Tested by these considerations we find no basis in the due process clause of the Fourteenth Amendment for condemning the provisions of the Agriculture and Markets Law here drawn into question.

The judgment is affirmed.

JUSTICE MCREYNOLDS dissented, with the concurrence of JUSTICES VAN DEVANTER, SUTHERLAND and BUTLER.

The exigency is of the kind which inevitably arises when one set of men continue to produce more than all others can buy. The distressing result to the producer followed his ill-advised but voluntary efforts. Similar situations occur in almost every business. If here we have an emergency sufficient to empower the legislature to fix sales prices, then whenever there is too much or too little of an essential thing—whether of milk or grain or pork or coal or shoes or clothes—constitutional provisions may be declared inoperative and the "anarchy and despotism" prefigured in *[Ex Parte Milligan]*, 71 U.S. 2 (1866), are at the door. The futility of such legislation in the circumstances is pointed out below.

Is the milk business so affected with public interest that the legislature may prescribe prices for sales by stores? This Court has approved the contrary view; has emphatically declared that a State lacks power to fix prices in similar private businesses.

Assuming that the views and facts reported by the Legislative Committee are correct, it appears to me wholly unreasonable to expect this legislation to accomplish the proposed end—increase of prices at the farm.

Not only does the statute interfere arbitrarily with the rights of the little grocer to conduct his business according to standards long accepted—complete destruction may follow; but it takes away the liberty of twelve million consumers to buy a necessity of life in an open market.

FOR DISCUSSION

Does *Nebbia* overrule *Munn v. Illinois* (94 U.S. 113, 1877)? How does the Supreme Court reach its conclusion that regulation of milk is permitted? Does it reject the *Munn* test or apply it and find that milk is cloaked with a public interest?

RELATED CASES

Wolff Packing Co. v. Court of Industrial Relations: 262 U.S. 522 (1923)

The only businesses affected with a public interest are (1) those operating under authority of a public grant of privileges to render public service, such as public utilities, (2) certain occupations with a distinct public interest attached, such as keepers of inns, and (3) those that have such a peculiar relation to the public that the owner has in effect granted the public an interest in that use. Here the packing business was held not to be a business under any of these categories.

Tyson and Bros. v. Banton: 273 U.S. 418 (1927)

To be "a business affected with a public interest," the business must have been so devoted to a public use that its use has been granted to the public. The selling of theater tickets is not such a business.

***Ribnik v. McBride:* 277 U.S. 350 (1928)**

A statute of New Jersey, attempting to confer on the commissioner of labor the power to fix the prices employment agency can charge for its services, is contrary to due process of law because the business is not one "affected with a public interest."

***Williams v. Standard Oil Co.:* 278 U.S. 235 (1929)**

The sale of gasoline is not a business in the "public interest" category, and therefore a Tennessee statute which conferred on a state officer the power to fix the sale price of gasoline is not valid.

***New State Ice Co. v. Liebmann:* 285 U.S. 262 (1932)**

Selling ice was held not to be a business affected with a public interest. Therefore, a state statute of Oklahoma requiring that a person desiring to enter this business secure a state certificate of convenience and necessity was ruled invalid.

***Olsen v. Nebraska:* 313 U.S. 236 (1941)**

A statute fixing the maximum compensation that an employment agency may collect is not a denial of due process of law. The Court in *Olsen* held that the test of affectation with a public interest had been dropped in *Nebbia v. New York*.

WEST COAST HOTEL CO. V. PARRISH

300 U.S. 379, 57 S.Ct. 578, 81 L.Ed. 703 (1937)

The state of Washington had by statute prohibited wages below a level adequate for the maintenance of women and minors. A commission was set up to establish standards of wages and conditions of labor for the protected groups. Elsie Parrish, a chambermaid, brought suit against the hotel to recover the difference between the wages paid her and the minimum wage fixed pursuant to the state law. The statute was attacked as repugnant to the Due Process Clause of the Fourteenth Amendment of the Constitution.

Vote: 5–4

CHIEF JUSTICE HUGHES delivered the opinion of the Court.

The principle which must control our decision is not in doubt. The constitutional provision invoked is the due process clause of the Fourteenth Amendment governing the States, as the due process clause invoked in the *Adkins v. Children's Hospital,* 261 U.S. 525 (1923), case governed Congress. In each case the violation alleged by those attacking minimum wage regulation for women is deprivation of freedom of contract. What is this freedom? The Constitution does not speak of freedom of contract. It speaks of liberty and prohibits the deprivation of liberty without due process of law. In prohibiting that deprivation the Constitution does not recognize an absolute and uncontrollable liberty. Liberty in each of its phases has its history and connotation. But the liberty safeguarded is liberty in a social organization which requires the protection of law against the evils which menace the health, safety, morals and welfare of the people. Liberty under the Constitution is thus necessarily subject to the restraints of due process, and regulation which is reasonable in relation to its subject and is adopted in the interests of the community is due process.

With full recognition of the earnestness and vigor which characterize the prevailing opinion in the *Adkins* case, we find it impossible to reconcile that ruling with these well-considered declarations. What can be closer to the public interest than the health of women and their protection from unscrupulous and overreaching employers? And if the protection of women is a legitimate end of the exercise of state power, how can it be said that the requirement of the payment of a minimum wage fairly fixed in order to meet the very necessities of existence is not an admissible means to that end? The legislature of the State was clearly entitled to consider the situation of women in employment, the fact that they are in the class receiving the least pay, that their bargaining power is relatively weak, and that they are the ready victims of those who would take advantage of their necessitous circumstances. The legislature was entitled to adopt measures to reduce the evils of the "sweating system," the exploiting of workers at wages so low as to be insufficient to meet the bare cost of living thus making their very helplessness the occasion of a most injurious competition. The legislature had the right to consider that its minimum wage requirements would be an important aid in carrying out its policy of protection. The adoption of similar requirements by many States evidences a deep-seated conviction both as to the presence of the evil and as to the means adapted to check it. Legislative response to that conviction cannot be regarded as arbitrary or capricious and that is all we have to decide. Even if the wisdom of the policy be regarded as debatable and its effects uncertain, still the legislature is entitled to its judgment.

There is an additional and compelling consideration which recent economic experience has brought into a strong light. The exploitation of a class of workers who are in an unequal position with respect to bargaining power and are thus relatively defenceless against the denial of a living wage is not only detrimental to their health and well being but casts a direct burden for their support upon the community. What these workers lose in wages the taxpayers are called upon to pay. The bare cost of living must be met. We may take judicial notice of the unparalleled demands for relief which arose during the recent period of depression and still continue to an alarming extent despite the degree of economic recovery which has been achieved. It is unnecessary to cite official statistics to establish what is of common knowledge through the length and breadth of the land. While in the instant case no factual brief has been presented, there is no reason to doubt that the State of Washington has encountered the same social problem that is present elsewhere. The community is not bound to provide what is in effect a subsidy for unconscionable employers. The community may direct its law-making power to correct the abuse which springs from their selfish disregard of the public interest. The argument that the legislation in question constitutes an arbitrary discrimination, because it does not extend to men, is unavailing. This Court has frequently held that the legislative authority, acting within its proper field, is not bound to extend its regulation to all cases which it might possibly reach. The legislature "is free to recognize degrees of harm and it may confine its restrictions to those classes of cases where the need is deemed to be clearest." If "the law presumably hits the evil where it is most felt, it is not to be overthrown because there are other instances to which it might have been applied." There is no "doctrinaire requirement" that the legislation should be couched in all embracing terms.

Our conclusion is that the case of *Adkins v. Children's Hospital* should be, and it is, overruled. The judgment of the Supreme Court of the State of Washington is affirmed.

JUSTICE SUTHERLAND dissented, with the concurrence of JUSTICES VAN DEVANTER, MCREYNOLDS, and BUTLER.

The principles and authorities relied upon to sustain the judgment, were considered in *Adkins v. Children's Hospital* and *Morehead v. New York ex rel. Tipaldo,* 298 U.S. 587 (1936), and their lack of application to cases like the one in hand was pointed out. . . .

Neither the statute involved in the *Adkins* case nor the Washington statute, so far as it is involved here, has the slightest relation to the capacity or earning power of the employee, to the number of hours which constitute the day's work, the character of the place where the work is to be done, or the circumstances or surroundings of the employment. The sole basis upon which the question of validity rests is the assumption that the employee is entitled to receive a sum of money sufficient to provide a living for her, keep her in health and preserve her morals. And as we pointed out at some length in that case, the question thus presented for the determination of the board cannot be solved by any general formula prescribed by a statutory bureau, since it is not a composite but an individual question to be answered for each individual, considered by herself. What we said further in that case is equally applicable here:

. . . The feature of this statute which, perhaps more than any other, puts upon it the stamp of invalidity is that it exacts from the employer an arbitrary payment for a purpose and upon a basis having no causal connection with his business, or the contract or the work the employee engages to do. The declared basis, as already pointed out, is not the value of the service rendered, but the extraneous circumstance that the employee needs to get a prescribed sum of money to insure her subsistence, health and morals. The ethical right of every worker, man or women, to a living wage may be conceded. One of the declared and important purposes of trade organizations is to secure it. And with that principle and with every legitimate effort to realize it in fact, no one can quarrel; but the fallacy of the proposed method of attaining it is that it assumes that every legitimate employer is bound at all events to furnish it. The moral requirement implicit in every contract of employment, *viz.*, that the amount to be paid and the service to be rendered shall bear to each other some relation of just equivalence, is completely ignored. The necessities of the employee are alone considered and these arise outside of the employment, are the same when there is no employment, and as great in one occupation as in another. A statute requiring an employer to pay in money, to pay at prescribed and regular intervals, to pay the value of the services rendered, even to pay with fair relation to the extent of the benefit obtained from the service, would be understandable. But a statute which prescribes payment without regard to any of these things and solely with relation to circumstances apart from the contract of employment, the business affected by it and the work done under it, is so clearly the product of a naked, arbitrary exercise of power that it cannot be allowed to stand under the Constitution of the United States.

Finally, it may be said that a statute absolutely fixing wages in the various industries at definite sums and forbidding employers and employees from contracting for any other than those designated, would probably not be thought to be constitutional. It is hard to see why the power to fix minimum wages does not connote a like power in respect of maximum wages. And yet, if both powers be exercised in such a way that the minimum and the maximum so nearly approach each other as to become substantially the same, the right to make any contract in respect of wages will have been completely abrogated.

FOR DISCUSSION

Does *Parrish* only overrule *Adkins*, or does it also extend to *Mugler v. Kansas* (123 U.S. 623, 1887)? Some claim it effectively overturned both, but does it reject the heightened scrutiny found in the latter?

RELATED CASES

Holden v. Hardy: 169 U.S. 366 (1898)

A statute of Utah fixed an eight-hour day for the employment of men in underground mines. The Court upheld the law as a proper exercise of state police power in light of the inequality of employers and employees in the making of labor contracts.

Morehead v. New York ex rel. Tipaldo: 298 U.S. 587 (1936)

A state is without power by any form of legislation to prohibit, change, or nullify contracts between employers and adult women workers as to the amount of wages to be paid. A state statute, therefore, which authorizes an administrative order prescribing minimum wages for women employees is a violation of the Due Process Clause of the Fourteenth Amendment.

***United States v. Darby Lumber Co.:* 312 U.S. 100 (1941)**

Here the Court upheld a federal statute prohibiting the shipment in interstate commerce of certain products and commodities produced in the United States under labor conditions which fail to conform to standards set up by the Act and further requiring employers to keep records of the operations of employees. The standards in the act referred to wages, hours, and child labor.

UNITED STATES V. CAROLENE PRODUCTS CO.

304 U.S. 144, 304 S.Ct. 778, 82 L.Ed. 1234 (1938)

The federal government prohibited the sale of filled milk, or skim milk mixed with fats. The law was challenged as a violation of the Commerce Clause.

Vote: 6–1 (Justice Brandeis not participating)

JUSTICE STONE delivered the opinion of the Court.

The question for decision is whether the "Filled Milk Act" of Congress of March 4, 1923, which prohibits the shipment in interstate commerce of skimmed milk compounded with any fat or oil other than milk fat, so as to resemble milk or cream, transcends the power of Congress to regulate interstate commerce or infringes the Fifth Amendment.

But such we think is not the purpose or construction of the statutory characterization of filled milk as injurious to health and as a fraud upon the public. There is no need to consider it here as more than a declaration of the legislative findings deemed to support and justify the action taken as a constitutional exertion of the legislative power, aiding informed judicial review, as do the reports of legislative committees, by revealing the rationale of the legislation. Even in the absence of such aids, the existence of facts supporting the legislative judgment is to be presumed, for regulatory legislation affecting ordinary commercial transactions is not to be pronounced unconstitutional unless in the light of the facts made known or generally assumed it is of such a character as to preclude the assumption that it rests upon some rational basis within the knowledge and experience of the legislators.*

FOR DISCUSSION

After *Carolene Products*, what level of scrutiny does the Court take toward economic regulation? Is it a return to the logic of *McCulloch v. Maryland* (17 U.S. 316, 1819) and a rational basis test?

---

* There may be narrower scope for operation of the presumption of constitutionality when legislation appears on its face to be within a specific prohibition of the Constitution, such as those of the first ten Amendments, which are deemed equally specific when held to be embraced within the Fourteenth. See *Stromberg v. California*, 283 U.S. 359 (1931); *Lovell v. Griffin*, 303 U.S. 444 (1938).

It is unnecessary to consider now whether legislation which restricts those political processes which can ordinarily be expected to bring about repeal of undesirable legislation, is to be subjected to more exacting judicial scrutiny under the general prohibitions of the Fourteenth Amendment than are most other types of legislation. Nor need we enquire whether similar considerations enter into the review of statutes directed at particular religious, or national, or racial minorities; whether prejudice against discrete and insular minorities may be a special condition, which tends seriously to curtail the operation of those political processes ordinarily to be relied upon to protect minorities, and which may call for a correspondingly more searching judicial inquiry.

FERGUSON V. SKRUPA

372 U.S. 726, 83 S.Ct. 1028, 10 L.Ed.2d 93 (1963)

The state of Kansas enacted a law making it illegal to engage in the business of debt adjustment. The law defined debt adjustment as any contract for a fee to help someone pay off their debts to third parties. The law was challenged as a violation of the Fourteenth Amendment.

Vote: 9–0

JUSTICE BLACK delivered the opinion of the Court.

In this case, properly here on appeal, we are asked to review the judgment of a three-judge District Court enjoining, as being in violation of the Due Process Clause of the Fourteenth Amendment, a Kansas statute making it a misdemeanor for any person to engage "in the business of debt adjusting" except as an incident to "the lawful practice of law in this state." The statute defines "debt adjusting" as "the making of a contract, express, or implied with a particular debtor whereby the debtor agrees to pay a certain amount of money periodically to the person engaged in the debt adjusting business who shall for a consideration distribute the same among certain specified creditors in accordance with a plan agreed upon."

The complaint, filed by appellee Skrupa doing business as "Credit Advisors," alleged that Skrupa was engaged in the business of "debt adjusting" as defined by the statute, that his business was a "useful and desirable" one, that his business activities were not "inherently immoral or dangerous" or in any way contrary to the public welfare, and that therefore the business could not be "absolutely prohibited" by Kansas. The three-judge court heard evidence by Skrupa tending to show the usefulness and desirability of his business and evidence by the state officials tending to show that "debt adjusting" lends itself to grave abuses against distressed debtors, particularly in the lower income brackets, and that these abuses are of such gravity that a number of States have strictly regulated "debt adjusting" or prohibited it altogether. The court found that Skrupa's business did fall within the Act's proscription and concluded, one judge dissenting, that the Act was prohibitory, not regulatory, but that even if construed in part as regulatory it was an unreasonable regulation of a "lawful business," which the court held amounted to a violation of the Due Process Clause of the Fourteenth Amendment. The court accordingly enjoined enforcement of the statute.

The only case discussed by the court below as support for its invalidation of the statute was *Commonwealth v. Stone,* 321 Mass. 471 (1947), in which the Superior Court of Pennsylvania struck down a statute almost identical to the Kansas act involved here. In *Stone* the Pennsylvania court held that the State could regulate, but could not prohibit, a "legitimate" business. Finding debt adjusting, called "budget planning" in the Pennsylvania statute, not to be "against the public interest" and concluding that it could "see no justification for such interference" with this business, the Pennsylvania court ruled that State's statute to be unconstitutional.

Both the District Court in the present case and the Pennsylvania court in *Stone* adopted the philosophy of *Adams v. Tanner,* 244 U.S. 590 (1917), and cases like it, that it is the province of courts to draw on their own views as to the morality, legitimacy, and usefulness of a particular business in order to decide whether a statute bears too heavily upon that business and by so doing violates due process. Under the system of government created by our Constitution, it is up to legislatures, not courts, to decide on the wisdom and utility of legislation. There was a time when the Due Process Clause was used by this Court to strike down laws which were thought unreasonable, that is, unwise or incompatible with some particular economic or social philosophy. In this manner the Due Process Clause was used, for example, to nullify laws prescribing maximum hours for work in bakeries, *Lochner v. New York,* 198 U.S. 45 (1905), outlawing "yellow dog" contracts, *Coppage v. Kansas,* 236 U.S. 1 (1915), setting minimum wages for women, and fixing the weight of loaves of bread. This intrusion by the judiciary into the realm of legislative value judgments was strongly objected to at the time, particularly by Mr. Justice Holmes and Mr. Justice Brandeis.

The doctrine that prevailed in *Lochner*, *Coppage*, *Adkins [v. Children's Hospital*, 261 U.S. 525 (1923)], *Jay Burns Baking Co. v. Bryan,* 264 US 504 (1924), and like cases—that due process authorizes courts to hold laws unconstitutional when they believe the legislature has acted unwisely—has long since been discarded. We have returned to the original constitutional proposition that courts do not substitute their social and economic beliefs for the judgment of legislative bodies, who are elected to pass laws. As this Court stated in a unanimous opinion in 1941, "We are not concerned with the wisdom, need, or appropriateness of the legislation." Legislative bodies have broad scope to experiment with economic problems, and this Court does not sit to "subject the state to an intolerable supervision hostile to the basic principles of our government and wholly beyond the protection which the general clause of the Fourteenth Amendment was intended to secure." It is now settled that States "have power to legislate against what are found to be injurious practices in their internal commercial and business affairs, so long as their laws do not run afoul of some specific federal constitutional prohibition, or of some valid federal law."

Reversed.

FOR DISCUSSION

What is left of substantive due process after *Skrupa*? Does the doctrine have any value or validity? Should courts be questioning economic regulation? What is left of the Framers' views on property? of Locke's?

LINGLE V. CHEVRON U.S.A. INC.

544 U.S. 528, 125 S.Ct. 2074, 161 L.Ed.2d 876 (2005)

Chevron Oil objected to a Hawaii law that set a cap on the maximum rate it could charge dealers renting company-owned service stations. The claim was that the law was an unconstitutional taking of private property in violation of the Fifth Amendment.

Vote: 9–0

JUSTICE O'CONNOR delivered the opinion of the Court.

On occasion, a would-be doctrinal rule or test finds its way into our case law through simple repetition of a phrase—however fortuitously coined. A quarter century ago, in *Agins v. City of Tiburon,* 447 U.S. 255 (1980), the Court declared that government regulation of private property "effects a taking if [such regulation] does not substantially advance legitimate state interests." Through reiteration in a half dozen or so decisions since *Agins,* this language has been ensconced in our Fifth Amendment takings jurisprudence.

In the case before us, the lower courts applied *Agins'* "substantially advances" formula to strike down a Hawaii statute that limits the rent that oil companies may charge to dealers who lease service stations owned by the companies. The lower courts held that the rent cap effects an uncompensated taking of private property in violation of the Fifth and Fourteenth Amendments because it does not substantially advance Hawaii's asserted interest in controlling retail gasoline prices. This case requires us to decide whether the "substantially advances" formula announced in *Agins* is an appropriate test for determining whether a regulation effects a Fifth Amendment taking. We conclude that it is not.

I

The State of Hawaii, whose territory comprises an archipelago of 132 islands clustered in the midst of the Pacific Ocean, is located over 1,600 miles from the U.S. mainland and ranks among the least populous of the 50 States. Because of Hawaii's small size and geographic isolation, its wholesale market for oil products is highly concentrated. When this lawsuit began in 1997, only two refineries and six gasoline wholesalers were doing business in the State. As of that time, respondent Chevron U.S.A. Inc. was the largest refiner and marketer of gasoline in Hawaii: It controlled 60 percent of the market for gasoline produced or refined in-state and 30 percent of the wholesale market on the State's most populous island, Oahu.

Gasoline is sold at retail in Hawaii from about 300 different service stations. About half of these stations are leased from oil companies by independent lessee-dealers, another 75 or so are owned and operated by "open" dealers, and the remainder are owned and operated by the oil companies. Chevron sells most of its product through 64 independent lessee-dealer stations. In a typical lessee-dealer arrangement, Chevron buys or leases land from a third party, builds a service station, and then leases the station to a dealer on a turnkey basis. Chevron charges the lessee-dealer a monthly rent, defined as a percentage of the dealer's margin on retail sales of gasoline and other goods. In addition, Chevron requires the lessee-dealer to enter into a supply contract, under which the dealer agrees to purchase from Chevron whatever is necessary to satisfy demand at the station for Chevron's product. Chevron unilaterally sets the wholesale price of its product.

The Hawaii Legislature enacted Act 257 in June 1997, apparently in response to concerns about the effects of market concentration on retail gasoline prices. The statute seeks to protect independent dealers by imposing certain restrictions on the ownership and leasing of service stations by oil companies. It prohibits oil companies from converting existing lessee-dealer stations to company-operated stations and from locating new company-operated stations in close proximity to existing dealer-operated stations. More importantly for present purposes, Act 257 limits the amount of rent that an oil company may charge a lessee-dealer to 15 percent of the dealer's gross profits from gasoline sales plus 15 percent of gross sales of products other than gasoline.

Thirty days after Act 257's enactment, Chevron sued the Governor and Attorney General of Hawaii in their official capacities (collectively Hawaii) in the United States District Court for the District of Hawaii, raising several federal constitutional challenges to the statute. As pertinent here, Chevron claimed that the statute's rent cap provision, on its face, effected a taking of Chevron's property in violation of the Fifth and Fourteenth Amendments. Chevron sought a declaration to this effect as well as an injunction against the application of the rent cap to its stations. Chevron swiftly moved for summary judgment on its takings claim, arguing that the rent cap does not substantially advance any legitimate government interest. Hawaii filed a cross-motion for summary judgment on all of Chevron's claims.

Finally, the "substantially advances" formula is not only *doctrinally* untenable as a takings test—its application as such would also present serious practical difficulties. The *Agins* formula can be read to demand heightened means-ends review of virtually any regulation of private property. If so interpreted, it would require courts to scrutinize the efficacy of a vast array of state and federal regulations—a task for which courts are not well suited. Moreover, it would empower—and might often require—courts to substitute their predictive judgments for those of elected legislatures and expert agencies.

Although the instant case is only the tip of the proverbial iceberg, it foreshadows the hazards of placing courts in this role. To resolve Chevron's takings claim, the District Court was required to choose between the views of two opposing economists as to whether Hawaii's rent control statute would help to prevent concentration and supracompetitive prices in the State's retail gasoline market. Finding one expert to be "more persuasive" than the other, the court concluded that the Hawaii Legislature's chosen regulatory strategy would not actually achieve its objectives. Along the way, the court determined that the State was not entitled to enact a prophylactic rent cap without actual evidence that oil companies had charged, or would charge, excessive rents. Based on these findings, the District Court enjoined further enforcement of Act 257's rent cap provision against Chevron. We find the proceedings below remarkable, to say the least, given that we have long eschewed such heightened scrutiny when addressing substantive due process challenges to government regulation. See, *e.g., Exxon Corp. v. Governor of Maryland*, 437 U.S. 117 (1978); *Ferguson v. Skrupa*, 372 U.S. 726 (1963). The reasons for deference to legislative judgments about the need for, and likely effectiveness of, regulatory actions are by now well established, and we think they are no less applicable here.

JUSTICE KENNEDY, concurring.

This separate writing is to note that today's decision does not foreclose the possibility that a regulation might be so arbitrary or irrational as to violate due process. The failure of a regulation to accomplish a stated or obvious objective would be relevant to that inquiry. Chevron voluntarily dismissed its due process claim without prejudice, however, and we have no occasion to consider whether Act 257 of the 1997 Hawaii Session Laws "represents one of the rare instances in which even such a permissive standard has been violated."

FOR DISCUSSION

Is there any substantive component to due process? Is it purely procedural? Should it be?

BMW OF NORTH AMERICA, INC. V. GORE

517 U.S. 559, 116 S.Ct. 1589, 134 L.Ed.2d 809 (1996)

A jury awarded an individual $4 million in punitive damages and $4,000 in compensatory damages as a result of finding that BMW had a policy of fixing, painting, and repairing new cars with minor damage and not informing the customers of the repairs. The auto dealer sued, claiming the punitive damages were excessive under the Fourteenth Amendment.

Vote: 5–4

JUSTICE STEVENS delivered the opinion of the Court.

The Due Process Clause of the Fourteenth Amendment prohibits a State from imposing a " 'grossly excessive' " punishment on a tortfeasor. The wrongdoing involved in this case was the decision by a national distributor of automobiles not to advise its dealers, and hence their customers, of predelivery damage to new cars when the cost of repair amounted to less than 3 percent of the car's suggested retail price. The question presented is whether a $2 million punitive damages award to the purchaser of one of these cars exceeds the constitutional limit.

I

In January 1990, Dr. Ira Gore, Jr. (respondent), purchased a black BMW sports sedan for $40,750.88 from an authorized BMW dealer in Birmingham, Alabama. After driving the car for approximately nine months, and without noticing any flaws in its appearance, Dr. Gore took the car to "Slick Finish," an independent detailer, to make it look " 'snazzier than it normally would appear.' " Mr. Slick, the proprietor, detected evidence that the car had been repainted. Convinced that he had been cheated, Dr. Gore brought suit against petitioner BMW of

North America (BMW), the American distributor of BMW automobiles. Dr. Gore alleged, *inter alia* [among other things], that the failure to disclose that the car had been repainted constituted suppression of a material fact. The complaint prayed for $500,000 in compensatory and punitive damages, and costs.

At trial, BMW acknowledged that it had adopted a nationwide policy in 1983 concerning cars that were damaged in the course of manufacture or transportation. If the cost of repairing the damage exceeded 3 percent of the car's suggested retail price, the car was placed in company service for a period of time and then sold as used. If the repair cost did not exceed 3 percent of the suggested retail price, however, the car was sold as new without advising the dealer that any repairs had been made. Because the $601.37 cost of repainting Dr. Gore's car was only about 1.5 percent of its suggested retail price, BMW did not disclose the damage or repair to the Birmingham dealer.

Dr. Gore asserted that his repainted car was worth less than a car that had not been refinished. To prove his actual damages of $4,000, he relied on the testimony of a former BMW dealer, who estimated that the value of a repainted BMW was approximately 10 percent less than the value of a new car that had not been damaged and repaired. To support his claim for punitive damages, Dr. Gore introduced evidence that since 1983 BMW had sold 983 refinished cars as new, including 14 in Alabama, without disclosing that the cars had been repainted before sale at a cost of more than $300 per vehicle. Using the actual damage estimate of $4,000 per vehicle, Dr. Gore argued that a punitive award of $4 million would provide an appropriate penalty for selling approximately 1,000 cars for more than they were worth.

In defense of its disclosure policy, BMW argued that it was under no obligation to disclose repairs of minor damage to new cars and that Dr. Gore's car was as good as a car with the original factory finish. It disputed Dr. Gore's assertion that the value of the car was impaired by the repainting and argued that this good-faith belief made a punitive award inappropriate. BMW also maintained that transactions in jurisdictions other than Alabama had no relevance to Dr. Gore's claim.

The jury returned a verdict finding BMW liable for compensatory damages of $4,000. In addition, the jury assessed $4 million in punitive damages, based on a determination that the nondisclosure policy constituted "gross, oppressive or malicious" fraud.

Because we believed that a review of this case would help to illuminate "the character of the standard that will identify unconstitutionally excessive awards" of punitive damages, we granted certiorari.

II

Punitive damages may properly be imposed to further a State's legitimate interests in punishing unlawful conduct and deterring its repetition. In our federal system, States necessarily have considerable flexibility in determining the level of punitive damages that they will allow in different classes of cases and in any particular case. Most States that authorize exemplary damages afford the jury similar latitude, requiring only that the damages awarded be reasonably necessary to vindicate the State's legitimate interests in punishment and deterrence. Only when an award can fairly be categorized as "grossly excessive" in relation to these interests does it enter the zone of arbitrariness that violates the Due Process Clause of the Fourteenth Amendment. For that reason, the federal excessiveness inquiry appropriately begins with an identification of the state interests that a punitive award is designed to serve. We therefore focus our attention first on the scope of Alabama's legitimate interests in punishing BMW and deterring it from future misconduct.

No one doubts that a State may protect its citizens by prohibiting deceptive trade practices and by requiring automobile distributors to disclose presale repairs that affect the value of a new car. But the States need not, and in fact do not, provide such protection in a uniform manner. Some States rely on the judicial process to formulate and enforce an appropriate disclosure requirement by applying principles of contract and tort law. Other States have enacted various forms of legislation that define the disclosure obligations of automobile manufacturers, distributors, and dealers. The result is a patchwork of rules representing the diverse policy judgments of lawmakers in 50 States.

That diversity demonstrates that reasonable people may disagree about the value of a full disclosure requirement. Some legislatures may conclude that affirmative disclosure requirements are unnecessary because the self-interest of those involved in the automobile trade in developing and maintaining the goodwill of their customers will motivate them to make voluntary disclosures or to refrain from selling cars that do not comply with self-imposed standards. Those legislatures that do adopt affirmative disclosure obligations may take into account the cost of government regulation, choosing to draw a line exempting minor repairs from such a requirement. In formulating a disclosure standard, States may also consider other goals, such as providing a "safe harbor" for automobile manufacturers, distributors, and dealers against lawsuits over minor repairs.

We think it follows from these principles of state sovereignty and comity that a State may not impose economic sanctions on violators of its laws with the intent of changing the tortfeasors' lawful conduct in other States. Before this Court Dr. Gore argued that the large punitive damages award was necessary to induce BMW to change the nationwide policy that it adopted in 1983. But by attempting to alter BMW's nationwide policy, Alabama would be infringing on the policy choices of other States. To avoid such encroachment, the economic penalties that a State such as Alabama inflicts on those who transgress its laws, whether the penalties take the form of legislatively authorized fines or judicially imposed punitive damages, must be supported by the State's interest in protecting its own consumers and its own economy. Alabama may insist that BMW adhere to a particular disclosure policy in that State. Alabama does not have the power, however, to punish BMW for conduct that was lawful where it occurred and that had no impact on Alabama or its residents. Nor may Alabama impose sanctions on BMW in order to deter conduct that is lawful in other jurisdictions.

In this case, we accept the Alabama Supreme Court's interpretation of the jury verdict as reflecting a computation of the amount of punitive damages "based in large part on conduct that happened in other jurisdictions." As the Alabama Supreme Court noted, neither the jury nor the trial court was presented with evidence that any of BMW's out-of-state conduct was unlawful. "The only testimony touching the issue showed that approximately 60% of the vehicles that were refinished were sold in states where failure to disclose the repair was not an unfair trade practice." The Alabama Supreme Court therefore properly eschewed reliance on BMW's out-of-state conduct and based its remitted award solely on conduct that occurred within Alabama. The award must be analyzed in the light of the same conduct, with consideration given only to the interests of Alabama consumers, rather than those of the entire Nation. When the scope of the interest in punishment and deterrence that an Alabama court may appropriately consider is properly limited, it is apparent—for reasons that we shall now address—that this award is grossly excessive.

III

Elementary notions of fairness enshrined in our constitutional jurisprudence dictate that a person receive fair notice not only of the conduct that will subject him to punishment, but also of the severity of the penalty that a State may impose. Three guideposts, each of which indicates that BMW did not receive adequate notice of the magnitude of the sanction that Alabama might impose for adhering to the nondisclosure policy adopted in 1983, lead us to the conclusion that the $2 million award against BMW is grossly excessive: the degree of reprehensibility of the nondisclosure; the disparity between the harm or potential harm suffered by Dr. Gore and his punitive damages award; and the difference between this remedy and the civil penalties authorized or imposed in comparable cases. We discuss these considerations in turn.

Degree of Reprehensibility

Perhaps the most important indicium of the reasonableness of a punitive damages award is the degree of reprehensibility of the defendant's conduct. As the Court stated nearly 150 years ago, exemplary damages imposed on a defendant should reflect "the enormity of his offense." This principle reflects the accepted view that some wrongs are more blameworthy than others. Thus, we have said that "nonviolent crimes are less serious than crimes marked by violence or the threat of violence." Similarly, "trickery and deceit" are more reprehensible than negligence.

In this case, none of the aggravating factors associated with particularly reprehensible conduct is present. The harm BMW inflicted on Dr. Gore was purely economic in nature. The presale refinishing of the car had no effect on its performance or safety features, or even its appearance for at least nine months after his purchase. BMW's conduct evinced no indifference to or reckless disregard for the health and safety of others. To be sure, infliction of economic injury, especially when done intentionally through affirmative acts of misconduct, or when the target is financially vulnerable, can warrant a substantial penalty. But this observation does not convert all acts that cause economic harm into torts that are sufficiently reprehensible to justify a significant sanction in addition to compensatory damages.

Ratio

The second and perhaps most commonly cited indicium of an unreasonable or excessive punitive damages award is its ratio to the actual harm inflicted on the plaintiff. The principle that exemplary damages must bear a "reasonable relationship" to compensatory damages has a long pedigree. Scholars have identified a number of early English statutes authorizing the award of multiple damages for particular wrongs. Some 65 different enactments during the period between 1275 and 1753 provided for double, treble, or quadruple damages.

The $2 million in punitive damages awarded to Dr. Gore by the Alabama Supreme Court is 500 times the amount of his actual harm as determined by the jury. Moreover, there is no suggestion that Dr. Gore or any other BMW purchaser was threatened with any additional potential harm by BMW's nondisclosure policy.

Of course, we have consistently rejected the notion that the constitutional line is marked by a simple mathematical formula, even one that compares actual *and potential* damages to the punitive award. Indeed, low awards of compensatory damages may properly support a higher ratio than high compensatory awards, if, for example, a particularly egregious act has resulted in only a small amount of economic damages. A higher ratio may also be justified in cases in which the injury is hard to detect or the monetary value of noneconomic harm might have been difficult to determine. It is appropriate, therefore, to reiterate our rejection of a categorical approach. Once again, "we return to what we said . . . in *Life Ins. Co. v. Haslip,* 499 U.S. 1 (1991): 'We need not, and indeed we cannot, draw a mathematical bright line between the constitutionally acceptable and the constitutionally unacceptable that would fit every case. We can say, however, that [a] general concer[n] of reasonableness . . . properly enter[s] into the constitutional calculus.' " In most cases, the ratio will be within a constitutionally acceptable range, and remittitur will not be justified on this basis. When the ratio is a breathtaking 500 to 1, however, the award must surely "raise a suspicious judicial eyebrow."

Sanctions for Comparable Misconduct

Comparing the punitive damages award and the civil or criminal penalties that could be imposed for comparable misconduct provides a third indicium of excessiveness. As Justice O'Connor has correctly observed, a reviewing court engaged in determining whether an award of punitive damages is excessive should "accord 'substantial deference' to legislative judgments concerning appropriate sanctions for the conduct at issue." In this case the $2 million economic sanction imposed on BMW is substantially greater than the statutory fines available in Alabama and elsewhere for similar malfeasance.

The maximum civil penalty authorized by the Alabama Legislature for a violation of its Deceptive Trade Practices Act is $2,000; other States authorize more severe sanctions, with the maxima ranging from $5,000 to $10,000. Significantly, some statutes draw a distinction between first offenders and recidivists; thus, in New York the penalty is $50 for a first offense and $250 for subsequent offenses. None of these statutes would provide an out-of-state distributor with fair notice that the first violation—or, indeed the first 14 violations—of its provisions might subject an offender to a multimillion dollar penalty. Moreover, at the time BMW's policy was first challenged, there does not appear to have been any judicial decision in Alabama or elsewhere indicating that application of that policy might give rise to such severe punishment.

The sanction imposed in this case cannot be justified on the ground that it was necessary to deter future misconduct without considering whether less drastic remedies could be expected to achieve that goal. The fact that a multimillion dollar penalty prompted a change in policy sheds no light on the question whether a lesser deterrent would have adequately protected the interests of Alabama consumers. In the absence of a history of noncompliance with known statutory requirements, there is no basis for assuming that a more modest sanction would not have been sufficient to motivate full compliance with the disclosure requirement imposed by the Alabama Supreme Court in this case.

IV

The fact that BMW is a large corporation rather than an impecunious individual does not diminish its entitlement to fair notice of the demands that the several States impose on the conduct of its business. Indeed, its status as an active participant in the national economy implicates the federal interest in preventing individual States from imposing undue burdens on interstate commerce. While each State has ample power to protect its own consumers, none may use the punitive damages deterrent as a means of imposing its regulatory policies on the entire Nation.

The judgment is reversed, and the case is remanded for further proceedings not inconsistent with this opinion.

It is so ordered.

JUSTICE SCALIA, with whom Justice Thomas joins, dissenting.

Today we see the latest manifestation of this Court's recent and increasingly insistent "concern about punitive damages that 'run wild.' " Since the Constitution does not make that concern any of our business, the Court's activities in this area are an unjustified incursion into the province of state governments.

In earlier cases that were the prelude to this decision, I set forth my view that a state trial procedure that commits the decision whether to impose punitive damages, and the amount, to the discretion of the jury, subject to some judicial review for "reasonableness," furnishes a defendant with all the process that is "due."

I do not regard the Fourteenth Amendment's Due Process Clause as a secret repository of substantive guarantees against "unfairness"—neither the unfairness of an excessive civil compensatory award, nor the unfairness of an "unreasonable" punitive award. What the Fourteenth Amendment's procedural guarantee assures is an opportunity to contest the reasonableness of a damages judgment in state court; but there is no federal guarantee a damages award actually *be* reasonable.

I

The most significant aspects of today's decision—the identification of a "substantive due process" right against a "grossly excessive" award, and the concomitant assumption of ultimate authority to decide anew a matter of "reasonableness" resolved in lower court proceedings—are of course not new. *Haslip* and *TXO Production Corp. v. Alliance Resources Corp.*, 509 U.S. 443 (1993), revived the notion, moribund since its appearance in the first years of this century, that the measure of civil punishment poses a question of constitutional dimension to be answered by this Court. Neither of those cases, however, nor any of the precedents upon which they relied, actually took the step of declaring a punitive award unconstitutional simply because it was "too big."

At the time of adoption of the Fourteenth Amendment, it was well understood that punitive damages represent the assessment by the jury, as the voice of the community, of the measure of punishment the defendant deserved. Today's decision, though dressed up as a legal opinion, is really no more than a disagreement with the community's sense of indignation or outrage expressed in the punitive award of the Alabama jury, as reduced by the State Supreme Court. It reflects not merely, as the concurrence candidly acknowledges, "a judgment about a matter of degree," but a judgment about the appropriate degree of indignation or outrage, which is hardly an analytical determination.

There is no precedential warrant for giving our judgment priority over the judgment of state courts and juries on this matter. The only support for the Court's position is to be found in a handful of errant federal cases, bunched within a few years of one other, which invented the notion that an unfairly severe civil sanction amounts to a violation of constitutional liberties.

JUSTICE GINSBURG, with whom CHIEF JUSTICE REHNQUIST joins, dissenting.

The Court, I am convinced, unnecessarily and unwisely ventures into territory traditionally within the States' domain, and does so in the face of reform measures recently adopted or currently under consideration in legislative arenas. The Alabama Supreme Court, in this case, endeavored to follow this Court's prior instructions; and, more recently, Alabama's highest court has installed further controls on awards of punitive damages. I would therefore leave the state court's judgment undisturbed, and resist unnecessary intrusion into an area dominantly of state concern.

GLOSSARY

Affected with a Public Interest: A legal doctrine developed by the Supreme Court in *Munn v. Illinois*. According to this doctrine, governments could engage in regulation of economic or property rights if the activity that invoked affected the public interest or good.

Bills of Attainder: Legislative punishments without benefit of a trial, prohibited in Article I, Secs. 9 and 10 of the U.S. Constitution.

Brandeis Brief: The presentation of sociological or other social science evidence in order to sustain or support legislation. The Brandeis brief is named after Louis Brandeis, who presented sociological data about the working conditions of women in *Muller v. Oregon* in order to convince the Court to uphold workplace regulations.

***Carolene Products* note four:** This note is found in *United States v. Carolene Products*; many regard its language as both proclaiming the end of the *Lochner* era protection for property rights and the beginning of the New Deal era of law, which placed a greater emphasis on the court defending individual rights.

Contracts Clause: Provision in Article I, Sec. 10, prohibiting states from abridging the freedom of contract.

Economic Due Process: A constitutional theory formulated by the Supreme Court used to invalidate government regulation of economic or property interests.

Ex Post Facto Laws: Retroactive criminal laws that seek either to punish individuals for actions that were not crimes when they were committed or that seek to increase the penalty over that which was in effect when they did so. Prohibited by Article I, Secs. 8 and 9 of the U.S. Constitution.

Heightened Scrutiny: A theory of judicial review first articulated in *Mugler v. Kansas* (1887) that stated that the Court would require the government to demonstrate a greater need to pass legislation when it affected property rights or the regulation of economic interests.

Laissez Faire: A French term generally referring to an economic philosophy that lets the free market operate with little or no government regulation or involvement.

Liberty of Contract: A theory of constitutional law formulated by the Court in cases such as *Lochner v. New York* (1905) and *Allgeyer v. State of Louisiana* (1897) used to invalidate efforts to regulate contracts or workplace conditions such as in terms of minimum wages or number of hours worked.

***Lochner* Era:** A name given by legal scholars to a period between the passage of the Fourteenth Amendment and the New Deal when the Supreme Court used various parts of the Constitution, but mostly the Due Process clause, to strike down laws that affected property rights or regulated the economy. The name is derived from the Supreme Court case *Lochner v. New York*.

No Taxation Without Representation: A principle cited by the American colonies explaining their opposition to taxation by the British Parliament, in which they were geographically unrepresented.

Popular Sovereignty: A notion, often associated with President Andrew Jackson, that emphasized universal white manhood suffrage and greater popular control over the government.

Punitive Damages: Damages assessed by a jury or a judge against a losing party in a civil case to punish them for the wrongdoing. In *BMW of North America, Inc. v. Gore* (1996) the Supreme Court stated that some punitive damages may be so excessive that they violate the Fourteenth Amendment.

State Police Powers: Powers over health, welfare, and morals that are considered to be reserved to the states and thus indirectly recognized in the Tenth Amendment.

Substantive Due Process: Substantive due process refers to using the Due Process Clause of the Fourteenth Amendment to invalidate economic legislation. Substantive due process states that there are certain things or activities the government cannot engage in. This is in contrast to procedural due process, which places limits on how government acts, such as requiring a hearing before taking action.

Vested Rights: Rights, particularly in reference to property, which are thought to be sacrosanct.

BIBLIOGRAPHY

Anderson, Terry L., and Fred S. McChesney. 2003. *Property Rights: Cooperation, Conflict, and the Law*. Princeton, NJ: Princeton University Press.

Aylmer, G. E. 1980. "The Meaning and Definition of 'Property' in Seventeenth Century England." *Past and Present,* Vol. 86, p. 93.

Baker, C. Edwin. 1986. "Property and Its Relation to Constitutionally Protected Liberty." *University of Pennsylvania Law Review,* Vol. 134, p. 741.

Barnett, Randy E. 2016. *Our Republican Constitution: Securing the Liberty and Sovereignty of We the People*. New York: Broadside Books.

Beard, Charles A. 1964. *An Economic Interpretation of the Constitution of the United States*. New York: Macmillan.

Bruchey, Stuart. 1980. "The Impact of Concern for the Security of Property Rights on the Legal System of the Early American Republic." *Wisconsin Law Review,* p. 1135.

Corwin, Edward S. 1948. *Liberty Against Government, The Rise, Flowering, and Decline of A Famous Juridical Concept*. Baton Rouge: Louisiana State University Press.

Corwin, Edwin S. 1955. *The Higher Law Background of American Constitutional Law*. Ithaca, NY: Cornell University Press.

Coyle, Dennis J. 1993. *Property Rights and the Constitution: Shaping Society Through Land Use Regulation*. Albany, NY: SUNY Press.

Currie, David P. 1985. *The Constitution in the Supreme Court: The First Hundred Years*, 1789–1888, Chicago: University of Chicago Press.

Currie, David P. 1990. *The Constitution in the Supreme Court: The Second Hundred Years*, 1888–1886. Chicago: University of Chicago Press.

Cushman, Barry. 1998. *Rethinking the New Deal Court: The Structure of a Constitutional Revolution*. New York: Oxford University Press.

Ely, James W., Jr. 1995. *The Chief Justiceship of Melville W. Fuller: 1888–1910*. Columbia: University of South Carolina Press.

Ely, James W. Jr. 1997. *The Guardian of Every Other Right: A Constitutional History of Property Rights*. New York: Oxford University Press.

Ely, James W. Jr. 2001. *Railroads and American Law*. Lawrence: University Press of Kansas.

Ely, James W., Jr. 2016. *The Contract Clause: A Constitutional History*. Lawrence: University Press of Kansas.

Epstein, Richard A. 1985. *Takings: Private Property and the Power of Eminent Domain*. Cambridge, MA: Harvard University Press.

Fischel, William A. 1995. *Regulatory Takings: Law, Economics, and Politics*. Cambridge, MA: Harvard University Press.

Frankfurter, Felix. 1964. *The Commerce Clause under Marshall, Taney and Waite*. Chicago: Quadrangle Books.

Gillman, Howard. 1993. *The Constitution Besieged: The Rise & Demise of Lochner Era Police Powers Jurisprudence*. Durham, NC: Duke University Press.

Gottlieb, Stephen E. 2000. *Morality Imposed: The Rehnquist Court and Liberty in America*. New York: New York University Press.

Hall, Kermit L. 1989. *The Magic Mirror: Law in American History*. New York: Oxford University Press.

Hill, G. Richard. 1993. *Regulatory Taking: The Limits of Land Use Controls*. Chicago: American Bar Association.

Horwitz, Morton J. 1977. *The Transformation of American Law: 1780–1860*. Cambridge, MA: Harvard University Press.

Horwitz, Morton J. 1992. *The Transformation of American Law: 1870–1960*. New York: Oxford University Press.

Hovenkamp, Herbert. 1988. "The Political Economy of Substantive Due Process." *Stanford Law Review,* Vol. 40, p. 379.

Hurst, James Willard. 1950. *The Growth of American Law*. Boston: Little, Brown.

Hurst, James Willard. 1956. *Laws and the Conditions of Freedom*. Madison: The University of Wisconsin Press.

Kahn, Ronald. 1994. *The Supreme Court and Constitutional Theory*: 1953–1993. Lawrence: University Press of Kansas.

Larkin, Paschal. 1930. *Property in the Eighteenth Century with Special Reference to England and Locke*. London: Cork University Press.

Leuchtenburg, William E. 1995. *The Supreme Court Reborn: The Constitutional Revolution in the Age of Roosevelt*. New York: Oxford University Press.

Levinson, Sanford. 2008. *Our Undemocratic Constitution: Where the Constitution Goes Wrong (And How We the People Can Correct It).* New York: Oxford University Press.

Levy, Leonard W. 1996. *A License to Steal: The Forfeiture of Property*. Chapel Hill: The University of North Carolina Press.

Michelman, Frank I. 1981. "Property as a Constitutional Right." 38 *Washington and Lee Law Review,* Vol. 38, p. 1097.

Nedelsky, Jennifer. 1994. *Private Property and the Limits of American Constitutionalism: The Madisonian Framework and Its Legacy*. Chicago: University of Chicago Press.

Nelson, William. 1979. *Americanization of the Common Law*. Cambridge, MA: Harvard University Press.

Paulsen, Monrad G. 1950. "The Persistence of Substantive Due Process in the States." *Minnesota Law Review,* Vol. 34, p. 91.

Pennock, J. Roland, and John W. Chapman. 1980. *Nomos XXII: Property*. New York: New York University Press.

Pound, Roscoe. 1938. *The Formative Era of American Law*. Glouchester, MA: Peter Smith.

Reeve, Andrew. 1986. *Property*. Atlantic Heights: New Jersey Humanities Press.

Ryan, Alan. 1984. *Property and Political Theory*. New York: Basil Blackwell.

Ryan, Alan. 1987. *Property*. Minneapolis: University of Minnesota Press.

Savage, David G. 1992. *Turning Right: The Making of the Rehnquist Supreme Court*. New York: John Wiley and Sons.

Segel, Jeffrey A, Harold J. Spaeth, and Sara C. Benesh. 2005. *The Supreme Court in the American Legal System*. New York: Cambridge University Press.

Schultz, David A. 1992. *Property, Power, and American Democracy*. New Brunswick, NJ: Transaction Publishers.

Siegan, Bernard H. 1980. *Economic Liberties and the Constitution*. Chicago: University of Chicago Press.

Siegan, Bernard H. 1987. *The Supreme Court's Constitution: An Inquiry into Judicial Review and its Impact on Society*. New Brunswick, NJ: Transactions, Inc.

Strong, Frank R. 1986. *Substantive Due Process: A Dichotomy of Sense and Nonsense*. Durham, NC: Carolina Academic Press.

Tushnet, Mark. 2003. *The New Constitutional Order*. Princeton, NJ: Princeton University Press.

White, G. Edward. 1991. *The Marshall Court & Cultural Change: 1815–1835*. New York: Oxford University Press.

White, G. Edward. 2000. *The Constitution and the New Deal*. Boston: Harvard University Press, 2000.

Wood, Stephen. 1968. *Constitutional Politics and the Progressive Era: Child Labor and the Law*. Chicago: University of Chicago Press.

Wright, Benjamin Fletcher. 1938. *The Contract Clause of the Constitution*. Cambridge, MA: Harvard University Press.

CHAPTER VI

Property Rights and Eminent Domain

Fifth Amendment:

. . . nor shall private property be taken for public use, without just compensation.

Timeline: Property Rights and Eminent Domain

1639 Massachusetts enacts the first eminent domain law in the colonies permitting the taking of private property for roads.

1690 John Locke publishes his *Second Treatise of Government.*

1776 American colonies declare their independence from England.

1777 Vermont enacts first Just Compensation Clause for private property taken by eminent domain.

1791 Fifth Amendment, including the Takings Clause, is ratified by the states and becomes part of the Constitution.

1820s States such as Massachusetts adopt Mill Acts.

1833 In *Barron v. Baltimore* the Supreme Court rules that the Bill of Rights, including the Fifth Amendment Just Compensation clause, does not apply to the states.

1868 Fourteenth Amendment is ratified.

1869 The first connection for the transcontinental railed road is completed in Promontory Summit, Utah.

1897 In *Chicago, B. & Q. R. Co. v. City of Chicago*, the Supreme Court rules that the Just Compensation Clause of the Fifth Amendment does apply to states.

1916 New York City adopts the first zoning laws in the United States.

1919 World War I ends.

1919 First rent control statutes enacted in the United States in New York, San Francisco, and Washington, D.C.

1921 Pennsylvania enacts the Kohler Act to prevent land subsistence due to mining.

1922 In *Pennsylvania v. Mahon*, the Supreme Court strikes down the Kohler Act and states that some forms of land use regulation might constitute a taking.

1926 In *Euclid v. Ambler Realty Co.*, the Court rules that zoning regulations do not constitute a taking under the Constitution.

1945 World War II ends.

1947 Levittown, New York, the first planned community in the United States, is developed.

1948 Robert Moses begins the construction of the Cross Bronx highway in Bronx, New York.

1948 1948 Housing Act enacted by Congress.

1954 In *Berman v. Parker*, the Supreme Court permits as a valid use the taking of private property in order to eliminate blight.

1956 The first contract for the development of the interstate highway system is signed.

1978 In *Penn Central v. New York*, the Court rules that a taking has not occurred unless it interferes with "significant investment-backed expectations."

1981 In *Poletown Neighborhood Council v. City of Detroit* the Michigan Supreme Court ruled that the taking of private property in order to promote economic development was a valid public use under the Michigan Constitution.

1982 In *Loretto v. Teleprompter Manhattan CATV Corp.*, the Court rules that any physical invasion of property constitutes a per se taking.

1984 In *Hawaii Housing Authority v. Midkiff*, the Supreme Court rules that the scope of the "public use" provision of the Fifth Amendment was as broad as the police powers of the state.

1987 In *Nollan v. California Coastal Commission*, the Court strikes down a state law giving the public a right to cross private property in order to access public beaches.

1987 The Court rules in *First English Evangelical Lutheran Church of Glendale v. County of Los Angeles* that even temporary moratoria on the use of property might constitute a compensable taking under the Fifth Amendment.

1992 In *Lucas v. South Carolina Coastal Council* the Supreme Court rules that regulations that deny owners all viable economic use of their property constitute a taking.

1994 In *Dolan v. City of Tigard*, the Supreme Court ruled that requiring owners to let the public use part of their property as a condition of getting a building permit constituted a taking.

2004 In *County of Wayne v. Hathcock*, the Michigan Supreme Court overturned Poletown and ruled that the promotion of economic development was not a valid public use under the Michigan Constitution.

2005 In *Kelo v. City of New London*, the Supreme Court ruled that the taking of a private home in order to promote economic development was a valid public use.

2013 In *Koontz v. St. Johns River Water Management District*, the Supreme Court rules that the denial of a land use permit because an owner refused to dedicate part of his property to the public or make a payment of money to fund projects on public lands constituted an uncompensated taking.

INTRODUCTION

Eminent domain is the inherent authority of governments to take private property for a variety of governmental purposes. The power dates back to Medieval England, where it was assumed that the crown ultimately had title or control over all property but allowed individuals to use it until such time as the government needed it for some public purpose, such as building roads. The power of eminent domain stands in contrast to the protection of property rights. If the king is free to take private property whenever he wants, then how protected are ownership rights? The protection of property, for some, such as English political philosopher John Locke in his *Second Treatise of Government*, is the chief goal of society. Locke's views on property, as well as many other features of his political theory, were extremely influential upon America and the constitutional founders. Thus, they sought some protections for property and limitations upon the use of eminent domain.

When the American colonies declared their independence from England, some of the earliest state constitutions contained eminent domain provisions. These constitutional provisions influenced the eventual adoption of the Fifth Amendment, which contains the eminent domain or **Takings Clause**. The Takings Clause actually refers to three separate requisites or elements that must be met for a valid exercise of eminent domain to occur. First, there must be a taking, or an acquisition of property. Second, the taking of the property must be for a **public use**. Finally, owners must receive **just compensation** for the property that has been taken. All three of these requirements have been the subject of significant constitutional adjudication and interpretation. This chapter's cases examine these three issues.

JUST COMPENSATION

While early state constitutions had eminent domain provisions, not all of them mandated that owners be compensated for property that had been acquired by the government. Lacking such a state requirement, the question became whether the Fifth Amendment Just Compensation Clause would require a state to compensate an owner for property taken by the government.

Barron v. Baltimore (32 U.S. 243, 1833) held that neither the Fifth Amendment nor the entire Bill of Rights served as a limit upon state behavior. In effect, states did not have to comply with the Just Compensation Clause. States were thus free to take property and not pay the owners. In fact, during the early nineteenth century, states such as Massachusetts adopted Mill Acts that provided for a flooding of adjacent property without compensation in order to build grist and grain mills. Some scholars have thus argued that economic development in the states was facilitated by the ability to take property and not pay compensation. It forced private individuals to bear the costs of economic development for the community.

Barron is normally read not in constitutional law but in civil rights/liberties courses as a way to highlight the limited application of the Bill of Rights to the states until the later part of the nineteenth century, when the Fourteenth Amendment Due Process Clause was first used to "incorporate" various provisions of the first ten amendments to be limits upon states. However, the case's significance in terms of property rights is also critical. It is one of those rare examples of the Marshall Court not coming to the defense of property rights.

Barron did not remain the law of the land too long. In *Chicago, B. & Q. R. Co. v. City of Chicago* (166 US 226, 1897), the Court modified by holding that the takings clause was inherent in the due process provision of the Fourteenth Amendment and mandated that the just compensation requirement is binding on states when they acquire property via eminent domain. *Chicago, B. & Q. R. Co.* is an often overlooked and underappreciated case. The reasons for that are many, not the least of which is the dense prose in which the decision is written. But the case would set in place a series of later decisions where the Court would eventually, over a sixty-year period, come to selectively incorporate or apply almost all of the Bill of Rights provisions to the individual states. This meant the states and local governments would have to pay just compensation for private property that was taken for a valid public use. This mandate begged two questions: What does just compensation entail in terms of an amount of dollars, and when does a taking occur?

The first question is not the subject of the cases in this chapter. But to answer the first question, the courts have consistently ruled that just compensation is paying the owner the fair market value for the property acquired, with this value determined in a variety of ways. In general, fair market value is the value of property that would be arrived at when a buyer and seller agree to a price at an "arm's length" negotiation. Another way to describe just compensation is to ask what a willing buyer would pay a willing seller for a piece of property. Courts also use a variety of appraisal methods to help determine what a piece of property is worth. One way is to look at the price of comparable sales of similar properties. Another is to ask what the replacement value of the property is, i.e., what would it cost to replace the property, such as by rebuilding it? Finally, judges may ask appraisers to look to what the income stream value of the property is. While these different appraisal methods are not the subject of this discussion, it is sufficient to know that the Supreme Court has stated that the Constitution requires that just compensation be paid for all property taken, with "just compensation" defined as the payment of fair market value.

Barron v. Baltimore

2 U.S. 243, 7 Peters 243, 8 L.Ed. 672 (1833)

In the process of paving certain streets around the waterfront, the city of Baltimore had diverted the course of some streams. The net result had been the deposit of silt and sediment around a wharf owned by Barron, making the water so shallow as to preclude use of the wharf. In a suit for $4500 in damages, using the provision of the Fifth Amendment of the Constitution that forbids deprivation of property without just compensation as a basis for his claim, Barron lost in the lower courts.

Vote: No dissent

Chief Justice Marshall delivered the opinion of the Court.

The Constitution was ordained and established by the people of the United States for themselves, for their own government, and not for the government of the individual States. Each State established a Constitution for itself, and, in that Constitution, provided such limitations and restrictions on the powers of its particular government as its judgment dictated. The people of the United States framed such a government for the United States as they supposed best adapted to their situation, and best calculated to their interests. The powers they conferred on this government were to be exercised by itself; and the limitations on power, if expressed in general terms, are naturally, and, we think, necessarily applicable to the government created by the instrument. They are limitations of power granted in the instrument itself; not of distinct governments, framed by different persons and for different purposes.

If these propositions be correct, the Fifth Amendment must be understood as restraining the power of the general government, not as applicable to the States. In their several constitutions they have imposed such restrictions on their respective governments as their own wisdom suggested; such as they deemed most proper for themselves. It is a subject on which they judge exclusively, and with which others interfere no further than they are supposed to have a common interest.

The counsel for the plaintiff in error insists that the Constitution was intended to secure the people of the several States against the undue exercise of power by their respective State governments; as well as against that which might be attempted by their general government. In support of this argument he relies on the inhibitions contained in the tenth section of the first article.

We think that section affords a strong if not a conclusive argument in support of the opinion already indicated by the court.

The preceding section contains restrictions which are obviously intended for the exclusive purpose of restraining the exercise of power by the departments of the general government. Some of them use language applicable only to Congress; others are expressed in general terms. The third clause, for example, declares that "no **bill of attainder** or ***ex post facto*** **law** shall be passed." No language can be more general; yet the demonstration is complete that it applies solely to the government of the United States. In addition to the general arguments furnished by the instrument itself, some of which have been already suggested, the succeeding section, the avowed purpose of which is to restrain State legislation, contains in terms the very prohibition. It declares that "no State shall pass any bill of attainder or *ex post facto* law." This provision, then, of the ninth section, however comprehensive its language, contains no restriction on state legislation. . . .

If the original Constitution, in the ninth and tenth sections of the first article, draws this plain and marked line of discrimination between the limitations it imposes on the powers of the general government, and on those of the States; if in every inhibition intended to act on State power, words are employed which directly express that intent,—some strong reason must be assigned for departing from this safe and judicious course in framing the amendments, before that departure can be assumed.

We search in vain for that reason.

. . . In almost every convention by which the Constitution was adopted, amendments to guard against the abuse of power were recommended. These amendments demanded security against the apprehended encroachments of the general government, not against those of the local governments.

FOR DISCUSSION

Does this decision mean that states are free to disregard the Bill of Rights and take property for any reason and without compensating the owner? What possible restrictions are there on states after this decision?

CHICAGO, B. & Q. R. CO. V. CITY OF CHICAGO

166 U.S. 226, 17 S.Ct. 581, 41 L.Ed. 979 (1897)

The City of Chicago used its power of eminent domain to condemn a right of way owned by the Chicago, Burlington & Quincy Railroad Company, a corporation of Illinois. In a jury trial to determine the compensation owned to the railroad company, a jury awarded it one dollar. The railroad company objected and appealed and the award was sustained. The case was appealed to the United States Supreme Court claiming a violation of Fourteenth Amendment Due Process clause.

Vote: No dissent

JUSTICE HARLAN delivered the opinion of the court.

The questions presented on this writ of error relate to the jurisdiction of this court to re-examine the final judgment of the supreme court of Illinois, and to certain rulings of the state court, which, it is alleged, were in disregard of that part of the fourteenth amendment declaring that no state shall deprive any person of his property without due process of law, or deny the equal protection of the laws to any person within its jurisdiction.

By an ordinance of the city council of Chicago approved October 9, 1880, it was ordained that Rockwell street, in that city, be opened and widened from West Eighteenth street to West Nineteenth street by condemning therefore, in accordance with the above act of April 10, 1872, certain parcels of land owned by individuals, and also certain parts of the right of way in that city of the Chicago, Burlington & Quincy Railroad Company, a corporation of Illinois.

In execution of that ordinance a petition was filed by the city, November 12, 1890, in the circuit court of Cook county, Ill., for the condemnation of the lots, pieces, or parcels of land and property proposed to be taken or damaged for the proposed improvement, and praying that the just compensation required for private property taken or damaged be ascertained by a jury.

The parties interested in the property described in the petition, including the Chicago, Burlington & Quincy Railroad Company, were admitted as defendants in the proceeding. In their verdict the jury fixed the just compensation to be paid to the respective individual owners of the lots, pieces, and parcels of land and property sought to be taken or damaged by the proposed improvements, and fixed one dollar as just compensation to the railroad company in respect of those parts of its right of way described in the city's petition as necessary to be used for the purposes of the proposed street.

Thereupon the railroad company moved for a new trial. The motion was overruled, and a final judgment was rendered in execution of the award by the jury. That judgment was affirmed by the supreme court of the state.

It is proper now to inquire whether the due process of law enjoined by the fourteenth amendment requires compensation to be made or adequately secured to the owner of private property taken for public use under the authority of a state. . . .

But if, as this court has adjudged, a legislative enactment, assuming arbitrarily to take the property of one individual and give it to another individual, would not be due process of law, as enjoined by the fourteenth amendment, it must be that the requirement of due process of law in that amendment is applicable to the direct appropriation by the state to public use, and without compensation, of the private property of the citizen. The legislature may prescribe a form of procedure to be observed in the taking of private property for public use, but it is not due process of law if provision be not made for compensation. Notice to the owner to appear in some judicial tribunal and show cause why his property shall not be taken for public use without compensation would be a mockery of justice. Due process of law as applied to judicial proceedings instituted for the taking of private property for public use means, therefore, such process as recognizes the right of the owner to be compensated if his property be wrested from him and transferred to the public. The mere form of the proceeding instituted against the owner, even if he be admitted to defend, cannot convert the process used into due process of law, if the necessary result be to deprive him of his property without compensation.

In *Fletcher v. Peck*, 10 U.S. 87 (1810), this court, speaking by Chief Justice Marshall, said: "It may well be doubted whether the nature of society and of government does not prescribe some limits to the legislative power; and, if any be prescribed, where are they to be found, if the property of an individual, fairly and honestly acquired, may be seized without compensation? To the legislature all legislative power is granted, but the question whether the act of transferring the property of an individual to the public be in the nature of legislative power is well worthy of serious reflection."

In *Citizens' Savings & Loan Ass'n v. City of Topeka*, 87 U.S. 655 (1874), Mr. Justice Miller, delivering the judgment of this court, after observing that there were private rights in every free government beyond the control of the state, and that a government, by whatever name it was called, under which the property of citizens was at the absolute disposition and unlimited control of any depository of power, was, after all, but a despotism, said: "The theory of our governments, state and national, is opposed to the deposit of unlimited power anywhere. The executive, the legislative, and the judicial branches of these governments are all of limited and defined powers. There are limitations on such power, which grow out of the essential nature of all free governments, implied reservations of individual rights, without which the social compact could not exist, and which are respected by all governments entitled to the name." No court, he said, would hesitate to adjudge void any statute declaring that "the homestead now owned by A. should no longer be his, but should henceforth be the property of B." In accordance with these principles it was held in that case that the property of the citizen could not be taken under the power of taxation to promote private objects, and, therefore, that a statute authorizing a town to issue its bonds in aid of a manufacturing enterprise of individuals was void because the object was a private, not a public, one.

In our opinion, a judgment of a state court, even if it be authorized by statute, whereby private property is taken for the state or under its direction for public use, without compensation made or secured to the owner, is, upon principle and authority, wanting in the due process of law required by the fourteenth amendment of the constitution of the United States, and the affirmance of such judgment by the highest court of the state is a denial by that state of a right secured to the owner by that instrument.

FOR DISCUSSION

Does this decision reverse *Barron v. Baltimore*? What is the basis of the Court finding that just compensation is required? Is it the Fourteenth Amendment or something else?

WHAT CONSTITUTES A TAKING?

Deciding what constitutes a **taking** is the subject of numerous court opinions. The Takings Clause is vague. While it states that it applies to private property, it is not clear that it applies to all forms of property or that all property interests come within the protection of the Fifth Amendment. The general assumption was that eminent domain applied to real property, that is, land, homes, and buildings. Yet in *West River Bridge v. Dix* (6 Howard 507, 1848), the Supreme Court ruled that all forms of property, including contracts, franchises, and even personal property, could be acquired by eminent domain. In the *City of Oakland v. Oakland Raiders* (646 P. 2d 835, Cal. 1982), the California Supreme Court ruled that a city could in theory use its power of eminent domain to condemn and acquire the property of a football team in order to prevent it from moving to another city. This use of eminent domain would permit the taking of individual contracts with athletes. In short, all forms of property, whether personal, real, tangible, or intangible, are subject to being taken by eminent domain.

But assume that the government does not actually take the physical or legal possession of property. What if instead the government decides to impose some restrictions on how individuals use their property? Can the government do that without having to pay compensation? The answer is that it depends, and resolving the question involves drawing a line between two government powers: eminent domain and police power.

Police power, as discussed in Chapter VII, is the inherent ability or authority of states to regulate the health, safety, welfare, and morals of the people. States have broad police power to protect individuals from numerous problems. In addition, the Supreme Court has ruled that individuals have no right to use their property in a way that causes a nuisance or hurts others. If they do, the government can use its police power to regulate the property to prevent the nuisance. If that regulatory power is used to abate a nuisance, no compensation is due to owners, even if it means that they are denied some use of their property. However, not all regulations are the same, and some may be more extensive than necessary to address a problem. How does one determine when a regulation has become so extensive that it effectively becomes what is called a **regulatory taking**? This is the subject of *Pennsylvania v. Mahon* (260 U.S. 393, 1922); in that case Justice Holmes stated that a regulation turns into a taking when it goes "too far."

The facts of *Mahon* are unique and are worth noting. Was the state of Pennsylvania really seeking to abate a public nuisance when it passed a law to limit underground mining into order to prevent the collapse of surface ground above? How many individuals was the legislation seeking to help? All this may be important to understanding the case. Holmes's test has remained influential to this day, but what it means for a regulation to go "too far" has generated significant controversy and debate because of its vagueness. Subsequent decisions would offer more clarity to the *Mahon* rule. Moreover, the ruling in this case suggested that a taking could occur even if there were no physical occupation of property. Mere regulation could rise to a taking.

The *Mahon* ruling opened up to owners a new remedy called inverse condemnation. If owners believed their property had been taken by a regulation, they could sue for damages or just compensation under inverse condemnation. *Mahon* should be contrasted to *Keystone Bituminous Coal Ass'n v. DeBenedictis* (480 U.S. 470, 1987), where in a 5–4 opinion, the Court rejected claims that a new state law almost identical to the one in *Mahon* constituted a regulatory taking. Here the Court found a public purpose in preventing subsidence, there was no loss of value to property, and, more importantly, unlike in *Mahon*, where only one home was protected against the collapse of the surface soil, more structures were protected by the new state law. The contrast between *Mahon* and *Keystone* perhaps lies in the number of individuals who were benefited by the act, with the latter involving a clear public good that may have been lacking in the former.

Another issue that surfaces in the interaction between police power and eminent domain involves land use **zoning**, which became popular in the early part of the twentieth century as communities sought to achieve two objectives. One objective was to maximize the best use of land and property, making them more efficient by, for example, placing certain types of functions or usages, such as factories, in the same area where they can share water, sewer, and electrical resources. A second purpose of zoning is to minimize nuisances and protect property values. It may very well be good for a community to have cement factories and single family homes, but not necessarily next to one another. The pollution and waste from the former may damage or hurt the property values of the latter. Thus, zoning is one way to separate the two different uses as a means of allowing both to coexist without affecting one another negatively.

The constitutional issue as far as zoning is concerned is whether it is a form of policy power regulation that has gone too far to effect a taking. This was the issue raised in *Euclid v. Ambler Realty Co* (272 U.S. 365, 1926). Zoning regulations limit what owners may do with their property. The Court concluded that zoning regulations are constitutional and generally do not constitute a form of a regulatory taking or inverse condemnation. *Euclid* is probably the leading case on zoning and land use. Only recently has the Court gone beyond the matters of safety, health, and morals to include aesthetic considerations as a proper basis for such legislation.

Penn Central Company v. City of New York (438 U.S. 104, 1978) is another important case in the history of defining a taking. Here the Court was looking at another aspect of land use or zoning law when it came to the question of a taking. At issue were historic preservation laws that, at least in the case, placed a limit on the right of the owner to use the airspace above his property for development purposes. The city of New York asserted two claims against assertions that the denial of this development was a taking. First, it argued that the promotion of aesthetic goals—historic preservation—was a valid police power function when it came to zoning. Second, the city argued that there was no taking here because one had to look at the overall value of the property when determining whether an owner had suffered a compensable loss. Penn Central claimed that it had suffered a loss because it had been denied a right to use a portion of its property—its airspace rights.

The Court ruled for the City of New York. First, it stated that not all forms of restrictions upon the use of property constitute a taking. Following *Mahon*, a taking occurs only when a regulation goes too far. Here, the Court suggested that the loss of investment-backed expectations constituted a taking. Second, following *Euclid*, not all zoning regulations were takings. In some cases, restrictions on airspace development or to promote aesthetic interests would be considered valid police power objectives. Finally, when evaluating whether a taking had occurred, one should look at the impact upon the property as a whole, and not upon specific segments of property. Thus, even though airspace development was limited, its loss should not be segmented off from the rest of the property when assessing the diminution of the value of the entire property. The critical point in *Penn Central* was as follows: a taking can occur if one loses significant **investment-backed expectations** in property. Physical invasion of property by the government is not necessary for there to be a taking. The *Penn Central* case is also frequently cited for two other major propositions related to eminent domain. First, the case upheld the promotion of aesthetics as a valid public use. In effect, communities could pass laws regulating the appearance of buildings without that constituting a taking. Second, when determining whether a taking had occurred one is to evaluate the property as a whole and not break it up into segments such as air right, the surface, of the subsurface.

Mahon and *Penn Central* raised timely questions about how regulations might affect a taking, and the Court sought to clarify the line between a taking and a use of the police power. Its answer in these cases did not settle the question regarding when a taking had occurred. The Court has continued to struggle with that question in several cases. First, in *Loretto v. Teleprompter Manhattan CATV Corp* (458 U.S. 419, 1982)., the Court articulated a clear per se rule: any physical invasion of private property by the government constituted a taking. In this case, providing access to a building to install a cable television cable without the owner's permission constituted a direct physical taking of property. Second, in *First English Evangelical Lutheran Church of Glendale v. County of Los Angeles* (482 U.S. 304, 1987), the Court established the rule that total temporary bans, such as moratoria, could rise to the level of a compensable taking under some circumstances. This was a significant case. Prior to *First English*, governments could issue moratoria on development of property lasting for years, claiming that they were studying potential changes in zoning laws or comprehensive plans, or, as in the case of *First English*, prevent owners from redeveloping their land after it had been flooded. Until *First English* the Court ruled that temporary takings, whether total or partial denial or use of property, were not compensable. This decision changed that, ruling that even short-term denial of the use of property may rise to a level of a taking.

Another question growing out of *Mahon* and then *Penn Central* was about the degree of denial of use of property one had to suffer before there was a taking. Phrased another way: How do we know when a regulation has gone too far or how large a loss to investment-backed expectations must occur for there to be a taking? *Nollan v. California Coastal Commission* (483 U.S. 825, 1987) and *Lucas v. South Carolina Coastal Council* (505 U.S. 1003, 1992) sought to answer this question. In *Nollan* the Court ruled that a state law granting the public a right of way across an owner's private property in order to provide access to the ocean and beach (which was public property) was a form of a taking. Writing for the Court, Justice Scalia invoked a familiar metaphor for property—that it was a **bundle of sticks**. This means that ownership is associated with many different rights, including the right to exclude others. Scalia and a majority of the Court believed that a loss of this right rose to a level of a taking.

In *Lucas* the Court looked at coastal regulations that prevented an owner from developing his property due to concerns about flooding. According to Scalia in *Lucas*, a taking occurs in one of two situations. First, if a regulation leads to a total loss of the value of the property, that is a **per se taking**. Second, if a land use regulation seeks to prevent a harm that was not already a restriction on the property at the time of its purchase (not in a total), it might also be a taking.

One issue left unanswered by *Nollan* was the degree of justification that a government had to provide if it wished to impose restrictions upon property. Specifically, *Nollan* involved a common practice of exactions, whereby owners, as a condition of receiving a permit to build or develop property, were required to perform some task, such as give the public access to the property. How far could the government condition development upon these exactions without it rising to a taking? *Dolan v. City of Tigard* (512 U.S. 374, 1994) sought to answer this question. In *Dolan* the Court had to address this issue of exactions. In a decision that many found surprising, the Court suggested that these exactions needed to be examined not under a normal rational basis standard but with a more heightened scrutiny that demanded some rough proportionality between the permit and the exaction required.

Does the majority opinion in *Dolan* represent a revival of property rights and a return to some form of heightened scrutiny for economic rights, and especially for a taking? Some have contended yes, whereas others see the holding as more limited to the special case of exactions. While the Court did not go to the level of strict scrutiny, the "rough proportionality" test here seemed to reintroduce some more heightened analysis to at least one form of government regulation.

Finally, building off of *Nollan* and *Dolan* was another question that was addressed in *Koontz v. St. Johns River Water Management District*, 568 U.S. ___, 133 S.Ct. 2586 (2013). Specifically, the issue was whether the government, here a state water management district, could deny an owner a land use permit because he refused either to dedicate part of his property to public use or pay for offsite public water management projects. Here the Court said no, arguing that there was effectively no difference in approving a land use permit conditioned upon an owner turning over part of his property for public use, as in *Nollan* and *Dolan*, or here, denying a permit because an owner refuses to do the same. Both situations can effect uncompensated takings. This is the case unless the government can show that there is some nexus or connection between the permit being requested (or denied) and the need for the owner to dedicate or turn over part of his property to public use or fund public projects. The significance of the *Koontz* decision is that it reinforces the legal principles of *Nollan* and *Dolan* that exactions from owners who seek land use permits will be given a special scrutiny. Does this represent additional protection for property owners or limits on government action?

PENNSYLVANIA COAL CO. V. MAHON

260 U.S. 393, 43 S.Ct. 158, 67 L.Ed. 322 (1922)

The state of Pennsylvania enacted a subsidence law entitled the Kohler Act in 1921 that aimed to prevent the surface land from collapsing as a result of underground mining. The Act required owners to maintain supports and limit the amount of coal mined. Mine owners challenged this requirement as a taking of their property under the Fifth and Fourteenth Amendments.

Vote: 8–1

JUSTICE HOLMES delivered the opinion of the Court.

This is a bill in equity brought by the defendants in error to prevent the Pennsylvania Coal Company from mining under their property in such way as to remove the supports and cause a subsidence of the surface and of their house. The bill sets out a deed executed by the Coal Company in 1878, under which the plaintiffs claim. The deed conveys the surface but in express terms reserves the right to remove all the coal under the same and the grantee takes the premises with the risk and waives all claim for damages that may arise from mining out the coal. But the plaintiffs say that whatever may have been the Coal Company's rights, they were taken away by an Act of Pennsylvania, approved May 27, 1921 (P. L. 1198), commonly known there as the Kohler Act. The Court of Common Pleas found that if not restrained the defendant would cause the damage to prevent which the bill was brought but denied an injunction, holding that the statute if applied to this case would be unconstitutional. On appeal the Supreme Court of the State agreed that the defendant had contract and property rights protected by the Constitution of the United States, but held that the statute was a legitimate exercise of the police power and directed a decree for the plaintiffs. A writ of error was granted bringing the case to this Court.

The statute forbids the mining of anthracite coal in such way as to cause the subsidence of, among other things, any structure used as a human habitation, with certain exceptions, including among them land where the surface is owned by the owner of the underlying coal and is distant more than one hundred and fifty feet from any improved property belonging to any other person. As applied to this case the statute is admitted to destroy previously existing rights of property and contract. The question is whether the police power can be stretched so far.

Government hardly could go on if to some extent values incident to property could not be diminished without paying for every such change in the general law. As long recognized some values are enjoyed under an implied limitation and must yield to the police power. But obviously the implied limitation must have its limits or the contract and due process clauses are gone. One fact for consideration in determining such limits is the extent of the diminution. When it reaches a certain magnitude, in most if not in all cases there must be an exercise of eminent domain and compensation to sustain the act. So the question depends upon the particular facts. The greatest weight is given to the judgment of the legislature but it always is open to interested parties to contend that the legislature has gone beyond its constitutional power.

This is the case of a single private house. No doubt there is a public interest even in this, as there is in every purchase and sale and in all that happens within the commonwealth. Some existing rights may be modified even in such a case. But usually in ordinary private affairs the public interest does not warrant much of this kind of interference. A source of damage to such a house is not a public nuisance even if similar damage is inflicted on others in different places. The damage is not common or public. The extent of the public interest is shown by the statute to be limited, since the statute ordinarily does not apply to land when the surface is owned by the owner of the coal. Furthermore, it is not justified as a protection of personal safety. That could be provided for by notice. Indeed the very foundation of this bill is that the defendant gave timely notice of its intent to mine under the house. On the other hand the extent of the taking is great. It purports to abolish what is recognized in Pennsylvania as an estate in land—a very valuable estate—and what is declared by the Court below to be a contract hitherto binding the plaintiffs. If we were called upon to deal with the plaintiffs' position alone we should think it clear that the statute does not disclose a public interest sufficient to warrant so extensive a destruction of the defendant's constitutionally protected rights.

It is our opinion that the act cannot be sustained as an exercise of the police power, so far as it affects the mining of coal under streets or cities in places where the right to mine such coal has been reserved. As said in a Pennsylvania case, "For practical purposes, the right to coal consists in the right to mine it." *Commonwealth v. Clearview Coal Co.*, 256 Pa. 328, 331. What makes the right to mine coal valuable is that it can be exercised with profit. To make it commercially impracticable to mine certain coal has very nearly the same effect for constitutional purposes as appropriating or destroying it. This we think that we are warranted in assuming that the statute does.

The general rule at least is that while property may be regulated to a certain extent, if regulation goes too far it will be recognized as a taking. It may be doubted how far exceptional cases, like the blowing up of a house to stop a conflagration, go—and if they go beyond the general rule, whether they do not stand as much upon tradition as upon principle. In general it is not plain that a man's misfortunes or necessities will justify his shifting the damages to his neighbor's shoulders. We are in danger of forgetting that a strong public desire to improve the public condition is not enough to warrant achieving the desire by a shorter cut than the constitutional way of paying for the change. As we already have said this is a question of degree—and therefore cannot be disposed of by general propositions. But we regard this as going beyond any of the cases decided by this Court. The late decisions upon laws dealing with the congestion of Washington and New York, caused by the war, dealt with laws intended to meet a temporary emergency and providing for compensation determined to be reasonable by an impartial board. They were to the verge of the law but fell far short of the present act.

Decree reversed.

JUSTICE BRANDEIS dissenting.

Every restriction upon the use of property imposed in the exercise of the police power deprives the owner of some right theretofore enjoyed, and is, in that sense, an abridgment by the state of rights in property without making compensation. But restriction imposed to protect the public health, safety or morals from dangers threatened is not a taking. The restriction here in question is merely the prohibition of a noxious use. The property so restricted remains in the possession of its owner. The state does not appropriate it or make any use of it. The state merely prevents the owner from making a use which interferes with paramount rights of the public. Whenever the use prohibited ceases to be noxious—as it may because of further change in local or social conditions—the restriction will have to be removed and the owner will again be free to enjoy his property as heretofore.

A prohibition of mining which causes subsidence of such structures and facilities is obviously enacted for a public purpose; and it seems, likewise, clear that mere notice of intention to mine would not in this connection secure the public safety. Yet it is said that these provisions of the act cannot be sustained as an exercise of the police power where the right to mine such coal has been reserved. The conclusion seems to rest upon the assumption that in order to justify such exercise of the police power there must be "an average reciprocity of advantage" as between the owner of the property restricted and the rest of the community; and that here such reciprocity is absent. Reciprocity of advantage is an important consideration, and may even be an essential, where the state's power is exercised for the purpose of conferring benefits upon the property of a neighborhood, as in drainage projects; or upon adjoining owners, as by party wall provisions. But where the police power is exercised, not to confer benefits upon property owners but to protect the public from detriment and danger, there is in my opinion, no room for considering reciprocity of advantage.

FOR DISCUSSION

What facts seemed to be important to Holmes's opinion that the law in question only sought to promote a private good? After this decision, is it clear when a regulation has gone "too far?" What facts would be important in making that determination?

RELATED CASE

***Keystone Bituminous Coal Ass'n v. DeBenedictis:* 480 U.S. 470 (1987).**

In a 5–4 opinion, the Court rejected claims that a state law almost identical to the one in *Mahon* constituted a regulatory taking.

EUCLID V. AMBLER REALTY CO.

272 U.S. 365, 47 S.Ct. 114, 71 L.Ed. 303 (1926)

The village of Euclid, Ohio, adopted a zoning ordinance restricting the use of land. The land owned by the Ambler Realty Co. was zoned residential and had been held for years by the owner with the prospect of developing it for industrial use. Since land for such use is of much greater value than land used for residential purposes, the ordinance was challenged as depriving the company of property without due process of law contrary to the Fourteenth Amendment.

Vote: 6–3

JUSTICE SUTHERLAND delivered the opinion of the Court:

The ordinance now under review, and all similar laws and regulations, must find their justification in some aspect of the police power, asserted for the public welfare. The line which in this field separates the legitimate from the illegitimate assumption of power is not capable of precise delimitation. It varies with circumstances and conditions. A regulatory zoning ordinance, which would be clearly valid as applied to the great cities, might be clearly invalid as applied to rural communities. In solving doubts, the maxim "*sic utere tuo ut alienum non laedas*," [one must use property in a fashion that does not harm the property of others] which lies at the foundation of so much of the common law of nuisances, ordinarily will furnish a fairly helpful clew. And the law of nuisances, likewise, may be consulted, not for the purpose of controlling, but for the helpful aid of its analogies in the process of ascertaining the scope of the power. Thus the question whether the power exists to forbid the erection of a building of a particular kind of for a particular use, like the question whether a particular thing is a nuisance, is to be determined, not by an abstract consideration of the building or of the thing considered apart, but by considering it in connection with the circumstances and the locality. A nuisance may merely be a right thing in the wrong place, like a pig in the parlor instead of the barnyard. If the validity of the legislative classification for zoning purpose be fairly debatable, the legislative judgment must be allowed to control.

The serious question in the case arises over the provisions of the ordinance excluding from residential districts apartment houses, business houses, retail stores and shops, and other like establishments. This question involves the validity of what is really the crux of the more recent zoning legislation, namely, the creation and maintenance of residential districts, from which business and trade of every sort, including hotels and apartment houses, are excluded. Upon that question this court has not thus far spoken. The decisions of the state courts are numerous and conflicting; but those which broadly sustain the power greatly outnumber those which deny it altogether or narrowly limit it, and it is very apparent that there is a constantly increasing tendency in the direction of the broader view.

It is true that when, if ever, the provisions set forth in the ordinance in tedious and minute detail, come to be concretely applied to particular premises, including those of the appellee, or to particular conditions, or to be considered in connection with specific complaints, some of them, or even many of them, may be found to be clearly arbitrary and unreasonable. But where the equitable remedy of injunction is sought, as it is here, not upon the ground of a present infringement or denial of a specific right, or of a particular injury in process of actual execution, but upon the broad ground that the mere existence and threatened enforcement of the ordinance, by materially and adversely affecting values and curtailing the opportunities of the market, constitute a present and irreparable injury, the court will not scrutinize its provisions, sentence by sentence, to ascertain by a process of piecemeal dissection whether there may be, here and there provisions of a minor character, or relating to matters of administration, or not shown to contribute to the injury complained of, which, if attacked separately, might not withstand the test of constitutionality. In respect of such provisions, of which specific complaint is not made, it cannot be said that the landowner has suffered or is threatened with an injury which entitles him to challenge their constitutionality.

What would be the effect of a restraint imposed by one or more of the innumerable provisions of the ordinance, considered apart, upon the value or marketability of the lands, is neither disclosed by the bill nor by the evidence, and we are afforded no basis, apart from mere speculation, upon which to rest a conclusion that it or they would have any appreciable effect upon those matters. Under these circumstances, therefore, it is enough for us to determine, as we do, that the ordinance in its general scope and dominant features, so far as its provisions are here involved, is a valid exercise of authority, leaving other provisions to be dealt with as cases arise directly involving them.

And this is in accordance with the traditional policy of this court. In the realm of constitutional law, especially, this court has perceived the embarrassment which is likely to result from an attempt to formulate rules or decide questions beyond the necessities of the immediate issue. It has preferred to follow the method of a gradual approach to the general by a systematically guarded application and extension of constitutional principles to particular cases as they arise, rather than by out of hand attempts to establish general rules to which future cases must be fitted. This process applies with peculiar force to the solution of questions arising under the due process clause of the Constitution as applied to the exercise of the flexible powers of police, with which we are here concerned.

Decree reversed.

JUSTICES VAN DEVANTER, MCREYNOLDS, and BUTLER dissented without reported opinion.

FOR DISCUSSION

What is the difference between the police and eminent domain powers? What goals does zoning seek to effect? If zoning laws prevent an owner from developing property, why is that not a taking?

RELATED CASES

***Chicago, B. & Q. Ry. Co. v. Drainage Commissioners:* 200 U.S. 561 (1906).**

It was not considered deprivation of property without due process or denial of equal protection of the laws to force a railroad to move a bridge and culvert and appurtenances in order to care for increased artificial drainage into a creek. The police power covers regulations (here by drainage commissioners) designed to promote the public convenience or the general prosperity.

***Reinman v. Little Rock:* 237 U.S. 171 (1915).**

A city ordinance making it unlawful to conduct the business of a livery stable in certain defined portions of that city was not unconstitutional as depriving an owner of a livery stable already established within that district of his property without due process of law or denying him equal protection of the law.

***Hadacheck v. Los Angeles:* 239 U.S. 394 (1915).**

A city ordinance prohibiting the manufacture of bricks within specified limits of the city is not unconstitutional as depriving an owner of a brick factory of his property without due process of law or denying him equal protection of the laws.

***Cusack Co. v. Chicago:* 242 U.S. 526 (1917).**

An ordinance of the city of Chicago prohibiting billboards over a certain size in residential areas without securing the written consent of a majority of the property owners on both sides of the street was valid as a proper exercise of the police power.

***St. Louis Poster Advertising Co. v. City of St. Louis:* 249 U.S. 269 (1919).**

Aesthetic considerations in zoning regulations are secondary to the main consideration of health, morals, and safety.

PENN CENTRAL TRANSPORTATION COMPANY v. CITY OF NEW YORK

438 U.S. 104, 98 S.Ct. 2646, 57 L.Ed.2d 631 (1978)

Under a New York City historic preservation law, Grand Central Terminal was designated an historic landmark. Under this law, owners were limited in their ability to build beyond a certain height. However, owners were able to transfer these airspace development rights to other property. The Penn Station Company sought to develop the airspace rights above Grand Central Terminal and was refused permission to do so. They challenged the denial as a taking.

Vote: 6–3

JUSTICE BRENNAN delivered the opinion of the Court.

The question presented is whether a city may, as part of a comprehensive program to preserve historic landmarks and historic districts, place restrictions on the development of individual historic landmarks—in addition to those imposed by applicable zoning ordinances—without effecting a "taking" requiring the payment of "just compensation." Specifically, we must decide whether the application of New York City's Landmarks Preservation Law to the parcel of land occupied by Grand Central Terminal has "taken" its owners' property in violation of the Fifth and Fourteenth Amendments.

I

A

Over the past 50 years, all 50 States and over 500 municipalities have enacted laws to encourage or require the preservation of buildings and areas with historic or aesthetic importance. These nationwide legislative efforts have been precipitated by two concerns. The first is recognition that, in recent years, large numbers of historic structures, landmarks, and areas have been destroyed without adequate consideration of either the values represented therein or the possibility of preserving the destroyed properties for use in economically productive ways. The second is a widely shared belief that structures with special historic, cultural, or architectural significance enhance the quality of life for all. Not only do these buildings and their workmanship represent the lessons of the past and embody precious features of our heritage, they serve as examples of quality for today. "[H]istoric conservation is but one aspect of the much larger problem, basically an environmental one, of enhancing—or perhaps developing for the first time—the quality of life for people."

New York City, responding to similar concerns and acting pursuant to a New York State enabling Act, adopted its Landmarks Preservation Law in 1965. The city acted from the conviction that "the standing of [New York City] as a world-wide tourist center and world capital of business, culture and government" would be threatened if legislation were not enacted to protect historic landmarks and neighborhoods from precipitate decisions to destroy or fundamentally alter their character. The city believed that comprehensive measures to safeguard desirable features of the existing urban fabric would benefit its citizens in a variety of ways: *e. g.*, fostering "civic pride in the beauty and noble accomplishments of the past"; protecting and enhancing "the city's attractions to tourists and visitors"; "support[ing] and stimul[ating] business and industry"; "strengthen[ing] the economy of the city"; and promoting "the use of historic districts, landmarks, interior landmarks and scenic landmarks for the education, pleasure and welfare of the people of the city." § 205–1.0(b).

B

This case involves the application of New York City's Landmarks Preservation Law to Grand Central Terminal (Terminal). The Terminal, which is owned by the Penn Central Transportation Co. and its affiliates

(Penn Central), is one of New York City's most famous buildings. Opened in 1913, it is regarded not only as providing an ingenious engineering solution to the problems presented by urban railroad stations, but also as a magnificent example of the French beaux-arts style.

The Terminal is located in midtown Manhattan. Its south facade faces 42d Street and that street's intersection with Park Avenue. At street level, the Terminal is bounded on the west by Vanderbilt Avenue, on the east by the Commodore Hotel, and on the north by the Pan-American Building. Although a 20-story office tower, to have been located above the Terminal, was part of the original design, the planned tower was never constructed. The Terminal itself is an eight-story structure which Penn Central uses as a railroad station and in which it rents space not needed for railroad purposes to a variety of commercial interests. The Terminal is one of a number of properties owned by appellant Penn Central in this area of midtown Manhattan. The others include the Barclay, Biltmore, Commodore, Roosevelt, and Waldorf-Astoria Hotels, the Pan-American Building and other office buildings along Park Avenue, and the Yale Club. At least eight of these are eligible to be recipients of development rights afforded the Terminal by virtue of landmark designation.

On August 2, 1967, following a public hearing, the Commission designated the Terminal a "landmark" and designated the "city tax block" it occupies a "landmark site." The Board of Estimate confirmed this action on September 21, 1967. Although appellant Penn Central had opposed the designation before the Commission, it did not seek judicial review of the final designation decision.

On January 22, 1968, appellant Penn Central, to increase its income, entered into a renewable 50-year lease and sublease agreement with appellant UGP Properties, Inc. (UGP), a wholly owned subsidiary of Union General Properties, Ltd., a United Kingdom corporation. Under the terms of the agreement, UGP was to construct a multistory office building above the Terminal. UGP promised to pay Penn Central $1 million annually during construction and at least $3 million annually thereafter. The rentals would be offset in part by a loss of some $700,000 to $1 million in net rentals presently received from concessionaires displaced by the new building.

Appellants UGP and Penn Central then applied to the Commission for permission to construct an office building atop the Terminal. Two separate plans, both designed by architect Marcel Breuer and both apparently satisfying the terms of the applicable zoning ordinance, were submitted to the Commission for approval. The first, Breuer I, provided for the construction of a 55-story office building, to be cantilevered above the existing facade and to rest on the roof of the Terminal. The second, Breuer II Revised, called for tearing down a portion of the Terminal that included the 42d Street facade, stripping off some of the remaining features of the Terminal's facade, and constructing a 53-story office building. The Commission denied a certificate of no exterior effect on September 20, 1968. Appellants then applied for a certificate of "appropriateness" as to both proposals. After four days of hearings at which over 80 witnesses testified, the Commission denied this application as to both proposals.

The Commission's reasons for rejecting certificates respecting Breuer II Revised are summarized in the following statement: "To protect a Landmark, one does not tear it down. To perpetuate its architectural features, one does not strip them off."

II

The issues presented by appellants are (1) whether the restrictions imposed by New York City's law upon appellants' exploitation of the Terminal site effect a "taking" of appellants' property for a public use within the meaning of the Fifth Amendment, which of course is made applicable to the States through the Fourteenth Amendment, and, (2), if so, whether the transferable development rights afforded appellants constitute "just compensation" within the meaning of the Fifth Amendment. We need only address the question whether a "taking" has occurred.

The first and fourth questions assume that there has been a taking and raise the problem whether, under the circumstances of this case, the transferable development rights constitute "just compensation." The second and third questions, on the other hand, are directed to the issue whether a taking has occurred.

A

Before considering appellants' specific contentions, it will be useful to review the factors that have shaped the jurisprudence of the Fifth Amendment injunction "nor shall private property be taken for public use, without just compensation." The question of what constitutes a "taking" for purposes of the Fifth Amendment has proved to be a problem of considerable difficulty. While this Court has recognized that the "Fifth Amendment's guarantee [is] designed to bar Government from forcing some people alone to bear public burdens which, in all fairness and justice, should be borne by the public as a whole," this Court, quite simply, has been unable to develop any "set formula" for determining when "justice and fairness" require that economic injuries caused by public action be compensated by the government, rather than remain disproportionately concentrated on a few persons.

In engaging in these essentially ad hoc, factual inquiries, the Court's decisions have identified several factors that have particular significance. The economic impact of the regulation on the claimant and, particularly, the extent to which the regulation has interfered with distinct investment-backed expectations are, of course, relevant considerations. A "taking" may more readily be found when the interference with property can be characterized as a physical invasion by government than when interference arises from some public program adjusting the benefits and burdens of economic life to promote the common good.

"Government hardly could go on if to some extent values incident to property could not be diminished without paying for every such change in the general law," *Pennsylvania Coal Co. v. Mahon,* 260 U.S. 393 (1922), and this Court has accordingly recognized, in a wide variety of contexts, that government may execute laws or programs that adversely affect recognized economic values. Exercises of the taxing power are one obvious example. A second are the decisions in which this Court has dismissed "taking" challenges on the ground that, while the challenged government action caused economic harm, it did not interfere with interests that were sufficiently bound up with the reasonable expectations of the claimant to constitute "property" for Fifth Amendment purposes.

More importantly for the present case, in instances in which a state tribunal reasonably concluded that "the health, safety, morals, or general welfare" would be promoted by prohibiting particular contemplated uses of land, this Court has upheld land-use regulations that destroyed or adversely affected recognized real property interests. Zoning laws are, of course, the classic example.

Zoning laws generally do not affect existing uses of real property, but "taking" challenges have also been held to be without merit in a wide variety of situations when the challenged governmental actions prohibited a beneficial use to which individual parcels had previously been devoted and thus caused substantial individualized harm. In that case, a state entomologist, acting pursuant to a state statute, ordered the claimants to cut down a large number of ornamental red cedar trees because they produced cedar rust fatal to apple trees cultivated nearby. Although the statute provided for recovery of any expense incurred in removing the cedars, and permitted claimants to use the felled trees, it did not provide compensation for the value of the standing trees or for the resulting decrease in market value of the properties as a whole. A unanimous Court held that this latter omission did not render the statute invalid. The Court held that the State might properly make "a choice between the preservation of one class of property and that of the other" and since the apple industry was important in the State involved, concluded that the State had not exceeded "its constitutional powers by deciding upon the destruction of one class of property [without compensation] in order to save another which, in the judgment of the legislature, is of greater value to the public."

Stated baldly, appellants' position appears to be that the only means of ensuring that selected owners are not singled out to endure financial hardship for no reason is to hold that any restriction imposed on individual landmarks pursuant to the New York City scheme is a "taking" requiring the payment of "just compensation." Agreement with this argument would, of course, invalidate not just New York City's law, but all comparable landmark legislation in the Nation. We find no merit in it.

It is true, as appellants emphasize, that both historic-district legislation and zoning laws regulate all properties within given physical communities whereas landmark laws apply only to selected parcels. But, contrary to appellants' suggestions, landmark laws are not like discriminatory, or "reverse spot," zoning: that is, a land-use decision which arbitrarily singles out a particular parcel for different, less favorable treatment than the neighboring ones. In contrast to discriminatory zoning, which is the antithesis of land-use control as part of some comprehensive plan, the New York City law embodies a comprehensive plan to preserve structures of historic or aesthetic interest wherever they might be found in the city, and as noted, over 400 landmarks and 31 historic districts have been designated pursuant to this plan.

Equally without merit is the related argument that the decision to designate a structure as a landmark "is inevitably arbitrary or at least subjective, because it is basically a matter of taste," thus unavoidably singling out individual landowners for disparate and unfair treatment. The argument has a particularly hollow ring in this case. For appellants not only did not seek judicial review of either the designation or of the denials of the certificates of appropriateness and of no exterior effect, but do not even now suggest that the Commission's decisions concerning the Terminal were in any sense arbitrary or unprincipled. But, in any event, a landmark owner has a right to judicial review of any Commission decision, and, quite simply, there is no basis whatsoever for a conclusion that courts will have any greater difficulty identifying arbitrary or discriminatory action in the context of landmark regulation than in the context of classic zoning or indeed in any other context.

Appellants' final broad-based attack would have us treat the law as an instance, like that in *United States v. Causby*, 328 U.S. 256 (1946), in which government, acting in an enterprise capacity, has appropriated part of their property for some strictly governmental purpose. Apart from the fact that *Causby* was a case of invasion of airspace that destroyed the use of the farm beneath and this New York City law has in nowise impaired the present use of the Terminal, the Landmarks Law neither exploits appellants' parcel for city purposes nor facilitates nor arises from any entrepreneurial operations of the city. The situation is not remotely like that in *Causby* where the airspace above the property was in the flight pattern for military aircraft. The Landmarks Law's effect is simply to prohibit appellants or anyone else from occupying portions of the airspace above the Terminal, while permitting appellants to use the remainder of the parcel in a gainful fashion. This is no more an appropriation of property by government for its own uses than is a zoning law prohibiting, for "aesthetic" reasons, two or more adult theaters within a specified area, or a safety regulation prohibiting excavations below a certain level.

Affirmed.

JUSTICE REHNQUIST, with whom the CHIEF JUSTICE BURGER, and JUSTICE STEVENS join, dissenting.

FOR DISCUSSION

What is an investment-backed expectation? Do not owners have a property interest in the airspace above their property? How high up does that right extend? Could airplane flights over property constitute a taking?

LORETTO V. TELEPROMPTER MANHATTAN CATV CORP.

458 U.S. 419, 102 S.Ct. 3164, 73 L.Ed.2d 868 (1982)

A New York State law permitted cable companies access to private buildings for the purpose of installing cable television equipment. Owners objected that permitting this access by a cable company and leaving of cable and other equipment constituted a Fifth Amendment taking. One building owner, Jean Loretto, brought suit in court, challenging the law as a regulatory taking.

Vote: 6–3

JUSTICE MARSHALL delivered the opinion of the Court. JUSTICE BLACKMUN dissented and filed and opinion in which JUSTICES BRENNAN and WHITE joined.

This case presents the question whether a minor but permanent physical occupation of an owner's property authorized by government constitutes a "taking" of property for which just compensation is due under the Fifth and Fourteenth Amendments of the Constitution. New York law provides that a landlord must permit a cable television company to install its cable facilities upon his property. In this case, the cable installation occupied portions of appellant's roof and the side of her building. The New York Court of Appeals ruled that this appropriation does not amount to a taking. Because we conclude that such a physical occupation of property is a taking, we reverse.

I

Appellant Jean Loretto purchased a five-story apartment building located at 303 West 105th Street, New York City, in 1971. The previous owner had granted appellees Teleprompter Corp. and Teleprompter Manhattan CATV (collectively Teleprompter) permission to install a cable on the building and the exclusive privilege of furnishing cable television (CATV) services to the tenants. The New York Court of Appeals described the installation as follows:

> On June 1, 1970 TelePrompter installed a cable slightly less than one-half inch in diameter and of approximately 30 feet in length along the length of the building about 18 inches above the roof top, and directional taps, approximately 4 inches by 4 inches by 4 inches, on the front and rear of the roof. By June 8, 1970 the cable had been extended another 4 to 6 feet and cable had been run from the directional taps to the adjoining building at 305 West 105th Street.

Teleprompter also installed two large silver boxes along the roof cables. The cables are attached by screws or nails penetrating the masonry at approximately two-foot intervals, and other equipment is installed by bolts.

Initially, Teleprompter's roof cables did not service appellant's building. They were part of what could be described as a cable "highway" circumnavigating the city block, with service cables periodically dropped over the front or back of a building in which a tenant desired service. Crucial to such a network is the use of so-called "crossovers"—cable lines extending from one building to another in order to reach a new group of tenants. Two years after appellant purchased the building, Teleprompter connected a "noncrossover" line—*i.e.*, one that provided CATV service to appellant's own tenants—by dropping a line to the first floor down the front of appellant's building.

Prior to 1973, Teleprompter routinely obtained authorization for its installations from property owners along the cable's route, compensating the owners at the standard rate of 5% of the gross revenues that Teleprompter realized from the particular property. To facilitate tenant access to CATV, the State of New York enacted § 828 of the Executive Law, effective January 1, 1973. Section 828 provides that a landlord may not "interfere with the installation of cable television facilities upon his property or premises," and may not demand payment from any tenant for permitting CATV, or demand payment from any CATV company "in excess of any amount which the [State Commission on Cable Television] shall, by regulation, determine to be reasonable." The landlord may, however, require the CATV company or the tenant to bear the cost of installation and to indemnify for any damage caused by the installation.

Appellant did not discover the existence of the cable until after she had purchased the building. She brought a class action against Teleprompter in 1976 on behalf of all owners of real property in the State on which Teleprompter has placed CATV components, alleging that Teleprompter's installation was a trespass and a taking without just compensation. She requested damages and injunctive relief. Appellee City of New York, which has granted Teleprompter an exclusive franchise to provide CATV within certain areas of Manhattan, intervened.

II

The Court of Appeals determined that § 828 serves the legitimate public purpose of "rapid development of and maximum penetration by a means of communication which has important educational and community aspects," and thus is within the State's police power. We have no reason to question that determination. It is a separate question, however, whether an otherwise valid regulation so frustrates property rights that compensation must be paid. See *Penn Central Transportation Co. v. New York City,* 438 U.S. 104 (1978). We conclude that a permanent physical occupation authorized by government is a taking without regard to the public interests that it may serve. Our constitutional history confirms the rule, recent cases do not question it, and the purposes of the Takings Clause compel its retention.

A

As *Penn Central* affirms, the Court has often upheld substantial regulation of an owner's use of his own property where deemed necessary to promote the public interest. At the same time, we have long considered a physical intrusion by government to be a property restriction of an unusually serious character for purposes of the Takings Clause. Our cases further establish that when the physical intrusion reaches the extreme form of a permanent physical occupation, a taking has occurred. In such a case, "the character of the government action" not only is an important factor in resolving whether the action works a taking but also is determinative.

When faced with a constitutional challenge to a permanent physical occupation of real property, this Court has invariably found a taking. As early as 1872, in *Pumpelly v. Green Bay Co.*, 80 U.S. 166, this Court held that the defendant's construction, pursuant to state authority, of a dam which permanently flooded plaintiff's property constituted a taking. A unanimous Court stated, without qualification, that "where real estate is actually invaded by superinduced additions of water, earth, sand, or other material, or by having any artificial structure placed on it, so as to effectually destroy or impair its usefulness, it is a taking, within the meaning of the Constitution."

Although this Court's most recent cases have not addressed the precise issue before us, they have emphasized that physical *invasion* cases are special and have not repudiated the rule that any permanent physical *occupation* is a taking. The cases state or imply that a physical invasion is subject to a balancing process, but they do not suggest that a permanent physical occupation would ever be exempt from the Takings Clause.

Penn Central Transportation Co. v. New York City, as noted above, contains one of the most complete discussions of the Takings Clause. The Court explained that resolving whether public action works a taking is ordinarily an ad hoc inquiry in which several factors are particularly significant—the economic impact of the regulation, the extent to which it interferes with investment-backed expectations, and the character of the governmental action The opinion does not repudiate the rule that a permanent physical occupation is a government action of such a unique character that it is a taking without regard to other factors that a court might ordinarily examine.

B

The historical rule that a permanent physical occupation of another's property is a taking has more than tradition to commend it. Such an appropriation is perhaps the most serious form of invasion of an owner's property interests. To borrow a metaphor, *cf. Andrus v. Allard*, 444 U.S. 51, 65–66 (1979), the government does not simply take a single "strand" from the "bundle" of property rights: it chops through the bundle, taking a slice of every strand.

Moreover, an owner suffers a special kind of injury when a *stranger* directly invades and occupies the owner's property. As Part II-A indicates, property law has long protected an owner's expectation that he will be relatively undisturbed at least in the possession of his property. To require, as well, that the owner permit another to exercise complete dominion literally adds insult to injury. Furthermore, such an occupation is qualitatively more severe than a regulation of the *use* of property, even a regulation that imposes affirmative duties on the owner, since the owner may have no control over the timing, extent, or nature of the invasion.

C

Teleprompter's cable installation on appellant's building constitutes a taking under the traditional test. The installation involved a direct physical attachment of plates, boxes, wires, bolts, and screws to the building, completely occupying space immediately above and upon the roof and along the building's exterior wall.

The judgment of the New York Court of Appeals is reversed, and the case is remanded for further proceedings not inconsistent with this opinion.

It is so ordered.

FOR DISCUSSION

Why should we not view the cable installation as simply a police power regulation? Does the cable really amount to a physical taking or invasion of property given how little the intrusion?

First English Evangelical Lutheran Church of Glendale v. County of Los Angeles

482 U.S. 304, 107 S.Ct. 2378, 96 L.Ed.2d 250 (1987)

Property owned by the First English Evangelical Lutheran Church was used by them as a campground. A forest fire on adjacent property created a flood hazard by permitting runoff from the adjacent property onto that owned by First English Evangelical Lutheran Church. The flood destroyed all of the structures on their property. In response to this flooding, the County of Los Angeles issued a moratorium that placed a temporary ban on rebuilding or building on any property that had been flooded. The Church challenged this moratorium as a regulatory taking.

Vote: 6–3

Chief Justice Rehnquist delivered the opinion of the Court, in which Justices Brennan, White, Marshall, Powell, and Scalia joined.

In this case the California Court of Appeal held that a landowner who claims that his property has been "taken" by a land-use regulation may not recover damages for the time before it is finally determined that the regulation constitutes a "taking" of his property. We disagree, and conclude that in these circumstances the Fifth and Fourteenth Amendments to the United States Constitution would require compensation for that period.

In 1957, appellant First English Evangelical Lutheran Church purchased a 21-acre parcel of land in a canyon along the banks of the Middle Fork of Mill Creek in the Angeles National Forest. The Middle Fork is the natural drainage channel for a watershed area owned by the National Forest Service. Twelve of the acres owned by the church are flat land, and contained a dining hall, two bunkhouses, a caretaker's lodge, an outdoor chapel, and a footbridge across the creek. The church operated on the site a campground, known as "Lutherglen," as a retreat center and a recreational area for handicapped children.

In July 1977, a forest fire denuded the hills upstream from Lutherglen, destroying approximately 3,860 acres of the watershed area and creating a serious flood hazard. Such flooding occurred on February 9 and 10, 1978, when a storm dropped 11 inches of rain in the watershed. The runoff from the storm overflowed the banks of the Mill Creek, flooding Lutherglen and destroying its buildings.

In response to the flooding of the canyon, appellee County of Los Angeles adopted Interim Ordinance No. 11,855 in January 1979. The ordinance provided that "[a] person shall not construct, reconstruct, place or enlarge any building or structure, any portion of which is, or will be, located within the outer boundary lines of the interim flood protection area located in Mill Creek Canyon. . . ." The ordinance was effective immediately because the county determined that it was "required for the immediate preservation of the public health and safety. . . ." The interim flood protection area described by the ordinance included the flat areas on either side of Mill Creek on which Lutherglen had stood.

The church filed a complaint in the Superior Court of California a little more than a month after the ordinance was adopted. As subsequently amended, the complaint alleged two claims against the county and the Los Angeles County Flood Control District. The first alleged that the defendants were liable under Cal.Govt. Code Ann. § 835 for dangerous conditions on their upstream properties that contributed to the flooding of Lutherglen. As a part of this claim, appellant also alleged that "Ordinance No. 11,855 denies [appellant] all use of Lutherglen." The second claim sought to recover from the Flood Control District in inverse condemnation and in tort for engaging in cloud seeding during the storm that flooded Lutherglen. Appellant sought damages under each count for loss of use of Lutherglen. The defendants moved to strike the portions of the complaint alleging that the county's ordinance denied all use of Lutherglen, on the view that the California Supreme Court's decision in *Agins v. Tiburon*, 447 U.S. 255 (1980).

In *Agins v. Tiburon,* the California Supreme Court decided that a landowner may not maintain an inverse condemnation suit in the courts of that State based upon a "regulatory" taking. Under this decision, then, compensation is not required until the challenged regulation or ordinance has been held excessive in an action for declaratory relief or a writ of mandamus and the government has nevertheless decided to continue the regulation in effect. Based on this decision, the trial court in the present case granted the motion to strike the allegation that the church had been denied all use of Lutherglen. It explained that "a careful re-reading of the *Agins* case persuades the Court that when an ordinance, even a non-zoning ordinance, deprives a person of the total use of his lands, his challenge to the ordinance is by way of declaratory relief or possibly mandamus." Because the appellant alleged a regulatory taking and sought only damages, the allegation that the ordinance denied all use of Lutherglen was deemed irrelevant.

Appellant asks us to hold that the California Supreme Court erred in *Agins v. Tiburon* in determining that the Fifth Amendment, as made applicable to the States through the Fourteenth Amendment, does not require compensation as a remedy for "temporary" regulatory takings—those regulatory takings which are ultimately invalidated by the courts. Four times this decade, we have considered similar claims and have found ourselves for one reason or another unable to consider the merits of the *Agins* rule. For the reasons explained below, however, we find the constitutional claim properly presented in this case, and hold that on these facts the

California courts have decided the compensation question inconsistently with the requirements of the Fifth Amendment.

II

Consideration of the compensation question must begin with direct reference to the language of the Fifth Amendment, which provides in relevant part that "private property [shall not] be taken for public use, without just compensation." As its language indicates, and as the Court has frequently noted, this provision does not prohibit the taking of private property, but instead places a condition on the exercise of that power. This basic understanding of the Amendment makes clear that it is designed not to limit the governmental interference with property rights *per se,* but rather to secure *compensation* in the event of otherwise proper interference amounting to a taking. Thus, government action that works a taking of property rights necessarily implicates the "constitutional obligation to pay just compensation."

In *Pumpelly v. Green Bay Co.,* 80 U.S. 166 (1871), construing a provision in the Wisconsin Constitution identical to the Just Compensation Clause, this Court said:

> It would be a very curious and unsatisfactory result, if . . . it shall be held that if the government refrains from the absolute conversion of real property to the uses of the public it can destroy its value entirely, can inflict irreparable and permanent injury to any extent, can, in effect, subject it to total destruction without making any compensation, because, in the narrowest sense of that word, it is not *taken* for the public use.

Later cases have unhesitatingly applied this principle.

While the California Supreme Court may not have actually disavowed this general rule in *Agins,* we believe that it has truncated the rule by disallowing damages that occurred prior to the ultimate invalidation of the challenged regulation. The California Supreme Court justified its conclusion at length in the *Agins* opinion, concluding that:

> In combination, the need for preserving a degree of freedom in the land-use planning function, and the inhibiting financial force which inheres in the inverse condemnation remedy, persuade us that on balance mandamus or declaratory relief rather than inverse condemnation is the appropriate relief under the circumstances.

We, of course, are not unmindful of these considerations, but they must be evaluated in the light of the command of the Just Compensation Clause of the Fifth Amendment. The Court has recognized in more than one case that the government may elect to abandon its intrusion or discontinue regulations. Similarly, a governmental body may acquiesce in a judicial declaration that one of its ordinances has effected an unconstitutional taking of property; the landowner has no right under the Just Compensation Clause to insist that a "temporary" taking be deemed a permanent taking. But we have not resolved whether abandonment by the government requires payment of compensation for the period of time during which regulations deny a landowner all use of his land.

In considering this question, we find substantial guidance in cases where the government has only temporarily exercised its right to use private property. In *United States v. Dow,* though rejecting a claim that the Government may not abandon condemnation proceedings, the Court observed that abandonment "results in an alteration in the property interest taken—from [one of] full ownership to one of temporary use and occupation. . . . In such cases compensation would be measured by the principles normally governing the taking of a right to use property temporarily. Each of the cases cited by the [*United States v. Dow,* 357 U.S. 17 (1958),] Court involved appropriation of private property by the United States for use during World War II. Though the takings were in fact "temporary," there was no question that compensation would be required for the

Government's interference with the use of the property; the Court was concerned in each case with determining the proper measure of the monetary relief to which the property holders were entitled.

These cases reflect the fact that "temporary" takings which, as here, deny a landowner all use of his property, are not different in kind from permanent takings, for which the Constitution clearly requires compensation. In the present case the interim ordinance was adopted by the County of Los Angeles in January 1979, and became effective immediately. Appellant filed suit within a month after the effective date of the ordinance and yet when the California Supreme Court denied a hearing in the case on October 17, 1985, the merits of appellant's claim had yet to be determined. The United States has been required to pay compensation for leasehold interests of shorter duration than this. The value of a leasehold interest in property for a period of years may be substantial, and the burden on the property owner in extinguishing such an interest for a period of years may be great indeed. Where this burden results from governmental action that amounted to a taking, the Just Compensation Clause of the Fifth Amendment requires that the government pay the landowner for the value of the use of the land during this period. Invalidation of the ordinance or its successor ordinance after this period of time, though converting the taking into a "temporary" one, is not a sufficient remedy to meet the demands of the Just Compensation Clause.

Here we must assume that the Los Angeles County ordinance has denied appellant all use of its property for a considerable period of years, and we hold that invalidation of the ordinance without payment of fair value for the use of the property during this period of time would be a constitutionally insufficient remedy. The judgment of the California Court of Appeal is therefore reversed, and the case is remanded for further proceedings not inconsistent with this opinion.

It is so ordered.

JUSTICE STEVENS, with whom JUSTICES BLACKMUN and O'CONNOR join as to Parts I and III, dissenting.

One thing is certain. The Court's decision today will generate a great deal of litigation. Most of it, I believe, will be unproductive. But the mere duty to defend the actions that today's decision will spawn will undoubtedly have a significant adverse impact on the land-use regulatory process. The Court has reached out to address an issue not actually presented in this case, and has then answered that self-imposed question in a superficial and, I believe, dangerous way.

Until today, we have repeatedly rejected the notion that all temporary diminutions in the value of property automatically activate the compensation requirement of the Takings Clause. In *Agins,* we held:

> The State Supreme Court correctly rejected the contention that the municipality's good-faith planning activities, which did not result in successful prosecution of an eminent domain claim, so burdened the appellants' enjoyment of their property as to constitute a taking. . . . Even if the appellants' ability to sell their property was limited during the pendency of the condemnation proceeding, the appellants were free to sell or develop their property when the proceedings ended. Mere fluctuations in value during the process of governmental decisionmaking, absent extraordinary delay, are "incidents of ownership. They cannot be considered as a 'taking' in the constitutional sense.

In my opinion, the question whether a "temporary taking" has occurred should not be answered by simply looking at the reason a temporary interference with an owner's use of his property is terminated. Litigation challenging the validity of a land-use restriction gives rise to a delay that is just as "normal" as an administrative procedure seeking a variance or an approval of a controversial plan. Just because a plaintiff can prove that a land-use restriction would constitute a taking if allowed to remain in effect permanently does not mean that he or she can also prove that its temporary application rose to the level of a constitutional taking.

FOR DISCUSSION

Was not the temporary ban on development in the interest of protecting the public and the owners? Should this justify the ban on development? What confusion will result from majority holding, according to the dissent? Are there ever any situations where a temporary ban on the use of property would be upheld as a valid police power regulation?

NOLLAN V. CALIFORNIA COASTAL COMMISSION

483 U.S. 825, 107 S.Ct. 3141, 97 L.Ed.2d 677 (1987)

Beachfront property up to the high-water mark is considered public property under California law. The Nollans owned property along the beach, and they sought a permit to demolish an existing building and build a new home on their land. As a condition of getting a building permit, they were required to grant an easement across their land to give the public access to the beach. The Nollans objected that this easement was an uncompensated taking, and they challenged the access requirement in court.

Vote: 5–4

JUSTICE SCALIA delivered the opinion of the Court, in which CHIEF JUSTICE REHNQUIST and JUSTICES WHITE, POWELL, and O'CONNOR joined.

James and Marilyn Nollan appeal from a decision of the California Court of Appeal ruling that the California Coastal Commission could condition its grant of permission to rebuild their house on their transfer to the public of an easement across their beachfront property. The California court rejected their claim that imposition of that condition violates the Takings Clause of the Fifth Amendment, as incorporated against the States by the Fourteenth Amendment. *Ibid.* We noted probable jurisdiction.

I

The Nollans own a beachfront lot in Ventura County, California. A quarter-mile north of their property is Faria County Park, an oceanside public park with a public beach and recreation area. Another public beach area, known locally as "the Cove," lies 1,800 feet south of their lot. A concrete seawall approximately eight feet high separates the beach portion of the Nollans' property from the rest of the lot. The historic mean high tide line determines the lot's oceanside boundary.

The Nollans originally leased their property with an option to buy. The building on the lot was a small bungalow, totaling 504 square feet, which for a time they rented to summer vacationers. After years of rental use, however, the building had fallen into disrepair, and could no longer be rented out.

The Nollans' option to purchase was conditioned on their promise to demolish the bungalow and replace it. In order to do so, under Cal.Pub.Res. Code Ann. §§ 30106, 30212, and 30600 (West 1986), they were required to obtain a coastal development permit from the California Coastal Commission. On February 25, 1982, they submitted a permit application to the Commission in which they proposed to demolish the existing structure and replace it with a three-bedroom house in keeping with the rest of the neighborhood.

The Nollans were informed that their application had been placed on the administrative calendar, and that the Commission staff had recommended that the permit be granted subject to the condition that they allow the public an easement to pass across a portion of their property bounded by the mean high tide line on one side, and their seawall on the other side. This would make it easier for the public to get to Faria County Park and the

Cove. The Nollans protested imposition of the condition, but the Commission overruled their objections and granted the permit subject to their recordation of a deed restriction granting the easement.

On June 3, 1982, the Nollans filed a petition for writ of administrative mandamus asking the Ventura County Superior Court to invalidate the access condition. They argued that the condition could not be imposed absent evidence that their proposed development would have a direct adverse impact on public access to the beach. The court agreed, and remanded the case to the Commission for a full evidentiary hearing on that issue.

On remand, the Commission held a public hearing, after which it made further factual findings and reaffirmed its imposition of the condition. It found that the new house would increase blockage of the view of the ocean, thus contributing to the development of "a 'wall' of residential structures" that would prevent the public "psychologically . . . from realizing a stretch of coastline exists nearby that they have every right to visit." The new house would also increase private use of the shorefront. These effects of construction of the house, along with other area development, would cumulatively "burden the public's ability to traverse to and along the shorefront." Therefore the Commission could properly require the Nollans to offset that burden by providing additional lateral access to the public beaches in the form of an easement across their property. The Commission also noted that it had similarly conditioned 43 out of 60 coastal development permits along the same tract of land, and that of the 17 not so conditioned, 14 had been approved when the Commission did not have administrative regulations in place allowing imposition of the condition, and the remaining 3 had not involved shorefront property.

II

Had California simply required the Nollans to make an easement across their beachfront available to the public on a permanent basis in order to increase public access to the beach, rather than conditioning their permit to rebuild their house on their agreeing to do so, we have no doubt there would have been a taking. To say that the appropriation of a public easement across a landowner's premises does not constitute the taking of a property interest but rather (as Justice Brennan contends) "a mere restriction on its use," is to use words in a manner that deprives them of all their ordinary meaning. Indeed, one of the principal uses of the eminent domain power is to assure that the government be able to require conveyance of just such interests, so long as it pays for them. Perhaps because the point is so obvious, we have never been confronted with a controversy that required us to rule upon it, but our cases' analysis of the effect of other governmental action leads to the same conclusion. We have repeatedly held that, as to property reserved by its owner for private use, "the right to exclude [others is] 'one of the most essential sticks in the bundle of rights that are commonly characterized as property.' " *Loretto v. Teleprompter Manhattan CATV Corp.,* 458 U.S. 419 (1982), quoting *Kaiser Aetna v. United States*, 444 U.S. 164 (1979). In *Loretto* we observed that where governmental action results in "[a] permanent physical occupation" of the property, by the government itself or by others "our cases uniformly have found a taking to the extent of the occupation, without regard to whether the action achieves an important public benefit or has only minimal economic impact on the owner." We think a "permanent physical occupation" has occurred, for purposes of that rule, where individuals are given a permanent and continuous right to pass to and fro, so that the real property may continuously be traversed, even though no particular individual is permitted to station himself permanently upon the premises.

Given, then, that requiring uncompensated conveyance of the easement outright would violate the Fourteenth Amendment, the question becomes whether requiring it to be conveyed as a condition for issuing a land-use permit alters the outcome. We have long recognized that land-use regulation does not effect a taking if it "substantially advance[s] legitimate state interests" and does not "den[y] an owner economically viable use of his land." ("[A] use restriction may constitute a 'taking' if not reasonably necessary to the effectuation of a substantial government purpose"). Our cases have not elaborated on the standards for determining what constitutes a "legitimate state interest" or what type of connection between the regulation and the state interest satisfies the requirement that the former "substantially advance" the latter. They have made clear, however, that a broad range of governmental purposes and regulations satisfies these requirements. The Commission argues that among these permissible purposes are protecting the public's ability to see the beach, assisting the public in overcoming the "psychological barrier" to using the beach created by a developed shorefront, and preventing congestion on the public beaches. We assume, without deciding, that this is so—in which case the Commission unquestionably would be able to deny the Nollans their permit outright if their new house (alone, or by reason of the cumulative impact produced in conjunction with other construction) would substantially impede these purposes, unless the denial would interfere so drastically with the Nollans' use of their property as to constitute a taking.

The Commission argues that a permit condition that serves the same legitimate police-power purpose as a refusal to issue the permit should not be found to be a taking if the refusal to issue the permit would not constitute a taking. We agree. Thus, if the Commission attached to the permit some condition that would have protected the public's ability to see the beach notwithstanding construction of the new house—for example, a height limitation, a width restriction, or a ban on fences—so long as the Commission could have exercised its police power (as we have assumed it could) to forbid construction of the house altogether, imposition of the condition would also be constitutional. Moreover (and here we come closer to the facts of the present case), the condition would be constitutional even if it consisted of the requirement that the Nollans provide a viewing spot on their property for passersby with whose sighting of the ocean their new house would interfere. Although such a requirement, constituting a permanent grant of continuous access to the property, would have to be considered a taking if it were not attached to a development permit, the Commission's assumed power to forbid construction of the house in order to protect the public's view of the beach must surely include the power to condition construction upon some concession by the owner, even a concession of property rights, that serves the same end. If a prohibition designed to accomplish that purpose would be a legitimate exercise of the police power rather than a taking, it would be strange to conclude that providing the owner an alternative to that prohibition which accomplishes the same purpose is not.

The evident constitutional propriety disappears, however, if the condition substituted for the prohibition utterly fails to further the end advanced as the justification for the prohibition. When that essential nexus is eliminated, the situation becomes the same as if California law forbade shouting fire in a crowded theater, but granted dispensations to those willing to contribute $100 to the state treasury. While a ban on shouting fire can be a core exercise of the State's police power to protect the public safety, and can thus meet even our stringent standards for regulation of speech, adding the unrelated condition alters the purpose to one which, while it may be legitimate, is inadequate to sustain the ban. Therefore, even though, in a sense, requiring a $100 tax contribution in order to shout fire is a lesser restriction on speech than an outright ban, it would not pass constitutional muster. Similarly here, the lack of nexus between the condition and the original purpose of the building restriction converts that purpose to something other than what it was. The purpose then becomes, quite simply, the obtaining of an easement to serve some valid governmental purpose, but without payment of compensation. Whatever may be the outer limits of "legitimate state interests" in the takings and land-use context, this is not one of them. In short, unless the permit condition serves the same governmental purpose as the development ban, the building restriction is not a valid regulation of land use but "an out-and-out plan of extortion."

Reversed.

JUSTICE BRENNAN, with whom JUSTICE MARSHALL joins, dissenting.

Appellants in this case sought to construct a new dwelling on their beach lot that would both diminish visual access to the beach and move private development closer to the public tidelands. The Commission reasonably concluded that such "buildout," both individually and cumulatively, threatens public access to the shore. It sought to offset this encroachment by obtaining assurance that the public may walk along the shoreline in order to gain access to the ocean. The Court finds this an illegitimate exercise of the police power, because it maintains that there is no reasonable relationship between the effect of the development and the condition imposed.

The first problem with this conclusion is that the Court imposes a standard of precision for the exercise of a State's police power that has been discredited for the better part of this century. Furthermore, even under the Court's cramped standard, the permit condition imposed in this case directly responds to the specific type of burden on access created by appellants' development. Finally, a review of those factors deemed most significant in takings analysis makes clear that the Commission's action implicates none of the concerns underlying the Takings Clause. The Court has thus struck down the Commission's reasonable effort to respond to intensified development along the California coast, on behalf of landowners who can make no claim that their reasonable expectations have been disrupted. The Court has, in short, given appellants a windfall at the expense of the public.

FOR DISCUSSION

The Court refers to property as a bundle of sticks. What rights are in this bundle? If any of those rights are taken or limited, does that constitute a taking according to Scalia? Is there something about the right to exclude here?

LUCAS V. SOUTH CAROLINA COASTAL COUNCIL

505 U.S. 1003, 112 S.Ct. 2886, 120 L.Ed.2d 798 (1992)

Lucas was denied a permit by the South Carolina Coastal Commission to build on two beachfront properties he had purchased. The reason for the denial was that the property was within a critical habitat area, and under the South Carolina Beachfront Management Act no permanent structures could be built in these areas. Lucas contended that the denial of ability to develop his property constituted a taking, and he challenged the denial of the permit in state court. A lower court had found that the Beachfront Act and the denial of the permit had rendered Lucas's property valueless.

Vote: 6–3

JUSTICE KENNEDY filed the opinion, concurring in the judgment.

JUSTICE SCALIA delivered the opinion of the Court.

In 1986, petitioner David H. Lucas paid $975,000 for two residential lots on the Isle of Palms in Charleston County, South Carolina, on which he intended to build single-family homes. In 1988, however, the South Carolina Legislature enacted the Beachfront Management Act, which had the direct effect of barring petitioner from erecting any permanent habitable structures on his two parcels. See § 48–39–290(A). A state trial court found that this prohibition rendered Lucas's parcels "valueless." This case requires us to decide whether the Act's dramatic effect on the economic value of Lucas's lots accomplished a taking of private property under the Fifth and Fourteenth Amendments requiring the payment of "just compensation." U.S. Const., Amdt. 5.

I

A

Carolina's expressed interest in intensively managing development activities in the so-called "coastal zone" dates from 1977 when, in the aftermath of Congress's passage of the federal Coastal Zone Management Act of 1972, 86 Stat. 1280, as amended, 16 U.S.C. § 1451 *et seq.,* the legislature enacted a Coastal Zone Management Act of its own. In its original form, the South Carolina Act required owners of coastal zone land that qualified as a "critical area" (defined in the legislation to include beaches and immediately adjacent sand dunes) to obtain a permit from the newly created South Carolina Coastal Council (Council) (respondent here) prior to committing the land to a "use other than the use the critical area was devoted to on [September 28, 1977]."

In the late 1970's, Lucas and others began extensive residential development of the Isle of Palms, a barrier island situated eastward of the city of Charleston. Toward the close of the development cycle for one residential subdivision known as "Beachwood East," Lucas in 1986 purchased the two lots at issue in this litigation for his own account. No portion of the lots, which were located approximately 300 feet from the beach, qualified as a "critical area" under the 1977 Act; accordingly, at the time Lucas acquired these parcels, he was not legally obliged to obtain a permit from the Council in advance of any development activity. His intention with respect to the lots was to do what the owners of the immediately adjacent parcels had already done: erect single-family residences. He commissioned architectural drawings for this purpose.

The Beachfront Management Act brought Lucas's plans to an abrupt end. Under that 1988 legislation, the Council was directed to establish a "baseline" connecting the landward-most "point[s] of erosion . . . during the past forty years" in the region of the Isle of Palms that includes Lucas's lots. In action not challenged here, the Council fixed this baseline landward of Lucas's parcels. That was significant, for under the Act construction of occupiable improvements was flatly prohibited seaward of a line drawn 20 feet landward of, and parallel to, the baseline. The Act provided no exceptions.

B

Lucas promptly filed suit in the South Carolina Court of Common Pleas, contending that the Beachfront Management Act's construction bar effected a taking of his property without just compensation. Lucas did not take issue with the validity of the Act as a lawful exercise of South Carolina's police power, but contended that the Act's complete extinguishment of his property's value entitled him to compensation regardless of whether the legislature had acted in furtherance of legitimate police power objectives. Following a bench trial, the court agreed. Among its factual determinations was the finding that "at the time Lucas purchased the two lots, both were zoned for single-family residential construction and . . . there were no restrictions imposed upon such use of the property by either the State of South Carolina, the County of Charleston, or the Town of the Isle of Palms." The trial court further found that the Beachfront Management Act decreed a permanent ban on construction insofar as Lucas's lots were concerned, and that this prohibition "deprive[d] Lucas of any reasonable economic use of the lots, . . . eliminated the unrestricted right of use, and render[ed] them valueless." The court thus concluded that Lucas's properties had been "taken" by operation of the Act, and it ordered respondent to pay "just compensation" in the amount of $1,232,387.50.

The Supreme Court of South Carolina reversed. It found dispositive what it described as Lucas's concession "that the Beachfront Management Act [was] properly and validly designed to preserve . . . South Carolina's beaches." Failing an attack on the validity of the statute as such, the court believed itself bound to accept the "uncontested . . . findings" of the South Carolina Legislature that new construction in the coastal zone—such as petitioner intended—threatened this public resource. The court ruled that when a regulation respecting the use of property is designed "to prevent serious public harm," no compensation is owing under the Takings Clause regardless of the regulation's effect on the property's value.

III

A

Prior to Justice Holmes's exposition in *Pennsylvania Coal Co. v. Mahon,* 260 U.S. 393 (1922), it was generally thought that the Takings Clause reached only a "direct appropriation" of property, or the functional equivalent of a "practical ouster of [the owner's] possession." Justice Holmes recognized in *Mahon,* however, that if the protection against physical appropriations of private property was to be meaningfully enforced, the government's power to redefine the range of interests included in the ownership of property was necessarily constrained by constitutional limits. If, instead, the uses of private property were subject to unbridled, uncompensated qualification under the police power, "the natural tendency of human nature [would be] to extend the qualification more and more until at last private property disappear[ed]." These considerations gave birth in that case to the oft-cited maxim that, "while property may be regulated to a certain extent, if regulation goes too far it will be recognized as a taking."

Nevertheless, our decision in *Mahon* offered little insight into when, and under what circumstances, a given regulation would be seen as going "too far" for purposes of the Fifth Amendment. In 70-odd years of succeeding "regulatory takings" jurisprudence, we have generally eschewed any " 'set formula' " for determining how far is too far, preferring to "engag[e] in . . . essentially ad hoc, factual inquiries." We have, however, described at least two discrete categories of regulatory action as compensable without case-specific inquiry into the public interest advanced in support of the restraint. The first encompasses regulations that compel the property owner to suffer a physical "invasion" of his property. In general (at least with regard to permanent invasions), no matter how minute the intrusion, and no matter how weighty the public purpose behind it, we have required compensation. For example, in *Loretto v. Teleprompter Manhattan CATV Corp.,* 458 U.S. 419 (1982), we determined that New York's law requiring landlords to allow television cable companies to emplace cable facilities in their apartment buildings constituted a taking, even though the facilities occupied at most only 1 1/2 cubic feet of the landlords' property.

The second situation in which we have found categorical treatment appropriate is where regulation denies all economically beneficial or productive use of land. See *Nollan v. California Coastal Comm'n,* 483 US 825 (1987). As we have said on numerous occasions, the Fifth Amendment is violated when land-use regulation "does not substantially advance legitimate state interests *or denies an owner economically viable use of his land.*"

We think, in short, that there are good reasons for our frequently expressed belief that when the owner of real property has been called upon to sacrifice *all* economically beneficial uses in the name of the common good, that is, to leave his property economically idle, he has suffered a taking.

B

The trial court found Lucas's two beachfront lots to have been rendered valueless by respondent's enforcement of the coastal-zone construction ban. Under Lucas's theory of the case, which rested upon our "no economically viable use" statements, that finding entitled him to compensation. Lucas believed it unnecessary to take issue with either the purposes behind the Beachfront Management Act, or the means chosen by the South Carolina Legislature to effectuate those purposes. The South Carolina Supreme Court, however, thought otherwise. In its view, the Beachfront Management Act was no ordinary enactment, but involved an exercise of South Carolina's "police powers" to mitigate the harm to the public interest that petitioner's use of his land might occasion. By neglecting to dispute the findings enumerated in the Act or otherwise to challenge the legislature's purposes, petitioner "concede[d] that the beach/dune area of South Carolina's shores is an extremely valuable public resource; that the erection of new construction, *inter alia,* contributes to the erosion and destruction of this public resource; and that discouraging new construction in close proximity to the beach/dune area is necessary to prevent a great public harm." In the court's view, these concessions brought petitioner's challenge within a long line of this Court's cases sustaining against Due Process and Takings Clause challenges the State's use of its "police powers" to enjoin a property owner from activities akin to public nuisances.

It is correct that many of our prior opinions have suggested that "harmful or noxious uses" of property may be proscribed by government regulation without the requirement of compensation. For a number of reasons, however, we think the South Carolina Supreme Court was too quick to conclude that that principle decides the present case. The "harmful or noxious uses" principle was the Court's early attempt to describe in theoretical terms why government may, consistent with the Takings Clause, affect property values by regulation without incurring an obligation to compensate—a reality we nowadays acknowledge explicitly with respect to the full scope of the State's police power.

The transition from our early focus on control of "noxious" uses to our contemporary understanding of the broad realm within which government may regulate without compensation was an easy one, since the distinction between "harm-preventing" and "benefit-conferring" regulation is often in the eye of the beholder. It is quite possible, for example, to describe in *either* fashion the ecological, economic, and esthetic concerns that inspired the South Carolina Legislature in the present case. One could say that imposing a servitude on Lucas's land is necessary in order to prevent his use of it from "harming" South Carolina's ecological resources; or, instead, in order to achieve the "benefits" of an ecological preserve. Whether one or the other of the competing characterizations will come to one's lips in a particular case depends primarily upon one's evaluation of the worth of competing uses of real estate. A given restraint will be seen as mitigating "harm" to the adjacent parcels or securing a "benefit" for them, depending upon the observer's evaluation of the relative importance of the use that the restraint favors. Whether Lucas's construction of single-family residences on his parcels should be described as bringing "harm" to South Carolina's adjacent ecological resources thus depends principally upon whether the describer believes that the State's use interest in nurturing those resources is so important that *any* competing adjacent use must yield.

When it is understood that "prevention of harmful use" was merely our early formulation of the police power justification necessary to sustain (without compensation) *any* regulatory diminution in value; and that the distinction between regulation that "prevents harmful use" and that which "confers benefits" is difficult, if not impossible, to discern on an objective, value-free basis; it becomes self-evident that noxious-use logic cannot serve as a touchstone to distinguish regulatory "takings"—which require compensation—from regulatory deprivations that do not require compensation. *A fortiori* the legislature's recitation of a noxious-use justification cannot be the basis for departing from our categorical rule that total regulatory takings must be compensated. If it were, departure would virtually always be allowed. The South Carolina Supreme Court's approach would essentially nullify *Mahon*'s affirmation of limits to the noncompensable exercise of the police power. Our cases provide no support for this: None of them that employed the logic of "harmful use" prevention to sustain a regulation involved an allegation that the regulation wholly eliminated the value of the claimant's land.

Where the State seeks to sustain regulation that deprives land of all economically beneficial use, we think it may resist compensation only if the logically antecedent inquiry into the nature of the owner's estate shows that the proscribed use interests were not part of his title to begin with. This accords, we think, with our "takings" jurisprudence, which has traditionally been guided by the understandings of our citizens regarding the content of, and the State's power over, the "bundle of rights" that they acquire when they obtain title to property. It seems to us that the property owner necessarily expects the uses of his property to be restricted, from time to time, by various measures newly enacted by the State in legitimate exercise of its police powers; "[a]s long recognized, some values are enjoyed under an implied limitation and must yield to the police power." *Pennsylvania Coal Co. v. Mahon*, 260 U.S. 393 (1922). And in the case of personal property, by reason of the State's traditionally high degree of control over commercial dealings, he ought to be aware of the possibility that new regulation might even render his property economically worthless (at least if the property's only economically productive use is sale or manufacture for sale). In the case of land, however, we think the notion pressed by the Council that title is somehow held subject to the "implied limitation" that the State may subsequently eliminate all economically valuable use is inconsistent with the historical compact recorded in the Takings Clause that has become part of our constitutional culture.

The judgment is reversed, and the case is remanded for proceedings not inconsistent with this opinion.

FOR DISCUSSION

When only 99 percent of the value of the property is lost by a regulation, does that constitute a per se taking? What does it mean for a limit to be placed in the deed at the time of sale? Why is this an important issue for the majority?

DOLAN V. CITY OF TIGARD

512 U.S. 374, 114 S.Ct. 2309, 129 L.Ed.2d 304 (1994)

Florence Dolan owned a plumbing and electric supply store located on Main Street in the central business district of the city of Tigard. She sought a permit from the city to expand the size of her business and to add new parking spots. However, as a condition of Dolan receiving the permit from the City, she was informed that she would be required to dedicate approximately 10 percent of her property to be used by the city for public drainage purposes. This drainage was deemed necessary because the property was located along a creek and in a floodplain. It was also required to meet some of the open space or green space requirements of the comprehensive development plan for the area. Dolan objected to the dedication, claiming it was an illegal taking of her property. She challenged the dedication or extraction in court.

Vote: 5–4

CHIEF JUSTICE REHNQUIST delivered the opinion of the Court.

Petitioner challenges the decision of the Oregon Supreme Court which held that the city of Tigard could condition the approval of her building permit on the dedication of a portion of her property for flood control and traffic improvements. (1993). We granted certiorari to resolve a question left open by our decision in *Nollan v. California Coastal Comm'n,* 483 US 825 (1987), of what is the required degree of connection between the exactions imposed by the city and the projected impacts of the proposed development.

I

The State of Oregon enacted a comprehensive land use management program in 1973. The program required all Oregon cities and counties to adopt new comprehensive land use plans that were consistent with the statewide planning goals. The plans are implemented by land use regulations which are part of an integrated hierarchy of legally binding goals, plans, and regulations. Pursuant to the State's requirements, the city of Tigard, a community of some 30,000 residents on the southwest edge of Portland, developed a comprehensive plan and codified it in its Community Development Code (CDC). The CDC requires property owners in the area zoned Central Business District to comply with a 15% open space and landscaping requirement, which limits total site coverage, including all structures and paved parking, to 85% of the parcel. After the completion of a transportation study that identified congestion in the Central Business District as a particular problem, the city adopted a plan for a pedestrian/bicycle pathway intended to encourage alternatives to automobile transportation for short trips. The CDC requires that new development facilitate this plan by dedicating land for pedestrian pathways where provided for in the pedestrian/bicycle pathway plan.

The city also adopted a Master Drainage Plan (Drainage Plan). The Drainage Plan noted that flooding occurred in several areas along Fanno Creek, including areas near petitioner's property. The Drainage Plan also established that the increase in impervious surfaces associated with continued urbanization would exacerbate these flooding problems. To combat these risks, the Drainage Plan suggested a series of improvements to the Fanno Creek Basin, including channel excavation in the area next to petitioner's property. Other recommendations included ensuring that the floodplain remains free of structures and that it be preserved as greenways to minimize flood damage to structures. The Drainage Plan concluded that the cost of these improvements should be shared based on both direct and indirect benefits, with property owners along the waterways paying more due to the direct benefit that they would receive.

Petitioner Florence Dolan owns a plumbing and electric supply store located on Main Street in the Central Business District of the city. The store covers approximately 9,700 square feet on the eastern side of a 1.67-acre parcel, which includes a gravel parking lot. Fanno Creek flows through the southwestern corner of the lot and along its western boundary. The year-round flow of the creek renders the area within the creek's 100-year floodplain virtually unusable for commercial development. The city's comprehensive plan includes the Fanno Creek floodplain as part of the city's greenway system.

Petitioner applied to the city for a permit to redevelop the site. Her proposed plans called for nearly doubling the size of the store to 17,600 square feet and paving a 39-space parking lot. The existing store, located on the opposite side of the parcel, would be razed in sections as construction progressed on the new building. In the second phase of the project, petitioner proposed to build an additional structure on the northeast side of the site for complementary businesses and to provide more parking. The proposed expansion and intensified use are consistent with the city's zoning scheme in the Central Business District.

The City Planning Commission (Commission) granted petitioner's permit application subject to conditions imposed by the city's CDC. The CDC establishes the following standard for site development review approval:

> Where landfill and/or development is allowed within and adjacent to the 100-year floodplain, the City shall require the dedication of sufficient open land area for greenway adjoining and within the floodplain. This area shall include portions at a suitable elevation for the construction of a pedestrian/bicycle pathway within the floodplain in accordance with the adopted pedestrian/bicycle plan.

Thus, the Commission required that petitioner dedicate the portion of her property lying within the 100-year floodplain for improvement of a storm drainage system along Fanno Creek and that she dedicate an additional 15-foot strip of land adjacent to the floodplain as a pedestrian/bicycle pathway. The dedication required by that condition encompasses approximately 7,000 square feet, or roughly 10% of the property. In accordance with city practice, petitioner could rely on the dedicated property to meet the 15% open space and landscaping requirement mandated by the city's zoning scheme.

II

The Takings Clause of the Fifth Amendment of the United States Constitution, made applicable to the States through the Fourteenth Amendment, provides: "Nor shall private property be taken for public use, without just compensation." One of the principal purposes of the Takings Clause is "to bar Government from forcing some people alone to bear public burdens which, in all fairness and justice, should be borne by the public as a whole." Without question, had the city simply required petitioner to dedicate a strip of land along Fanno Creek for public use, rather than conditioning the grant of her permit to redevelop her property on such a dedication, a taking would have occurred. Such public access would deprive petitioner of the right to exclude others, "one of the most essential sticks in the bundle of rights that are commonly characterized as property."

On the other side of the ledger, the authority of state and local governments to engage in land use planning has been sustained against constitutional challenge as long ago as our decision in *Village of Euclid v. Ambler Realty Co.*, 272 U.S. 365 (1926). "Government hardly could go on if to some extent values incident to property could not be diminished without paying for every such change in the general law." A land use regulation does not effect a taking if it "substantially advance[s] legitimate state interests" and does not "den[y] an owner economically viable use of his land."

The sort of land use regulations discussed in the cases just cited, however, differ in two relevant particulars from the present case. First, they involved essentially legislative determinations classifying entire areas of the city, whereas here the city made an adjudicative decision to condition petitioner's application for a building permit on an individual parcel. Second, the conditions imposed were not simply a limitation on the use petitioner might make of her own parcel, but a requirement that she deed portions of the property to the city. In *Nollan,* we held that governmental authority to exact such a condition was circumscribed by the Fifth and Fourteenth Amendments. Under the well-settled doctrine of "unconstitutional conditions," the government may not require a person to give up a constitutional right—here the right to receive just compensation when property is taken for a public use—in exchange for a discretionary benefit conferred by the government where the benefit sought has little or no relationship to the property.

Petitioner contends that the city has forced her to choose between the building permit and her right under the Fifth Amendment to just compensation for the public easements. Petitioner does not quarrel with the city's authority to exact some forms of dedication as a condition for the grant of a building permit, but challenges the showing made by the city to justify these exactions. She argues that the city has identified "no special benefits" conferred on her, and has not identified any "special quantifiable burdens" created by her new store that would justify the particular dedications required from her which are not required from the public at large.

III

In evaluating petitioner's claim, we must first determine whether the "essential nexus" exists between the "legitimate state interest" and the permit condition exacted by the city. If we find that a nexus exists, we must then decide the required degree of connection between the exactions and the projected impact of the proposed development. We were not required to reach this question in *Nollan,* because we concluded that the connection did not meet even the loosest standard. Here, however, we must decide this question.

B

The second part of our analysis requires us to determine whether the degree of the exactions demanded by the city's permit conditions bears the required relationship to the projected impact of petitioner's proposed development. Here the Oregon Supreme Court deferred to what it termed the "city's unchallenged factual findings" supporting the dedication conditions and found them to be reasonably related to the impact of the expansion of petitioner's business.

The city required that petitioner dedicate "to the City as Greenway all portions of the site that fall within the existing 100-year floodplain [of Fanno Creek] . . . and all property 15 feet above [the floodplain] boundary." In addition, the city demanded that the retail store be designed so as not to intrude into the greenway area. The city relies on the Commission's rather tentative findings that increased storm water flow from petitioner's property "can only add to the public need to manage the [floodplain] for drainage purposes" to support its conclusion that the "requirement of dedication of the floodplain area on the site is related to the applicant's plan to intensify development on the site."

The city made the following specific findings relevant to the pedestrian/bicycle pathway:

> In addition, the proposed expanded use of this site is anticipated to generate additional vehicular traffic thereby increasing congestion on nearby collector and arterial streets. Creation of a convenient, safe pedestrian/bicycle pathway system as an alternative means of transportation could offset some of the traffic demand on these nearby streets and lessen the increase in traffic congestion.

The question for us is whether these findings are constitutionally sufficient to justify the conditions imposed by the city on petitioner's building permit. Since state courts have been dealing with this question a good deal longer than we have, we turn to representative decisions made by them.

In some States, very generalized statements as to the necessary connection between the required dedication and the proposed development seem to suffice. We think this standard is too lax to adequately protect petitioner's right to just compensation if her property is taken for a public purpose.

Other state courts require a very exacting correspondence, described as the "specifi[c] and uniquely attributable" test. Under this standard, if the local government cannot demonstrate that its exaction is directly proportional to the specifically created need, the exaction becomes "a veiled exercise of the power of eminent domain and a confiscation of private property behind the defense of police regulations." We do not think the Federal Constitution requires such exacting scrutiny, given the nature of the interests involved.

A number of state courts have taken an intermediate position, requiring the municipality to show a "reasonable relationship" between the required dedication and the impact of the proposed development. Typical is the Supreme Court of Nebraska's opinion in *Simpson v. North Platte,* 206 Neb. 240, 292 N.W.2d 297 (1980), where that court stated:

> The distinction, therefore, which must be made between an appropriate exercise of the police power and an improper exercise of eminent domain is whether the requirement has some reasonable relationship or nexus to the use to which the property is being made or is merely being used as an excuse for taking property simply because at that particular moment the landowner is asking the city for some license or permit.

Thus, the court held that a city may not require a property owner to dedicate private property for some future public use as a condition of obtaining a building permit when such future use is not "occasioned by the construction sought to be permitted."

Some form of the reasonable relationship test has been adopted in many other jurisdictions. . . .

We think the "reasonable relationship" test adopted by a majority of the state courts is closer to the federal constitutional norm than either of those previously discussed. But we do not adopt it as such, partly because the term "reasonable relationship" seems confusingly similar to the term "rational basis" which describes the minimal level of scrutiny under the Equal Protection Clause of the Fourteenth Amendment. We think a term such as "rough proportionality" best encapsulates what we hold to be the requirement of the Fifth Amendment. No precise mathematical calculation is required, but the city must make some sort of individualized determination that the required dedication related both in nature and extent to the impact of the proposed development.

IV

Cities have long engaged in the commendable task of land use planning, made necessary by increasing urbanization, particularly in metropolitan areas such as Portland. The city's goals of reducing flooding hazards and traffic congestion, and providing for public greenways, are laudable, but there are outer limits to how this may be done. "A strong public desire to improve the public condition [will not] warrant achieving the desire by a shorter cut than the constitutional way of paying for the change." *Pennsylvania Coal Co. v. Mahon,* 260 U.S. 393 (1922).

The judgment of the Supreme Court of Oregon is reversed, and the case is remanded for further proceedings not inconsistent with this opinion.

It is so ordered.

JUSTICE STEVENS, with whom Justices Blackmun and Ginsburg join, dissenting.

II

It is not merely state cases, but our own cases as well, that require the analysis to focus on the impact of the city's action on the entire parcel of private property. In *Penn Central Transp. Co. v. New York City,* 438 U.S. 104 (1978), we stated that takings jurisprudence "does not divide a single parcel into discrete segments and attempt to determine whether rights in a particular segment have been entirely abrogated." Instead, this Court focuses "both on the character of the action and on the nature and extent of the interference with rights in the parcel as a whole." *Andrus v. Allard*, 444 U.S. 51 (1979), reaffirmed the nondivisibility principle outlined in *Penn Central,* stating that "[a]t least where an owner possesses a full 'bundle' of property rights, the destruction of one 'strand' of the bundle is not a taking, because the aggregate must be viewed in its entirety." Although limitation of the right to exclude others undoubtedly constitutes a significant infringement upon property ownership, *Kaiser Aetna v. United States,* 444 US 164 (1979), restrictions on that right do not alone constitute a taking, and do not do so in any event unless they "unreasonably impair the value or use" of the property.

The Court's narrow focus on one strand in the property owner's bundle of rights is particularly misguided in a case involving the development of commercial property.

The exactions associated with the development of a retail business are likewise a species of business regulation that heretofore warranted a strong presumption of constitutional validity.

The Court's assurances that its "rough proportionality" test leaves ample room for cities to pursue the "commendable task of land use planning,"—even twice avowing that "[n]o precise mathematical calculation is required"—are wanting given the result that test compels here. Under the Court's approach, a city must not only "quantify its findings," and make "individualized determination[s]" with respect to the nature *and* the extent of the relationship between the conditions and the impact, but also demonstrate "proportionality." The correct inquiry should instead concentrate on whether the required nexus is present and venture beyond considerations of a condition's nature or germaneness only if the developer establishes that a concededly germane condition is so grossly disproportionate to the proposed development's adverse effects that it manifests motives other than land use regulation on the part of the city. The heightened requirement the Court imposes on cities is even more unjustified when all the tools needed to resolve the questions presented by this case can be garnered from our existing case law.

FOR DISCUSSION

Is the rough proportionality test a new form of substantive due process? What does the test require, and when must it be used? Does this test make it harder or more difficult for a local government to require owners to agree to limits on their property as a condition to receiving building permits?

KOONTZ V. ST. JOHNS RIVER WATER MANAGEMENT DISTRICT

568 U.S. ___, 133 S.Ct. 2586, 186 L.Ed.2d 697 (2013)

Landowner sued in a Florida court a state water management district, alleging its denial of land use permits unless he funded offsite projects on public lands effected a taking without just compensation. The lower state courts held in favor of the landowner, the state supreme court reversed, and the U.S. Supreme Court reversed and remanded.

Vote: 5–4

JUSTICE ALITO delivered the opinion of the Court, in which ROBERTS, SCALIA, KENNEDY, and THOMAS joined.

Our decisions in *Nollan v. California Coastal Comm'n,* 483 U.S. 825 (1987), and *Dolan v. City of Tigard,* 512 U.S. 374, (1994), provide important protection against the misuse of the power of land-use regulation. In those cases, we held that a unit of government may not condition the approval of a land-use permit on the owner's relinquishment of a portion of his property unless there is a "nexus" and "rough proportionality" between the government's demand and the effects of the proposed land use. In this case, the St. Johns River Water Management District (District) believes that it circumvented *Nollan* and *Dolan* because of the way in which it structured its handling of a permit application submitted by Coy Koontz, Sr., whose estate is represented in this Court by Coy Koontz, Jr. The District did not approve his application on the condition that he surrender an interest in his land. Instead, the District, after suggesting that he could obtain approval by signing over such an interest, denied his application because he refused to yield. The Florida Supreme Court blessed this maneuver and thus effectively interred those important decisions. Because we conclude that *Nollan* and *Dolan* cannot be evaded in this way, the Florida Supreme Court's decision must be reversed.

I

A

In 1972, petitioner purchased an undeveloped 14.9-acre tract of land on the south side of Florida State Road 50, a divided four-lane highway east of Orlando. The property is located less than 1,000 feet from that road's intersection with Florida State Road 408, a tolled expressway that is one of Orlando's major thoroughfares.

A drainage ditch runs along the property's western edge, and high-voltage power lines bisect it into northern and southern sections. The combined effect of the ditch, a 100-foot wide area kept clear for the power lines, the highways, and other construction on nearby parcels is to isolate the northern section of petitioner's property from any other undeveloped land. Although largely classified as wetlands by the State, the northern section drains well; the most significant standing water forms in ruts in an unpaved road used to access the power lines. The natural topography of the property's southern section is somewhat more diverse, with a small creek, forested uplands, and wetlands that sometimes have water as much as a foot deep. A wildlife survey found evidence of animals that often frequent developed areas: raccoons, rabbits, several species of bird, and a turtle. The record also indicates that the land may be a suitable habitat for opossums.

The same year that petitioner purchased his property, Florida enacted the Water Resources Act, which divided the State into five water management districts and authorized each district to regulate "construction that connects to, draws water from, drains water into, or is placed in or across the waters in the state." Under the Act, a landowner wishing to undertake such construction must obtain from the relevant district a Management and Storage of Surface Water (MSSW) permit, which may impose "such reasonable conditions" on the permit as are "necessary to assure" that construction will "not be harmful to the water resources of the district."

In 1984, in an effort to protect the State's rapidly diminishing wetlands, the Florida Legislature passed the Warren S. Henderson Wetlands Protection Act, which made it illegal for anyone to "dredge or fill in, on, or over surface waters" without a Wetlands Resource Management (WRM) permit. Under the Henderson Act, permit applicants are required to provide "reasonable assurance" that proposed construction on wetlands is "not contrary to the public interest," as defined by an enumerated list of criteria. Consistent with the Henderson Act, the St. Johns River Water Management District, the district with jurisdiction over petitioner's land, requires that permit applicants wishing to build on wetlands offset the resulting environmental damage by creating, enhancing, or preserving wetlands elsewhere.

Petitioner decided to develop the 3.7-acre northern section of his property, and in 1994 he applied to the District for MSSW and WRM permits. Under his proposal, petitioner would have raised the elevation of the northernmost section of his land to make it suitable for a building, graded the land from the southern edge of the building site down to the elevation of the high-voltage electrical lines, and installed a dry-bed pond for retaining and gradually releasing stormwater runoff from the building and its parking lot. To mitigate the environmental effects of his proposal, petitioner offered to foreclose any possible future development of the approximately 11-acre southern section of his land by deeding to the District a conservation easement on that portion of his property.

The District considered the 11-acre conservation easement to be inadequate, and it informed petitioner that it would approve construction only if he agreed to one of two concessions. First, the District proposed that petitioner reduce the size of his development to 1 acre and deed to the District a conservation easement on the remaining 13.9 acres. To reduce the development area, the District suggested that petitioner could eliminate the dry-bed pond from his proposal and instead install a more costly subsurface stormwater management system beneath the building site. The District also suggested that petitioner install retaining walls rather than gradually sloping the land from the building site down to the elevation of the rest of his property to the south.

In the alternative, the District told petitioner that he could proceed with the development as proposed, building on 3.7 acres and deeding a conservation easement to the government on the remainder of the property, if he also agreed to hire contractors to make improvements to District-owned land several miles away. Specifically, petitioner could pay to replace culverts on one parcel or fill in ditches on another. Either of those projects would have enhanced approximately 50 acres of District-owned wetlands. When the District asks permit applicants to fund offsite mitigation work, its policy is never to require any particular offsite project, and it did not do so here. Instead, the District said that it "would also favorably consider" alternatives to its suggested offsite mitigation projects if petitioner proposed something "equivalent."

Believing the District's demands for mitigation to be excessive in light of the environmental effects that his building proposal would have caused, petitioner filed suit in state court. Among other claims, he argued that he was entitled to relief under Fla. Stat. § 373.617(2), which allows owners to recover "monetary damages" if a state agency's action is "an unreasonable exercise of the state's police power constituting a taking without just compensation."

II

A

We have said in a variety of contexts that "the government may not deny a benefit to a person because he exercises a constitutional right." for example, we held that a public college would violate a professor's freedom of speech if it declined to renew his contract because he was an outspoken critic of the college's administration. And in *Memorial Hospital v. Maricopa County,* 415 U.S. 250, 94 S.Ct. 1076, 39 L.Ed.2d 306 (1974), we concluded that a county impermissibly burdened the right to travel by extending healthcare benefits only to those indigent sick who had been residents of the county for at least one year. Those cases reflect an overarching principle, known as the unconstitutional conditions doctrine, that vindicates the Constitution's enumerated rights by preventing the government from coercing people into giving them up.

Nollan and *Dolan* "involve a special application" of this doctrine that protects the Fifth Amendment right to just compensation for property the government takes when owners apply for land-use permits. Our decisions in those cases reflect two realities of the permitting process. The first is that land-use permit applicants are especially vulnerable to the type of coercion that the unconstitutional conditions doctrine prohibits because the government often has broad discretion to deny a permit that is worth far more than property it would like to take. By conditioning a building permit on the owner's deeding over a public right-of-way, for example, the government can pressure an owner into voluntarily giving up property for which the Fifth Amendment would otherwise require just compensation. So long as the building permit is more valuable than any just compensation the owner could hope to receive for the right-of-way, the owner is likely to accede to the government's demand, no matter how unreasonable. Extortionate demands of this sort frustrate the Fifth Amendment right to just compensation, and the unconstitutional conditions doctrine prohibits them.

A second reality of the permitting process is that many proposed land uses threaten to impose costs on the public that dedications of property can offset. Where a building proposal would substantially increase traffic congestion, for example, officials might condition permit approval on the owner's agreement to deed over the land needed to widen a public road. Respondent argues that a similar rationale justifies the exaction at issue here: petitioner's proposed construction project, it submits, would destroy wetlands on his property, and in order to compensate for this loss, respondent demands that he enhance wetlands elsewhere. Insisting that landowners internalize the negative externalities of their conduct is a hallmark of responsible land-use policy, and we have long sustained such regulations against constitutional attack.

Nollan and *Dolan* accommodate both realities by allowing the government to condition approval of a permit on the dedication of property to the public so long as there is a "nexus" and "rough proportionality" between the property that the government demands and the social costs of the applicant's proposal. Our precedents thus enable permitting authorities to insist that applicants bear the full costs of their proposals while still forbidding the government from engaging in "out-and-out . . . extortion" that would thwart the Fifth Amendment right to just compensation. (internal quotation marks omitted). Under *Nollan* and *Dolan* the government may choose whether and how a permit applicant is required to mitigate the impacts of a proposed development, but it may not leverage its legitimate interest in mitigation to pursue governmental ends that lack an essential nexus and rough proportionality to those impacts.

B

The principles that undergird our decisions in *Nollan* and *Dolan* do not change depending on whether the government *approves* a permit on the condition that the applicant turn over property or *denies* a permit because the applicant refuses to do so. We have often concluded that denials of governmental benefits were impermissible under the unconstitutional conditions doctrine. In so holding, we have recognized that regardless of whether the government ultimately succeeds in pressuring someone into forfeiting a constitutional right, the unconstitutional conditions doctrine forbids burdening the Constitution's enumerated rights by coercively withholding benefits from those who exercise them.

That is not to say, however, that there is *no* relevant difference between a consummated taking and the denial of a permit based on an unconstitutionally extortionate demand. Where the permit is denied and the condition is never imposed, nothing has been taken. While the unconstitutional conditions doctrine recognizes that this *burdens* a constitutional right, the Fifth Amendment mandates a particular *remedy*—just compensation—only for takings. In cases where there is an excessive demand but no taking, whether money damages are available is not a question of federal constitutional law but of the cause of action—whether state or federal—on which the landowner relies. Because petitioner brought his claim pursuant to a state law cause of action, the

Court has no occasion to discuss what remedies might be available for a *Nollan/Dolan* unconstitutional conditions violation either here or in other cases.

III

We turn to the Florida Supreme Court's alternative holding that petitioner's claim fails because respondent asked him to spend money rather than give up an easement on his land. A predicate for any unconstitutional conditions claim is that the government could not have constitutionally ordered the person asserting the claim to do what it attempted to pressure that person into doing. For that reason, we began our analysis in both *Nollan* and *Dolan* by observing that if the government had directly seized the easements it sought to obtain through the permitting process, it would have committed a *per se* taking. The Florida Supreme Court held that petitioner's claim fails at this first step because the subject of the exaction at issue here was money rather than a more tangible interest in real property.

We note as an initial matter that if we accepted this argument it would be very easy for land-use permitting officials to evade the limitations of *Nollan* and *Dolan*. Because the government need only provide a permit applicant with one alternative that satisfies the nexus and rough proportionality standards, a permitting authority wishing to exact an easement could simply give the owner a choice of either surrendering an easement or making a payment equal to the easement's value. Such so-called "in lieu of" fees are utterly commonplace, and they are functionally equivalent to other types of land use exactions. For that reason and those that follow, we reject respondent's argument and hold that so-called "monetary exactions" must satisfy the nexus and rough proportionality requirements of *Nollan* and *Dolan*.

A

In *Eastern Enterprises* the United States retroactively imposed on a former mining company an obligation to pay for the medical benefits of retired miners and their families. A four-Justice plurality concluded that the statute's imposition of retroactive financial liability was so arbitrary that it violated the Takings Clause. Although Justice KENNEDY concurred in the result on due process grounds, he joined four other Justices in dissent in arguing that the Takings Clause does not apply to government-imposed financial obligations that "d[o] not operate upon or alter an identified property interest." Relying on the concurrence and dissent in *Eastern Enterprises,* respondent argues that a requirement that petitioner spend money improving public lands could not give rise to a taking.

Respondent's argument rests on a mistaken premise. Unlike the financial obligation in *Eastern Enterprises,* the demand for money at issue here did "operate upon . . . an identified property interest" by directing the owner of a particular piece of property to make a monetary payment. In this case, unlike *Eastern Enterprises,* the monetary obligation burdened petitioner's ownership of a specific parcel of land. In that sense, this case bears resemblance to our cases holding that the government must pay just compensation when it takes a lien—a right to receive money that is secured by a particular piece of property. The fulcrum this case turns on is the direct link between the government's demand and a specific parcel of real property. Because of that direct link, this case implicates the central concern of *Nollan* and *Dolan*: the risk that the government may use its substantial power and discretion in land-use permitting to pursue governmental ends that lack an essential nexus and rough proportionality to the effects of the proposed new use of the specific property at issue, thereby diminishing without justification the value of the property.

In this case, moreover, petitioner does not ask us to hold that the government can commit a *regulatory* taking by directing someone to spend money. As a result, we need not apply *Penn Central*'s "essentially ad hoc, factual inquir[y],", at all, much less extend that "already difficult and uncertain rule" to the "vast category of cases" in which someone believes that a regulation is too costly. Instead, petitioner's claim rests on the more limited proposition that when the government commands the relinquishment of funds linked to a specific, identifiable property interest such as a bank account or parcel of real property, a "*per se* [takings] approach" is the proper mode of analysis under the Court's precedent.

Finally, it bears emphasis that petitioner's claim does not implicate "normative considerations about the wisdom of government decisions." We are not here concerned with whether it would be "arbitrary or unfair" for respondent to order a landowner to make improvements to public lands that are nearby. Whatever the wisdom of such a policy, it would transfer an interest in property from the landowner to the government. For that reason, any such demand would amount to a *per se* taking similar to the taking of an easement or a lien.

B

Respondent and the dissent argue that if monetary exactions are made subject to scrutiny under *Nollan* and *Dolan,* then there will be no principled way of distinguishing impermissible land-use exactions from property taxes. See *post,* at 2607–2608. We think they exaggerate both the extent to which that problem is unique to the land-use permitting context and the practical difficulty of distinguishing between the power to tax and the power to take by eminent domain.

It is beyond dispute that "[t]axes and user fees . . . are not 'takings.'" We said as much in *County of Mobile v. Kimball,* 102 U.S. 691, 703, (1881), and our cases have been clear on that point ever since. This case therefore does not affect the ability of governments to impose property taxes, user fees, and similar laws and regulations that may impose financial burdens on property owners.

At the same time, we have repeatedly found takings where the government, by confiscating financial obligations, achieved a result that could have been obtained by imposing a tax. . .Two facts emerge from those cases. The first is that the need to distinguish taxes from takings is not a creature of our holding today that monetary exactions are subject to scrutiny under *Nollan* and *Dolan*. Rather, the problem is inherent in this Court's long-settled view that property the government could constitutionally demand through its taxing power can also be taken by eminent domain.

Second, our cases show that teasing out the difference between taxes and takings is more difficult in theory than in practice.

The same dynamic is at work in this case because Florida law greatly circumscribes respondent's power to tax. If respondent had argued that its demand for money was a tax, it would have effectively conceded that its denial of petitioner's permit was improper under Florida law. Far from making that concession, respondent has maintained throughout this litigation that it considered petitioner's money to be a substitute for his deeding to the public a conservation easement on a larger parcel of undeveloped land.

This case does not require us to say more. We need not decide at precisely what point a land-use permitting charge denominated by the government as a "tax" becomes "so arbitrary . . . that it was not the exertion of taxation but a confiscation of property." For present purposes, it suffices to say that despite having long recognized that "the power of taxation should not be confused with the power of eminent domain," we have had little trouble distinguishing between the two.

C

We hold that the government's demand for property from a land-use permit applicant must satisfy the requirements of *Nollan* and *Dolan* even when the government denies the permit and even when its demand is for money. The Court expresses no view on the merits of petitioner's claim that respondent's actions here failed to comply with the principles set forth in this opinion and those two cases. The Florida Supreme Court's judgment is reversed, and this case is remanded for further proceedings not inconsistent with this opinion.

It is so ordered.

JUSTICE KAGAN with whom JUSTICE GINSBURG, JUSTICE BREYER, and JUSTICE SOTOMAYOR join, dissenting.

In the paradigmatic case triggering review under *Nollan v. California Coastal Comm'n,* and *Dolan v. City of Tigard,*, the government approves a building permit on the condition that the landowner relinquish an interest in real property, like an easement. The significant legal questions that the Court resolves today are whether *Nollan* and *Dolan* also apply when that case is varied in two ways. First, what if the government does not approve the permit, but instead demands that the condition be fulfilled before it will do so? Second, what if the condition entails not transferring real property, but simply paying money? This case also raises other, more fact-specific issues I will address: whether the government here imposed any condition at all, and whether petitioner Coy Koontz suffered any compensable injury.

I think the Court gets the first question it addresses right. The *Nollan-Dolan* standard applies not only when the government approves a development permit conditioned on the owner's conveyance of a property interest (*i.e.,* imposes a condition subsequent), but also when the government denies a permit until the owner meets the condition (*i.e.,* imposes a condition precedent). That means an owner may challenge the denial of a permit on the ground that the government's condition lacks the "nexus" and "rough proportionality" to the development's social costs that *Nollan* and *Dolan* require. Still, the condition-subsequent and condition-precedent situations differ in an important way. When the government grants a permit subject to the relinquishment of real property, and that condition does not satisfy *Nollan* and *Dolan,* then the government has taken the property and must pay just compensation under the Fifth Amendment. But when the government denies a permit because an owner has refused to accede to that same demand, nothing has actually been taken. The owner is entitled to have the improper condition removed; and he may be entitled to a monetary remedy created by state law for imposing such a condition; but he cannot be entitled to constitutional compensation for a taking of property. So far, we all agree.

Our core disagreement concerns the second question the Court addresses. The majority extends *Nollan* and *Dolan* to cases in which the government conditions a permit not on the transfer of real property, but instead on the payment or expenditure of money. That runs roughshod over *Eastern Enterprises v. Apfel,* 524 U.S. 498, (1998), which held that the government may impose ordinary financial obligations without triggering the Takings Clause's protections. The boundaries of the majority's new rule are uncertain. But it threatens to subject a vast array of land-use regulations, applied daily in States and localities throughout the country, to heightened constitutional scrutiny. I would not embark on so unwise an adventure, and would affirm the Florida Supreme Court's decision.

FOR DISCUSSION

Does *Koontz* represent a change in the law from *Nollan* and *Dolan* or is it as the majority argues, simply applying the same principle and effectively closes a loophole in the law that allows the government to get around the holdings in these two cases? Is this case a major victory for property owners?

WHAT IS A VALID PUBLIC USE?

The final requirement of the Takings Clause is that the use of eminent domain must secure a valid public use.

Colonial and early American uses of eminent domain were confined mainly to the building of roads, schools, and other public buildings. In some cases, eminent domain furthered economic development, but generally, while the eminent domain power was established and accepted, little discussion about the meaning of public use occurred. Moreover, the Fifth Amendment Takings Clause did not apply to the states until 1897; thus, unless local state constitutions had a public use stipulation, states were not limited by federal constitutional standards. In 1776 only two state constitutions had a public use clause in their constitutions, and it was not until the 1830s that most states had such a stipulation attached to eminent domain. Because the federal courts did not become very involved with public use and eminent domain questions until the last quarter of the nineteenth century, local state courts were crucial in constructing the public use meaning, subject to local conditions.

As a rule, the federal courts have also given great deference to local determinations of public use. Since the nineteenth century the Supreme Court never held a use to be private when a local court had already declared it to be public. There is only one case, *Missouri Pacific Railway Company v. Nebraska* (164 U.S. 403, 1896), in the nineteenth century where the Supreme Court reversed a lower court on this question. Justice Holmes, in *Strickley v. Highland Boy Mining Company* (200 U.S. 527, 1905), underscored this point, indicating that if eminent domain statutes of a state are constitutional, the Supreme Court would "follow the construction of the state court." As a result of the deference, public use has taken on various meanings.

The term "public use" has been defined both narrowly and more broadly to mean "used by the public," "promoting the general welfare," for the "welfare of the public," the "public good," "public advantage," the "public benefit," "public utility or necessity," and as actions "enlarging resources," "promoting productive power," "conducive to commercial prosperity," and "furthering an important public policy." Narrow conceptions of the term public use have stipulated that the public in some way be given access to or use of the property taken, whereas the broader definitions of the term do not require that the public actually use the property as long as its acquisition serves the public good. Examples of takings for the narrow public good include the use of eminent domain for projects such as highways, schools, public buildings, and parks. Rarely have these types of public uses been controversial. In addition, using eminent domain to abate a nuisance has also been common and accepted. However, the use of eminent domain to serve a larger public good, such as furthering economic development, or that results in the transfer of private property from one owner to another has generated controversy.

Berman v. Parker (348 U.S. 26, 1954) is a landmark case in which many see the Court as having first expanded the concept of public use beyond the more traditional notions. Here the Court first used the concept of blight as a public use justification for eminent domain. While this case arose in the District of Columbia, the federal government has power there comparable to that in each of the states, so presumably the same argument could be used for state action. The case was significant because of the vague notion of blight. Even if one's property was not blighted but was located within an area that was, the *Berman* decision provided justification for the taking of the property.

However broadly *Berman* expanded the concept of what constituted a valid public use, *Hawaii Housing Authority v. Midkiff* (467 U.S. 229, 1984) was even more significant. Here the Court upheld a Hawaii law allowing for the breakup and redistribution of land from large estates into smaller parcels of property. In a unanimous opinion upholding the law, Justice O'Connor provided an expansive definition of public use to be coterminous with a state's police power. This suggested to many that there was no limit to the use of eminent domain and that the courts would no longer question what is a valid public use. This decision came on the heels of *Poletown Neighborhood Council v. City of Detroit* (304 N.W. 2d. 455, Mich. 1981), which upheld the use of eminent domain to condemn 465 acres of land, remove 3,500 people, and take 1,176 buildings, including 144 businesses, 3 schools, 16 churches, and one cemetery, in order to provide land for the General Motors Corporation. The case is often understood as establishing a precedent that permits as a valid public use the taking of private property from one party and giving it to another in order to promote economic development. *Poletown* was condemned by both property rights activists and liberals who saw communities and neighborhoods being attacked. The decision produced fear among property rights and community advocates that property rights no longer would receive any serious constitutional protection. However, this fear proved premature, as the next two cases (and reaction to them) demonstrated.

County of Wayne v. Hathcock (684 N.W.2d 765, 2004) is a Michigan State Supreme Court decision that overturned the *Poletown* ruling by deciding that a taking of private property from one and giving to another for economic development reasons violated the state constitution. It was a major victory for property owners, but the decision affected only Michigan law. Within a few weeks of the *Hathcock* decision in 2004, the Supreme Court announced it was taking the next case, *Kelo v. City of New London* (545 U.S. 469, 2005), raising hope among many that it might modify *Midkiff* or *Berman* and adopt a narrower conception of public use that precluded the use of eminent domain for economic development purposes. The Court failed to do so, and reaction to *Kelo* was swift and loud.

Many read the Stevens opinion as opening up economic development as a new justification for the use of eminent domain. Others, as Stevens pointed out, merely ruled in a way consistent with existing precedent that had already allowed takings for this purpose. Few noticed or believed that the majority opinion's efforts to distinguish a valid public use from a private taking by connecting the former to a local comprehensive plan (showing a public purpose to the taking) provided a sufficient basis for defending ownership rights. Instead, criticism centered on Justice Stevens' statement that local governments could adopt more narrow restrictions of public use if they wish, and many also pointed to the dissents by Justices O'Connor and Thomas, noting the "eminent domain abuse" inflicted upon the poor and people of color. As a result, many state and local governments adopted laws either banning the taking of private property for economic development purposes or imposing more procedural, evidentiary, or compensation requirements if certain types of property were taken for this purpose.

Overall, the use of eminent domain is an extraordinary and controversial tool of the government. Its use raises critical questions about government power, individual rights, and the ability of the Constitution to mediate the boundaries between the two.

BERMAN V. PARKER

348 U.S. 26, 75 S.Ct. 98, 99 L.Ed. 27 (1954)

The District of Columbia Redevelopment Act was challenged as involving improper taking of property. The Act created a land agency with power to prepare a comprehensive plan for the elimination and prevention of slums and substandard housing conditions. The appellants, owners of an unblighted store, objected to the appropriation of their property for the purposes of this project. They claimed that the taking did not secure a valid public use.

Vote: 8–0

JUSTICE DOUGLAS delivered the opinion of the Court:

The power of Congress over the District of Columbia includes all the legislative powers which a state may exercise over its affairs. We deal, in other words, with what traditionally has been known as the police power. An attempt to define its reach or trace its outer limits is fruitless, for each case must turn on its own facts. The definition is essentially the product of legislative determinations addressed to the purposes of government, purposes neither abstractly nor historically capable of complete definition. Subject to specific constitutional limitations, when the legislature has spoken, the public interest has been declared in terms well-nigh conclusive. In such cases the legislature, not the judiciary, is the main guardian of the public needs to be served by social legislation, whether it be Congress legislating concerning the District of Columbia or the States legislating concerning local affairs. This principle admits of no exception merely because the power of eminent domain is involved. The role of the judiciary in determining whether that power is being exercised for a public purpose is an extremely narrow one.

We do not sit to determine whether a particular housing project is or is not desirable. The concept of the public welfare is broad and inclusive. The values it represents are spiritual as well as physical, aesthetic as well as monetary. It is within the power of the legislature to determine that the community should be beautiful as well as healthy, spacious as well as clean, well-balanced as well as carefully patrolled. In the present case, the Congress and its authorized agencies have made determinations that take into account a wide variety of values. It is not for us to reappraise them. If those who govern the District of Columbia decide that the Nation's capital should be beautiful as well as sanitary, there is nothing in the Fifth Amendment that stands in the way.

Once the object is within the authority of Congress, the right to realize it through the exercise of eminent domain is clear. For the power of eminent domain is merely the means to the end. Once the object is within the authority of Congress, the means by which it will be attained is also for Congress to determine. Here one of the means chosen is the use of private enterprise for redevelopment of the area. It is not for the courts to oversee the choice of the boundary line nor to sit in review on the size of a particular project area. Once the question of the public purpose has been decided, the amount and character of land to be taken for the project and the need for a particular tract to complete the integrated plan rests in the discretion of the legislative branch.

The rights of these property owners are satisfied when they receive that just compensation which the Fifth Amendment exacts as the price of the taking.

The judgment of the District Court, as modified by this opinion, is affirmed.

Affirmed.

NOTE

Due to the death of Justice Jackson, the Court had only eight members sitting at this time.

FOR DISCUSSION

Would it matter to the Court if the property were actually blighted or in need of repair? What role does the Court say the judiciary should have when it comes to making public use determinations? Who gets to say what a valid public use is? Who gets to decide if property is really blighted?

HAWAII HOUSING AUTHORITY V. MIDKIFF

467 U.S. 229, 104 S.Ct. 2321, 81 L.Ed.2d 186 (1984)

In Hawaii the state and federal governments owned almost 49 percent of the land, with another 47 percent in the hands of only 72 private landowners. In order to address the concentration of land ownership, the state of Hawaii enacted the Land Reform Act of 1967. This Act allowed for the use of eminent domain to take many of the large private tracts, break them up into smaller parcels, and then sell them to homeowners living on these tracts. The owners of these large tracks claimed that this use of eminent domain to take their land and transfer it to other primate individuals was unconstitutional since the condemnation was not for a valid public use.

Vote: 9–0

JUSTICE O'CONNOR delivered the opinion of the Court.

The Fifth Amendment of the United States Constitution provides, in pertinent part, that "private property [shall not] be taken for public use, without just compensation." These cases present the question whether the Public Use Clause of that Amendment, made applicable to the States through the Fourteenth Amendment, prohibits the State of Hawaii from taking, with just compensation, title in real property from lessors and transferring it to lessees in order to reduce the concentration of ownership of fees simple in the State. We conclude that it does not.

I

A

The Hawaiian Islands were originally settled by Polynesian immigrants from the western Pacific. These settlers developed an economy around a feudal land tenure system in which one island high chief, the ali'i nui, controlled the land and assigned it for development to certain subchiefs. The subchiefs would then reassign the land to other lower ranking chiefs, who would administer the land and govern the farmers and other tenants working it. All land was held at the will of the ali'i nui and eventually had to be returned to his trust. There was no private ownership of land.

Beginning in the early 1800's, Hawaiian leaders and American settlers repeatedly attempted to divide the lands of the kingdom among the crown, the chiefs, and the common people. These efforts proved largely unsuccessful, however, and the land remained in the hands of a few. In the mid-1960's, after extensive hearings, the Hawaii Legislature discovered that, while the State and Federal Governments owned almost 49% of the State's land, another 47% was in the hands of only 72 private landowners. The legislature further found that 18 landholders, with tracts of 21,000 acres or more, owned more than 40% of this land and that on Oahu, the most urbanized of the islands, 22 landowners owned 72.5% of the fee simple titles. The legislature concluded that concentrated land ownership was responsible for skewing the State's residential fee simple market, inflating land prices, and injuring the public tranquility and welfare.

To redress these problems, the legislature decided to compel the large landowners to break up their estates. The legislature considered requiring large landowners to sell lands which they were leasing to homeowners. However, the landowners strongly resisted this scheme, pointing out the significant federal tax liabilities they would incur. Indeed, the landowners claimed that the federal tax laws were the primary reason they previously had chosen to lease, and not sell, their lands. Therefore, to accommodate the needs of both lessors and lessees, the Hawaii Legislature enacted the Land Reform Act of 1967 (Act), Haw.Rev.Stat., ch. 516, which created a mechanism for condemning residential tracts and for transferring ownership of the condemned fees simple to existing lessees. By condemning the land in question, the Hawaii Legislature intended to make the land sales involuntary, thereby making the federal tax consequences less severe while still facilitating the redistribution of fees simple.

Under the Act's condemnation scheme, tenants living on single-family residential lots within developmental tracts at least five acres in size are entitled to ask the Hawaii Housing Authority (HHA) to condemn the property on which they live. When 25 eligible tenants, or tenants on half the lots in the tract, whichever is less, file appropriate applications, the Act authorizes HHA to hold a public hearing to determine whether acquisition by the State of all or part of the tract will "effectuate the public purposes" of the Act. § 516–22. If HHA finds that these public purposes will be served, it is authorized to designate some or all of the lots in the tract for acquisition. It then acquires, at prices set either by condemnation trial or by negotiation between lessors and lessees, the former fee owners' full "right, title, and interest" in the land.

III

A

The starting point for our analysis of the Act's constitutionality is the Court's decision in *Berman v. Parker*, 348 U.S. 26 (1954). In *Berman*, the Court held constitutional the District of Columbia Redevelopment Act of 1945. That Act provided both for the comprehensive use of the eminent domain power to redevelop slum areas and for the possible sale or lease of the condemned lands to private interests. In discussing whether the takings authorized by that Act were for a "public use," the Court stated:

We deal, in other words, with what traditionally has been known as the police power. An attempt to define its reach or trace its outer limits is fruitless, for each case must turn on its own facts. The definition is essentially the product of legislative determinations addressed to the purposes of government, purposes neither abstractly nor historically capable of complete definition. Subject to specific constitutional limitations, when the legislature has spoken, the public interest has been declared in terms well-nigh conclusive. In such cases the legislature, not the judiciary, is the main guardian of the public needs to be served by social legislation, whether it be Congress legislating concerning the District of Columbia . . . or the States legislating concerning local affairs. . . This principle admits of no exception merely because the power of eminent domain is involved. . . .

The Court explicitly recognized the breadth of the principle it was announcing, noting:

> Once the object is within the authority of Congress, the right to realize it through the exercise of eminent domain is clear. For the power of eminent domain is merely the means to the end. . . . Once the object is within the authority of Congress, the means by which it will be attained is also for Congress to determine. Here one of the means chosen is the use of private enterprise for redevelopment of the area. Appellants argue that this makes the project a taking from one businessman for the benefit of another businessman. But the means of executing the project are for Congress and Congress alone to determine, once the public purpose has been established.

The "public use" requirement is thus coterminous with the scope of a sovereign's police powers.

There is, of course, a role for courts to play in reviewing a legislature's judgment of what constitutes a public use, even when the eminent domain power is equated with the police power. But the Court in *Berman* made clear that it is "an extremely narrow" one. In short, the Court has made clear that it will not substitute its judgment for a legislature's judgment as to what constitutes a public use "unless the use be palpably without reasonable foundation."

On this basis, we have no trouble concluding that the Hawaii Act is constitutional. The people of Hawaii have attempted, much as the settlers of the original 13 Colonies did, to reduce the perceived social and economic evils of a land oligopoly traceable to their monarchs. The land oligopoly has, according to the Hawaii Legislature, created artificial deterrents to the normal functioning of the State's residential land market and forced thousands of individual homeowners to lease, rather than buy, the land underneath their homes. Regulating oligopoly and the evils associated with it is a classic exercise of a State's police powers.

FOR DISCUSSION

How broad is eminent domain authority after this decision? Is there anything that would not constitute a valid public use? What is the difference between the police and eminent domain powers after this decision? Does O'Connor permit any role for the judiciary in questioning public use decisions? Are there any limits on the type of property or reason for the taking? Are uses of eminent domain that take property from one private individual and give it to another permitted as a result of the *Midkiff* decision?

County of Wayne v. Hathcock

471 Mich. 445, 684 N.W.2d 765 (Mich., 2004)

Wayne County in Michigan sought to use eminent domain to build an industrial park. The Hathcocks, owners of one of the properties being acquired for this project, objected, claiming that the taking of the property and giving it to another private party for economic development purposes violated the Michigan constitution. They challenged the taking in state court.

Judge Young delivered the opinion of the court.

We are presented again with a clash of two bedrock principles of our legal tradition: the sacrosanct right of individuals to dominion over their private property, on the one hand and, on the other, the state's authority to condemn private property for the commonwealth. In this case, Wayne County would use the power of eminent domain to condemn defendants' real properties for the construction of a 1,300-acre business and technology park. This proposed commercial center is intended to reinvigorate the struggling economy of southeastern Michigan by attracting businesses, particularly those involved in developing new technologies, to the area.

Defendants argue that this exercise of the power of eminent domain is neither authorized by statute nor permitted under article 10 of the 1963 Michigan Constitution, which requires that any condemnation of private property advance a "public use." Both the Wayne Circuit Court and the Court of Appeals rejected these arguments—compelled, in no small measure, by this Court's opinion in *Poletown Neighborhood Council v. Detroit,* 304 N.W.2d 455, 410 Mich. 616 (1981). We granted leave in this case to consider the legality of the proposed condemnations under MCL 213.23 and art. 10, § 2 of our 1963 Constitution.

We conclude that, although these condemnations are authorized by MCL 213.23, they do not pass constitutional muster under art. 10, § 2 of our 1963 constitution. Section 2 permits the exercise of the power of eminent domain only for a "public use." In this case, Wayne County intends to transfer the condemned properties to private parties in a manner wholly inconsistent with the common understanding of "public use" at the time our Constitution was ratified. Therefore, we reverse the judgment of the Court of Appeals and remand the case to the Wayne Circuit Court for entry of summary disposition in defendants' favor.

I

Facts and Procedural History

In April 2001, plaintiff Wayne County initiated actions to condemn nineteen parcels of land immediately south of Metropolitan Airport. The owners of those parcels, defendants in the present actions, maintain that these condemnations lack statutory authorization and exceed constitutional bounds.

This dispute has its roots in recent renovations of Metropolitan Airport. The county's $2 billion construction program produced a new terminal and jet runway and, consequently, raised concerns that noise from increased air traffic would plague neighboring landowners. In an effort to obviate such problems, the county, funded by a partial grant of $21 million from the Federal Aviation Administration (FAA), began a program of purchasing neighboring properties through voluntary sales. Eventually, the county purchased approximately five hundred acres in nonadjacent plots scattered in a checkerboard pattern throughout an area south of Metropolitan Airport.

Wayne County's agreement with the FAA provided that any properties acquired through the noise abatement program were to be put to economically productive use. In order to fulfill this mandate, the county, through its Jobs and Economic Development Department, developed the idea of constructing a large business and technology park with a conference center, hotel accommodations, and a recreational facility. Thus, the "Pinnacle Project" was born.

The Pinnacle Project calls for the construction of a state-of-the-art business and technology park in a 1,300-acre area adjacent to Metropolitan Airport. The county avers that the Pinnacle Project will

> create thousands of jobs, and tens of millions of dollars in tax revenue, while broadening the County's tax base from predominantly industrial to a mixture of industrial, service and technology. The Pinnacle Project will enhance the image of the County in the development community, aiding in its transformation from a high industrial area, to that of an arena ready to meet the needs of the 21st century. This cutting-edge development will attract national and international businesses, leading to accelerated economic growth and revenue enhancement.

According to expert testimony at trial, it is anticipated that the Pinnacle Project will create thirty thousand jobs and add $350 million in tax revenue for the county.

The county planned to construct the business and technology park in a 1,300-acre area that included the five hundred acres purchased under the federally funded noise abatement program. Because the county needed to acquire more land within the project area, it began anew to solicit voluntary sales from area landowners. This round of sales negotiations enabled the county to purchase an additional five hundred acres within the project area.

Having acquired over one thousand acres, the county determined that an additional forty-six parcels distributed in a checkerboard fashion throughout the project area were needed for the business and technology park. The county apparently determined that further efforts to negotiate additional voluntary sales would be futile and decided instead to invoke the power of eminent domain. Thus, on July 12, 2000, the Wayne County Commission adopted a Resolution of Necessity and Declaration of Taking (Resolution of Necessity) authorizing the acquisition of the remaining three hundred acres needed for the Pinnacle Project.

The remaining properties were appraised as required by the Uniform Condemnation Procedures Act (UCPA), and the county issued written offers based on these appraisals to the property owners. Twenty-seven more property owners accepted these offers and sold their parcels to the county. But according to the county's estimates, nineteen additional parcels were still needed for the Pinnacle Project. These properties, owned by defendants, are the subject of the present condemnation actions.

In late April 2001, plaintiff initiated condemnation actions under the UCPA. In response, each property owner filed a motion to review the necessity of the proposed condemnations. They argued, first, that the county lacked statutory authority to exercise the power of eminent domain in this manner. Second, defendants contended that acquisition of the subject properties was not necessary as required by statute. Finally, they challenged the constitutionality of these condemnation actions, maintaining that the Pinnacle Project would not serve a public purpose.

An evidentiary hearing on the consolidated cases was held over four weeks in the Wayne Circuit Court. On December 19, 2001, the trial court affirmed the county's determination of necessity. The court held that the takings were authorized by MCL 213.23, that the county did not abuse its discretion in determining that condemnation was necessary, and that the Pinnacle Project served a public purpose as defined by *Poletown*. The trial court denied defendants' motions for reconsideration on January 24, 2002.

Defendants appealed the matter to the Court of Appeals, which granted leave on April 24, 2003. The Court of Appeals affirmed the trial court's decision. The panel concluded that the proposed condemnations passed statutory and constitutional muster under MCL 213.21 *et seq.* and our *Poletown* decision. Judge Murray, joined by Judge Fitzgerald, concurred with Presiding Judge O'Connell, but opined that *Poletown* was poorly reasoned, wrongly decided, and ripe for reversal by this Court. . . .

B. Art 10, § 2

Art. 10, § 2 of Michigan's 1963 Constitution provides that "[p]rivate property shall not be taken for public use without just compensation therefor being first made or secured in a manner prescribed by law." Plaintiffs contend that the proposed condemnations are not "for public use," and therefore are not within constitutional bounds. Accordingly, our analysis must now focus on the "public use" requirement of Art. 10, § 2.

1. "Public Use" as a Legal Term of Art

"Public use" is a legal term of art every bit as complex as "just compensation." It has reappeared as a positive limit on the state's power of eminent domain in Michigan's constitutions of 1850, 1908, and 1963, and each invocation of "public use" has been followed by litigation over the precise contours of this language. Consequently, this Court has weighed in repeatedly on the meaning of this legal term of art. We can uncover the common understanding of art. 10, § 2 only by delving into this body of case law, and thereby determining the "common understanding" among those sophisticated in the law at the time of the Constitution's ratification.

This case does not require that this Court cobble together a single, comprehensive definition of "public use" from our pre-1963 precedent and other relevant sources. The question presented here is a fairly discrete one: are the condemnation of defendants' properties and the subsequent transfer of those properties to private entities pursuant to the Pinnacle Project consistent with the common understanding of "public use" at ratification? For the reasons stated below, we answer that question in the negative.

2. "Public Use" and Private Ownership

When our Constitution was ratified in 1963, it was well-established in this Court's eminent domain jurisprudence that the constitutional "public use" requirement was not an absolute bar against the transfer of condemned property to private entities. It was equally clear, however, that the constitutional "public use" requirement worked to prohibit the state from transferring condemned property to private entities for a *private* use. Thus, this Court's eminent domain jurisprudence—at least that portion concerning the reasons for which the state may condemn private property—has focused largely on the area between these poles.

Justice Ryan's *Poletown* dissent accurately describes the factors that distinguish takings in the former category from those in the latter according to our pre-1963 eminent domain jurisprudence. Accordingly, we conclude that the transfer of condemned property is a "public use" when it possess one of the three characteristics in our pre-1963 case law identified by Justice Ryan.

The foregoing indicates that the transfer of condemned property to a private entity, seen through the eyes of an individual sophisticated in the law at the time of ratification of our 1963 Constitution, would be appropriate in one of three contexts: (1) where "public necessity of the extreme sort" requires collective action; (2) where the property remains subject to public oversight after transfer to a private entity; and (3) where the property is selected because of "facts of independent public significance," rather than the interests of the private entity to which the property is eventually transferred.

3. *Poletown,* the Pinnacle Project, and Public Use

The exercise of eminent domain at issue here—the condemnation of defendants' properties for the Pinnacle Project and the subsequent transfer of those properties to private entities—implicates none of the saving elements noted by our pre-1963 eminent domain jurisprudence.

The Pinnacle Project's business and technology park is certainly not an enterprise "whose very *existence* depends on the use of land that can be assembled only by the coordination central government alone is capable of achieving." To the contrary, the landscape of our country is flecked with shopping centers, office parks, clusters of hotels, and centers of entertainment and commerce. We do not believe, and plaintiff does not contend, that these constellations required the exercise of eminent domain or any other form of collective public action for their formation.

Second, the Pinnacle Project is not subject to public oversight to ensure that the property continues to be used for the commonwealth after being sold to private entities. Rather, plaintiff intends for the private entities purchasing defendants' properties to pursue their own financial welfare with the single-mindedness expected of any profit-making enterprise. The public benefit arising from the Pinnacle Project is an epiphenomenon of the eventual property owners' collective attempts at profit maximization. No formal mechanisms exist to ensure that the businesses that would occupy what are now defendants' properties will continue to contribute to the health of the local economy.

Finally, there is nothing about the *act* of condemning defendants' properties that serves the public good in this case. The only public benefits cited by plaintiff arise after the lands are acquired by the government and put to private use. Thus, the present case is quite unlike *In Re Slum Clearance*, 331 Mich 714, 50 NW2d 340 (1951), because there are no facts of independent public significance (such as the need to promote health and safety) that might justify the condemnation of defendants' lands.

We can only conclude, therefore, that no one sophisticated in the law at the 1963 Constitution's ratification would have understood "public use" to permit the condemnation of defendants' properties for the construction of a business and technology park owned by private entities. Therefore, the condemnations proposed in this case are unconstitutional under art. 10, § 2.

[T]he *Poletown* majority concluded, for the first time in the history of our eminent domain jurisprudence, that a generalized economic benefit was sufficient under art. 10, § 2 to justify the transfer of condemned property to a private entity. Before *Poletown,* we had never held that a private entity's pursuit of profit was a "public use" for constitutional takings purposes simply because one entity's profit maximization contributed to the health of the general economy.

Justice Cooley considered a similar proposition well over a century ago and held that incidental benefits to the economy did not justify the exercise of eminent domain for private, water-powered mills:

> The statute [allowing the condemnation of private property for the construction of private powermills] appears to have been drawn with studious care to avoid any requirement that the person availing himself of its provisions shall consult any interest except his own, and it therefore seems perfectly manifest that when a public use is spoken of in this statute nothing further is intended than that the use shall be one that, in the opinion of the commission or jury, will in some manner advance the public interest. But incidentally every lawful business does this.

Justice Cooley was careful to point out that the Court was not ruling out the possibility that "incidental benefits to the public" might, in some cases, "justify an exercise of the right of eminent domain." But Wayne County has not directed us to a single case, other than *Poletown,* holding that a vague economic benefit stemming from a private profit-maximizing enterprise is a "public use."

Every business, every productive unit in society, does, as Justice Cooley noted, contribute in some way to the commonwealth. To justify the exercise of eminent domain solely on the basis of the fact that the use of that property by a private entity seeking its own profit might contribute to the economy's health is to render impotent our constitutional limitations on the government's power of eminent domain. *Poletown's* "economic benefit" rationale would validate practically *any* exercise of the power of eminent domain on behalf of a private entity. After all, if one's ownership of private property is forever subject to the government's determination that another private party would put one's land to better use, then the ownership of real property is perpetually threatened by the expansion plans of any large discount retailer, "megastore," or the like. Indeed, it is for precisely this reason that this Court has approved the transfer of condemned property to private entities only when certain other conditions—those identified in our pre-1963 eminent domain jurisprudence in Justice Ryan's *Poletown* dissent—are present.

Because *Poletown's* conception of a public use—that of "alleviating unemployment and revitalizing the economic base of the community"—has no support in the Court's eminent domain jurisprudence before the Constitution's ratification, its interpretation of "public use" in art. 10, § 2 cannot reflect the common understanding of that phrase among those sophisticated in the law at ratification. Consequently, the *Poletown* analysis provides no legitimate support for the condemnations proposed in this case and, for the reasons stated above, is overruled.

We conclude that the condemnations proposed in this case do not pass constitutional muster because they do not advance a public use as required by Const. 1963, art. 10, § 2. Accordingly, this case is remanded to the Wayne Circuit Court for entry of summary disposition in defendants' favor.

FOR DISCUSSION

Why did the court reverse *Poletown*? What is the exact issue that the court is objecting to in this case? Did the court say that all takings for economic development purposes violated the state constitution? In what situations may property be taken from one private party and given to another?

KELO V. CITY OF NEW LONDON

545 U.S. 469, 125 S.Ct. 2655, 162 L.Ed.2d 439 (2005)

The city of New London had created a development plan for the economic redevelopment of its city, including the creation of an industrial park with Pfizer Pharmaceuticals as the main tenant in the facility. The development broke the development plan and property into different parcels and uses. The Kelos owned a house located within the area designated for parking in this development plan. Their house was slated for acquisition by eminent domain. They challenged the taking as a violation of public use provisions under the U.S. and Connecticut constitutions. They lost in the Connecticut supreme court and appealed.

Vote: 5–4

JUSTICE STEVENS delivered the opinion of the Court, in which JUSTICES KENNEDY, SOUTER, GINSBURG, and BREYER joined.

In 2000, the city of New London approved a development plan that, in the words of the Supreme Court of Connecticut, was "projected to create in excess of 1,000 jobs, to increase tax and other revenues, and to revitalize an economically distressed city, including its downtown and waterfront areas." In assembling the land needed for this project, the city's development agent has purchased property from willing sellers and proposes to use the power of eminent domain to acquire the remainder of the property from unwilling owners in exchange for just compensation. The question presented is whether the city's proposed disposition of this property qualifies as a "public use" within the meaning of the Takings Clause of the Fifth Amendment to the Constitution.

I

The city of New London (hereinafter City) sits at the junction of the Thames River and the Long Island Sound in southeastern Connecticut. Decades of economic decline led a state agency in 1990 to designate the

City a "distressed municipality." In 1996, the Federal Government closed the Naval Undersea Warfare Center, which had been located in the Fort Trumbull area of the City and had employed over 1,500 people. In 1998, the City's unemployment rate was nearly double that of the State, and its population of just under 24,000 residents was at its lowest since 1920.

These conditions prompted state and local officials to target New London, and particularly its Fort Trumbull area, for economic revitalization. To this end, respondent New London Development Corporation (NLDC), a private nonprofit entity established some years earlier to assist the City in planning economic development, was reactivated. In January 1998, the State authorized a $5.35 million bond issue to support the NLDC's planning activities and a $10 million bond issue toward the creation of a Fort Trumbull State Park. In February, the pharmaceutical company Pfizer Inc. announced that it would build a $300 million research facility on a site immediately adjacent to Fort Trumbull; local planners hoped that Pfizer would draw new business to the area, thereby serving as a catalyst to the area's rejuvenation. After receiving initial approval from the city council, the NLDC continued its planning activities and held a series of neighborhood meetings to educate the public about the process. In May, the city council authorized the NLDC to formally submit its plans to the relevant state agencies for review. Upon obtaining state-level approval, the NLDC finalized an integrated development plan focused on 90 acres of the Fort Trumbull area.

The Fort Trumbull area is situated on a peninsula that juts into the Thames River. The area comprises approximately 115 privately owned properties, as well as the 32 acres of land formerly occupied by the naval facility (Trumbull State Park now occupies 18 of those 32 acres). The development plan encompasses seven parcels. Parcel 1 is designated for a waterfront conference hotel at the center of a "small urban village" that will include restaurants and shopping. This parcel will also have marinas for both recreational and commercial uses. A pedestrian "riverwalk" will originate here and continue down the coast, connecting the waterfront areas of the development. Parcel 2 will be the site of approximately 80 new residences organized into an urban neighborhood and linked by public walkway to the remainder of the development, including the state park. This parcel also includes space reserved for a new U.S. Coast Guard Museum. Parcel 3, which is located immediately north of the Pfizer facility, will contain at least 90,000 square feet of research and development office space. Parcel 4A is a 2.4-acre site that will be used either to support the adjacent state park, by providing parking or retail services for visitors, or to support the nearby marina. Parcel 4B will include a renovated marina, as well as the final stretch of the riverwalk. Parcels 5, 6, and 7 will provide land for office and retail space, parking, and water-dependent commercial uses.

The NLDC intended the development plan to capitalize on the arrival of the Pfizer facility and the new commerce it was expected to attract. In addition to creating jobs, generating tax revenue, and helping to "build momentum for the revitalization of downtown New London," the plan was also designed to make the City more attractive and to create leisure and recreational opportunities on the waterfront and in the park.

The city council approved the plan in January 2000, and designated the NLDC as its development agent in charge of implementation. The city council also authorized the NLDC to purchase property or to acquire property by exercising eminent domain in the City's name. The NLDC successfully negotiated the purchase of most of the real estate in the 90-acre area, but its negotiations with petitioners failed. As a consequence, in November 2000, the NLDC initiated the condemnation proceedings that gave rise to this case.

II

Petitioner Susette Kelo has lived in the Fort Trumbull area since 1997. She has made extensive improvements to her house, which she prizes for its water view. Petitioner Wilhelmina Dery was born in her Fort Trumbull house in 1918 and has lived there her entire life. Her husband Charles (also a petitioner) has lived in the house since they married some 60 years ago. In all, the nine petitioners own 15 properties in Fort

Trumbull—4 in parcel 3 of the development plan and 11 in parcel 4A. Ten of the parcels are occupied by the owner or a family member; the other five are held as investment properties. There is no allegation that any of these properties is blighted or otherwise in poor condition; rather, they were condemned only because they happen to be located in the development area.

In December 2000, petitioners brought this action in the New London Superior Court. They claimed, among other things, that the taking of their properties would violate the "public use" restriction in the Fifth Amendment. After a 7-day bench trial, the Superior Court granted a permanent restraining order prohibiting the taking of the properties located in parcel 4A (park or marina support). It, however, denied petitioners relief as to the properties located in parcel 3 (office space).

III

Two polar propositions are perfectly clear. On the one hand, it has long been accepted that the sovereign may not take the property of *A* for the sole purpose of transferring it to another private party *B,* even though *A* is paid just compensation. On the other hand, it is equally clear that a State may transfer property from one private party to another if future "use by the public" is the purpose of the taking; the condemnation of land for a railroad with common-carrier duties is a familiar example. Neither of these propositions, however, determines the disposition of this case.

As for the first proposition, the City would no doubt be forbidden from taking petitioners' land for the purpose of conferring a private benefit on a particular private party. Nor would the City be allowed to take property under the mere pretext of a public purpose, when its actual purpose was to bestow a private benefit. The takings before us, however, would be executed pursuant to a "carefully considered" development plan. The trial judge and all the members of the Supreme Court of Connecticut agreed that there was no evidence of an illegitimate purpose in this case. Therefore, as was true of the statute challenged in *Midkiff,* the City's development plan was not adopted "to benefit a particular class of identifiable individuals."

On the other hand, this is not a case in which the City is planning to open the condemned land—at least not in its entirety—to use by the general public. Nor will the private lessees of the land in any sense be required to operate like common carriers, making their services available to all comers. But although such a projected use would be sufficient to satisfy the public use requirement, this "Court long ago rejected any literal requirement that condemned property be put into use for the general public." Indeed, while many state courts in the mid-19th century endorsed "use by the public" as the proper definition of public use, that narrow view steadily eroded over time. Not only was the "use by the public" test difficult to administer (*e.g.,* what proportion of the public need have access to the property? at what price?), but it proved to be impractical given the diverse and always evolving needs of society. Accordingly, when this Court began applying the Fifth Amendment to the States at the close of the 19th century, it embraced the broader and more natural interpretation of public use as "public purpose." Thus, in a case upholding a mining company's use of an aerial bucket line to transport ore over property it did not own, Justice Holmes' opinion for the Court stressed "the inadequacy of use by the general public as a universal test." We have repeatedly and consistently rejected that narrow test ever since.

The disposition of this case therefore turns on the question whether the City's development plan serves a "public purpose." Without exception, our cases have defined that concept broadly, reflecting our longstanding policy of deference to legislative judgments in this field.

In *Berman v. Parker,* 348 U.S. 26 (1954), this Court upheld a redevelopment plan targeting a blighted area of Washington, D.C., in which most of the housing for the area's 5,000 inhabitants was beyond repair. Under the plan, the area would be condemned and part of it utilized for the construction of streets, schools, and other public facilities. The remainder of the land would be leased or sold to private parties for the purpose of redevelopment, including the construction of low-cost housing.

The owner of a department store located in the area challenged the condemnation, pointing out that his store was not itself blighted and arguing that the creation of a "better balanced, more attractive community" was not a valid public use. Writing for a unanimous Court, Justice Douglas refused to evaluate this claim in isolation, deferring instead to the legislative and agency judgment that the area "must be planned as a whole" for the plan to be successful. The Court explained that "community redevelopment programs need not, by force of the Constitution, be on a piecemeal basis—lot by lot, building by building."

In *Hawaii Housing Authority v. Midkiff,* 467 U.S. 229 (1984), the Court considered a Hawaii statute whereby fee title was taken from lessors and transferred to lessees (for just compensation) in order to reduce the concentration of land ownership. We unanimously upheld the statute and rejected the Ninth Circuit's view that it was "a naked attempt on the part of the state of Hawaii to take the property of A and transfer it to B solely for B's private use and benefit." Reaffirming *Berman's* deferential approach to legislative judgments in this field, we concluded that the State's purpose of eliminating the "social and economic evils of a land oligopoly" qualified as a valid public use. Our opinion also rejected the contention that the mere fact that the State immediately transferred the properties to private individuals upon condemnation somehow diminished the public character of the taking. "[I]t is only the taking's purpose, and not its mechanics," we explained, that matters in determining public use.

IV

Those who govern the City were not confronted with the need to remove blight in the Fort Trumbull area, but their determination that the area was sufficiently distressed to justify a program of economic rejuvenation is entitled to our deference. The City has carefully formulated an economic development plan that it believes will provide appreciable benefits to the community, including—but by no means limited to—new jobs and increased tax revenue. As with other exercises in urban planning and development, the City is endeavoring to coordinate a variety of commercial, residential, and recreational uses of land, with the hope that they will form a whole greater than the sum of its parts. To effectuate this plan, the City has invoked a state statute that specifically authorizes the use of eminent domain to promote economic development. Given the comprehensive character of the plan, the thorough deliberation that preceded its adoption, and the limited scope of our review, it is appropriate for us, as it was in *Berman,* to resolve the challenges of the individual owners, not on a piecemeal basis, but rather in light of the entire plan. Because that plan unquestionably serves a public purpose, the takings challenged here satisfy the public use requirement of the Fifth Amendment.

To avoid this result, petitioners urge us to adopt a new bright-line rule that economic development does not qualify as a public use. Putting aside the unpersuasive suggestion that the City's plan will provide only purely economic benefits, neither precedent nor logic supports petitioners' proposal. Promoting economic development is a traditional and long accepted function of government. There is, moreover, no principled way of distinguishing economic development from the other public purposes that we have recognized. In our cases upholding takings that facilitated agriculture and mining, for example, we emphasized the importance of those industries to the welfare of the States in question. It would be incongruous to hold that the City's interest in the economic benefits to be derived from the development of the Fort Trumbull area has less of a public character than any of those other interests. Clearly, there is no basis for exempting economic development from our traditionally broad understanding of public purpose.

Petitioners contend that using eminent domain for economic development impermissibly blurs the boundary between public and private takings. Again, our cases foreclose this objection. Quite simply, the government's pursuit of a public purpose will often benefit individual private parties.

It is further argued that without a bright-line rule nothing would stop a city from transferring citizen *A*'s property to citizen *B* for the sole reason that citizen *B* will put the property to a more productive use and thus pay more taxes. Such a one-to-one transfer of property, executed outside the confines of an integrated development plan, is not presented in this case. While such an unusual exercise of government power would certainly raise a suspicion that a private purpose was afoot, the hypothetical cases posited by petitioners can be confronted if and when they arise. They do not warrant the crafting of an artificial restriction on the concept of public use.

Just as we decline to second-guess the City's considered judgments about the efficacy of its development plan, we also decline to second-guess the City's determinations as to what lands it needs to acquire in order to effectuate the project. "It is not for the courts to oversee the choice of the boundary line nor to sit in review on the size of a particular project area. Once the question of the public purpose has been decided, the amount and character of land to be taken for the project and the need for a particular tract to complete the integrated plan rests in the discretion of the legislative branch."

In affirming the City's authority to take petitioners' properties, we do not minimize the hardship that condemnations may entail, notwithstanding the payment of just compensation. We emphasize that nothing in our opinion precludes any State from placing further restrictions on its exercise of the takings power. Indeed, many States already impose "public use" requirements that are stricter than the federal baseline. Some of these requirements have been established as a matter of state constitutional law*, while others are expressed in state eminent domain statutes that carefully limit the grounds upon which takings may be exercised. As the submissions of the parties and their *amici* make clear, the necessity and wisdom of using eminent domain to promote economic development are certainly matters of legitimate public debate. This Court's authority, however, extends only to determining whether the City's proposed condemnations are for a "public use" within the meaning of the Fifth Amendment to the Federal Constitution. Because over a century of our case law interpreting that provision dictates an affirmative answer to that question, we may not grant petitioners the relief that they seek.

The judgment of the Supreme Court of Connecticut is affirmed.

It is so ordered.

JUSTICE O'CONNOR, with whom CHIEF JUSTICE REHNQUIST and JUSTICES SCALIA and THOMAS join, dissenting.

Over two centuries ago, just after the Bill of Rights was ratified, Justice Chase wrote:

> An ACT of the Legislature (for I cannot call it a law) contrary to the great first principles of the social compact, cannot be considered a rightful exercise of legislative authority. . . . A few instances will suffice to explain what I mean. . . . [A] law that takes property from A. and gives it to B: It is against all reason and justice, for a people to entrust a Legislature with SUCH powers; and, therefore, it cannot be presumed that they have done it.

Today the Court abandons this long-held, basic limitation on government power. Under the banner of economic development, all private property is now vulnerable to being taken and transferred to another private owner, so long as it might be upgraded—*i.e.*, given to an owner who will use it in a way that the legislature deems more beneficial to the public—in the process. To reason, as the Court does, that the incidental public benefits resulting from the subsequent ordinary use of private property render economic development takings "for public use" is to wash out any distinction between private and public use of property—and thereby effectively to delete the words "for public use" from the Takings Clause of the Fifth Amendment. Accordingly I respectfully dissent.

---

* See, *e.g.*, *County of Wayne v. Hathcock*, 471 Mich. 445, 684 N.W.2d 765 (2004).

I

While the Takings Clause presupposes that government can take private property without the owner's consent, the just compensation requirement spreads the cost of condemnations and thus "prevents the public from loading upon one individual more than his just share of the burdens of government." The public use requirement, in turn, imposes a more basic limitation, circumscribing the very scope of the eminent domain power: Government may compel an individual to forfeit her property for the *public's* use, but not for the benefit of another private person. This requirement promotes fairness as well as security.

Where is the line between "public" and "private" property use? We give considerable deference to legislatures' determinations about what governmental activities will advantage the public. But were the political branches the sole arbiters of the public-private distinction, the Public Use Clause would amount to little more than hortatory fluff. An external, judicial check on how the public use requirement is interpreted, however limited, is necessary if this constraint on government power is to retain any meaning.

Our cases have generally identified three categories of takings that comply with the public use requirement, though it is in the nature of things that the boundaries between these categories are not always firm. Two are relatively straightforward and uncontroversial. First, the sovereign may transfer private property to public ownership—such as for a road, a hospital, or a military base. Second, the sovereign may transfer private property to private parties, often common carriers, who make the property available for the public's use—such as with a railroad, a public utility, or a stadium. But "public ownership" and "use-by-the-public" are sometimes too constricting and impractical ways to define the scope of the Public Use Clause. Thus we have allowed that, in certain circumstances and to meet certain exigencies, takings that serve a public purpose also satisfy the Constitution even if the property is destined for subsequent private use.

This case returns us for the first time in over 20 years to the hard question of when a purportedly "public purpose" taking meets the public use requirement. It presents an issue of first impression: Are economic development takings constitutional? I would hold that they are not.

JUSTICE THOMAS, dissenting.

IV

The consequences of today's decision are not difficult to predict, and promise to be harmful. So-called "urban renewal" programs provide some compensation for the properties they take, but no compensation is possible for the subjective value of these lands to the individuals displaced and the indignity inflicted by uprooting them from their homes. Allowing the government to take property solely for public purposes is bad enough, but extending the concept of public purpose to encompass any economically beneficial goal guarantees that these losses will fall disproportionately on poor communities. Those communities are not only systematically less likely to put their lands to the highest and best social use, but are also the least politically powerful. If ever there were justification for intrusive judicial review of constitutional provisions that protect "discrete and insular minorities," *United States v. Carolene Products Co.*, 304 U.S. 144 (1938), surely that principle would apply with great force to the powerless groups and individuals the Public Use Clause protects. The deferential standard this Court has adopted for the Public Use Clause is therefore deeply perverse. It encourages "those citizens with disproportionate influence and power in the political process, including large corporations and development firms" to victimize the weak.

FOR DISCUSSION

Some claim that after *Kelo* there were no limits on takings. Is that correct? What limits does Justice Stevens suggest? What role do comprehensive plans or local law have in limiting takings for economic development purposes?

How does Justice O'Connor reconcile her dissent here with her majority opinion in *Midkiff*? Why does Justice Thomas object to the taking here? Some also claimed that *Kelo* made new law, ruling for the first time ever that the promotion of economic development was a valid public use. Is that an accurate description of the Stevens' opinion?

RELATED CASE

***Horne v. Department of Agriculture:* 569 U.S. ___, 133 S.Ct. 2053 (2013).**

In a 9–0 opinion the Supreme Court ruled that raisin growers might be able to challenge as a taking a percentage of their crop to fund marketing programs under the Agricultural Marketing Agreement Act of 1937 (AMAA).

GLOSSARY

Bundle of Sticks: This metaphor is used by legal scholars to describe all of the different rights associated with property ownership. To own property means one has a bundle of different rights, including the right to exclude others from using one's property.

Bill of Attainder: A legislative action that declares an individual or group of people guilty of a crime, such as treason, and punishing them without providing a trial or due process. The Constitution bans such laws.

Eminent Domain: Eminent domain is the power of the government to take property for a public use.

Ex Post Facto Law: A law that retroactively changes the legal consequences of a behavior. For instance, an action that was committed legally at the time, after the passage of an ex post facto law could be punished. The Constitution states these types of laws are unconstitutional.

Extractions: The conditioning of a government permit based upon owners dedicating part of their property to be used by the public. In *Dolan v. City of Tigard* the Court stated that it would examine extractions as a form of a taking with greater level of scrutiny than other forms of property regulation.

Investment-Backed Expectations: This concept refers to a test the Court uses to determine if a taking has occurred. In *Pennsylvania Central v. New York* the Court stated that a taking may have occurred when there was a loss of investment-backed expectations.

Just Compensation: The amount of money the government or a condemnor constitutionally must pay an owner when the latter's property is taken by eminent domain. Just compensation is generally considered to be the fair market value of the property.

Per Se Taking: Actions undertaken by the government that are automatically considered to be acts of eminent domain. In *Loretto v. Teleprompter Manhattan CATV Corp.*, the Court stated that a physical invasion of the property was a per se taking, and in *Lucas v. South Carolina Coastal Council* it ruled that a total deprivation of the value of the property would also constitute a taking.

Public Use: Public use refers to one of the stipulations or requirements that an act of eminent domain must serve in order to be considered constitutional. A taking for a private use is not permitted under the Fifth Amendment of the Constitution. Ascertaining what constitutes a valid public use is a matter often debated by members of the Supreme Court, as in cases such as *Kelo v. City of New London* and *Hawaii Housing Authority v. Midkiff.*

Regulatory Taking: According to cases such as *Pennsylvania v. Mahon*, a regulatory taking occurs when the normal police power authority of a state goes "too far" in limiting property rights such that it effectively becomes a taking of private property.

Taking: The acquisition of property by the government. A taking may occur if the government takes legal or physical control of property. It may also effect a taking if some forms of regulation are too extensive or if it renders some property valueless. The Supreme Court has constructed numerous tests to define what constitutes a taking.

Takings Clause: The Takings Clause refers to the Fifth Amendment clause that defines the limitations on eminent domain authority.

Temporary Taking: A taking by the government for a short period of time. In *First English Evangelical Lutheran Church of Glendale v. County of Los Angeles*, the Court stated that temporary takings were compensable under the Fifth and Fourteenth Amendments.

Zoning: Zoning refers to laws, generally at the local level, that determine how owners may use their property. Zoning laws may indicate whether an owner can use property for residential or commercial use. Zoning was constitutionally upheld in *Euclid v. Ambler Realty*.

SELECTED BIBLIOGRAPHY

Berger, Lawrence. 1978. "The Public Use Requirement in Eminent Domain." *Oregon Law Review,* Vol. 57, p. 203246.

Corwin, Edwin S. 1955. *The Higher Law Background of American Constitutional Law*. Ithaca, NY: Cornell University Press.

Currie, David P. 1985. *The Constitution in the Supreme Court: The First Hundred Years*, 1789–1888. Chicago: University of Chicago Press.

Currie, David P. 1990. *The Constitution in the Supreme Court: The Second Hundred Years*, 1888–1886. Chicago: University of Chicago Press.

Ely, James W., Jr. 1997. *The Guardian of Every Other Right: A Constitutional History of Property Rights*. New York: Oxford University Press.

Epstein, Richard A. 1985. *Takings: Private Property and the Power of Eminent Domain*. Cambridge, MA: Harvard University Press.

Gillman, Howard. 1993. *The Constitution Besieged: The Rise & Demise of Lochner Era Police Powers Jurisprudence*. Durham, NC: Duke University Press.

Grant, J. A. C. 1930–31. "The 'Higher Law' Background of the Law of Eminent Domain." *Wisconsin Law Review,* Vol. 6, p. 67–89.

Hurst, James Willard. 1950. *The Growth of American Law*. Boston: Little, Brown.

Hurst, James Willard. 1956. *Laws and the Conditions of Freedom*. Madison: The University of Wisconsin Press.

King, Martin J. 1972. "Rex Non Potest Peccare??? The Decline and Fall of the Public Use Limitation on Eminent Domain." *Dickinson Law Review,* Vol. 76, p. 266–281.

Landry, Mark C. 1985. "The Public Use Requirement in Eminent Domain—A Requiem." *Tulane Law Review,* Vol. 60, p. 419–435.

Lewis, John. 1909. *A Treatise on the Law of Eminent Domain in the United States*. Chicago: Callaghan.

Meidinger, Errol E. 1980. "The 'Public Uses' of Eminent Domain: History and Policy." *Environmental Law,* Vol. 11, p. 1–66.

Paul, Ellen Frankel. 1988. *Property Rights and Eminent Domain.* New Brunswick, NJ: Transaction Publishers.

Sax, Joseph L. 1964. "Takings and the Police Power." *The Yale Law Journal,* Vol. 74, p. 36–76.

Schultz, David A. 1992. *Property, Power, and American Democracy.* New Brunswick, NJ: Transaction Publishers.

Schultz, David A. 2009. *Evicted! Property Rights and Eminent Domain.* Westport CT: Praeger Press.

Somin, Ilya, 2015. *The Grasping Hand: Kelo v. City of New London and the Limits of Eminent Domain.* Chicago: University of Chicago Press.

Stoebuck, William B. 1972. "A General Theory of Eminent Domain." *Washington Law Review,* Vol. 47, pp. 553–608.

Treanor, William Michael. 1985. "The Origins and Original Significance of the Just Compensation Clause of the Fifth Amendment." *The Yale Law Journal,* Vol. 94, pp. 694–716.

CHAPTER VII

State Authority in a Federal System

Timeline: The States and Commerce Power

1807 Robert Fulton begins the first commercial steamship route in the United States.

1821 Maryland enacts a law requiring all importers to have a state license to do business.

1827 In *Brown v. Maryland*, the United States Supreme Court rules that states may not tax products while they remain in their original package.

1828 Andrew Jackson is elected as president.

1837 In *City of New York v. Miln* the Supreme Court rules that states uniquely have the police power to pass laws to protect the health, safety, welfare, and morals of its citizens.

1851 The Supreme Court rules in *Cooley v. Board of Wardens* that in the absence of congressional legislation, states have the authority to regulate commerce that is local in nature.

1860 Abraham Lincoln is elected as president.

1861 Start of the Civil War begins.

1865 Civil War ends.

1886 In *Coe v. Errol* the Supreme Court rules that states can regulate commerce until products are thrust into the stream of interstate commerce.

1929 Stock Market Crash and the beginning of the Great Depression.

1932 Franklin Roosevelt is elected as president.

1933 Start of the New Deal.

1933 Congress adopts the Agricultural Adjustment Act.

1937 The Supreme Court upheld in *Henneford v. Silas Mason Co., Inc.*, a state tax on chattels purchased out of state but used within the Washington State.

1938 The Supreme Court rules in *South Carolina State Highway Department v. Barnwell Brothers, Inc.*, that states a state can regulate the height and width of vehicles that use its roads without violating the Commerce Clause.

1939 Smith Act is adopted.

1941 The Supreme Court rules in *Edwards v. California* that a state law limiting individuals from migrating into California violated the Commerce Clause.

1945 The Supreme Court in *Southern Pacific v. Arizona*, declares a state law that limited the number of cars that could be attached to a train as a violation of the Commerce Clause.

1945 WW World War II ends; Cold War begins.

1945 Franklin Delano Roosevelt dies; Harry Truman becomes president.

1948 The Supreme Court in *Hood v. Dumond* declared declares a violation of the Commerce Clause New York State's refusal to issue a license to allow an out-of-state milk company to open up another receiving depot in New York so that it could purchase milk.

1950 Senator Joseph McCarthy gives speech alleging that U.S. government is being infiltrated by communist spies.

1951 In *Dean Milk Co. v. City of Madison* the Supreme Court strikes down a state law requiring all milk sold in Wisconsin to be pasteurized within five miles of Madison.

1956 In *Pennsylvania v. Nelson* the Supreme Court rules that a state law seeking to punish espionage was preempted by federal law.

1968 Richard Nixon is elected as president.

1970 The first Earth Day is observed.

1972 Congress adopts the Clean Water Act.

1974 Nixon resigns; Gerald Ford becomes president.

1977 In *Complete Auto Transit v. Brady* the Supreme Court upholds a state system to apportion tax on a business operating in interstate commerce but also operating within a specific state.

1978 In *Philadelphia v. New Jersey* the Court struck strikes down a state law preventing the shipment of trash and waste out-of-state as a violation of the Commerce Clause.

1978 The Supreme Court ruled rules in *Baldwin v. Fish & Game Commission of Montana* that Montana did not violate the Commerce Clause when it charged in-state and out-of-state residents a different fee to hunt elk.

1980 In *Reeves v. Stake* the Supreme Court rules that it was not a violation of the Commerce Clause for the state of South Dakota to favor its residents over nonresidents in the sale of concrete in its own state-owned facility.

Ronald Reagan is elected as president.

1987 The Supreme Court rules in *California v. Cabazon Band of Mission Indians* that absent federal authorization, a state cannot regulate bingo activities on an Indian reservation.

1988 Congress adopts the Indian Gaming Regulatory Act.

1992 Bill Clinton is elected as president.

1993 In *Quill v. North Dakota* the Supreme Court rules that the Commerce Clause prevents states from requiring an out-of-state business that does mail sales to its state to collect sales tax on purchases made by its residents.

1994 Microsoft Explorer is invented.

1994 Amazon.com founded.

2000 George W. Bush is elected as president.

2005 The Supreme Court in *Granholm v. Heald*, strikes down a state law banning out-of-state mail delivery of wine into Michigan.

2015 The Supreme Court rules in *Comptroller of Treasury of Maryland v. Wynne* that the Dormant Commerce Clause prevents a state from refusing to give a taxpayer credit for taxes paid to another state.

Article I, Sec. 8:

The Congress shall have Power To . . . To regulate Commerce with foreign Nations, and among the several States, and with the Indian Tribes. . . ."

—Article I, Section 8, Clause 3.

INTRODUCTION

One of the very great difficulties encountered under the Articles of Confederation was the inability of the central government to control interstate commerce and the virtual anarchy resulting from the efforts of the states to regulate it. Instead, states often acted like sovereign nations, engaging in protectionist or retaliatory measures against one another. To address these problems, the constitutional Framers vested in Congress the power to regulate interstate commerce. At least in theory this clause resolved the problem of states seeking to interfere with interstate commerce or engaging in protectionist legislation. Yet the question remained: Did the Commerce Clause foreclose all state regulation or interference with interstate commerce? More specifically, what was the line that the Commerce clause imposed that separated permissible state action to regulate its own internal affairs or economy, to address or abate problems, or to tax and raise revenue for its own operations? Perhaps no other constitutional question or problem has been as enduring or as vexing for the Supreme Court as that separating interstate versus **intrastate commerce**. While Chapter III examined this issue from the perspective of national legislative power, this chapter analyzes the topic from a different direction, looking instead at what powers states possess within the federal union.

This issue of state commerce power was adjudicated for the first time in *Gibbons v. Ogden* (9 Wheat. 1, 1824), when both the question of the extent of federal power and the question of restrictions on the states in commerce were before the Court. This decision was unclear as to whether it created an exclusive power for the federal government or simply admitting no power for the states to act when the federal government has acted. Yet changes in the economy, such as the emergence of railroads, shipping along the rivers and newly-built canals, and increased demands to sort out the problems the growth of the American economy presented, placed state and federal regulation of the economy into conflict.

In *Cooley v. Board of Wardens* (53 U.S. 299, 1851) the Court clarified when Congress's power was exclusive and when it was not, leaving room for the states to act when there were diverse local conditions and Congress had not stepped in to regulate. Thus, as a result of both *Gibbons* and *Cooley*, it was clear that both the federal government and the states could act in the realm of interstate commerce. The question was when and what were the dividing lines of authority between them.

This chapter examines the "other side" of the Commerce Clause. It examines what powers remain in the hands of state governments when it comes to regulating commerce. It demonstrates that states do have an important role when it comes to regulating commerce and the economy.

DRAWING THE LINES BETWEEN STATE AND FEDERAL COMMERCE POWER

Once there is established the proposition that the entire realm of commerce is divided between state and federal governments, it immediately raises the question where the line of division is to be drawn in a practical sense. Where does state jurisdiction for tax and regulatory purposes end and then begin again after the interstate journey? Where does state power begin in the case of an article imported from abroad? These are the questions the Court attempted to answer in *New York v. Miln* (36 U.S. 102, 1837), *Brown v. Maryland* (25 U.S. 419, 1827), *Cooley v. Board of Wardens,* and *Coe v. Errol* (116 U.S. 517, 1886). As you read these cases, ask yourself several questions: Has the Court defined a clear and manageable rule for drawing a line between state and federal responsibility? What are the reasons states are offering for passing their legislation? Are these reasons legitimate, or are they efforts to engage in protectionism?

New York v. Miln develops the legal concept of **police power** as an importance attribute of state sovereignty. The police power may be described as the inherent power of states to regulate for the health, safety, welfare, and morals of its citizens. Only states have police power; the federal government does not. As *New York v. Miln* pointed out, this power does not always conflict with the commerce power of the federal government. Instead, states may be able to legislate to protect their citizens even in circumstances where it may affect the commerce power of the federal government. Sorting out the respective spheres of authority between the state and federal governments has occupied the Supreme Court's agenda for much of its history. The police power, as subsequent cases below will show, allows states to regulate even in cases where its actions might interfere with federal Commerce Clause authority.

Brown v. Maryland is the "**original package**" case and involves a partial solution to the problem of relinquishment of federal control to state control. There is a difference in this as between foreign and interstate commerce. In the former, the beginning of state control—either taxation or regulation—is delayed until the package in which the product is shipped is broken open or is sold. In the latter, taxation by the state can begin as soon as the article in question arrives at its destination. Only state regulation is delayed until the package is opened or sold. Justice Marshall's statement in *Brown v. Maryland* that he supposed the original package doctrine to apply "to importations from a sister state" as well as to foreign imports was treated as dictum and state taxation permitted after an article coming from another state had "come to rest."

Brown was also decided before the *Willson* and *Miln* decisionsand before the Court recognized or articulated the police power doctrine. As you read the case, ask yourself why could not the license requirements in *Brown* could not be defined or described as a valid police power action? What is the asserted interest that Maryland would have had in adopting such a regulation? If *Brown* had come to the Court after *Miln*, do you think the case would have been decided differently?

Cooley v. Board of Wardens was an important case modifying the decision in *Gibbons.* As a result of *Gibbons v. Ogden*, there was no question that in case of conflicting state and federal commercial regulations the federal would prevail. There remained, however, the question of the validity of state regulations of foreign or interstate commerce, in the absence of federal regulation. The answer of the Court in *Cooley*, which has come to be known as the "**Cooley doctrine**," is that wherever a matter of commerce requires uniform regulation in all areas of the country, this it is a matter of exclusive federal jurisdiction—what has been called "**selective exclusiveness.**" On the other hand, some aspects of commerce permit, and even require, a diversity of treatment to meet local differences. These can be regulated by the states in the absence of legislation by Congress. The test is really the balance of state and federal interests. A state may pass laws affecting interstate commerce when Congress has not acted on a matter that requires regulation for the public welfare, when it is a matter on which there need not be uniform legislation for the entire country, and when the state laws involve no discrimination against or impose no undue burden on interstate commerce.

Within *Cooley* one also finds the origin of another important Supreme Court doctrine—the **dormant commerce clause**. This theory maintains that states, even in the absence of congressional action, may not take any action that burdens or discriminates against interstate commerce. While Justices such as Antonin Scalia were highly critical of this theory, the concept of the dormant Commerce Clause has been a frequently used doctrine to strike down state regulations. The very practical question of when interstate commerce begins and ends too also requires a practical answer. When control over the whole scheme of commerce is divided between federal and state governments, the determination of where the lines of division of such control are must certainly be regarded as important. On both sides of a potential or real interstate commerce action there are areas of overlapping state and federal power. *Coe v. Errol* draws a very nice line on the end of state control at the beginning of interstate commerce. According to that decision, states can continue to tax or regulate items until the point when they are thrust into the stream of interstate commerce. Once that happens, then they become subject to federal control. However, as will be noted repeatedly, this does not preclude the operation of federal controls at a much earlier time. To some extent, at the other end of the "journey," state control may begin before complete federal jurisdiction has been relinquished.

Among the lessons that *Coe* teaches is that mere intention to send goods in interstate commerce is not enough to exempt such goods from state control. Only when the goods in question are finally committed to the interstate journey by being placed in the hands of a common carrier does state power cease. In a discipline such as public law, which seems to avoid "pat" answers and rules of thumb, this case comes very close to being just that.

However, what if a product passes through a state en route to another destination? Does a state have police power authority to regulate it while passing through the state, or is this merely a matter for federal regulation? While interstate commerce means something is crossing state lines, it is still within a state for a period of time, and should not a state have some ability to regulate a product if it needs to protect public safety? Goods pass through states all the time via highways and rail lines. When are regulations really meant to promote safety versus, and when are they simply efforts to extort taxes or other benefits that might hurt interstate commerce? Thus, in some situations, states may continue to regulate interstate commerce so as long as it is for valid police power reasons—to protect the health, safety, welfare, or morals of its citizens. The issue then is to determine when such regulation is genuine and not a burden on interstate commerce. Ascertaining both may be a matter of balancing state and federal interests.

One of the factors that must be considered in all such instances is the balance of legitimate state power against the needed freedom of interstate commerce. In *South Carolina State Highway Department v. Barnwell Brothers, Inc.* (303 U.S. 177, 1938) the Court had to address whether a state could regulate the weight and width of vehicles that use its roads in order to promote public safety when there were no federal regulations in effect and when other states had less restrictive standards. The Court upheld the state rules. It specifically noted the absence of federal action addressing the issue of vehicle height and weight and argued that states possess valid police power authority to regulate its roads.

In *Southern Pacific v. Arizona* (325 U.S. 761, 1945) the Court rejected a state law that limited the number of cars that could be attached to a train. Here the Court found that the state action burdened interstate commerce. It held that not only was the balance in favor of the invalidity of the proposed state regulation but also that this (the number of cars on a train) was a matter that required uniform regulation in accordance with the "Cooley rule." *Southern Pacific* also emphasizes the distinction the Court has made between state regulations that affect commerce by highway and by railroad. The Court, as noted in *Barnwell*, has been much more tolerant of highway regulation, basically because of the great "local concern" about the use of a state's highways, a concern that does not find the same expression where railroads are concerned, presumably because of the proprietary interest of the states in highways. The Court in *Southern Pacific* specifically stated that there was no intention to overrule *Barnwell.* Is the distinction between regulation of railroads and highways persuasive? Why should states have more leeway to regulate one as opposed to another? In addition, is there any way to distinguish legitimate police power regulation from either improper interference with interstate commerce or hidden efforts to favor state interests or industries at the expense of out-of-state ones? Perhaps one distinction, and that one which the Commerce Clause was set up to address, was to prevent states from engaging in protectionism or parochialism. By that, the Commerce Clause's core goal is to prevent states from favoring their own businesses by discriminating against out-of-state entities. What is called for is a test that seeks to smoke out legitimate police power activity from mere parochialism or **protectionist measures** that impose a **discriminatory burden on interstate commerce.**

In *Pike v. Bruce Church, Inc.* (397 U.S. 137, 1970) Justice Stewart for the Court devised a balancing test for determining when a state may regulate interstate commerce to protect local police power interests.

> [W]here the statute regulates evenhandedly to effectuate a legitimate local public interest, and its effects on interstate commerce are only incidental, it will be upheld unless the burden imposed on such commerce is clearly excessive in relation to the putative local benefits. If a legitimate local purpose is found, then the question becomes one of degree. And the extent of the burden that will be tolerated will, of course, depend on the nature of the local interest involved, and on whether it could be promoted as well with a lesser impact on interstate activities.

This test seeks to weigh local interests against the burdens on interstate commerce to determine if the regulation will be upheld. It also requires the Court to ascertain whether an asserted local interest is in fact legitimate. Does this test offer any guidance towards for clarifying the line between state and federal control over interstate commerce?

In cases such as *Dean Milk Co. v. City of Madison* (340 U.S. 349, 1951) the determining factor is that it often involves discrimination against interstate commerce, not the burdening of the commerce itself. Look at the case and ask what was it the State of Wisconsin was really doing when it required all milk to be pasteurized within five miles of Madison? What is the burden on out out-of of-state milk producers versus those in state? Were there not both discrimination and a burden on interstate commerce? In the application of the "balance test," the power of the state to safeguard local health was overruled in *Dean Milk* because the particular regulation was not necessary for the exercise of such state power. The Court held that there are other ways of safeguarding public health in this situation. A state cannot legislate away interstate competition. The discrimination in *Dean* against Illinois producers conjured up shades of the Articles of Confederation era.

The dairy industry seemed, at least at one time, to be a popular subject for economic regulation and protectionism as states enacted laws to protect their own cows and farmers. *Hood v. DuMond H. P. Hood and Sons v. DuMond* (336 U.S. 525, 1949) is an example. Here New York State refused to issue a license to allow an out-of-state milk company to open up another receiving depot in New York so that it could purchase milk. New York justified the license denial because it claimed that this new facility would upset the milk market in the state. The Court found the license denial a burden on interstate commerce. Cases such as *Hood* demonstrate that a state cannot hinder free shipment of goods out of that state as a means of protecting local industry. Also for this purpose (as opposed to safety on highways), a state cannot use its licensing power to restrict competition of common carriers in interstate commerce. *Hood v. Dumond* involves an application of the "undue burden" formula, which again seeks to determine if the state regulation unconstitutionally interferes with interstate commerce.

In addition to discriminating against cows, states often do the same when it comes to people. During the Dust Bowl-Depression era of the 1930s, many individuals left states such as Oklahoma and headed for California in search of jobs and better opportunities. John Steinbeck's novel *The Grapes of Wrath* offers a particularly good description of this phenomenon. But as individuals flocked to California, the state adopted laws making it more difficult for poverty-stricken persons to take up residence there. The official concern was to prevent additional burdens on state resources. Unofficially, it may have been discrimination. *Edwards v. California* (314 U.S. 160, 1941) considers whether a state can protect its borders to limit immigration, especially of the indigent.

The exercise of state police power in such a way as to hinder or obstruct interstate commerce is invalid. This is especially true where alternative means are available to the state for the care of the general welfare. A state cannot indulge in economic or social isolation. A state may impose quarantine on interstate commerce in instances where a person or an article poses a real danger to general health or safety. The obvious objective of California's "anti-Okie" law was to hold down California's relief costs. The Court held that not only is care of the needy a national problem but there is also a right of interstate travel. A state cannot erect barriers.

Ordinarily, many would not think of the shipment of solid waste and trash as a form of interstate commerce, but it is, as evidenced by *Philadelphia v. New Jersey* (437 U.S. 617, 1978). States generally do not want dumps or trash within their borders and seek to pass laws to limit pollution. Why was New Jersey's law not viewed as a legitimate police power activity to prevent pollution? Could New Jersey have enacted its own laws preventing dumping or landfills within its own borders? If so, why could it not also limit more garbage from coming into its state?

At the heart of the majority opinion is a distinction between a state acting as a regulator versus acting in its capacity as a **market participant**. If acting in the former, it must play fair and it may not favor its citizens over non-nonresidents. However, if a state is acting as a market participant, it may choose to whom it wishes to sell to (subject to civil rights limits), even if it means it favors citizens or non-noncitizens. This distinction is at the heart of why and how state universities may charge different tuitions based on state residency. Is the market participant rule different from the police power justification for the regulation of interstate commerce? Why should states be allowed to discriminate against interstate commerce simply because they are acting as employer or market participant? *Reeves v. Stake* (447 U.S. 429, 1980) appears to open the door to an entirely different set of actions that discriminate against interstate commerce. Here the Court permitted South Dakota as a market participant and operator of a cement company to favor its own residents at the expense of out-of-state entities. What if the state decides to enter the waste-hauling or dairy businesses? Would the Court be willing to change its perspective on discriminating against out-of-state businesses?

Baldwin v. Fish & Game Commission of Montana (436 U.S. 371, 1978) is an Equal Protection and Privileges and Immunities Clause case, but it involves issues similar to that those raised by the Commerce Clause. Could the State of Montana set different hunting license fees for residents and nonresidents? The Court said yes. Is *Baldwin* a decision based more on the police power or market participant exception to the Commerce Clause? The Court seems to assert that the state owns the elk and therefore can restrict hunting, but it also seems to be invoking a regulatory claim in terms of the state seeking to protect scare resources. Why is this argument more acceptable here than with in the case of New Jersey and its efforts to restrict waste from being brought into the state? Do not both arguments rest on the same principle?

California v. Cabazon Band of Mission Indians (480 U.S. 202, 1987) ventures into state authority to regulate activities within its borders as they affect Native Americans. Specifically, the State of California sought to regulate bingo activities on Indian reservations within its borders. The Court, in a very controversial opinion, struck the California regulation, holding that in the absence of federal authority, states could not regulate activities such as this on reservations. As a result of this decision, Congress the next year adopted the **Indian Gaming Regulatory Act of 1988 (IGRA).** The decision limited *Cabazon*'s holding, and it created three classes of games that could operate on Indian reservations. The first class included traditional Indian games, which could not be regulated by states. The second class was low-stakes games, which could be regulated on Indian reservations the same way as elsewhere in a state. Finally, for high-stakes games, IGRA stipulated that tribes and states should negotiate a compact under the supervision of the Interior Department. As a result of IGRA, many states have reached compacts with Indian tribes regarding, for example, the division of revenue between the states and the tribes. Finally, both IGRA and *Cabazon* state that a specific type of tribal gaming cannot be banned if it is otherwise permitted in the state. For those states that operate their own gaming for revenue purposes, they may not ban Indian gaming to eliminate competition. In enacting IGRA, what was Congress seeking to accomplish? Also, when *Cabazon* was decided, think about the fact that many states were beginning to operate their own lotteries and gambling to generate state revenue. Do states view tribal gaming as a rival or competitor that is similar to an out-of-state business?

If at one time states often fought over milk, perhaps now it is wine and alcohol. Many states such as New York and Michigan are anxious to protect their new or growing wineries. *Granholm v. Heald* (544 U.S. 460, 2005) is an example of this effort. How different is the issue at stake in *Heald* different from that in *Dean* and *Hood*? What was the interest Michigan was asserting to ban out out-of-state shipment of wine into its state? Was it health and safety or something else? The Court did not see much difference in between wine in *Heald* between wine and milk from in *Dean* and *Hood* even though alcohol is historically subject to more regulation than milk.

Heald is a challenging case because it implicates the world of e-commerce, or commerce that is undertaken over the Web or the Internet. To what extent has the Internet changed the debate on the state regulation of interstate commerce? Web sales or activities such as gaming and sale of prescription drugs, for example, pose new difficulties for state regulation in terms of drawing the lines between their state and federal authority to act. If a business does not physically exist in a state but ships products via the Web into it, how legally (and practically) can a state legally (and practically) regulate that product?

Preemption of state law by the federal government is partly grounded in the Commerce Clause, but also in the Supremacy Clause, (Article VI, Section Sec. 2) of the Constitution. Why should not states not also be allowed to criminalize certain activity that the federal government already addresses? In many areas of criminal law, both the state and federal government have laws on the same topic, placing defendants at risk of prosecution from either governmental entity. Why was the state prohibited from acting in *Pennsylvania v. Nelson* (350 U.S. 497, 1956)? In reading *Pennsylvania v. Nelson*, ask if the Court's reasoning is persuasive in the sense that the federal government has so occupied the field that it has left no room for state action.

MAYOR, ALDERMEN AND COMMONALTY OF CITY OF NEW YORK V. MILN

36 U.S. 102, 11 Pet. 102, 9 L.Ed. 648 (1837)

New York passed a law requiring ships' masters to provide a passenger manifest, post security for indigent passengers, and to remove aliens considered to be undesirable. The law was challenged as a violation of the Commerce Clause because it interfered with the authority of the federal government to regulate shipping into and out of the United States.

Vote: 6–1

JUSTICE BARBOUR delivered the opinion of the Court.

This case comes before this court upon a certificate of division of the circuit court of the United States for the southern district of New York. It was an action of debt, brought in that court, by the plaintiff, to recover of the defendant, as consignee of the ship called the *Emily*, the amount of certain penalties imposed by a statute of New York, passed February 11th, 1824, entitled, "an act concerning passengers in vessels coming to the port of

New York." The statute, amongst other things, enacts, that every master or commander of any ship or other vessel, arriving at the port of New York, from any country out of the United States, or from any other of the United States than the state of New York, shall, within twenty-four hours after the arrival of such ship or vessel in the said port, make a report in writing, on oath or affirmation, to the mayor of the city of New York, or, in case of his sickness or absence, to the recorder of the said city, of the name, place of birth, and last legal settlement, age and occupation, of every person who shall have been brought as a passenger in such ship or vessel, on her last voyage from any country out of the United States into the port of New York or any of the United States, and from any of the United States other than the state of New York, to the city of New York, and of all passengers who shall have landed, or been suffered or permitted to land, from such ship or vessel, at any place, during such her last voyage, or have been put on board, or suffered or permitted to go on board, of any other ship or vessel, with the intention of proceeding to the said city, under the penalty on such master or commander, and the owner or owners, consignee or consignees of such ship or vessel, severally and respectively, of $75 for every person neglected to be reported as aforesaid, and for every person whose name, place of birth, and last legal settlement, age and occupation, or either or any of such particulars, shall be falsely reported as aforesaid; to be used for and recovered as therein provided.

The declaration alleges, that the defendant was consignee of the ship *Emily*, of which a certain William Thompson was master; and that in the month of August 1829, said Thompson, being master of such ship, did arrive with the same in the port of New York, from a country out of the United States, and that one hundred passengers were brought in said ship, on her then last voyage, from a country out of the United States, into the port of New York; and that the said master did not make the report required by the statute, as before recited. The defendant demurred to the declaration. The plaintiff joined in the demurrer, and the following point, on a division of the court, was thereupon certified to this court, viz: " 'That the act of the legislature of New York, mentioned in the plaintiff's declaration, assumes to regulate trade and commerce between the port of New York and foreign ports, and is unconstitutional and void.'."

It is contended by the counsel for the defendant, that the act in question is a regulation of commerce; that the power to regulate commerce is, by the constitution of the United States, granted to congress; that this power is exclusive, and that consequently, the act is a violation of the constitution of the United States.

On the part of the plaintiff, it is argued, that an affirmative grant of power previously existing in the states to congress, is not exclusive; except, 1st, where it is so expressly declared in terms, by the clause giving the power; or 2d, where a similar power is prohibited to the states; or 3d, where the power in the states would be repugnant to, and incompatible with, a similar power in congress; that this power falls within neither of these predicaments; that it is not, in terms, declared to be exclusive; that it is not prohibited to the states; and that it is not repugnant to, nor incompatible with, a similar power in congress; and that having pre-existed in the states, they, therefore, have a concurred power in relation to the subject; and that the act in question would be valid, even if it were a regulation of commerce, it not contravening any regulation made by congress. But they deny that it is a regulation of commerce; on the contrary, they assert, that it is a mere regulation of internal police, a power over which is not granted to congress; and which, therefore, as well upon the true construction of the constitution, as by force of the tenth amendment to that instrument, is reserved to, and resides in, the several states.

We shall not enter into any examination of the question, whether the power to regulate commerce, be or be not exclusive of the states, because the opinion which we have formed renders it unnecessary: in other words, we are of opinion, that the act is not a regulation of commerce, but of police; and that being thus considered, it was passed in the exercise of a power which rightfully belonged to the states.

That the state of New York possessed power to pass this law, before the adoption of the constitution of the United States, might probably be taken as a truism, without the necessity of proof. But as it may tend to present it in a clearer point of view, we will quote a few passages from a standard writer upon public law, showing the origin and character of this power. Vattel, book 2, ch. 7, § 94.— ' "The sovereign may forbid the entrance of his territory, either to foreigners in general, or in particular cases, or to certain persons, or for certain particular purposes, according as he may think it advantageous to the state.'." . . . " 'Since the lord of the territory may, whenever he thinks proper, forbid its being entered, he has, no doubt, a power to annex what conditions he pleases, to the permission to enter.'." The power then of New York to pass this law having undeniably existed at the formation of the constitution, the simple inquiry is, whether by that instrument is was taken from the states, and granted to congress; for if it were not, it yet remains with them.

If, as we think, it be a regulation, not of commerce, but police; then it is not taken from the states. To decide this, let us examine its purpose, the end to be attained, and the means of its attainment. It is apparent, from the whole scope of the law, that the object of the legislature was, to prevent New York from being burdened by an influx of persons brought thither in ships, either from foreign countries, or from any other of the states; and for that purpose, a report was required of the names, places of birth, &c., of all passengers, that the necessary steps might be taken by the city authorities, to prevent them from becoming chargeable as paupers. Now, we hold, that both the end and the means here used, are within the competency of the states, since a portion of their powers were surrendered to the federal government. Let us see, what powers are left with the states. The Federalist, No 45, speaking of this subject, says, the powers reserved to the several states, all extend to all the objects, which in the ordinary course of affairs, concern the lives, liberties and properties of the people; and the internal order, improvement and prosperity of the state. And this court, in the case of *Gibbons v. Ogden*, 9 Wheat. 203 (1924), which will hereafter be more particularly noticed, in speaking of the inspection laws of the states, say, they form a portion of that immense mass of legislation which embraces everything within the territory of a state, not surrendered to the general government, all which can be most advantageously exercised by the states themselves. Inspection laws, quarantine laws, health laws of every description, as well as laws for regulating the internal commerce of a state, and those which respect turnpike-roads, ferries, &c., are component parts of this mass.

Now, if the act in question be tried by reference to the delineation of power laid down in the preceding quotations, it seems to us, that we are necessarily brought to the conclusion, that it falls within its limits. There is no aspect in which it can be viewed, in which it transcends them. If we look at the place of its operation, we find it to be within the territory, and therefore, within the jurisdiction of New York. If we look at the person on whom it operates, he is found within the same territory and jurisdiction. If we look at the persons for whose benefit it was passed, they are the people of New York, for whose protection and welfare the legislature of that state are authorized and in duty bound to provide. If we turn our attention to the purpose to be attained, it is to secure that very protection, and to provide for that very welfare. If we examine the means by which these ends are proposed to be accomplished, they bear a just, natural and appropriate relation to those ends.

From this it appears, that whilst a state is acting within the legitimate scope of its power, as to the end to be attained, it may use whatsoever means, being appropriate to that end, it may think fit; although they may be the same, or so nearly the same, as scarcely to be distinguishable from those adopted by congress, acting under a different power; subject, only, say the court, to this limitation, that in the event of collision, the law of the state must yield to the law of congress. The court must be understood, of course, as meaning that the law of congress is passed upon a subject within the sphere of its power. Even, then, if the section of the act in question could be considered as partaking of the nature of a commercial regulation, the principle here laid down would save it from condemnation, if no such collision exist.

FOR DISCUSSION

How broad is the police power? Does it mean that states can enact any legislation to protect their citizens? When does this power face a limit from the Commerce Clause or from other parts of the Constitution?

BROWN V. MARYLAND

25 U.S. 419, 12 Wheat. 419, 6 L.Ed. 678 (1827)

Maryland, by statute of 1821, provided that all importers of goods had to secure a state license. Brown, an importer, was indicted for selling a package of dry goods in the form in which it was imported, without a license. This was challenged as an interference with foreign commerce, which was vested in the federal government by the Constitution. The state contended that this was an occupational tax.

Vote: 6–1

CHIEF JUSTICE MARSHALL delivered the opinion of the Court:

The constitutional prohibition on the States to lay a duty on imports, a prohibition which a vast majority of them must feel an interest in preserving, may certainly come in conflict with their acknowledged power to tax persons and property within their territory. The power, and the restriction on it, though quite distinguishable when they do not approach each other, may yet, like the intervening colours between white and black, approach so nearly as to perplex the understanding, as colours perplex the vision in marking the distinction between them. Yet the distinction exists, and must be marked as the cases arise. Till they do arise, it might be premature to state any rule as being universal in its application. It is sufficient for the present to say, generally, that when the importer has so acted upon the thing imported, that it has become incorporated and mixed up with the mass of property in the country, it has, perhaps, lost its distinctive character as an import, and has become subject to the taxing power of the State; but while remaining the property of the importer, in his warehouse, in the original form or package in which it was imported, a tax upon it is too plainly a duty on imports to escape the prohibition in the Constitution.

So a tax on the occupation of an importer is, in like manner, a tax on importation. It must add to the price of the article, and be paid by the consumer, or by the importer himself, in like manner as a direct duty on the article itself would be made. This the State has not a right to do, because it is prohibited by the Constitution.

We think, then, that the act, under which the plaintiffs in error were indicted, is repugnant to that article of the Constitution which declares, that "no State shall lay any impost or duties on imports or exports."

. . . Is it also repugnant to that clause in the Constitution which empowers "Congress to regulate commerce with foreign nations, and among the several States, and with the Indian tribes"? . . .

If the principles we have stated be correct, the result to which they conduct us cannot be mistaken. Any penalty inflicted on the importer or selling the article in his character of importer, must be in opposition to the act of Congress which authorizes importation. Any charge on the introduction and incorporation of the articles into and with the mass of property in the country, must be hostile to the power given to Congress to regulate commerce, since an essential part of that regulation, and principal object of it, is to prescribe the regular means for accomplishing that introduction and incorporation.

It may be proper to add, that we suppose the principles laid down in this case, to apply equally to importations from a sister State. We do not mean to give any opinion on a tax discriminating between foreign and domestic articles.

JUSTICE THOMPSON dissented:

It is very obvious that this law can, in no manner whatever, affect the commercial intercourse between the states; it applies purely to the internal trade of the state of Maryland. The defendants were merchants, trading in the city of Baltimore. The indictment describes them as such, and alleges the sale to have been in that place; and nothing appears to warrant an inference, that the package of goods sold was not intended for consumption at that place; and the law has no relation whatever to goods intended for transportation to another state.

It appears to me, that no other sound and practical rule can be adopted, than to consider the external commerce as ending with the importation of the foreign article; and the importation is complete, as soon as the goods are introduced in the country, according to the provisions of the revenue laws, with the intention of being sold here for consumption, or for the purpose of internal and domestic trade, and the duties paid or secured. And this is the light in which this question has been considered by this and other courts of the United States. This, it will be perceived, does not embrace foreign merchandise intended for exportation, and not for consumption; nor articles intended for commerce between the states; but such as are intended for domestic trade within the state: and it is to such articles only that the law of Maryland extends. I cannot, therefore, think, that this law at all interferes with the power of Congress to regulate commerce; nor does it, according to my understanding of the Constitution, violate that provision, which declares that no state shall, without the consent of Congress, lay any imposts or duties on imports or exports, except what may be absolutely necessary for executing its inspection laws.

This law seems to have been treated as if it imposed a tax or duty upon the importer, or the importation. It certainly admits of no such construction. It is a charge upon the wholesale dealer, whoever he may be, and to operate upon the sale, and not upon the importation.

FOR DISCUSSION

Does the original package doctrine offer a viable line to distinguish federal from state commerce authority? Could an article of commerce not stay in its original package the entire journey across the country? If so, would that allow one or more states to regulate its shipment?

RELATED CASES

***Walling v. Jacksonville Paper Co.:* 317 U.S. 564 (1943).**

When goods are brought through interstate commerce to a wholesale company, placing the goods temporarily in a warehouse for later delivery to local customers, who specifically ordered the goods, does not change the interstate commerce aspect of the goods. The goods are in interstate commerce "until they reach the customer for whom they are intended."

***Hooven and Allison Co. v. Evatt:* 324 U.S. 652 (1945).**

Hemp and other fibers imported from the Philippines and placed in the importer's warehouse, without their being used or sold, for a period of three years are still immune from state taxation.

***Department of Revenue v. James B. Beam Distilling Co.*: 377 U.S. 341 (1964).**

A state tax on whisky produced in Scotland and shipped to Kentucky, which retained its character as an import in the original package, was clearly proscribed by the export-import clause of the Constitution (Article I, Section Sec. 10, Clause para. 2), which was not, insofar as intoxicants are concerned, repealed by the Twenty-First Amendment.

COOLEY V. BOARD OF WARDENS

53 U.S. 299, 12 How. 299, 13 L.Ed. 996 (1851)

The state of Pennsylvania had, by statutory enactment, provided that ships bound to or from a foreign destination must engage a local pilot. Enforcement of the monetary penalties for violation of the regulations was placed in the hands of the Board of Wardens of the Port of Philadelphia. Cooley violated the regulations but claimed that the statute was an invasion of the exclusive authority over interstate and foreign commerce vested in Congress by the Constitution.

Vote: 7–2

JUSTICE CURTIS delivered the opinion of the Court.

Now, the power to regulate commerce, embraces a vast field, containing not only many, but exceedingly various subjects, quite unlike in their nature: some imperatively demanding a single uniform rule, operating equally on the commerce of the United States in every port; and some, like the subject now in question, as imperatively demanding that diversity, which alone can meet the local necessities of navigation.

Either absolutely to affirm, or deny, that the nature of this power requires exclusive legislation by Congress, is to lose sight of the nature of the subjects of this power, and to assert concerning all of them, what is really applicable but to a part. Whatever subjects of this power are in their nature national, or admit only of one uniform system, or plan of regulation, may justly be said to be of such a nature as to require exclusive legislation by Congress. That this cannot be affirmed of laws for the regulation of pilots and pilotage is plain. The Act of 1789 contains a clear and authoritative declaration by the first Congress, that the nature of this subject is such, that until Congress should find it necessary to exert its power, it should be left to the legislation of the States; that it is local and not national; that it is likely to be the best provided for, not by one system, or plan of regulations, but by as many as the legislative discretion of the several states should deem applicable to the local peculiarities of the ports within their limits.

It is the opinion of a majority of the court that the mere grant to Congress of the power to regulate commerce, did not deprive the States of power to regulate pilots, and that although Congress has legislated on this subject, its legislation manifests an intention, with a single exception, not to regulate this subject, but to leave its regulation to the several States. To these precise questions, which are all we are called on to decide, this opinion must be understood to be confined. It does not extend to the question what other subjects, under the commercial power, are within the exclusive control of Congress, or may be regulated by the States in the absence of all congressional legislation; nor to the general question, how far any regulation of a subject by Congress may be deemed to operate as an exclusion of all legislation by the States upon the same subject.

JUSTICE DANIEL concurred:

The true question here is, whether the power to enact pilot laws is appropriate and necessary, or rather most appropriate and necessary to the State or the federal governments. It being conceded that this power has been exercised by the States from their very dawn of existence; that it can be practically and beneficially applied by the local authorities only; it being conceded, as it must be, that the power to pass pilot laws, as such, has not been in any express terms delegated to Congress, and does not necessarily conflict with the right to establish commercial regulations, I am forced to conclude that this is an original and inherent power in the States, and not one to be merely tolerated, or held subject to the sanctions of the Federal government.

JUSTICE MCLEAN dissented, with the concurrence of JUSTICE WAYNE:

That a State may regulate foreign commerce, or commerce among the States, is a doctrine which has been advanced by individual judges of this court; but never before, I believe, has such a power been sanctioned by the decision of this court. In this case, the power to regulate pilots is admitted to belong to the commercial power of Congress; and yet it is held, that a State, by virtue of its inherent power, may regulate the subject, until such regulation shall be annulled by Congress. This is the principle established by this decision. Its language is guarded, in order to apply the decision only to the case before the court. But such restrictions can never operate, so as to render the principle inapplicable to other cases. And it is in this light that the decision is chiefly to be regretted.

FOR DISCUSSION

Under the doctrine of selective exclusiveness, where is the line between what a state versus what the federal government can regulate? Are there some aspects of commerce that states cannot regulate, regardless of whether or not the federal government acts or takes action? Is the *Cooley* doctrine, in your opinion, an improvement upon the original package doctrine?

RELATED CASES

***DiSanto v. Pennsylvania:* 273 U.S. 34 (1927).**

A state statute providing for the licensing of all persons selling steamship tickets on transportation to or from foreign countries, other than railroad or steamship companies, was held to infringe on the Commerce Clause. The sale of tickets by travel agents was a part of commerce, so licensing was a direct burden on commerce.

***California v. Thompson:* 313 U.S. 109 (1941).**

A statute of the state provided for the licensing and bonding of transportation agents selling interstate bus transportation. In the absence of regulation by Congress, the Court held this not to be a burden on interstate commerce. Thus the *DiSanto* case was overruled. (*California v. Thompson* has a good listing of regulations affecting commerce that have been upheld by the Court.) The purpose of the statute was to prevent fraud, peculiarly a subject of local concern, so it was a proper exercise of police power.

***City of Burbank v. Lockheed Air Terminal, Inc.:* 411 U.S. 624 (1973).**

An ordinance of the city of Burbank, California, made it unlawful for a so-called pure jet aircraft to take off from the Hollywood-Burbank Airport between 11:00 PM. and 7:00 A.M. The Court held that the interdependence of the factors of safety and efficiency requires a uniform and exclusive system of federal regulation if the congressional objectives underlying the Federal Aviation Act are to be fulfilled. Fractionalized local control of the timing of takeoffs and landings would severely limit the flexibility of the Federal Aviation Administration (FAA) in controlling air traffic flow. While there is no express provision of preemption of federal authority in the statute, "It is the pervasive nature of the scheme of federal regulation of aircraft noise that leads us to conclude that there is preemption."

COE V. ERROL

116 U.S. 517, 6 S.Ct. 475, 29 L.Ed. 715 (1886)

A supply of logs had been cut in Maine by Edward Coe and floated down the Androscoggin River, which flows through New Hampshire on the way to Lewiston, Maine. During this process the logs were frozen in the river within the limits of the town of Errol, New Hampshire. A number of other logs had been cut in New Hampshire and had been taken to the banks of the river in Errol to await the spring thaw. These logs were then to be floated down the river to Maine. The town of Errol attempted to tax both sets of logs, and this was challenged as a tax on interstate commerce.

Vote: 9–0

JUSTICE BRADLEY delivered the opinion of the Court.

The question for us to consider, therefore, is, whether the products of a State (in this case timber cut in its forests) are liable to be taxed like other property within the State, though intended for exportation to another State, and partially prepared for that purpose by being deposited at a place of shipment, such products being owned by persons residing in another State.

We have no difficulty in disposing of the last condition of the question, namely, the fact (if it be a fact) that the property was owned by persons residing in another State; for, if not exempt from taxation for other reasons, it cannot be exempt by reason of being owned by non-residents of the State.

We recur, then, to a consideration of the question freed from this limitation: Are the products of a State, though intended for exportation to another State, and partially prepared for that purpose by being deposited at a place or port of shipment within the State, liable to be taxed like other property within the State? This question does not present the predicament of goods in course of transportation through a State, though detained for a time within the State by low water or other causes of delay, as was the case of the logs cut in the State of Maine, the tax on which was abated by the Supreme Court of New Hampshire. Such goods are already in the course of commercial transportation, and are clearly under the protection of the Constitution. And so, we think, would the goods in question be when actually started in the course of transportation to another State, or delivered to a carrier for such transportation. There must be a point of time when they cease to be governed exclusively by the domestic law and begin to be governed and protected by the national law of commercial regulation, and that moment seems to us to be a legitimate one for this purpose, in which they commence their final movement for transportation from the State of their origin to that of their destination. When the products of the farm or the forest are collected and brought in from the surrounding country to a town or station serving as an entrepót [port] for that particular region, whether on a river or a line of railroad, such products are not yet exports, nor are they in process of exportation, nor is exportation begun until they are committed to the common carrier for transportation out of the State to the State of their destination, or have started on their ultimate passage to that State. Until then it is reasonable to regard them as not only within the State of their origin, but as a part of the general mass of property of that State, subject to its jurisdiction, and liable to taxation there, if not taxed by reason or their being intended for exportation, but taxed without any discrimination, in the usual way and manner in which such property is taxed in the State.

But no definite rule has been adopted with regard to the point of time at which the taxing power of the State ceases as to goods exported to a foreign country or to another State. What we have already said, however, in relation to the products of a State intended for exportation to another State will indicate the view which seems to use the sound one on that subject, namely, that such goods do not cease to be part of the general mass of property of the State, subject, as such, to its jurisdiction, and to taxation in the usual way, until they have been shipped, or entered with a common carrier for transportation to another State, or have been started upon such transportation in a continuous route or journey. We think that this must be the true rule on the subject. It seems to us untenable to hold that a crop or a herd is exempt from taxation merely because it is, by its owner, intended for exportation. If such were the rule in many States there would be nothing but the lands and real estate to bear the taxes.

These conditions we understand to have been complied with in the present case. At all events there is no evidence to show that the taxes were not imposed in the regular and ordinary way. As the presumption, so far as mode and manner are concerned, is always in favor of, and not against, official acts, the want of evidence to the contrary must be regarded as evidence in favor of the regularity of the assessment in this case.

The judgment of the Supreme Court of New Hampshire is *Affirmed.*

FOR DISCUSSION

Where does the stream of commerce begin and end? When do products begin their journey into interstate commerce? Is it when they cross state borders, or does it start even earlier than that?

RELATED CASES

***State Freight Tax Case* (*Reading R.R. v. Pennsylvania*): 15 Wall. 232 (1873).**

A state tax based on the tonnage of freight carried by a common carrier was held to be an unreasonable burden on interstate commerce. Goods actually in interstate commerce are immune from taxation by a state.

SOUTH CAROLINA STATE HIGHWAY DEPARTMENT V. BARNWELL BROTHERS, INC.

303 U.S. 177, 58 S.Ct. 510, 82 L.Ed. 734 (1938)

A statute of South Carolina set the gross weight limit for motor trucks and semi-trailer trucks at 20,000 pounds and a width limit of ninety inches. These regulations are stricter than those of neighboring states. In fact, most trucks in interstate commerce are wider and carry a greater gross weight. The statute was attacked as imposing a burden on interstate commerce.

Vote: 7–0

JUSTICE STONE delivered the opinion of the Court.

While the constitutional grant to Congress of power to regulate interstate commerce has been held to operate of its own force to curtail state power in some measure, it did not forestall all state action affecting interstate commerce. Ever since *Willson v. Black-Bird Creek Marsh Co.,* 2 Pet. 245 (1829), and *Cooley v. Board of Wardens,* 12 How. 299 (1829), it has been recognized that there are matters of local concern, the regulation of which unavoidably involves some regulation of interstate commerce but which, because of their local character and their number and diversity, may never be fully dealt with by Congress. Notwithstanding the commerce clause, such regulation in the absence of Congressional action has for the most part been left to the states by the decision of this Court, subject to the other applicable constitutional restraints.

The commerce clause, by its own force, prohibits discrimination against interstate commerce, whatever its form or method, and the decisions of this Court have recognized that there is scope for its like operation when state legislation nominally of local concern is in point of fact aimed at interstate commerce, or by its necessary operation is a means of gaining a local benefit by throwing the attendant burdens on those without the state. It was to end these practices that the commerce clause was adopted.

But the present case affords no occasion for saying that the bare possession of power by Congress to regulate the interstate traffic forces the states to conform to standards which Congress might, but has not adopted, or curtails their power to take measures to insure the safety and conservation of their highways which may be applied to like traffic moving intrastate. Few subjects of state regulation are so peculiarly of local concern as is the use of state highways. There are few, local regulation of which is so inseparable from a substantial effect on interstate commerce. Unlike the railroads, local highways are built, owned and maintained by the state or its municipal subdivisions. The state has a primary and immediate concern in their safe and economical administration. The present regulations, or any others of like purpose, if they are to accomplish their end, must be applied alike to interstate and intrastate traffic both moving in large volume over the highways. The fact that they affect alike shippers in interstate and intrastate commerce in large number within as well as without the state is a safeguard against their abuse.

From the beginning it has been recognized that a state can, if it sees fit, build and maintain its own highways, canals and railroads and that in the absence of Congressional action their regulation is peculiarly within its competence, even though interstate commerce is materially affected

In the absence of such legislation the judicial function, under the commerce clause as well as the Fourteenth Amendment, stops with the inquiry whether the state legislature in adopting regulations such as the present has acted within its province, and whether the means of regulation chosen are reasonably adapted to the end sought.

The regulatory measures taken by South Carolina are within its legislative power. They do not infringe the Fourteenth Amendment, and the resulting burden on interstate commerce is not forbidden.

Reversed.

JUSTICES CARDOZO and REED took no part in this case.

FOR DISCUSSION

At what point does a legitimate police power activity of a state cross the line and place a burden on interstate commerce? If there is a legitimate need by a state to regulate, should that necessarily be considered a violation of the Commerce Clause? What factors may need to be considered when assessing the constitutionality of a specific state regulation?

RELATED CASES

***Hendrick v. Maryland:* 235 U.S. 610 (1915).**

The power of a state to regulate the use of motor vehicles on its highways extends to nonresidents as well as to residents. This power includes the right to exact reasonable fees for special facilities afforded as well as reasonable provisions to insure safety.

***Clark v. Poor:* 274 U.S. 554 (1927).**

A tax levied by Ohio on commercial trucks, the proceeds of which are used for highway policing and maintenance, was upheld as applied to trucks engaged in interstate commerce as not imposing an illegal burden on such commerce. The tax was not discriminatory or prohibitive.

***Sprout v. City of South Bend:* 277 U.S. 163 (1928).**

A city tax levied on all buses passing through the city and which that makes no distinction between those engaged in interstate or intrastate commerce or both is invalid. The tax was not based on city costs or the value of the use of the streets.

***Kassell v. Consolidated Freightways Corporation,*: 450 U.S. 662 (1981).**

The Supreme Court ruled that an Iowa rule banning the use of "double" tractor traile-trucks on its state's interstates violated the Commerce Clause. The Court ruled that the ban discriminated against out-of-state truckers, and it rejected the argument by the state that the ban was adopted to promote safety.

SOUTHERN PACIFIC CO. V. ARIZONA

325 U.S. 761, 65 S.Ct. 1515, 89 L.Ed. 1915 (1945)

The Arizona Train Limit Law of 1912 made it unlawful for any person or corporation to operate within the state a railroad train of more than fourteen passenger or seventy freight cars, with a money penalty provided for each violation of the Act. Suit was brought by the state against the railroad to recover the penalties for violation of the statute. The defense maintained that the statute violated the commerce Commerce Clause as well as conflicting and conflicted with federal legislation.

Vote: 7–2

CHIEF JUSTICE STONE delivered the opinion of the Court.

Although the commerce clause conferred on the national government power to regulate commerce, its possession of the power does not exclude all state power of regulation. Ever since *Willson v. Black-Bird Creek Marsh Co.,* 2 Pet. 245 (1829), and *Cooley v. Board of Wardens,* 12 How. 299 (1852), it has been recognized that, in the absence of conflicting legislation by Congress, there is a residuum of power in the state to make laws governing matters of local concern which nevertheless in some measure affect interstate commerce or even, to some extent, regulate it.

But ever since *Gibbons v. Ogden,* 9 Wheat. 1 (1824), the states have not been deemed to have authority to impede substantially the free flow of commerce from state to state, or to regulate those phases of the national commerce which, because of the need of national uniformity, demand that their regulation, if any, be prescribed by a single authority. Whether or not this long recognized distribution of power between the national and the state governments is predicated upon the implications of the commerce clause itself or upon the presumed intention of Congress, where Congress has not spoken the result is the same.

For a hundred years it has been accepted constitutional doctrine that the commerce clause, without the aid of congressional legislation, thus affords some protection from state legislation inimical to the national commerce, and that in such cases, where Congress has not acted, this Court, and not the state legislature, is under the commerce clause the final arbiter between the competing demands of state and national interests.

Congress has undoubted power to redefine the distribution of power over interstate commerce. It may either permit the states to regulate the commerce in a manner which would otherwise not be permissible or exclude state regulation even of matters of peculiarly local concern which nevertheless affect interstate commerce.

But in general Congress has left it to the courts to formulate the rules thus interpreting the commerce clause in its application, doubtless because it has appreciated the destructive consequences to the commerce of the nation if their protection were withdrawn and has been aware that in their application state laws will not be invalidated without the support of relevant factual material which will "afford a sure basis" for an informed judgment. Meanwhile, Congress has accommodated its legislation, as have the states, to these rules as an established feature of our constitutional system. There has thus been left to the states wide scope for the regulation of matters of local state concern, even though it in some measure affects the commerce, provided it does not materially restrict the free flow of commerce across state lines, or interfere with it in matters with respect to which uniformity of regulation is of predominant national concern.

Hence the matters for ultimate determination here are the nature and extent of the burden which the state regulation of interstate trains, adopted as a safety measure, imposes on interstate commerce, and whether the relative weights of the state and national interests involved are such as to make inapplicable the rule, generally observed, that the free flow of interstate commerce and its freedom from local restraints in matters requiring uniformity of regulation are interests safeguarded by the commerce clause from state interference.

The findings show that the operation of long trains, that is trains of more than fourteen passenger and more than seventy freight cars, is standard practice over the main lines of the railroads of the United States, and that, if the length of trains is to be regulated at all, national uniformity in the regulation adopted, such as only Congress can prescribe, is practically indispensable to the operation of an efficient and economical national railway system.

In Arizona, approximately 93% of the freight traffic and 95% of the passenger traffic is interstate. Because of the Train Limit Law appellant is required to haul over 30% more trains in Arizona that than would otherwise have been necessary. The record shows a definite relationship between operating costs and the length of trains, the increase in length resulting in a reduction of operating costs per car. The additional costs cost of operation of trains complying with the Train Limit Law in Arizona amounts for the two railroads traversing that state to about $1,000,000 a year. The reduction in train lengths also impedes efficient operation.

The unchallenged findings leave no doubt that the Arizona Train Limit Law imposes a serious burden on the interstate commerce conducted by appellant. It materially impedes the movement of appellant's interstate trains through that state and interposes a substantial obstruction to the national policy proclaimed by Congress, to promote adequate, economical and efficient railway transportation service.

The principle that, without controlling Congressional action, a state may not regulate interstate commerce so as substantially to affect its flow or deprive it of needed uniformity in its regulation is not to be avoided by "simply invoking the convenient apologetics of the police power."

Here we conclude that the state does go too far. Its regulation of train lengths, admittedly obstructive to interstate train operation, and having a seriously adverse effect on transportation efficiency and economy, passes beyond what is plainly essential for safety since it does not appear that it will lessen rather than increase the danger of accident.

JUSTICE RUTLEDGE concurred without separate opinion.

JUSTICE BLACK dissented:

Under those circumstances, the determination of whether it is in the interest of society for the length of trains to be governmentally regulated is a matter of public policy. Someone must fix that policy—either the Congress, or the state, or the courts. A century and a half of constitutional history and government admonishes this court to leave that choice to the elected legislative representatives of the people themselves, where it properly belongs both on democratic principles and the requirements of efficient government.

JUSTICE DOUGLAS dissented:

I have expressed my doubts whether the courts should intervene in situations like the present and strike down state legislation on the grounds that it burdens interstate commerce. *McCarroll v. Dixie Greyhound Lines,* 309 U.S. 176, 183–189 (1940). My view has been that the courts should intervene only where the state legislation discriminated against interstate commerce or was out of harmony with laws which Congress had enacted.

FOR DISCUSSION

Why would a state want to regulate the length of a train? Would not such a regulation be burdensome to trains travelling traveling across country, especially if each state mandated a different length? How could Congress fix this problem?

RELATED CASES

***Southern Railway Co. v. King:* 217 U.S. 524 (1910).**

The Court held valid a Georgia statute requiring trains not to exceed a certain speed at highway crossings on the basis that there was no unreasonable interference with interstate commerce. There was no real showing of burden on commerce, obstruction, or delay. This was called the "blow-post law" because of warning posts near crossings.

***Seaboard Air Line Ry. Co. v. Blackwell:* 244 U.S. 310 (1917).**

A Georgia statute limiting the speed of trains at road crossings was held invalid as an unreasonable burden on interstate commerce in a case where there were 124 grade crossings in 123 miles between Atlanta and the South Carolina state line. A 4½-hour run was extended to 10½ hours. This was not the same statute as in *King.*

***McCarroll v. Dixie Greyhound Lines:* 309 U.S. 176 (1940).**

A tax imposed by Arkansas on gasoline in excess of twenty gallons carried into the state in the tanks of motor vehicles, to be used as fuel by these vehicles, in excess of twenty gallons was declared void as a burden on interstate commerce.

***Terminal R.R. Association v. Brotherhood:* 318 U.S. 1 (1943).**

In the absence of federal legislation which that is in conflict or which that occupies the field, it is within the authority of a state, in the interests of the health and safety of employees, to require a railroad to provide cabooses on trains within the state on designated runs, even though some of the runs are across state lines and the requirement increases the cost of interstate transportation. This case came out of East St. Louis, Illinois.

DEAN MILK CO. V. MADISON

340 U.S. 349, 71 S.Ct. 295, 95 L.Ed. 329 (1951)

The city of Madison, Wisconsin, enacted an ordinance regarding the sale of milk and milk products. One section of the ordinance prohibited the sale in Madison of pasteurized milk processed and bottled at any plant more than five miles distant from the center of the city. The other section required that all sources of supply of milk be within a twenty-five-mile radius of the center of the city. Dean Milk Co. challenged the ordinance as an unconstitutional violation of the commerce clause and the Fourteenth Amendment. The Supreme Court of Wisconsin upheld the section establishing the five-mile limit on pasteurization. As to the twenty-five-mile limitation, the Court ordered the complaint dismissed for want of a justiciable controversy. The milk company was engaged in interstate business, with purchases and sales of milk in both Illinois and Wisconsin. Its processing plants were located in Illinois, more than five miles from Madison.

Vote: 6–3

JUSTICE CLARK delivered the opinion of the Court.

This is not an instance in which an enactment falls because of federal legislation which, as a proper exercise of paramount national power over commerce, excludes measures which might otherwise be within the police power of the states.

There is no pertinent national regulation by the Congress, and statutes enacted for the District of Columbia indicate that Congress has recognized the appropriateness of local regulation of the sale of fluid milk. It is not contended, however, that Congress has authorized the regulation before us.

Nor can there be objection to the avowed purpose of this enactment. We also assume that since Congress has not spoken to the contrary, the subject matter of the ordinance lies within the sphere of state regulation even though interstate commerce may be affected.

But this regulation, like the provision invalidated in *Baldwin v. Seelig, Inc.,* 294 U.S. 511 (1935), in practical effect excludes from distribution in Madison wholesome milk produced and pasteurized in Illinois. "The importer may keep his milk or drink it, but sell it he may not." In thus erecting an economic barrier protecting a major local industry against competition from without the State, Madison plainly discriminates against interstate commerce. This it cannot do, even in the exercise of its unquestioned power to protect the health and safety of its people, if reasonable nondiscriminatory alternatives, adequate to conserve local interests, are available. A different view, that the ordinance is valid simply because it professes to be a health measure, would mean that the Commerce Clause of itself imposes no limitations on state action: other than those laid down by the Due Process Clause, save for the rare instance where a state artlessly discloses an avowed purpose to discriminate against interstate goods. Our issue then is whether the discrimination inherent in the Madison ordinance can be justified in view of the character of the local interests and the available methods of protecting them.

It appears that reasonable and adequate alternatives are available. If the City of Madison prefers to rely upon its own officials for inspection of distant milk sources, such inspection is readily open to it without hardship for it could charge the actual and reasonable cost of such inspection to the importing producers and processors. Moreover; appellee Health Commissioner of Madison testified that as proponent of the local milk ordinance he had submitted the provisions here in controversy and an alternative proposal based on § 11 of the Model Milk Ordinance recommended by the United States Public Health Service. The model provision imposes no geographical limitation on location of milk sources and processing plants but excludes from the municipality milk not produced and pasteurized conformably to standards as high as those enforced by the receiving city.

To permit Madison to adopt a regulation not essential for the protection of local health interests and placing a discriminatory burden on interstate commerce would invite a multiplication of preferential trade areas destructive of the very purpose of the Commerce Clause.

For these reasons we conclude that the judgment below sustaining the five-mile provision as to pasteurization must be reversed.

The Supreme Court of Wisconsin thought it was unnecessary to pass upon the validity of the twenty-five-mile limitation, apparently in part for the reason that this issue was made academic by its decision upholding the five-mile section. In view of our conclusion as to the latter provision, a determination of appellant's contention as to the other section is now necessary. As to this issue, therefore, we vacate the judgment below and remand for further proceedings not inconsistent with principles announced in this opinion.

JUSTICE BLACK dissented, with the concurrence of JUSTICES MINTON and DOUGLAS.

I disagree with the Court's premises, reasoning, and judgment.

(1) This ordinance does not exclude wholesome milk coming from Illinois or anywhere else. It does require that all milk sold in Madison must be pasteurized within five miles of the center of the city. But there was no finding in the state courts, nor evidence to justify a finding there or here, that appellant, Dean Milk Company, is unable to have its milk pasteurized within the defined geographical area.

(2) Characterization of § 7.21 as a "discriminatory burden" on interstate commerce is merely a statement of the Court's result, which I think incorrect.

(3) This health regulation should not be invalidated merely because the Court believes that alternative milk-inspection methods might insure the cleanliness and healthfulness of Dean's Illinois milk. I find it difficult to explain why the Court uses the "reasonable alternative" concept to protect trade when today it refuses to apply the same principle to protect freedom of speech. No case is cited, and I have found none, in which a bona fide health law was struck down on the ground that some other method of safeguarding health would be as good as, or better than, the one the Court was called on to review. In my view, to use this ground now elevates the right to traffic in commerce for profit above the power of the people to guard the purity of their daily diet of milk.

From what this record shows, and from what it fails to show, I do not think that either of the alternatives suggested by the Court [that Madison require milk processors to pay reasonable inspection fees at the milk supply sources and that Madison adopt § 11 of the Model Milk Ordinance] would assure the people of Madison as pure a supply of milk as they receive under their own ordinance. On this record I would uphold the Madison law. At the very least, however, I would not invalidate it without giving the parties a chance to present evidence and get findings on the ultimate issues the Court thinks crucial—namely, the relative merits of the Madison ordinance and the alternatives suggested by the Court today.

FOR DISCUSSION

What was Wisconsin really seeking to do by the passage of this law? What if all the milk or dairy inspectors were located in Madison? Would that make a difference? What if to comply with this decision, the state had to place inspectors around the state? Perhaps such an option might cost a lot of money. Thus, maybe it is more convenient and less burdensome on the state to have the inspections in Madison. Is this not a legitimate or reasonable explanation for the law?

RELATED CASES

***Mintz v. Baldwin:* 289 U.S. 346 (1933).**

A New York statute required that cattle brought into the state for dairy or breeding purposes be certified as being free from Bang's disease by the chief sanitary officer of the state of origin. Those that had been federally inspected were exempt. This was held not to be contrary to federal statutes or to be a burden on interstate commerce.

***Head v. New Mexico Board of Examiners in Optometry:* 374 U.S. 424 (1963).**

A New Mexico statute prohibited the publication in New Mexico of a certain type of advertising by optometrists. The application of this to a Texas optometrist's advertising was held not to impose a constitutionally prohibited burden in interstate commerce. This was a valid exercise of state police power with no requirement of uniformity. Legislation may affect interstate commerce without burdening it.

***Joseph E. Seagram and Sons, Inc. v. Hostetter:* 384 U.S. 35 (1966).**

A New York State requirement that liquor prices to domestic wholesalers and retailers be as low as prices offered elsewhere in the country is not an unconstitutional burden on interstate commerce. Wide latitude is given to the states under the Twenty-first Amendment to regulate liquor introduced into a state from outside the state. However, this does not prevent enforcement of the Sherman Act against a conspiracy to raise prices.

H. P. HOOD AND SONS V. DUMOND

336 U.S. 525, 69 S.Ct. 657, 93 L.Ed. 865 (1949)

The Hood Company distributed milk in Massachusetts after securing its supply in New York State. Hood wished to expand operations, but the company was denied the license to do this by the New York Commissioner of Agriculture and Markets. The reason for the refusal was a fear that consumers in New York State would not have adequate supplies. The order was challenged as an obstruction to interstate commerce.

Vote: 5–4

JUSTICE JACKSON delivered the opinion of the Court.

This distinction between the power of the State to shelter its people from menaces to their health or safety and from fraud, even when those dangers emanate from interstate commerce, and its lack of power to retard, burden or constrict the flow of such commerce for their economic advantage, is one deeply rooted in both our history and our law.

This principle that our economic unit is the Nation, which alone has the gamut of powers necessary to control of the economy including the vital power of erecting customs barriers against foreign competition, has as its corollary that the states are not separable economic units.

Our system, fostered by the Commerce Clause, is that every farmer and every craftsman shall be encouraged to produce by the certainty that he will have free access to every market in the Nation, that no home embargoes will withhold his export, and no foreign state will by customs duties or regulations exclude them. Likewise, every consumer may look to the free competition from every producing area in the Nation to protect him from exploitation by any. Such was the vision of the Founders; such has been the doctrine of this Court which has given it reality.

Since the statute as applied violates the Commerce Clause and is not authorized by federal legislation pursuant to that Clause, it cannot stand. The judgment is reversed and the cause remanded for proceedings not inconsistent with this opinion.

JUSTICE BLACK dissented, joined by JUSTICE MURPHY.

The language of this state Act is not discriminatory, the legislative history shows it was not so intended, and the commissioner has not administered it with a hostile eye. The Act must stand or fall on this basis notwithstanding the overtones of the Court's opinion. If petitioner and other interstate milk dealers are to be placed above and beyond this law, it must be done solely on this Court's new constitutional formula which bars a state from protecting itself against local destructive competitive practices so far as they are indulged in by dealers who ship their milk into other states.

It is always a serious thing for this Court to strike down a statewide law. . . .

It is more serious when the state law falls under a new rule which will inescapably narrow the area in which states can regulate and control local business practices found inimical to the public welfare. The gravity of striking down state regulations is immeasurably increased when it results as here in leaving a no-man's land immune from any effective regulation whatever.

JUSTICE FRANKFURTER dissented, joined by JUSTICE RUTLEDGE.

If the Court's opinion has meaning beyond deciding this case in isolation, its effect is to hold that no matter how important to the internal economy of a State may be the prevention of destructive competition, and no matter how unimportant the interstate commerce affected, a State cannot as a means of preventing such competition deny an applicant access to a market within the State if that applicant happens to intend the out-of-state shipment of the product that he buys. I feel constrained to dissent because I cannot agree in treating what is essentially a problem of striking a balance between competing interests as an exercise in absolutes. Nor does it seem to me that such a problem should be disposed of on a record from which we cannot tell what weights to put in which side of the scales.

FOR DISCUSSION

Why is it not a reasonable objective for a state to want to protect its own businesses? Why does the Commerce Clause prevent that? Or does it always?

EDWARDS V. CALIFORNIA

314 U.S. 160, 62 S.Ct. 164, 86 L.Ed. 119 (1941)

Edwards, a citizen of the United States and a resident of California, had taken Frank Duncan, his wife's brother, from Spur, Texas, to Marysville, California. Edwards was aware that Duncan, a United States citizen and a resident of Texas, was an indigent person. When he left Texas he had about twenty dollars, all of which had been spent by the time he reached Marysville. Edwards was accused of violation of the Welfare and Institutions Code of California, which provided that any person who knowingly brings into the state a nonresident indigent person is guilty of a misdemeanor. This statute was called the "anti-Okie" law because of the large number of indigent persons from Oklahoma going to California during the Dust Bowl days of the 1930s. This was challenged as an improper exercise of state police power.

Vote: 9–0

JUSTICE BYRNES delivered the opinion of the Court.

It is frequently the case that a State might gain a momentary respite from the pressure of events by the simple expedient of shutting its gates to the outside world. But, in the words of Mr. Justice Cardozo, "The Constitution was framed under the dominion of a political philosophy less parochial in range. It was framed upon the theory that the peoples of the several States must sink or swim together, and that in the long run prosperity and salvation are in union and not division." *Baldwin v. Seelig,* 294 U.S. 511 (1935).

It is difficult to conceive of a statute more squarely in conflict with this theory than the section challenged here. Its express purpose and inevitable effect is to prohibit the transportation of indigent persons across the California border. The burden upon interstate commerce is intended and immediate; it is the plain and sole function of the statute. Moreover, the indigent non-residents who are the real victims of the statute are deprived of the opportunity to exert political pressure upon the California legislature in order to obtain a change in policy. We think this statute must fail under any known test of the validity of State interference with interstate commerce.

The prohibition against transporting indigent non-residents into one State is an open invitation to retaliatory measures, and the burdens upon the transportation of such persons become cumulative. Moreover, it would be a virtual impossibility for migrants and those who transport them to acquaint themselves with the peculiar rules of admission of many States. "This Court has repeatedly declared that the grant [the commerce clause] established the immunity of interstate commerce from the control of the States respecting all those subjects embraced within the grant which are of such a nature as to demand that, if regulated at all, their regulation must be prescribed by a single authority." *Milk Control Board v. Eisenberg Farm Products,* 306 U.S. 346 (1939). We are of the opinion that the transportation of indigent persons from State to State clearly falls within this class of subjects. The scope of congressional power to deal with this problem we are not now called upon to decide.

Whether an able-bodied but unemployed person like Duncan is a "pauper" within the historical meaning of the term is open to considerable doubt. But assuming that the term is applicable to him and to persons similarly situated, we do not consider ourselves bound by the language referred to. *City of New York v. Miln,* 36 U.S. 102, was decided in 1837. Whatever may have been the notion then prevailing, we do not think that it will now be seriously contended that because a person is without employment and without funds he constitutes a "moral pestilence." Poverty and immorality are not synonymous.

We are of the opinion that Section 2615 is not a valid exercise of the police power of California, that it imposes an unconstitutional burden upon interstate commerce, and that the conviction under it cannot be sustained. In the view we have taken it is unnecessary to decide whether the section is repugnant to other provisions of the Constitution.

Reversed.

[Justice Douglas concurred, and was joined by Justices Black and Murphy. He contended that "The right to move freely from State to State is an incident of *national* citizenship protected by the privileges and immunities clause of the Fourteenth Amendment against State interference."]

JUSTICE JACKSON concurred.

I concur in the result reached by the Court, and I agree that the grounds of its decision are permissible ones under applicable authorities. But the migrations of a human being, of whom it is charged that he possesses nothing that can be sold and has no wherewithal to buy, do not fit easily into my notions as to what is commerce. To hold that the measure of his rights is the commerce clause is likely to result eventually either in distorting the commercial law or in denaturing human rights. I turn, therefore, away from principles by which commerce is regulated to that clause of the Constitution by virtue of which Duncan is a citizen of the United States and which forbids any state to abridge his privileges or immunities as such.

While instances of valid "privileges or immunities" must be but few, I am convinced that this is one. I do not ignore or belittle the difficulties of what has been characterized by this Court as an "almost forgotten" clause. But the difficulty of the task does not excuse us from giving these general and abstract words whatever of specific content and concreteness they will bear as we mark out their application, case by case. That is the method of the common law, and it has been the method of this Court with other no less general statements in our fundamental law. This Court has not been timorous about giving concrete meaning to such obscure and vagrant phrases as "due process," "general welfare," "equal protection," or even "commerce among the several States." But it has always hesitated to give any real meaning to the privileges and immunities clause lest it improvidently give too much.

FOR DISCUSSION

What if a state was significantly overpopulated or it lacked the water or other resources, should it be able to place limits on immigration into its state? Could there ever be a compelling reason for a state to restrict migration?

RELATED CASES

***Madden v. Kentucky:* 309 U.S. 83 (1940).**

It is not a violation of due process or equal protection for a state to impose a higher tax on out-of-state bank deposits than it imposes on in-state deposits. The right to deposit money in banks is not a privilege of national citizenship. This case overruled *Colgate v. Harvey,* 296 U.S. 404 (1935).

***Shapiro v. Thompson:* 394 U.S. 618 (1969).**

Absent a compelling state interest, it is a violation of the Equal Protection Clause of the Fourteenth Amendment and the Due Process Clause of the Fifth Amendment (as applied to state and federal governments, respectively) to classify by length of residence persons as to eligibility to receive welfare assistance. This discriminates, and it imposes on the constitutional right to travel. The decision in this case may well have resulted indirectly from *Edwards.*

CITY OF PHILADELPHIA V. NEW JERSEY

437 U.S. 617, 98 S.Ct. 2531, 57 L.Ed.2d 475 (1978)

The State of New Jersey enacted a law banning the shipment of solid or liquid waste into its borders. The law was enacted to limit pollution in the state, regulate landfills, and promote public health. Landfill operators, as well as the City of Philadelphia, challenged the law as a violation of the Commerce Clause.

Vote: 7–2

JUSTICE STEWART delivered the opinion of the Court.

A New Jersey law prohibits the importation of most "solid or liquid waste which originated or was collected outside the territorial limits of the State." In this case we are required to decide whether this statutory prohibition violates the Commerce Clause of the United States Constitution.

I

The statutory provision in question is ch. 363 of 1973 N.J. Laws, which took effect in early 1974. In pertinent part it provides:

> "No person shall bring into this State any solid or liquid waste which originated or was collected outside the territorial limits of the State, except garbage to be fed to swine in the State of New Jersey, until the commissioner [of the State Department of Environmental Protection] shall determine that such action can be permitted without endangering the public health, safety and welfare and has promulgated regulations permitting and regulating the treatment and disposal of such waste in this State."

Immediately affected by these developments were the operators of private landfills in New Jersey, and several cities in other States that had agreements with these operators for waste disposal. They brought suit against New Jersey and its Department of Environmental Protection in state court, attacking the statute and regulations on a number of state and federal grounds

We agree with the New Jersey court that the state law has not been pre-empted by federal legislation. The dispositive question, therefore, is whether the law is constitutionally permissible in light of the Commerce Clause of the Constitution.

II

Before it addressed the merits of the appellants' claim, the New Jersey Supreme Court questioned whether the interstate movement of those wastes banned by ch. 363 is "commerce" at all within the meaning of the Commerce Clause. Any doubts on that score should be laid to rest at the outset.

The state court expressed the view that there may be two definitions of "commerce" for constitutional purposes. When relied on "to support some exertion of federal control or regulation," the Commerce Clause permits "a very sweeping concept" of commerce. But when relied on "to strike down or restrict state legislation," that Clause and the term "commerce" have a "much more confined reach."

The state court reached this conclusion in an attempt to reconcile modern Commerce Clause concepts with several old cases of this Court holding that States can prohibit the importation of some objects because they "are not legitimate subjects of trade and commerce." These articles include items "which, on account of their existing condition, would bring in and spread disease, pestilence, and death, such as rags or other substances infected with the germs of yellow fever or the virus of small-pox, or cattle or meat or other provisions that are diseased or decayed, or otherwise, from their condition and quality, unfit for human use or consumption." The state court found that ch. 363 as narrowed by the state regulations, banned only "those wastes which can[not] be put to effective use," and therefore those wastes were not commerce at all, unless "the mere transportation and disposal of valueless waste between states constitutes interstate commerce within the meaning of the constitutional provision."

We think the state court misread our cases, and thus erred in assuming that they require a two-tiered definition of commerce. In saying that innately harmful articles "are not legitimate subjects of trade and commerce," the *Bowman* [*v. Chicago & Northwestern Ry. Co.*, 125 U.S. 465 (1888),] Court was stating its conclusion, not the starting point of its reasoning. All objects of interstate trade merit Commerce Clause protection; none is excluded by definition at the outset. In *Bowman* and similar cases, the Court held simply that because the articles' worth in interstate commerce was far outweighed by the dangers inhering in their very movement, States could prohibit their transportation across state lines. Hence, we reject the state court's suggestion that the banning of "valueless" out-of-state wastes by ch. 363 implicates no constitutional protection. Just as Congress has power to regulate the interstate movement of these wastes, States are not free from constitutional scrutiny when they restrict that movement.

III

A

Although the Constitution gives Congress the power to regulate commerce among the States, many subjects of potential federal regulation under that power inevitably escape congressional attention "because of their local character and their number and diversity." In the absence of federal legislation, these subjects are open to control by the States so long as they act within the restraints imposed by the Commerce Clause itself. The bounds of these restraints appear nowhere in the words of the Commerce Clause, but have emerged gradually in the decisions of this Court giving effect to its basic purpose. That broad purpose was well expressed by Mr. Justice Jackson in his opinion for the Court in *H. P. Hood & Sons, Inc. v. Du Mond*, 336 U.S. 525 (1949).

> "This principle that our economic unit is the Nation, which alone has the gamut of powers necessary to control of the economy, including the vital power of erecting customs barriers against foreign competition, has as its corollary that the states are not separable economic units. As the Court said in *Baldwin v. Seelig*, 294 U.S. 511 (1935), " 'what is ultimate is the principle that one state in its dealings with another may not place itself in a position of economic isolation.' " "

The opinions of the Court through the years have reflected an alertness to the evils of "economic isolation" and protectionism, while at the same time recognizing that incidental burdens on interstate commerce may be unavoidable when a State legislates to safeguard the health and safety of its people. Thus, where simple economic protectionism is effected by state legislation, a virtually *per se* rule of invalidity has been erected. The clearest example of such legislation is a law that overtly blocks the flow of interstate commerce at a State's borders. But where other legislative objectives are credibly advanced and there is no patent discrimination against interstate trade, the Court has adopted a much more flexible approach, the general contours of which were outlined in *Pike v. Bruce Church, Inc.*, 397 U.S. 137 (1970):

> "Where the statute regulates evenhandedly to effectuate a legitimate local public interest, and its effects on interstate commerce are only incidental, it will be upheld unless the burden imposed on such commerce is clearly excessive in relation to the putative local benefits. If a legitimate local purpose is found, then the question becomes one of degree. And the extent of the burden that will be tolerated will of course depend on the nature of the local interest involved, and on whether it could be promoted as well with a lesser impact on interstate activities."

The crucial inquiry, therefore, must be directed to determining whether ch. 363 is basically a protectionist measure, or whether it can fairly be viewed as a law directed to legitimate local concerns, with effects upon interstate commerce that are only incidental.

B

The purpose of ch. 363 is set out in the statute itself as follows:

> "The Legislature finds and determines that that . . . the volume of solid and liquid waste continues to rapidly increase, that the treatment and disposal of these wastes continues to pose an even greater threat to the quality of the environment of New Jersey, that the available and appropriate land fill sites within the State are being diminished, that the environment continues to be threatened by the treatment and disposal of waste which originated or was collected outside the State, and that the public health, safety and welfare require that the treatment and disposal within this State of all wastes generated outside of the State be prohibited."

The New Jersey Supreme Court accepted this statement of the state legislature's purpose. The state court additionally found that New Jersey's existing landfill sites will be exhausted within a few years; that to go on using these sites or to develop new ones will take a heavy environmental toll, both from pollution and from loss of scarce open lands; that new techniques to divert waste from landfills to other methods of disposal and resource recovery processes are under development, but that these changes will require time; and finally, that " "the extension of the lifespan of existing landfills, resulting from the exclusion of out-of-state waste, may be of crucial importance in preventing further virgin wetlands or other undeveloped lands from being devoted to landfill purposes."." Based on these findings, the court concluded that ch. 363 was designed to protect, not the State's economy, but its environment, and that its substantial benefits outweigh its "slight" burden on interstate commerce.

The appellants strenuously contend that ch. 363, "while outwardly cloaked 'in the currently fashionable garb of environmental protection,' is actually no more than a legislative effort to suppress competition and stabilize the cost of solid waste disposal for New Jersey residents." They cite passages of legislative history suggesting that the problem addressed by ch. 363 is primarily financial: Stemming the flow of out-of-state waste into certain landfill sites will extend their lives, thus delaying the day when New Jersey cities must transport their waste to more distant and expensive sites.

The appellees, on the other hand, deny that ch. 363 was motivated by financial concerns or economic protectionism. In the words of their brief, "[n]o New Jersey commercial interests stand to gain advantage over competitors from outside the state as a result of the ban on dumping out-of-state waste." Noting that New Jersey landfill operators are among the plaintiffs, the appellee's brief argues that "[t]he complaint is not that New Jersey has forged an economic preference for its own commercial interests, but rather that it has denied a small group of its entrepreneurs an economic opportunity to traffic in waste in order to protect the health, safety and welfare of the citizenry at large."

This dispute about ultimate legislative purpose need not be resolved, because its resolution would not be relevant to the constitutional issue to be decided in this case. Contrary to the evident assumption of the state court and the parties, the evil of protectionism can reside in legislative means as well as legislative ends. Thus, it does not matter whether the ultimate aim of ch. 363 is to reduce the waste disposal costs of New Jersey residents or to save remaining open lands from pollution, for we assume New Jersey has every right to protect its residents' pocketbooks as well as their environment. And it may be assumed as well that New Jersey may pursue those ends by slowing the flow of all waste into the State's remaining landfills, even though interstate commerce may incidentally be affected. But whatever New Jersey's ultimate purpose, it may not be accomplished by discriminating against articles of commerce coming from outside the State unless there is some reason, apart from their origin, to treat them differently. Both on its face and in its plain effect, ch. 363 violates this principle of nondiscrimination.

The New Jersey law at issue in this case falls squarely within the area that the Commerce Clause puts off limits to state regulation. On its face, it imposes on out-of-state commercial interests the full burden of conserving the State's remaining landfill space. It is true that in our previous cases the scarce natural resource was itself the article of commerce, whereas here the scarce resource and the article of commerce are distinct. But that difference is without consequence. In both instances, the State has overtly moved to slow or freeze the flow of commerce for protectionist reasons. It does not matter that the State has shut the article of commerce inside the State in one case and outside the State in the other. What is crucial is the attempt by one State to isolate itself from a problem common to many by erecting a barrier against the movement of interstate trade.

The appellees argue that not all laws which facially discriminate against out-of-state commerce are forbidden protectionist regulations. In particular, they point to quarantine laws, which this Court has repeatedly upheld even though they appear to single out interstate commerce for special treatment. In the appellees' view, ch. 363 is analogous to such health-protective measures, since it reduces the exposure of New Jersey residents to the allegedly harmful effects of landfill sites.

It is true that certain quarantine laws have not been considered forbidden protectionist measures, even though they were directed against out-of-state commerce. But those quarantine laws banned the importation of articles such as diseased livestock that required destruction as soon as possible because their very movement risked contagion and other evils. Those laws thus did not discriminate against interstate commerce as such, but simply prevented traffic in noxious articles, whatever their origin.

The New Jersey statute is not such a quarantine law. There has been no claim here that the very movement of waste into or through New Jersey endangers health, or that waste must be disposed of as soon and as close to its point of generation as possible. The harms caused by waste are said to arise after its disposal in landfill sites, and at that point, as New Jersey concedes, there is no basis to distinguish out-of-state waste from domestic waste. If one is inherently harmful, so is the other. Yet New Jersey has banned the former while leaving its landfill sites open to the latter. The New Jersey law blocks the importation of waste in an obvious effort to saddle those outside the State with the entire burden of slowing the flow of refuse into New Jersey's remaining landfill sites. That legislative effort is clearly impermissible under the Commerce Clause of the Constitution.

Today, cities in Pennsylvania and New York find it expedient or necessary to send their waste into New Jersey for disposal, and New Jersey claims the right to close its borders to such traffic. Tomorrow, cities in New Jersey may find it expedient or necessary to send their waste into Pennsylvania or New York for disposal, and those States might then claim the right to close their borders. The Commerce Clause will protect New Jersey in the future, just as it protects her neighbors now, from efforts by one State to isolate itself in the stream of interstate commerce from a problem shared by all. The judgment is

Reversed.

JUSTICE REHNQUIST, with whom CHIEF JUSTICE BURGER joins, dissenting.

A growing problem in our Nation is the sanitary treatment and disposal of solid waste. For many years, solid waste was incinerated. Because of the significant environmental problems attendant on incineration, however, this method of solid waste disposal has declined in use in many localities, including New Jersey. "Sanitary" landfills have replaced incineration as the principal method of disposing of solid waste. In ch. 363 of the 1973 N.J. Laws, the State of New Jersey legislatively recognized the unfortunate fact that landfills also present extremely serious health and safety problems. First, in New Jersey, "virtually all sanitary landfills can be expected to produce leachate, a noxious and highly polluted liquid which is seldom visible and frequently pollutes ground and surface waters." The natural decomposition process which occurs in landfills also produces large quantities of methane and thereby presents a significant explosion hazard. Landfills can also generate "health hazards caused by rodents, fires and scavenger birds" and, "needless to say, do not help New Jersey's aesthetic appearance nor New Jersey's noise or water or air pollution problems."

The health and safety hazards associated with landfills present appellees with a currently unsolvable dilemma. Other, hopefully safer, methods of disposing of solid wastes are still in the development stage and cannot presently be used. But appellees obviously cannot completely stop the tide of solid waste that its citizens will produce in the interim. For the moment, therefore, appellees must continue to use sanitary landfills to dispose of New Jersey's own solid waste despite the critical environmental problems thereby created.

The question presented in this case is whether New Jersey must also continue to receive and dispose of solid waste from neighboring States, even though these will inexorably increase the health problems discussed above. The Court answers this question in the affirmative. New Jersey must either prohibit *all* landfill operations, leaving itself to cast about for a presently nonexistent solution to the serious problem of disposing of the waste generated within its own borders, or it must accept waste from every portion of the United States, thereby multiplying the health and safety problems which would result if it dealt only with such wastes generated within the State. Because past precedents establish that the Commerce Clause does not present appellees with such a Hobson's choice, I dissent.

The Court recognizes, that States can prohibit the importation of items

> " 'which, on account of their existing condition, would bring in and spread disease, pestilence, and death, such as rags or other substances infected with the germs of yellow fever or the virus of small-pox, or cattle or meat or other provisions that are diseased or decayed or otherwise, from their condition and quality, unfit for human use or consumption.'

As the Court points out, such "quarantine laws have not been considered forbidden protectionist measures, *even though they were directed against out-of-state commerce.*" (emphasis added).

In my opinion, these cases are dispositive of the present one. Under them, New Jersey may require germ-infected rags or diseased meat to be disposed of as best as possible within the State, but at the same time prohibit the *importation* of such items for disposal at the facilities that are set up within New Jersey for disposal of such material generated *within* the State. The physical fact of life that New Jersey must somehow dispose of its own noxious items does not mean that it must serve as a depository for those of every other State. Similarly, New Jersey should be free under our past precedents to prohibit the importation of solid waste because of the health and safety problems that such waste poses to its citizens. The fact that New Jersey continues to, and indeed must continue to, dispose of its own solid waste does not mean that New Jersey may not prohibit the importation of even more solid waste into the State. I simply see no way to distinguish solid waste, on the record of this case, from germ-infected rags, diseased meat, and other noxious items.

FOR DISCUSSION

Instead of banning the shipment of waste into the state, could the citizens of New Jersey have required a permit or attached special conditions about disposal of waste in their state? What if the state required special landfills or other protections to ensure the trash was not toxic, for example?

RELATED CASE

United Haulers Ass'n, Inc. v. Oneida-Herkimer Solid Waste Management: **127 S.Ct. 1786 (2007).**

The Court ruled that a county ordinance that required all waste both in- and out-of-state haulers to bring waste to a state-created public benefit corporation did not discriminate against the dormant Commerce Clause.

REEVES V. STAKE

447 U.S. 429, 100 S.Ct. 2271, 65 L.Ed.2d 244 (1980)

The State of South Dakota operated its own cement plant and generally sold both to residents and non-nonresidents. During a time when there was a shortage, the state decided to limit sales to residents. Non-Nonresidents objected, and they challenged the law as a violation of the Commerce Clause.

Vote: 5–4

JUSTICE BLACKMUN delivered the opinion of the Court.

The issue in this case is whether, consistent with the Commerce Clause, U.S. Const., Art. I, § 8, cl. 3, the State of South Dakota, in a time of shortage, may confine the sale of the cement it produces solely to its residents.

I

In 1919, South Dakota undertook plans to build a cement plant. The project, a product of the State's then prevailing Progressive political movement, was initiated in response to recent regional cement shortages that "interfered with and delayed both public and private enterprises," and that were "threatening the people of this state." In 1920, the South Dakota Cement Commission anticipated "[t]hat there would be a ready market for the entire output of the plant within the state." The plant, however, located at Rapid City, soon produced more cement than South Dakotans could use. Over the years, buyers in no less than nine nearby States purchased cement from the State's plant.

The plant's list of out-of-state cement buyers included petitioner Reeves, Inc. Reeves is a ready-mix concrete distributor organized under Wyoming law and with facilities in Buffalo, Gillette, and Sheridan, Wyo. From the beginning of its operations in 1958, and until 1978, Reeves purchased about 95% of its cement from the South Dakota plant. In 1977, its purchases were $1,172,000. In turn, Reeves has supplied three northwestern Wyoming counties with more than half their ready-mix concrete needs. For 20 years the relationship between Reeves and the South Dakota cement plant was amicable, uninterrupted, and mutually profitable.

As the 1978 construction season approached, difficulties at the plant slowed production. Meanwhile, a booming construction industry spurred demand for cement both regionally and nationally. The plant found itself unable to meet all orders. Faced with the same type of "serious cement shortage" that inspired the plant's construction, the Commission "reaffirmed its policy of supplying all South Dakota customers first and to honor all contract commitments, with the remaining volume allocated on a first come, first served basis."

Reeves, which had no pre-existing long-term supply contract, was hit hard and quickly by this development. On June 30, 1978, the plant informed Reeves that it could not continue to fill Reeves' orders, and on July 5, it turned away a Reeves truck. Unable to find another supplier, Reeves was forced to cut production by 76% in mid-July.

On July 19, Reeves brought this suit against the Commission, challenging the plant's policy of preferring South Dakota buyers, and seeking injunctive relief. After conducting a hearing and receiving briefs and affidavits, the District Court found no substantial issue of material fact and permanently enjoined the Commission's practice. The court reasoned that South Dakota's "hoarding" was inimical to the national free market envisioned by the Commerce Clause.

We granted Reeves' petition for certiorari to consider once again the impact of the Commerce Clause on state proprietary activity.

II

A

Hughes v. Alexandria Scrap Corp., 426 U.S. 794 (1976), concerned a Maryland program designed to remove abandoned automobiles from the State's roadways and junkyards. To encourage recycling, a "bounty" was offered for every Maryland-titled junk car converted into scrap. Processors located both in and outside Maryland were eligible to collect these subsidies. The legislation, as initially enacted in 1969, required a processor seeking a bounty to present documentation evidencing ownership of the wrecked car. This requirement however, did not apply to "hulks," inoperable automobiles over eight years old. In 1974, the statute was amended to extend documentation requirements to hulks, which comprised a large majority of the junk cars being processed. Departing from prior practice, the new law imposed more exacting documentation requirements on out-of-state than in-state processors. By making it less remunerative for suppliers to transfer vehicles outside Maryland, the reform triggered a "precipitate decline in the number of bounty-eligible hulks supplied to appellee's [Virginia] plant from Maryland sources." Indeed, "[t]he practical effect was substantially the same as if Maryland had withdrawn altogether the availability of bounties on hulks delivered by unlicensed suppliers to licensed non-Maryland processors."

Invoking the Commerce Clause, a three-judge District Court struck down the legislation. It observed that the amendment imposed "substantial burdens upon the free flow of interstate commerce," and reasoned that the discriminatory program was not the least disruptive means of achieving the State's articulated objective.

This Court reversed. It recognized the persuasiveness of the lower court's analysis if the inherent restrictions of the Commerce Clause were deemed applicable. In the Court's view, however, *Alexandria Scrap* did not involve "the kind of action with which the Commerce Clause is concerned." Unlike prior cases voiding state laws inhibiting interstate trade, "Maryland has not sought to prohibit the flow of hulks, or to regulate the conditions under which it may occur. Instead, it has entered into the market itself to bid up their price," . . . "as a purchaser, in effect, of a potential article of interstate commerce," and has restricted "its trade to its own citizens or businesses within the State."

Having characterized Maryland as a market participant, rather than as a market regulator, the Court found no reason to "believe the Commerce Clause was intended to require independent justification for [the State's] action." The Court couched its holding in unmistakably broad terms. "Nothing in the purposes animating the Commerce Clause prohibits a State, in the absence of congressional action, from participating in the market and exercising the right to favor its own citizens over others."

B

The basic distinction drawn in *Alexandria Scrap* between States as market participants and States as market regulators makes good sense and sound law. As that case explains, the Commerce Clause responds principally to state taxes and regulatory measures impeding free private trade in the national marketplace. There is no indication of a constitutional plan to limit the ability of the States themselves to operate freely in the free market.

Restraint in this area is also counseled by considerations of state sovereignty, the role of each State " 'as guardian and trustee for its people,' " and "the long recognized right of trader or manufacturer, engaged in an entirely private business, freely to exercise his own independent discretion as to parties with whom he will deal." Moreover, state proprietary activities may be, and often are, burdened with the same restrictions imposed on private market participants. Evenhandedness suggests that, when acting as proprietors, States should similarly share existing freedoms from federal constraints, including the inherent limits of the Commerce Clause. Finally, as this case illustrates, the competing considerations in cases involving state proprietary action often will be subtle, complex, politically charged, and difficult to assess under traditional Commerce Clause analysis. Given these factors, *Alexandria Scrap* wisely recognizes that, as a rule, the adjustment of interests in this context is a task better suited for Congress than this Court.

III

South Dakota, as a seller of cement, unquestionably fits the "market participant" label more comfortably than a State acting to subsidize local scrap processors. Thus, the general rule of *Alexandria Scrap* plainly applies here. Petitioner argues, however, that the exemption for marketplace participation necessarily admits of exceptions. While conceding that possibility, we perceive in this case no sufficient reason to depart from the general rule.

C

We conclude, then, that the arguments for invalidating South Dakota's resident-preference program are weak at best. Whatever residual force inheres in them is more than offset by countervailing considerations of policy and fairness. Reversal would discourage similar state projects, even though this project demonstrably has served the needs of state residents and has helped the entire region for more than a half century. Reversal also would rob South Dakota of the intended benefit of its foresight, risk, and industry. Under these circumstances, there is no reason to depart from the general rule of *Alexandria Scrap*.

The judgment of the United States Court of Appeals is affirmed.

It is so ordered.

JUSTICE POWELL, with whom JUSTICES BRENNAN, WHITE, and STEVENS join, dissenting.

The South Dakota Cement Commission has ordered that in times of shortage the state cement plant must turn away out-of-state customers until all orders from South Dakotans are filled. This policy represents precisely the kind of economic protectionism that the Commerce Clause was intended to prevent.* The Court, however, finds no violation of the Commerce Clause, solely because the State produces the cement. I agree with the Court that the State of South Dakota may provide cement for its public needs without violating the Commerce Clause. But I cannot agree that South Dakota may withhold its cement from interstate commerce in order to benefit private citizens and businesses within the State.

I

The need to ensure unrestricted trade among the States created a major impetus for the drafting of the Constitution. "The power over commerce . . . was one of the primary objects for which the people of America adopted their government." Indeed, the Constitutional Convention was called after an earlier convention on trade and commercial problems proved inconclusive. C. Beard, *An Economic Interpretation of the Constitution* 61–63 (1935); S. Bloom, *History of the Formation of the Union Under the Constitution* 14–15 (1940). In the subsequent debate over ratification, Alexander Hamilton emphasized the importance of unrestricted interstate commerce:

> "An unrestrained intercourse between the States themselves will advance the trade of each, by an interchange of their respective productions. Commercial enterprise will have much greater scope, from the diversity in the productions of different States. When the staple of one fails . . . it can call to its aid the staple of another." *The Federalist, No. 11,* p. 71 (J. Cooke ed., 1961) (A. Hamilton); see *id., No. 42*, p. 283 (J. Madison).

The Commerce Clause has proved an effective weapon against protectionism. The Court has used it to strike down limitations on access to local goods, be they animal, *Hughes v. Oklahoma*, 441 U.S. 322 (1979), (minnows); vegetable, *Pike v. Bruce Church, Inc.*, 397 U.S. 137 (1970), (cantaloupes); or mineral, *Pennsylvania v. West Virginia*, 262 U.S. 553 (1923), (natural gas). Only this Term, the Court held unconstitutional a Florida statute designed to exclude out-of-state investment advisers. As we observed in *Hughes v. Alexandria Scrap Corp.*, [426 U.S. 794 (1976),] "this Nation is a common market in which state lines cannot be made barriers to the free flow of both raw materials and finished goods in response to the economic laws of supply and demand."

This case presents a novel constitutional question. The Commerce Clause would bar legislation imposing on private parties the type of restraint on commerce adopted by South Dakota. Conversely, a private business constitutionally could adopt a marketing policy that excluded customers who come from another State. This

* By "protectionism," I refer to state policies designed to protect private economic interests within the State from the forces of the interstate market. I would exclude from this term policies relating to traditional governmental functions, such as education, and subsidy programs like the one at issue in *Alexandria Scrap*.

case falls between those polar situations. The State, through its Commission, engages in a commercial enterprise and restricts its own interstate distribution. The question is whether the Commission's policy should be treated like state regulation of private parties or like the marketing policy of a private business.

The application of the Commerce Clause to this case should turn on the nature of the governmental activity involved. If a public enterprise undertakes an "integral operatio[n] in areas of traditional governmental functions," the Commerce Clause is not directly relevant. If, however, the State enters the private market and operates a commercial enterprise for the advantage of its private citizens, it may not evade the constitutional policy against economic Balkanization.

The Court holds that South Dakota, like a private business, should not be governed by the Commerce Clause when it enters the private market. But precisely because South Dakota is a State, it cannot be presumed to behave like an enterprise " " 'engaged in an entirely private business.' " A State frequently will respond to market conditions on the basis of political rather than economic concerns. To use the Court's terms, a State may attempt to act as a "market regulator" rather than a "market participant." In that situation, it is a pretense to equate the State with a private economic actor. State action burdening interstate trade is no less state action because it is accomplished by a public agency authorized to participate in the private market.

II

The threshold issue is whether South Dakota has undertaken integral government operations in an area of traditional governmental functions, or whether it has participated in the marketplace as a private firm. If the latter characterization applies, we also must determine whether the State Commission's marketing policy burdens the flow of interstate trade. This analysis highlights the differences between the state action here and that before the Court in *Alexandria Scrap*.

A

In *Alexandria Scrap*, a Virginia scrap processor challenged a Maryland program to pay bounties for every junk car registered in Maryland that was converted into scrap. The program imposed more onerous documentation standards on non-Maryland processors, thereby diverting Maryland "hulks" to in-state processors. The Virginia plaintiff argued that this diversion burdened interstate commerce.

As the Court today notes, *Alexandria Scrap* determined that Maryland's bounty program constituted direct state participation in the market for automobile hulks. But the critical question—the second step in the opinion's analysis—was whether the bounty program constituted an impermissible burden on interstate commerce. Recognizing that the case did not fit neatly into conventional Commerce Clause theory, we found no burden on commerce.

B

Unlike the market subsidies at issue in *Alexandria Scrap*, the marketing policy of the South Dakota Cement Commission has cut off interstate trade.* The State can raise such a bar when it enters the market to supply its own needs. In order to ensure an adequate supply of cement for public uses, the State can withhold from interstate commerce the cement needed for public projects.

The State, however, has no parallel justification for favoring private, in-state customers over out-of-state customers. In response to political concerns that likely would be inconsequential to a private cement producer, South Dakota has shut off its cement sales to customers beyond its borders. That discrimination constitutes a

* One distinction between a private and a governmental function is whether the activity is supported with general tax funds, as was the case for the reprocessing program in *Alexandria Scrap*, or whether it is financed by the revenues it generates. In this case, South Dakota's cement plant has supported itself for many years. There is thus no need to consider the question whether a state-subsidized business could confine its sales to local residents.

direct barrier to trade "of the type forbidden by the Commerce Clause, and involved in previous cases." The effect on interstate trade is the same as if the state legislature had imposed the policy on private cement producers. The Commerce Clause prohibits this severe restraint on commerce.

III

I share the Court's desire to preserve state sovereignty. But the Commerce Clause long has been recognized as a limitation on that sovereignty, consciously designed to maintain a national market and defeat economic provincialism. The Court today approves protectionist state policies. In the absence of contrary congressional action, those policies now can be implemented as long as the State itself directly participates in the market.

By enforcing the Commerce Clause in this case, the Court would work no unfairness on the people of South Dakota. They still could reserve cement for public projects and share in whatever return the plant generated. They could not, however, use the power of the State to furnish themselves with cement forbidden to the people of neighboring States.

The creation of a free national economy was a major goal of the States when they resolved to unite under the Federal Constitution. The decision today cannot be reconciled with that purpose.

FOR DISCUSSION

Why can states as market participants discriminate? How do does one draw the line between the state acting as a market participant and acting in its traditional governmental role? Are there any limits you think states should face even if operating as a market participant? Should they be allowed to discriminate against interstate commerce?

RELATED CASES

United Building & Construction Trades Council v. Mayor and Council of Camden: **465 U.S. 208 (1984).**

The Court upheld a city requirement that at least 40% percent of the workers on construction projects be residents. Because Camden was acting as a market participant, it was permitted to impose this quota on hiring.

White v. Massachusetts Council of Construction: **460 U.S. 204 (1983).**

Because the State was acting as a market participant, the Court upheld a state requirement that at least half of all workers on construction projects be Massachusetts citizens.

BALDWIN V. FISH AND GAME COMMISSION OF MONTANA

436 U.S. 371, 98 S.Ct. 1852, 56 L.Ed.2d 354 (1978)

The State of Montana enacted a law charging non-nonresidents a higher fee to obtain a hunting license than required of residents. Out-of-state hunters objected and challenged the law.

Vote: 6–3

JUSTICE BLACKMUN delivered the opinion of the Court.

This case presents issues, under the Privileges and Immunities Clause of the Constitution's Art. IV, § 2, and the Equal Protection Clause of the Fourteenth Amendment, as to the constitutional validity of disparities, as between residents and nonresidents, in a State's hunting license system.

I

Appellant Lester Baldwin is a Montana resident. He also is an outfitter holding a state license as a hunting guide. The majority of his customers are nonresidents who come to Montana to hunt elk and other big game. Appellants Carlson, Huseby, Lee and Moris are residents of Minnesota. They have hunted big game, particularly elk, in Montana in past years and wish to continue to do so.

In 1975, the five appellants, disturbed by the difference in the kinds of Montana elk-hunting licenses available to nonresidents, as contrasted with those available to residents of the State, and by the difference in the fees the nonresident and the resident must pay for their respective licenses, instituted the present federal suit for declaratory and injunctive relief and for reimbursement, in part, of fees already paid. The defendants were the Fish and Game Commission of the State of Montana, the Commission's director, and its five commissioners. The complaint challenged the Montana elk-hunting licensing scheme specifically, and asserted that, as applied to nonresidents, it violated the Constitution's Privileges and Immunities Clause, Art. IV, § 2, and the Equal Protection Clause of the Fourteenth Amendment. A three-judge District Court was convened and, by a divided vote, entered judgment denying all relief to the plaintiff-appellants. We noted probable jurisdiction.*

II

The relevant facts are not in any real controversy and many of them are agreed:

For the 1975 hunting season, a Montana resident could purchase a license solely for elk for $4. The nonresident, however, in order to hunt elk, was required to purchase a combination license at a cost of $151; this entitled him to take one elk and two deer.

For the 1976 season, the Montana resident could purchase a license solely for elk for $9. The nonresident, in order to hunt elk was required to purchase a combination license at a cost of $225; this entitled him to take one elk, one deer, one black bear, and game birds, and to fish with hook and line. A resident was not required to buy any combination of licenses, but if he did, the cost to him of all the privileges granted by the nonresident combination license was $30. The nonresident thus paid 7½ times as much as the resident, and if the nonresident wished to hunt only elk, he paid 25 times as much as the resident.

Montana maintains significant populations of big game, including elk, deer, and antelope. Its elk population is one of the largest in the United States. Elk are prized by big-game hunters who come from near and far to pursue the animals for sport.**

The quest for big game has grown in popularity. During the 10-year period from 1960 to 1970 licenses issued by Montana increased by approximately 67% for residents and by approximately 530% for nonresidents.***

IV

Privileges and immunities. Appellants strongly urge here that the Montana licensing scheme for the hunting of elk violates the Privileges and Immunities Clause of Art. IV, § 2, of our Constitution. That Clause is not one the contours of which have been precisely shaped by the process and wear of constant litigation and judicial interpretation over the years since 1789. If there is any significance in the fact, the Clause appears in the so-called States' Relations Article, the same Article that embraces the Full Faith and Credit Clause, the Extradition

* We note, in passing, that most States charge nonresidents more than residents for hunting licenses.

** Approximately 43,500 nonresident hunting licenses for deer and elk were issued during [1974–1975]. The District Court found that elk hunting is recreational in nature and, "except for a few residents who live in exactly the right place," expensive. There was testimony that for a typical seven-day elk hunt a nonresident spends approximately $1,250 *exclusive* of outfitter's fee and the hunting license. Thus, while the nonresident combination license fee is not insubstantial, it appears to be a lesser part of the overall expense of the elk hunt.

*** The number of nonresident hunters has not yet reached the 17,000 limit. There are no similar numerical limitations on resident elk or deer licenses.

Clause (also in § 2), the provisions for the admission of new States, the Territory and Property Clause, and the Guarantee Clause. Historically, it has been overshadowed by the appearance in 1868 of similar language in § 1 of the Fourteenth Amendment, and by the continuing controversy and consequent litigation that attended that Amendment's enactment and its meaning and application.

The Privileges and Immunities Clause originally was not isolated from the Commerce Clause, now in the Constitution's Art. I, § 8. In the Articles of Confederation, where both Clauses have their source, the two concepts were together in the fourth Article. Their separation may have been an assurance against an anticipated narrow reading of the Commerce Clause.

Perhaps because of the imposition of the Fourteenth Amendment upon our constitutional consciousness and the extraordinary emphasis that the Amendment received, it is not surprising that the contours of Art. IV, § 2, cl. 1, are not well developed, and that the relationship, if any, between the Privileges and Immunities Clause and the "privileges or immunities" language of the Fourteenth Amendment is less than clear. We are, nevertheless, not without some pronouncements by this Court as to the Clause's significance and reach. There are at least three general comments that deserve mention:

The first is that of Mr. Justice Field, writing for a unanimous Court in *Paul v. Virginia*, 75 U.S. 168 (1869). He emphasized nationalism, the proscription of discrimination, and the assurance of equality of all citizens within any State:

> "It was undoubtedly the object of the clause in question to place the citizens of each State upon the same footing with citizens of other States, so far as the advantages resulting from citizenship in those States are concerned. It relieves them from the disabilities of alienage in other States; it inhibits discriminating legislation against them by other States; it gives them the right of free ingress into other States, and egress from them; it insures to them in other States the same freedom possessed by the citizens of those States in the acquisition and enjoyment of property and in the pursuit of happiness; and it secures to them in other States the equal protection of their laws. It has been justly said that no provision in the Constitution has tended so strongly to constitute the citizens of the United States one people as this."

The second came 70 years later when Mr. Justice Roberts, writing for himself and Mr. Justice Black in *Hague v. CIO*, 307 U.S. 496 (1939), summed up the history of the Clause and pointed out what he felt to be the difference in analysis in the earlier cases from the analysis in later ones:

"As has been said, prior to the adoption of the Fourteenth Amendment, there had been no constitutional definition of citizenship of the United States, or of the rights, privileges, and immunities secured thereby or springing therefrom.

"At one time it was thought that this section recognized a group of rights which, according to the jurisprudence of the day, were classed as 'natural rights'; and that the purpose of the section was to create rights of citizens of the United States by guaranteeing the citizens of every State the recognition of this group of rights by every other State. Such was the view of Justice Washington.

"While this description of the civil rights of the citizens of the States has been quoted with approval, it has come to be the settled view that Article IV, § 2, does not import that a citizen of one State carries with him into another fundamental privileges and immunities which come to him necessarily by the mere fact of his citizenship in the State first mentioned, but, on the contrary, that in any State every citizen of any other State is to have the same privileges and immunities which the citizens of that State enjoy. The section, in effect, prevents a State from discriminating against citizens of other States in favor of its own."

The third and most recent general pronouncement is that authored by Mr. Justice Marshall for a nearly unanimous Court in *Austin v. New Hampshire,* 420 U.S. 656 (1975), stressing the Clause's "norm of comity" and the Framers' concerns:

> "The Clause thus establishes a norm of comity without specifying the particular subjects as to which citizens of one State coming within the jurisdiction of another are guaranteed equality of treatment. The origins of the Clause do reveal, however, the concerns of central import to the Framers. During the preconstitutional period, the practice of some States denying to outlanders the treatment that its citizens demanded for themselves was widespread. The fourth of the Articles of Confederation was intended to arrest this centrifugal tendency with some particularity. . . .
>
> * * *
>
> "The discriminations at which this Clause was aimed were by no means eradicated during the short life of the Confederation, and the provision was carried over into the comity article of the Constitution in briefer form but with no change of substance or intent, unless it was to strengthen the force of the Clause in fashioning a single nation."

When the Privileges and Immunities Clause has been applied to specific cases, it has been interpreted to prevent a State from imposing unreasonable burdens on citizens of other States in their pursuit of common callings within the State, *Ward v. Maryland,* 79 U.S. 418 (1870); in the ownership and disposition of privately held property within the State, *Blake v. McClung,* 172 U.S. 239 (1898); and in access to the courts of the State, *Canadian Northern R. Co. v. Eggen*, 252 U.S. 553 (1920).

It has not been suggested, however, that state citizenship or residency may never be used by a State to distinguish among persons. Suffrage, for example, always has been understood to be tied to an individual's identification with a particular State. No one would suggest that the Privileges and Immunities Clause requires a State to open its polls to a person who declines to assert that the State is the only one where he claims a right to vote. The same is true as to qualification for an elective office of the State. Nor must a State always apply all its laws or all its services equally to anyone, resident or nonresident, who may request it so to do. Some distinctions between residents and nonresidents merely reflect the fact that this is a Nation composed of individual States, and are permitted; other distinctions are prohibited because they hinder the formation, the purpose, or the development of a single Union of those States. Only with respect to those "privileges" and "immunities" bearing upon the vitality of the Nation as a single entity must the State treat all citizens, resident and nonresident, equally. Here we must decide into which category falls a distinction with respect to access to recreational big-game hunting.

Many of the early cases embrace the concept that the States had complete ownership over wildlife within their boundaries, and, as well, the power to preserve this bounty for their citizens alone. It was enough to say "that in regulating the use of the common property of the citizens of [a] state, the legislature is [not] bound to extend to the citizens of all the other states the same advantages as are secured to their own citizens." *Corfield v. Coryell*, 6 Fed. Cas. 546, C.C.E.D.Pa. 1823). It appears to have been generally accepted that although the States were obligated to treat all those within their territory equally in most respects, they were not obliged to share those things they held in trust for their own people. In *Corfield*, a case the Court has described as "the first, and long the leading, explication of the [Privileges and Immunities] Clause," Mr. Justice Washington, sitting as Circuit Justice, although recognizing that the States may not interfere with the "right of a citizen of one state to pass through, or to reside in any other state, for purposes of trade, agriculture, professional pursuits, or otherwise; to claim the benefit of the writ of habeas corpus; to institute and maintain actions of any kind in the courts of the state; to take, hold and dispose of property, either real or personal," nonetheless concluded that access to oyster beds determined to be owned by New Jersey could be limited to New Jersey residents. This holding, and the conception of state sovereignty upon which it relied, formed the basis for similar decisions during later years of the 19th century. In *Geer v. Connecticut,* 161 U.S. 519 (1896), a case dealing with Connecticut's authority to limit the disposition of game birds taken within its boundaries, the Court roundly rejected the contention "that a State cannot allow its own people the enjoyment of the benefits of the property belonging to them in common, without at the same time permitting the citizens of other States to participate in that which they do not own."

In more recent years, however, the Court has recognized that the States' interest in regulating and controlling those things they claim to "own," including wildlife, is by no means absolute. States may not compel the confinement of the benefits of their resources, even their wildlife, to their own people whenever such hoarding and confinement impedes interstate commerce. *Foster-Fountain Packing Co. v. Haydel,* 278 U.S. 1 (1928). Nor does a State's control over its resources preclude the proper exercise of federal power. And a State's interest in its wildlife and other resources must yield when, without reason, it interferes with a nonresident's right to pursue a livelihood in a State other than his own, a right that is protected by the Privileges and Immunities Clause.

Appellants contend that the doctrine on which *Corfield, McCready v. Virginia,* 94 U.S. 391 (1876), and *Geer* all relied has no remaining vitality. We do not agree. Only last Term, in referring to the "ownership" or title language of those cases and characterizing it "as no more than a 19th-century legal fiction," the Court pointed out that that language nevertheless expressed " 'the importance to its people that a State have power to preserve and regulate the exploitation of an important resource.' " The fact that the State's control over wildlife is not exclusive and absolute in the face of federal regulation and certain federally protected interests does not compel the conclusion that it is meaningless in their absence.

We need look no further than decisions of this Court to know that this is so. It is true that in *Toomer v. Witsell,* 334 U.S. 385 (1948), the Court in 1948 struck down a South Carolina statute requiring nonresidents of the State to pay a license fee of $2,500 for each commercial shrimp boat, and residents to pay a fee of only $25, and did so on the ground that the statute violated the Privileges and Immunities Clause. Less than three years, however, after the decision in *Toomer,* so heavily relied upon by appellants here, the Court dismissed for the want of a substantial federal question an appeal from a decision of the Supreme Court of South Dakota holding that the *total* exclusion from that State of nonresident hunters of migratory waterfowl was justified by the State's assertion of a special interest in wildlife that qualified as a substantial reason for the discrimination. In that case South Dakota had proved that there was real danger that the flyways, breeding grounds, and nursery for ducks and geese would be subject to excessive hunting and possible destruction by nonresident hunters lured to the State by an abundance of pheasants.

Does the distinction made by Montana between residents and nonresidents in establishing access to elk hunting threaten a basic right in a way that offends the Privileges and Immunities Clause? Merely to ask the question seems to provide the answer. We repeat much of what already has been said above: Elk hunting by nonresidents in Montana is a recreation and a sport. In itself—wholly apart from license fees—it is costly and obviously available only to the wealthy nonresident or to the one so taken with the sport that he sacrifices other values in order to indulge in it and to enjoy what it offers. It is not a means to the nonresident's livelihood. The mastery of the animal and the trophy are the ends that are sought; appellants are not totally excluded from these. The elk supply, which has been entrusted to the care of the State by the people of Montana, is finite and must be carefully tended in order to be preserved.

Appellants' interest in sharing this limited resource on more equal terms with Montana residents simply does not fall within the purview of the Privileges and Immunities Clause. Equality in access to Montana elk is not basic to the maintenance or well-being of the Union. Appellants do not—and cannot—contend that they are deprived of a means of a livelihood by the system or of access to any part of the State to which they may seek to travel. We do not decide the full range of activities that are sufficiently basic to the livelihood of the Nation that the States may not interfere with a nonresident's participation therein without similarly interfering with a resident's participation. Whatever rights or activities may be "fundamental" under the Privileges and Immunities Clause, we are persuaded, and hold, that elk hunting by nonresidents in Montana is not one of them.

V

Equal protection. Appellants urge, too, that distinctions drawn between residents and nonresidents are not permissible under the Equal Protection Clause of the Fourteenth Amendment when used to allocate access to recreational hunting. Appellees argue that the State constitutionally should be able to charge nonresidents, who are not subject to the State's general taxing power, more than it charges it residents, who are subject to that power and who already have contributed to the programs that make elk hunting possible. Appellees also urge that Montana, as a State, has made sacrifices in its economic development, and therefore in its tax base, in order to preserve the elk and other wildlife within the State and that this, too, must be counted, along with actual tax revenues spent, when computing the fair share to be paid by nonresidents. We need not commit ourselves to any particular method of computing the cost to the State of maintaining an environment in which elk can survive in order to find the State's efforts rational, and not invidious, and therefore not violative of the Equal Protection Clause.

The judgment of the District Court is affirmed.

It is so ordered.

JUSTICE BRENNAN, with whom JUSTICES WHITE and MARSHALL join, dissenting.

Far more troublesome than the Court's narrow holding—elk hunting in Montana is not a privilege or immunity entitled to protection under Art. IV, § 2, cl. 1, of the Constitution—is the rationale of the holding that Montana's elk-hunting licensing scheme passes constitutional muster. The Court concludes that because elk hunting is not a "basic and essential activit[y], interference with which would frustrate the purposes of the formation of the Union," the Privileges and Immunities Clause of Art. IV, § 2—"The Citizens of each State shall be entitled to all Privileges and Immunities of Citizens in the several States"—does not prevent Montana from irrationally, wantonly, and even invidiously discriminating against nonresidents seeking to enjoy natural treasures it alone among the 50 States possesses. I cannot agree that the Privileges and Immunities Clause is so impotent a guarantee that such discrimination remains wholly beyond the purview of that provision.

I think the time has come to confirm explicitly that which has been implicit in our modern privileges and immunities decisions, namely that an inquiry into whether a given right is "fundamental" has no place in our analysis of whether a State's discrimination against nonresidents—who "are not represented in the [discriminating] State's legislative halls"—violates the Clause. Rather, our primary concern is the State's justification for its discrimination. Drawing from the principles announced in *Toomer* and *Mullaney*, a State's discrimination against nonresidents is permissible where (1) the presence or activity of nonresidents is the source or cause of the problem or effect with which the State seeks to deal, and (2) the discrimination practiced against nonresidents bears a substantial relation to the problem they present. Although a State has no burden to prove that its laws are not violative of the Privileges and Immunities Clause, its mere assertion that the discrimination practiced against nonresidents is justified by the peculiar problem nonresidents present will not prevail in the face of a prima facie showing that the discrimination is not supportable on the asserted grounds. This requirement that a State's unequal treatment of nonresidents be reasoned and suitably tailored furthers the federal interest in ensuring that "a norm of comity," prevails throughout the Nation while simultaneously guaranteeing to the States the needed leeway to draw viable distinctions between their citizens and those of other States.

II

It is clear that under a proper privileges and immunities analysis Montana's discriminatory treatment of nonresident big-game hunters in this case must fall. Putting aside the validity of the requirement that nonresident hunters desiring to hunt elk must purchase a combination license that resident elk hunters need not buy, there are three possible justifications for charging nonresident elk hunters an amount at least 7.5 times the fee imposed on resident big-game hunters. The first is conservation. The State did not attempt to assert this as a justification for its discriminatory licensing scheme in the District Court, and apparently does not do so here. Indeed, it is difficult to see how it could consistently with the first prong of a modern privileges and immunities analysis. First, there is nothing in the record to indicate that the influx of nonresident hunters created a special danger to Montana's elk or to any of its other wildlife species. In the most recent year for which statistics are available, 1974–1975, there were 198,411 resident hunters in Montana and only 31,406 nonresident hunters. Nonresidents thus constituted only 13% of all hunters pursuing their sport in the State.

The second possible justification for the fee differential Montana imposes on nonresident elk hunters—the one presented in the District Court and principally relied upon here—is a cost justification. Appellants have never contended that the Privileges and Immunities Clause requires that identical fees be assessed residents and nonresidents. They recognize that *Toomer* and *Mullaney* allow additional charges to be made on nonresidents based on both the added enforcement costs the presence of nonresident hunters imposes on Montana and the State's conservation expenditures supported by resident-borne taxes. Their position throughout this litigation has been that the higher fee extracted from nonresident elk hunters is not a valid effort by Montana to recoup state expenditures on their behalf, but a price gouged from those who can satisfactorily pursue their avocation in no other State in the Union. The licensing scheme, appellants contend, is simply an attempt by Montana to shift the costs of its conservation efforts, however commendable they may be, onto the shoulders of nonresidents who are powerless to help themselves at the ballot box.

The third possible justification for Montana's licensing scheme, the doctrine of *McCready v. Virginia*, is actually no justification at all, but simply an assertion that a State "owns" the wildlife within its borders in trust for its citizens and may therefore do with it what it pleases.

In unjustifiably discriminating against nonresident elk hunters, Montana has not "exercised its police power in conformity with the Constitution." The State's police power interest in its wildlife cannot override the appellants' constitutionally protected privileges and immunities right. I respectfully dissent and would reverse.*

FOR DISCUSSION

Given this case, do you understand how or why states can charge different tuition at public colleges and universities for in-state versus out-of-state students?

---

* Because I find Montana's elk-hunting licensing scheme unconstitutional under the Privileges and Immunities Clause of Art. IV, § 2, I find it unnecessary to determine whether the scheme would pass equal protection scrutiny. In any event, where a State discriminates *solely* on the basis of noncitizenship or nonresidency in the State, see n. 1, *supra*, it is my view that the Equal Protection Clause affords a discriminatee no greater protection than the Privileges and Immunities Clause.

CALIFORNIA V. CABAZON BAND OF MISSION INDIANS

480 U.S. 202, 107 S.Ct. 1083, 94 L.Ed.2d 244 (1987)

The State of California sought to regulate bingo games that were being conducted on Indian reservations. While bingo was not illegal in the state, a California law required that bingo games be operated and staffed by members of non-nonprofit charities who could not be paid for their services. The Cabazon Band challenged the regulation.

Vote: 6–3

JUSTICE WHITE delivered the opinion of the Court.

The Cabazon and Morongo Bands of Mission Indians, federally recognized Indian Tribes, occupy reservations in Riverside County, California. Each Band, pursuant to an ordinance approved by the Secretary of the Interior, conducts bingo games on its reservation. The Cabazon Band has also opened a card club at which draw poker and other card games are played. The games are open to the public and are played predominantly by non-Indians coming onto the reservations. The games are a major source of employment for tribal members, and the profits are the Tribes' sole source of income. The State of California seeks to apply to the two Tribes Cal. Penal Code Ann. § 326.5. That statute does not entirely prohibit the playing of bingo but permits it when the games are operated and staffed by members of designated charitable organizations who may not be paid for their services. Profits must be kept in special accounts and used only for charitable purposes; prizes may not exceed $250 per game. Asserting that the bingo games on the two reservations violated each of these restrictions, California insisted that the Tribes comply with state law. Riverside County also sought to apply its local Ordinance No. 558, regulating bingo, as well as its Ordinance No. 331, prohibiting the playing of draw poker and the other card games.

The Tribes sued the county in Federal District Court seeking a declaratory judgment that the county had no authority to apply its ordinances inside the reservations and an injunction against their enforcement. The State intervened, the facts were stipulated, and the District Court granted the Tribes' motion for summary judgment, holding that neither the State nor the county had any authority to enforce its gambling laws within the reservations. The Court of Appeals for the Ninth Circuit affirmed, the State and the county appealed, and we postponed jurisdiction to the hearing on the merits.

I

The Court has consistently recognized that Indian tribes retain "attributes of sovereignty over both their members and their territory," and that "tribal sovereignty is dependent on, and subordinate to, only the Federal Government, not the States." It is clear, however, that state laws may be applied to tribal Indians on their reservations if Congress has expressly so provided. Here, the State insists that Congress has twice given its express consent: first in Pub.L. 280 in 1953, 67 Stat. 588, as amended, and second in the Organized Crime Control Act in 1970. We disagree in both respects.

In Pub.L. 280, Congress expressly granted six States, including California, jurisdiction over specified areas of Indian country within the States and provided for the assumption of jurisdiction by other States. In § 2, California was granted broad criminal jurisdiction over offenses committed by or against Indians within all Indian country within the State. Section 4's grant of civil jurisdiction was more limited. In *Bryan v. Itasca County,* 426 U.S. 373 (1976), we interpreted § 4 to grant States jurisdiction over private civil litigation involving reservation Indians in state court, but not to grant general civil regulatory authority. We held, therefore, that Minnesota could not apply its personal property tax within the reservation. Congress' primary concern in enacting Pub.L. 280 was combating lawlessness on reservations. The Act plainly was not intended to effect total assimilation of Indian tribes into mainstream American society. We recognized that a grant to States of general civil regulatory power over Indian reservations would result in the destruction of tribal institutions and values. Accordingly, when a State seeks to enforce a law within an Indian reservation under the authority of Pub.L. 280, it must be determined whether the law is criminal in nature, and thus fully applicable to the reservation under § 2, or civil in nature, and applicable only as it may be relevant to private civil litigation in state court.

The Minnesota personal property tax at issue in *Bryan* was unquestionably civil in nature. The California bingo statute is not so easily categorized. California law permits bingo games to be conducted only by charitable and other specified organizations, and then only by their members who may not receive any wage or profit for doing so; prizes are limited and receipts are to be segregated and used only for charitable purposes. Violation of any of these provisions is a misdemeanor. California insists that these are criminal laws which Pub.L. 280 permits it to enforce on the reservations.

Following its earlier decision in *Barona Group of Capitan Grande Band of Mission Indians, San Diego County, Cal. v. Duffy*, 694 F.2d 1185 (CA 9 1982), which also involved the applicability of § 326.5 of the California Penal Code to Indian reservations, the Court of Appeals rejected this submission. In *Barona,* applying what it thought to be the civil/criminal dichotomy drawn in *Bryan v. Itasca County*, the Court of Appeals drew a distinction between state "criminal/prohibitory" laws and state "civil/regulatory" laws: if the intent of a state law is generally to prohibit certain conduct, it falls within Pub.L. 280's grant of criminal jurisdiction, but if the state law generally permits the conduct at issue, subject to regulation, it must be classified as civil/regulatory and Pub.L. 280 does not authorize its enforcement on an Indian reservation. The shorthand test is whether the conduct at issue violates the State's public policy. Inquiring into the nature of § 326.5, the Court of Appeals held that it was regulatory rather than prohibitory. This was the analysis employed, with similar results, by the Court of Appeals for the Fifth Circuit in *Seminole Tribe of Florida v. Butterworth*, 658 F.2d 310 (1981), which the Ninth Circuit found persuasive.

There is surely a fair basis for its conclusion. California does not prohibit all forms of gambling. California itself operates a state lottery, and daily encourages its citizens to participate in this state-run gambling. California also permits parimutuel horse-race betting. Although certain enumerated gambling games are prohibited under Cal.Penal Code Ann. § 330, games not enumerated, including the card games played in the Cabazon card club, are permissible. The Tribes assert that more than 400 card rooms similar to the Cabazon card club flourish in California, and the State does not dispute this fact. Also, as the Court of Appeals noted, bingo is legally sponsored by many different organizations and is widely played in California. There is no effort to forbid the playing of bingo by any member of the public over the age of 18. Indeed, the permitted bingo games *must* be open to the general public. Nor is there any limit on the number of games which eligible organizations may operate, the receipts which they may obtain from the games, the number of games which a participant may play, or the amount of money which a participant may spend, either per game or in total. In light of the fact that California permits a substantial amount of gambling activity, including bingo, and actually promotes gambling through its state lottery, we must conclude that California regulates rather than prohibits gambling in general and bingo in particular.

California argues, however, that high stakes, *unregulated* bingo, the conduct which attracts organized crime, is a misdemeanor in California and may be prohibited on Indian reservations. But that an otherwise regulatory law is enforceable by criminal as well as civil means does not necessarily convert it into a criminal law within the meaning of Pub.L. 280. Otherwise, the distinction between § 2 and § 4 of that law could easily be avoided and total assimilation permitted. This view, adopted here and by the Fifth Circuit in the *Butterworth* case, we find persuasive. Accordingly, we conclude that Pub.L. 280 does not authorize California to enforce Cal.Penal Code Ann. § 326.5 within the Cabazon and Morongo Reservations.

California and Riverside County also argue that the Organized Crime Control Act (OCCA) authorizes the application of their gambling laws to the tribal bingo enterprises. The OCCA makes certain violations of state and local gambling laws violations of federal law. The Court of Appeals rejected appellants' argument, relying on its earlier decisions in *United States v. Farris*, 77 F.3d 391 (11th Cir.1996), and *Barona Group of Capitan Grande Band of Mission Indians, San Diego County, Cal. v. Duffy*, 694 F.2d 1185 (CA 9 1982). The court explained that whether a tribal activity is "a violation of the law of a state" within the meaning of OCCA depends on whether it violates the "public policy" of the State, the same test for application of state law under Pub.L. 280, and similarly concluded that bingo is not contrary to the public policy of California.

The Court of Appeals for the Sixth Circuit has rejected this view. *United States v. Dakota*, 796 F.2d 186 (1986). Since the OCCA standard is simply whether the gambling business is being operated in "violation of the law of a State," there is no basis for the regulatory/prohibitory distinction that it agreed is suitable in construing and applying Pub.L. 280. And because enforcement of OCCA is an exercise of federal rather than state authority, there is no danger of state encroachment on Indian tribal sovereignty. This latter observation exposes the flaw in appellants' reliance on OCCA. That enactment is indeed a federal law that, among other things, defines certain federal crimes over which the district courts have exclusive jurisdiction. There is nothing in OCCA indicating that the States are to have any part in enforcing federal criminal laws or are authorized to make arrests on Indian reservations that in the absence of OCCA they could not effect. We are not informed of any federal efforts to employ OCCA to prosecute the playing of bingo on Indian reservations, although there are more than 100 such enterprises currently in operation, many of which have been in existence for several years, for the most part with the encouragement of the Federal Government. Whether or not, then, the Sixth Circuit is right and the Ninth Circuit wrong about the coverage of OCCA, a matter that we do not decide, there is no warrant for California to make arrests on reservations and thus, through OCCA, enforce its gambling laws against Indian tribes.

II

We conclude that the State's interest in preventing the infiltration of the tribal bingo enterprises by organized crime does not justify state regulation of the tribal bingo enterprises in light of the compelling federal and tribal interests supporting them. State regulation would impermissibly infringe on tribal government, and this conclusion applies equally to the county's attempted regulation of the Cabazon card club. We therefore affirm the judgment of the Court of Appeals and remand the case for further proceedings consistent with this opinion.

It is so ordered.

JUSTICE STEVENS, with whom JUSTICES O'CONNOR and SCALIA join, dissenting.

Unless and until Congress exempts Indian-managed gambling from state law and subjects it to federal supervision, I believe that a State may enforce its laws prohibiting high-stakes gambling on Indian reservations within its borders. Congress has not pre-empted California's prohibition against high-stakes bingo games and the Secretary of the Interior plainly has no authority to do so. While gambling provides needed employment and income for Indian tribes, these benefits do not, in my opinion, justify tribal operation of currently unlawful commercial activities. Accepting the majority's reasoning would require exemptions for cockfighting, tattoo parlors, nude dancing, houses of prostitution, and other illegal but profitable enterprises. As the law now stands, I believe tribal entrepreneurs, like others who might derive profits from catering to non-Indian customers, must obey applicable state laws.

I respectfully dissent.

FOR DISCUSSION

Does this opinion mean that states can never regulate Indian affairs? Can they ever regulate activities that take place on Indian reservations? Could a reservation set a lower age limit lower than the state for smoking or the consumption of alcohol?

GRANHOLM V. HEALD

544 U.S. 460, 125 S.Ct. 1885, 161 L.Ed.2d 796 (2005)

Both the states of Michigan and New York banned the shipment of wine into their states from out-of-state wineries. Distributors objected, claiming a violation of the Commerce Clause because the ban on shipping did not apply to in-state wineries.

Vote: 5–4

JUSTICE KENNEDY delivered the opinion of the Court.

These consolidated cases present challenges to state laws regulating the sale of wine from out-of-state wineries to consumers in Michigan and New York. The details and mechanics of the two regulatory schemes differ, but the object and effect of the laws are the same: to allow in-state wineries to sell wine directly to consumers in that State but to prohibit out-of-state wineries from doing so, or, at the least, to make direct sales impractical from an economic standpoint. It is evident that the object and design of the Michigan and New York statutes is to grant in-state wineries a competitive advantage over wineries located beyond the States' borders.

We hold that the laws in both States discriminate against interstate commerce in violation of the Commerce Clause, Art. I, § 8, cl. 3, and that the discrimination is neither authorized nor permitted by the Twenty-first Amendment. Accordingly, we affirm the judgment of the Court of Appeals for the Sixth Circuit, which invalidated the Michigan laws; and we reverse the judgment of the Court of Appeals for the Second Circuit, which upheld the New York laws.

II

A

Time and again this Court has held that, in all but the narrowest circumstances, state laws violate the Commerce Clause if they mandate "differential treatment of in-state and out-of-state economic interests that benefits the former and burdens the latter." *Oregon Waste Systems, Inc. v. Department of Environmental Quality of Ore.*, 511 U.S. 93 (1994). This rule is essential to the foundations of the Union. The mere fact of nonresidence should not foreclose a producer in one State from access to markets in other States. *H.P. Hood & Sons, Inc. v. Du Mond,* 336 U.S. 525 (1949). States may not enact laws that burden out-of-state producers or shippers simply to give a competitive advantage to in-state businesses. This mandate "reflect[s] a central concern of the Framers that was an immediate reason for calling the Constitutional Convention: the conviction that in order to succeed, the new Union would have to avoid the tendencies toward economic Balkanization that had plagued relations among the Colonies and later among the States under the Articles of Confederation."

The rule prohibiting state discrimination against interstate commerce follows also from the principle that States should not be compelled to negotiate with each other regarding favored or disfavored status for their own citizens. States do not need, and may not attempt, to negotiate with other States regarding their mutual economic interests. U.S. Const., Art. I, § 10, cl. 3. Rivalries among the States are thus kept to a minimum, and a proliferation of trade zones is prevented.

Laws of the type at issue in the instant cases contradict these principles. They deprive citizens of their right to have access to the markets of other States on equal terms. The perceived necessity for reciprocal sale privileges risks generating the trade rivalries and animosities, the alliances and exclusivity, that the Constitution and, in particular, the Commerce Clause were designed to avoid. State laws that protect local wineries have led to the enactment of statutes under which some States condition the right of out-of-state wineries to make direct wine sales to in-state consumers on a reciprocal right in the shipping State. California, for example, passed a reciprocity law in 1986, retreating from the State's previous regime that allowed unfettered direct shipments from out-of-state wineries.

Prior to 1986, all but three States prohibited direct-shipments of wine. The obvious aim of the California statute was to open the interstate direct-shipping market for the State's many wineries. The current patchwork of laws—with some States banning direct shipments altogether, others doing so only for out-of-state wines, and still others requiring reciprocity—is essentially the product of an ongoing, low-level trade war. Allowing States to discriminate against out-of-state wine "invite[s] a multiplication of preferential trade areas destructive of the very purpose of the Commerce Clause." *Dean Milk Co. v. Madison,* 340 U.S. 349 (1951).

B

The discriminatory character of the Michigan system is obvious. Michigan allows in-state wineries to ship directly to consumers, subject only to a licensing requirement. Out-of-state wineries, whether licensed or not, face a complete ban on direct shipment. The differential treatment requires all out-of-state wine, but not all in-state wine, to pass through an in-state wholesaler and retailer before reaching consumers. These two extra layers of overhead increase the cost of out-of-state wines to Michigan consumers. The cost differential, and in some cases the inability to secure a wholesaler for small shipments, can effectively bar small wineries from the Michigan market.

The New York regulatory scheme differs from Michigan's in that it does not ban direct shipments altogether. Out-of-state wineries are instead required to establish a distribution operation in New York in order to gain the privilege of direct-shipment. This, though, is just an indirect way of subjecting out-of-state wineries, but not local ones, to the three-tier system. New York and those allied with its interests defend the scheme by arguing that an out-of-state winery has the same access to the State's consumers as in-state wineries: All wine must be sold through a licensee fully accountable to New York; it just so happens that in order to become a licensee, a winery must have a physical presence in the State. There is some confusion over the precise steps out-of-state wineries must take to gain access to the New York market, in part because no winery has run the State's regulatory gauntlet. New York's argument, in any event, is unconvincing.

The New York scheme grants in-state wineries access to the State's consumers on preferential terms. The suggestion of a limited exception for direct shipment from out-of-state wineries does nothing to eliminate the discriminatory nature of New York's regulations. In-state producers, with the applicable licenses, can ship directly to consumers from their wineries. Out-of-state wineries must open a branch office and warehouse in New York, additional steps that drive up the cost of their wine. For most wineries, the expense of establishing a bricks-and-mortar distribution operation in 1 State, let alone all 50, is prohibitive. It comes as no surprise that not a single out-of-state winery has availed itself of New York's direct-shipping privilege. We have "viewed with particular suspicion state statutes requiring business operations to be performed in the home State that could more efficiently be performed elsewhere." *Pike v. Bruce Church, Inc.,* 397 U.S. 137 (1970). New York's in-state presence requirement runs contrary to our admonition that States cannot require an out-of-state firm "to become a resident in order to compete on equal terms." *Halliburton Oil Well Cementing Co. v. Reily,* 373 US 64 (1963).

These cases advanced two distinct principles. First, the Court held that the Commerce Clause prevented States from discriminating against imported liquor. In *Walling v. Michigan,* 116 U.S. 446 (1886), for example, the Court invalidated a Michigan tax that discriminated against liquor imports by exempting sales of local products. The Court held that States were not free to pass laws burdening only out-of-state products:

> "A discriminating tax imposed by a State operating to the disadvantage of the products of other States when introduced into the first mentioned State, is, in effect, a regulation in restraint of commerce among the States, and as such is a usurpation of the power conferred by the Constitution upon the Congress of the United States." 116 U.S., at 455.

Second, the Court held that the Commerce Clause prevented States from passing facially neutral laws that placed an impermissible burden on interstate commerce. For example, in *Bowman v. Chicago & Northwestern R. Co.,* 125 U.S. 465 (1888), the Court struck down an Iowa statute that required all liquor importers to have a permit. *Bowman* and its progeny rested in part on the since-rejected original-package doctrine. Under this doctrine, goods shipped in interstate commerce were immune from state regulation while in their original package. As the Court explained in *Vance v. W.A. Vandercook Co.,* 170 U.S. 438 (1898):

> "The power to ship merchandise from one State into another carries with it, as an incident, the right in the receiver of the goods to sell them in the original packages, any state regulation to the contrary notwithstanding; that is to say, that the goods received by Interstate Commerce remain under the shelter of the Interstate Commerce clause of the Constitution, until by a sale in the original package they have been commingled with the general mass of property in the State."

JUSTICE STEVENS with whom JUSTICE O'CONNOR joins, dissenting.

Congress' power to regulate commerce among the States includes the power to authorize the States to place burdens on interstate commerce. Absent such congressional approval, a state law may violate the unwritten rules described as the "dormant Commerce Clause" either by imposing an undue burden on both out-of-state and local producers engaged in interstate activities or by treating out-of-state producers less favorably than their local competitors. A state law totally prohibiting the sale of an ordinary article of commerce might impose an even more serious burden on interstate commerce. If Congress may nevertheless authorize the States to enact such laws, surely the people may do so through the process of amending our Constitution.

The New York and Michigan laws challenged in these cases would be patently invalid under well-settled dormant Commerce Clause principles if they regulated sales of an ordinary article of commerce rather than wine. But ever since the adoption of the Eighteenth Amendment and the Twenty-first Amendment, our Constitution has placed commerce in alcoholic beverages in a special category. Section 2 of the Twenty-first Amendment expressly provides that "[t]he transportation or importation into any State, Territory, or possession of the United States for delivery or use therein of intoxicating liquors, in violation of the laws thereof, is hereby prohibited."

FOR DISCUSSION

Would it make a difference if New York or Michigan did not allow for Internet or mail sales of wine even from wineries within their own borders?

PENNSYLVANIA V. NELSON

350 U.S. 497, 76 S.Ct. 477, 100 L.Ed. 640 (1956)

Steve Nelson, an admitted member of the Communist Party, had been convicted of violating the Pennsylvania Sedition Act. He challenged the validity of the state statute insofar as it proscribed sedition against the government of the United States, the offense with which he was charged. The federal government had previously regulated in this arena in 1940 through the Alien Registration of Smith Act.

This case is found in chapter II, page 112.

RELATED CASES

***Pacific Gas & Electric Company v. State Energy Resources Conservation and Development Commission:* 461 U.S. 190 (1983).**

The Court ruled in a 9–0 opinion that Congress's authority under the Atomic Energy Act to regulate the safety of nuclear reactors did not preclude a state from making citing decisions based upon economic reasons.

***Chamber of Commerce of U.S. v. Whiting:* 563 U.S. 582, 131 S.Ct. 1968 (2011).**

The Court ruled 5–3 that an Arizona law that required employers to verify citizenship status of employees was not preempted by federal immigration law.

***Arizona v. Inter Tribal Council of Arizona, Inc.:* 570 U.S. ___, 133 S.Ct. 2247 (2013).**

The Supreme Court by a vote of 7–2 ruled that a state law requiring voters to present proof of citizenship when they registered to vote was preempted by the National Voter Registration Act (NVRA).

STATE TAXATION

Fourteenth Amendment, Article I:

. . . "nor shall any State deprive any person of life, liberty, or property, without due process of law; nor deny to any person within its jurisdiction the equal protection of the laws."

—Fourteenth Amendment, Article I.

Article I, Sec. 8, para 3:

[The Congress shall have the Power] 'To regulate Commerce with foreign Nations, and among the several States, and with the Indian Tribes. . . ."

—Article I, Section 8, Clause 3.

Article IV, Sec. 2:

"The Citizens of each State shall be entitled to all Privileges and Immunities of Citizens in the several States."

—Article IV, Section 2.

"[T]he power to tax involves the power to destroy." So stated Chief Justice John Marshall in his famous *McCulloch v. Maryland* (17 U.S. 316, 1819) decision striking down a state tax on the Bank of the United States. While the individual states have broad authority on their own to tax in order to raise revenue for their own purposes, such a power is not unlimited. For instance, there are limits on taxing power imposed by the laws and constitutions of the different states. All of them have rules and often constitutional amendments that proscribe the types of taxes that can be imposed or how they might be levied. But second, there are also limits on their states' ability to tax that are imposed upon them by the United States Constitution. In *McCulloch* the Supremacy Clause was the reason cited precluding Maryland from taxing the Bank of the United States, but there are also other constitutional clauses involved, specifically, the Commerce, Due Process, Equal Protection, and Privileges and Immunities Clauses. These four clauses preclude a state from taxing in such a way that they it discriminates against out-of-state businesses or individuals or acts in a way that inappropriately interferes with interstate commerce. If states can avoid these problems, the Supreme Court has generally given states broad leeway to tax.

For example, there is no debate that states are able to tax the income of individuals who reside or domicile within their borders, but they may also tax, according to the Court in *Shaffer v. Carter* (252 U.S. 37, 1920) the income of individuals sourced or earned within their borders. Professional sports athletes are often required to pay income taxes in every state where in which they play their sports. Finally, in some circumstances, states may also be able to tax nonresidents working outside their borders if an individual elects to work out of state instead of working at a business that is located within the taxing state.

For many years the main constitutional problems with state taxation revolved around the issue of intergovernmental tax immunities. If *McCulloch* stood for the proposition that states could not tax the federal government, was the reverse not also true? Was the federal government precluded by, perhaps by the Tenth Amendment, from taxing state governments? In *Collector v. Day* (8 U.S. 113, 1871) the Supreme Court ruled invalid a federal income tax on the salary of a state judge. Yet in *Helvering v. Gerhardt* (304 U.S. 405, 1938) the Court held that the United States could levy nondiscriminatory taxes on the incomes of most state employees.

The next year, in *Graves v. New York ex rel. O'Keefe* (306 U.S. 467, 1939) the Court upheld the imposition of a state income tax on a federal employee. As a result of *Graves*, intergovernmental tax immunity precluded only those taxes that were imposed directly on one sovereign government by the other, or that discriminated against a sovereign.

But the *Graves* doctrine dissolved in *State of New York v. United States* (326 U.S. 572, 1946) when the Court upheld an excise tax on the sale of bottled water by a corporation operated by an individual state. Finally, in *South Carolina v. Baker* (485 U.S. 505, 1988) the Court ruled that a nondiscriminatory tax on the interest earned on state bonds did not violate the Tenth Amendment. For now, at least, the concept question of intergovernmental tax immunity seems to be on hold.

A second problem facing involving state taxation arises as a result of living in a federal system. At one point are state efforts to tax discriminatory? Can states tax products that are part of interstate commerce? In *Brown v. Maryland* (25 U.S. 419, 1827), as discussed above, the Supreme Court ruled that states could not tax products located in interstate commerce if products were still in their original package. Another question has been asked: Can states tax their own individuals and businesses at one rate and out-of-state ones at a different rate? In addition, if a business or a taxpayer is operating in several states, how are taxes to be apportioned? By that, what income can be used as a basis for a state levying a tax? These are some of the questions the cases to follow here address.

Henneford v. Silas Mason Co., Inc. (300 U.S. 577, 1937) involved a state tax on chattels purchased out of state but used within the Washington State. The Court upheld the tax, stating that it did not discriminate against interstate commerce because the goods were at the end of interstate commerce and now had been incorporated into Washington's commerce. If *Coe* said states could tax and regulate until the point when goods were sent on the journey into interstate commerce, *Henneford* seems to state that once they rest on the other end of their journey and come to rest in a state, they can again be taxed. Unfortunately, this case did not resolve or clarify the problems associated with the taxation of income located within interstate commerce. Instead, it was located in middle of a host of cases where the Court sought to construct apportionment rules regarding how much a state could tax of an activity or business that was engaging in interstate commerce, with a portion of that activity operating within its borders, a state could tax.

In *Henneford* the Court found that there was no burden on interstate commerce. But the case has led to a distinction between two types of taxes states may impose: "use" and "sales." Sales taxes are imposed when goods are sold within a state. For example, there may be a five 5 percent tax on the sale of cars, household good, clothes, or electronic items. A use tax is similar to a sales tax, except it is on the sale of goods from an out out-of-state merchant to a citizen within a state. To clarify, if I were to buy a television set at a store in my state, I may be required to pay a five 5 percent sales tax. But if I buy it from an out out-of-state company, I may still be required to pay a five 5 percent use tax. Most states impose both sales and use taxes. However, states cannot require all businesses to collect use taxes. If a business has a physical presence, such as a store, in a state, then it can be required to collect the use tax also.

In general, the Supreme Court has permitted states to impose a use tax without violating the Commerce Clause. Not only is a use tax on goods that have been carried through interstate commerce valid if nondiscriminatory, but a company engaged in interstate trade which has branches in the taxing state may be taxed on goods sent into that state on the basis of benefits received from the state. The basic principle is that goods can be subject to the state's normal taxes on arrival at destination through interstate commerce.

The above discussion has led to two constitutional issues that the courts have had to address. The first is in general, how to tax entities that do business in a specific state and also are engaged in interstate commerce? Second, when does a state have jurisdiction over an entity such that it can require it to collect use taxes? The Court has struggled with both of these questions, and the Court has offered several answers to this question.

In *Woodruff v. Parham* (8 Wall. 123, 1869) Alabama's sales tax on goods sold at auction in the packages in which they were sent through interstate commerce was upheld. The Court held that goods from another state are not "imports" under the terms of the Constitution, and taxes affecting them are valid unless discriminatory so as to burden interstate commerce. The word "import" in Article I, Section Sec. 10, Clause para. 2 was held to mean "from abroad," and here the sale was local. In *Plumley v. Massachusetts* (55 U.S. 461, 1894) a state statute prohibiting the sale of oleomargarine colored to resemble butter was upheld even though the product was from another state and sold in the original package. The Court ruled in *Austin v. Tennessee* (179 U.S. 343, 1900) that when cigarettes were shipped into a state in packages of ten, loose in open baskets, the Court held that these were not the "original packages" in which cigarettes were usually shipped. The state statute forbidding the sale of cigarettes was upheld. But in *Cook v. Marshall County* (196 U.S. 261, 1905) the Justices held that when cigarette packages often were shipped loose in a freight car, the Court also held that the "original package doctrine" did not apply and upheld an Iowa tax on cigarettes. No baskets were used in this instance.

In *Adams Express Co. v. Ohio State Auditors* (166 U.S. 185, 1897) the Court said that a state may tax a corporation engaged in interstate business on the state's proportionate share of both the tangible and intangible property of the corporation located within the state. In *New York Central & M. R. R. Co. v. Miller* (202 U.S. 584, 1906) it ruled that all of the railroad's cars were taxable in New York as the state of domicile. The cars were outside the state at irregular intervals, and the same cars did not make every trip. The state of origin, New York, was regarded as the permanent situs of the property. In *Western Union Telegraph Co. v. Kansas ex rel. Coleman* (216 U.S. 1, 1910) the Court held that even though a foreign (out-of-state) corporation can be excluded from the state, if it is admitted it cannot be forced, as a condition to doing intrastate business, to submit to a percentage tax on its total capitalization. This would be a denial of due process because of the taking of property beyond the jurisdiction of the state as well as an indirect burden on interstate commerce by placing a burden on domestic commerce in a situation where the two are inseparable. This case established the "unconstitutional conditions" doctrine, that is, a state cannot impose conditions which are themselves unconstitutional.

In *Northwest Airlines v. Minnesota* (322 U.S. 292, 1944) the Court ruled that Minnesota's tax of all of Northwest Airlines' fleet of planes, all of which were in Minnesota from time to time during the taxable year, was valid. Specifically, a state personal property tax may be applied to the entire fleet of airplanes of a corporation incorporated under the laws of the state, which had its principal place of business in the state, which used a city within the state for its home port, and none of whose planes were continuously without the state during the whole tax year, even though its planes operated in interstate commerce, without violation of the Commerce Clause or the Due Process Clause. This decision applied to airplanes a rule applied to ships—the "home port" rule. The Court applied the "home port theory" and noted that "No other State can claim to tax as the State of the legal domicile as well as the home State of the fleet, as a business fact. No other State is the State which gave Northwest the power to be as well as the power to function as Northwest functions in Minnesota; no other State could impose a tax that derives from the significant legal relation of creator and creature and the practical consequences of that relation in this case. On the basis of rights which Minnesota alone originated and Minnesota continues to safeguard, she alone can tax the personality which is permanently attributable to Minnesota and to no other State."

In *Braniff Airways v. Nebraska Board* (347 U.S. 590, 1954) the Court found Nebraska could assess an ad valorem tax on the flight equipment of an interstate carrier when that tax was fairly apportioned and there was adequate contact within the state by the carrier. Here the carrier made eighteen stops a day, and approximately one-tenth of its revenue was derived from the pick-up and discharge of Nebraska freight and passengers. The tax was not deemed to be a burden on interstate commerce. Whether an instrumentality of commerce has a sufficient tax situs within a state to allow it to be taxed is a due process question. States other than that of the corporate domicile can tax instrumentalities of commerce on an apportioned basis.

In *Spector Motor Service v. O'Connor* (340 U.S. 602, 1951) The Supreme Court ruled that a state may not tax a business simply on the basis of operating within the former's borders without violating the Commerce clause. But then in *Central R. Co. v. Pennsylvania* (370 U.S. 607, 1962) the Court ruled that Pennsylvania could impose a property tax on the freight cars of a railway whose tracks were entirely in Pennsylvania except, but that the railroad could obtain an exemption for that portion of its freight cars which were being taxed by another state, here New Jersey, because the cars were used regularly in that state. Pennsylvania was the domiciliary state.

Finally, in *Norfolk & Western Railroad Co. v. Tax Commission* (390 U.S. 317, 1968) the Court ruled invalid the tax formula of Missouri as a violation of the Commerce Clause and of due process. The formula was founded on an apportionment based on the percentage of miles of operation within the state. The company established that a great proportion of its rolling stock was never within the state and that the tax was unfair and confiscatory when computed as it had been.

Collectively, the above rulings created confusion over state taxation. But after decades of confusion, *Complete Auto Transit, Inc., v. Brady* (430 U.S. 274, 1977) offered clarity to the issue regarding how to apportion taxes when businesses are engaged in interstate commerce. According to the rule constructed in *Complete Auto Transit, Inc., v. Brady*, states may tax the income of entities doing business in several states. They may do so, so as long as the business has a substantial nexus or presence in the state, and the tax is fairly apportioned based on the percentage of the sales, income, or other factors, such as property derived from, or sourced, or located within that state.

While *Brady* addressed and clarified one issue, it left another open. Specifically, what did it mean to have a substantial nexus within a state? The rise of catalog and now Internet sales by out-of-state companies raises a new issue regarding the collection of sales taxes. This especially became an issue with the funding of Amazon.com n 1994 which heralded in a new era of significant on-line sale of goods. States are permitted to levy a tax on the sale of items within their borders. In addition, in order to ease enforcement of this requirement, they can also require businesses to collect these taxes directly from the consumer at the point of sale. States can also mandate that citizens of theirs making purchases from out-of-state companies through the mail or over the telephone are be required to pay a use tax. However, in *National Bellas Hess, Inc. v. Department of Revenue of Illinois* (386 U.S. 753, 1967) the Supreme Court ruled that the Commerce and Due Process Clauses precluded states from requiring these businesses to collect these use taxes. However, by the early 1990s the percentage of purchases coming from catalog or out-of-state sales had so dramatically increased, and states alleged they were losing so much uncollected revenue as a result, that some though thought it was ripe to challenge the *National Bellas Hess* rule.

Quill v. North Dakota (504 U.S. 298, 1992) offered some hope to states. If Congress so authorized it, the dormant Commerce Clause restriction on mandating the collection of use taxes could be lifted. Thus far Congress has not acted. Since the time the *Quill* case was decided, e-commerce, representing sales off on the Web and Internet, have has only accelerated the amount of purchases from out-of-state vendors who maintain no physical presence in a state. Estimates are that states are losing millions if not billions of dollars of use tax per year as a result.

One last challenge states are confronting is seen in *Comptroller of Treasury of Maryland v. Wynne,* 575 U.S. ___, 135 S.Ct. 1787 (2015), the problem of tax commuters and tax credits to other states. Increasing more and more individuals work across different jurisdictions or states, such as professional sports players. But there are also individuals who have a primary residence in one state and a vacation or secondary home in another state. Or some individuals simply have income being produced in another state. Individuals have tax obligations to all these states where their income is earned or sourced. Potentially it creates a problem of double taxation and the constitutional question is whether states must credit individuals for taxes they pay in another? In *Wynne* the Court said yes, invoking the Dormant Commerce Clause. The case is significant because as many states face pressures to cut taxes or as tax bases decline for a variety of reasons, tax collectors are loath to want to credit taxpayers for what they have paid out to another state. Simply put, it means less revenue for the former state. Thus, both technology and increased taxpayer mobility are creating dual problems for states as they seek to collect tax revenues.

HENNEFORD V. SILAS MASON CO., INC.

300 U.S. 577, 57 S.Ct. 524, 81 L.Ed. 814 (1937)

A statute of the state of Washington levied a tax of 2 percent of the purchase price on the use of chattels. This was not to apply to any tangible personal property already subjected to as great or a greater tax by Washington or any other state. This tax was challenged as a violation of the commerce clause. The company was a contractor on the Grand Coulee Dam on the Columbia River and had brought machinery and materials into the state.

Vote: 7–2

JUSTICE CARDOZO delivered the opinion of the Court.

. . . (1) The tax is not upon the operations of interstate commerce, but upon the privilege of use after commerce is at an end.

Things acquired or transported in interstate commerce may be subjected to a property tax, non-discriminatory in its operation, when they have become part of the common mass of property within the state of destination. . . . This is so, indeed, though they are still in the original packages. . . . For like reasons they may be subjected, when once they are at rest, to a non-discriminatory tax upon use or enjoyment. . . . The privilege of use is only one attribute, among many, of the bundle of privileges that make up property or ownership. . . . A state is at liberty, if it pleases, to tax them all collectively, or to separate the faggots and lay the charge distributively. Calling the tax an excise when it is laid solely upon the use . . . does not make the power to impose it less, for anything the commerce clause has to say of its validity, than calling it a property tax and laying it on ownership. "A non-discriminatory tax upon local sales . . . has never been regarded as imposing a direct burden upon interstate commerce and has no greater or different effect upon that commerce than a general property tax to which all those enjoying the protection of the State may be subjected." *Eastern Air Transport, Inc. v. South Carolina Tax Commission,* 285 U.S. 147 (1932). A tax upon the privilege of use or storage when the chattel used or stored has ceased to be in transit is now an impost so common that its validity has been withdrawn from the arena of debate. . . .

(2) The tax upon the use after the property is at rest is not so measured or conditioned as to hamper the transactions of interstate commerce or discriminate against them.

Equality is the theme that runs through all the sections of the statute. There shall be a tax upon the use, but subject to an offset if another use or sales tax has been paid for the same thing. This is true where the offsetting tax became payable to Washington by reason of purchase or use within the state. It is true in exactly the same measure where the offsetting tax has been paid to another state by reason of use or purchase there. No one who uses property in Washington after buying it at retail is to be exempt from a tax upon the privilege of enjoyment except to the extent that he has paid a use or sales tax somewhere. Everyone who has paid a use or sales tax anywhere, or, more accurately, in any state, is to that extent to be exempt from the payment of another tax in Washington.

. . . A state, for many purposes, is to be reckoned as a self-contained unit, which may frame its own system of burdens and exemptions without heeding systems elsewhere. If there are limits to that power, there is no need to mark them now. It will be time enough to mark them when a taxpayer paying in the state of origin is compelled to pay again in the state of destination. This statute by its framework avoids that possibility. The offsetting allowance has been conceded, whether the concession was necessary or not, and thus the system has been divested of any semblance of inequality or prejudice. A taxing act is not invalid because its exemptions are more generous than the state would have been free to make them by exerting the full measure of her power. . . .

The interlocutory injunction was erroneously granted, and the decree must be reversed.

JUSTICE MCREYNOLDS and JUSTICE BUTLER dissented.

FOR DISCUSSION

How does the Court draw a distinction between when a tax is permitted or not? Is it the same type of test as is used to distinguish between the use of the police power and burdens on interstate commerce?

COMPLETE AUTO TRANSIT, INC. V. BRADY

430 U.S. 274, 97 S.Ct. 1076, 51 L.Ed.2d 326 (1977)

The State of Mississippi sought to impose and collect taxes against Complete Auto Transit, Inc., a company doing business in that state and others. The company complained that the taxing formula used by Mississippi violated the commerce clause. Complete Auto Transit lost its argument and appeals, bringing the case to the Supreme Court.

Vote: 9–0

JUSTICE BLACKMUN delivered the opinion of the Court.

Once again we are presented with " 'the perennial problem of the validity of a state tax for the privilege of carrying on within a state, certain activities' activities' related to a corporation's operation of an interstate business."

I

The taxes in question are sales taxes assessed by the Mississippi State Tax Commission against the appellant, Complete Auto Transit, Inc., for the period from August 1, 1968, through July 31, 1972. The assessments were made pursuant to the following Mississippi statutes:

> 'There is hereby levied and assessed and shall be collected, privilege taxes for the privilege of engaging or continuing in business or doing business within this state to be determined by the application of rates against gross proceeds of sales or gross income or values, as the case may be, as provided in the following sections.
>
> 'Upon every person operating a pipeline, railroad, airplane, bus, truck, or any other transportation business for the transportation of persons or property for compensation or hire between points within this State, there is hereby levied, assessed, and shall be collected, a tax equal to five per cent of the gross income of such business . . . .' s. . . . § 10109(2), as amended.

Any person liable for the tax is required to add it to the gross sales price and, " 'insofar as practicable,' " to collect it at the time the sales price is collected. § 10117, as amended.

Appellant is a Michigan corporation engaged in the business of transporting motor vehicles by motor carrier for General Motors Corporation. General Motors assembles outside Mississippi vehicles that are destined for dealers within the State. The vehicles are then shipped by rail to Jackson, Miss., where, usually within 48 hours, they are loaded onto appellant's trucks and transported by appellant to the Mississippi dealers. Appellant is paid on a contract basis for the transportation from the railhead to the dealers.

By letter dated October 5, 1971, the Mississippi Tax Commission informed appellant that it was being assessed taxes and interest totaling $122,160.59 for the sales of transportation services during the three-year period from August 1, 1968, through July 31, 1971. Remittance within 10 days was requested. By similar letter dated December 28, 1972, the Commission advised appellant of an assessment of $42,990.89 for the period from August 1, 1971, through July 31, 1972. Appellant paid the assessments under protest and, in April 1973, pursuant to s 10121.1, as amended, of the 1942 Code (now s 27–65–47 of the 1972 Code), instituted the present refund action in the Chancery Court of the First Judicial District of Hinds County.

Appellant claimed that its transportation was but one part of an interstate movement, and that the taxes assessed and paid were unconstitutional as applied to operations in interstate commerce. The Chancery Court, in an unreported opinion, sustained the assessments.

Over the years, the Court has applied this practical analysis in approving many types of tax that avoided running afoul of the prohibition against taxing the "privilege of doing business," but in each instance it has refused to overrule the prohibition. Under the present state of the law, the Spector rule, as it has come to be known, has no relationship to economic realities. Rather it stands only as a trap for the unwary draftsman.

II

The modern origin of the Spector rule may be found in *Freeman v. Hewit,* 329 US 249 (1946). At issue in *Freeman* was the application of an Indiana tax upon " 'the receipt of the entire gross income' income" of residents and domiciliaries. Indiana sought to impose this tax on income generated when a trustee of an Indiana estate instructed his local stockbroker to sell certain securities. The broker arranged with correspondents in New York to sell the securities on the New York Stock Exchange. The securities were sold, and the New York brokers, after deducting expenses and commission, transmitted the proceeds to the Indiana broker who in turn delivered them, less his commission, to the trustee. The Indiana Supreme Court sustained the tax, but this Court reversed.

Mr. Justice Frankfurter, speaking for five Members of the Court, announced a blanket prohibition against any state taxation imposed directly on an interstate transaction. He explicitly deemed unnecessary to the decision of the case any showing of discrimination against interstate commerce or error in apportionment of the tax. He recognized that a State could constitutionally tax local manufacture, impose license taxes on corporations doing business in the State, tax property within the State, and tax the privilege of residence in the State and measure the privilege by net income, including that derived from interstate commerce. Nevertheless, a direct tax on interstate sales, even if fairly apportioned and nondiscriminatory, was held to be unconstitutional per se.

The prohibition against state taxation of the "privilege" of engaging in commerce that is interstate was reaffirmed in *Spector Motor Service v. O'Connor*, 340 U.S. 602 (1951), a case similar on its facts to the instant case. The taxpayer there was a Missouri corporation engaged exclusively in interstate trucking. Some of its shipments originated or terminated in Connecticut. Connecticut imposed on a corporation a "tax or excise upon its franchise for the privilege of carrying on or doing business within the state," measured by apportioned net income. Spector brought suit in federal court to enjoin collection of the tax as applied to its activities. The District Court issued the injunction. The Second Circuit reversed. This Court, with three Justices in dissent, in turn reversed the Court of Appeals and held the tax unconstitutional as applied.

The Court recognized that "where a taxpayer is engaged both in intrastate and interstate commerce, a state may tax the privilege of carrying on intrastate business and, within reasonable limits, may compute the amount of the charge by applying the tax rate to a fair proportion of the taxpayer's business done within the state, including both interstate and intrastate." It held, nevertheless, that a tax on the "privilege" of doing business is unconstitutional if applied against what is exclusively interstate commerce. The dissenters argued, on the other hand, that there is no constitutional difference between an "exclusively interstate" business and a "mixed" business, and that a fairly apportioned and nondiscriminatory tax on either type is not prohibited by the Commerce Clause.

The unsatisfactory operation of the *Spector* rule is well demonstrated by our recent case of *Colonial Pipeline Co. v. Traigle,* 421 U.S. 100 (1975). Colonial was a Delaware corporation with an interstate pipeline running through Louisiana for approximately 258 miles. It maintained a work force and pumping stations in Louisiana to keep the pipeline flowing, but it did no intrastate business in that State. In 1962, Louisiana imposed on Colonial a franchise tax for "the privilege of carrying on or doing business" in the State. The Louisiana Court of Appeal invalidated the tax as violative of the rule of *Spector.* The Supreme Court of Louisiana refused review. The Louisiana Legislature, perhaps recognizing that it had run afoul of a rule of words rather than a rule of substance, then redrafted the statute to levy the tax, as an alternative incident, on the "qualification to carry on or do business in this state or the actual doing of business within this state in a corporate form." Again, the Court of Appeal held the tax unconstitutional as applied to the appellant. But this time the Louisiana Supreme Court upheld the new tax.

By a 7-to-1 vote, this Court affirmed. No question had been raised as to the propriety of the apportionment of the tax, and no claim was made that the tax was discriminatory. The Court noted that the tax was imposed on that aspect of interstate commerce to which the State bore a special relation, and that the State bestowed powers, privileges, and benefits sufficient to support a tax on doing business in the corporate form in Louisiana. Accordingly, on the authority of Memphis Gas, the tax was held to be constitutional. The Court distinguished *Spector* on the familiar ground that it involved a tax on the privilege of carrying on interstate commerce, while the Louisiana Legislature, in contrast, had worded the statute at issue "narrowly to confine the impost to one related to appellant's activities within the State in the corporate form."

III

In this case, of course, we are confronted with a situation like that presented in Spector. The tax is labeled a privilege tax "for the privilege of . . . doing business" in Mississippi, s 10105 of the State's 1942 Code, as amended, and the activity taxed is, or has been assumed to be, interstate commerce. We note again that no claim is made that the activity is not sufficiently connected to the State to justify a tax, or that the tax is not fairly related to benefits provided the taxpayer, or that the tax discriminates against interstate commerce, or that the tax is not fairly apportioned.

The view of the Commerce Clause that gave rise to the rule of Spector perhaps was not without some substance. Nonetheless, the possibility of defending it in the abstract does not alter the fact that the Court has rejected the proposition that interstate commerce is immune from state taxation:

> It is a truism that the mere act of carrying on business in interstate commerce does not exempt a corporation from state taxation. 'It was not the purpose of the commerce clause to relieve those engaged in interstate commerce from their just share of state tax burden even though it increases the cost of doing business.

Not only has the philosophy underlying the rule been rejected, but the rule itself has been stripped of any practical significance. If Mississippi had called its tax one on "net income" or on the "going concern value" of appellant's business, the *Spector* rule could not invalidate it. There is no economic consequence that follows necessarily from the use of the particular words, "privilege of doing business," and a focus on that formalism merely obscures the question whether the tax produces a forbidden effect. Simply put, the *Spector* rule does not address the problems with which the Commerce Clause is concerned.* Accordingly, we now reject the rule of *Spector Motor Service, Inc. v. O'Connor*, that a state tax on the "privilege of doing business" is per se unconstitutional when it is applied to interstate commerce, and that case is overruled.

There being no objection to Mississippi's tax on appellant except that it was imposed on nothing other than the "privilege of doing business" that is interstate, the judgment of the Supreme Court of Mississippi is affirmed.

It is so ordered.

FOR DISCUSSION

What factors may a state consider when it taxes a business engaged in interstate commerce that also does business within its borders? If you were a state official, how would you tax professional sports teams that travel to your state? Would you tax a team and its players based on the number of games they played in your state, the number of days they are in your state, or some other rule? Why are states so interested in taxing professional sports players?

QUILL CORPORATION V. NORTH DAKOTA

504 U.S. 298, 112 S.Ct. 1904, 119 L.Ed.2d 91 (1992)

Quill was an out-of-state business that shipped products to customers within North Dakota even though it did not maintain a physical presence in that state. North Dakota sought to require the company to impose and collect a use tax on products sold in the state. The North Dakota Supreme Court upheld the tax, and Quill appealed.

Vote: 8–1

JUSTICE STEVENS delivered the opinion of the Court.

This case, like *National Bellas Hess, Inc. v. Department of Revenue of Ill.*, 386 U.S. 753 (1967), involves a State's attempt to require an out-of-state mail-order house that has neither outlets nor sales representatives in the State to collect and pay a use tax on goods purchased for use within the State. In *Bellas Hess* we held that a similar Illinois statute violated the Due Process Clause of the Fourteenth Amendment and created an unconstitutional burden on interstate commerce. In particular, we ruled that a "seller whose only connection with customers in the State is by common carrier or the United States mail" lacked the requisite minimum contacts with the State.

* It might be argued that "privilege" taxes, by focusing on the doing of business, are easily tailored to single out interstate businesses and subject them to effects forbidden by the Commerce Clause, and that, therefore, "privilege" taxes should be subjected to a per se rule against their imposition on interstate business. Yet property taxes also may be tailored to differentiate between property used in transportation and other types of property; an income tax could use different rates for different types of business; and a tax on the "privilege of doing business in corporate form" could be made to change with the nature of the corporate activity involved. Any tailored tax of this sort creates an increased danger of error in apportionment, of discrimination against interstate commerce, and of a lack of relationship to the services provided by the State. A tailored tax, however accomplished, must receive the careful scrutiny of the courts to determine whether it produces a forbidden effect on interstate commerce. We perceive no reason, however, why a tax on the "privilege of doing business" should be viewed as creating a qualitatively different danger so as to require a per se rule of unconstitutionality.

It might also be argued that adoption of a rule of absolute immunity for interstate commerce (a rule that would, of course, go beyond *Spector*) would relieve this Court of difficult judgments that on occasion will have to be made. We believe, however, that administrative convenience, in this instance, is insufficient justification for abandoning the principle that "interstate commerce may be made to pay its way."

In this case, the Supreme Court of North Dakota declined to follow *Bellas Hess* because "the tremendous social, economic, commercial, and legal innovations" of the past quarter-century have rendered its holding "obsole[te]." Having granted certiorari, we must either reverse the State Supreme Court or overrule *Bellas Hess*. While we agree with much of the state court's reasoning, we take the former course.

I

Quill is a Delaware corporation with offices and warehouses in Illinois, California, and Georgia. None of its employees work or reside in North Dakota, and its ownership of tangible property in that State is either insignificant or nonexistent. Quill sells office equipment and supplies; it solicits business through catalogs and flyers, advertisements in national periodicals, and telephone calls. Its annual national sales exceed $200 million, of which almost $1 million are made to about 3,000 customers in North Dakota. It is the sixth largest vendor of office supplies in the State. It delivers all of its merchandise to its North Dakota customers by mail or common carrier from out-of-state locations.

As a corollary to its sales tax, North Dakota imposes a use tax upon property purchased for storage, use, or consumption within the State. North Dakota requires every "retailer maintaining a place of business in" the State to collect the tax from the consumer and remit it to the State. In 1987, North Dakota amended the statutory definition of the term "retailer" to include "every person who engages in regular or systematic solicitation of a consumer market in th[e] state." State regulations in turn define "regular or systematic solicitation" to mean three or more advertisements within a 12-month period. Thus, since 1987, mail-order companies that engage in such solicitation have been subject to the tax even if they maintain no property or personnel in North Dakota.

Quill has taken the position that North Dakota does not have the power to compel it to collect a use tax from its North Dakota customers. Consequently, the State, through its Tax Commissioner, filed this action to require Quill to pay taxes (as well as interest and penalties) on all such sales made after July 1, 1987. The trial court ruled in Quill's favor, finding the case indistinguishable from *Bellas Hess*; specifically, it found that because the State had not shown that it had spent tax revenues for the benefit of the mail-order business, there was no " "nexus to allow the state to define retailer in the manner it chose."

The North Dakota Supreme Court reversed, concluding that "wholesale changes" in both the economy and the law made it inappropriate to follow *Bellas Hess* today. The principal economic change noted by the court was the remarkable growth of the mail-order business "from a relatively inconsequential market niche" in 1967 to a "goliath" with annual sales that reached "the staggering figure of $183.3 billion in 1989." Moreover, the court observed, advances in computer technology greatly eased the burden of compliance with a "welter of complicated obligations" imposed by state and local taxing authorities (quoting *Bellas Hess*).

Equally important, in the court's view, were the changes in the "legal landscape." With respect to the Commerce Clause, the court emphasized that *Complete Auto Transit, Inc. v. Brady*, 430 U.S. 274 (1977), rejected the line of cases holding that the direct taxation of interstate commerce was impermissible and adopted instead a "consistent and rational method of inquiry [that focused on] the practical effect of [the] challenged tax." This and subsequent rulings, the court maintained, indicated that the Commerce Clause no longer mandated the sort of physical-presence nexus suggested in *Bellas Hess*.

Similarly, with respect to the Due Process Clause, the North Dakota court observed that cases following *Bellas Hess* had not construed "minimum contacts" to require physical presence within a State as a prerequisite to the legitimate exercise of state power. The state court then concluded that "the Due Process requirement of a 'minimal connection' to establish nexus is encompassed within the *Complete Auto* test" and that the relevant inquiry under the latter test was whether "the state has provided some protection, opportunities, or benefit for which it can expect a return."

Turning to the case at hand, the state court emphasized that North Dakota had created "an economic climate that fosters demand for" Quill's products, maintained a legal infrastructure that protected that market, and disposed of 24 tons of catalogs and flyers mailed by Quill into the State every year. Based on these facts, the court concluded that Quill's "economic presence" in North Dakota depended on services and benefits provided by the State and therefore generated "a constitutionally sufficient nexus to justify imposition of the purely administrative duty of collecting and remitting the use tax."

II

As in a number of other cases involving the application of state taxing statutes to out-of-state sellers, our holding in *Bellas Hess* relied on both the Due Process Clause and the Commerce Clause. Although the "two claims are closely related," *Bellas Hess,* the Clauses pose distinct limits on the taxing powers of the States. Accordingly, while a State may, consistent with the Due Process Clause, have the authority to tax a particular taxpayer, imposition of the tax may nonetheless violate the Commerce Clause.

The two constitutional requirements differ fundamentally, in several ways. The Due Process Clause and the Commerce Clause reflect different constitutional concerns. Moreover, while Congress has plenary power to regulate commerce among the States and thus may authorize state actions that burden interstate commerce, it does not similarly have the power to authorize violations of the Due Process Clause. Thus, although we have not always been precise in distinguishing between the two, the Due Process Clause and the Commerce Clause are analytically distinct.

"Due process" and "commerce clause" conceptions are not always sharply separable in dealing with these problems. . . . To some extent they overlap. If there is a want of due process to sustain the tax, by that fact alone any burden the tax imposes on the commerce among the states becomes "undue." But, though overlapping, the two conceptions are not identical. There may be more than sufficient factual connections, with economic and legal effects, between the transaction and the taxing state to sustain the tax as against due process objections. Yet it may fall because of its burdening effect upon the commerce. And, although the two notions cannot always be separated, clarity of consideration and of decision would be promoted if the two issues are approached, where they are presented, at least tentatively as if they were separate and distinct, not intermingled ones.

III

The Due Process Clause "requires some definite link, some minimum connection, between a state and the person, property or transaction it seeks to tax," and that the "income attributed to the State for tax purposes must be rationally related to 'values connected with the taxing State.' " Here, we are concerned primarily with the first of these requirements. Prior to *Bellas Hess,* we had held that that requirement was satisfied in a variety of circumstances involving use taxes. For example, the presence of sales personnel in the State or the maintenance of local retail stores in the State justified the exercise of that power because the seller's local activities were "plainly accorded the protection and services of the taxing State." The furthest extension of that power was recognized in *Scripto, Inc. v. Carson*, 362 US 207 (1960), in which the Court upheld a use tax despite the fact that all of the seller's in-state solicitation was performed by independent contractors. These cases all involved some sort of physical presence within the State, and in *Bellas Hess* the Court suggested that such presence was not only sufficient for jurisdiction under the Due Process Clause, but also necessary. We expressly declined to obliterate the "sharp distinction . . . between mail-order sellers with retail outlets, solicitors, or property within a State, and those who do no more than communicate with customers in the State by mail or common carrier as a part of a general interstate business."

Our due process jurisprudence has evolved substantially in the 25 years since *Bellas Hess,* particularly in the area of judicial jurisdiction. Building on the seminal case of *International Shoe Co. v. Washington*, 326 U.S. 310 (1945), we have framed the relevant inquiry as whether a defendant had minimum contacts with the jurisdiction "such that the maintenance of the suit does not offend 'traditional notions of fair play and substantial justice.'" In that spirit, we have abandoned more formalistic tests that focused on a defendant's "presence" within a State in favor of a more flexible inquiry into whether a defendant's contacts with the forum made it reasonable, in the context of our federal system of Government, to require it to defend the suit in that State. In *Shaffer v. Heitner*, the Court extended the flexible approach that *International Shoe* had prescribed for purposes of *in personam* jurisdiction to *in rem* jurisdiction, concluding that "all assertions of state-court jurisdiction must be evaluated according to the standards set forth in *International Shoe* and its progeny."

Applying these principles, we have held that if a foreign corporation purposefully avails itself of the benefits of an economic market in the forum State, it may subject itself to the State's *in personam* jurisdiction even if it has no physical presence in the State. As we explained in *Burger King Corp. v. Rudzewicz*, 471 U.S. 462 (1985),

> Jurisdiction in these circumstances may not be avoided merely because the defendant did not *physically* enter the forum State. Although territorial presence frequently will enhance a potential defendant's affiliation with a State and reinforce the reasonable foreseeability of suit there, it is an inescapable fact of modern commercial life that a substantial amount of business is transacted solely by mail and wire communications across state lines, thus obviating the need for physical presence within a State in which business is conducted. So long as a commercial actor's efforts are "purposefully directed" toward residents of another State, we have consistently rejected the notion that an absence of physical contacts can defeat personal jurisdiction there.

Comparable reasoning justifies the imposition of the collection duty on a mail-order house that is engaged in continuous and widespread solicitation of business within a State. Such a corporation clearly has "fair warning that [its] activity may subject [it] to the jurisdiction of a foreign sovereign." *Shaffer v. Heitner*, 433 U.S. 186 (1977). In "modern commercial life" it matters little that such solicitation is accomplished by a deluge of catalogs rather than a phalanx of drummers: The requirements of due process are met irrespective of a corporation's lack of physical presence in the taxing State. Thus, to the extent that our decisions have indicated that the Due Process Clause requires physical presence in a State for the imposition of duty to collect a use tax, we overrule those holdings as superseded by developments in the law of due process.

In this case, there is no question that Quill has purposefully directed its activities at North Dakota residents, that the magnitude of those contacts is more than sufficient for due process purposes, and that the use tax is related to the benefits Quill receives from access to the State. We therefore agree with the North Dakota Supreme Court's conclusion that the Due Process Clause does not bar enforcement of that State's use tax against Quill.

IV

Article I, § 8, cl. 3, of the Constitution expressly authorizes Congress to "regulate Commerce with foreign Nations, and among the several States." It says nothing about the protection of interstate commerce in the absence of any action by Congress. Nevertheless, as Justice Johnson suggested in his concurring opinion in *Gibbons v. Ogden*, 22 U.S. 1 (1824), the Commerce Clause is more than an affirmative grant of power; it has a negative sweep as well. The Clause, in Justice Stone's phrasing, "by its own force" prohibits certain state actions that interfere with interstate commerce.

Our interpretation of the "negative" or "dormant" Commerce Clause has evolved substantially over the years, particularly as that Clause concerns limitations on state taxation powers. Our early cases, beginning with *Brown v. Maryland*, 25 U.S. 419 (1827), swept broadly, and in *Leloup v. Port of Mobile*, 127 U.S. 640 (1888), we declared that "no State has the right to lay a tax on interstate commerce in any form." We later narrowed that rule and distinguished between direct burdens on interstate commerce, which were prohibited, and indirect burdens, which generally were not and subsequent decisions rejected this formal, categorical analysis and adopted a "multiple-taxation doctrine" that focused not on whether a tax was "direct" or "indirect" but rather on whether a tax subjected interstate commerce to a risk of multiple taxation. However, in *Freeman v. Hewit*, [329 U.S. 249 (1946),] we embraced again the formal distinction between direct and indirect taxation, invalidating Indiana's imposition of a gross receipts tax on a particular transaction because that application would "impos[e] a direct tax on interstate sales." Most recently, in *Complete Auto Transit, Inc. v. Brady,* 430 U.S. 274 (1977), we renounced the *Freeman* approach as "attaching constitutional significance to a semantic difference." We expressly overruled one of *Freeman's* progeny, *Spector Motor Service, Inc. v. O'Connor*, 340 US 602 (1951), which held that a tax on "the privilege of doing interstate business" was unconstitutional, while recognizing that a differently denominated tax with the same economic effect would not be unconstitutional.

Bellas Hess was decided in 1967, in the middle of this latest rally between formalism and pragmatism. Contrary to the suggestion of the North Dakota Supreme Court, this timing does not mean that *Complete Auto* rendered *Bellas Hess* "obsolete." *Complete Auto* rejected *Freeman* and *Spector's* formal distinction between "direct" and "indirect" taxes on interstate commerce because that formalism allowed the validity of statutes to hinge on "legal terminology," "draftsmanship and phraseology." *Bellas Hess* did not rely on any such labeling of taxes and therefore did not automatically fall with *Freeman* and its progeny.

While contemporary Commerce Clause jurisprudence might not dictate the same result were the issue to arise for the first time today, *Bellas Hess* is not inconsistent with *Complete Auto* and our recent cases. Under *Complete Auto*'s four-part test, we will sustain a tax against a Commerce Clause challenge so long as the "tax [1] is applied to an activity with a substantial nexus with the taxing State, [2] is fairly apportioned, [3] does not discriminate against interstate commerce, and [4] is fairly related to the services provided by the State." *Bellas Hess* concerns the first of these tests and stands for the proposition that a vendor whose only contacts with the taxing State are by mail or common carrier lacks the "substantial nexus" required by the Commerce Clause.

The State of North Dakota relies less on *Complete Auto* and more on the evolution of our due process jurisprudence. The State contends that the nexus requirements imposed by the Due Process and Commerce Clauses are equivalent and that if, as we concluded above, a mail-order house that lacks a physical presence in the taxing State nonetheless satisfies the due process "minimum contacts" test, then that corporation also meets the Commerce Clause "substantial nexus" test. We disagree. Despite the similarity in phrasing, the nexus requirements of the Due Process and Commerce Clauses are not identical. The two standards are animated by different constitutional concerns and policies.

Due process centrally concerns the fundamental fairness of governmental activity. Thus, at the most general level, the due process nexus analysis requires that we ask whether an individual's connections with a State are substantial enough to legitimate the State's exercise of power over him. We have, therefore, often identified "notice" or "fair warning" as the analytic touchstone of due process nexus analysis. In contrast, the Commerce Clause and its nexus requirement are informed not so much by concerns about fairness for the individual defendant as by structural concerns about the effects of state regulation on the national economy. Under the Articles of Confederation, state taxes and duties hindered and suppressed interstate commerce; the Framers intended the Commerce Clause as a cure for these structural ills. It is in this light that we have interpreted the negative implication of the Commerce Clause. Accordingly, we have ruled that that Clause prohibits discrimination against interstate commerce

The *Complete Auto* analysis reflects these concerns about the national economy. The second and third parts of that analysis, which require fair apportionment and non-discrimination, prohibit taxes that pass an unfair share of the tax burden onto interstate commerce. The first and fourth prongs, which require a substantial nexus and a relationship between the tax and state-provided services, limit the reach of state taxing authority so as to ensure that state taxation does not unduly burden interstate commerce. Thus, the "substantial nexus" requirement is not, like due process' "minimum contacts" requirement, a proxy for notice, but rather a means for limiting state burdens on interstate commerce. Accordingly, contrary to the State's suggestion, a corporation may have the "minimum contacts" with a taxing State as required by the Due Process Clause, and yet lack the "substantial nexus" with that State as required by the Commerce Clause.

Moreover, a bright-line rule in the area of sales and use taxes also encourages settled expectations and, in doing so, fosters investment by businesses and individuals. Indeed, it is not unlikely that the mail-order industry's dramatic growth over the last quarter century is due in part to the bright-line exemption from state taxation created in *Bellas Hess*.

Notwithstanding the benefits of bright-line tests, we have, in some situations, decided to replace such tests with more contextual balancing inquiries. . . .

[A]lthough in our cases subsequent to *Bellas Hess* and concerning other types of taxes we have not adopted a similar bright-line, physical-presence requirement, our reasoning in those cases does not compel that we now reject the rule that *Bellas Hess* established in the area of sales and use taxes. To the contrary, the continuing value of a bright-line rule in this area and the doctrine and principles of *stare decisis* indicate that the *Bellas Hess* rule remains good law. For these reasons, we disagree with the North Dakota Supreme Court's conclusion that the time has come to renounce the bright-line test of *Bellas Hess*.

This aspect of our decision is made easier by the fact that the underlying issue is not only one that Congress may be better qualified to resolve, but also one that Congress has the ultimate power to resolve. No matter how we evaluate the burdens that use taxes impose on interstate commerce, Congress remains free to disagree with our conclusions. Indeed, in recent years Congress has considered legislation that would "overrule" the *Bellas Hess* rule. Its decision not to take action in this direction may, of course, have been dictated by respect for our holding in *Bellas Hess* that the Due Process Clause prohibits States from imposing such taxes, but today we have put that problem to rest. Accordingly, Congress is now free to decide whether, when, and to what extent the States may burden interstate mail-order concerns with a duty to collect use taxes.

Indeed, even if we were convinced that *Bellas Hess* was inconsistent with our Commerce Clause jurisprudence, "this very fact [might] giv[e us] pause and counse[l] withholding our hand, at least for now. Congress has the power to protect interstate commerce from intolerable or even undesirable burdens." In this situation, it may be that "the better part of both wisdom and valor is to respect the judgment of the other branches of the Government."

The judgment of the Supreme Court of North Dakota is reversed, and the case is remanded for further proceedings not inconsistent with this opinion.

It is so ordered.

JUSTICE WHITE, concurring in part and dissenting in part.

Today the Court repudiates that aspect of our decision in National Bellas Hess, Inc. v. Department of Revenue of Ill., which restricts, under the Due Process Clause of the Fourteenth Amendment, the power of the States to impose use tax collection responsibilities on out-of-state mail-order businesses that do not have a "physical presence" in the State. The Court stops short, however, of giving Bellas Hess the complete burial it justly deserves. In my view, the Court should also overrule that part of Bellas Hess which justifies its holding under the Commerce Clause. I, therefore, respectfully dissent from Part IV.

I

In Part IV of its opinion, the majority goes to some lengths to justify the *Bellas Hess* physical-presence requirement under our Commerce Clause jurisprudence. I am unpersuaded by its interpretation of our cases. In *Bellas Hess,* the majority placed great weight on the interstate quality of the mail-order sales, stating that "it is difficult to conceive of commercial transactions more exclusively interstate in character than the mail order transactions here involved." As the majority correctly observes, the idea of prohibiting States from taxing "exclusively interstate" transactions had been an important part of our jurisprudence for many decades, ranging intermittently from such cases as *Case of State Freight Tax,* 82 U.S. 232 (1872), through *Freeman v. Hewit*, and *Spector Motor Service, Inc. v. O'Connor.* But though it recognizes that *Bellas Hess* was decided amidst an upheaval in our Commerce Clause jurisprudence, in which we began to hold that "a State, with proper drafting, may tax exclusively interstate commerce so long as the tax does not create any effect forbidden by the Commerce Clause," *Complete Auto Transit, Inc. v. Brady,* the majority draws entirely the wrong conclusion from this period of ferment.

The Court attempts to paint *Bellas Hess* in a different hue from *Freeman* and *Spector* because the former "did not rely" on labeling taxes that had "direct" and "indirect" effects on interstate commerce. Thus, the Court concludes, *Bellas Hess* "did not automatically fall with *Freeman* and its progeny" in our decision in Complete Auto. I am unpersuaded by this attempt to distinguish *Bellas Hess* from *Freeman* and *Spector*, both of which were repudiated by this Court. What we disavowed in *Complete Auto* was not just the "formal distinction between 'direct' and 'indirect' taxes on interstate commerce," but also the whole notion underlying the *Bellas Hess* physical-presence rule—that "interstate commerce is immune from state taxation."

II

The Court next launches into an uncharted and treacherous foray into differentiating between the "nexus" requirements under the Due Process and Commerce Clauses. The Court explains that the Commerce Clause nexus requirement is not "like due process' 'minimum contacts' requirement, a proxy for notice, but rather a means for limiting state burdens on interstate commerce." This is very curious, because parts two and three of the *Complete Auto* test, which require fair apportionment and nondiscrimination in order that interstate commerce not be unduly burdened, now appear to become the animating features of the nexus requirement, which is the first prong of the *Complete Auto* inquiry. The Court freely acknowledges that there is no authority for this novel interpretation of our cases and that we have never before found, as we do in this case, sufficient contacts for due process purposes but an insufficient nexus under the Commerce Clause.

The cases from which the *Complete Auto* Court derived the nexus requirement in its four-part test convince me that the issue of "nexus" is really a due process fairness inquiry. . . .

. . . When the Court announced its four-part synthesis in *Complete Auto,* the nexus requirement was definitely traceable to concerns grounded in the Due Process Clause, and not the Commerce Clause, as the Court's discussion of the doctrinal antecedents for its rule made clear. For the Court now to assert that our Commerce Clause jurisprudence supports a separate notion of nexus is without precedent or explanation.

Even were there to be such an independent requirement under the Commerce Clause, there is no relationship between the physical-presence/nexus rule the Court retains and Commerce Clause considerations that allegedly justify it. Perhaps long ago a seller's "physical presence" was a sufficient part of a trade to condition imposition of a tax on such presence. But in today's economy, physical presence frequently has very little to do with a transaction a State might seek to tax. Wire transfers of money involving billions of dollars occur every day; purchasers place orders with sellers by fax, phone, and computer linkup; sellers ship goods by air, road, and sea through sundry delivery services without leaving their place of business. It is certainly true that the days of the door-to-door salesperson are not gone. Nevertheless, an out-of-state direct marketer derives numerous commercial benefits from the State in which it does business. These advantages include laws establishing sound local banking institutions to support credit transactions; courts to ensure collection of the purchase price from the seller's customers; means of waste disposal from garbage generated by mail-order solicitations; and creation and enforcement of consumer protection laws, which protect buyers and sellers alike, the former by ensuring that they will have a ready means of protecting against fraud, and the latter by creating a climate of consumer confidence that inures to the benefit of reputable dealers in mail-order transactions. To create, for the first time, a nexus requirement under the Commerce Clause independent of that established for due process purposes is one thing; to attempt to justify an anachronistic notion of physical presence in economic terms is quite another.

III

The illogic of retaining the physical-presence requirement in these circumstances is palpable. Under the majority's analysis, and our decision in *National Geographic Society v. California Bd. of Equalization,* 430 U.S. 551 (1977), an out-of-state seller with one salesperson in a State would be subject to use tax collection burdens on its entire mail-order sales even if those sales were unrelated to the salesperson's solicitation efforts. By contrast, an out-of-state seller in a neighboring State could be the dominant business in the putative taxing State, creating the greatest infrastructure burdens and undercutting the State's home companies by its comparative price advantage in selling products free of use taxes, and yet not have to collect such taxes if it lacks a physical presence in the taxing State. The majority clings to the physical-presence rule not because of any logical relation to fairness or any economic rationale related to principles underlying the Commerce Clause, but simply out of the supposed convenience of having a bright-line rule. I am less impressed by the convenience of such adherence than the unfairness it produces. Here, convenience should give way.

Also very questionable is the rationality of perpetuating a rule that creates an interstate tax shelter for one form of business—mail-order sellers—but no countervailing advantage for its competitors. If the Commerce Clause was intended to put businesses on an even playing field, the majority's rule is hardly a way to achieve that goal. Indeed, arguably even under the majority's explanation for its "Commerce Clause nexus" requirement, the unfairness of its rule on retailers other than direct marketers should be taken into account. I would think that protectionist rules favoring a $180-billion-a-year industry might come within the scope of such "structural concerns."

FOR DISCUSSION

After this decision, could Congress authorize or permit states to tax mail order or Internet businesses that do not have a physical presence within their borders? Under what authority? After this case, is the dormant Commerce Clause alive or dead?

RELATED CASE

Lunding v. New York Tax Appeals Tribunal: **522 U.S. 287 (1998).**

In a 6–3 opinion the Court ruled that the State of New York violated the Privileges and Immunities Clause of Art. 4 sec. 2 when it denied non-nonresidents an alimony tax deduction that was available to state residents.

COMPTROLLER OF TREASURY OF MARYLAND V. WYNNE

575 U.S. ___, 135 S.Ct. 1787, 191 L.Ed.2d 813 (2015)

Maryland taxpayers challenged assessment by state comptroller of county income tax without a credit for payment of out-of-state income taxes as a violation of the Commerce Clause. A tax court ruled in their favor. The Circuit Court, reversed and remanded. On appeal, the Maryland Court of Appeals, affirmed the Circuit Court's decision, and certiorari was granted.

Vote: 7–2

JUSTICE ALITO wrote for the Court.

We have long held that States cannot subject corporate income to tax schemes similar to Maryland's, and we see no reason why income earned by individuals should be treated less favorably. Maryland admits that its law has the same economic effect as a state tariff, the quintessential evil targeted by the dormant Commerce Clause. We therefore affirm the decision of Maryland's highest court and hold that this feature of the State's tax scheme violates the Federal Constitution.

II

A

The Commerce Clause grants Congress power to "regulate Commerce . . . among the several States." Art. I, § 8, cl. 3. These "few simple words . . . reflected a central concern of the Framers that was an immediate reason for calling the Constitutional Convention: the conviction that in order to succeed, the new Union would have to avoid the tendencies toward economic Balkanization that had plagued relations among the Colonies and later among the States under the Articles of Confederation." Although the Clause is framed as a positive grant of power to Congress, "we have consistently held this language to contain a further, negative command, known as the dormant Commerce Clause, prohibiting certain state taxation even when Congress has failed to legislate on the subject."

Under our precedents, the dormant Commerce Clause precludes States from "discriminat[ing] between transactions on the basis of some interstate element." This means, among other things, that a State "may not tax a transaction or incident more heavily when it crosses state lines than when it occurs entirely within the State." "Nor may a State impose a tax which discriminates against interstate commerce either by providing a direct commercial advantage to local business, or by subjecting interstate commerce to the burden of 'multiple taxation.' "

B

Our existing dormant Commerce Clause cases all but dictate the result reached in this case by Maryland's highest court. Three cases involving the taxation of the income of domestic corporations are particularly instructive.

In *J.D. Adams Mfg. Co. v. Storen,* 304 U.S. 307, 58 S.Ct. 913, 82 L.Ed. 1365 (1938), Indiana taxed the income of every Indiana resident (including individuals) and the income that every nonresident derived from sources within Indiana. The State levied the tax on income earned by the plaintiff Indiana corporation on sales made out of the State. Holding that this scheme violated the dormant Commerce Clause, we explained that the "vice of the statute" was that it taxed, "without apportionment, receipts derived from activities in interstate commerce." If these receipts were also taxed by the States in which the sales occurred, we warned, interstate commerce would be subjected "to the risk of a double tax burden to which intrastate commerce is not exposed, and which the commerce clause forbids."

The next year, in *Gwin, White & Prince, Inc. v. Henneford,* 305 U.S. 434 (1939), we reached a similar result. In that case, the State of Washington taxed all the income of persons doing business in the State. Washington levied that tax on income that the plaintiff Washington corporation earned in shipping fruit from Washington to other States and foreign countries. This tax, we wrote, "discriminates against interstate commerce, since it imposes upon it, merely because interstate commerce is being done, the risk of a multiple burden to which local commerce is not exposed."

In the third of these cases involving the taxation of a domestic corporation, *Central Greyhound Lines, Inc. v. Mealey,* 334 U.S. 653 (1948), New York sought to tax the portion of a domiciliary bus company's gross receipts that were derived from services provided in neighboring States. Noting that these other States might also attempt to tax this portion of the company's gross receipts, the Court held that the New York scheme violated the dormant Commerce Clause because it imposed an "unfair burden" on interstate commerce.

In all three of these cases, the Court struck down a state tax scheme that might have resulted in the double taxation of income earned out of the State and that discriminated in favor of intrastate over interstate economic activity. Maryland's tax scheme is unconstitutional for similar reasons.

For these reasons, the judgment of the Court of Appeals of Maryland is affirmed.

It is so ordered.

JUSTICE SCALIA, with whom JUSTICE THOMAS joins as to Parts I and II, dissenting.

The Court holds unconstitutional Maryland's refusal to give its residents full credits against income taxes paid to other States. It does this by invoking the negative Commerce Clause, a judge-invented rule under which judges may set aside state laws that they think impose too much of a burden upon interstate commerce. I join the principal dissent, which demonstrates the incompatibility of this decision with our prior negative Commerce Clause cases. Incompatibility, however, is not the test for me—though what is incompatible with our cases *a fortiori* fails my test as well. The principal purpose of my writing separately is to point out how wrong our negative Commerce Clause jurisprudence is in the first place, and how well today's decision illustrates its error.

I

The fundamental problem with our negative Commerce Clause cases is that the Constitution does not contain a negative Commerce Clause. It contains only a Commerce Clause. Unlike the negative Commerce Clause adopted by the judges, the real Commerce Clause adopted by the People merely empowers Congress to "regulate Commerce with foreign Nations, and among the several States, and with the Indian Tribes." Art. I, § 8, cl. 3. The Clause says nothing about prohibiting state laws that burden commerce. Much less does it say anything about authorizing judges to set aside state laws *they believe* burden commerce. The clearest sign that the negative Commerce Clause is a judicial fraud is the utterly illogical holding that congressional consent enables States to enact laws that would otherwise constitute impermissible burdens upon interstate commerce.

FOR DISCUSSION

Does *Wynne* give a constitutional right of individuals against double taxation? Could Congress authorize or permit states not to give credit to taxes paid in other states?

GLOSSARY

***Cooley* Doctrine:** A legal doctrine developed by the Supreme Court in *Cooley v. Board of Wardens* (1851) that permits state governments to regulate local commerce. It is also referred to as selective exclusiveness. The test is meant to draw a line between federal and state authority to regulate commerce.

***Complete Auto Transit, Inc. v. Brady* Test:** A multipart test formulated by the Court in *Complete Auto Transit, Inc., v. Brady* (1977) to determine when and how a state may tax a business operating in several states.

Discriminatory Burden on Interstate Commerce: Actions taken by a government that interfere with interstate commerce that are not legitimate acts of its police. This may include efforts to regulate wine sales that favor in-state businesses or limits on the length of trucks on highways.

Dormant Commerce Clause: A theory of constitutional law fashioned by the Supreme Court that bars states from certain types of activity that affect interstate commerce even if Congress has not prohibited it.

Government as a Market Participant: Activity of a government such as a state when it acts as an employer or a producer of a good or service. In acting as a market participant as opposed to being in its governmental role, a government may have more leeway to engage in some types of practices, such as favoring its own citizens at the expense of out-of-state residents.

Indian Gaming Regulatory Act of 1988: A law passed by Congress after the Supreme Court decision of *California v. Cabazon Band of Mission Indians* (1983) to regulate Indian gambling between tribes and states.

Intrastate Commerce: Commerce that takes place within one state or commerce that stands outside of the scope of regulation by the federal government. States have the authority to regulate intrastate commerce. Over time the Supreme Court has formulated various tests to distinguish intrastate commerce from interstate commerce.

Original Package Doctrine: A theory devised by the Supreme Court in *Brown v. Maryland* (1827) indicating that states could not require products in interstate commerce to be taxed if they were still in their original package. The purpose of this now discredited doctrine was to determine at what point states had the authority to regulate commercial activity.

Police Power: The authority of states to legislate for the health, safety, welfare, and morals of their residents.

Preemption: Occupation of a field of policy or issue by Congress that is so broad and pervasive that it prevents states from legislating on that topic for the same reasons that Congress did.

Protectionist Measures: Measures enacted by states to protect their own businesses by discriminating against out-of state businesses.

Selective Exclusiveness: A doctrine devised by the Supreme Court in *Cooley v. Board of Wardens* that states that regulations of commerce that require national uniformity can only be made by the federal government. Even if Congress has not acted, the states cannot act because such regulation is exclusively the domain of Congress. But where there are diverse local conditions, the states may act to regulate commerce in the absence of congressional regulation. Thus Congress's commerce power is that of selective exclusiveness.

SELECTED BIBLIOGRAPHY

Beer, Samuel H. 1993. *To Make a Nation: The Rediscovery of American Federalism*. Cambridge, MA: The Belknap Press of Harvard University Press.

Belz, Herman, Winfred Harbison, and Alfred H. Kelly. 1991. *The American Constitution, Its Origins and Development*, 2 vol. 7th ed. New York: W.W. Norton & Company.

Brunori, David. 1998. *The Future of State Taxation*. Washington, D.C.: Urban Institute Press.

Corwin, Edward S. 1936. *The Commerce Power Versus States' Rights*. Princeton, N.J.: Princeton University Press; London: H. Milford, Oxford University Press.

Currie, David P. 1985. *The Constitution in the Supreme Court: The First Hundred Years*, 1789–1888. Chicago: University of Chicago Press.

Currie, David P. 1990. *The Constitution in the Supreme Court: The Second Hundred Years*, 1888–1886. Chicago: University of Chicago Press.

Hellerstein, Jerome R., and Walter Hellerstein. 1997. *State and Local Taxation: Cases and Materials*. St. Paul, MN: Westgroup.

LaCroix, Alison L., 2010. *The Ideological Origins of American Federalism.* Cambridge, Mass.: Harvard University Press.

Leuchtenburg, William E. 1995. *The Supreme Court Reborn: The Constitutional Revolution in the Age of Roosevelt.* New York: Oxford University Press.

Mandelker, Daniel, et al. 2006. *State and Local Government in a Federal System.* Charlottesville, VA: LexisNexis.

Miller, William G. 2008. *Faith Reason, and Consent: Legislating Morality in Early American States.* New York: LFB Scholarly Publishing.

Simon, James F. 2003. *What Kind of Nation: Thomas Jefferson, John Marshall, and the Epic Struggle to Create a United States.* New York: Simon & Schuster Adult Publishing Group.

Valente, William D., et al. 2001. *Cases and Materials on State and Local Government Law.* St Paul, MN: West Group.

White, G. Edward. 1991. *The Marshall Court & Cultural Change: 1815–1835.* New York: Oxford University Press.

White, G. Edward. 2000. *The Constitution and the New Deal.* Boston: Harvard University Press, 2000.

Williams, Robert F. 2006. *State Constitutional Law: Cases and Materials.* Charlottesville, VA: LexisNexis.

CHAPTER VIII

Federal Power in Foreign Affairs

Timeline: Foreign Affairs and the Constitution

1776 United States colonies declare their independence from England.

1781 British General Cornwallis surrenders to George Washington at Yorktown, Virginia.

1783 Treaty of Paris signed between the United States and England, formally ending the Revolutionary War.

1831 In *Cherokee Nation v. Georgia* the Supreme Court refuses to issue an injunction halting the state of Georgia from expelling Indians from their borders.

1832 In *Worcester v. Georgia* the Supreme Court strikes down a state law regulating the behavior of non-Indians who live and work on Indian reservations.

1860 Abraham Lincoln is elected president of the United States.

1861 The shelling of Fort Sumter marks the beginning of the Civil War.

1863 In *The Prize Cases* the Supreme Court upholds the authority of the president to issue a blockade of ports located in the states of the Confederacy.

1866 In *Ex parte Milligan* the Supreme Court rules that military courts do not have the authority to try a civilian so long as the federal courts remain open within an area.

1914 World War I begins in Europe.

1917 The United States enters World War I.

1918 In the *Selective Draft Law Cases* the Supreme Court upholds a congressional military conscription act requiring service of all male citizens between the ages of twenty-one and thirty.

1919 World War I ends with the signing of the Treaty of Versailles.

1920 League of Nations created, without the United States joining as a member.

1920 In *Missouri v. Holland* the Court upholds a federal treaty that regulates the migratory birds between Canada and the United States over state objections that it violated its power.

1933 Adolph Hitler becomes chancellor of Germany.

1936 In *United States v. Curtiss-Wright Export Corporation*, the Court upholds an act of Congress empowering the president to embargo the shipment of articles of war to countries engaged in armed conflict.

1937 In *United States v. Belmont* the Supreme Court upholds an executive agreement between the president and the Soviet Union to address debts owed to U.S. citizens and corporations that were unpaid as a result of the 1917 Russian Revolution.

1939 Germany invades Poland, starting World War II.

1941 Japanese attack the U.S. naval base Pearl Harbor in Hawaii, and the United States enters World War II.

1944 In *Korematsu v. United States* the Supreme Court upholds an executive order relocating Japanese Americans living on the West Coast to internment camps.

1944 In *Ex parte Endo* the Supreme Court grants a habeas corpus request from a Japanese American citizen interned in a detention camp.

1945 President Truman orders the detonation of two atomic bombs in Japan, ending World War II.

1952 In *Youngstown Sheet and Tube v. Sawyer*, the Supreme Court declares that President Truman lacks the authority to seize steel mills to prevent a labor strike in order to prevent a disruption in production during the Korean War.

1964 North Vietnamese allegedly attack United States ships in the Gulf of Tonkin off the coast of North Vietnam.

1964 Gulf of Tonkin Resolution adopted by the two houses of Congress authorizing the president to "repel any armed attack against the forces of the United States and to prevent further aggression" in Vietnam.

1967 In *Mitchell v. United States* and *Mora v. McNamara*, the Supreme Court refuses to hear a case questioning the constitutionality of the Vietnam War.

1979 In *Goldwater v. Carter* a majority of the Supreme Court decides that a case brought questioning the authority of the president to cancel without Senate approval a defense treaty between the United States and Taiwan is either a political question or is not ripe for review.

1979 Iranian nationals raid the United States embassy in Tehran and take fifty-two Americans hostage.

1980 Ronald Reagan is elected president.

1981 American hostages in Iran are released the same day Ronald Reagan is sworn in as president.

1981 In *Dames & Moore v. Regan* the Supreme Court upholds an executive agreement with the president ending the Iranian hostage crisis and negotiating the settlement of debts between Iran and the United States.

1990 In *Perpich v. Department of Defense* the Supreme Court rejects claims by a state governor that his permission is needed before the president can deploy the National Guard for training outside of the United States.

2001 September 11 terrorist attacks on the United States.

2001 Authorization to Use Military Force by Congress declares that the "President is authorized to use all necessary and appropriate force against those nations, organizations, or persons he determines planned, authorized, committed, or aided the terrorist attacks that occurred on September 11, 2001."

2002 The Bush Administration designated the military base at Guantanamo Bay, Cuba to be a detention facility for individuals captured and suspected as being terrorists.

2004 In *Hamdi v. Rumsfeld* the Supreme Court rules that an American citizen cannot be held indefinitely on American soil without a right to habeas corpus review.

2005 In *Hamdan v. Rumsfeld* the Court rules that a Yemeni national held at Guantanamo Bay was entitled to habeas review of his detention and trial before a special military commission.

2008 In *Medellín v. Texas* the Supreme Court rules that the president could not order a state to give a Mexican national a new trial because it had failed to honor the terms of a treaty negotiated between that country and the United States.

2008 In *Boumediene v. Bush* the Court rules that the Military Commissions Act of 2006 (MCA), which sought to preclude courts from having habeas jurisdiction over detained aliens determined to be enemy combatants, provided inadequate substitution for habeas and that individuals detained at Guantanamo Bay were entitled to have civil courts review their detentions.

2016 The Obama Administration clarifies it policy for the use of military drones against suspected terrorists outside of US borders, including those who are American citizens.

Article II, Sec. 2:

The President shall be Commander in Chief of the Army and Navy of the United States, and of the Militia of the several States, when called into the actual Service of the United States. . . ."

Article I, Sec. 8:

The Congress shall have Power . . .

To declare War, grant Letters of Marque and Reprisal, and make Rules concerning Captures on Land and Water;

To raise and support Armies, but no Appropriation of Money to that Use shall be for a longer Term than two Years;

To provide and maintain a Navy;

To make Rules for the Government and Regulation of the land and naval Forces;

To provide for calling forth the Militia to execute the Laws of the Union, suppress Insurrections and repel Invasions; . . .

INTRODUCTION

The Constitution is textually rich with clauses in Article I and Article II that address matters of foreign policy and war and peace. There are numerous reasons for this. First, the American colonial experience with England and King George III raised concerns about the possibility that an executive could abuse his military and war-making powers. Second, under the Articles of Confederation the national government was weak, leading to situations where individual states effectively undertook their own foreign policies, often in ways inconsistent with the national government or other states. Finally, the decentralized nature of the Articles, along with the federalism of the new government created under the 1787 Constitution, demanded that there be clear lines of authority both between the states and national government, but also between Congress and the newly independent president.

If one examines the text of the Constitution, the number of clauses that define congressional as opposed to presidential power in the area of foreign policy and war-making powers seem to suggest that the former was meant to be the preeminent institution in these areas. Historical analysis also confirms this point. Over the years, presidents have increasingly taken control over foreign policy into their own hands. President Franklin Roosevelt, for example, carried the exercise of such prerogatives to a new level. Early in his first term, Congress had passed a resolution authorizing the president to regulate the exportation of arms and munitions of war to the point of complete embargo if he found certain specified conditions to exist.

That the federal government may exercise only powers granted by the terms of the Constitution is a truism of public law. However, the federal government operates not only internally but in foreign affairs as well, and it has come to be accepted doctrine that the strict doctrine of delegated powers applies to the federal government only in the field of domestic affairs. Since the federal government is the only entity in the United States recognized to carry on international relations, it must have plenary power in this field in dealing with the nations of the world. This was confirmed in *United States v. Curtiss-Wright Export Corp.* (299 U.S. 304, 1936), where the Court granted significant authority to the president and the national government to act in the field of foreign affairs.

The operation of foreign and military policy thus poses at least three constitutional dilemmas. The first involves the application of the constitutional division of labor in foreign as opposed to domestic relations. How do the principles of checks and balances and separation of powers apply when it comes to international affairs, especially those that take place outside the borders of the United States? A second question addresses the issue of national emergencies: When the country is at war, does the Constitution afford either the president or Congress special or extraordinary powers that are not expressly defined in its text?

Finally, a third constitutional dilemma lies at the intersection between the powers of Congress under Article I and presidential power under Article II. Under Article I, Sec. 8, Congress is given the **power to declare war**, raise and support armies and a navy, and undertake a host of other activities related to war and foreign policy. Under Article II, Sec. 2, the president is **commander in chief** of the army and navy (armed forces). This dual authority over war-making and foreign policy powers leaves open critical questions regarding when or where the power of Congress ends and that of the president begins. For example, does the president have inherent constitutional authority to start a war, deploy troops to defend the United States from attack, or undertake other military activities? In a world with nuclear capacities and international terrorism—especially since the attacks and events of 9/11—the issue became more pronounced in terms of the ability of the president to respond to an attack and, if necessary, deploy nuclear missiles in a matter of minutes, perhaps in the absence of congressional authorization or consultation. While the Vietnam War in the 1960s and 1970s and the terrorist attacks of September 11, 2001, brought up many constitutional issues testing the war-making powers of the two branches, the scope of presidential power to deploy troops goes far back in American history.

The cases in this chapter examine these three questions. They seek to define the division of labor between Congress and the president in the area of foreign and military affairs. The cases are also meant to describe how the Constitution addresses issues such as international law and its application to the United States, the ability of the courts to review matters addressing military and foreign policy issues, and the role that states may still retain in this area. Overall, as will become clear from examining these decisions, the role of the Constitution in deciding foreign policy raises difficult and often controversial legal issues.

INDIAN AFFAIRS

The relationship between Native Americans, the United States government, and the states is complicated. Indian territories in the United States are considered separate sovereign entities, and thus interaction between the United States and Native American tribes can be considered a type of foreign policy. The question remains whether state law can apply or regulate activities on tribal reservations. *Cherokee Nation v. the State of Georgia* (30 U.S. 1, 1931) and *Worcester v. Georgia* (31 U.S. 515, 1832) offer contrasting views on this question and on the role of the federal government in mediating disputes between states and sovereign tribes.

Cherokee Nation is important for both what the Court decided and what it did not. It held that Indians are sovereign, but not foreign sovereigns. Did that make them more like the other states? The Court was not clear. Second, the Court refused to hear their dispute, essentially ruling the matter to be a political question or dispute that would best be handled by Congress or the president. In essentially ruling this dispute a political question by saying it had no jurisdiction to hear the case, the Supreme Court established a precedent when it came to foreign affairs that could remain for quite some time . . . at least in theory. That precedent was that matters of foreign affairs, especially those involving military issues, were to be considered political questions resolved not by the judiciary but by Congress and the president. However, as other cases in this chapter will show, the political question doctrine often posed merely an intermittent or occasional limit upon the Court's involvement in foreign affairs.

In contrast to its decision in *Cherokee Nation*, the Court in *Worcester v. Georgia* did act, ruling that states could not impose their laws upon tribes because of the latter's sovereignty. In this case, Georgia could not evict several white missionaries from tribal lands because they had violated a state law. Chief Justice Marshall in *Worcester* articulated a theory of state-federal-tribal relations that remains good law to this day. This case is famous in part because the federal government was ordered to enforce this act. President Andrew Jackson allegedly retorted: "John Marshall has made his decision, now let him enforce it." Does the Court develop a clear theory of the relationship between states and tribes? How does the reasoning compare to the 1987 *California v. Cabazon Band of Mission Indians* (480 U.S. 202) decision (see Chapter VII, page 597)?

As a result of concern about due process rights in Indian territory, Congress passed in 1968 the Indian Civil Rights Act, which afforded ten rights that tribal governments could not violate. These included prohibitions against violations of freedom of speech, assembly, and religion, unreasonable searches and seizures, and cruel and unusual punishment.

THE CHEROKEE NATION V. THE STATE OF GEORGIA

30 U.S. 1, 5 Pet. 1, 8 L.Ed. 25 (1831)

The state of Georgia passed a series of laws that expelled members of the Cherokee Nation from their land. Members of the tribe traveled to Washington, D.C., and sought help from Congress to intervene on their behalf. When that effort failed, they sought original jurisdiction from the Supreme Court, requesting an injunction to order Georgia to halt their expulsion.

Vote: 6–2

JUSTICE JOHNSON delivered the opinion of the Court.

This bill is brought by the Cherokee nation, praying an injunction to restrain the state of Georgia from the execution of certain laws of that state, which, as is alleged, go directly to annihilate the Cherokees as a political society, and to seize, for the use of Georgia, the lands of the nation which have been assured to them by the United States in solemn treaties repeatedly made and still in force.

Before we can look into the merits of the case, a preliminary inquiry presents itself. Has this court jurisdiction of the cause?

The third article of the constitution describes the extent of the judicial power. The second section closes an enumeration of the cases to which it is extended, with "controversies" "between a state or the citizens thereof, and foreign states, citizens, or subjects." A subsequent clause of the same section gives the supreme court original jurisdiction in all cases in which a state shall be a party. The party defendant may then unquestionably be sued in this court. May the plaintiff sue in it? Is the Cherokee nation a foreign state in the sense in which that term is used in the constitution?

The counsel for the plaintiffs have maintained the affirmative of this proposition with great earnestness and ability. So much of the argument as was intended to prove the character of the Cherokees as a state, as a distinct political society, separated from others, capable of managing its own affairs and governing itself, has, in the opinion of a majority of the judges, been completely successful. They have been uniformly treated as a state from the settlement of our country. The numerous treaties made with them by the United States recognize them as a people capable of maintaining the relations of peace and war, of being responsible in their political character for any violation of their engagements, or for any aggression committed on the citizens of the United States by any individual of their community. Laws have been enacted in the spirit of these treaties. The acts of our government plainly recognize the Cherokee nation as a state, and the courts are bound by those acts.

A question of much more difficulty remains. Do the Cherokees constitute a foreign state in the sense of the constitution?

The counsel have shown conclusively that they are not a state of the union, and have insisted that individually they are aliens, not owing allegiance to the United States. An aggregate of aliens composing a state must, they say, be a foreign state. Each individual being foreign, the whole must be foreign.

This argument is imposing, but we must examine it more closely before we yield to it. The condition of the Indians in relation to the United States is perhaps unlike that of any other two people in existence. In the general, nations not owing a common allegiance are foreign to each other. The term *foreign nation* is, with strict propriety, applicable by either to the other. But the relation of the Indians to the United States is marked by peculiar and cardinal distinctions which exist no where else.

The Indian territory is admitted to compose a part of the United States. In all our maps, geographical treatises, histories, and laws, it is so considered. In all our intercourse with foreign nations, in our commercial regulations, in any attempt at intercourse between Indians and foreign nations, they are considered as within the jurisdictional limits of the United States, subject to many of those restraints which are imposed upon our own citizens. They acknowledge themselves in their treaties to be under the protection of the United States; they admit that the United States shall have the sole and exclusive right of regulating the trade with them, and managing all their affairs as they think proper; and the Cherokees in particular were allowed by the treaty of Hopewell, which preceded the constitution, "to send a deputy of their choice, whenever they think fit, to congress." Treaties were made with some tribes by the state of New York, under a then unsettled construction of the confederation, by which they ceded all their lands to that state, taking back a limited grant to themselves, in which they admit their dependence.

Though the Indians are acknowledged to have an unquestionable, and, heretofore, unquestioned right to the lands they occupy, until that right shall be extinguished by a voluntary cession to our government; yet it may well be doubted whether those tribes which reside within the acknowledged boundaries of the United States can, with strict accuracy, be denominated foreign nations. They may, more correctly, perhaps, be denominated domestic dependent nations. They occupy a territory to which we assert a title independent of their will, which must take effect in point of possession when their right of possession ceases. Meanwhile they are in a state of pupilage. Their relation to the United States resembles that of a ward to his guardian.

They look to our government for protection; rely upon its kindness and its power; appeal to it for relief to their wants; and address the president as their great father. They and their country are considered by foreign nations, as well as by ourselves, as being so completely under the sovereignty and dominion of the United States, that any attempt to acquire their lands, or to form a political connexion with them, would be considered by all as an invasion of our territory, and an act of hostility.

These considerations go far to support the opinion, that the framers of our constitution had not the Indian tribes in view, when they opened the courts of the union to controversies between a state or the citizens thereof, and foreign states.

In considering this subject, the habits and usages of the Indians, in their intercourse with their white neighbours, ought not to be entirely disregarded. At the time the constitution was framed, the idea of appealing to an American court of justice for an assertion of right or a redress of wrong, had perhaps never entered the mind of an Indian or of his tribe. Their appeal was to the tomahawk, or to the government. This was well understood by the statesmen who framed the constitution of the United States, and might furnish some reason for omitting to enumerate them among the parties who might sue in the courts of the union. Be this as it may, the peculiar relations between the United States and the Indians occupying our territory are such, that we should feel much difficulty in considering them as designated by the term *foreign state*, were there no other part of the constitution which might shed light on the meaning of these words. But we think that in construing them, considerable aid is furnished by that clause in the eighth section of the third article; which empowers congress to "regulate commerce with foreign nations, and among the several states, and with the Indian tribes."

In this clause they are as clearly contradistinguished by a name appropriate to themselves, from foreign nations, as from the several states composing the union. They are designated by a distinct appellation; and as this appellation can be applied to neither of the others, neither can the appellation distinguishing either of the others be in fair construction applied to them. The objects, to which the power of regulating commerce might be directed, are divided into three distinct classes—foreign nations, the several states, and Indian tribes. When forming this article, the convention considered them as entirely distinct. We cannot assume that the distinction was lost in framing a subsequent article, unless there be something in its language to authorize the assumption.

The counsel for the plaintiffs contend that the words "Indian tribes" were introduced into the article, empowering congress to regulate commerce, for the purpose of removing those doubts in which the management of Indian affairs was involved by the language of the ninth article of the confederation. Intending to give the whole power of managing those affairs to the government about to be instituted, the convention conferred it explicitly; and omitted those qualifications which embarrassed the exercise of it as granted in the confederation. This may be admitted without weakening the construction which has been intimated. Had the Indian tribes been foreign nations, in the view of the convention, this exclusive power of regulating intercourse with them might have been, and most probably would have been, specifically given, in language indicating that idea, not in language contradistinguishing them from foreign nations. Congress might have been empowered "to regulate commerce with foreign nations, including the Indian tribes, and among the several states." This language would have suggested itself to statesmen who considered the Indian tribes as foreign nations, and were yet desirous of mentioning them particularly.

It has been also said, that the same words have not necessarily the same meaning attached to them when found in different parts of the same instrument: their meaning is controlled by the context. This is undoubtedly true. In common language the same word has various meanings, and the peculiar sense in which it is used in any sentence is to be determined by the context. This may not be equally true with respect to proper names. *Foreign nations* is a general term, the application of which to Indian tribes, when used in the American constitution, is at best extremely questionable. In one article in which a power is given to be exercised in regard to foreign nations generally, and to the Indian tribes particularly, they are mentioned as separate in terms clearly contra-distinguishing them from each other. We perceive plainly that the constitution in this article does not comprehend Indian tribes in the general term "foreign nations," not we presume because a tribe may not be a nation, but because it is not foreign to the United States. When, afterwards, the term "foreign state" is introduced, we cannot impute to the convention the intention to desert its former meaning, and to comprehend Indian tribes within it, unless the context force that construction on us. We find nothing in the context, and nothing in the subject of the article, which leads to it.

The court has bestowed its best attention on this question, and, after mature deliberation, the majority is of opinion that an Indian tribe or nation within the United States is not a foreign state in the sense of the constitution, and cannot maintain an action in the courts of the United States.

If it be true that the Cherokee nation have rights, this is not the tribunal in which those rights are to be asserted. If it be true that wrongs have been inflicted, and that still greater are to be apprehended, this is not the tribunal which can redress the past or prevent the future.

The motion for an injunction is denied.

JUSTICE BALDWIN, concurring.

As jurisdiction is the first question which must arise in every cause, I have confined my examination of this, entirely to that point, and that branch of it which relates to the capacity of the plaintiffs to ask the interposition of this court. I concur in the opinion of the court in dismissing the bill, but not for the reasons assigned.

In my opinion there is no plaintiff in this suit; and this opinion precludes any examination into the merits of the bill, or the weight of any minor objections. My judgment stops me at the threshold, and forbids me to examine into the acts complained of.

Indians have rights of occupancy to their lands as sacred as the fee-simple, absolute title of the whites; but they are only rights of occupancy, incapable of alienation, or being held by any other than common right without permission from the government. In *Fletcher vs. Peck*, this court decided that the Indian occupancy was not absolutely repugnant to a seisin in fee in Georgia, that she had good right to grant land so occupied, that it was within the state, and could be held by purchasers under a law subject only to extinguishment of the Indian title. In the case of *Johnson vs. M'Intosh*, 8 Wheaton 543(1823), the nature of the Indian title to land on this continent, throughout its whole extent, was most ably and elaborately considered; leading to conclusions satisfactory to every jurist, clearly establishing that from the time of discovery under the royal government, the colonies, the states, the confederacy and this union, their tenure was the same occupancy, their rights occupancy and nothing more; that the ultimate absolute fee, jurisdiction and sovereignty was in the government, subject only to such rights; that grants vested soil and dominion, and the powers of government, whether the land granted was vacant or occupied by Indians.

JUSTICE THOMPSON, dissenting.

Entertaining different views of the questions now before us in this case, and having arrived at a conclusion different from that of a majority of the court, and considering the importance of the case and the constitutional principle involved in it; I shall proceed, with all due respect for the opinion of others, to assign the reasons upon which my own has been formed.

. . . By the constitution of the United States it is declared (Art. 3, § 2), that the judicial power shall extend to all cases in law and equity, arising under this constitution, the laws of the United States, and treaties made or which shall be made under their authority; &c. to controversies between two or more states, &c. and between a state or the citizens thereof; and foreign states, citizens or subjects.

The controversy in the present case is alleged to be between a foreign state, and one of the states of the union; and does not, therefore, come within the eleventh amendment of the constitution, which declares that the judicial power of the United States, shall not be construed to extend to any suit in law or equity commenced or prosecuted against one of the United States by citizens of another state, or by citizens or subjects of any foreign state. This amendment does not, therefore, extend to suits prosecuted against one of the United States by a foreign state. The constitution further provides, that in all cases where a state shall be a party, the supreme court shall have original jurisdiction. Under these provisions in the constitution, the complainants have filed their bill in this court, in the character of a foreign state, against the state of Georgia; praying an injunction to restrain that state from committing various alleged violations of the property of the nation, claimed under the laws of the United States, and treaties made with the Cherokee nation.

That a state of this union may be sued by a foreign state, when a proper case exists and is presented, is too plainly and expressly declared in the constitution to admit of doubt; and the first inquiry is, whether the Cherokee nation is a foreign state within the sense and meaning of the constitution.

The terms *state* and *nation* are used in the law of nations, as well as in common parlance, as importing the same thing; and imply a body of men, united together, to procure their mutual safety and advantage by means of their union. Such a society has its affairs and interests to manage; it deliberates, and takes resolutions in common, and thus becomes a moral person, having an understanding and a will peculiar to itself, and is susceptible of obligations and laws. Nations being composed of men naturally free and independent, and who, before the establishment of civil societies, live together in the state of nature, nations or sovereign states; are to be considered as so many free persons, living together in a state of nature. Every nation that governs itself, under what form soever, without any dependence on a foreign power, is a sovereign state. Its rights are naturally the same as those of any other state. Such are moral persons who live together in a natural society, under the law of nations. It is sufficient if it be really sovereign and independent: that is, it must govern itself by its own authority and laws.

We ought, therefore, to reckon in the number of sovereigns those states that have bound themselves to another more powerful, although by an unequal alliance. The conditions of these unequal alliances may be infinitely varied; but whatever they are, provided the inferior ally reserves to itself the sovereignty or the right to govern its own body, it ought to be considered an independent state. Consequently, a weak state, that, in order to provide for its safety, places itself under the protection of a more powerful one, without stripping itself of the right of government and sovereignty, does not cease on this account to be placed among the sovereigns who acknowledge no other power. Tributary and feudatory states do not thereby cease to be sovereign and independent states, so long as self government, and sovereign and independent authority is left in the administration of the state.

Testing the character and condition of the Cherokee Indians by these rules, it is not perceived how it is possible to escape the conclusion, that they form a sovereign state. They have always been dealt with as such by the government of the United States; both before and since the adoption of the present constitution. They have been admitted and treated as a people governed solely and exclusively by their own laws, usages, and customs within their own territory, claiming and exercising exclusive dominion over the same; yielding up by treaty, from time to time, portions of their land, but still claiming absolute sovereignty and self government over what remained unsold. And this has been the light in which they have, until recently, been considered from the earliest settlement of the country by the white people. And indeed, I do not understand it is denied by a majority of the court, that the Cherokee Indians form a sovereign state according to the doctrine of the law of nations; but that, although a sovereign state, they are not considered a foreign state within the meaning of the constitution.

FOR DISCUSSION

What does it mean for the Indians to be considered a sovereign nation? Constitutionally, are states precluded from interacting with Indian tribes? Should Indians be viewed differently from other sovereign nations? Given Johnson's opinion, can you ever envision the courts hearing claims between states and Indians?

WORCESTER V. GEORGIA

31 U.S. 515, 6 Pet. 515, 8 L.Ed. 483 (1832)

The state of Georgia had a law requiring whites who lived on Indian territory to obtain a license to do so. When seven missionaries living on Cherokee land refused to secure the licenses, they were arrested. They challenged the licensing requirement, arguing that Georgia had no authority to pass laws regulating behavior on Indian reservations.

Vote: 6–1

CHIEF JUSTICE MARSHALL delivered the opinion of the Court.

This cause, in every point of view in which it can be placed, is of the deepest interest.

The defendant is a state, a member of the union, which has exercised the powers of government over a people who deny its jurisdiction, and are under the protection of the United States.

The plaintiff is a citizen of the state of Vermont, condemned to hard labour for four years in the penitentiary of Georgia; under colour of an act which he alleges to be repugnant to the constitution, laws, and treaties of the United States.

The legislative power of a state, the controlling power of the constitution and laws of the United States, the rights, if they have any, the political existence of a once numerous and powerful people, the personal liberty of a citizen, are all involved in the subject now to be considered.

The defendant in the state court appeared in proper person, and filed the following plea:

> And the said Samuel A. Worcester, in his own proper person, comes and says, that this court ought not to take further cognizance of the action and prosecution aforesaid, because, he says, that, on the 15th day of July in the year 1831, he was, and still is, a resident in the Cherokee nation; and that the said supposed crime or crimes, and each of them, were committed, if committed at all, at the town of New Echota, in the said Cherokee nation, out of the jurisdiction of this court, and not in the county Gwinnett, or elsewhere, within the jurisdiction of this court: and this defendant saith, that he is a citizen of the state of Vermont, one of the United States of America, and that he entered the aforesaid Cherokee nation in the capacity of a duly authorised missionary of the American Board of Commissioners for Foreign Missions, under the authority of the president of the United States, and has not since been required by him to leave it: that he was, at the time of his arrest, engaged in preaching the gospel to the Cherokee Indians, and in translating the sacred scriptures into their language, with the permission and approval of the said Cherokee nation, and in accordance with the humane policy of the government of the United States for the civilization and improvement of the Indians; and that his residence there, for this purpose, is the residence charged in the aforesaid indictment; and this defendant further saith, that this prosecution the state of Georgia ought not to have or maintain, because, he saith, that several treaties have, from time to time, been entered into

between the United States and the Cherokee nation of Indians, [The Court cites twelve treaties from 1785 to 1819] all which treaties have been duly ratified by the senate of the United States of America; and, by which treaties, the United States of America acknowledge the said Cherokee nation to be a sovereign nation, authorised to govern themselves, and all persons who have settled within their territory, free from any right of legislative interference by the several states composing the United States of America, in reference to acts done within their own territory; and, by which treaties, the whole of the territory now occcupied by the Cherokee nation, on the east of the Mississippi, has been solemnly guarantied to them; all of which treaties are existing treaties at this day, and in full force. By these treaties, and particularly by the treaties of Hopewell and Holston, the aforesaid territory is acknowledged to lie without the jurisdiction of the several states composing the union of the United States; and, it is thereby specially stipulated, that the citizens of the United States shall not enter the aforesaid territory, even on a visit, without a passport from the governor of a state, or from some one duly authorised thereto, by the president of the United States: all of which will more fully and at large appear, by reference to the aforesaid treaties. And this defendant saith, that the several acts charged in the bill of indictment were done, or omitted to be done, if at all, within the said territory so recognized as belonging to the said nation, and so, as aforesaid, held by them, under the guarantee of the United States: that, for those acts, the defendant is not amenable to the laws of Georgia, nor to the jurisdiction of the courts of the said state; and that the laws of the state of Georgia, which profess to add the said territory to the several adjacent counties of the said state, and to extend the laws of Georgia over the said territory, and persons inhabiting the same; and, in particular, the act on which this indictment against this defendant is grounded, to wit, "an act entitled an act to prevent the exercise of assumed and arbitrary power, by all persons, under pretext of authority from the Cherokee Indians, and their laws, and to prevent white persons from residing within that part of the chartered limits of Georgia occupied by the Cherokee Indians, and to provide a guard for the protection of the gold mines, and to enforce the laws of the state within the aforesaid territory," are repugnant to the aforesaid treaties; which, according to the constitution of the United States, compose a part of the supreme law of the land; and that these laws of Georgia are, therefore, unconstitutional, void, and of no effect; that the said laws of Georgia are also unconstitutional and void, because they impair the obligation of the various contracts formed by and between the aforesaid Cherokee nation and the said United States of America, as above recited: also, that the said laws of Georgia are unconstitutional and void, because they interfere with, and attempt to regulate and control the intercourse with the said Cherokee nation, which, by the said constitution, belongs exclusively to the congress of the United States; and because the said laws are repugnant to the statute of the United States, passed on the ___ day of March 1802, entitled "an act to regulate trade and intercourse with the Indian tribes, and to preserve peace on the frontiers:" and that, therefore, this court has no jurisdiction to cause this defendant to make further or other answer to the said bill of indictment, or further to try and punish this defendant for the said supposed offence or offences alleged in the bill of indictment, or any of them: and, therefore, this defendant prays judgment whether he shall be held bound to answer further to said indictment.

This plea was overruled by the court. And the prisoner, being arraigned, plead not guilty. The jury found a verdict against him, and the court sentenced him to hard labour, in the penitentiary, for the term of four years.

By overruling this plea, the court decided that the matter it contained was not a bar to the action. The plea, therefore, must be examined, for the purpose of determining whether it makes a case which brings the party within the provisions of the twenty-fifth section of the "act to establish the judicial courts of the United States."

The plea avers, that the residence, charged in the indictment, was under the authority of the president of the United States, and with the permission and approval of the Cherokee nation. That the treaties, subsisting between the United States, and the Cherokees, acknowledge their right as a sovereign nation to govern themselves and all persons who have settled within their territory, free from any right of legislative interference by the several states composing the United States of America. That the act under which the prosecution was instituted is repugnant to the said treaties, and is, therefore, unconstitutional and void. That the said act is, also, unconstitutional; because it interferes with, and attempts to regulate and control, the intercourse with the Cherokee nation, which belongs, exclusively, to congress; and, because, also, it is repugnant to the statute of the United States, entitled "an act to regulate trade and intercourse with the Indian tribes, and to preserve peace on the frontiers."

It enacts that "all white persons, residing within the limits of the Cherokee nation on the 1st day of March next, or at any time thereafter, without a license or permit from his excellency the governor, or from such agent as his excellency the governor shall authorise to grant such permit or license, and who shall not have taken the oath hereinafter required, shall be guilty of a high misdemeanour, and, upon conviction thereof, shall be punished by confinement to the penitentiary, at hard labour, for a term not less than four years."

The eleventh section authorises the governor, should he deem it necessary for the protection of the mines, or the enforcement of the laws in force within the Cherokee nation, to raise and organize a guard."

The thirteenth section enacts, "that the said guard or any member of them, shall be, and they are hereby authorised and empowered to arrest any person legally charged with or detected in a violation of the laws of this state, and to convey, as soon as practicable, the person so arrested, before a justice of the peace, judge of the superior, or justice of inferior court of this state, to be dealt with according to law.' "

The extra-territorial power of every legislature being limited in its action, to its own citizens or subjects, the very passage of this act is an assertion of jurisdiction over the Cherokee nation, and of the rights and powers consequent on jurisdiction.

The first step, then, in the inquiry, which the constitution and laws impose on this court, is an examination of the rightfulness of this claim.

America, separated from Europe by a wide ocean, was inhabited by a distinct people, divided into separate nations, independent of each other and of the rest of the world, having institutions of their own, and governing themselves by their own laws. It is difficult to comprehend the proposition, that the inhabitants of either quarter of the globe could have rightful original claims of dominion over the inhabitants of the other, or over the lands they occupied; or that the discovery of either by the other should give the discoverer rights in the country discovered, which annulled the pre-existing rights of its ancient possessors.

After lying concealed for a series of ages, the enterprise of Europe, guided by nautical science, conducted some of her adventurous sons into this western world. They found it in possession of a people who had made small progress in agriculture or manufactures, and whose general employment was war, hunting, and fishing.

Did these adventurers, by sailing along the coast, and occasionally landing on it, acquire for the several governments to whom they belonged, or by whom they were commissioned, a rightful property in the soil, from the Atlantic to the Pacific; or rightful dominion over the numerous people who occupied it? Or has nature, or the great Creator of all things, conferred these rights over hunters and fishermen, on agriculturists and manufacturers?

But power, war, conquest, give rights, which, after possession, are conceded by the world; and which can never be controverted by those on whom they descend. We proceed, then, to the actual state of things, having glanced at their origin; because holding it in our recollection might shed some light on existing pretensions.

The great maritime powers of Europe discovered and visited different parts of this continent at nearly the same time. The object was too immense for any one of them to grasp the whole; and the claimants were too powerful to submit to the exclusive or unreasonable pretensions of any single potentate. To avoid bloody conflicts, which might terminate disastrously to all, it was necessary for the nations of Europe to establish some principle which all would acknowledge, and which should decide their respective rights as between themselves. This principle, suggested by the actual state of things, was, "that discovery gave title to the government by whose subjects or by whose authority it was made, against all other European governments, which title might be consummated by possession."

This principle, acknowledged by all Europeans, because it was the interest of all to acknowledge it, gave to the nation making the discovery, as its inevitable consequence, the sole right of acquiring the soil and of making settlements on it. It was an exclusive principle which shut out the right of competition among those who had agreed to it; not one which could annul the previous rights of those who had not agreed to it. It regulated the right given by discovery among the European discoverers; but could not affect the rights of those already in possession, either as aboriginal occupants, or as occupants by virtue of a discovery made before the memory of man. It gave the exclusive right to purchase, but did not found that right on a denial of the right of the possessor to sell.

The relation between the Europeans and the natives was determined in each case by the particular government which asserted and could maintain this pre-emptive privilege in the particular place. The United States succeeded to all the claims of Great Britain, both territorial and political; but no attempt, so far as is known, has been made to enlarge them. So far as they existed merely in theory, or were in their nature only exclusive of the claims of other European nations, they still retain their original character, and remain dormant. So far as they have been practically exerted, they exist in fact, are understood by both parties, are asserted by the one, and admitted by the other.

The general views of Great Britain, with regard to the Indians, were detailed by Mr Stuart, superintendent of Indian affairs, in a speech delivered at Mobile, in presence of several persons of distinction, soon after the peace of 1763. Towards the conclusion he says, "lastly, I inform you that it is the king's order to all his governors and subjects, to treat Indians with justice and humanity, and to forbear all encroachments on the territories allotted to them; accordingly, all individuals are prohibited from purchasing any of your lands; but, as you know that, as your white brethren cannot feed you when you visit them unless you give them ground to plant, it is expected that you will cede lands to the king for that purpose. But, whenever you shall be pleased to surrender any of your territories to his majesty, it must be done, for the future, at a public meeting of your nation, when the governors of the provinces, or the superintendent shall be present, and obtain the consent of all your people. The boundaries of your hunting grounds will be accurately fixed, and no settlement permitted to be made upon them. As you may be assured that all treaties with your people will be faithfully kept, so it is expected that you, also, will be careful strictly to observe them."

During the war of the revolution, the Cherokees took part with the British. After its termination, the United States, though desirous of peace, did not feel its necessity so strongly as while the war continued. Their political situation being changed, they might very well think it advisable to assume a higher tone, and to impress on the Cherokees the same respect for congress which was before felt for the king of Great Britain. This may account for the language of the treaty of Hopewell. There is the more reason for supposing that the Cherokee chiefs were not very critical judges of the language, from the fact that every one makes his mark; no chief was capable of signing his name. It is probable the treaty was interpreted to them.

The treaty is introduced with the declaration, that "the commissioners plenipotentiary of the United States give peace to all the Cherokees, and receive them into the favour and protection of the United States of America, on the following conditions."

When the United States gave peace, did they not also receive it? Were not both parties desirous of it? If we consult the history of the day, does it not inform us that the United States were at least as anxious to obtain it as the Cherokees? We may ask, further: did the Cherokees come to the seat of the American government to solicit peace; or, did the American commissioners go to them to obtain it? The treaty was made at Hopewell, not at New York. The word "give," then, has no real importance attached to it.

The first and second articles stipulate for the mutual restoration of prisoners, and are of course equal.

The third article acknowledges the Cherokees to be under the protection of the United States of America, and of no other power.

This stipulation is found in Indian treaties, generally. It was introduced into their treaties with Great Britain; and may probably be found in those with other European powers. Its origin may be traced to the nature of their connexion with those powers; and its true meaning is discerned in their relative situation.

The same stipulation entered into with the United States, is undoubtedly to be construed in the same manner. They receive the Cherokee nation into their favor and protection. The Cherokees acknowledge themselves to be under the protection of the United States, and of no other power. Protection does not imply the destruction of the protected. The manner in which this stipulation was understood by the American government, is explained by the language and acts of our first president.

The fourth article draws the boundary between the Indians and the citizens of the United States. But, in describing this boundary, the term "allotted" and the term "hunting ground" are used.

From the commencement of our government, congress has passed acts to regulate trade and intercourse with the Indians; which treat them as nations, respect their rights, and manifest a firm purpose to afford that protection which treaties stipulate. All these acts, and especially that of 1802, which is still in force, manifestly consider the several Indian nations as distinct political communities, having territorial boundaries, within which their authority is exclusive, and having a right to all the lands within those boundaries, which is not only acknowledged, but guarantied by the United States.

The Indian nations had always been considered as distinct, independent political communities, retaining their original natural rights, as the undisputed possessors of the soil, from time immemorial, with the single exception of that imposed by irresistible power, which excluded them from intercourse with any other European potentate than the first discoverer of the coast of the particular region claimed: and this was a restriction which those European potentates imposed on themselves, as well as on the Indians. The very term "nation," so generally applied to them, means "a people distinct from others." The constitution, by declaring treaties already made, as well as those to be made, to be the supreme law of the land, has adopted and sanctioned the previous treaties with the Indian nations, and consequently admits their rank among those powers who are capable of making treaties. The words "treaty" and "nation" are words of our own language, selected in our diplomatic and legislative proceedings, by ourselves, having each a definite and well understood meaning. We have applied them to Indians, as we have applied them to the other nations of the earth. They are applied to all in the same sense.

The Cherokee nation, then, is a distinct community occupying its own territory, with boundaries accurately described, in which the laws of Georgia can have no force, and which the citizens of Georgia have no right to enter, but with the assent of the Cherokees themselves, or in conformity with treaties, and with the acts of congress. The whole intercourse between the United States and this nation, is, by our constitution and laws, vested in the government of the United States.

The act of the state of Georgia, under which the plaintiff in error was prosecuted, is consequently void, and the judgment a nullity. Can this court revise, and reverse it?

If the objection to the system of legislation, lately adopted by the legislature of Georgia, in relation to the Cherokee nation, was confined to its extra-territorial operation, the objection, though complete, so far as respected mere right, would give this court no power over the subject.

But it goes much further. If the review which has been taken be correct, and we think it is, the acts of Georgia are repugnant to the constitution, laws, and treaties of the United States.

They interfere forcibly with the relations established between the United States and the Cherokee nation, the regulation of which, according to the settled principles of our constitution, are committed exclusively to the government of the union.

They are in direct hostility with treaties, repeated in a succession of years, which mark out the boundary that separates the Cherokee country from Georgia; guaranty to them all the land within their boundary; solemnly pledge the faith of the United States to restrain their citizens from trespassing on it; and recognize the pre-existing power of the nation to govern itself.

They are in equal hostility with the acts of congress for regulating this intercourse, and giving effect to the treaties.

The forcible seizure and abduction of the plaintiff in error, who was residing in the nation with its permission, any by authority of the president of the United States, is also a violation of the acts which authorise the chief magistrate to exercise this authority.

FOR DISCUSSION

What facts distinguish this case from Johnson's ruling in the previous one? Why is the Court willing to decide this case? Constitutionally, is there a difference? Are Indian affairs exclusively a federal matter?

RELATED CASES

***Williams v. Lee:* 358 U.S. 217 (1959).**

The Court ruled that tribal courts have exclusive jurisdiction in civil matters involving their tribal members that arise from disputes arising out of Indian country.

***Central Machinery Company v. Arizona State Tax Commission:* 448 U.S. 160 (1980).**

The Court held that federal Indian law preempts the levying of state taxes on businesses in Indian territory.

***Santa Clara Pueblo v. Martinez:* 436 U.S. 49 (1978).**

The Court ruled that tribal sovereignty included sovereign immunity against lawsuits.

PRESIDENTIAL POWER

Debates since the Vietnam War and the terrorist attacks of 9/11 about presidential power in foreign affairs actually have a precedent in the early days of American history. Defenders of executive power often point to a statement by John Marshall (not in his capacity as chief justice) that the president is the "sole organ" in foreign affairs. In so doing, defenders of presidential power look to the Commander-in-Chief Clause as support for executive supremacy in foreign and military affairs. They also note that the president, unlike Congress, may be able to act quickly to respond to emergencies. Conversely, defenders of congressional supremacy or authority point to the text of the Constitution, which gives more explicit foreign and military power to the Congress than to the president. They also cite debates at the time of the writing of the Constitution, which tend to suggest that the Framers favored giving more authority in foreign affairs to Congress than to the president.

Many of the major issues testing the intersection between presidential and congressional authority in this area first arose during the Civil War. At that time, important questions about the presidential power of Abraham Lincoln to embargo ships and try individuals for conspiring against the Union North, among other asserted powers, were first raised before the courts.

Immediately after the fall of Fort Sumter in April of 1861, President Lincoln ordered a blockade of all southern ports. As a result of the enforcement of this blockade, four ships were seized and taken to port to be held as prizes. In *The Prize Cases* (67 U.S. 635, 1963) the owners of the ships contended that the seizure was illegal since a blockade was a belligerent act and could not be undertaken in the absence of a declaration of war by Congress. In permitting President Lincoln to act, the Court made a distinction between "declaring" war and "making" or "conducting" war. This phraseology was changed at the Constitutional Convention.

The Court also draws upon international law in helping it to understand presidential power. In doing this, the Court engaged in what has recently become a controversial issue. Specifically, what is the status of international law in relation to the Constitution and American law? Some argue that American courts should not cite foreign law and that it is not binding upon the United States, except in rare circumstances when it opts to import it into domestic law. Others contend that it is binding on the United States and that it can change legal obligations and perhaps even the Constitution. This debate is pursued in the *Missouri v. Holland* (252 U.S. 416, 1920) case.

Ex parte Milligan (71 U.S. 2, 1866) is another Civil War era precedent that has assumed renewed importance in light of the war on terrorism begun by President George Bush after the events of 9/11. In *Milligan* the military used its courts to try a civilian who sought to steal guns and attack the United States. He was tried, found guilty, and sentenced to hang. However, he appealed his case to the Supreme Court, seeking habeas corpus review of his trial and conviction. The Court ruled in his favor, arguing that unless the civilian courts were not functioning, a civilian could not be tried in military courts. The decision placed tight limits on when habeas corpus could be suspended (it was permitted here), but it also placed even tighter restrictions on when, where, and who could be tried in what type of courts. *Milligan* would become a critical precedent often debated when terrorist suspects were detained as enemy combatants at the U.S. Naval Base at Guantánamo Bay in Cuba and denied habeas relief by the president and Congress.

United States v. Curtiss-Wright Export Corporation (299 U.S. 304, 1936) raises important constitutional questions. The Court distinguishes between federal activities in domestic matters and those in foreign affairs. The former are strictly limited by the doctrine of delegated powers and the Tenth Amendment. The latter are plenary powers and brook no interference on the part of the states. In the area of foreign relations, the power belongs to the federal government. Included here are such matters as the powers of Congress, the power of the president, and limitations on Congress such as delegation of legislative power. Only the federal government has the powers of external sovereignty. The states are unknown in the field of international relations. Only the federal government may speak there, and the president is its chief spokesperson—the voice of America.

The conduct of foreign relations, at least according to the *Curtiss-Wright* Court, is an inherent power of the federal government under international law. There are no limitations on it in the Constitution except such incidentals as the procedure for the making of treaties. Also, Article I, Section 10 of the U.S. Constitution forbids states from entering the field of foreign relations. The opinion in *Curtiss-Wright* does not authorize the president to act contrary to a statute. However, the precedent may allow the president to claim extraconstitutional powers or authority in foreign affairs. Can he make this claim absent congressional authorization? Could Congress authorize the president to exercise authority in foreign affairs that separation of powers would not normally permit domestically? Note also Sutherland's thesis about the states and the passage of foreign policy power to the national government. Does it leave room for states in foreign policy? It seems to suggest that the Tenth

Amendment is not a bar in foreign affairs. Is that accurate? In 2008 the Court in *Medellín v. Texas* (552 U.S. 491, 2008) disagreed with that assertion.

Finally, much of the opinion is dictum (i.e., incidental remarks that are *not* law and *not* binding. Moreover, the statement by the Court in *Curtiss-Wright* that international powers were transmitted to the central government by the British Crown may not be entirely historically accurate, but this point is not basic to the decision. The fact is that the federal government has complete control over international matters.

Youngstown Sheet and Tube v. Sawyer (343 U.S. 579, 1952) also known as the "Steel Seizure" case, may be one of the most influential cases on foreign policy in the Court's history—at least it has become so. While the Court struck down President Truman's effort to nationalize the steel industry in order to avert a strike and the interruption of steel production during the Korean War, the case is not read as detrimental to presidential power and authority. The various opinions describe legal scenarios that might support significant presidential power in foreign policy matters, or at least issues that take place beyond U.S. borders. It is important to read the opinion as providing an outline for what types of foreign policy authority the president does have. Most importantly, Justice Jackson's opinion is often the most cited part of the *Youngstown* decision. It describes a tripartite division of presidential power in foreign affairs depending on whether the chief executive is acting alone or with or against congressional approval. Presidents from Lyndon Johnson to George Bush cite it to support their military adventures, especially when they can point to congressional resolutions endorsing their actions. It seems to suggest, following *Curtiss-Wright*, that Congress can augment presidential power in foreign affairs by authorizing the chief executive to act. But as you read the Jackson opinion, think about the limits to that authorization. For example, can Congress authorize the president to act in a way contrary to the Constitution?

Conversely, how far can Congress go in limiting presidential power in matters traditionally considered within the prerogative of the President? If Jackson's tripart analysis in *Sawyer* is correct, one would think that Congress could impose some limits. However look at *Zivotofsky ex rel. Zivotofsky v. Kerry*, ___ U.S. ___, 135 S.Ct. 2076 (2015), where Congress passed a law directing the executive branch how to designate on passports the country of origin or birth for those from Jerusalem. The case, in affirming presidential power to recognize countries diplomatically, draws upon Art. II, § 3 (as well as his role in negotiating treaties) of the Constitution, which textually commits to the president the authority to receive ambassadors and other public ministers, to endorse a view that seems to create a distinct role or set of powers for the president that Congress cannot erode or encroach upon.

Foreign and defense policy in the United States is also complicated by the federal nature of the American political system. While the federal government is supreme in the field of both foreign and defense policy, it may not act in ways that are contrary to the Constitution. One potential limitation is the Tenth Amendment and federalism. The extent to which states limit federal authority is often a contentious political and legal matter. *Curtiss-Wright* suggested that the Tenth Amendment is not a bar to foreign policy actions. Similarly, look at both *Perpich v. Department of Defense* (496 U.S. 334, 1990) and *Missouri v. Holland* (252 U.S. 416, 1920). Both cases again suggest that states have but a small role in foreign affairs. Governors and states cannot generally act in ways contrary to determinations by the president of the national government. Holmes's language in *Holland* is expansive, and it frightened many. It suggested that treaties, as the supreme law of the land, could serve to amend the Constitution, including in the area of federalism, regarding the relationship between the states and the federal government. However, the next decision questions this claim and calms fears.

How far can treaties or the president go in binding states under international law? While the Court may be prepared to give the president a significant amount of leeway to act in foreign affairs, clearly this power is not unlimited, and it does not look as if the situation reflected in *Holland* was as dire as some critics thought. Whatever fears *Holland* may have raised, *Medellín v. Texas* might stand for the reverse proposition. Why couldn't the president require Texas to comply with an international agreement? Does the case suggest that in fact federalism might actually limit presidential foreign policy authority? If so, under what circumstances? How can one reconcile *Medellín* with *Holland*, *Perpich*, and the dicta in *Curtiss-Wright*?

Congressional Authority to Raise and Support Armies

Article I, Section 8, clause 12 empowers Congress to "raise and support Armies" along with clause 13 which authorizes it to "provide and maintain a Navy." The Supreme Court has afforded Congress significant deference in defining the scope of these powers to maintain the military. One area where this deference appears is in its power to conscript or draft individuals to serve in the military.

It took well over a hundred years and several wars for the power of Congress to conscript individuals for military service to be challenged, although conscription had been used in only one war prior to World War I. Both the restricted use of the power and the rather obvious basis in the constitutional provision for raising armies and providing a navy probably explain this delay in a test case. The *Selective Draft Law Cases* (245 U.S. 366, 1918) seemed to raise every conceivable challenge to the exercise of the power of drafting, and the Court resolved in favor of the power. The Court also denied that this power encroached on the power of the states over the militia, and it denied that exemptions from the draft extended to the clergy and the recognition of conscientious objectors involved "establishment of religion. During the Vietnam War many individuals objected not only to the constitutionality of the conflict but also sought to escape from being drafted by claiming conscientious objector status, *i.e.,* claiming religious objections from the war. While in cases such as in *United States v. Seeger,* 380 U.S. 163 (1965) the Court allowed for an expansive concept of what constituted as religious beliefs to qualify for designation as a conscientious objector, in *Gillette v. United States*, 401 U.S. 437 (1971) the Court said that in order to secure a religious objection to serving in the military one had to show that he opposed all wars and not just a specific one, thereby limiting or narrowing the grounds that would classify one as a conscientious objector.

From World War II though the end of the Vietnam War, the United States government required males to register for the draft and potentially be conscripted into serving in the military. After the Vietnam War ended, the United States government ended the draft and registration by 1973. However, in 1980, after the Soviet Union had invaded Afghanistan in late 1979, President Carter issued Presidential Proclamation 4771 reinstating the requirement that young men born on or after January 1, 1960 register with the Selective Service System. In *Rostker v. Goldberg* (453 U.S. 57, 1981) the Court rejected claims that excluding women from registering violated the Equal Protection clause as a form of sex-based discrimination. Critical to their decision was the fact that women were excluded from combat positions. This policy of excluding women from combat positions has now been reversed as of December 2015, raising questions about the possible constitutionality of excluding women from registration. In subsequent cases such as *National Coalition for Men v. Selective Service System*, (No. 13–56690. Argued and Submitted Dec. 8, 2015. Filed Feb. 19, 2016), a court held that a challenge to the exclusion could proceed.

In order to encourage men to register with the Selective Service System they need to present proof of registration in order to be eligible for federal financial aid. The Solomon Amendment required men to certify that they had registered. *In Selective Service System v. Minnesota Public Interest Research Group*, 468 U.S. 841 104 (1984), the Supreme Court rejected claims that this certification constituted either a Bill of a Attainder or a violation of the Fifth Amendment right against self-incrimination.

Finally, while campaigning for president in 1992 Bill Clinton promised to allow for gays and lesbians to serve opening in the military. Previous policy had barred them from serving. In a compromise President Clinton signed what was known as the "Don't Ask, Don't tell" law that allowed gays and lesbians to serve in the military so long they were not open. The law was challenged several times, and sustained in *Richenberg v. Perry,* 97 F.3d 256 (8th Cir. 1996); *Thomasson v. Perry*, 80 F.3d 915 (4th Cir. 1996); *Able v. United States,* 155 F.3d 628 (2d Cir.

1998); *Cook v. Gates*, 528 F.3d 42 (1st Cir. 2008), and *Holmes v. California National Guard*, 124 F.3d 1126 (9th Cir. 1998). In 2010 the law was repealed.

Overall, the Supreme Court has given significant constitutional deference to Congress and the President to determine how to raise and maintain the military, including determining who may be called upon to serve.

The Legal Effect of Executive Agreements

Until the twentieth century an executive agreement was held not to be a part of "the supreme law of the land," as indicated in Article VI of the Constitution. The executive agreement has always been recognized as a valid international arrangement, but it was not regarded as enforceable in domestic courts. A hint of what was to come was given by the Court in *Altman and Company v. United States* (224 U.S. 583, 1912). But it was not until 1937, in *United States v. Belmont* (301 U.S. 324, 1937) that the Court distinctly placed executive agreements on the same legal level with treaties. This decision was followed five years later by a corollary case, *United States v. Pink* (315 U.S. 203, 1942).

The importance of *Belmont* seems to have been overlooked by many persons. With the addition of *Pink*, executive agreements assume a new legal status and are now to be regarded in the same legal light as treaties, part of the supreme law of the land against which state law cannot prevail. There remains the question of conflict between an executive agreement and federal law. This question has not been definitively answered, but the best authority seems to be that an executive agreement cannot supersede a federal statute or a treaty.

In other cases, the Court made clear the point that the judiciary is to stay clear of the field of foreign relations. Further, as noted in *Curtiss-Wright*, the doctrine of separation of powers is not applied with particular earnestness in the matter of foreign affairs. Congress has almost complete freedom to permit the president to exercise whatever discretion it may see fit. Many executive agreements have been entered into pursuant to statutory authority, such as the modification of tariff schedules under the Trade Agreement Act of 1934 and the Trade Expansion Act of 1962. Other trade agreements, such as the North American Free Trade Agreement (NAFTA) of 1994, while treaties, have also been pursued or negotiated as if they were executive agreements in the sense of the president asking for "fast-track" authority to negotiate them subject to minimal congressional debate or oversight.

THE PRIZE CASES

67 U.S. 635, 2 Black 635, 17 L.Ed. 459 (1863)

At the outbreak of the Civil War in 1861, President Lincoln established a blockade of ports of the southern Confederacy. At this time Congress had taken no action on the matter. U.S. navy ships confiscated cargoes of ships that had been carrying cargoes to the southern ports during the blockade, and their owners sued to recover damages.

Vote: 5–4

JUSTICE GRIER delivered the opinion of the Court.

There are certain propositions of law which must necessarily affect the ultimate decision of these cases, and many others, which it will be proper to discuss and decide before we notice the special facts peculiar to each.

They are, *first.* Had the President a right to institute a blockade of ports in possession of persons in armed rebellion against the Government, on the principles of international law, as known and acknowledged among civilized States?

Second. Was the property of persons domiciled or residing within those States a proper subject of capture on the sea as "enemies' property"?

That a blockade *de facto* actually existed, and was formally declared and notified by the President on the 27th and 30th of April, 1861, is an admitted fact in these cases.

That the President, as the Executive Chief of the Government and Commander-in-Chief of the Army and Navy, was the proper person to make such notification, has not been, and cannot be disputed.

As a civil war is never publicly proclaimed, *eo nomine,* against insurgents, its actual existence is a fact in our domestic history which the Court is bound to notice and to know.

By the Constitution, Congress alone has the power to declare a national or foreign war. It cannot declare war against a State or any number of States, by virtue of any clause in the Constitution. The Constitution confers on the President the whole Executive power. He is bound to take care that the laws be faithfully executed. He is Commander-in-Chief of the Army and Navy of the United States, and of the militia of the several States when called into the actual service of the United States. He has no power to initiate or declare a war either against a foreign nation or a domestic State. But by the Acts of Congress of February 28th, 1795, and 3d of March, 1807, he is authorized to call out the militia and use the military and naval forces of the United States in case of invasion by foreign nations, and to suppress insurrection against the government of a State or of the United States.

If a war be made by invasion of a foreign nation, the President is not only authorized but bound to resist force by force. He does not initiate the war, but is bound to accept the challenge without waiting for any special legislative authority. And whether the hostile party be a foreign invader, or States organized in rebellion, it is none the less a war, although the declaration of it be "*unilateral*."

This greatest of civil wars was not gradually developed by popular commotion, tumultuous assemblies, or local unorganized insurrections. However long may have been its previous conception, it nevertheless sprung forth suddenly from the parent brain, a Minerva in the full panoply of *war.* The President was bound to meet it in the shape it presented itself, without waiting for Congress to baptize it with a name; and no name given to it by him or them could change the fact.

Whether the President in fulfilling his duties, as Commander-in-Chief, in suppressing an insurrection, has met with such armed hostile resistance, and a civil war of such alarming proportions as will compel him to accord to them the character of belligerents, is a question to be decided *by him,* and this Court must be governed by the decisions and acts of the political department of the Government to which this power was entrusted. "He must determine what degree of force the crisis demands." The proclamation of blockade is itself official and conclusive evidence to the Court that a state of war existed which demanded and authorized a recourse to such a measure, under the circumstances peculiar to the case.

On this first question therefore we are of the opinion that the President had the right *jure belli,* to institute a blockade of ports in possession of the States in rebellion, which neutrals are bound to regard.

II.

We come now to the consideration of the second question. What is included in the term "*enemies' property*"?

Is the property of all persons residing within the territory of the States now in rebellion, captured on the high seas, to be treated as "enemies' property" whether the owner be in arms against the Government or not?

The right of one belligerent not only to coerce the other by direct force, but also to cripple his resources by the seizure or destruction of his property, is a necessary result of a state of war. Money and wealth, the products of agriculture and commerce, are said to be the sinews of war, and as necessary in its conduct as numbers and physical force. Hence it is, that the laws of war recognize the right of a belligerent to cut these sinews of the power of the enemy, by capturing his property on the high seas. . . .

Whether property be liable to capture as "enemies' property" does not in any manner depend on the personal allegiance of the owner. "It is the illegal traffic that stamps it as 'enemies' property.' It is of no consequence whether it belongs to an ally or a citizen. . . . The owner, *pro hac vice,* is an enemy." . . .

The produce of the soil of the hostile territory, as well as other property engaged in the commerce of the hostile power, as the source of its wealth and strength, are always regarded as legitimate prize, without regard to the domicile of the owner, and much more so if he reside or trade within their territory.

NOTE

Justice Nelson dissented with the concurrence of Chief Justice Taney, Justice Catron, and Justice Clifford. They denied the power of the president, in this connection, noting that

> . . . the President does not possess the power under the Constitution to declare war or recognize its existence within the meaning of the law of nations, which carries with it belligerent rights, and thus change the country and all its citizens from a state of peace to a state of war; that this power belongs exclusively to the Congress of the United States, and, consequently, that the President had no power to set on foot a blockade under the law of nations, and that the capture of the vessel and cargo in this case, and in all cases before us in which the capture occurred before the 13th of July, 1861, for breach of blockade, or as enemies' property, are illegal and void, and that the decrees of condemnation should be reversed and the vessel and cargo restored.

FOR DISCUSSION

What is the basis for the constitutional power that the president has here? What does the Court identify? Is the power magnified or enhanced during war or hostilities?

RELATED CASES

Jecker v. Montgomery: 13 Howard 498 (1851).

The president cannot establish a prize court in conquered territory; these courts must be established by Congress. A U.S. ship was accused of trading with the enemy in the war with Mexico. The prize court was at Monterey in California. This is the only case where the Court has so held.

Ex parte Quirin: 317 U.S. 1 (1942).

The Court upheld the jurisdiction of the military commission named by the president to try German saboteurs. The president had acted under a federal statute. The Court decided that the provisions of the Fifth and Sixth Amendments do not apply to trials for offenses against the law of war. This case was decided at a special session of the Court. The saboteurs were German citizens.

EX PARTE MILLIGAN

71 U.S. 2, 18 L.Ed. 281, 4 Wall. 2 (1866)

Lambdin Milligan, a civilian joined by several other Confederate supporters, planned to steal union supplies in Indiana and use them to invade prisoner-of-war camps. When their plot was discovered, they were arrested and tried in a military court even though other civilian courts were open and operating at the time. They were convicted and sentenced to hang. They contested the jurisdiction of the military courts over them.

Vote: 9–0

JUSTICE DAVIS delivered the opinion of the court.

On the 10th day of May, 1865, Lambdin P. Milligan presented a petition to the Circuit Court of the United States for the District of Indiana, to be discharged from an alleged unlawful imprisonment. The case made by the petition is this: Milligan is a citizen of the United States; has lived for twenty years in Indiana; and, at the time of the grievances complained of, was not, and never had been in the military or naval service of the United States. On the 5th day of October, 1864, while at home, he was arrested by order of General Alvin P. Hovey, commanding the military district of Indiana; and has ever since been kept in close confinement.

On the 21st day of October, 1864, he was brought before a military commission, convened at Indianapolis, by order of General Hovey, tried on certain charges and specifications; found guilty, and sentenced to be hanged; and the sentence ordered to be executed on Friday, the 19th day of May, 1865.

On the 2d day of January, 1865, after the proceedings of the military commission were at an end, the Circuit Court of the United States for Indiana met at Indianapolis and empanelled a grand jury, who were charged to inquire whether the laws of the United States had been violated; and, if so, to make presentments. The court adjourned on the 27th day of January, having, prior thereto, discharged from further service the grand jury, who did not find any bill of indictment or make any presentment against Milligan for any offence whatever; and, in fact, since his imprisonment, no bill of indictment has been found or presentment made against him by any grand jury of the United States.

Milligan insists that said military commission had no jurisdiction to try him upon the charges preferred, or upon any charges whatever; because he was a citizen of the United States and the State of Indiana, and had not been, since the commencement of the late Rebellion, a resident of any of the States whose citizens were arrayed against the government, and that the right of trial by jury was guaranteed to him by the Constitution of the United States.

The prayer of the petition was, that under the act of Congress, approved March 3d, 1863, entitled, "An act relating to *habeas corpus* and regulating judicial proceedings in certain cases," he may be brought before the court, and either turned over to the proper civil tribunal to be proceeded against according to the law of the land or discharged from custody altogether.

With the petition were filed the order for the commission, the charges and specifications, the findings of the court, with the order of the War Department reciting that the sentence was approved by the President of the United States, and directing that it be carried into execution without delay. The petition was presented and filed in open court by the counsel for Milligan; at the same time the District Attorney of the United States for Indiana appeared, and, by the agreement of counsel, the application was submitted to the court. The opinions of the judges of the Circuit Court were opposed on three questions, which are certified to the Supreme Court:

1st. " 'On the facts stated in said petition and exhibits, ought a writ of *habeas corpus* to be issued?"

2d. "On the facts stated in said petition and exhibits, ought the said Lambdin P. Milligan to be discharged from custody as in said petition prayed?"

3d. "Whether, upon the facts stated in said petition and exhibits, the military commission mentioned therein had jurisdiction legally to try and sentence said Milligan in manner and form as in said petition and exhibits is stated?"

The importance of the main question presented by this record cannot be overstated; for it involves the very framework of the government and the fundamental principles of American liberty.

The controlling question in the case is this: Upon the *facts* stated in Milligan's petition, and the exhibits filed, had the military commission mentioned in it *jurisdiction*, legally, to try and sentence him? Milligan, not a resident of one of the rebellious states, or a prisoner of war, but a citizen of Indiana for twenty years past, and never in the military or naval service, is, while at his home, arrested by the military power of the United States, imprisoned, and, on certain criminal charges preferred against him, tried, convicted, and sentenced to be hanged by a military commission, organized under the direction of the military commander of the military district of Indiana. Had this tribunal the *legal* power and authority to try and punish this man?

No graver question was ever considered by this court, nor one which more nearly concerns the rights of the whole people; for it is the birthright of every American citizen when charged with crime, to be tried and punished according to law. The power of punishment is, alone through the means which the laws have provided for that purpose, and if they are ineffectual, there is an immunity from punishment, no matter how great an offender the individual may be, or how much his crimes may have shocked the sense of justice of the country, or endangered its safety. By the protection of the law human rights are secured; withdraw that protection, and they are at the mercy of wicked rulers. or the clamor of an excited people. If there was law to justify this military trial, it is not our province to interfere; if there was not, it is our duty to declare the nullity of the whole proceedings. The decision of this question does not depend on argument or judicial precedents, numerous and highly illustrative as they are. These precedents inform us of the extent of the struggle to preserve liberty and to relieve those in civil life from military trials.

The founders of our government were familiar with the history of that struggle; and secured in a written constitution every right which the people had wrested from power during a contest of ages. By that Constitution and the laws authorized by it this question must be determined. The provisions of that instrument on the administration of criminal justice are too plain and direct, to leave room for misconstruction or doubt of their true meaning. Those applicable to this case are found in that clause of the original Constitution which says, "That the trial of all crimes, except in case of impeachment, shall be by jury;" and in the fourth, fifth, and sixth articles of the amendments. The fourth proclaims the right to be secure in person and effects against unreasonable search and seizure; and directs that a judicial warrant shall not issue "without proof of probable cause supported by oath or affirmation." The fifth declares "that no person shall be held to answer for a capital or otherwise infamous crime unless on presentment by a grand jury, except in cases arising in the land or naval forces, or in the militia, when in actual service in time of war or public danger, nor be deprived of life, liberty, or property, without due process of law." And the sixth guarantees the right of trial by jury, in such manner and with such regulations that with upright judges, impartial juries, and an able bar, the innocent will be saved and the guilty punished. It is in these words: "In all criminal prosecutions the accused shall enjoy the right to a speedy and public trial by an impartial jury of the state and district wherein the crime shall have been committed, which district shall have been previously ascertained by law, and to be informed of the nature and cause of the accusation, to be confronted with the witnesses against him, to have compulsory process for obtaining witnesses in his favor, and to have the assistance of counsel for his defence." These securities for personal liberty thus embodied, were such as wisdom and experience had demonstrated to be necessary for the protection of those accused of crime. And so strong was the sense of the country of their importance, and so jealous were the people that these rights, highly prized, might be denied them by implication, that when the original Constitution was proposed for adoption it encountered severe opposition; and, but for the belief that it would be so amended as to embrace them, it would never have been ratified.

Time has proven the discernment of our ancestors; for even these provisions, expressed in such plain English words, that it would seem the ingenuity of man could not evade them, are *now*, after the lapse of more than seventy years, sought to be avoided. Those great and good men foresaw that troublous times would arise, when rulers and people would become restive under restraint, and seek by sharp and decisive measures to accomplish ends deemed just and proper; and that the principles of constitutional liberty would be in peril, unless established by irrepealable law. The history of the world had taught them that what was done in the past might be attempted in the future. The Constitution of the United States is a law for rulers and people, equally in war and in peace, and covers with the shield of its protection all classes of men, at all times, and under all circumstances. No doctrine, involving more pernicious consequences, was ever invented by the wit of man than that any of its provisions can be suspended during any of the great exigencies of government. Such a doctrine leads directly to anarchy or despotism, but the theory of necessity on which it is based is false; for the government, within the Constitution, has all the powers granted to it, which are necessary to preserve its existence; as has been happily proved by the result of the great effort to throw off its just authority.

Have any of the rights guaranteed by the Constitution been violated in the case of Milligan? and if so, what are they?

. . . One of the plainest constitutional provisions was, therefore, infringed when Milligan was tried by a court not ordained and established by Congress, and not composed of judges appointed during good behavior.

Why was he not delivered to the Circuit Court of Indiana to be proceeded against according to law? No reason of necessity could be urged against it; because Congress had declared penalties against the offences charged, provided for their punishment, and directed that court to hear and determine them. And soon after this military tribunal was ended, the Circuit Court met, peacefully transacted its business, and adjourned. It needed no bayonets to protect it, and required no military aid to execute its judgments. It was held in a state, eminently distinguished for patriotism, by judges commissioned during the Rebellion, who were provided with juries, upright, intelligent, and selected by a marshal appointed by the President. The government had no right to conclude that Milligan, if guilty, would not receive in that court merited punishment; for its records disclose that it was constantly engaged in the trial of similar offences, and was never interrupted in its administration of criminal justice. If it was dangerous, in the distracted condition of affairs, to leave Milligan unrestrained of his liberty, because he "conspired against the government, afforded aid and comfort to rebels, and incited the people to insurrection," the *law* said arrest him, confine him closely, render him powerless to do further mischief; and then present his case to the grand jury of the district, with proofs of his guilt, and, if indicted, try him according to the course of the common law. If this had been done, the Constitution would have been vindicated, the law of 1863 enforced, and the securities for personal liberty preserved and defended.

Another guarantee of freedom was broken when Milligan was denied a trial by jury. The great minds of the country have differed on the correct interpretation to be given to various provisions of the Federal Constitution; and judicial decision has been often invoked to settle their true meaning; but until recently no one ever doubted that the right of trial by jury was fortified in the organic law against the power of attack. It is *now* assailed; but if ideas can be expressed in words, and language has any meaning, *this right*—one of the most valuable in a free country—is preserved to every one accused of crime who is not attached to the army, or navy, or militia in actual service. The sixth amendment affirms that "in all criminal prosecutions the accused shall enjoy the right to a speedy and public trial by an impartial jury," language broad enough to embrace all persons and cases; but the fifth, recognizing the necessity of an indictment, or presentment, before any one can be held to answer for high crimes, "*excepts* cases arising in the land or naval forces, or in the militia, when in actual service, in time of war or public danger;" and the framers of the Constitution, doubtless, meant to limit the right of trial by jury, in the sixth amendment, to those persons who were subject to indictment or presentment in the fifth.

The discipline necessary to the efficiency of the army and navy, required other and swifter modes of trial than are furnished by the common law courts; and, in pursuance of the power conferred by the Constitution, Congress has declared the kinds of trial, and the manner in which they shall be conducted, for offences committed while the party is in the military or naval service. Every one connected with these branches of the public service is amenable to the jurisdiction which Congress has created for their government, and, while thus serving, surrenders his right to be tried by the civil courts. *All other persons*, citizens of states where the courts are open, if charged with crime, are guaranteed the inestimable privilege of trial by jury. This privilege is a vital principle, underlying the whole administration of criminal justice; it is not held by sufference, and cannot be frittered away on any plea of state or political necessity. When peace prevails, and the authority of the government is undisputed, there is no difficulty of preserving the safeguards of liberty; for the ordinary modes of trial are never neglected, and no one wishes it otherwise; but if society is disturbed by civil commotion—if the passions of men are aroused and the restraints of law weakened, if not disregarded—these safeguards need, and should receive, the watchful care of those intrusted with the guardianship of the Constitution and laws. In no other way can we transmit to posterity unimpaired the blessings of liberty, consecrated by the sacrifices of the Revolution.

It is claimed that martial law covers with its broad mantle the proceedings of this military commission. The proposition is this: that in a time of war the commander of an armed force (if in his opinion the exigencies of the country demand it, and of which he is to judge), has the power, within the lines of his military district, to suspend all civil rights and their remedies, and subject citizens as well as soldiers to the rule of *his will*; and in the exercise of his lawful authority cannot be restrained, except by his superior officer or the President of the United States.

If this position is sound to the extent claimed, then when war exists, foreign or domestic, and the country is subdivided into military departments for mere convenience, the commander of one of them can, if he chooses, within his limits, on the plea of necessity, with the approval of the Executive, substitute military force for and to the exclusion of the laws, and punish all persons, as he thinks right and proper, without fixed or certain rules.

The statement of this proposition shows its importance; for, if true, republican government is a failure, and there is an end of liberty regulated by law. Martial law, established on such a basis, destroys every guarantee of the Constitution, and effectually renders the "military independent of and superior to the civil power"—the attempt to do which by the King of Great Britain was deemed by our fathers such an offence, that they assigned it to the world as one of the causes which impelled them to declare their independence. Civil liberty and this kind of martial law cannot endure together; the antagonism is irreconcilable; and, in the conflict, one or the other must perish.

This nation, as experience has proved, cannot always remain at peace, and has no right to expect that it will always have wise and humane rulers, sincerely attached to the principles of the Constitution. Wicked men, ambitious of power, with hatred of liberty and contempt of law, may fill the place once occupied by Washington and Lincoln; and if this right is conceded, and the calamities of war again befall us, the dangers to human liberty are frightful to contemplate. If our fathers had failed to provide for just such a contingency, they would have been false to the trust reposed in them. They knew—the history of the world told them—the nation they were founding, be its existence short or long, would be involved in war; how often or how long continued, human foresight could not tell; and that unlimited power, wherever lodged at such a time, was especially hazardous to freemen. For this, and other equally weighty reasons, they secured the inheritance they had fought to maintain, by incorporating in a written constitution the safeguards which *time* had proved were essential to its preservation.

Not one of these safeguards can the President, or Congress, or the Judiciary disturb, except the one concerning the writ of *habeas corpus*.

It is difficult to see how the *safety* for the country required martial law in Indiana. If any of her citizens were plotting treason, the power of arrest could secure them, until the government was prepared for their trial, when the courts were open and ready to try them. It was as easy to protect witnesses before a civil as a military tribunal; and as there could be no wish to convict, except on sufficient legal evidence, surely an ordained and establish court was better able to judge of this than a military tribunal composed of gentlemen not trained to the profession of the law.

It follows, from what has been said on this subject, that there are occasions when martial rule can be properly applied. If, in foreign invasion or civil war, the courts are actually closed, and it is impossible to administer criminal justice according to law, *then*, on the theatre of active military operations, where war really prevails, there is a necessity to furnish a substitute for the civil authority, thus overthrown, to preserve the safety of the army and society; and as no power is left but the military, it is allowed to govern by martial rule until the laws can have their free course. As necessity creates the rule, so it limits its duration; for, if this government is continued *after* the courts are reinstated, it is a gross usurpation of power. Martial rule can never exist where the courts are open, and in the proper and unobstructed exercise of their jurisdiction. It is also confined to the locality of actual war. Because, during the late Rebellion it could have been enforced in Virginia, where the national authority was overturned and the courts driven out, it does not follow that it should obtain in Indiana, where that authority was never disputed, and justice was always administered. And so in the case of a foreign invasion, martial rule may become a necessity in one state, when, in another, it would be "mere lawless violence."

Congress has the power not only to raise and support and govern armies but to declare war. It has, therefore, the power to provide by law for carrying on war. This power necessarily extends to all legislation essential to the prosecution of war with vigor and success, except such as interferes with the command of the forces and the conduct of campaigns. That power and duty belong to the President as commander-in-chief. Both these powers are derived from the Constitution, but neither is defined by that instrument. Their extent must be determined by their nature, and by the principles of our institutions.

The power to make the necessary laws is in Congress; the power to execute in the President. Both powers imply many subordinate and auxiliary powers. Each includes all authorities essential to its due exercise. But neither can the President, in war more than in peace, intrude upon the proper authority of Congress, nor Congress upon the proper authority of the President. Both are servants of the people, whose will is expressed in the fundamental law. Congress cannot direct the conduct of campaigns, nor can the President, or any commander under him, without the sanction of Congress, institute tribunals for the trial and punishment of offences, either of soldiers or civilians, unless in cases of a controlling necessity, which justifies what it compels, or at least insures acts of indemnity from the justice of the legislature.

We by no means assert that Congress can establish and apply the laws of war where no war has been declared or exists.

Where peace exists the laws of peace must prevail. What we do maintain is, that when the nation is involved in war, and some portions of the country are invaded, and all are exposed to invasion, it is within the power of Congress to determine in what states or district such great and imminent public danger exists as justifies the authorization of military tribunals for the trial of crimes and offences against the discipline or security of the army or against the public safety.

In Indiana, for example, at the time of the arrest of Milligan and his co-conspirators, it is established by the papers in the record, that the state was a military district, was the theatre of military operations, had been actually invaded, and was constantly threatened with invasion. It appears, also, that a powerful secret association, composed of citizens and others, existed within the state, under military organization, conspiring against the draft, and plotting insurrection, the liberation of the prisoners of war at various depots, the seizure of the state and national arsenals, armed cooperation with the enemy, and war against the national government.

We cannot doubt that, in such a time of public danger, Congress had power, under the Constitution, to provide for the organization of a military commission, and for trial by that commission of persons engaged in this conspiracy. The fact that the Federal courts were open was regarded by Congress as a sufficient reason for not exercising the power; but that fact could not deprive Congress of the right to exercise it. Those courts might be open and undisturbed in the execution of their functions, and yet wholly incompetent to avert threatened danger, or to punish, with adequate promptitude and certainty, the guilty conspirators.

We think that the power of Congress, in such times and in such localities, to authorize trials for crimes against the security and safety of the national forces, may be derived from its constitutional authority to raise and support armies and to declare war, if not from its constitutional authority to provide for governing the national forces.

We have no apprehension that this power, under our American system of government, in which all official authority is derived from the people, and exercised under direct responsibility to the people, is more likely to be abused than the power to regulate commerce, or the power to borrow money. And we are unwilling to give our assent by silence to expressions of opinion which seem to us calculated, though not intended, to cripple the constitutional powers of the government, and to augment the public dangers in times of invasion and rebellion.

Mr. Justice Wayne, Mr. Justice Swayne, and Mr. Justice Miller concur with me in these views.

FOR DISCUSSION

Under what conditions, if any, could a president use military courts to try civilians in the United States? Could the president use such courts to try noncitizens in the United States? Is this case more about the Article II power of the president or the Article III power of the federal courts? When could habeas corpus be suspended?

UNITED STATES V. CURTISS-WRIGHT EXPORT CORP.

299 U.S. 304, 57 S.Ct. 216, 81 L.Ed. 255 (1936)

Congress had passed a joint resolution empowering the president to embargo the shipment of articles of war to countries engaged in armed conflict when, in his judgment, such action would be in the interest of the resolution, which applied to sales within the United States. The president forbade sales to the principals in the Chaco war between Bolivia and Paraguay. The Curtiss-Wright Export Corp. sold arms of war (aircraft machine guns) to Bolivia and was charged with violation of the act of Congress and the president's order. The corporation challenged the validity of the act, claiming that it was an illegal delegation of power to the president.

Vote: 7–1

JUSTICE SUTHERLAND delivered the opinion of the Court:

Whether, if the Joint Resolution had related solely to internal affairs, it would be open to the challenge that it constituted an unlawful delegation of legislative power to the Executive, we find it unnecessary to determine. The whole aim of the resolution is to affect a situation entirely external to the United States, and falling within the category of foreign affairs. The determination which we are called to make, therefore, is whether the Joint

Resolution, as applied to that situation, is vulnerable to attack under the rule that forbids a delegation of the lawmaking power. In other words, assuming (but not deciding) that the challenged delegation, if it were confined to internal affairs, would be invalid, may it nevertheless be sustained on the ground that its exclusive aim is to afford a remedy for a hurtful condition within foreign territory?

It will contribute to the elucidation of the question if we first consider the differences between the powers of the Federal government in respect of foreign or external affairs and those in respect of domestic or internal affairs. That there are differences between them, and that these differences are fundamental, may not be doubted.

The two classes of powers are different, both in respect of their origin and their nature. The broad statement that the Federal government can exercise no powers except those specifically enumerated in the Constitution, and such implied powers as are necessary and proper to carry into effect the enumerated powers, is categorically true only in respect of our internal affairs. In that field, the primary purpose of the Constitution was to carve from the general mass of legislative powers *then possessed by the states* such portions as it was thought desirable to vest in the Federal government, leaving those not included in the enumeration still in the states. *Carter v. Carter Coal Co.* (298 U.S. 238, 1936). That this doctrine applies only to powers which the states had is self-evident. And since the states severally never possessed international powers, such powers could not have been carved from the mass of state powers but obviously were transmitted to the United States from some other source. During the colonial period, those powers were possessed exclusively by and were entirely under the control of the Crown. By the Declaration of Independence, "the Representatives of the United States of America" declared the United (not the several) Colonies to be free and independent states, and as such to have "full Power to levy War, conclude Peace, contract Alliances, establish Commerce and to do all other Acts and Things which Independent States may of right do."

As a result of the separation from Great Britain by the colonies, acting as a unit, the powers of external sovereignty passed from the Crown not to the colonies severally, but to the colonies in their collective and corporate capacity as the United States of America. Even before the Declaration, the colonies were a unit in foreign affairs, acting through a common agency—namely, the Continental Congress, composed of delegates from the thirteen colonies. That agency exercised the powers of war and peace, raised an army, created a navy, and finally adopted the Declaration of Independence. Rulers come and go; governments end and forms of government change; but sovereignty survives. A political society cannot endure without a supreme will somewhere. Sovereignty is never held in suspense. When, therefore, the external sovereignty of Great Britain in respect of the colonies ceased, it immediately passed to the Union. That fact was given practical application almost at once. The treaty of peace, made on September 3, 1783, was concluded between his Britannic Majesty and the "United States of America."

The Union existed before the Constitution, which was ordained and established among other things to form "a more perfect Union." Prior to that event it is clear that the Union, declared by the Articles of Confederation to be "perpetual," was the sole possessor of external sovereignty, and in the Union it remained without change save in so far as the Constitution in express terms qualified its exercise. It results that the investment of the Federal government with the powers of external sovereignty did not depend upon the affirmative grants of the Constitution. The powers to declare and wage war, to conclude peace, to make treaties, to maintain diplomatic relations with other sovereignties, if they had never been mentioned in the Constitution, would have vested in the Federal government as necessary concomitants of nationality. Neither the Constitution nor the laws passed in pursuance of it have any force in foreign territory unless in respect of our own citizens; and operations of the nation in such territory must be governed by treaties, international understandings and compacts, and the principles of international law. As a member of the family of nations, the right and power of the United States in that field are equal to the right and power of the other members of the international family.

It is important to bear in mind that we are here dealing not alone with an authority vested in the President by an exertion of legislative power, but with such an authority plus the very delicate, plenary and exclusive power of the President as the sole organ of the Federal government in the field of international relations—a power which does not require as a basis for its exercise an act of Congress, but which, of course, like every other governmental power, must be exercised in subordination to the applicable provisions of the Constitution. It is quite apparent that if, in the maintenance of our international relations, embarrassment—perhaps serious embarrassment—is to be avoided and success for our aims achieved, congressional legislation which is to be made effective throughout negotiation and inquiry within the international field must often accord to the President a degree of discretion and freedom from statutory restriction which would not be admissible were domestic affairs alone involved. Moreover, he, not Congress, has the better opportunity of knowing the conditions which prevail in foreign countries, and especially is this true in time of war. He has his confidential sources of information. He has his agents in the form of diplomatic, consular and other officials. Secrecy in respect of information gathered by them may be highly necessary, and the premature disclosure of it productive of harmful results.

In the light of the foregoing observations, it is evident that this court should not be in haste to apply a general rule which will have the effect of condemning legislation like that under review as constituting an unlawful delegation of legislative power. The principles which justify such legislation find overwhelming support in the unbroken legislative practice which has prevailed almost from the inception of the national government to the present day.

Practically every volume of the United States Statutes contains one or more acts or joint resolutions of Congress authorizing action by the President in respect of subjects affecting foreign relations, which either leave the exercise of the power to his unrestricted judgment, or provide a standard far more general than that which has always been considered requisite with regard to domestic affairs

A legislative practice such as we have here, evidenced not by only occasional instances, but marked by the movement of a steady stream for a century and a half of time, goes a long way in the direction of proving the presence of unassailable ground for the constitutionality of the practice, to be found in the origin and history of the power involved, or in its nature, or in both combined.

The judgment of the court below must be reversed and the cause remanded for further proceedings in accordance with the foregoing opinion.

Reversed.

JUSTICE MCREYNOLDS does not agree. He is of opinion that the court below reached the right conclusion and its judgment ought to be affirmed. [There is no further report beyond this statement of dissent.]

JUSTICE STONE took no part in the consideration or decision of this case.

FOR DISCUSSION

Justice Sutherland's discussion in this case regarding the passing of foreign policy power from England after America's independence is often referred to as the **Sutherland thesis.** According to the **Sutherland thesis**, who possesses foreign policy authority in the United States? Is this a power of the presidency or Congress? What clauses in the Constitution support the Sutherland thesis? What clauses oppose it? Given Sutherland's claims, does the president have unlimited or sole authority in foreign affairs?

RELATED CASES

Jones v. United States: **137 U.S. 202 (1890).**

The United States, under general international law, may acquire territory by discovery and occupation. The Court here was taking judicial notice of general international law. Involved here was a guano island that had been discovered by a United States citizen. Jones had committed murder on the island. For offenses against federal law outside a state, Congress can prescribe the place of trial.

Fong Yue Ting v. United States: **149 U.S. 698 (1893).**

The power of Congress to expel or exclude aliens is an aspect of the plenary control over international relations, which is an inherent and inalienable right of every sovereign and independent nation. This power is vested in the political departments of government. Immigration legislation is based on this. Deportation was held not to be a criminal punishment.

YOUNGSTOWN SHEET AND TUBE CO. V. SAWYER (THE STEEL SEIZURE CASE)

343 U.S. 579, 72 S.Ct. 863, 96 L.Ed. 1153 (1952)

In 1951 a dispute arose between steel management and labor over the provisions of new collective bargaining agreements. Lengthy conferences failed to settle the difficulties. In December of 1951 the United Steel Workers of America served notice of an intention to strike at the expiration of agreements on December 31. The Federal Mediation and Conciliation Service was unsuccessful in its intervention. Then the president referred the matter to the federal Wage Stabilization Board, and this likewise failed. Finally, the union announced a nationwide strike to begin on April 9, 1952. Because of the importance of steel to national defense, President Truman ordered Secretary of Commerce Sawyer to seize the steel mills and to keep them operating. On April 30 Judge Pine of the United States District Court of the District of Columbia granted a preliminary injunction enjoining Sawyer from continuing the seizure. While the president could not be made subject to such judicial process, his subordinates could. The Supreme Court, with unusual speed, handed down this decision on June 2, 1952. While a member of the Cabinet was the defendant, it was really presidential action that was in question.

Vote: 6–3

JUSTICE BLACK delivered the opinion of the Court.

We are asked to decide whether the President was acting within his constitutional power when he issued an order directing the Secretary of Commerce to take possession of and operate most of the Nation's steel mills. The mill owners argue that the President's order amounts to lawmaking, a legislative function which the Constitution has expressly confided to the Congress and not to the President. The Government's position is that the order was made on findings of the President that his action was necessary to avert a national catastrophe which would inevitably result from a stoppage of steel production, and that in meeting this grave emergency the President was acting within the aggregate of his constitutional powers as the Nation's Chief Executive and the Commander in Chief of the Armed Forces of the United States.

The President's power, if any, to issue the order must stem either from an act of Congress or from the Constitution itself. There is no statute that expressly authorizes the President to take possession of property as he did here. Nor is there any act of Congress to which our attention has been directed from which such a power can fairly be implied. Indeed, we do not understand the Government to rely on statutory authorization for this seizure. There are two statutes which do authorize the President to take both personal and real property under certain conditions. [The Selective Service Act of 1948 and the Defense Production Act of 1950.] However, the Government admits that these conditions were not met and that the President's order was not rooted in either of them. The Government refers to the seizure provisions of one of these statutes (§ 201 (b) of the Defense Production Act) as "much too cumbersome, involved, and time-consuming for the crisis which was at hand."

Moreover, the use of the seizure technique to solve labor disputes in order to prevent work stoppages was not only unauthorized by any congressional enactment; prior to this controversy, Congress had refused to adopt that method of settling labor disputes. When the Taft-Hartley Act was under consideration in 1947, Congress rejected an amendment which would have authorized such governmental seizures in cases of emergency. Apparently it was thought that the technique of seizure, like that of compulsory arbitration, would interfere with the process of collective bargaining. Consequently, the plan Congress adopted in that Act did not provide for seizure under any circumstances. Instead, the plan sought to bring about settlements by use of the customary devices of mediation, conciliation, investigation by boards of inquiry, and public reports. In some instances temporary injunctions were authorized to provide cooling-off periods. All this failing, unions were left free to strike after a secret vote by employees as to whether they wished to accept their employers' final settlement offer.

It is clear that if the President had authority to issue the order he did, it must be found in some provisions of the Constitution. And it is not claimed that express constitutional language grants this power to the President. The contention is that presidential power should be implied from the aggregate of his powers under the Constitution. Particular reliance is placed on provisions in Article Two which say that "The executive Power shall be vested in a President"; that "he shall take care that the laws be faithfully executed"; and that he "shall be Commander in Chief of the Army and Navy of the United States."

The order cannot properly be sustained as an exercise of the President's military power as Commander in Chief of the Armed Forces. The Government attempts to do so by citing a number of cases upholding broad powers in military commanders engaged in day-to-day fighting in a theater of war. Such cases need not concern us here. Even though "theater of war" be an expanding concept, we cannot with faithfulness to our constitutional system hold that the Commander in Chief of the Armed Forces has the ultimate power as such to take possession of private property in order to keep labor disputes from stopping production. This is a job for the Nation's lawmakers, not for its military authorities.

Nor can the seizure order be sustained because of the several constitutional provisions that grant executive power to the President. In the framework of our Constitution the President's power to see that the laws are faithfully executed refutes the idea that he is to be a lawmaker. The Constitution limits his functions in the lawmaking process to the recommending of laws he thinks wise and the vetoing of laws he thinks bad. And the Constitution is neither silent nor equivocal about who shall make laws which the President is to execute. The first section of the first article says that "All legislative Powers herein granted shall be vested in a Congress of the United States. . . ."

The President's order does not direct that a congressional policy be executed in a manner prescribed by Congress—it directs that a presidential policy be executed in a manner prescribed by the President. The preamble of the order itself, like that of many statutes, sets out reasons why the President believes certain policies should be adopted, proclaims these policies as rules of conduct to be followed, and again, like a statute, authorizes a government official to promulgate additional rules and regulations consistent with the policy proclaimed and needed to carry the policy into execution. The power of Congress to adopt such public policies as those proclaimed by the order is beyond question. It can authorize the taking of private property for public use.

The Founders of this Nation entrusted the lawmaking power to the Congress alone in both good and bad times. It would do no good to recall the historical events, the fears of power and the hopes for freedom that lay behind their choice. Such a review would but confirm our holding that this seizure order cannot stand. The judgment of the District Court is

Affirmed.

JUSTICE FRANKFURTER concurred.

A scheme of government like ours no doubt at times feels the lack of power to act with complete, all-embracing, swiftly moving authority. No doubt a government with distributed authority, subject to be challenged in the courts of laws, at least long enough to consider and adjudicate the challenge, labors under restrictions from which other governments are free. It has not been our tradition to envy such governments. In any event our government was designed to have such restrictions. The price was deemed not too high in view of the safeguards which these restrictions afford.

JUSTICE DOUGLAS concurred.

There can be no doubt that the emergency which caused the President to seize these steel plants was one that bore heavily on the country. But the emergency did not create power; it merely marked an occasion when power should be exercised. And the fact that it was necessary that measures be taken to keep steel in production does not mean that the President, rather than the Congress, had the constitutional authority to act. The Congress, as well as the President, is trustee of the national welfare. The President can act more quickly than the Congress. The President with the armed services at his disposal can move with force as well as with speed. All executive power—from the reign of ancient kings to the rule of modern dictators—has the outward appearance of efficiency.

Legislative action may indeed often be cumbersome, time-consuming, and apparently inefficient. But as Mr. Justice Brandeis stated in his dissent in *Myers v. United States,* 272 U.S. 52 (1926):

> The doctrine of the separation of powers was adopted by the Convention of 1787, not to promote efficiency but to preclude the exercise of arbitrary power. The purpose was, not to avoid friction, but, by means of the inevitable friction incident to the distribution of the governmental powers among three departments, to save the people from autocracy.

We therefore cannot decide this case by determining which branch of government can deal most expeditiously with the present crisis. The answer must depend on the allocation of powers under the Constitution. That in turn requires an analysis of the conditions giving rise to the seizure and of the seizure itself.

We pay a price for our system of checks and balances, for the distribution of power among the three branches of government. It is a price that today may seem exorbitant to many. Today a kindly President uses the seizure power to effect a wage increase and to keep the steel furnaces in production. Yet tomorrow another President might use the same power to prevent a wage increase, to curb trade unionists, to regiment labor as oppressively as industry thinks it has been regimented by this seizure.

JUSTICE JACKSON, concurring in the judgment and opinion of the Court.

That comprehensive and undefined presidential powers hold both practical advantages and grave dangers for the country will impress anyone who has served as legal adviser to a President in time of transition and public anxiety. While an interval of detached reflection may temper teachings of that experience, they probably are a more realistic influence on my views than the conventional materials of judicial decision which seem unduly to accentuate doctrine and legal fiction. But as we approach the question of presidential power, we half overcome mental hazards by recognizing them. The opinions of judges, no less than executives and publicists, often suffer the infirmity of confusing the issue of a power's validity with the cause it is invoked to promote, of confounding the permanent executive office with its temporary occupant. The tendency is strong to emphasize transient results upon policies—such as wages or stabilization—and lose sight of enduring consequences upon the balanced power structure of our Republic.

A judge, like an executive adviser, may be surprised at the poverty of really useful and unambiguous authority applicable to concrete problems of executive power as they actually present themselves. Just what our forefathers did envision, or would have envisioned had they foreseen modern conditions, must be divined from materials almost as enigmatic as the dreams Joseph was called upon to interpret for Pharaoh. A century and a half of partisan debate and scholarly speculation yields no net result but only supplies more or less apt quotations from respected sources on each side of any question. They largely cancel each other. And court decisions are indecisive because of the judicial practice of dealing with the largest questions in the most narrow way.

The actual art of governing under our Constitution does not and cannot conform to judicial definitions of the power of any of its branches based on isolated clauses or even single Articles torn from context. While the Constitution diffuses power the better to secure liberty, it also contemplates that practice will integrate the dispersed powers into a workable government. It enjoins upon its branches separateness but interdependence, autonomy but reciprocity. Presidential powers are not fixed but fluctuate, depending upon their disjunction or conjunction with those of Congress. We may well begin by a somewhat over-simplified grouping of practical situations in which a President may doubt, or others may challenge, his powers, and by distinguishing roughly the legal consequences of this factor of relativity.

1. When the President acts pursuant to an express or implied authorization of Congress, his authority is at its maximum, for it includes all that he possesses in his own right plus all that Congress can delegate. In these circumstances, and in these only, may he be said (for what it may be worth) to personify the federal sovereignty. If his act is held unconstitutional under these circumstances, it usually means that the Federal Government, as an undivided whole, lacks power. A seizure executed by the President pursuant to an Act of Congress would be supported by the strongest of presumptions and the widest latitude of judicial interpretation, and the burden of persuasion would rest heavily upon any who might attack it.

> It is in this class of cases that we find the broadest recent statements of presidential power, including those relied on here. *United States v. Curtiss-Wright Export Corp.*, 299 U.S. 304 (1936), involved, not the question of the President's power to act without congressional authority, but the question of his right to act under and in accord with an Act of Congress. The constitutionality of the Act under which the President had proceeded was assailed on the ground that it delegated legislative powers to the President. Much of the Court's opinion is dictum, but the ***ratio decidendi*** is contained in the following language:
>
> > When the President is to be authorized by legislation to act in respect of a matter intended to affect a situation in foreign territory, the legislator properly bears in mind the important consideration that the form of the President's action—or, indeed, whether he shall act at all—may well depend, among other things, upon the nature of the confidential information which he has or may thereafter receive, or upon the effect which his action may have upon our foreign relations. This consideration, in connection with what we have already said on the subject, discloses the unwisdom of requiring Congress in this field of governmental power to lay down narrowly definite standards by which the President is to be governed. As this court said in *Mackenzie v. Hare*, 239 U.S. 299, 311 (1915), "As a government, the United States is invested with all the attributes of sovereignty. As it has the character of nationality it has the powers of nationality, especially those which concern its relations and intercourse with other countries. We should hesitate long before limiting or embarrassing such powers."

That case does not solve the present controversy. It recognized internal and external affairs as being in separate categories, and held that the strict limitation upon congressional delegations of power to the President over internal affairs does not apply with respect to delegations of power in external affairs. It was intimated that the President might act in external affairs without congressional authority, but not that he might act contrary to an Act of Congress.

2. When the President acts in absence of either a congressional grant or denial of authority, he can only rely upon his own independent powers, but there is a zone of twilight in which he and Congress may have concurrent authority, or in which its distribution is uncertain. Therefore, congressional inertia, indifference or quiescence may sometimes, at least as a practical matter, enable, if not invite, measures on independent presidential responsibility. In this area, any actual test of power is likely to depend on the imperatives of events and contemporary imponderables rather than on abstract theories of law.*

3. When the President takes measures incompatible with the expressed or implied will of Congress, his power is at its lowest ebb, for then he can rely only upon his own constitutional powers minus any constitutional powers of Congress over the matter. Courts can sustain exclusive Presidential control in such a case only be disabling the Congress from acting upon the subject.** Presidential claim to a power at once so conclusive and preclusive must be scrutinized with caution, for what is at stake is the equilibrium established by our constitutional system.

JUSTICE BURTON concurred.

The controlling fact here is that Congress, within its constitutionally delegated power, has prescribed for the President specific procedures, exclusive of seizure, for his use in meeting the present type of emergency. Congress has reserved to itself the right to determine where and when to authorize the seizure of property in meeting such an emergency. Under these circumstances, the President's order of April 8 invaded the jurisdiction of Congress. It violated the essence of the principle of the separation of governmental powers. Accordingly, the injunction against its effectiveness should be sustained.

JUSTICE CLARK concurred:

I conclude th[at] where Congress has laid down specific procedures to deal with the type of crisis confronting the President, he must follow those procedures in meeting the crisis; but that in the absence of such action by Congress, the President's independent power to act depends upon the gravity of the situation confronting the nation. I cannot sustain the seizure in question because here, Congress had prescribed methods to be followed by the President in meeting the emergency at hand.

JUSTICE VINSON dissented and was joined by JUSTICES REED and MINTON.

Much of the argument in this case has been directed at straw men. We do not now have before us the case of a President acting solely on the basis of his own notions of the public welfare. Nor is there any question of unlimited executive power in this case. The President himself closed the door to any such claim when he sent his Message to Congress stating his purpose to abide by any action of Congress, whether approving or disapproving his seizure action. Here, the President immediately made sure that Congress was fully informed of the temporary action he had taken only to preserve the legislative programs from destruction until Congress could act.

* Since the Constitution implies that the writ of habeas corpus may be suspended in certain circumstances but does not say by whom, President Lincoln asserted and maintained it as an executive function in the face of judicial challenge and doubt.

** President Roosevelt's effort to remove a Federal Trade Commissioner was found to be contrary to the policy of Congress and impinging upon an area of congressional control, and so his removal power was cut down accordingly.

The absence of a specific statute authorizing seizure of the steel mills as a mode of executing the laws—both the military procurement program and the anti-inflation program—has not until today been thought to prevent the President from executing the laws. Unlike an administrative commission confined to the enforcement of the statute under which it was created, or the head of a department when administering a particular statute, the President is a constitutional officer charged with taking care that a "mass of legislation" be executed. Flexibility as to mode of execution to meet critical situations is a matter of practical necessity.

FOR DISCUSSION

According to Jackson, does the president have more authority in foreign affairs overseas than within the United States? Could congressional authorization expand the president's constitutional power? Could congressional action limit the president's constitutional power?

PERPICH V. DEPARTMENT OF DEFENSE

496 U.S. 334, 110 S.Ct. 2418, 110 L.Ed.2d 312 (1990)

Rudy Perpich, governor of Minnesota, objected to President Ronald Reagan ordering the Minnesota National Guard to report for training outside of the United States pursuant to authority given him by Congress. The governor objected to deployment of the Guard for exercises in Guatemala as part of a military exercise to oppose the leaders in Nicaragua. Perpich contested the deployment of the Guard, contending that the president needed the permission of the governor.

Vote: 9–0

JUSTICE STEVENS delivered the opinion for a unanimous Court.

The question presented is whether the Congress may authorize the President to order members of the National Guard to active duty for purposes of training outside the United States during peacetime without either the consent of a State Governor or the declaration of a national emergency.

A gubernatorial consent requirement that had been enacted in 1952 was partially repealed in 1986 by the "Montgomery Amendment," which provides:

Sec. 101. When used in this Act—

(c) "Active duty for training" means full-time duty in the active military service of the United States for training purposes.

[Section 233] (c) At any time, any unit and the members thereof, or any member not assigned to a unit organized for the purpose of serving as such, in an active status in any reserve component may, by competent authority, be ordered to and required to perform active duty or active duty for training, without his consent, for not to exceed fifteen days annually: *Provided,* That units and members of the National Guard of the United States or the Air National Guard of the United States shall not be ordered to or required to serve on active duty in the service of the United States pursuant to this subsection without the consent of the Governor of the State or Territory concerned, or the Commanding General of the District of Columbia National Guard.

(d) A member of a reserve component may, by competent authority, be ordered to active duty or active duty for training at any time with his consent: *Provided,* That no member of the National Guard

> of the United States or Air National Guard of the United States shall be so ordered without the consent of the Governor or other appropriate authority of the State, Territory, or District of Columbia concerned.

These provisions, as amended, are now codified at 10 U.S.C. §§ 672(b) and 672(d).

> The consent of a Governor described in subsections (b) and (d) may not be withheld (in whole or in part) with regard to active duty outside the United States, its territories, and its possessions, because of any objection to the location, purpose, type, or schedule of such active duty.

In this litigation the Governor of Minnesota and the State of Minnesota (hereinafter collectively referred to as the Governor), challenge the constitutionality of that amendment. The Governor contends that it violates the Militia Clauses of the Constitution.*

In his complaint the Governor alleged that pursuant to a state statute the Minnesota National Guard is the organized militia of the State of Minnesota and that pursuant to a federal statute members of that militia "are also members of either the Minnesota unit of the Air National Guard of the United States or the Minnesota unit of the Army National Guard of the United States (hereinafter collectively referred to as the 'National Guard of the United States')." The complaint further alleged that the Montgomery Amendment had prevented the Governor from withholding his consent to a training mission in Central America for certain members of the Minnesota National Guard in January 1987, and prayed for an injunction against the implementation of any similar orders without his consent.

I

Two conflicting themes, developed at the Constitutional Convention and repeated in debates over military policy during the next century, led to a compromise in the text of the Constitution and in later statutory enactments. On the one hand, there was a widespread fear that a national standing Army posed an intolerable threat to individual liberty and to the sovereignty of the separate States, while, on the other hand, there was a recognition of the danger of relying on inadequately trained soldiers as the primary means of providing for the common defense. Thus, Congress was authorized both to raise and support a national Army and also to organize "the Militia."

In the early years of the Republic, Congress did neither. In 1792, it did pass a statute that purported to establish "an Uniform Militia throughout the United States," but its detailed command that every able-bodied male citizen between the ages of 18 and 45 be enrolled therein and equip himself with appropriate weaponry was virtually ignored for more than a century, during which time the militia proved to be a decidedly unreliable fighting force. The statute was finally repealed in 1901. It was in that year that President Theodore Roosevelt declared: "Our militia law is obsolete and worthless." The process of transforming "the National Guard of the several States" into an effective fighting force then began.

The Dick Act divided the class of able-bodied male citizens between 18 and 45 years of age into an "organized militia" to be known as the National Guard of the several States, and the remainder of which was

---

* Two clauses of Article I—clauses 15 and 16 of § 8—are commonly described as "the Militia Clause" or "the Militia Clauses." They provide:

> The Congress shall have Power . . .
>
> . . . .
>
> To provide for calling forth the Militia to execute the Laws of the Union, suppress Insurrections and repel Invasions;
>
> To provide for organizing, arming, and disciplining, the Militia, and for governing such Part of them as may be employed in the Service of the United States, reserving to the States respectively, the Appointment of the Officers, and the Authority of training the Militia according to the discipline prescribed by Congress."

then described as the "reserve militia," and which later statutes have termed the "unorganized militia." The statute created a table of organization for the National Guard conforming to that of the Regular Army, and provided that federal funds and Regular Army instructors should be used to train its members. It is undisputed that Congress was acting pursuant to the Militia Clauses of the Constitution in passing the Dick Act. Moreover, the legislative history of that Act indicates that Congress contemplated that the services of the organized militia would "be rendered only upon the soil of the United States or of its Territories." In 1908, however, the statute was amended to provide expressly that the Organized Militia should be available for service "either within or without the territory of the United States."

During World War I, the President exercised the power to draft members of the National Guard into the Regular Army. That power, as well as the power to compel civilians to render military service, was upheld in the *Selective Draft Law Cases,* 245 U.S. 366 (1918). Specifically, in those cases, and in *Cox v. Wood*, 247 US 3 (1918), the Court held that the plenary power to raise armies was "not qualified or restricted by the provisions of the militia clause."

The draft of the individual members of the National Guard into the Army during World War I virtually destroyed the Guard as an effective organization. The draft terminated the members' status as militiamen, and the statute did not provide for a restoration of their prewar status as members of the Guard when they were mustered out of the Army. This problem was ultimately remedied by the 1933 amendments to the 1916 Act. Those amendments created the "two overlapping but distinct organizations" described by the District Court—the National Guard of the various States and the National Guard of the United States.

Since 1933 all persons who have enlisted in a State National Guard unit have simultaneously enlisted in the National Guard of the United States. In the latter capacity they became a part of the Enlisted Reserve Corps of the Army, but unless and until ordered to active duty in the Army, they retained their status as members of a separate State Guard unit. Under the 1933 Act, they could be ordered into active service whenever Congress declared a national emergency and authorized the use of troops in excess of those in the Regular Army.

Until 1952 the statutory authority to order National Guard units to active duty was limited to periods of national emergency. In that year, Congress broadly authorized orders to "active duty or active duty for training" without any emergency requirement, but provided that such orders could not be issued without gubernatorial consent. The National Guard units have under this plan become a sizable portion of the Nation's military forces; for example, "the Army National Guard provides 46 percent of the combat units and 28 percent of the support forces of the Total Army." Apparently gubernatorial consents to training missions were routinely obtained until 1985, when the Governor of California refused to consent to a training mission for 450 members of the California National Guard in Honduras, and the Governor of Maine shortly thereafter refused to consent to a similar mission. Those incidents led to the enactment of the Montgomery Amendment and this litigation ensued.

II

The Governor's attack on the Montgomery Amendment relies in part on the traditional understanding that "the Militia" can only be called forth for three limited purposes that do not encompass either foreign service or nonemergency conditions, and in part on the express language in the second Militia Clause reserving to the States "the Authority of training the Militia." The Governor does not, however, challenge the authority of Congress to create a dual enlistment program. Nor does the Governor claim that membership in a State Guard unit—or any type of state militia—creates any sort of constitutional immunity from being drafted into the Federal Armed Forces. Indeed, it would be ironic to claim such immunity when every member of the Minnesota National Guard has voluntarily enlisted, or accepted a commission as an officer, in the National Guard of the United States and thereby become a member of the Reserve Corps of the Army.

The unchallenged validity of the dual enlistment system means that the members of the National Guard of Minnesota who are ordered into federal service with the National Guard of the United States lose their status as members of the state militia during their period of active duty. If that duty is a training mission, the training is performed by the Army in which the trainee is serving, not by the militia from which the member has been temporarily disassociated. "Each member of the Army National Guard of the United States or the Air National Guard of the United States who is ordered to active duty is relieved from duty in the National Guard of his State or Territory, or of Puerto Rico or the District of Columbia, as the case may be, from the effective date of his order to active duty until he is relieved from that duty."

This view of the constitutional issue was presupposed by our decision in the *Selective Draft Law Cases*. Although the Governor is correct in pointing out that those cases were decided in the context of an actual war, the reasoning in our opinion was not so limited. After expressly noting that the 1916 Act had incorporated members of the National Guard into the National Army, the Court held that the Militia Clauses do not constrain the powers of Congress "to provide for the common Defence," to "raise and support Armies," to "make Rules for the Government and Regulation of the land and naval Forces," or to enact such laws as "shall be necessary and proper" for executing those powers The Court instead held that, far from being a limitation on those powers, the Militia Clauses are—as the constitutional text plainly indicates—additional grants of power to Congress.

The first empowers Congress to call forth the militia "to execute the Laws of the Union, suppress Insurrections and repel Invasions." We may assume that Attorney General Wickersham was entirely correct in reasoning that when a National Guard unit retains its status as a state militia, Congress could not "impress" the entire unit for any other purpose. Congress did, however, authorize the President to call forth the entire membership of the Guard into federal service during World War I, even though the soldiers who fought in France were not engaged in any of the three specified purposes. Membership in the Militia did not exempt them from a valid order to perform federal service, whether that service took the form of combat duty or training for such duty. The congressional power to call forth the militia may in appropriate cases supplement its broader power to raise armies and provide for the common defense and general welfare, but it does not limit those powers.

The second Militia Clause enhances federal power in three additional ways. First, it authorizes Congress to provide for "organizing, arming and disciplining the Militia." It is by congressional choice that the available pool of citizens has been formed into organized units. Over the years, Congress has exercised this power in various ways, but its current choice of a dual enlistment system is just as permissible as the 1792 choice to have the members of the militia arm themselves. Second, the Clause authorizes Congress to provide for governing such part of the militia as may be employed in the service of the United States. Surely this authority encompasses continued training while on active duty. Finally, although the appointment of officers "and the Authority of training the Militia" is reserved to the States respectively, that limitation is, in turn, limited by the words "according to the discipline prescribed by Congress." If the discipline required for effective service in the Armed Forces of a global power requires training in distant lands, or distant skies, Congress has the authority to provide it. The subordinate authority to perform the actual training prior to active duty in the federal service does not include the right to edit the discipline that Congress may prescribe for Guard members after they are ordered into federal service.

The Governor argues that this interpretation of the Militia Clauses has the practical effect of nullifying an important state power that is expressly reserved in the Constitution. We disagree. It merely recognizes the supremacy of federal power in the area of military affairs. The Federal Government provides virtually all of the funding, the materiel, and the leadership for the State Guard units. The Minnesota unit, which includes about 13,000 members, is affected only slightly when a few dozen, or at most a few hundred, soldiers are ordered into active service for brief periods of time. Neither the State's basic training responsibility, nor its ability to rely on its own Guard in state emergency situations, is significantly affected. Indeed, if the federal training mission were to interfere with the State Guard's capacity to respond to local emergencies, the Montgomery Amendment would permit the Governor to veto the proposed mission. Moreover, Congress has provided by statute that in addition to its National Guard, a State may provide and maintain at its own expense a defense force that is exempt from being drafted into the Armed Forces of the United States. As long as that provision remains in effect, there is no basis for an argument that the federal statutory scheme deprives Minnesota of any constitutional entitlement to a separate militia of its own.

In light of the Constitution's more general plan for providing for the common defense, the powers allowed to the States by existing statutes are significant. As has already been mentioned, several constitutional provisions commit matters of foreign policy and military affairs to the exclusive control of the National Government. This Court in *Tarble's Case*, 80 US 397 (1871), had occasion to observe that the constitutional allocation of powers in this realm gave rise to a presumption that federal control over the Armed Forces was exclusive. Were it not for the Militia Clauses, it might be possible to argue on like grounds that the constitutional allocation of powers precluded the formation of organized state militia. The Militia Clauses, however, subordinate any such structural inferences to an express permission while also subjecting state militia to express federal limitations.

We thus conclude that the Montgomery Amendment is not inconsistent with the Militia Clauses. In so doing, we of course do not pass upon the relative virtues of the various political choices that have frequently altered the relationship between the Federal Government and the States in the field of military affairs. This case does not raise any question concerning the wisdom of the gubernatorial veto established in 1952 or of its partial repeal in 1986. We merely hold that because the former was not constitutionally compelled, the Montgomery Amendment is constitutionally valid.

The judgment of the Court of Appeals is affirmed.

FOR DISCUSSION

After *Perpich*, do governors have any authority to refuse the deployment of National Guard troops if the president calls them into service? Why does the Court reject federalism concerns here?

MISSOURI V. HOLLAND

252 U.S. 416, 40 S.Ct. 382, 64 L.Ed. 641 (1920)

The United States and Great Britain in 1916 had entered into a **treaty** for the protection of migratory birds in the United States and Canada. The treaty included a provision that the contracting powers would enact legislation to implement the purposes of the treaty. Congress in 1918 enacted a statute, The Migratory Bird Treaty Act, forbidding the killing, capturing, or sale of the protected birds except in accordance with regulations established by the secretary of agriculture. Missouri challenged the action as an invasion of state powers and sued to enjoin a federal game warden from carrying out the provisions of the statute and the regulations of the secretary of agriculture.

This case is excerpted in Chapter Two, 110.

DISCUSSION

Could the president and Congress use the treaty-making authority to change a state's representation in the Senate? Given the opinion by Holmes, are there any limits to the treaty-making power? Is federalism limited by the treaty power?

ZIVOTOFSKY EX REL. ZIVOTOFSKY V. KERRY

___ U.S. ___, 135 S.Ct. 2076, 192 L.Ed.2d 83 (2015)

A minor child born in Jerusalem sought through his parents to have his passport mark his country of birth as Israel. He sought declaratory and injunctive relief against Secretary of State John Kerry, contending that Foreign Relations Authorization Act (FRAA) permitted this passport designation. The United States District Court for the District of Columbia dismissed the case. The United States Court of Appeals for the District of Columbia Circuit, reversed and remanded for further development of the record. On remand, the District Court again dismissed and the Court of Appeals affirmed. The Supreme Court vacated and remanded. On remand the Court of Appeals affirmed, the Supreme Court granted certiorari and affirmed.

Vote 6–3

JUSTICE KENNEDY wrote for the Court joined by GINSBURG, SOTOMAYOR, and KAGAN.

JUSTICE BREYER filed concurring opinion.

JUSTICE THOMAS filed opinion concurring in part and dissenting in part.

CHIEF JUSTICE ROBERTS filed dissenting opinion, in which JUSTICE ALITO joined.

JUSTICE SCALIA filed dissenting opinion, in which CHIEF JUSTICE ROBERTS and JUSTICE ALITO joined.

The Court addresses two questions to resolve the interbranch dispute now before it. First, it must determine whether the President has the exclusive power to grant formal recognition to a foreign sovereign. Second, if he has that power, the Court must determine whether Congress can command the President and his Secretary of State to issue a formal statement that contradicts the earlier recognition. The statement in question here is a congressional mandate that allows a United States citizen born in Jerusalem to direct the President and Secretary of State, when issuing his passport, to state that his place of birth is "Israel."

I

A

Jerusalem's political standing has long been, and remains, one of the most sensitive issues in American foreign policy, and indeed it is one of the most delicate issues in current international affairs. In 1948, President Truman formally recognized Israel in a signed statement of "recognition." That statement did not recognize Israeli sovereignty over Jerusalem. Over the last 60 years, various actors have sought to assert full or partial sovereignty over the city, including Israel, Jordan, and the Palestinians. Yet, in contrast to a consistent policy of formal recognition of Israel, neither President Truman nor any later United States President has issued an official statement or declaration acknowledging any country's sovereignty over Jerusalem. Instead, the Executive Branch has maintained that " 'the status of Jerusalem . . . should be decided not unilaterally but in consultation with all concerned.' "

The President's position on Jerusalem is reflected in State Department policy regarding passports and consular reports of birth abroad. Understanding that passports will be construed as reflections of American policy, the State Department's Foreign Affairs Manual instructs its employees, in general, to record the place of birth on a passport as the "country [having] present sovereignty over the actual area of birth.". If a citizen objects to the country listed as sovereign by the State Department, he or she may list the city or town of birth rather than the country. The FAM, however, does not allow citizens to list a sovereign that conflicts with Executive Branch policy. Because the United States does not recognize any country as having sovereignty over Jerusalem, the FAM instructs employees to record the place of birth for citizens born there as "Jerusalem."

In 2002, Congress passed the Act at issue here, the Foreign Relations Authorization Act. Section 214 of the Act is titled "United States Policy with Respect to Jerusalem as the Capital of Israel." The subsection that lies at the heart of this case, § 214(d), addresses passports. That subsection seeks to override the FAM by allowing citizens born in Jerusalem to list their place of birth as "Israel." Titled "Record of Place of Birth as Israel for Passport Purposes," § 214(d) states "[f]or purposes of the registration of birth, certification of nationality, or issuance of a passport of a United States citizen born in the city of Jerusalem, the Secretary shall, upon the request of the citizen or the citizen's legal guardian, record the place of birth as Israel."

When he signed the Act into law, President George W. Bush issued a statement declaring his position that § 214 would, "if construed as mandatory rather than advisory, impermissibly interfere with the President's constitutional authority to formulate the position of the United States, speak for the Nation in international affairs, and determine the terms on which recognition is given to foreign states." The President concluded, "U.S. policy regarding Jerusalem has not changed."

B

In 2002, petitioner Menachem Binyamin Zivotofsky was born to United States citizens living in Jerusalem. In December 2002, Zivotofsky's mother visited the American Embassy in Tel Aviv to request both a passport and a consular report of birth abroad for her son. She asked that his place of birth be listed as " 'Jerusalem, Israel.' " The Embassy clerks explained that, pursuant to State Department policy, the passport would list only "Jerusalem.". Zivotofsky's parents objected and, as his guardians, brought suit on his behalf in the United States District Court for the District of Columbia, seeking to enforce § 214(d).

II

In considering claims of Presidential power this Court refers to Justice Jackson's familiar tripartite framework from *Youngstown Sheet & Tube Co. v. Sawyer*. The framework divides exercises of Presidential power into three categories: First, when "the President acts pursuant to an express or implied authorization of Congress, his authority is at its maximum, for it includes all that he possesses in his own right plus all that Congress can delegate." Second, "in absence of either a congressional grant or denial of authority" there is a "zone of twilight in which he and Congress may have concurrent authority," and where "congressional inertia, indifference or quiescence may" invite the exercise of executive power. Finally, when "the President takes measures incompatible with the expressed or implied will of Congress . . . he can rely only upon his own constitutional powers minus any constitutional powers of Congress over the matter.". To succeed in this third category, the President's asserted power must be both "exclusive" and "conclusive" on the issue.

In this case the Secretary contends that § 214(d) infringes on the President's exclusive recognition power by "requiring the President to contradict his recognition position regarding Jerusalem in official communications with foreign sovereigns." Brief for Respondent 48. In so doing the Secretary acknowledges the President's power is "at its lowest ebb." *Youngstown*. Because the President's refusal to implement § 214(d) falls into Justice Jackson's third category, his claim must be "scrutinized with caution," and he may rely solely on powers the Constitution grants to him alone.

To determine whether the President possesses the exclusive power of recognition the Court examines the Constitution's text and structure, as well as precedent and history bearing on the question.

A

Recognition is a "formal acknowledgement" that a particular "entity possesses the qualifications for statehood" or "that a particular regime is the effective government of a state." Restatement (Third) of Foreign Relations Law of the United States § 203, Comment *a,* p. 84 (1986). Recognition is often effected by an express "written or oral declaration." 1 J. Moore, Digest of International Law § 27, p. 73 (1906) (Moore). It may also be implied—for example, by concluding a bilateral treaty or by sending or receiving diplomatic agents.; I. Brownlie, Principles of Public International Law 93 (7th ed. 2008) (Brownlie).

Legal consequences follow formal recognition. Recognized sovereigns may sue in United States courts, and may benefit from sovereign immunity when they are sued. The actions of a recognized sovereign committed within its own territory also receive deference in domestic courts under the act of state doctrine. Recognition at international law, furthermore, is a precondition of regular diplomatic relations. Recognition is thus "useful, even necessary," to the existence of a state.

Despite the importance of the recognition power in foreign relations, the Constitution does not use the term "recognition," either in Article II or elsewhere. The Secretary asserts that the President exercises the recognition power based on the Reception Clause, which directs that the President "shall receive Ambassadors and other public Ministers." Art. II, § 3. As Zivotofsky notes, the Reception Clause received little attention at the Constitutional Convention. In fact, during the ratification debates, Alexander Hamilton claimed that the power to receive ambassadors was "more a matter of dignity than of authority," a ministerial duty largely "without consequence." The Federalist No. 69, p. 420 (C. Rossiter ed. 1961).

At the time of the founding, however, prominent international scholars suggested that receiving an ambassador was tantamount to recognizing the sovereignty of the sending state. It is a logical and proper inference, then, that a Clause directing the President alone to receive ambassadors would be understood to acknowledge his power to recognize other nations.

This in fact occurred early in the Nation's history when President Washington recognized the French Revolutionary Government by receiving its ambassador. After this incident the import of the Reception Clause became clear—causing Hamilton to change his earlier view. He wrote that the Reception Clause "includes th[e power] of judging, in the case of a revolution of government in a foreign country, whether the new rulers are competent organs of the national will, and ought to be recognised, or not." As a result, the Reception Clause provides support, although not the sole authority, for the President's power to recognize other nations.

The inference that the President exercises the recognition power is further supported by his additional Article II powers. It is for the President, "by and with the Advice and Consent of the Senate," to "make Treaties, provided two thirds of the Senators present concur." Art. II, § 2, cl. 2. In addition, "he shall nominate, and by and with the Advice and Consent of the Senate, shall appoint Ambassadors" as well as "other public Ministers and Consuls.".

As a matter of constitutional structure, these additional powers give the President control over recognition decisions. At international law, recognition may be effected by different means, but each means is dependent upon Presidential power. In addition to receiving an ambassador, recognition may occur on "the conclusion of a bilateral treaty," or the "formal initiation of diplomatic relations," including the dispatch of an ambassador. The President has the sole power to negotiate treaties, see *United States v. Curtiss-Wright Export Corp.,* 299 U.S. 304, 319, 57 S.Ct. 216, 81 L.Ed. 255 (1936), and the Senate may not conclude or ratify a treaty without Presidential action. The President, too, nominates the Nation's ambassadors and dispatches other diplomatic agents. Congress may not send an ambassador without his involvement. Beyond that, the President himself has the power to open diplomatic channels simply by engaging in direct diplomacy with foreign heads of state and their ministers. The Constitution thus assigns the President means to effect recognition on his own initiative. Congress, by contrast, has no constitutional power that would enable it to initiate diplomatic relations with a foreign nation. Because these specific Clauses confer the recognition power on the President, the Court need not consider whether or to what extent the Vesting Clause, which provides that the "executive Power" shall be vested in the President, provides further support for the President's action here. Art. II, § 1, cl. 1.

The text and structure of the Constitution grant the President the power to recognize foreign nations and governments. The question then becomes whether that power is exclusive. The various ways in which the President may unilaterally effect recognition—and the lack of any similar power vested in Congress—suggest that it is. So, too, do functional considerations. Put simply, the Nation must have a single policy regarding which governments are legitimate in the eyes of the United States and which are not. Foreign countries need to know, before entering into diplomatic relations or commerce with the United States, whether their ambassadors will be received; whether their officials will be immune from suit in federal court; and whether they may initiate lawsuits here to vindicate their rights. These assurances cannot be equivocal.

As described in more detail below, the President since the founding has exercised this unilateral power to recognize new states—and the Court has endorsed the practice. Texts and treaties on international law treat the President's word as the final word on recognition. In light of this authority all six judges who considered this case in the Court of Appeals agreed that the President holds the exclusive recognition power.

In foreign affairs, as in the domestic realm, the Constitution "enjoins upon its branches separateness but interdependence, autonomy but reciprocity." *Youngstown,* 343 U.S., at 635, 72 S.Ct. 863 (Jackson, J., concurring). Although the President alone effects the formal act of recognition, Congress' powers, and its central role in making laws, give it substantial authority regarding many of the policy determinations that precede and follow the act of recognition itself. If Congress disagrees with the President's recognition policy, there may be consequences. Formal recognition may seem a hollow act if it is not accompanied by the dispatch of an ambassador, the easing of trade restrictions, and the conclusion of treaties. And those decisions require action by the Senate or the whole Congress.

In practice, then, the President's recognition determination is just one part of a political process that may require Congress to make laws. The President's exclusive recognition power encompasses the authority to acknowledge, in a formal sense, the legitimacy of other states and governments, including their territorial bounds. Albeit limited, the exclusive recognition power is essential to the conduct of Presidential duties. The formal act of recognition is an executive power that Congress may not qualify. If the President is to be effective in negotiations over a formal recognition determination, it must be evident to his counterparts abroad that he speaks for the Nation on that precise question.

A clear rule that the formal power to recognize a foreign government subsists in the President therefore serves a necessary purpose in diplomatic relations. All this, of course, underscores that Congress has an important role in other aspects of foreign policy, and the President may be bound by any number of laws Congress enacts. In this way ambition counters ambition, ensuring that the democratic will of the people is observed and respected in foreign affairs as in the domestic realm. See The Federalist No. 51, p. 322 (J. Madison).

B

No single precedent resolves the question whether the President has exclusive recognition authority and, if so, how far that power extends. In part that is because, until today, the political branches have resolved their disputes over questions of recognition. The relevant cases, though providing important instruction, address the division of recognition power between the Federal Government and the States, or between the courts and the political branches—not between the President and Congress. As the parties acknowledge, some isolated statements in those cases lend support to the position that Congress has a role in the recognition process. In the end, however, a fair reading of the cases shows that the President's role in the recognition process is both central and exclusive.

During the administration of President Van Buren, in a case involving a dispute over the status of the Falkland Islands, the Court noted that "when the executive branch of the government" assumes "a fact in regard to the sovereignty of any island or country, it is conclusive on the judicial department." Once the President has made his determination, it "is enough to know, that in the exercise of his constitutional functions, he has decided the question. Having done this under the responsibilities which belong to him, it is obligatory on the people and government of the Union." Later, during the 1930's and 1940's, the Court addressed issues surrounding President Roosevelt's decision to recognize the Soviet Government of Russia. In *United States v. Belmont,* 301 U.S. 324, 57 S.Ct. 758, 81 L.Ed. 1134 (1937), and *Pink,* 315 U.S. 203, 62 S.Ct. 552, 86 L.Ed. 796, New York state courts declined to give full effect to the terms of executive agreements the President had concluded in negotiations over recognition of the Soviet regime. In particular the state courts, based on New York public policy, did not treat assets that had been seized by the Soviet Government as property of Russia and declined to turn those assets over to the United States. The Court stated that it "may not be doubted" that "recognition, establishment of diplomatic relations, . . . and agreements with respect thereto" are "within the competence of the President." In these matters, "the Executive ha[s] authority to speak as the sole organ of th [e] government.". The Court added that the President's authority "is not limited to a determination of the government to be recognized. It includes the power to determine the policy which is to govern the question of recognition." Thus, New York state courts were required to respect the executive agreements.

It is true, of course, that *Belmont* and *Pink* are not direct holdings that the recognition power is exclusive. Those cases considered the validity of executive agreements, not the initial act of recognition. The President's determination in those cases did not contradict an Act of Congress. And the primary issue was whether the executive agreements could supersede state law. Still, the language in *Pink* and *Belmont,* which confirms the President's competence to determine questions of recognition, is strong support for the conclusion that it is for the President alone to determine which foreign governments are legitimate.

The Secretary now urges the Court to define the executive power over foreign relations in even broader terms. He contends that under the Court's precedent the President has "exclusive authority to conduct diplomatic relations," along with "the bulk of foreign-affairs powers." In support of his submission that the President has broad, undefined powers over foreign affairs, the Secretary quotes *United States v. Curtiss-Wright Export Corp.,* which described the President as "the sole organ of the federal government in the field of international relations." This Court declines to acknowledge that unbounded power. A formulation broader than the rule that the President alone determines what nations to formally recognize as legitimate—and that he consequently controls his statements on matters of recognition—presents different issues and is unnecessary to the resolution of this case.

The *Curtiss-Wright* case does not extend so far as the Secretary suggests. In *Curtiss-Wright,* the Court considered whether a congressional delegation of power to the President was constitutional. Congress had passed a joint resolution giving the President the discretion to prohibit arms sales to certain militant powers in South America. The resolution provided criminal penalties for violation of those orders. The Court held that the delegation was constitutional, reasoning that Congress may grant the President substantial authority and discretion in the field of foreign affairs. Describing why such broad delegation may be appropriate, the opinion stated:

> "In this vast external realm, with its important, complicated, delicate and manifold problems, the President alone has the power to speak or listen as a representative of the nation. He *makes* treaties with the advice and consent of the Senate; but he alone negotiates. Into the field of negotiation the

Senate cannot intrude; and Congress itself is powerless to invade it. As Marshall said in his great argument of March 7, 1800, in the House of Representatives, 'The President is the sole organ of the nation in its external relations, and its sole representative with foreign nations.' "

This description of the President's exclusive power was not necessary to the holding of *Curtiss-Wright*—which, after all, dealt with congressionally authorized action, not a unilateral Presidential determination. Indeed, *Curtiss-Wright* did not hold that the President is free from Congress' lawmaking power in the field of international relations. The President does have a unique role in communicating with foreign governments, as then-Congressman John Marshall acknowledged. But whether the realm is foreign or domestic, it is still the Legislative Branch, not the Executive Branch, that makes the law.

In a world that is ever more compressed and interdependent, it is essential the congressional role in foreign affairs be understood and respected. For it is Congress that makes laws, and in countless ways its laws will and should shape the Nation's course. The Executive is not free from the ordinary controls and checks of Congress merely because foreign affairs are at issue. It is not for the President alone to determine the whole content of the Nation's foreign policy.

That said, judicial precedent and historical practice teach that it is for the President alone to make the specific decision of what foreign power he will recognize as legitimate, both for the Nation as a whole and for the purpose of making his own position clear within the context of recognition in discussions and negotiations with foreign nations. Recognition is an act with immediate and powerful significance for international relations, so the President's position must be clear. Congress cannot require him to contradict his own statement regarding a determination of formal recognition.

C

Having examined the Constitution's text and this Court's precedent, it is appropriate to turn to accepted understandings and practice.

From the first Administration forward, the President has claimed unilateral authority to recognize foreign sovereigns. For the most part, Congress has acquiesced in the Executive's exercise of the recognition power. On occasion, the President has chosen, as may often be prudent, to consult and coordinate with Congress. As Judge Tatel noted in this case, however, "the most striking thing" about the history of recognition "is what is absent from it: a situation like this one," where Congress has enacted a statute contrary to the President's formal and considered statement concerning recognition.

The first debate over the recognition power arose in 1793, after France had been torn by revolution. Once the Revolutionary Government was established, Secretary of State Jefferson and President Washington, without consulting Congress, authorized the American Ambassador to resume relations with the new regime. Soon thereafter, the new French Government proposed to send an ambassador, Citizen Genet, to the United States. Members of the President's Cabinet agreed that receiving Genet would be a binding and public act of recognition. They decided, however, both that Genet should be received and that consultation with Congress was not necessary. Congress expressed no disagreement with this position, and Genet's reception marked the Nation's first act of recognition—one made by the President alone.

President Lincoln, too, sought to coordinate with Congress when he requested support for his recognition of Liberia and Haiti. In his first annual message to Congress he said he could see no reason "why we should persevere longer in withholding our recognition of the independence and sovereignty of Hayti and Liberia.". Nonetheless, he was "[u]nwilling" to "inaugurate a novel policy in regard to them without the approbation of Congress.". In response Congress concurred in the President's recognition determination and enacted a law appropriating funds to appoint diplomatic representatives to the two countries—leaving, as usual, the actual dispatch of ambassadors and formal statement of recognition to the President.

Three decades later, the branches again were able to reach an accord, this time with regard to Cuba. In 1898, an insurgency against the Spanish colonial government was raging in Cuba. President McKinley determined to ask Congress for authorization to send armed forces to Cuba to help quell the violence. Although McKinley thought Spain was to blame for the strife, he opposed recognizing either Cuba or its insurgent government. At first, the House proposed a resolution consistent with McKinley's wishes. The Senate countered with a resolution that authorized the use of force but that did recognize both Cuban independence and the insurgent government. *Id.,* at 3993. When the Senate's version reached the House, the House again rejected the language recognizing Cuban independence. *Id.,* at 4017. The resolution went to Conference, which, after debate, reached a compromise. The final resolution stated "the people of the Island of Cuba are, and of right ought to be, free and independent," but made no mention of recognizing a new Cuban Government. Act of Apr. 20, 1898, 30 Stat. 738. Accepting the compromise, the President signed the joint resolution.

For the next 80 years, "[P]residents consistently recognized new states and governments without any serious opposition from, or activity in, Congress." The next debate over recognition did not occur until the late 1970's. It concerned China.

President Carter recognized the People's Republic of China (PRC) as the government of China, and derecognized the Republic of China, located on Taiwan. As to the status of Taiwan, the President "acknowledge[d] the Chinese position" that "Taiwan is part of China," but he did not accept that claim. The President proposed a new law defining how the United States would conduct business with Taiwan. After extensive revisions, Congress passed, and the President signed, the Taiwan Relations Act, 93 Stat. 14 (1979) (codified as amended at 22 U.S.C. §§ 3301–3316). The Act (in a simplified summary) treated Taiwan as if it were a legally distinct entity from China—an entity with which the United States intended to maintain strong ties.

Throughout the legislative process, however, no one raised a serious question regarding the President's exclusive authority to recognize the PRC—or to decline to grant formal recognition to Taiwan. Rather, Congress accepted the President's recognition determination as a completed, lawful act; and it proceeded to outline the trade and policy provisions that, in its judgment, were appropriate in light of that decision.

This history confirms the Court's conclusion in the instant case that the power to recognize or decline to recognize a foreign state and its territorial bounds resides in the President alone.

III

As the power to recognize foreign states resides in the President alone, the question becomes whether § 214(d) infringes on the Executive's consistent decision to withhold recognition with respect to Jerusalem.

Section 214(d) requires that, in a passport or consular report of birth abroad, "the Secretary shall, upon the request of the citizen or the citizen's legal guardian, record the place of birth as Israel" for a "United States citizen born in the city of Jerusalem." That is, § 214(d) requires the President, through the Secretary, to identify citizens born in Jerusalem who so request as being born in Israel. But according to the President, those citizens were not born in Israel. As a matter of United States policy, neither Israel nor any other country is acknowledged as having sovereignty over Jerusalem. In this way, § 214(d) "directly contradicts" the "carefully calibrated and longstanding Executive branch policy of neutrality toward Jerusalem."

If the power over recognition is to mean anything, it must mean that the President not only makes the initial, formal recognition determination but also that he may maintain that determination in his and his agent's statements. This conclusion is a matter of both common sense and necessity. If Congress could command the President to state a recognition position inconsistent with his own, Congress could override the President's recognition determination. Under international law, recognition may be effected by "written or oral declaration of the recognizing state." In addition an act of recognition must "leave no doubt as to the intention to grant it."

Thus, if Congress could alter the President's statements on matters of recognition or force him to contradict them, Congress in effect would exercise the recognition power.

If Congress may not pass a law, speaking in its own voice, that effects formal recognition, then it follows that it may not force the President himself to contradict his earlier statement. That congressional command would not only prevent the Nation from speaking with one voice but also prevent the Executive itself from doing so in conducting foreign relations.

The judgment of the Court of Appeals for the District of Columbia Circuit is

Affirmed.

JUSTICE BREYER, concurring.

I continue to believe that this case presents a political question inappropriate for judicial resolution. But because precedent precludes resolving this case on political question grounds, I join the Court's opinion.

FOR DISCUSSION

Does the majority opinion here affirm the idea that the president is the sole organ in foreign affairs? Does the analysis here conflict with the arguments that Justice Jackson articulated about presidential power in the *Youngstown* case?

MEDELLÍN V. TEXAS

552 U.S. 491, 128 S.Ct. 1346, 170 L.Ed.2d 190 (2008)

José Ernesto Medellín was a Mexican national convicted of murder and sentenced to death in Texas. He then exhausted his habeas corpus and appeals in state and federal courts. The International Court of Justice (ICJ) ruled in *Case Concerning Avena and Other Mexican Nationals* (*Avena*) that the United States had violated Article 36(1)(b) of the Vienna Convention on Consular Relations (Vienna Convention or Convention) by failing to inform fifty-one named Mexican nationals, including Medellín, of their Vienna Convention rights. President Bush then issued a memorandum declaring that the United States would "discharge its international obligations" under Avena "by having State courts give effect to the decision." Medellín used the ICJ decision and Bush's memorandum as the basis for a new habeas petition in state court. The Texas Court of Criminal Appeals dismissed the appeal, contending that neither the Avena opinion nor Bush's memo could serve to circumvent the state's limits on habeas petitions.

Vote: 6–3

CHIEF JUSTICE ROBERTS delivered the opinion of the Court.

Petitioner José Ernesto Medellín, who had been convicted and sentenced in Texas state court for murder, is one of the 51 Mexican nationals named in the *Case Concerning Avena and Other Mexican Nationals (Mexico v. U.S.)*, 2004 I.C.J. 12 (Judgment of Mar. 31) *(Avena)* decision. Relying on the International Court of Justice's decision and the President's Memorandum, Medellín filed an application for a writ of habeas corpus in state court. The Texas Court of Criminal Appeals dismissed Medellín's application as an abuse of the writ under state law, given Medellín's failure to raise his Vienna Convention claim in a timely manner under state law. We granted certiorari to decide two questions. *First,* is the ICJ's judgment in *Avena* directly enforceable as domestic law in a state court in the United States? *Second,* does the President's Memorandum independently require the States to provide review and reconsideration of the claims of the 51 Mexican nationals named in *Avena* without regard to state procedural default rules? We conclude that neither *Avena* nor the President's Memorandum constitutes directly enforceable federal law that pre-empts state limitations on the filing of successive habeas petitions. We therefore affirm the decision below.

I

In 1969, the United States, upon the advice and consent of the Senate, ratified the Vienna Convention on Consular Relations (Vienna Convention or Convention) and the Optional Protocol Concerning the Compulsory Settlement of Disputes to the Vienna Convention (Optional Protocol or Protocol). The preamble to the Convention provides that its purpose is to "contribute to the development of friendly relations among nations." Toward that end, Article 36 of the Convention was drafted to "facilitat[e] the exercise of consular functions." It provides that if a person detained by a foreign country "so requests, the competent authorities of the receiving State shall, without delay, inform the consular post of the sending State" of such detention, and "inform the [detainee] of his righ[t]" to request assistance from the consul of his own state.

The Optional Protocol provides a venue for the resolution of disputes arising out of the interpretation or application of the Vienna Convention. Under the Protocol, such disputes "shall lie within the compulsory jurisdiction of the International Court of Justice" and "may accordingly be brought before the [ICJ] . . . by any party to the dispute being a Party to the present Protocol.'

II

Medellín first contends that the ICJ's judgment in *Avena* constitutes a "binding" obligation on the state and federal courts of the United States. He argues that "by virtue of the Supremacy Clause, the treaties requiring compliance with the *Avena* judgment are *already* the 'Law of the Land' by which all state and federal courts in this country are 'bound.' " Accordingly, Medellín argues, *Avena* is a binding federal rule of decision that pre-empts contrary state limitations on successive habeas petitions.

No one disputes that the *Avena* decision—a decision that flows from the treaties through which the United States submitted to ICJ jurisdiction with respect to Vienna Convention disputes—constitutes an *international* law obligation on the part of the United States. But not all international law obligations automatically constitute binding federal law enforceable in United States courts. The question we confront here is whether the *Avena* judgment has automatic *domestic* legal effect such that the judgment of its own force applies in state and federal courts.

This Court has long recognized the distinction between treaties that automatically have effect as domestic law, and those that—while they constitute international law commitments—do not by themselves function as binding federal law. The distinction was well explained by Chief Justice Marshall's opinion in *Foster v. Neilson,* 2 Pet. 253, 315 (1829), overruled on other grounds, *United States v. Percheman,* 7 Pet. 51 (1833), which held that a treaty is "equivalent to an act of the legislature," and hence self-executing, when it "operates of itself without the aid of any legislative provision." When, in contrast, "[treaty] stipulations are not self-executing they can only be enforced pursuant to legislation to carry them into effect." *Whitney v. Robertson,* 124 U.S. 190, 194 (1888). In sum, while treaties "may comprise international commitments . . . they are not domestic law unless Congress has either enacted implementing statutes or the treaty itself conveys an intention that it be 'self-executing' and is ratified on these terms." *Igartúa De La Rosa v. United States,* 417 F.3d 145, 150 (C.A.1 2005).

Medellín and his *amici* nonetheless contend that the Optional Protocol, United Nations Charter, and ICJ Statute supply the "relevant obligation" to give the *Avena* judgment binding effect in the domestic courts of the United States. Because none of these treaty sources creates binding federal law in the absence of implementing legislation, and because it is uncontested that no such legislation exists, we conclude that the *Avena* judgment is not automatically binding domestic law.

III

Medellín next argues that the ICJ's judgment in *Avena* is binding on state courts by virtue of the President's February 28, 2005 Memorandum. The United States contends that while the *Avena* judgment does not of its own force require domestic courts to set aside ordinary rules of procedural default, that judgment became the law of the land with precisely that effect pursuant to the President's Memorandum and his power "to establish binding rules of decision that preempt contrary state law." Accordingly, we must decide whether the President's declaration alters our conclusion that the *Avena* judgment is not a rule of domestic law binding in state and federal courts.

A

The United States maintains that the President's constitutional role "uniquely qualifies" him to resolve the sensitive foreign policy decisions that bear on compliance with an ICJ decision and "to do so expeditiously." We do not question these propositions. In this case, the President seeks to vindicate United States interests in ensuring the reciprocal observance of the Vienna Convention, protecting relations with foreign governments, and demonstrating commitment to the role of international law. These interests are plainly compelling.

Such considerations, however, do not allow us to set aside first principles. The President's authority to act, as with the exercise of any governmental power, "must stem either from an act of Congress or from the Constitution itself." *Youngstown Sheet & Tube Co. v. Sawyer,* 343 US 579 (1952); *Dames & Moore v. Regan*, 453 U.S. 654 (1981).

Justice Jackson's familiar tripartite scheme provides the accepted framework for evaluating executive action in this area. First, "[w]hen the President acts pursuant to an express or implied authorization of Congress, his authority is at its maximum, for it includes all that he possesses in his own right plus all that Congress can delegate." *Youngstown,* 343 U.S., at 635 (Jackson, J., concurring). Second, "[w]hen the President acts in absence of either a congressional grant or denial of authority, he can only rely upon his own independent powers, but there is a zone of twilight in which he and Congress may have concurrent authority, or in which its distribution is uncertain." In this circumstance, Presidential authority can derive support from "congressional inertia, indifference or quiescence." Finally, "[w]hen the President takes measures incompatible with the expressed or implied will of Congress, his power is at its lowest ebb," and the Court can sustain his actions "only by disabling the Congress from acting upon the subject."

B

The United States marshals two principal arguments in favor of the President's authority "to establish binding rules of decision that preempt contrary state law." The Solicitor General first argues that the relevant treaties give the President the authority to implement the *Avena* judgment and that Congress has acquiesced in the exercise of such authority. The United States also relies upon an "independent" international dispute-resolution power wholly apart from the asserted authority based on the pertinent treaties. Medellín adds the additional argument that the President's Memorandum is a valid exercise of his power to take care that the laws be faithfully executed.

1

The United States maintains that the President's Memorandum is authorized by the Optional Protocol and the U.N. Charter. That is, because the relevant treaties "create an obligation to comply with *Avena,*" they "*implicitly* give the President authority to implement that treaty-based obligation." As a result, the President's Memorandum is well grounded in the first category of the *Youngstown* framework.

We disagree. The President has an array of political and diplomatic means available to enforce international obligations, but unilaterally converting a non-self-executing treaty into a self-executing one is not among them.

The responsibility for transforming an international obligation arising from a non-self-executing treaty into domestic law falls to Congress. As this Court has explained, when treaty stipulations are "not self-executing they can only be enforced pursuant to legislation to carry them into effect."

The requirement that Congress, rather than the President, implement a non-self-executing treaty derives from the text of the Constitution, which divides the treaty-making power between the President and the Senate. The Constitution vests the President with the authority to "make" a treaty. Art. II, § 2. If the Executive determines that a treaty should have domestic effect of its own force, that determination may be implemented "in mak[ing]" the treaty, by ensuring that it contains language plainly providing for domestic enforceability. If the treaty is to be self-executing in this respect, the Senate must consent to the treaty by the requisite two-thirds vote, consistent with all other constitutional restraints.

Once a treaty is ratified without provisions clearly according it domestic effect, however, whether the treaty will ever have such effect is governed by the fundamental constitutional principle that " '[t]he power to make the necessary laws is in Congress; the power to execute in the President.' " As already noted, the terms of a non-self-executing treaty can become domestic law only in the same way as any other law—through passage of legislation by both Houses of Congress, combined with either the President's signature or a congressional override of a Presidential veto. Indeed, "the President's power to see that the laws are faithfully executed refutes the idea that he is to be a lawmaker." *Youngstown,* 343 U.S., at 587.

A non-self-executing treaty, by definition, is one that was ratified with the understanding that it is not to have domestic effect of its own force. That understanding precludes the assertion that Congress has implicitly authorized the President—acting on his own—to achieve precisely the same result. We therefore conclude, given the absence of congressional legislation, that the non-self-executing treaties at issue here did not "express[ly] or implied[ly]" vest the President with the unilateral authority to make them self-executing. Accordingly, the President's Memorandum does not fall within the first category of the *Youngstown* framework.

Indeed, the preceding discussion should make clear that the non-self-executing character of the relevant treaties not only refutes the notion that the ratifying parties vested the President with the authority to unilaterally make treaty obligations binding on domestic courts, but also implicitly prohibits him from doing so. When the President asserts the power to "enforce" a non-self-executing treaty by unilaterally creating domestic law, he acts in conflict with the implicit understanding of the ratifying Senate. His assertion of authority, insofar as it is based on the pertinent non-self-executing treaties, is therefore within Justice Jackson's third category, not the first or even the second.

Each of the two means described above for giving domestic effect to an international treaty obligation under the Constitution—for making law—requires joint action by the Executive and Legislative Branches: The Senate can ratify a self-executing treaty "ma[de]" by the Executive, or, if the ratified treaty is not self-executing, Congress can enact implementing legislation approved by the President. It should not be surprising that our Constitution does not contemplate vesting such power in the Executive alone. As Madison explained in *The Federalist No. 47*, under our constitutional system of checks and balances, "[t]he magistrate in whom the whole executive power resides cannot of himself make a law." That would, however, seem an apt description of the asserted executive authority unilaterally to give the effect of domestic law to obligations under a non-self-executing treaty.

The United States nonetheless maintains that the President's Memorandum should be given effect as domestic law because "this case involves a valid Presidential action in the context of Congressional 'acquiescence'." Under the *Youngstown* tripartite framework, congressional acquiescence is pertinent when the President's action falls within the second category—that is, when he "acts in absence of either a congressional grant or denial of authority." Here, however, as we have explained, the President's effort to accord domestic effect to the *Avena* judgment does not meet that prerequisite.

In any event, even if we were persuaded that congressional acquiescence could support the President's asserted authority to create domestic law pursuant to a non-self-executing treaty, such acquiescence does not exist here. The United States first locates congressional acquiescence in Congress's failure to act following the President's resolution of prior ICJ controversies. A review of the Executive's actions in those prior cases, however, cannot support the claim that Congress acquiesced in this particular exercise of Presidential authority, for none of them remotely involved transforming an international obligation into domestic law and thereby displacing state law.

JUSTICE BREYER, with whom JUSTICES SOUTER and GINSBURG join, dissenting.

The Constitution's Supremacy Clause provides that "all Treaties . . . which shall be made . . . under the Authority of the United States, shall be the supreme Law of the Land; and the Judges in every State shall be bound thereby." Art. VI, cl. 2. The Clause means that the "courts" must regard "a treaty . . . as equivalent to an act of the legislature, whenever it operates of itself without the aid of any legislative provision." *Foster v. Neilson,* 2 Pet. 253, 314 (1829).

In the *Avena* case the International Court of Justice (ICJ) (interpreting and applying the Vienna Convention on Consular Relations) issued a judgment that requires the United States to reexamine certain criminal proceedings in the cases of 51 Mexican nationals. The question here is whether the ICJ's *Avena* judgment is enforceable now as a matter of domestic law, *i.e.*, whether it "operates of itself without the aid" of any further legislation.

The United States has signed and ratified a series of treaties obliging it to comply with ICJ judgments in cases in which it has given its consent to the exercise of the ICJ's adjudicatory authority. Specifically, the United States has agreed to submit, in this kind of case, to the ICJ's "compulsory jurisdiction" for purposes of "compulsory settlement." And it agreed that the ICJ's judgments would have "binding force . . . between the parties and in respect of [a] particular case." President Bush has determined that domestic courts should enforce this particular ICJ judgment. And Congress has done nothing to suggest the contrary. Under these circumstances, I believe the treaty obligations, and hence the judgment, resting as it does upon the consent of the United States to the ICJ's jurisdiction, bind the courts no less than would "an act of the [federal] legislature."

FOR DISCUSSION

Does *Medellín* respond to *Holland*? Does *Medellín* demonstrate that federalism and states' rights are not dead when it comes to foreign affairs and treaties? Could a treaty be used to alter the basic federal structure of the United States? How far can presidents go in using international law to direct states to do something they do not wish to do?

UNITED STATES V. BELMONT

301 U.S. 324, 57 S.Ct. 758, 81 L.Ed. 1134 (1937)

A sum of money had been deposited by a Russian corporation, Petrograd Metal Works, with August Belmont, a private banker doing business in New York City. In 1918 the Soviet government by decree liquidated the corporation and nationalized and appropriated all of its assets, including the deposit account with Belmont. In 1933 the Soviet government assigned to the United States government all accounts due to the Soviet government from American nationals. This arrangement was established by means of an executive agreement between the two governments, the Litvinov Assignment. The Soviet government was recognized by the United

States on November 16, 1933. This confiscation of property was challenged as being contrary to the public policy of the state of New York, the situs of the bank deposit.

Vote: 9–0

JUSTICE SUTHERLAND delivered the opinion of the Court:

We take judicial notice of the fact that coincident with the assignment set forth in the complaint, the President recognized the Soviet Government, and normal diplomatic relations were established between that government and the Government of the United States, followed by an exchange of ambassadors. The effect of this was to validate, so far as this country is concerned, all acts of the Soviet Government here involved from the commencement of its existence. The recognition, establishment of diplomatic relations, the assignment, and agreements with respect thereto, were all parts of one transaction, resulting in an international compact between the two governments. That the negotiations, acceptance of the assignment and agreements and understandings in respect thereof were within the competence of the President may not be doubted. Governmental power over internal affairs is distributed between the national government and the several states. Governmental power over external affairs is not distributed, but is vested exclusively in the national government. And in respect of what was done here, the Executive had authority to speak as the sole organ of that government. The assignment and the agreements in connection therewith did not, as in the case of treaties, as that term is used in the treaty making clause of the Constitution (Article II, § 2), require the advice and consent of the Senate.

A treaty signifies "a compact made between two or more independent nations, with a view to the public welfare." But an international compact, as this was, is not always a treaty which requires the participation of the Senate. There are many such compacts, of which a protocol, *a modus vivendi* [a temporary agreement until conflicting parties can resolve their differences], a postal convention, and agreements like that now under consideration are illustrations. The distinction was pointed out by this court in [*Altman & Co. v. United States*, 224 U.S. 583 (1912),] which arose under § 3 of the Tariff Act of 1897, authorizing the President to conclude commercial agreements with foreign countries in certain specified matters. We held that although this might not be a treaty requiring ratification by the Senate, it was a compact negotiated and proclaimed under the authority of the President, and as such was a "treaty" within the meaning of the Circuit Court of Appeals Act, the construction of which might be reviewed upon direct appeal to this court.

Plainly, the external powers of the United States are to be exercised without regard to state laws or policies. The supremacy of a treaty in this respect has been recognized from the beginning. Mr. Madison, in the Virginia Convention, said that if a treaty does not supersede existing state laws, as far as they contravene its operation, the treaty would be ineffective. "To counteract it by the supremacy of the state laws, would bring on the Union the just charge of national perfidy, and involve us in war." And while this rule in respect of treaties is established by the express language of clause 2, Article Six, of the Constitution, the same rule would result in the case of all international compacts and agreements from the very fact that complete power over international affairs is in the national government and is not and cannot be subject to any curtailment or interference on the part of the several states. In respect of all international negotiations and compacts, and in respect of our foreign relations generally, state lines disappear. As to such purposes the State of New York does not exist. Within the field of its powers, whatever the United States rightfully undertakes, it necessarily has warrant to consummate. And when judicial authority is invoked in aid of such consummation, state constitutions, state Jaws, and state policies are irrelevant to the inquiry and decision. It is inconceivable that any of them can be interposed as an obstacle to the effective operation of a federal constitutional power.

FOR DISCUSSION

Do executive agreements enjoy the same constitutional status as do treaties? What is the difference between the two? Why would a president ever resort to a treaty if the same goals could be accomplished with an executive agreement?

RELATED CASE

United States v. Pink: **315 U.S. 203 (1942).**

A treaty is a part of the "law of the land" under the supremacy clause of the Constitution. Such international compacts and agreements as the Litvinov Assignment have a similar dignity. Thus, a treaty and an executive agreement were held to be legally equal. The result of this decision was that Russian law was put above New York law, that is, state policy as declared by the courts. Pink was state superintendent of insurance. Thus, an executive agreement can be enforced internally. No consideration was given by the Court to the question of taking property for public use without just compensation.

SELECTIVE DRAFT LAW CASES (ARVER V. UNITED STATES)

245 U.S. 366, 38 S.Ct. 159, 62 L.Ed. 349 (1918)

In 1917 Congress enacted a military conscription act that required service of all male citizens between the ages of twenty-one and thirty. Certain exceptions were provided. All persons liable to service under the act were required to register at a time appointed by the president. Arver and others were convicted of failure to register, and their defense was the alleged unconstitutionality of the act of Congress.

Vote: 9–0

CHIEF JUSTICE WHITE delivered the opinion of the Court.

The possession of authority to enact the statute must be found in the clauses of the Constitution giving Congress power "to declare war; to raise and support armies, but no appropriation of money to that use shall be for a longer term than two years; to make rules for the government and regulation of the land and naval forces." Article One, § 8. And of course the powers conferred by these provisions like all other powers given carry with them as provided by Constitution the authority "to make all laws which shall be necessary and proper for carrying into execution the foregoing powers." Article One, § 8.

As the mind cannot conceive an army without the men to compose it, on the face of the Constitution the objection that it does not give power to provide for such men would seem to be too frivolous for further notice. It is said, however, and since under the Constitution as originally framed state citizenship was primary and United States citizenship but derivative and dependent thereon, therefore the power conferred upon Congress to raise armies was only coterminous with United States citizenship and could not be exerted so as to cause that citizenship to lose its dependent character and dominate state citizenship. But the proposition simply denies to Congress the power to raise armies which the Constitution gives. That power by the very terms of the Constitution, being delegated, is supreme. Article Six. In truth the contention simply assails the wisdom of the framers of the Constitution in conferring authority on Congress and in not retaining it as it was under the Confederation in the several States. Further it is said, the right to provide is not denied by calling for volunteer enlistments, but it does not and cannot include the power to exact enforced military duty by the citizen. This however but challenges the existence of all power, for a governmental power which has no sanction to it and which therefore can only be exercised provided the citizen consents to its exertion is in no substantial sense a power. It is argued, however, that although this is abstractly true, it is not concretely so because as compelled military service is repugnant to a free government and in conflict with all the great guarantees of the Constitution as to individual liberty, it must be assumed that the authority to raise armies was intended to be limited to the right to call an army into existence counting alone upon the willingness of the citizen to do his duty in time of public need, that is, in time of war. But the premise of this proposition is so devoid of foundation that it leaves not even a shadow of ground upon which to base the conclusion.

When the Constitution came to be formed it may not be disputed that one of the recognized necessities for its adoption was the want of power in Congress to raise an army and the dependence upon the States for their quotas. In supplying the power it was manifestly intended to give it all and leave none to the States, since besides the delegation to Congress of authority to raise armies the Constitution prohibited the States, without the consent of Congress, from keeping troops in time of peace or engaging in war. Article One, § 10.

Thus sanctioned as is the act before us by the text of the Constitution, and by its significance as read in the light of the fundamental principles with which the subject is concerned, by the power recognized and carried into effect in many civilized countries, by the authority and practice of the colonies before the Revolution, and of the States under the Confederation and of the Government since the formation of the Constitution, the want of merit in the contentions that the act in the particulars which we have been previously called upon to consider was beyond the constitutional power of Congress, is manifest.

Finally, as we are unable to conceive upon what theory the exaction by government from the citizen of the performance of his supreme and noble duty of contributing to the defense of the rights and honor of the nation, as the result of a war declared by the great representative body of the people, can be said to be the imposition of voluntary servitude in violation of the prohibitions of the Thirteenth Amendment, we are constrained to the conclusion that the contention to that effect is refuted by its mere statement.

Affirmed.

FOR DISCUSSION

What formal requirements must be met for Congress to institute a draft for the army? Must there be a declared war, or could Congress institute a peacetime draft if it deemed one necessary?

RELATED CASES

***Cox v. Wood:* 247 U.S. 3 (1918).**

Congress may conscript for military duty outside the territorial limits of the United States. The militia clause, relating to the use of troops within the United States, should not be read as a limitation upon the war power.

***United States v. Williams:* 302 U.S. 46 (1937).**

Where parents consent to the enlistment of their son on the condition that he carry war risk insurance, the failure of the son to maintain and continue that insurance is not chargeable to the United States government, since Congress nowhere confers upon parents the right to condition their son's enlistment.

***United States v. O'Brien:* 391 U.S. 367 (1968).**

Federal law prohibits knowing destruction or mutilation of Selective Service registration certificates. This statute does not abridge free speech and is a proper exercise of the military power of Congress to raise and support armies.

ROSTKER V. GOLDBERG

453 U.S. 57, 101 S.Ct. 2646, 69 L.Ed.2d 478 (1981)

In 1980, shortly after the Soviet invasion of Afghanistan, the Military Selective Service Act (MSSA) was reactivated to require registration of all male citizens between the ages of eighteen and twenty-six in case of a need for a national military draft. Despite President Carter's recommendation that the MSSA be amended to allow for the registration and possible conscription of women, after a long debate Congress declined to expand the scope of the act. A lawsuit initiated by several young men in 1971 was heard before the federal district court of the Eastern District of Pennsylvania. The court struck down the act, ruling that it violated the Due Process Clause of the Fifth Amendment.

Vote: 6–3

JUSTICE REHNQUIST delivered the opinion of the Court.

I

[Reviews congressional authority to institute the draft and the history of this particular measure.]

II

The case arises in the context of Congress' authority over national defense and military affairs, and perhaps in no other area has the Court accorded Congress greater deference. In rejecting the registration of women, Congress explicitly relied upon its constitutional powers under Art. I, § 8, cls. 12–14.

This Court has consistently recognized Congress' "broad constitutional power" to raise and regulate armies and navies, *Schlesinger v. Ballard*, 419 U.S. 498, 510 (1975).

In *Schlesinger v. Ballard*, the Court considered a due process challenge, brought by males, to the Navy policy of according females a longer period than males in which to attain promotions necessary to continued service. The Court distinguished previous gender-based discriminations held unlawful in *Reed v. Reed*, 404 U.S. 71 (1971), and *Frontiero v. Richardson*, 411 U.S. 677 (1973). In those cases, the classifications were based on "overbroad generalizations." In the case before it, however, the Court noted:

> [The] different treatment of men and women naval officers . . . reflects, not archaic and overbroad generalizations, but, instead, the demonstrable fact that male and female line officers in the Navy are not similarly situated with respect to opportunities for professional service. Appellee has not challenged the current restrictions on women officers' participation in combat and in most sea duty. Id., at 508.

In light of the combat restrictions, women did not have the same opportunities for promotion as men, and therefore it was not unconstitutional for Congress to distinguish between them.

None of this is to say that Congress is free to disregard the Constitution when it acts in the area of military affairs. In that area, as any other, Congress remains subject to the limitations of the Due Process Clause; *Hamilton v. Kentucky Distilleries & Warehouse Co.*, 251 U.S. 146, 156 (1919), but the tests and limitations to be applied may differ because of the military context. We of course do not abdicate our ultimate responsibility to decide the constitutional question, but simply recognize that the Constitution itself requires such deference to congressional choice.

III

This case is quite different from several of the gender-based discrimination cases we have considered in that, despite appellees' assertions, Congress did not act "unthinkingly" or "reflexively and not for any considered reason." The question of registering women for the draft not only received considerable national attention and was the subject of wide-ranging public debate, but also was extensively considered by Congress in hearings, floor debate, and in committee. Hearings held by both Houses of Congress in response to the President's request for authorization to register women adduced extensive testimony and evidence concerning the issue.

The foregoing clearly establishes that the decision to exempt women from registration was not the " 'accidental by-product of a traditional way of thinking about females.' " *Califano v. Webster*, 430 U.S. 313, 320 (1977) (quoting *Califano v. Goldfarb*, 430 U.S. 199, 223 (1977) (Stevens, J., concurring in judgment)). The issue was considered at great length, and Congress clearly expressed its purpose and intent.

Congress determined that any future draft, which would be facilitated by the registration scheme, would be characterized by a need for combat troops. The Senate Report explained, in a specific finding later adopted by both Houses, that "[if] mobilization were to be ordered in a wartime scenario, the primary manpower need would be for combat replacements." S. Rep. No. 96–826, p. 160 (1980). The purpose of registration, therefore, was to prepare for a draft of combat troops.

Women as a group, however, unlike men as a group, are not eligible for combat. The restrictions on the participation of women in combat in the Navy and Air Force are statutory. Under 10 U S.C. § 6015 (1976 ed., Supp. III), "women may not be assigned to duty on vessels or in aircraft that are engaged in combat missions," and under 10 U.S.C. § 8549 female members of the Air Force "may not be assigned to duty in aircraft engaged in combat missions." The Army and Marine Corps preclude the use of women in combat as a matter of established policy. Congress specifically recognized and endorsed the exclusion of women from combat in exempting women from registration.

The existence of the combat restrictions clearly indicates the basis for Congress' decision to exempt women from registration. The purpose of registration was to prepare for a draft of combat troops. Since women are excluded from combat, Congress concluded that they would not be needed in the event of a draft, and therefore decided not to register them.

Although the military experts who testified in favor of registering women uniformly opposed the actual drafting of women, there was testimony that in the event of a draft of 650,000 the military could absorb some 80,000 female inductees. The 80,000 would be used to fill noncombat positions, freeing men to go to the front. In relying on this testimony in striking down the MSSA, the District Court palpably exceeded its authority when it ignored Congress' considered response to this line of reasoning.

. . . Congress simply did not consider it worth the added burdens of including women in draft and registration plans.

Congress also concluded that whatever the need for women for noncombat roles during mobilization, whether 80,000 or less, it could be met by volunteers.

Most significantly, Congress determined that staffing noncombat positions with women during a mobilization would be positively detrimental to the important goal of military flexibility.

In sum, Congress carefully evaluated the testimony that 80,000 women conscripts could be usefully employed in the event of a draft and rejected it in the permissible exercise of its constitutional responsibility. The District Court was quite wrong in undertaking an independent evaluation of this evidence, rather than adopting an appropriately deferential examination of Congress' evaluation of that evidence.

In light of the foregoing, we conclude that Congress acted well within its constitutional authority when it authorized the registration of men, and not women, under the Military Selective Service Act. The decision of the District Court holding otherwise is accordingly Reversed.

FOR DISCUSSION

On December 3, 2015 the United States Department of Defense announced that it would open up all military occupations to women, including those in combat. Does this change in policy now question the reasoning in *Rostker*?

SELECTIVE SERVICE SYSTEM V. MINNESOTA PUBLIC INTEREST RESEARCH GROUP

468 U.S. 841, 104 S.Ct. 3348, 82 L.Ed.2d 632 (1984)

A public interest group representing four males challenged the constitutionality of statute otherwise known as the Solomon Amendment, denying federal financial aid to male students who failed to register for the draft. The United States District Court for the District of Minnesota found the statute unconstitutional, and the Supreme Court reversed.

Vote: 6–2

CHIEF JUSTICE BURGER delivered the opinion of the Court.

We noted probable jurisdiction to decide (a) whether § 12(f) of the Military Selective Service Act, 96 Stat. 748, 50 U.S.C.App. § 462(f), which denies federal financial assistance under Title IV of the Higher Education Act of 1965 to male students who fail to register for the draft under the Military Selective Service Act, is a bill of attainder; and (b) whether § 12(f) compels those students who elect to request federal aid to incriminate themselves in violation of the Fifth Amendment.

I

Section 3 of the Military Selective Service Act, 62 Stat. 605, as amended, empowers the President to require every male citizen and male resident alien between the ages of 18 and 26 to register for the draft. Section 12 of that Act imposes criminal penalties for failure to register. On July 2, 1980, President Carter issued a Proclamation requiring young men to register within 30 days of their 18th birthday.

Appellee students (hereafter appellees) are anonymous individuals who were required to register before September 1, 1982. On September 8, Congress enacted the Department of Defense Authorization Act of 1983, Pub.L. 97–252, 96 Stat. 718. Section 1113(a) of that Act added § 12(f) to the Military Selective Service Act. Section 12(f)(1) provides that any person who is required to register and fails to do so "in accordance with any proclamation" issued under the Military Selective Service Act "shall be ineligible for any form of assistance or benefit provided under title IV of the Higher Education Act of 1965." Section 1113(f)(2) requires applicants for Title IV assistance to file with their institutions of higher education a statement attesting to their compliance with the draft registration law and regulations issued under it. Sections 1113(f)(3) and (4) require the Secretary of Education, in agreement with the Director of Selective Service, to prescribe methods for verifying such statements of compliance and to issue implementing regulations.

Regulations issued in final form on April 11, 1983 provide that no applicant may receive Title IV aid unless he files a statement of compliance certifying that he is registered with the Selective Service or that, for a specified reason, he is not required to register. The regulations allow a student who has not previously registered, although required to do so, to establish eligibility for Title IV aid by registering, filing a statement of registration compliance, and, if required, verifying that he is registered. The statement of compliance does not require the applicant to state the date that he registered.

In November 1982 the Minnesota Public Interest Research Group filed a complaint in the United States District Court for the District of Minnesota seeking to enjoin the operation of § 12(f). The District Court dismissed the Minnesota Group for lack of standing but allowed three anonymous students to intervene as plaintiffs. The intervenors alleged that they reside in Minnesota, that they need financial aid to pursue their educations, that they intend to apply for Title IV assistance, and that they are legally required to register with the Selective Service but have failed to do so. This suit was informally consolidated with a separate action brought by three other anonymous students making essentially the same allegations as the intervenors.

In March 1983 the District Court granted a preliminary injunction restraining the Selective Service System from enforcing § 12(f). After finding that appellees had demonstrated a threat of irreparable injury, the court held that appellees were likely to succeed on the merits. First, the District Court thought it likely that § 12(f) was a Bill of Attainder. The court interpreted the statutory bar to student aid as applicable to students who registered late. Thus interpreted, the statute "clearly singles out an ascertainable group based on past conduct" and "legislatively determines the guilt of this ascertainable group." Doe v. Selective Service System,. The court viewed the denial of aid as punishment within the meaning of the Bill of Attainder Clause because it "deprives students of the practical means to achieve the education necessary to pursue many vocations in our society." Second, the District Court found it likely that § 12(f) violated appellees' Fifth Amendment privilege against compelled self-incrimination. In the District Court's view, the statement of compliance required by § 12(f) compels students who have not registered for the draft and need financial aid to confess to the fact of nonregistration, which is a crime.

On June 16, 1983, the District Court entered a permanent, nationwide injunction against the enforcement of § 1113. The court held that the regulations making late registrants eligible for aid were inconsistent with the statute and concluded that the statute was an unconstitutional attainder. It also held the statute to violate appellees' constitutional privilege against compelled self-incrimination.

On June 29, we stayed the District Court's June 16 order pending the timely docketing and final disposition of this appeal. We noted probable jurisdiction and we reverse.

II

The District Court held that § 1113 falls within the category of congressional actions that Art. I, § 9, cl. 3, of the Constitution bars by providing that "[n]o Bill of Attainder . . . shall be passed." A bill of attainder was most recently described by this Court as "a law that legislatively determines guilt and inflicts punishment upon an identifiable individual without provision of the protections of a judicial trial." The Government argues that § 1113 does not satisfy any of these three requirements, i.e., specification of the affected persons, punishment, and lack of a judicial trial.

A

In forbidding bills of attainder, the draftsmen of the Constitution sought to prohibit the ancient practice of the Parliament in England of punishing without trial "specifically designated persons or groups." Historically, bills of attainder generally named the persons to be punished. However, "[t]he singling out of an individual for legislatively prescribed punishment constitutes an attainder whether the individual is called by name or described in terms of conduct which, because it is past conduct, operates only as a designation of particular persons.". When past activity serves as "a point of reference for the ascertainment of particular persons ineluctably designated by the legislature" for punishment.

In Cummings the Court struck down a provision of the Missouri post-Civil War Reconstruction Constitution that barred persons from various professions unless they stated under oath that they had not given aid or comfort to persons engaged in armed hostility to the United States and had never " 'been a member of, or connected with, any order, society, or organization, inimical to the government of the United States.' " Id., at

279. The Court recognized that the oath was required, not "as a means of ascertaining whether parties were qualified" for their professions, id., at 320, but rather to effect a punishment for having associated with the Confederacy. Although the State Constitution did not mention the persons or groups required to take the oath by name, the Court concluded that in creating a qualification having no possible relation to their fitness for their chosen professions, the Constitution was intended "to reach the person, not the calling." Ibid.

The District Court in this case viewed § 12(f) as comparable to the provisions of the Reconstruction laws declared unconstitutional in Cummings and Garland, because it thought the statute singled out nonregistrants and made them ineligible for aid based on their past conduct, i.e., failure to register. To understand the District Court's analysis, it is necessary to turn to its construction of the statute. The court noted that § 12(f) disqualifies applicants for financial assistance unless they have registered "in accordance with any proclamation issued under [§ 3 of the Military Selective Service Act]," and that Proclamation No. 4771 requires those born after January 1, 1963, to register within 30 days of their 18th birthday. See 3 CFR 82 (1981). In the court's view, the language of § 12(f), coupled with the Proclamation's 30-day registration requirement, precluded late registrants from qualifying for Title IV aid. Having construed § 12(f) as precluding late registration, the District Court read the statute to be retrospective, in that it denies financial assistance to an identifiable group—nonregistrants—based on their past conduct. The District Court acknowledged that implementing regulations would allow students who had not previously registered to become eligible for Title IV benefits by registering, see 34 CFR § 668.27(b)(1) (1983), but the court declared those regulations to be void because they conflicted with what the District Court viewed as § 12(f)'s requirement of registration within the time prescribed by Proclamation No. 4771.

We reject the District Court's view that § 12(f) requires registration within the time fixed by Proclamation No. 4771. That view is plainly inconsistent with the structure of § 12(f) and with the legislative history. Subsection (f)(4) of the statute requires the Secretary of Education to issue regulations providing that "any person" to whom the Secretary proposes to deny Title IV assistance shall be given notice of the proposed denial and "not less than thirty days" after such notice to "establis[h] that he has complied with the registration requirement." 50 U.S.C. § 462(f)(4). The statute clearly gives nonregistrants 30 days after receiving notice that they are ineligible for Title IV aid to register for the draft and qualify for aid. See 34 CFR § 668.27(b)(1) (1983). To require registration within the time fixed by the Presidential Proclamation would undermine this provision allowing "any person" 30 days after notification to establish compliance with the registration requirement. This was clearly a grace period.

The District Court also ignored the relevant legislative history. Congress' purpose in enacting § 12(f) was to encourage registration by those who must register, but have not yet done so. Proponents of the legislation emphasized that those failing to register timely can qualify for aid by registering late.[5] The District Court failed to take account of this legislative purpose.

Because it allows late registration, § 12(f) is clearly distinguishable from the provisions struck down in Cummings and Garland. Cummings and Garland dealt with absolute barriers to entry into certain professions for those who could not file the required loyalty oaths; no one who had served the Confederacy could possibly comply, for his status was irreversible. By contrast, § 12(f)'s requirements, far from irreversible, can be met readily by either timely or late filing. "Far from attaching to . . . past and ineradicable actions," ineligibility for Title IV benefits "is made to turn upon continuingly contemporaneous fact" which a student who wants public assistance can correct.

B

Even if the specificity element were deemed satisfied by § 12(f), the statute would not necessarily implicate the Bill of Attainder Clause. The proscription against bills of attainder reaches only statutes that inflict punishment on the specified individual or group. In determining whether a statute inflicts punishment within the proscription against bills of attainder, our holdings recognize that the severity of a sanction is not determinative of its character as punishment. That burdens are placed on citizens by federal authority does not make those burdens punishment. Conversely, legislative intent to encourage compliance with the law does not establish that a statute is merely the legitimate regulation of conduct. Punishment is not limited solely to retribution for past events, but may involve deprivations inflicted to deter future misconduct. It is thus apparent that, though the governing criteria for an attainder may be readily indicated, "each case has turned on its own highly particularized context."

In deciding whether a statute inflicts forbidden punishment, we have recognized three necessary inquiries: (1) whether the challenged statute falls within the historical meaning of legislative punishment; (2) whether the statute, "viewed in terms of the type and severity of burdens imposed, reasonably can be said to further nonpunitive legislative purposes"; and (3) whether the legislative record "evinces a congressional intent to punish." We conclude that under these criteria § 12(f) is not a punitive bill of attainder.

III

Appellees assert that § 12(f) violates the Fifth Amendment by compelling nonregistrants to acknowledge that they have failed to register timely when confronted with certifying to their schools that they have complied with the registration law. Pointing to the fact that the willful failure to register within the time fixed by Proclamation No. 4771 is a criminal offense punishable under §§ 12(a) and (b), they contend that § 12(f) requires them—since in fact they have not registered—to confess to a criminal act and that this is "compulsion" in violation of their Fifth Amendment rights.

However, a person who has not registered clearly is under no compulsion to seek financial aid; if he has not registered, he is simply ineligible for aid. Since a nonregistrant is bound to know that his application for federal aid would be denied, he is in no sense under any "compulsion" to seek that aid. He has no reason to make any statement to anyone as to whether or not he has registered.

IV

We conclude that § 12(f) does not violate the proscription against bills of attainder. Nor have appellees raised a cognizable claim under the Fifth Amendment.

The judgment of the District Court is Reversed.

JUSTICE BLACKMUN took no part in the decision of this case.

JUSTICE BRENNAN, dissenting.

For the reasons stated in Part II of Justice MARSHALL's dissenting opinion, I too would affirm the judgment of the District Court on the ground that § 12(f) of the Military Selective Service Act, as added by § 1113(a) of the Department of Defense Authorization Act of 1983, compels those students seeking financial aid who have not registered with the Selective Service in timely fashion to incriminate themselves and thereby violates the Fifth Amendment.

JUSTICE MARSHALL, dissenting.

II

I do not have to disagree with the majority that § 12(f) does not violate the constitutional prohibition against bills of attainder. That holding depends on construing the statute to permit late registration,, which in turn depends on construing Congress' intent as encouragement of compliance with the Selective Service registration requirement. The majority emphasizes the "nonpunitive spirit" of the legislation implicit in the fact that Congress "allowed all nonregistrants to qualify for Title IV aid simply by registering late." Congress did not, however, grant immunity from criminal prosecution for that act of late registration. Absent such a grant, § 12(f) must be struck because it compels self-incrimination.

The Fifth Amendment privilege against coerced self-incrimination extends to every means of government information gathering. In our regulatory state, the line between permissible conditioning of the Government's taxing and spending power and impermissible Government coercion of information that presents a real threat of self-incrimination is not easy to identify. But I am confident the line has been crossed here.

I do not take issue with the majority's conclusion, that the Title IV application process itself does not require a student to divulge incriminating information to the educational institution. The neutrality of this compliance verification system is central to the majority's acceptance of the permissible, regulatory purpose of the statute. However, our inquiry cannot stop there. Although § 12(f) does not coerce an admission of nonregistration, it does coerce registration with the Selective Service System, and hence individual reporting of self-incriminatory information directly to the Federal Government.

If appellees were to register with Selective Service now so that they could submit statements of compliance to obtain financial aid for their schooling, they would still be in violation of federal law, for, by registering late, they would not have submitted to registration "in accordance with any proclamation" issued under § 3 of the Military Selective Service Act, Failure to comply with Selective Service registration requirements within 30 days of one's 18th birthday is a felony, punishable by imprisonment for up to five years and/or a fine of up to $10,000.

A student who registers late provides the Government with two crucial links in the chain of evidence necessary to prosecute him criminally. First, he supplies the Government with proof of two elements of a violation: his birth date and date of registration. Second, and perhaps more importantly, he calls attention to the fact that he is one of the 674,000 young men in technical violation of the Military Selective Service Act. Armed with these data, the Government need prove only that the student "knowingly" failed to register at the time prescribed by law in order to obtain a conviction. When students, such as appellees in this case, have acknowledged their awareness of their legal duty to register, the Government could prosecute the commission of a felony.

FOR DISCUSSION

Since this decision was issued, college tuition has increased dramatically and there are few students who can attend school without seeking financial assistance. Given this, is it really a voluntary option for male students not to register for the draft?

THE SCOPE OF THE TREATY POWER

Treatises are referred to in two places in the Constitution. First, in Article II, the president, subject to two-thirds approval by the Senate, may negotiate treaties with other nations. Second, in Article VI, treaties are grouped with the Constitution in the Supremacy Clause as part of the highest legal authority in the country. Both of these clauses have spurred constitutional questions and litigation. As noted in *Medellín v. Texas* (552 U.S. 491, 2008), not all treaties are automatically binding. Some are self-executing, while others require further congressional action for them to take effect. In either case, as *Missouri v. Holland* (252 U.S. 416, 1920) points out, they are part of the "supreme law of the land" with the Constitution. The issues posed in these two questions is under what conditions treaties are enforceable parts of the American law and how far can they go in altering the constitutional structure of the United States, both internationally and domestically.

Article II, Sec. 2:

He shall have power, by and with the Advice and Consent of the Senate, to make Treaties, provided two thirds of the Senators present concur; and he shall nominate, and by and with the Advice and Consent of the Senate, shall appoint Ambassadors, other public Ministers and Consuls. . . .

Article VI:

This Constitution, and the Laws of the United States which shall be made in Pursuance thereof; and all Treaties made, or which shall be made, under the Authority of the United States, shall be the supreme Law of the Land. . . .

Prior to *Missouri v. Holland* the Supreme Court adjudicated several cases involving treaties. For example, in *Foster v. Neilson* (2 Pet. 253, 1829), Chief Justice Marshall held for the Court that the determination of an international boundary involving the United States is a political rather than a legal question, and on this matter the courts must accept the judgment of the political departments. In *Hauenstein v. Lynham* (100 U.S. 483, 1880), the Court upheld a treaty between the United States and Switzerland against a statute of Virginia. The latter provided that real property in Virginia of aliens who died intestate should escheat to the state. The treaty gave the heirs the right to sell such property and to withdraw the proceeds. This treaty was held to be self-executing. The property involved was located in Richmond. Hauenstein was a citizen of Switzerland, and Lynham an official of Virginia. In *Whitney v. Robertson* (124 U.S. 190, 1888), it was ruled that a treaty and a federal statute are on the same plane of legal equality: "When the two relate to the same subject, the courts will always endeavor to construe them so as to give effect to both, if that can be done without violating the language of either; but if the two are inconsistent, the one last in date will control the other." The Court reached the same conclusion in the *Chinese Exclusion Cases (Chae Chan Ping v. United States)* (130 U.S. 581, 1889). In *Geofroy v. Riggs* (133 U.S. 258, 1890), the Court stated that a treaty may not be contrary to the Constitution, but any matter that is properly the subject of negotiation with a foreign country may be the subject of a treaty. Here a treaty with France referred to "states of the Union," but the Court gave a liberal interpretation to the term "states" and included the District of Columbia. Therefore, French citizens could inherit land in the United States from a U.S. citizen. In this instance, Geofroy was the French citizen and Riggs the American. Finally, in *United States v. Shauver* (214 F. 154, 1914), a district court judge held that Congress cannot attempt to regulate migratory birds under an alleged or implied police power as the federal government does not have title to the birds. Title rests in the state for all of the people of that state.

Missouri v. Holland raised shouts of concerns when decided. Holmes's language implied that treaties could de facto amend the Constitution and alter the domestic lines of authority between states and the national government in the United States. It need hardly be mentioned that the potential under the *Missouri v. Holland* decision has never been realized. Under this decision a treaty need only be made under the authority of the United States. The subject matter of the treaty need be only in the general realm of matters properly the subject of an international arrangement. By contrast, a statute must be made in pursuance of the Constitution; there must be some specific basis for the action. Thus, in the *Missouri* case, Congress had attempted by statute to regulate the killing of migratory birds. Two lower federal courts held the statute void as being beyond the powers delegated to Congress (*United States v. Shauver* 214 Fed. 154, 1914; *United States v. McCullagh,* 221 Fed. 288, 1915). Later, after the treaty, legislation passed by Congress in implementation of the treaty was upheld. Thus, within limits, there can be the results of de facto amendment of the Constitution by means of a treaty that will require or authorize statutory implementation. In the light of the doctrine of the *Belmont* and *Pink* decisions read earlier, presumably the same would be true of an executive agreement. However, no treaty or executive agreement can deprive persons of rights guaranteed in the Constitution.

By the terms of Article VI of the Constitution, a properly ratified treaty is part of the supreme law of the land. No state law can generally prevail against a treaty. But one clear exception is *Medellín v. Texas*. Here the principles of federalism prevailed over an international agreement entered into by the United States government. Does this decision represent repudiation of the *Holland* dicta? What federalism limits are placed on foreign policy decision making? How can *Medellín, Holland,* and *Perpich* be reconciled?

If treaties can be approved only with the advice and consent of the Senate, is their approval also needed when the president decides to nullify one? This question was raised in *Goldwater v. Carter*, 444 U.S. 996 (1979). The Court seems to say no. Why? Why did the Court let President Carter terminate the defense treaty with Taiwan without seeking Senate approval?

MISSOURI V. HOLLAND

252 U.S. 416, 40 S.Ct. 382, 64 L.Ed. 641 (1920)

See Chapter II, page 110.

RELATED CASES

***Ware v. Hylton:* 3 Dall. 199 (1796).**

A statute of Virginia cannot deny a British subject rights established by the Jay Treaty between the United States and Britain. The rights involved here concerned the payments of debts by Americans to British subjects. Ware represented British subjects, and Hylton represented U.S. citizens. The statute had been passed in 1777 during the Revolutionary War. The Jay Treaty of 1794 was held to be retroactive and thus nullified the state law and action taken under it. There is no such thing as dual federalism in foreign relations.

***Reid v. Covert:* 354 U.S. 1 (1957).**

Civilian dependents who are accompanying members of the armed forces cannot be made subject by Congress to court-martial for capital offenses committed in another country, even though such prosecution has been recognized in a treaty with that country. A portion of the treaty, the Status of Forces Agreement, was held invalid. Here a wife, Covert, had murdered her husband. Reid was Superintendent of the District of Columbia jail. (See Vol. II.) delete the cross-reference.

***Wilson v. Girard:* 354 U.S. 524 (1957).**

The status-of-forces treaty between the United States and Japan, including the discretionary waiver of criminal jurisdiction to Japan over members of the United States armed forces, is not contrary to the Constitution. This jurisdiction was set by the administrative agreement implementing the 1952 treaty. It was agreed that at the time of the incident, Girard, an American soldier, was engaged in an official exercise. He was accused of causing the death of a Japanese woman in Japan by firing a grenade launcher. Charles Wilson was secretary of defense. The Court denied an injunction, and Girard was turned over to Japanese authorities for trial. Upon conviction he was given a light sentence.

GOLDWATER V. CARTER

444 U.S. 996, 100 S.Ct. 533, 62 L.Ed.2d 428 (1979)

President Jimmy Carter nullified the Sino-American Mutual Defense Treaty, which the United States had signed with Taiwan. The treaty was broken as part of an agreement to give diplomatic recognition to the People's Republic of China. Several members of Congress, including Senator Barry Goldwater, objected, claiming that since the Senate had to ratify a treaty, a president could not nullify it on his own.

Vote: 9–0

ORDER

The petition for a writ of certiorari is granted. The judgment of the Court of Appeals is vacated and the case is remanded to the District Court with directions to dismiss the complaint.

JUSTICE POWELL, concurring.

Although I agree with the result reached by the Court, I would dismiss the complaint as not ripe for judicial review.

This Court has recognized that an issue should not be decided if it is not ripe for judicial review. Prudential considerations persuade me that a dispute between Congress and the President is not ready for judicial review unless and until each branch has taken action asserting its constitutional authority.

Differences between the President and the Congress are commonplace under our system. The differences should, and almost invariably do, turn on political rather than legal considerations. The Judicial Branch should not decide issues affecting the allocation of power between the President and Congress until the political branches reach a constitutional impasse. Otherwise, we would encourage small groups or even individual Members of Congress to seek judicial resolution of issues before the normal political process has the opportunity to resolve the conflict.

MR. JUSTICE MARSHALL concurs in the result.

MR. JUSTICE WHITE and MR. JUSTICE BLACKMUN join in the grant of the petition for a writ of certiorari but would set the case for argument and give it plenary consideration.

In this case, a few Members of Congress claim that the President's action in terminating the treaty with Taiwan has deprived them of their constitutional role with respect to a change in the supreme law of the land. Congress has taken no official action. In the present posture of this case, we do not know whether there ever will be an actual confrontation between the Legislative and Executive Branches. Although the Senate has considered a resolution declaring that Senate approval is necessary for the termination of any mutual defense treaty, no final vote has been taken on the resolution. Moreover, it is unclear whether the resolution would have retroactive effect. It cannot be said that either the Senate or the House has rejected the President's claim. If the Congress chooses not to confront the President, it is not our task to do so. I therefore concur in the dismissal of this case.

II

Mr. Justice Rehnquist suggests, however, that the issue presented by this case is a nonjusticiable political question which can never be considered by this Court. I cannot agree. In my view, reliance upon the political-question doctrine is inconsistent with our precedents. As set forth in the seminal case of *Baker v. Carr*, 369 U.S. 186 (1962), the doctrine incorporates three inquiries: (i) Does the issue involve resolution of questions committed by the text of the Constitution to a coordinate branch of Government? (ii) Would resolution of the question demand that a court move beyond areas of judicial expertise? (iii) Do prudential considerations counsel against judicial intervention? In my opinion the answer to each of these inquiries would require us to decide this case if it were ready for review.

First, the existence of "a textually demonstrable constitutional commitment of the issue to a coordinate political department," turns on an examination of the constitutional provisions governing the exercise of the power in question. No constitutional provision explicitly confers upon the President the power to terminate treaties. Further, Art. II, § 2, of the Constitution authorizes the President to make treaties with the advice and consent of the Senate. Article VI provides that treaties shall be a part of the supreme law of the land. These provisions add support to the view that the text of the Constitution does not unquestionably commit the power to terminate treaties to the President alone.

Second, there is no "lack of judicially discoverable and manageable standards for resolving" this case; nor is a decision impossible "without an initial policy determination of a kind clearly for nonjudicial discretion." We are asked to decide whether the President may terminate a treaty under the Constitution without congressional approval. Resolution of the question may not be easy, but it only requires us to apply normal principles of interpretation to the constitutional provisions at issue. The present case involves neither review of the President's activities as Commander in Chief nor impermissible interference in the field of foreign affairs. Such a case would arise if we were asked to decide, for example, whether a treaty required the President to order troops into a foreign country. But "it is error to suppose that every case or controversy which touches foreign relations lies beyond judicial cognizance." This case "touches" foreign relations, but the question presented to us concerns only the constitutional division of power between Congress and the President.

A simple hypothetical demonstrates the confusion that I find inherent in Mr. Justice Rehnquist's opinion concurring in the judgment. Assume that the President signed a mutual defense treaty with a foreign country and announced that it would go into effect despite its rejection by the Senate. Under Mr. Justice Rehnquist's analysis that situation would present a political question even though Art. II, § 2, clearly would resolve the dispute. Although the answer to the hypothetical case seems self-evident because it demands textual rather than interstitial analysis, the nature of the legal issue presented is no different from the issue presented in the case before us. In both cases, the Court would interpret the Constitution to decide whether congressional approval is necessary to give a Presidential decision on the validity of a treaty the force of law. Such an inquiry demands no special competence or information beyond the reach of the Judiciary

Finally, the political-question doctrine rests in part on prudential concerns calling for mutual respect among the three branches of Government. Thus, the Judicial Branch should avoid "the potentiality of embarrassment [that would result] from multifarious pronouncements by various departments on one question." Similarly, the doctrine restrains judicial action where there is an "unusual need for unquestioning adherence to a political decision already made."

If this case were ripe for judicial review, none of these prudential considerations would be present. Interpretation of the Constitution does not imply lack of respect for a coordinate branch. If the President and the Congress had reached irreconcilable positions, final disposition of the question presented by this case would eliminate, rather than create, multiple constitutional interpretations. The specter of the Federal Government brought to a halt because of the mutual intransigence of the President and the Congress would require this Court to provide a resolution pursuant to our duty " 'to say what the law is.' " *United States v. Nixon*, 418 U.S. 683, 703 (1974), quoting *Marbury v. Madison*, 1 Cranch 137, 177 (1803).

III

In my view, the suggestion that this case presents a political question is incompatible with this Court's willingness on previous occasions to decide whether one branch of our Government has impinged upon the power of another. Under the criteria enunciated in *Baker v. Carr*, we have the responsibility to decide whether both the Executive and Legislative Branches have constitutional roles to play in termination of a treaty. If the Congress, by appropriate formal action, had challenged the President's authority to terminate the treaty with Taiwan, the resulting uncertainty could have serious consequences for our country. In that situation, it would be the duty of this Court to resolve the issue.

JUSTICE REHNQUIST, with whom CHIEF JUSTICE BURGER, and JUSTICES STEWART and STEVENS join, concurring in the judgment.

I am of the view that the basic question presented by the petitioners in this case is "political" and therefore nonjusticiable because it involves the authority of the President in the conduct of our country's foreign relations and the extent to which the Senate or the Congress is authorized to negate the action of the President.

I believe . . . that the controversy in the instant case is a nonjusticiable political dispute that should be left for resolution by the Executive and Legislative Branches of the Government. Here, while the Constitution is express as to the manner in which the Senate shall participate in the ratification of a treaty, it is silent as to that body's participation in the abrogation of a treaty.

In light of the absence of any constitutional provision governing the termination of a treaty, and the fact that different termination procedures may be appropriate for different treaties, the instant case in my view also "must surely be controlled by political standards."

The present case differs in several important respects from *Youngstown Sheet & Tube Co. v. Sawyer,* 343 U.S. 579 (1952), cited by petitioners as authority both for reaching the merits of this dispute and for reversing the Court of Appeals. In *Youngstown,* private litigants brought a suit contesting the President's authority under his war powers to seize the Nation's steel industry, an action of profound and demonstrable domestic impact. Here, by contrast, we are asked to settle a dispute between coequal branches of our Government, each of which has resources available to protect and assert its interests, resources not available to private litigants outside the judicial forum. Moreover, as in [*United States v. Curtiss-Wright Export Corp.,* 299 U.S. 304 (1936)], the effect of this action, as far as we can tell, is "entirely external to the United States, and [falls] within the category of foreign affairs."

Having decided that the question presented in this action is nonjusticiable, I believe that the appropriate disposition is for this Court to vacate the decision of the Court of Appeals and remand with instructions for the District Court to dismiss the complaint.

JUSTICE BLACKMUN, with whom JUSTICE WHITE joins, dissenting in part.

In my view, the time factor and its importance are illusory; if the President does not have the power to terminate the treaty (a substantial issue that we should address only after briefing and oral argument), the notice of intention to terminate surely has no legal effect. It is also indefensible, without further study, to pass on the issue of justiciability or on the issues of standing or ripeness. While I therefore join in the grant of the petition for certiorari, I would set the case for oral argument and give it the plenary consideration it so obviously deserves.

JUSTICE BRENNAN, dissenting.

I respectfully dissent from the order directing the District Court to dismiss this case, and would affirm the judgment of the Court of Appeals insofar as it rests upon the President's well-established authority to recognize, and withdraw recognition from, foreign governments. In stating that this case presents a nonjusticiable "political question," Mr. Justice Rehnquist, in my view, profoundly misapprehends the political-question principle as it applies to matters of foreign relations. Properly understood, the political-question doctrine restrains courts from reviewing an exercise of foreign policy judgment by the coordinate political branch to which authority to make that judgment has been "constitutional[ly] commit[ted]." But the doctrine does not pertain when a court is faced with the *antecedent* question whether a particular branch has been constitutionally designated as the repository of political decisionmaking power. The issue of decisionmaking authority must be resolved as a matter of constitutional law, not political discretion; accordingly, it falls within the competence of the courts.

The constitutional question raised here is prudently answered in narrow terms. Abrogation of the defense treaty with Taiwan was a necessary incident to Executive recognition of the Peking Government, because the defense treaty was predicated upon the now-abandoned view that the Taiwan Government was the only legitimate political authority in China. Our cases firmly establish that the Constitution commits to the President alone the power to recognize, and withdraw recognition from, foreign regimes That mandate being clear, our judicial inquiry into the treaty rupture can go no further.

FOR DISCUSSION

Where does the Court locate the constitutional power of the president to cancel treaties? Does the president have unlimited discretion to cancel them? If the president is the sole organ in foreign affairs, does he or she have the final word regarding what a treaty means and what its obligations entail?

THE PRESIDENT AS COMMANDER IN CHIEF

Article II of the Constitution makes the President **commander in chief** of the armed forces. The scope of what this grant of authority means first arose during the Civil War, testing the limits of Abraham Lincoln's powers.

The Prize Cases (67 U.S. 635, 1863), which were discussed earlier, examine the president's commander-in-chief powers. Here the Court gave expansive authority to the president's decision to act and order the blockade. The second instance when presidential commander-in-chief powers were tested involved Franklin Roosevelt during World War II. In *Korematsu v. United States* (323 U.S. 214, 1944) the Court upheld the constitutionality of the Japanese relocation program. It ruled that the relocation of Japanese Americans to special camps was permissible under executive authority in the Constitution. The case, while a plus for presidential power, was a mixed blessing for civil libertarians. While the Court declared that policies targeting individuals based on their race would be given special scrutiny, it nonetheless still permitted this relocation despite what many now consider to be obvious racist motives and hysteria that overshadowed any real concerns about loyalty and security. *Korematsu* was decided after *Hirabayashi v. United States* (320 U.S. 81, 1943), where, writing for the Court, Chief Justice Stone held valid curfew regulations for persons of Japanese ancestry as a proper military measure to prevent espionage and sabotage. The Court noted that "in time of war residents having ethnic affiliation with an invading enemy may be a greater source of danger than those of a different ancestry."

Ex parte Mitsuye Endo (323 U.S. 283, 1944) reaches a different holding when it comes to presidential power to detain individuals. Justice Douglas ruled that an American citizen of Japanese ancestry who had been in custody in a war relocation center could no longer be detained and must be unconditionally released after his loyalty had been conceded. The purpose was to protect the war effort against possible sabotage, and when that purpose had been achieved, those involved had to be released. This case, decided the same day as *Korematsu*, arose out of the relocation center at Tule Lake, California.

In *Korematsu*, *Hirabayashi*, and *Endo* the Court refused to rule on the basic constitutional issues of the relocation, confinement, and segregation program for Japanese Americans. Undoubtedly, the Court was influenced by what it felt was military necessity in the view of those in charge at the time. The racial aspects of the program made the whole thing especially unfortunate. The only question under consideration was the right of the military to evacuate persons. The war power was used, rather than martial law. If the latter had been used, all citizens would have been subject to it, and the principles set down by *Milligan* might have been brought into the situation. All of these cases, however, speak to important issues regarding presidential war-making power.

The president has considerable discretion in the use of the armed forces as the commander in chief. But the president also appears to have broad powers even when it comes to the use of diplomatic skills to address foreign policy matters. In *Dames & Moore v. Regan* (453 U.S. 654, 1981), at issue is the scope of the president's authority to negotiate an agreement to resolve an international dispute. Here it involved President Carter negotiating an agreement to end the Iranian hostage crisis. The Court draws upon Justice Jackson's tripartite analysis of presidential power to support part of the agreement. However, the Court also looks to inherent presidential authority to act on his or her own to settle claims with the Iranian government. Could Congress have prevented the president from acting here? What does the Court seem to suggest?

Issues such as those raised in *Dames & Moore* test the boundary between the authority of Congress and the president in the field of foreign and military affairs. While the Constitution does provide significant language regarding the authority of the two branches, the exact lines regarding what a president can do in military affairs as commander in chief versus the powers reserved to Congress to declare war and raise an army and navy, for example, are not clear. Could the president commit the United States to a war or deploy troops without congressional authorization?

Because this type of action can influence policy in obvious ways, the importance of this single power—of deploying troops as commander in chief—can hardly be overemphasized. It is interesting to note that Justice Jackson in his dissenting opinion in *Korematsu* stated that he regarded war as an extraconstitutional activity. Does such a power really exist when the Constitution is supposed to be an enabling document that only grants power? Alexander Hamilton once argued that if the Constitution does not grant a specific power, it does not exist. Even if such a power is not extraconstitutional, another question is how far can the president go in acting as commander in chief to protect the United States against a possible attack? While many would say the president's authority would allow for the defensive deployment of troops, a bigger issue is for how long and how many troops could be committed? Once committed, does Congress have any say over the conduct of the war? If in fact the United States is attacked and the president seeks congressional authorization to act, short of a formal declaration of war, what is the extent of the commitment that is permissible under the Constitution? These are just some of the questions raised by the Vietnam War.

As a result of an alleged attack on U.S. ships in the Gulf of Tonkin off the coast of North Vietnam, President Lyndon Johnson sought congressional approval to respond to the aggression. (The authenticity of the attack on American ships has become a matter of historical contention.) The **Gulf of Tonkin Resolution** was Congress's response, leading up to the eventual deployment of several hundreds of thousands of troops in Vietnam and Indo-China for nearly a decade. One immediate constitutional question that emerged was whether the war was legal. If this war was unconstitutional, because it was not accompanied by a formal congressional declaration of war, one had to ask if the president as commander in chief, under the analysis set up by Justice Jackson's analysis in *Youngstown*, could authorize this military action? Finally, if the war was not constitutional, was the draft conscripting individuals into the military unconstitutional?

Mitchell v. United States (386 U.S. 972, 1967) and *Mora v. McNamara* (389 U.S. 934, 1967) addressed some of these questions. In both cases the Court refused to hear the claims of a **conscientious objector** fighting the draft who argued that the Vietnam War violated international law. Why? Were these political questions, or did the Court believe that the president had the authority to act either as a result of inherent Article II authority or because of congressional authorization? Should the Court have heard the case? Subsequently, in *Massachusetts v. Laird* (400 U.S. 886, 1970), in a memorandum decision the Court refused to rule on the constitutionality of United States action in Indochina. By refusing to take the case, the Court in effect affirmed a circuit court of appeals decision in which the lower court had held that Congress had implicitly acknowledged the existence of the Vietnam War by the passage of the Tonkin Gulf Resolution, appropriations of money, and the implementation of the Selective Service.

These three decisions failed to address the constitutional questions about presidential versus congressional lines of authority in military affairs. Under the terms of the Constitution the Congress determines the size, organization, and rules of the armed forces, makes appropriations for the military, formally declares war, and exercises certain powers in connection with the state militia. But the *use* of the military is basically a function of the president as commander in chief. Because the Court did not act, Congress sought to define the lines of authority in military affairs. The **War Powers Act of 1973**, passed by Congress over a presidential veto, sought to restrict the president's power to use the armed forces for hostile purposes outside the United States without the approval of Congress. According to the Act, the president may deploy troops for up to sixty days and then for an additional thirty days, if needed. Congress, however, by majority votes of both bodies, can require the president to bring the troops home sooner. There are two problems with the Act. First, it requires the president to invoke it, and since its adoption presidents have been mostly unwilling to do so. Second, many argue that the Act itself is unconstitutional. Some contend that the two-house vote by Congress to bring troops home is a legislative veto that is unconstitutional under *INS v. Chadha* (463 U.S. 919, 1983). However, that case only struck down a one-house veto. Others argue that the Act encroaches on either presidential or congressional authority.

For the foreseeable future it does not look like the Act will be challenged in court. In part this is because of the difficulty of finding someone with standing whom the judiciary will recognize. Whatever its fate, the War Powers Act is an attempt to fill in the constitutional grey area defining what presidents and Congress can do in foreign military affairs.

THE PRIZE CASES

67 U.S. 635, 2 Black 635, 17 L.Ed. 459 (1863)

See p. 643 above.

KOREMATSU V. UNITED STATES

323 U.S. 214, 65 S.Ct. 193, 89 L.Ed. 194 (1944)

Korematsu, an American citizen by birth of Japanese descent, was convicted of violation of an order that directed all persons of Japanese ancestry to evacuate an area in California to be transferred to war relocation centers. Of approximately 112,000 persons affected, about 70,000 were reported as having been born in the United States. This order was issued in pursuance of an executive order based on an act of Congress. The power of Congress to do this was challenged.

Vote: 6–3

JUSTICE BLACK delivered the opinion of the Court.

In the instant case prosecution of the petitioner was begun by information charging violation of an Act of Congress, of March 21, 1942, 56 Stat. 173, which provides that whoever shall enter, remain in, leave, or commit any act in any military area or military zone prescribed, under the authority of an Executive order of the President, by the Secretary of War, or by any military commander designated by the Secretary of War, contrary to the restrictions applicable to any such area or zone or contrary to the order of the Secretary of War or any such military commander, shall, if it appears that he knew or should have known of the existence and extent of the restrictions or order and that his act was in violation thereof, be guilty of a misdemeanor and upon conviction shall be liable to a fine of not to exceed $5,000 or to imprisonment for not more than one year, or both, for each offense.

Exclusion Order No.34, which the petitioner knowingly and admittedly violated, was one of a number of military orders and proclamations, all of which were substantially based upon Executive Order No.9066, 7 Fed. Reg. 1407. That order, issued after we were at war with Japan, declared that "the successful prosecution of the war requires every possible protection against espionage and against sabotage to national-defense material, national-defense premises, and national-defense utilities."

One of the series of orders and proclamations, a curfew order, which like the exclusion order here was promulgated pursuant to Executive Order 9066, subjected all persons of Japanese ancestry in prescribed West Coast military areas to remain in their residences from 8 p.m. to 6 a.m. As is the case with the exclusion order here, that prior curfew order was designed as a "protection against espionage and against sabotage." In *Kiyoshi Hirabayashi v. United States,* 320 U.S. 81 (1943), we sustained a conviction obtained for violation of the curfew order. The Hirabayashi conviction and this one thus rest on the same 1942 Congressional Act and the same basic executive and military orders, all of which orders were aimed at the twin dangers of espionage and sabotage.

The 1942 Act was attacked in the Hirabayashi case as an unconstitutional delegation of power; it was contended that the curfew order and other orders on which it rested were beyond the war powers of the Congress, the military authorities and of the President, as Commander-in-Chief of the Army; and finally that to apply the curfew order against none but citizens of Japanese ancestry amounted to a constitutionally prohibited discrimination solely on account of race. To these questions, we gave the serious consideration which their importance justified. We upheld the curfew order as an exercise of the power of the government to take steps necessary to prevent espionage and sabotage in an area threatened by Japanese attack.

In the light of the principles we announced in the *Hirabayashi* case, we are unable to conclude that it was beyond the war power of Congress and the Executive to exclude those of Japanese ancestry from the West Coast war area at the time they did. True, exclusion from the area in which one's home is located is a far greater deprivation than constant confinement to the home from 8 p.m. to 6 a.m. Nothing short of apprehension by the proper military authorities of the gravest imminent danger to the public safety can constitutionally justify either. But exclusion from a threatened area, no less than curfew, has a definite and close relationship to the prevention of espionage and sabotage. The military authorities, charged with the primary responsibility of defending our shores, concluded that curfew provided inadequate protection and ordered exclusion. They did so, as pointed out in our Hirabayashi opinion, in accordance with Congressional authority to the military to say who should, and who should not, remain in the threatened areas.

It is said that we are dealing here with the case of imprisonment of a citizen in a concentration camp solely because of his ancestry, without evidence or inquiry concerning his loyalty and good disposition towards the United States. Our task would be simple, our duty clear, were this a case involving the imprisonment of a loyal citizen in a concentration camp because of racial prejudice. Regardless of the true nature of the assembly and relocation centers—and we deem it unjustifiable to call them concentration camps with all the ugly connotations that term implies—we are dealing specifically with nothing but an exclusion order. To cast this case into outlines of racial prejudice, without reference to the real military dangers which were presented, merely confuses the issue. Korematsu was not excluded from the Military Area because of hostility to him or his race. He was excluded because we are at war with the Japanese Empire, because the properly constituted military authorities feared an invasion of our West Coast and felt constrained to take proper security measures, because they decided that the military urgency of the situation demanded that all citizens of Japanese ancestry be segregated from the West Coast temporarily, and finally, because Congress, reposing its confidence in this time of war in our military leaders—as inevitably it must—determined that they should have the power to do just this. There was evidence of disloyalty on the part of some, the military authorities considered that the need for action was great, and time was short. We cannot—by availing ourselves of the calm perspective of hindsight—now say that at that time these actions were unjustified.

Affirmed.

JUSTICE FRANKFURTER concurred:

The provisions of the Constitution which confer on the Congress and the President powers to enable this country to wage war are as much part of the Constitution as provisions looking to a nation at peace. And we have had recent occasion to quote approvingly the statement of former Chief Justice Hughes that the war power of the Government is "the power to wage war successfully." *Hirabayashi v. United States*. Therefore, the validity of action under the war power must be judged wholly in the context of war. That action is not to be stigmatized as lawless because like action in times of peace would be lawless. To talk about a military order that expresses an allowable judgment of war needs by those entrusted with the duty of conducting war as "an unconstitutional order" is to suffuse a part of the Constitution with an atmosphere of unconstitutionality. The respective spheres of action of military authorities and of judges are of course very different. But within their sphere, military authorities are no more outside the bounds of obedience to the Constitution than are judges within theirs. To recognize that military orders are "reasonably expedient military precautions" in time of war and yet to deny them constitutional legitimacy makes of the Constitution an instrument for dialectic subtleties not reasonably to be attributed to the hard-headed Framers, of whom a majority had had actual participation in war.

JUSTICE ROBERTS dissented.

I dissent, because I think the indisputable facts exhibit a clear violation of Constitutional rights.

This is not a case of keeping people off the streets at night as was *Kiyoshi Hirabayashi v. United States*, nor a case of temporary exclusion of a citizen from an area for his own safety or that of the community, nor a case of offering him an opportunity to go temporarily out of an area where his presence might cause danger to himself or to his fellows. On the contrary, it is the case of convicting a citizen as a punishment for not submitting to imprisonment in a concentration camp, based on his ancestry, and solely because of his ancestry, without evidence or inquiry concerning his loyalty and good disposition towards the United States. If this be a correct statement of the facts disclosed by this record, and facts of which we take judicial notice, I need hardly labor the conclusion that Constitutional rights have been violated.

I would reverse the judgment of conviction.

JUSTICE MURPHY dissented:

No adequate reason is given for the failure to treat these Japanese-Americans on an individual basis by holding investigations and hearings to separate the loyal from the disloyal, as was done in the case of persons of German and Italian ancestry. It is asserted merely that the loyalties of this group "were unknown and time was of the essence." Yet nearly four months elapsed after Pearl Harbor before the first exclusion order was issued; nearly eight months went by until the last order was issued; and the last of these "subversive" persons was not actually removed until almost eleven months had elapsed. Leisure and deliberation seem to have been more of the essence than speed. And the fact that conditions were not such as to warrant a declaration of martial law adds strength to the belief that the factors of time and military necessity were not as urgent as they have been represented to be.

I dissent, therefore, from this legalization of racism. Racial discrimination in any form and in any degree has no justifiable part whatever in our democratic way of life. It is unattractive in any setting but it is utterly revolting among a free people who have embraced the principles set forth in the Constitution of the United States. All residents of this nation are kin in some way by blood or culture to a foreign land. Yet they are primarily and necessarily a part of the new and distinct civilization of the United States. They must accordingly be treated at all times as the heirs of the American experiment and as entitled to all the rights and freedoms guaranteed by the Constitution.

JUSTICE JACKSON dissented:

But if we cannot confine military expedients by the Constitution, neither would I distort the Constitution to approve all that the military may deem expedient. That is what the Court appears to be doing, whether consciously or not. I cannot say, from any evidence before me, that the orders of General DeWitt were not reasonably expedient military precautions, nor could I say that they were. But even if they were permissible military procedures, I deny that it follows that they are constitutional. If, as the Court holds, it does follow, then we may as well say that any military order will be constitutional and have done with it.

I should hold that a civil court cannot be made to enforce an order which violates constitutional limitations even if it is a reasonable exercise of military authority. The courts can exercise only the judicial power, can apply only law, and must abide by the Constitution, or they cease to be civil courts and become instruments of military policy.

Of course the existence of a military power resting on force, so vagrant, so centralized, so necessarily heedless of the individual, is an inherent threat to liberty. But I would not lead people to rely on this Court for a review that seems to me wholly delusive. The military reasonableness of these orders can only be determined by military superiors. If the people ever let command of the war power fall into irresponsible and unscrupulous hands, the courts wield no power equal to its restraint. The chief restraint upon those who command the physical forces of the country, in the future as in the past, must be their responsibility to the political judgments of their contemporaries and to the moral judgments of history.

My duties as a justice as I see them do not require me to make a military judgment as to whether General DeWitt's evacuation and detention program was a reasonable military necessity. I do not suggest that the courts should have attempted to interfere with the Army in carrying out its task. But I do not think they may be asked to execute a military expedient that has no place in law under the Constitution. I would reverse the judgment and discharge the prisoner.

FOR DISCUSSION

What was the compelling government interest that justified the internment of the Japanese Americans? Did the Supreme Court simply defer to the president because of war hysteria or fears? What, if anything, did those interned do wrong, or was it guilt by association?

RELATED CASES

***Martin v. Mott:* 12 Wheat. 19 (1827).**

The president, under the act of 1795, was justified in calling out the militia. "The authority to decide whether the exigency has arisen, belongs exclusively to the President." This is a political matter and is not justiciable.

***Luther v. Borden:* 7 Howard I (1849).**

The president, in taking steps to support militarily the charter government in Rhode Island, had indicated his judgment as to which government was "republican" in form. No court can question a decision by the president to call out the militia.

EX PARTE ENDO

323 U.S. 283, 65 S.Ct. 208, 89 L.Ed. 243 (1944)

Mitsuye Endo was an American citizen of Japanese origin who in 1942, pursuant to an executive order, was evacuated from his home in California to a relocation camp. She filed for habeas corpus in federal court; it was denied at the district and court of appeals levels.

Vote: 9–0

JUSTICE DOUGLAS delivered the opinion of the Court.

Mitsuye Endo, hereinafter designated as the appellant, is an American citizen of Japanese ancestry. She was evacuated from Sacramento, California, in 1942, pursuant to certain military orders which we will presently discuss, and was removed to the Tule Lake War Relocation Center located at Newell, Modoc County, California. In July, 1942, she filed a petition for a writ of habeas corpus in the District Court of the United States for the Northern District of California, asking that she be discharged and restored to liberty. That petition was denied by the District Court in July, 1943, and an appeal was prefected to the Circuit Court of Appeals in August, 1943. Shortly thereafter appellant was transferred from the Tule Lake Relocation Center to the Central Utah Relocation Center located at Topaz, Utah, where she is presently detained. The certificate of questions of law was filed here on April 22, 1944, and on May 8, 1944, we ordered the entire record to be certified to this Court. It does not appear that any respondent was ever served with process or appeared in the proceedings. But the United States Attorney for the Northern District of California argued before the District Court that the petition should not be granted. And the Solicitor General argued the case here.

The history of the evacuation of Japanese aliens and citizens of Japanese ancestry from the Pacific coastal regions, following the Japanese attack on our Naval Base at Pearl Harbor on December 7, 1941, and the declaration of war against Japan on December 8, 1941, has been reviewed in *Kiyoshi Hirabayashi v. United States,* 320 U.S. 81 (1943). On February 19, 1942, the President promulgated Executive Order No. 9066. It recited that "the successful prosecution of the war requires every possible protection against espionage and against sabotage to national defense material, national-defense premises, and national-defense utilities as defined in Section 4, Act of April 20, 1918, 40 Stat. 533, as amended by the Act of November 30, 1940, 54 Stat. 1220, and the Act of August 21, 1941, 55 Stat. 655 (U.S.C., Title 50, Sec. 104)." And it authorized and directed "the Secretary of War, and the Military Commanders whom he may from time to time designate, whenever he or any designated Commander deems such action necessary or desirable, to prescribe military areas in such places and of such extent as he or the appropriate Military Commander may determine, from which any or all persons may be excluded, and with respect to which, the right of any person to enter, remain in, or leave shall be subject to whatever restrictions the Secretary of War or the appropriate Military Commander may impose in his discretion. The Secretary of War is hereby authorized to provide for residents of any such area who are excluded therefrom, such transportation, food, shelter, and other accommodations as may be necessary, in the judgment of the Secretary of War or the said Military Commander, and until other arrangements are made, to accomplish the purpose of this order."

Lt. General J. L. De Witt, Military Commander of the Western Defense Command, was designated to carry out the duties prescribed by that Executive Order. On March 2, 1942, he promulgated Public Proclamation No. 1 which recited that the entire Pacific Coast of the United States "by its geographical location is particularly subject to attack, to attempted invasion by the armed forces of nations with which the United States is now at war, and, in connection therewith, is subject to espionage and acts of sabotage, thereby requiring the adoption of military measures necessary to establish safeguards against such enemy operations." It designated certain Military Areas and Zones in the Western Defense Command and announced that certain persons might subsequently be excluded from these areas. On March 16, 1942, General De Witt promulgated Public Proclamation No. 2 which contained similar recitals and designated further Military Areas and Zones.

On March 18, 1942, the President promulgated Executive Order No. 9102 which established in the Office for Emergency Management of the Executive Office of the President the War Relocation Authority. It recited that it was made "in order to provide for the removal from designated areas of persons whose removal is necessary in the interests of national security." It provided for a Director and authorized and directed him to "formulate and effectuate a program for the removal, from the areas designated from time to time by the Secretary of War or appropriate military commander under the authority of Executive Order No. 9066 of February 19, 1942, of the persons or classes of persons designated under such Executive Order, and for their relocation, maintenance, and supervision." The Director was given the authority, among other things, to prescribe regulations necessary or desirable to promote effective execution of the program.

Congress shortly enacted legislation which, as we pointed out in Kiyoshi Hirabayashi v. United States, ratified and confirmed Executive Order No. 9066, which provided: "That whoever shall enter, remain in, leave, or commit any act in any military area or military zone prescribed, under the authority of an Executive order of the President, by the Secretary of War, or by any military commander designated by the Secretary of War, contrary to the restrictions applicable to any such area or zone or contrary to the order of the Secretary of War or any such military commander, shall, if it appears that he knew or should have known of the existence and extent of the restrictions or order and that his act was in violation thereof, be guilty of a misdemeanor and upon conviction shall be liable to a fine of not to exceed $5,000 or to imprisonment for not more than one year, or both, for each offense."

Beginning on March 24, 1942, a series of 108 Civilian Exclusion Orders were issued by General De Witt pursuant to Public Proclamation Nos. 1 and 2. Appellant's exclusion was effected by Civilian Exclusion Order No. 52, dated May 7, 1942. It ordered that "all persons of Japanese ancestry, both alien and non-alien" be excluded from Sacramento, California, beginning at noon on May 16, 1942. Appellant was evacuated to the Sacramento Assembly Center on May 15, 1942, and was transferred from there to the Tule Lake Relocation Center on June 19, 1942.

The program of the War Relocation Authority is said to have three main features: (1) the maintenance of Relocation Centers as interim places of residence for evacuees; (2) the segregation of loyal from disloyal evacuees; (3) the continued detention of the disloyal and so far as possible the relocation of the loyal in selected communities. In connection with the latter phase of its work the War Relocation Authority established a procedure for obtaining leave from Relocation Centers.

Application for leave clearance is required. An investigation of the applicant is made for the purpose of ascertaining "the probable effect upon the war program and upon the public peace and security of issuing indefinite leave" to the applicant. The grant of leave clearance does not authorize departure from the Relocation Center. Application for indefinite leave must also be made. Indefinite leave may be granted under 14 specified conditions. For example, it may be granted (1) where the applicant proposes to accept an employment offer or an offer of support that has been investigated and approved by the Authority; or (2) where the applicant does not intend to work but has "adequate financial resources to take care of himself" and a Relocation Officer has investigated and approved "public sentiment at his proposed destination", or (3) where the applicant has made arrangements to live at a hotel or in a private home approved by a Relocation Officer while arranging for employment; or (4) where the applicant proposes to accept employment by a federal or local governmental agency; or (5) where the applicant is going to live with designated classes of relatives.

But even if an applicant meets those requirements, no leave will issue when the proposed place of residence or employment is within a locality where it has been ascertained that "community sentiment is unfavorable" or when the applicant plans to go to an area which has been closed by the Authority to the issuance of indefinite leave. Nor will such leave issue if the area where the applicant plans to reside or work is one which has not been cleared for relocation. Moreover, the applicant agrees to give the Authority prompt notice of any change of employment or residence. And the indefinite leave which is granted does not permit entry into a prohibited military area, including those from which these people were evacuated.

Mitsuye Endo made application for leave clearance on February 19, 1943, after the petition was filed in the District Court. Leave clearance was granted her on August 16, 1943. But she made no application for indefinite leave.

Her petition for a writ of habeas corpus alleges that she is a loyal and law-abiding citizen of the United States, that no charge has been made against her, that she is being unlawfully detained, and that she is confined in the Relocation Center under armed guard and held there against her will.

It is conceded by the Department of Justice and by the War Relocation Authority that appellant is a loyal and law-abiding citizen. They make no claim that she is detained on any charge or that she is even suspected of disloyalty. Moreover, they do not contend that she may be held any longer in the Relocation Center. They concede that it is beyond the power of the War Relocation Authority to detain citizens against whom no charges of disloyalty or subversiveness have been made for a period longer than that necessary to separate the loyal from the disloyal and to provide the necessary guidance for relocation. But they maintain that detention for an additional period after leave clearance has been granted is an essential step in the evacuation program.

First. We are of the view that Mitsuye Endo should be given her liberty. In reaching that conclusion we do not come to the underlying constitutional issues which have been argued. For we conclude that, whatever power the War Relocation Authority may have to detain other classes of citizens, it has no authority to subject citizens who are concededly loyal to its leave procedure.

It should be noted at the outset that we do not have here a question such as was presented in *Ex parte Milligan*, 71 U.S. 2 (1866), or in *Ex parte Quirin*, 317 U.S. 1 (1942), where the jurisdiction of military tribunals to try persons according to the law of war was challenged in habeas corpus proceedings. Mitsuye Endo is detained by a civilian agency, the War Relocation Authority, not by the military. Moreover, the evacuation program was not left exclusively to the military; the Authority was given a large measure of responsibility for its execution and Congress made its enforcement subject to civil penalties by the Act of March 21, 1942. Accordingly, no questions of military law are involved.

Such power of detention as the Authority has stems from Executive Order No. 9066. That order is the source of the authority delegated by General De Witt in his letter of August 11, 1942. And Executive Order No. 9102 which created the War Relocation Authority purported to do no more than to implement the program authorized by Executive Order No. 9066.

We approach the construction of Executive Order No. 9066 as we would approach the construction of legislation in this field. That Executive Order must indeed be considered along with the Act of March 21, 1942, which ratified and confirmed it (*Kiyoshi Hirabayashi v. United States*) as the Order and the statute together laid such basis as there is for participation by civil agencies of the federal government in the evacuation program. Broad powers frequently granted to the President or other executive officers by Congress so that they may deal with the exigencies of war time problems have been sustained. And the Constitution when it committed to the Executive and to Congress the exercise of the war power necessarily gave them wide scope for the exercise of judgment and discretion so that war might be waged effectively and successfully. At the same time, however, the Constitution is as specific in its enumeration of many of the civil rights of the individual as it is in its enumeration of the powers of his government. Thus it has prescribed procedural safeguards surrounding the arrest, detention and conviction of individuals. Some of these are contained in the Sixth Amendment, compliance with which is essential if convictions are to be sustained. And the Fifth Amendment provides that no person shall be deprived of liberty (as well as life or property) without due process of law. Moreover, as a further safeguard against invasion of the basic civil rights of the individual it is provided in Art. I, Sec. 9 of the Constitution that "The Privilege of the Writ of Habeas Corpus shall not be suspended, unless when in Cases of Rebellion or Invasion the public Safety may require it."

We mention these constitutional provisions not to stir the constitutional issues which have been argued at the bar but to indicate the approach which we think should be made to an Act of Congress or an order of the Chief Executive that touches the sensitive area of rights specifically guaranteed by the Constitution. This Court has quite consistently given a narrower scope for the operation of the presumption of constitutionality when legislation appeared on its face to violate a specific prohibition of the Constitution. We have likewise favored that interpretation of legislation which gives it the greater chance of surviving the test of constitutionality. Those analogies are suggestive here. We must assume that the Chief Executive and members of Congress, as well as the courts, are sensitive to and respectful of the liberties of the citizen. In interpreting a war-time measure we must assume that their purpose was to allow for the greatest possible accommodation between those liberties and the exigencies of war. We must assume, when asked to find implied powers in a grant of legislative or executive authority, that the law makers intended to place no greater restraint on the citizen than was clearly and unmistakably indicated by the language they used.

A citizen who is concededly loyal presents no problem of espionage or sabotage. Loyalty is a matter of the heart and mind not of race, creed, or color. He who is loyal is by definition not a spy or a saboteur. When the power to detain is derived from the power to protect the war effort against espionage and sabotage, detention which has no relationship to that objective is unauthorized.

Nor may the power to detain an admittedly loyal citizen or to grant him a conditional release be implied as a useful or convenient step in the evacuation program, whatever authority might be implied in case of those whose loyalty was not conceded or established. If we assume (as we do) that the original evacuation was justified, its lawful character was derived from the fact that it was an espionage and sabotage measure, not that there was community hostility to this group of American citizens. The evacuation program rested explicitly on the former ground not on the latter as the underlying legislation shows. The authority to detain a citizen or to grant him a conditional release as protection against espionage or sabotage is exhausted at least when his loyalty is conceded. If we held that the authority to detain continued thereafter, we would transform an espionage or sabotage measure into something else. That was not done by Executive Order No. 9066 or by the Act of March 21, 1942, which ratified it. What they did not do we cannot do. Detention which furthered the campaign against espionage and sabotage would be one thing. But detention which has no relationship to that campaign is of a distinct character. Community hostility even to loyal evacuees may have been (and perhaps still is) a serious problem. But if authority for their custody and supervision is to be sought on that ground, the Act of March 21, 1942, Executive Order No. 9066, and Executive Order No. 9102, offer no support. And none other is advanced. To read them that broadly would be to assume that the Congress and the President intended that this discriminatory action should be taken against these people wholly on account of their ancestry even though the government conceded their loyalty to this country. We cannot make such an assumption. As the President has said of these loyal citizens: "Americans of Japanese ancestry, like those of many other ancestries, have shown that they can, and want to, accept our institutions and work loyally with the rest of us, making their own valuable contribution to the national wealth and well-being. In vindication of the very ideals for which we are fighting this war it is important to us to maintain a high standard of fair, considerate, and equal treatment for the people of this minority as of all other minorities."

Mitsuye Endo is entitled to an unconditional release by the War Relocation Authority.

Second. The question remains whether the District Court has jurisdiction to grant the writ of habeas corpus because of the fact that while the case was pending in the Circuit Court of Appeals appellant was moved from the Tule Lake Relocation Center in the Northern District of California where she was originally detained to the Central Utah Relocation Center in a different district and circuit.

That question is not colored by any purpose to effectuate a removal in evasion of the habeas corpus proceedings. It appears that appellant's removal to Utah was part of a general segregation program involving many of these people and was in no way related to this pending case. Moreover, there is no suggestion that there is no one within the jurisdiction of the District Court who is responsible for the detention of appellant and who would be an appropriate respondent. We are indeed advised by the Acting Secretary of the Interior that if the writ issues and is directed to the Secretary of the Interior or any official of the War Relocation Authority (including an assistant director whose office is at San Francisco, which is in the jurisdiction of the District Court), the corpus of appellant will be produced and the court's order complied with in all respects. Thus it would seem that the case is not moot.

In *United States ex rel. Innes v. Crystal*, 319 U.S. 755 (1943), the relator challenged a judgment of court martial by habeas corpus. The District Court denied his petition and the Circuit Court of Appeals affirmed that order. After that decision and before his petition for certiorari was filed here, he was removed from the custody of the Army to a federal penitentiary in a different district and circuit. The sole respondent was the commanding officer. Only an order directed to the warden of the penitentiary could effectuate his discharge and the warden as well as the prisoner was outside the territorial jurisdiction of the District Court. We therefore held the cause moot. There is no comparable situation here.

The fact that no respondent was ever served with process or appeared in the proceedings is not important. The United States resists the issuance of a writ. A cause exists in that state of the proceedings and an appeal lies from denial of a writ without the appearance of a respondent. *Ex parte Milligan*, 71 U.S. 2 (1866),.

Hence, so far as presently appears, the cause is not moot and the District Court has jurisdiction to act unless the physical presence of appellant in that district is essential.

We need not decide whether the presence of the person detained within the territorial jurisdiction of the District Court is prerequisite to filing a petition for a writ of habeas corpus. We only hold that the District Court acquired jurisdiction in this case and that the removal of Mitsuye Endo did not cause it to lose jurisdiction where a person in whose custody she is remains within the district.

There are expressions in some of the cases which indicate that the place of confinement must be within the court's territorial jurisdiction in order to enable it to issue the writ. But we are of the view that the court may act if there is a respondent within reach of its process who has custody of the petitioner. As Judge Cooley stated in *Matter of Jackson*, 15 Mich. 417, 439, 440 (1867): "The important fact to be observed in regard to the mode of procedure upon this writ is, that it is directed to, and served upon, not the person confined, but his jailer. It does not reach the former except through the latter. The officer or person who serves it does not unbar the prison doors, and set the prisoner free, but the court relieves him by compelling the oppressor to release his constraint. The whole force of the writ is spent upon the respondent."

The judgment is reversed and the cause is remanded to the District Court for proceedings in conformity with this opinion.

Reversed.

JUSTICE MURPHY, concurring.

I join in the opinion of the Court, but I am of the view that detention in Relocation Centers of persons of Japanese ancestry regardless of loyalty is not only unauthorized by Congress or the Executive but is another example of the unconstitutional resort to racism inherent in the entire evacuation program. As stated more fully in my dissenting opinion in *Fred Toyosaburo Korematsu v. United States*, 323 U.S. 214 (1944), racial discrimination of this nature bears no reasonable relation to military necessity and is utterly foreign to the ideals and traditions of the American people.

JUSTICE ROBERTS.

I concur in the result but I cannot agree with the reasons stated in the opinion of the court for reaching that result.

As in *Korematsu v. United States*, the court endeavors to avoid constitutional issues which are necessarily involved. The opinion, at great length, attempts to show that neither the executive nor the legislative arm of the Government authorized the detention of the relator.

I conclude, therefore, that the court is squarely faced with a serious constitutional question,—whether the relator's detention violated the guarantees of the Bill of Rights of the federal Constitution and especially the guarantee of due process of law. There can be but one answer to that question. An admittedly loyal citizen has been deprived of her liberty for a period of years. Under the Constitution she should be free to come and go as she pleases. Instead, her liberty of motion and other innocent activities have been prohibited and conditioned. She should be discharged.

FOR DISCUSSION

How does one explain the difference between the *Korematsu* and *Endo* decisions? Constitutionally, were different issues at stake? Why did the Court not defer to the president here as it did in *Korematsu*?

DAMES & MOORE V. REGAN

453 U.S. 654, 101 S.Ct. 2972, 69 L.Ed.2d 918 (1981)

After the Iranian government had taken Americans hostage in 1979, President Jimmy Carter ordered all of that country's assets located in American banks to be frozen. Subsequently, in securing the hostages' release, the president negotiated a deal that provided for any legal claims by American nationals against Iran to be suspended in American courts and transferred to a special tribunal. Dames & Moore, an American company with claims against Iran, objected and challenged this agreement in court.

Vote: 8–1

JUSTICE REHNQUIST delivered the opinion of the Court.

The questions presented by this case touch fundamentally upon the matter in which our Republic is to be governed. Throughout the nearly two centuries of our Nation's existence under the Constitution, this subject has generated considerable debate. We have had the benefit of commentators such as John Jay, Alexander Hamilton, and James Madison writing in The Federalist Papers at the Nation's very inception, the benefit of astute foreign observers of our system such as Alexis deTocqueville and James Bryce writing during the first century of the Nation's existence, and the benefit of many other treatises as well as more than 400 volumes of reports of decisions of this Court. As these writings reveal it is doubtless both futile and perhaps dangerous to find any epigrammatical explanation of how this country has been governed. Indeed, as Justice Jackson noted, "[a] judge . . . may be surprised at the poverty of really useful and unambiguous authority applicable to concrete problems of executive power as they actually present themselves." *Youngstown Sheet & Tube Co. v. Sawyer*, 343 U.S. 579 (1952).

Our decision today will not dramatically alter this situation, for the Framers "did not make the judiciary the overseer of our government." We are confined to a resolution of the dispute presented to us. That dispute involves various Executive Orders and regulations by which the President nullified attachments and liens on Iranian assets in the United States, directed that these assets be transferred to Iran, and suspended claims against Iran that may be presented to an International Claims Tribunal. This action was taken in an effort to comply with an Executive Agreement between the United States and Iran. We granted certiorari before judgment in this case, and set an expedited briefing and argument schedule, because lower courts had reached conflicting conclusions on the validity of the President's actions and, as the Solicitor General informed us, unless the Government acted by July 19, 1981, Iran could consider the United States to be in breach of the Executive Agreement.

But before turning to the facts and law which we believe determine the result in this case, we stress that the expeditious treatment of the issues involved by all of the courts which have considered the President's actions makes us acutely aware of the necessity to rest decision on the narrowest possible ground capable of deciding the case. *Ashwander v. TVA*, 297 U.S. 288, 347 (1936) (Brandeis, J., concurring). This does not mean that reasoned analysis may give way to judicial fiat. It does mean that the statement of Justice Jackson—that we decide difficult cases presented to us by virtue of our commissions, not our competence—is especially true here. We attempt to lay down no general "guidelines" covering other situations not involved here, and attempt to confine the opinion only to the very questions necessary to decision of the case.

Perhaps it is because it is so difficult to reconcile the foregoing definition of Art. III judicial power with the broad range of vitally important day-to-day questions regularly decided by Congress or the Executive, without either challenge or interference by the Judiciary, that the decisions of the Court in this area have been rare, episodic, and afford little precedential value for subsequent cases. The tensions present in any exercise of executive power under the tri-partite system of Federal Government established by the Constitution have been reflected in opinions by Members of this Court more than once. The Court stated in *United States v. Curtiss-Wright Export Corp.*, 299 U.S. 304, 319–320 (1936):

> [W]e are here dealing not alone with an authority vested in the President by an exertion of legislative power, but with such an authority plus the very delicate, plenary and exclusive power of the President as the sole organ of the federal government in the field of international relations—a power which does not require as a basis for its exercise an act of Congress, but which, of course, like every other governmental power, must be exercised in subordination to the applicable provisions of the Constitution.

And yet 16 years later, Justice Jackson in his concurring opinion in *Youngstown Sheet & Tube Co. v. Sawyer*, 343 U.S. 579 (1952), which both parties agree brings together as much combination of analysis and common sense as there is in this area, focused not on the "plenary and exclusive power of the President" but rather responded to a claim of virtually unlimited powers for the Executive by noting:

> The example of such unlimited executive power that must have most impressed the forefathers was the prerogative exercised by George III, and the description of its evils in the Declaration of Independence leads me to doubt that they were creating their new Executive in his image.

As we now turn to the factual and legal issues in this case, we freely confess that we are obviously deciding only one more episode in the never-ending tension between the President exercising the executive authority in a world that presents each day some new challenge with which he must deal and the Constitution under which we all live and which no one disputes embodies some sort of system of checks and balances.

I

On November 4, 1979, the American Embassy in Tehran was seized and our diplomatic personnel were captured and held hostage. In response to that crisis, President Carter, acting pursuant to the International Emergency Economic Powers Act, 91 Stat. 1626, 50 U.S.C. §§ 1701–1706 (1976 ed., Supp. III) (hereinafter IEEPA), declared a national emergency on November 14, 1979, and blocked the removal or transfer of "all property and interests in property of the Government of Iran, its instrumentalities and controlled entities and the Central Bank of Iran which are or become subject to the jurisdiction of the United States. . . ." President Carter authorized the Secretary of the Treasury to promulgate regulations carrying out the blocking order. On November 15, 1979, the Treasury Department's Office of Foreign Assets Control issued a regulation providing that "[u]nless licensed or authorized . . . any attachment, judgment, decree, lien, execution, garnishment, or other judicial process is null and void with respect to any property in which on or since [November 14, 1979,] there existed an interest of Iran." The regulations also made clear that any licenses or authorizations granted could be "amended, modified, or revoked at any time."

On November 26, 1979, the President granted a general license authorizing certain judicial proceedings against Iran but which did not allow the "entry of any judgment or of any decree or order of similar or analogous effect. . . ." On December 19, 1979, a clarifying regulation was issued stating that "the general authorization for judicial proceedings contained in § 535.504(a) includes pre-judgment attachment."

On December 19, 1979, petitioner Dames & Moore filed suit in the United States District Court for the Central District of California against the Government of Iran, the Atomic Energy Organization of Iran, and a number of Iranian banks. In its complaint, petitioner alleged that its wholly owned subsidiary, Dames & Moore International, was a party to a written contract with the Atomic Energy Organization, and that the subsidiary's entire interest in the contract had been assigned to petitioner. Under the contract, the subsidiary was to conduct site studies for a proposed nuclear power plant in Iran. As provided in the terms of the contract, the Atomic Energy Organization terminated the agreement for its own convenience on June 30, 1979. Petitioner contended, however, that it was owed $3,436,694.30 plus interest for services performed under the contract prior to the date of termination. The District Court issued orders of attachment directed against property of the defendants, and the property of certain Iranian banks was then attached to secure any judgment that might be entered against them.

On January 20, 1981, the Americans held hostage were released by Iran pursuant to an Agreement entered into the day before and embodied in two Declarations of the Democratic and Popular Republic of Algeria. The Agreement stated that "[i]t is the purpose of [the United States and Iran] . . . to terminate all litigation as between the Government of each party and the nationals of the other, and to bring about the settlement and termination of all such claims through binding arbitration." In furtherance of this goal, the Agreement called for the establishment of an Iran-United States Claims Tribunal which would arbitrate any claims not settled within six months. Awards of the Claims Tribunal are to be "final and binding" and "enforceable . . . in the courts of any nation in accordance with its laws." Under the Agreement, the United States is obligated

> to terminate all legal proceedings in United States courts involving claims of United States persons and institutions against Iran and its state enterprises, to nullify all attachments and judgments obtained therein, to prohibit all further litigation based on such claims, and to bring about the termination of such claims through binding arbitration.

In addition, the United States must "act to bring about the transfer" by July 19, 1981, of all Iranian assets held in this country by American banks. One billion dollars of these assets will be deposited in a security account in the Bank of England, to the account of the Algerian Central Bank, and used to satisfy awards rendered against Iran by the Claims Tribunal.

On January 19, 1981, President Carter issued a series of Executive Orders implementing the terms of the agreement. These Orders revoked all licenses permitting the exercise of "any right, power, or privilege" with regard to Iranian funds, securities, or deposits; "nullified" all non-Iranian interests in such assets acquired subsequent to the blocking order of November 14, 1979; and required those banks holding Iranian assets to transfer them "to the Federal Reserve Bank of New York, to be held or transferred as directed by the Secretary of the Treasury."

On February 24, 1981, President Reagan issued an Executive Order in which he "ratified" the January 19th Executive Orders. Moreover, he "suspended" all "claims which may be presented to the . . . Tribunal" and provided that such claims "shall have no legal effect in any action now pending in any court of the United States." The suspension of any particular claim terminates if the Claims Tribunal determines that it has no jurisdiction over that claim; claims are discharged for all purposes when the Claims Tribunal either awards some recovery and that amount is paid, or determines that no recovery is due.

Meanwhile, on January 27, 1981, petitioner moved for summary judgment in the District Court against the Government of Iran and the Atomic Energy Organization, but not against the Iranian banks. The District Court granted petitioner's motion and awarded petitioner the amount claimed under the contract plus interest. Thereafter, petitioner attempted to execute the judgment by obtaining writs of garnishment and execution in state court in the State of Washington, and a sheriff's sale of Iranian property in Washington was noticed to satisfy the judgment. However, by order of May 28, 1981, as amended by order of June 8, the District Court stayed execution of its judgment pending appeal by the Government of Iran and the Atomic Energy Organization. The District Court also ordered that all prejudgment attachments obtained against the Iranian defendants be vacated and that further proceedings against the bank defendants be stayed in light of the Executive Orders discussed above.

On April 28, 1981, petitioner filed this action in the District Court for declaratory and injunctive relief against the United States and the Secretary of the Treasury, seeking to prevent enforcement of the Executive Orders and Treasury Department regulations implementing the Agreement with Iran. In its complaint, petitioner alleged that the actions of the President and the Secretary of the Treasury implementing the Agreement with Iran were beyond their statutory and constitutional powers and, in any event, were unconstitutional to the extent they adversely affect petitioner's final judgment against the Government of Iran and the Atomic Energy Organization, its execution of that judgment in the State of Washington, its prejudgment attachments, and its ability to continue to litigate against the Iranian banks. On May 28, 1981, the District Court denied petitioner's motion for a preliminary injunction and dismissed petitioner's complaint for failure to state a claim upon which relief could be granted. Prior to the District Court's ruling, the United States Courts of Appeals for the First and the District of Columbia Circuits upheld the President's authority to issue the Executive Orders and regulations challenged by petitioner.

II

The parties and the lower courts, confronted with the instant questions, have all agreed that much relevant analysis is contained in *Youngstown*. Justice Black's opinion for the Court in that case, involving the validity of President Truman's effort to seize the country's steel mills in the wake of a nationwide strike, recognized that "[t]he President's power, if any, to issue the order must stem either from an act of Congress or from the Constitution itself." Justice Jackson's concurring opinion elaborated in a general way the consequences of different types of interaction between the two democratic branches in assessing Presidential authority to act in any given case. When the President acts pursuant to an express or implied authorization from Congress, he exercises not only his powers but also those delegated by Congress. In such a case the executive action "would be supported by the strongest of presumptions and the widest latitude of judicial interpretation, and the burden of persuasion would rest heavily upon any who might attack it."

When the President acts in the absence of congressional authorization he may enter "a zone of twilight in which he and Congress may have concurrent authority, or in which its distribution is uncertain." In such a case the analysis becomes more complicated, and the validity of the President's action, at least so far as separation-of-powers principles are concerned, hinges on a consideration of all the circumstances which might shed light on the views of the Legislative Branch toward such action, including "congressional inertia, indifference or quiescence." Finally, when the President acts in contravention of the will of Congress, "his power is at its lowest ebb," and the Court can sustain his actions "only by disabling the Congress from acting upon the subject."

Although we have in the past found and do today find Justice Jackson's classification of executive actions into three general categories analytically useful, we should be mindful of Justice Holmes' admonition, quoted by Justice Frankfurter in *Youngstown*, that "[t]he great ordinances of the Constitution do not establish and divide fields of black and white." *Springer v. Philippine Islands*, 277 U.S. 189, 209 (1928) (dissenting opinion). Justice Jackson himself recognized that his three categories represented "a somewhat over-simplified grouping," 343 U.S., at 635, and it is doubtless the case that executive action in any particular instance falls, not neatly in one of three pigeonholes, but rather at some point along a spectrum running from explicit congressional authorization to explicit congressional prohibition. This is particularly true as respects cases such as the one before us, involving responses to international crises the nature of which Congress can hardly have been expected to anticipate in any detail.

III

In nullifying post-November 14, 1979, attachments and directing those persons holding blocked Iranian funds and securities to transfer them to the Federal Reserve Bank of New York for ultimate transfer to Iran, President Carter cited five sources of express or inherent power. The Government, however, has principally relied on § 203 of the IEEPA, as authorization for these actions. Section 1702(a)(1) provides in part:

> At the times and to the extent specified in section 1701 of this title, the President may, under such regulations as he may prescribe, by means of instructions, licenses, or otherwise—
>
> (A) investigate, regulate, or prohibit—
>
> (i) any transactions in foreign exchange,
>
> (ii) transfers of credit or payments between, by, through, or to any banking institution, to the extent that such transfers or payments involve any interest of any foreign country or a national thereof,
>
> (iii) the importing or exporting of currency or securities, and
>
> (B) investigate, regulate, direct and compel, nullify, void, prevent or prohibit, any acquisition, holding, withholding, use, transfer, withdrawal, transportation, importation or exportation of, or dealing in, or exercising any right, power, or privilege with respect to, or transactions involving, any property in which any foreign country or a national thereof has any interest;
>
> by any person, or with respect to any property, subject to the jurisdiction of the United States.

Because the President's action in nullifying the attachments and ordering the transfer of the assets was taken pursuant to specific congressional authorization, it is "supported by the strongest of presumptions and the widest latitude of judicial interpretation, and the burden of persuasion would rest heavily upon any who might attack it." *Youngstown*, 343 U.S., at 637 (Jackson, J., concurring). Under the circumstances of this case, we cannot say that petitioner has sustained that heavy burden. A contrary ruling would mean that the Federal Government as a whole lacked the power exercised by the President, and that we are not prepared to say.

IV

Although we have concluded that the IEEPA constitutes specific congressional authorization to the President to nullify the attachments and order the transfer of Iranian assets, there remains the question of the President's authority to suspend claims pending in American courts. Such claims have, of course, an existence apart from the attachments which accompanied them. In terminating these claims through Executive Order No. 12294 the President purported to act under authority of both the IEEPA and 22 U.S.C. § 1732, the so-called "Hostage Act."*

We conclude that although the IEEPA authorized the nullification of the attachments, it cannot be read to authorize the suspension of the claims. The claims of American citizens against Iran are not in themselves transactions involving Iranian property or efforts to exercise any rights with respect to such property. An *in personam* lawsuit, although it might eventually be reduced to judgment and that judgment might be executed upon, is an effort to establish liability and fix damages and does not focus on any particular property within the jurisdiction. The terms of the IEEPA therefore do not authorize the President to suspend claims in American courts

We are reluctant to conclude that this provision constitutes specific authorization to the President to suspend claims in American courts. Although the broad language of the Hostage Act suggests it may cover this case, there are several difficulties with such a view. The legislative history indicates that the Act was passed in response to a situation unlike the recent Iranian crisis. Congress in 1868 was concerned with the activity of certain countries refusing to recognize the citizenship of naturalized Americans traveling abroad, and repatriating such citizens against their will. These countries were not interested in returning the citizens in exchange for any sort of ransom. This also explains the reference in the Act to imprisonment "in violation of the rights of American citizenship." Although the Iranian hostage-taking violated international law and common decency, the hostages were not seized out of any refusal to recognize their American citizenship—they were seized precisely *because of* their American citizenship. The legislative history is also somewhat ambiguous on the question whether Congress contemplated Presidential action such as that involved here or rather simply reprisals directed against the offending foreign country and *its* citizens.

Concluding that neither the IEEPA nor the Hostage Act constitutes specific authorization of the President's action suspending claims, however, is not to say that these statutory provisions are entirely irrelevant to the question of the validity of the President's action. We think both statutes highly relevant in the looser sense of indicating congressional acceptance of a broad scope for executive action in circumstances such as those presented in this case.

Crucial to our decision today is the conclusion that Congress has implicitly approved the practice of claim settlement by executive agreement. This is best demonstrated by Congress' enactment of the International Claims Settlement Act of 1949. The Act had two purposes: (1) to allocate to United States nationals funds received in the course of an executive claims settlement with Yugoslavia, and (2) to provide a procedure whereby funds resulting from future settlements could be distributed. To achieve these ends Congress created the International Claims Commission, now the Foreign Claims Settlement Commission, and gave it jurisdiction to make final and binding decisions with respect to claims by United States nationals against settlement funds.

By creating a procedure to implement future settlement agreements, Congress placed its stamp of approval on such agreements. Indeed, the legislative history of the Act observed that the United States was seeking

* Judge Mikva, in his separate opinion in *American Int'l Group, Inc. v. Islamic Republic of Iran*, 657 F.2d 430, 452 (1981), argued that the moniker "Hostage Act" was newly coined for purposes of this litigation. Suffice it to say that we focus on the language of 22 U.S.C. § 1732, not any shorthand description of it. See W. Shakespeare, *Romeo and Juliet*, Act II, scene 2, line 43 ("What's in a name?").

settlements with countries other than Yugoslavia and that the bill contemplated settlements of a similar nature in the future.

In addition to congressional acquiescence in the President's power to settle claims, prior cases of this Court have also recognized that the President does have some measure of power to enter into executive agreements without obtaining the advice and consent of the Senate. In *United States v. Pink*, 315 US 203 (1942), for example, the Court upheld the validity of the Litvinov Assignment, which was part of an Executive Agreement whereby the Soviet Union assigned to the United States amounts owed to it by American nationals so that outstanding claims of other American nationals could be paid.

The judgment of the District Court is accordingly affirmed, and the mandate shall issue forthwith.

It is so ordered.

JUSTICE STEVENS, concurring in part.

In my judgment the possibility that requiring this petitioner to prosecute its claim in another forum will constitute an unconstitutional "taking" is so remote that I would not address the jurisdictional question considered in Part V of the Court's opinion. However, I join the remainder of the opinion.

FOR DISCUSSION

What if Congress had not endorsed the president's actions here? Would the Court have taken a different approach to the agreement? How critical was Congress's assent in this situation?

Vietnam and Presidential War Powers

The American military involvement in Vietnam was controversial in many ways. Many argued that the conflict was illegal because Congress never formally declared war. Others alleged that it violated international law. President Johnson cited the Gulf of Tonkin Resolution, which was adopted by Congress to support the escalation and deployment of troops into Vietnam. The resolution was adopted by Congress after an alleged attack on U.S. ships by the North Vietnamese in the Gulf of Tonkin in 1964.

Efforts to challenge the legality of the Vietnam War went to federal courts, but with little resolution of the matter, as they ruled that the issue of the constitutionality of the war was a nonjusticiable political question.

Joint Resolution of Congress

H.J. RES 1145 August 7, 1964

Resolved by the Senate and House of Representatives of the United States of America in Congress assembled,

That the Congress approves and supports the determination of the President, as Commander in Chief, to take all necessary measures to repel any armed attack against the forces of the United States and to prevent further aggression.

Section 2. The United States regards as vital to its national interest and to world peace the maintenance of international peace and security in southeast Asia. Consonant with the Constitution of the United States and the Charter of the United Nations and in accordance with its obligations under the Southeast Asia Collective Defense Treaty, the United States is, therefore, prepared, as the President determines, to take all necessary steps, including the use of armed force, to assist any member or protocol state of the Southeast Asia Collective Defense Treaty requesting assistance in defense of its freedom.

Section 3. This resolution shall expire when the President shall determine that the peace and security of the area is reasonably assured by international conditions created by action of the United Nations or otherwise, except that it may be terminated earlier by concurrent resolution of the Congress.

MITCHELL V. UNITED STATES

386 U.S. 972, 87 S.Ct. 1162, 18 L.Ed.2d 132 (1967)

David Mitchell was drafted and ordered to report to a military induction center. He refused, contending that the Vietnam War was illegal under international law and treaties. He was convicted of failing to report to the draft board and was sentenced to five years in prison. He appealed his conviction.

Vote: 8–1

Petition for writ of certiorari to the United States Court of Appeals for the Second Circuit.

Denied.

JUSTICE DOUGLAS dissents.

Petitioner did not report for induction as ordered, was indicted, convicted, and sentenced to five years imprisonment and his conviction was affirmed. His defense was that the "war" in Vietnam was being conducted in violation of various treaties to which we were a signatory especially the Treaty of London of August 8, 1945, 59 Stat. 1544, which in Article 6(a) declares that "waging of a war of aggression" is a "crime against peace" imposing "individual responsibility." Article 8 provides:

> The fact that the Defendant acted pursuant to order of his Government or of a superior shall not free him from responsibility, but may be considered in mitigation of punishment if the Tribunal determines that justice so requires.

Petitioner claimed that the "war" in Vietnam was a "war of aggression" within the meaning of the Treaty of London and that Article 8 makes him responsible for participating in it even though he is ordered to do.

Mr. Justice Jackson, the United States prosecutor at Nuremberg, stated: "If certain acts in violation of treaties are crimes, they are crimes whether the United States does them or whether Germany does them, and we are not prepared to lay down a rule of criminal conduct against others which we would not be willing to have invoked against us."

Article VI, cl. 2 of the Constitution states that "treaties" are a part of "the supreme law of the land; and the Judges in every State shall be bound thereby."

There is a considerable body of opinion that our actions in Vietnam constitute the waging of an aggressive "war"

This case presents the questions:

(1) whether the Treaty of London is a treaty within the meaning of Art. VI, cl. 2;

(2) whether the question as to the waging of an aggressive "war" is in the context of this criminal prosecution a justiciable question;

(3) whether the Vietnam episode is a "war" in the sense of the Treaty;

(4) whether petitioner has standing to raise the question;

(5) whether, if he has, it may be tendered as a defense in this criminal case or in amelioration of the punishment.

These are extremely sensitive and delicate questions. But they should, I think, be answered. Even those who think that the Nuremberg judgments were unconstitutional by our guarantee relating to *ex post facto laws* would have to take a different view of the Treaty of London that purports to lay down a standard of future conduct for all the signatories.

I intimate no opinion on the merits. But I think the petition for certiorari should be granted. We have here a recurring question in present-day Selective Service cases.

MORA V. MCNAMARA

389 U.S. 934, 88 S.Ct. 282, 19 L.Ed. 287 (1967)

Dennis Mora and two other individuals already serving in the military refused orders to deploy to Vietnam. They claimed that the war in Vietnam was an illegal act of aggression under treaty and international law.

Vote: 7–2

Petition for writ of certiorari to the United States Court of Appeals for the District of Columbia Circuit.

Denied.

JUSTICE STEWART, with whom Justice Douglas joins, dissenting.

The petitioners were drafted into the United States Army in late 1965, and six months later were ordered to a West Coast replacement station for shipment to Vietnam. They brought this suit to prevent the Secretary of Defense and the Secretary of the Army from carrying out those orders, and requested a declaratory judgment that the present United States military activity in Vietnam is "illegal." The District Court dismissed the suit, and the Court of Appeals affirmed.

There exist in this case questions of great magnitude. Some are akin to those referred to by Mr. Justice Douglas in *Mitchell v. United States*, But there are others:

I. Is the present United States military activity in Vietnam a "war" within the meaning of Article I, Section 8, Clause 11 of the Constitution?

II. If so, may the Executive constitutionally order the petitioners to participate in that military activity, when no war has been declared by the Congress?

III. Of what relevance to Question II are the present treaty obligations of the United States?

IV. Of what relevance to Question II is the joint Congressional ("Tonkin Bay") Resolution of August 10, 1964?

(a) Do present United States military operations fall within the terms of the Joint Resolution?

(b) If the Joint Resolution purports to give the Chief Executive authority to commit United States forces to armed conflict limited in scope only by his own absolute discretion, is the

> Resolution a constitutionally impermissible delegation of all or part of Congress' power to declare war?

These are large and deeply troubling questions. Whether the Court would ultimately reach them depends, of course, upon the resolution of serious preliminary issues of justiciability. We cannot make these problems go away simply by refusing to hear the case of three obscure Army privates. I intimate not even tentative views upon any of these matters, but I think the Court should squarely face them by granting certiorari and setting this case for oral argument.

JUSTICE DOUGLAS, with whom JUSTICE STEWART concurs, dissenting.

The questions posed by Mr. Justice Stewart cover the wide range of problems which the Senate Committee on Foreign Relations recently explored, in connection with the SEATO Treaty of February 19, 1955, and the Tonkin Gulf Resolution.

Mr. Katzenbach, representing the Administration, testified that he did not regard the Tonkin Gulf Resolution to be "a declaration of war" and that while the Resolution was not "constitutionally necessary" it was "politically, from an international viewpoint and from a domestic viewpoint, extremely important." He added:

> The use of the phrase "to declare war" as it was used in the Constitution of the United States had a particular meaning in terms of the events and the practices which existed at the time it was adopted.
>
> [I]t was recognized by the Founding Fathers that the President might have to take emergency action to protect the security of the United States, but that if there was going to be another use of the armed forces of the United States, that was a decision which Congress should check the Executive on, which Congress should support. It was for that reason that the phrase was inserted in the Constitution.
>
> Now, over a long period of time, . . . there have been many uses of the military forces of the United States for a variety of purposes without a congressional declaration of war. But it would be fair to say that most of these were relatively minor uses of force. . . .
>
> A declaration of war would not, I think, correctly reflect the very limited objectives of the United States with respect to Vietnam. It would not correctly reflect our efforts there, what we are trying to do, the reasons why we are there, to use an outmoded phraseology, to declare war.

The view that Congress was intended to play a more active role in the initiation and conduct of war than the above statements might suggest has been espoused by Senator Fulbright, quoting Thomas Jefferson who said:

> We have already given in example one effectual check to the Dog of war by transferring the power of letting him loose from the Executive to the Legislative body, from those who are to spend to those who are to pay.

These opposed views are reflected in the *Prize Cases*, 67 U.S. 635 (1863), a five-to-four decision rendered in 1863. Mr. Justice Grier, writing for the majority, emphasized the arguments for strong presidential powers. Justice Nelson, writing for the minority of four, read the Constitution more strictly, emphasizing that what is war in actuality may not constitute war in the constitutional sense. During all subsequent periods in our history—through the Spanish-American War, the Boxer Rebellion, two World Wars, Korea, and now Vietnam—the two points of view urged in the *Prize Cases* have continued to be voiced.

A host of problems is raised. Does the President's authority to repel invasions and quiet insurrections, his powers in foreign relations and his duty to execute faithfully the laws of the United States, including its treaties, justify what has been threatened of petitioners? What is the relevancy of the Gulf of Tonkin Resolution and the yearly appropriations in support of the Vietnam effort?

The London Treaty, the SEATO Treaty, the Kellogg-Briand Pact, and Article 39 of Chapter VII of the UN Charter deal with various aspects of wars of "aggression." Do any of them embrace hostilities in Vietnam, or give rights to individuals affected to complain, or in other respects give rise to justiciable controversies?

There are other treaties or declarations that could be cited. Perhaps all of them are wide of the mark. There are sentences in our opinions which, detached from their context, indicate that what is happening is none of our business:

> Certainly it is not the function of the Judiciary to entertain private litigation—even by a citizen—which challenges the legality, the wisdom, or the propriety of the Commander-in-Chief in sending our armed forces abroad or to any particular region. *Johnson v. Eisentrager*, 339 U.S. 763 (1950).

We do not, of course, sit as a committee of oversight or supervision. What resolutions the President asks and what the Congress provides are not our concern. With respect to the Federal Government, we sit only to decide actual cases or controversies within judicial cognizance that arise as a result of what the Congress or the President or a judge does or attempts to do to a person or his property.

In *Ex parte Milligan*, 71 U.S. 2 (1866), the Court relieved a person of the death penalty imposed by a military tribunal, holding that only a civilian court had power to try him for the offense charged. Speaking of the purpose of the Founders in providing constitutional guarantees, the Court said:

> They knew . . . the nation they were founding, be its existence short or long, would be involved in war; how often or how long continued, human foresight could not tell; and that unlimited power, wherever lodged at such a time, was especially hazardous to freemen. For this, and other equally weighty reasons, they secured the inheritance they had fought to maintain, by incorporating in a written constitution the safeguards which *time* had proved were essential to its preservation. Not one of these safeguards can the President, or Congress, or the Judiciary disturb, except the one concerning the writ of *habeas corpus*.

The fact that the political branches are responsible for the threat to petitioners' liberty is not decisive. As Mr. Justice Holmes said in *Nixon v. Herndon*, 273 U.S. 536 (1927),

> The objection that the subject matter of the suit is political is little more than a play upon words. Of course the petition concerns political action but it alleges and seeks to recover for private damage. That private damage may be caused by such political action and may be recovered for in a suit at law hardly has been doubted for over two hundred years, since *Ashby v. White*, (1703) 1 Sm LC (13th Edn) 253, and has been recognized by this Court.

These petitioners should be told whether their case is beyond judicial cognizance. If it is not, we should then reach the merits of their claims, on which I intimate no views whatsoever.

FOR DISCUSSION

Why did the Supreme Court refuse to hear both *Mora* and *Mitchell*? Why should the legality of a war be viewed as a political question? What is the constitutional check upon an illegal war? Is there a political check?

PRESIDENTIAL POWER IN A POST-9/11 WORLD

The terrorist attacks on September 11, 2001, were significant blows to the American psyche and its security. The events, sometimes compared to the Japanese attack on Pearl Harbor on December 7, 1941, or the North Vietnamese attacks on U.S. ships in the Gulf of Tonkin in 1964, demanded that the United States react. As with Vietnam, Congress adopted a resolution—the **Authorization for Use of Military Force (AUMF)**—empowering the president to take appropriate action to respond. As had been the case during the Vietnam War, President George Bush argued that even without congressional approval, both his powers as commander in chief and his authority as the chief executive gave him the requisite authority to respond to the terrorist acts and to protect American security.

Specifically, beyond congressional or legislative authorization, four Justice Department memoranda also asserted inherent presidential power to respond to terrorism. The first and most important of these is the September 25, 2001, memorandum describing presidential war-making powers. As an assistant attorney general and legal advisor to the president, John C. Yoo wrote a memorandum that formed the legal basis for nearly all of the Bush administration's later arguments to Congress and to the courts as to why the president had the legal authority to conduct a war on terrorism. This memorandum's arguments, more forcefully developed in Yoo's book, *The Powers of War and Peace: The Constitution and Foreign Affairs After 9/11* (2005), are repeated in a second legal opinion of January 22, 2002, addressing the treatment of al Qaeda and Taliban detainees. The third memorandum, dated August 1, 2002, reviewed the classification and treatment of al Qaeda held outside the United States; the fourth was a January 19, 2006, Department of Justice memorandum supporting President Bush's decision to order the warrantless wiretapping of telephone conversations by the National Security Agency. These four memoranda, taken together, frame the Bush administration's arguments for its foreign policy and national security authority post-9/11. They provided the legal justification for President Bush to claim that he could disregard international law and treaties, and constitutional and statutory prohibitions, when it comes to the treatment and questioning of suspected terrorists or when it comes to pursuing national security actions.

The Yoo September 2001 memorandum argues that the president has extensive inherent authority to use force against terrorists. To substantiate this claim, Yoo relies upon the judicial and executive construction of the Constitution, recent practice and tradition, and finally congressional enactments authorizing use of force. First, in terms of the structure of the Constitution, Yoo draws heavily upon the Founders' constitutional intent, especially as interpreted by Alexander Hamilton in the *Federalist Papers*. For example, Yoo argues that:

> The text, structure and history of the Constitution establish that the Founders entrusted the President with the primary responsibility, and therefore the power, to use military force in situations of emergency. Article II, Section 2 states that the "President shall be Commander in Chief of the Army and Navy of the United States, and of the Militia of the several States, when called into the actual Service of the United States." U.S. Const. art. II, § 2, cl. 1. He is further vested with all of "the executive Power" and the duty to execute the laws. U.S. Const. art. II, § 1. These powers give the President broad constitutional authority to use military force in response to threats to the national security and foreign policy of the United States. During the period leading up to the Constitution's ratification, the power to initiate hostilities and to control the escalation of conflict had been long understood to rest in the hands of the executive branch.

For Yoo, the text of the Constitution vests "full control" of military powers in the president to direct military operations, even absent congressional declarations of war. The basis for this claim rests upon a specific view of the presidency, again attributed to Hamilton, that asserts that the constitutional text creates a unified executive power or presidency. This unified conception of the presidency, along with the conveyance of executive power in the president, and a historical view of war powers and foreign policy activity as an executive function, gives this office the *exclusive* power that it has in national security and defense issues.

Second, judicial and executive construction, according to the Yoo memorandum, also endorses a strong view of presidential power in national security issues. In terms of executive construction, part II of the memorandum outlines numerous occasions where the attorney general or the Justice Department has supported presidential supremacy if not exclusivity in this policy area. For example, Yoo cites opinions of Attorneys General William Barr, Frank Murphy, and Thomas Gregory as arguing that the president had inherent constitutional authority to commit troops overseas or to take military action without congressional approval in anticipation of events that would eventually lead to World Wars I and II. Furthermore, the judiciary has endorsed these executive readings of the Constitution. For example, in *Mitchell v. Laird*, a district court, in ruling on the constitutionality of the Vietnam War, stated that "there are some types of war which without Congressional approval, the President may begin to wage: for example, he may respond immediately without such approval to a belligerent attack."

Appeal to practice and tradition is a third argument offered to support presidential exclusivity in national security matters. Specifically, Yoo refers to what he claims are at least 125 times in American history where troops have been committed overseas by the president without congressional approval. This deference to presidential authority is a reflection, for Yoo, of the practical needs of the Constitution to afford flexibility in assigning responsibility in the area of national security. Finally, Yoo points both to the War Powers Resolution and the September 18, 2001, congressional resolution as also demonstrating "Congress's acceptance of the President's unilateral war powers in an emergency situation like that created by the September 11 incidents." Invoking Justice Jackson's famous concurrence in *Youngstown Sheet & Tube Co.* that presidential power in foreign affairs is at its maximum when given legislative support by Congress, these two acts of Congress clearly endorse the idea that the president has broad if not exclusive and unlimited power to acts in foreign affairs and national security matters.

What are the overall implications of the Yoo memoranda? First, as asserted in the conclusion, Yoo argues that the president has "plenary constitutional power" to take military action, as he deems appropriate, to respond to terrorist attacks. This power is inherent, regardless of what Congress authorized in either the War Powers or September 18 resolution. As subsequently articulated in Yoo's book, the president has total control over foreign and military powers, with Congress confined merely to either terminating funding or authorization for the military if it disapproves of what the executive branch does. Yoo's memorandum proposes a theory of a unified executive and president with strict separation of powers, again leaving no room for Congress or the courts in the field of national security. In the conclusion of the memorandum, Yoo also states that the president can deploy troops not just to retaliate but to prevent future attacks, thereby providing the rationale for the Bush administration's claim of "anticipatory self-defense" and the invasions of Afghanistan and Iraq. Finally, the memorandum suggests and actually does state that there appears to be no limit to presidential power in the field of national security, thereby setting the stage for expansion of chief executive authority to make claims for expanded capacity to act beyond the text of the Constitution.

The presidential powers described in the Yoo memorandum are invoked in three subsequent memoranda. Reclassification of captured al Qaeda and Taliban members as "enemy combatants" is justified by giving the president inherent power to interpret and suspend treaties, including the Geneva Convention (III). The same logic allows the president to interpret what constitutes torture under the Convention Against Torture. Finally, the authority of the president to order wiretapping of telephones without warrants and apparently outside the requirements of the Foreign Intelligence Surveillance Act (FISA) rests upon the September 18 congressional resolution augmenting and authorizing him to use his inherent power to act in the name of national security.

Collectively, the four memoranda make the case for what has become the doctrine of the unitary executive. Under this theory, the president has broad authority to act in military and foreign affairs to the exclusion of congressional and judicial oversight or interference. Yoo contends that the Constitution, history, and practice all endorse the preeminence of presidential power in foreign affairs and national security issues, leaving Congress only the powers of the purse and deauthorizing the military if it wishes to check the executive branch. Many argue that this theory lacks constitutional support and that Yoo's history and analysis fail to support his claims.

The next cases examine how the Supreme Court has treated claims of presidential foreign and defense authority since 9/11. They discuss the status of AUMF within Justice Jackson's *Youngstown* tripartite schema on presidential power, and, to a lesser extent, they explore the inherent powers of the president under Article II.

In *Rasul v. Bush* (545 U.S. 466, 2004) the Court ruled that aliens being held in confinement at the American military base in Guantanamo Bay, Cuba, were entitled to have a federal court hear challenges to their detention under the federal habeas corpus statute. In *Hamdi v. Rumsfeld* (542 U.S. 507, 2004) the Court ruled that an American citizen could not be held indefinitely on American soil without a right to habeas corpus review. In *Hamdan v. Rumsfeld* (548 U.S. 557, 2006) the Supreme Court ruled that a Yemeni national held at Guantanamo Bay was entitled to habeas review of his detention and trial before a special military commission. The Court ruled that the Detainee Treatment Act of 2005 (DTA), which sought to deny habeas review to any alien detained at this facility, did not apply to persons whose cases were in the courts at the time the Act was adopted. Both of these cases skirted the unitary executive theory and the question of whether the president has inherent authority as commander in chief to undertake these actions. In addition, the Court seems somewhat skeptical that AUMF provided the needed authority for the president to act. Instead, other constitutional limitations applied and limited how the executive branch and, perhaps, even the government can undertake the war on terrorism.

Finally, post *Hamdan*, Congress adopted the Military Commissions Act of 2006 (MCA), which sought to preclude courts from having habeas jurisdiction over detained aliens determined to be enemy combatants. In *Boumediene v. Bush*, 553 U.S.723 (2008), the Court ruled that the MCA provided inadequate substitution for habeas and that individuals detained at Guantanamo Bay were entitled to have civil courts review their detentions. This case examined the authority of Congress and the president under the **Suspension Clause** to limit or deny habeas review for detainees in Cuba. Thus, by the time of *Boumediene*, Bush had lost all of his major cases before the Supreme Court testing the limits of presidential authority to act in military and foreign affairs. The decisions seem to suggest a thinning or limiting of inherent or extraconstitutional presidential power, including in time of emergency.

Contrary to the assertions of some, the Constitution does apply to foreign and military affairs. *Curtiss-Wright*, *Holland*, and Jackson's views in *Youngstown* suggest that the interpretation of the Constitution abroad may be different than when it is applied domestically. But there is also no question that even abroad the text of the Constitution defines some outer limits regarding how foreign and military affairs are conducted. The lines between presidential-congressional and federal-state authority still have not been completely resolved. But few would argue that issues regarding foreign and military affairs are not governed by the Constitution, or that the president or the national government have powers here that are not enumerated in the law. In that regard, many recent decisions seem to suggest that the deference the Court gave to the president and Congress during the Civil War, World War II, and the Vietnam War is diminishing. Is it possible that the Supreme Court should review and perhaps accept cases in the area of foreign affairs? Recent case law suggests that the Court is not shying away from ruling on matters in this subject area.

SECTION 1. SHORT TITLE.

This joint resolution may be cited as the 'Authorization for Use of Military Force'.

SEC. 2. AUTHORIZATION FOR USE OF UNITED STATES ARMED FORCES.

(a) IN GENERAL—That the President is authorized to use all necessary and appropriate force against those nations, organizations, or persons he determines planned, authorized, committed, or aided the terrorist attacks that occurred on September 11, 2001, or harbored such organizations or persons, in order to prevent any future acts of international terrorism against the United States by such nations, organizations or persons.

(b) War Powers Resolution Requirements—

(1) SPECIFIC STATUTORY AUTHORIZATION—Consistent with section 8(a)(1) of the War Powers Resolution, the Congress declares that this section is intended to constitute specific statutory authorization within the meaning of section 5(b) of the War Powers Resolution.

(2) APPLICABILITY OF OTHER REQUIREMENTS—Nothing in this resolution supercedes any requirement of the War Powers Resolution.

Approved September 18, 2001.

Authorization for Use of Military Force September 18, 2001

Public Law 107–40 [S. J. RES. 23]

107th CONGRESS

JOINT RESOLUTION

To authorize the use of United States Armed Forces against those responsible for the recent attacks launched against the United States.

Whereas, on September 11, 2001, acts of treacherous violence were committed against the United States and its citizens; and

Whereas, such acts render it both necessary and appropriate that the United States exercise its rights to self-defense and to protect United States citizens both at home and abroad; and

Whereas, in light of the threat to the national security and foreign policy of the United States posed by these grave acts of violence; and

Whereas, such acts continue to pose an unusual and extraordinary threat to the national security and foreign policy of the United States; and

Whereas, the President has authority under the Constitution to take action to deter and prevent acts of international terrorism against the United States: Now, therefore, be it

Resolved by the Senate and House of Representatives of the United States of America in Congress assembled

Another issue that has emerged in the last few years is the use of drones in the battle against terrorists. Drones are unmanned aircraft navigated autonomously or remotely by computer. They have become useful tools, especially when armed, to kill individuals who are suspected terrorists, without directly deploying humans or troops. Drones during the George Bush and then the Barack Obama presidencies became a powerful tool of the military. However, their use raises many legal questions. For one, does their use violate international law either in terms of violating the sovereign territory of another country, or do they contravene international humanitarian law? A second question is in regards to the constitutionality of their use, especially when they target U.S. citizens abroad. There is no question that the president could not order the killing of a U.S. citizen located in the United States. Yet could the president order the use of a drone outside of American borders to kill a U.S. citizen? Could Congress authorize this? This is a significant constitutional and legal question yet to be resolved, raising questions regarding possible violation of the Fourth and Fifth Amendment, as well as whether an order to kill an American citizen is a Bill of Attainder. So far, legal efforts to examine this question have been rejected by the Courts such as in *Nasser Al-Aulaqi, as personal representative of the Estates of Anwar Al-Aulaqi and Abdulrahman Al-Aulaqi v. Panetta,* Civil Action No. 12–1192 (RMC) (April 4, 2014).

On July 1, 2016, President Obama issued an Executive Order (reprinted below) that outlines the policy regarding the use of drones, with an emphasis upon trying to minimize civilian casualties. It contains review and consultation policies as part of a process to address this problem. The executive order is largely silent on how it addresses the constitutional issues when drones are used against US citizens. Would non-U.S. citizens be able to raise either international of US constitutional law claims in US courts to challenge the use of drones against them? These too are important legal questions yet to be resolved.

EXECUTIVE ORDER 13732 OF JULY 1, 2016

United States Policy on Pre- and Post-Strike Measures To Address Civilian Casualties in U.S. Operations Involving the Use of Force

By the authority vested in me as President by the Constitution and the laws of the United States of America, I hereby direct as follows:

Section 1. Purpose. United States policy on civilian casualties resulting from U.S. operations involving the use of force in armed conflict or in the exercise of the Nation's inherent right of self-defense is based on our national interests, our values, and our legal obligations. As a Nation, we are steadfastly committed to complying with our obligations under the law of armed conflict, including those that address the protection of civilians, such as the fundamental principles of necessity, humanity, distinction, and proportionality.

The protection of civilians is fundamentally consistent with the effective, efficient, and decisive use of force in pursuit of U.S. national interests. Minimizing civilian casualties can further mission objectives; help maintain the support of partner governments and vulnerable populations, especially in the conduct of counterterrorism and counterinsurgency operations; and enhance the legitimacy and sustainability of U.S. operations critical to our national security. As a matter of policy, the United States therefore routinely imposes certain heightened policy standards that are more protective than the requirements of the law of armed conflict that relate to the protection of civilians.

Civilian casualties are a tragic and at times unavoidable consequence of the use of force in situations of armed conflict or in the exercise of a state's inherent right of self-defense. The U.S. Government shall maintain and promote best practices that reduce the likelihood of civilian casualties, take appropriate steps when such casualties occur, and draw lessons from our operations to further enhance the protection of civilians.

Sec. 2. Policy. In furtherance of U.S. Government efforts to protect civilians in U.S. operations involving the use of force in armed conflict or in the exercise of the Nation's inherent right of self-defense, and with a view toward enhancing such efforts, relevant departments and agencies (agencies) shall continue to take certain measures in present and future operations.

(a) In particular, relevant agencies shall, consistent with mission objectives and applicable law, including the law of armed conflict:

(i) train personnel, commensurate with their responsibilities, on compliance with legal obligations and policy guidance that address the protection of civilians and on implementation of best practices that reduce the likelihood of civilian casualties, including through exercises, pre-deployment training, and simulations of complex operational environments that include civilians;

(ii) develop, acquire, and field intelligence, surveillance, and reconnaissance systems that, by enabling more accurate battlespace awareness, contribute to the protection of civilians;

(iii) develop, acquire, and field weapon systems and other technological capabilities that further enable the discriminate use of force in different operational contexts;

(iv) take feasible precautions in conducting attacks to reduce the likelihood of civilian casualties, such as providing warnings to the civilian population (unless the circumstances do not permit), adjusting the timing of attacks, taking steps to ensure military objectives and civilians are clearly distinguished, and taking other measures appropriate to the circumstances; and

(v) conduct assessments that assist in the reduction of civilian casualties by identifying risks to civilians and evaluating efforts to reduce risks to civilians.

(b) In addition to the responsibilities above, relevant agencies shall also, as appropriate and consistent with mission objectives and applicable law, including the law of armed conflict:

(i) review or investigate incidents involving civilian casualties, including by considering relevant and credible information from all available sources, such as other agencies, partner governments, and nongovernmental organizations, and take measures to mitigate the likelihood of future incidents of civilian casualties;

(ii) acknowledge U.S. Government responsibility for civilian casualties and offer condolences, including ex gratia payments, to civilians who are injured or to the families of civilians who are killed;

(iii) engage with foreign partners to share and learn best practices for reducing the likelihood of and responding to civilian casualties, including through appropriate training and assistance; and

(iv) maintain channels for engagement with the International Committee of the Red Cross and other nongovernmental organizations that operate in conflict zones and encourage such organizations to assist in efforts to distinguish between military objectives and civilians, including by appropriately marking protected facilities, vehicles, and personnel, and by providing updated information on the locations of such facilities and personnel.

Sec. 3. Report on Strikes Undertaken by the U.S. Government Against Terrorist Targets Outside Areas of Active Hostilities. (a) The Director of National Intelligence (DNI), or such other official as the President may designate, shall obtain from relevant agencies information about the number of strikes undertaken by the U.S. Government against terrorist targets outside areas of active hostilities from January 1, 2016, through December 31, 2016, as well as assessments of combatant and non-combatant deaths resulting from those strikes, and publicly release an unclassified summary of such information no later than May 1, 2017. By May 1 of each subsequent year, as consistent with the need to protect sources and methods, the DNI shall publicly release a report with the same information for the preceding calendar year.

(b) The annual report shall also include information obtained from relevant agencies regarding the general sources of information and methodology used to conduct these assessments and, as feasible and appropriate, shall address the general reasons for discrepancies between post-strike assessments from the U.S. Government and credible reporting from nongovernmental organizations regarding non-combatant deaths resulting from strikes undertaken by the U.S. Government against terrorist targets outside areas of active hostilities.

(c) In preparing a report under this section, the DNI shall review relevant and credible post-strike all-source reporting, including such information from nongovernmental sources, for the purpose of ensuring that this reporting is available to and considered by relevant agencies in their assessment of deaths.

(d) The Assistant to the President for National Security Affairs may, as appropriate, request that the head of any relevant agency conduct additional reviews related to the intelligence assessments of deaths from strikes against terrorist targets outside areas of active hostilities.

Sec. 4. Periodic Consultation. In furtherance of the policies and practices set forth in this order, the Assistant to the President for National Security Affairs, through the National Security Council staff, will convene agencies with relevant defense, counterterrorism, intelligence, legal, civilian protection, and technology expertise to consult on civilian casualty trends, consider potential improvements to U.S. Government civilian casualty mitigation efforts, and, as appropriate, report to the Deputies and Principals Committees, consistent with Presidential Policy Directive 1 or its successor. Specific incidents will not be considered in this context, and will continue to be examined within relevant chains of command.

Sec. 5. General Provisions. (a) The policies and practices set forth above are not intended to alter, and shall be implemented consistent with, the authority and responsibility of commanders and other U.S. personnel to execute their mission as directed by the President or other appropriate authorities, which necessarily includes the inherent right of self-defense and the maintenance of good order and discipline among U.S. personnel. No part of this order modifies the chain of command of the U.S. Armed Forces or the authority of U.S. commanders.

(b) No part of this order modifies priorities in the collection of intelligence or the development, acquisition, or fielding of weapon systems and other technological capabilities.

(c) No part of this order shall prejudice or supplant established procedures pertaining to administrative or criminal investigative or judicial processes in the context of the military justice system or other applicable law and regulation.

(d) The policies set forth in this order are consistent with existing U.S. obligations under international law and are not intended to create new international legal obligations; nor shall anything in this order be construed to derogate from obligations under applicable law, including the law of armed conflict.

(e) This order is not intended to, and does not, create any right or benefit, substantive or procedural, enforceable at law or in equity by any party against the United States, its departments, agencies, or entities, its officers, employees, or agents, or any other person.

HAMDI V. RUMSFELD

542 U.S. 507, 124 S.Ct. 2633, 159 L.Ed. 2d 578 (2004)

Esam Hamdi was an American citizen captured in Afghanistan and held as an enemy combatant under presidential order. He was suspected of being a terrorist with ties to the Taliban. While initially he was detained at the American Naval Base in Guantanamo Bay, Cuba, he was eventually transferred to a military facility in the United States. His father filed a writ of habeas corpus for him in Virginia, and the district court granted it, only to have the Fourth Circuit overturn it.

Vote: 6–3

JUSTICE O'CONNOR announced the judgment of the Court and delivered an opinion, in which CHIEF JUSTICE REHNQUIST, and JUSTICES KENNEDY and BREYER join.

At this difficult time in our Nation's history, we are called upon to consider the legality of the Government's detention of a United States citizen on United States soil as an "enemy combatant" and to address the process that is constitutionally owed to one who seeks to challenge his classification as such. The United States Court of Appeals for the Fourth Circuit held that petitioner's detention was legally authorized and that he was entitled to no further opportunity to challenge his enemy-combatant label. We now vacate and remand. We hold that although Congress authorized the detention of combatants in the narrow circumstances alleged here, due process demands that a citizen held in the United States as an enemy combatant be given a meaningful opportunity to contest the factual basis for that detention before a neutral decisionmaker.

On September 11, 2001, the al Qaeda terrorist network used hijacked commercial airliners to attack prominent targets in the United States. Approximately 3,000 people were killed in those attacks. One week later, in response to these "acts of treacherous violence," Congress passed a resolution authorizing the President to "use all necessary and appropriate force against those nations, organizations, or persons he determines planned, authorized, committed, or aided the terrorist attacks" or "harbored such organizations or persons, in order to prevent any future acts of international terrorism against the United States by such nations, organizations or persons." Authorization for Use of Military Force ("the AUMF"), 115 Stat. 224. Soon thereafter, the President ordered United States Armed Forces to Afghanistan, with a mission to subdue al Qaeda and quell the Taliban regime that was known to support it.

This case arises out of the detention of a man whom the Government alleges took up arms with the Taliban during this conflict. His name is Yaser Esam Hamdi. Born in Louisiana in 1980, Hamdi moved with his family to Saudi Arabia as a child. By 2001, the parties agree, he resided in Afghanistan. At some point that year, he was seized by members of the Northern Alliance, a coalition of military groups opposed to the Taliban government, and eventually was turned over to the United States military. The Government asserts that it initially detained and interrogated Hamdi in Afghanistan before transferring him to the United States Naval Base in Guantanamo Bay in January 2002. In April 2002, upon learning that Hamdi is an American citizen, authorities transferred him to a naval brig in Norfolk, Virginia, where he remained until a recent transfer to a brig in Charleston, South Carolina. The Government contends that Hamdi is an "enemy combatant," and that this status justifies holding him in the United States indefinitely—without formal charges or proceedings—unless and until it makes the determination that access to counsel or further process is warranted.

In June 2002, Hamdi's father, Esam Fouad Hamdi, filed the present petition for a writ of habeas corpus under 28 U.S.C. § 2241 in the Eastern District of Virginia, naming as petitioners his son and himself as next friend. The elder Hamdi alleges in the petition that he has had no contact with his son since the Government took custody of him in 2001, and that the Government has held his son "without access to legal counsel or notice of any charges pending against him." The petition contends that Hamdi's detention was not legally authorized. It argues that, "[a]s an American citizen, . . . Hamdi enjoys the full protections of the Constitution," and that Hamdi's detention in the United States without charges, access to an impartial tribunal, or assistance of counsel "violated and continue[s] to violate the Fifth and Fourteenth Amendments to the United States Constitution." The habeas petition asks that the court, among other things, (1) appoint counsel for Hamdi; (2) order respondents to cease interrogating him; (3) declare that he is being held in violation of the Fifth and Fourteenth Amendments; (4) "[t]o the extent Respondents contest any material factual allegations in this Petition, schedule an evidentiary hearing, at which Petitioners may adduce proof in support of their allegations"; and (5) order that Hamdi be released from his "unlawful custody."

II

The threshold question before us is whether the Executive has the authority to detain citizens who qualify as "enemy combatants." There is some debate as to the proper scope of this term, and the Government has never provided any court with the full criteria that it uses in classifying individuals as such. It has made clear, however, that, for purposes of this case, the "enemy combatant" that it is seeking to detain is an individual who, it alleges, was " 'part of or supporting forces hostile to the United States or coalition partners' " in Afghanistan and who " 'engaged in an armed conflict against the United States' " there. We therefore answer only the narrow question before us: whether the detention of citizens falling within that definition is authorized.

The Government maintains that no explicit congressional authorization is required, because the Executive possesses plenary authority to detain pursuant to Article II of the Constitution. We do not reach the question whether Article II provides such authority, however, because we agree with the Government's alternative position, that Congress has in fact authorized Hamdi's detention, through the AUMF.

The AUMF authorizes the President to use "all necessary and appropriate force" against "nations, organizations, or persons" associated with the September 11, 2001, terrorist attacks. There can be no doubt that individuals who fought against the United States in Afghanistan as part of the Taliban, an organization known to have supported the al Qaeda terrorist network responsible for those attacks, are individuals Congress sought to target in passing the AUMF. We conclude that detention of individuals falling into the limited category we are considering, for the duration of the particular conflict in which they were captured, is so fundamental and accepted an incident to war as to be an exercise of the "necessary and appropriate force" Congress has authorized the President to use.

The capture and detention of lawful combatants and the capture, detention, and trial of unlawful combatants, by "universal agreement and practice," are "important incident[s] of war." *Ex parte Quirin*, 317 U.S. 1, at 28 (1942). The purpose of detention is to prevent captured individuals from returning to the field of battle and taking up arms once again. Naqvi, Doubtful Prisoner-of-War Status, 84 *Int'l Rev. Red Cross* 571, 572 (2002) ("[C]aptivity in war is 'neither revenge, nor punishment, but solely protective custody, the only purpose of which is to prevent the prisoners of war from further participation in the war' ") (quoting decision of Nuremberg Military Tribunal, reprinted in 41 Am. J. Int'l L. 172, 229 (1947)); W. Winthrop, Military Law and Precedents 788 (rev.2d ed. 1920) ("The time has long passed when 'no quarter' was the rule on the battlefield. . . . It is now recognized that 'Captivity is neither a punishment nor an act of vengeance,' but 'merely a temporary detention which is devoid of all penal character.' . . . 'A prisoner of war is no convict; his imprisonment is a simple war measure.' "

There is no bar to this Nation's holding one of its own citizens as an enemy combatant. In *Quirin*, one of the detainees, Haupt, alleged that he was a naturalized United States citizen. We held that "[c]itizens who associate themselves with the military arm of the enemy government, and with its aid, guidance and direction enter this country bent on hostile acts, are enemy belligerents within the meaning of . . . the law of war." While Haupt was tried for violations of the law of war, nothing in *Quirin* suggests that his citizenship would have precluded his mere detention for the duration of the relevant hostilities. Instructions for the Government of Armies of the United States in the Field, Gen. Order No. 100 (1863), reprinted in 2 Lieber, Miscellaneous Writings, p. 273 (contemplating, in code binding the Union Army during the Civil War, that "captured rebels" would be treated "as prisoners of war"). Nor can we see any reason for drawing such a line here. A citizen, no less than an alien, can be "part of or supporting forces hostile to the United States or coalition partners" and "engaged in an armed conflict against the United States," such a citizen, if released, would pose the same threat of returning to the front during the ongoing conflict.

In light of these principles, it is of no moment that the AUMF does not use specific language of detention. Because detention to prevent a combatant's return to the battlefield is a fundamental incident of waging war, in permitting the use of "necessary and appropriate force," Congress has clearly and unmistakably authorized detention in the narrow circumstances considered here.

Hamdi contends that the AUMF does not authorize indefinite or perpetual detention. Certainly, we agree that indefinite detention for the purpose of interrogation is not authorized. Further, we understand Congress' grant of authority for the use of "necessary and appropriate force" to include the authority to detain for the duration of the relevant conflict, and our understanding is based on longstanding law-of-war principles. If the practical circumstances of a given conflict are entirely unlike those of the conflicts that informed the development of the law of war, that understanding may unravel. But that is not the situation we face as of this date. Active combat operations against Taliban fighters apparently are ongoing in Afghanistan. See, *e.g.*, Constable, U.S. Launches New Operation in Afghanistan, *Washington Post*, Mar. 14, 2004, p. A22 (reporting that 13,500 United States troops remain in Afghanistan, including several thousand new arrivals). The United States may detain, for the duration of these hostilities, individuals legitimately determined to be Taliban combatants who "engaged in an armed conflict against the United States." If the record establishes that United States troops are still involved in active combat in Afghanistan, those detentions are part of the exercise of "necessary and appropriate force," and therefore are authorized by the AUMF.

Ex parte Milligan, 71 U.S. 2 (1866), does not undermine our holding about the Government's authority to seize enemy combatants, as we define that term today. In that case, the Court made repeated reference to the fact that its inquiry into whether the military tribunal had jurisdiction to try and punish Milligan turned in large part on the fact that Milligan was not a prisoner of war, but a resident of Indiana arrested while at home there. That fact was central to its conclusion. Had Milligan been captured while he was assisting Confederate soldiers by carrying a rifle against Union troops on a Confederate battlefield, the holding of the Court might well have been different. The Court's repeated explanations that Milligan was not a prisoner of war suggest that had these different circumstances been present he could have been detained under military authority for the duration of the conflict, whether or not he was a citizen.

III

Even in cases in which the detention of enemy combatants is legally authorized, there remains the question of what process is constitutionally due to a citizen who disputes his enemy-combatant status. Hamdi argues that he is owed a meaningful and timely hearing and that "extra judicial detention [that] begins and ends with the submission of an affidavit based on third-hand hearsay" does not comport with the Fifth and Fourteenth Amendments. The Government counters that any more process than was provided below would be both unworkable and "constitutionally intolerable." Our resolution of this dispute requires a careful examination both of the writ of habeas corpus, which Hamdi now seeks to employ as a mechanism of judicial review, and of the Due Process Clause, which informs the procedural contours of that mechanism in this instance.

A

Though they reach radically different conclusions on the process that ought to attend the present proceeding, the parties begin on common ground. All agree that, absent suspension, the writ of habeas corpus remains available to every individual detained within the United States. U.S. Const., Art. I, § 9, cl. 2 ("The Privilege of the Writ of Habeas Corpus shall not be suspended, unless when in Cases of Rebellion or Invasion the public Safety may require it"). Only in the rarest of circumstances has Congress seen fit to suspend the writ. At all other times, it has remained a critical check on the Executive, ensuring that it does not detain individuals except in accordance with law. See *INS v. St. Cyr*, 533 U.S. 289, 301 (2001). All agree suspension of the writ has not occurred here. Thus, it is undisputed that Hamdi was properly before an Article III court to challenge his detention under 28 U.S.C. § 2241. Further, all agree that § 2241 and its companion provisions provide at least a skeletal outline of the procedures to be afforded a petitioner in federal habeas review. Most notably, § 2243 provides that "the person detained may, under oath, deny any of the facts set forth in the return or allege any other material facts," and § 2246 allows the taking of evidence in habeas proceedings by deposition, affidavit, or interrogatories.

C

The Government's second argument requires closer consideration. This is the argument that further factual exploration is unwarranted and inappropriate in light of the extraordinary constitutional interests at stake. Under the Government's most extreme rendition of this argument, "[r]espect for separation of powers and the limited institutional capabilities of courts in matters of military decision-making in connection with an ongoing conflict" ought to eliminate entirely any individual process, restricting the courts to investigating only whether legal authorization exists for the broader detention scheme. At most, the Government argues, courts should review its determination that a citizen is an enemy combatant under a very deferential "some evidence" standard. Under this review, a court would assume the accuracy of the Government's articulated basis for Hamdi's detention, as set forth in the Mobbs Declaration, and assess only whether that articulated basis was a legitimate one.

In response, Hamdi emphasizes that this Court consistently has recognized that an individual challenging his detention may not be held at the will of the Executive without recourse to some proceeding before a neutral tribunal to determine whether the Executive's asserted justifications for that detention have basis in fact and warrant in law. He argues that the Fourth Circuit inappropriately "ceded power to the Executive during wartime to define the conduct for which a citizen may be detained, judge whether that citizen has engaged in the proscribed conduct, and imprison that citizen indefinitely," and that due process demands that he receive a hearing in which he may challenge the Mobbs Declaration and adduce his own counter evidence. The District Court, agreeing with Hamdi, apparently believed that the appropriate process would approach the process that accompanies a criminal trial. It therefore disapproved of the hearsay nature of the Mobbs Declaration and anticipated quite extensive discovery of various military affairs. Anything less, it concluded, would not be "meaningful judicial review."

Both of these positions highlight legitimate concerns. And both emphasize the tension that often exists between the autonomy that the Government asserts is necessary in order to pursue effectively a particular goal and the process that a citizen contends he is due before he is deprived of a constitutional right. The ordinary mechanism that we use for balancing such serious competing interests, and for determining the procedures that are necessary to ensure that a citizen is not "deprived of life, liberty, or property, without due process of law," U.S. Const., Amdt. 5, is the test that we articulated in *Mathews v. Eldridge,* 424 U.S. 319 (1976). *Mathews* dictates that the process due in any given instance is determined by weighing "the private interest that will be affected by the official action" against the Government's asserted interest, "including the function involved" and the burdens the Government would face in providing greater process. The *Mathews* calculus then contemplates a judicious balancing of these concerns, through an analysis of "the risk of an erroneous deprivation" of the private interest if the process were reduced and the "probable value, if any, of additional or substitute safeguards." We take each of these steps in turn.

1

It is beyond question that substantial interests lie on both sides of the scale in this case. Hamdi's "private interest . . . affected by the official action," is the most elemental of liberty interests—the interest in being free from physical detention by one's own government. ("Freedom from bodily restraint has always been at the core of the liberty protected by the Due Process Clause from arbitrary governmental action").

Nor is the weight on this side of the *Mathews* scale offset by the circumstances of war or the accusation of treasonous behavior, for "[i]t is clear that commitment for *any* purpose constitutes a significant deprivation of liberty that requires due process protection," *Jones v. United States,* 463 U.S. 354, 361 (1983), and at this stage in the *Mathews* calculus, we consider the interest of the *erroneously* detained individual. Indeed, as *amicus* briefs from media and relief organizations emphasize, the risk of erroneous deprivation of a citizen's liberty in the absence of sufficient process here is very real. Moreover, as critical as the Government's interest may be in detaining those who actually pose an immediate threat to the national security of the United States during ongoing international conflict, history and common sense teach us that an unchecked system of detention carries the potential to become a means for oppression and abuse of others who do not present that sort of threat. Because we live in a society in which "[m]ere public intolerance or animosity cannot constitutionally justify the deprivation of a person's physical liberty," our starting point for the *Mathews v. Eldridge* analysis is unaltered by the allegations surrounding the particular detainee or the organizations with which he is alleged to have associated. We reaffirm today the fundamental nature of a citizen's right to be free from involuntary confinement by his own government without due process of law, and we weigh the opposing governmental interests against the curtailment of liberty that such confinement entails.

2

On the other side of the scale are the weighty and sensitive governmental interests in ensuring that those who have in fact fought with the enemy during a war do not return to battle against the United States. As discussed above, the law of war and the realities of combat may render such detentions both necessary and appropriate, and our due process analysis need not blink at those realities. Without doubt, our Constitution recognizes that core strategic matters of warmaking belong in the hands of those who are best positioned and most politically accountable for making them. *Department of Navy v. Egan*, 484 U.S. 518, 530 (1988) (noting the reluctance of the courts "to intrude upon the authority of the Executive in military and national security affairs"); *Youngstown Sheet & Tube Co. v. Sawyer*, 343 U.S. 579, 587 (1952) (acknowledging "broad powers in military commanders engaged in day-to-day fighting in a theater of war").

3

We therefore hold that a citizen-detainee seeking to challenge his classification as an enemy combatant must receive notice of the factual basis for his classification, and a fair opportunity to rebut the Government's factual assertions before a neutral decisionmaker. "For more than a century the central meaning of procedural due process has been clear: 'Parties whose rights are to be affected are entitled to be heard; and in order that they may enjoy that right they must first be notified.' It is equally fundamental that the right to notice and an opportunity to be heard 'must be granted at a meaningful time and in a meaningful manner.' " These essential constitutional promises may not be eroded.

At the same time, the exigencies of the circumstances may demand that, aside from these core elements, enemy combatant proceedings may be tailored to alleviate their uncommon potential to burden the Executive at a time of ongoing military conflict. Hearsay, for example, may need to be accepted as the most reliable available evidence from the Government in such a proceeding. Likewise, the Constitution would not be offended by a presumption in favor of the Government's evidence, so long as that presumption remained a rebuttable one and fair opportunity for rebuttal were provided. Thus, once the Government puts forth credible evidence that the habeas petitioner meets the enemy-combatant criteria, the onus could shift to the petitioner to rebut that evidence with more persuasive evidence that he falls outside the criteria. A burden-shifting scheme of this sort would meet the goal of ensuring that the errant tourist, embedded journalist, or local aid worker has a chance to prove military error while giving due regard to the Executive once it has put forth meaningful support for its conclusion that the detainee is in fact an enemy combatant. In the words of *Mathews,* process of this sort would sufficiently address the "risk of erroneous deprivation" of a detainee's liberty interest while eliminating certain procedures that have questionable additional value in light of the burden on the Government.

In sum, while the full protections that accompany challenges to detentions in other settings may prove unworkable and inappropriate in the enemy-combatant setting, the threats to military operations posed by a basic system of independent review are not so weighty as to trump a citizen's core rights to challenge meaningfully the Government's case and to be heard by an impartial adjudicator.

D

In so holding, we necessarily reject the Government's assertion that separation of powers principles mandate a heavily circumscribed role for the courts in such circumstances. Indeed, the position that the courts must forgo any examination of the individual case and focus exclusively on the legality of the broader detention scheme cannot be mandated by any reasonable view of separation of powers, as this approach serves only to *condense* power into a single branch of government. We have long since made clear that a state of war is not a blank check for the President when it comes to the rights of the Nation's citizens. Whatever power the United States Constitution envisions for the Executive in its exchanges with other nations or with enemy organizations in times of conflict, it most assuredly envisions a role for all three branches when individual liberties are at stake. Likewise, we have made clear that, unless Congress acts to suspend it, the Great Writ of habeas corpus allows the Judicial Branch to play a necessary role in maintaining this delicate balance of governance, serving as an important judicial check on the Executive's discretion in the realm of detentions. Thus, while we do not question that our due process assessment must pay keen attention to the particular burdens faced by the Executive in the context of military action, it would turn our system of checks and balances on its head to suggest that a citizen could not make his way to court with a challenge to the factual basis for his detention by his government, simply because the Executive opposes making available such a challenge. Absent suspension of the writ by Congress, a citizen detained as an enemy combatant is entitled to this process.

JUSTICE SCALIA, with whom Justice Stevens joins, dissenting.

Petitioner, a presumed American citizen, has been imprisoned without charge or hearing in the Norfolk and Charleston Naval Brigs for more than two years, on the allegation that he is an enemy combatant who bore arms against his country for the Taliban. His father claims to the contrary, that he is an inexperienced aid worker caught in the wrong place at the wrong time. This case brings into conflict the competing demands of national security and our citizens' constitutional right to personal liberty. Although I share the Court's evident unease as it seeks to reconcile the two, I do not agree with its resolution.

Where the Government accuses a citizen of waging war against it, our constitutional tradition has been to prosecute him in federal court for treason or some other crime. Where the exigencies of war prevent that, the Constitution's Suspension Clause, Art. I, § 9, cl. 2, allows Congress to relax the usual protections temporarily. Absent suspension, however, the Executive's assertion of military exigency has not been thought sufficient to permit detention without charge. No one contends that the congressional Authorization for Use of Military Force, on which the Government relies to justify its actions here, is an implementation of the Suspension Clause. Accordingly, I would reverse the decision below.

I

The very core of liberty secured by our Anglo-Saxon system of separated powers has been freedom from indefinite imprisonment at the will of the Executive. Blackstone stated this principle clearly:

> Of great importance to the public is the preservation of this personal liberty: for if once it were left in the power of any, the highest, magistrate to imprison arbitrarily whomever he or his officers thought proper. . . . there would soon be an end of all other rights and immunities. . . . To bereave a man of life, or by violence to confiscate his estate, without accusation or trial, would be so gross and notorious an act of despotism, as must at once convey the alarm of tyranny throughout the whole kingdom. But confinement of the person, by secretly hurrying him to gaol, where his sufferings are unknown or forgotten; is a less public, a less striking, and therefore a more dangerous engine of arbitrary government. . . .
>
> To make imprisonment lawful, it must either be, by process from the courts of judicature, or by warrant from some legal officer, having authority to commit to prison; which warrant must be in writing, under the hand and seal of the magistrate, and express the causes of the commitment, in order to be examined into (if necessary) upon a *habeas corpus*. If there be no cause expressed, the gaoler is not bound to detain the prisoner. For the law judges in this respect, . . . that it is unreasonable to send a prisoner, and not to signify withal the crimes alleged against him.

These words were well known to the Founders. Hamilton quoted from this very passage in *The Federalist No. 84*. The two ideas central to Blackstone's understanding—due process as the right secured, and habeas corpus as the instrument by which due process could be insisted upon by a citizen illegally imprisoned—found expression in the Constitution's Due Process and Suspension Clauses.

The gist of the Due Process Clause, as understood at the founding and since, was to force the Government to follow those common-law procedures traditionally deemed necessary before depriving a person of life, liberty, or property. When a citizen was deprived of liberty because of alleged criminal conduct, those procedures typically required committal by a magistrate followed by indictment and trial. The Due Process Clause "in effect affirms the right of trial according to the process and proceedings of the common law."

These due process rights have historically been vindicated by the writ of habeas corpus. In England before the founding, the writ developed into a tool for challenging executive confinement. It was not always effective. For example, in *Darnel's Case*, 3 How. St. Tr. 1 (K.B.1627), King Charles I detained without charge several individuals for failing to assist England's war against France and Spain. The prisoners sought writs of habeas corpus, arguing that without specific charges, "imprisonment shall not continue on for a time, but for ever; and the subjects of this kingdom may be restrained of their liberties perpetually." The Attorney General replied that the Crown's interest in protecting the realm justified imprisonment in "a matter of state . . . not ripe nor timely" for the ordinary process of accusation and trial. The court denied relief, producing widespread outrage, and Parliament responded with the Petition of Right, accepted by the King in 1628, which expressly prohibited imprisonment without formal charges.

The writ of habeas corpus was preserved in the Constitution—the only common-law writ to be explicitly mentioned. See Art. I, § 9, cl. 2. Hamilton lauded "the establishment of the writ of *habeas corpus*" in his Federalist defense as a means to protect against "the practice of arbitrary imprisonments . . . in all ages, [one of] the favourite and most formidable instruments of tyranny." Indeed, availability of the writ under the new Constitution (along with the requirement of trial by jury in criminal cases, see Art. III, § 2, cl. 3) was his basis for arguing that additional, explicit procedural protections were unnecessary. See *The Federalist No. 83*.

II

The allegations here, of course, are no ordinary accusations of criminal activity. Yaser Esam Hamdi has been imprisoned because the Government believes he participated in the waging of war against the United States. The relevant question, then, is whether there is a different, special procedure for imprisonment of a citizen accused of wrongdoing *by aiding the enemy in wartime.*

Our Federal Constitution contains a provision explicitly permitting suspension, but limiting the situations in which it may be invoked: "The privilege of the Writ of Habeas Corpus shall not be suspended, unless when in Cases of Rebellion or Invasion the public Safety may require it." Art. I, § 9, cl. 2. Although this provision does not state that suspension must be effected by, or authorized by, a legislative act, it has been so understood, consistent with English practice and the Clause's placement in Article I.

The Suspension Clause was by design a safety valve, the Constitution's only "express provision for exercise of extraordinary authority because of a crisis," *Youngstown Sheet & Tube Co. v. Sawyer.*

A view of the Constitution that gives the Executive authority to use military force rather than the force of law against citizens on American soil flies in the face of the mistrust that engendered these provisions.

JUSTICE THOMAS, dissenting.

The Executive Branch, acting pursuant to the powers vested in the President by the Constitution and with explicit congressional approval, has determined that Yaser Hamdi is an enemy combatant and should be detained. This detention falls squarely within the Federal Government's war powers, and we lack the expertise and capacity to second-guess that decision. As such, petitioners' habeas challenge should fail, and there is no reason to remand the case. The plurality reaches a contrary conclusion by failing adequately to consider basic principles of the constitutional structure as it relates to national security and foreign affairs and by using the balancing scheme of *Mathews v. Eldridge*. I do not think that the Federal Government's war powers can be balanced away by this Court. Arguably, Congress could provide for additional procedural protections, but until it does, we have no right to insist upon them. But even if I were to agree with the general approach the plurality takes, I could not accept the particulars. The plurality utterly fails to account for the Government's compelling interests and for our own institutional inability to weigh competing concerns correctly. I respectfully dissent.

FOR DISCUSSION

Compare the Scalia and Stevens dissent to that of Thomas. How do their dissents differ? Were Stevens and Scalia willing to support the president? Why do they disagree with the majority? Why does Thomas? Do any of the justices argue that the president has inherent authority to act to detain? What is the legal status of AUMF?

HAMDAN V. RUMSFELD

548 U.S. 557, 126 S.Ct. 2749, 165 L.Ed.2d 723 (2006)

Salim Hamdan was a Yemeni citizen who was captured by the American military in Afghanistan. He was relocated to the American facility in Guantanamo Bay and ordered to face trial as a suspected terrorist. The trial would take place before a military tribunal organized pursuant to an executive order of the president. Hamdan argued that the trial was illegal, violating both international law and the U.S. Uniform Code of Military Justice.

Vote: 5–3 (Justice Roberts did not participate)

JUSTICE STEVENS announced the judgment of the Court and delivered the opinion of the Court with respect to Parts I through IV, Parts VI through VI-D-iii, Part VI-D-v, and Part VII, and an opinion with respect to Parts V and VI-D-iv, in which JUSTICES SOUTER, GINSBURG, and BREYER join.

Petitioner Salim Ahmed Hamdan, a Yemeni national, is in custody at an American prison in Guantanamo Bay, Cuba. In November 2001, during hostilities between the United States and the Taliban (which then governed Afghanistan), Hamdan was captured by militia forces and turned over to the U.S. military. In June 2002, he was transported to Guantanamo Bay. Over a year later, the President deemed him eligible for trial by military commission for then-unspecified crimes. After another year had passed, Hamdan was charged with one count of conspiracy "to commit . . . offenses triable by military commission."

Hamdan filed petitions for writs of habeas corpus and mandamus to challenge the Executive Branch's intended means of prosecuting this charge. He concedes that a court-martial constituted in accordance with the Uniform Code of Military Justice (UCMJ) would have authority to try him. His objection is that the military commission the President has convened lacks such authority, for two principal reasons: First, neither congressional Act nor the common law of war supports trial by this commission for the crime of conspiracy—an offense that, Hamdan says, is not a violation of the law of war. Second, Hamdan contends, the procedures that the President has adopted to try him violate the most basic tenets of military and international law, including the principle that a defendant must be permitted to see and hear the evidence against him.

The District Court granted Hamdan's request for a writ of habeas corpus. The Court of Appeals for the District of Columbia Circuit reversed. Recognizing, as we did over a half-century ago, that trial by military commission is an extraordinary measure raising important questions about the balance of powers in our constitutional structure, *Ex parte Quirin*, 317 U.S. 1 (1942), we granted certiorari.

For the reasons that follow, we conclude that the military commission convened to try Hamdan lacks power to proceed because its structure and procedures violate both the UCMJ and the Geneva Conventions. Four of us also conclude, see Part V, that the offense with which Hamdan has been charged is not an "offens[e] that by . . . the law of war may be tried by military commissions."

I

On September 11, 2001, agents of the al Qaeda terrorist organization hijacked commercial airplanes and attacked the World Trade Center in New York City and the national headquarters of the Department of Defense in Arlington, Virginia. Americans will never forget the devastation wrought by these acts. Nearly 3,000 civilians were killed.

Congress responded by adopting a Joint Resolution authorizing the President to "use all necessary and appropriate force against those nations, organizations, or persons he determines planned, authorized, committed, or aided the terrorist attacks . . . in order to prevent any future acts of international terrorism against the United States by such nations, organizations or persons." Authorization for Use of Military Force (AUMF). Acting pursuant to the AUMF, and having determined that the Taliban regime had supported al Qaeda, the President ordered the Armed Forces of the United States to invade Afghanistan. In the ensuing hostilities, hundreds of individuals, Hamdan among them, were captured and eventually detained at Guantanamo Bay.

On November 13, 2001, while the United States was still engaged in active combat with the Taliban, the President issued a comprehensive military order intended to govern the "Detention, Treatment, and Trial of Certain Non-Citizens in the War Against Terrorism," (hereinafter November 13 Order or Order). Those subject to the November 13 Order include any noncitizen for whom the President determines "there is reason to believe" that he or she (1) "is or was" a member of al Qaeda or (2) has engaged or participated in terrorist activities aimed at or harmful to the United States. Any such individual "shall, when tried, be tried by military commission for any and all offenses triable by military commission that such individual is alleged to have committed, and may be punished in accordance with the penalties provided under applicable law, including imprisonment or death." The November 13 Order vested in the Secretary of Defense the power to appoint military commissions to try individuals subject to the Order, but that power has since been delegated to John D. Altenberg, Jr., a retired Army major general and longtime military lawyer who has been designated "Appointing Authority for Military Commissions."

On July 3, 2003, the President announced his determination that Hamdan and five other detainees at Guantanamo Bay were subject to the November 13 Order and thus triable by military commission. In December 2003, military counsel was appointed to represent Hamdan. Two months later, counsel filed demands for charges and for a speedy trial pursuant to Article 10 of the UCMJ. On February 23, 2004, the legal adviser to the Appointing Authority denied the applications, ruling that Hamdan was not entitled to any of the protections of the UCMJ. Not until July 13, 2004, after Hamdan had commenced this action in the United States District Court for the Western District of Washington, did the Government finally charge him with the offense for which, a year earlier, he had been deemed eligible for trial by military commission.

The charging document, which is unsigned, contains 13 numbered paragraphs. The first two paragraphs recite the asserted bases for the military commission's jurisdiction—namely, the November 13 Order and the President's July 3, 2003, declaration that Hamdan is eligible for trial by military commission. The next nine paragraphs, collectively entitled "General Allegations," describe al Qaeda's activities from its inception in 1989 through 2001 and identify Osama bin Laden as the group's leader. Hamdan is not mentioned in these paragraphs.

Only the final two paragraphs, entitled "Charge: Conspiracy," contain allegations against Hamdan. Paragraph 12 charges that "from on or about February 1996 to on or about November 24, 2001," Hamdan "willfully and knowingly joined an enterprise of persons who shared a common criminal purpose and conspired and agreed with [named members of al Qaeda] to commit the following offenses triable by military commission: attacking civilians; attacking civilian objects; murder by an unprivileged belligerent; and terrorism." There is no allegation that Hamdan had any command responsibilities, played a leadership role, or participated in the planning of any activity.

Paragraph 13 lists four "overt acts" that Hamdan is alleged to have committed sometime between 1996 and November 2001 in furtherance of the "enterprise and conspiracy": (1) he acted as Osama bin Laden's "bodyguard and personal driver," "believ[ing]" all the while that bin Laden "and his associates were involved in" terrorist acts prior to and including the attacks of September 11, 2001; (2) he arranged for transportation of, and actually transported, weapons used by al Qaeda members and by bin Laden's bodyguards (Hamdan among them); (3) he "drove or accompanied [O]sama bin Laden to various al Qaida-sponsored training camps, press conferences, or lectures," at which bin Laden encouraged attacks against Americans; and (4) he received weapons training at al Qaeda-sponsored camps.

After this formal charge was filed, the United States District Court for the Western District of Washington transferred Hamdan's habeas and mandamus petitions to the United States District Court for the District of Columbia. Meanwhile, a Combatant Status Review Tribunal (CSRT) convened pursuant to a military order issued on July 7, 2004, decided that Hamdan's continued detention at Guantanamo Bay was warranted because he was an "enemy combatant."* Separately, proceedings before the military commission commenced.

On November 8, 2004, however, the District Court granted Hamdan's petition for habeas corpus and stayed the commission's proceedings. It concluded that the President's authority to establish military commissions extends only to "offenders or offenses triable by military [commission] under the law of war," that the law of war includes the Geneva Convention (III); that Hamdan is entitled to the full protections of the Third Geneva Convention until adjudged, in compliance with that treaty, not to be a prisoner of war; and that, whether or not Hamdan is properly classified as a prisoner of war, the military commission convened to try him was established in violation of both the UCMJ and Common Article 3 of the Third Geneva Convention because it had the power to convict based on evidence the accused would never see or hear.

The Court of Appeals for the District of Columbia Circuit reversed. Like the District Court, the Court of Appeals declined the Government's invitation to abstain from considering Hamdan's challenge. On the merits, the panel rejected the District Court's further conclusion that Hamdan was entitled to relief under the Third Geneva Convention. All three judges agreed that the Geneva Conventions were not "judicially enforceable," and two thought that the Conventions did not in any event apply to Hamdan. In other portions of its opinion, the court concluded that our decision in *Quirin* foreclosed any separation-of-powers objection to the military commission's jurisdiction, and held that Hamdan's trial before the contemplated commission would violate neither the UCMJ nor U.S. Armed Forces regulations intended to implement the Geneva Conventions.

---

* An "enemy combatant" is defined by the military order as "an individual who was part of or supporting Taliban or al Qaeda forces, or associated forces that are engaged in hostilities against the United States or its coalition partners." Memorandum from Deputy Secretary of Defense Paul Wolfowitz re: Order Establishing Combatant Status Review Tribunal § *a* (Jul. 7, 2004), available at http://www.defenselink.mil/news/Jul2004/d20040707review.pdf (all Internet materials as visited November 5, 2009, and available in Clerk of Court's case file).

On November 7, 2005, we granted certiorari to decide whether the military commission convened to try Hamdan has authority to do so, and whether Hamdan may rely on the Geneva Conventions in these proceedings.

II

On February 13, 2006, the Government filed a motion to dismiss the writ of certiorari. The ground cited for dismissal was the recently enacted Detainee Treatment Act of 2005 (DTA).

The DTA, which was signed into law on December 30, 2005, addresses a broad swath of subjects related to detainees. It places restrictions on the treatment and interrogation of detainees in U.S. custody, and it furnishes procedural protections for U.S. personnel accused of engaging in improper interrogation. It also sets forth certain "PROCEDURES FOR STATUS REVIEW OF DETAINEES OUTSIDE THE UNITED STATES." § 1005. Subsections (a) through (d) of § 1005 direct the Secretary of Defense to report to Congress the procedures being used by CSRTs to determine the proper classification of detainees held in Guantanamo Bay, Iraq, and Afghanistan, and to adopt certain safeguards as part of those procedures.

Subsection (e) of § 1005, which is entitled "JUDICIAL REVIEW OF DETENTION OF ENEMY COMBATANTS," supplies the basis for the Government's jurisdictional argument. The subsection contains three numbered paragraphs. The first paragraph amends the judicial code as follows:

> "(1) IN GENERAL.—Section 2241 of title 28, United States Code, is amended by adding at the end the following: . . .
>
> " '(e) Except as provided in section 1005 of the Detainee Treatment Act of 2005, no court, justice, or judge shall have jurisdiction to hear or consider—
>
> " '(1) an application for a writ of habeas corpus filed by or on behalf of an alien detained by the Department of Defense at Guantanamo Bay, Cuba; or
>
> " '(2) any other action against the United States or its agents relating to any aspect of the detention by the Department of Defense of an alien at Guantanamo Bay, Cuba, who—
>
> " '(A) is currently in military custody; or
>
> " '(B) has been determined by the United States Court of Appeals for the District of Columbia Circuit in accordance with the procedures set forth in section 1005(e) of the Detainee Treatment Act of 2005 to have been properly detained as an enemy combatant.' "

The Government argues that §§ 1005(e)(1) and 1005(h) had the immediate effect, upon enactment, of repealing federal jurisdiction not just over detainee habeas actions yet to be filed but also over any such actions then pending in any federal court—including this Court. Accordingly, it argues, we lack jurisdiction to review the Court of Appeals' decision below.

Hamdan objects to this theory on both constitutional and statutory grounds. Principal among his constitutional arguments is that the Government's preferred reading raises grave questions about Congress' authority to impinge upon this Court's appellate jurisdiction, particularly in habeas cases. Support for this argument is drawn from *Ex parte Yerger*, 8 Wall. 85 (1869), in which, having explained that "the denial to this court of appellate jurisdiction" to consider an original writ of habeas corpus would "greatly weaken the efficacy of the writ," we held that Congress would not be presumed to have effected such denial absent an unmistakably clear statement to the contrary.

Hamdan also suggests that, if the Government's reading is correct, Congress has unconstitutionally suspended the writ of habeas corpus.

We find it unnecessary to reach either of these arguments. Ordinary principles of statutory construction suffice to rebut the Government's theory—at least insofar as this case, which was pending at the time the DTA was enacted, is concerned.

The Government acknowledges that only paragraphs (2) and (3) of subsection (e) are expressly made applicable to pending cases, but argues that the omission of paragraph (1) from the scope of that express statement is of no moment. This is so, we are told, because Congress' failure to expressly reserve federal courts' jurisdiction over pending cases erects a presumption against jurisdiction, and that presumption is rebutted by neither the text nor the legislative history of the DTA.

The first part of this argument is not entirely without support in our precedents. We have in the past "applied intervening statutes conferring or ousting jurisdiction, whether or not jurisdiction lay when the underlying conduct occurred or when the suit was filed." *Landgraf v. USI Film Products,* 511 U.S. 244, 274 (1994) (citing *Bruner v. United States,* 343 U.S. 112 (1952) that these cases have applied is more accurately viewed as the nonapplication of another presumption—viz., the presumption against retroactivity—in certain limited circumstances. If a statutory provision "would operate retroactively" as applied to cases pending at the time the provision was enacted, then "our traditional presumption teaches that it does not govern absent clear congressional intent favoring such a result." *Landgraf,* 511 U.S., at 280. We have explained, however, that, unlike other intervening changes in the law, a jurisdiction-conferring or jurisdiction-stripping statute usually "takes away no substantive right but simply changes the tribunal that is to hear the case." *Hallowell v. Commons,* 239 U.S. 506, at 508 (1916). If that is truly all the statute does, no retroactivity problem arises because the change in the law does not "impair rights a party possessed when he acted, increase a party's liability for past conduct, or impose new duties with respect to transactions already completed." *Landgraf,* 511 U.S., at 280. And if a new rule has no retroactive effect, the presumption against retroactivity will not prevent its application to a case that was already pending when the new rule was enacted.

That does not mean, however, that all jurisdiction-stripping provision—or even all such provisions that truly lack retroactive effec—must apply to cases pending at the time of their enactment. "[N]ormal rules of construction," including a contextual reading of the statutory language, may dictate otherwise. A familiar principle of statutory construction, relevant both in *Lindh v. Murphy,* 521 U.S. 320 (1997), and here, is that a negative inference may be drawn from the exclusion of language from one statutory provision that is included in other provisions of the same statute. The Court in *Lindh* relied on this reasoning to conclude that certain limitations on the availability of habeas relief imposed by AEDPA applied only to cases filed after that statute's effective date. Congress' failure to identify the temporal reach of those limitations, which governed noncapital cases, stood in contrast to its express command in the same legislation that new rules governing habeas petitions in capital cases "apply to cases pending on or after the date of enactment." That contrast, combined with the fact that the amendments at issue "affect[ed] substantive entitlement to relief," warranted drawing a negative inference.

We note that statements made by Senators preceding passage of the Act lend further support to what the text of the DTA and its drafting history already make plain. Senator Levin, one of the sponsors of the final bill, objected to earlier versions of the Act's "effective date" provision that would have made subsection (e)(1) applicable to pending cases. See, *e.g.,* 151 Cong. Rec. S12667 (Nov. 10, 2005) (amendment proposed by Sen. Graham that would have rendered what is now subsection (e)(1) applicable to "any application or other action that is pending on or after the date of the enactment of this Act"). Senator Levin urged adoption of an alternative amendment that "would apply only to new habeas cases filed after the date of enactment.

While statements attributed to the final bill's two other sponsors, Senators Graham and Kyl, arguably contradict Senator Levin's contention that the final version of the Act preserved jurisdiction over pending habeas cases, those statements appear to have been inserted into the Congressional Record *after* the Senate debate. All statements made during the debate itself support Senator Levin's understanding that the final text of the DTA would not render subsection (e)(1) applicable to pending cases. The statements that Justice Scalia cites as evidence to the contrary construe *subsection (e)(3)* to strip this Court of jurisdiction, a construction that the Government has expressly disavowed in this litigation. The inapposite November 14, 2005, statement of Senator Graham, which Justice Scalia cites as evidence of that Senator's "assumption that pending cases are covered," follows directly after the uncontradicted statement of his co-sponsor, Senator Levin, assuring members of the Senate that "the amendment will not strip the courts of jurisdiction over [pending] cases."

The Government's second objection is that applying subsections (e)(2) and (e)(3) but not (e)(1) to pending cases "produces an absurd result" because it grants (albeit only temporarily) dual jurisdiction over detainees' cases in circumstances where the statute plainly envisions that the District of Columbia Circuit will have "*exclusive*" and immediate jurisdiction over such cases. But the premise here is faulty; subsections (e)(2) and (e)(3) grant jurisdiction only over actions to "determine the validity of any final decision" of a CSRT or commission. Because Hamdan, at least, is not contesting any "final decision" of a CSRT or military commission, his action does not fall within the scope of subsection (e)(2) or (e)(3). There is, then, no absurdity.

For these reasons, we deny the Government's motion to dismiss.

III

Relying on our decision in *Schlesinger v. Councilman*, 420 U.S. 738 (1975), the Government argues that, even if we have statutory jurisdiction, we should apply the "judge-made rule that civilian courts should await the final outcome of on-going military proceedings before entertaining an attack on those proceedings." Like the District Court and the Court of Appeals before us, we reject this argument.

In *Councilman,* an army officer on active duty was referred to a court-martial for trial on charges that he violated the UCMJ by selling, transferring, and possessing marijuana. Objecting that the alleged offenses were not " 'service connected,' " the officer filed suit in Federal District Court to enjoin the proceedings. He neither questioned the lawfulness of courts-martial or their procedures nor disputed that, as a serviceman, he was subject to court-martial jurisdiction. His sole argument was that the subject matter of his case did not fall within the scope of court-martial authority. The District Court granted his request for injunctive relief, and the Court of Appeals affirmed.

We granted certiorari and reversed. We did not reach the merits of whether the marijuana charges were sufficiently "service connected" to place them within the subject-matter jurisdiction of a court-martial. Instead, we concluded that, as a matter of comity, federal courts should normally abstain from intervening in pending court-martial proceedings against members of the Armed Forces, and further that there was nothing in the particular circumstances of the officer's case to displace that general rule.

[T]wo considerations of comity together favor abstention pending completion of ongoing court-martial proceedings against service personnel. First, military discipline and, therefore, the efficient operation of the Armed Forces are best served if the military justice system acts without regular interference from civilian courts. Second, federal courts should respect the balance that Congress struck between military preparedness and fairness to individual service members when it created "an integrated system of military courts and review procedures, a critical element of which is the Court of Military Appeals, consisting of civilian judges 'completely removed from all military influence or persuasion. . . .' " Just as abstention in the face of ongoing state criminal proceedings is justified by our expectation that state courts will enforce federal rights, so abstention in the face of ongoing court-martial proceedings is justified by our expectation that the military court system established by Congress—with its substantial procedural protections and provision for appellate review by independent civilian judges—"will vindicate servicemen's constitutional rights."

The same cannot be said here; indeed, neither of the comity considerations identified in *Councilman* weighs in favor of abstention in this case. First, Hamdan is not a member of our Nation's Armed Forces, so concerns about military discipline do not apply. Second, the tribunal convened to try Hamdan is not part of the integrated system of military courts, complete with independent review panels, that Congress has established. Unlike the officer in *Councilman,* Hamdan has no right to appeal any conviction to the civilian judges of the Court of Military Appeals (now called the United States Court of Appeals for the Armed Forces. Instead, under Dept. of Defense Military Commission Order No. 1 (Commission Order No. 1), which was issued by the President on March 21, 2002, and amended most recently on August 31, 2005, and which governs the procedures for Hamdan's commission, any conviction would be reviewed by a panel consisting of three military officers designated by the Secretary of Defense. Commission Order No. 1 § 6(H)(4). Commission Order No. 1 provides that appeal of a review panel's decision may be had only to the Secretary of Defense himself, § 6(H)(5), and then, finally, to the President, § 6(H)(6).

We have no doubt that the various individuals assigned review power under Commission Order No. 1 would strive to act impartially and ensure that Hamdan receive all protections to which he is entitled. Nonetheless, these review bodies clearly lack the structural insulation from military influence that characterizes the Court of Appeals for the Armed Forces, and thus bear insufficient conceptual similarity to state courts to warrant invocation of abstention principles.

In sum, neither of the two comity considerations underlying our decision to abstain in *Councilman* applies to the circumstances of this case. Instead, this Court's decision in *Quirin* is the most relevant precedent. In *Quirin,* seven German saboteurs were captured upon arrival by submarine in New York and Florida. The President convened a military commission to try the saboteurs, who then filed habeas corpus petitions in the United States District Court for the District of Columbia challenging their trial by commission. We granted the saboteurs' petition for certiorari to the Court of Appeals before judgment. Far from abstaining pending the conclusion of military proceedings, which were ongoing, we convened a special Term to hear the case and expedited our review. That course of action was warranted, we explained, "[i]n view of the public importance of the questions raised by [the cases] and of the duty which rests on the courts, in time of war as well as in time of peace, to preserve unimpaired the constitutional safeguards of civil liberty, and because in our opinion the public interest required that we consider and decide those questions without any avoidable delay."

As the Court of Appeals here recognized, *Quirin* "provides a compelling historical precedent for the power of civilian courts to entertain challenges that seek to interrupt the processes of military commissions." The circumstances of this case, like those in *Quirin,* simply do not implicate the "obligations of comity" that, under appropriate circumstances, justify abstention.

Finally, the Government has identified no other "important countervailing interest" that would permit federal courts to depart from their general "duty to exercise the jurisdiction that is conferred upon them by Congress." To the contrary, Hamdan and the Government both have a compelling interest in knowing in advance whether Hamdan may be tried by a military commission that arguably is without any basis in law and operates free from many of the procedural rules prescribed by Congress for courts-martial—rules intended to safeguard the accused and ensure the reliability of any conviction. While we certainly do not foreclose the possibility that abstention may be appropriate in some cases seeking review of ongoing military commission proceedings (such as military commissions convened on the battlefield), the foregoing discussion makes clear that, under our precedent, abstention is not justified here. We therefore proceed to consider the merits of Hamdan's challenge.

IV

The military commission, a tribunal neither mentioned in the Constitution nor created by statute, was born of military necessity. Though foreshadowed in some respects by earlier tribunals like the Board of General

Officers that General Washington convened to try British Major John Andre for spying during the Revolutionary War, the commission "as such" was inaugurated in 1847. As commander of occupied Mexican territory, and having available to him no other tribunal, General Winfield Scott that year ordered the establishment of both " '*military commissions*' " to try ordinary crimes committed in the occupied territory and a "*council of war*" to try offenses against the law of war. When the exigencies of war next gave rise to a need for use of military commissions, during the Civil War, the dual system favored by General Scott was not adopted. Instead, a single tribunal often took jurisdiction over ordinary crimes, war crimes, and breaches of military orders alike. As further discussed below, each aspect of that seemingly broad jurisdiction was in fact supported by a separate military exigency. Generally, though, the need for military commissions during this period—as during the Mexican War—was driven largely by the then very limited jurisdiction of courts-martial: "The *occasion* for the military commission arises principally from the fact that the jurisdiction of the court-martial proper, in our law, is restricted by statute almost exclusively to members of the military force and to certain specific offences defined in a written code."

Exigency alone, of course, will not justify the establishment and use of penal tribunals not contemplated by Article I, § 8 and Article III, § 1 of the Constitution unless some other part of that document authorizes a response to the felt need. See *Ex parte Milligan,* 4 Wall. 2, 121 (1866) ("Certainly no part of the judicial power of the country was conferred on [military commissions]"); *Ex parte Vallandigham,* 1 Wall. 243, 251 (1864); see also *Quirin,* 317 U.S., at 25 ("Congress and the President, like the courts, possess no power not derived from the Constitution"). And that authority, if it exists, can derive only from the powers granted jointly to the President and Congress in time of war.

The Constitution makes the President the "Commander in Chief" of the Armed Forces, Art. II, § 2, cl. 1, but vests in Congress the powers to "declare War . . . and make Rules concerning Captures on Land and Water," Art. I, § 8, cl. 11, to "raise and support Armies," cl. 12, to "define and punish . . . Offences against the Law of Nations," cl. 10, and "To make Rules for the Government and Regulation of the land and naval Forces," cl. 14. The interplay between these powers was described by Chief Justice Chase in the seminal case of *Ex parte Milligan.*

Whether Chief Justice Chase was correct in suggesting that the President may constitutionally convene military commissions "without the sanction of Congress" in cases of "controlling necessity" is a question this Court has not answered definitively, and need not answer today. For we held in *Quirin* that Congress had, through Article of War 15, sanctioned the use of military commissions in such circumstances.

We have no occasion to revisit *Quirin*'s controversial characterization of Article of War 15 as congressional authorization for military commissions. Contrary to the Government's assertion, however, even *Quirin* did not view the authorization as a sweeping mandate for the President to "invoke military commissions when he deems them necessary." Rather, the *Quirin* Court recognized that Congress had simply preserved what power, under the Constitution and the common law of war, the President had had before 1916 to convene military commissions—with the express condition that the President and those under his command comply with the law of war. That much is evidenced by the Court's inquiry, *following* its conclusion that Congress had authorized military commissions, into whether the law of war had indeed been complied with in that case.

The Government would have us dispense with the inquiry that the *Quirin* Court undertook and find in either the AUMF or the DTA specific, overriding authorization for the very commission that has been convened to try Hamdan. Neither of these congressional Acts, however, expands the President's authority to convene military commissions. First, while we assume that the AUMF activated the President's war powers, and that those powers include the authority to convene military commissions in appropriate circumstances, there is nothing in the text or legislative history of the AUMF even hinting that Congress intended to expand or alter the authorization set forth in Article 21 of the UCMJ. Likewise, the DTA cannot be read to authorize this commission. Although the DTA, unlike either Article 21 or the AUMF, was enacted after the President had convened Hamdan's commission, it contains no language authorizing that tribunal or any other at Guantanamo Bay. The DTA obviously "recognize[s]" the existence of the Guantanamo Bay commissions in the weakest sense, because it references some of the military orders governing them and creates limited judicial review of their "final decision[s]." But the statute also pointedly reserves judgment on whether "the Constitution and laws of the United States are applicable" in reviewing such decisions and whether, if they are, the "standards and procedures" used to try Hamdan and other detainees actually violate the "Constitution and laws."

Together, the UCMJ, the AUMF, and the DTA at most acknowledge a general Presidential authority to convene military commissions in circumstances where justified under the "Constitution and laws," including the law of war. Absent a more specific congressional authorization, the task of this Court is, as it was in *Quirin*, to decide whether Hamdan's military commission is so justified. It is to that inquiry we now turn.

V

Quirin is the model the Government invokes most frequently to defend the commission convened to try Hamdan. That is both appropriate and unsurprising. Since Guantanamo Bay is neither enemy-occupied territory nor under martial law, the law-of-war commission is the only model available. At the same time, no more robust model of executive power exists; *Quirin* represents the high-water mark of military power to try enemy combatants for war crimes.

The classic treatise penned by Colonel William Winthrop, whom we have called "the 'Blackstone of Military Law,' " describes at least four preconditions for exercise of jurisdiction by a tribunal of the type convened to try Hamdan. First, "[a] military commission, (except where otherwise authorized by statute), can legally assume jurisdiction only of offenses committed within the field of the command of the convening commander." The "field of command" in these circumstances means the "theatre of war." Second, the offense charged "must have been committed within the period of the war." No jurisdiction exists to try offenses "committed either before or after the war." Third, a military commission not established pursuant to martial law or an occupation may try only "[i]ndividuals of the enemy's army who have been guilty of illegitimate warfare or other offences in violation of the laws of war" and members of one's own army "who, in time of war, become chargeable with crimes or offences not cognizable, or triable, by the criminal courts or under the Articles of war." Finally, a law-of-war commission has jurisdiction to try only two kinds of offense: "Violations of the laws and usages of war cognizable by military tribunals only," and "[b]reaches of military orders or regulations for which offenders are not legally triable by court-martial under the Articles of war."

The charge against Hamdan, described in detail in Part I, alleges a conspiracy extending over a number of years, from 1996 to November 2001. All but two months of that more than 5-year-long period preceded the attacks of September 11, 2001, and the enactment of the AUMF—the Act of Congress on which the Government relies for exercise of its war powers and thus for its authority to convene military commissions. Neither the purported agreement with Osama bin Laden and others to commit war crimes, nor a single overt act, is alleged to have occurred in a theater of war or on any specified date after September 11, 2001. None of the overt acts that Hamdan is alleged to have committed violates the law of war.

At a minimum, the Government must make a substantial showing that the crime for which it seeks to try a defendant by military commission is acknowledged to be an offense against the law of war. That burden is far from satisfied here. The crime of "conspiracy" has rarely if ever been tried as such in this country by any law-of-war military commission not exercising some other form of jurisdiction, and does not appear in either the Geneva Conventions or the Hague Conventions—the major treaties on the law of war.

If anything, *Quirin* supports Hamdan's argument that conspiracy is not a violation of the law of war. Not only did the Court pointedly omit any discussion of the conspiracy charge, but its analysis of Charge I placed special emphasis on the *completion* of an offense; it took seriously the saboteurs' argument that there can be no violation of a law of war—at least not one triable by military commission—without the actual commission of or attempt to commit a "hostile and warlike act."

Finally, international sources confirm that the crime charged here is not a recognized violation of the law of war. As observed above, none of the major treaties governing the law of war identifies conspiracy as a violation thereof. And the only "conspiracy" crimes that have been recognized by international war crimes tribunals (whose jurisdiction often extends beyond war crimes proper to crimes against humanity and crimes against the peace) are conspiracy to commit genocide and common plan to wage aggressive war, which is a crime against the peace and requires for its commission actual participation in a "concrete plan to wage war."

In sum, the sources that the Government and Justice Thomas rely upon to show that conspiracy to violate the law of war is itself a violation of the law of war in fact demonstrate quite the opposite. Far from making the requisite substantial showing, the Government has failed even to offer a "merely colorable" case for inclusion of conspiracy among those offenses cognizable by law-of-war military commission. Because the charge does not support the commission's jurisdiction, the commission lacks authority to try Hamdan.

Hamdan is charged not with an overt act for which he was caught redhanded in a theater of war and which military efficiency demands be tried expeditiously, but with an *agreement* the inception of which long predated the attacks of September 11, 2001 and the AUMF. That may well be a crime, but it is not an offense that "by the law of war may be tried by military commissio[n]."

VI

Whether or not the Government has charged Hamdan with an offense against the law of war cognizable by military commission, the commission lacks power to proceed. The UCMJ conditions the President's use of military commissions on compliance not only with the American common law of war, but also with the rest of the UCMJ itself, insofar as applicable, and with the "rules and precepts of the law of nations," *Quirin*, 317 U.S., at 28—including, the four Geneva Conventions signed in 1949. The procedures that the Government has decreed will govern Hamdan's trial by commission violate these laws.

D

The procedures adopted to try Hamdan also violate the Geneva Conventions. The Court of Appeals dismissed Hamdan's Geneva Convention challenge on three independent grounds: (1) the Geneva Conventions are not judicially enforceable; (2) Hamdan in any event is not entitled to their protections; and (3) even if he is entitled to their protections, *Councilman* abstention is appropriate. Judge Williams, concurring, rejected the second ground but agreed with the majority respecting the first and the last. As we explained in Part III, the abstention rule applied in *Councilman* is not applicable here. And for the reasons that follow, we hold that neither of the other grounds the Court of Appeals gave for its decision is persuasive.

Where, as here, no emergency prevents consultation with Congress, judicial insistence upon that consultation does not weaken our Nation's ability to deal with danger. To the contrary, that insistence strengthens the Nation's ability to determine—through democratic means—how best to do so. The Constitution places its faith in those democratic means. Our Court today simply does the same.

JUSTICE THOMAS, with whom JUSTICE SCALIA joins, and with whom JUSTICE ALITO joins in all but Parts I, II–C–1, and III–B–2, dissenting.

For the reasons set forth in Justice Scalia's dissent, it is clear that this Court lacks jurisdiction to entertain petitioner's claims. The Court having concluded otherwise, it is appropriate to respond to the Court's resolution of the merits of petitioner's claims because its opinion openly flouts our well-established duty to respect the Executive's judgment in matters of military operations and foreign affairs. The Court's evident belief that *it* is qualified to pass on the "[m]ilitary necessity," of the Commander in Chief's decision to employ a particular form of force against our enemies is so antithetical to our constitutional structure that it simply cannot go unanswered. I respectfully dissent.

I

Our review of petitioner's claims arises in the context of the President's wartime exercise of his commander-in-chief authority in conjunction with the complete support of Congress. Accordingly, it is important to take measure of the respective roles the Constitution assigns to the three branches of our Government in the conduct of war.

As I explained in *Hamdi v. Rumsfeld*, 542 U.S. 507 (2004), the structural advantages attendant to the Executive Branch—namely, the decisiveness, " 'activity, secrecy, and dispatch' " that flow from the Executive's " 'unity,' "(dissenting opinion) (quoting *The Federalist No. 70*) (A. Hamilton)—led the Founders to conclude that the "President ha[s] primary responsibility—along with the necessary power—to protect the national security and to conduct the Nation's foreign relations." Consistent with this conclusion, the Constitution vests in the President "[t]he executive Power," Art. II, § 1, provides that he "shall be Commander in Chief" of the Armed Forces, § 2, and places in him the power to recognize foreign governments, § 3. This Court has observed that these provisions confer upon the President broad constitutional authority to protect the Nation's security in the manner he deems fit. Congress, to be sure, has a substantial and essential role in both foreign affairs and national security. But "Congress cannot anticipate and legislate with regard to every possible action the President may find it necessary to take or every possible situation in which he might act," and "[s]uch failure of Congress . . . does not, 'especially . . . in the areas of foreign policy and national security,' imply 'congressional disapproval' of action taken by the Executive." *Dames & Moore v. Regan,* 453 U.S. 654, 678 (1981) (quoting *Haig v. Agee,* 453 U.S. 280, 291 (1981)). Rather, in these domains, the fact that Congress has provided the President with broad authorities does not imply—and the Judicial Branch should not infer—that Congress intended to deprive him of particular powers not specifically enumerated.

When "the President acts pursuant to an express or implied authorization from Congress," his actions are " 'supported by the strongest of presumptions and the widest latitude of judicial interpretation, and the burden of persuasion . . . rest[s] heavily upon any who might attack it.' " Accordingly, in the very context that we address today, this Court has concluded that "the detention and trial of petitioners—ordered by the President in the declared exercise of his powers as Commander in Chief of the Army in time of war and of grave public danger—are not to be set aside by the courts without the clear conviction that they are in conflict with the Constitution or laws of Congress constitutionally enacted." *Ex parte Quirin.*

Under this framework, the President's decision to try Hamdan before a military commission for his involvement with al Qaeda is entitled to a heavy measure of deference. In the present conflict, Congress has authorized the President "to use all necessary and appropriate force against those nations, organizations, or persons *he determines* planned, authorized, committed, or aided the terrorist attacks that occurred on September 11, 2001 . . . in order to prevent any future acts of international terrorism against the United States by such nations, organizations or persons." Authorization for Use of Military Force (AUMF). As a plurality of the Court observed in *Hamdi*, the "capture, detention, and *trial* of unlawful combatants, by 'universal agreement and practice,' are 'important incident[s] of war,' " *Hamdi v. Rumsfeld*, 542 U.S. 507, at 518 (2004) (quoting *Quirin*), and are therefore "an exercise of the 'necessary and appropriate force' Congress has authorized the President to use." *Hamdi*, 542 U.S., at 518 (Thomas, J., dissenting). *Hamdi*'s observation that military commissions are included within the AUMF's authorization is supported by this Court's previous recognition that "[a]n important incident to the conduct of war is the adoption of measures by the military commander, not only to repel and defeat the enemy, but to seize and subject to disciplinary measures those enemies who, in their attempt to thwart or impede our military effort, have violated the law of war."

FOR DISCUSSION

What is the constitutional objection the majority has with military commissions trying the detainees at Guantanamo Bay, Cuba? Why could the president not order their trials heard before these commissions?

RELATED CASES

***Rasul v. Bush:* 545 U.S. 466 (2004).**

Issued the same day as *Hamdi*, the Supreme Court ruled that aliens being held in confinement at the American military base in Guantanamo Bay, Cuba, were entitled to have a federal court hear challenges to their detention under the federal habeas corpus statute.

***Rumsfeld v. Padilla:* 542 U.S. at 426 (2004).**

This is the third of three Supreme Court decisions ruling that an individual being held in detention by the United States as a suspected terrorist must receive a hearing. José Padilla was an American citizen detained in Chicago by the Bush administration after he had returned from Pakistan. He was then transported to New York and placed in federal custody under a warrant issued by a grand jury investigating the 9/11 terrorist attacks. Padilla obtained a lawyer and sought to contest his detention. While his motion was pending, the Bush administration designated him an enemy combatant and placed him in military custody in South Carolina. He was so designated because the government believed that he wished to set off a "dirty bomb" in the United States in cooperation with or at the behest of al Qaeda. The Bush administration justified his detention based both on the president's power as commander in chief and the congressional AUMF of September 18, 2001. Padilla sought habeas review in New York (Southern District), naming as respondents President Bush, Secretary Rumsfeld, and Melanie A. Marr, commander of the South Carolina facility. The government sought dismissal of the petition, claiming that only Marr was a proper respondent and that the New York court lacked jurisdiction to hear the case.

The district court ruled that the president could detain him and that the Court had jurisdiction to hear the habeas petition. The Court of Appeals reversed, holding both that the secretary of defense was the appropriate respondent for habeas and that the president had no authority to detain Padilla militarily.

The Supreme Court reversed, deciding only the jurisdictional issues in the case and not whether the president has the authority to detain Padilla. Writing for the Court, Chief Justice Rehnquist indicated that the federal habeas law was clear in stating that the appropriate respondent is "the person who has custody over [the petitioner]." This respondent or person must be the one who could actually produce the detained individual before the court. The respondent is also the one who has direct physical control over the person filing the habeas petition. Since only Marr had this type of relationship to Padilla, only she, and not Bush or Rumsfield, was the proper habeas respondent.

BOUMEDIENE V. BUSH

553 U.S. 723, 128 S.Ct. 2229, 171 L.Ed.2d 41 (2008)

After the terrorist attacks against the United States on September 11, 2001, President Bush designated that aliens detained as enemy combatants should be held at the United States Naval Base at Guantanamo Bay, Cuba. According to a presidential order, these enemy combatants would not be tried in civilian courts, but instead would be tried in special military courts. In Rasul v. Bush in 2004, the Supreme Court ruled that aliens being held in confinement at Guantanamo Bay were entitled to have a federal court hear challenges to their detention under the federal habeas corpus statute. As a result of this decision, Congress enacted a statute, the Detainee Treatment Act of 2005 (DTA), which provided certain procedures for review of the detainees' status. Congress also adopted the Military Commissions Act of 2006 (MCA), which suspended the writ of habeas corpus for detainees at Guantanamo Bay. Boumediene and others challenged their detention at this facility, claiming that their denial of habeas corpus violated the Suspension Clause, Art. I, § 9, cl. 2, of the Constitution. Lower courts granted motions by the United States government to dismiss the case.

Vote: 5–4

JUSTICE KENNEDY delivered the opinion of the Court, in which JUSTICES STEVENS, SOUTER, GINSBURG, and BREYER joined.

Petitioners present a question not resolved by our earlier cases relating to the detention of aliens at Guantanamo: whether they have the constitutional privilege of habeas corpus, a privilege not to be withdrawn except in conformance with the Suspension Clause, Art. I, § 9, cl. 2. We hold these petitioners do have the habeas corpus privilege. We do not address whether the President has authority to detain these petitioners nor do we hold that the writ must issue. These and other questions regarding the legality of the detention are to be resolved in the first instance by the District Court.

III

In deciding the constitutional questions now presented we must determine whether petitioners are barred from seeking the writ or invoking the protections of the Suspension Clause either because of their status, *i.e.*, petitioners' designation by the Executive Branch as enemy combatants, or their physical location, *i.e.*, their presence at Guantanamo Bay. The Government contends that noncitizens designated as enemy combatants and detained in territory located outside our Nation's borders have no constitutional rights and no privilege of habeas corpus. Petitioners contend they do have cognizable constitutional rights and that Congress, in seeking to eliminate recourse to habeas corpus as a means to assert those rights, acted in violation of the Suspension Clause.

We begin with a brief account of the history and origins of the writ. Our account proceeds from two propositions. First, protection for the privilege of habeas corpus was one of the few safeguards of liberty specified in a Constitution that, at the outset, had no Bill of Rights. In the system conceived by the Framers the writ had a centrality that must inform proper interpretation of the Suspension Clause. Second, to the extent there were settled precedents or legal commentaries in 1789 regarding the extraterritorial scope of the writ or its application to enemy aliens, those authorities can be instructive for the present cases.

A

The Framers viewed freedom from unlawful restraint as a fundamental precept of liberty, and they understood the writ of habeas corpus as a vital instrument to secure that freedom. Experience taught, however, that the common-law writ all too often had been insufficient to guard against the abuse of monarchial power. That history counseled the necessity for specific language in the Constitution to secure the writ and ensure its place in our legal system.

Magna Carta decreed that no man would be imprisoned contrary to the law of the land. Important as the principle was, the Barons at Runnymede prescribed no specific legal process to enforce it. Holdsworth tells us, however, that gradually the writ of habeas corpus became the means by which the promise of Magna Carta was fulfilled.

The development was painstaking, even by the centuries-long measures of English constitutional history. The writ was known and used in some form at least as early as the reign of Edward I. Yet at the outset it was used to protect not the rights of citizens but those of the King and his courts. The early courts were considered agents of the Crown, designed to assist the King in the exercise of his power. Thus the writ, while it would become part of the foundation of liberty for the King's subjects, was in its earliest use a mechanism for securing compliance with the King's laws. Over time it became clear that by issuing the writ of habeas corpus common-law courts sought to enforce the King's prerogative to inquire into the authority of a jailer to hold a prisoner.

Even so, from an early date it was understood that the King, too, was subject to the law. As the writers said of Magna Carta, "it means this, that the king is and shall be below the law." And, by the 1600's, the writ was deemed less an instrument of the King's power and more a restraint upon it.

Still, the writ proved to be an imperfect check. Even when the importance of the writ was well understood in England, habeas relief often was denied by the courts or suspended by Parliament. Denial or suspension occurred in times of political unrest, to the anguish of the imprisoned and the outrage of those in sympathy with them.

A notable example from this period was *Darnel's Case,* 3 How. St. Tr. 1 (K.B.1627). The events giving rise to the case began when, in a display of the Stuart penchant for authoritarian excess, Charles I demanded that Darnel and at least four others lend him money. Upon their refusal, they were imprisoned. The prisoners sought a writ of habeas corpus; and the King filed a return in the form of a warrant signed by the Attorney General. The court held this was a sufficient answer and justified the subjects' continued imprisonment.

There was an immediate outcry of protest. The House of Commons promptly passed the Petition of Right, which condemned executive "imprison[ment] without any cause" shown, and declared that "no freeman in any such manner as is before mencioned [shall] be imprisoned or deteined." Yet a full legislative response was long delayed. The King soon began to abuse his authority again, and Parliament was dissolved. When Parliament reconvened in 1640, it sought to secure access to the writ by statute. The Act of 1640 expressly authorized use of the writ to test the legality of commitment by command or warrant of the King or the Privy Council. Civil strife and the Interregnum soon followed, and not until 1679 did Parliament try once more to secure the writ, this time through the Habeas Corpus Act of 1679. The Act, which later would be described by Blackstone as the "stable bulwark of our liberties," established procedures for issuing the writ; and it was the model upon which the habeas statutes of the 13 American Colonies were based.

This history was known to the Framers. It no doubt confirmed their view that pendular swings to and away from individual liberty were endemic to undivided, uncontrolled power. The Framers' inherent distrust of governmental power was the driving force behind the constitutional plan that allocated powers among three independent branches. This design serves not only to make Government accountable but also to secure individual liberty. Because the Constitution's separation-of-powers structure, like the substantive guarantees of the Fifth and Fourteenth Amendments, see *Yick Wo v. Hopkins*, 118 U.S. 356 (1886), protects persons as well as citizens, foreign nationals who have the privilege of litigating in our courts can seek to enforce separation-of-powers principles.

That the Framers considered the writ a vital instrument for the protection of individual liberty is evident from the care taken to specify the limited grounds for its suspension: "The Privilege of the Writ of Habeas Corpus shall not be suspended, unless when in Cases of Rebellion or Invasion the public Safety may require it." Art. I, § 9, cl. 2. The word "privilege" was used, perhaps, to avoid mentioning some rights to the exclusion of others. (Indeed, the only mention of the term "right" in the Constitution, as ratified, is in its clause giving Congress the power to protect the rights of authors and inventors. See Art. I, § 8, cl. 8.)

Surviving accounts of the ratification debates provide additional evidence that the Framers deemed the writ to be an essential mechanism in the separation-of-powers scheme. In a critical exchange with Patrick Henry at the Virginia ratifying convention Edmund Randolph referred to the Suspension Clause as an "exception" to the "power given to Congress to regulate courts." A resolution passed by the New York ratifying convention made clear its understanding that the Clause not only protects against arbitrary suspensions of the writ but also guarantees an affirmative right to judicial inquiry into the causes of detention.

In our own system the Suspension Clause is designed to protect against these cyclical abuses. The Clause protects the rights of the detained by a means consistent with the essential design of the Constitution. It ensures that, except during periods of formal suspension, the Judiciary will have a time-tested device, the writ, to maintain the "delicate balance of governance" that is itself the surest safeguard of liberty. The separation-of-powers doctrine, and the history that influenced its design, therefore must inform the reach and purpose of the Suspension Clause.

IV

Drawing from its position that at common law the writ ran only to territories over which the Crown was sovereign, the Government says the Suspension Clause affords petitioners no rights because the United States does not claim sovereignty over the place of detention.

Guantanamo Bay is not formally part of the United States. And under the terms of the lease between the United States and Cuba, Cuba retains "ultimate sovereignty" over the territory while the United States exercises "complete jurisdiction and control." Under the terms of the 1934 Treaty, however, Cuba effectively has no rights as a sovereign until the parties agree to modification of the 1903 Lease Agreement or the United States abandons the base.

A

The Court has discussed the issue of the Constitution's extraterritorial application on many occasions. These decisions undermine the Government's argument that, at least as applied to noncitizens, the Constitution necessarily stops where *de jure* sovereignty ends.

Fundamental questions regarding the Constitution's geographic scope first arose at the dawn of the 20th century when the Nation acquired noncontiguous Territories: Puerto Rico, Guam, and the Philippines—ceded to the United States by Spain at the conclusion of the Spanish-American War—and Hawaii—annexed by the United States in 1898. At this point Congress chose to discontinue its previous practice of extending constitutional rights to the territories by statute.

In a series of opinions later known as the *Insular Cases,* the Court addressed whether the Constitution, by its own force, applies in any territory that is not a State. See *De Lima v. Bidwell,* 182 U.S. 1 (1901); *Dooley v. United States,* 182 U.S. 222 (1901); *Armstrong v. United States,* 182 U.S. 243 (1901); *Downes v. Bidwell,* 182 U.S. 244 (1901); *Hawaii v. Mankichi,* 190 U.S. 197 (1903); *Dorr v. United States,* 195 U.S. 138 (1904). The Court held that the Constitution has independent force in these territories, a force not contingent upon acts of legislative grace.

These concerns have particular bearing upon the Suspension Clause question in the cases now before us, for the writ of habeas corpus is itself an indispensable mechanism for monitoring the separation of powers. The test for determining the scope of this provision must not be subject to manipulation by those whose power it is designed to restrain.

C

The United States Naval Station at Guantanamo Bay consists of 45 square miles of land and water. The base has been used, at various points, to house migrants and refugees temporarily. At present, however, other than the detainees themselves, the only long-term residents are American military personnel, their families, and a small number of workers. The detainees have been deemed enemies of the United States. At present, dangerous as they may be if released, they are contained in a secure prison facility located on an isolated and heavily fortified military base.

There is no indication, furthermore, that adjudicating a habeas corpus petition would cause friction with the host government. No Cuban court has jurisdiction over American military personnel at Guantanamo or the enemy combatants detained there. While obligated to abide by the terms of the lease, the United States is, for all practical purposes, answerable to no other sovereign for its acts on the base. Were that not the case, or if the detention facility were located in an active theater of war, arguments that issuing the writ would be "impracticable or anomalous" would have more weight.

It is true that before today the Court has never held that noncitizens detained by our Government in territory over which another country maintains *de jure* sovereignty have any rights under our Constitution. But the cases before us lack any precise historical parallel. They involve individuals detained by executive order for the duration of a conflict that, if measured from September 11, 2001, to the present, is already among the longest wars in American history. The detainees, moreover, are held in a territory that, while technically not part of the United States, is under the complete and total control of our Government. Under these circumstances the lack of a precedent on point is no barrier to our holding.

We hold that Art. I, § 9, cl. 2, of the Constitution has full effect at Guantanamo Bay. If the privilege of habeas corpus is to be denied to the detainees now before us, Congress must act in accordance with the requirements of the Suspension Clause. This Court may not impose a *de facto* suspension by abstaining from these controversies. The MCA does not purport to be a formal suspension of the writ; and the Government, in its submissions to us, has not argued that it is. Petitioners, therefore, are entitled to the privilege of habeas corpus to challenge the legality of their detention.

V

In light of this holding the question becomes whether the statute stripping jurisdiction to issue the writ avoids the Suspension Clause mandate because Congress has provided adequate substitute procedures for habeas corpus. The Government submits there has been compliance with the Suspension Clause because the DTA review process in the Court of Appeals provides an adequate substitute.

A

Our case law does not contain extensive discussion of standards defining suspension of the writ or of circumstances under which suspension has occurred. This simply confirms the care Congress has taken throughout our Nation's history to preserve the writ and its function. Indeed, most of the major legislative enactments pertaining to habeas corpus have acted not to contract the writ's protection but to expand it or to hasten resolution of prisoners' claims.

B

We do not endeavor to offer a comprehensive summary of the requisites for an adequate substitute for habeas corpus. We do consider it uncontroversial, however, that the privilege of habeas corpus entitles the prisoner to a meaningful opportunity to demonstrate that he is being held pursuant to "the erroneous application or interpretation" of relevant law. And the habeas court must have the power to order the conditional release of an individual unlawfully detained—though release need not be the exclusive remedy and is not the appropriate one in every case in which the writ is granted.

Indeed, common-law habeas corpus was, above all, an adaptable remedy. Its precise application and scope changed depending upon the circumstances. It appears the common-law habeas court's role was most extensive in cases of pretrial and noncriminal detention, where there had been little or no previous judicial review of the cause for detention. Notably, the black-letter rule that prisoners could not controvert facts in the jailer's return was not followed (or at least not with consistency) in such cases.

There is evidence from 19th-century American sources indicating that, even in States that accorded strong ***res judicata*** [a matter already resolved by a court and cannot be decided again] effect to prior adjudications, habeas courts in this country routinely allowed prisoners to introduce exculpatory evidence that was either unknown or previously unavailable to the prisoner.

Accordingly, where relief is sought from a sentence that resulted from the judgment of a court of record, as was the case in *Ex parte Watkins*, 3 Pet. 193 (1830), and indeed in most federal habeas cases, considerable deference is owed to the court that ordered confinement.

Where a person is detained by executive order, rather than, say, after being tried and convicted in a court, the need for collateral review is most pressing. A criminal conviction in the usual course occurs after a judicial hearing before a tribunal disinterested in the outcome and committed to procedures designed to ensure its own independence. These dynamics are not inherent in executive detention orders or executive review procedures. In this context the need for habeas corpus is more urgent. The intended duration of the detention and the reasons for it bear upon the precise scope of the inquiry. Habeas corpus proceedings need not resemble a criminal trial, even when the detention is by executive order. But the writ must be effective. The habeas court must have sufficient authority to conduct a meaningful review of both the cause for detention and the Executive's power to detain.

To determine the necessary scope of habeas corpus review, therefore, we must assess the CSRT process, the mechanism through which petitioners' designation as enemy combatants became final. Whether one characterizes the CSRT process as direct review of the Executive's battlefield determination that the detainee is an enemy combatant—as the parties have and as we do—or as the first step in the collateral review of a battlefield determination makes no difference in a proper analysis of whether the procedures Congress put in place are an adequate substitute for habeas corpus. What matters is the sum total of procedural protections afforded to the detainee at all stages, direct and collateral.

Petitioners identify what they see as myriad deficiencies in the CSRTs. The most relevant for our purposes are the constraints upon the detainee's ability to rebut the factual basis for the Government's assertion that he is an enemy combatant. As already noted, see Part IV-C, at the CSRT stage the detainee has limited means to find or present evidence to challenge the Government's case against him. He does not have the assistance of counsel and may not be aware of the most critical allegations that the Government relied upon to order his detention.

Even if we were to assume that the CSRTs satisfy due process standards, it would not end our inquiry. Habeas corpus is a collateral process that exists, in Justice Holmes' words, to "cu[t] through all forms and g[o] to the very tissue of the structure. It comes in from the outside, not in subordination to the proceedings, and although every form may have been preserved opens the inquiry whether they have been more than an empty shell." Even when the procedures authorizing detention are structurally sound, the Suspension Clause remains applicable and the writ relevant.

Although we make no judgment as to whether the CSRTs, as currently constituted, satisfy due process standards, we agree with petitioners that, even when all the parties involved in this process act with diligence and in good faith, there is considerable risk of error in the tribunal's findings of fact. This is a risk inherent in any process that, in the words of the former Chief Judge of the Court of Appeals, is "closed and accusatorial." And given that the consequence of error may be detention of persons for the duration of hostilities that may last a generation or more, this is a risk too significant to ignore.

For the writ of habeas corpus, or its substitute, to function as an effective and proper remedy in this context, the court that conducts the habeas proceeding must have the means to correct errors that occurred during the CSRT proceedings. This includes some authority to assess the sufficiency of the Government's evidence against the detainee. It also must have the authority to admit and consider relevant exculpatory evidence that was not introduced during the earlier proceeding. Federal habeas petitioners long have had the means to supplement the record on review, even in the postconviction habeas setting.

C

We now consider whether the DTA allows the Court of Appeals to conduct a proceeding meeting these standards.

The DTA does not explicitly empower the Court of Appeals to order the applicant in a DTA review proceeding released should the court find that the standards and procedures used at his CSRT hearing were insufficient to justify detention. This is troubling. Yet, for present purposes, we can assume congressional silence permits a constitutionally required remedy. In that case it would be possible to hold that a remedy of release is impliedly provided for. The DTA might be read, furthermore, to allow the petitioners to assert most, if not all, of the legal claims they seek to advance, including their most basic claim: that the President has no authority under the AUMF to detain them indefinitely. (Whether the President has such authority turns on whether the AUMF authorizes—and the Constitution permits—the indefinite detention of "enemy combatants" as the Department of Defense defines that term. Thus a challenge to the President's authority to detain is, in essence, a challenge to the Department's definition of enemy combatant, a "standard" used by the CSRTs in petitioners' cases.) At oral argument, the Solicitor General urged us to adopt both these constructions, if doing so would allow MCA § 7 to remain intact.

The absence of a release remedy and specific language allowing AUMF challenges are not the only constitutional infirmities from which the statute potentially suffers, however. The more difficult question is whether the DTA permits the Court of Appeals to make requisite findings of fact. The DTA enables petitioners to request "review" of their CSRT determination in the Court of Appeals, but the "Scope of Review" provision confines the Court of Appeals' role to reviewing whether the CSRT followed the "standards and procedures" issued by the Department of Defense and assessing whether those "standards and procedures" are lawful. § 1005(e)(C), *ibid.* Among these standards is "the requirement that the conclusion of the Tribunal be supported by a preponderance of the evidence . . . allowing a rebuttable presumption in favor of the Government's evidence."

Assuming the DTA can be construed to allow the Court of Appeals to review or correct the CSRT's factual determinations, as opposed to merely certifying that the tribunal applied the correct standard of proof, we see no way to construe the statute to allow what is also constitutionally required in this context: an opportunity for the detainee to present relevant exculpatory evidence that was not made part of the record in the earlier proceedings.

On its face the statute allows the Court of Appeals to consider no evidence outside the CSRT record. In the parallel litigation, however, the Court of Appeals determined that the DTA allows it to order the production of all " 'reasonably available information in the possession of the U.S. Government bearing on the issue of whether the detainee meets the criteria to be designated as an enemy combatant,' " regardless of whether this evidence was put before the CSRT. For present purposes, however, we can assume that the Court of Appeals was correct that the DTA allows introduction and consideration of relevant exculpatory evidence that was "reasonably available" to the Government at the time of the CSRT but not made part of the record. Even so, the DTA review proceeding falls short of being a constitutionally adequate substitute, for the detainee still would have no opportunity to present evidence discovered after the CSRT proceedings concluded.

Under the DTA the Court of Appeals has the power to review CSRT determinations by assessing the legality of standards and procedures. This implies the power to inquire into what happened at the CSRT hearing and, perhaps, to remedy certain deficiencies in that proceeding. But should the Court of Appeals determine that the CSRT followed appropriate and lawful standards and procedures, it will have reached the limits of its jurisdiction. There is no language in the DTA that can be construed to allow the Court of Appeals to admit and consider newly discovered evidence that could not have been made part of the CSRT record because it was unavailable to either the Government or the detainee when the CSRT made its findings. This evidence, however, may be critical to the detainee's argument that he is not an enemy combatant and there is no cause to detain him.

By foreclosing consideration of evidence not presented or reasonably available to the detainee at the CSRT proceedings, the DTA disadvantages the detainee by limiting the scope of collateral review to a record that may not be accurate or complete. In other contexts, *e.g.*, in post-trial habeas cases where the prisoner already has had a full and fair opportunity to develop the factual predicate of his claims, similar limitations on the scope of habeas review may be appropriate.

VI

A

In light of our conclusion that there is no jurisdictional bar to the District Court's entertaining petitioners' claims the question remains whether there are prudential barriers to habeas corpus review under these circumstances.

The Government argues petitioners must seek review of their CSRT determinations in the Court of Appeals before they can proceed with their habeas corpus actions in the District Court. As noted earlier, in other contexts and for prudential reasons this Court has required exhaustion of alternative remedies before a prisoner can seek federal habeas relief. Most of these cases were brought by prisoners in state custody.

The real risks, the real threats, of terrorist attacks are constant and not likely soon to abate. The ways to disrupt our life and laws are so many and unforeseen that the Court should not attempt even some general catalogue of crises that might occur. Certain principles are apparent, however. Practical considerations and exigent circumstances inform the definition and reach of the law's writs, including habeas corpus. The cases and our tradition reflect this precept.

In cases involving foreign citizens detained abroad by the Executive, it likely would be both an impractical and unprecedented extension of judicial power to assume that habeas corpus would be available at the moment the prisoner is taken into custody. If and when habeas corpus jurisdiction applies, as it does in these cases, then proper deference can be accorded to reasonable procedures for screening and initial detention under lawful and proper conditions of confinement and treatment for a reasonable period of time. Domestic exigencies, furthermore, might also impose such onerous burdens on the Government that here, too, the Judicial Branch would be required to devise sensible rules for staying habeas corpus proceedings until the Government can comply with its requirements in a responsible way. Here, as is true with detainees apprehended abroad, a relevant consideration in determining the courts' role is whether there are suitable alternative processes in place to protect against the arbitrary exercise of governmental power.

The cases before us, however, do not involve detainees who have been held for a short period of time while awaiting their CSRT determinations. Were that the case, or were it probable that the Court of Appeals could complete a prompt review of their applications, the case for requiring temporary abstention or exhaustion of alternative remedies would be much stronger. These qualifications no longer pertain here. In some of these cases six years have elapsed without the judicial oversight that habeas corpus or an adequate substitute demands. And there has been no showing that the Executive faces such onerous burdens that it cannot respond to habeas corpus actions. To require these detainees to complete DTA review before proceeding with their habeas corpus actions would be to require additional months, if not years, of delay. The first DTA review applications were filed over a year ago, but no decisions on the merits have been issued. While some delay in fashioning new procedures is unavoidable, the costs of delay can no longer be borne by those who are held in custody. The detainees in these cases are entitled to a prompt habeas corpus hearing.

Our decision today holds only that the petitioners before us are entitled to seek the writ; that the DTA review procedures are an inadequate substitute for habeas corpus; and that the petitioners in these cases need not exhaust the review procedures in the Court of Appeals before proceeding with their habeas actions in the District Court. The only law we identify as unconstitutional is MCA § 7, 28 U.S.C.A. § 2241(e). Accordingly, both the DTA and the CSRT process remain intact. Our holding with regard to exhaustion should not be read to imply that a habeas court should intervene the moment an enemy combatant steps foot in a territory where the writ runs. The Executive is entitled to a reasonable period of time to determine a detainee's status before a court entertains that detainee's habeas corpus petition. The CSRT process is the mechanism Congress and the President set up to deal with these issues. Except in cases of undue delay, federal courts should refrain from entertaining an enemy combatant's habeas corpus petition at least until after the Department, acting via the CSRT, has had a chance to review his status.

It is so ordered.

CHIEF JUSTICE ROBERTS, with whom JUSTICES SCALIA, THOMAS, and ALITO join, dissenting.

Today the Court strikes down as inadequate the most generous set of procedural protections ever afforded aliens detained by this country as enemy combatants. The political branches crafted these procedures amidst an ongoing military conflict, after much careful investigation and thorough debate. The Court rejects them today out of hand, without bothering to say what due process rights the detainees possess, without explaining how the statute fails to vindicate those rights, and before a single petitioner has even attempted to avail himself of the law's operation. And to what effect? The majority merely replaces a review system designed by the people's representatives with a set of shapeless procedures to be defined by federal courts at some future date. One cannot help but think, after surveying the modest practical results of the majority's ambitious opinion, that this decision is not really about the detainees at all, but about control of federal policy regarding enemy combatants.

The majority is adamant that the Guantanamo detainees are entitled to the protections of habeas corpus—its opinion begins by deciding that question. I regard the issue as a difficult one, primarily because of the unique and unusual jurisdictional status of Guantanamo Bay. I nonetheless agree with Justice Scalia's analysis of our precedents and the pertinent history of the writ, and accordingly join his dissent. The important point for me, however, is that the Court should have resolved these cases on other grounds. Habeas is most fundamentally a procedural right, a mechanism for contesting the legality of executive detention. The critical threshold question in these cases, prior to any inquiry about the writ's scope, is whether the system the political branches designed protects whatever rights the detainees may possess. If so, there is no need for any additional process, whether called "habeas" or something else.

JUSTICE SCALIA, with whom CHIEF JUSTICE ROBERTS and JUSTICES THOMAS, and ALITO join, dissenting.

Today, for the first time in our Nation's history, the Court confers a constitutional right to habeas corpus on alien enemies detained abroad by our military forces in the course of an ongoing war. The Chief Justice's dissent, which I join, shows that the procedures prescribed by Congress in the Detainee Treatment Act provide the essential protections that habeas corpus guarantees; there has thus been no suspension of the writ, and no basis exists for judicial intervention beyond what the Act allows. My problem with today's opinion is more fundamental still: The writ of habeas corpus does not, and never has, run in favor of aliens abroad; the Suspension Clause thus has no application, and the Court's intervention in this military matter is entirely *ultra vires* [beyond the power of legal authority].

I

America is at war with radical Islamists. The enemy began by killing Americans and American allies abroad: 241 at the Marine barracks in Lebanon, 19 at the Khobar Towers in Dhahran, 224 at our embassies in Dar es Salaam and Nairobi, and 17 on the *USS Cole* in Yemen. On September 11, 2001, the enemy brought the battle to American soil, killing 2,749 at the Twin Towers in New York City, 184 at the Pentagon in Washington, D.C., and 40 in Pennsylvania. It has threatened further attacks against our homeland; one need only walk about buttressed and barricaded Washington, or board a plane anywhere in the country, to know that the threat is a serious one. Our Armed Forces are now in the field against the enemy, in Afghanistan and Iraq. Last week, 13 of our countrymen in arms were killed.

The game of bait-and-switch that today's opinion plays upon the Nation's Commander in Chief will make the war harder on us. It will almost certainly cause more Americans to be killed. That consequence would be tolerable if necessary to preserve a time-honored legal principle vital to our constitutional Republic. But it is this Court's blatant *abandonment* of such a principle that produces the decision today. The President relied on our settled precedent in *Johnson v. Eisentrager,* 339 U.S. 763 (1950), when he established the prison at Guantanamo Bay for enemy aliens. Citing that case, the President's Office of Legal Counsel advised him "that the great weight of legal authority indicates that a federal district court could not properly exercise habeas jurisdiction over an alien detained at [Guantanamo Bay]." Had the law been otherwise, the military surely would not have transported prisoners there, but would have kept them in Afghanistan, transferred them to another of our foreign military bases, or turned them over to allies for detention. Those other facilities might well have been worse for the detainees themselves.

In the long term, then, the Court's decision today accomplishes little, except perhaps to reduce the well-being of enemy combatants that the Court ostensibly seeks to protect. In the short term, however, the decision is devastating. At least 30 of those prisoners hitherto released from Guantanamo Bay have returned to the battlefield. But others have succeeded in carrying on their atrocities against innocent civilians. In one case, a detainee released from Guantanamo Bay masterminded the kidnapping of two Chinese dam workers, one of whom was later shot to death when used as a human shield against Pakistani commandoes. Another former detainee promptly resumed his post as a senior Taliban commander and murdered a United Nations engineer and three Afghan soldiers. Still another murdered an Afghan judge. It was reported only last month that a released detainee carried out a suicide bombing against Iraqi soldiers in Mosul, Iraq.

These, mind you, were detainees whom *the military* had concluded were not enemy combatants. Their return to the kill illustrates the incredible difficulty of assessing who is and who is not an enemy combatant in a foreign theater of operations where the environment does not lend itself to rigorous evidence collection. Astoundingly, the Court today raises the bar, requiring military officials to appear before civilian courts and defend their decisions under procedural and evidentiary rules that go beyond what Congress has specified. As The Chief Justice's dissent makes clear, we have no idea what those procedural and evidentiary rules are, but they will be determined by civil courts and (in the Court's contemplation at least) will be more detainee-friendly than those now applied, since otherwise there would no reason to hold the congressionally prescribed procedures unconstitutional. If they impose a higher standard of proof (from foreign battlefields) than the current procedures require, the number of the enemy returned to combat will obviously increase.

But even when the military has evidence that it can bring forward, it is often foolhardy to release that evidence to the attorneys representing our enemies. And one escalation of procedures that the Court *is* clear about is affording the detainees increased access to witnesses (perhaps troops serving in Afghanistan?) and to classified information. During the 1995 prosecution of Omar Abdel Rahman, federal prosecutors gave the names of 200 unindicted co-conspirators to the "Blind Sheik's" defense lawyers; that information was in the hands of Osama Bin Laden within two weeks. In another case, trial testimony revealed to the enemy that the United States had been monitoring their cellular network, whereupon they promptly stopped using it, enabling more of them to evade capture and continue their atrocities.

II

A

The Suspension Clause of the Constitution provides: "The Privilege of the Writ of Habeas Corpus shall not be suspended, unless when in Cases of Rebellion or Invasion the public Safety may require it." Art. I, § 9, cl. 2. As a court of law operating under a written Constitution, our role is to determine whether there is a conflict between that Clause and the Military Commissions Act. A conflict arises only if the Suspension Clause preserves the privilege of the writ for aliens held by the United States military as enemy combatants at the base in Guantanamo Bay, located within the sovereign territory of Cuba.

We have frequently stated that we owe great deference to Congress's view that a law it has passed is constitutional. That is especially so in the area of foreign and military affairs.

C

What drives today's decision is neither the meaning of the Suspension Clause, nor the principles of our precedents, but rather an inflated notion of judicial supremacy. The Court says that if the extraterritorial applicability of the Suspension Clause turned on formal notions of sovereignty, "it would be possible for the political branches to govern without legal constraint" in areas beyond the sovereign territory of the United States. That cannot be, the Court says, because it is the duty of this Court to say what the law is. It would be difficult to imagine a more question-begging analysis. "The very foundation of the power of the federal courts to declare Acts of Congress unconstitutional lies in the power and duty of those courts to decide cases and controversies *properly before them*."

III

[I]t is clear that the original understanding of the Suspension Clause was that habeas corpus was not available to aliens abroad, as Judge Randolph's thorough opinion for the court below detailed.

The Suspension Clause reads: "The Privilege of the Writ of Habeas Corpus shall not be suspended, unless when in Cases of Rebellion or Invasion the public Safety may require it." U.S. Const., Art. I, § 9, cl. 2. The proper course of constitutional interpretation is to give the text the meaning it was understood to have at the time of its adoption by the people. That course is especially demanded when (as here) the Constitution limits the power of Congress to infringe upon a pre-existing common-law right. The nature of the writ of habeas corpus that cannot be suspended must be defined by the common-law writ that was available at the time of the founding.

It is entirely clear that, at English common law, the writ of habeas corpus did not extend beyond the sovereign territory of the Crown.

In sum, *all* available historical evidence points to the conclusion that the writ would not have been available at common law for aliens captured and held outside the sovereign territory of the Crown. Despite three opening briefs, three reply briefs, and support from a legion of *amici*, petitioners have failed to identify a single case in the history of Anglo-American law that supports their claim to jurisdiction. The Court finds it significant that there is no recorded case *denying* jurisdiction to such prisoners either. But a case standing for the remarkable proposition that the writ could issue to a foreign land would surely have been reported, whereas a case denying such a writ for lack of jurisdiction would likely not. At a minimum, the absence of a reported case either way leaves unrefuted the voluminous commentary stating that habeas was confined to the dominions of the Crown.

What history teaches is confirmed by the nature of the limitations that the Constitution places upon suspension of the common-law writ. It can be suspended only "in Cases of Rebellion or Invasion." Art. I, § 9, cl. 2. The latter case (invasion) is plainly limited to the territory of the United States; and while it is conceivable that a rebellion could be mounted by American citizens abroad, surely the overwhelming majority of its occurrences would be domestic. If the extraterritorial scope of habeas turned on flexible, "functional" considerations, as the Court holds, why would the Constitution limit its suspension almost entirely to instances of domestic crisis? Surely there is an even greater justification for suspension in foreign lands where the United States might hold prisoners of war during an ongoing conflict. And correspondingly, there is less threat to liberty when the Government suspends the writ's (supposed) application in foreign lands, where even on the most extreme view prisoners are entitled to fewer constitutional rights. It makes no sense, therefore, for the Constitution generally to forbid suspension of the writ abroad if indeed the writ has application there.

Today the Court warps our Constitution in a way that goes beyond the narrow issue of the reach of the Suspension Clause, invoking judicially brainstormed separation-of-powers principles to establish a manipulable "functional" test for the extraterritorial reach of habeas corpus (and, no doubt, for the extraterritorial reach of other constitutional protections as well). It blatantly misdescribes important precedents, most conspicuously Justice Jackson's opinion for the Court in *Johnson v. Eisentrager.* It breaks a chain of precedent as old as the common law that prohibits judicial inquiry into detentions of aliens abroad absent statutory authorization. And, most tragically, it sets our military commanders the impossible task of proving to a civilian court, under whatever standards this Court devises in the future, that evidence supports the confinement of each and every enemy prisoner.

The Nation will live to regret what the Court has done today. I dissent.

FOR DISCUSSION

President Bush and other supporters of executive authority argue that 9/11 changed everything, including how we should think about presidential power in the face of terrorism. Do *Hamdi, Hamdan, Rasul, Padilla,* and *Boumediene* suggest that the Supreme Court is ready to go along with this assertion? Has the Court directly ruled on inherent president authority as commander-in-chief? Under what circumstances could the president suspend habeas corpus?

GLOSSARY

Authorization to Use Military Force: A joint resolution adopted by Congress after the terrorist attacks on September 11, 2001, authoring the president to take appropriate action to repel future terrorist attacks. The resolution was invoked by President George W. Bush to support a variety of presidential actions. However, the Supreme Court, in cases such as *Hamdi v. Rumsfeld* and *Rasul v. Bush*, was been unwilling to let this resolution support presidential orders to detain suspected terrorists without some type of court hearing.

Commander in Chief: Article II power given to the president of the United States to be the civilian head of the armed forces. Constitutionally, the issue is what powers are associated with being commander in chief versus the powers assigned to Congress in defense and foreign policy under Article I.

Constitution Abroad: In *United States v. Curtiss-Wright Export Corporation*, the Supreme Court suggested that the division of powers assigned to Congress and the president may not necessarily apply the same way in foreign matters. This doctrine seems to suggest broad powers for the president to act in international affairs.

Executive Agreements: In *United States v. Belmont* and *United States v. Pink*, the Supreme Court ruled that agreements the president negotiates with other countries have the force of law.

Gulf of Tonkin Resolution: This was a joint resolution adopted by Congress after U.S. ships were supposedly attacked by North Vietnam in 1964. The resolution gave the president authority to take appropriate action to repel the attacks and defend the United States. Supporters of presidential power point to this resolution as the legal basis for Presidents Johnson and Nixon's escalation of the war in Vietnam. Critics argued that the Resolution did not support this action and contended that the Vietnam War was illegal. In cases such as *Mora v. McNamara*, the Supreme Court refused to adjudicate the constitutionality of the war, ruling it a political question.

Indian Affairs: In Article I, Section 8, clause 4, Congress is given the authority to regulate commerce with Indian tribes. The Supreme Court has interpreted this clause as giving the federal government exclusive authority to negotiate or regulate Indian affairs, while giving states minimal power in this area.

Power to Declare War: In Article I, Sec. 8, cl. 11 of the Constitution, Congress is given the authority to declare war. In several Vietnam War era cases, the Supreme Court refused to offer a ruling regarding what it meant to declare war, and it also refused to rule on whether the conflict in Vietnam was a constitutional war.

Presidential Power in Foreign Affairs: According to Justice Jackson's concurrence in *Youngstown v. Sawyer*, presidential power in foreign affairs can be classified into a tripartite distinction depending on whether the president is acting with, without, or contrary to congressional approval. Jackson's distinction has become precedent in assessing presidential power in foreign and defense matters, and it seems to suggest that Congress can augment Article II power of the executive branch.

Ratio Decidendi: The reason for the decision.

Suspension Cause: The Suspension Clause refers to Article I, Sec. 9, cl. 2 of the Constitution, which states that the writ of habeas corpus cannot be suspended except under certain circumstances. The terms and conditions under which a suspension may occur has been the source of significant constitutional debate since the terrorist attacks of 9/11.

Sutherland Thesis: The Sutherland Thesis refers to a claim by Justice Sutherland in *United States v. Curtiss-Wright Export Corporation* that the president was "the sole organ" (or person constitutionally responsible) in foreign affairs and that the power of foreign affairs passed to him from the states after the Revolutionary War.

Treaties: Treaties are agreements with other countries negotiated by the executive branch that must be approved by a two-thirds vote of the Senate. Once approved, they do not need Senate approval to be nullified. Treaties, according to Article VI of the Constitution, are the "supreme law of the land" along with the Constitution and other federal laws.

War Powers Act: Adopted by Congress in 1973, the War Powers Act allows the president to deploy troops for a finite amount of time without Congress's authorization. However, a resolution adopted by both houses of Congress can compel the president to withdraw the troops. The Act was passed to limit presidential power to commit the country to military action. Many argue that the Act is unconstitutional.

SELECTED BIBLIOGRAPHY

Abraham, Henry J., 2008. *Justices, Presidents and Senators: A History of the U.S. Supreme Court Appointments from Washington to Bush II*, 5th ed., Lanham, MD. Rowman & Littlefield Publishers, Inc.

Baum, Lawrence, 2016. *The Supreme Court*, 12th ed. Thousand Oaks, CA: Sage.

Brenner, Saul, and Harold J. Spaeth. 1995. *Stare Indecisis: The Alteration of Precedent on the Supreme Court, 1946–1992.* New York: Cambridge University Press.

Campbell, Tom. 2004. *Separation of Powers in Practice.* Palo Alto, CA: Stanford University Press.

Cheney, Timothy D. 1998. *Who Makes the Law: The Supreme Court, Congress, the States, and Society.* Upper Saddle River, NJ: Prentice Hall.

Edelson, Chris. 2013. *Emergency Presidential Power: From the Drafting of the Constitution to the War on Terror.* Madison: University of Wisconsin Press.

Ely, John Hart. 1996. *On Constitutional Ground.* Princeton, NJ: Princeton University Press.

Fallon, Jr., Richard H. 2004. *The Dynamic Constitution: An Introduction to American Constitutional Law.* Cambridge, UK: Cambridge University Press

Fisher, Louis. 1997. *Constitutional Conflicts Between Congress and the President*, 4th ed. Lawrence: University Press of Kansas.

Fisher, Louis. 1998. *The Politics of Shared Power: Congress and the Executive*, 4th ed. College Station: Texas A&M University Press.

Fisher, Louis. 2008. *The Constitution and 9/11: Recurring Threats to America's Freedoms.* Lawrence, KS: University Press of Kansas.

Griffin, Stephen M. 2013. *Long Wars and the Constitution.* Cambridge: Harvard University Press.

Henkin, Louis. 1990. *Constitutionalism, Democracy, and Foreign Affairs.* New York: Columbia University Press.

Hendrickson, Ryan C. 2015. *Obama at War: Congress and the Imperial Presidency.* Lexington, Kentucky: University Press of Kentucky.

Ivers, Gregg, and Kevin T. McGuire. 2004. *Creating Constitutional Change: Clashes over Power and Liberty in the Supreme Court.* Charlottesville, VA: University of Virginia Press.

Ramsey, Michael D. 2007. *The Constitution's Text in Foreign Affairs.* Cambridge, MA: Harvard University Press.

Van Geel, T. R. 2004. *Understanding Supreme Court Opinions,* 4th ed. New York: Longman.

Whittington, Keith E. 1999. *Constitutional Construction: Divided Powers and Constitutional Meaning.* Cambridge, MA: Harvard University Press.

Whittington, Keith E. 1999. *Constitutional Interpretation: Textual Meaning, Original Intent, and Judicial Review.* Lawrence, KS: University Press of Kansas.

Yoo, John C. 2005. *The Powers of War and Peace: The Constitution and Foreign Affairs After 9/11.* Chicago: University of Chicago Press.

CHAPTER IX

The Citizen and the Political Process

Timeline: Citizens and the American Election Process

1870 Fifteenth Amendment adopted, banning discrimination in voting based on race, color, or slavery.

1875 In *Minor v. Happersett* the Supreme Court rules that women, while citizens, do not have the right to vote because voting is not a privilege or immunity of United States citizenship guaranteed by the Fourteenth Amendment.

1877 Reconstruction ends as northern troops are withdrawn from the South.

1896 *Plessy v. Ferguson* affirms the doctrine of "separate but equal," authorizing racial segregation that had begun from Reconstruction forward.

1907 Congress passes the Tillman Act baring corporations from making political contributions to candidates for federal office.

1913 Thirteenth Amendment adopted, granting citizens the right to vote for United States senators.

1920 Nineteenth Amendment adopted, banning discrimination in voting based on sex.

1924 Congress adopts Indian Citizenship Bill of 1924 giving Native Americans the right to vote.

1941 In *United States v. Classic* the Supreme Court rules that the Constitution grants individuals the right to vote in federal elections for members of the House of Representatives.

1944 In *Smith v. Allwright* the Supreme Court rules that political parties may not exclude individuals from participating in primaries based on race, ending the practice of "white primaries."

1946 In *Colegrove v. Green* the Court rules that reapportionment is a nonjusticiable political question.

1947 Congress passes the Labor Management Relations Act (Taft-Hartley) that prevents corporations and labor unions from expending money to influence federal elections.

1959 In *Lassiter v. Northampton County Bd. of Elections* the Court rules that literacy tests as a requirement for voting do not violate the Constitution.

1960 In *Gomillion v. Lightfoot* the Court rules that challenges to reapportionment based on the Fifteenth Amendment are justiciable.

1962 In *Baker v. Carr* the Supreme Court overrules *Colegrove*, holding that reapportionment is justiciable.

1964 Twenty-Fourth Amendment adopted, banning poll taxes.

1964 In *Reynolds v. Sims* the Supreme Court rules that state legislative malapportionment violates the Fourteenth Amendment.

1965 Congress adopts the 1965 Voting Rights Act.

1966 *Harper v. Virginia Board of Elections* rules that individuals under the Equal Protection Clause of the Fourteenth Amendment have a right to vote in state elections without having to pay a poll tax, which the Court strikes down

1970 *Oregon v. Mitchell* rules that while Congress can lower the voting age in federal elections to age 18, it may not do so for state elections.

1971 Twenty-Sixth Amendment adopted, lowering the voting age to 18.

1972 In *Bullock v. Carter*, the Court rules that candidate filing fees are unconstitutional.

1972 Break-in at the National Democratic Headquarters at the Watergate building in Washington, D.C.

1974 In *Richardson v. Ramirez* the Supreme Court upholds the constitutionality of felon disenfranchisement laws.

1974 Congress amends the Federal Election Campaign Act (FECA) to provide for public funding in presidential races.

1976 In *Buckley v. Valeo* the Supreme Court upholds, in part, and declares unconstitutional, in part, the 1974 FECA.

1976 In *Skafte v. Rorex* the Colorado Supreme Court upholds a law barring aliens from voting in local elections.

1983 In *Anderson v. Celebrezze* the Court declares unconstitutional state laws that restrict the ability of third-party candidates to get on the ballot.

1986 In *Munro v. Socialist Workers Party* the Supreme Court upholds a state law requiring a third or minor party to secure 1 percent of the vote or its equivalent in signatures in order to appear on the general election ballot.

1986 In *Davis v. Bandemer* the Supreme Court declares partisan gerrymandering to be a justiciable question.

1990 In *Rutan v. Republican Party of Illinois* the Supreme Court declares the use of party affiliation by the government to determine hiring, firing, or other employment decisions unconstitutional.

1992 In *Burson v. Freeman* the Supreme Court upholds a state law banning political campaigning within 100 feet of a polling place on election day.

1992 In *Burdick v. Takushi* the Court upholds a state law banning the writing in of candidate names in a general election.

1993 In *Shaw v. Reno* the Supreme Court declares the use of race in redistricting to be subject to strict scrutiny.

1995 In *McIntyre v. Ohio* the Court declares that the First Amendment protects the right of individuals to engage in anonymous political speech.

2000 In *Nixon v. Shrink Missouri Government PAC* the Supreme Court upholds a state law imposing $250 contribution limits on candidates for state office.

2000 In *Bush v. Gore* the Supreme Court ends the 2000 presidential election in Florida, ruling that the four county recounts of presidential ballots violated the Equal Protection Clause.

2000 In *California Democratic Party v. Jones* the Supreme Court declares unconstitutional a state law creating a blanket primary system in California to choose party nominees.

2002 Congress adopts the Bipartisan Campaign Reform Act (BCRA).

2003 In *McConnell v. FEC* the Supreme Court upholds the major provisions of the BCRA.

2006 In *League of United Latin American Citizens v. Perry*, the Supreme Court rules that partisan gerrymandering violates the Constitution, but it is unable to offer a standard to determine when such a gerrymander occurred.

2006 In *Randall v. Sorrell* the Supreme Court declares Vermont's political campaign expenditure limits unconstitutional.

2008 In *Crawford v. Marion County Election Board* the Supreme Court upholds an Indiana voter identification law, rejecting a facial challenge to the law.

2010 In *Citizens United v. Federal Election Commission* the Supreme Court strikes down the Taft-Hartley provision banning corporations and labor unions from making independent expenditures to influence federal elections.

2014 In *McCutcheon v. Federal election Commission* the Supreme Court strikes down as unconstitutional aggregate contribution limits that were initially adopted in 1974.

INTRODUCTION

One of the most basic of the privileges of citizenship is that of participation in free and fair elections. In no other way can our claim to democracy be made effective. Only when the officials of government are reminded periodically that the electorate is ultimately in control can there be assurance of true consideration of the welfare of the whole people.

At the center of making American democracy work are the constitutional provisions regulating the political process. These are rules regarding who can vote in elections, but they encompass more than that. They include provisions regarding the eligibility of those who can run for Congress or the presidency, the Electoral College and the selection of the president, and the grants of authority to Congress and the states to regulate elections. But even more broadly, the field of election law, which has grown dramatically in the last decade or so, also addresses the rights of political parties, the financing of campaigns and elections, reapportionment and the drawing of district lines, and a host of other rules and regulations, all defining how the political process operates.

One might think that the conduct of campaigns and elections is not a matter for the courts to decide. But given that the right to vote and many of these other issues implicate constitutional rights or questions, it is no surprise that the courts eventually intervene. As Alexis de Tocqueville remarked in *Democracy in America*: "There is hardly a political question in the United States which does not sooner or later turn into a judicial one. Consequently the language of everyday party-political controversy has to be borrowed from legal phraseology and conceptions." Thus, the Supreme Court has become a powerful and influential voice in the field of election law and the regulation of the political process. While for many this role is necessary to protect minorities from the tyranny of the majority, others see the courts as venturing into a political thicket (as Justice Frankfurter once stated) and incorrectly influencing the outcome of elections (as some allege the Supreme Court did during the 2000 presidential election).

This chapter examines some of the major decisions that the Supreme Court and other courts have addressed regarding the rights of citizens in the political process. Dominating these efforts are decisions by the judiciary to give effect to the overarching principles and values of the Constitution that seek to respect the principles of majority rule through electoral democracy while at the same time trying to protect the rights of minorities. Questions that the Court has addressed include whether there is a constitutional right to vote, whether that right may be limited, and who is entitled to vote. But the election law cases here also extend to asking questions about the scope of associational rights of political parties, whether money contributed or expended for political purposes is protected speech under the First Amendment, and what rules should be imposed when reapportioning legislative and other districts. Finally, the cases here look at what role partisanship or race can serve in districting, and how votes are to be read when interpreting ballots. Overall, the cases in this chapter cover a wide range of issues governing, in effect, how the American democracy operates.

THE RIGHT TO VOTE

Article I, Sec. 2, cl. 1:

The House of Representatives shall be composed of Members chosen every second Year by the People of the several States . . .

First Amendment:

Congress shall make no law . . . abridging the freedom of speech . . .

Elections are critical to the maintenance of a democracy, and the selection of one's representatives is the hallmark of representative democracy. The chant of "no taxation without representation" at the Boston Tea Party was as much a protest against taxes as it was a demand that the American colonies be allowed to elect and select their own representatives. Given this concern with the alleged abuses by the British government, one would think that the constitutional Framers would have addressed franchise rights.

The Constitution does not explicitly mention the right to vote. Instead, at the time of its writing, franchise rights were determined by the states. In general, state laws limited franchise to white male property owners over the age of 21 who were of a specific religious faith. In some cases, the religious qualification required one to be a Protestant, in others it excluded clergy. The Constitution's apparent silence on voting rights led critics such as historian Charles Beard and former Supreme Court Justice Thurmond Marshall to describe it as originally undemocratic. For Marshall:

> For a sense of the evolving nature of the Constitution we need look no further than the first three words of the document's preamble: "We the People." When the Founding Fathers used this phrase in 1787, they did not have in mind the majority of America's citizens. "We the People" included, in the words of the Framers, "the whole Number of free Persons." On a matter so basic as the right to vote, for example, Negro slaves were excluded, although they were counted for representational purposes at three-fifths each. Women did not gain the right to vote for over a hundred and thirty years.

According to Marshall, it would take "several amendments, a civil war, and momentous social transformation" before the right to vote began even remotely to approximate the promise that "We the People" held out.

Beginning in the 1820s the right to vote began to expand. Property qualifications were dropped and replaced with what was seen as a more democratic and fair poll tax during the Jackson era. The end of the Civil War marked the passage of the Fourteenth and Fifteenth Amendments granting African Americans—at least males—the right to vote. At the same time suffragette activists such as Elizabeth Cady Stanton and Susan B. Anthony advocated that women should have the right to vote. Eventually in 1920 the adoption of the

Nineteenth Amendment did that. Earlier, in 1913, the Seventeenth Amendment gave citizens the right to vote for U.S. senators. Then in 1971, during the height of the Vietnam War, adoption of the Twenty-sixth Amendment lowered the voting age to eighteen in state and federal elections. These constitutional amendments, plus the adoption of the Twenty-fourth Amendment in 1964 banning poll taxes, the Indian Citizenship Bill of 1924 giving Native Americans the right to vote, and the 1965 Voting Rights Act outlawing certain discriminatory voting practices directed against minorities, all further protected voting rights.

But while there is an American tradition marked by an expansion of franchise, Alexander Keyssar notes another one characterized by efforts to deny the right to vote. There are repeated periods in American history during which efforts were made to disenfranchise voters or to scare them away from the polls. For example, after the Civil War many in the South used Jim Crow laws, poll taxes, literacy tests, grandfather laws, and not-so-subtle means such as lynchings, cross burnings, and other techniques to prevent newly freed slaves from voting. The battle for the ballot box has definitely been long and often violent.

Today, while nearly every adult citizen age 18 or older has the right to vote, not everyone exercises this right. In presidential races often only half of those eligible to vote do so, while in some local elections only as few as 5 or 10 percent of the eligible voters participate. Compared to many major European countries, the United States has a low voter turnout, with the profile of the average voter still looking much like someone who could legally vote in 1787, except in the demographic of gender.

While the Constitution and Congress have addressed voting rights, the basic determination of who possesses suffrage is still largely a matter for the states to determine. Constitutional amendments and federal laws have somewhat limited this discretion of the states, but it is still a matter of prime state concern. This is not to say that the federal government is excluded from the field, and over a period of years the Court has been occupied attempting to determine the exact extent to which state power over the entire field of voting has been delimited by these amendments, which, as indicated, basically act as a restriction on certain state suffrage activities while leaving the positive determinations of voting to the states.

Minor v. Happersett (88 U.S. 162, 1874) is the first important case the Supreme Court decided regarding the right to vote. Here a woman sought to challenge a state law preventing her from voting. The Court upheld the state law. In so doing the Court acknowledged that women were citizens but that citizenship, as a form of a privilege or immunity under the Fourteenth Amendment, did not grant them the right to vote. The decision thus set a constitutional pattern for the future, delinking voting and citizenship, ruling that not every citizen has an inherent constitutional right to vote. Instead, voting rights may be limited. The Nineteenth Amendment, which was adopted in 1920, overturned the *Minor v. Happersett* decision.

Nineteenth Amendment:

The right of citizens of the United States to vote shall not be denied or abridged by the United States or by any State on account of sex.

Article I, Sec. 4, cl. 1:

The Times, Places and Manner of holding Elections for Senators and Representatives, shall be prescribed in each State by the Legislature thereof; but the Congress may at any time by Law make or alter such Regulations, except as to the Places of Chusing Senators."

In Article I, Sec. 4, Congress is empowered to determine the times, places, and manner of holding congressional elections. Congress has seen fit to determine only the times and the manner. However, a series of decisions by the Supreme Court from the 1920s to the 1950s called the "white primary cases" tested the right to vote against party autonomy. The issue here was whether primaries and caucuses were elections that could be regulated. The legal arguments over this have had a long and stormy history. In 1921 in *Newberry v. United States* (256 U.S. 232, 1921) the Court held that a party primary was not an election in a constitutional sense and that therefore Congress could not control primaries. Following this the Texas legislature prohibited the participation of African Americans in that state's Democratic Party primaries. In *Nixon v. Herndon* (273 U.S. 536, 1927) the Court held this violative of the Equal Protection Clause of the Fourteenth Amendment. Then the Texas legislature empowered the executive committee of a party to determine qualifications for voting in that party's primary. The Democratic Party committee thereupon restricted participation in its primary to white Democrats. In *Nixon v. Condon* (286 U.S. 73, 1932) the Court voided this as being in effect state action and subject to the Equal Protection Clause.

In a new approach the state convention of the Texas Democratic Party adopted a resolution in 1932 providing that only white citizens qualified to vote should be eligible for membership in the Democratic Party and entitled to take part in its activities and deliberations. This action the Court in *Grovey v. Townsend* (295 U.S. 45, 1935) upheld as legal. The reasoning was that the voluntary action of the state party convention did not involve the state government while determination by the party's executive committee acting under authority of a state statute did involve the state and did therefore invoke constitutional restrictions. A few years later the Supreme Court decided the *United States v. Classic* (313 U.S. 299, 1941) and *Smith v. Allwright* (321 U.S. 649, 1944) cases.

Classic and *Smith* are important cases for several reasons. First, *Classic* for the first time recognizes that the right to vote, at least for members of the House of Representatives, is located in Article I, Sec. 2. Locating a constitutional text to support the right to vote in state elections is more problematic. In *Harper v. Virginia State Board of Elections* (383 U.S. 663, 1966) in striking down the imposition of a poll tax in state elections, the Supreme Court ruled that the right to vote in state elections was located in the First Amendment by way of the Fourteenth Amendment's Due Process and Equal Protection Clauses.

Second, both *Classic* and *Smith* argued that whatever associational rights political parties may have, they did not extend to discriminating against African Americans. The issue of party rights versus the rights of individuals to participate is examined in this chapter in the discussion of party rights.

Fourteenth Amendment, Sec. 1:

No State shall . . . deny to any person within its jurisdiction the equal protection of the laws."

Twenty-fourth Amendment, Sec. 1:

The right of citizens of the United States to vote in any primary or other election for President or Vice President, for electors for President or Vice President, or for Senator or Representative in Congress, shall not be denied or abridged by the United States or any State by reason of failure to pay any poll tax or other tax.

In *Harper v. Virginia Board of Elections* the Court ruled that the right to vote in state elections is located in the First Amendment. In doing so the justices ruled that a fee that had to be paid in order to vote—a poll tax—was unconstitutional. Subsequently, with the adoption of the Twenty-fourth Amendment, poll taxes are now unconstitutional. However, what does the ban on poll taxes include? Would it extend to costs associated with registering to vote, such as obtaining photo identification? This is the question addressed in *Crawford v. Marion County Election Board* (553 U.S. 181, 2008) where the Court ruled that a state law requiring the production of government-issued photo identification when voting in person did not violate the constitutional right to vote. Effectively, the costs associated with securing this identification did not constitute a poll tax.

If *Happersett* delinked voting from citizenship, should voting be limited to United States citizens? In some places, such as New York City, resident aliens have been allowed to vote in local elections. Aliens are required to pay taxes, may serve in the military, and are subject to all the laws that citizens are. Lacking the right to vote, they appear to be a classic discrete and insular minority subject to persecution by the tyranny of the majority. Should the Constitution guarantee them the right to vote? While the Supreme Court has not addressed this issue, at least one lower court has. In *Skafte v. Rorex* (553 P.2d 830, 191 Colo. 399, 1976) the Colorado Supreme Court rejected claims that denying noncitizens the right to vote violated the Constitution. In effect, the Constitution did not grant or protect the right of noncitizens to vote.

After the Civil War newly enfranchised African Americans were given the right to vote. They elected members to Congress and state legislatures, but the end of Reconstruction brought in a wave of Jim Crow laws meant to discourage them from voting. Some techniques were violent, such as lynchings and cross-burnings by groups like the Ku Klux Klan, whereas others were more subtle in nature. Grandfather laws denied one the right to vote unless one's grandfather could have voted, felon disenfranchisement laws prevent those convicted of crimes from voting, poll taxes imposed fees, and literacy tests were used to ostensibly fulfill the goal of ensuring that only those who could read and write and who knew something about the political process did in fact vote. All of these tests were used primarily against African Americans. In *Lassiter v. Northampton County Board of Elections*, (360 U.S. 45, 1959) the Court upheld the use of literacy tests in North Carolina, contending that the state had an interest in ensuring that citizens were educated and knowledgeable about the issues. Moreover, note how the Court upheld use of the literacy test even while the state exempted those who could vote before 1867, or their descendants, from having to take it. This reference is to an obvious grandfather's clause.

The Court did not strike down the use of a literacy test even though its adoption was part of the Jim Crow laws adopted by North Carolina. The Court seems to have an important interest in a state wishing to ensure its citizens are literate when voting. Do you agree? Should a voter be required to read and write as a condition of voting? Speak English? Know some basic facts about American government? If yes, what should voters know?

The literacy test shown here is one used in the South in the 1950s. The test was administered mostly to African Americans, who had to score 100 percent correct to be entitled to register to vote. Do you think knowledge of these constitutional facts is necessary to being an informed voter? Do you think an individual who could not read or write could still make a meaningful electoral choice?

Alabama Literacy Test (circa 1950s)

1. A person appointed to the U.S. Supreme Court is appointed for a term of __________.
2. If a person is indicted for a crime, name two rights which that person has.
3. Cases tried before a court of law are of what two types?
4. If no candidate for president receives a majority of the electoral vote, who decides who will become president?
5. If no candidate for vice president receives a majority of the electoral vote, the vice president is selected by the Senate. True or false?
6. If an effort to impeach the president of the United States is made, who presides at the trial?
7. If the two houses of Congress cannot decide on adjournment, who sets the time?
8. A president elected in November takes office the following year on what date?
9. Of the original 13 states, the one with the largest representation in Congress was:
10. The Constitution limits the size of the District of Columbia to:

Many states take away the right to vote when a person is convicted of a crime. This right is not restored until one has completed a sentence. In some cases, restoration of voting rights is not automatic, and in other situations, such as in Florida, conviction of a felony results in a lifetime loss of voting rights. Does the Constitution prevent ex-felons from being denied the right to vote? Despite subsequent efforts to challenge felon disenfranchisement laws, the ***Richardson v. Ramirez*** (418 U.S. 24, 1974) ruling is still precedent, and it allows states to take away the right to vote temporarily or even permanently. In the last few years some states have loosened their disenfranchisement laws, but many millions of individuals, mostly members of racial minorities, have temporarily or permanently lost their right to vote.

Fourteenth Amendment, Sec. 2:

But when the right to vote at any election for the choice of electors for President and Vice-President of the United States, Representatives in Congress, the Executive and Judicial officers of a State, or the members of the Legislature thereof, is denied to any of the male inhabitants of such State, being twenty-one years of age, and citizens of the United States, or in any way abridged, except for participation in rebellion, or other crime, the basis of representation therein shall be reduced in the proportion which the number of such male citizens shall bear to the whole number of male citizens twenty-one years of age in such State.

If one is old enough to be drafted and die in Vietnam, shouldn't one be allowed to vote? That logic was compelling enough to move Congress by statute to lower the voting age from 21 to 18 in national and state elections. Its authority to do that was tested in *Oregon v. Mitchell* (400 U.S. 112, 1970). Here the Court found that while the federal government could lower the voting age in federal elections, it could not do so in state elections. The decision portended the prospect of two different voting ages for state versus federal elections. The Twenty-sixth Amendment partially overturned the *Mitchell* case, extending the right to vote to eighteen-year-olds in national and state elections.

The legacy of *Classic*, *Reynolds*, and *Harper* is that these three cases stand for the proposition that voting is a fundamental right that must be subject to strict scrutiny. Collectively, these cases would seem to suggest that interference with, or regulation of the fundamental right to vote must be subject to strict scrutiny, and that only if a compelling governmental interest is asserted that overwrites it may it be limited. But note how the language of the Fifteenth, Nineteenth, and Twenty-sixth Amendments does not actually guarantee the right to vote. Instead, it merely states that the right to vote may not be denied on account of race, gender, and age. Given this phrasing, do these amendments affirmatively protect franchise rights, or is such a right conditional, as is the choice to given aliens the right to vote? In many ways, the right to vote in the United States appears very qualified. However, the Court itself has created some confusion about this point, as demonstrated in *Burdick v. Takushi* (504 U.S. 428, 1992) where it upheld a state law banning citizens from naming write-in candidates during a general election. The Court here created a two-tier test: Regulations that imposed a severe burden on voting rights would be subject to strict scrutiny, whereas other, more routine regulations of voting, those that are perhaps more administrative, would be examined from a more rational basis or balancing of interests test.

It was this latter test that was used in *Crawford v. Marion County Election Board,* 553 U.S. 181 (2008), to uphold photo identification laws. Perhaps no issue has been more controversial in American politics and election law than the subject of voter fraud. After the disputed 2000 presidential election where there were questions about the fairness and accuracy of the voting laws in Florida, a partisan divide emerged where many came to believe that in-person voter fraud was a significant issue affecting the outcome of elections. As a result, many states adopted laws mandating some type of voter photo identification to be able to vote in person. These laws were often adopted, as in the case of Indiana, even though there were no proven cases of such type of fraud in that state. Despite the lack of evidence of in-person voter in personification or fraud and claims that such a law could potentially disenfranchise the poor, students, the elderly, and racial minorities, the Supreme Court in *Crawford* upheld the law. The challenge to the Indiana law as a **facial challenge**. A facial challenge is one where the constitutionality of a law is challenged, claiming that no matter the law is enforced it is unconstitutional. This is in contrast to suit known as an **applied challenge**, arguing that the law as applied or enforced is unconstitutional. In *Crawford* the Court rejected the claim that the voter ID was facially invalid, but it held out in a footnote that future challenges to such laws could be brought as applied if one could show the ID requirements were burdensome, especially to specific groups, such as people of color.

An intense political and legal battle across the country has been waged since the 2008 *Crawford* decision between Republicans who generally support voter ID laws and Democrats who oppose them. Leading up the to 2016 presidential election several federal courts struck down voter ID laws and other voting barriers in states such as Texas, North Carolina, Wisconsin, and North Dakota. State courts, such as in Missouri in *Weinschenk v. State*, 203 S.W.3d 201 (Mo. 2006), used its own state constitution to invalidate a voter ID requirement. These voter ID requirements continue to be controversial, including questions to whether they constitute a form of voter suppression or a legitimate means to ensure fair elections.

The constitutional right to vote also implicates another set of issues. The first is protection or enforcement of that right, the second issue is ensuring that only those who are eligible do in fact vote. As noted earlier, prior to the end of the civil War and the passage of the Fifteenth Amendment African-Americans could note vote. The Fifteenth Amendment, as part of Reconstruction, gave freed (males) slaves the rights to vote. Females would have to wait for the Nineteenth Amendment in 1920 to secure this right. During Reconstruction federal enforcement of voting rights lead to a significant rise in the number of African-Americans voting and serving in office across the south. But with the end of Reconstruction in 1877 (as part of a deal to settle the disputed 1876 presidential election where Democrats ceded the presidency to the Republican Rutherford Hayes in return for a withdrawal of federal troops in the South) the Jim Crow era began and Blacks effectively were disenfranchised across the South, and often across other parts of the country.

The Civil rights movement of the 1950s led by individuals such as Martin Luther King, Jr. crossed many dimensions to address many grievances, but central to his campaign was the push for a real and effective right to vote. The culmination of that battle was the 1965 Voting Rights Act (VRA), subsequently reauthorized several times in 1970, 1975, 1982, and 2006. In brief, the purpose of the VRA was to outlaw and prevent discriminatory voting practices by prohibiting certain states or covered jurisdictions from diluting the right to vote (Section 2 of the VRA) and to require some jurisdictions to preclear any changes they wished to make that affected voting (Section 5). As Chief Justice Earl Warren declared in *Allen v. State Board of Elections*, 393 U.S. 544 (1969): "The Voting Rights Act was aimed at the subtle, as well as the obvious, state regulations which have the effect of denying citizens their right to vote because of their race." The VRA recognized, as the Court had declared earlier in *United States* v. *Mosley*, 238 U.S. 383, 386 (1915): "We regard it as equally unquestionable that the right to have one's vote counted is as open to protection by Congress as the right to put a ballot in a box."

The VRA is a complex piece of legislation that has been adjudicated several times. It would take an entirely separate book to cover the history of the case law surrounding the law. Its overall constitutionality was upheld in *Katzenbach v. Morgan*, 384 U.S. 641 (1966). The central features, as noted above, are Sections 2 and 5. In particular Section 5, as noted above, required some political jurisdictions to preclear with the Attorney General any changes they wished to make with their voting procedures. The specific jurisdictions subject to preclearance were determined by Section 4, which outlined, based on Congressional hearings back when the original VRA was adopted in 1965, discriminatory voting criteria that would force preclearance. Roughly speaking, the Section 4 criteria included many of the states, counties, or jurisdictions in the former Confederacy of the South.

The VRA had had a dramatic impact on increasing voting among people of color, and in electing minority officials. Chandler Davidson's *Quiet Revolution in the South: The Impact of the Voting Rights Act, 1965–1990* and Charles S. Bullock, III, Ronald Keith Gaddie, and Justin J. Wert, *The Rise and Fall of the Voting Rights Act* offer excellent accounts of its impact. Some point to the election of Barack Obama as proof that the VRA was a success, and that it was no longer needed. By the second decade of the twenty-first century critics grew louder in arguing that the law was not only outdated but perhaps even unconstitutional in its singling out some jurisdictions for preclearance.

In *Shelby County, Alabama v. Holder*, 570 U.S ___ (2013), Shelby County was covered by the Voting Rights Act and it was required to seek preclearance from the Justice Department or the D.C. District Court to prove that any changes to its voting laws were not discriminatory. Shelby County challenged as unconstitutional the coverage formula under the VRA which determined which jurisdictions were required to preclear. Shelby County argued that Congress's Fifteenth Amendment enforcement powers, under which the VRA was passed, is outweighed by a state's rights under the Tenth Amendment. Congress, in reauthorizing the VRA in 2007, used outdated data to support Section 5 and therefore the pre-clearance requirements are disproportionate to the authority the federal government has to enforce this act. The Supreme Court by a 5–4 majority declared that the coverage formula of Section 4 unconstitutional, thereby effectively voiding Section 5 pre-clearance. The Court ruled that Section 5 limits on state sovereignty could not be justified by voting data and evidence that was outdated. Pre-clearance could only be justified based upon current or present voting statistics, and the Court contended that voter registration and voting patterns no longer demonstrated that there was a "blight of racial discrimination in voting" across the South that needed to be prevented or addressed by pre-clearance. The majority decision overlooked, as the dissent argued, the hundreds of voting changes that the Justice Department refused to pre-clear, and it also ignored how the threat of pre-clearance had deterred other forms of racial discrimination when it came to voting.

Shelby County's critics argued that the decision undermined a powerful tool to protect voting rights. The VRA had been used to challenge voter identification provisions in Texas, and some have argued that it has freed up other states to pass discriminatory laws that hurt voting rights. Republicans and Democrats in Congress have been stalemated in their ability to amend the VRA in light of *Shelby County*, and how the voiding of Section 4 (and effectively Section 5) will impact minority voting rights in the future is a subject of major partisan contention.

Another issue that crosses voting rights and federalism is in respect to ensuring that only U.S. citizens vote. As the 2012 and 2016 presidential elections revealed, the issue of immigration is also a hotly contested partisan issue. Generally, Democrats want to pass immigration reform to make it easier for individuals to enter the country, and there is also support to make it easier for those already in the country without proper documentation to remain in the United States. The impasse over immigration reform led President Obama in 2015 to issue an executive order that would allow many of these individuals to remain legally in the country. But as discussed in chapter IV, the federal courts enjoined the president from acting.

But even before the 2012 and 2016 presidential elections there was criticism by many that the federal government was not doing enough to address illegal immigration into the United States. While Article I, Section 8 of the Constitution textually commits to Congress the authority to establish rules regulating naturalization, some states, in particular Arizona, have contended that they should be able to act to address this issue too. While this general debate on federalism and immigration is discussed more fully in chapter twi, one aspect of that issue addresses voting rights. Specifically, may a state require proof of citizenship when individuals are registering to vote in federal elections. This was the issue raised in *Arizona v. Inter Tribal Council of Arizona, Inc.*, 570 U.S. ___, 133 S.Ct. 2247 (2013). Here the Supreme Court struck down a state law which required proof of citizenship. The Court invoked in part Article I, Section 4 of the Constitution, granting Congress the power to displace state regulation of the time, manner, and place of federal elections. The decision did not preempt the ability of states perhaps to require proof of citizenship for its own elections and certainly the decision did not ultimately resolve the debate either on immigration, voter fraud, or the enforcement of voting rights.

By the time one finishes the right-to-vote cases one should ask how fundamental that right is? Given how the Constitution is phrased, the Court's opinions, and the fact that half of Americans do not vote, what does it say about this right and under what circumstances it can be limited?

MINOR V. HAPPERSETT

88 U.S. 162, 22 L.Ed. 627 (1875)

Virginia Minor challenged a Missouri state law that limited the right to vote to males. Minor sought to register to vote but was denied because of her gender. She challenged the law as a violation under the Fourteenth Amendment.

Vote: Unanimous

CHIEF JUSTICE WAITE delivered the opinion of the Court.

The question is presented in this case, whether, since the adoption of the fourteenth amendment, a woman, who is a citizen of the United States and of the State of Missouri, is a voter in that State, notwithstanding the provision of the constitution and laws of the State, which confine the right of suffrage to men alone. We might, perhaps, decide the case upon other grounds, but this question is fairly made. From the opinion we find that it was the only one decided in the court below, and it is the only one which has been argued here. The case was undoubtedly brought to this court for the sole purpose of having that question decided by us, and in view of the evident propriety there is of having it settled, so far as it can be by such a decision, we have concluded to waive all other considerations and proceed at once to its determination.

It is contended that the provisions of the constitution and laws of the State of Missouri which confine the right of suffrage and registration therefor to men, are in violation of the Constitution of the United States, and therefore void. The argument is, that as a woman, born or naturalized in the United States and subject to the jurisdiction thereof, is a citizen of the United States and of the State in which she resides, she has the right of suffrage as one of the privileges and immunities of her citizenship, which the State cannot by its laws or constitution abridge.

There is no doubt that women may be citizens. They are persons, and by the fourteenth amendment "all persons born or naturalized in the United States and subject to the jurisdiction thereof" are expressly declared to be "citizens of the United States and of the State wherein they reside." But, in our opinion, it did not need this amendment to give them that position. Before its adoption the Constitution of the United States did not in terms prescribe who should be citizens of the United States or of the several States, yet there were necessarily such citizens without such provision. There cannot be a nation without a people. The very idea of a political community, such as a nation is, implies an association of persons for the promotion of their general welfare. Each one of the persons associated becomes a member of the nation formed by the association. He owes it allegiance and is entitled to its protection. Allegiance and protection are, in this connection, reciprocal obligations. The one is a compensation for the other; allegiance for protection and protection for allegiance.

But if more is necessary to show that women have always been considered as citizens the same as men, abundant proof is to be found in the legislative and judicial history of the country. Thus, by the Constitution, the judicial power of the United States is made to extend to controversies between citizens of different States. Under this it has been uniformly held that the citizenship necessary to give the courts of the United States jurisdiction of a cause must be affirmatively shown on the record. Its existence as a fact may be put in issue and tried. If found not to exist the case must be dismissed.

Notwithstanding this the records of the courts are full of cases in which the jurisdiction depends upon the citizenship of women, and not one can be found, we think, in which objection was made on that account. Certainly none can be found in which it has been held that women could not sue or be sued in the courts of the United States. Again, at the time of the adoption of the Constitution, in many of the States (and in some probably now) aliens could not inherit or transmit inheritance. There are a multitude of cases to be found in which the question has been presented whether a woman was or was not an alien, and as such capable or incapable of inheritance, but in no one has it been insisted that she was not a citizen because she was a woman. On the contrary, her right to citizenship has been in all cases assumed. The only question has been whether, in the particular case under consideration, she had availed herself of the right.

In the legislative department of the government similar proof will be found. Thus, in the pre-emption laws, a widow, "being a citizen of the United States," is allowed to make settlement on the public lands and purchase upon the terms specified, and women, "being citizens of the United States." are permitted to avail themselves of the benefit of the homestead law.

If the right of suffrage is one of the necessary privileges of a citizen of the United States, then the constitution and laws of Missouri confining it to men are in violation of the Constitution of the United States, as amended, and consequently void. The direct question is, therefore, presented whether all citizens are necessarily voters.

The Constitution does not define the privileges and immunities of citizens. For that definition we must look elsewhere. In this case we need not determine what they are, but only whether suffrage is necessarily one of them.

It certainly is nowhere made so in express terms. The United States has no voters in the States of its own creation. The elective officers of the United States are all elected directly or indirectly by State voters. The members of the House of Representatives are to be chosen by the people of the States, and the electors in each State must have the qualifications requisite for electors of the most numerous branch of the State legislature. Senators are to be chosen by the legislatures of the States, and necessarily the members of the legislature required to make the choice are elected by the voters of the State. Each State must appoint in such manner, as the legislature thereof may direct, the electors to elect the President and Vice-President. The times, places, and manner of holding elections for Senators and Representatives are to be prescribed in each State by the legislature thereof; but Congress may at any time, by law, make or alter such regulations, except as to the place of choosing Senators. It is not necessary to inquire whether this power of supervision thus given to Congress is sufficient to authorize any interference with the State laws prescribing the qualifications of voters, for no such interference has ever been attempted. The power of the State in this particular is certainly supreme until Congress acts.

The amendment did not add to the privileges and immunities of a citizen. It simply furnished an additional guaranty for the protection of such as he already had. No new voters were necessarily made by it. Indirectly it may have had that effect, because it may have increased the number of citizens entitled to suffrage under the constitution and laws of the States, but it operates for this purpose, if at all, through the States and the State laws, and not directly upon the citizen.

It is clear, therefore, we think, that the Constitution has not added the right of suffrage to the privileges and immunities of citizenship as they existed at the time it was adopted. This makes it proper to inquire whether suffrage was coextensive with the citizenship of the States at the time of its adoption. If it was, then it may with force be argued that suffrage was one of the rights which belonged to citizenship, and in the enjoyment of which every citizen must be protected. But if it was not, the contrary may with propriety be assumed.

Being unanimously of the opinion that the Constitution of the United States does not confer the right of suffrage upon any one, and that the constitutions and laws of the several States which commit that important trust to men alone are not necessarily void, we

AFFIRM THE JUDGMENT.

FOR DISCUSSION

Should voting be considered a right of citizenship? Should all citizens over a certain age automatically be granted the right to vote? What restrictions, if any, do you think should be placed on the right to vote?

UNITED STATES V. CLASSIC

313 U.S. 299, 61 S.Ct. 1031, 85 L.Ed. 1368 (1941)

As in many states, Louisiana statutes provided for a primary election, at public expense, to nominate candidates for representatives in Congress. In such a primary, Classic and other commissioners of elections willfully altered and falsely counted and certified the ballots of voters cast in the primary election. They were convicted of violation of the Federal Criminal Code, which prohibits attempts to deprive citizens of their rights or privileges under the Constitution or laws of the United States. The Court had before it the question whether voting in such a primary and having one's vote counted is a constitutional right under the Criminal Code.

Vote: 5–3

JUSTICE STONE delivered the opinion of the Court.

The primary in Louisiana is an integral part of the procedure for the popular choice of Congressman. The right of qualified voters to vote at the congressional primary in Louisiana and to have their ballots counted is thus the right to participate in that choice.

We come then to the question whether that right is one secured by the Constitution. Section 2 of Article One commands that Congressmen shall be chosen by the people of the several states by electors, the qualifications of which it prescribes. The right of the people to choose, whatever its appropriate constitutional limitations, where in other respects it is defined, and the mode of its exercise is prescribed by state action in conformity to the Constitution, is a right established and guaranteed by the Constitution and hence is one secured by it to those citizens and inhabitants of the state entitled to exercise the right. . . . While, in a loose sense, the right to vote for representatives in Congress is sometimes spoken of as a right derived from the states, . . . this statement is true only in the sense that the states are authorized by the Constitution, to legislate on the subject as provided by Section 2 of Article One, to the extent that Congress has not restricted state action by the exercise of its powers to regulate elections under Section 4 and its more general power under Article One, Section 8, Clause 18 of the Constitution "to make all laws which shall be necessary and proper for carrying into execution the foregoing powers." . . .

Obviously included within the right to choose, secured by the Constitution, is the right of qualified voters within a state to cast their ballots and have them counted at congressional elections. This Court has consistently held that this is a right secured by the Constitution. . . . And since the constitutional command is without restriction or limitation, the right, unlike those guaranteed by the Fourteenth and Fifteenth Amendments, is secured against the action of individuals as well as of states.

But we are now concerned with the question whether the right to choose at a primary election, a candidate for election as representative, is embraced in the right to choose representatives secured by Article One, Section 2. We may assume that the framers of the Constitution in adopting that section, did not have specifically in mind the selection and elimination of candidates for Congress by the direct primary any more than they contemplated the application of the commerce clause to interstate telephone, telegraph and wireless communication which are concededly within it. But in determining whether a provision of the Constitution applies to a new subject matter, it is of little significance that it is one with which the framers were not familiar. For in setting up an enduring framework of government they undertook to carry out for the indefinite future and in all the vicissitudes of the changing affairs of men, those fundamental purposes which the instrument itself discloses. Hence we read its words, not as we read legislative codes which are subject to continuous revision with the changing course of events, but as the revelation of the great purposes which were intended to be achieved by the Constitution as a continuing instrument of government. . . . If we remember that "it is a Constitution we are expounding," we cannot rightly prefer, of the possible meanings of its words, that which will defeat rather than effectuate the constitutional purpose.

That the free choice by the people of representatives in Congress, subject only to the restrictions to be found in Sections 2 and 4 of Article One and elsewhere in the Constitution, was one of the great purposes of our constitutional scheme of government cannot be doubted. We cannot regard it as any the less the constitutional purpose or its words as any the less guaranteeing the integrity of that choice when a state, exercising its privilege in the absence of congressional action, changes the mode of choice from a single step, a general election, to two, of which the first is the choice at a primary of those candidates from whom, as a second step, the representative in Congress is to be chosen at the election.

Nor can we say that that choice which the Constitution protects is restricted to the second step because Section 4 of Article One, as a means of securing a free choice of representatives by the people, has authorized Congress to regulate the manner of elections, without making any mention of primary elections. For we think that the authority of Congress, given by Section 4, includes the authority to regulate primary elections when, as in this case, they are a step in the exercise by the people of their choice of representatives in Congress. . . .

The right to participate in the choice of representatives for Congress includes, as we have said, the right to cast a ballot and to have it counted at the general election whether for the successful candidate or not. Where the state law has made the primary an integral part of the procedure of choice, or where in fact the primary effectively controls the choice, the right of the elector to have his ballot counted at the primary, is likewise included in the right protected by Article One, Section 2.

If a right secured by the Constitution may be infringed by the corrupt failure to include the vote at a primary in the official count, it is not significant that the primary, like the voting machine, was unknown when Section 19 was adopted. Abuse of either may infringe the right and therefore violate Section 19.

The right of the voters at the primary to have their votes counted is, as we have stated, a right or privilege secured by the Constitution, and to this Section 20 also gives protection. The alleged acts of appellees were committed in the course of their performance of duties under the Louisiana statute requiring them to count the ballots, to record the result of the count, and to certify the result of the election. Misuse of power, possessed by virtue of state law, is action taken "under color of" state law.

Here the acts of appellees infringed the constitutional right and deprived the voters of the benefit of it within the meaning of Section 20.

Reversed.

CHIEF JUSTICE HUGHES took no part in the hearing or decision of this case. JUSTICE DOUGLAS dissented, with the concurrence of JUSTICES BLACK and MURPHY.

I agree with most of the views expressed in the opinion of the Court. And it is with diffidence that I dissent from the result there reached.

The disagreement centers on the meaning of § 19 of the Criminal Code, which protects every right secured by the Constitution. The right to vote at a final Congressional election and the right to have one's vote counted in such an election have been held to be protected by § 19. . . . Yet I do not think that the principles of those cases should be, or properly can be, extended to primary elections. To sustain this indictment we must so extend them. But when we do, we enter perilous territory.

We should ever be mindful that "before a man can be punished, his case must be plainly and unmistakably within the statute." *United States v. Lacher*, 134 U.S. 624, 628, 1890. That admonition is reemphasized here by the fact that § 19 imposes not only a fine of $5,000 and ten years in prison, but also makes him who is convicted "ineligible to any office, or place of honor, profit or trust created by the Constitution or laws of the United States." It is not enough for us to find in the vague penumbra of a statute some offense about which Congress could have legislated, and then to particularize it as a crime because it is highly offensive. . . . Civil liberties are too dear to permit conviction for crimes which are only implied and which can be spelled out only by adding inference to inference.

Section 19 does not purport to be an exercise by Congress of its power to regulate primaries. It merely penalizes conspiracies "to injure, oppress, threaten, or intimidate any citizen in the free exercise or enjoyment of any right or privilege secured to him by the Constitution or laws of the United States." Thus, it does no more than refer us to the Constitution for the purpose of determining whether or not the right to vote in a primary is secured. Hence we must do more than find in the Constitution the power of Congress to afford that protection. We must find that protection on the face of the Constitution itself.

Article One, § 4 specifies the machinery whereby the times, places and manner of holding elections shall be established and controlled. Article One, § 2 provides that representatives shall be "chosen" by the people. But for purposes of the criminal law as contrasted to the interpretation of the Constitution as the source of the implied power of Congress, I do not think that those provisions in absence of specific legislation by Congress protect the primary election or the nominating convention. While they protected the right to vote, and the right to have one's vote counted, at the final election, as held in the Yarbrough and Mosley cases, they certainly do not per se extend to all acts which in their indirect or incidental effect restrain, restrict, or interfere with that choice.

FOR DISCUSSION

Where exactly does the Constitution guarantee the right to vote according to the Court in *Classic*? How broad is this right? Is it a right to vote in both federal and state elections? What offices does it include?

SMITH V. ALLWRIGHT

321 U.S. 649, 64 S.Ct. 757, 88 L.Ed. 987 (1944)

Dr. Lonnie Smith was an African-American citizen in Harris County (Houston), Texas. He sought to vote in the Democratic Party primary and election officials refused to give him a ballot because of his race. During the 1930s and 1940s Texas was essentially a one party state, with the Democratic primary effectively determining who would win the general election. Smith challenged the decision not to give him a ballot, claiming that it violated his right to vote under the Fourteenth, Fifteenth, and Seventeenth Amendments.

Vote: 8–1

JUSTICE REED delivered the opinion of the Court.

This writ of certiorari brings here for review a claim for damages in the sum of $5,000 on the part of petitioner, a Negro citizen of the 48th precinct of Harris County, Texas, for the refusal of respondents, election and associate election judges, respectively, of that precinct, to give petitioner a ballot or to permit him to cast a ballot in the primary election of July 27, 1940, for the nomination of Democratic candidates for the United States Senate and House of Representatives, and Governor and other state officers. The refusal is alleged to have been solely because of the race and color of the proposed voter.

The actions of respondents are said to violate §§ 31 and 43 of Title 8 of the United States Code, 8 U.S.C. §§ 31 and 43, in that petitioner was deprived of rights secured by §§ 2 and 4 of Article I and the Fourteenth, Fifteenth and Seventeenth Amendments to the United States Constitution. The suit was filed in the District Court of the United States for the Southern District of Texas, which had jurisdiction under Judicial Code § 24, subsection 14.

The District Court denied the relief sought, and the Circuit Court of Appeals quite properly affirmed its action on the authority of *Grovey v. Townsend*, 295 US 45 (1935). We granted the petition for certiorari to resolve a claimed inconsistency between the decision in the *Grovey* case and that of *United States v. Classic,* 313 U.S. 299 (1941).

The State of Texas by its Constitution and statutes provides that every person, if certain other requirements are met which are not here in issue, qualified by residence in the district or county "shall be deemed a qualified elector." Primary elections for United States Senators, Congressmen and state officers are provided for by Chapters Twelve and Thirteen of the statutes. Under these chapters, the Democratic Party was required to hold the primary which was the occasion of the alleged wrong to petitioner. These nominations are to be made by the qualified voters of the party.

The Democratic Party of Texas is held by the Supreme Court of that state to be a "voluntary association," *Bell v. Hill,* 123 Tex. 531, 534, protected by § 27 of the Bill of Rights, Art. 1, Constitution of Texas, from interference by the state except that:

In the interest of fair methods and a fair expression by their members of their preferences in the selection of their nominees, the State may regulate such elections by proper laws.

That court stated further:

> Since the right to organize and maintain a political party is one guaranteed by the Bill of Rights of this state, it necessarily follows that every privilege essential or reasonably appropriate to the exercise of that right is likewise guaranteed, including, of course, the privilege of determining the policies of the party and its membership. Without the privilege of determining the policy of a political association and its membership, the right to organize such an association would be a mere mockery. We think these rights, that is, the right to determine the membership of a political party and to determine its policies, of necessity are to be exercised by the State Convention of such party, and cannot, under any circumstances, be conferred upon a state or governmental agency.

The Democratic Party, on May 24, 1932, in a state convention adopted the following resolution, which has not since been "amended, abrogated, annulled or avoided":

> Be it resolved that all white citizens of the State of Texas who are qualified to vote under the Constitution and laws of the State shall be eligible to membership in the Democratic Party and, as such, entitled to participate in its deliberations.

It was by virtue of this resolution that the respondents refused to permit the petitioner to vote.

Texas is free to conduct her elections and limit her electorate as she may deem wise, save only as her action may be affected by the prohibitions of the United States Constitution or in conflict with powers delegated to and exercised by the National Government. The Fourteenth Amendment forbids a state from making or enforcing any law which abridges the privileges or immunities of citizens of the United States and the Fifteenth Amendment specifically interdicts any denial or abridgement by a state of the right of citizens to vote on account of color. Respondents appeared in the District Court and the Circuit Court of Appeals and defended on the ground that the Democratic party of Texas is a voluntary organization, with members banded together for the purpose of selecting individuals of the group representing the common political beliefs as candidates in the general election. As such a voluntary organization, it was claimed, the Democratic Party is free to select its own membership and limit to whites participation in the party primary. Such action, the answer asserted, does not violate the Fourteenth, Fifteenth or Seventeenth Amendment, as officers of government cannot be chosen at primaries, and the Amendments are applicable only to general elections, where governmental officers are actually elected. Primaries, it is said, are political party affairs, handled by party, not governmental, officers. No appearance for respondents is made in this Court. Arguments presented here by the Attorney General of Texas and the Chairman of the State Democratic Executive Committee of Texas, as *amici curiae,* urged substantially the same grounds as those advanced by the respondents.

The right of a Negro to vote in the Texas primary has been considered heretofore by this Court. The first case was *Nixon v. Herndon,* 273 U.S. 536 (1927). At that time, 1924, the Texas statute declared "in no event shall a Negro be eligible to participate in a Democratic party primary election . . . in the State of Texas." Nixon was refused the right to vote in a Democratic primary, and brought a suit for damages against the election officers. It was urged to this Court that the denial of the franchise the Nixon violated his Constitutional rights under the Fourteenth and Fifteenth Amendments. Without consideration of the Fifteenth, this Court held that the action of Texas in denying the ballot to Negroes by statute was in violation of the equal protection clause of the Fourteenth Amendment, and reversed the dismissal of the suit.

The legislature of Texas reenacted the article, but gave the State Executive Committee of a party the power to prescribe the qualifications of its members for voting or other participation. This article remains in the statutes. The State Executive Committee of the Democratic party adopted a resolution that white Democrats and none other might participate in the primaries of that party. Nixon was refused again the privilege of voting in a primary, and again brought suit for damages. This Court again reversed the dismissal of the suit for the reason that the Committee action was deemed to be State action, and invalid as discriminatory under the Fourteenth Amendment. The test was said to be whether the Committee operated as representative of the State in the discharge of the State's authority. *Nixon v. Condon,* 286 U.S. 73 (1932). The question of the inherent power of a political party in Texas "without restraint by any law to determine its own membership" was left open.

The statutes of Texas relating to primaries and the resolution of the Democratic party of Texas extending the privileges of membership to white citizens only are the same in substance and effect today as they were when *Grovey v. Townsend* was decided by a unanimous Court. The question as to whether the exclusionary action of the party was the action of the State persists as the determinative factor. In again entering upon consideration of the inference to be drawn as to state action from a substantially similar factual situation, it should be noted that *Grovey v. Townsend* upheld exclusion of Negroes from primaries through the denial of party membership by a party convention. A few years before, this Court refused approval of exclusion by the State Executive Committee of the party. A different result was reached on the theory that the Committee action was state authorized, and the Convention action was unfettered by statutory control. Such a variation in the result from so slight a change in form influences us to consider anew the legal validity of the distinction which has resulted in barring Negroes from participating in the nominations of candidates of the Democratic party in Texas. Other precedents of this Court forbid the abridgement of the right to vote. *United States v. Reese*, 92 US 214 (1876); *Neal v. Delaware*, 103 US 370 (1880); *Guinn v. United States*, 238 U.S. 347 (1915); *Myers v. Anderson*, 238 US 368 (1915); *Lane v. Wilson*, 307 US 268 (1939).

It may now be taken as a postulate that the right to vote in such a primary for the nomination of candidates without discrimination by the State, like the right to vote in a general election, is a right secured by the Constitution. *United States v. Classic*; *Myers v. Anderson*; *Ex parte Yarbrough*, 110 US 651 (1884). By the terms of the Fifteenth Amendment, that right may not be abridged by any state on account of race. Under our Constitution, the great privilege of the ballot may not be denied a man by the State because of his color.

We think that this statutory system for the selection of party nominees for inclusion on the general election ballot makes the party which is required to follow these legislative directions an agency of the state in so far as it determines the participants in a primary election. The party takes its character as a state agency from the duties imposed upon it by state statutes; the duties do not become matters of private law because they are performed by a political party. The plan of the Texas primary follows substantially that of Louisiana, with the exception that, in Louisiana, the state pays the cost of the primary, while Texas assesses the cost against candidates. In numerous instances, the Texas statutes fix or limit the fees to be charged. Whether paid directly by the state or through state requirements, it is state action which compels. When primaries become a part of the machinery for choosing officials, state and national, as they have here, the same tests to determine the character of discrimination or abridgement should be applied to the primary as are applied to the general election. If the state requires a certain electoral procedure, prescribes a general election ballot made up of party nominees so chosen and limits the choice of the electorate in general elections for state offices, practically speaking, to those whose names appear on such a ballot, it endorses, adopts and enforces the discrimination against Negroes, practiced by a party entrusted by Texas law with the determination of the qualifications of participants in the primary. This is state action within the meaning of the Fifteenth Amendment. *Guinn v. United States.*

The United States is a constitutional democracy. Its organic law grants to all citizens a right to participate in the choice of elected officials without restriction by any state because of race. This grant to the people of the opportunity for choice is not to be nullified by a state through casting its electoral process in a form which permits a private organization to practice racial discrimination in the election. Constitutional rights would be of little value if they could be thus indirectly denied. *Lane v. Wilson.*

FOR DISCUSSION

According to the Court, when does a political party become subject to the Constitution? Are parties private associations, or are they state actors? Today, could a political party refuse to admit individuals based on their gender? Their gender orientation? Their political views? Does the right to vote include the right to participate in the activities of a party, including a primary?

RELATED CASES

Breedlove v. Suttles: **302 U.S. 277 (1937).**

A state poll tax as a precondition to voting does not deny equal protection nor does it violate the Fifteenth or Nineteenth Amendments.

United States v. Raines: **362 U.S. 17 (1960).**

Discrimination by state officials, within the course of their official duties, against the voting rights of citizens, on grounds of race or color, is subject to the ban of the Fifteenth Amendment, and legislation designed to deal with such discrimination is appropriate legislation under it.

Harman v. Forssenius: **380 U.S. 528 (1965).**

For federal elections the Twenty-fourth Amendment abolished the poll tax as a prerequisite for voting, and no equivalent or milder substitute may be imposed. Here the substitute under Virginia law was the filing of a witnessed or notarized certificate of residence six months before the federal election.

South Carolina v. Katzenbach: **383 U.S. 301 (1966).**

The Voting Rights Act of 1965 providing for a temporary suspension of a state's voting tests or devices, review of new voting rules, and federal examiners to qualify applicants for registration are means Congress may use to effectuate the constitutional prohibition of racial discrimination in voting. The Fifteenth Amendment supersedes contrary exertions of state power.

HARPER V. VIRGINIA STATE BOARD OF ELECTIONS

383 U.S. 663, 86 S.Ct. 1079, 16 L.Ed.2d 169 (1966)

The state of Virginia imposed a fee of $1.50 on individuals seeking to vote. Annie Harper challenged the fee, but the case was dismissed. The court cited *Breedlove v. Suttles* (302 U.S. 277, 1937), where a state poll tax as a precondition to voting was held not to deny equal protection or to violate the Fifteenth or Nineteenth Amendment.

Vote: 6–3

JUSTICE DOUGLAS delivered the opinion of the Court.

These are suits by Virginia residents to have declared unconstitutional Virginia's poll tax. The three-judge District Court, feeling bound by our decision in *Breedlove v. Suttles*, 302 U.S. 277 (1937), dismissed the complaint. The cases came here on appeal and we noted probable jurisdiction.

Section 173 of Virginia's Constitution directs the General Assembly to levy an annual poll tax not exceeding $1.50 on every resident of the State 21 years of age and over (with exceptions not relevant here). One dollar of the tax is to be used by state officials "exclusively in aid of the public free schools" and the remainder is to be returned to the counties for general purposes. Section 18 of the Constitution includes payment of poll taxes as a precondition for voting. Section 20 provides that a person must "personally" pay all state poll taxes for the three years preceding the year in which he applies for registration. By § 21 the poll tax must be paid at least six months prior to the election in which the voter seeks to vote. Since the time for election of state officials varies, the six months' deadline will vary, election from election. The poll tax is often assessed along with the personal property tax. Those who do not pay a personal property tax are not assessed for a poll tax, it being their responsibility to take the initiative and request to be assessed. Enforcement of poll taxes takes the form of disenfranchisement of those who do not pay, § 22 of the Virginia Constitution providing that collection of delinquent poll taxes for a particular year may not be enforced by legal proceedings until the tax for that year has become three years delinquent.

While the right to vote in federal elections is conferred by Art. I, § 2, of the Constitution (*United States v. Classic*, 313 US 299 (1941)), the right to vote in state elections is nowhere expressly mentioned. It is argued that the right to vote in state elections is implicit, particularly by reason of the First Amendment, and that it may not constitutionally be conditioned upon the payment of a tax or fee. We do not stop to canvass the relation between voting and political expression. For it is enough to say that once the franchise is granted to the electorate, lines may not be drawn which are inconsistent with the Equal Protection Clause of the Fourteenth Amendment. That is to say, the right of suffrage "is subject to the imposition of state standards which are not discriminatory and which do not contravene any restriction that Congress, acting pursuant to its constitutional powers, has imposed." *Lassiter v. Northampton County Board of Elections*, 360 U.S. 45 (1959). We were speaking there of a state literacy test which we sustained, warning that the result would be different if a literacy test, fair on its face, were used to discriminate against a class. But the Lassiter case does not govern the result here, because, unlike a poll tax, the "ability to read and write has some relation to standards designed to promote intelligent use of the ballot."

We conclude that a State violates the Equal Protection Clause of the Fourteenth Amendment whenever it makes the affluence of the voter or payment of any fee an electoral standard. Voter qualifications have no relation to wealth nor to paying or not paying this or any other tax. Our cases demonstrate that the Equal Protection Clause of the Fourteenth Amendment restrains the States from fixing voter qualifications which invidiously discriminate. Thus without questioning the power of a State to impose reasonable residence restrictions on the availability of the ballot, we held in *Carrington v. Rash*, 380 U.S. 89 (1965), that a State may not deny the opportunity to vote to a bona fide resident merely because he is a member of the armed services. "By forbidding a soldier ever to controvert the presumption of non-residence, the Texas Constitution imposes an invidious discrimination in violation of the Fourteenth Amendment." Previously we had said that neither homesite nor occupation "affords a permissible basis for distinguishing between qualified voters within the State." We think the same must be true of requirements of wealth or affluence or payment of a fee.

FOR DISCUSSION

Other than a direct payment of money to vote, should any other factors be considered as a form of a poll tax? Should the costs of voter registration or obtaining proper identification, for example, be considered a form of a poll tax?

SKAFTE V. ROREX

553 P.2d 830, 191 Colo. 399 (1976)

Peter Skafte was a resident alien living in Colorado. State law barred anyone except citizens from voting in elections. He challenged the Colorado law barring resident aliens from voting in local elections. He claimed it violated his Fourteenth Amendment rights, and the state Supreme Court accepted review.

Vote: Unanimous

CHIEF JUSTICE PRINGLE delivered the opinion of the court.

The appellant, Peter Skafte, a permanent resident alien, brought this suit in Boulder County District Court, seeking a declaratory judgment that the Colorado statutes which deny aliens the right to vote in school elections are unconstitutional. The appellant also sought appropriate injunctive relief. Specifically, the appellant claimed that such a limitation violates the Equal Protection Clause and Due Process Clause of the Fourteenth Amendment, and the Supremacy Clause of Article VI of the United States Constitution. The district court granted summary judgment in favor of the appellee, the Boulder County Clerk, holding the statutory provisions constitutional. We affirm.

The appellant attempted to register for a school election with the Boulder County Clerk and permission to do so was denied by the appellee for the sole reason that the appellant was not a United States citizen. This denial was based on 1971 Perm.Supp., C.R.S.1963, 123–31–1(3) and 1965 Perm.Supp., C.R.S.1963, 123–31–6(2). Section 123–31–1(3) defines an elector for the purposes of school elections as a "person who is legally qualified to register to vote for state officers at general elections" and who meets residency requirements. Section 123–31–6(2) provides that registration requirements for school elections "shall be the same as those governing general elections." Consequently, the substantive and procedural requirements concerning general elections are incorporated into school elections. Under C.R.S.1963, 49–3–1(1) (b), one qualification that electors must meet is that of United States citizenship.

I.

The appellant asserts that the statutes prohibiting permanent resident aliens from voting in school elections violate the Equal Protection Clause.

A.

At the outset, the registrar contends that the Equal Protection Clause has no application to the issue in this case. For this proposition, she relies on section 2 of the Fourteenth Amendment. Section 2 provides, in part:

> (W)hen the right to vote at any election for the choice of electors for President and Vice President of the United States, Representatives in Congress, the Executive and Judicial officers of a State, or the members of the Legislature thereof, is denied to any of the male inhabitants of such state, being twenty-one years of age, And citizens of the United States, or in any way abridged, except for participation in rebellion or other crime, the basis of representation therein shall be reduced in the

proportion which the number of such male citizens shall bear to the whole number of male citizens twenty-one years of age in such State.

The registrar argues that section 2 makes the Equal Protection Clause of the Fourteenth Amendment inapplicable to this case, since the specific wording of the section shows that those adopting the Fourteenth Amendment considered citizenship a valid classification in legislation dealing with the franchise. We do not agree with this contention.

Local school elections are not contained in the types of elections expressly listed in section 2. Moreover, the implicit sanction of a citizenship requirement contained in section 2 for the elections there listed does not warrant a conclusion that the Equal Protection Clause is inapplicable in the instant case. Indeed, the United States Supreme Court has rejected the general proposition that section 2 was intended to supplant the Equal Protection Clause in the area of voting rights.

Nevertheless, we do believe that section 2 is helpful in deciding the constitutional questions raised in this appeal. The section demonstrates, as an historical matter, that the requirement of citizenship to exercise the franchise was assumed to be a valid one at the time the Fourteenth Amendment was adopted. Hence, in deciding the constitutional issues in this case, we are mindful of the language of section 2.

B.

The appellant asserts that the alienage classification created here requires strict judicial scrutiny. The United States Supreme Court has consistently used language suggesting that citizenship with respect to the franchise is not a suspect classification and that therefore the compelling interest test does not apply.

C.

We hold that the state's citizenship requirements for a school district election do not contravene the Equal Protection Clause of the Fourteenth Amendment. The state has a rational interest in limiting participation in government to those persons within the political community. Aliens are not a part of the political community.

The United States Supreme Court has recognized a state's valid interest in establishing a government and in limiting participation in that government to those within the concept of a political community. The Supreme Court has noted that "alienage itself is a factor that reasonably could be employed in defining 'political community.' " Indeed, the Court has further stated that "implicit in many of this Court's voting rights decisions is the notion that citizenship is a permissible criterion for limiting such rights."

The appellant contends that this justification satisfies the Equal Protection requirement only as it pertains to voting in General elections. He contends, however, that a school election is a "special interest" election, and therefore the proposition that a citizenship requirement is valid for general elections does not apply.

We believe that a school election is an election which falls within the class of cases prohibiting aliens from voting contemplated by the Supreme Court. We point out that school districts are governmental entities. Elections involving local government units "have always been a major aspect of our system, and their responsible and responsive operation is today of increasing importance to the quality of life of more and more of our citizens." Further, in *Kramer v. Union Free School District No. 15*, 395 U.S. 621 (1969), the Supreme Court indicated that school elections are elections involving participation by the political community.

Moreover, voting in school elections involves participation in the decision making process of the polity, a factor which indicates the "general" nature of such elections. It is in fact a determination of participation or not in the government policy-making process which often has been crucial in deciding cases contesting alienage classifications. The Supreme Court in In Re Griffiths held unconstitutional a requirement that bar examinees be citizens. The court noted that the acts of a lawyer "hardly involve matters of state policy" and that the status of holding a license to practice law does not "place one so close to the core of the political process as to make him a formulator of government policy."

The administration of school districts, however, does involve one matters of "state policy" and entails the formulation of such policy. Therefore, voting in school elections constitutes participation in the government policy-making process.

II.

Next, the appellant contends that the prohibition against voting placed upon resident aliens creates a conclusive presumption in violation of the Due Process Clause of the Fourteenth Amendment.

The statutes do not create an irrebuttable presumption. There is no fact presumed from the status of alienage; rather, the legislature intended to prohibit aliens from voting, and the classification exactly achieves that purpose. The statutes do not purport to be concerned with prohibiting from voting persons with some common trait, which trait is conclusively presumed from the status of alienage. Instead, the statutes only purport to exclude aliens from voting. Thus, they do not create a conclusive presumption.*

While it is true that the state interest justifying the classification on equal protection grounds includes a concern for loyalty, awareness of United States laws and customs, and the extent to which voters are informed about political affairs, these interests are not equivalent with the purpose of the statute. To hold otherwise would turn the conclusive presumption doctrine into a "virtual engine of destruction for countless legislative judgments which have heretofore been thought wholly consistent with the Fifth and Fourteenth Amendments to the Constitution."

FOR DISCUSSION

Should citizenship be a necessary condition for voting? Recall in *Minor* that the Court ruled that while women were citizens, they were not entitled to vote. Does the decision in this case follow the logic of *Minor*? If resident aliens are not entitled to vote, should they not also be exempt from having to pay taxes?

LASSITER V. NORTHAMPTON COUNTY BD. OF ELECTIONS

360 U.S. 45, 79 S.Ct. 985, 3 L.Ed.2d 1072 (1959)

The state of North Carolina required individuals to pass a literacy test before being allowed to register to vote. This requirement was challenged under the Fourteenth, Fifteenth, and Seventeenth Amendments.

---

* In *Mourning v. Family Publications Service, Inc.*, 411 U.S. 356 (1973), the Supreme Court sustained the constitutionality of a regulation in the Truth and Lending Act which made disclosure provisions applicable whenever credit is offered to a consumer for which a finance charge is imposed or which is payable in more than four installments. The Court rejected the argument that the regulation conclusively presumed that debts payable in more than four installments necessarily included a finance charge, stating:

> The rule does not presume that all creditors who are within its ambit assess finance charges, but, rather, imposes a disclosure requirement on all members of a defined class in order to discourage evasion by a substantial portion of that class. 411 U.S. at 377.

Vote: 9–0

JUSTICE DOUGLAS delivered the opinion of the Court.

This controversy started in a Federal District Court. Appellant, a Negro citizen of North Carolina, sued to have the literacy test for voters prescribed by that State declared unconstitutional and void. A three-judge court was convened. That court noted that the literacy test was part of a provision of the North Carolina Constitution that also included a grandfather clause. It said that the grandfather clause plainly would be unconstitutional under *Guinn v. United States*, 238 U.S. 347 (1915). It noted, however, that the North Carolina statute which enforced the registration requirements contained in the State Constitution had been superseded by a 1957 Act and that the 1957 Act does not contain the grandfather clause or any reference to it. But being uncertain as to the significance of the 1957 Act and deeming it wise to have all administrative remedies under that Act exhausted before the federal court acted, it stayed its action, retaining jurisdiction for a reasonable time to enable appellant to exhaust her administrative remedies and obtain from the state courts an interpretation of the statute in light of the State Constitution.

Thereupon the instant case was commenced. It started as an administrative proceeding. Appellant applied for registration as a voter. Her registration was denied by the registrar because she refused to submit to a literacy test as required by the North Carolina statute.* She appealed to the County Board of Elections. On the de novo hearing before that Board appellant again refused to take the literacy test and she was again denied registration for that reason. She appealed to the Superior Court which sustained the Board against the claim that the requirement of the literacy test violated the Fourteenth, Fifteenth, and Seventeenth Amendments of the Federal Constitution. Preserving her federal question, she appealed to the North Carolina Supreme Court which affirmed the lower court.

The literacy test is a part of § 4 of Art. VI of the North Carolina Constitution. That test is contained in the first sentence of § 4. The second sentence contains a so-called grandfather clause. The entire § 4 reads as follows:

> Every person presenting himself for registration shall be able to read and write any section of the Constitution in the English language. But no male person who was, on January 1, 1867, or at any time prior thereto, entitled to vote under the laws of any state in the United states wherein he then resided, and no lineal descendant of any such person, shall be denied the right to register and vote at any election in this State by reason of his failure to possess the educational qualifications herein prescribed: Provided, he shall have registered in accordance with the terms of this section prior to December 1, 1908. The General Assembly shall provide for the registration of all persons, entitled to vote without the educational qualifications herein prescribed, and shall, on or before November 1, 1908, provide for the making of a permanent record of such registration, and all persons so registered shall forever thereafter have the right to vote in all elections by the people in this State, unless disqualified under section 2 of this article.

Originally Art. VI contained in § 5 the following provision:

> 'That this amendment to the Constitution is presented and adopted as one indivisible plan for the regulation of the suffrage, with the intent and purpose to so connect the different parts, and to make them so dependent upon each other, that the whole shall stand or fall together.

---

* This Act, passed in 1957, provides in § 163–28 as follows:

> Every person presenting himself for registration shall be able to read and write any section of the Constitution of North Carolina in the English language. It shall be the duty of each registrar to administer the provisions of this section.

Sections 163–28.1, 163–28.2, and 163–28.3 provide the administrative remedies pursued in this case.

But the North Carolina Supreme Court in the instant case held that a 1945 amendment to Article VI freed it of the indivisibility clause. That amendment rephrased § 1 of Art. VI to read as follows: "Every person born in the United States, and every person who has been naturalized, twenty-one years of age, and possessing the qualifications set out in this Article, shall be entitled to vote." That court said that "one of those qualifications" was the literacy test contained in § 4 of Art. VI; and that the 1945 amendment "had the effect of incorporating and adopting anew the provisions as to the qualifications required o a voter as set out in Article VI, freed of the indivisibility clause of the 1902 amendment. And the way was made clear for the General Assembly to act."

In 1957 the Legislature rewrote General Statutes § 163–28 as we have noted. Prior to that 1957 amendment § 163–28 perpetuated the grandfather clause contained in § 4 of Art. VI of the Constitution and § 163–32 established a procedure for registration to effectuate it. But the 1957 amendment contained a provision that "All laws and clauses of laws in conflict with this Act are hereby repealed." The federal three-judge court ruled that this 1957 amendment eliminated the grandfather clause from the statute.

The Attorney General of North Carolina, in an amicus brief, agrees that the grandfather clause contained in Art. VI is in conflict with the Fifteenth Amendment. Appellee maintains that the North Carolina Supreme Court ruled that the invalidity of that part of Art. VI does not impair the remainder of Art. VI since the 1945 amendment to Art. VI freed it of its indivisibility clause. Under that view Art. VI would impose the same literacy test as that imposed by the 1957 statute and neither would be linked with the grandfather clause which, though present in print, is separable from the rest and void. We so read the opinion of the North Carolina Supreme Court.

Appellant argues that that is not the end of the problem presented by the grandfather clause. There is a provision in the General Statutes for permanent registration in some counties. Appellant points out that although the cut-off date in the grandfather clause was December 1, 1908, those who registered before then might still be voting. If they were allowed to vote without taking a literacy test and if appellant were denied the right to vote unless she passed it, members of the white race would receive preferential privileges of the ballot contrary to the command of the Fifteenth Amendment. That would be analogous to the problem posed in the classic case of *Yick Wo v. Hopkins*, 118 U.S. 356 (1886), where an ordinance unimpeachable on its face was applied in such a way as to violate the guarantee of equal protection contained in the Fourteenth Amendment. But this issue of discrimination in the actual operation of the ballot laws of North Carolina has not been framed in the issues presented for the state court litigation. So we do not reach it. But we mention it in passing so that it may be clear that nothing we say or do here will prejudice appellant in tendering that issue in the federal proceedings which await the termination of this state court litigation.

We come then to the question whether a State may consistently with the Fourteenth and Seventeenth Amendments apply a literacy test to all voters irrespective of race or color. The Court in *Guinn v. United States*, disposed of the question in a few words, " 'No time need be spent on the question of the validity of the literacy test, considered alone, since, as we have seen its establishment was but the exercise by the state of a lawful power vested in it not subject to our supervision, and indeed, its validity is admitted."

The States have long been held to have broad powers to determine the conditions under which the right of suffrage may be exercised, Pope v. Williams; Mason v. State of Missouri, absent of course the discrimination which the Constitution condemns. Article I, § 2 of the Constitution in its provision for the election of members of the House of Representatives and the Seventeenth Amendment in its provision for the election of Senators provide that officials will be chosen "by the People." Each provision goes on to state that "the Electors in each State shall the Qualifications requisite for Electors of the most numerous Branch of the State Legislature." So while the right of suffrage is established and guaranteed by the Constitution it is subject to the imposition of state standards which are not discriminatory and which do not contravene any restriction that Congress acting pursuant to its constitutional powers, has imposed. See *United States v. Classic*, 313 U.S. 299 (1941). While § 2 of the Fourteenth Amendment, which provides for apportionment of Representatives among the States according to their respective numbers counting the whole number of persons in each State (except Indians not taxed), speaks of "the right to vote," the right protected "refers to the right to vote as established by the laws and constitution of the state." *McPherson v. Blacker*, 146 U.S. 1, 39 (1892).

We do not suggest that any standards which a State desires to adopt may be required of voters. But there is wide scope for exercise of its jurisdiction. Residence requirements, age, previous criminal record are obvious examples indicating factors which a State may take into consideration in determining the qualifications of voters. The ability to read and write likewise has some relation to standards designed to promote intelligent use of the ballot. Literacy and illiteracy are neutral on race, creed, color, and sex, as reports around the world show. Literacy and intelligence are obviously not synonymous. Illiterate people may be intelligent voters. Yet in our society where newspapers, periodicals, books, and other printed matter canvass and debate campaign issues, a State might conclude that only those who are literate should exercise the franchise. It was said last century in Massachusetts that a literacy test was designed to insure an "independent and intelligent" exercise of the right of suffrage. We do not sit in judgment on the wisdom of that policy. We cannot say, however, that it is not an allowable one measured by constitutional standards.

Of course a literacy test, fair on its face, may be employed to perpetuate that discrimination which the Fifteenth Amendment was designed to uproot. No such influence is charged here. On the other hand, a literacy test may be unconstitutional on its face. In *Davis v. Schnell*, D.C., 81 F.Supp. 872, 873, affirmed 336 U.S. 933 (1949), the test was the citizen's ability to "understand and explain" an article of the Federal Constitution. The legislative setting of that provision and the great discretion it vested in the registrar made clear that a literacy requirement was merely a device to make racial discrimination easy. We cannot make the same inference here. The present requirement, applicable to members of all races, is that the prospective voter "be able to read and write any section of the Constitution of North Carolina in the English language." That seems to us to be one fair way of determining whether a person is literate, not a calculated scheme to lay springes for the citizen. Certainly we cannot condemn it on its face as a device unrelated to the desire of North Carolina to raise the standards for people of all races who cast the ballot.

Affirmed.

FOR DISCUSSION

What reason did the Court give for permitting a state to require literacy tests as a condition for voting? Do you think some type of basic civics knowledge ought to be required to vote? What knowledge should it be? Should individuals who pass a college-level American politics class be deemed to have the required knowledge to vote?

RELATED CASES

Williams v. Mississippi: **170 U.S. 213 (1898).**

A state statute requiring persons desiring to vote to show a receipt for the payment of poll tax as well as the ability to read, understand, and interpret reasonably the state constitution was held not to deny the privilege of voting on the basis of race or color.

Guinn v. United States: **238 U.S. 347 (1915).**

An Oklahoma statute established literacy tests for voting but exempted from the test those persons who were themselves, or whose ancestors were, entitled to vote on January 1, 1866. This was the so-called "grandfather clause." The Court held this to be in violation of the Fifteenth Amendment.

RICHARDSON V. RAMIREZ

418 U.S. 24, 94 S.Ct. 2655, 41 L.Ed.2d 551 (1974)

The state of California barred ex-felons from voting. Three individuals who were convicted of felonies sought to register to vote after their release from prison. They were denied registration and challenged the law under the Fourteenth Amendment.

Vote: 6–3

JUSTICE REHNQUIST delivered the opinion of the Court.

The three individual respondents in this case were convicted of felonies and have completed the service of their respective sentences and paroles. They filed a petition for a writ of mandate in the Supreme Court of California to compel California county election officials to register them as voters. They claimed, on behalf of themselves and others similarly situated, that application to them of the provisions of the California Constitution and implementing statutes which disenfranchised persons convicted of an "infamous crime" denied them the right to equal protection of the laws under the Federal Constitution. The Supreme Court of California held that "as applied to all ex-felons whose terms of incarceration and parole have expired, the provisions of article II and article XX, section 11, of the California Constitution denying the right of suffrage to persons convicted of crime, together with the several sections of the Elections Code implementing that disqualification violate the equal protection clause of the Fourteenth Amendment." *Ramirez v. Brown*, 9 Cal.3d 199 (1973). We granted certiorari.

Article XX, § 11, of the California Constitution has provided since its adoption in 1879 that "(l)aws shall be made" to exclude from voting persons convicted of bribery, perjury, forgery, malfeasance in office, "or other high crimes." At the time respondents were refused registration, former Art, II, § 1, of the California Constitution provided in part that "no alien ineligible to citizenship, no idiot, no insane person, no person convicted of any infamous crime, no person hereafter convicted of the embezzlement or misappropriation of public money, and no person who shall not be able to read the Constitution in the English language and write his or her name, shall ever exercise the privileges of an elector in this State." Sections 310 and 321 of the California Elections Code provide that an affidavit of registration shall show whether the affiant has been convicted of "a felony which disqualifies (him) from voting." Sections 383, 389, and 390 direct the county clerk to cancel the registration of all voters who have been convicted of "any infamous crime or of the embezzlement or misappropriation of any public money." Sections 14240 and 14246 permit a voter's qualifications to be challenged on the ground that he has been convicted of "a felony" or of "the embezzlement or misappropriation of public money." California provides by statute for restoration of the right to vote to persons convicted of crime either by court order after the completion of probation, or, if a prison term was served, by executive pardon after completion of rehabilitation proceedings. California also provides a procedure by which a person refused registration may obtain judicial review of his disqualification.

Each of the individual respondents was convicted of one or more felonies, and served some time in jail or prison followed by a successfully terminated parole. Respondent Ramirez was convicted in Texas; respondents Lee and Gill were convicted in California. When Ramirez applied to register to vote in San Luis Obispo County, the County Clerk refused to allow him to register. The Monterey County Clerk refused registration to respondent Lee, and the Stanislaus County Registrar of Voters (hereafter also included in references to clerks) refused registration to respondent Gill.

All three respondents were refused registration because of their felony convictions.

In May 1972 respondents filed a petition for a writ of mandate in the Supreme Court of California, invoking its original jurisdiction. They named as defendants below the three election officials of San Luis Obispo, Monterey, and Stanislaus Counties who had refused to allow them to register, "individually and as representatives of the class of all other County Clerks and Registrars of Voters who have the duty of determining for their respective counties whether any ex-felon will be denied the right to vote." The petition for a writ of mandate challenged the constitutionality of respondents' exclusion from the voting rolls on two grounds. First, it was contended that California's denial of the franchise to the class of ex-felons could no longer withstand scrutiny under the Equal Protection Clause of the Fourteenth Amendment. Relying on the Court's recent voting-rights cases, respondents argued that a compelling state interest must be found to justify exclusion of a class from the franchise, and that California could assert no such interest with respect to ex-felons. Second, respondents contended that application of the challenged California constitutional and statutory provisions by election officials of the State's 58 counties was so lacking in uniformity as to deny them due process and "geographical equal protection." They appended a report by respondent California Secretary of State, and the questionnaires returned by county election officials on which it was based. The report concluded that there was wide variation in the county election officials' interpretation of the challenged voting exclusions. The Supreme Court of California upheld the first contention and therefore did not reach the second one.

II

Unlike most claims under the Equal Protection Clause, for the decision of which we have only the language of the Clause itself as it is embodied in the Fourteenth Amendment, respondents' claim implicates not merely the language of the Equal Protection Clause of § 1 of the Fourteenth Amendment, but also the provisions of the less familiar § 2 of the Amendment:

> Representatives shall be apportioned among the several States according to their respective numbers, counting the whole number of persons in each State, excluding Indians not taxed. But when the right to vote at any election for the choice of electors for President and Vice President of the United States, Representatives in Congress, the Executive and Judicial officers of a State, or the members of the Legislature thereof, is denied to any of the male inhabitants of such State, being twenty-one years of age, and citizens of the United States, or in any way abridged, *except for participation in rebellion, or other crime*, the basis of representation therein shall be reduced in the proportion which the number of such male citizens shall bear to the whole number of male citizens twenty-one years of age in such State.

Petitioner contends that the italicized language of § 2 expressly exempts from the sanction of that section disenfranchisement grounded on prior conviction of a felony. She goes on to argue that those who framed and adopted the Fourteenth Amendment could not have intended to prohibit outright in § 1 of that Amendment that which was expressly exempted from the lesser sanction of reduced representation imposed by § 2 of the Amendment. This argument seems to us a persuasive one unless it can be shown that the language of § 2, "except for participation in rebellion, or other crime," was intended to have a different meaning than would appear from its face.

The problem of interpreting the "intention" of a constitutional provision is, as countless cases of this Court recognize, a difficult one. Not only are there deliberations of congressional committees and floor debates in the House and Senate, but an amendment must thereafter be ratified by the necessary number of States. The legislative history bearing on the meaning of the relevant language of § 2 is scant indeed; the framers of the Amendment were primarily concerned with the effect of reduced representation upon the States, rather than with the two forms of disenfranchisement which were exempted from that consequence by the language with which we are concerned here. Nonetheless, what legislative history there is indicates that this language was intended by Congress to mean what it says.

A predecessor of § 2 was contained in an earlier draft of the proposed amendment, which passed the House of Representatives, but was defeated in the Senate early in 1866. The Joint Committee of Fifteen of Reconstruction then reconvened, and for a short period in April 1866, revised and redrafted what ultimately became the Fourteenth Amendment. The Journal of that Committee's proceedings shows only what motions were made and how the various members of the Committee voted on the motions; it does not indicate the nature or content of any of the discussion in the Committee. While the Journal thus enables us to trace the evolution of the draft language in the Committee, it throws only indirect light on the intention or purpose of those who drafted § 2. See B. Kendrick, *Journal of the Joint Committee of Fifteen on Reconstruction* 104–120 (1914).

We do know that the particular language of § 2 upon which petitioner relies was first proposed by Senator Williams of Oregon to a meeting of the Joint Committee on April 28, 1866. Senator Williams moved to strike out what had been § 3 of the earlier version of the draft, and to insert in place thereof the following:

> Representatives shall be apportioned among the several states which may be included within this Union according to their respective numbers, counting the whole number of persons in each State excluding Indians not taxed. But whenever in any State the elective franchise shall be denied to any portion of its male citizens, not less than twenty-one years of age, or in any way abridged, except for participation in rebellion or other crime, the basis of representation in such State shall be reduced in the proportion which the number of such male citizens shall bear to the whole number of male citizens not less than twenty-one years of age.

The Joint Committee approved this proposal by a lopsided margin, and the draft Amendment was reported to the House floor with no change in the language of § 2.

Throughout the floor debates in both the House and the Senate, in which numerous changes of language in § 2 were proposed, the language "except for participation in rebellion, or other crime" was never altered. The language of § 2 attracted a good deal of interest during the debates, but most of the discussion was devoted to its foreseeable consequences in both the Northern and Southern States, and to arguments as to its necessity or wisdom. What little comment there was on the phrase in question here supports a plain reading of it.

Congressman Bingham of Ohio, who was one of the principal architects of the Fourteenth Amendment and an influential member of the Committee of Fifteen, commented with respect to § 2 as follows during the floor debates in the House:

> The second section of the amendment simply provides for the equalization of representation among all the States of the Union, North, South, East, and West. It makes no discrimination. New York has a colored population of fifty thousand. By this section, if that great State discriminates against her colored population as to the elective franchise, (except in cases of crime,) she loses to that extent her representative power in Congress. So also will it be with every other State. Cong.Globe, 39th Cong., 1st Sess., 2543 (1866).

Two other Representatives who spoke to the question made similar comments. Representative Eliot of Massachusetts commented in support of the enactment of § 2 as follows:

> 'Manifestly no State should have its basis of national representation enlarged by reason of a portion of citizens within its borders to which the elective franchise is denied. If political power shall be lost because of such denial, not imposed because of participation in rebellion or other crime, it is to be hoped that political interests may work in the line of justice, and that the end will be the impartial enfranchisement of all citizens not disqualified by crime.

Representative Eckley of Ohio made this observation:

> Under a congressional act persons convicted of a crime against the laws of the United States, the penalty for which is imprisonment in the penitentiary, are now and always have been disfranchised, and a pardon did not restore them unless the warrant of pardon so provided.
>
> . . . But suppose the mass of the people of a State are pirates, counterfeiters, or other criminals, would gentlemen be willing to repeal the laws now in force in order to give them an opportunity to land their piratical crafts and come on shore to assist in the election of a President or members of Congress because they are numerous? And let it be borne in mind that these latter offenses are only crimes committed against property; that of treason is against the nation, against the whole people—the highest known to the law.

Further light is shed on the understanding of those who framed and ratified the Fourteenth Amendment, and thus on the meaning of § 2, by the fact that at the time of the adoption of the Amendment, 29 States had provisions in their constitutions which prohibited, or authorized the legislature to prohibit, exercise of the franchise by persons convicted of felonies or infamous crimes.

JUSTICE MARSHALL, with whom JUSTICE BRENNAN joins, dissenting.

The Court today holds that a State may strip ex-felons who have fully paid their debt to society of their fundamental right to vote without running afoul of the Fourteenth Amendment. This result is, in my view, based on an unsound historical analysis which already has been rejected by this Court. In straining to reach that result, I believe that the Court has also disregarded important limitations on its jurisdiction. For these reasons, I respectfully dissent.

III

In my view, the disenfranchisement of ex-felons must be measured against the requirements of the Equal Protection Clause of § 1 of the Fourteenth Amendment. That analysis properly begins with the observation that because the right to vote "is of the essence of a democratic society, and any restrictions on that right strike at the heart of representative government," *Reynolds v. Sims*, 377 U.S. 533 (1964), voting is a "fundamental" right. As we observed in *Dunn v. Blumstein*, 405 US 330 (1972),

> There is no need to repeat now the labors undertaken in earlier cases to analyze (the) right to vote and to explain in detail the judicial role in reviewing state statutes that selectively distribute the franchise. In decision after decision, this Court has made clear that a citizen has a constitutionally protected right to participate in elections on an equal basis with other citizens in the jurisdiction. See, e.g., *Evans v. Cornman,* 398 US 419 (1970); *Kramer v. Union Free School District*, 395 U.S. 621 (1969); *Cipriano v. City of Houma*, 395 US 701 (1969); *Harper v. Virginia Board of Elections*, 383 U.S. 663 (1966); *Carrington v. Rash*, 380 U.S. 89 (1965); *Reynolds v. Sims.*

We concluded: "(I)f a challenge statute grants the right to vote to some citizens and denies the franchise to others, 'the Court must determine whether the exclusions are necessary to promote a compelling state interest.' "

To determine that the compelling-state-interest test applies to the challenged classification is, however, to settle only a threshold question. "Compelling state interest" is merely a shorthand description of the difficult process of balancing individual and state interests that the Court must embark upon when faced with a classification touching on fundamental rights. Our other equal protection cases give content to the nature of that balance. The State has the heavy burden of showing, first, that the challenged disenfranchisement is necessary to a legitimate and substantial state interest; second, that the classification is drawn with precision—that it does not exclude too many people who should not and need not be excluded; and, third, that there are no other reasonable ways to achieve the State's goal with a lesser burden on the constitutionally protected interest.

I think it clear that the State has not met its burden of justifying the blanket disenfranchisement of former felons presented by this case. There is certainly no basis for asserting that ex-felons have any less interest in the democratic process than any other citizen. Like everyone else, their daily lives are deeply affected and changed by the decisions of government. See *Kramer*. As the Secretary of State of California observed in his memorandum to the Court in support of respondents in this case:

> It is doubtful whether the state can demonstrate either a compelling or rational policy interest in denying former felons the right to vote. The individuals involved in the present case are persons who have fully paid their debt to society. They are as much affected by the actions of government as any other citizens, and have as much of a right to participate in governmental decision-making. Furthermore, the denial of the right to vote to such persons is a hindrance to the efforts of society to rehabilitate former felons and convert them into law-abiding and productive citizens.

It is argued that disenfranchisement is necessary to prevent vote frauds. Although the State has a legitimate and, in fact, compelling interest in preventing election fraud, the challenged provision is not sustainable on that ground. First, the disenfranchisement provisions are patently both overinclusive and underinclusive. The provision is not limited to those who have demonstrated a marked propensity for abusing the ballot by violating election laws. Rather, it encompasses all former felons and there has been no showing that ex-felons generally are any more likely to abuse the ballot than the remainder of the population. In contrast, many of those convicted of violating election laws are treated as misdemeanants and are not barred from voting at all. It seems clear that the classification here is not tailored to achieve its articulated goal, since it crudely excludes large numbers of otherwise qualified voters.

Moreover, there are means available for the State to prevent voting fraud which are far less burdensome on the constitutionally protected right to vote. As we said in *Dunn*, the State "has at its disposal a variety of criminal laws that are more than adequate to detect and deter whatever fraud may be feared." The California court's catalogue of that State's penal sanctions for election fraud surely demonstrates that there are adequate alternatives to disenfranchisement.

> Today the Elections Code punishes at least 76 different acts as felonies, in 33 separate sections; at least 60 additional acts are punished as misdemeanors, in 40 separate sections; and 14 more acts are declared to be felony-misdemeanors. Among this plethora of offenses we take particular note, in the present connection, of the felony sanctions against fraudulent registrations, buying and selling of votes intimidating voters by threat or bribery, voting twice, or fraudulently voting without being entitled to do so, or impersonating another voter, fraud or forgery in casting absentee ballots, tampering with voting machines or ballot boxes, forging or altering election returns (§§ 29100–29103), and so interfering " 'with the officers holding an election or conducting a canvass, or with the voters lawfully exercising their rights of voting at an election, as to prevent the election or canvass from being fairly held and lawfully conducted."

Given the panoply of criminal offenses available to deter and to punish electoral misconduct, as well as the statutory reforms and technological changes which have transformed the electoral process in the last century, election fraud may no longer be a serious danger.

FOR DISCUSSION

How do the dissents justify their interpretations of the same clause of the Fourteenth Amendment? Which do you find more persuasive? What does the Fourteenth Amendment really say about felon disenfranchisement?

OREGON V. MITCHELL

400 U.S. 112, 91 S.Ct. 260, 27 L.Ed.2d 272 (1970)

Congress passed a law lowering the voting age from 21 to 18 in national and state elections. The state of Oregon sued John Mitchell, the United States Attorney General, claiming the law was unconstitutional as applied to state and local elections.

Vote: 5–4

JUSTICE BLACK, announcing the judgments of the Court in an opinion expressing his own view of the cases. Five Justices agreed that Congress could lower the voting age for federal elections, with JUSTICES HARLAN, STEWART, BLACKMUN, and CHIEF JUSTICE BURGER dissenting.

In these suits certain States resist compliance with the Voting Rights Act Amendments of 1970, Pub.L. 91–285, 84 Stat. 314, because they believe that the Act takes away from them powers reserved to the States by the Constitution to control their own elections. By its terms the Act does three things. First: It lowers the minimum age of voters in both state and federal elections from 21 to 18. Second: Based upon a finding by Congress that literacy tests have been used to discriminate against voters on account of their color, the Act enforces the Fourteenth and Fifteenth Amendments by barring the use of such tests in all elections, state and national, for a five-year period. Third: The Act forbids States from disqualifying voters in national elections for presidential and vice-presidential electors because they have not met state residency requirements.

For the reasons set out in Part I of this opinion, I believe Congress can fix the age of voters in national elections, such as congressional, senatorial, vice-presidential and presidential elections, but cannot set the voting age in state and local elections. For reasons expressed in separate opinions, my Brothers Douglas, Brennan, White, and Marshall join me in concluding that Congress can enfranchise 18-year-old citizens in national elections, but dissent from the judgment that Congress cannot extend the franchise to 18-year-old citizens in state and local elections. For reasons expressed in separate opinions, my Brothers The Chief Justice, Harlan, Stewart, and Blackmun join me in concluding that Congress cannot interfere with the age for voters set by the States for state and local elections. They, however, dissent from the judgment that Congress can control voter qualifications in federal elections. In summary, it is the judgment of the Court that the 18-year-old vote provisions of the Voting Rights Act Amendments of 1970 are constitutional and enforceable insofar as they pertain to federal elections and unconstitutional and unenforceable insofar as they pertain to state and local elections.

I

The Framers of our Constitution provided in Art. I, § 2, that members of the House of Representatives should be elected by the people and that the voters for Representatives should have "the Qualifications requisite for Electors of the most numerous Branch of the State Legislature." Senators were originally to be elected by the state legislatures, but under the Seventeenth Amendment Senators are also elected by the people, and voters for Senators have the same qualifications as voters for Representatives. In the very beginning the responsibility of the States for setting the qualifications of voters in congressional elections was made subject to the power of Congress to make or alter such regulations, if it deemed it advisable to do so. This was done in Art. I, § 4, of the Constitution which provides:

> The Times, Places and Manner of holding Elections for Senators and Representatives, shall be prescribed in each State by the Legislature thereof; but the Congress may at any time by Law make or alter such Regulations, except as to the Places of chusing Senators.

Moreover, the power of Congress to make election regulations in national elections is augmented by the Necessary and Proper Clause. See *McCulloch v. Maryland*, 17 U.S. 4 Wheat. 316 (1819). In *United States v. Classic*, 313 U.S. 299 (1941), where the Court upheld congressional power to regulate party primaries, Mr. Justice Stone speaking for the Court construed the interrelation of these clauses of the Constitution, stating:

> While, in a loose sense, the right to vote for representatives in Congress is sometimes spoken of as a right derived from the states . . . this statement is true only in the sense that the states are authorized by the Constitution, to legislate on the subject as provided by § 2 of Art. I, to the extent that Congress has not restricted state action by the exercise of its powers to regulate elections under § 4 and its more general power under Article I, § 8, clause 18 of the Constitution "To make all laws which shall be necessary and proper for carrying into execution the foregoing powers."
>
> The breadth of power granted to Congress to make or alter election regulations in national elections, including the qualifications of voters, is demonstrated by the fact that the Framers of the Constitution and the state legislatures which ratified it intended to grant to Congress the power to lay out or alter the boundaries of the congressional districts. In the ratifying conventions speakers "argued that the power given Congress in Art. I, § 4, was meant to be used to vindicate the people's right to equality of representation in the House," and that Congress would "most probably . . . lay the state off into districts." And in *Colegrove v. Green*, 328 U.S. 549 (1946), no Justice of this Court doubted Congress' power to rearrange the congressional districts according to population; the fight in that case revolved about the judicial power to compel redistricting.

Surely no voter qualification was more important to the Framers than the geographical qualification embodied in the concept of congressional districts. The Framers expected Congress to use this power to eradicate "rotten boroughs," and Congress has in fact used its power to prevent States from electing all Congressmen at large. There can be no doubt that the power to alter congressional district lines is vastly more significant in its effect than the power to permit 18-year-old citizens to go to the polls and vote in all federal elections.

Any doubt about the powers of Congress to regulate congressional elections, including the age and other qualifications of the voters, should be dispelled by the opinion of this Court in *Smiley v. Holm*, 285 US 355 (1932). There, Chief Justice Hughes writing for a unanimous Court discussed the scope of congressional power under § 4 at some length. He said:

> 'The subject matter is the "times, places and manner of holding elections for senators and representatives." It cannot be doubted that these comprehensive words embrace authority to provide a complete code for congressional elections, not only as to times and places, but in relation to notices, registration, supervision of voting, protection of voters, prevention of fraud and corrupt practices, counting of votes, duties of inspectors and canvassers, and making and publication of election returns; in short, to enact the numerous requirements as to procedure and safeguards which experience shows are necessary in order to enforce the fundamental right involved.
>
> This view is confirmed by the second clause of Article I, § 4, which provides that "the Congress may at any time by law make or alter such regulations," with the single exception stated. The phrase "such regulations" plainly refers to regulations of the same general character that the legislature of the State is authorized to prescribe with respect to congressional elections. In exercising this power, the Congress may supplement these state regulations or may substitute its own. It 'has a general supervisory power over the whole subject.'

In short, the Constitution allotted to the States the power to make laws regarding national elections, but provided that if Congress became dissatisfied with the state laws, Congress could alter them. A newly created national government could hardly have been expected to survive without the ultimate power to rule itself and to fill its offices under its own laws.

On the other hand, the Constitution was also intended to preserve to the States the power that even the Colonies had to establish and maintain their own separate and independent governments, except insofar as the Constitution itself commands otherwise. My Brother Harlan has persuasively demonstrated that the Framers of the Constitution intended the States to keep for themselves, as provided in the Tenth Amendment, the power to regulate elections. My major disagreement with my Brother Harlan is that, while I agree as to the States' power to regulate the elections of their own officials, I believe, contrary to his view, that Congress has the final authority over federal elections. No function is more essential to the separate and independent existence of the States and their governments than the power to determine within the limits of the Constitution the qualifications of their own voters for state, county, and municipal offices and the nature of their own machinery for filling local public offices.

Moreover, Art. I, § 2, is a clear indication that the Framers intended the States to determine the qualifications of their own voters for state offices, because those qualifications were adopted for federal offices unless Congress directs otherwise under Art. I, § 4. It is a plain fact of history that the Framers never imagined that the national Congress would set the qualifications for voters in every election from President to local constable or village alderman. It is obvious that the whole Constitution reserves to the States the power to set voter qualifications in state and local elections, except to the limited extent that the people through constitutional amendments have specifically narrowed the powers of the States. Amendments Fourteen, Fifteen, Nineteen, and Twenty-four, each of which has assumed that the States had general supervisory power over state elections, are examples of express limitations on the power of the States to govern themselves. And the Equal Protection Clause of the Fourteenth Amendment was never intended to destroy the States' power to govern themselves, making the Nineteenth and Twenty-fourth Amendments superfluous. My brother Brennan's opinion, if carried to its logical conclusion, would, under the guise of insuring equal protection, blot out all state power, leaving the 50 States as little more than impotent figureheads. In interpreting what the Fourteenth Amendment means, the Equal Protection Clause should not be stretched to nullify the States' powers over elections which they had before the Constitution was adopted and which they have retained throughout our history.

In enacting the 18-year-old vote provisions of the Act now before the Court, Congress made no legislative findings that the 21-year-old vote requirement was used by the States to disenfranchise voters on account of race. I seriously doubt that such a finding, if made, could be supported by substantial evidence. Since Congress has attempted to invade an area preserved to the States by the Constitution without a foundation for enforcing the Civil War Amendments' ban on racial discrimination, I would hold that Congress has exceeded its powers in attempting to lower the voting age in state and local elections. On the other hand, where Congress legislates in a domain not exclusively reserved by the Constitution to the States, its enforcement power need not be tied so closely to the goal of eliminating discrimination on account of race.

To invalidate part of the Voting Rights Act Amendments of 1970, however, does not mean that the entire Act must fall or that the constitutional part of the 18-year-old vote provision cannot be given effect. In passing the Voting Rights Act Amendments of 1970, Congress recognized that the limits of its power under the Enforcement Clauses were largely undetermined, and therefore included a broad severability provision:

JUSTICE DOUGLAS, dissenting.

I dissent from the judgments of the Court insofar as they declare § 302 of the Voting Rights Act, 84 Stat. 318, unconstitutional as applied to state elections and concur in the judgments as they affect federal elections, but for different reasons. I rely on the Equal Protection Clause and on the Privileges and Immunities Clause of the Fourteenth Amendment.

The grant of the franchise to 18-year-olds by Congress is in my view valid across the board.

The powers granted Congress by § 5 of the Fourteenth Amendment to "enforce" the Equal Protection Clause are "the same broad powers expressed in the Necessary and Proper Clause, Art. I, § 8, cl. 18." *Katzenbach v. Morgan*, 384 U.S. 641 (1966). As we stated in that case, "Correctly viewed, s 5 is a positive grant of legislative power authorizing Congress to exercise its discretion in determining whether and what legislation is needed to secure the guarantees of the Fourteenth Amendment."

Congress might well conclude that a reduction in the voting age from 21 to 18 was needed in the interest of equal protection. The Act itself brands the denial of the franchise to 18-year-olds as "a particularly unfair treatment of such citizens in view of the national defense responsibilities imposed" on them. The fact that only males are drafted while the vote extends to females as well is not relevant, for the female component of these families or prospective families is also caught up in war and hit hard by it. Congress might well believe that men and women alike should share the fateful decision.

It is said, why draw the line at 18? Why not 17? Congress can draw lines and I see no reason why it cannot conclude that 18-year-olds have that degree of maturity which entitles them to the franchise. They are "generally considered by American law to be mature enough to contract, to marry, to drive an automobile, to own a gun, and to be responsible for criminal behavior as an adult." Moreover, we are advised that under state laws, mandatory school attendance does not, as a matter of practice, extend beyond the age of 18. On any of these items the States, of course, have leeway to raise or lower the age requirements. But voting is "a fundamental matter in a free and democratic society," *Reynolds v. Sims*, 377 U.S. 533 (1964). Where "fundamental rights and liberties are asserted under the Equal Protection Clause, classifications which might invade or restrain them must be closely scrutinized and carefully confined." *Harper v. Virginia State Board of Elections*, 383 U.S. 663 (1966). There we were speaking of state restrictions on those rights. Here we are dealing with the right of Congress to "enforce" the principles of equality enshrined in the Fourteenth Amendment. The right to "enforce" granted by § 5 of that Amendment is, as noted, parallel with the Necessary and Proper Clause whose reach Chief Justice Marshall described in *McCulloch v. Maryland*: "Let the end be legitimate, let it be within the scope of the constitution, and all means which are appropriate, which are plainly adapted to that end, which are not prohibited, but consist with the letter and spirit of the constitution, are constitutional."

FOR DISCUSSION

Could the federal government lower the voting age to 16 in its own elections? Should the voting age be lowered to age 16? Some believe so. The Twenty-sixth Amendment partially overturned the *Mitchell* case, extending the right to vote to 18-year-olds in state as well as in national elections.

As a result of the *Mitchell* decision Congress and the states adopted the Twenty-Sixth Amendment. Congress proposed the Amendment in March 1971 and it was ratified by the required three-fourths of the states in a matter of four months. The amendment lowered the voting age to eighteen in all federal, state, and local elections in the United States.

Twenty-sixth Amendment, Sec. 1: The right of citizens of the United States, who are eighteen years of age or older, to vote, shall not be denied or abridged by the United States or by any State on account of age.

BURDICK V. TAKUSHI

504 U.S. 428, 112 S.Ct. 2059, 119 L.Ed.2d 245 (1992)

The state of Hawaii prohibited write-in votes in general elections. The law was challenged as a violation of the First Amendment.

Vote: 6–3

JUSTICE WHITE delivered the opinion of the Court.

The issue in this case is whether Hawaii's prohibition on write in voting unreasonably infringes upon its citizens' rights under the First and Fourteenth Amendments. Petitioner contends that the Constitution requires Hawaii to provide for the casting, tabulation, and publication of write in votes. The Court of Appeals for the Ninth Circuit disagreed, holding that the prohibition, taken as part of the State's comprehensive election scheme, does not impermissibly burden the right to vote. We affirm.

Petitioner is a registered voter in the city and County of Honolulu. In 1986, only one candidate filed nominating papers to run for the seat representing petitioner's district in the Hawaii House of Representatives. Petitioner wrote to state officials inquiring about Hawaii's write in voting policy and received a copy of an opinion letter issued by the Hawaii Attorney General's Office stating that the State's election law made no provision for write in voting.

Petitioner then filed this lawsuit, claiming that he wished to vote in the primary and general elections for a person who had not filed nominating papers and that he wished to vote in future elections for other persons whose names were not and might not appear on the ballot.

The United States District Court for the District of Hawaii concluded that the ban on write in voting violated petitioner's First Amendment right of expression and association and entered a preliminary injunction ordering respondents to provide for the casting and tallying of write in votes in the November 1986 general election. The District Court denied a stay pending appeal.

The Court of Appeals entered the stay and vacated the judgment of the District Court, reasoning that consideration of the federal constitutional question raised by petitioner was premature because "neither the plain language of Hawaii statutes nor any definitive judicial interpretation of those statutes establishes that the Hawaii legislature has enacted a ban on write in voting." *Burdick* v. *Takushi,* 846 F. 2d 587, 588 (CA9 1988). Accordingly, the Court of Appeals ordered the District Court to abstain, see *Railroad Comm'n of Tex.* v. *Pullman Co.,* 312 U.S. 496 (1941), until state courts had determined whether Hawaii's election laws permitted write in voting. On remand, the District Court certified the following three questions to the Supreme Court of Hawaii:

> "(1) Does the Constitution of the State of Hawaii require Hawaii's election officials to permit the casting of write in votes and require Hawaii's election officials to count and publish write in votes?
>
> "(2) Do Hawaii's election laws require Hawaii's election officials to permit the casting of write in votes and require Hawaii's election officials to count and publish write in votes?
>
> "(3) Do Hawaii's election laws permit, but not require, Hawaii's election officials to allow voters to cast write in votes and to count and publish write in votes?"

Hawaii's high court answered "No" to all three questions, holding that Hawaii's election laws barred write in voting and that these measures were consistent with the State's Constitution. The United States District Court then granted petitioner's renewed motion for summary judgment and injunctive relief, but entered a stay pending appeal.

The Court of Appeals again reversed, holding that Hawaii was not required to provide for write in votes:

> Although the prohibition on write in voting places some restrictions on [petitioner's] rights of expression and association, that burden is justified in light of the ease of access to Hawaii's ballots, the alternatives available to [petitioner] for expressing his political beliefs, the State's broad powers to regulate elections, and the specific interests advanced by the State.

In so ruling, the Ninth Circuit expressly declined to follow an earlier decision regarding write in voting by the Court of Appeals for the Fourth Circuit. We granted certiorari to resolve the disagreement on this important question.

Petitioner proceeds from the erroneous assumption that a law that imposes any burden upon the right to vote must be subject to strict scrutiny. Our cases do not so hold.

It is beyond cavil that "voting is of the most fundamental significance under our constitutional structure." It does not follow, however, that the right to vote in any manner and the right to associate for political purposes through the ballot are absolute. The Constitution provides that States may prescribe "[t]he Times, Places and Manner of holding Elections for Senators and Representatives," Art. I, § 4, cl. 1, and the Court therefore has recognized that States retain the power to regulate their own elections. Common sense, as well as constitutional law, compels the conclusion that government must play an active role in structuring elections; "as a practical matter, there must be a substantial regulation of elections if they are to be fair and honest and if some sort of order, rather than chaos, is to accompany the democratic processes." *Scorer* v. *Brown,* 415 U.S. 724, 730 (1974).

Election laws will invariably impose some burden upon individual voters. Each provision of a code, "whether it governs the registration and qualifications of voters, the selection and eligibility of candidates, or the voting process itself, inevitably affects—at least to some degree—the individual's right to vote and his right to associate with others for political ends." *Anderson* v. *Celebrezze*, 460 U.S. 780, 788 (1983). Consequently, to subject every voting regulation to strict scrutiny and to require that the regulation be narrowly tailored to advance a compelling state interest, as petitioner suggests, would tie the hands of States seeking to assure that elections are operated equitably and efficiently. Accordingly, the mere fact that a State's system "creates barriers tending to limit the field of candidates from which voters might choose does not of itself compel close scrutiny."

Instead, as the full Court agreed in *Anderson,* a more flexible standard applies. A court considering a challenge to a state election law must weigh "the character and magnitude of the asserted injury to the rights protected by the First and Fourteenth Amendments that the plaintiff seeks to vindicate" against "the precise interests put forward by the State as justifications for the burden imposed by its rule," taking into consideration "the extent to which those interests make it necessary to burden the plaintiff's rights." Under this standard, the rigorousness of our inquiry into the propriety of a state election law depends upon the extent to which a challenged regulation burdens First and Fourteenth Amendment rights. Thus, as we have recognized when those rights are subjected to "severe" restrictions, the regulation must be "narrowly drawn to advance a state interest of compelling importance." *Norman* v. *Reed,* 502 U.S. (1992). But when a state election law provision imposes only "reasonable, nondiscriminatory restrictions" upon the First and Fourteenth Amendment rights of voters, "the State's important regulatory interests are generally sufficient to justify" the restrictions. We apply this standard in considering petitioner's challenge to Hawaii's ban on write in ballots.

There is no doubt that the Hawaii election laws, like all election regulations, have an impact on the right to vote, but it can hardly be said that the laws at issue here unconstitutionally limit access to the ballot by party or independent candidates or unreasonably interfere with the right of voters to associate and have candidates of their choice placed on the ballot. Indeed, petitioners understandably do not challenge the manner in which the State regulates candidate access to the ballot. To obtain a position on the November general election ballot, a candidate must participate in Hawaii's open primary, "in which all registered voters may choose in which party primary to vote." The State provides three mechanisms through which a voter's candidate of choice may appear on the primary ballot.

First, a party petition may be filed 150 days before the primary by any group of persons who obtain the signatures of one percent of the State's registered voters. Then, 60 days before the primary, candidates must file nominating papers certifying, among other things, that they will qualify for the office sought and that they are members of the party that they seek to represent in the general election. The nominating papers must contain the signatures of a specified number of registered voters: 25 for candidates for statewide or federal office; 15 for state legislative and county races. The winner in each party advances to the general election. Thus, if a party forms around the candidacy of a single individual and no one else runs on that party ticket, the individual will be elected at the primary and win a place on the November general election ballot.

The second method through which candidates may appear on the Hawaii primary ballot is the established party route. Established parties that have qualified by petition for three consecutive elections and received a specified percentage of the vote in the preceding election may avoid filing party petitions for 10 years. The Democratic, Republican, and Libertarian Parties currently meet Hawaii's criteria for established parties. Like new party candidates, established party contenders are required to file nominating papers 60 days before the primary.

The third mechanism by which a candidate may appear on the ballot is through the designated nonpartisan ballot. Nonpartisans may be placed on the nonpartisan primary ballot simply by filing nominating papers containing 15 to 25 signatures, depending upon the office sought, 60 days before the primary. To advance to the general election, a nonpartisan must receive 10 percent of the primary vote or the number of votes that was sufficient to nominate a partisan candidate, whichever number is lower. During the 10 years preceding the filing of this action, 8 of 26 nonpartisans who entered the primary obtained slots on the November ballot.

Although Hawaii makes no provision for write in voting in its primary or general elections, the system outlined above provides for easy access to the ballot until the cutoff date for the filing of nominating petitions, two months before the primary. Consequently, any burden on voters' freedom of choice and association is borne only by those who fail to identify their candidate of choice until days before the primary. But in *Scorer* v. *Brown,* we gave little weight to "the interest the candidate and his supporters may have in making a late rather than an early decision to seek independent ballot status." We think the same reasoning applies here and therefore conclude that any burden imposed by Hawaii's write in vote prohibition is a very limited one. "To conclude otherwise might sacrifice the political stability of the system of the State, with profound consequences for the entire citizenry, merely in the interest of particular candidates and their supporters having instantaneous access to the ballot."

Accordingly, we have repeatedly upheld reasonable, politically neutral regulations that have the effect of channeling expressive activity at the polls. Petitioner offers no persuasive reason to depart from these precedents. Reasonable regulation of elections *does not* require voters to espouse positions that they do not support; it *does* require them to act in a timely fashion if they wish to express their views in the voting booth. And there is nothing content based about a flat ban on all forms of write in ballots.

The appropriate standard for evaluating a claim that a state law burdens the right to vote is set forth in *Anderson.* Applying that standard, we conclude that, in light of the adequate ballot access afforded under Hawaii's election code, the State's ban on write in voting imposes only a limited burden on voters' rights to make free choices and to associate politically through the vote.

Hawaii's interest in "avoid[ing] the possibility of unrestrained factionalism at the general election," provides adequate justification for its ban on write in voting in November. The primary election is "an integral part of the entire election process," and the State is within its rights to reserve "[t]he general election ballot for major struggles [and] not a forum for continuing intraparty feuds." The prohibition on write in voting is a legitimate means of averting divisive sore loser candidacies. Hawaii further promotes the two stage, primary general election process of winnowing out candidates, by permitting the unopposed victors in certain primaries to be designated office holders. This focuses the attention of voters upon contested races in the general election. This would not be possible, absent the write in voting ban.

Hawaii also asserts that its ban on write in voting at the primary stage is necessary to guard against "party raiding." Party raiding is generally defined as "the organized switching of blocs of voters from one party to another in order to manipulate the outcome of the other party's primary election." Petitioner suggests that, because Hawaii conducts an open primary, this is not a cognizable interest. We disagree. While voters may vote on any ticket in Hawaii's primary, the State requires that party candidates be "member[s] of the party," and prohibits candidates from filing "nomination papers both as a party candidate and as a nonpartisan candidate." Hawaii's system could easily be circumvented in a party primary election by mounting a write in campaign for a person who had not filed in time or who had never intended to run for election. It could also be frustrated at the general election by permitting write in votes for a loser in a party primary or for an independent who had failed to get sufficient votes to make the general election ballot. The State has a legitimate interest in preventing these sorts of maneuvers, and the write in voting ban is a reasonable way of accomplishing this goal.

We think these legitimate interests asserted by the State are sufficient to outweigh the limited burden that the write in voting ban imposes upon Hawaii's voters.

We think that Hawaii's prohibition on write in voting, considered as part of an electoral scheme that provides constitutionally sufficient ballot access, does not impose an unconstitutional burden upon the First and Fourteenth Amendment rights of the State's voters. Accordingly, the judgment of the Court of Appeals is affirmed.

It is so ordered.

JUSTICE KENNEDY, with whom JUSTICES BLACKMUN and STEVENS join, dissenting.

The question before us is whether Hawaii can enact a total ban on write in voting. The majority holds that it can, finding that Hawaii's ballot access rules impose no serious limitations on the right to vote. Indeed, the majority in effect adopts a presumption that prohibitions on write in voting are permissible if the State's ballot access laws meet constitutional standards. I dissent because I disagree with the presumption, as well as the majority's specific conclusion that Hawaii's ban on write in voting is constitutional.

The record demonstrates the significant burden that Hawaii's write in ban imposes on the right of voters such as petitioner to vote for the candidates of their choice. In the election that triggered this lawsuit, petitioner did not wish to vote for the one candidate who ran for state representative in his district. Because he could not write in the name of a candidate he preferred, he had no way to cast a meaningful vote. Petitioner's dilemma is a recurring, frequent phenomenon in Hawaii because of the State's ballot access rules and the circumstance that one party, the Democratic Party, is predominant. It is critical to understand that petitioner's case is not an isolated example of a restriction on the free choice of candidates. The very ballot access rules the Court cites as mitigating his injury in fact compound it systemwide.

Given that so many Hawaii voters are dissatisfied with the choices available to them, it is hard to avoid the conclusion that at least some voters would cast write in votes for other candidates if given this option. The write in ban thus prevents these voters from participating in Hawaii elections in a meaningful manner.

This evidence also belies the majority's suggestion that Hawaii voters are presented with adequate electoral choices because Hawaii makes it easy to get on the official ballot. To the contrary, Hawaii's ballot access laws taken as a whole impose a significant impediment to third party or independent candidacies. The majority suggests that it is easy for new parties to petition for a place on the primary ballot because they must obtain the signatures of only one percent of the State's registered voters. This ignores the difficulty presented by the early deadline for gathering these signatures: 150 days (5 months) before the primary election. Meeting this deadline requires considerable organization at an early stage in the election, a condition difficult for many small parties to meet.

With this background, I turn to the legal principles that control this case. At the outset, I agree with the first premise in the majority's legal analysis. The right at stake here is the right to cast a meaningful vote for the candidate of one's choice. Petitioner's right to freedom of expression is not implicated. His argument that the First Amendment confers upon citizens the right to cast a protest vote and to have government officials count and report this vote is not persuasive. As the majority points out, the purpose of casting, counting, and recording votes is to elect public officials, not to serve as a general forum for political expression.

I agree as well with the careful statement the Court gives of the test to be applied in this case to determine if the right to vote has been constricted. As the Court phrases it, we must "weigh 'the character and magnitude of the asserted injury to the rights protected by the First and Fourteenth Amendments that the plaintiff seeks to vindicate' against 'the precise interests put forward by the State as justifications for the burden imposed by its rule,' taking into consideration 'the extent to which those interests make it necessary to burden the plaintiff's rights.' " I submit the conclusion must be that the write in ban deprives some voters of any substantial voice in selecting candidates for the entire range of offices at issue in a particular election.

FOR DISCUSSION

Should not the right to vote include writing in the name of any candidate you want? Could a state ban write-in votes in primaries? Note the two-tier test for regulation of voting that the Court articulates in *Burdick*. What types of actions should fit into either level or category?

CRAWFORD V. MARION COUNTY ELECTION BD.

553 U.S. 181, 128 S.Ct. 1610, 170 L.Ed.2d 574 (2008)

In order to address the problems of alleged voter fraud, the state of Indiana enacted a law mandating that individuals voting in person at the polls present government-issued identification (such as a drivers license) before being allowed to vote. Individuals who could not present such identification would be allowed to cast a provisional ballot, which would be counted once an approved ID was presented. The law did not require individuals voting by absentee ballot to present proof of identity. The government-issued identification cards would be issued free to individuals who needed them. Several individuals and groups challenged the voter identification requirement, claiming it was a form of a poll tax and that it violated the First Amendment.

Vote: 6–3

JUSTICE STEVENS announced the judgment of the Court and delivered an opinion, in which CHIEF JUSTICE ROBERTS and JUSTICE KENNEDY joined.

At issue in these cases is the constitutionality of an Indiana statute requiring citizens voting in person on election day, or casting a ballot in person at the office of the circuit court clerk prior to election day, to present photo identification issued by the government.

Referred to as either the "Voter ID Law" or "SEA 483," the statute applies to in-person voting at both primary and general elections. The requirement does not apply to absentee ballots submitted by mail, and the statute contains an exception for persons living and voting in a state-licensed facility such as a nursing home. A voter who is indigent or has a religious objection to being photographed may cast a provisional ballot that will be counted only if she executes an appropriate affidavit before the circuit court clerk within 10 days following the election. A voter who has photo identification but is unable to present that identification on election day may file a provisional ballot that will be counted if she brings her photo identification to the circuit county clerk's office within 10 days. No photo identification is required in order to register to vote, and the State offers free photo identification to qualified voters able to establish their residence and identity.

Promptly after the enactment of SEA 483 in 2005, the Indiana Democratic Party and the Marion County Democratic Central Committee (Democrats) filed suit in the Federal District Court for the Southern District of Indiana against the state officials responsible for its enforcement, seeking a judgment declaring the Voter ID Law invalid and enjoining its enforcement. A second suit seeking the same relief was brought on behalf of two elected officials and several nonprofit organizations representing groups of elderly, disabled, poor, and minority voters. The cases were consolidated, and the State of Indiana intervened to defend the validity of the statute.

The complaints in the consolidated cases allege that the new law substantially burdens the right to vote in violation of the Fourteenth Amendment; that it is neither a necessary nor appropriate method of avoiding election fraud; and that it will arbitrarily disfranchise qualified voters who do not possess the required identification and will place an unjustified burden on those who cannot readily obtain such identification.

After discovery, District Judge Barker prepared a comprehensive 70-page opinion explaining her decision to grant defendants' motion for summary judgment. She found that petitioners had "not introduced evidence of a single, individual Indiana resident who will be unable to vote as a result of SEA 483 or who will have his or her right to vote unduly burdened by its requirements." She rejected "as utterly incredible and unreliable" an expert's report that up to 989,000 registered voters in Indiana did not possess either a driver's license or other acceptable photo identification. She estimated that as of 2005, when the statute was enacted, around 43,000 Indiana residents lacked a state-issued driver's license or identification card.

A divided panel of the Court of Appeals affirmed.

I

In *Harper v. Virginia Bd. of Elections*, 383 U.S. 663 (1966), the Court held that Virginia could not condition the right to vote in a state election on the payment of a poll tax of $1.50. We rejected the dissenters' argument that the interest in promoting civic responsibility by weeding out those voters who did not care enough about public affairs to pay a small sum for the privilege of voting provided a rational basis for the tax. Applying a stricter standard, we concluded that a State "violates the Equal Protection Clause of the Fourteenth Amendment whenever it makes the affluence of the voter or payment of any fee an electoral standard." We used the term "invidiously discriminate" to describe conduct prohibited under that standard, noting that we had previously held that while a State may obviously impose "reasonable residence restrictions on the availability of the ballot," it "may not deny the opportunity to vote to a bona fide resident merely because he is a member of the armed services." Although the State's justification for the tax was rational, it was invidious because it was irrelevant to the voter's qualifications.

Thus, under the standard applied in *Harper*, even rational restrictions on the right to vote are invidious if they are unrelated to voter qualifications. In *Anderson v. Celebrezze*, 460 U.S. 780 (1983), however, we confirmed the general rule that "evenhanded restrictions that protect the integrity and reliability of the electoral process itself" are not invidious and satisfy the standard set forth in *Harper*. Rather than applying any "litmus test" that would neatly separate valid from invalid restrictions, we concluded that a court must identify and evaluate the interests put forward by the State as justifications for the burden imposed by its rule, and then make the "hard judgment" that our adversary system demands.

In later election cases we have followed *Anderson*'s balancing approach. Thus, in *Norman v. Reed*, 502 U.S. 279 (1992), after identifying the burden Illinois imposed on a political party's access to the ballot, we "called for the demonstration of a corresponding interest sufficiently weighty to justify the limitation," and concluded that the "severe restriction" was not justified by a narrowly drawn state interest of compelling importance. Later, in *Burdick v. Takushi,* 504 U.S. 428 (1992), we applied *Anderson*'s standard for " 'reasonable, nondiscriminatory restrictions,' " 504 U.S., at 434, and upheld Hawaii's prohibition on write-in voting despite the fact that it prevented a significant number of "voters from participating in Hawaii elections in a meaningful manner." We reaffirmed *Anderson*'s requirement that a court evaluating a constitutional challenge to an election regulation weigh the asserted injury to the right to vote against the " 'precise interests put forward by the State as justifications for the burden imposed by its rule.' "

In neither *Norman* nor *Burdick* did we identify any litmus test for measuring the severity of a burden that a state law imposes on a political party, an individual voter, or a discrete class of voters. However slight that burden may appear, as *Harper* demonstrates, it must be justified by relevant and legitimate state interests "sufficiently weighty to justify the limitation." We therefore begin our analysis of the constitutionality of Indiana's statute by focusing on those interests.

II

The State has identified several state interests that arguably justify the burdens that SEA 483 imposes on voters and potential voters. While petitioners argue that the statute was actually motivated by partisan concerns and dispute both the significance of the State's interests and the magnitude of any real threat to those interests, they do not question the legitimacy of the interests the State has identified. Each is unquestionably relevant to the State's interest in protecting the integrity and reliability of the electoral process.

The first is the interest in deterring and detecting voter fraud. The State has a valid interest in participating in a nationwide effort to improve and modernize election procedures that have been criticized as antiquated and inefficient. The State also argues that it has a particular interest in preventing voter fraud in response to a problem that is in part the product of its own maladministration—namely, that Indiana's voter registration rolls include a large number of names of persons who are either deceased or no longer live in Indiana. Finally, the State relies on its interest in safeguarding voter confidence. Each of these interests merits separate comment.

Election Modernization

Two recently enacted federal statutes have made it necessary for States to reexamine their election procedures. Both contain provisions consistent with a State's choice to use government-issued photo identification as a relevant source of information concerning a citizen's eligibility to vote.

In the National Voter Registration Act of 1993 (NVRA), Congress established procedures that would both increase the number of registered voters and protect the integrity of the electoral process. The statute requires state motor vehicle driver's license applications to serve as voter registration applications. While that requirement has increased the number of registered voters, the statute also contains a provision restricting States' ability to remove names from the lists of registered voters. These protections have been partly responsible for inflated lists of registered voters. For example, evidence credited by Judge Barker estimated that as of 2004 Indiana's voter rolls were inflated by as much as 41.4%, and data collected by the Election Assistance Committee in 2004 indicated that 19 of 92 Indiana counties had registration totals exceeding 100% of the 2004 voting-age population.

In HAVA, Congress required every State to create and maintain a computerized statewide list of all registered voters. HAVA also requires the States to verify voter information contained in a voter registration application and specifies either an "applicant's driver's license number" or "the last 4 digits of the applicant's social security number" as acceptable verifications. If an individual has neither number, the State is required to assign the applicant a voter identification number.

HAVA also imposes new identification requirements for individuals registering to vote for the first time who submit their applications by mail. If the voter is casting his ballot in person, he must present local election officials with written identification, which may be either "a current and valid photo identification" or another form of documentation such as a bank statement or paycheck. If the voter is voting by mail, he must include a copy of the identification with his ballot. A voter may also include a copy of the documentation with his application or provide his driver's license number or Social Security number for verification. Finally, in a provision entitled "Fail-safe voting," HAVA authorizes the casting of provisional ballots by challenged voters.

Of course, neither HAVA nor NVRA required Indiana to enact SEA 483, but they do indicate that Congress believes that photo identification is one effective method of establishing a voter's qualification to vote and that the integrity of elections is enhanced through improved technology. That conclusion is also supported by a report issued shortly after the enactment of SEA 483 by the Commission on Federal Election Reform chaired by former President Jimmy Carter and former Secretary of State James A. Baker III, which is a part of the record in these cases. In the introduction to their discussion of voter identification, they made these pertinent comments:

> A good registration list will ensure that citizens are only registered in one place, but election officials still need to make sure that the person arriving at a polling site is the same one that is named on the registration list. In the old days and in small towns where everyone knows each other, voters did not need to identify themselves. But in the United States, where 40 million people move each year, and in urban areas where some people do not even know the people living in their own apartment building let alone their precinct, some form of identification is needed.
>
> There is no evidence of extensive fraud in U.S. elections or of multiple voting, but both occur, and it could affect the outcome of a close election. The electoral system cannot inspire public confidence if no safeguards exist to deter or detect fraud or to confirm the identity of voters. Photo identification cards currently are needed to board a plane, enter federal buildings, and cash a check. Voting is equally important.

Voter Fraud

The only kind of voter fraud that SEA 483 addresses is in-person voter impersonation at polling places. The record contains no evidence of any such fraud actually occurring in Indiana at any time in its history. Moreover, petitioners argue that provisions of the Indiana Criminal Code punishing such conduct as a felony provide adequate protection against the risk that such conduct will occur in the future. It remains true, however, that flagrant examples of such fraud in other parts of the country have been documented throughout this Nation's history by respected historians and journalists, that occasional examples have surfaced in recent years, and that Indiana's own experience with fraudulent voting in the 2003 Democratic primary for East Chicago Mayor—though perpetrated using absentee ballots and not in-person fraud—demonstrate that not only is the risk of voter fraud real but that it could affect the outcome of a close election.

There is no question about the legitimacy or importance of the State's interest in counting only the votes of eligible voters. Moreover, the interest in orderly administration and accurate recordkeeping provides a sufficient justification for carefully identifying all voters participating in the election process. While the most effective method of preventing election fraud may well be debatable, the propriety of doing so is perfectly clear.

In its brief, the State argues that the inflation of its voter rolls provides further support for its enactment of SEA 483. The record contains a November 5, 2000, newspaper article asserting that as a result of NVRA and "sloppy record keeping," Indiana's lists of registered voters included the names of thousands of persons who had either moved, died, or were not eligible to vote because they had been convicted of felonies. The conclusion that Indiana has an unusually inflated list of registered voters is supported by the entry of a consent decree in litigation brought by the Federal Government alleging violations of NVRA. Even though Indiana's own negligence may have contributed to the serious inflation of its registration lists when SEA 483 was enacted, the fact of inflated voter rolls does provide a neutral and nondiscriminatory reason supporting the State's decision to require photo identification.

Safeguarding Voter Confidence

Finally, the State contends that it has an interest in protecting public confidence "in the integrity and legitimacy of representative government." While that interest is closely related to the State's interest in preventing voter fraud, public confidence in the integrity of the electoral process has independent significance, because it encourages citizen participation in the democratic process. As the Carter-Baker Report observed, the "electoral system cannot inspire public confidence if no safeguards exist to deter or detect fraud or to confirm the identity of voters."

III

States employ different methods of identifying eligible voters at the polls. Some merely check off the names of registered voters who identify themselves; others require voters to present registration cards or other documentation before they can vote; some require voters to sign their names so their signatures can be compared with those on file; and in recent years an increasing number of States have relied primarily on photo identification. A photo identification requirement imposes some burdens on voters that other methods of identification do not share. For example, a voter may lose his photo identification, may have his wallet stolen on the way to the polls, or may not resemble the photo in the identification because he recently grew a beard. Burdens of that sort arising from life's vagaries, however, are neither so serious nor so frequent as to raise any question about the constitutionality of SEA 483; the availability of the right to cast a provisional ballot provides an adequate remedy for problems of that character.

The burdens that are relevant to the issue before us are those imposed on persons who are eligible to vote but do not possess a current photo identification that complies with the requirements of SEA 483. The fact that most voters already possess a valid driver's license, or some other form of acceptable identification, would not save the statute under our reasoning in *Harper*, if the State required voters to pay a tax or a fee to obtain a new photo identification. But just as other States provide free voter registration cards, the photo identification cards issued by Indiana's BMV are also free. For most voters who need them, the inconvenience of making a trip to the BMV, gathering the required documents, and posing for a photograph surely does not qualify as a substantial burden on the right to vote, or even represent a significant increase over the usual burdens of voting.

Both evidence in the record and facts of which we may take judicial notice, however, indicate that a somewhat heavier burden may be placed on a limited number of persons. They include elderly persons born out-of-state, who may have difficulty obtaining a birth certificate; persons who because of economic or other personal limitations may find it difficult either to secure a copy of their birth certificate or to assemble the other required documentation to obtain a state-issued identification; homeless persons; and persons with a religious objection to being photographed. If we assume, as the evidence suggests, that some members of these classes were registered voters when SEA 483 was enacted, the new identification requirement may have imposed a special burden on their right to vote.

The severity of that burden is, of course, mitigated by the fact that, if eligible, voters without photo identification may cast provisional ballots that will ultimately be counted. To do so, however, they must travel to the circuit court clerk's office within 10 days to execute the required affidavit. It is unlikely that such a requirement would pose a constitutional problem unless it is wholly unjustified. And even assuming that the burden may not be justified as to a few voters, that conclusion is by no means sufficient to establish petitioners' right to the relief they seek in this litigation.

IV

Petitioners ask this Court, in effect, to perform a unique balancing analysis that looks specifically at a small number of voters who may experience a special burden under the statute and weighs their burdens against the State's broad interests in protecting election integrity. Petitioners urge us to ask whether the State's interests justify the burden imposed on voters who cannot afford or obtain a birth certificate and who must make a second trip to the circuit court clerk's office after voting. But on the basis of the evidence in the record it is not possible to quantify either the magnitude of the burden on this narrow class of voters or the portion of the burden imposed on them that is fully justified.

First, the evidence in the record does not provide us with the number of registered voters without photo identification; Judge Barker found petitioners' expert's report to be "utterly incredible and unreliable." Much of the argument about the numbers of such voters comes from extrarecord, postjudgment studies, the accuracy of which has not been tested in the trial court.

Further, the deposition evidence presented in the District Court does not provide any concrete evidence of the burden imposed on voters who currently lack photo identification. The record includes depositions of two case managers at a day shelter for homeless persons and the depositions of members of the plaintiff organizations, none of whom expressed a personal inability to vote under SEA 483. A deposition from a named plaintiff describes the difficulty the elderly woman had in obtaining an identification card, although her testimony indicated that she intended to return to the BMV since she had recently obtained her birth certificate and that she was able to pay the birth certificate fee.

Judge Barker's opinion makes reference to six other elderly named plaintiffs who do not have photo identifications, but several of these individuals have birth certificates or were born in Indiana and have not indicated how difficult it would be for them to obtain a birth certificate. One elderly named plaintiff stated that she had attempted to obtain a birth certificate from Tennessee, but had not been successful, and another testified that he did not know how to obtain a birth certificate from North Carolina. The elderly in Indiana, however, may have an easier time obtaining a photo identification card than the nonelderly, and although it may not be a completely acceptable alternative, the elderly in Indiana are able to vote absentee without presenting photo identification.

The record says virtually nothing about the difficulties faced by either indigent voters or voters with religious objections to being photographed. While one elderly man stated that he did not have the money to pay for a birth certificate, when asked if he did not have the money or did not wish to spend it, he replied, "both." From this limited evidence we do not know the magnitude of the impact SEA 483 will have on indigent voters in Indiana. The record does contain the affidavit of one homeless woman who has a copy of her birth certificate, but was denied a photo identification card because she did not have an address. But that single affidavit gives no indication of how common the problem is.

In sum, on the basis of the record that has been made in this litigation, we cannot conclude that the statute imposes "excessively burdensome requirements" on any class of voters. See *Scorer v. Brown,* 415 U.S. 724, 738 (1974).

JUSTICE SOUTER, with whom JUSTICE GINSBURG joins, dissenting.

Indiana's "Voter ID Law" threatens to impose nontrivial burdens on the voting right of tens of thousands of the State's citizens, and a significant percentage of those individuals are likely to be deterred from voting. The statute is unconstitutional under the balancing standard of *Burdick v. Takushi*: a State may not burden the right to vote merely by invoking abstract interests, be they legitimate, or even compelling, but must make a particular, factual showing that threats to its interests outweigh the particular impediments it has imposed. The State has made no such justification here, and as to some aspects of its law, it has hardly even tried. I therefore respectfully dissent from the Court's judgment sustaining the statute.

II

Under *Burdick*, "the rigorousness of our inquiry into the propriety of a state election law depends upon the extent to which a challenged regulation burdens First and Fourteenth Amendment rights," upon an assessment of the "character and magnitude of the asserted [threatened] injury."

A

The first set of burdens shown in these cases is the travel costs and fees necessary to get one of the limited variety of federal or state photo identifications needed to cast a regular ballot under the Voter ID Law. The travel is required for the personal visit to a license branch of the Indiana Bureau of Motor Vehicles (BMV), which is demanded of anyone applying for a driver's license or nondriver photo identification. The need to travel to a BMV branch will affect voters according to their circumstances, with the average person probably viewing it as nothing more than an inconvenience. Poor, old, and disabled voters who do not drive a car, however, may find the trip prohibitive, witness the fact that the BMV has far fewer license branches in each county than there are voting precincts. Marion County, for example, has over 900 active voting precincts, yet only 12 BMV license branches; in Lake County, there are 565 active voting precincts, to match up with only 8 BMV locations; and Allen County, with 309 active voting precincts, has only 3 BMV license branches. The same pattern holds in counties with smaller populations. Brown County has 12 active voter precincts, and only one BMV office; while there were 18 polling places available in Fayette County's 2007 municipal primary, there was only 1 BMV license branch; and Henry County, with 42 polling places approved for 2008 elections, has only 1 BMV office.

The burden of traveling to a more distant BMV office rather than a conveniently located polling place is probably serious for many of the individuals who lack photo identification. They almost certainly will not own cars, and public transportation in Indiana is fairly limited. According to a report published by Indiana's Department of Transportation in August 2007, 21 of Indiana's 92 counties have no public transportation system at all, and as of 2000, nearly 1 in every 10 voters lived within 1 of these 21 counties. Among the counties with some public system, 21 provide service only within certain cities, and 32 others restrict public transportation to regional county service, leaving only 18 that offer countywide public transportation. State officials recognize the effect that travel costs can have on voter turnout, as in Marion County, for example, where efforts have been made to "establis[h] most polling places in locations even more convenient than the statutory minimum," in order to "provid[e] for neighborhood voting." Although making voters travel farther than what is convenient for most and possible for some does not amount to a "severe" burden under *Burdick*, that is no reason to ignore the burden altogether. It translates into an obvious economic cost (whether in work time lost, or getting and paying for transportation) that an Indiana voter must bear to obtain an ID.

For those voters who can afford the roundtrip, a second financial hurdle appears: in order to get photo identification for the first time, they need to present " 'a birth certificate, a certificate of naturalization, U.S. veterans photo identification, U.S. military photo identification, or a U.S. passport.' " As the lead opinion says, the two most common of these documents come at a price: Indiana counties charge anywhere from $3 to $12 for a birth certificate (and in some other States the fee is significantly higher), and that same price must usually be paid for a first-time passport, since a birth certificate is required to prove U.S. citizenship by birth. The total fees for a passport, moreover, are up to about $100. So most voters must pay at least one fee to get the ID necessary to cast a regular ballot. As with the travel costs, these fees are far from shocking on their face, but in the *Burdick* analysis it matters that both the travel costs and the fees are disproportionately heavy for, and thus disproportionately likely to deter, the poor, the old, and the immobile.

B

The law allows these voters who lack the necessary ID to sign the poll book and cast a provisional ballot. As the lead opinion recognizes, though, *ante,* at 1621, that is only the first step; to have the provisional ballot counted, a voter must then appear in person before the circuit court clerk or county election board within 10 days of the election, to sign an affidavit attesting to indigency or religious objection to being photographed (or to present an ID at that point). Unlike the trip to the BMV (which, assuming things go smoothly, needs to be made only once every four years for renewal of nondriver photo identification), this one must be taken every time a poor person or religious objector wishes to vote, because the State does not allow an affidavit to count in successive elections. And unlike the trip to the BMV (which at least has a handful of license branches in the more populous counties), a county has only one county seat. Forcing these people to travel to the county seat every time they try to vote is particularly onerous for the reason noted already, that most counties in Indiana either lack public transportation or offer only limited coverage.

That the need to travel to the county seat each election amounts to a high hurdle is shown in the results of the 2007 municipal elections in Marion County, to which Indiana's Voter ID Law applied. Thirty-four provisional ballots were cast, but only two provisional voters made it to the County Clerk's Office within the 10 days.

All of this suggests that provisional ballots do not obviate the burdens of getting photo identification. And even if that were not so, the provisional-ballot option would be inadequate for a further reason: the indigency exception by definition offers no relief to those voters who do not consider themselves (or would not be considered) indigent but as a practical matter would find it hard, for nonfinancial reasons, to get the required ID (most obviously the disabled).

C

Indiana's Voter ID Law thus threatens to impose serious burdens on the voting right, even if not "severe" ones, and the next question under *Burdick* is whether the number of individuals likely to be affected is significant as well. Record evidence and facts open to judicial notice answer yes.

Although the District Court found that petitioners failed to offer any reliable empirical study of numbers of voters affected we may accept that court's rough calculation that 43,000 voting-age residents lack the kind of identification card required by Indiana's law. The District Court made that estimate by comparing BMV records reproduced in petitioners' statistician's report with U.S. Census Bureau figures for Indiana's voting-age population in 2004, and the State does not argue that these raw data are unreliable.

The upshot is this. Tens of thousands of voting-age residents lack the necessary photo identification. A large proportion of them are likely to be in bad shape economically. The Voter ID Law places hurdles in the way of either getting an ID or of voting provisionally, and they translate into nontrivial economic costs. There is accordingly no reason to doubt that a significant number of state residents will be discouraged or disabled from voting.

JUSTICE BREYER, dissenting.

Indiana's statute requires registered voters to present photo identification at the polls. It imposes a burden upon some voters, but it does so in order to prevent fraud, to build confidence in the voting system, and thereby to maintain the integrity of the voting process. In determining whether this statute violates the Federal Constitution, I would balance the voting-related interests that the statute affects, asking "whether the statute burdens any one such interest in a manner out of proportion to the statute's salutary effects upon the others (perhaps, but not necessarily, because of the existence of a clearly superior, less restrictive alternative)." Applying this standard, I believe the statute is unconstitutional because it imposes a disproportionate burden upon those eligible voters who lack a driver's license or other statutorily valid form of photo ID.

FOR DISCUSSION

What evidence does the Court offer to sustain the photo identification law? Are you persuaded by the evidence? What burdens are placed on the right to vote with the identification requirements? Was the problem for those challenging the law that they lacked evidence of burden on voters? Take a look at the footnote 20 for the majority opinion?

RELATED CASES

***North Carolina State Conference of NAACP v. McCrory:* ___ F.3d ___ (4th Cir. 2016), 2016 WL 4053033.**

Federal Court of Appeals strikes down as a violation of the Fourteenth and Fifteenth Amendments and the Voting Rights Act claiming that the voter photo identification law and other restrictions on voting had an intent to discriminate against racial minorities.

***Veasey v. Abbott:* ___ F.3d. ___ (5th Cir. 2016).**

Federal Court of Appeals struck down and enjoined enforcement of a state voter identification law ruling that it was racially discriminatory under the Voting Rights Act.

SHELBY COUNTY, ALABAMA V. HOLDER

570 U.S ___, 133 S.Ct. 2612, 186 L.Ed.2d 651 (2013)

Shelby County was covered by the Voting Rights Act which required it to seek preclearance from the Justice Department or the D.C. District Court to prove that any changes to its voting laws were not discriminatory. Shelby County challenged as unconstitutional the coverage formula under the VRA which determined which jurisdictions were required to preclear. The United States District Court for the District of Columbia, entered summary judgment for Attorney General and the Court of Appeals affirmed. The Supreme Court overturned the Court of Appeals, declaring the coverage formula unconstitutional.

Vote 5–4

CHIEF JUSTICE ROBERTS wrote for the Court and was joined by SCALIA, KENNEDY, THOMAS, and ALITO, JUSTICE THOMAS filed concurring opinion.

JUSTICE GINSBURG filed dissenting opinion in which JUSTICES BREYER, SOTOMAYOR, and KAGAN joined.

The Voting Rights Act of 1965 employed extraordinary measures to address an extraordinary problem. Section 5 of the Act required States to obtain federal permission before enacting any law related to voting—a drastic departure from basic principles of federalism. And § 4 of the Act applied that requirement only to some States—an equally dramatic departure from the principle that all States enjoy equal sovereignty. This was strong medicine, but Congress determined it was needed to address entrenched racial discrimination in voting, "an insidious and pervasive evil which had been perpetuated in certain parts of our country through unremitting and ingenious defiance of the Constitution." As we explained in upholding the law, "exceptional conditions can justify legislative measures not otherwise appropriate." Reflecting the unprecedented nature of these measures, they were scheduled to expire after five years.

Nearly 50 years later, they are still in effect; indeed, they have been made more stringent, and are now scheduled to last until 2031. There is no denying, however, that the conditions that originally justified these measures no longer characterize voting in the covered jurisdictions. By 2009, "the racial gap in voter registration and turnout [was] lower in the States originally covered by § 5 than it [was] nationwide." Since that time, Census Bureau data indicate that African-American voter turnout has come to exceed white voter turnout in five of the six States originally covered by § 5, with a gap in the sixth State of less than one half of one percent.

At the same time, voting discrimination still exists; no one doubts that. The question is whether the Act's extraordinary measures, including its disparate treatment of the States, continue to satisfy constitutional requirements. As we put it a short time ago, "the Act imposes current burdens and must be justified by current needs."

I

A

The Fifteenth Amendment was ratified in 1870, in the wake of the Civil War. It provides that "[t]he right of citizens of the United States to vote shall not be denied or abridged by the United States or by any State on account of race, color, or previous condition of servitude," and it gives Congress the "power to enforce this article by appropriate legislation."

"The first century of congressional enforcement of the Amendment, however, can only be regarded as a failure." In the 1890s, Alabama, Georgia, Louisiana, Mississippi, North Carolina, South Carolina, and Virginia began to enact literacy tests for voter registration and to employ other methods designed to prevent African-Americans from voting. Congress passed statutes outlawing some of these practices and facilitating litigation against them, but litigation remained slow and expensive, and the States came up with new ways to discriminate as soon as existing ones were struck down. Voter registration of African-Americans barely improved.

Inspired to action by the civil rights movement, Congress responded in 1965 with the Voting Rights Act. Section 2 was enacted to forbid, in all 50 States, any "standard, practice, or procedure . . . imposed or applied . . . to deny or abridge the right of any citizen of the United States to vote on account of race or color." The current version forbids any "standard, practice, or procedure" that "results in a denial or abridgement of the right of any citizen of the United States to vote on account of race or color." Both the Federal Government and individuals have sued to enforce, and injunctive relief is available in appropriate cases to block voting laws from going into effect, Section 2 is permanent, applies nationwide, and is not at issue in this case.

Other sections targeted only some parts of the country. At the time of the Act's passage, these "covered" jurisdictions were those States or political subdivisions that had maintained a test or device as a prerequisite to voting as of November 1, 1964, and had less than 50 percent voter registration or turnout in the 1964 Presidential election. Such tests or devices included literacy and knowledge tests, good moral character requirements, the need for vouchers from registered voters, and the like. A covered jurisdiction could "bail out" of coverage if it had not used a test or device in the preceding five years "for the purpose or with the effect of denying or abridging the right to vote on account of race or color." In 1965, the covered States included Alabama, Georgia, Louisiana, Mississippi, South Carolina, and Virginia. The additional covered subdivisions included 39 counties in North Carolina and one in Arizona.

In those jurisdictions, § 4 of the Act banned all such tests or devices. Section 5 provided that no change in voting procedures could take effect until it was approved by federal authorities in Washington, D.C.—either the Attorney General or a court of three judges. A jurisdiction could obtain such "preclearance" only by proving that the change had neither "the purpose [nor] the effect of denying or abridging the right to vote on account of race or color.".

Sections 4 and 5 were intended to be temporary; they were set to expire after five years. In *South Carolina v. Katzenbach,* we upheld the 1965 Act against constitutional challenge, explaining that it was justified to address "voting discrimination where it persists on a pervasive scale."

In 1970, Congress reauthorized the Act for another five years, and extended the coverage formula in § 4(b) to jurisdictions that had a voting test and less than 50 percent voter registration or turnout as of 1968. That swept in several counties in California, New Hampshire, and New York. also extended the ban in § 4(a) on tests and devices nationwide.

In 1975, Congress reauthorized the Act for seven more years, and extended its coverage to jurisdictions that had a voting test and less than 50 percent voter registration or turnout as of 1972.Congress also amended the definition of "test or device" to include the practice of providing English-only voting materials in places where over five percent of voting-age citizens spoke a single language other than English. As a result of these amendments, the States of Alaska, Arizona, and Texas, as well as several counties in California, Florida, Michigan, New York, North Carolina, and South Dakota, became covered jurisdictions. Congress correspondingly amended sections 2 and 5 to forbid voting discrimination on the basis of membership in a language minority group, in addition to discrimination on the basis of race or color. Finally, Congress made the nationwide ban on tests and devices permanent.

In 1982, Congress reauthorized the Act for 25 years, but did not alter its coverage formula. Congress did, however, amend the bailout provisions, allowing political subdivisions of covered jurisdictions to bail out. Among other prerequisites for bailout, jurisdictions and their subdivisions must not have used a forbidden test or device, failed to receive preclearance, or lost a § 2 suit, in the ten years prior to seeking bailout.

We upheld each of these reauthorizations against constitutional challenge.

In 2006, Congress again reauthorized the Voting Rights Act for 25 years, again without change to its coverage formula. Fannie Lou Hamer, Rosa Parks, and Coretta Scott King Voting Rights Act Reauthorization and Amendments Act. Congress also amended § 5 to prohibit more conduct than before. Section 5 now forbids voting changes with "any discriminatory purpose" as well as voting changes that diminish the ability of citizens, on account of race, color, or language minority status, "to elect their preferred candidates of choice."

Shortly after this reauthorization, a Texas utility district brought suit, seeking to bail out from the Act's coverage and, in the alternative, challenging the Act's constitutionality. A three-judge District Court explained that only a State or political subdivision was eligible to seek bailout under the statute, and concluded that the utility district was not a political subdivision, a term that encompassed only "counties, parishes, and voter-registering subunits." The District Court also rejected the constitutional challenge. *Id.,* at 283.

We reversed. We explained that " 'normally the Court will not decide a constitutional question if there is some other ground upon which to dispose of the case.' " Concluding that "underlying constitutional concerns," among other things, "compel[led] a broader reading of the bailout provision," we construed the statute to allow the utility district to seek bailout. In doing so we expressed serious doubts about the Act's continued constitutionality.

We explained that § 5 "imposes substantial federalism costs" and "differentiates between the States, despite our historic tradition that all the States enjoy equal sovereignty." We also noted that "[t]hings have changed in the South. Voter turnout and registration rates now approach parity. Blatantly discriminatory evasions of federal decrees are rare. And minority candidates hold office at unprecedented levels." Finally, we questioned whether the problems that § 5 meant to address were still "concentrated in the jurisdictions singled out for preclearance."

Eight Members of the Court subscribed to these views, and the remaining Member would have held the Act unconstitutional. Ultimately, however, the Court's construction of the bailout provision left the constitutional issues for another day.

II

In *Northwest Austin,* we stated that "the Act imposes current burdens and must be justified by current needs." And we concluded that "a departure from the fundamental principle of equal sovereignty requires a showing that a statute's disparate geographic coverage is sufficiently related to the problem that it targets.". These basic principles guide our review of the question before us.

A

The Constitution and laws of the United States are "the supreme Law of the Land." U.S. Const., Art. VI, cl. 2. State legislation may not contravene federal law. The Federal Government does not, however, have a general right to review and veto state enactments before they go into effect. A proposal to grant such authority to "negative" state laws was considered at the Constitutional Convention, but rejected in favor of allowing state laws to take effect, subject to later challenge under the Supremacy Clause.

Outside the strictures of the Supremacy Clause, States retain broad autonomy in structuring their governments and pursuing legislative objectives. Indeed, the Constitution provides that all powers not specifically granted to the Federal Government are reserved to the States or citizens. This "allocation of powers in our federal system preserves the integrity, dignity, and residual sovereignty of the States." But the federal balance "is not just an end in itself: Rather, federalism secures to citizens the liberties that derive from the diffusion of sovereign power.". (internal quotation marks omitted).

More specifically, " 'the Framers of the Constitution intended the States to keep for themselves, as provided in the Tenth Amendment, the power to regulate elections.' " Of course, the Federal Government retains significant control over federal elections. For instance, the Constitution authorizes Congress to establish the time and manner for electing Senators and Representatives. Art. I, § 4, cl. 1. But States have "broad powers to determine the conditions under which the right of suffrage may be exercised." And "[e]ach State has the power to prescribe the qualifications of its officers and the manner in which they shall be chosen." Drawing lines for congressional districts is likewise "primarily the duty and responsibility of the State."

Not only do States retain sovereignty under the Constitution, there is also a "fundamental principle of *equal* sovereignty" among the States. Over a hundred years ago, this Court explained that our Nation "was and is a union of States, equal in power, dignity and authority." *Coyle v. Smith,* 221 U.S. 559, 567, 31 S.Ct. 688, 55 L.Ed. 853 (1911). Indeed, "the constitutional equality of the States is essential to the harmonious operation of the scheme upon which the Republic was organized." *Coyle* concerned the admission of new States, and *Katzenbach* rejected the notion that the principle operated as a *bar* on differential treatment outside that context. At the same time, as we made clear in *Northwest Austin,* the fundamental principle of equal sovereignty remains highly pertinent in assessing subsequent disparate treatment of States.

The Voting Rights Act sharply departs from these basic principles. It suspends "*all* changes to state election law—however innocuous—until they have been precleared by federal authorities in Washington, D.C." States must beseech the Federal Government for permission to implement laws that they would otherwise have the right to enact and execute on their own, subject of course to any injunction in a § 2 action. The Attorney General has 60 days to object to a preclearance request, longer if he requests more information. If a State seeks preclearance from a three-judge court, the process can take years.

And despite the tradition of equal sovereignty, the Act applies to only nine States (and several additional counties). While one State waits months or years and expends funds to implement a validly enacted law, its neighbor can typically put the same law into effect immediately, through the normal legislative process. Even if a noncovered jurisdiction is sued, there are important differences between those proceedings and preclearance proceedings; the preclearance proceeding "not only switches the burden of proof to the supplicant jurisdiction, but also applies substantive standards quite different from those governing the rest of the nation."

All this explains why, when we first upheld the Act in 1966, we described it as "stringent" and "potent." We recognized that it "may have been an uncommon exercise of congressional power," but concluded that "legislative measures not otherwise appropriate" could be justified by "exceptional conditions." We have since noted that the Act "authorizes federal intrusion into sensitive areas of state and local policymaking," and represents an "extraordinary departure from the traditional course of relations between the States and the Federal Government," As we reiterated in *Northwest Austin,* the Act constitutes "extraordinary legislation otherwise unfamiliar to our federal system."

B

In 1966, we found these departures from the basic features of our system of government justified. The "blight of racial discrimination in voting" had "infected the electoral process in parts of our country for nearly a century." Several States had enacted a variety of requirements and tests "specifically designed to prevent" African-Americans from voting. Case-by-case litigation had proved inadequate to prevent such racial discrimination in voting, in part because States "merely switched to discriminatory devices not covered by the federal decrees," "enacted difficult new tests," or simply "defied and evaded court orders." Shortly before enactment of the Voting Rights Act, only 19.4 percent of Africa-Americans of voting age were registered to vote in Alabama, only 31.8 percent in Louisiana, and only 6.4 percent in Mississippi. Those figures were roughly 50 percentage points or more below the figures for whites.

In short, we concluded that "[u]nder the compulsion of these unique circumstances, Congress responded in a permissibly decisive manner." We also noted then and have emphasized since that this extraordinary legislation was intended to be temporary, set to expire after five years

At the time, the coverage formula—the means of linking the exercise of the unprecedented authority with the problem that warranted it—made sense. We found that "Congress chose to limit its attention to the geographic areas where immediate action seemed necessary." The areas where Congress found "evidence of actual voting discrimination" shared two characteristics: "the use of tests and devices for voter registration, and a voting rate in the 1964 presidential election at least 12 points below the national average." We explained that "[t]ests and devices are relevant to voting discrimination because of their long history as a tool for perpetrating the evil; a low voting rate is pertinent for the obvious reason that widespread disenfranchisement must inevitably affect the number of actual voters.". We therefore concluded that "the coverage formula [was] rational in both practice and theory.". It accurately reflected those jurisdictions uniquely characterized by voting discrimination "on a pervasive scale," linking coverage to the devices used to effectuate discrimination and to the resulting disenfranchisement. The formula ensured that the "stringent remedies [were] aimed at areas where voting discrimination ha[d] been most flagrant."

C

Nearly 50 years later, things have changed dramatically. Shelby County contends that the preclearance requirement, even without regard to its disparate coverage, is now unconstitutional. Its arguments have a good deal of force. In the covered jurisdictions, "[v]oter turnout and registration rates now approach parity. Blatantly discriminatory evasions of federal decrees are rare. And minority candidates hold office at unprecedented levels." The tests and devices that blocked access to the ballot have been forbidden nationwide for over 40 years.

Those conclusions are not ours alone. Congress said the same when it reauthorized the Act in 2006, writing that "[s]ignificant progress has been made in eliminating first generation barriers experienced by minority voters, including increased numbers of registered minority voters, minority voter turnout, and minority representation in Congress, State legislatures, and local elected offices." The House Report elaborated that "the number of African-Americans who are registered and who turn out to cast ballots has increased significantly over the last 40 years, particularly since 1982," and noted that "[i]n some circumstances, minorities register to vote and cast ballots at levels that surpass those of white voters." That Report also explained that there have been "significant increases in the number of African-Americans serving in elected offices"; more specifically, there has been approximately a 1,000 percent increase since 1965 in the number of African-American elected officials in the six States originally covered by the Voting Rights Act.

The following chart, compiled from the Senate and House Reports, compares voter registration numbers from 1965 to those from 2004 in the six originally covered States. These are the numbers that were before Congress when it reauthorized the Act in 2006:

	1965			2004		
	White	Black	Gap	White	Black	Gap
Alabama	69.2	19.3	49.9	73.8	72.9	0.9
Georgia	62.[6]	27.4	35.2	63.5	64.2	-0.7
Louisiana	80.5	31.6	48.9	75.1	71.1	4.0
Mississippi	69.9	6.7	63.2	72.3	76.1	-3.8
South Carolina	75.7	37.3	38.4	74.4	71.1	3.3
Virginia	61.1	38.3	22.8	68.2	57.4	10.8

The 2004 figures come from the Census Bureau. Census Bureau data from the most recent election indicate that African-American voter turnout exceeded white voter turnout in five of the six States originally covered by § 5, with a gap in the sixth State of less than one half of one percent. See Dept. of Commerce, Census Bureau, Reported Voting and Registration, by Sex, Race and Hispanic Origin, for States. The preclearance statistics are also illuminating. In the first decade after enactment of § 5, the Attorney General objected to 14.2 percent of proposed voting changes. H. R Rep. No. 109–478, at 22. In the last decade before reenactment, the Attorney General objected to a mere 0.16 percent.

There is no doubt that these improvements are in large part *because of* the Voting Rights Act. The Act has proved immensely successful at redressing racial discrimination and integrating the voting process. During the "Freedom Summer" of 1964, in Philadelphia, Mississippi, three men were murdered while working in the area to register African-American voters. On "Bloody Sunday" in 1965, in Selma, Alabama, police beat and used tear gas against hundreds marching in support of African-American enfranchisement. Today both of those towns are governed by African-American mayors. Problems remain in these States and others, but there is no denying that, due to the Voting Rights Act, our Nation has made great strides.

Yet the Act has not eased the restrictions in § 5 or narrowed the scope of the coverage formula in § 4(b) along the way. Those extraordinary and unprecedented features were reauthorized—as if nothing had changed. In fact, the Act's unusual remedies have grown even stronger. When Congress reauthorized the Act in 2006, it did so for another 25 years on top of the previous 40—a far cry from the initial five-year period. Congress also expanded the prohibitions in § 5.

Respondents do not deny that there have been improvements on the ground, but argue that much of this can be attributed to the deterrent effect of § 5, which dissuades covered jurisdictions from engaging in discrimination that they would resume should § 5 be struck down. Under this theory, however, § 5 would be effectively immune from scrutiny; no matter how "clean" the record of covered jurisdictions, the argument could always be made that it was deterrence that accounted for the good behavior.

The provisions of § 5 apply only to those jurisdictions singled out by § 4. We now consider whether that coverage formula is constitutional in light of current conditions.

III

A

When upholding the constitutionality of the coverage formula in 1966, we concluded that it was "rational in both practice and theory." The formula looked to cause (discriminatory tests) and effect (low voter registration and turnout), and tailored the remedy (preclearance) to those jurisdictions exhibiting both.

By 2009, however, we concluded that the "coverage formula raise[d] serious constitutional questions." As we explained, a statute's "current burdens" must be justified by "current needs," and any "disparate geographic coverage" must be "sufficiently related to the problem that it targets." The coverage formula met that test in 1965, but no longer does so.

Coverage today is based on decades-old data and eradicated practices. The formula captures States by reference to literacy tests and low voter registration and turnout in the 1960s and early 1970s. But such tests have been banned nationwide for over 40 years. And voter registration and turnout numbers in the covered States have risen dramatically in the years since. Racial disparity in those numbers was compelling evidence justifying the preclearance remedy and the coverage formula. There is no longer such a disparity.

In 1965, the States could be divided into two groups: those with a recent history of voting tests and low voter registration and turnout, and those without those characteristics. Congress based its coverage formula on that distinction. Today the Nation is no longer divided along those lines, yet the Voting Rights Act continues to treat it as if it were.

B

The Government's defense of the formula is limited. First, the Government contends that the formula is "reverse-engineered": Congress identified the jurisdictions to be covered and *then* came up with criteria to describe them. Brief for Federal Respondent 48–49. Under that reasoning, there need not be any logical relationship between the criteria in the formula and the reason for coverage; all that is necessary is that the formula happen to capture the jurisdictions Congress wanted to single out.

The Government falls back to the argument that because the formula was relevant in 1965, its continued use is permissible so long as any discrimination remains in the States Congress identified back then—regardless of how that discrimination compares to discrimination in States unburdened by coverage. Brief for Federal

Respondent 49–50. This argument does not look to "current political conditions,", but instead relies on a comparison between the States in 1965. That comparison reflected the different histories of the North and South. It was in the South that slavery was upheld by law until uprooted by the Civil War, that the reign of Jim Crow denied African-Americans the most basic freedoms, and that state and local governments worked tirelessly to disenfranchise citizens on the basis of race. The Court invoked that history—rightly so—in sustaining the disparate coverage of the Voting Rights Act in 1966.

But history did not end in 1965. By the time the Act was reauthorized in 2006, there had been 40 more years of it. In assessing the "current need [ ]" for a preclearance system that treats States differently from one another today, that history cannot be ignored. During that time, largely because of the Voting Rights Act, voting tests were abolished, disparities in voter registration and turnout due to race were erased, and African-Americans attained political office in record numbers. And yet the coverage formula that Congress reauthorized in 2006 ignores these developments, keeping the focus on decades-old data relevant to decades-old problems, rather than current data reflecting current needs.

The Fifteenth Amendment commands that the right to vote shall not be denied or abridged on account of race or color, and it gives Congress the power to enforce that command. The Amendment is not designed to punish for the past; its purpose is to ensure a better future. To serve that purpose, Congress—if it is to divide the States—must identify those jurisdictions to be singled out on a basis that makes sense in light of current conditions. It cannot rely simply on the past. We made that clear in *Northwest Austin,* and we make it clear again today.

C

In defending the coverage formula, the Government, the intervenors, and the dissent also rely heavily on data from the record that they claim justify disparate coverage. Congress compiled thousands of pages of evidence before reauthorizing the Voting Rights Act. The court below and the parties have debated what that record shows—they have gone back and forth about whether to compare covered to noncovered jurisdictions as blocks, how to disaggregate the data State by State, how to weigh § 2 cases as evidence of ongoing discrimination, and whether to consider evidence not before Congress, among other issues. Regardless of how to look at the record, however, no one can fairly say that it shows anything approaching the "pervasive," "flagrant," "widespread," and "rampant" discrimination that faced Congress in 1965, and that clearly distinguished the covered jurisdictions from the rest of the Nation at that time.

But a more fundamental problem remains: Congress did not use the record it compiled to shape a coverage formula grounded in current conditions. It instead reenacted a formula based on 40-year-old facts having no logical relation to the present day. The dissent relies on "second-generation barriers," which are not impediments to the casting of ballots, but rather electoral arrangements that affect the weight of minority votes. That does not cure the problem. Viewing the preclearance requirements as targeting such efforts simply highlights the irrationality of continued reliance on the § 4 coverage formula, which is based on voting tests and access to the ballot, not vote dilution. We cannot pretend that we are reviewing an updated statute, or try our hand at updating the statute ourselves, based on the new record compiled by Congress. Contrary to the dissent's contention, see *post,* at 2644, we are not ignoring the record; we are simply recognizing that it played no role in shaping the statutory formula before us today.

The judgment of the Court of Appeals is reversed.

It is so ordered.

JUSTICE THOMAS, concurring.

I join the Court's opinion in full but write separately to explain that I would find § 5 of the Voting Rights Act unconstitutional as well.

JUSTICE GINSBURG, with whom JUSTICE BREYER, JUSTICE SOTOMAYOR, and JUSTICE KAGAN join, dissenting.

In the Court's view, the very success of § 5 of the Voting Rights Act demands its dormancy. Congress was of another mind. Recognizing that large progress has been made, Congress determined, based on a voluminous record, that the scourge of discrimination was not yet extirpated. The question this case presents is who decides whether, as currently operative, § 5 remains justifiable, this Court, or a Congress charged with the obligation to enforce the post-Civil War Amendments "by appropriate legislation." With overwhelming support in both Houses, Congress concluded that, for two prime reasons, § 5 should continue in force, unabated. First, continuance would facilitate completion of the impressive gains thus far made; and second, continuance would guard against backsliding. Those assessments were well within Congress' province to make and should elicit this Court's unstinting approbation.

I

"[V]oting discrimination still exists; no one doubts that." *Ante,* at 2619. But the Court today terminates the remedy that proved to be best suited to block that discrimination. The Voting Rights Act of 1965 (VRA) has worked to combat voting discrimination where other remedies had been tried and failed. Particularly effective is the VRA's requirement of federal preclearance for all changes to voting laws in the regions of the country with the most aggravated records of rank discrimination against minority voting rights.

Although the VRA wrought dramatic changes in the realization of minority voting rights, the Act, to date, surely has not eliminated all vestiges of discrimination against the exercise of the franchise by minority citizens. Jurisdictions covered by the preclearance requirement continued to submit, in large numbers, proposed changes to voting laws that the Attorney General declined to approve, auguring that barriers to minority voting would quickly resurface were the preclearance remedy eliminated. Congress also found that as "registration and voting of minority citizens increas[ed], other measures may be resorted to which would dilute increasing minority voting strength.".

Second-generation barriers come in various forms. One of the blockages is racial gerrymandering, the redrawing of legislative districts in an "effort to segregate the races for purposes of voting." Another is adoption of a system of at-large voting in lieu of district-by-district voting in a city with a sizable black minority. By switching to at-large voting, the overall majority could control the election of each city council member, effectively eliminating the potency of the minority's votes. Grofman & Davidson, The Effect of Municipal Election Structure on Black Representation in Eight Southern States, in Quiet Revolution in the South 301, 319 (C. Davidson & B. Grofman eds. 1994) (hereinafter Quiet Revolution). A similar effect could be achieved if the city engaged in discriminatory annexation by incorporating majority-white areas into city limits, thereby decreasing the effect of VRA-occasioned increases in black voting. Whatever the device employed, this Court has long recognized that vote dilution, when adopted with a discriminatory purpose, cuts down the right to vote as certainly as denial of access to the ballot.

In response to evidence of these substituted barriers, Congress reauthorized the VRA for five years in 1970, for seven years in 1975, and for 25 years in 1982. *Ante,* at 2620–2621. Each time, this Court upheld the reauthorization as a valid exercise of congressional power. *Ante,* at 2620. As the 1982 reauthorization approached its 2007 expiration date, Congress again considered whether the VRA's preclearance mechanism remained an appropriate response to the problem of voting discrimination in covered jurisdictions.

In the long course of the legislative process, Congress "amassed a sizable record." The House and Senate Judiciary Committees held 21 hearings, heard from scores of witnesses, received a number of investigative reports and other written documentation of continuing discrimination in covered jurisdictions. In all, the legislative record Congress compiled filled more than 15,000 pages. H.R. Rep. 109–478, at 5, 11–12; S. Rep. 109–295, at 2–4, 15. The compilation presents countless "examples of flagrant racial discrimination" since the last reauthorization; Congress also brought to light systematic evidence that "intentional racial discrimination in voting remains so serious and widespread in covered jurisdictions that section 5 preclearance is still needed."

After considering the full legislative record, Congress made the following findings: The VRA has directly caused significant progress in eliminating first-generation barriers to ballot access, leading to a marked increase in minority voter registration and turnout and the number of minority elected officials. 2006 Reauthorization § 2(b)(1). But despite this progress, "second generation barriers constructed to prevent minority voters from fully participating in the electoral process" continued to exist, as well as racially polarized voting in the covered jurisdictions, which increased the political vulnerability of racial and language minorities in those jurisdictions. Extensive "[e]vidence of continued discrimination," Congress concluded, "clearly show[ed] the continued need for Federal oversight" in covered jurisdictions. The overall record demonstrated to the federal lawmakers that, "without the continuation of the Voting Rights Act of 1965 protections, racial and language minority citizens will be deprived of the opportunity to exercise their right to vote, or will have their votes diluted, undermining the significant gains made by minorities in the last 40 years."

Based on these findings, Congress reauthorized preclearance for another 25 years, while also undertaking to reconsider the extension after 15 years to ensure that the provision was still necessary and effective. The question before the Court is whether Congress had the authority under the Constitution to act as it did.

II

In answering this question, the Court does not write on a clean slate. It is well established that Congress' judgment regarding exercise of its power to enforce the Fourteenth and Fifteenth Amendments warrants substantial deference. The VRA addresses the combination of race discrimination and the right to vote, which is "preservative of all rights." When confronting the most constitutionally invidious form of discrimination, and the most fundamental right in our democratic system, Congress' power to act is at its height.

The basis for this deference is firmly rooted in both constitutional text and precedent. The Fifteenth Amendment, which targets precisely and only racial discrimination in voting rights, states that, in this domain, "Congress shall have power to enforce this article by appropriate legislation." In choosing this language, the Amendment's framers invoked Chief Justice Marshall's formulation of the scope of Congress' powers under the Necessary and Proper Clause:

"Let the end be legitimate, let it be within the scope of the constitution, and *all means which are appropriate, which are plainly adapted to that end,* which are not prohibited, but consist with the letter and spirit of the constitution, are constitutional." *McCulloch v. Maryland,* 4 Wheat. 316, 421, 4 L.Ed. 579 (1819) (emphasis added). It cannot tenably be maintained that the VRA, an Act of Congress adopted to shield the right to vote from racial discrimination, is inconsistent with the letter or spirit of the Fifteenth Amendment, or any provision of the Constitution read in light of the Civil War Amendments. Nowhere in today's opinion, or in *Northwest Austin,* is there clear recognition of the transformative effect the Fifteenth Amendment aimed to achieve. Notably, "the Founders' first successful amendment told Congress that it could 'make no law' over a certain domain"; in contrast, the Civil War Amendments used "language [that] authorized transformative new federal statutes to uproot all vestiges of unfreedom and inequality" and provided "sweeping enforcement powers . . . to enact 'appropriate' legislation targeting state abuses."

FOR DISCUSSION

Do you think that the VRA preclearance provisions need to be reauthorized given the changes in voting and office holding among people of color since the original adoption of the Act in 1965? Did the election of Barack Obama as president prove that the VRA is no longer needed? Since the *Shelby County* decision, do you see voting rights as being less protected than before? If current voting data and trends had been offered and used by Congress, would the Court have invalidated the Section 4 criteria?

ARIZONA V. INTER TRIBAL COUNCIL OF ARIZONA, INC.

570 U.S. ___, 133 S.Ct. 2247, 186 L.Ed.2d 239 (2013)

Arizona residents and non-profits challenged a state law requiring voters to present proof of citizenship when they registered to vote and to present identification when they voted on election day, claiming that the proof of citizenship requirement was preempted by National Voter Registration Act (NVRA). The District Court held for the state, the Ninth Circuit affirmed and reversed in part. The Supreme Court affirmed.

Vote 7–2

JUSTICE SCALIA wrote for the court.

KENNEDY filed a concurrence and THOMAS and ALITO dissented.

The National Voter Registration Act requires States to "accept and use" a uniform federal form to register voters for federal elections. The contents of that form (colloquially known as the Federal Form) are prescribed by a federal agency, the Election Assistance Commission. The Federal Form developed by the EAC does not require documentary evidence of citizenship; rather, it requires only that an applicant aver, under penalty of perjury, that he is a citizen. Arizona law requires voter-registration officials to "reject" any application for registration, including a Federal Form, that is not accompanied by concrete evidence of citizenship. The question is whether Arizona's evidence-of-citizenship requirement, as applied to Federal Form applicants, is pre-empted by the Act's mandate that States "accept and use" the Federal Form.

I

Over the past two decades, Congress has erected a complex superstructure of federal regulation atop state voter-registration systems. The National Voter Registration Act of 1993 (NVRA), "requires States to provide simplified systems for registering to vote in *federal* elections." The Act requires each State to permit prospective voters to "register to vote in elections for Federal office" by any of three methods: simultaneously with a driver's license application, in person, or by mail.

This case concerns registration by mail. Section 1973gg–2(a)(2) of the Act requires a State to establish procedures for registering to vote in federal elections "by mail application pursuant to section 1973gg–4 of this title." Section 1973gg–4, in turn, requires States to "accept and use" a standard federal registration form. The Election Assistance Commission is invested with rulemaking authority to prescribe the contents of that Federal Form. § 1973gg–7(a)(1). The EAC is explicitly instructed, however, to develop the Federal Form "in consultation with the chief election officers of the States." The Federal Form thus contains a number of state-specific instructions, which tell residents of each State what additional information they must provide and where they must submit the form. Each state-specific instruction must be approved by the EAC before it is included on the Federal Form.

To be eligible to vote under Arizona law, a person must be a citizen of the United States. This case concerns Arizona's efforts to enforce that qualification. In 2004, Arizona voters adopted Proposition 200, a ballot initiative designed in part "to combat voter fraud by requiring voters to present proof of citizenship when they register to vote and to present identification when they vote on election day." Proposition 200 amended the State's election code to require county recorders to "reject any application for registration that is not accompanied by satisfactory evidence of United States citizenship." The proof-of-citizenship requirement is satisfied by (1) a photocopy of the applicant's passport or birth certificate, (2) a driver's license number, if the license states that the issuing authority verified the holder's U.S. citizenship, (3) evidence of naturalization, (4) tribal identification, or (5) "[o]ther documents or methods of proof . . . established pursuant to the Immigration Reform and Control Act of 1986." The EAC did not grant Arizona's request to include this new requirement among the state-specific instructions for Arizona on the Federal Form. App. 225. Consequently, the Federal Form includes a statutorily required attestation, subscribed to under penalty of perjury, that an Arizona applicant meets the State's voting requirements (including the citizenship requirement), but does not require concrete evidence of citizenship.

II

The Elections Clause, Art. I, § 4, cl. 1, provides:

> "The Times, Places and Manner of holding Elections for Senators and Representatives, shall be prescribed in each State by the Legislature thereof; but the Congress may at any time by Law make or alter such Regulations, except as to the places of chusing Senators."

The Clause empowers Congress to pre-empt state regulations governing the "Times, Places and Manner" of holding congressional elections. The question here is whether the federal statutory requirement that States "accept and use" the Federal Form pre-empts Arizona's state-law requirement that officials "reject" the application of a prospective voter who submits a completed Federal Form unaccompanied by documentary evidence of citizenship.

A

The Elections Clause has two functions. Upon the States it imposes the duty ("*shall* be prescribed") to prescribe the time, place, and manner of electing Representatives and Senators; upon Congress it confers the power to alter those regulations or supplant them altogether. This grant of congressional power was the Framers' insurance against the possibility that a State would refuse to provide for the election of representatives to the Federal Congress. "[E]very government ought to contain in itself the means of its own preservation," and "an exclusive power of regulating elections for the national government, in the hands of the State legislatures, would leave the existence of the Union entirely at their mercy. They could at any moment annihilate it by neglecting to provide for the choice of persons to administer its affairs." The Federalist No. 59, pp. 362–363 (C. Rossiter ed. 1961) (A. Hamilton) (emphasis deleted). That prospect seems fanciful today, but the widespread, vociferous opposition to the proposed Constitution made it a very real concern in the founding era.

The Clause's substantive scope is broad. "Times, Places, and Manner," we have written, are "comprehensive words," which "embrace authority to provide a complete code for congressional elections," including, as relevant here and as petitioners do not contest, regulations relating to "registration." (recounts) (primaries). In practice, the Clause functions as "a default provision; it invests the States with responsibility for the mechanics of congressional elections, but only so far as Congress declines to pre-empt state legislative choices." The power of Congress over the "Times, Places and Manner" of congressional elections "is paramount, and may be exercised at any time, and to any extent which it deems expedient; and so far as it is exercised, and no farther, the regulations effected supersede those of the State which are inconsistent therewith."

B

The straightforward textual question here is whether Ariz.Rev.Stat. Ann. § 16–166(F), which requires state officials to "reject" a Federal Form unaccompanied by documentary evidence of citizenship, conflicts with the NVRA's mandate that Arizona "accept and use" the Federal Form. If so, the state law, "so far as the conflict extends, ceases to be operative." In Arizona's view, these seemingly incompatible obligations can be read to operate harmoniously: The NVRA, it contends, requires merely that a State receive the Federal Form willingly and use that form as one element in its (perhaps lengthy) transaction with a prospective voter.

Taken in isolation, the mandate that a State "accept and use" the Federal Form is fairly susceptible of two interpretations. It might mean that a State must accept the Federal Form as a complete and sufficient registration application; or it might mean that the State is merely required to receive the form willingly and use it *somehow* in its voter registration process. Both readings—"receive willingly" and "accept as sufficient"—are compatible with the plain meaning of the word "accept." See 1 Oxford English Dictionary 70 (2d ed. 1989) ("To take or receive (a thing offered) willingly"; "To receive as sufficient or adequate"); Webster's New International Dictionary 14 (2d ed. 1954) ("To receive (a thing offered to or thrust upon one) with a consenting mind"; "To receive with favor; to approve"). And we take it as self-evident that the "elastic" verb "use," read in isolation, is broad enough to encompass Arizona's preferred construction. In common parlance, one might say that a restaurant accepts and uses credit cards even though it requires customers to show matching identification when making a purchase.

"Words that can have more than one meaning are given content, however, by their surroundings." And reading "accept" merely to denote willing receipt seems out of place in the context of an official mandate to accept and use something for a given purpose. The implication of such a mandate is that its object is to be accepted *as sufficient* for the requirement it is meant to satisfy. For example, a government *diktat* that "civil servants shall accept government IOUs for payment of salaries" does not invite the response, "sure, we'll accept IOUs—if you pay us a ten percent down payment in cash." Many federal statutes contain similarly phrased commands, and they contemplate more than mere willing receipt.

Arizona's reading is also difficult to reconcile with neighboring provisions of the NVRA. Section 1973gg–6(a)(1)(B) provides that a State shall "ensure that any eligible applicant is registered to vote in an election . . . if the *valid voter registration form* of the applicant is postmarked" not later than a specified number of days before the election. (Emphasis added.) Yet Arizona reads the phrase "accept and use" in § 1973gg–4(a)(1) as permitting it to *reject* a completed Federal Form if the applicant does not submit additional information required by state law. That reading can be squared with Arizona's obligation under § 1973gg–6(a)(1) only if a completed Federal Form is not a "valid voter registration form," which seems unlikely. The statute empowers the EAC to create the Federal Form, § 1973gg–7(a), requires the EAC to prescribe its contents within specified limits, § 1973gg–7(b), and requires States to "accept and use" it, § 1973gg–4(a)(1). It is improbable that the statute envisions a completed copy of the form it takes such pains to create as being anything less than "valid."

The Act also authorizes States, "*[i]n addition to* accepting and using the" Federal Form, to create their own, state-specific voter-registration forms, which can be used to register voters in both state and federal elections. These state-developed forms may require information the Federal Form does not. (For example, unlike the Federal Form, Arizona's registration form includes Proposition 200's proof-of-citizenship requirement. This permission works in tandem with the requirement that States "accept and use" the Federal Form. States retain the flexibility to design and use their own registration forms, but the Federal Form provides a backstop: No matter what procedural hurdles a State's own form imposes, the Federal Form guarantees that a simple means of registering to vote in federal elections will be available. Arizona's reading would permit a State to demand of Federal Form applicants every additional piece of information the State requires on its state-specific form. If that is so, the Federal Form ceases to perform any meaningful function, and would be a feeble means of "increas[ing] the number of eligible citizens who register to vote in elections for Federal office."

III

Arizona contends, however, that its construction of the phrase "accept and use" is necessary to avoid a conflict between the NVRA and Arizona's constitutional authority to establish qualifications (such as citizenship) for voting. Arizona is correct that the Elections Clause empowers Congress to regulate *how* federal elections are held, but not *who* may vote in them. The Constitution prescribes a straightforward rule for the composition of the federal electorate. Article I, § 2, cl. 1, provides that electors in each State for the House of Representatives "shall have the Qualifications requisite for Electors of the most numerous Branch of the State Legislature," and the Seventeenth Amendment adopts the same criterion for senatorial elections. Cf. also Art. II, § 1, cl. 2 ("Each State shall appoint, in such Manner as the Legislature thereof may direct," presidential electors). One cannot read the Elections Clause as treating implicitly what these other constitutional provisions regulate explicitly. "It is difficult to see how words could be clearer in stating what Congress can control and what it cannot control. Surely nothing in these provisions lends itself to the view that voting qualifications in federal elections are to be set by Congress."

Prescribing voting qualifications, therefore, "forms no part of the power to be conferred upon the national government" by the Elections Clause, which is "expressly restricted to the regulation of the *times,* the *places,* and the *manner* of elections." The Federalist No. 60, at 371 (A. Hamilton); see also *id.,* No. 52, at 326 (J. Madison). This allocation of authority sprang from the Framers' aversion to concentrated power. A Congress empowered to regulate the qualifications of its own electorate, Madison warned, could "by degrees subvert the Constitution." 2 Records of the Federal Convention of 1787, p. 250 (M. Farrand rev. 1966). At the same time, by tying the federal franchise to the state franchise instead of simply placing it within the unfettered discretion of state legislatures, the Framers avoided "render[ing] too dependent on the State governments that branch of the federal government which ought to be dependent on the people alone." The Federalist No. 52, at 326 (J. Madison).

Since the power to establish voting requirements is of little value without the power to enforce those requirements, Arizona is correct that it would raise serious constitutional doubts if a federal statute precluded a State from obtaining the information necessary to enforce its voter qualifications. If, but for Arizona's interpretation of the "accept and use" provision, the State would be precluded from obtaining information necessary for enforcement, we would have to determine whether Arizona's interpretation, though plainly not the best reading, is at least a possible one. Happily, we are spared that necessity, since the statute provides another means by which Arizona may obtain information needed for enforcement.

Section 1973gg–7(b)(1) of the Act provides that the Federal Form "may require only such identifying information (including the signature of the applicant) and other information (including data relating to previous registration by the applicant), as is necessary to enable the appropriate State election official to assess the eligibility of the applicant and to administer voter registration and other parts of the election process." At oral argument, the United States expressed the view that the phrase "may require only" in § 1973gg–7(b)(1) means that the EAC "*shall require* information that's necessary, but may only require that information." That is to say, § 1973gg–7(b)(1) acts as both a ceiling and a floor with respect to the contents of the Federal Form. We need not consider the Government's contention that despite the statute's statement that the EAC "may" require on the Federal Form information "necessary to enable the appropriate State election official to assess the eligibility of the applicant," other provisions of the Act indicate that such action is statutorily required. That is because we think that—by analogy to the rule of statutory interpretation that avoids questionable constitutionality—validly conferred discretionary executive authority is properly exercised (as the Government has proposed) to avoid serious constitutional doubt. That is to say, it is surely permissible if not requisite for the Government to say that necessary information which *may* be required *will* be required.

Since, pursuant to the Government's concession, a State may request that the EAC alter the Federal Form to include information the State deems necessary to determine eligibility, and may challenge the EAC's rejection of that request in a suit under the Administrative Procedure Act, no constitutional doubt is raised by giving the "accept and use" provision of the NVRA its fairest reading. That alternative means of enforcing its constitutional power to determine voting qualifications remains open to Arizona here. In 2005, the EAC divided 2-to-2 on the request by Arizona to include the evidence-of-citizenship requirement among the state-specific instructions on the Federal Form, which meant that no action could be taken, see 42 U.S.C. § 15328 ("Any action which the Commission is authorized to carry out under this chapter may be carried out only with the approval of at least three of its members"). Arizona did not challenge that agency action (or rather inaction) by seeking APA review in federal court, but we are aware of nothing that prevents Arizona from renewing its request. Should the EAC's inaction persist, Arizona would have the opportunity to establish in a reviewing court that a mere oath will not suffice to effectuate its citizenship requirement and that the EAC is therefore under a nondiscretionary duty to include Arizona's concrete evidence requirement on the Federal Form. Arizona might also assert (as it has argued here) that it would be arbitrary for the EAC to refuse to include Arizona's instruction when it has accepted a similar instruction requested by Louisiana.

We hold that 42 U.S.C. § 1973gg–4 precludes Arizona from requiring a Federal Form applicant to submit information beyond that required by the form itself. Arizona may, however, request anew that the EAC include such a requirement among the Federal Form's state-specific instructions, and may seek judicial review of the EAC's decision under the Administrative Procedure Act.

The judgment of the Court of Appeals is affirmed.

FOR DISCUSSION

Is there anything Congress can do to prevent states from requiring proof of citizenship to vote in state elections? If not and if states do require this proof, what impact do you think it will have on how state and federal elections are administered? Will it create a two-tier election process where states hold separate elections for their own and federal offices?

Article I, Sec. 2, cl. 3:

The actual Enumeration shall be made within three Years after the first Meeting of the Congress of the United States, and within every subsequent Term of ten Years, in such Manner as they shall by Law direct.

REAPPORTIONMENT AND REDISTRICTING

The Constitution mandates a **decennial census**. The purpose of the census is, in part, to determine the population of states and therefore the allocation of seats for Congress. But how should new congressional district lines and, for that matter, state legislative lines be drawn? This is one of the most vexing and important questions in politics. Legislatures, entrusted with the duty to draw both, have often resorted to a variety of tricks when engaging in **reapportionment**. They do so because the drawing of district lines can have an impact on who is elected and who has power. From the earliest days of the American republic, efforts have been undertaken to manipulate district lines. In the early nineteenth century Elbridge Gerry, a signer of the

Declaration of Independence and later governor in Massachusetts, sought to draw lines in a way that would benefit him. One district, which looked like a salamander, led a newspaper to coin the term "**gerrymander**" to describe the process of drawing district lines to favor a specific group, such as incumbents.

While such a practice has deep roots in American history, is the practice unconstitutional or simply an accepted fact of politics? Is it also an issue that the courts should address?

Colegrove v. Green (328 U.S. 549, 1946) reiterates the traditional view of the Court that reapportionment and redistricting of legislative bodies is a politica1 matter and not a justiciable question. The case is notable for Justice Frankfurter's observation that the Court should not get involved in the "political thicket" and for Justice Black's dissent, in which he maintained that deliberate legislative discrimination in a matter such as this was denial of equal protection. Yet the *Colgrove* decision did not stand long. A few years later in *Gomillion v. Lightfoot* (364 U.S. 339, 1960) Justice Frankfurter found that racial gerrymandering could be challenged under the Fifteenth Amendment. Sixteen years later in *Baker v. Carr* (369 U.S. 186, 1962) majority and minority positions were reversed. Justice Rutledge had voted with the majority in *Colegrove* because he thought this view was the lesser of two evils. The presumption of the Court seemed to be that Congress under Article I, Sec. 4 has the power to redistrict states. But now, writing for the majority, Justice Brennan in *Baker* overruled *Colgrove* and stated that redistricting was a justiciable question that could be heard by the courts. It left to later cases what standards were to be used to judge where gerrymandering had occurred.

Reynolds v. Sims (377 U.S. 533, 1963) along with *Gray v. Sanders* (372 U.S. 368, 1963) and *Westbury v. Sanders* (376 U.S. 1, 1964) established the principle that all districts must adhere to the "**one person, one vote**" standard. More exactly, in Westbury the Court said the standard must be one person, one vote, "as nearly as is practicable." While one-person, one-vote was the official mathematical standard, the Court applied it differently to congressional versus state and local government seats. In *Kirkpatrick v. Preisler* (394 U.S. 526, 1969), *White v. Weiser* (412 U.S. 783, 1973), and most notably *Karcher v. Daggett* (462 U.S. 725, 1983), the Court ruled that mathematical equality was mandated for congressional districts. Although subsequently in *Tennant v. Jefferson County Commission*, 133 S.Ct. 3 (2012) the Court ruled that a 4,871-person variance among congressional districts within a states did not violate the *Wesbury* "as nearly as is practicable" standard. When it came to apportionment of state and local government seats, the Court seemed more willing to tolerate some variance—10 percent from the least to the most populous districts—if needed to prevent the dividing up of subunits of government (*Abate v. Mundt*, 403 U.S. 182, 184–5, 1971; *Mahan v. Howell*, 410 U.S. 315, 323–4, 1973; and *Gaffney v. Cummings*, 412 U.S. 735, 740–41, 1973) (*permitting* the deviations under the Equal Protection Clause).

After *Reynolds* the general assumption was that one person, one vote and the drawing of district lines was meant to be based on the total population within a state, and not based on the population which votes. Yet in *Evenwel v. Abbott*, 136 S.Ct. 1120 (2016), the Supreme Court was confronted with this question. Plaintiffs argued that the Texas state senate lines should be based on equal voters per district, not total population. Using total population amounted to a dilution of voting rights, where some districts represented far more voters than others. The Court unanimously rejected the plaintiff's argument, saying that states were free to use total population as the basis of drawing district lines.

When redistricting is undertaken, population, respect for local subdivisions, and the shape and compactness of the district are considered traditional redistricting criteria that may be considered when lines are drawn. As *Gomillion* pointed out, race may not normally be considered when drawing lines. However, the passage of the 1965 **Voting Rights Act** (VRA), as well as subsequent amendments to it, sought to increase both the voting registration and turnout of people of color, as well as minority candidates. The VRA included a requirement that seats for office should be created in a way that makes it possible for people of color to elect their own representatives. These seats were called **majority-minority seats** because the racial makeup of voters might need to be considered when district lines were drawn. The question posed here is whether this use of race was unconstitutional, even though it was aimed at increasing minority turnout and representation. As early as *United Jewish Organizations of Williamsburg, Inc. v. Carey* (430 U.S. 144, 1977), the Supreme Court seems to suggest that the use of race could be considered when drawing district lines if the goal were to preserve communities of interest and maximize minority representation. In that case, the breaking up of Jewish communities was permitted to draw lines to enhance African-American representation. But how far could race, even with the VRA, be considered when drawing district lines?

Fifteenth Amendment, Sec. 1:

The right of citizens of the United States to vote shall not be denied or abridged by the United States or by any State on account of race, color, or previous condition of servitude.

Shaw v. Reno, 509 U.S. 630 (1993), mandated that strict scrutiny be used when race was employed for redistricting purposes. Justice O'Connor's language, that appearances matter, suggested that if the shape of districts could not be explained but for race, then the presumption was that race was a factor when drawing the lines. The *Shaw* majority suggested that redistricting should be race neutral. Is that the best way to promote the representation of people of color? Does *Shaw* mean that race may never be used in the drawing of district lines? In subsequent cases such as *Shaw v. Hunt* (517 U.S. 899, 1996) and *Bush v. Vera* (517 U.S. 952, 1996), the Court seemed to suggest that. *Hunt* was the follow-up case after *Reno*, and it again struck down the North Carolina redistricting plan. However, in *Hunt v. Cromartie* (526 U.S. 541, 1999), the Court did uphold the a third redistricting schema in North Carolina, ruling that race could be used if it is a proxy for partisanship. Does this decision back away from the hard line against the use of race in *Reno*?

Is the use of political party or partisanship a legitimate criterion to use when redistricting? Some argue that the use of party affiliation when drawing lines, especially if the purpose is to favor one political party at the expense of another, amounts to an unconstitutional **partisan gerrymander**. Addressing partisan gerrymandering has been the object of three Supreme Court decisions that have done no more than muddle the issues. In all three cases, the Equal Protection Clause was the primary constitutional hook for the litigation.

First, in *Davis v. Bandamer* (478 U.S. 109, 1986), Indiana Democrats contested the constitutionality of a 1981 state redistricting plan. The specific allegation was that the plan drew legislative lines and seats so as to disadvantage Democrats. It did so by dividing up cities such as South Bend in arguably unusual ways. The Democrats filed suit, contending that these districts violated their rights under the Fourteenth Amendment Equal Protection Clause. The district court had ruled in favor of the Democrats, in part, because of evidence and testimony suggesting that the Republican Party had in fact drawn the lines to favor their own. When the case reached the Supreme Court, a central issue was whether this was a justiciable controversy under the Equal Protection Clause. The Court held that it was.

Yet while the case was deemed justiciable, the Court also articulated several stipulations that had to be met to sustain a political gerrymandering claim. First, there had to be proof of intentional discrimination against the one party, here, the Democrats. Second, "a group's electoral power is not unconstitutionally diminished by the simple fact of an apportionment scheme that makes winning elections more difficult. A failure of proportional representation alone does not constitute impermissible discrimination under the equal protection clause." Instead, the Court stated that the political process must frustrate political activity in a systematic fashion.

> As in individual district cases, an equal protection violation may be found only where the electoral system substantially disadvantages certain voters in their opportunity to influence the political process effectively. In this context, such a finding of unconstitutionality must be supported by evidence of continued frustration of the will of a majority of the voters or effective denial to a minority of voters of a fair chance to influence the political process.

Finally, the Court contended that showing frustration or dilution of political influence in one election was also insufficient. Instead, it would need to be shown that it took place over several elections. In sum, to support a constitutional claim for partisan gerrymandering, the *Bandamer* Court stated that one would have to demonstrate intentional discrimination against a party that systematically frustrated and diluted their ability to influence the political process across several elections.

In *Vieth v. Jubelirer* (541 U.S. 267, 2004) at issue was the constitutionality of a Pennsylvania districting plan that drew the seats for its congressional delegation after the 2000 census. Prior to the census the state had twenty-one representatives, but after 2000 it was only entitled to nineteen seats. Republicans controlled both houses of the Pennsylvania legislature as well as the governor's office. State Democrats contended that the district lines drawn violated Article I, Secs. 2 and 4, and the Equal Protection Clause, thereby constituting both a violation of the one-person, one-vote standard and, more importantly here, a partisan gerrymander. The district court dismissed the partisan or political gerrymandering claim (with some of the other issues addressed or resolved in other litigation in the case), and it was appealed to the Supreme Court.

In a split decision, a four-person plurality opinion written by Justice Scalia reviewed the history of partisan gerrymandering in the United States, concluding that such a practice went back to the early days of the republic. Given this history, there had also been numerous efforts to address it. Justice Scalia argued that the standards for addressing partisan gerrymandering in *Bandamer* had proved unworkable.

Overall, a four-justice plurality ruled that partisan gerrymanders were not justiciable and therefore in the case before them the claims of the Democrats should be rejected. However, five Justices agreed that the Democrats had not proved that a partisan gerrymander existed in the case before them and that this type of issue was not justiciable. Justice Kennedy concurred that there was no partisan gerrymander here, but he refused to go along with overruling *Bandamer.* He agreed that neutral rules for resolving and adjudicating partisan gerrymanders were needed, but he did not agree with the majority that it would never be possible to find them. This thus created a five-justice majority to reject the plaintiffs' claims. Five justices in several dissents, including Kennedy, refused to overrule *Bandamer,* continuing to make partisan gerrymanders justiciable issues. The dissenters could not agree on what constituted acceptable or manageable standards for adjudicating a partisan gerrymander dispute. The hope was that *League of United Latin American Citizens v. Perry (LULAC)* (548 U.S. 399, 2006) would do that, but it did not. In *LULAC* the Court again failed to reverse *Davis.* It also failed to find a manageable standard to govern or address partisan gerrymandering, and it rejected claims that mid-decade redistricting was unconstitutional. By the time one finishes *LULAC,* one can literally see the Court throwing its hands up, saying partisan gerrymandering is problem, but not knowing what to do about it.

Criticism that state legislatures cannot redistrict in a non-partisan or fair fashion has prompted not just judicial remedies, but in some cases the voters have taken that power away and given it to independent redistricting commissions. The argument for some is that is it a conflict of interest or simply improper for state legislatures to draw their own boundaries, or, as some say, for elected officials to pick their own voters. In Arizona voters through a ballot measure created a redistricting commission that took away the power from the legislature to draw the boundaries. Members of the State Legislature challenged the ballot proposition, arguing that it violated the Elections Clause of United States Constitution, (Article I, Section 4, clause 1). In a closely divided 5–4 opinion the Court rejected the challenge in *Arizona State Legislature v. Arizona Independent Redistricting Commission,* 135 S.Ct. 2652 (2015). Its decision turned on a careful reading and interpretation of what the word "legislature" referred to or meant to the constitutional framers, as well as on legislative history both in Congress and in Arizona. The decision may facilitate movement in other states to create similar commissions and break the impasse on partisan gerrymandering that the Court left after the *LULAC* decision.

COLEGROVE V. GREEN

328 U.S. 549, 66 S.Ct. 1198, 90 L.Ed. 1432 (1946)

Suit was brought by residents of a congressional district in Illinois with a larger population than other districts in the state to restrain the officials of the state from carrying on an election in which representatives were to be elected from these districts. The contention was that the congressional districts lacked compactness of territory and approximate equality of population.

Vote: 4–3

JUSTICE FRANKFURTER delivered the opinion of the Court:

We are of opinion that the petitioners ask of this Court what is beyond its competence to grant. This is one of those demands on judicial power which cannot be met by verbal fencing about "jurisdiction." It must be resolved by considerations on the basis of which this Court, from time to time, has refused to intervene in controversies. It has refused to do so because due regard for the effective working of our Government revealed this issue to be of a peculiarly political nature and therefore not meet for judicial determination.

The short of it is that the Constitution has conferred upon Congress exclusive authority to secure fair representation by the States in the popular House and left to that House determination whether States have fulfilled their responsibility. If Congress failed in exercising its powers, whereby standards of fairness are offended, the remedy ultimately lies with the people. Whether Congress faithfully discharges its duty or not, the subject has been committed to the exclusive control of Congress. An aspect of government from which the judiciary, in view of what is involved, has been excluded by the clear intention of the Constitution cannot be entered by the federal courts because Congress may have been in default in exacting from States obedience to its mandate.

To sustain this action would cut very deep into the very being of Congress. Courts ought not to enter this political thicket. The remedy for unfairness in districting is to secure State legislatures that will apportion properly, or to invoke the ample powers of Congress. The Constitution has many commands that are not enforceable by courts because they clearly fall outside the conditions and purposes that circumscribe judicial action. Thus, "on Demand of the executive Authority," Article Four, Section 2, of a State it is the duty of a sister State to deliver up a fugitive from justice. But the fulfillment of this duty cannot be judicially enforced. *Kentucky v. Dennison,* 65 U.S. 66 (1860). The duty to see to it that the laws are faithfully executed cannot be brought under legal compulsion. *Mississippi v. Johnson,* 71 U.S. 475 (1867). Violation of the great guaranty of a republican form of government in States cannot be challenged in the courts. *Pacific Teleph. & Teleg. Co. v. Oregon,* 223 U.S. 118 (1912). The Constitution has left the performance of many duties in our governmental scheme to depend on the fidelity of the executive and legislative action and, ultimately, on the vigilance of the people in exercising their political rights.

Dismissal of the complaint is affirmed.

NOTE

Justice Jackson did not sit in this case because of his attendance at the Nuremberg War Crimes trials. Chief Justice Stone had died shortly before the decision.

JUSTICE RUTLEDGE concurred.

. . . Assuming that the controversy is justiciable, I think the cause is of so delicate a character, in view of the considerations above noted, that the jurisdiction should be exercised only in the most compelling circumstances.

As a matter of legislative attention, whether by Congress or the General Assembly, the case made by the complaint is strong. But the relief it seeks pitches this Court into delicate relation to the functions of state officials and Congress, compelling them to take action which heretofore they have declined to take voluntarily or to accept the alternative of electing representatives from Illinois at large in the forthcoming elections.

The shortness of the time remaining makes it doubtful whether action could, or would, be taken in time to secure for petitioners the effective relief they seek. To force them to share in an election at large might bring greater equality of voting right. It would also deprive them and all other Illinois citizens of representation by districts which the prevailing policy of Congress commands.

The right here is not absolute. And the cure sought may be worse than the disease.

JUSTICE BLACK dissented, with the concurrence of JUSTICES DOUGLAS and MURPHY:

. . . It is difficult for me to see why the 1901 State Apportionment Act does not deny appellants equal protection of the laws. The failure of the Legislature to reapportion the Congressional election districts for forty years, despite census figures indicating great changes in the distribution of the population, has resulted in election districts the population of which range from 112,000 to 900,000. One of the appellants lives in a district of more than 900,000 people. His vote is consequently much less effective than that of each of the citizens living in the district of 112,000. And such a gross inequality in the voting power of citizens irrefutably demonstrates a complete lack of effort to make an equitable apportionment. The 1901 State Apportionment Act if applied to the next election would thus result in a wholly indefensible discrimination against appellants and all other voters in heavily populated districts. The equal protection clause of the Fourteenth Amendment forbids such discrimination. It does not permit the States to pick out certain qualified citizens or groups of citizens and deny them the right to vote at all. No one would deny that the equal protection clause would also prohibit a law that would expressly give certain citizens a half-vote and others a full vote. The probable effect of the 1901 State Apportionment Act in the coming election will be that certain citizens, and among them the appellants, will in some instances have votes only one-ninth as effective in choosing representatives to Congress as the votes of other citizens. Such discriminatory legislation seems to me exactly the kind that the equal protection clause was introduced to prohibit.

FOR DISCUSSION

If redistricting is a political question, how will voters remedy their complaints? What options do they have?

RELATED CASES

***Fergus v. Marks:* 321 Ill. 510 (1926).**

State courts cannot compel a state legislature to reapportion the state into districts from which members of the state Senate will be elected. Such actions would be violations of the constitutionally imposed separation of powers. The legislature "is responsible to the people for a failure to perform that duty."

***Cook v. Fortson:* 329 U.S. 675 (1946).**

In this case the Supreme Court directed a district court to dismiss a petition by a candidate who had received the majority of the popular vote in an election. The petitioner was seeking to enjoin compliance with the Georgia county unit rule in selecting a party nominee for Congress.

***MacDougall v. Green:* 335 U.S. 281 (1948).**

An Illinois statute that requires a distribution of signatures of voters on a petition to nominate candidates for a new political party among at least fifty counties of the state is not a denial of equal protection.

***South v. Peters:* 339 U.S. 276 (1950).**

In Georgia, a county unit system allots each county a number of votes that range from two to six depending on population. The distribution amounts to discrimination in favor of the rural counties and resultant discrimination against urban African-American populations. Within each county the "electoral vote" goes to the candidate who receives the greatest popular vote. The Court refused to rule on the legality of this system, holding that this was a political issue "arising from a state's geographical distribution of electoral strength among its political subdivisions."

GOMILLION V. LIGHTFOOT

364 U.S. 339, 81 S.Ct. 125, 5 L.Ed.2d 110 (1960)

The state of Alabama in 1957 redrew the district lines in Tuskegee with a twenty-eight-sided figure such that it eliminated almost all African Americans, including many well-educated African American faculty members at Tuskegee Institute, from a district. The redistricting was challenged as a violation of the Fifteenth Amendment.

Vote: 9–0

JUSTICE FRANKFURTER delivered the opinion of the Court.

This litigation challenges the validity, under the United States Constitution, of Local Act No. 140, passed by the Legislature of Alabama in 1957, redefining the boundaries of the City of Tuskegee. Petitioners, Negro citizens of Alabama who were, at the time of this redistricting measure, residents of the City of Tuskegee, brought an action in the United States District Court for the Middle District of Alabama for a declaratory judgment that Act 140 is unconstitutional, and for an injunction to restrain the Mayor and officers of Tuskegee and the officials of Macon County, Alabama, from enforcing the Act against them and other Negroes similarly situated. Petitioners' claim is that enforcement of the statute, which alters the shape of Tuskegee from a square to an uncouth twenty-eight-sided figure, will constitute a discrimination against them in violation of the Due Process and Equal Protection Clauses of the Fourteenth Amendment to the Constitution and will deny them the right to vote in defiance of the Fifteenth Amendment.

The respondents moved for dismissal of the action for failure to state a claim upon which relief could be granted and for lack of jurisdiction of the District Court. The court granted the motion, stating, "This Court has no control over, no supervision over, and no power to change any boundaries of municipal corporations fixed by a duly convened and elected legislative body, acting for the people in the State of Alabama."

At this stage of the litigation we are not concerned with the truth of the allegations, that is, the ability of petitioners to sustain their allegations by proof. The sole question is whether the allegations entitle them to make good on their claim that they are being denied rights under the United States Constitution. The complaint, charging that Act 140 is a device to disenfranchise Negro citizens, alleges the following facts: Prior to Act 140 the City of Tuskegee was square in shape; the Act transformed it into a strangely irregular twenty-eight-sided figure as indicated in the diagram appended to this opinion. The essential inevitable effect of this redefinition of Tuskegee's boundaries is to remove from the city all save four or five of its 400 Negro voters while not removing a single white voter or resident. The result of the Act is to deprive the Negro petitioners discriminatorily of the benefits of residence in Tuskegee, including, inter alia, the right to vote in municipal elections.

These allegations, if proven, would abundantly establish that Act 140 was not an ordinary geographic redistricting measure even within familiar abuses of gerrymandering. If these allegations upon a trial remained uncontradicted or unqualified, the conclusion would be irresistible, tantamount for all practical purposes to a mathematical demonstration, that the legislation is solely concerned with segregating white and colored voters by fencing Negro citizens out of town so as to deprive them of their pre-existing municipal vote.

It is difficult to appreciate what stands in the way of adjudging a statute having this inevitable effect invalid in light of the principles by which this Court must judge, and uniformly has judged, statutes that, howsoever speciously defined, obviously discriminate against colored citizens. "The (Fifteenth) Amendment nullifies sophisticated as well as simple-minded modes of discrimination."

The complaint amply alleges a claim of racial discrimination. Against this claim the respondents have never suggested, either in their brief or in oral argument, any countervailing municipal function which Act 140 is designed to serve. The respondents invoke generalities expressing the State's unrestricted power-unlimited, that is, by the United States Constitution-to establish, destroy, or reorganize by contraction or expansion its political subdivisions, to wit, cities, counties, and other local units. We freely recognize the breadth and importance of this aspect of the State's political power.

In short, the cases that have come before this Court regarding legislation by States dealing with their political subdivisions fall into two classes: (1) those in which it is claimed that the State, by virtue of the prohibition against impairment of the obligation of contract (Art. I, § 10) and of the Due Process Clause of the Fourteenth Amendment, is without power to extinguish, or alter the boundaries of, an existing municipality; and (2) in which it is claimed that the State has no power to change the identity of a municipality whereby citizens of a pre-existing municipality suffer serious economic disadvantage.

Neither of these claims is supported by such a specific limitation upon State power as confines the States under the Fifteenth Amendment. As to the first category, it is obvious that the creation of municipalities—clearly a political act—does not come within the conception of a contract under the Dartmouth College case. *Trustees of Dartmouth College v. Woodward*, 17 U.S. (4 Wheat.) 518 (1819). As to the second, if one principle clearly emerges from the numerous decisions of this Court dealing with taxation it is that the Due Process Clause affords no immunity against mere inequalities in tax burdens, nor does it afford protection against their increase as an indirect consequence of a State's exercise of its political powers.

This line of authority conclusively shows that the Court has never acknowledged that the States have power to do as they will with municipal corporations regardless of consequences. Legislative control of municipalities, no less than other state power, lies within the scope of relevant limitations imposed by the United States Constitution. If all this is so in regard to the constitutional protection of contracts, it should be equally true that, to paraphrase, such power, extensive though it is, is met and overcome by the Fifteenth Amendment to the

Constitution of the United States, which forbids a State from passing any law which deprives a citizen of his vote because of his race. The opposite conclusion, urged upon us by respondents, would sanction the achievement by a State of any impairment of voting rights whatever so long as it was cloaked in the garb of the realignment of political subdivisions. 'It is inconceivable that guaranties embedded in the Constitution of the United States may thus be manipulated out of existence.

The respondents find another barrier to the trial of this case in *Colegrove v. Green*, 328 U.S. 549 (1946). In that case the Court passed on an Illinois law governing the arrangement of congressional districts within that State. The complaint rested upon the disparity of population between the different districts which rendered the effectiveness of each individual's vote in some districts far less than in others. This disparity came to pass solely through shifts in population between 1901, when Illinois organized its congressional districts, and 1946, when the complaint was lodged. During this entire period elections were held under the districting scheme devised in 1901. The Court affirmed the dismissal of the complaint on the ground that it presented a subject not meet for adjudication. The decisive facts in this case, which at this stage must be taken as proved, are wholly different from the considerations found controlling in *Colegrove*.

That case involved a complaint of discriminatory apportionment of congressional districts. The appellants in *Colegrove* complained only of a dilution of the strength of their votes as a result of legislative inaction over a course of many years. The petitioners here complain that affirmative legislative action deprives them of their votes and the consequent advantages that the ballot affords. When a legislature thus singles out a readily isolated segment of a racial minority for special discriminatory treatment, it violates the Fifteenth Amendment. In no case involving unequal weight in voting distribution that has come before the Court did the decision sanction a differentiation on racial lines whereby approval was given to unequivocal withdrawal of the vote solely from colored citizens. Apart from all else, these considerations lift this controversy out of the so-called 'political' arena and into the conventional sphere of constitutional litigation.

In sum, as Mr. Justice Holmes remarked, when dealing with a related situation, in *Nixon v. Herndon*, 273 U.S. 536 (1927), "Of course the petition concerns political action," but "The objection that the subject-matter of the suit is political is little more than a play upon words." A statute which is alleged to have worked unconstitutional deprivations of petitioners' rights is not immune to attack simply because the mechanism employed by the legislature is a redefinition of municipal boundaries. According to the allegations here made, the Alabama Legislature has not merely redrawn the Tuskegee city limits with incidental inconvenience to the petitioners; it is more accurate to say that it has deprived the petitioners of the municipal franchise and consequent rights and to that end it has incidentally changed the city's boundaries. While in form this is merely an act redefining metes and bounds, if the allegations are established, the inescapable human effect of this essay in geometry and geography is to despoil colored citizens, and only colored citizens, of their theretofore enjoyed voting rights. That was no *Colegrove v. Green*.

When a State exercises power wholly within the domain of state interest, it is insulated from federal judicial review. But such insulation is not carried over when state power is used as an instrument for circumventing a federally protected right. The petitioners are entitled to prove their allegations at trial.

For these reasons, the principal conclusions of the District Court and the Court of Appeals are clearly erroneous and the decision below must be reversed.

Reversed.

JUSTICE WHITTAKER, concurring.

I concur in the Court's judgment, but not in the whole of its opinion. It seems to me that the decision should be rested not on the Fifteenth Amendment, but rather on the Equal Protection Clause of the Fourteenth Amendment to the Constitution.

FOR DISCUSSION

How does Justice Frankfurter distinguish his decision in this case from the previous one in *Colgrove*? Constitutionally, why is the Court willing to hear the latter and not the former?

BAKER V. CARR

369 U.S. 186, 82 S.Ct. 691, 7 L.Ed. 2d 663 (1962)

This was a civil action brought to redress an alleged deprivation of federal constitutional rights. A 1901 statute of Tennessee had been the most recent apportionment of members of the state's general assembly, and the contention was that this did not provide for a proper representation of the voters of the state. The constitution of the state provides for decennial reapportionment. Because of the growth and redistribution of the state's population after 1901, the apportionment in force was challenged as denying equal protection to voters under the Fourteenth Amendment. The federal district court dismissed the case for lack of jurisdiction of the subject matter.

Vote: 6–2

JUSTICE BRENNAN delivered the opinion of the Court:

In light of the District Court's treatment of the case, we hold today only (a) that the court possessed jurisdiction of the subject matter; (b) that a justiciable cause of action is stated upon which appellants would be entitled to appropriate relief; and (c) because appellees raise the issue before this Court, that the appellants have standing to challenge the Tennessee apportionment statutes. Beyond noting that we have no cause at this stage to doubt the District Court will be able to fashion relief if violations of constitutional rights are found, it is improper now to consider what remedy would be most appropriate if appellants prevail at the trial.

[*Jurisdiction of the Subject Matter.*] The District Court was uncertain whether our cases withholding federal judicial relief rested upon a lack of federal jurisdiction or upon the inappropriateness of the subject matter for judicial consideration—what we have designated "nonjusticiability." The distinction between the two grounds is significant. In the instance of nonjusticiability, consideration of the cause is not wholly and immediately foreclosed; rather, the Court's inquiry necessarily proceeds to the point of deciding whether the duty asserted can be judicially identified and its breach judicially determined, and whether protection for the right asserted can be judicially molded. In the instance of lack of jurisdiction the cause either does not "arise under" the Federal Constitution, laws or treaties (or fall within one of the other enumerated categories of Article Three, § 2), or is not a "case or controversy" within the meaning of that section; or the cause is not one described by any jurisdictional statute. Our conclusion that this cause presents no nonjusticiable "political question" settles the only possible doubt that it is a case or controversy. Under the present heading of "Jurisdiction of the Subject Matter" we hold only that the matter set forth in the complaint does arise under the Constitution and is within 28 U.S.C. § 1343.

Article Three, § 2 of the Federal Constitution provides that "the judicial Power shall extend to all Cases, in Law and Equity, arising under this Constitution, the Laws of the United States, and Treaties made, or which shall be made, under their Authority." It is clear that the cause of action is one which "arises under" the Federal Constitution. The complaint alleges that the 1901 statute effects an apportionment that deprives the appellants of the equal protection of the Jaws in violation of the Fourteenth Amendment.

Since the complaint plainly sets forth a case arising under the Constitution, the subject matter is within the federal judicial power defined in Article Three, § 2, and so within the power of Congress to assign to the jurisdiction of the District Courts. Congress has exercised that power in 28 U.S.C. § 1343 (3).

We hold that the District Court has jurisdiction of the subject matter of the federal constitutional claim asserted in the complaint.

[*Standing.*] A federal court cannot "pronounce any statute, wither of a state or of the United States, void, because irreconcilable with the constitution, except as it is called upon to adjudge the legal rights of litigants in actual controversies." *Liverpool, N. Y. & P. Steamship Co. v. Commissioners of Emigration,* 113 U.S. 33, 39 (1885). Have the appellants alleged such a personal stake in the outcome of the controversy as to assure that concrete adverseness which sharpens the presentation of issues upon which the court so largely depends for illumination of difficult constitutional questions? This is the gist of the question of standing. It is, of course, a question of federal law.

The complaint was filed by residents of Davidson, Hamilton, Knox, Montgomery, and Shelby Counties. Each is a person allegedly qualified to vote for members of the General Assembly representing his county. These appellants sued "on their own behalf and on behalf of all qualified voters of their respective counties, and further, on behalf of all voters of the State of Tennessee who are similarly situated." The appellees are the Tennessee Secretary of State, Attorney General, Coordinator of Elections, and members of the State Board of Elections; the members of the State Board are sued in their own right and also as representatives of the County Election Commissioners whom they appoint.

We hold that the appellants do have standing to maintain this suit. Our decisions plainly support this conclusion. Many of the cases have assumed rather than articulated the premise in deciding the merits of similar claims. And *Colegrove v. Green* squarely held that voters who allege facts showing disadvantage to themselves as individuals have standing to sue. A number of cases decided after *Colegrove* recognized the standing of the voters there involved to bring those actions.

[*Justiciability.*] In holding that the subject matter of this suit was not justiciable, the District Court relied on *Colegrove v. Green* and subsequent *per curiam* cases. The court stated: "From a review of these decisions there can be no doubt that the federal rule is that the federal courts will not intervene in cases of this type to compel legislative reapportionment." We understand the District Court to have read the cited cases as compelling the conclusion that since the appellants sought to have a legislative apportionment held unconstitutional, their suit presented a "political question" and was therefore nonjusticiable. We hold that this challenge to an apportionment presents no nonjusticiable "political question." The cited cases do not hold the contrary

The nonjusticiability of a political question is primarily a function of the separation of powers. Much confusion results from the capacity of the "political question" label to obscure the need for case-by-case inquiry. Deciding whether a matter has in any measure been committed by the Constitution to another branch of government, or whether the action of that branch exceeds whatever authority has been committed, is itself a delicate exercise in constitutional interpretation, and is a responsibility of this Court as ultimate interpreter of the Constitution.

The question here is the consistency of state action with the Federal Constitution. We have no question decided, or to be decided, by a political branch of government coequal with this Court. Nor do we risk embarrassment of our government abroad, or grave disturbance at home if we take issue with Tennessee as to the constitutionality of her action here challenged. Nor need the appellants, in order to succeed in this action, ask the Court to enter upon policy determinations for which judicially manageable standards are lacking. Judicial standards under the Equal Protection Clause are well developed and familiar, and it has been open to courts since the enactment of the Fourteenth Amendment to determine if on the particular facts they must, that a discrimination reflects *no* policy, but simply arbitrary and capricious action.

We conclude that the complaint's allegations of a denial of equal protection prevent a justiciable constitutional cause of action upon which appellants are entitled to a trial and a decision. The right asserted is within the reach of judicial protection under the Fourteenth Amendment.

The judgment of the District Court is reversed and the cause is remanded for further proceedings consistent with this opinion.

Reversed and remanded.

JUSTICE WHITTAKER did not participate in the decision of this case.

JUSTICE DOUGLAS concurred:

There is no doubt that the federal courts have jurisdiction of controversies concerning voting rights. The Civil Rights Act gives them authority to redress the deprivation "under color of any state law" of any "right, privilege or immunity secured by the Constitution of the United States or by any Act of Congress providing for equal rights of citizens."

With the exceptions of *Colegrove v. Green*; *MacDougall v. Green,* 335 U.S. 281 (1948); *South v. Peters,* 339 U.S. 276 (1950), and the decisions they spawned, the Court has never thought that protection of voting rights was beyond judicial cognizance. Today's treatment of those cases removes the only impediment to judicial cognizance of the claims stated in the present complaint.

The justiciability of the present claims being established, any relief accorded can be fashioned in the light of well-known principles of equity.

JUSTICE CLARK concurred:

Although I find the Tennessee apportionment statute offends the Equal Protection Clause, I would not consider intervention by this Court into so delicate a field if there were any other relief available to the people of Tennessee. But the majority of the people of Tennessee have no "practical Opportunities for exerting their political weight at the polls" to correct the existing "invidious discrimination." Tennessee has no initiative and referendum. I have searched diligently for other "practical opportunities" present under the law. I find none other than through the federal courts. The majority of the voters have been caught up in a legislative strait jacket. Tennessee has an "informed, civically militant electorate" and "an aroused popular conscience," but it does not sear "the conscience of the people's representatives." This is because the legislative policy has riveted the present seats in the Assembly to their respective constituencies, and by the votes of their incumbents a reapportionment of any kind is prevented. The people have been rebuffed at the hands of the Assembly; they have tried the constitutional convention route, but since the call must originate in the Assembly it, too, has been fruitless. They have tried Tennessee courts with the same result, and Governors have fought the tide only to flounder. It is said that there is recourse in Congress and perhaps that may be, but from a practical standpoint this is without substance. To date Congress has never undertaken such a task in any State. We therefore must conclude that the people of Tennessee are stymied and without judicial intervention will be saddled with the present discrimination in the affairs of their state government.

In view of the detailed study that the Court has given this problem, it is unfortunate that a decision is not reached on the merits. The majority appears to hold, at least *sub silentio,* that an invidious discrimination is present, but it remands to the three-judge court for it to make what is certain to be that formal determination. It is true that Tennessee has not filed a formal answer. However, it has filed voluminous papers and made extended arguments supporting its position. At no time has it been able to contradict the appellants' factual claims; it has offered no rational explanation for the present apportionment; indeed, it has indicated that there are none known to it. As I have emphasized, the case proceeded to the point before the three-judge court that it was able to find an invidious discrimination factually present, and the State has not contested that holding here. In view of all this background I doubt if anything more can be offered or will be gained by the State on remand, other than time. Nevertheless, not being able to muster a court to dispose of the case on the merits, I concur in the opinion of the majority and acquiesce in the decision to remand.

It is well for this Court to practice self-restraint and discipline in constitutional adjudication, but never in its history have those principles received sanction where the national rights of so many have been so clearly infringed for so long a time. National respect for the courts is more enhanced through the forthright enforcement of those rights rather than by rendering them nugatory through the interposition of subterfuges. In my view the ultimate decision today is in the greatest tradition of this Court.

JUSTICE STEWART concurred:

The separate writings of my dissenting and concurring Brothers stray so far from the subject of today's decision as to convey, I think, a distressingly inaccurate impression of what the Court decides. For that reason, I think it appropriate, in joining the opinion of the Court, to emphasize in a few words what the opinion does and does not say.

The Court today decides three things and no more: "(a) that the court possessed jurisdiction of the subject matter; (b) that a justiciable cause of action is stated upon which appellants would be entitled to appropriate relief; and (c) that the appellants have standing to challenge the Tennessee apportionment statutes."

But the merits of this case are not before us now. The defendants have not yet had an opportunity to be heard in defense of the State's system of apportionment; indeed, they have not yet even filed an answer to the complaint. As in other cases, the proper place for the trial is in the trial court, not here.

JUSTICE FRANKFURTER, whom JUSTICE HARLAN joined, dissented:

The Court today reverses a uniform course of decision established by a dozen cases, including one by which the very claim now sustained was unanimously rejected only five years ago. The impressive body of rulings thus cast aside reflected the equally uniform course of our political history regarding the relationship between population and legislative representation—a wholly different matter from denial of the franchise to individuals because of race, color, religion or sex. Such a massive repudiation of the experience of our whole past in asserting destructively novel judicial power demands a detailed analysis of the role of this Court in our constitutional scheme. Disregard of inherent limits in the effective exercise of the Court's "judicial Power" not only presages the futility of judicial intervention in the essentially political conflict of forces by which the relation between population and representation has time out of mind been and now is determined. It may well impair the Court's position as the ultimate organ of "the supreme Law of the Land" in that vast range of legal problems, often strongly entangled in popular feeling, on which this Court must pronounce. The Court's authority—possessed neither of the purse nor the sword—ultimately rests on sustained public confidence in its moral sanction. Such feeling must be nourished by the Court's complete detachment, in fact and in appearance, from political entanglements and by abstention from injecting itself into the clash of political forces in political settlements.

We were soothingly told at the bar of this Court that we need not worry about the kind of remedy a court could effectively fashion once the abstract constitutional right to have courts pass on a state-wide system of electoral districting is recognized as a matter of judicial rhetoric, because legislatures would heed the Court's admonition. This is not only an euphoric hope. It implies a sorry confession of judicial impotence in place of a frank acknowledgment that there is not under our Constitution a judicial remedy for every political mischief, for every undesirable exercise of legislative power. The Framers carefully and with deliberate forethought refused so to enthrone the judiciary. In this situation, as in others of like nature, appeal for relief does not belong here. Appeal must be to an informed, civically militant electorate. In a democratic society like ours, relief must come through an aroused popular conscience that sears the conscience of the people's representatives. In any event there is nothing judicially more unseemly nor more self-defeating than for this Court to make *in terrorem* pronouncements [with the purpose of frightening], to indulge in merely empty rhetoric, sounding a word of promise to the ear, sure to be disappointing to the hope.

This is the latest in the series of cases in which the Equal Protection and Due Process Clauses of the Fourteenth Amendment have been invoked in federal courts as restrictions upon the power of the States to allocate electoral weight among the voting populations of their various geographical subdivisions.

Of course it is important to recognize particular, relevant diversities among comprehensively similar situations. Appellants seek to distinguish several of this Court's prior decisions on one or another ground—*Colegrove v. Green* on the ground that congressional, not state legislative, apportionment was involved; *Remmey v. Smith*, 342 U.S. 916 (1952), on the ground that state judicial remedies had not been tried; *Radford v. Gary*, 352 U.S. 991 (1957), on the ground that Oklahoma has the initiative, whereas Tennessee does not. It would only darken counsel to discuss the relevance and significance of each of these assertedly distinguishing factors here and in the context of this entire line of cases.

The *Colegrove* doctrine, in the form in which repeated decisions have settled it, was not an innovation. It represents long judicial thought and experience. From its earliest opinions this Court has consistently recognized a class of controversies which do not lend themselves to judicial standards and judicial remedies. To classify the various instances as "political questions" is rather a form of stating this conclusion than revealing of analysis.

What, then, is this question of legislative apportionment? Appellants invoke the right to vote and to have their votes counted: But they are permitted to vote and their votes are counted. They go to the polls, they cast their ballots, they send their representatives to the state councils. Their complaint is simply that the representatives are not sufficiently numerous or powerful—in short, that Tennessee has adopted a basis of representation with which they are dissatisfied. Talk of "debasement" or "dilution" is circular talk. One cannot speak of "debasement" or "dilution" of the value of a vote until there is first defined a standard of reference as to what a vote should be worth. What is actually asked of the Court in this case is to choose among competing bases of representation—ultimately, really, among competing theories of political philosophy—in order to establish an appropriate frame of government for the State of Tennessee and thereby for all the States of the Union.

They would make the Equal Protection Clause the charter of adjudication, asserting that the equality which it guarantees comports, if not the assurance of equal weight to every voter's vote, at least the basic conception that representation ought to be proportionate to population, a standard by reference to which the reasonableness of apportionment plans may be judged.

To find such a political conception legally enforceable in the broad and unspecific guarantee of equal protection is to rewrite the Constitution. See *Luther v. Borden,* 48 U.S. 1 (1849). Certainly, "equal protection" is no more secure a foundation for judicial judgment of the permissibility of varying forms of representative government than is "Republican Form." Indeed since "equal protection of the laws" can only mean an equality of persons standing in the same relation to whatever governmental action is challenged, the determination whether treatment is equal presupposes a determination concerning the nature of the relationship. This, with respect to apportionment, means an inquiry into the theoretic base of representation in an acceptably republican state. For a court could not determine the equal-protection issue without in fact first determining the Republican-Form issue, simply because what is reasonable for equal protection purposes will depend upon what frame of government, basically, is allowed. To divorce "equal protection" from "Republican Form" is to talk about half a question.

The notion that representation proportioned to the geographic spread of population is so universally accepted as a necessary element of equality between man and man that it must be taken to be the standard of a political equality preserved by the Fourteenth Amendment—that it is, in appellants' words "the basic principle of representative government"—is, to put it bluntly, not true. However desirable and however desired by some among the great political thinkers and framers of our government, it has never been generally practiced, today or in the past.

Although the District Court had jurisdiction in the very restricted sense of power to determine whether it could adjudicate the claim, the case is of that class of political controversy which, by the nature of its subject, is unfit for federal judicial action. The judgment of the District Court, in dismissing the complaint for failure to state a claim on which relief can be granted, should therefore be affirmed.

Dissenting opinion of JUSTICE HARLAN, whom JUSTICE FRANKFURTER joined:

The dissenting opinion of Mr. Justice Frankfurter, in which I join, demonstrates the abrupt departure the majority makes from judicial history by putting the federal courts into this area of state concerns—an area which, in this instance, the Tennessee state courts themselves have refused to enter.

It does not detract from his opinion to say that the panorama of judicial history it unfolds, though evincing a steadfast underlying principle of keeping the federal courts out of these domains, has a tendency, because of variants in expression to becloud analysis in a given case. With due respect to the majority, I think that has happened here.

Once one cuts through the thicket of discussion devoted to "jurisdiction," "standing," "justiciability," and "political question," there emerges a straightforward issue which, in my view, is determinative of this case. Does the complaint disclose a violation of a federal constitutional right, in other words, a claim over which a United States District Court would have jurisdiction under 28 U.S.C. § 1343(3) and 42 U.S.C. § 1983. The majority opinion does not actually discuss this basic question, but, as one concurring Justice observes, seems to decide it "*sub silentio*." However, in my opinion, appellants' allegations, accepting all of them as true, do not, parsed down or as a whole, show an infringement by Tennessee of any rights assured by the Fourteenth Amendment. Accordingly, I believe the complaint should have been dismissed for "failure to state a claim upon which relief can be granted." Fed. Rules Civ. Proc. rule 12 (b) (6).

It is at once essential to recognize this case for what it is. The issue here relates not to a method of state electoral apportionment by which seats in the *federal* House of Representatives are allocated, but solely to the right of a State to fix the basis of representation in its *own* legislature. Until it is first decided to what extent that right is limited by the Federal Constitution, and whether what Tennessee has done or failed to do in this instance runs afoul of any such limitation, we need not reach the issues of "justiciability" or "political question" or any of the other considerations which in such cases as *Colegrove v. Green* led the Court to decline to adjudicate a challenge to a state apportionment affecting seats in the federal House of Representatives, in the absence of a controlling Act of Congress.

I can find nothing in the Equal Protection Clause or elsewhere in the Federal Constitution which expressly or impliedly supports the view that state legislatures must be so structured as to reflect with approximate equality the voice of every voter. Not only is that proposition refuted by history, as shown by my Brother Frankfurter, but it strikes deep into the heart of our federal system. Its acceptance would require us to turn our backs on the regard which this Court has always shown for the judgment of state legislatures and courts on matters of basically local concern.

FOR DISCUSSION

What is left of the political question doctrine after *Baker v. Carr*? Is reapportionment a political thicket into which the judiciary should enter? What did the Court actually decide in *Baker*? Did it declare anything unconstitutional?

REYNOLDS V. SIMS

377 U.S. 533, 84 S.Ct. 1362, 12 L.Ed.2d 506 (1963)

The Alabama constitution provided that each county receive one state representative. This mandate resulted in some districts having more than forty times the voters as others. This apportionment schema was challenged under the Fourteenth Amendment.

Vote: 8–1

CHIEF JUSTICE WARREN delivered the opinion of the Court.

Involved in these cases are an appeal and two cross-appeals from a decision of the Federal District Court for the Middle District of Alabama holding invalid, under the Equal Protection Clause of the Federal Constitution, the existing and two legislative proposed plans for the apportionment of seats in the two houses of the Alabama Legislature, and ordering into effect a temporary reapportionment plan comprised of parts of the proposed but judicially disapproved measures.

II.

Undeniably the Constitution of the United States protects the right of all qualified citizens to vote, in state as well as in federal elections. A consistent line of decisions by this Court in cases involving attempts to deny or restrict the right of suffrage has made this indelibly clear. It has been repeatedly recognized that all qualified voters have a constitutionally protected right to vote, *Ex parte Yarbrough*, 110 US 651 (1884), and to have their votes counted, *United States v. Mosley*, 238 US 383 (1915). In *Mosley* the Court stated that it is "as equally unquestionable that the right to have one's vote counted is as open to protection as the right to put a ballot in a box." The right to vote can neither be denied outright, *Guinn v. United States*, 238 U.S. 347 (1915), *Lane v. Wilson*, 307 US 268 (1939), nor destroyed by alteration of ballots, see *United States v. Classic*, 313 US 299 (1941), nor diluted by ballot-box stuffing *Ex parte Siebold*, 100 US 371 (1880), *United States v. Saylor*, 322 U.S. 385 (1944). As the Court stated in *Classic*, "Obviously included within the right to choose, secured by the Constitution, is the right of qualified voters within a state to cast their ballots and have them counted. Racially based gerrymandering, *Gomillion v. Lightfoot*, 364 U.S. 339 (1960), and the conducting of white primaries, *Nixon v. Herndon*, 273 U.S. 536 (1927), *Nixon v. Condon*, 286 U.S. 73 (1932), *Smith v. Allwright*, 321 U.S. 649 (1944), *Terry v. Adams*, 345 US 461 (1953), both of which result in denying to some citizens their right to vote, have been held to be constitutionally impermissible. And history has seen a continuing expansion of the scope of the right of suffrage in this country. The right to vote freely for the candidate of one's choice is of the essence of a democratic society, and any restrictions on that right strike at the heart of representative government. And the right of suffrage can be denied by a debasement or dilution of the weight of a citizen's vote just as effectively as by wholly prohibiting the free exercise of the franchise.

In *Wesberry v. Sanders*, 376 U.S. 1 (1964), decided earlier this Term, we held that attacks on the constitutionality of congressional districting plans enacted by state legislatures do not present nonjusticiable questions and should not be dismissed generally for "want of equity." We determine that the constitutional test for the validity of congressional districting schemes was one of substantial equality of population among the various districts established by a state legislature for the election of members of the Federal House of Representatives.

In that case we decided that an apportionment of congressional seats which "contracts the value of some votes and expands that of others" is unconstitutional, since "the Federal Constitution intends that when qualified voters elect members of Congress each vote be given as much weight as any other vote." We concluded that the constitutional prescription for election of members of the House of Representatives " 'by the People,'' construed in its historical context, "means that as nearly as is practicable one man's vote in a congressional election is to be worth as much as another's." We further stated:

> It would defeat the principle solemnly embodied in the Great Compromise—equal representation in the House for equal numbers of people—for us to hold that, within the States, legislatures may draw the lines of congressional districts in such a way as to give some voters a greater voice in choosing a Congressman than others.

We found further, in *Wesberry*, that "our Constitution's plain objective" was that " 'of making equal representation for equal numbers of people the fundamental goal." We concluded by stating:

> No right is more precious in a free country than that of having a voice in the election of those who make the laws under which, as good citizens, we must live. Other rights, even the most basic, are illusory if the right to vote is undermined. Our Constitution leaves no room for classification of people in a way that unnecessarily abridges this right.

Gray and *Wesberry* are of course not dispositive of or directly controlling on our decision in these cases involving state legislative apportionment controversies. Admittedly, those decisions, in which we held that, in statewide and in congressional elections, one person's vote must be counted equally with those of all other voters in a State, were based on different constitutional considerations and were addressed to rather distinct problems. But neither are they wholly inapposite. *Gray*, though not determinative here since involving the weighting of votes in statewide elections, established the basic principle of equality among voters within a State, and held that voters cannot be classified, constitutionally, on the basis of where they live, at least with respect to voting in statewide elections. And our decision in *Wesberry* was of course grounded on that language of the Constitution which prescribes that members of the Federal House of Representatives are to be chosen "by the People," while attacks on state legislative apportionment schemes, such as that involved in the instant cases, are principally based on the Equal Protection Clause of the Fourteenth Amendment. Nevertheless, *Wesberry* clearly established that the fundamental principle of representative government in this country is one of equal representation for equal numbers of people, without regard to race, sex, economic status, or place of residence within a State. Our problem, then, is to ascertain, in the instant cases, whether there are any constitutionally cognizable principles which would justify departures from the basic standard of equality among voters in the apportionment of seats in state legislatures.

A predominant consideration in determining whether a State's legislative apportionment scheme constitutes an invidious discrimination violative of rights asserted under the Equal Protection Clause is that the rights allegedly impaired are individual and personal in nature. While the result of a court decision in a state legislative apportionment controversy may be to require the restructuring of the geographical distribution of seats in a state legislature, the judicial focus must be concentrated upon ascertaining whether there has been any discrimination against certain of the State's citizens which constitutes an impermissible impairment of their constitutionally protected right to vote. Like *Skinner v. Oklahoma*, 316 U.S. 535 (1942), such a case "touches a sensitive and important area of human rights,' and 'involves one of the basic civil rights of man," presenting questions of alleged "invidious discriminations . . . against groups or types of individuals in violation of the constitutional guaranty of just and equal laws," Undoubtedly, the right of suffrage is a fundamental matter in a free and democratic society. Especially since the right to exercise the franchise in a free and unimpaired manner is preservative of other basic civil and political rights, any alleged infringement of the right of citizens to vote must be carefully and meticulously scrutinized. Almost a century ago, in *Yick Wo v. Hopkins*, 118 U.S. 356 (1886), the Court referred to "the political franchise of voting" as "a fundamental political right, because preservative of all rights."

FOR DISCUSSION

What standard for redistricting should be used as a result of *Reynolds*? What did the Court mandate? What did it disallow? May geography ever be considered when drawing district lines?

RELATED CASES

***Gray v. Sanders:* 372 U.S. 368 (1963).**

Georgia's county-unit system as a basis for counting votes in a Democratic primary election violates the Equal Protection Clause of the Fourteenth Amendment. The practical effect of this system is that the vote of each citizen counts for less and less as the population of his county increases, and a combination of the units from the counties having the smallest population gives counties having one-third of the total population of the state a clear majority of county votes.

***Wesberry v. Sanders:* 376 U.S. 1 (1964).**

The constitutional requirement in Article I, Sec. 2, that representatives be chosen by the people of the several states means that as nearly as practicable one man's vote in a congressional election is to be worth as much as another's.

***Wright v. Rockefeller:* 376 U.S. 52 (1964).**

It was not shown that the challenged part of the New York state congressional districting act was the product of "state contrivance" to segregate on the basis of race or place of origin.

***Avery v. Midland County, Texas:* 390 U.S. 474 (1968).**

The Constitution permits no substantial variation from equal protection in drawing districts for units of local government having general governmental powers over the entire geographic area served by the body. The Court also mandated under the Equal Protection Clause that the one-person, one-vote, standard also be extended to local government units.

***Kirkpatrick v. Preisler:* 394 U.S. 526 (1969).**

The command of Article I, Sec. 2 that states create congressional districts which provide equal representation for equal numbers of people (and the "as nearly as practicable" test) permits only the limited population variances which are unavoidable despite a good-faith effort to achieve absolute equality, or for which justification is shown.

***Kramer v. Union Free School District:* 395 U.S. 621 (1969).**

A statutory provision that only such electors as own or lease taxable real property within the school district or are parents of children enrolled in the local public schools can vote in school district elections is void as violating equal protection. See also *Cipriano v. City of Houma,* 395 U.S. 701, 1969.

EVENWEL V. ABBOTT

136 S.Ct. 1120, 194 L.Ed.2d 291 (2016)

Voters challenged a state redistricting plan drawing a State Senate map based upon equal voters in each district. They argued that the districts should be drawn based upon equal number of voters and sought an injunction to prevent use of the current plan. The case was brought in district court, then referred to a three judge district court dismissed the suit. The Supreme Court took the case and affirmed.

Vote 8–0

JUSTICE GINSBURG delivered the opinion of the Court.

Texas, like all other States, draws its legislative districts on the basis of total population. Plaintiffs-appellants are Texas voters; they challenge this uniform method of districting on the ground that it produces unequal districts when measured by voter-eligible population. Voter-eligible population, not total population, they urge, must be used to ensure that their votes will not be devalued in relation to citizens' votes in other districts. We hold, based on constitutional history, this Court's decisions, and longstanding practice, that a State may draw its legislative districts based on total population.

I

A

This Court long resisted any role in overseeing the process by which States draw legislative districts. "The remedy for unfairness in districting," the Court once held, "is to secure State legislatures that will apportion properly, or to invoke the ample powers of Congress." "Courts ought not to enter this political thicket," as Justice Frankfurter put it.

Judicial abstention left pervasive malapportionment unchecked. In the opening half of the 20th century, there was a massive population shift away from rural areas and toward suburban and urban communities. Nevertheless, many States ran elections into the early 1960's based on maps drawn to equalize each district's population as it was composed around 1900. Other States used maps allocating a certain number of legislators to each county regardless of its population. These schemes left many rural districts significantly underpopulated in comparison with urban and suburban districts. But rural legislators who benefited from malapportionment had scant incentive to adopt new maps that might put them out of office.

The Court confronted this ingrained structural inequality in *Baker v. Carr.* That case presented an equal protection challenge to a Tennessee state-legislative map that had not been redrawn since 1901. See also *id.,* at 192, 82 S.Ct. 691 (observing that, in the meantime, there had been "substantial growth and redistribution" of the State's population). Rather than steering clear of the political thicket yet again, the Court held for the first time that malapportionment claims are justiciable.

Although the Court in *Baker* did not reach the merits of the equal protection claim, *Baker*'s justiciability ruling set the stage for what came to be known as the one-person, one-vote principle. Just two years after *Baker,* in *Wesberry v. Sanders,.* the Court invalidated Georgia's malapportioned congressional map, under which the population of one congressional district was "two to three times" larger than the population of the others. Relying on Article I, § 2, of the Constitution, the Court required that congressional districts be drawn with equal populations. Later that same Term, in *Reynolds v. Sims,,* the Court upheld an equal protection challenge to Alabama's malapportioned state-legislative maps. "[T]he Equal Protection Clause," the Court concluded, "requires that the seats in both houses of a bicameral state legislature must be apportioned on a population basis." *Wesberry* and *Reynolds* together instructed that jurisdictions must design both congressional and state-legislative districts with equal populations, and must regularly reapportion districts to prevent malapportionment.

Over the ensuing decades, the Court has several times elaborated on the scope of the one-person, one-vote rule. States must draw congressional districts with populations as close to perfect equality as possible. But, when drawing state and local legislative districts, jurisdictions are permitted to deviate somewhat from perfect population equality to accommodate traditional districting objectives, among them, preserving the integrity of political subdivisions, maintaining communities of interest, and creating geographic compactness. Where the maximum population deviation between the largest and smallest district is less than 10%, the Court has held, a state or local legislative map presumptively complies with the one-person, one-vote rule. Maximum deviations above 10% are presumptively impermissible.

In contrast to repeated disputes over the permissibility of deviating from perfect population equality, little controversy has centered on the population base jurisdictions must equalize. On rare occasions, jurisdictions have relied on the registered-voter or voter-eligible populations of districts. But, in the overwhelming majority of cases, jurisdictions have equalized total population, as measured by the decennial census. Today, all States use total-population numbers from the census when designing congressional and state-legislative districts, and only seven States adjust those census numbers in any meaningful way.

B

Appellants challenge that consensus. After the 2010 census, Texas redrew its State Senate districts using a total-population baseline. At the time, Texas was subject to the preclearance requirements of § 5 of the Voting Rights Act of 1965. 52 U.S.C. § 10304 (requiring jurisdictions to receive approval from the U.S. Department of Justice or the U.S. District Court for the District of Columbia before implementing certain voting changes). Once it became clear that the new Senate map, S148, would not receive preclearance in advance of the 2012 elections, the U.S. District Court for the Western District of Texas drew an interim Senate map, S164, which also equalized the total population of each district. On direct appeal, this Court observed that the District Court had failed to "take guidance from the State's recently enacted plan in drafting an interim plan," and therefore vacated the District Court's map.

The District Court, on remand, again used census data to draw districts so that each included roughly the same size total population. Texas used this new interim map, S172, in the 2012 elections, and, in 2013, the Texas Legislature adopted S172 as the permanent Senate map. See App. to Brief for Texas Senate Hispanic Caucus et al. as *Amici Curiae* 5 (reproducing the current Senate map). The permanent map's maximum total-population deviation is 8.04%, safely within the presumptively permissible 10% range. But measured by a voter-population baseline—eligible voters or registered voters—the map's maximum population deviation exceeds 40%.

Appellants Sue Evenwel and Edward Pfenninger live in Texas Senate districts (one and four, respectively) with particularly large eligible- and registered-voter populations. Contending that basing apportionment on total population dilutes their votes in relation to voters in other Senate districts, in violation of the one-person, one-vote principle of the Equal Protection Clause.

II

The parties and the United States advance different positions in this case. As they did before the District Court, appellants insist that the Equal Protection Clause requires jurisdictions to draw state and local legislative districts with equal voter-eligible populations, thus protecting "voter equality," *i.e.*, "the right of eligible voters to an equal vote." To comply with their proposed rule, appellants suggest, jurisdictions should design districts based on citizen-voting-age-population (CVAP) data from the Census Bureau's American Community Survey (ACS), an annual statistical sample of the U.S. population. Texas responds that jurisdictions may, consistent with the Equal Protection Clause, design districts using any population baseline—including total population and voter-eligible population—so long as the choice is rational and not invidiously discriminatory. Although its use of total-population data from the census was permissible, Texas therefore argues, it could have used ACS CVAP data instead. Sharing Texas' position that the Equal Protection Clause does not mandate use of voter-eligible population, the United States urges us not to address Texas' separate assertion that the Constitution allows States to use alternative population baselines, including voter-eligible population. Equalizing total population, the United States maintains, vindicates the principle of representational equality by "ensur[ing] that the voters in each district have the power to elect a representative who represents the same number of constituents as all other representatives."

In agreement with Texas and the United States, we reject appellants' attempt to locate a voter-equality mandate in the Equal Protection Clause. As history, precedent, and practice demonstrate, it is plainly permissible for jurisdictions to measure equalization by the total population of state and local legislative districts.

A

We begin with constitutional history. At the time of the founding, the Framers confronted a question analogous to the one at issue here: On what basis should congressional districts be allocated to States? The Framers' solution, now known as the Great Compromise, was to provide each State the same number of seats in the Senate, and to allocate House seats based on States' total populations. "Representatives and direct Taxes," they wrote, "shall be apportioned among the several States which may be included within this Union, *according to their respective Numbers*." U.S. Const., Art. I, § 2, cl. 3. "It is a fundamental principle of the proposed constitution," James Madison explained in the Federalist Papers, "that as the aggregate number of representatives allotted to the several states, is to be . . . founded on the aggregate number of inhabitants; so, the right of choosing this allotted number in each state, is to be exercised by such part of the inhabitants, as the state itself may designate." The Federalist No. 54, p. 284 (G. Carey & J. McClellan eds. 2001). In other words, the basis of *representation* in the House was to include all inhabitants—although slaves were counted as only three-fifths of a person—even though States remained free to deny many of those inhabitants the right to participate in the selection of their representatives. Endorsing apportionment based on total population, Alexander Hamilton declared: "There can be no truer principle than this—that every individual of the community at large has an equal right to the protection of government." 1 Records of the Federal Convention of 1787, p. 473 (M. Farrand ed. 1911).

When debating what is now the Fourteenth Amendment, Congress reconsidered the proper basis for apportioning House seats. Concerned that Southern States would not willingly enfranchise freed slaves, and aware that "a slave's freedom could swell his state's population for purposes of representation in the House by one person, rather than only three-fifths," the Framers of the Fourteenth Amendment considered at length the possibility of allocating House seats to States on the basis of voter population.

In December 1865, Thaddeus Stevens, a leader of the Radical Republicans, introduced a constitutional amendment that would have allocated House seats to States "according to their respective legal voters"; in addition, the proposed amendment mandated that "[a] true census of the legal voters shall be taken at the same time with the regular census." Cong. Globe, 39th Cong., 1st Sess., 10 (1866). Supporters of apportionment based on voter population employed the same voter-equality reasoning that appellants now echo.

Voter-based apportionment proponents encountered fierce resistance from proponents of total-population apportionment. Much of the opposition was grounded in the principle of representational equality. "As an abstract proposition," argued Representative James G. Blaine, a leading critic of allocating House seats based on voter population, "no one will deny that population is the true basis of representation; for women, children, and other non-voting classes may have as vital an interest in the legislation of the country as those who actually deposit the ballot."

The product of these debates was § 2 of the Fourteenth Amendment, which retained total population as the congressional apportionment base. See U.S. Const., Amdt. 14, § 2 ("Representatives shall be apportioned among the several States according to their respective numbers, counting the whole number of persons in each State, excluding Indians not taxed."). Introducing the final version of the Amendment on the Senate floor, Senator Jacob Howard explained:

"[The] basis of representation is numbers . . .; that is, the whole population except untaxed Indians and persons excluded by the State laws for rebellion or other crime. . . . The committee adopted numbers as the most just and satisfactory basis, and this is the principle upon which the Constitution itself was originally framed, that the basis of representation should depend upon numbers; and such, I think, after all, is the safest and most secure principle upon which the Government can rest. Numbers, not voters; numbers, not property; this is the theory of the Constitution." Cong. Globe, 39th Cong., 1st Sess., 2766–2767 (1866).

Appellants ask us to find in the Fourteenth Amendment's Equal Protection Clause a rule inconsistent with this "theory of the Constitution." But, as the Court recognized in *Wesberry,* this theory underlies not just the method of allocating House seats to States; it applies as well to the method of apportioning legislative seats within States. "The debates at the [Constitutional] Convention," the Court explained, "make at least one fact abundantly clear: that when the delegates agreed that the House should represent 'people,' they intended that in allocating Congressmen the number assigned to each state should be determined solely by the number of inhabitants." "While it may not be possible to draw congressional districts with mathematical precision," the Court acknowledged, "that is no excuse for ignoring our Constitution's plain objective of making equal representation for *equal numbers of people* the fundamental goal for the House of Representatives." It cannot be that the Fourteenth Amendment calls for the apportionment of congressional districts based on total population, but simultaneously prohibits States from apportioning their own legislative districts on the same basis.

B

Consistent with constitutional history, this Court's past decisions reinforce the conclusion that States and localities may comply with the one-person, one-vote principle by designing districts with equal total populations. Quoting language from those decisions that, in appellants' view, supports the principle of equal voting power—and emphasizing the phrase "one-person, one-vote"—appellants contend that the Court had in mind, and constantly meant, that States should equalize the voter-eligible population of districts. See *Reynolds,* 377 U.S., at 568, 84 S.Ct. 1362 ("[A]n individual's right to vote for State legislators is unconstitutionally impaired when its weight is in a substantial fashion diluted when compared with votes of citizens living on other parts of the State.")

For every sentence appellants quote from the Court's opinions, one could respond with a line casting the one-person, one-vote guarantee in terms of equality of representation, not voter equality. In *Reynolds,* for instance, the Court described "the fundamental principle of representative government in this country" as "one of equal representation for equal numbers of people." And the Court has suggested, repeatedly, that districting based on total population serves *both* the State's interest in preventing vote dilution *and* its interest in ensuring equality of representation.

Moreover, from *Reynolds* on, the Court has consistently looked to total-population figures when evaluating whether districting maps violate the Equal Protection Clause by deviating impermissibly from perfect population equality. See Brief for Appellees 29–31 (collecting cases brought under the Equal Protection Clause). Appellants point to no instance in which the Court has determined the permissibility of deviation based on eligible- or registered-voter data. It would hardly make sense for the Court to have mandated voter equality *sub silentio* and then used a total-population baseline to evaluate compliance with that rule. More likely, we think, the Court has always assumed the permissibility of drawing districts to equalize total population.

C

What constitutional history and our prior decisions strongly suggest, settled practice confirms. Adopting voter-eligible apportionment as constitutional command would upset a well-functioning approach to districting that all 50 States and countless local jurisdictions have followed for decades, even centuries. Appellants have shown no reason for the Court to disturb this longstanding use of total population. As the Framers of the Constitution and the Fourteenth Amendment comprehended, representatives serve all residents, not just those eligible or registered to vote. Nonvoters have an important stake in many policy debates—children, their parents, even their grandparents, for example, have a stake in a strong public-education system—and in receiving constituent services, such as help navigating public-benefits bureaucracies. By ensuring that each representative is subject to requests and suggestions from the same number of constituents, total-population apportionment promotes equitable and effective representation.

In sum, the rule appellants urge has no mooring in the Equal Protection Clause. The Texas Senate map, we therefore conclude, complies with the requirements of the one-person, one-vote principle. Because history, precedent, and practice suffice to reveal the infirmity of appellants' claims, we need not and do not resolve whether, as Texas now argues, States may draw districts to equalize voter-eligible population rather than total population.

For the reasons stated, the judgment of the United States District Court for the Western District of Texas is

Affirmed.

FOR DISCUSSION

Did the Supreme Court mandate that total population is required as the basis of drawing district lines? Could or should states be allowed to use total voting population and if it did what problems might ensue?

SHAW V. RENO

509 U.S. 630, S. Ct. 2816, 125 L. Ed. 2d 511 (1993)

Following the 1990 census, the state of North Carolina redrew its congressional and legislative districts. In order to comply with the mandates of the Voting Rights Act, the state legislature drew one congressional district to create a "majority-minority" seat. The United States Justice Department informed the state that a second majority-minority seat should also be created. After the state redistricted to provide for it, white voters challenged it as a violation of their Fourteenth Amendment rights.

Vote: 5–4

JUSTICE O'CONNOR delivered the opinion of the Court, in which CHIEF JUSTICE REHNQUIST and JUSTICES SCALIA, KENNEDY, and THOMAS joined.

This case involves two of the most complex and sensitive issues this Court has faced in recent years: the meaning of the constitutional "right" to vote, and the propriety of race-based state legislation designed to benefit members of historically disadvantaged racial minority groups. As a result of the 1990 census, North Carolina became entitled to a 12th seat in the United States House of Representatives. The General Assembly enacted a reapportionment plan that included one majority-black congressional district. After the Attorney General of the United States objected to the plan pursuant to § 5 of the Voting Rights Act of 1965, the General Assembly passed new legislation creating a second majority-black district. Appellants allege that the revised plan, which contains district boundary lines of dramatically irregular shape, constitutes an unconstitutional racial gerrymander. The question before us is whether appellants have stated a cognizable claim.

I

The voting age population of North Carolina is approximately 78% white, 20% black, and 1% Native American; the remaining 1% is predominantly Asian. The black population is relatively dispersed; blacks constitute a majority of the general population in only 5 of the State's 100 counties. Geographically, the State divides into three regions: the eastern Coastal Plain, the central Piedmont Plateau, and the western mountains. The largest concentrations of black citizens live in the Coastal Plain, primarily in the northern part. The General Assembly's first redistricting plan contained one majority-black district centered in that area of the State.

Forty of North Carolina's one hundred counties are covered by § 5 of the Voting Rights Act of 1965, 42 U.S.C. § 1973c, which prohibits a jurisdiction subject to its provisions from implementing changes in a "standard, practice, or procedure with respect to voting" without federal authorization. The jurisdiction must obtain either a judgment from the United States District Court for the District of Columbia declaring that the proposed change "does not have the purpose and will not have the effect of denying or abridging the right to vote on account of race or color" or administrative preclearance from the Attorney General. Because the General Assembly's reapportionment plan affected the covered counties, the parties agree that § 5 applied. The State chose to submit its plan to the Attorney General for preclearance.

The Attorney General, acting through the Assistant Attorney General for the Civil Rights Division, interposed a formal objection to the General Assembly's plan. The Attorney General specifically objected to the configuration of boundary lines drawn in the south-central to southeastern region of the State. In the Attorney General's view, the General Assembly could have created a second majority-minority district "to give effect to black and Native American voting strength in this area" by using boundary lines "no more irregular than [those] found elsewhere in the proposed plan," but failed to do so for "pretextual reasons."

Under § 5, the State remained free to seek a declaratory judgment from the District Court for the District of Columbia notwithstanding the Attorney General's objection. It did not do so. Instead, the General Assembly enacted a revised redistricting plan, that included a second majority-black district. The General Assembly located the second district not in the south-central to southeastern part of the State, but in the north-central region along Interstate 85.

The first of the two majority-black districts contained in the revised plan, District 1, is somewhat hook shaped. Centered in the northeast portion of the State, it moves southward until it tapers to a narrow band; then, with finger-like extensions, it reaches far into the southern-most part of the State near the South Carolina border. District 1 has been compared to a "Rorschach ink-blot test," *Shaw v. Barr,* 808 F.Supp. 461, 476 (EDNC 1992) (Voorhees, C.J., concurring in part and dissenting in part), and a "bug splattered on a windshield," *Wall Street Journal,* Feb. 4, 1992, p. A14.

The second majority-black district, District 12, is even more unusually shaped. It is approximately 160 miles long and, for much of its length, no wider than the I-85 corridor. It winds in snakelike fashion through tobacco country, financial centers, and manufacturing areas "until it gobbles in enough enclaves of black neighborhoods." Northbound and southbound drivers on I-85 sometimes find themselves in separate districts in one county, only to "trade" districts when they enter the next county. Of the 10 counties through which District 12 passes, 5 are cut into 3 different districts; even towns are divided. At one point the district remains contiguous only because it intersects at a single point with two other districts before crossing over them. One state legislator has remarked that " '[i]f you drove down the interstate with both car doors open, you'd kill most of the people in the district.' "

Appellants contended that the General Assembly's revised reapportionment plan violated several provisions of the United States Constitution, including the Fourteenth Amendment. They alleged that the General Assembly deliberately "create[d] two Congressional Districts in which a majority of black voters was concentrated arbitrarily—without regard to any other considerations, such as compactness, contiguousness, geographical boundaries, or political subdivisions" with the purpose "to create Congressional Districts along racial lines" and to assure the election of two black representatives to Congress. Appellants sought declaratory and injunctive relief against the state appellees. They sought similar relief against the federal appellees, arguing, alternatively, that the federal appellees had misconstrued the Voting Rights Act or that the Act itself was unconstitutional.

II

A

"The right to vote freely for the candidate of one's choice is of the essence of a democratic society. . . ." *Reynolds v. Sims,* 377 U.S. 533 (1964). For much of our Nation's history, that right sadly has been denied to many because of race. The Fifteenth Amendment, ratified in 1870 after a bloody Civil War, promised unequivocally that "[t]he right of citizens of the United States to vote" no longer would be "denied or abridged . . . by any State on account of race, color, or previous condition of servitude." U.S. Const., Amdt. 15, § 1.

But "[a] number of states . . . refused to take no for an answer and continued to circumvent the fifteenth amendment's prohibition through the use of both subtle and blunt instruments, perpetuating ugly patterns of pervasive racial discrimination." Blumstein, Defining and Proving Race Discrimination: Perspectives on the Purpose Vs. Results Approach from the Voting Rights Act, 69 Va.L.Rev. 633, 637 (1983). Ostensibly race-neutral devices such as literacy tests with "grandfather" clauses and "good character" provisos were devised to deprive black voters of the franchise. Another of the weapons in the States' arsenal was the racial gerrymander—"the deliberate and arbitrary distortion of district boundaries . . . for [racial] purposes." In the 1870's, for example, opponents of Reconstruction in Mississippi "concentrated the bulk of the black population in a 'shoestring' Congressional district running the length of the Mississippi River, leaving five others with white majorities." Some 90 years later, Alabama redefined the boundaries of the city of Tuskegee "from a square to an uncouth twenty-eight-sided figure" in a manner that was alleged to exclude black voters, and only black voters, from the city limits. *Gomillion v. Lightfoot,* 364 U.S. 339 (1960).

Alabama's exercise in geometry was but one example of the racial discrimination in voting that persisted in parts of this country nearly a century after ratification of the Fifteenth Amendment. In some States, registration of eligible black voters ran 50% behind that of whites. Congress enacted the Voting Rights Act of 1965 as a dramatic and severe response to the situation. The Act proved immediately successful in ensuring racial minorities access to the voting booth; by the early 1970's, the spread between black and white registration in several of the targeted Southern States had fallen to well below 10%.

But it soon became apparent that guaranteeing equal access to the polls would not suffice to root out other racially discriminatory voting practices. Drawing on the "one person, one vote" principle, this Court recognized that "[t]he right to vote can be affected by a *dilution* of voting power as well as by an absolute prohibition on casting a ballot." Where members of a racial minority group vote as a cohesive unit, practices such as multimember or at-large electoral systems can reduce or nullify minority voters' ability, as a group, "to elect the candidate of their choice." Accordingly, the Court held that such schemes violate the Fourteenth Amendment when they are adopted with a discriminatory purpose and have the effect of diluting minority voting strength. Congress, too, responded to the problem of vote dilution. In 1982, it amended § 2 of the Voting Rights Act to prohibit legislation that *results* in the dilution of a minority group's voting strength, regardless of the legislature's intent.

B

It is against this background that we confront the questions presented here. In our view, the District Court properly dismissed appellants' claims against the federal appellees. Our focus is on appellants' claim that the State engaged in unconstitutional racial gerrymandering. That argument strikes a powerful historical chord: It is unsettling how closely the North Carolina plan resembles the most egregious racial gerrymanders of the past.

An understanding of the nature of appellants' claim is critical to our resolution of the case. In their complaint, appellants did not claim that the General Assembly's reapportionment plan unconstitutionally "diluted" white voting strength. They did not even claim to be white. Rather, appellants' complaint alleged that the deliberate segregation of voters into separate districts on the basis of race violated their constitutional right to participate in a "color-blind" electoral process.

Despite their invocation of the ideal of a "color-blind" Constitution, see *Plessy v. Ferguson,* appellants appear to concede that race-conscious redistricting is not always unconstitutional. That concession is wise: This Court never has held that race-conscious state decisionmaking is impermissible in *all* circumstances. What appellants object to is redistricting legislation that is so extremely irregular on its face that it rationally can be viewed only as an effort to segregate the races for purposes of voting, without regard for traditional districting principles and without sufficiently compelling justification. For the reasons that follow, we conclude that appellants have stated a claim upon which relief can be granted under the Equal Protection Clause.

III

A

The Equal Protection Clause provides that "[n]o State shall . . . deny to any person within its jurisdiction the equal protection of the laws." U.S. Const., Amdt. 14, § 1. Its central purpose is to prevent the States from purposefully discriminating between individuals on the basis of race. Laws that explicitly distinguish between individuals on racial grounds fall within the core of that prohibition.

No inquiry into legislative purpose is necessary when the racial classification appears on the face of the statute. Classifications of citizens solely on the basis of race "are by their very nature odious to a free people whose institutions are founded upon the doctrine of equality." They threaten to stigmatize individuals by reason of their membership in a racial group and to incite racial hostility. ("[E]ven in the pursuit of remedial objectives, an explicit policy of assignment by race may serve to stimulate our society's latent race consciousness, suggesting the utility and propriety of basing decisions on a factor that ideally bears no relationship to an individual's worth or needs"). Accordingly, we have held that the Fourteenth Amendment requires state legislation that expressly distinguishes among citizens because of their race to be narrowly tailored to further a compelling governmental interest

These principles apply not only to legislation that contains explicit racial distinctions, but also to those "rare" statutes that, although race neutral, are, on their face, "unexplainable on grounds other than race."

B

Appellants contend that redistricting legislation that is so bizarre on its face that it is "unexplainable on grounds other than race," *Village of Arlington Heights v. Metropolitan Housing Development Corp,* 429 U.S. 252 (1977), demands the same close scrutiny that we give other state laws that classify citizens by race. Our voting rights precedents support that conclusion.

In *Guinn v. United States,* 238 U.S. 347, 357 (1915), the Court invalidated under the Fifteenth Amendment a statute that imposed a literacy requirement on voters but contained a "grandfather clause" applicable to individuals and their lineal descendants entitled to vote "on [or prior to] January 1, 1866.". The determinative consideration for the Court was that the law, though ostensibly race neutral, on its face "embod[ied] no exercise of judgment and rest[ed] upon no discernible reason" other than to circumvent the prohibitions of the Fifteenth Amendment. In other words, the statute was invalid because, on its face, it could not be explained on grounds other than race.

Put differently, we believe that reapportionment is one area in which appearances do matter. A reapportionment plan that includes in one district individuals who belong to the same race, but who are otherwise widely separated by geographical and political boundaries, and who may have little in common with one another but the color of their skin, bears an uncomfortable resemblance to political apartheid. It reinforces the perception that members of the same racial group—regardless of their age, education, economic status, or the community in which they live—think alike, share the same political interests, and will prefer the same candidates at the polls. We have rejected such perceptions elsewhere as impermissible racial stereotypes. By perpetuating such notions, a racial gerrymander may exacerbate the very patterns of racial bloc voting that majority-minority districting is sometimes said to counteract.

The message that such districting sends to elected representatives is equally pernicious. When a district obviously is created solely to effectuate the perceived common interests of one racial group, elected officials are more likely to believe that their primary obligation is to represent only the members of that group, rather than their constituency as a whole. This is altogether antithetical to our system of representative democracy. As Justice Douglas explained in his dissent in *Wright v. Rockefeller*, 376 U.S. 52 (1964), nearly 30 years ago:

> Here the individual is important, not his race, his creed, or his color. The principle of equality is at war with the notion that District A must be represented by a Negro, as it is with the notion that District B must be represented by a Caucasian, District C by a Jew, District D by a Catholic, and so on. . . . That system, by whatever name it is called, is a divisive force in a community, emphasizing differences between candidates and voters that are irrelevant in the constitutional sense. . . .

When racial or religious lines are drawn by the State, the multiracial, multireligious communities that our Constitution seeks to weld together as one become separatist; antagonisms that relate to race or to religion rather than to political issues are generated; communities seek not the best representative but the best racial or religious partisan. Since that system is at war with the democratic ideal, it should find no footing here.

For these reasons, we conclude that a plaintiff challenging a reapportionment statute under the Equal Protection Clause may state a claim by alleging that the legislation, though race-neutral on its face, rationally cannot be understood as anything other than an effort to separate voters into different districts on the basis of race, and that the separation lacks sufficient justification. It is unnecessary for us to decide whether or how a reapportionment plan that, on its face, can be explained in nonracial terms successfully could be challenged. Thus, we express no view as to whether "the intentional creation of majority-minority districts, without more," always gives rise to an equal protection claim. We hold only that, on the facts of this case, appellants have stated a claim sufficient to defeat the state appellees' motion to dismiss.

V

Racial classifications of any sort pose the risk of lasting harm to our society. They reinforce the belief, held by too many for too much of our history, that individuals should be judged by the color of their skin. Racial classifications with respect to voting carry particular dangers. Racial gerrymandering, even for remedial purposes, may balkanize us into competing racial factions; it threatens to carry us further from the goal of a political system in which race no longer matters—a goal that the Fourteenth and Fifteenth Amendments embody, and to which the Nation continues to aspire. It is for these reasons that race-based districting by our state legislatures demands close judicial scrutiny.

In this case, the Attorney General suggested that North Carolina could have created a reasonably compact second majority-minority district in the south-central to southeastern part of the State. We express no view as to whether appellants successfully could have challenged such a district under the Fourteenth Amendment. We also do not decide whether appellants' complaint stated a claim under constitutional provisions other than the Fourteenth Amendment. Today we hold only that appellants have stated a claim under the Equal Protection Clause by alleging that the North Carolina General Assembly adopted a reapportionment scheme so irrational on its face that it can be understood only as an effort to segregate voters into separate voting districts because of their race, and that the separation lacks sufficient justification. If the allegation of racial gerrymandering remains uncontradicted, the District Court further must determine whether the North Carolina plan is narrowly tailored to further a compelling governmental interest. Accordingly, we reverse the judgment of the District Court and remand the case for further proceedings consistent with this opinion.

It is so ordered.

JUSTICE WHITE, with whom JUSTICES BLACKMUN and STEVENS join, dissenting.

The facts of this case mirror those presented in *United Jewish Organizations of Williamsburgh, Inc. v. Carey (UJO)*, 430 US 144 (1977), where the Court rejected a claim that creation of a majority-minority district violated the Constitution, either as a *per se* matter or in light of the circumstances leading to the creation of such a district. Of particular relevance, five of the Justices reasoned that members of the white majority could not plausibly argue that their influence over the political process had been unfairly canceled or that such had been the State's intent. Accordingly, they held that plaintiffs were not entitled to relief under the Constitution's Equal Protection Clause. On the same reasoning, I would affirm the District Court's dismissal of appellants' claim in this instance.

FOR DISCUSSION

Should race ever be used when drawing district lines? Does O'Connor's decision preclude this? Is there any difference in the use of race in this case versus that in *Gomillion*?

LEAGUE OF UNITED LATIN AMERICAN CITIZENS V. PERRY

548 U.S. 399, 126 S.Ct. 2594, 165 L.Ed.2d 609 (2006)

Following the 2000 census Texas was unable to draw its district lines and it fell to the courts to do that. In the 2002 elections Republicans took control of both houses of the Texas legislature, and they redrew the legislative lines again, resulting in significant gains for their party in the 2004 congressional elections. This second mid-decade redistricting, and the districts that were produced, were challenged under the Fourteenth Amendment as a partisan gerrymander.

Vote: 5–4

JUSTICE KENNEDY announced the judgment of the Court with respect to Parts II–A and III, in which JUSTICES STEVENS, SOUTER, GINSBERG, and BREYER joined, an opinion with respect to Parts I and IV, in which CHIEF JUSTICE ROBERTS and JUSTICE ALITO joined, an opinion with respect to Parts II–B and II–C, and an opinion with respect to Part II–D, in which JUSTICES SOUTER and GINSBERG joined. JUSTICE STEVENS filed an opinion concurring in part and dissenting in part, in which JUSTICE BREYER joined as to Parts I and II.

These four consolidated cases are appeals from a judgment entered by the United States District Court for the Eastern District of Texas. Convened as a three-judge court under 28 U.S.C. § 2284, the court heard appellants' constitutional and statutory challenges to a 2003 enactment of the Texas State Legislature that drew new district lines for the 32 seats Texas holds in the United States House of Representatives.

Appellants contend the new plan is an unconstitutional partisan gerrymander and that the redistricting statewide violates § 2 of the Voting Rights Act of 1965, 79 Stat. 437, as amended, 42 U.S.C. § 1973. Appellants also contend that the use of race and politics in drawing lines of specific districts violates the First Amendment and the Equal Protection Clause of the Fourteenth Amendment. The three-judge panel, consisting of Circuit Judge Higginbotham and District Judges Ward and Rosenthal, brought considerable experience and expertise to the instant case, based on their knowledge of the State's people, history, and geography. Judges Higginbotham and Ward, moreover, had served on the three-judge court that drew the plan the Texas Legislature replaced in 2003, so they were intimately familiar with the history and intricacies of the cases.

We affirm the District Court's dispositions on the statewide political gerrymandering claims and the Voting Rights Act claim against District 24. We reverse and remand on the Voting Rights Act claim with respect to District 23. Because we do not reach appellants' race-based equal protection claim or the political gerrymandering claim as to District 23, we vacate the judgment of the District Court on these claims.

I

To set out a proper framework for the case, we first recount the history of the litigation and recent districting in Texas. An appropriate starting point is not the reapportionment in 2000 but the one from the census in 1990.

The 1990 census resulted in a 30-seat congressional delegation for Texas, an increase of 3 seats over the 27 representatives allotted to the State in the decade before. In 1991 the Texas Legislature drew new district lines. At the time, the Democratic Party controlled both houses in the state legislature, the governorship, and 19 of the State's 27 seats in Congress. Yet change appeared to be on the horizon. In the previous 30 years the Democratic Party's post-Reconstruction dominance over the Republican Party had eroded, and by 1990 the Republicans received 47% of the statewide vote, while the Democrats received 51%.

Faced with a Republican opposition that could be moving toward majority status, the state legislature drew a congressional redistricting plan designed to favor Democratic candidates. Using then-emerging computer technology to draw district lines with artful precision, the legislature enacted a plan later described as the "shrewdest gerrymander of the 1990s."

Although the 1991 plan was enacted by the state legislature, Democratic Congressman Martin Frost was acknowledged as its architect. The 1991 plan "carefully constructs democratic districts 'with incredibly convoluted lines' and packs 'heavily Republican' suburban areas into just a few districts." Voters who considered this unfair and unlawful treatment sought to invalidate the 1991 plan as an unconstitutional partisan gerrymander, but to no avail. The 1991 plan realized the hopes of Democrats and the fears of Republicans with respect to the composition of the Texas congressional delegation. The 1990's were years of continued growth for the Texas Republican Party, and by the end of the decade it was sweeping elections for statewide office. Nevertheless, despite carrying 59% of the vote in statewide elections in 2000, the Republicans only won 13 congressional seats to the Democrats' 17.

These events likely were not forgotten by either party when it came time to draw congressional districts in conformance with the 2000 census and to incorporate two additional seats for the Texas delegation. The Republican Party controlled the governorship and the State Senate; it did not yet control the State House of Representatives, however. As so constituted, the legislature was unable to pass a redistricting scheme, resulting in litigation and the necessity of a court-ordered plan to comply with the Constitution's one-person, one-vote requirement.

As we have said, two members of the three-judge court that drew Plan 1151C later served on the three-judge court that issued the judgment now under review. Thus we have the benefit of their candid comments concerning the redistricting approach taken in the *Balderas v. Texas,* 536 U.S. 919 (2002), litigation. Conscious that the primary responsibility for drawing congressional districts is given to political branches of government, and hesitant to "und[o] the work of one political party for the benefit of another," the three-judge *Balderas* court sought to apply "only 'neutral' redistricting standards" when drawing Plan 1151C. Once the District Court applied these principles—such as placing the two new seats in high-growth areas, following county and voting precinct lines, and avoiding the pairing of incumbents—"the drawing ceased, leaving the map free of further change except to conform it to one-person, one-vote." Under Plan 1151C, the 2002 congressional elections resulted in a 17-to-15 Democratic majority in the Texas delegation, compared to a 59% to 40% Republican majority in votes for statewide office in 2000. Reflecting on the *Balderas* Plan, the District Court in *Henderson v. Perry,* 399 F. Supp. 2d 756 (2005), was candid to acknowledge "[t]he practical effect of this effort was to leave the 1991 Democratic Party gerrymander largely in place as a 'legal' plan."

The continuing influence of a court-drawn map that "perpetuated much of [the 1991] gerrymander," was not lost on Texas Republicans when, in 2003, they gained control of the State House of Representatives and, thus, both houses of the legislature. The Republicans in the legislature "set out to increase their representation in the congressional delegation." After a protracted partisan struggle, during which Democratic legislators left the State for a time to frustrate quorum requirements, the legislature enacted a new congressional districting map in October 2003. It is called Plan 1374C. The 2004 congressional elections did not disappoint the plan's drafters. Republicans won 21 seats to the Democrats' 11, while also obtaining 58% of the vote in statewide races against the Democrats' 41%. Soon after Texas enacted Plan 1374C, appellants challenged it in court, alleging a host of constitutional and statutory violations. Initially, the District Court entered judgment against appellants on all their claims.

II

A

Based on two similar theories that address the mid-decade character of the 2003 redistricting, appellants now argue that Plan 1374C should be invalidated as an unconstitutional partisan gerrymander. In *Davis v. Bandemer,* 478 U.S. 109 (1986), the Court held that an equal protection challenge to a political gerrymander presents a justiciable case or controversy, but there was disagreement over what substantive standard to apply. A plurality of the Court in *Vieth v. Jubelirer,* 541 U.S. 267 (2004), would have held such challenges to be nonjusticiable political questions, but a majority declined to do so. We do not revisit the justiciability holding but do proceed to examine whether appellants' claims offer the Court a manageable, reliable measure of fairness for determining whether a partisan gerrymander violates the Constitution.

C

Appellants claim that Plan 1374C, enacted by the Texas Legislature in 2003, is an unconstitutional political gerrymander. A decision, they claim, to effect mid-decennial redistricting, when solely motivated by partisan objectives, violates equal protection and the First Amendment because it serves no legitimate public purpose and burdens one group because of its political opinions and affiliation. The mid-decennial nature of the redistricting, appellants say, reveals the legislature's sole motivation. Unlike *Vieth,* where the legislature acted in the context of a required decennial redistricting, the Texas Legislature voluntarily replaced a plan that itself was designed to comply with new census data. Because Texas had "no constitutional obligation to act at all" in 2003, it is hardly surprising, according to appellants, that the District Court found "[t]here is little question but that the single-minded purpose of the Texas Legislature in enacting Plan 1374C was to gain partisan advantage" for the Republican majority over the Democratic minority.

A rule, or perhaps a presumption, of invalidity when a mid-decade redistricting plan is adopted solely for partisan motivations is a salutary one, in appellants' view, for then courts need not inquire about, nor parties prove, the discriminatory effects of partisan gerrymandering—a matter that has proved elusive since *Bandemer*. Adding to the test's simplicity is that it does not quibble with the drawing of individual district lines but challenges the decision to redistrict at all.

For a number of reasons, appellants' case for adopting their test is not convincing. To begin with, the state appellees dispute the assertion that partisan gain was the "sole" motivation for the decision to replace Plan 1151C. There is some merit to that criticism, for the pejorative label overlooks indications that partisan motives did not dictate the plan in its entirety. The legislature does seem to have decided to redistrict with the sole purpose of achieving a Republican congressional majority, but partisan aims did not guide every line it drew. As the District Court found, the contours of some contested district lines were drawn based on more mundane and local interests. The state appellees also contend, and appellants do not contest, that a number of line-drawing requests by Democratic state legislators were honored.

Evaluating the legality of acts arising out of mixed motives can be complex, and affixing a single label to those acts can be hazardous, even when the actor is an individual performing a discrete act. When the actor is a legislature and the act is a composite of manifold choices, the task can be even more daunting. Appellants' attempt to separate the legislature's sole motive for discarding Plan 1151C from the complex of choices it made while drawing the lines of Plan 1374C seeks to avoid that difficulty. We are skeptical, however, of a claim that seeks to invalidate a statute based on a legislature's unlawful motive but does so without reference to the content of the legislation enacted.

Even setting this skepticism aside, a successful claim attempting to identify unconstitutional acts of partisan gerrymandering must do what appellants' sole-motivation theory explicitly disavows: show a burden, as measured by a reliable standard, on the complainants' representational rights. For this reason, a majority of the Court rejected a test proposed in *Vieth* that is markedly similar to the one appellants present today.

The sole-intent standard offered here is no more compelling when it is linked to the circumstance that Plan 1374C is mid-decennial legislation. The text and structure of the Constitution and our case law indicate there is nothing inherently suspect about a legislature's decision to replace mid-decade a court-ordered plan with one of its own. And even if there were, the fact of mid-decade redistricting alone is no sure indication of unlawful political gerrymanders. Under appellants' theory, a highly effective partisan gerrymander that coincided with decennial redistricting would receive less scrutiny than a bumbling, yet solely partisan, mid-decade redistricting. More concretely, the test would leave untouched the 1991 Texas redistricting, which entrenched a party on the verge of minority status, while striking down the 2003 redistricting plan, which resulted in the majority Republican Party capturing a larger share of the seats. A test that treats these two similarly effective power plays in such different ways does not have the reliability appellants ascribe to it.

Furthermore, compared to the map challenged in *Vieth,* which led to a Republican majority in the congressional delegation despite a Democratic majority in the statewide vote, Plan 1374C can be seen as making the party balance more congruent to statewide party power. To be sure, there is no constitutional requirement of proportional representation, and equating a party's statewide share of the vote with its portion of the congressional delegation is a rough measure at best. Nevertheless, a congressional plan that more closely reflects the distribution of state party power seems a less likely vehicle for partisan discrimination than one that entrenches an electoral minority. By this measure, Plan 1374C can be seen as fairer than the plan that survived in *Vieth* and the two previous Texas plans—all three of which would pass the modified sole-intent test that Plan 1374C would fail.

In the absence of any other workable test for judging partisan gerrymanders, one effect of appellants' focus on mid-decade redistricting could be to encourage partisan excess at the outset of the decade, when a legislature redistricts pursuant to its decennial constitutional duty and is then immune from the charge of sole-motivation. If mid-decade redistricting were barred or at least subject to close judicial oversight, opposition legislators would also have every incentive to prevent passage of a legislative plan and try their luck with a court that might give them a better deal than negotiation with their political rivals.

D

Appellants' second political gerrymandering theory is that mid-decade redistricting for exclusively partisan purposes violates the one-person, one-vote requirement. They observe that population variances in legislative districts are tolerated only if they "are unavoidable despite a good-faith effort to achieve absolute equality, or for which justification is shown." Working from this unchallenged premise, appellants contend that, because the population of Texas has shifted since the 2000 census, the 2003 redistricting, which relied on that census, created unlawful interdistrict population variances.

To distinguish the variances in Plan 1374C from those of ordinary, 3-year-old districting plans or belatedly drawn court-ordered plans, appellants again rely on the voluntary, mid-decade nature of the redistricting and its partisan motivation. Appellants do not contend that a decennial redistricting plan would violate equal representation three or five years into the decade if the State's population had shifted substantially. As they must, they concede that States operate under the legal fiction that their plans are constitutionally apportioned throughout the decade, a presumption that is necessary to avoid constant redistricting, with accompanying costs and instability.

In sum, we disagree with appellants' view that a legislature's decision to override a valid, court-drawn plan mid-decade is sufficiently suspect to give shape to a reliable standard for identifying unconstitutional political gerrymanders. We conclude that appellants have established no legally impermissible use of political classifications. For this reason, they state no claim on which relief may be granted for their statewide challenge.

FOR DISCUSSION

What is the status of partisan gerrymanders after *LULAC*? Are they still justiciable? What will the Court do about them? Why did the Court not rule that mid-decade reapportionment was unconstitutional or a sign of partisan gerrymandering?

ARIZONA STATE LEGISLATURE V. ARIZONA INDEPENDENT REDISTRICTING COMMISSION

135 S.Ct. 2652, 192 L.Ed.2d 704 (2015)

Arizona voters through a ballot initiative created an independent commission which replaced the state legislature as the body responsible for drawing congressional district lines. Members of the State Legislature challenged the ballot proposition, arguing that it violated the Elections Clause of United States Constitution, and injunction against use of commission maps for any future congressional election. A three judge panel rejected the claims and the Supreme Court affirmed.

Vote 5–4

JUSTICE GINSBURG wrote for the Court and was joined by

CHIEF JUSTICE ROBERTS filed dissenting opinion in which JUSTICE SCALIA, JUSTICE THOMAS, and JUSTICE ALITO joined.

JUSTICE SCALIA filed dissenting opinion in which JUSTICE THOMAS joined.

JUSTICE THOMAS filed dissenting opinion in which JUSTICE SCALIA joined.

JUSTICE GINSBURG delivered the opinion of the Court.

This case concerns an endeavor by Arizona voters to address the problem of partisan gerrymandering—the drawing of legislative district lines to subordinate adherents of one political party and entrench a rival party in power. "[P]artisan gerrymanders," this Court has recognized, "[are incompatible] with democratic principles." *Vieth v. Jubelirer,* 541 U.S. 267, 292 (2004) Even so, the Court in *Vieth* did not grant relief on the plaintiffs' partisan gerrymander claim. The plurality held the matter nonjusticiable Justice Kennedy found no standard workable in that case, but left open the possibility that a suitable standard might be identified in later litigation.

In 2000, Arizona voters adopted an initiative, Proposition 106, aimed at "ending the practice of gerrymandering and improving voter and candidate participation in elections." Proposition 106 amended Arizona's Constitution to remove redistricting authority from the Arizona Legislature and vest that authority in an independent commission, the Arizona Independent Redistricting Commission (AIRC or Commission). After the 2010 census, as after the 2000 census, the AIRC adopted redistricting maps for congressional as well as state legislative districts.

The Arizona Legislature challenged the map the Commission adopted in January 2012 for congressional districts. Recognizing that the voters could control redistricting for state legislators, the Arizona Legislature sued the AIRC in federal court seeking a declaration that the Commission and its map for congressional districts violated the "Elections Clause" of the U.S. Constitution. That Clause, critical to the resolution of this case, provides:

> "The Times, Places and Manner of holding Elections for Senators and Representatives, shall be prescribed in each State by the Legislature thereof; but the Congress may at any time by Law make or alter such Regulations. . . ." Art. I, § 4, cl. 1.

The Arizona Legislature's complaint alleged that "[t]he word 'Legislature' in the Elections Clause means [specifically and only] the representative body which makes the laws of the people." The Legislature urges, the Clause precludes resort to an independent commission, created by initiative, to accomplish redistricting. The AIRC responded that, for Elections Clause purposes, "the Legislature" is not confined to the elected representatives; rather, the term encompasses all legislative authority conferred by the State Constitution, including initiatives adopted by the people themselves.

We now affirm the District Court's judgment. We hold, first, that the Arizona Legislature, having lost authority to draw congressional districts, has standing to contest the constitutionality of Proposition 106. Next, we hold that lawmaking power in Arizona includes the initiative process, and that both § 2a(c) and the Elections Clause permit use of the AIRC in congressional districting in the same way the Commission is used in districting for Arizona's own Legislature.

I

A

Direct lawmaking by the people was "virtually unknown when the Constitution of 1787 was drafted." There were obvious precursors or analogues to the direct lawmaking operative today in several States, notably, New England's town hall meetings and the submission of early state constitutions to the people for ratification. But it was not until the turn of the 20th century, as part of the Progressive agenda of the era, that direct lawmaking by the electorate gained a foothold, largely in Western States.

The two main "agencies of direct legislation" are the initiative and the referendum. The initiative operates entirely outside the States' representative assemblies; it allows "voters [to] petition to propose statutes or constitutional amendments to be adopted or rejected by the voters at the polls." While the initiative allows the electorate to adopt positive legislation, the referendum serves as a negative check. It allows "voters [to] petition to refer a legislative action to the voters [for approval or disapproval] at the polls." "The initiative [thus] corrects sins of omission" by representative bodies, while the "referendum corrects sins of commission."

In 1898, South Dakota took the pathmarking step of affirming in its Constitution the people's power "directly [to] control the making of all ordinary laws" by initiative and referendum. In 1902, Oregon became the first State to adopt the initiative as a means, not only to enact ordinary laws, but also to amend the State's Constitution. By 1920, the people in 19 States had reserved for themselves the power to initiate ordinary lawmaking, and, in 13 States, the power to initiate amendments to the State's Constitution. Those numbers increased to 21 and 18, respectively, by the close of the 20th century.

B

For the delegates to Arizona's constitutional convention, direct lawmaking was a "principal issu[e]." J. Leshy, The Arizona State Constitution 8–9 (2d ed. 2013) (hereinafter Leshy). By a margin of more than three to one, the people of Arizona ratified the State's Constitution, which included, among lawmaking means, initiative and referendum provisions. In the runup to Arizona's admission to the Union in 1912, those provisions generated no controversy.

In particular, the Arizona Constitution "establishes the electorate [of Arizona] as a coordinate source of legislation" on equal footing with the representative legislative body. The initiative, housed under the article of the Arizona Constitution concerning the "Legislative Department" and the section defining the State's "legislative authority," reserves for the people "the power to propose laws and amendments to the constitution." The Arizona Constitution further states that "[a]ny law which may be enacted by the Legislature under this Constitution may be enacted by the people under the Initiative." Accordingly, "[g]eneral references to the power of the 'legislature' " in the Arizona Constitution "include the people's right (specified in Article IV, part 1) to bypass their elected representatives and make laws directly through the initiative."

C

Proposition 106, vesting redistricting authority in the AIRC, was adopted by citizen initiative in 2000 against a "background of recurring redistricting turmoil" in Arizona. Redistricting plans adopted by the Arizona Legislature sparked controversy in every redistricting cycle since the 1970's, and several of those plans were rejected by a federal court or refused preclearance by the Department of Justice under the Voting Rights Act of 1965.

Aimed at "ending the practice of gerrymandering and improving voter and candidate participation in elections," App. 50, Proposition 106 amended the Arizona Constitution to remove congressional redistricting authority from the state legislature, lodging that authority, instead, in a new entity, the AIRC. The AIRC convenes after each census, establishes final district boundaries, and certifies the new districts to the Arizona

Secretary of State. The legislature may submit nonbinding recommendations to the AIRC, and is required to make necessary appropriations for its operation. The highest ranking officer and minority leader of each chamber of the legislature each select one member of the AIRC from a list compiled by Arizona's Commission on Appellate Court Appointments. The four appointed members of the AIRC then choose, from the same list, the fifth member, who chairs the Commission. A Commission's tenure is confined to one redistricting cycle; each member's time in office "expire[s] upon the appointment of the first member of the next redistricting commission."

II

We turn first to the threshold question: Does the Arizona Legislature have standing to bring this suit? Trained on "whether the plaintiff is [a] proper party to bring [a particular lawsuit,]" standing is "[o]ne element" of the Constitution's case-or-controversy limitation on federal judicial authority, expressed in Article III of the Constitution. "To qualify as a party with standing to litigate," the Arizona Legislature "must show, first and foremost," injury in the form of " 'invasion of a legally protected interest' that is 'concrete and particularized' and 'actual or imminent.' " The Legislature's injury also must be "fairly traceable to the challenged action" and "redressable by a favorable ruling."

The Arizona Legislature maintains that the Elections Clause vests in it "primary responsibility" for redistricting. To exercise that responsibility, the Legislature urges, it must have at least the opportunity to engage (or decline to engage) in redistricting before the State may involve other actors in the redistricting process. Proposition 106, which gives the AIRC binding authority over redistricting, regardless of the Legislature's action or inaction, strips the Legislature of its alleged prerogative to initiate redistricting. That asserted deprivation would be remedied by a court order enjoining the enforcement of Proposition 106. Although we conclude that the Arizona Legislature does not have the exclusive, constitutionally guarded role it asserts,, one must not "confus[e] weakness on the merits with absence of Article III standing."

III

On the merits, we instructed the parties to address this question: Do the Elections Clause of the United States Constitution and 2 U.S.C. § 2a(c) permit Arizona's use of a commission to adopt congressional districts? The Elections Clause is set out at the start of this opinion. Section 2a(c) provides:

> "Until a State is redistricted in the manner provided by the law thereof after any apportionment, the Representatives to which such State is entitled under such apportionment shall be elected in the following manner: [setting out five federally prescribed redistricting procedures]."

A

Davis v. Hildebrant involved an amendment to the Constitution of Ohio vesting in the people the right, exercisable by referendum, to approve or disapprove by popular vote any law enacted by the State's legislature. A 1915 Act redistricting the State for the purpose of congressional elections had been submitted to a popular vote, resulting in disapproval of the legislature's measure. State election officials asked the State's Supreme Court to declare the referendum void. That court rejected the request, holding that the referendum authorized by Ohio's Constitution, "was a part of the legislative power of the State," and "nothing in [federal statutory law] or in [the Elections Clause] operated to the contrary." This Court affirmed the Ohio Supreme Court's judgment. In upholding the state court's decision, we recognized that the referendum was "part of the legislative power" in Ohio, legitimately exercised by the people to disapprove the legislation creating congressional districts. For redistricting purposes, *Hildebrant* thus established, "the Legislature" did not mean the representative body alone. Rather, the word encompassed a veto power lodged in the people. (Elections Clause does not bar "treating the referendum as part of the legislative power for the purpose of apportionment, where so ordained by the state constitutions and laws").

Hawke v. Smith involved the Eighteenth Amendment to the Federal Constitution. Ohio's Legislature had ratified the Amendment, and a referendum on that ratification was at issue. Reversing the Ohio Supreme Court's decision upholding the referendum, we held that "ratification by a State of a constitutional amendment is not an act of legislation within the proper sense of the word." Instead, Article V governing ratification had lodged in "the legislatures of three-fourths of the several States" sole authority to assent to a proposed amendment. The Court contrasted the ratifying function, exercisable exclusively by a State's legislature, with "the ordinary business of legislation." *Davis v. Hildebrant,* the Court explained, involved the enactment of legislation, *i.e.,* a redistricting plan, and properly held that "the referendum [was] part of the legislative authority of the State for [that] purpose."

Smiley v. Holm raised the question whether legislation purporting to redistrict Minnesota for congressional elections was subject to the Governor's veto. The Minnesota Supreme Court had held that the Elections Clause placed redistricting authority exclusively in the hands of the State's legislature, leaving no role for the Governor. We reversed that determination and held, for the purpose at hand, Minnesota's legislative authority includes not just the two houses of the legislature; it includes, in addition, a make-or-break role for the Governor. In holding that the Governor's veto counted, we distinguished instances in which the Constitution calls upon state legislatures to exercise a function other than lawmaking. State legislatures, we pointed out, performed an "electoral" function "in the choice of United States Senators under Article I, section 3, prior to the adoption of the Seventeenth Amendment," a "ratifying" function for "proposed amendments to the Constitution under Article V," as explained in *Hawke v. Smith,* and a "consenting" function "in relation to the acquisition of lands by the United States under Article I, section 8, paragraph 17."

In contrast to those other functions, we observed, redistricting "involves lawmaking in its essential features and most important aspect." Lawmaking, we further noted, ordinarily "must be in accordance with the method which the State has prescribed for legislative enactments." In Minnesota, the State's Constitution had made the Governor "part of the legislative process." And the Elections Clause, we explained, respected the State's choice to include the Governor in that process, although the Governor could play no part when the Constitution assigned to "the Legislature" a ratifying, electoral, or consenting function. Nothing in the Elections Clause, we said, "attempt[ed] to endow the legislature of the State with power to enact laws in any manner other than that in which the constitution of the State ha[d] provided that laws shall be enacted."

In sum, our precedent teaches that redistricting is a legislative function, to be performed in accordance with the State's prescriptions for lawmaking, which may include the referendum and the Governor's veto. The exercise of the initiative, we acknowledge, was not at issue in our prior decisions. But as developed below, we see no constitutional barrier to a State's empowerment of its people by embracing that form of lawmaking.

B

We take up next the statute the Court asked the parties to address, 2 U.S.C. § 2a(c), a measure modeled on the Reapportionment Act Congress passed in 1911, Act of Aug. 8 (1911 Act), ch. 5, § 4, 37 Stat. 14. Section 2a(c), we hold, permits use of a commission to adopt Arizona's congressional districts.

From 1862 through 1901, the decennial congressional apportionment Acts provided that a State would be required to follow federally prescribed procedures for redistricting unless "the legislature" of the State drew district lines. *E.g.,* Act of July 14, 1862, ch. 170, 12 Stat. 572; Act of Jan. 16, 1901, ch. 93, § 4, 31 Stat. 734. In drafting the 1911 Act, Congress focused on the fact that several States had supplemented the representative legislature mode of lawmaking with a direct lawmaking role for the people, through the processes of initiative (positive legislation by the electorate) and referendum (approval or disapproval of legislation by the electorate). 47 Cong. Rec. 3508 (statement of Sen. Burton). To accommodate that development, the 1911 Act eliminated the statutory reference to redistricting by the state "legislature" and instead directed that, if a State's apportionment of Representatives increased, the State should use the Act's default procedures for redistricting "until such State shall be redistricted *in the manner provided by the laws thereof*." Ch. 5, § 4, 37 Stat. 14 (emphasis added).

Some Members of Congress questioned whether the language change was needed. In their view, existing apportionment legislation (referring to redistricting by a State's "legislature") "suffic[ed] to allow, whatever the law of the State may be, the people of that State to control [redistricting]." 47 Cong. Rec. 3507 (statement of Sen. Shively); cf. *Shiel v. Thayer,* Bartlett Contested Election Cases, H.R. Misc. Doc. No. 57, 38th Cong., 2d Sess., 351 (1861) (view of House Committee of Elections Member Dawes that Art. I, § 4's reference to "the Legislature" meant simply the "constituted authorities, through whom [the State] choose[s] to speak," prime among them, the State's Constitution, "which rises above . . . all legislative action"). Others anticipated that retaining the reference to "the legislature" would "condem [n] . . . any [redistricting] legislation by referendum or by initiative." 47 Cong. Rec. 3436 (statement of Sen. Burton). In any event, proponents of the change maintained, "[i]n view of the very serious evils arising from gerrymanders," Congress should not "take any chances in [the] matter.". "[D]ue respect to the rights, to the established methods, and to the laws of the respective States," they urged, required Congress "to allow them to establish congressional districts in whatever way they may have provided by their constitution and by their statutes."(statement of Sen. Works).

As this Court observed in *Hildebrant,* "the legislative history of th[e] [1911 Act] leaves no room for doubt [about why] the prior words were stricken out and the new words inserted." The change was made to safeguard to "each State full authority to employ in the creation of congressional districts its own laws and regulations." 47 Cong. Rec. 3437 (statement of Sen. Burton). The 1911 Act, in short, left the question of redistricting "to the laws and methods of the States. If they include initiative, it is included."

While the 1911 Act applied only to reapportionment following the 1910 census, Congress used virtually identical language when it enacted § 2a(c) in 1941. See Act of Nov. 15, 1941, ch. 470, 55 Stat. 761–762. Section 2a(c) sets forth congressional-redistricting procedures operative only if the State, "after any apportionment," had not redistricted "in the manner provided by the law thereof." The 1941 provision, like the 1911 Act, thus accorded full respect to the redistricting procedures adopted by the States. So long as a State has "redistricted in the manner provided by the law thereof"—as Arizona did by utilizing the independent commission procedure called for by its Constitution—the resulting redistricting plan becomes the presumptively governing map.

C

We note, preliminarily, that dictionaries, even those in circulation during the founding era, capaciously define the word "legislature." Samuel Johnson defined "legislature" simply as "[t]he power that makes laws." 2 A Dictionary of the English Language (1st ed. 1755); *ibid.* (6th ed. 1785); (10th ed. 1792); (12th ed. 1802). Thomas Sheridan's dictionary defined "legislature" exactly as Dr. Johnson did: "The power that makes laws." 2 A Complete Dictionary of the English Language (4th ed. 1797). Noah Webster defined the term precisely that way as well. Compendious Dictionary of the English Language 174 (1806). And Nathan Bailey similarly defined "legislature" as "the Authority of making Laws, or Power which makes them." An Universal Etymological English Dictionary (20th ed. 1763).

As to the "power that makes laws" in Arizona, initiatives adopted by the voters legislate for the State just as measures passed by the representative body do. See Ariz. Const., Art. IV, pt. 1, § 1 ("The legislative authority of the state shall be vested in the legislature, consisting of a senate and a house of representatives, but the people reserve the power to propose laws and amendments to the constitution and to enact or reject such laws and amendments at the polls, independently of the legislature."). As well in Arizona, the people may delegate their legislative authority over redistricting to an independent commission just as the representative body may choose to do.

1

The dominant purpose of the Elections Clause, the historical record bears out, was to empower Congress to override state election rules, not to restrict the way States enact legislation. As this Court explained in *Arizona v. Inter Tribal Council of Ariz., Inc.*, 570 U.S. ___, 133 S.Ct. 2247, 186 L.Ed.2d 239 (2013), the Clause "was the Framers' insurance against the possibility that a State would refuse to provide for the election of representatives to the Federal Congress." *Id.*, at ___, 133 S.Ct., at 2253 (citing The Federalist No. 59, pp. 362–363 (C. Rossiter ed. 1961) (A. Hamilton)).

The Clause was also intended to act as a safeguard against manipulation of electoral rules by politicians and factions in the States to entrench themselves or place their interests over those of the electorate. As Madison urged, without the Elections Clause, "[w]henever the State Legislatures had a favorite measure to carry, they would take care so to mould their regulations as to favor the candidates they wished to succeed." 2 Records of the Federal Convention 241 (M. Farrand rev. 1966). Madison spoke in response to a motion by South Carolina's delegates to strike out the federal power. Those delegates so moved because South Carolina's coastal elite had malapportioned their legislature, and wanted to retain the ability to do so. See J. Rakove, Original Meanings: Politics and Ideas in the Making of the Constitution 223–224 (1996). The problem Madison identified has hardly lessened over time. Conflict of interest is inherent when "legislators dra[w] district lines that they ultimately have to run in."

Arguments in support of congressional control under the Elections Clause were reiterated in the public debate over ratification. Theophilus Parsons, a delegate at the Massachusetts ratifying convention, warned that "when faction and party spirit run high," a legislature might take actions like "mak[ing] an unequal and partial division of the states into districts for the election of representatives." Debate in Massachusetts Ratifying Convention (16–17, 21 Jan. 1788), in 2 The Founders' Constitution 256 (P. Kurland & R. Lerner eds. 1987). Timothy Pickering of Massachusetts similarly urged that the Clause was necessary because "the State governments *may* abuse their power, and regulate . . . elections in such manner as would be highly inconvenient to the people." Letter to Charles Tillinghast (24 Dec. 1787). He described the Clause as a way to "ensure to the *people* their rights of election."

While attention focused on potential abuses by state-level politicians, and the consequent need for congressional oversight, the legislative processes by which the States could exercise their initiating role in regulating congressional elections occasioned no debate. That is hardly surprising. Recall that when the Constitution was composed in Philadelphia and later ratified, the people's legislative prerogatives—the initiative and the referendum—were not yet in our democracy's arsenal. The Elections Clause, however, is not reasonably read to disarm States from adopting modes of legislation that place the lead rein in the people's hands.

4

Banning lawmaking by initiative to direct a State's method of apportioning congressional districts would do more than stymie attempts to curb partisan gerrymandering, by which the majority in the legislature draws district lines to their party's advantage. It would also cast doubt on numerous other election laws adopted by the initiative method of legislating.

The people, in several States, functioning as the lawmaking body for the purpose at hand, have used the initiative to install a host of regulations governing the "Times, Places and Manner" of holding federal elections. Art. I, § 4. For example, the people of California provided for permanent voter registration, specifying that "no amendment by the Legislature shall provide for a general biennial or other periodic reregistration of voters." Cal. Elec.Code Ann. § 2123 (West 2003). The people of Ohio banned ballots providing for straight-ticket voting along party lines. Ohio Const., Art. V, § 2a. The people of Oregon shortened the deadline for voter registration to 20 days prior to an election. Ore. Const., Art. II, § 2. None of those measures permit the state legislatures to override the people's prescriptions. The Arizona Legislature's theory—that the lead role in regulating federal elections cannot be wrested from "the Legislature," and vested in commissions initiated by the people—would endanger all of them.

The list of endangered state elections laws, were we to sustain the position of the Arizona Legislature, would not stop with popular initiatives. Almost all state constitutions were adopted by conventions and ratified by voters at the ballot box, without involvement or approval by "the Legislature." Core aspects of the electoral process regulated by state constitutions include voting by "ballot" or "secret ballot," voter registration, absentee voting, vote counting, and victory thresholds. Again, the States' legislatures had no hand in making these laws and may not alter or amend them.

The importance of direct democracy as a means to control election regulations extends beyond the particular statutes and constitutional provisions installed by the people rather than the States' legislatures. The very prospect of lawmaking by the people may influence the legislature when it considers (or fails to consider) election-related measures. Turning the coin, the legislature's responsiveness to the people its members represent is hardly heightened when the representative body can be confident that what it does will not be overturned or modified by the voters themselves.

For the reasons stated, the judgment of the United States District Court for the District of Arizona is

Affirmed.

CHIEF JUSTICE ROBERTS, with whom JUSTICE SCALIA, JUSTICE THOMAS, and JUSTICE ALITO join, dissenting.

Just over a century ago, Arizona became the second State in the Union to ratify the Seventeenth Amendment. That Amendment transferred power to choose United States Senators from "the Legislature" of each State, Art. I, § 3, to "the people thereof." The Amendment resulted from an arduous, decades-long campaign in which reformers across the country worked hard to garner approval from Congress and three-quarters of the States.

What chumps! Didn't they realize that all they had to do was interpret the constitutional term "the Legislature" to mean "the people"? The Court today performs just such a magic trick with the Elections Clause. Art. I, § 4. That Clause vests *2678 congressional redistricting authority in "the Legislature" of each State. An Arizona ballot initiative transferred that authority from "the Legislature" to an "Independent Redistricting Commission." The majority approves this deliberate constitutional evasion by doing what the proponents of the Seventeenth Amendment dared not: revising "the Legislature" to mean "the people."

The Court's position has no basis in the text, structure, or history of the Constitution, and it contradicts precedents from both Congress and this Court. The Constitution contains seventeen provisions referring to the "Legislature" of a State, many of which cannot possibly be read to mean "the people." Indeed, several provisions expressly distinguish "the Legislature" from "the People." See Art. I, § 2. This Court has accordingly defined "the Legislature" in the Elections Clause as "*the representative body* which ma[kes] the laws of the people."

The majority largely ignores this evidence, relying instead on disconnected observations about direct democracy, a contorted interpretation of an irrelevant statute, and naked appeals to public policy. Nowhere does the majority explain how a constitutional provision that vests redistricting authority in "the Legislature" permits a State to wholly exclude "the Legislature" from redistricting. Arizona's Commission might be a noble endeavor—although it does not seem so "independent" in practice—but the "fact that a given law or procedure is efficient, convenient, and useful . . . will not save it if it is contrary to the Constitution." No matter how concerned we may be about partisanship in redistricting, this Court has no power to gerrymander the Constitution. I respectfully dissent.

FOR DISCUSSION

Does the *Arizona Independent Redistricting Commission* endorse the use of independent redistricting commissions? Will they be able to address the partisan gerrymandering problem? Who are or what is a "legislature" as a result of the case?

POLITICAL PARTIES AND BALLOT ACCESS

There is a 1960s Leslie Gore song—"It's My Party and I'll Cry if I Want to." In some ways the song speaks to the jurisprudence of political parties. They generally have broad leeway under the First Amendment freedom of association and "peaceable assembly" clausees to govern their own internal affairs by determining who may participate in their business. But is this authority unlimited? Could they create a party for whites or males only? Could Democrats invite independents in or prevent Republicans from participating in their conventions, primaries, or caucuses? Could states, in an effort to increase voter turnout or eliminate discrimination, mandate who may participate? These are some of the questions raised when party associational rights are considered.

In *Smith v. Allwright*, 321 U.S. 649 (1944), the Court viewed political parties not always as private agents but as occasionally state actors who can be regulated. In this case, a party primary is treated as state action for the purposes of ruling that banning African Americans from their proceedings violated the Constitution. It appears from this decision that parties cannot engage in some types of discrimination, but not all types of discrimination are forbidden. For example, could a party refuse admission or membership to members from another party or decide to impose an ideological litmus test? Conversely, could party members from another party participate in events, such as a primary or convention?

First, in *Tashjian v. Republican Party of Connecticut* (479 U.S. 208, 1986), the Court ruled that a state **closed primary** law, which required individuals to be a member of a party to participate in its primaries, was unconstitutional. Here, the Connecticut Republican Party wished to invite independents to participate in their primaries. But the Court's ruling meant that the party can determine whom it wishes to participate in their primaries. Then, in *Eu v. San Francisco County Democratic Central Committee* (489 U.S. 214, 1989), California law precluding elected officials from endorsing candidates for office was declared a violation of the First Amendment. In the case excerpted in this section, *California Democratic Party v. Jones* (530 U.S. 567, 2000) the Court struck down a state ballot measure creating a **blanket primary** system where voters, regardless of their party affiliation, could vote in primaries for candidates of any party affiliation. The Court ruled that such a measure violated the **associational rights of the party** (which raises the interesting question of who is the party and who may speak for it) not to affiliate with individuals with whom they do not wish to associate. The *Jones* opinion seems to stand in sharp contrast to *Allwright*, suggesting that parties are more private than public entities and therefore insulated from state regulation.

However, while party rights appeared to reach a highpoint in *Jones*, in *Washington State Grange v. Washington State Republican Party*, 552 U.S. 542 (2008) by a 7–2 vote, the Supreme Court upheld a state of Washington law that identifies candidates by party affiliation on the primary ballot, lets voters select any candidate, and declares that the two candidates who receive the most votes, regardless of affiliation, will proceed to have their names advanced to the general election. Political parties had objected to the law, claiming that their First Amendment rights under *Jones* had been violated. The Court rejected this, claiming that party associational rights were not burdened.

Another way to look at party rights is in terms of **ballot access**. Three cases included in this chapter speak to this issue. In *Bullock v. Carter* (405 U.S. 134, 1972) the Court struck down a Texas law requiring the payment of a filing fee to appear on a ballot. Such fees, the court ruled, burdened the rights of poor candidates. As a result of this decision, states generally give candidates the option of filing fees or gathering signatures on a petition as a way of securing ballot access. The *Bullock* case, however, raises another important question: Is there a constitutional right to appear on the ballot? Should any individual be allowed to appear on any ballot for any election, or should there be some minimum threshold that needs to be met? Perhaps there needs to be some minimum number of voters who support the candidate before one should be allowed on the ballot? The simple answer is that while a candidate has a First Amendment right to run for office, the right to appear on a general election ballot is limited by state interests to prevent voter confusion.

This question about ballot access is important because it looks to how laws may inhibit or discourage third parties or alternative candidates in the electoral process. For example, in 1980, Republican Illinois Congressman John Anderson ran for president but lost the nomination to Ronald Reagan. He then decided to run as an independent for president. However, like Alabama Governor George Wallace before him, who decided to run for president as a third-party candidate in 1968, Anderson faced numerous state laws that appeared to block his efforts, forcing him to go to court in many states to secure ballot access. In *Anderson v. Celebrezze* (460 U.S. 780, 1983) the Court appeared to agree that many of these laws were burdensome obstacles. The Court here articulated one of the tests now used to judge whether ballot access laws are unfair or burdensome to the candidate. John Anderson's presidential run was unsuccessful, but successful legal challenges made later campaigns by Ross Perot in 1992 and Ralph Nader in 2000 possible.

Finally, take a look at *Munro v. Socialist Workers Party* (479 U.S. 189, 1986). Here the question was whether a state law requiring a minor or third party to secure 1 percent of the vote in the primary in order to appear on the general election ballot violated its constitutional rights. The Court said no. Here the Court indicated that the 1 percent was sufficient to secure the state interests of protecting the major parties and preventing confusion. As you read the case, consider whether the current election laws favor the two major parties at the expense of third parties. Is such favoritism permissible?

SMITH V. ALLWRIGHT

321 U.S. 649, 64 S.Ct. 757, 88 L.Ed. 987 (1944)

See pages 768–771.

FOR DISCUSSION

What is the argument the Court gives for why the party cannot exclude Smith? Should parties ever be allowed to discriminate? Should they be allowed to determine their membership?

RELATED CASES

***Nixon v. Herndon:* 273 U.S. 536 (1927).**

A Texas statute prohibiting participation by African Americans in Democratic Party primaries violated the Equal Protection Clause of the Fourteenth Amendment.

***Nixon v. Condon:* 286 U.S. 73 (1932).**

When a Texas state statute empowers the state executive committee of a party to prescribe the qualifications of that party's members for voting or other participation, and a resolution of that committee bars African Americans from the primaries, that action by the committee is representative of the state in the discharge of the state's authority. Since the state could not deny equal protection, this was an unconstitutional act.

***Grovey v. Townsend:* 295 U.S. 45 (1935).**

A resolution of the Texas state convention of the Democratic Party resulted in barring all African Americans from the Democratic Party primaries. The Court held a state convention of a party to be a private organization and not an organization of the state. Therefore, there was no basis for applying the Fourteenth and Fifteenth Amendments.

***Lane v. Wilson:* 307 U.S. 268 (1939).**

An Oklahoma statute in 1916 provided for a registration period for voting of twelve days but exempted from the registration those who had voted in the 1914 election when the "grandfather clause" was effective. The Court held that the provisions of the law as well as the practical difficulties in the administration of the law amounted to discrimination under the Fifteenth Amendment.

CALIFORNIA DEMOCRATIC PARTY V. JONES

530 U.S. 567, 120 S.Ct. 2402, 147 L.Ed.2d 502 (2000)

The voters of California passed a ballot initiative mandating that the political parties use a blanket primary system when selecting party nominees. A blanket primary is one where voters can select their choice for each office, regardless of the party affiliation of the candidates. This is in contrast to an open primary system where voters can vote in whatever primary they wish (but only in one), regardless of their party affiliation. The California Republican and Democratic Parties challenged the blanket primary as a violation of their First and Fourteenth Amendment rights.

Vote: 7–2

JUSTICE SCALIA delivered the opinion of the Court.

This case presents the question whether the State of California may, consistent with the First Amendment to the United States Constitution, use a so-called "blanket" primary to determine a political party's nominee for the general election.

I

Under California law, a candidate for public office has two routes to gain access to the general ballot for most state and federal elective offices. He may receive the nomination of a qualified political party by winning its primary, or he may file as an independent by obtaining (for a statewide race) the signatures of one percent of the State's electorate or (for other races) the signatures of three percent of the voting population of the area represented by the office in contest.

Until 1996, to determine the nominees of qualified parties California held what is known as a "closed" partisan primary, in which only persons who are members of the political party—*i.e.*, who have declared affiliation with that party when they register to vote, can vote on its nominee. In 1996 the citizens of California adopted by initiative Proposition 198. Promoted largely as a measure that would "weaken" party "hard-liners" and ease the way for "moderate problem-solvers," Proposition 198 changed California's partisan primary from a closed primary to a blanket primary. Under the new system, "[a]ll persons entitled to vote, including those not affiliated with any political party, shall have the right to vote . . . for any candidate regardless of the candidate's political affiliation." Whereas under the closed primary each voter received a ballot limited to candidates of his own party, as a result of Proposition 198 each voter's primary ballot now lists every candidate regardless of party affiliation and allows the voter to choose freely among them. It remains the case, however, that the candidate of each party who wins the greatest number of votes "is the nominee of that party at the ensuing general election."

Petitioners in this case are four political parties—the California Democratic Party, the California Republican Party, the Libertarian Party of California, and the Peace and Freedom Party—each of which has a rule prohibiting persons not members of the party from voting in the party's primary. Petitioners brought suit in the United States District Court for the Eastern District of California against respondent California Secretary of State, alleging, that California's blanket primary violated their First Amendment rights of association, and seeking declaratory and injunctive relief. The group Californians for an Open Primary, also respondent, intervened as a party defendant. The District Court recognized that the new law would inject into each party's primary substantial numbers of voters unaffiliated with the party. It further recognized that this might result in selection of a nominee different from the one party members would select, or at the least cause the same nominee to commit himself to different positions. Nevertheless, the District Court held that the burden on petitioners' rights of association was not a severe one, and was justified by state interests ultimately reducing to this: "enhanc[ing] the democratic nature of the election process and the representativeness of elected officials." The Ninth Circuit, adopting the District Court's opinion as its own, affirmed. We granted certiorari.

II

Respondents rest their defense of the blanket primary upon the proposition that primaries play an integral role in citizens' selection of public officials. As a consequence, they contend, primaries are public rather than private proceedings, and the States may and must play a role in ensuring that they serve the public interest. Proposition 198, respondents conclude, is simply a rather pedestrian example of a State's regulating its system of elections.

We have recognized, of course, that States have a major role to play in structuring and monitoring the election process, including primaries. We have considered it "too plain for argument," for example, that a State may require parties to use the primary format for selecting their nominees, in order to assure that intraparty competition is resolved in a democratic fashion. Similarly, in order to avoid burdening the general election ballot with frivolous candidacies, a State may require parties to demonstrate "a significant modicum of support" before allowing their candidates a place on that ballot. Finally, in order to prevent "party raiding"—a process in which dedicated members of one party formally switch to another party to alter the outcome of that party's primary—a State may require party registration a reasonable period of time before a primary election.

What we have not held, however, is that the processes by which political parties select their nominees are, as respondents would have it, wholly public affairs that States may regulate freely. To the contrary, we have continually stressed that when States regulate parties' internal processes they must act within limits imposed by the Constitution. In this regard, respondents' reliance on *Smith* v. *Allwright* and *Terry* v. *Adams*, 345 US 461 (1953), is misplaced. In *Allwright*, we invalidated the Texas Democratic Party's rule limiting participation in its primary to whites; in *Terry*, we invalidated the same rule promulgated by the Jaybird Democratic Association, a "self-governing voluntary club." These cases held only that, when a State prescribes an election process that gives a special role to political parties, it "endorses, adopts and enforces the discrimination against Negroes," that the parties (or, in the case of the Jaybird Democratic Association, organizations that are "part and parcel" of the parties, bring into the process—so that the parties' discriminatory action becomes state action under the Fifteenth Amendment. They do not stand for the proposition that party affairs are public affairs, free of First Amendment protections-and our later holdings make that entirely clear. Representative democracy in any populous unit of governance is unimaginable without the ability of citizens to band together in promoting among the electorate candidates who espouse their political views. The formation of national political parties was almost concurrent with the formation of the Republic itself. See Cunningham, The Jeffersonian Republican Party, in 1 *History of U.S. Political Parties* 239, 241 (A. Schlesinger ed., 1973). Consistent with this tradition, the Court has recognized that the First Amendment protects "the freedom to join together in furtherance of common political beliefs," *Tashjian v. Republican Party Of Connecticut,* 479 U.S. 208 (1986), which "necessarily presupposes the freedom to identify the people who constitute the association, and to limit the association to those people only," *Democratic Party v. Wisconsin ex rel. La Follette,* 450 US 107 (1981). That is to say, a corollary of the right to associate is the right not to associate. " 'Freedom of association would prove an empty guarantee if associations could not limit control over their decisions to those who share the interests and persuasions that underlie the association's being.' "

In no area is the political association's right to exclude more important than in the process of selecting its nominee. That process often determines the party's positions on the most significant public policy issues of the day, and even when those positions are predetermined it is the nominee who becomes the party's ambassador to the general electorate in winning it over to the party's views. Some political parties—such as President Theodore Roosevelt's Bull Moose Party, the La Follette Progressives of 1924, the Henry Wallace Progressives of 1948, and the George Wallace American Independent Party of 1968—are virtually inseparable from their nominees (and tend not to outlast them). See generally E. Kruschke, *Encyclopedia of Third Parties in the United States* (1991).

Unsurprisingly, our cases vigorously affirm the special place the First Amendment reserves for, and the special protection it accords, the process by which a political party "select[s] a standard bearer who best represents the party's ideologies and preferences." The moment of choosing the party's nominee, we have said, is "the crucial juncture at which the appeal to common principles may be translated into concerted action, and hence to political power in the community." *Tashjian,* 479 U.S., at 216; see also *id.*, at 235–236 (Scalia, J., dissenting) ("The ability of the members of the Republican Party to select their own candidate ... unquestionably implicates an associational freedom"). . . .

In *La Follette*, the State of Wisconsin conducted an open presidential preference primary. Although the voters did not select the delegates to the Democratic Party's National Convention directly—they were chosen later at caucuses of party members—Wisconsin law required these delegates to vote in accord with the primary results. Thus allowing nonparty members to participate in the selection of the party's nominee conflicted with the Democratic Party's rules. We held that, whatever the strength of the state interests supporting the open primary itself, they could not justify this "substantial intrusion into the associational freedom of members of the National Party."

California's blanket primary violates the principles set forth in these cases. Proposition 198 forces political parties to associate with—to have their nominees, and hence their positions, determined by—those who, at best, have refused to affiliate with the party, and, at worst, have expressly affiliated with a rival. In this respect, it is qualitatively different from a closed primary. Under that system, even when it is made quite easy for a voter to change his party affiliation the day of the primary, and thus, in some sense, to "cross over," at least he must formally *become a member of the party;* and once he does so, he is limited to voting for candidates of that party.

The evidence in this case demonstrates that under California's blanket primary system, the prospect of having a party's nominee determined by adherents of an opposing party is far from remote—indeed, it is a clear and present danger. For example, in one 1997 survey of California voters 37 percent of Republicans said that they planned to vote in the 1998 Democratic gubernatorial primary, and 20 percent of Democrats said they planned to vote in the 1998 Republican United States Senate primary. Those figures are comparable to the results of studies in other States with blanket primaries. One expert testified, for example, that in Washington the number of voters crossing over from one party to another can rise to as high as 25 percent, and another that only 25 to 33 percent of all Washington voters limit themselves to candidates of one party throughout the ballot. The impact of voting by nonparty members is much greater upon minor parties, such as the Libertarian Party and the Peace and Freedom Party. In the first primaries these parties conducted following California's implementation of Proposition 198, the total votes cast for party candidates in some races was more than *double* the total number of *registered party members*. The record also supports the obvious proposition that these substantial numbers of voters who help select the nominees of parties they have chosen not to join often have policy views that diverge from those of the party faithful. The 1997 survey of California voters revealed significantly different policy preferences between party members and primary voters who "crossed over" from another party. One expert went so far as to describe it as "inevitable [under Proposition 198] that parties will be forced in some circumstances to give their official designation to a candidate who's not preferred by a majority or even plurality of party members."

In sum, Proposition 198 forces petitioners to adulterate their candidate-selection process-the "basic function of a political party," by opening it up to persons wholly unaffiliated with the party. Such forced association has the likely outcome—indeed, in this case the *intended* outcome—of changing the parties' message. We can think of no heavier burden on a political party's associational freedom. Proposition 198 is therefore unconstitutional unless it is narrowly tailored to serve a compelling state interest.

FOR DISCUSSION

What is a blanket primary? Why did the rights of the voters to vote not outweigh the associational rights of the party? Could one not consider voters to be party members?

RELATED CASES

***Timmons v. Twin Cities Area New Party:* 520 U.S. 351 (1997).**

Ruled that a state law banning fusion or cross-party endorsements of candidates did not violate the First Amendment.

***Tashjian v. Republican Party of Connecticut:* 479 U.S.208 (1986).**

The Court ruled that a state closed primary law, which required individuals to be a member of a party to participate in its primaries, was unconstitutional. Here, the Connecticut Republican Party wished to invite independents to participate in their primaries.

***Eu v. San Francisco County Democratic Central Committee:* 489 U.S. 214 (1989).**

A California law precluding elected officials from endorsing candidates for office was declared a violation of the First Amendment.

***Democratic Party of the United States v. Wisconsin:* 450 U.S. 107 (1981).**

The Wisconsin Democratic Party allowed non-party members to participate in its primary, contrary to national Democratic Party rules. The state party challenged the decision of the national party to refuse to seat their delegates. The Supreme Court ruled that the First Amendment Freedom of Association Clause protected the decision of the national party to refuse to seat the state party delegates.

Washington State Grange v. Washington State Republican Party

552 U.S. 442, 128 S.Ct. 1184, 170 L.Ed.2d 151 (2008)

State political parties challenged a ballot proposition creating a modified blanket primary system in the state of Washington. The law would allow voters, regardless of party affiliation, to select candidates in a primary regardless of party label. The top two vote getters for each office would then appear on the general election ballot.

Vote 7–2

Justice Thomas delivered the opinion of the Court, in which Chief Justice Roberts, and Justices Stevens, Souter, Ginsburg, Breyer, and Alito joined.

Justice Thomas delivered the opinion of the Court.

In 2004, voters in the State of Washington passed an initiative changing the State's primary election system. The People's Choice Initiative of 2004, or Initiative 872 (I-872), provides that candidates for office shall be identified on the ballot by their self-designated "party preference"; that voters may vote for any candidate; and that the top two votegetters for each office, regardless of party preference, advance to the general election. The Court of Appeals for the Ninth Circuit held I-872 facially invalid as imposing an unconstitutional burden on state political parties' First Amendment rights. Because I-872 does not on its face impose a severe burden on political parties' associational rights, and because respondents' arguments to the contrary rest on factual assumptions about voter confusion that can be evaluated only in the context of an as-applied challenge, we reverse.

I

For most of the past century, Washington voters selected nominees for state and local offices using a blanket primary. From 1935 until 2003, the State used a blanket primary that placed candidates from all parties on one ballot and allowed voters to select a candidate from any party. Under this system, the candidate who won a plurality of votes within each major party became that party's nominee in the general election.

California used a nearly identical primary in its own elections until our decision in *California Democratic Party v. Jones*, 530 U.S. 567 (2000). In *Jones,* four political parties challenged California's blanket primary, arguing that it unconstitutionally burdened their associational rights by forcing them to associate with voters who did not share their beliefs. We agreed and struck down the blanket primary as inconsistent with the First Amendment. In so doing, we emphasized the importance of the nomination process as " 'the crucial juncture at which the appeal to common principles may be translated into concerted action, and hence to political power in the community.' " California's blanket primary, we concluded, severely burdened the parties' freedom of association because it forced them to allow nonmembers to participate in selecting the parties' nominees. That the parties retained the right to endorse their preferred candidates did not render the burden any less severe, as "[t]here is simply no substitute for a party's selecting its own candidates."

Because California's blanket primary severely burdened the parties' associational rights, we subjected it to strict scrutiny, carefully examining each of the state interests offered by California in support of its primary system. We rejected as illegitimate three of the asserted interests: "producing elected officials who better represent the electorate," "expanding candidate debate beyond the scope of partisan concerns," and ensuring "the right to an effective vote" by allowing nonmembers of a party to vote in the majority party's primary in " 'safe' " districts. We concluded that the remaining interests—promoting fairness, affording voters greater choice, increasing voter participation, and protecting privacy—were not compelling on the facts of the case.

Even if they were, the partisan California primary was not narrowly tailored to further those interests because a nonpartisan blanket primary, in which the top two votegetters advance to the general election regardless of party affiliation, would accomplish each of those interests without burdening the parties' associational rights. The nonpartisan blanket primary had "all the characteristics of the partisan blanket primary, save the constitutionally crucial one: Primary voters [were] not choosing a party's nominee."

After our decision in *Jones,* the Court of Appeals for the Ninth Circuit struck down Washington's primary as "materially indistinguishable from the California scheme." The Washington State Grange promptly proposed I-872 as a replacement. It passed with nearly 60% of the vote and became effective in December 2004.

Under I-872, all elections for "partisan offices" are conducted in two stages: a primary and a general election. To participate in the primary, a candidate must file a "declaration of candidacy" form, on which he declares his "major or minor party preference, or independent status." Each candidate and his party preference (or independent status) is in turn designated on the primary election ballot. A political party cannot prevent a candidate who is unaffiliated with, or even repugnant to, the party from designating it as his party of preference. In the primary election, voters may select "any candidate listed on the ballot, regardless of the party preference of the candidates or the voter."

The candidates with the highest and second-highest vote totals advance to the general election, regardless of their party preferences. Thus, the general election may pit two candidates with the same party preference against one another. Each candidate's party preference is listed on the general election ballot, and may not be changed between the primary and general elections.

Immediately after the State enacted regulations to implement I-872, the Washington State Republican Party filed suit against a number of county auditors challenging the law on its face. The party contended that the new system violates its associational rights by usurping its right to nominate its own candidates and by forcing it to associate with candidates it does not endorse. The Washington State Democratic Central Committee and Libertarian Party of Washington State joined the suit as plaintiffs. The Washington State Grange joined as a defendant, and the State of Washington was substituted for the county auditors as defendant. The United States District Court for the Western District of Washington granted the political parties' motions for summary judgment and enjoined the implementation of I-872.

The Court of Appeals affirmed. It held that the I-872 primary severely burdens the political parties' associational rights because the party-preference designation on the ballot creates a risk that primary winners will be perceived as the parties' nominees and produces an "impression of associatio[n]" between a candidate and his party of preference even when the party does not associate, or wish to be associated, with the candidate. The Court of Appeals noted a "constitutionally significant distinction between ballots and other vehicles for political expression," reasoning that the risk of perceived association is particularly acute when ballots include party labels because such labels are typically used to designate candidates' views on issues of public concern. And it determined that the State's interests underlying I-872 were not sufficiently compelling to justify the severe burden on the parties' association. Concluding that the provisions of I-872 providing for the party-preference designation on the ballot were not severable, the court struck down I-872 in its entirety.

We granted certiorari to determine whether I-872, on its face, violates the political parties' associational rights.

II

Respondents object to I-872 not in the context of an actual election, but in a facial challenge. Under *United States v. Salerno,* 481 U.S. 739 (1987), a plaintiff can only succeed in a facial challenge by "establish[ing] that no set of circumstances exists under which the Act would be valid," *i.e.,* that the law is unconstitutional in all of its applications. While some Members of the Court have criticized the *Salerno* formulation, all agree that a facial challenge must fail where the statute has a " 'plainly legitimate sweep.' " Washington's primary system survives under either standard, as we explain below. In determining whether a law is facially invalid, we must be careful not to go beyond the statute's facial requirements and speculate about "hypothetical" or "imaginary" cases. The State has had no opportunity to implement I-872, and its courts have had no occasion to construe the law in the context of actual disputes arising from the electoral context, or to accord the law a limiting construction to avoid constitutional questions. Exercising judicial restraint in a facial challenge "frees the Court not only from unnecessary pronouncement on constitutional issues, but also from premature interpretations of statutes in areas where their constitutional application might be cloudy."

Facial challenges are disfavored for several reasons. Claims of facial invalidity often rest on speculation. As a consequence, they raise the risk of "premature interpretation of statutes on the basis of factually barebones records." Facial challenges also run contrary to the fundamental principle of judicial restraint that courts should neither " 'anticipate a question of constitutional law in advance of the necessity of deciding it' " nor " 'formulate a rule of constitutional law broader than is required by the precise facts to which it is to be applied.' " *Ashwander v. TVA,* 297 U.S. 288, 347 (1936) (Brandeis, J., concurring). Finally, facial challenges threaten to short circuit the democratic process by preventing laws embodying the will of the people from being implemented in a manner consistent with the Constitution. We must keep in mind that " '[a] ruling of unconstitutionality frustrates the intent of the elected representatives of the people.' " It is with these principles in view that we turn to the merits of respondents' facial challenge to I-872.

A

The States possess a " 'broad power to prescribe the "Times, Places and Manner of holding Elections for Senators and Representatives," Art. I, § 4, cl. 1, which power is matched by state control over the election process for state offices.' " This power is not absolute, but is "subject to the limitation that [it] may not be exercised in a way that violates . . . specific provisions of the Constitution." In particular, the State has the " 'responsibility to observe the limits established by the First Amendment rights of the State's citizens,' " including the freedom of political association.

Election regulations that impose a severe burden on associational rights are subject to strict scrutiny, and we uphold them only if they are "narrowly tailored to serve a compelling state interest." If a statute imposes only modest burdens, however, then "the State's important regulatory interests are generally sufficient to justify reasonable, nondiscriminatory restrictions" on election procedures. *Anderson v. Celebrezze,* 460 U.S. 780 (1983). "Accordingly, we have repeatedly upheld reasonable, politically neutral regulations that have the effect of channeling expressive activity at the polls."

The parties do not dispute these general principles; rather, they disagree about whether I-872 severely burdens respondents' associational rights. That disagreement begins with *Jones.* Petitioners argue that the I-872 primary is indistinguishable from the alternative *Jones* suggested would be constitutional. In *Jones* we noted that a nonpartisan blanket primary, where the top two votegetters proceed to the general election regardless of their party, was a less restrictive alternative to California's system because such a primary does not nominate candidates. (The nonpartisan blanket primary "has all the characteristics of the partisan blanket primary, save the constitutionally crucial one: Primary voters are not choosing a party's nominee"). Petitioners are correct that we assumed that the nonpartisan primary we described in *Jones* would be constitutional. But that is not dispositive here because we had no occasion in *Jones* to determine whether a primary system that indicates each candidate's party preference on the ballot, in effect, chooses the parties' nominees.

That question is now squarely before us. Respondents argue that I-872 is unconstitutional under *Jones* because it has the same "constitutionally crucial" infirmity that doomed California's blanket primary: it allows primary voters who are unaffiliated with a party to choose the party's nominee. Respondents claim that candidates who progress to the general election under I-872 will become the *de facto* nominees of the parties they prefer, thereby violating the parties' right to choose their own standard-bearers and altering their messages. They rely on our statement in *Jones* reaffirming "the special place the First Amendment reserves for, and the special protection it accords, the process by which a political party 'select[s] a standard bearer who best represents the party's ideologies and preferences.' "

The flaw in this argument is that, unlike the California primary, the I-872 primary does not, by its terms, choose parties' nominees. The essence of nomination—the choice of a party representative—does not occur under I-872. The law never refers to the candidates as nominees of any party, nor does it treat them as such. To the contrary, the election regulations specifically provide that the primary "does not serve to determine the nominees of a political party but serves to winnow the number of candidates to a final list of two for the general election." The top two candidates from the primary election proceed to the general election regardless of their party preferences. Whether parties nominate their own candidates outside the state-run primary is simply irrelevant. In fact, parties may now nominate candidates by whatever mechanism they choose because I-872 repealed Washington's prior regulations governing party nominations.

Respondents counter that, even if the I-872 primary does not actually choose parties' nominees, it nevertheless burdens their associational rights because voters will assume that candidates on the general election ballot are the nominees of their preferred parties. This brings us to the heart of respondents' case—and to the fatal flaw in their argument. At bottom, respondents' objection to I-872 is that voters will be confused by candidates' party-preference designations. Respondents' arguments are largely variations on this theme. Thus, they argue that even if voters do not assume that candidates on the general election ballot are the nominees of their parties, they will at least assume that the parties associate with, and approve of, them. This, they say, compels them to associate with candidates they do not endorse, alters the messages they wish to convey, and forces them to engage in counterspeech to disassociate themselves from the candidates and their positions on the issues.

We reject each of these contentions for the same reason: They all depend, not on any facial requirement of I-872, but on the possibility that voters will be confused as to the meaning of the party-preference designation. But respondents' assertion that voters will misinterpret the party-preference designation is sheer speculation. It "depends upon the belief that voters can be 'misled' by party labels. But '[o]ur cases reflect a greater faith in the ability of individual voters to inform themselves about campaign issues.' " There is simply no basis to presume that a well-informed electorate will interpret a candidate's party-preference designation to mean that the candidate is the party's chosen nominee or representative or that the party associates with or approves of the candidate. See *New York State Club Assn., Inc. v. City of New York,* 487 U.S. 1, 13–14 (1988) (rejecting a facial challenge to a law regulating club membership and noting that "[w]e could hardly hold otherwise on the record before us, which contains no specific evidence on the characteristics of *any* club covered by the [l]aw"). This strikes us as especially true here, given that it was the voters of Washington themselves, rather than their elected representatives, who enacted I-872.

Of course, it is *possible* that voters will misinterpret the candidates' party-preference designations as reflecting endorsement by the parties. But these cases involve a facial challenge, and we cannot strike down I-872 on its face based on the mere possibility of voter confusion. Because respondents brought their suit as a facial challenge, we have no evidentiary record against which to assess their assertions that voters will be confused. Indeed, because I-872 has never been implemented, we do not even have ballots indicating how party preference will be displayed. It stands to reason that whether voters will be confused by the party-preference designations will depend in significant part on the form of the ballot. The Court of Appeals assumed that the ballot would not place abbreviations like " 'D' " and " 'R,' " or " 'Dem.' " and " 'Rep.' " after the names of candidates, but would instead "clearly state that a particular candidate 'prefers' a particular party." It thought that even such a clear statement did too little to eliminate the risk of voter confusion.

But we see no reason to stop there. As long as we are speculating about the form of the ballot-and we can do no more than speculate in this facial challenge-we must, in fairness to the voters of the State of Washington who enacted I-872 and in deference to the executive and judicial officials who are charged with implementing it, ask whether the ballot could conceivably be printed in such a way as to eliminate the possibility of widespread voter confusion and with it the perceived threat to the First Amendment.

It is not difficult to conceive of such a ballot. For example, petitioners propose that the actual I-872 ballot could include prominent disclaimers explaining that party preference reflects only the self-designation of the candidate and not an official endorsement by the party. They also suggest that the ballots might note preference in the form of a candidate statement that emphasizes the candidate's personal determination rather than the party's acceptance of the candidate, such as "my party preference is the Republican Party." Additionally, the State could decide to educate the public about the new primary ballots through advertising or explanatory materials mailed to voters along with their ballots. We are satisfied that there are a variety of ways in which the State could implement I-872 that would eliminate any real threat of voter confusion. And without the specter of widespread voter confusion, respondents' arguments about forced association and compelled speech fall flat.

Our conclusion that these implementations of I-872 would be consistent with the First Amendment is fatal to respondents' facial challenge. See *Schall v. Martin,* 467 U.S. 253, 264 (1984) (a facial challenge fails where "at least some" constitutional applications exist). Each of their arguments rests on factual assumptions about voter confusion, and each fails for the same reason: In the absence of evidence, we cannot assume that Washington's voters will be misled. That factual determination must await an as-applied challenge. On its face, I-872 does not impose any severe burden on respondents' associational rights.

B

Because we have concluded that I-872 does not severely burden respondents, the State need not assert a compelling interest. The State's asserted interest in providing voters with relevant information about the candidates on the ballot is easily sufficient to sustain I-872.

III

Respondents ask this Court to invalidate a popularly enacted election process that has never been carried out. Immediately after implementing regulations were enacted, respondents obtained a permanent injunction against the enforcement of I-872. The First Amendment does not require this extraordinary and precipitous nullification of the will of the people. Because I-872 does not on its face provide for the nomination of candidates or compel political parties to associate with or endorse candidates, and because there is no basis in this facial challenge for presuming that candidates' party-preference designations will confuse voters, I-872 does not on its face severely burden respondents' associational rights. We accordingly hold that I-872 is facially constitutional. The judgment of the Court of Appeals is reversed.

It is so ordered.

CHIEF JUSTICE ROBERTS, with whom JUSTICE ALITO joins, concurring.

I share Justice Scalia's concern that permitting a candidate to identify his political party preference on an official election ballot—regardless of whether the candidate is endorsed by the party or is even a member—may effectively force parties to accept candidates they do not want, amounting to forced association in violation of the First Amendment.

I do think, however, that whether voters *perceive* the candidate and the party to be associated is relevant to the constitutional inquiry. Our other forced-association cases indicate as much.

Voter perceptions matter, and if voters do not actually believe the parties and the candidates are tied together, it is hard to see how the parties' associational rights are adversely implicated.

After all, individuals frequently claim to favor this or that political party; these preferences, without more, do not create an unconstitutional forced association.

But because respondents brought this challenge before the State of Washington had printed ballots for use under the new primary regime, we have no idea what those ballots will look like. Petitioners themselves emphasize that the content of the ballots in the pertinent respect is yet to be determined.

If the ballot is designed in such a manner that no reasonable voter would believe that the candidates listed there are nominees or members of, or otherwise associated with, the parties the candidates claimed to "prefer," the I-872 primary system would likely pass constitutional muster. I cannot say on the present record that it would be impossible for the State to design such a ballot. Assuming the ballot is so designed, voters would not regard the listed candidates as "party" candidates, any more than someone saying "I like Campbell's soup" would be understood to be associated with Campbell's. Voters would understand that the candidate does not speak on the party's behalf or with the party's approval. On the other hand, if the ballot merely lists the candidates' preferred parties next to the candidates' names, or otherwise fails clearly to convey that the parties and the candidates are not necessarily associated, the I-872 system would not survive a First Amendment challenge.

JUSTICE SCALIA, with whom JUSTICE KENNEDY joins, dissenting.

The electorate's perception of a political party's beliefs is colored by its perception of those who support the party; and a party's defining act is the selection of a candidate and advocacy of that candidate's election by conferring upon him the party's endorsement. When the state-printed ballot for the general election causes a party to be associated with candidates who may not fully (if at all) represent its views, it undermines both these vital aspects of political association. The views of the self-identified party supporter color perception of the party's message, and that self-identification on the ballot, with no space for party repudiation or party identification of its own candidate, impairs the party's advocacy of its standard bearer. Because Washington has not demonstrated that this severe burden upon parties' associational rights is narrowly tailored to serve a compelling interest—indeed, because it seems to me Washington's only plausible interest is precisely to reduce the effectiveness of political parties—I would find the law unconstitutional.

FOR DISCUSSION

Does *Washington State Grange* effectively overrule *Jones*? How does the Court distinguish the two cases? What evidence did those challenging the law offer to claim the law was unconstitutional?

BULLOCK V. CARTER

405 U.S. 134, 92 S.Ct. 849, 31 L.Ed.2d 92 (1972)

The state of Texas imposed a filing fee for candidates wishing to run for office. A candidate for a local office challenged the fee requirement, claiming a violation of the First Amendment.

Vote: 7–0

CHIEF JUSTICE BURGER delivered the opinion of the Court, in which all Members joined except JUSTICES POWELL and REHNQUIST, who took no part in the consideration or decision of the case.

Under Texas law, a candidate must pay a filing fee as a condition to having his name placed on the ballot in a primary election. The constitutionality of the Texas filing-fee system is the subject of this appeal from the judgment of a three-judge District Court.

Appellee Pate met all qualifications to be a candidate in the May 2, 1970, Democratic primary for the office of County Commissioner of Precinct Four for El Paso County, except that he was unable to pay the $1,424.60 assessment required of candidates in that primary.

Appellee Wischkaemper sought to be placed on the Democratic primary ballot as a candidate for County Judge in Tarrant County, but he was unable to pay the $6,300 assessment for candidacy for that office. Appellee Carter wished to be a Democratic candidate for Commissioner of the General Land Office; his application was not accompanied by the required $1,000 filing fee.

After being denied places on the Democratic primary ballots in their respective counties, these appellees instituted separate actions in the District Court challenging the validity of the Texas filing-fee system. Their actions were consolidated, and a three-judge District Court was convened pursuant to 28 U.S.C. 2281 and 2284. Appellee Jenkins was permitted to intervene as a voter on his claimed desire to vote for Wischkaemper, and appellee Guzman and others were permitted to intervene as voters desiring to cast their ballots for Pate. On April 3, 1970, the District Court ordered that Wischkaemper and Pate be permitted to participate in the primary conducted on May 2, 1970, without pre-payment of filing fees. Following a hearing on the merits, the three-judge court declared the Texas filing-fee scheme unconstitutional and enjoined its enforcement. A direct appeal was taken under 28 U.S.C. 1253, and we noted probable jurisdiction.

Under the Texas statute, payment of the filing fee is an absolute prerequisite to a candidate's participation in a primary election. There is no alternative procedure by which a potential candidate who is unable to pay the fee can get on the primary ballot by way of petitioning voters, and write-in votes are not permitted in primary elections for public office. Any person who is willing and able to pay the filing fee and who meets the basic eligibility requirements for holding the office sought can run in a primary.

Candidates for most district, county, and precinct offices must pay their filing fee to the county executive committee of the political party conducting the primary; the committee also determines the amount of the fee. The party committee must make an estimate of the total cost of the primary and apportion it among the various candidates "as in their judgment is just and equitable." The committee's judgment is to be guided by "the importance, emolument, and term of office for which the nomination is to be made." In counties with populations of one million or more, candidates for offices of two-year terms can be assessed up to 10% of their aggregate annual salary, and candidates for offices of four-year terms can be assessed up to 15% of their aggregate annual salary. In smaller counties there are no such percentage limitations.

The threshold question to be resolved is whether the filing-fee system should be sustained if it can be shown to have some rational basis, or whether it must withstand a more rigid standard of review.

In *Harper v. Virginia Board of Elections*, 383 U.S. 663 (1966), the Court held that Virginia's imposition of an annual poll tax not exceeding $1.50 on residents over the age of 21 was a denial of equal protection. Subjecting the Virginia poll tax to close scrutiny, the Court concluded that the placing of even a minimal price on the exercise of the right to vote constituted an invidious discrimination. The problem presented by candidate filing fees is not the same, of course, and we must determine whether the strict standard of review of the Harper case should be applied.

The initial and direct impact of filing fees is felt by aspirants for office, rather than voters, and the Court has not heretofore attached such fundamental status to candidacy as to invoke a rigorous standard of review. However, the rights of voters and the rights of candidates do not lend themselves to neat separation; laws that affect candidates always have at least some theoretical, correlative effect on voters. Of course, not every limitation or incidental burden on the exercise of voting rights is subject to a stringent standard of review. Texas does not place a condition on the exercise of the right to vote, nor does it quantitatively dilute votes that have been cast. Rather, the Texas system creates barriers to candidate access to the primary ballot, thereby tending to limit the field of candidates from which voters might choose. The existence of such barriers does not of itself compel close scrutiny. In approaching candidate restrictions, it is essential to examine in a realistic light the extent and nature of their impact on voters.

Unlike a filing-fee requirement that most candidates could be expected to fulfill from their own resources or at least through modest contributions, the very size of the fees imposed under the Texas system gives it a patently exclusionary character. Many potential office seekers lacking both personal wealth and affluent backers are in every practical sense precluded from seeking the nomination of their chosen party, no matter how qualified they might be, and no matter how broad or enthusiastic their popular support. The effect of this exclusionary mechanism on voters is neither incidental nor remote. Not only are voters substantially limited in their choice of candidates, but also there is the obvious likelihood that this limitation would fall more heavily on the less affluent segment of the community, whose favorites may be unable to pay the large costs required by the Texas system. To the extent that the system requires candidates to rely on contributions from voters in order to pay the assessments, a phenomenon that can hardly be rare in light of the size of the fees, it tends to deny some voters the opportunity to vote for a candidate of their choosing; at the same time it gives the affluent the power to place on the ballot their own names or the names of persons they favor. Appellants do not dispute that this is endemic to the system. This disparity in voting power based on wealth cannot be described by reference to discrete and precisely defined segments of the community as is typical of inequities challenged under the Equal Protection Clause, and there are doubtless some instances of candidates representing the views of voters of modest means who are able to pay the required fee. But we would ignore reality were we not to recognize that this system falls with unequal weight on voters, as well as candidates, according to their economic status.

Because the Texas filing-fee scheme has a real and appreciable impact on the exercise of the franchise, and because this impact is related to the resources of the voters supporting a particular candidate, we conclude, as in Harper, that the laws must be "closely scrutinized" and found reasonably necessary to the accomplishment of legitimate state objectives in order to pass constitutional muster.

Since the State has failed to establish the requisite justification for this filing-fee system, we hold that it results in a denial of equal protection of the laws. It must be emphasized that nothing herein is intended to cast doubt on the validity of reasonable candidate filing fees or licensing fees in other contexts. By requiring candidates to shoulder the costs of conducting primary elections through filing fees and by providing no reasonable alternative means of access to the ballot, the State of Texas has erected a system that utilizes the criterion of ability to pay as a condition to being on the ballot, thus excluding some candidates otherwise qualified and denying an undetermined number of voters the opportunity to vote for candidates of their choice. These salient features of the Texas system are critical to our determination of constitutional invalidity.

FOR DISCUSSION

Does *Bullock* support the claim that individuals have a constitutional right to appear on the ballot? Would there have been anything wrong with charging candidates or parties a small administrative fee in order to cover the costs of appearing on the ballot?

ANDERSON V. CELEBREZZE

460 U.S. 780, 103 S.Ct. 1564, 75 L.Ed.2d 547 (1983)

In 1980 Congressman John Anderson ran for the Republican presidential nomination but lost to Ronald Reagan. He then decided to run as an independent and sought to get his name on the ballots across the fifty states. In the state of Ohio he faced a requirement that as an independent candidate he had to file his nominating petition in March for the general election in November. This March date would have been before the Republican primary or presidential nomination process was completed. He challenged the Ohio law imposing petition signature and filing deadline requirements.

Vote: 5–4

JUSTICE STEVENS delivered the opinion of the Court.

On April 24, 1980, petitioner John Anderson announced that he was an independent candidate for the office of President of the United States. Thereafter, his supporters—by gathering the signatures of registered voters, filing required documents, and submitting filing fees—were able to meet the substantive requirements for having his name placed on the ballot for the general election in November 1980 in all 50 States and the District of Columbia. On April 24, however, it was already too late for Anderson to qualify for a position on the ballot in Ohio and certain other States because the statutory deadlines for filing a statement of candidacy had already passed. The question presented by this case is whether Ohio's early filing deadline placed an unconstitutional burden on the voting and associational rights of Anderson's supporters.

The facts are not in dispute. On May 16, 1980, Anderson's supporters tendered a nominating petition containing approximately 14,500 signatures and a statement of candidacy to respondent Celebrezze, the Ohio Secretary of State. These documents would have entitled Anderson to a place on the ballot if they had been filed on or before March 20, 1980. Respondent refused to accept the petition solely because it had not been filed within the time required by 3513.25.7 of the Ohio Revised Code. Three days later Anderson and three voters, two registered in Ohio and one in New Jersey, commenced this action in the United States District Court for the Southern District of Ohio, challenging the constitutionality of Ohio's early filing deadline for independent candidates. The District Court granted petitioners' motion for summary judgment and ordered respondent to place Anderson's name on the general election ballot.

I

The impact of candidate eligibility requirements on voters implicates basic constitutional rights. Writing for a unanimous Court in *NAACP v. Alabama ex rel. Patterson*, 357 U.S. 449, 460 (1958), Justice Harlan stated that it "is beyond debate that freedom to engage in association for the advancement of beliefs and ideas is an inseparable aspect of the 'liberty' assured by the Due Process Clause of the Fourteenth Amendment, which embraces freedom of speech." In our first review of Ohio's electoral scheme,), this Court explained the interwoven strands of "liberty" affected by ballot access restrictions:

> In the present situation the state laws place burdens on two different, although overlapping, kinds of rights—the right of individuals to associate for the advancement of political beliefs, and the right of qualified voters, regardless of their political persuasion, to cast their votes effectively. Both of these rights, of course, rank among our most precious freedoms.

As we have repeatedly recognized, voters can assert their preferences only through candidates or parties or both. "It is to be expected that a voter hopes to find on the ballot a candidate who comes near to reflecting his policy preferences on contemporary issues." The right to vote is "heavily burdened" if that vote may be cast only for major-party candidates at a time when other parties or other candidates are "clamoring for a place on the ballot." The exclusion of candidates also burdens voters' freedom of association, because an election campaign is an effective platform for the expression of views on the issues of the day, and a candidate serves as a rallying point for likeminded citizens.

Although these rights of voters are fundamental, not all restrictions imposed by the States on candidates' eligibility for the ballot impose constitutionally suspect burdens on voters' rights to associate or to choose among candidates. We have recognized that, "as a practical matter, there must be a substantial regulation of elections if they are to be fair and honest and if some sort of order, rather than chaos, is to accompany the democratic processes." To achieve these necessary objectives, States have enacted comprehensive and sometimes complex election codes. Each provision of these schemes, whether it governs the registration and qualifications of voters, the selection and eligibility of candidates, or the voting process itself, inevitably affects—at least to some degree—the individual's right to vote and his right to associate with others for political ends. Nevertheless, the State's important regulatory interests are generally sufficient to justify reasonable, nondiscriminatory restrictions.

Constitutional challenges to specific provisions of a State's election laws therefore cannot be resolved by any "litmus-paper test" that will separate valid from invalid restrictions. Instead, a court must resolve such a challenge by an analytical process that parallels its work in ordinary litigation. It must first consider the character and magnitude of the asserted injury to the rights protected by the First and Fourteenth Amendments that the plaintiff seeks to vindicate. It then must identify and evaluate the precise interests put forward by the State as justifications for the burden imposed by its rule. In passing judgment, the Court must not only determine the legitimacy and strength of each of those interests, it also must consider the extent to which those interests make it necessary to burden the plaintiff's rights. Only after weighing all these factors is the reviewing court in a position to decide whether the challenged provision is unconstitutional. The results of this evaluation will not be automatic; as we have recognized, there is "no substitute for the hard judgments that must be made."

FOR DISCUSSION

How difficult should it be to appear on a ballot before it violates the Constitution? What factors need to be considered under the test described in the *Anderson* case?

RELATED CASES

***Williams v. Rhodes:* 393 U.S. 23 (1968).**

The Supreme Court ordered the state of Ohio to place third-party presidential candidate George Wallace on the general election ballot. It rejected state arguments that the complex ballot access laws were justified by the state's interest in preserving the two-party system.

***Scorer v. Brown:* 415 U.S. 724 (1974).**

This decision upheld a California "sore-loser" law, which prevented an individual from running as a third-party candidate if in the past year he or she had been affiliated with another party.

MUNRO V. SOCIALIST WORKERS PARTY

479 U.S. 189, 107 S.Ct. 533, 93 L.Ed.2d 499 (1986)

The state of Washington required third- or minority party candidates to secure at least 1 percent of the vote in a primary for them to appear on the general election ballot. The Socialist Workers Party objected, claiming it violated their First Amendment rights.

Vote: 7–2

JUSTICE WHITE delivered the opinion of the Court.

The State of Washington requires that a minor-party candidate for partisan office receive at least 1% of all votes cast for that office in the State's primary election before the candidate's name will be placed on the general election ballot. The question for decision is whether this statutory requirement, as applied to candidates for statewide offices, violates the First and Fourteenth Amendments to the United States Constitution. The Court of Appeals for the Ninth Circuit declared the provision unconstitutional. We reverse.

While there is no "litmus-paper test" for deciding a case like this, ibid., it is now clear that States may condition access to the general election ballot by a minor-party or independent candidate upon a showing of a modicum of support among the potential voters for the office. In *Jenness v. Fortson*, 403 U.S. 431 (1971), the Court unanimously rejected a challenge to Georgia's election statutes that required independent candidates and minor-party candidates, in order to be listed on the general election ballot, to submit petitions signed by at least 5% of the voters eligible to vote in the last election for the office in question. Primary elections were held only for those political organizations whose candidate received 20% or more of the vote at the last gubernatorial or Presidential election. The Court's opinion observed that "[t]here is surely an important state interest in requiring some preliminary showing of a significant modicum of support before printing the name of a political organization's candidate on the ballot—the interest, if no other, in avoiding confusion, deception, and even frustration of the democratic process at the general election." And, in *American Party of Texas v. White*, 415 U.S. 767 (1974), candidates of minor political parties in Texas were required to demonstrate support by persons numbering at least 1% of the total vote cast for Governor at the last preceding general election. Candidates could secure the requisite number of petition signatures at precinct nominating conventions and by supplemental petitions following the conventions. Voters signing these supplemental petitions had to swear under oath that they had not participated in another party's primary election or nominating process. In rejecting a First Amendment challenge to the 1% requirement, we asserted that the State's interest in preserving the integrity of the electoral process and in regulating the number of candidates on the ballot was compelling and reiterated the holding in *Jenness* that a State may require a preliminary showing of significant support before placing a candidate on the general election ballot.

We have never required a State to make a particularized showing of the existence of voter confusion, ballot over-crowding, [479 U.S. 189, 195] or the presence of frivolous candidacies prior to the imposition of reasonable restrictions on ballot access. In *Jenness v. Fortson* we conducted no inquiry into the sufficiency and quantum of the data supporting the reasons for Georgia's 5% petition-signature requirement. In *American Party of Texas v. White*, we upheld the 1% petition-signature requirement, asserting that the "State's admittedly vital interests are sufficiently implicated to insist that political parties appearing on the general ballot demonstrate a significant, measurable quantum of community support." And, in *Storer v. Brown*, 415 U.S. 724 (1974), we upheld California's statutory provisions that denied ballot access to an independent candidate if the candidate had been affiliated with any political party within one year prior to the immediately preceding primary election. We recognized that California had a "compelling" interest in maintaining the integrity of its political processes, and that the disaffiliation requirement furthered this interest and was therefore valid, even though it was an absolute bar to attaining a ballot position. We asserted that "[i]t appears obvious to us that the one-year disaffiliation provision furthers the State's interest in the stability of its political system." There is no indication that we held California to the burden of demonstrating empirically the objective effects on political stability that were produced by the 1-year disaffiliation requirement.

To require States to prove actual voter confusion, ballot overcrowding, or the presence of frivolous candidacies as a predicate to the imposition of reasonable ballot access restrictions would invariably lead to endless court battles over the sufficiency of the "evidence" marshaled by a State to prove the predicate. Such a requirement would necessitate that a State's political system sustain some level of damage before the legislature could take corrective action. Legislatures, we think, should be permitted to respond to potential deficiencies in the electoral process with foresight rather than reactively, provided that the response is reasonable and does not significantly impinge on constitutionally protected rights.

Washington has chosen a vehicle by which minor-party candidates must demonstrate voter support that serves to promote the very First Amendment values that are threatened by overly burdensome ballot access restrictions. It can hardly be said that Washington's voters are denied freedom of association because they must channel their expressive activity into a campaign at the primary as opposed to the general election. It is true that voters must make choices as they vote at the primary, but there are no state-imposed obstacles impairing voters in the exercise of their choices. Washington simply has not substantially burdened the "availability of political opportunity."

Jenness and *American Party* rejected challenges to ballot access restrictions that were based on a candidate's showing of voter support, notwithstanding the fact that the systems operated to foreclose a candidate's access to any statewide ballot. Here, because Washington affords a minor-party candidate easy access to the primary election ballot and the opportunity for the candidate to wage a ballot-connected campaign, we conclude that the magnitude of 29.18.110's effect on constitutional rights is slight when compared to the restrictions we upheld in *Jenness* and *American Party*. Accordingly, Washington did not violate the Constitution by denying appellee Peoples a position on the general election ballot on November 8, 1983.

The judgment of the Court of Appeals for the Ninth Circuit is therefore reversed.

JUSTICE MARSHALL, with whom JUSTICE BRENNAN joins, dissenting.

Limitations on ballot access burden two fundamental rights: "the right of individuals to associate for the advancement of political beliefs, and the right of qualified voters, regardless of their political persuasion, to cast their votes effectively." These fundamental rights are implicated most clearly where minor-party access to the ballot is restricted. As we noted in *Illinois Board of Elections v. Socialist Workers Party*, 440 U.S. 173 (1979), "[t]he States' interest in screening out frivolous candidates must be considered in light of the significant role that third parties have played in the political development of the Nation."

The minor party's often unconventional positions broaden political debate, expand the range of issues with which the electorate is concerned, and influence the positions of the majority, in some instances ultimately becoming majority positions. And its very existence provides an outlet for voters to express dissatisfaction with the candidates or platforms of the major parties. Notwithstanding the crucial role minor parties play in the American political arena, the Court holds today that the associational rights of minor parties and their supporters are not unduly burdened by a ballot access statute that, in practice, completely excludes minor parties from participating in statewide general elections.

FOR DISCUSSION

Does the government have a compelling interest in maintaining the two-party system? Does such an interest not discriminate against minor parties? Do major and minor parties have different rights?

CAMPAIGN FINANCE AND REGULATION

Money, as former California politician Jesse Unruh once said, is the "mother's milk of politics." So much about politics, or at least campaigns and elections, involves money. It costs money to run for office or communicate a message, necessitating in most if not all parts of the United States that candidates, political parties, and other groups both raise and spend money to achieve their political objectives. However, while money is critical to political success and can be a valuable tool for many purposes, it also potentially corrupts the political system as it raises the possibility of bribery and extortion. Dating back to the days when George Washington was a candidate for the Virginia Assembly and there were allegations that he spent too much money on rum that he gave to voters, there has been a fear that money posed dangers to the political process.

Beginning in the Jacksonian Era of the 1820s, the **spoils system** ushered in an era of politics and campaigning in which donors gave in the hope of receiving favors and jobs if candidates were elected. Federal and state government jobs were freely traded for contributions and support, and often these offices served as a basis of funding campaigns, as salaries were often "assessed" to help pay for political expenses. But beginning in the 1880s with the passage of the first civil service act and then into the Progressive Era of the early twentieth century, efforts were made to reform the spoils system and limit the role of money in politics.

For example, in 1907, Congress, at the urging of President Theodore Roosevelt, passed the **Tillman Act,** which banned corporations from giving money to federal campaigns. In 1925 Congress passed the Federal Corrupt Practices Act, which banned political assessments. This Act was upheld in *U.S. v. Wurzbach* (280 U.S. 396, 1930). Then, in the 1947 Taft-Hartley Act, labor unions were banned from expending money for the purposes of trying to affect a federal election. The Labor Management Act of 1947, otherwise now as the Taft-Hartley Act, barred corporations and labor unions from making independent expenditures in federal elections.

Throughout the 1950s, and more so in the 1960s and early 1970s, Congress sought to reform the way in which campaigns are funded and conducted. Efforts were undertaken to impose contribution or expenditure limits, to provide public financing, or to increase disclosure requirements on donors and campaigns. These efforts mostly failed. However, when revelations of President Nixon's 1972 fund-raising scandals surfaced, it gave new life to the cause of campaign finance reform, resulting in the adoption of the 1974 amendments to the **Federal Election Campaign Act** (FECA). These amendments provided for a major overhaul of federal elections and included spending and contribution limits, disclosure rules, public financing, and the creation of a new federal agency to regulate campaign activity.

Yet these amendments raised significant constitutional questions that persist to today. For example, given the importance of money to campaigns, was money speech for the purposes of the First Amendment? Or could the government impose expenditure or contribution limits in order to equalize the political playing field and make elections more competitive? These are the core questions that dominate much of the debate on campaign finance issues from the 1970s through today.

Buckley v. Valeo (424 U.S. 1, 1976) is arguably the most important case in the field of campaign finance reform. It did not say that money is speech, but it did say that money contributed or expended for political purposes raises important free speech concerns. The Court then distinguishes contributions from expenditures, finding that limits on the former were permissible in order to prevent corruption or its appearance. This corruption stemmed from the concern about how money could be exchanged for political favors. However, while abating corruption or its appearance was found to be a compelling governmental interest that could justify limits on contributions, the absence of such a possibility for corruption precluded expenditure limits. The Court thus seemed to give more constitutional protection to the latter than to contributions.

Many, if not all, of the most important comments in *Buckley* appear in footnotes: see footnotes, 18, 52, and 65, for example. The Court holds out in note 65 that voluntary public financing of campaigns is possible and would permit expenditure limits. What is express advocacy? Footnote 52, referring to what came to be called the "magic words," provided a way for corporations and unions to communicate their political views in federal elections without being limited by the Tillman and Taft-Hartley Acts. So long as political ads lacked the magic words, they were considered issue advocacy and therefore protected under the First Amendment. This language would be the target of later laws, such as **McCain-Feingold or the Bipartisan Campaign Reform Act of 2002** (BCRA), when it sought to close several federal loopholes that allowed unions, corporations, and other groups to spend money despite bans being in place.

A 1975 opinion by the FEC also opened up a new hole in FECA regulations. It ruled that a corporation could expend money to solicit contributions from employees and stockholders. More importantly, the decision opened the way for unions and corporations eventually to give money to political parties for the purposes of voter registration, to get out the vote, and for party building. These exceptions allowed for a dramatic increase in the amount of money these groups could spend. Thus, *Buckley*, the 1975 FEC opinion, and other Court cases created a new distinction in the law between hard and soft money. Hard money constituted regulated and disclosed contributions to candidates; soft money was unregulated (in terms of dollar amounts) to parties. The problem of soft money would grow until the passage of BCRA.

One of the issues growing out of *Buckley* was in regard to the evidence needed to sustain either contribution or expenditure limits. When *Buckley* stated that abating corruption or its appearance was a compelling interest, how much evidence of either did the government need to produce to sustain regulations? In addition, how low could contribution limits be set? These questions are posed in *Nixon v. Shrink Missouri Government PAC* (528 U.S. 377, 2000).

Some argue that *Shrink* lowered the evidentiary burden necessary to sustain a contribution limit and that it established new and lesser burdens to regulate money in politics. As you read the opinion, ask yourself if the Court lowered the burden or instead reversed the burden, shifting the presumption that contribution limits were valid unless shown they were not. Also note how the Court upheld quite low contribution limits and appeared to define an outer limit to these limits.

In addition to contribution limits, *Buckley* upheld disclosure requirements. This disclosure included the name of the contributor, employer, the amount of the contribution, and, for campaigns, expenditures. Disclosure was upheld to promote detecting fraud, among other purposes. But did *Buckley* mean that disclosure could always be mandated or required? Could individuals not engage in anonymous political speech, much like Publius did with the *Federalist Papers* in 1787? *McIntyre v. Ohio* (514 U.S. 334, 1995) seems to stand for the proposition that individuals have a constitutional right to engage in anonymous political speech. But how far does that ruling extend? Does it protect anonymous speech for groups? The Court has never clarified the scope of its ruling here.

In part to stem the dramatic increase of money being spent for political purposes in the 1980s and 1990s, and to address many of the loopholes and problems in the law caused by *Buckley* and subsequent Supreme Court decisions, Senators Russ Feingold and John McCain worked for nearly a decade to achieve passage of the Bipartisan Campaign Reform Act of 2002 ("BCRA" or "McCain-Feingold Act"). BCRA sought to close the **soft money** loophole, redefine the line between express and issue advocacy, improve disclosure, and place some limits on the ability of wealthy candidates to use their money to affect elections. A summary chart of major BCRA provisions is provided in this chapter on page 887.

BCRA was a controversial piece of legislation challenged by numerous groups who argued that it violated their First Amendment rights. The Court of Appeals upheld parts of the act in a decision that was in excess of 1,500 pages. To the surprise of many, when the Supreme Court ruled in *McConnell v. FEC* (540 U.S. 93, 2003), it upheld almost all of the major provisions. With the exception of one provision, all of BCRA was upheld. A summary chart of the Court's ruling is found on page 902. The net result of the decision was to uphold the soft money ban and to endorse the closing of the express versus issue advocacy distinction that *Buckley* had created in footnote 52.

After the *McConnell* decision, many critics of *Buckley* thought that the Court might be prepared to overturn that decision and uphold expenditure limits and even lower contribution limits than were permitted in the *Shrink* case. Vermont, in an effort to limit the impact of money in politics, passed Public Act 64, which imposed both expenditure and contribution limits. *Randall v. Sorrell* (548 U.S. 230, 2006) was seen as a test of the viability of *Buckley* and of the new chief justice, John Roberts, and associate justice, Samuel Alito. Supporters of campaign finance reform believed that the *McConnell* decision signaled that *Buckley* was possibly ripe for a challenge and that perhaps even expenditure limits would be sustained. Thus, when Vermont enacted both low contribution limits and expenditures limits, and the Second Circuit Court of Appeals affirmed as an *en banc* decision, the belief was that the time to reverse *Buckley* was at hand. However, for campaign finance advocates, the *McConnell* victory was short-lived. The new Court under Justice Roberts was less sympathetic to campaign finance than the Rehnquist Court had been.

In *Randall v. Sorrell* the Court reaffirmed *Buckley* and its framework, again striking down expenditure limits and here rejecting the contribution limits. In doing both, the Court drew both upon the *Shrink* and *Buckley* standards. The fate of BCRA and campaign finance seems very much in question now. After *Sorrell* in *Federal Election Commission v. Wisconsin Right to Life Committee* (551 U.S. 449, 2007), the Court ruled that as applied, the one-month ban on political ads or communication prior to an election violated the First Amendment. This decision effectively reinstated the express and issue advocacy distinction found in *Buckley*. Then, in *Davis v. Federal Election Commission* (554 U.S. 724, 2008), the Court struck down the provision of BCRA known as the "millionaire's amendment," which sought to offset expenditures made by wealthy candidates. Between these decisions and the nearly $750 million in contributions to Barack Obama's 2008 presidential campaign as a result of his decision to opt out of the presidential public financing system, the future of public financing is very much in doubt.

In *McConnell v. Federal Election Commission,* the Supreme Court upheld almost all of the major provisions of BCRA (Bipartisan Campaign Reform Act or McCain-Feingold). This included one provision that banned electioneering communication within 30/60 days before a primary or general election. But after that decision, three members of the Court—Chief Justice Rehnquist and Justices O'Connor and Souter—had left and were replaced by Chief Justice Roberts and Justices Alito and Sotomayor. In its first few years the Roberts Court appeared less sympathetic to campaign finance reform laws, rejecting expenditure and contribution limits in *Randall v. Sorrell* and the millionaires' provision in *Wisconsin Right-to-Life v. Federal Election Commission*, 551 U.S. 449 (2007). Both of the decisions put into question how the Roberts Court would view other parts of BCRA or campaign finance regulations if confronted with either.

In *Citizens United v.* Federal Election Commission, the Court, 557 U.S. 310 (2010), by a 5–4 majority, struck down one of the major provisions of BCRA, the ban on electioneering communication. The decision was controversial because, in part, the plaintiff in the case did not originally seek to challenge the constitutionality of the provision, it only occurred as a result of the Court asking for a rehearing and briefing of the case for that purpose. Second, the majority opinion overturned two precedents and appeared to challenge at least 60 years of what was thought of as settled law regulating corporate (and labor union) spending in federal elections that went back to Taft-Hartley. The decision was controversial in the discussion and analysis of precedent and what value it served in judicial review. Third, the decision seemed to suggest that corporations had the same political rights as citizens, raising the possibility that the Court might also revisit a 1907 law banning corporate contributions to candidates. Finally, as a result of the decision, the fear was that new money would flood into campaigns, just as the 2010 campaign season was ready to start. While the focus of the decision was on a federal regulation on corporate express advocacy independent expenditures, it also addressed regulations on labor union expenditures. The decision, besides invalidating federal law, also affected many states which had similar rules.

Shortly after *Citizens United* was decided a court permitted in *Speechnow.org. v.* FEC, 599 F.3d. 686 (D.C. Cir. 2010 (en banc)), unlimited contributions by corporations and unions to independent expenditure only political action committees, thereby creating what has now has come to be known as Super PACS. Normally contributions to PACS are limited because they can also contribute to candidates. But if the PACs do not directly contribute to candidates but only make independent expenditures then unions and corporations can make unlimited donations to them. The rise of Super PACS thus is a result of *Citizens United* and *Speechnow*, and have become a major presence in the elections since 2010, with many studies suggesting a dramatic rise in corporate spending in campaigns and elections. This spending, at least at the federal level, is mostly through independent expenditures, and not by candidates, leaving many of those seeking office feeling like they do not have enough money to counteract the messages—often negative—that these independent expenditures take.

But the Roberts' Court had also issued several other campaign finance decisions of consequence. In an effort to address the growing influence of independent expenditures and the cost of campaigns, have provided for public financing. The Supreme Court upheld voluntary public financing in *Buckley*. Generally, these schemes are financed by voluntary check offs on forms when citizens pay their state taxes (or on the federal tax form to finance the presidential voluntarily public financing system). Candidates would then be able to access these funds if they meet certain criteria such as agree to abide by spending limits or if they have raised some initial matching funds to qualify for matching public dollars. Arizona went further—allowing for candidates for state office who accept public financing to receive additional money from the State in direct response to the campaign activities of privately financed candidates and independent expenditure groups. Once a set spending limit is exceeded, a publicly financed candidate receives roughly one dollar for every dollar spent by an opposing privately financed candidate. The publicly financed candidate also receives roughly one dollar for every dollar spent by independent expenditure groups to support the privately financed candidate, or to oppose the publicly financed candidate. The idea behind this Arizona law was not to place candidates at a financial disadvantage simply because they accepted public funding. However, in *Arizona Free Enterprise Club's Freedom Club PAC v. Bennett,* 564 U.S. 721 (2011), the Supreme Court in a 5–4 decision concluded that this matching system violated the First Amendment in that it chilled the free speech rights of those who might wish to make expenditures but feared that if they did so public dollars would be used to counteract their speech.

In *McCutcheon v. Federal Election Commission,* 134 S.Ct. 1434 (2014) another 5–4 Roberts Court opinion struck down yet another campaign finance regulation—aggregate contribution limits. The 1974 FECA amendments included not only direct contribution limit to candidates and PACS but also an overall aggregate cap on the total amount of money an individual could donate to federal candidates for office and Political Action Committees. After subsequently amended again by the 2002 Bipartisan Campaign Reform Act in the 2011–12 election cycle that cap was $123,200. Shaun McCutcheon had contributed to 16 different federal candidates and wanted to contribute to another 12 but could not because of the aggregate contribute limit. He successfully challenged the aggregate contribution limit.

Chief Justice Roberts, in writing for the Court, argued first that the original *Buckley* decision did not adequately address the issue of aggregate limits—noting the court only devoted a paragraph to them—and that aggregate limits did not overall serve or promote the compelling governmental interest of addressing the reality or appearance of quid pro quo correction. In language cited by many, the Chief Justice declared that: "Spending large sums of money in connection with elections, but not in connection with an effort to control the exercise of an officeholder's official duties, does not give rise to such *quid pro quo* corruption. Nor does the possibility that an individual who spends large sums may garner "influence over or access to" elected officials or political parties." For those who see money as a form of speech they celebrated the decision as an important First Amendment victory while for those who see money as a political evil this dicta suggested that the Court was blind to the realities of how exchanging money for special access or influence to elected officials or policy makers is in fact a major source of political corruption.

BUCKLEY V. VALEO

424 U.S. 1, 96 S.Ct. 612, 46 L.Ed.2d 659 (1976)

In 1976 Congress amended the Federal Election and Campaign Act (FECA). The amendments imposed, among other provisions, contributions to candidates for office as spending limits on campaigns and on third-party groups. FECA also called for disclosure of all contributions of more than $200, it created the Federal Election Commission, and it established a voluntary public financing system for presidential candidates funded by a check-off system on federal tax returns. Several individuals and groups challenged the 1974 FECA amendments as a violation of the First Amendment.

Vote: Per curiam

These appeals present constitutional challenges to the key provisions of the Federal Election Campaign Act of 1971 (Act), and related provisions of the Internal Revenue Code of 1954, all as amended in 1974.

The Court of Appeals, in sustaining the legislation in large part against various constitutional challenges, 2 viewed it as "by far the most comprehensive reform legislation [ever] passed by Congress concerning the election of the President, Vice-President, and members of Congress." The statutes at issue summarized in broad terms, contain the following provisions: (a) individual political contributions are limited to $1,000 to any single candidate per election, with an overall annual limitation of $25,000 by any contributor; independent expenditures by individuals and groups "relative to a clearly identified candidate" are limited to $1,000 a year; campaign spending by candidates for various federal offices and spending for national conventions by political parties are subject to prescribed limits; (b) contributions and expenditures above certain threshold levels must be reported and publicly disclosed; (c) a system for public funding of Presidential campaign activities is established by Subtitle H of the Internal Revenue Code; 3 and (d) a Federal Election Commission is established to administer and enforce the legislation.

The Act's contribution and expenditure limitations operate in an area of the most fundamental First Amendment activities. Discussion of public issues and debate on the qualifications of candidates are integral to the operation of the system of government established by our Constitution. The First Amendment affords the broadest protection to such political expression in order "to assure [the] unfettered interchange of ideas for the bringing about of political and social changes desired by the people." Although First Amendment protections are not confined to "the exposition of ideas," "there is practically universal agreement that a major purpose of that Amendment was to protect the free discussion of governmental affairs, of course includ[ing] discussions of candidates." This no more than reflects our "profound national commitment to the principle that debate on public issues should be uninhibited, robust, and wide-open." In a republic where the people are sovereign, the ability of the citizenry to make informed choices among candidates for office is essential, for the identities of those who are elected will inevitably shape the course that we follow as a nation. As the Court observed in

Monitor Patriot Co. v. Roy, 401 US 265 (1971), "it can hardly be doubted that the constitutional guarantee has its fullest and most urgent application precisely to the conduct of campaigns for political office."

The First Amendment protects political association as well as political expression. The constitutional right of association explicated in *NAACP v. Alabama*, 357 U.S. 449 (1958), stemmed from the Court's recognition that "[e]ffective advocacy of both public and private points of view, particularly controversial ones, is undeniably enhanced by group association." Subsequent decisions have made clear that the First and Fourteenth Amendments guarantee " 'freedom to associate with others for the common advancement of political beliefs and ideas,' " a freedom that encompasses " '[t]he right to associate with the political party of one's choice.' "

It is with these principles in mind that we consider the primary contentions of the parties with respect to the Act's limitations upon the giving and spending of money in political campaigns. Those conflicting contentions could not more sharply define the basic issues before us. Appellees contend that what the Act regulates is conduct, and that its effect on speech and association is incidental at most. Appellants respond that contributions and expenditures are at the very core of political speech, and that the Act's limitations thus constitute restraints on First Amendment liberty that are both gross and direct.

We cannot share the view that the present Act's contribution and expenditure limitations are comparable to the restrictions on conduct upheld in *United States v. O'Brien,* 391 U.S. 367 (1968). The expenditure of money simply cannot be equated with such conduct as destruction of a draft card. Some forms of communication made possible by the giving and spending of money involve speech alone, some involve conduct primarily, and some involve a combination of the two. Yet this Court has never suggested that the dependence of a communication on the expenditure of money operates itself to introduce a non speech element or to reduce the exacting scrutiny required by the First Amendment. . . . [T]he Court contrasted picketing and parading with a newspaper comment and a telegram by a citizen to a public official. The parading and picketing activities were said to constitute conduct "intertwined with expression and association," whereas the newspaper comment and the telegram were described as a "pure form of expression" involving "free speech alone" rather than "expression mixed with particular conduct."

Even if the categorization of the expenditure of money as conduct were accepted, the limitations challenged here would not meet the *O'Brien* test because the governmental interests advanced in support of the Act involve "suppressing communication." The interests served by the Act include restricting the voices of people and interest groups who have money to spend and reducing the overall scope of federal election campaigns. Although the Act does not focus on the ideas expressed by persons or groups subject to its regulations, it is aimed in part at equalizing the relative ability of all voters to affect electoral outcomes by placing a ceiling on expenditures for political expression by citizens and groups. Unlike *O'Brien*, where the Selective Service System's administrative interest in the preservation of draft cards was wholly unrelated to their use as a means of communication, it is beyond dispute that the interest in regulating the alleged "conduct" of giving or spending money "arises in some measure because the communication allegedly integral to the conduct is itself thought to be harmful."

Nor can the Act's contribution and expenditure limitations be sustained, as some of the parties suggest, by reference to the constitutional principles reflected in such decisions as *Cox v. Louisiana*, 379 U.S. 536 (1965); *Adderley v. Florida*, 385 U.S. 39 (1966); and *Kovacs v. Cooper*, 336 U.S. 77 (1949). Those cases stand for the proposition that the government may adopt reasonable time, place, and manner regulations, which do not discriminate among speakers or ideas, in order to further an important governmental interest unrelated to the restriction of communication. In contrast to *O'Brien*, where the method of expression was held to be subject to prohibition, *Cox*, *Adderley*, and *Kovacs* involved place or manner restrictions on legitimate modes of expression—picketing, parading, demonstrating, and using a soundtruck. The critical difference between this case and those time, place, and manner cases is that the present Act's contribution and expenditure limitations impose direct quantity restrictions on political communication and association by persons, groups, candidates, and political parties in addition to any reasonable time, place, and manner regulations otherwise imposed.

A restriction on the amount of money a person or group can spend on political communication during a campaign necessarily reduces the quantity of expression by restricting the number of issues discussed, the depth of their exploration, and the size of the audience reached.*

This is because virtually every means of communicating ideas in today's mass society requires the expenditure of money. The distribution of the humblest handbill or leaflet entails printing, paper, and circulation costs. Speeches and rallies generally necessitate hiring a hall and publicizing the event. The electorate's increasing dependence on television, radio, and other mass media for news and information has made these expensive modes of communication indispensable instruments of effective political speech.

The Act's contribution and expenditure limitations also impinge on protected associational freedoms. Making a contribution, like joining a political party, serves to affiliate a person with a candidate. In addition, it enables like-minded persons to pool their resources in furtherance of common political goals. The Act's contribution ceilings thus limit one important means of associating with a candidate or committee, but leave the contributor free to become a member of any political association and to assist personally in the association's efforts on behalf of candidates. And the Act's contribution limitations permit associations and candidates to aggregate large sums of money to promote effective advocacy. By contrast, the Act's $1,000 limitation on independent expenditures "relative to a clearly identified candidate" precludes most associations from effectively amplifying the voice of their adherents, the original basis for the recognition of First Amendment protection of the freedom of association. The Act's constraints on the ability of independent associations and candidate campaign organizations to expend resources on political expression "is simultaneously an interference with the freedom of [their] adherents."

In sum, although the Act's contribution and expenditure limitations both implicate fundamental First Amendment interests, its expenditure ceilings impose significantly more severe restrictions on protected freedoms of political expression and association than do its limitations on financial contributions.

It is unnecessary to look beyond the Act's primary purpose—to limit the actuality and appearance of corruption resulting from large individual financial contributions—in order to find a constitutionally sufficient justification for the $1,000 contribution limitation. Under a system of private financing of elections, a candidate lacking immense personal or family wealth must depend on financial contributions from others to provide the resources necessary to conduct a successful campaign. The increasing importance of the communications media and sophisticated mass-mailing and polling operations to effective campaigning make the raising of large sums of money an ever more essential ingredient of an effective candidacy. To the extent that large contributions are given to secure a political quid pro quo from current and potential office holders, the integrity of our system of representative democracy is undermined. Although the scope of such pernicious practices can never be reliably ascertained, the deeply disturbing examples surfacing after the 1972 election demonstrate that the problem is not an illusory one.

Of almost equal concern as the danger of actual quid pro quo arrangements is the impact of the appearance of corruption stemming from public awareness of the opportunities for abuse inherent in a regime of large individual financial contributions. In *CSC v. Letter Carriers*, 413 US 548 (1973), the Court found that the danger to "fair and effective government" posed by partisan political conduct on the part of federal employees charged with administering the law was a sufficiently important concern to justify broad restrictions on the employees' right of partisan political association. Here, as there, Congress could legitimately conclude that the avoidance of

* Being free to engage in unlimited political expression subject to a ceiling on expenditures is like being free to drive an automobile as far and as often as one desires on a single tank of gas.

the appearance of improper influence "is also critical if confidence in the system of representative Government is not to be eroded to a disastrous extent."

The Act's expenditure ceilings impose direct and substantial restraints on the quantity of political speech. The most drastic of the limitations restricts individuals and groups, including political parties that fail to place a candidate on the ballot, to an expenditure of $1,000 "relative to a clearly identified candidate during a calendar year." Other expenditure ceilings limit spending by candidates, their campaigns, and political parties in connection with election campaigns. It is clear that a primary effect of these expenditure limitations is to restrict the quantity of campaign speech by individuals, groups, and candidates. The restrictions, while neutral as to the ideas expressed, limit political expression "at the core of our electoral process and of the First Amendment freedoms."

The discussion in Part I-A, explains why the Act's expenditure limitations impose far greater restraints on the freedom of speech and association than do its contribution limitations. The markedly greater burden on basic freedoms caused by 608 (e) (1) thus cannot be sustained simply by invoking the interest in maximizing the effectiveness of the less intrusive contribution limitations. Rather, the constitutionality of 608 (e) (1) turns on whether the governmental interests advanced in its support satisfy the exacting scrutiny applicable to limitations on core First Amendment rights of political expression.

The constitutional deficiencies described in *Thomas v. Collins*, 323 U.S. 516 (1945), can be avoided only by reading 608 (e) (1) as limited to communications that include explicit words of advocacy of election or defeat of a candidate, much as the definition of "clearly identified" in 608 (e) (2) requires that an explicit and unambiguous reference to the candidate appear as part of the communication.

This is the reading of the provision suggested by the non-governmental appellees in arguing that "[f]unds spent to propagate one's views on issues without expressly calling for a candidate's election or defeat are thus not covered." We agree that in order to preserve the provision against invalidation on vagueness grounds, 608 (e) (1) must be construed to apply only to expenditures for communications that in express terms advocate the election or defeat of a clearly identified candidate for federal office.*

We find that the governmental interest in preventing corruption and the appearance of corruption is inadequate to justify 608 (e) (1)'s ceiling on independent expenditures. First, assuming, arguendo, that large independent expenditures pose the same dangers of actual or apparent quid pro quo arrangements as do large contributions, 608 (e) (1) does not provide an answer that sufficiently relates to the elimination of those dangers. Unlike the contribution limitations' total ban on the giving of large amounts of money to candidates, 608 (e) (1) prevents only some large expenditures. So long as persons and groups eschew expenditures that in express terms advocate the election or defeat of a clearly identified candidate, they are free to spend as much as they want to promote the candidate and his views. The exacting interpretation of the statutory language necessary to avoid unconstitutional vagueness thus undermines the limitation's effectiveness as a loophole-closing provision by facilitating circumvention by those seeking to exert improper influence upon a candidate or office-holder. It would naively underestimate the ingenuity and resourcefulness of persons and groups desiring to buy influence to believe that they would have much difficulty devising expenditures that skirted the restriction on express advocacy of election or defeat but nevertheless benefited the candidate's campaign. Yet no substantial societal interest would be served by a loophole-closing provision designed to check corruption that permitted unscrupulous persons and organizations to expend unlimited sums of money in order to obtain improper influence over candidates for elective office.

---

* This construction would restrict the application of 608 (e) (1) to communications containing express words of advocacy of election or defeat, such as "vote for," "elect," "support," "cast your ballot for," "Smith for Congress," "vote against," "defeat," "reject."

Second, quite apart from the shortcomings of 608 (e) (1) in preventing any abuses generated by large independent expenditures, the independent advocacy restricted by the provision does not presently appear to pose dangers of real or apparent corruption comparable to those identified with large campaign contributions. The parties defending 608 (e) (1) contend that it is necessary to prevent would-be contributors from avoiding the contribution limitations by the simple expedient of paying directly for media advertisements or for other portions of the candidate's campaign activities. They argue that expenditures controlled by or coordinated with the candidate and his campaign might well have virtually the same value to the candidate as a contribution and would pose similar dangers of abuse. Yet such controlled or coordinated expenditures are treated as contributions rather than expenditures under the Act.

Section 608 (b)'s contribution ceilings rather than 608 (e) (1)'s independent expenditure limitation prevent attempts to circumvent the Act through prearranged or coordinated expenditures amounting to disguised contributions. By contrast, 608 (e) (1) limits expenditures for express advocacy of candidates made totally independently of the candidate and his campaign. Unlike contributions, such independent expenditures may well provide little assistance to the candidate's campaign and indeed may prove counterproductive. The absence of prearrangement and coordination of an expenditure with the candidate or his agent not only undermines the value of the expenditure to the candidate, but also alleviates the danger that expenditures will be given as a *quid pro quo* for improper commitments from the candidate. Rather than preventing circumvention of the contribution limitations, 608 (e) (1) severely restricts all independent advocacy despite its substantially diminished potential for abuse.

While the independent expenditure ceiling thus fails to serve any substantial governmental interest in stemming the reality or appearance of corruption in the electoral process, it heavily burdens core First Amendment expression. For the First Amendment right to " 'speak one's mind on all public institutions' " includes the right to engage in " 'vigorous advocacy' no less than 'abstract discussion.' " Advocacy of the election or defeat of candidates for federal office is no less entitled to protection under the First Amendment than the discussion of political policy generally or advocacy of the passage or defeat of legislation.

It is argued, however, that the ancillary governmental interest in equalizing the relative ability of individuals and groups to influence the outcome of elections serves to justify the limitation on express advocacy of the election or defeat of candidates imposed by 608 (e) (1)'s expenditure ceiling. But the concept that government may restrict the speech of some elements of our society in order to enhance the relative voice of others is wholly foreign to the First Amendment, which was designed "to secure 'the widest possible dissemination of information from diverse and antagonistic sources,' " and " 'to assure unfettered interchange of ideas for the bringing about of political and social changes desired by the people.' " The First Amendment's protection against governmental abridgment of free expression cannot properly be made to depend on a person's financial ability to engage in public discussion.

The ceiling on personal expenditures by candidates on their own behalf, like the limitations on independent expenditures contained in 608 (e) (1), imposes a substantial restraint on the ability of persons to engage in protected First Amendment expression.

The candidate, no less than any other person, has a First Amendment right to engage in the discussion of public issues and vigorously and tirelessly to advocate his own election and the election of other candidates. Indeed, it is of particular importance that candidates have the unfettered opportunity to make their views known so that the electorate may intelligently evaluate the candidates' personal qualities and their positions on vital public issues before choosing among them on election day. Mr. Justice Brandeis' observation that in our country "public discussion is a political duty."

The campaign expenditure ceilings appear to be designed primarily to serve the governmental interests in reducing the allegedly skyrocketing costs of political campaigns. Appellees and the Court of Appeals stressed statistics indicating that spending for federal election campaigns increased almost 300% between 1952 and 1972 in comparison with a 57.6% rise in the consumer price index during the same period. Appellants respond that during these years the rise in campaign spending lagged behind the percentage increase in total expenditures for commercial advertising and the size of the gross national product. In any event, the mere growth in the cost of federal election campaigns in and of itself provides no basis for governmental restrictions on the quantity of campaign spending and the resulting limitation on the scope of federal campaigns. The First Amendment denies government the power to determine that spending to promote one's political views is wasteful, excessive, or unwise. In the free society ordained by our Constitution it is not the government, but the people—individually as citizens and candidates and collectively as associations and political committees—who must retain control over the quantity and range of debate on public issues in a political campaign.*

Unlike the overall limitations on contributions and expenditures, the disclosure requirements impose no ceiling on campaign-related activities. But we have repeatedly found that compelled disclosure, in itself, can seriously infringe on privacy of association and belief guaranteed by the First Amendment.

As we have seen, group association is protected because it enhances "[e]ffective advocacy." The right to join together "for the advancement of beliefs and ideas," is diluted if it does not include the right to pool money through contributions, for funds are often essential if "advocacy" is to be truly or optimally "effective." Moreover, the invasion of privacy of belief may be as great when the information sought concerns the giving and spending of money as when it concerns the joining of organizations, for "[f]inancial transactions can reveal much about a person's activities, associations, and beliefs."

Our past decisions have not drawn fine lines between contributors and members but have treated them interchangeably. In *Bates v. Little Rock*, 361 U.S. 516 (1960), for example, we applied the principles of *NAACP v. Alabama*, 357 U.S. 449 (1958), and reversed convictions for failure to comply with a city ordinance that required the disclosure of "dues, assessments, and contributions paid, by whom and when paid." . . . (setting aside a contempt conviction of an organization official who refused to disclose names of those who made bulk purchases of books sold by the organization).

The strict test established by *NAACP v. Alabama* is necessary because compelled disclosure has the potential for substantially infringing the exercise of First Amendment rights. But we have acknowledged that there are governmental interests sufficiently important to outweigh the possibility of infringement, particularly when the "free functioning of our national institutions" is involved.

The governmental interests sought to be vindicated by the disclosure requirements are of this magnitude. They fall into three categories. First, disclosure provides the electorate with information "as to where political campaign money comes from and how it is spent by the candidate" in order to aid the voters in evaluating those who seek federal office. It allows voters to place each candidate in the political spectrum more precisely than is often possible solely on the basis of party labels and campaign speeches. The sources of a candidate's financial support also alert the voter to the interests to which a candidate is most likely to be responsive and thus facilitate predictions of future performance in office.

Second, disclosure requirements deter actual corruption and avoid the appearance of corruption by exposing large contributions and expenditures to the light of publicity. This exposure may discourage those who would use money for improper purposes either before or after the election. A public armed with information about a candidate's most generous supporters is better able to detect any post-election special favors that may be given in return. And, as we recognized in *Burroughs v. United States*, 290 U.S. 534 (1934), Congress could

---

* For the reasons discussed in Part III, Congress may engage in public financing of election campaigns and may condition acceptance of public funds on an agreement by the candidate to abide by specified expenditure limitations. Just as a candidate may voluntarily limit the size of the contributions he chooses to accept, he may decide to forgo private fundraising and accept public funding.

reasonably conclude that full disclosure during an election campaign tends "to prevent the corrupt use of money to affect elections." In enacting these requirements it may have been mindful of Mr. Justice Brandeis' advice:

> Publicity is justly commended as a remedy for social and industrial diseases. Sunlight is said to be the best of disinfectants; electric light the most efficient policeman.

Third, and not least significant, recordkeeping, reporting, and disclosure requirements are an essential means of gathering the data necessary to detect violations of the contribution limitations described above.

The disclosure requirements, as a general matter, directly serve substantial governmental interests. In determining whether these interests are sufficient to justify the requirements we must look to the extent of the burden that they place on individual rights.

It is undoubtedly true that public disclosure of contributions to candidates and political parties will deter some individuals who otherwise might contribute. In some instances, disclosure may even expose contributors to harassment or retaliation. These are not insignificant burdens on individual rights, and they must be weighed carefully against the interests which Congress has sought to promote by this legislation. In this process, we note and agree with appellants' concession that disclosure requirements—certainly in most applications—appear to be the least restrictive means of curbing the evils of campaign ignorance and corruption that Congress found to exist.

FOR DISCUSSION

Is money speech? What does the *Buckley* Court say in regard to the relationship between money and the First Amendment? In addition, what interests did the Court say support restrictions on political contributions? Are there any interests that would support restrictions on expenditures?

RELATED CASES

***First National Bank v. Bellotti:* 435 U.S. 765 (1978).**

The Court ruled unconstitutional a Massachusetts law banning corporations from expending money to influence a ballot initiative.

***FEC v. Massachusetts Citizens Concerned for Life:* 479 U.S. 238 (1986).**

The ban on corporate contributions does not apply to ideological not for profit corporations

***Austin v. Michigan Chamber of Commerce:* 494 U.S. 652 (1990).**

Upheld a limit on corporate expenditures that required separate segregated funds. In effect, corporations could not expend their own treasury money to affect elections but had to set up a separate PAC.

***Colorado Republican Federal Campaign Committee v. FEC:* 518 U.S. 605 (1996).**

Struck down the ban on party-independent expenditures.

***Colorado Republican Federal Campaign Committee v. FEC:* 533 U.S. 31 (2001).**

Upheld a ban on party expenditures coordinated with candidates.

***FEC v. Beaumont:* 539 U.S. 146 (2003).**

The federal bar on corporations contributing directly to candidates for federal office is not unconstitutional when applied to nonprofit advocacy corporations.

Buckley v. Valeo and FECA (Major Provisions)

1974 Federal Election Campaign Act (FECA) Provision	*Buckley v. Valeo* decision
Contribution limits $1,000 annual limit on individual contributions to a single federal candidate $25,000 annual limit on total individual contributions to federal candidates $5,000 annual limit on political action committee contributions to a single federal candidate	Court upholds all contribution limits ruling that the compelling government interest in preventing *quid pro quo* corruption or its appearance outweighs any First Amendment free speech rights.
Expenditure Limits $1,000 annual limit on individual expenditures "Relative to a Clearly Identified Candidate"	Court rejects all expenditure limits ruling that the compelling governmental interest in preventing corruption or its appearance does not outweigh any First Amendment free speech rights (the concerns of corruption are not the same with expenditures as they are with contributions).
Limits on Expenditure of Personal or Family Money $50,000 limit on expenditure of personal or family money in a presidential/vice-presidential race $35,000 limit on expenditure of personal or family money in a senate race $25,000 limit on expenditure of personal or family money in a House of Representatives race	Court rejects all expenditure limits ruling that the compelling governmental interest in preventing corruption or its appearance does not outweigh any First Amendment free speech rights (the concerns of corruption are not the same with expenditures as they are with contributions).
Overall Expenditure Limits on Campaigns $10,000,000 primary and $20,000,000 overall expenditure cap on presidential candidates. Caps on Senate and House campaigns pegged to the state populations.	Court rejects all mandatory expenditure limits ruling that the compelling governmental interest in preventing corruption or its appearance does not outweigh any First Amendment free speech rights (the concerns of corruption are not the same with expenditures as they are with contributions). Voluntary expenditure limits are constitutional if tied to participation in a voluntary public financing system.
Disclosure Requirements All political committees that receive or make total aggregate contributions or expenditures of $1,000 or more are required to file reports on contributions and expenditures All contributions greater than $10 require donor's name	Upholds all disclosure requirements against First Amendment objections. The Court states that disclosure helps: 1) tell the public where money comes from and how it is spent; 2) deter corruption or its appearance; and 3) record keeping necessary to ensure compliance with the law.

All aggregate contributions of individuals greater than $100 require donor's name, occupation, and place of business.	
Presidential Election Campaign Fund A voluntary check off on federal tax forms to create a federal fund to finance presidential campaigns Voluntary federal financing to presidential candidates who meet certain fundraising requirements Federal financing for primaries and party conventions	Upholds voluntary checkoff and financing as not a violation of the First Amendment (No one is being compelled to give and no one is compelled to accept the funds).
Federal Election Commission Creation of an eight-person Federal Election Commission to enforce federal elections campaign finance laws	Several of the powers of the FEC declared unconstitutional under Article II, section 2, clause 2 (The Appointments clause) because these duties must be performed by officers of the United States and cannot be delegated to this commission.

NIXON V. SHRINK MISSOURI GOVERNMENT PAC

528 U.S. 377, 120 S.Ct. 897, 145 L.Ed.2d 886 (2000)

The state of Missouri imposed contribution limits on candidates for state office, with some limits as low as $250 for state house candidates. These limits were challenged as a violation of the First Amendment since they were significantly less than the $1,000 limit upheld in Buckley.

Vote: 6–3

JUSTICE SOUTER delivered the opinion for the Court.

Precision about the relative rigor of the standard to review contribution limits was not a pretense of the *Buckley v. Valeo,* 424 U.S. 1 (1976), *per curiam* opinion. To be sure, in addressing the speech claim, we explicitly rejected both *O'Brien* intermediate scrutiny for communicative action, see *United States v. O'Brien,* 391 U.S. 367 (1968), and the similar standard applicable to merely time, place, and manner restrictions. In distinguishing these tests, the discussion referred generally to "the exacting scrutiny required by the First Amendment," *Buckley v. Valeo*, 424 U.S., at 16, and added that " 'the constitutional guarantee has its fullest and most urgent application precisely to the conduct of campaigns for political office.' "

We then, however, drew a line between expenditures and contributions, treating expenditure restrictions as direct restraints on speech, which nonetheless suffered little direct effect from contribution limits:

[A] limitation upon the amount that any one person or group may contribute to a candidate or political committee entails only a marginal restriction upon the contributor's ability to engage in free communication. A contribution serves as a general expression of support for the candidate and his views, but does not communicate the underlying basis for the support. The quantity of communication by the contributor does not increase perceptibly with the size of his contribution, since the expression rests solely on the undifferentiated symbolic act of contributing. At most, the size of the contribution provides a very rough index of the intensity of the contributor's support for the candidate. A limitation on the amount of money a person may give to a candidate or campaign organization thus involves little direct restraint on his political communication, for it permits the symbolic expression of support evidenced by a contribution but does not in any way infringe the contributor's freedom to discuss candidates and issues.

We thus said, in effect, that limiting contributions left communication significantly unimpaired.

We flagged a similar difference between expenditure and contribution limitations in their impacts on the association right. While an expenditure limit "precludes most associations from effectively amplifying the voice of their adherents," (thus interfering with the freedom of the adherents as well as the association), the contribution limits "leave the contributor free to become a member of any political association and to assist personally in the association's efforts on behalf of candidates," While we did not then say in so many words that different standards might govern expenditure and contribution limits affecting associational rights, we have since then said so explicitly in *Federal Election Comm'n v. Massachusetts Citizens for Life, Inc.,* 479 U.S. 238, 259–260 (1986): "We have consistently held that restrictions on contributions require less compelling justification than restrictions on independent spending." It has, in any event, been plain ever since *Buckley* that contribution limits would more readily clear the hurdles before them. Thus, under *Buckley*'s standard of scrutiny, a contribution limit involving "significant interference" with associational rights could survive if the Government demonstrated that contribution regulation was "closely drawn" to match a "sufficiently important interest," though the dollar amount of the limit need not be "fine tun[ed]."

While we did not attempt to parse distinctions between the speech and association standards of scrutiny for contribution limits, we did make it clear that those restrictions bore more heavily on the associational right than on freedom to speak. We consequently proceeded on the understanding that a contribution limitation surviving a claim of associational abridgment would survive a speech challenge as well, and we held the standard satisfied by the contribution limits under review.

"[T]he prevention of corruption and the appearance of corruption," was found to be a "constitutionally sufficient justification." . . .

"Of almost equal concern as the danger of actual *quid pro quo* arrangements is the impact of the appearance of corruption stemming from public awareness of the opportunities for abuse inherent in a regime of large individual financial contributions. . . . Congress could legitimately conclude that the avoidance of the appearance of improper influence 'is also critical . . . if confidence in the system of representative Government is not to be eroded to a disastrous extent.' "

In speaking of "improper influence" and "opportunities for abuse" in addition to "*quid pro quo* arrangements," we recognized a concern not confined to bribery of public officials, but extending to the broader threat from politicians too compliant with the wishes of large contributors. These were the obvious points behind our recognition that the Congress could constitutionally address the power of money "to influence governmental action" in ways less "blatant and specific" than bribery.

The quantum of empirical evidence needed to satisfy heightened judicial scrutiny of legislative judgments will vary up or down with the novelty and plausibility of the justification raised. *Buckley* demonstrates that the dangers of large, corrupt contributions and the suspicion that large contributions are corrupt are neither novel nor implausible. The opinion noted that "the deeply disturbing examples surfacing after the 1972 election demonstrate that the problem [of corruption] is not an illusory one." Although we did not ourselves marshal the evidence in support of the congressional concern, we referred to "a number of the abuses" detailed in the Court of Appeals's decision, which described how corporations, well-financed interest groups, and rich individuals had made large contributions, some of which were illegal under existing law, others of which reached at least the verge of bribery. The evidence before the Court of Appeals described public revelations by the parties in question more than sufficient to show why voters would tend to identify a big donation with a corrupt purpose.

While *Buckley*'s evidentiary showing exemplifies a sufficient justification for contribution limits, it does not speak to what may be necessary as a minimum. As to that, respondents are wrong in arguing that in the years since *Buckley* came down we have "supplemented" its holding with a new requirement that governments enacting contribution limits must " 'demonstrate that the recited harms are real, not merely conjectural,' " We have never accepted mere conjecture as adequate to carry a First Amendment burden, and *Colorado Republican Federal Campaign Committee v. FEC,* 518 U.S. 604 (1996), did not deal with a government's burden to justify limits on contributions. Although the principal opinion in that case charged the Government with failure to show a real risk of corruption, the issue in question was limits on independent expenditures by political parties, which the principal opinion expressly distinguished from contribution limits: "limitations on independent expenditures are less directly related to preventing corruption" than contributions are. In that case, the "constitutionally significant fact" that there was no "coordination between the candidate and the source of the expenditure" kept the principal opinion "from assuming, absent convincing evidence to the contrary, that [a limitation on expenditures] is necessary to combat a substantial danger of corruption of the electoral system." *Colorado Republican* thus goes hand in hand with *Buckley*, not toe to toe.

FOR DISCUSSION

Did *Shrink* lower the evidentiary burden necessary to sustain a contribution limit? Many argued that it did. In addition, what evidence can be offered to support a limit on campaign contributions?

MCINTYRE V. OHIO

514 U.S. 334, 120 S.Ct. 897, 145 L.Ed.2d 886 (1995)

Margaret McIntyre leafleted parked cars and individuals attending a public meeting expressing her opposition to a proposed school bonds levy. The leaflets were unsigned, in violation of an Ohio law banning the distribution of unsigned leaflets. Ms. McIntyre, and then her estate after she died, challenged the law as a violation of her First Amendment rights.

Vote: 6–3

JUSTICE STEVENS delivered the opinion of the Court.

On April 27, 1988, Margaret McIntyre distributed leaflets to persons attending a public meeting at the Blendon Middle School in Westerville, Ohio. At this meeting, the superintendent of schools planned to discuss an imminent referendum on a proposed school tax levy. The leaflets expressed Mrs. McIntyre's opposition to the levy. There is no suggestion that the text of her message was false, misleading, or libelous. She had composed and printed it on her home computer and had paid a professional printer to make additional copies. Some of the handbills identified her as the author; others merely purported to express the views of "CONCERNED PARENTS AND TAX PAYERS." Except for the help provided by her son and a friend, who placed some of the leaflets on car windshields in the school parking lot, Mrs. McIntyre acted independently.

While Mrs. McIntyre distributed her handbills, an official of the school district, who supported the tax proposal, advised her that the unsigned leaflets did not conform to the Ohio election laws. Undeterred, Mrs. McIntyre appeared at another meeting on the next evening and handed out more of the handbills.

The proposed school levy was defeated at the next two elections, but it finally passed on its third try in November 1988. Five months later, the same school official filed a complaint with the Ohio Elections

Commission charging that Mrs. McIntyre's distribution of unsigned leaflets violated § 3599.09(A) of the Ohio Code. The Commission agreed and imposed a fine of $100.

The Franklin County Court of Common Pleas reversed. Finding that Mrs. McIntyre did not "mislead the public nor act in a surreptitious manner," the court concluded that the statute was unconstitutional as applied to her conduct. The Ohio Court of Appeals, by a divided vote, reinstated the fine. Notwithstanding doubts about the continuing validity of a 1922 decision of the Ohio Supreme Court upholding the statutory predecessor of § 3599.09(A), the majority considered itself bound by that precedent. The dissenting judge thought that our intervening decision in *Talley* v. *California*, 362 U.S. 60 (1960), in which we invalidated a city ordinance prohibiting all anonymous leafletting, compelled the Ohio court to adopt a narrowing construction of the statute to save its constitutionality.

The Ohio Supreme Court affirmed by a divided vote. The majority distinguished Mrs. McIntyre's case from *Talley* on the ground that § 3599.09(A) "has as its purpose the identification of persons who distribute materials containing false statements." The Ohio court believed that such a law should be upheld if the burdens imposed on the First Amendment rights of voters are "*reasonable*" and "*nondiscriminatory*." Under that standard, the majority concluded that the statute was plainly valid:

> The minor requirement imposed by R.C. 3599.09 that those persons producing campaign literature identify themselves as the source thereof neither impacts the content of their message nor significantly burdens their ability to have it disseminated. This burden is more than counterbalanced by the state interest in providing the voters to whom the message is directed with a mechanism by which they may better evaluate its validity. Moreover, the law serves to identify those who engage in fraud, libel or false advertising. Not only are such interests sufficient to overcome the minor burden placed upon such persons, these interests were specifically acknowledged in *First National Bank of Boston v. Bellotti*[, 435 U.S. 765 (1978), to be regulations of the sort which would survive constitutional scrutiny.

In dissent, Justice Wright argued that the statute should be tested under a more severe standard because of its significant effect "on the ability of individual citizens to freely express their views in writing on political issues." He concluded that § 3599.09(A) "is not narrowly tailored to serve a compelling state interest and is, therefore, unconstitutional as applied to McIntyre."

Indeed, as we have explained on many prior occasions, the category of speech regulated by the Ohio statute occupies the core of the protection afforded by the First Amendment:

> "Discussion of public issues and debate on the qualifications of candidates are integral to the operation of the system of government established by our Constitution. The First Amendment affords the broadest protection to such political expression in order 'to assure [the] unfettered interchange of ideas for the bringing about of political and social changes desired by the people.' Although First Amendment protections are not confined to 'the exposition of ideas,' 'there is practically universal agreement that a major purpose of that Amendment was to protect the free discussion of governmental affairs, of course includ[ing] discussions of candidates.' This no more than reflects our 'profound national commitment to the principle that debate on public issues should be uninhibited, robust, and wide open.' In a republic where the people are sovereign, the ability of the citizenry to make informed choices among candidates for office is essential, for the identities of those who are elected will inevitably shape the course that we follow as a nation. As the Court observed in *Monitor Patriot Co.* v. *Roy*, 401 U.S. 265, 272 (1971), 'it can hardly be doubted that the constitutional guarantee has its fullest and most urgent application precisely to the conduct of campaigns for political office.' "

Of course, core political speech need not center on a candidate for office. The principles enunciated in *Buckley* extend equally to issue based elections such as the school tax referendum that Mrs. McIntyre sought to influence through her handbills. Indeed, the speech in which Mrs. McIntyre engaged—handing out leaflets in the advocacy of a politically controversial viewpoint—is the essence of First Amendment expression. That this advocacy occurred in the heat of a controversial referendum vote only strengthens the protection afforded to Ms. McIntyre's expression: urgent, important, and effective speech can be no less protected than impotent speech, lest the right to speak be relegated to those instances when it is least needed. No form of speech is entitled to greater constitutional protection than Mrs. McIntyre's.

When a law burdens core political speech, we apply "exacting scrutiny," and we uphold the restriction only if it is narrowly tailored to serve an overriding state interest. Our precedents thus make abundantly clear that the Ohio Supreme Court applied a significantly more lenient standard than is appropriate in a case of this kind.

VI

Under our Constitution, anonymous pamphleteering is not a pernicious, fraudulent practice, but an honorable tradition of advocacy and of dissent. Anonymity is a shield from the tyranny of the majority. See generally J. S. Mill, On Liberty, in *On Liberty and Considerations on Representative Government* 1, 3–4 (R. McCallum ed. 1947). It thus exemplifies the purpose behind the Bill of Rights, and of the First Amendment in particular: to protect unpopular individuals from retaliation—and their ideas from suppression—at the hand of an intolerant society. The right to remain anonymous may be abused when it shields fraudulent conduct. But political speech by its nature will sometimes have unpalatable consequences, and, in general, our society accords greater weight to the value of free speech than to the dangers of its misuse. Ohio has not shown that its interest in preventing the misuse of anonymous election related speech justifies a prohibition of all uses of that speech. The State may, and does, punish fraud directly. But it cannot seek to punish fraud indirectly by indiscriminately outlawing a category of speech, based on its content, with no necessary relationship to the danger sought to be prevented. One would be hard pressed to think of a better example of the pitfalls of Ohio's blunderbuss approach than the facts of the case before us.

The judgment of the Ohio Supreme Court is reversed.

FOR DISCUSSION

McIntyre seems to stand for the proposition that individuals have a constitutional right to engage in anonymous political speech. But how far does that ruling extend? Does it protect anonymous speech for groups?

Major Provisions of the Bipartisan Campaign Reform Act of 2002
("BCRA" or "McCain-Feingold Act")

a. **§ 323 (a) National Ban on Soft Money**

i. Bans national political parties and their agents from soliciting, receiving, directing, or spending any funds that are not subject to FECA's limitations, prohibitions, or reporting requirements.

b. **§ 323 (b) State and Local Party Soft Money Ban**

i. Prohibits state and local party committees from using soft money to engage in "federal election activity."

ii. "FEDERAL ELECTION ACTIVITY" is

(1) Voter registration activity 120 days before a federal election; or

(2) Voter identification, GOTV (Get out the vote), and generic campaign activity conducted with an election in which a federal candidate appears on the ballot; or

(3) Any public communication that refers to a clearly identified federal candidate who appears on ballot and which promotes, supports, attacks, or opposes the candidate; or

(4) The services of any state committee employee who devotes more than 255 of compensated time in connection with a federal election.

iii. **§ 323 (b) (2) Levin exception to the soft money ban**

(1) State and local party committees may pay for certain federal election activities with allocated ratio of hard money and Levin funds.

(a) State and local party committees may pay for (a) and (b):

(i) So long as there is no refer to a clearly identified federal candidate;

(ii) Any broadcast communication must refer to a clearly identified state or local candidate

(iii) No contributor can donate more than $10,000 per year to a single committee's Levin fund;

(iv) Levin funds allocated portion of hard money funds must be raised by the state and local committee that spends them;

(v) Committees can team up with other national, state, and local committees to raise the hard money portion.

c. **§ 323 (c) Fundraising costs**

i. National, state, and local parties must use federally-regulated funds to raise money for federal election activities.

d. **§ 323 (d) Ban on national, state, and local party committees soliciting for non-profits**

i. Ban on national, state, and local party committees and officials soliciting for, or making or directing contributions to § 501 (c) tax exempt organizations that make expenditures in connection with a federal election, or to § 527 entities other than a political committee or a state or local political committee.

e. **§ 323 (e) Ban on federal officeholders candidates from soliciting soft money.**

i. Forbids federal candidates and officeholders from soliciting, receiving, directing,, transferring, or spending soft money in connection with a federal elections, and also limits the ability to do so for state and local elections.

f. **§ 323 (f) Ban on state/local officeholders candidates from soliciting soft money to influence federal elections.**

i. Forbids state and local candidates and officeholders from raising and spending soft money to fund ads and other "political communications" to promote or attack federal candidates.

g. **§ 201 Express and Issue Advocacy**

i. Disclosure for "Electioneering communication"

(1) "ELECTIONEERING COMMUNICATION" is defined as:

(a) Any broadcast, cable, or satellite which:

(i) refers to a clearly identified candidate for federal office; **and**

(ii) which is made:

1) 60 days before a general election or

2) 30 days before a convention or primary; **and**

(iii) targeted at the relevant electorate; **and**

1) Must be received by 50,000 or more individuals in that electorate.

h. **§ 304 (f) (5) Disclosure of executory contracts**

i. Disclosure of executory contracts when a person makes disbursements totally more than $10,000 in any calendar year to pay for electioneering communication.

i. **§ 202 Coordination**

i. Disbursements for electioneering communication that are coordinated with a party or candidate will be treated as contributions to, and expenditures by that candidate or party.

j. **§ 203 Ban on corporate/union treasury funds for electioneering communication.**

i. Corporate and union general treasury funds may not be used for electioneering communication

ii. Snowe-Jeffords exception

(1) Would have allowed some exceptions to the § 203 ban for some non-profits but the Wellstone Amendment effectively erases that exception.

k. **§ 204 Ban on non-profit treasury funds for electioneering communication.**

i. Prohibits all non *Massachusetts Citizens Concerned for Life* (MCFL) organizations from using general treasury fund to pay for electioneering communication.

l. **§ 212 Mandatory individual disclosure for independent expenditures**

i. Mandatory disclosure for persons making independent expenditures of $1,000 or more 20 days before any election.

m. **§ 213 Parties to choose between independent and coordinated expenditures**

i. Requires political parties to choose between making coordinated and independent expenditures during the post nomination, pre election period.

n. **§ 311 Candidate authorization of political communications**

i. Mandatory disclosure electioneering communications disbursements

(1) "I am John Kerry (or George Bush) and I approve of this ad."

o. **§ 318 Ban political contributions from minors**

i. Forbids individuals 17 and younger from making contributions to parties and candidates.

McConnell v. Federal Election Commission

540 U.S. 93, 124 S.Ct. 619, 157 L.Ed.2d 491 (2003)

The Bipartisan Campaign Reform Act of 2002 (BCRA) amended the Federal Election Campaign Act of 1971 (FECA) and the Communications Act of 1934. Among other things, it placed limits on soft money political contributions and issue ads. BCRA was challenged by several groups and members of Congress, and in a 1,500-page-plus Court of Appeals decision it was largely upheld. The case was appealed to the United States Supreme Court, with oral arguments held in September 2003. The decision was released in December 2003. The Supreme Court opinion was several hundred pages long, making it one of the longest opinions ever issued.

Vote: 5–4

Justices Stevens and O'Connor delivered the opinion of the Court with respect to BCRA Titles I and II, in which Justices Souter, Ginsburg, and Breyer joined. Chief Justice Rehnquist delivered the opinion of the Court with respect to BCRA Titles III and IV, in which Justices O'Connor, Scalia, Kennedy, and Souter joined, in which Justices Stevens, Ginsburg, and Breyer joined except with respect to BCRA § 305, and in which Justice Thomas joined with respect to BCRA §§ 304, 305, 307, 316, 319, and 403(b). Justice Breyer delivered the opinion of the Court with respect to BCRA Title V, in which Justices Stevens, O'Connor, Souter, and Ginsburg joined.

Justice Stevens and Justice O'Connor delivered the Opinion of the Court with respect to BCRA Titles I and II.

More than a century ago the "sober-minded Elihu Root" advocated legislation that would prohibit political contributions by corporations in order to prevent " 'the great aggregations of wealth, from using their corporate funds, directly or indirectly,' " to elect legislators who would " 'vote for their protection and the advancement of their interests as against those of the public.' " " In Root's opinion, such legislation would " 'strik[e] at a constantly growing evil which has done more to shake the confidence of the plain people of small means of this country in our political institutions than any other practice which has ever obtained since the foundation of our Government.' " The Congress of the United States has repeatedly enacted legislation endorsing Root's judgment.

BCRA is the most recent federal enactment designed "to purge national politics of what was conceived to be the pernicious influence of 'big money' campaign contributions. As Justice Frankfurter explained in his opinion for the Court in *United States v. Automobile Workers*, 352 U.S. 567 (1957), the first such enactment responded to President Theodore Roosevelt's call for legislation forbidding all contributions by corporations " 'to any political committee or for any political purpose.' " In his annual message to Congress in December 1905, President Roosevelt stated that " 'directors should not be permitted to use stockholders' money' " for political purposes, and he recommended that " 'a prohibition' " on corporate political contributions " 'would be, as far as it went, an effective method of stopping the evils aimed at in corrupt practices acts.' " The resulting 1907 statute completely banned corporate contributions of "money . . . in connection with" any federal election. Congress soon amended the statute to require the public disclosure of certain contributions and expenditures and to place "maximum limits on the amounts that congressional candidates could spend in seeking nomination and election."

In 1925 Congress extended the prohibition of "contributions" "to include 'anything of value,' and made acceptance of a corporate contribution as well as the giving of such a contribution a crime." During the debates preceding that amendment, a leading Senator characterized " 'the apparent hold on political parties which business interests and certain organizations seek and sometimes obtain by reason of liberal campaign contributions' " as " 'one of the great political evils of the time.' " We upheld the amended statute against a constitutional challenge, observing that "[t]he power of Congress to protect the election of President and Vice President from corruption being clear, the choice of means to that end presents a question primarily addressed to the judgment of Congress."

Congress' historical concern with the "political potentialities of wealth" and their "untoward consequences for the democratic process," has long reached beyond corporate money. During and shortly after World War II, Congress reacted to the "enormous financial outlays" made by some unions in connection with national elections. Congress first restricted union contributions in the Hatch Act, and it later prohibited "union contributions in connection with federal elections . . . altogether." Congress subsequently extended that prohibition to cover unions' election-related expenditures as well as contributions, and it broadened the coverage of federal campaigns to include both primary and general elections. Labor Management Relations Act, 1947 (Taft-Hartley Act). During the consideration of those measures, legislators repeatedly voiced their concerns regarding the pernicious influence of large campaign contributions. As we noted in a unanimous opinion recalling this history, Congress' "careful legislative adjustment of the federal electoral laws, in a 'cautious advance, step by step,' to account for the particular legal and economic attributes of corporations and labor organizations warrants considerable deference."

In early 1972 Congress continued its steady improvement of the national election laws by enacting FECA. As first enacted, that statute required disclosure of all contributions exceeding $100 and of expenditures by candidates and political committees that spent more than $1,000 per year. It also prohibited contributions made in the name of another person and by Government contractors. The law ratified the earlier prohibition on the use of corporate and union general treasury funds for political contributions and expenditures, but it expressly permitted corporations and unions to establish and administer separate segregated funds. As the 1972 Presidential elections made clear, however, FECA's passage did not deter unseemly fundraising and campaign practices. Evidence of those practices persuaded Congress to enact the Federal Election Campaign Act Amendments of 1974. Reviewing a constitutional challenge to the amendments, the Court of Appeals for the District of Columbia Circuit described them as "by far the most comprehensive . . . reform legislation [ever] passed by Congress concerning the election of the President, Vice-President and members of Congress." The 1974 amendments closed the loophole that had allowed candidates to use an unlimited number of political committees for fundraising purposes and thereby to circumvent the limits on individual committees' receipts and disbursements. They also limited individual political contributions to any single candidate to $1,000 per election, with an overall annual limitation of $25,000 by any contributor; imposed ceilings on spending by candidates and political parties for national conventions; required reporting and public disclosure of contributions and expenditures exceeding certain limits; and established the Federal Election Commission (FEC) to administer and enforce the legislation. The Court of Appeals upheld the 1974 amendments almost in their entirety. It concluded that the clear and compelling interest in preserving the integrity of the electoral process provided a sufficient basis for sustaining the substantive provisions of the Act. The court's opinion relied heavily on findings that large contributions facilitated access to public officials and described methods of evading the contribution limits that had enabled contributors of massive sums to avoid disclosure

The Court of Appeals upheld the provisions establishing contribution and expenditure limitations on the theory that they should be viewed as regulations of conduct rather than speech. This Court, however, concluded that each set of limitations raised serious—though different—concerns under the First Amendment. We treated the limitations on candidate and individual expenditures as direct restraints on speech, but we observed that the contribution limitations, in contrast, imposed only "a marginal restriction upon the contributor's ability to engage in free communication." Considering the "deeply disturbing examples" of corruption related to candidate contributions discussed in the Court of Appeals' opinion, we determined that limiting contributions served an interest in protecting "the integrity of our system of representative democracy." In the end, the Act's primary purpose—"to limit the actuality and appearance of corruption resulting from large individual financial contributions"—provided "a constitutionally sufficient justification for the $1,000 contribution limitation."

We prefaced our analysis of the $1,000 limitation on expenditures by observing that it broadly encompassed every expenditure " 'relative to a clearly identified candidate.' " To avoid vagueness concerns we construed that phrase to apply only to "communications that in express terms advocate the election or defeat of a clearly identified candidate for federal office." We concluded, however, that as so narrowed, the provision would not provide effective protection against the dangers of *quid pro quo* arrangements, because persons and groups could eschew expenditures that expressly advocated the election or defeat of a clearly identified candidate while remaining "free to spend as much as they want to promote the candidate and his views." We also rejected the argument that the expenditure limits were necessary to prevent attempts to circumvent the Act's contribution limits, because FECA already treated expenditures controlled by or coordinated with the candidate as contributions, and we were not persuaded that independent expenditures posed the same risk of real or apparent corruption as coordinated expenditures. We therefore held that Congress' interest in preventing real or apparent corruption was inadequate to justify the heavy burdens on the freedoms of expression and association that the expenditure limits imposed.

We upheld all of the disclosure and reporting requirements in the Act that were challenged on appeal to this Court after finding that they vindicated three important interests: providing the electorate with relevant information about the candidates and their supporters; deterring actual corruption and discouraging the use of money for improper purposes; and facilitating enforcement of the prohibitions in the Act. In order to avoid an overbreadth problem, however, we placed the same narrowing construction on the term "expenditure" in the disclosure context that we had adopted in the context of the expenditure limitations. Thus, we construed the reporting requirement for persons making expenditures of more than $100 in a year "to reach only funds used for communications that expressly advocate the election or defeat of a clearly identified candidate."

Our opinion in *Buckley* addressed issues that primarily related to contributions and expenditures by individuals, since none of the parties challenged the prohibition on contributions by corporations and labor unions. We noted, however, that the statute authorized the use of corporate and union resources to form and administer segregated funds that could be used for political purposes.

Three important developments in the years after our decision in *Buckley* persuaded Congress that further legislation was necessary to regulate the role that corporations, unions, and wealthy contributors play in the electoral process. As a preface to our discussion of the specific provisions of BCRA, we comment briefly on the increased importance of "soft money," the proliferation of "issue ads," and the disturbing findings of a Senate investigation into campaign practices related to the 1996 federal elections.

Soft Money

Under FECA, "contributions" must be made with funds that are subject to the Act's disclosure requirements and source and amount limitations. Such funds are known as "federal" or "hard" money. FECA defines the term "contribution," however, to include only the gift or advance of anything of value "made by any person for the purpose of influencing any election for *Federal* office." Donations made solely for the purpose of influencing state or local elections are therefore unaffected by FECA's requirements and prohibitions. As a result, prior to the enactment of BCRA, federal law permitted corporations and unions, as well as individuals who had already made the maximum permissible contributions to federal candidates, to contribute "nonfederal money"—also known as "soft money"—to political parties for activities intended to influence state or local elections.

Shortly after *Buckley* was decided, questions arose concerning the treatment of contributions intended to influence both federal and state elections. Although a literal reading of FECA's definition of "contribution" would have required such activities to be funded with hard money, the FEC ruled that political parties could fund mixed-purpose activities—including get-out-the-vote drives and generic party advertising—in part with soft money. In 1995 the FEC concluded that the parties could also use soft money to defray the costs of "legislative advocacy media advertisements," even if the ads mentioned the name of a federal candidate, so long as they did not expressly advocate the candidate's election or defeat.

As the permissible uses of soft money expanded, the amount of soft money raised and spent by the national political parties increased exponentially. Of the two major parties' total spending, soft money accounted for 5% ($21.6 million) in 1984, 11% ($45 million) in 1988, 16% ($80 million) in 1992, 30% ($272 million) in 1996, and 42% ($498 million) in 2000. The national parties transferred large amounts of their soft money to the state parties, which were allowed to use a larger percentage of soft money to finance mixed-purpose activities under FEC rules. In the year 2000, for example, the national parties diverted $280 million—more than half of their soft money—to state parties.

Many contributions of soft money were dramatically larger than the contributions of hard money permitted by FECA. For example, in 1996 the top five corporate soft-money donors gave, in total, more than $9 million in nonfederal funds to the two national party committees. In the most recent election cycle the political parties raised almost $300 million—60% of their total soft-money fundraising—from just 800 donors, each of which contributed a minimum of $120,000. Moreover, the largest corporate donors often made substantial contributions to both parties. Such practices corroborate evidence indicating that many corporate contributions were motivated by a desire for access to candidates and a fear of being placed at a disadvantage in the legislative process relative to other contributors, rather than by ideological support for the candidates and parties.

Not only were such soft-money contributions often designed to gain access to federal candidates, but they were in many cases solicited by the candidates themselves. Candidates often directed potential donors to party committees and tax-exempt organizations that could legally accept soft money. For example, a federal legislator running for reelection solicited soft money from a supporter by advising him that even though he had already " 'contributed the legal maximum' " to the campaign committee, he could still make an additional contribution to a joint program supporting federal, state, and local candidates of his party. Such solicitations were not uncommon.

The solicitation, transfer, and use of soft money thus enabled parties and candidates to circumvent FECA's limitations on the source and amount of contributions in connection with federal elections.

II

BCRA's central provisions are designed to address Congress' concerns about the increasing use of soft money and issue advertising to influence federal elections. Title I regulates the use of soft money by political parties, officeholders, and candidates. Title II primarily prohibits corporations and labor unions from using general treasury funds for communications that are intended to, or have the effect of, influencing the outcome of federal elections.

III

Title I is Congress' effort to plug the soft-money loophole. The cornerstone of Title I is new FECA § 323(a), which prohibits national party committees and their agents from soliciting, receiving, directing, or spending any soft money. In short, § 323(a) takes national parties out of the soft-money business.

The remaining provisions of new FECA § 323 largely reinforce the restrictions in § 323(a). New FECA § 323(b) prevents the wholesale shift of soft-money influence from national to state party committees by prohibiting state and local party committees from using such funds for activities that affect federal elections. These "Federal election activit[ies]," defined in new FECA § 301(20)(A), are almost identical to the mixed-purpose activities that have long been regulated under the FEC's pre-BCRA allocation regime New FECA § 323(d) reinforces these soft-money restrictions by prohibiting political parties from soliciting and donating funds to tax-exempt organizations that engage in electioneering activities. New FECA § 323(e) restricts federal candidates and officeholders from receiving, spending, or soliciting soft money in connection with federal elections and limits their ability to do so in connection with state and local elections. Finally, new FECA § 323(f) prevents circumvention of the restrictions on national, state, and local party committees by prohibiting state and local candidates from raising and spending soft money to fund advertisements and other public communications that promote or attack federal candidates.

Plaintiffs mount a facial First Amendment challenge to new FECA § 323, as well as challenges based on the Elections Clause, U.S. Const., Art. I, § 4, principles of federalism, and the equal protection component of the Due Process Clause. We address these challenges in turn.

A

In *Buckley* and subsequent cases, we have subjected restrictions on campaign expenditures to closer scrutiny than limits on campaign contributions. In these cases we have recognized that contribution limits, unlike limits on expenditures, "entai[l] only a marginal restriction upon the contributor's ability to engage in free communication."

We have recognized that contribution limits may bear "more heavily on the associational right than on freedom to speak," since contributions serve "to affiliate a person with a candidate" and "enabl[e] like-minded persons to pool their resources." Unlike expenditure limits, however, which "preclud[e] most associations from effectively amplifying the voice of their adherents," contribution limits both "leave the contributor free to become a member of any political association and to assist personally in the association's efforts on behalf of candidates," and allow associations "to aggregate large sums of money to promote effective advocacy." The "overall effect" of dollar limits on contributions is "merely to require candidates and political committees to raise funds from a greater number of persons." Thus, a contribution limit involving even " 'significant interference' " with associational rights is nevertheless valid if it satisfies the "lesser demand" of being " 'closely drawn' " to match a " 'sufficiently important interest.' "

Our treatment of contribution restrictions reflects more than the limited burdens they impose on First Amendment freedoms. It also reflects the importance of the interests that underlie contribution limits—interests in preventing "both the actual corruption threatened by large financial contributions and the eroding of public confidence in the electoral process through the appearance of corruption." We have said that these interests directly implicate " 'the integrity of our electoral process, and, not less, the responsibility of the individual citizen for the successful functioning of that process.' " Because the electoral process is the very "means through which a free society democratically translates political speech into concrete governmental action," contribution limits, like other measures aimed at protecting the integrity of the process, tangibly benefit public participation in public debate. For that reason, when reviewing Congress' decision to enact contribution limits, "there is no place for a strong presumption against constitutionality, of the sort often thought to accompany the words 'strict scrutiny.' " The less rigorous standard of review we have applied to contribution limits (*Buckley*'s "closely drawn" scrutiny) shows proper deference to Congress' ability to weigh competing constitutional interests in an area in which it enjoys particular expertise. It also provides Congress with sufficient room to anticipate and respond to concerns about circumvention of regulations designed to protect the integrity of the political process.

New FECA § 323(a)'s Restrictions on National Party Committees

The core of Title I is new FECA § 323(a), which provides that "national committee[s] of a political party . . . may not solicit, receive, or direct to another person a contribution, donation, or transfer of funds or any other thing of value, or spend any funds, that are not subject to the limitations, prohibitions, and reporting requirements of this Act." The prohibition extends to "any officer or agent acting on behalf of such a national committee, and any entity that is directly or indirectly established, financed, maintained, or controlled by such a national committee."

The main goal of § 323(a) is modest. In large part, it simply effects a return to the scheme that was approved in *Buckley* and that was subverted by the creation of the FEC's allocation regime, which permitted the political parties to fund federal electioneering efforts with a combination of hard and soft money. Under that allocation regime, national parties were able to use vast amounts of soft money in their efforts to elect federal candidates. Consequently, as long as they directed the money to the political parties, donors could contribute large amounts of soft money for use in activities designed to influence federal elections. New § 323(a) is designed to put a stop to that practice.

Governmental Interests Underlying New FECA § 323(a)

The Government defends § 323(a)'s ban on national parties' involvement with soft money as necessary to prevent the actual and apparent corruption of federal candidates and officeholders. Our cases have made clear that the prevention of corruption or its appearance constitutes a sufficiently important interest to justify political contribution limits. We have not limited that interest to the elimination of cash-for-votes exchanges. In *Buckley,* we expressly rejected the argument that antibribery laws provided a less restrictive alternative to FECA's contribution limits, noting that such laws "deal[t] with only the most blatant and specific attempts of those with money to influence governmental action." Thus, "[i]n speaking of 'improper influence' and 'opportunities for abuse' in addition to '*quid pro quo* arrangements,' we [have] recognized a concern not confined to bribery of public officials, but extending to the broader threat from politicians too compliant with the wishes of large contributors."

Of "almost equal" importance has been the Government's interest in combating the appearance or perception of corruption engendered by large campaign contributions. Take away Congress' authority to regulate the appearance of undue influence and "the cynical assumption that large donors call the tune could jeopardize the willingness of voters to take part in democratic governance." And because the First Amendment does not require Congress to ignore the fact that "candidates, donors, and parties test the limits of the current law," these interests have been sufficient to justify not only contribution limits themselves, but laws preventing the circumvention of such limits.

"The quantum of empirical evidence needed to satisfy heightened judicial scrutiny of legislative judgments will vary up or down with the novelty and plausibility of the justification raised." The idea that large contributions to a national party can corrupt or, at the very least, create the appearance of corruption of federal candidates and officeholders is neither novel nor implausible. For nearly 30 years, FECA has placed strict dollar limits and source restrictions on contributions that individuals and other entities can give to national, state, and local party committees for the purpose of influencing a federal election. The premise behind these restrictions has been, and continues to be, that contributions to a federal candidate's party in aid of that candidate's campaign threaten to create—no less than would a direct contribution to the candidate—a sense of obligation. This is particularly true of contributions to national parties, with which federal candidates and officeholders enjoy a special relationship and unity of interest. This close affiliation has placed national parties in a unique position, "whether they like it or not," to serve as "agents for spending on behalf of those who seek to produce obligated officeholders."

The question for present purposes is whether large *soft-money* contributions to national party committees have a corrupting influence or give rise to the appearance of corruption. Both common sense and the ample record in these cases confirm Congress' belief that they do. As set forth above, the FEC's allocation regime has invited widespread circumvention of FECA's limits on contributions to parties for the purpose of influencing federal elections. Under this system, corporate, union, and wealthy individual donors have been free to contribute substantial sums of soft money to the national parties, which the parties can spend for the specific purpose of influencing a particular candidate's federal election. It is not only plausible, but likely, that candidates would feel grateful for such donations and that donors would seek to exploit

The evidence in the record shows that candidates and donors alike have in fact exploited the soft-money loophole, the former to increase their prospects of election and the latter to create debt on the part of officeholders, with the national parties serving as willing intermediaries. Thus, despite FECA's hard-money limits on direct contributions to candidates, federal officeholders have commonly asked donors to make soft-money donations to national and state committees " 'solely in order to assist federal campaigns,' " including the officeholder's own. Parties kept tallies of the amounts of soft money raised by each officeholder, and "the amount of money a Member of Congress raise[d] for the national political party committees often affect[ed] the amount the committees g[a]ve to assist the Member's campaign." Donors often asked that their contributions be credited to particular candidates, and the parties obliged, irrespective of whether the funds were hard or soft. National party committees often teamed with individual candidates' campaign committees to create joint fundraising committees, which enabled the candidates to take advantage of the party's higher contribution limits while still allowing donors to give to their preferred candidate. Even when not participating directly in the fundraising, federal officeholders were well aware of the identities of the donors: National party committees would distribute lists of potential or actual donors, or donors themselves would report their generosity to officeholders.

Particularly telling is the fact that, in 1996 and 2000, more than half of the top 50 soft-money donors gave substantial sums to *both* major national parties, leaving room for no other conclusion but that these donors were seeking influence, or avoiding retaliation, rather than promoting any particular ideology.

The evidence from the federal officeholders' perspective is similar. For example, one former Senator described the influence purchased by nonfederal donations as follows:

> Too often, Members' first thought is not what is right or what they believe, but how it will affect fundraising. Who, after all, can seriously contend that a $100,000 donation does not alter the way one thinks about—and quite possibly votes on—an issue? . . . When you don't pay the piper that finances your campaigns, you will never get any more money from that piper. Since money is the mother's milk of politics, you never want to be in that situation (quoting declaration of former Sen. Alan Simpson).

By bringing soft-money donors and federal candidates and officeholders together, "[p]arties are thus necessarily the instruments of some contributors whose object is not to support the party's message or to elect party candidates across the board, but rather to support a specific candidate for the sake of a position on one narrow issue, or even to support any candidate who will be obliged to the contributors."

Plaintiffs argue that without concrete evidence of an instance in which a federal officeholder has actually switched a vote (or, presumably, evidence of a specific instance where the public believes a vote was switched). Congress has not shown that there exists real or apparent corruption. But the record is to the contrary. The evidence connects soft money to manipulations of the legislative calendar, leading to Congress' failure to enact, among other things, generic drug legislation, tort reform, and tobacco legislation. To claim that such actions do not change legislative outcomes surely misunderstands the legislative process.

More importantly, plaintiffs conceive of corruption too narrowly. Our cases have firmly established that Congress' legitimate interest extends beyond preventing simple cash-for-votes corruption to curbing "undue influence on an officeholder's judgment, and the appearance of such influence." Many of the "deeply disturbing examples" of corruption cited by this Court in *Buckley,* to justify FECA's contribution limits were not episodes of vote buying, but evidence that various corporate interests had given substantial donations to gain access to high-level government officials. Even if that access did not secure actual influence, it certainly gave the "appearance of such influence."

The record in the present cases is replete with similar examples of national party committees peddling access to federal candidates and officeholders in exchange for large soft-money donations. As one former Senator put it:

> Special interests who give large amounts of soft money to political parties do in fact achieve their objectives. They do get special access. Sitting Senators and House Members have limited amounts of time, but they make time available in their schedules to meet with representatives of business and unions and wealthy individuals who gave large sums to their parties. These are not idle chit-chats about the philosophy of democracy. . . . Senators are pressed by their benefactors to introduce legislation, to amend legislation, to block legislation, and to vote on legislation in a certain way (quoting declaration of former Sen. Warren Rudman).

So pervasive is this practice that the six national party committees actually furnish their own menus of opportunities for access to would-be soft-money donors, with increased prices reflecting an increased level of access. For example, the DCCC offers a range of donor options, starting with the $10,000-per-year Business Forum program, and going up to the $100,000-per-year National Finance Board program. The latter entitles the donor to bimonthly conference calls with the Democratic House leadership and chair of the DCCC, complimentary invitations to all DCCC fundraising events, two private dinners with the Democratic House leadership and ranking Members, and two retreats with the Democratic House leader and DCCC chair in Telluride, Colorado, and Hyannisport, Massachusetts. Similarly, "the RNC's donor programs offer greater access to federal office holders as the donations grow larger, with the highest level and most personal access offered to the largest soft money donors."

Despite this evidence and the close ties that candidates and officeholders have with their parties, Justice Kennedy would limit Congress' regulatory interest *only* to the prevention of the actual or apparent *quid pro quo* corruption "inherent in" contributions made directly to, contributions made at the express behest of, and expenditures made in coordination with, a federal officeholder or candidate. Regulation of any other donation or expenditure—regardless of its size, the recipient's relationship to the candidate or officeholder, its potential impact on a candidate's election, its value to the candidate, or its unabashed and explicit intent to purchase influence—would, according to Justice Kennedy, simply be out of bounds. This crabbed view of corruption, and particularly of the appearance of corruption, ignores precedent, common sense, and the realities of political fundraising exposed by the record in this litigation.

In sum, there is substantial evidence to support Congress' determination that large soft-money contributions to national political parties give rise to corruption and the appearance of corruption.

New FECA § 323(a)'s Restriction on Spending and Receiving Soft Money

Section 323(a), like the remainder of § 323, regulates contributions, not activities. As the record demonstrates, it is the close relationship between federal officeholders and the national parties, as well as the means by which parties have traded on that relationship, that have made all large soft-money contributions to national parties suspect.

As one expert noted, " '[t]here is no meaningful separation between the national party committees and the public officials who control them.' " The national committees of the two major parties are both run by, and largely composed of, federal officeholders and candidates. Indeed, of the six national committees of the two major parties, four are composed entirely of federal officeholders.

The nexus between national parties and federal officeholders prompted one of Title I's framers to conclude:

> Because the national parties operate at the national level, and are inextricably intertwined with federal officeholders and candidates, who raise the money for the national party committees, there is a close connection between the funding of the national parties and the corrupting dangers of soft money on the federal political process. The only effective way to address this [soft-money] problem of corruption is to ban entirely all raising and spending of soft money by the national parties (statement of Rep. Shays).

Given this close connection and alignment of interests, large soft-money contributions to national parties are likely to create actual or apparent indebtedness on the part of federal officeholders, regardless of how those funds are ultimately used.

This close affiliation has also placed national parties in a position to sell access to federal officeholders in exchange for soft-money contributions that the party can then use for its own purposes. Access to federal officeholders is the most valuable favor the national party committees are able to give in exchange for large donations. The fact that officeholders comply by donating their valuable time indicates either that officeholders place substantial value on the soft-money contribution themselves, without regard to their end use, or that national committees are able to exert considerable control over federal officeholders. Either way, large soft-money donations to national party committees are likely to buy donors preferential access to federal officeholders no matter the ends to which their contributions are eventually put. As discussed above, Congress had sufficient grounds to regulate the appearance of undue influence associated with this practice. The Government's strong interests in preventing corruption, and in particular the appearance of corruption, are thus sufficient to justify subjecting all donations to national parties to the source, amount, and disclosure limitations of FECA.

New FECA § 323(a)'s Restriction on Soliciting or Directing Soft Money

Plaintiffs also contend that § 323(a)'s prohibition on national parties' soliciting or directing soft-money contributions is substantially overbroad. The reach of the solicitation prohibition, however, is limited. It bars only solicitations of soft money by national party committees and by party officers in their official capacities. The committees remain free to solicit hard money on their own behalf, as well as to solicit hard money on behalf of state committees and state and local candidates. They also can contribute hard money to state committees and to candidates. In accordance with FEC regulations, furthermore, officers of national parties are free to solicit soft money in their individual capacities, or, if they are also officials of state parties, in that capacity.

This limited restriction on solicitation follows sensibly from the prohibition on national committees' receiving soft money. The same observations that led us to approve the latter compel us to reach the same conclusion regarding the former. A national committee is likely to respond favorably to a donation made at its request regardless of whether the recipient is the committee itself or another entity. This principle accords with common sense and appears elsewhere in federal laws.

Accordingly, we affirm the judgment of the District Court insofar as it upheld §§ 323(e) and 323(f). We reverse the judgment of the District Court insofar as it invalidated §§ 323(a), 323(b), and 323(d).

IV

Title II of BCRA, entitled "Noncandidate Campaign Expenditures," is divided into two subtitles: "Electioneering Communications" and "Independent and Coordinated Expenditures." We consider each challenged section of these subtitles in turn.

BCRA § 201's Definition of "Electioneering Communications"

The first section of Title II, § 201, comprehensively amends FECA § 304, which requires political committees to file detailed periodic financial reports with the FEC. The amendment coins a new term, "electioneering communications," to replace the narrowing construction of FECA's disclosure provisions adopted by this Court in *Buckley*. As discussed further below, that construction limited the coverage of FECA's disclosure requirement to communications expressly advocating the election or defeat of particular candidates. By contrast, the term "electioneering communication" is not so limited, but is defined to encompass any "broadcast, cable, or satellite communication" that

> "(I) refers to a clearly identified candidate for Federal office;
>
> "(II) is made within—
>
> "(aa) 60 days before a general, special, or runoff election for the office sought by the candidate; or
>
> "(bb) 30 days before a primary or preference election, or a convention or caucus of a political party that has authority to nominate a candidate, for the office sought by the candidate; and
>
> "(III) in the case of a communication which refers to a candidate for an office other than President or Vice President, is targeted to the relevant electorate."

New FECA § 304(f)(3)(C) further provides that a communication is " 'targeted to the relevant electorate' " if it "can be received by 50,000 or more persons" in the district or State the candidate seeks to represent.

In addition to setting forth this definition, BCRA's amendments to FECA § 304 specify significant disclosure requirements for persons who fund electioneering communications. BCRA's use of this new term is not, however, limited to the disclosure context: A later section of the Act (BCRA § 203, which amends FECA § 316(b)(2)) restricts corporations' and labor unions' funding of electioneering communications. Plaintiffs challenge the constitutionality of the new term as it applies in both the disclosure and the expenditure contexts.

The major premise of plaintiffs' challenge to BCRA's use of the term "electioneering communication" is that *Buckley* drew a constitutionally mandated line between express advocacy and so-called issue advocacy, and that speakers possess an inviolable First Amendment right to engage in the latter category of speech. Thus, plaintiffs maintain, Congress cannot constitutionally require disclosure of, or regulate expenditures for, "electioneering communications" without making an exception for those "communications" that do not meet *Buckley*'s definition of express advocacy.

That position misapprehends our prior decisions, for the express advocacy restriction was an endpoint of statutory interpretation, not a first principle of constitutional law. In *Buckley* we began by examining then-18 U.S.C. § 608(e)(1) (1970 ed., Supp. IV), which restricted expenditures " 'relative to a clearly identified candidate,' " and we found that the phrase " 'relative to' " was impermissibly vague. We concluded that the vagueness deficiencies could "be avoided only by reading § 608(e)(1) as limited to communications that include explicit words of advocacy of election or defeat of a candidate." We provided examples of words of express advocacy, such as " 'vote for,' 'elect,' 'support,' . . . 'defeat,' [and] 'reject,' " and those examples eventually gave rise to what is now known as the "magic words" requirement.

We then considered FECA's disclosure provisions, including 2 U.S.C. § 431(f) (1970 ed., Supp. IV), which defined " 'expenditur[e]' " to include the use of money or other assets " 'for the purpose of . . . influencing' " a federal election. Finding that the "ambiguity of this phrase" posed "constitutional problems," we noted our "obligation to construe the statute, if that can be done consistent with the legislature's purpose, to avoid the shoals of vagueness." To insure that the reach" of the disclosure requirement was "not impermissibly broad, we construe[d] 'expenditure' for purposes of that section in the same way we construed the terms of § 608(e)—to reach only funds used for communications that expressly advocate the election or defeat of a clearly identified candidate."

Thus, a plain reading of *Buckley* makes clear that the express advocacy limitation, in both the expenditure and the disclosure contexts, was the product of statutory interpretation rather than a constitutional command. In narrowly reading the FECA provisions in *Buckley* to avoid problems of vagueness and overbreadth, we nowhere suggested that a statute that was neither vague nor overbroad would be required to toe the same express advocacy line.

In short, the concept of express advocacy and the concomitant class of magic words were born of an effort to avoid constitutional infirmities. We have long " 'rigidly adhered' " to the tenet " 'never to formulate a rule of constitutional law broader than is required by the precise facts to which it is to be applied.' " Consistent with that principle, our decisions in *Buckley* and [*FEC v. Massachusetts Citizens For Life, Inc.*, 479 U.S. 238 (1986) (*MCFL*)] were specific to the statutory language before us; they in no way drew a constitutional boundary that forever fixed the permissible scope of provisions regulating campaign-related speech.

Nor are we persuaded, independent of our precedents, that the First Amendment erects a rigid barrier between express advocacy and so-called issue advocacy. That notion cannot be squared with our longstanding recognition that the presence or absence of magic words cannot meaningfully distinguish electioneering speech from a true issue ad. Indeed, the unmistakable lesson from the record in this litigation, as all three judges on the District Court agreed, is that *Buckley*'s magic-words requirement is functionally meaningless. Not only can advertisers easily evade the line by eschewing the use of magic words, but they would seldom choose to use such words even if permitted. And although the resulting advertisements do not urge the viewer to vote for or against a candidate in so many words, they are no less clearly intended to influence the election. *Buckley*'s express advocacy line, in short, has not aided the legislative effort to combat real or apparent corruption, and Congress enacted BCRA to correct the flaws it found in the existing system.

Finally we observe that new FECA § 304(f)(3)'s definition of "electioneering communication" raises none of the vagueness concerns that drove our analysis in *Buckley*. The term "electioneering communication" applies only (1) to a broadcast (2) clearly identifying a candidate for federal office, (3) aired within a specific time period, and (4) targeted to an identified audience of at least 50,000 viewers or listeners. These components are both easily understood and objectively determinable. Thus, the constitutional objection that persuaded the Court in *Buckley* to limit FECA's reach to express advocacy is simply inapposite here.

For the foregoing reasons, we affirm the District Court's judgment finding the plaintiffs' challenges to BCRA § 305, § 307, and the millionaire provisions nonjusticiable, striking down as unconstitutional BCRA § 318, and upholding BCRA § 311. The judgment of the District Court is *Affirmed.*

JUSTICE SCALIA, concurring with respect to BCRA Titles III and IV, dissenting with respect to BCRA Titles I and V, and concurring in the judgment in part and dissenting in part with respect to BCRA Title II.

This is a sad day for the freedom of speech. Who could have imagined that the same Court which, within the past four years, has sternly disapproved of restrictions upon such inconsequential forms of expression as virtual child pornography, tobacco advertising, dissemination of illegally intercepted communications, and sexually explicit cable programming would smile with favor upon a law that cuts to the heart of what the First Amendment is meant to protect: the right to criticize the government. For that is what the most offensive provisions of this legislation are all about. We are governed by Congress, and this legislation prohibits the criticism of Members of Congress by those entities most capable of giving such criticism loud voice: national political parties and corporations, both of the commercial and the not-for-profit sort. It forbids pre-election criticism of incumbents by corporations, even not-for-profit corporations, by use of their general funds; and forbids national-party use of "soft" money to fund "issue ads" that incumbents find so offensive.

To be sure, the legislation is evenhanded: It similarly prohibits criticism of the candidates who oppose Members of Congress in their reelection bids. But as everyone knows, this is an area in which evenhandedness is not fairness. If *all* electioneering were evenhandedly prohibited, incumbents would have an enormous advantage. Likewise, if incumbents and challengers are limited to the same quantity of electioneering, incumbents are favored. In other words, *any* restriction upon a type of campaign speech that is equally available to challengers and incumbents tends to favor incumbents.

Beyond that, however, the present legislation *targets* for prohibition certain categories of campaign speech that are particularly harmful to incumbents. Is it accidental, do you think, that incumbents raise about three times as much "hard money"—the sort of funding generally *not* restricted by this legislation—as do their challengers? Or that lobbyists (who seek the favor of incumbents) give 92 percent of their money in "hard" contributions? Is it an oversight, do you suppose, that the so-called "millionaire provisions" raise the contribution limit for a candidate running against an individual who devotes to the campaign (as challengers often do) great personal wealth, but do not raise the limit for a candidate running against an individual who devotes to the campaign (as incumbents often do) a massive election "war chest"? And is it mere happenstance, do you estimate, that national-party funding, which is severely limited by the Act, is more likely to assist cash-strapped challengers than flush-with-hard-money incumbents? Was it unintended, by any chance, that incumbents are free personally to receive some soft money and even to solicit it for other organizations, while national parties are not?

I wish to address three fallacious propositions that might be thought to justify some or all of the provisions of this legislation—only the last of which is explicitly embraced by the principal opinion for the Court, but all of which underlie, I think, its approach to these cases.

(a) Money is Not Speech

It was said by congressional proponents of this legislation, that since this legislation regulates nothing but the expenditure of money for speech, as opposed to speech itself, the burden it imposes is not subject to full First Amendment scrutiny; the government may regulate the raising and spending of campaign funds just as it regulates other forms of conduct, such as burning draft cards, or camping out on the National Mall. That proposition has been endorsed by one of the two authors of today's principal opinion: "The right to use one's own money to hire gladiators, [and] to fund 'speech by proxy,' . . . [are] property rights . . . not entitled to the same protection as the right to say what one pleases." Until today, however, that view has been categorically rejected by our jurisprudence. As we said in *Buckley,* "this Court has never suggested that the dependence of a communication on the expenditure of money operates itself to introduce a nonspeech element or to reduce the exacting scrutiny required by the First Amendment."

Our traditional view was correct, and today's cavalier attitude toward regulating the financing of speech (the "exacting scrutiny" test of *Buckley* is not uttered in any majority opinion, and is not observed in the ones from which I dissent) frustrates the fundamental purpose of the First Amendment. In any economy operated on even the most rudimentary principles of division of labor, effective public communication requires the speaker to make use of the services of others. An author may write a novel, but he will seldom publish and distribute it himself. A freelance reporter may write a story, but he will rarely edit, print, and deliver it to subscribers. To a government bent on suppressing speech, this mode of organization presents opportunities: Control any cog in the machine, and you can halt the whole apparatus. License printers, and it matters little whether authors are still free to write. Restrict the sale of books, and it matters little who prints them. Predictably, repressive regimes have exploited these principles by attacking all levels of the production and dissemination of ideas. In response to this threat, we have interpreted the First Amendment broadly.

Division of labor requires a means of mediating exchange, and in a commercial society, that means is supplied by money. The publisher pays the author for the right to sell his book; it pays its staff who print and assemble the book; it demands payments from booksellers who bring the book to market. This, too, presents opportunities for repression: Instead of regulating the various parties to the enterprise individually, the government can suppress their ability to coordinate by regulating their use of money. What good is the right to print books without a right to buy works from authors? Or the right to publish newspapers without the right to pay deliverymen? The right to speak would be largely ineffective if it did not include the right to engage in financial transactions that are the incidents of its exercise.

This is not to say that *any* regulation of money is a regulation of speech. The government may apply general commercial regulations to those who use money for speech if it applies them evenhandedly to those who use money for other purposes. But where the government singles out money used to fund speech as its legislative object, it is acting against speech as such, no less than if it had targeted the paper on which a book was printed or the trucks that deliver it to the bookstore.

History and jurisprudence bear this out. The best early examples derive from the British efforts to tax the press after the lapse of licensing statutes by which the press was first regulated. The Stamp Act of 1712 imposed levies on all newspapers, including an additional tax for each advertisement. It was a response to unfavorable war coverage, "obvious[ly] . . . designed to check the publication of those newspapers and pamphlets which depended for their sale on their cheapness and sensationalism." It succeeded in killing off approximately half the newspapers in England in its first year. In 1765, Parliament applied a similar Act to the Colonies. The colonial Act likewise placed exactions on sales and advertising revenue, the latter at 2s. per advertisement, which was "by any standard . . . excessive, since the publisher himself received only from 3 to 5s. and still less for repeated insertions." The founding generation saw these taxes as grievous incursions on the freedom of the press.

We have kept faith with the Founders' tradition by prohibiting the selective taxation of the press. And we have done so whether the tax was the product of illicit motive or not. These press-taxation cases belie the claim that regulation of money used to fund speech is not regulation of speech itself. A tax on a newspaper's advertising revenue does not prohibit anyone from saying anything; it merely appropriates part of the revenue that a speaker would otherwise obtain. That is even a step short of totally prohibiting advertising revenue—

which would be analogous to the total prohibition of certain campaign-speech contributions in the present cases. Yet it is unquestionably a violation of the First Amendment.

Many other cases exemplify the same principle that an attack upon the funding of speech is an attack upon speech itself. In *Schaumburg v. Citizens for a Better Environment,* 444 U.S. 620 (1980), we struck down an ordinance limiting the amount charities could pay their solicitors. In *Simon & Schuster, Inc. v. Members of N.Y. State Crime Victims Bd.*, 502 U.S. 105 (1991), we held unconstitutional a state statute that appropriated the proceeds of criminals' biographies for payment to the victims. And in *Rosenberger v. Rector and Visitors of Univ. of Va.,* 515 U.S. 819 (1995), we held unconstitutional a university's discrimination in the disbursement of funds to speakers on the basis of viewpoint. Most notable, perhaps, is our famous opinion in *New York Times Co. v. Sullivan,* 376 U.S. 254 (1964), holding that paid advertisements in a newspaper were entitled to full First Amendment protection.

It should be obvious, then, that a law limiting the amount a person can spend to broadcast his political views is a direct restriction on speech. That is no different from a law limiting the amount a newspaper can pay its editorial staff or the amount a charity can pay its leafletters. It is equally clear that a limit on the amount a candidate can *raise* from any one individual for the purpose of speaking is also a direct limitation on speech. That is no different from a law limiting the amount a publisher can accept from any one shareholder or lender, or the amount a newspaper can charge any one advertiser or customer.

MCCONNELL V. FEDERAL ELECTION COMMISSION RULING ON BCRA

BCRA Provision	***McConnell v. FEC* decision**
§ 323 (a) National Ban on Soft Money	Upheld under *Buckley v. Valeo* standard for contributions that restrictions are permitted to address corruption or its appearance both in terms of *quid pro quo* and the broader sense of influence on officerholder's judgment under *Colorado Republican II.* *Nixon v. Shrink Missouri* governs the evidentiary burden to be met. Overbreadth arguments rejected.
§323 (b) State and Local Party Soft Money Ban	Upheld under *Buckley*
"FEDERAL ELECTION ACTIVITY" definition	Upheld
§323 (b) (2) Levin exception to the soft money ban	Upheld under *Buckley* and *Colorado II* (not every restriction on parties is unconstitutional)
§323 (c) Fundraising costs	Upheld
§323 (d) Ban on national, state, and local party committees soliciting for nonprofits	Upheld as a valid anticircumventure measure
§323 (e) Ban on federal officeholders candidates from soliciting soft money	Upheld as a valid anticircumventure measure
§323 (f) Ban on state/local officeholders candidates from soliciting soft money to influence federal elections.	Upheld as a valid anticircumventure measure

§201 Express and Issue Advocacy "ELECTIONEERING COMMUNICATION" definition	Upheld as a reasonable modification of the *Buckley* "magic words" distinctions between express and issue advocacy
§304 (f) (5) Disclosure of executory contracts	Upheld under *Buckley* standards for disclosure as necessary to: 1) informing the electorate; 2) deterring actual corruption or its appearance; and 3) gather information to enforce other provisions of the law
§202 Coordination between candidate or party	Upheld under *Buckley* and permissible for Congress to regulate
§203 Ban on corporate/union treasury funds for electioneering communication	Upheld under *F.E.C. v. Beaumont*
§212 Mandatory individual disclosure for independent expenditures	Court says it is moot since §201 was upheld
§213 Parties to chose between independent and coordinated expenditures	Unconstitutional under *Buckley*
§311 Candidate authorization of political communications	Upheld
§318 Ban political contributions from minors	Unconstitutional under *Tinker v. Des Moines Independent Community School District*

FOR DISCUSSION

Does the *McConnell* opinion suggest that the Court is prepared to accept all form of limits on contributions? Is *Buckley* still viable as precedent? How can the disclosure requirements in this case be reconciled with *McIntyre*?

RELATED CASE

***Federal Election Commission v. Wisconsin Right to Life Committee:* 551 U.S. (2007).**

The Court ruled that, as applied, the one-month ban on political ads or communication prior to an election violated the First Amendment. This decision effectively reinstated the express and issue advocacy distinction found in *Buckley*.

RANDALL V. SORRELL

548 U.S. 230, 126 S.Ct. 2479, 165 L.Ed.2d 482 (2006)

Vermont imposed both expenditure limits on campaigns and contribution limits to state candidates. The limits for the latter were as low as $200. The expenditure limits were determined by the office a candidate was running for. Both the contribution and expenditure limits were challenged as unconstitutional. The Second Circuit upheld the law, ruling, among other things, that the state had a compelling interest in limiting the amount of time that candidates could spend raising money.

Vote: 6–3

JUSTICE BREYER announced the judgment of the Court and delivered an opinion, in which CHIEF JUSTICE ROBERTS joined, and in which JUSTICE ALITO joined as to all but Parts II–B–1 and II–B–2.

We here consider the constitutionality of a Vermont campaign finance statute that limits both (1) the amounts that candidates for state office may spend on their campaigns (expenditure limitations) and (2) the amounts that individuals, organizations, and political parties may contribute to those campaigns (contribution limitations). We hold that both sets of limitations are inconsistent with the First Amendment. Well-established precedent makes clear that the expenditure limits violate the First Amendment. The contribution limits are unconstitutional because in their specific details (involving low maximum levels and other restrictions) they fail to satisfy the First Amendment's requirement of careful tailoring. That is to say, they impose burdens upon First Amendment interests that (when viewed in light of the statute's legitimate objectives) are disproportionately severe.

I

A

Prior to 1997, Vermont's campaign finance law imposed no limit upon the amount a candidate for state office could spend. It did, however, impose limits upon the amounts that individuals, corporations, and political committees could contribute to the campaign of such a candidate. Individuals and corporations could contribute no more than $1,000 to any candidate for state office. Political committees, excluding political parties, could contribute no more than $3,000. The statute imposed no limit on the amount that political parties could contribute to candidates.

In 1997, Vermont enacted a more stringent campaign finance law, Pub. Act No. 64, codified at Vt. Stat. Ann., Tit. 17, § 2801 *et seq.* (2002) (hereinafter Act or Act 64), the statute at issue here. Act 64, which took effect immediately after the 1998 elections, imposes mandatory expenditure limits on the total amount a candidate for state office can spend during a "two-year general election cycle," *i.e.,* the primary plus the general election, in approximately the following amounts: governor, $300,000; lieutenant governor, $100,000; other statewide offices, $45,000; state senator, $4,000 (plus an additional $2,500 for each additional seat in the district); state representative (two-member district), $3,000; and state representative (single member district), $2,000. These limits are adjusted for inflation in odd-numbered years based on the Consumer Price Index. Incumbents seeking reelection to statewide office may spend no more than 85% of the above amounts, and incumbents seeking reelection to the State Senate or House may spend no more than 90% of the above amounts. The Act defines "[e]xpenditure" broadly to mean the

> payment, disbursement, distribution, advance, deposit, loan or gift of money or anything of value, paid or promised to be paid, for the purpose of influencing an election, advocating a position on a public question, or supporting or opposing one or more candidates.

With certain minor exceptions, expenditures over $50 made on a candidate's behalf by others count against the candidate's expenditure limit if those expenditures are "intentionally facilitated by, solicited by or approved by" the candidate's campaign. These provisions apply so as to count against a campaign's expenditure limit any spending by political parties or committees that is coordinated with the campaign and benefits the candidate. And any party expenditure that "primarily benefits six or fewer candidates who are associated with the political party" is "presumed" to be coordinated with the campaign and therefore to count against the campaign's expenditure limit.

Act 64 also imposes strict contribution limits. The amount any single individual can contribute to the campaign of a candidate for state office during a "two-year general election cycle" is limited as follows: governor, lieutenant governor, and other statewide offices, $400; state senator, $300; and state representative, $200. Unlike its expenditure limits, Act 64's contribution limits are not indexed for inflation.

B

The petitioners are individuals who have run for state office in Vermont, citizens who vote in Vermont elections and contribute to Vermont campaigns, and political parties and committees that participate in Vermont politics. Soon after Act 64 became law, they brought this lawsuit in Federal District Court against the respondents, state officials charged with enforcement of the Act. Several other private groups and individual citizens intervened in the District Court proceedings in support of the Act and are joined here as respondents as well.

The District Court agreed with the petitioners that the Act's expenditure limits violate the First Amendment. The court also held unconstitutional the Act's limits on the contributions of political parties to candidates. At the same time, the court found the Act's other contribution limits constitutional. *Landell v. Sorrell,* 118 F.Supp.2d 459 (Vt.2000).

Both sides appealed. A divided panel of the Court of Appeals for the Second Circuit held that *all* of the Act's contribution limits are constitutional. It also held that the Act's expenditure limits may be constitutional. It found those limits supported by two compelling interests, namely, an interest in preventing corruption or the appearance of corruption and an interest in limiting the amount of time state officials must spend raising campaign funds. The Circuit then remanded the case to the District Court with instructions to determine whether the Act's expenditure limits were narrowly tailored to those interests.

The petitioners and respondents all sought certiorari. They asked us to consider the constitutionality of Act 64's expenditure limits, its contribution limits, and a related definitional provision. We agreed to do so.

II

We turn first to the Act's expenditure limits. Do those limits violate the First Amendment's free speech guarantees?

A

In *Buckley v. Valeo,* 424 U.S. 1 (1976), the Court considered the constitutionality of the Federal Election Campaign Act of 1971 (FECA), a statute that, much like the Act before us, imposed both expenditure and contribution limitations on campaigns for public office. The Court, while upholding FECA's contribution limitations as constitutional, held that the statute's expenditure limitations violated the First Amendment.

Buckley stated that both kinds of limitations "implicate fundamental First Amendment interests." It noted that the Government had sought to justify the statute's infringement on those interests in terms of the need to prevent "corruption and the appearance of corruption." In the Court's view, this rationale provided sufficient justification for the statute's contribution limitations, but it did not provide sufficient justification for the expenditure limitations.

The Court explained that the basic reason for this difference between the two kinds of limitations is that expenditure limitations "impose significantly more severe restrictions on protected freedoms of political expression and association than" do contribution limitations. Contribution limitations, though a "marginal restriction upon the contributor's ability to engage in free communication," nevertheless leave the contributor "fre[e] to discuss candidates and issues." Expenditure limitations, by contrast, impose "[a] restriction on the amount of money a person or group can spend on political communication during a campaign." They thereby necessarily "reduc[e] the quantity of expression by restricting the number of issues discussed, the depth of their exploration, and the size of the audience reached." Indeed, the freedom "to engage in unlimited political expression subject to a ceiling on expenditures is like being free to drive an automobile as far and as often as one desires on a single tank of gasoline."

The Court concluded that "[n]o governmental interest that has been suggested is sufficient to justify the restriction on the quantity of political expression imposed by" the statute's expenditure limitations. It decided that the Government's primary justification for expenditure limitations, preventing corruption and its appearance, was adequately addressed by the Act's contribution limitations and disclosure requirements. The Court also considered other governmental interests advanced in support of expenditure limitations. It rejected each. Consequently, it held that the expenditure limitations were "constitutionally invalid."

Over the last 30 years, in considering the constitutionality of a host of different campaign finance statutes, this Court has repeatedly adhered to *Buckley's* constraints, including those on expenditure limits.

B

1

The respondents recognize that, in respect to expenditure limits, *Buckley* appears to be a controlling—and unfavorable—precedent. They seek to overcome that precedent in two ways. First, they ask us in effect to overrule *Buckley*. Post-*Buckley* experience, they believe, has shown that contribution limits (and disclosure requirements) alone cannot effectively deter corruption or its appearance; hence experience has undermined an assumption underlying that case. Indeed, the respondents have devoted several pages of their briefs to attacking *Buckley*'s holding on expenditure limits. Second, in the alternative, they ask us to limit the scope of *Buckley* significantly by distinguishing *Buckley* from the present case. They advance as a ground for distinction a justification for expenditure limitations that, they say, *Buckley* did not consider, namely that such limits help to protect candidates from spending too much time raising money rather than devoting that time to campaigning among ordinary voters. We find neither argument persuasive.

2

The Court has often recognized the "fundamental importance" of *stare decisis,* the basic legal principle that commands judicial respect for a court's earlier decisions and the rules of law they embody. The Court has pointed out that *stare decisis* " 'promotes the evenhanded, predictable, and consistent development of legal principles, fosters reliance on judicial decisions, and contributes to the actual and perceived integrity of the judicial process.' " *Stare decisis* thereby avoids the instability and unfairness that accompany disruption of settled legal expectations. For this reason, the rule of law demands that adhering to our prior case law be the norm. Departure from precedent is exceptional, and requires "special justification." This is especially true where, as here, the principle has become settled through iteration and reiteration over a long period of time.

We can find here no such special justification that would require us to overrule *Buckley*. Subsequent case law has not made *Buckley* a legal anomaly or otherwise undermined its basic legal principles. We cannot find in the respondents' claims any demonstration that circumstances have changed so radically as to undermine *Buckley*'s critical factual assumptions. The respondents have not shown, for example, any dramatic increase in corruption or its appearance in Vermont; nor have they shown that expenditure limits are the only way to attack that problem. At the same time, *Buckley* has promoted considerable reliance. Congress and state legislatures have used *Buckley* when drafting campaign finance laws. And, as we have said, this Court has followed *Buckley,* upholding and applying its reasoning in latter cases. Overruling *Buckley* now would dramatically undermine this reliance on our settled precedent.

For all these reasons, we find this a case that fits the *stare decisis* norm. And we do not perceive the strong justification that would be necessary to warrant overruling so well established a precedent. We consequently decline the respondents' invitation to reconsider *Buckley*.

III

We turn now to a more complex question, namely the constitutionality of Act 64's contribution limits. The parties, while accepting *Buckley*'s approach, dispute whether, despite *Buckley*'s general approval of statutes that limit campaign contributions, Act 64's contribution limits are so severe that in the circumstances its particular limits violate the First Amendment.

A

As with the Act's expenditure limits, we begin with *Buckley*. In that case, the Court upheld the $1,000 contribution limit before it. *Buckley* recognized that contribution limits, like expenditure limits, "implicate fundamental First Amendment interests," namely, the freedoms of "political expression" and "political association." But, unlike expenditure limits (which "necessarily reduc[e] the quantity of expression by restricting the number of issues discussed, the depth of their exploration, and the size of the audience reached,") contribution limits "involv[e] little direct restraint on" the contributor's speech. They do restrict "one aspect of the contributor's freedom of political association," namely, the contributor's ability to support a favored candidate, but they nonetheless "permi[t] the symbolic expression of support evidenced by a contribution," and they do "not in any way infringe the contributor's freedom to discuss candidates and issues."

Since *Buckley*, the Court has consistently upheld contribution limits in other statutes. The Court has recognized, however, that contribution limits might *sometimes* work more harm to protected First Amendment interests than their anticorruption objectives could justify. And individual Members of the Court have expressed concern lest too low a limit magnify the "reputation-related or media-related advantages of incumbency and thereby insulat[e] legislators from effective electoral challenge."

B

Following *Buckley*, we must determine whether Act 64's contribution limits prevent candidates from "amassing the resources necessary for effective [campaign] advocacy," whether they magnify the advantages of incumbency to the point where they put challengers to a significant disadvantage; in a word, whether they are too low and too strict to survive First Amendment scrutiny. In answering these questions, we recognize, as *Buckley* stated, that we have "no scalpel to probe" each possible contribution level. We cannot determine with any degree of exactitude the precise restriction necessary to carry out the statute's legitimate objectives. In practice, the legislature is better equipped to make such empirical judgments, as legislators have "particular expertise" in matters related to the costs and nature of running for office. Thus ordinarily we have deferred to the legislature's determination of such matters.

Nonetheless, as *Buckley* acknowledged, we must recognize the existence of some lower bound. At some point the constitutional risks to the democratic electoral process become too great. After all, the interests underlying contribution limits, preventing corruption and the appearance of corruption, "directly implicate the integrity of our electoral process."

We find those danger signs present here. As compared with the contribution limits upheld by the Court in the past, and with those in force in other States, Act 64's limits are sufficiently low as to generate suspicion that they are not closely drawn. The Act sets its limits per election cycle, which includes both a primary and a general election. Thus, in a gubernatorial race with both primary and final election contests, the Act's contribution limit amounts to $200 per election per candidate (with significantly lower limits for contributions to candidates for State Senate and House of Representatives.) These limits apply both to contributions from individuals and to contributions from political parties, whether made in cash or in expenditures coordinated (or presumed to be coordinated) with the candidate.

These limits are well below the limits this Court upheld in *Buckley*. Indeed, in terms of real dollars *(i.e.,* adjusting for inflation), the Act's $200 per election limit on individual contributions to a campaign for governor is slightly more than one-twentieth of the limit on contributions to campaigns for federal office before the Court in *Buckley*. Adjusted to reflect its value in 1976 (the year *Buckley* was decided), Vermont's contribution limit on campaigns for statewide office (including governor) amounts to $113.91 per 2-year election cycle, or roughly $57 per election, as compared to the $1,000 per election limit on individual contributions at issue in *Buckley*. (The adjusted value of Act 64's limit on contributions from political parties to candidates for statewide office, again $200 per candidate per election, is just over one one-hundredth of the comparable limit before the Court in *Buckley,* $5,000 per election.) Yet Vermont's gubernatorial district—the entire State—is no smaller than the House districts to which *Buckley*'s limits applied. In 1976, the average congressional district contained a population of about 465,000. Indeed, Vermont's population is 621,000—about one-third *larger*. Moreover, considered as a whole, Vermont's contribution limits are the lowest in the Nation. Act 64 limits contributions to candidates for statewide office (including governor) to $200 per candidate per election. We have found no State that imposes a lower per election limit. Indeed, we have found only seven States that impose limits on contributions to candidates for statewide office at or below $500 per election, more than twice Act 64's limit

Finally, Vermont's limit is well below the lowest limit this Court has previously upheld, the limit of $1,075 per election (adjusted for inflation every two years) for candidates for Missouri state auditor. The comparable Vermont limit of roughly $200 per election, not adjusted for inflation, is less than one-sixth of Missouri's current inflation-adjusted limit ($1,275).

In sum, Act 64's contribution limits are substantially lower than both the limits we have previously upheld and comparable limits in other States. These are danger signs that Act 64's contribution limits may fall outside tolerable First Amendment limits. We consequently must examine the record independently and carefully to determine whether Act 64's contribution limits are "closely drawn" to match the State's interests.

C

Our examination of the record convinces us that, from a constitutional perspective, Act 64's contribution limits are too restrictive. We reach this conclusion based not merely on the low dollar amounts of the limits themselves, but also on the statute's effect on political parties and on volunteer activity in Vermont elections. *Taken together*, Act 64's substantial restrictions on the ability of candidates to raise the funds necessary to run a competitive election, on the ability of political parties to help their candidates get elected, and on the ability of individual citizens to volunteer their time to campaigns show that the Act is not closely drawn to meet its objectives. In particular, five factors together lead us to this decision.

First, the record suggests, though it does not conclusively prove, that Act 64's contribution limits will significantly restrict the amount of funding available for challengers to run competitive campaigns.

For another thing, the petitioners' expert witnesses produced evidence and analysis showing that Vermont political parties (particularly the Republican Party) "target" their contributions to candidates in competitive races, that those contributions represent a significant amount of total candidate funding in such races, and that the contribution limits will cut the parties' contributions to competitive races dramatically.

Second, Act 64's insistence that political parties abide by *exactly* the same low contribution limits that apply to other contributors threatens harm to a particularly important political right, the right to associate in a political party

Third, the Act's treatment of volunteer services aggravates the problem. Like its federal statutory counterpart, the Act excludes from its definition of "contribution" all "services provided without compensation by individuals volunteering their time on behalf of a candidate."

The absence of some such exception may matter in the present context, where contribution limits are very low. That combination, low limits and no exceptions, means that a gubernatorial campaign volunteer who makes four or five round trips driving across the State performing volunteer activities coordinated with the campaign can find that he or she is near, or has surpassed, the contribution limit.

Fourth, unlike the contribution limits we upheld in *Shrink*, Act 64's contribution limits are not adjusted for inflation. Its limits decline in real value each year.

Fifth, we have found nowhere in the record any special justification that might warrant a contribution limit so low or so restrictive as to bring about the serious associational and expressive problems that we have described.

JUSTICE THOMAS, with whom Justice Scalia joins, concurring in the judgment.

Although I agree with the plurality that Vt. Stat. Ann., Tit. 17, § 2801 *et seq.* (2002)(Act 64), is unconstitutional, I disagree with its rationale for striking down that statute. Invoking *stare decisis,* the plurality rejects the invitation to overrule *Buckley v. Valeo*. It then applies *Buckley* to invalidate the expenditure limitations and, less persuasively, the contribution limitations. I continue to believe that *Buckley* provides insufficient protection to political speech, the core of the First Amendment. The illegitimacy of *Buckley* is further underscored by the continuing inability of the Court (and the plurality here) to apply *Buckley* in a coherent and principled fashion. As a result, *stare decisis* should pose no bar to overruling *Buckley* and replacing it with a standard faithful to the First Amendment. Accordingly, I concur only in the judgment.

JUSTICE STEVENS, dissenting.

Justice Breyer and Justice Souter debate whether the *per curiam* decision in *Buckley v. Valeo* forecloses any constitutional limitations on candidate expenditures. This is plainly an issue on which reasonable minds can disagree. The *Buckley* Court never explicitly addressed whether the pernicious effects of endless fundraising can serve as a compelling state interest that justifies expenditure limits, yet its silence, in light of the record before it, suggests that it implicitly treated this proposed interest insufficient. Assuming this to be true, however, I am convinced that *Buckley*'s holding on expenditure limits is wrong, and that the time has come to overrule it.

To begin with, *Buckley*'s holding on expenditure limits itself upset a long-established practice. For the preceding 65 years, congressional races had been subject to statutory limits on both expenditures and contributions. See 37 Stat. 28; Federal Corrupt Practices Act of 1925, 43 Stat. 1073; Federal Election Campaign Finance Act of 1971, 86 Stat. 5; Federal Election Campaign Act Amendments of 1974, 88 Stat. 1263; *United States v. Automobile Workers*, 352 U.S. 567 (1957); *McConnell v. Federal Election Comm'n*, 540 U.S. 93 (2003). As the Court of Appeals had recognized in *Buckley v. Valeo,* our earlier jurisprudence provided solid support for treating these limits as permissible regulations of conduct rather than speech. While *Buckley*'s holding on contribution limits was consistent with this backdrop, its holding on expenditure limits "involve[d] collision with a prior doctrine more embracing in its scope, intrinsically sounder, and verified by experience."

FOR DISCUSSION

How does the Court apply *Buckley* in *Sorrell*? Does it overrule it or modify it in any way? What is the status of contribution and expenditure limits after this case? Are limits on the latter essentially unconstitutional? How low can contribution limits be set before they are considered unconstitutional?

CITIZENS UNITED V. FEDERAL ELECTION COMMISSION

558 U.S. 310, 130 S.Ct. 876, 175 L.Ed. 2d. 753 (2010)

Citizens United was a non-profit company that sought to promote a documentary/movie entitled Hillary. The movie was critical of Senator Hillary Clinton and her 2008 presidential campaign. To promote the documentary Citizens United wanted to produce and air brief ads indicating it was available on video-on-demand. Because of concern that these ads would be in violation of BCRA, Citizens United challenged applicability of one section of the Act addressing electioneering communications. Citizens United lost in lower court and after an initial hearing before the Supreme Court, parties were asked to brief arguments regarding its constitutionality. This decision occurred after the second hearing. The facts in the case are described in more detail by Justice Kennedy.

Vote 5–4

KENNEDY, J., delivered the opinion of the Court, in which ROBERTS., and SCALIA and ALITO, joined, in which THOMAS joined as to all but Part IV, and in which STEVENS, GINSBURG, BREYER, and SOTOMAYOR, joined as to Part IV.

JUSTICE KENNEDY delivered the opinion of the Court.

Federal law prohibits corporations and unions from using their general treasury funds to make independent expenditures for speech defined as an "electioneering communication" or for speech expressly advocating the election or defeat of a candidate. 2 U.S.C. § 441b. Limits on electioneering communications were upheld in *McConnell v. Federal Election Comm'n,* 540 U.S. 93 (2003). The holding of *McConnell* rested to a large extent on an earlier case, *Austin v. Michigan Chamber of Commerce. Austin* had held that political speech may be banned based on the speaker's corporate identity.

In this case we are asked to reconsider *Austin* and, in effect, *McConnell.* We agree with that conclusion and hold that *stare decisis* does not compel the continued acceptance of *Austin.* The Government may regulate corporate political speech through disclaimer and disclosure requirements, but it may not suppress that speech altogether. We turn to the case now before us.

I

A

Citizens United is a nonprofit corporation. It brought this action in the United States District Court for the District of Columbia. A three-judge court later convened to hear the cause. The resulting judgment gives rise to this appeal.

Citizens United has an annual budget of about $12 million. Most of its funds are from donations by individuals; but, in addition, it accepts a small portion of its funds from for-profit corporations.

In January 2008, Citizens United released a film entitled *Hillary: The Movie.* We refer to the film as *Hillary.* It is a 90-minute documentary about then-Senator Hillary Clinton, who was a candidate in the Democratic Party's 2008 Presidential primary elections. *Hillary* mentions Senator Clinton by name and depicts interviews with political commentators and other persons, most of them quite critical of Senator Clinton. *Hillary* was released in theaters and on DVD, but Citizens United wanted to increase distribution by making it available through video-on-demand.

To implement the proposal, Citizens United was prepared to pay for the video-on-demand; and to promote the film, it produced two 10-second ads and one 30-second ad for *Hillary.* Each ad includes a short (and, in our view, pejorative) statement about Senator Clinton, followed by the name of the movie and the movie's Website address. Citizens United desired to promote the video-on-demand offering by running advertisements on broadcast and cable television.

B

Before the Bipartisan Campaign Reform Act of 2002 (BCRA), federal law prohibited-and still does prohibit-corporations and unions from using general treasury funds to make direct contributions to candidates or independent expenditures that expressly advocate the election or defeat of a candidate, through any form of media, in connection with certain qualified federal elections.

C

Citizens United wanted to make *Hillary* available through video-on-demand within 30 days of the 2008 primary elections. It feared, however, that both the film and the ads would be covered by § 441b's ban on corporate-funded independent expenditures, thus subjecting the corporation to civil and criminal penalties under § 437g. In December 2007, Citizens United sought declaratory and injunctive relief against the FEC. It argued that (1) § 441b is unconstitutional as applied to *Hillary;* and (2) BCRA's disclaimer and disclosure requirements, BCRA §§ 201 and 311, are unconstitutional as applied to *Hillary* and to the three ads for the movie.

II

Before considering whether *Austin* should be overruled, we first address whether Citizens United's claim that § 441b cannot be applied to *Hillary* may be resolved on other, narrower grounds.

A

Citizens United contends that § 441b does not cover *Hillary,* as a matter of statutory interpretation, because the film does not qualify as an "electioneering communication."

B

Citizens United next argues that § 441b may not be applied to *Hillary* under the approach taken in *WRTL*. *McConnell* decided that § 441b(b)(2)'s definition of an "electioneering communication" was facially constitutional insofar as it restricted speech that was "the functional equivalent of express advocacy" for or against a specific candidate. 540 U.S., at 206, 124 S.Ct. 619. *WRTL* then found an unconstitutional application of § 441b where the speech was not "express advocacy or its functional equivalent." As explained by THE CHIEF JUSTICE's controlling opinion in *WRTL*, the functional-equivalent test is objective: "a court should find that [a communication] is the functional equivalent of express advocacy only if [it] is susceptible of no reasonable interpretation other than as an appeal to vote for or against a specific candidate."

Under this test, *Hillary* is equivalent to express advocacy. The movie, in essence, is a feature-length negative advertisement that urges viewers to vote against Senator Clinton for President. In light of historical footage, interviews with persons critical of her, and voiceover narration, the film would be understood by most viewers as an extended criticism of Senator Clinton's character and her fitness for the office of the Presidency. The narrative may contain more suggestions and arguments than facts, but there is little doubt that the thesis of the film is that she is unfit for the Presidency. The movie concentrates on alleged wrongdoing during the Clinton administration, Senator Clinton's qualifications and fitness for office, and policies the commentators predict she would pursue if elected President. It calls Senator Clinton "Machiavellian," and asks whether she is "the most qualified to hit the ground running if elected President,". The narrator reminds viewers that "Americans have never been keen on dynasties" and that "a vote for Hillary is a vote to continue 20 years of a Bush or a Clinton in the White House,"

Citizens United argues that *Hillary* is just "a documentary film that examines certain historical events." We disagree. The movie's consistent emphasis is on the relevance of these events to Senator Clinton's candidacy for President. The narrator begins by asking "could [Senator Clinton] become the first female President in the history of the United States?" And the narrator reiterates the movie's message in his closing line: "Finally, before America decides on our next president, voters should need no reminders of . . . what's at stake-the well being and prosperity of our nation."

As the District Court found, there is no reasonable interpretation of *Hillary* other than as an appeal to vote against Senator Clinton. Under the standard stated in *McConnell* and further elaborated in *WRTL*, the film qualifies as the functional equivalent of express advocacy.

C

Citizens United further contends that § 441b should be invalidated as applied to movies shown through video-on-demand, arguing that this delivery system has a lower risk of distorting the political process than do television ads. On what we might call conventional television, advertising spots reach viewers who have chosen a channel or a program for reasons unrelated to the advertising. With video-on-demand, by contrast, the viewer selects a program after taking "a series of affirmative steps": subscribing to cable; navigating through various menus; and selecting the program.

While some means of communication may be less effective than others at influencing the public in different contexts, any effort by the Judiciary to decide which means of communications are to be preferred for the particular type of message and speaker would raise questions as to the courts' own lawful authority. Substantial questions would arise if courts were to begin saying what means of speech should be preferred or disfavored. And in all events, those differentiations might soon prove to be irrelevant or outdated by technologies that are in rapid flux.

Courts, too, are bound by the First Amendment. We must decline to draw, and then redraw, constitutional lines based on the particular media or technology used to disseminate political speech from a particular speaker. It must be noted, moreover, that this undertaking would require substantial litigation over an extended time, all to interpret a law that beyond doubt discloses serious First Amendment flaws. The interpretive process itself would create an inevitable, pervasive, and serious risk of chilling protected speech pending the drawing of fine distinctions that, in the end, would themselves be questionable. First Amendment standards, however, "must give the benefit of any doubt to protecting rather than stifling speech."

D

Though it is true that the Court should construe statutes as necessary to avoid constitutional questions, the series of steps suggested would be difficult to take in view of the language of the statute. In addition to those difficulties the Government's suggestion is troubling for still another reason. The Government does not say that it agrees with the interpretation it wants us to consider. Presumably it would find textual difficulties in this approach too. The Government, like any party, can make arguments in the alternative; but it ought to say if there is merit to an alternative proposal instead of merely suggesting it. This is especially true in the context of the First Amendment. As the Government stated, this case "would require a remand" to apply a *de minimis* standard. Applying this standard would thus require case-by-case determinations. But archetypical political speech would be chilled in the meantime. " 'First Amendment freedoms need breathing space to survive.' " We decline to adopt an interpretation that requires intricate case-by-case determinations to verify whether political speech is banned, especially if we are convinced that, in the end, this corporation has a constitutional right to speak on this subject.

E

As the foregoing analysis confirms, the Court cannot resolve this case on a narrower ground without chilling political speech, speech that is central to the meaning and purpose of the First Amendment. It is not judicial restraint to accept an unsound, narrow argument just so the Court can avoid another argument with broader implications. Indeed, a court would be remiss in performing its duties were it to accept an unsound principle merely to avoid the necessity of making a broader ruling. Here, the lack of a valid basis for an alternative ruling requires full consideration of the continuing effect of the speech suppression upheld in *Austin.*

When the statute now at issue came before the Court in *McConnell,* both the majority and the dissenting opinions considered the question of its facial validity. The holding and validity of *Austin* were essential to the reasoning of the *McConnell* majority opinion, which upheld BCRA's extension of § 441b. *McConnell* permitted federal felony punishment for speech by all corporations, including nonprofit ones, that speak on prohibited subjects shortly before federal elections. Four Members of the *McConnell* Court would have overruled *Austin,* including Chief Justice Rehnquist, who had joined the Court's opinion in *Austin* but reconsidered that conclusion.

The *McConnell* majority considered whether the statute was facially invalid. An as-applied challenge was brought in *Wisconsin Right to Life, Inc. v. Federal Election Comm'n,* and the Court confirmed that the challenge could be maintained. Then, in *WRTL*, the controlling opinion of the Court not only entertained an as-applied challenge but also sustained it. Three Justices noted that they would continue to maintain the position that the record in *McConnell* demonstrated the invalidity of the Act on its face. The controlling opinion in *WRTL*, which refrained from holding the statute invalid except as applied to the facts then before the Court, was a careful attempt to accept the essential elements of the Court's opinion in *McConnell,* while vindicating the First Amendment arguments made by the *WRTL* parties.

As noted above, Citizens United's narrower arguments are not sustainable under a fair reading of the statute. In the exercise of its judicial responsibility, it is necessary then for the Court to consider the facial validity of § 441b. Any other course of decision would prolong the substantial, nation-wide chilling effect caused by § 441b's prohibitions on corporate expenditures.

III

The First Amendment provides that "Congress shall make no law . . . abridging the freedom of speech." Laws enacted to control or suppress speech may operate at different points in the speech process. The following are just a few examples of restrictions that have been attempted at different stages of the speech process-all laws found to be invalid: restrictions requiring a permit at the outset, imposing a burden by impounding proceeds on receipts or royalties,; seeking to exact a cost after the speech occurs, and subjecting the speaker to criminal penalties.

The law before us is an outright ban, backed by criminal sanctions. Section 441b makes it a felony for all corporations-including nonprofit advocacy corporations-either to expressly advocate the election or defeat of candidates or to broadcast electioneering communications within 30 days of a primary election and 60 days of a general election. Thus, the following acts would all be felonies under § 441b: The Sierra Club runs an ad, within the crucial phase of 60 days before the general election, that exhorts the public to disapprove of a Congressman who favors logging in national forests; the National Rifle Association publishes a book urging the public to vote for the challenger because the incumbent U.S. Senator supports a handgun ban; and the American Civil Liberties Union creates a Web site telling the public to vote for a Presidential candidate in light of that candidate's defense of free speech. These prohibitions are classic examples of censorship.

Section 441b is a ban on corporate speech notwithstanding the fact that a PAC created by a corporation can still speak. A PAC is a separate association from the corporation. So the PAC exemption from § 441b's expenditure ban, § 441b(b)(2), does not allow corporations to speak. Even if a PAC could somehow allow a corporation to speak-and it does not-the option to form PACs does not alleviate the First Amendment problems with § 441b. PACs are burdensome alternatives; they are expensive to administer and subject to extensive regulations. For example, every PAC must appoint a treasurer, forward donations to the treasurer promptly, keep detailed records of the identities of the persons making donations, preserve receipts for three years, and file an organization statement and report changes to this information within 10 days.

PACs have to comply with these regulations just to speak. This might explain why fewer than 2,000 of the millions of corporations in this country have PACs. PACs, furthermore, must exist before they can speak. Given the onerous restrictions, a corporation may not be able to establish a PAC in time to make its views known regarding candidates and issues in a current campaign.

Section 441b's prohibition on corporate independent expenditures is thus a ban on speech. As a "restriction on the amount of money a person or group can spend on political communication during a campaign," that statute "necessarily reduces the quantity of expression by restricting the number of issues discussed, the depth of their exploration, and the size of the audience reached."

Speech is an essential mechanism of democracy, for it is the means to hold officials accountable to the people. The right of citizens to inquire, to hear, to speak, and to use information to reach consensus is a precondition to enlightened self-government and a necessary means to protect it.

For these reasons, political speech must prevail against laws that would suppress it, whether by design or inadvertence. Laws that burden political speech are "subject to strict scrutiny."

Quite apart from the purpose or effect of regulating content, moreover, the Government may commit a constitutional wrong when by law it identifies certain preferred speakers. By taking the right to speak from some and giving it to others, the Government deprives the disadvantaged person or class of the right to use speech to strive to establish worth, standing, and respect for the speaker's voice. The Government may not by these means deprive the public of the right and privilege to determine for itself what speech and speakers are worthy of consideration. The First Amendment protects speech and speaker, and the ideas that flow from each.

We find no basis for the proposition that, in the context of political speech, the Government may impose restrictions on certain disfavored speakers. Both history and logic lead us to this conclusion.

A

1

The Court has recognized that First Amendment protection extends to corporations.

This protection has been extended by explicit holdings to the context of political speech. Under the rationale of these precedents, political speech does not lose First Amendment protection "simply because its source is a corporation." The Court has thus rejected the argument that political speech of corporations or other associations should be treated differently under the First Amendment simply because such associations are not "natural persons."

At least since the later part of the 19th century, the laws of some States and of the United States imposed a ban on corporate direct contributions to candidates. Yet not until 1947 did Congress first prohibit independent expenditures by corporations and labor unions in § 304 of the Labor Management Relations Act 1947. For almost three decades thereafter, the Court did not reach the question whether restrictions on corporate and union expenditures are constitutional.

2

In *Buckley,* the Court addressed various challenges to the Federal Election Campaign Act of 1971 (FECA) as amended in 1974. These amendments created 18 U.S.C. § 608(e), an independent expenditure ban separate from § 610 that applied to individuals as well as corporations and labor unions.

Before addressing the constitutionality of § 608(e)'s independent expenditure ban, *Buckley* first upheld § 608(b), FECA's limits on direct contributions to candidates. The *Buckley* Court recognized a "sufficiently important" governmental interest in "the prevention of corruption and the appearance of corruption." This followed from the Court's concern that large contributions could be given "to secure a political *quid pro quo.*"

The *Buckley* Court explained that the potential for *quid pro quo* corruption distinguished direct contributions to candidates from independent expenditures. The Court emphasized that "the independent expenditure ceiling . . . fails to serve any substantial governmental interest in stemming the reality or appearance of corruption in the electoral process."

Notwithstanding this precedent, Congress recodified § 610's corporate and union expenditure ban at 2 U.S.C. § 441b four months after *Buckley* was decided. Section 441b is the independent expenditure restriction challenged here.

Less than two years after *Buckley, Bellotti,* reaffirmed the First Amendment principle that the Government cannot restrict political speech based on the speaker's corporate identity. *Bellotti* could not have been clearer when it struck down a state-law prohibition on corporate independent expenditures related to referenda issues.

It is important to note that the reasoning and holding of *Bellotti* did not rest on the existence of a viewpoint-discriminatory statute. It rested on the principle that the Government lacks the power to ban corporations from speaking.

Bellotti did not address the constitutionality of the State's ban on corporate independent expenditures to support candidates. In our view, however, that restriction would have been unconstitutional under *Bellotti*'s central principle: that the First Amendment does not allow political speech restrictions based on a speaker's corporate identity. See *ibid.*

3

Thus the law stood until *Austin. Austin* "uph[eld] a direct restriction on the independent expenditure of funds for political speech for the first time in [this Court's] history." There, the Michigan Chamber of Commerce sought to use general treasury funds to run a newspaper ad supporting a specific candidate. Michigan law, however, prohibited corporate independent expenditures that supported or opposed any candidate for state office. A violation of the law was punishable as a felony. The Court sustained the speech prohibition.

To bypass *Buckley* and *Bellotti,* the *Austin* Court identified a new governmental interest in limiting political speech: an antidistortion interest. *Austin* found a compelling governmental interest in preventing "the corrosive and distorting effects of immense aggregations of wealth that are accumulated with the help of the corporate form and that have little or no correlation to the public's support for the corporation's political ideas."

B

The Court is thus confronted with conflicting lines of precedent: a pre- *Austin* line that forbids restrictions on political speech based on the speaker's corporate identity and a post- *Austin* line that permits them. No case before *Austin* had held that Congress could prohibit independent expenditures for political speech based on the speaker's corporate identity. Before *Austin* Congress had enacted legislation for this purpose, and the Government urged the same proposition before this Court.

1

Austin's antidistortion rationale would produce the dangerous, and unacceptable, consequence that Congress could ban political speech of media corporations.

C

Our precedent is to be respected unless the most convincing of reasons demonstrates that adherence to it puts us on a course that is sure error. "Beyond workability, the relevant factors in deciding whether to adhere to the principle of *stare decisis* include the antiquity of the precedent, the reliance interests at stake, and of course whether the decision was well reasoned." We have also examined whether "experience has pointed up the precedent's shortcomings."

These considerations counsel in favor of rejecting *Austin,* which itself contravened this Court's earlier precedents in *Buckley* and *Bellotti.*

For the reasons above, it must be concluded that *Austin* was not well reasoned.

Rapid changes in technology-and the creative dynamic inherent in the concept of free expression-counsel against upholding a law that restricts political speech in certain media or by certain speakers. Today, 30-second television ads may be the most effective way to convey a political message. Soon, however, it may be that Internet sources, such as blogs and social networking Web sites, will provide citizens with significant information about political candidates and issues. Yet, § 441b would seem to ban a blog post expressly advocating the election or defeat of a candidate if that blog were created with corporate funds. The First Amendment does not permit Congress to make these categorical distinctions based on the corporate identity of the speaker and the content of the political speech.

No serious reliance interests are at stake. As the Court stated in *Payne v. Tennessee,* 501 U.S. 808, 828 (1991), reliance interests are important considerations in property and contract cases, where parties may have acted in conformance with existing legal rules in order to conduct transactions. Here, though, parties have been prevented from acting-corporations have been banned from making independent expenditures. Legislatures may have enacted bans on corporate expenditures believing that those bans were constitutional. This is not a compelling interest for *stare decisis.* If it were, legislative acts could prevent us from overruling our own precedents, thereby interfering with our duty "to say what the law is." *Marbury v. Madison,* 1 Cranch 137, 177, 2 L.Ed. 60 (1803).

Due consideration leads to this conclusion: *Austin,* should be and now is overruled. We return to the principle established in *Buckley* and *Bellotti* that the Government may not suppress political speech on the basis of the speaker's corporate identity. No sufficient governmental interest justifies limits on the political speech of nonprofit or for-profit corporations.

D

Austin is overruled, so it provides no basis for allowing the Government to limit corporate independent expenditures.

Given our conclusion we are further required to overrule the part of *McConnell* that upheld BCRA § 203's extension of § 441b's restrictions on corporate independent expenditures.

The judgment of the District Court is reversed with respect to the constitutionality of 2 U.S.C. § 441b's restrictions on corporate independent expenditures. The judgment is affirmed with respect to BCRA's disclaimer and disclosure requirements. The case is remanded for further proceedings consistent with this opinion.

It is so ordered.

CHIEF JUSTICE ROBERTS, with whom JUSTICE ALITO joins, concurring.

The Government urges us in this case to uphold a direct prohibition on political speech. It asks us to embrace a theory of the First Amendment that would allow censorship not only of television and radio broadcasts, but of pamphlets, posters, the Internet, and virtually any other medium that corporations and unions might find useful in expressing their views on matters of public concern. Its theory, if accepted, would empower the Government to prohibit newspapers from running editorials or opinion pieces supporting or opposing candidates for office, so long as the newspapers were owned by corporations-as the major ones are. First Amendment rights could be confined to individuals, subverting the vibrant public discourse that is at the foundation of our democracy.

The Court properly rejects that theory, and I join its opinion in full. The First Amendment protects more than just the individual on a soapbox and the lonely pamphleteer. I write separately to address the important principles of judicial restraint and *stare decisis* implicated in this case.

I

Judging the constitutionality of an Act of Congress is "the gravest and most delicate duty that this Court is called upon to perform." Because the stakes are so high, our standard practice is to refrain from addressing constitutional questions except when necessary to rule on particular claims before us. See *Ashwander v. TVA,* 297 U.S. 288, 346–348 (1936) (Brandeis, J., concurring).

It is only because the majority rejects Citizens United's statutory claim that it proceeds to consider the group's various constitutional arguments, beginning with its narrowest claim (that *Hillary* is not the functional equivalent of express advocacy) and proceeding to its broadest claim (that *Austin v. Michigan Chamber of Commerce,* 494 U.S. 652, 110 S.Ct. 1391, 108 L.Ed.2d 652 (1990) should be overruled). This is the same order of operations followed by the controlling opinion in *Federal Election Comm'n v. Wisconsin Right to Life, Inc.* There the appellant was able to prevail on its narrowest constitutional argument because its broadcast ads did not qualify as the functional equivalent of express advocacy; there was thus no need to go on to address the broader claim that *McConnell v. Federal Election Comm'n,* should be overruled. This case is different-not, as the dissent suggests, because the approach taken in *WRTL* has been deemed a "failure," *post,* at 935, but because, in the absence of any valid narrower ground of decision, there is no way to avoid Citizens United's broader constitutional argument.

The dissent advocates an approach to addressing Citizens United's claims that I find quite perplexing. It presumably agrees with the majority that Citizens United's narrower statutory and constitutional arguments lack merit-otherwise its conclusion that the group should lose this case would make no sense. Despite agreeing that these narrower arguments fail, however, the dissent argues that the majority should nonetheless latch on to one of them in order to avoid reaching the broader constitutional question of whether *Austin* remains good law. It even suggests that the Court's failure to adopt one of these concededly meritless arguments is a sign that the majority is not "serious about judicial restraint."

This approach is based on a false premise: that our practice of avoiding unnecessary (and unnecessarily broad) constitutional holdings somehow trumps our obligation faithfully to interpret the law. It should go without saying, however, that we cannot embrace a narrow ground of decision simply because it is narrow; it must also be right. Thus while it is true that "[i]f it is not necessary to decide more, it is necessary not to decide more,"(internal quotation marks omitted), sometimes it *is* necessary to decide more. There is a difference between judicial restraint and judicial abdication. When constitutional questions are "indispensably necessary" to resolving the case at hand, "the court must meet and decide them."

Because it is necessary to reach Citizens United's broader argument that *Austin* should be overruled, the debate over whether to consider this claim on an as-applied or facial basis strikes me as largely beside the point.

Citizens United has standing-it is being injured by the Government's enforcement of the Act. Citizens United has a constitutional claim-the Act violates the First Amendment, because it prohibits political speech. The Government has a defense-the Act may be enforced, consistent with the First Amendment, against corporations. Whether the claim or the defense prevails is the question before us.

II

The text and purpose of the First Amendment point in the same direction: Congress may not prohibit political speech, even if the speaker is a corporation or union. What makes this case difficult is the need to confront our prior decision in *Austin.*

A

Fidelity to precedent-the policy of *stare decisis*-is vital to the proper exercise of the judicial function. "*Stare decisis* is the preferred course because it promotes the evenhanded, predictable, and consistent development of legal principles, fosters reliance on judicial decisions, and contributes to the actual and perceived integrity of the judicial process." For these reasons, we have long recognized that departures from precedent are inappropriate in the absence of a "special justification."

At the same time, *stare decisis* is neither an "inexorable command," *Lawrence v. Texas,* 539 U.S. 558, 577, 123 S.Ct. 2472, 156 L.Ed.2d 508 (2003), nor "a mechanical formula of adherence to the latest decision," *Helvering v. Hallock,* 309 U.S. 106, 119, 60 S.Ct. 444, 84 L.Ed. 604 (1940), especially in constitutional cases. If it were, segregation would be legal, minimum wage laws would be unconstitutional, and the Government could wiretap ordinary criminal suspects without first obtaining warrants. As the dissent properly notes, none of us has viewed *stare decisis* in such absolute terms.

Stare decisis is instead a "principle of policy." When considering whether to reexamine a prior erroneous holding, we must balance the importance of having constitutional questions *decided* against the importance of having them *decided right.*

In conducting this balancing, we must keep in mind that *stare decisis* is not an end in itself. Its greatest purpose is to serve a constitutional ideal-the rule of law. It follows that in the unusual circumstance when fidelity to any particular precedent does more to damage this constitutional ideal than to advance it, we must be more willing to depart from that precedent.

Thus, for example, if the precedent under consideration itself departed from the Court's jurisprudence, returning to the " 'intrinsically sounder' doctrine established in prior cases" may "better serv[e] the values of *stare decisis* than would following [the] more recently decided case inconsistent with the decisions that came before it." Abrogating the errant precedent, rather than reaffirming or extending it, might better preserve the law's coherence and curtail the precedent's disruptive effects.

Likewise, if adherence to a precedent actually impedes the stable and orderly adjudication of future cases, its *stare decisis* effect is also diminished. This can happen in a number of circumstances, such as when the precedent's validity is so hotly contested that it cannot reliably function as a basis for decision in future cases, when its rationale threatens to upend our settled jurisprudence in related areas of law, and when the precedent's underlying reasoning has become so discredited that the Court cannot keep the precedent alive without jury-rigging new and different justifications to shore up the original mistake.

B

These considerations weigh against retaining our decision in *Austin.* First, as the majority explains, that decision was an "aberration" insofar as it departed from the robust protections we had granted political speech in our earlier cases. *Austin* undermined the careful line that *Buckley* drew to distinguish limits on contributions to candidates from limits on independent expenditures on speech.

Austin's reasoning was-and remains-inconsistent with *Buckley*'s explicit repudiation of any government interest in "equalizing the relative ability of individuals and groups to influence the outcome of elections."

Austin was also inconsistent with *Bellotti*'s clear rejection of the idea that "speech that otherwise would be within the protection of the First Amendment loses that protection simply because its source is a corporation."

Second, the validity of *Austin*'s rationale-itself adopted over two "spirited dissents," The simple fact that one of our decisions remains controversial is, of course, insufficient to justify overruling it. But it does undermine the precedent's ability to contribute to the stable and orderly development of the law. In such circumstances, it is entirely appropriate for the Court-which in this case is squarely asked to reconsider *Austin*'s validity for the first time-to address the matter with a greater willingness to consider new approaches capable of restoring our doctrine to sounder footing.

Third, the *Austin* decision is uniquely destabilizing because it threatens to subvert our Court's decisions even outside the particular context of corporate express advocacy. The First Amendment theory underlying *Austin*'s holding is extraordinarily broad. *Austin*'s logic would authorize government prohibition of political speech by a category of speakers in the name of equality-a point that most scholars acknowledge (and many celebrate), but that the dissent denies.

JUSTICE STEVENS, with whom JUSTICE GINSBURG, JUSTICE BREYER, and JUSTICE SOTOMAYOR join, concurring in part and dissenting in part.

The real issue in this case concerns how, not if, the appellant may finance its electioneering. Citizens United is a wealthy nonprofit corporation that runs a political action committee (PAC) with millions of dollars in assets. Under the Bipartisan Campaign Reform Act of 2002 (BCRA), it could have used those assets to televise and promote *Hillary: The Movie* wherever and whenever it wanted to. It also could have spent unrestricted sums to broadcast *Hillary* at any time other than the 30 days before the last primary election. Neither Citizens United's nor any other corporation's speech has been "banned." All that the parties dispute is whether Citizens United had a right to use the funds in its general treasury to pay for broadcasts during the 30-day period. The notion that the First Amendment dictates an affirmative answer to that question is, in my judgment, profoundly misguided. Even more misguided is the notion that the Court must rewrite the law relating to campaign expenditures by *for-profit* corporations and unions to decide this case.

The basic premise underlying the Court's ruling is its iteration, and constant reiteration, of the proposition that the First Amendment bars regulatory distinctions based on a speaker's identity, including its "identity" as a corporation. While that glittering generality has rhetorical appeal, it is not a correct statement of the law. Nor does it tell us when a corporation may engage in electioneering that some of its shareholders oppose. It does not even resolve the specific question whether Citizens United may be required to finance some of its messages with the money in its PAC. The conceit that corporations must be treated identically to natural persons in the political sphere is not only inaccurate but also inadequate to justify the Court's disposition of this case.

In the context of election to public office, the distinction between corporate and human speakers is significant. Although they make enormous contributions to our society, corporations are not actually members of it. They cannot vote or run for office. Because they may be managed and controlled by nonresidents, their interests may conflict in fundamental respects with the interests of eligible voters. The financial resources, legal structure, and instrumental orientation of corporations raise legitimate concerns about their role in the electoral process. Our lawmakers have a compelling constitutional basis, if not also a democratic duty, to take measures designed to guard against the potentially deleterious effects of corporate spending in local and national races.

The majority's approach to corporate electioneering marks a dramatic break from our past. Congress has placed special limitations on campaign spending by corporations ever since the passage of the Tillman Act in 1907. We have unanimously concluded that this "reflects a permissible assessment of the dangers posed by those entities to the electoral process," and have accepted the "legislative judgment that the special characteristics of the corporate structure require particularly careful regulation." The Court today rejects a century of history when it treats the distinction between corporate and individual campaign spending as an invidious novelty born of *Austin v. Michigan Chamber of Commerce,* Relying largely on individual dissenting opinions, the majority blazes through our precedents, overruling or disavowing a body of case law.

In his landmark concurrence in *Ashwander v. TVA,* Justice Brandeis stressed the importance of adhering to rules the Court has "developed . . . for its own governance" when deciding constitutional questions.

I

The Court's ruling threatens to undermine the integrity of elected institutions across the Nation. The path it has taken to reach its outcome will, I fear, do damage to this institution. Before turning to the question whether to overrule *Austin* and part of *McConnell,* it is important to explain why the Court should not be deciding that question.

Scope of the Case

The first reason is that the question was not properly brought before us. In declaring § 203 of BCRA facially unconstitutional on the ground that corporations' electoral expenditures may not be regulated any more stringently than those of individuals, the majority decides this case on a basis relinquished below, not included in the questions presented to us by the litigants, and argued here only in response to the Court's invitation. This procedure is unusual and inadvisable for a court.

" 'It is only in exceptional cases coming here from the federal courts that questions not pressed or passed upon below are reviewed,. ' " The appellant in this case did not so much as assert an exceptional circumstance, and one searches the majority opinion in vain for the mention of any. That is unsurprising, for none exists.

Setting the case for reargument was a constructive step, but it did not cure this fundamental problem. Essentially, five Justices were unhappy with the limited nature of the case before us, so they changed the case to give themselves an opportunity to change the law.

Narrower Grounds

It is all the more distressing that our colleagues have manufactured a facial challenge, because the parties have advanced numerous ways to resolve the case that would facilitate electioneering by nonprofit advocacy corporations such as Citizens United, without toppling statutes and precedents.

Consider just three of the narrower grounds of decision that the majority has bypassed. First, the Court could have ruled, on statutory grounds, that a feature-length film distributed through video-on-demand does not qualify as an "electioneering communication" under § 203 of BCRA, 2 U.S.C. § 441b.

Second, the Court could have expanded the *MCFL* exemption to cover § 501(c)(4) nonprofits that accept only a *de minimis* amount of money from for-profit corporations.

Finally, let us not forget Citizens United's as-applied constitutional challenge. Precisely because Citizens United looks so much like the *MCFL* organizations we have exempted from regulation, while a feature-length video-on-demand film looks so unlike the types of electoral advocacy Congress has found deserving of regulation, this challenge is a substantial one. As the appellant's own arguments show, the Court could have easily limited the breadth of its constitutional holding had it declined to adopt the novel notion that speakers and speech acts must always be treated identically-and always spared expenditures restrictions-in the political realm. Yet the Court nonetheless turns its back on the as-applied review process that has been a staple of campaign finance litigation since *Buckley v. Valeo.*

II

The final principle of judicial process that the majority violates is the most transparent: *stare decisis.* I am not an absolutist when it comes to *stare decisis,* in the campaign finance area or in any other. No one is. But if this principle is to do any meaningful work in supporting the rule of law, it must at least demand a significant justification, beyond the preferences of five Justices, for overturning settled doctrine. "[A] decision to overrule should rest on some special reason over and above the belief that a prior case was wrongly decided." No such justification exists in this case, and to the contrary there are powerful prudential reasons to keep faith with our precedents.

The Court's central argument for why *stare decisis* ought to be trumped is that it does not like *Austin.* The opinion "was not well reasoned," our colleagues assert, and it conflicts with First Amendment principles. This, of course, is the Court's merits argument, the many defects in which we will soon consider. I am perfectly willing to concede that if one of our precedents were dead wrong in its reasoning or irreconcilable with the rest of our doctrine, there would be a compelling basis for revisiting it.

Perhaps in recognition of this point, the Court supplements its merits case with a smattering of assertions. The Court proclaims that "*Austin* is undermined by experience since its announcement." This is a curious claim to make in a case that lacks a developed record. The majority has no empirical evidence with which to substantiate the claim; we just have its *ipse dixit* that the real world has not been kind to *Austin.* Nor does the majority bother to specify in what sense *Austin* has been "undermined."

The majority also contends that the Government's hesitation to rely on *Austin*'s antidistortion rationale "diminishe[s]" "the principle of adhering to that precedent." Why it diminishes the value of *stare decisis* is left unexplained. We have never thought fit to overrule a precedent because a litigant has taken any particular tack. Nor should we. Our decisions can often be defended on multiple grounds, and a litigant may have strategic or case-specific reasons for emphasizing only a subset of them. Members of the public, moreover, often rely on our bottom-line holdings far more than our precise legal arguments; surely this is true for the legislatures that have been regulating corporate electioneering since *Austin.* The task of evaluating the continued viability of precedents falls to this Court, not to the parties.

Although the majority opinion spends several pages making these surprising arguments, it says almost nothing about the standard considerations we have used to determine *stare decisis* value, such as the antiquity of the precedent, the workability of its legal rule, and the reliance interests at stake.

We have recognized that "*[s]tare decisis* has special force when legislators or citizens 'have acted in reliance on a previous decision, for in this instance overruling the decision would dislodge settled rights and expectations or require an extensive legislative response.' " *Stare decisis* protects not only personal rights involving property or contract but also the ability of the elected branches to shape their laws in an effective and coherent fashion. Today's decision takes away a power that we have long permitted these branches to exercise. State legislatures have relied on their authority to regulate corporate electioneering, confirmed in *Austin,* for more than a century. The Federal Congress has relied on this authority for a comparable stretch of time, and it specifically relied on *Austin* throughout the years it spent developing and debating BCRA. The total record it compiled was *100,000 pages* long. Pulling out the rug beneath Congress after affirming the constitutionality of § 203 six years ago shows great disrespect for a coequal branch.

Beyond the reliance interests at stake, the other *stare decisis* factors also cut against the Court. Considerations of antiquity are significant for similar reasons. *McConnell* is only six years old, but *Austin* has been on the books for two decades, and many of the statutes called into question by today's opinion have been on the books for a half-century or more. The Court points to no intervening change in circumstances that warrants revisiting *Austin.*

Certainly nothing relevant has changed since we decided *WRTL* two Terms ago. And the Court gives no reason to think that *Austin* and *McConnell* are unworkable.

In fact, no one has argued to us that *Austin*'s rule has proved impracticable, and not a single for-profit corporation, union, or State has asked us to overrule it.

In the end, the Court's rejection of *Austin* and *McConnell* comes down to nothing more than its disagreement with their results. Virtually every one of its arguments was made and rejected in those cases, and the majority opinion is essentially an amalgamation of resuscitated dissents. The only relevant thing that has changed since *Austin* and *McConnell* is the composition of this Court. Today's ruling thus strikes at the vitals of *stare decisis*. . .

III

The novelty of the Court's procedural dereliction and its approach to *stare decisis* is matched by the novelty of its ruling on the merits. The ruling rests on several premises. First, the Court claims that *Austin* and *McConnell* have "banned" corporate speech. Second, it claims that the First Amendment precludes regulatory distinctions based on speaker identity, including the speaker's identity as a corporation. Third, it claims that *Austin* and *McConnell* were radical outliers in our First Amendment tradition and our campaign finance jurisprudence. Each of these claims is wrong.

The So-Called "Ban"

Pervading the Court's analysis is the ominous image of a "categorical ba[n]" on corporate speech. Indeed, the majority invokes the specter of a "ban" on nearly every page of its opinion. This characterization is highly misleading, and needs to be corrected.

In fact it already has been. Our cases have repeatedly pointed out that, "[c]ontrary to the [majority's] critical assumptions," the statutes upheld in *Austin* and *McConnell* do "not impose an *absolute* ban on all forms of corporate political spending." For starters, both statutes provide exemptions for PACs, separate segregated funds established by a corporation for political purposes. "The ability to form and administer separate segregated funds," we observed in *McConnell,* "has provided corporations and unions with a constitutionally sufficient opportunity to engage in express advocacy. That has been this Court's unanimous view."

Under BCRA, any corporation's "stockholders and their families and its executive or administrative personnel and their families" can pool their resources to finance electioneering communications. A significant and growing number of corporations avail themselves of this option.

The laws upheld in *Austin* and *McConnell* leave open many additional avenues for corporations' political speech. Like numerous statutes, it exempts media companies' news stories, commentaries, and editorials from its electioneering restrictions, in recognition of the unique role played by the institutional press in sustaining public debate.

Identity-Based Distinctions

The second pillar of the Court's opinion is its assertion that "the Government cannot restrict political speech based on the speaker's . . . identity."

The Government routinely places special restrictions on the speech rights of students, prisoners, members of the Armed Forces, foreigners, and its own employees When such restrictions are justified by a legitimate governmental interest, they do not necessarily raise constitutional problems. In contrast to the blanket rule that the majority espouses, our cases recognize that the Government's interests may be more or less compelling with respect to different classes of speakers,

The same logic applies to this case with additional force because it is the identity of corporations, rather than individuals, that the Legislature has taken into account. As we have unanimously observed, legislatures are entitled to decide "that the special characteristics of the corporate structure require particularly careful regulation" in an electoral context. Not only has the distinctive potential of corporations to corrupt the electoral process long been recognized, but within the area of campaign finance, corporate spending is also "furthest from the core of political expression, since corporations' First Amendment speech and association interests are derived largely from those of their members and of the public in receiving information."

If taken seriously, our colleagues' assumption that the identity of a speaker has *no* relevance to the Government's ability to regulate political speech would lead to some remarkable conclusions. Such an assumption would have accorded the propaganda broadcasts to our troops by "Tokyo Rose" during World War II the same protection as speech by Allied commanders. More pertinently, it would appear to afford the same protection to multinational corporations controlled by foreigners as to individual Americans.

In short, the Court dramatically overstates its critique of identity-based distinctions, without ever explaining why corporate identity demands the same treatment as individual identity. Only the most wooden approach to the First Amendment could justify the unprecedented line it seeks to draw.

Our First Amendment Tradition

A third fulcrum of the Court's opinion is the idea that *Austin* and *McConnell* are radical outliers, "aberration[s]," in our First Amendment tradition. The Court has it exactly backwards. It is today's holding that is the radical departure from what had been settled First Amendment law. To see why, it is useful to take a long view.

1. *Original Understandings*

Let us start from the beginning. The Court invokes "ancient First Amendment principles," to defend today's ruling, yet it makes only a perfunctory attempt to ground its analysis in the principles or understandings of those who drafted and ratified the Amendment. Perhaps this is because there is not a scintilla of evidence to support the notion that anyone believed it would preclude regulatory distinctions based on the corporate form. To the extent that the Framers' views are discernible and relevant to the disposition of this case, they would appear to cut strongly against the majority's position.

This is not only because the Framers and their contemporaries conceived of speech more narrowly than we now think of it, but also because they held very different views about the nature of the First Amendment right and the role of corporations in society. Those few corporations that existed at the founding were authorized by grant of a special legislative charter.

The individualized charter mode of incorporation reflected the "cloud of disfavor under which corporations labored" in the early years of this Nation.

The Framers thus took it as a given that corporations could be comprehensively regulated in the service of the public welfare. Unlike our colleagues, they had little trouble distinguishing corporations from human beings, and when they constitutionalized the right to free speech in the First Amendment, it was the free speech of individual Americans that they had in mind. While individuals might join together to exercise their speech rights, business corporations, at least, were plainly not seen as facilitating such associational or expressive ends.

As a matter of original expectations, then, it seems absurd to think that the First Amendment prohibits legislatures from taking into account the corporate identity of a sponsor of electoral advocacy. As a matter of original meaning, it likewise seems baseless-unless one evaluates the First Amendment's "principles," at such a high level of generality that the historical understandings of the Amendment cease to be a meaningful constraint on the judicial task. This case sheds a revelatory light on the assumption of some that an impartial judge's application of an originalist methodology is likely to yield more determinate answers, or to play a more decisive role in the decisional process, than his or her views about sound policy.

IV

Having explained why this is not an appropriate case in which to revisit *Austin* and *McConnell* and why these decisions sit perfectly well with "First Amendment principles," I come at last to the interests that are at stake. The majority recognizes that *Austin* and *McConnell* may be defended on anticorruption, antidistortion, and shareholder protection rationales. It badly errs both in explaining the nature of these rationales, which overlap and complement each other, and in applying them to the case at hand.

The Anticorruption Interest

Undergirding the majority's approach to the merits is the claim that the only "sufficiently important governmental interest in preventing corruption or the appearance of corruption" is one that is "limited to *quid pro quo* corruption." *Ante,* at 909–910. This is the same "crabbed view of corruption" that was espoused by Justice KENNEDY in *McConnell* and squarely rejected by the Court in that case. While it is true that we have not always spoken about corruption in a clear or consistent voice, the approach taken by the majority cannot be right, in my judgment. It disregards our constitutional history and the fundamental demands of a democratic society.

On numerous occasions we have recognized Congress' legitimate interest in preventing the money that is spent on elections from exerting an " 'undue influence on an officeholder's judgment' " and from creating " 'the appearance of such influence,' " beyond the sphere of *quid pro quo* relationships. Bribery may be the paradigm case. But the difference between selling a vote and selling access is a matter of degree, not kind. And selling access is not qualitatively different from giving special preference to those who spent money on one's behalf. Corruption operates along a spectrum, and the majority's apparent belief that *quid pro quo* arrangements can be neatly demarcated from other improper influences does not accord with the theory or reality of politics. It certainly does not accord with the record Congress developed in passing BCRA, a record that stands as a remarkable testament to the energy and ingenuity with which corporations, unions, lobbyists, and politicians may go about scratching each other's backs-and which amply supported Congress' determination to target a limited set of especially destructive practices.

Our "undue influence" cases have allowed the American people to cast a wider net through legislative experiments designed to ensure, to some minimal extent, "that officeholders will decide issues . . . on the merits or the desires of their constituencies," and not "according to the wishes of those who have made large financial contributions"-or expenditures-"valued by the officeholder."

Quid Pro Quo *Corruption*

There is no need to take my side in the debate over the scope of the anticorruption interest to see that the Court's merits holding is wrong. Even under the majority's "crabbed view of corruption," the Government should not lose this case.

"The importance of the governmental interest in preventing [corruption through the creation of political debts] has never been doubted." Even in the cases that have construed the anticorruption interest most narrowly, we have never suggested that such *quid pro quo* debts must take the form of outright vote buying or bribes, which have long been distinct crimes. Rather, they encompass the myriad ways in which outside parties may induce an officeholder to confer a legislative benefit in direct response to, or anticipation of, some outlay of money the parties have made or will make on behalf of the officeholder. It has likewise never been doubted that "[o]f almost equal concern as the danger of actual *quid pro quo* arrangements is the impact of the appearance of corruption." In theory, our colleagues accept this much. As applied to BCRA § 203, however, they conclude "[t]he anticorruption interest is not sufficient to displace the speech here in question."

The majority appears to think it decisive that the BCRA record does not contain "direct examples of votes being exchanged for . . . expenditures." It would have been quite remarkable if Congress had created a record detailing such behavior by its own Members. Proving that a specific vote was exchanged for a specific expenditure has always been next to impossible: Elected officials have diverse motivations, and no one will acknowledge that he sold a vote. Yet, even if "[i]ngratiation and access . . . are not corruption" themselves, *ibid.,* they are necessary prerequisites to it; they can create both the opportunity for, and the appearance of, *quid pro quo* arrangements. The influx of unlimited corporate money into the electoral realm also creates new opportunities for the mirror image of *quid pro quo* deals: threats, both explicit and implicit. Starting today, corporations with large war chests to deploy on electioneering may find democratically elected bodies becoming much more attuned to their interests. The majority both misreads the facts and draws the wrong conclusions when it suggests that the BCRA record provides "only scant evidence that independent expenditures . . . ingratiate," and that, "in any event," none of it matters.

The insight that even technically independent expenditures can be corrupting in much the same way as direct contributions is bolstered by our decision last year in *Caperton v. A.T. Massey Coal Co.,* 556 U.S. ____, 129 S.Ct. 2252, 173 L.Ed.2d 1208 (2009). In that case, Don Blankenship, the chief executive officer of a corporation with a lawsuit pending before the West Virginia high court, spent large sums on behalf of a particular candidate, Brent Benjamin, running for a seat on that court. "In addition to contributing the $1,000 statutory maximum to Benjamin's campaign committee, Blankenship donated almost $2.5 million to 'And For The Sake Of The Kids,' " a § 527 corporation that ran ads targeting Benjamin's opponent. *Id.,* at ____, 129 S.Ct., at 2257. "This was not all. Blankenship spent, in addition, just over $500,000 on independent expenditures . . . ' "to support . . . Brent Benjamin." ' " *Id.,* at ____, 129 S.Ct., at 2257 (second alteration in original). Applying its common sense, this Court accepted petitioners' argument that Blankenship's "pivotal role in getting Justice Benjamin elected created a constitutionally intolerable probability of actual bias" when Benjamin later declined to recuse himself from the appeal by Blankenship's corporation. *Id.,* at ____, 129 S.Ct., at 2262. "Though n[o] . . . bribe or criminal influence" was involved, we recognized that "Justice Benjamin would nevertheless feel a debt of gratitude to Blankenship for his extraordinary efforts to get him elected." *Ibid.* "The difficulties of inquiring into actual bias," we further noted, "simply underscore the need for objective rules," *id.,* at ____, 129 S.Ct., at 2263-rules which will perforce turn on the appearance of bias rather than its actual existence.

In *Caperton,* then, we accepted the premise that, at least in some circumstances, independent expenditures on candidate elections will raise an intolerable specter of *quid pro quo* corruption.

Austin and Corporate Expenditures

Just as the majority gives short shrift to the general societal interests at stake in campaign finance regulation, it also overlooks the distinctive considerations raised by the regulation of *corporate* expenditures. The majority fails to appreciate that *Austin*'s antidistortion rationale is itself an anticorruption rationale, tied to the special concerns raised by corporations. Understood properly, "antidistortion" is simply a variant on the classic governmental interest in protecting against improper influences on officeholders that debilitate the democratic process.

1. *Antidistortion*

The fact that corporations are different from human beings might seem to need no elaboration, except that the majority opinion almost completely elides it. *Austin* set forth some of the basic differences. Unlike natural persons, corporations have "limited liability" for their owners and managers, "perpetual life," separation of ownership and control, "and favorable treatment of the accumulation and distribution of assets . . . that enhance their ability to attract capital and to deploy their resources in ways that maximize the return on their shareholders' investments." Unlike voters in U.S. elections, corporations may be foreign controlled. Unlike other interest groups, business corporations have been "effectively delegated responsibility for ensuring society's economic welfare"; they inescapably structure the life of every citizen. " '[T]he resources in the treasury of a business corporation,' "

It might also be added that corporations have no consciences, no beliefs, no feelings, no thoughts, no desires. Corporations help structure and facilitate the activities of human beings, to be sure, and their "personhood" often serves as a useful legal fiction. But they are not themselves members of "We the People" by whom and for whom our Constitution was established.

These basic points help explain why corporate electioneering is not only more likely to impair compelling governmental interests, but also why restrictions on that electioneering are less likely to encroach upon First Amendment freedoms.

It is an interesting question "who" is even speaking when a business corporation places an advertisement that endorses or attacks a particular candidate. Presumably it is not the customers or employees, who typically have no say in such matters. It cannot realistically be said to be the shareholders, who tend to be far removed from the day-to-day decisions of the firm and whose political preferences may be opaque to management. Perhaps the officers or directors of the corporation have the best claim to be the ones speaking, except their fiduciary duties generally prohibit them from using corporate funds for personal ends. Some individuals associated with the corporation must make the decision to place the ad, but the idea that these individuals are thereby fostering their self-expression or cultivating their critical faculties is fanciful. It is entirely possible that the corporation's electoral message will *conflict* with their personal convictions. Take away the ability to use general treasury funds for some of those ads, and no one's autonomy, dignity, or political equality has been impinged upon in the least.

2. *Shareholder Protection*

There is yet another way in which laws such as § 203 can serve First Amendment values. Interwoven with *Austin*'s concern to protect the integrity of the electoral process is a concern to protect the rights of shareholders from a kind of coerced speech: electioneering expenditures that do not "reflec [t] [their] support." When corporations use general treasury funds to praise or attack a particular candidate for office, it is the shareholders, as the residual claimants, who are effectively footing the bill. Those shareholders who disagree with the corporation's electoral message may find their financial investments being used to undermine their political convictions.

V

Today's decision is backwards in many senses. It elevates the majority's agenda over the litigants' submissions, facial attacks over as-applied claims, broad constitutional theories over narrow statutory grounds, individual dissenting opinions over precedential holdings, assertion over tradition, absolutism over empiricism, rhetoric over reality. Our colleagues have arrived at the conclusion that *Austin* must be overruled and that § 203 is facially unconstitutional only after mischaracterizing both the reach and rationale of those authorities, and after bypassing or ignoring rules of judicial restraint used to cabin the Court's lawmaking power. Their conclusion that the societal interest in avoiding corruption and the appearance of corruption does not provide an adequate justification for regulating corporate expenditures on candidate elections relies on an incorrect description of that interest, along with a failure to acknowledge the relevance of established facts and the considered judgments of state and federal legislatures over many decades.

In a democratic society, the longstanding consensus on the need to limit corporate campaign spending should outweigh the wooden application of judge-made rules. The majority's rejection of this principle "elevate[s] corporations to a level of deference which has not been seen at least since the days when substantive due process was regularly used to invalidate regulatory legislation thought to unfairly impinge upon established economic interests." *Bellotti,* 435 U.S., at 817, n. 13, 98 S.Ct. 1407 (White, J., dissenting). At bottom, the Court's opinion is thus a rejection of the common sense of the American people, who have recognized a need to prevent corporations from undermining self-government since the founding, and who have fought against the distinctive corrupting potential of corporate electioneering since the days of Theodore Roosevelt. It is a strange time to repudiate that common sense. While American democracy is imperfect, few outside the majority of this Court would have thought its flaws included a dearth of corporate money in politics.

I would affirm the judgment of the District Court.

JUSTICE THOMAS, concurring in part and dissenting in part.

I join all but Part IV of the Court's opinion.

Political speech is entitled to robust protection under the First Amendment. Section 203 of the Bipartisan Campaign Reform Act of 2002 (BCRA) has never been reconcilable with that protection. By striking down § 203, the Court takes an important first step toward restoring full constitutional protection to speech that is "indispensable to the effective and intelligent use of the processes of popular government." *McConnell v. Federal Election Comm'n,* 540 U.S. 93 (2003) (THOMAS, J., concurring in part, concurring in judgment in part, and dissenting in part) (internal quotation marks omitted). I dissent from Part IV of the Court's opinion, however, because the Court's constitutional analysis does not go far enough. The disclosure, disclaimer, and reporting requirements in BCRA §§ 201 and 311 are also unconstitutional.

FOR DISCUSSION

What value and role do the different opinions assign to precedent? What grounds do they offer for when precedent should be upheld versus rejected? At one point Chief Justice Roberts asserts that: "There is a difference between judicial restraint and judicial abdication." Do you find his distinction valid here? Does the majority offer persuasive arguments for overruling its decisions in *Austin* and *McConnell*?

Do you think the Constitution should treat different speakers differently? Specifically, should corporations be treated differently in the electoral process from ordinary persons?

RELATED CASE

***Speechnow.org. v. FEC,* 599 F.3d 686 (D.C. Cir. 2010 (en banc):**

Following *Citizens United,* an en banc panel of the D.C. Circuit Court of Appeals ruled that individual contribution limits to Speechnow, a non-profit corporation which did not contribute money to candidates or candidates and only made independent expenditures, was a violation of the First Amendment.

ARIZONA FREE ENTERPRISE CLUB'S FREEDOM CLUB PAC V. BENNETT

564 U.S. 721, 131 S.Ct. 2806, 180 L.Ed.2d 664 (2011)

Vote: 5–4

A summary is presented in the first paragraph of the decision below.

CHIEF JUSTICE ROBERTS writing for the Court and joined by SCALIA, KENNEDY, THOMAS, and ALITO. KAGAN, J., filed a dissenting opinion, in which GINSBURG, BREYER, and SOTOMAYOR, joined.

Under Arizona law, candidates for state office who accept public financing can receive additional money from the State in direct response to the campaign activities of privately financed candidates and independent expenditure groups. Once a set spending limit is exceeded, a publicly financed candidate receives roughly one dollar for every dollar spent by an opposing privately financed candidate. The publicly financed candidate also receives roughly one dollar for every dollar spent by independent expenditure groups to support the privately financed candidate, or to oppose the publicly financed candidate. We hold that Arizona's matching funds scheme substantially burdens protected political speech without serving a compelling state interest and therefore violates the First Amendment.

II

"Discussion of public issues and debate on the qualifications of candidates are integral to the operation" of our system of government. As a result, the First Amendment " 'has its fullest and most urgent application' to speech uttered during a campaign for political office." "Laws that burden political speech are" accordingly "subject to strict scrutiny, which requires the Government to prove that the restriction furthers a compelling interest and is narrowly tailored to achieve that interest."

Applying these principles, we have invalidated government-imposed restrictions on campaign expenditures, restraints on independent expenditures applied to express advocacy groups, limits on uncoordinated political party expenditures, and regulations barring unions, nonprofit and other associations, and corporations from making independent expenditures for electioneering communication.

At the same time, we have subjected strictures on campaign-related speech that we have found less onerous to a lower level of scrutiny and upheld those restrictions. For example, after finding that the restriction at issue was "closely drawn" to serve a "sufficiently important interest," we have upheld government-imposed limits on contributions to candidates, caps on coordinated party expenditures, and requirements that political funding sources disclose their identities.

Although the speech of the candidates and independent expenditure groups that brought this suit is not directly capped by Arizona's matching funds provision, those parties contend that their political speech is substantially burdened by the state law in the same way that speech was burdened by the law we recently found invalid in *Davis v. Federal Election Comm'n,*. In *Davis,* we considered a First Amendment challenge to the so-called "Millionaire's Amendment" of the Bipartisan Campaign Reform Act of 2002,. Under that Amendment, if a candidate for the United States House of Representatives spent more than $350,000 of his personal funds, "a new, asymmetrical regulatory scheme [came] into play." The opponent of the candidate who exceeded that limit was permitted to collect individual contributions up to $6,900 per contributor—three times the normal contribution limit of $2,300. The candidate who spent more than the personal funds limit remained subject to the original contribution cap. Davis argued that this scheme "burden[ed] his exercise of his First Amendment right to make unlimited expenditures of his personal funds because" doing so had "the effect of enabling his opponent to raise more money and to use that money to finance speech that counteract[ed] and thus diminishe[d] the effectiveness of Davis' own speech."

In addressing the constitutionality of the Millionaire's Amendment, we acknowledged that the provision did not impose an outright cap on a candidate's personal expenditures. We nonetheless concluded that the Amendment was unconstitutional because it forced a candidate "to choose between the First Amendment right to engage in unfettered political speech and subjection to discriminatory fundraising limitations." Any candidate who chose to spend more than $350,000 of his own money was forced to "shoulder a special and potentially significant burden" because that choice gave fundraising advantages to the candidate's adversary. *Ibid.* We determined that this constituted an "unprecedented penalty" and "impose[d] a substantial burden on the exercise of the First Amendment right to use personal funds for campaign speech," and concluded that the Government had failed to advance any compelling interest that would justify such a burden.

A

1

The logic of *Davis* largely controls our approach to this case. Much like the burden placed on speech in *Davis,* the matching funds provision "imposes an unprecedented penalty on any candidate who robustly exercises [his] First Amendment right[s]." Under that provision, "the vigorous exercise of the right to use personal funds to finance campaign speech" leads to "advantages for opponents in the competitive context of electoral politics."

Once a privately financed candidate has raised or spent more than the State's initial grant to a publicly financed candidate, each personal dollar spent by the privately financed candidate results in an award of almost one additional dollar to his opponent. That plainly forces the privately financed candidate to "shoulder a special and potentially significant burden" when choosing to exercise his First Amendment right to spend funds on behalf of his candidacy. If the law at issue in *Davis* imposed a burden on candidate speech, the Arizona law unquestionably does so as well.

The penalty imposed by Arizona's matching funds provision is different in some respects from the penalty imposed by the law we struck down in *Davis.* But those differences make the Arizona law *more* constitutionally problematic, not less. First, the penalty in *Davis* consisted of raising the contribution limits for one of the candidates. The candidate who benefited from the increased limits still had to go out and raise the funds. He may or may not have been able to do so. The other candidate, therefore, faced merely the possibility that his opponent would be able to raise additional funds, through contribution limits that remained subject to a cap. And still the Court held that this was an "unprecedented penalty," a "special and potentially significant burden" that had to be justified by a compelling state interest—a rigorous First Amendment hurdle., Here the benefit to the publicly financed candidate is the direct and automatic release of public money. That is a far heavier burden than in *Davis.*

Second, depending on the specifics of the election at issue, the matching funds provision can create a multiplier effect. In the Arizona Fourth District House election previously discussed, if the spending cap were exceede d, each dollar spent by the privately funded candidate would result in an additional dollar of campaign funding to each of that candidate's publicly financed opponents. In such a situation, the matching funds provision forces privately funded candidates to fight a political hydra of sorts. Each dollar they spend generates two adversarial dollars in response. Again, a markedly more significant burden than in *Davis.*

Third, unlike the law at issue in *Davis,* all of this is to some extent out of the privately financed candidate's hands. Even if that candidate opted to spend less than the initial public financing cap, any spending by independent expenditure groups to promote the privately financed candidate's election—regardless whether such support was welcome or helpful—could trigger matching funds. What is more, that state money would go directly to the publicly funded candidate to use as he saw fit. That disparity in control—giving money directly to a publicly financed candidate, in response to independent expenditures that cannot be coordinated with the privately funded candidate—is a substantial advantage for the publicly funded candidate. That candidate can allocate the money according to his own campaign strategy, which the privately financed candidate could not do with the independent group expenditures that triggered the matching funds.

The burdens that this regime places on independent expenditure groups are akin to those imposed on the privately financed candidates themselves. Just as with the candidate the independent group supports, the more money spent on that candidate's behalf or in opposition to a publicly funded candidate, the more money the publicly funded candidate receives from the State. And just as with the privately financed candidate, the effect of a dollar spent on election speech is a guaranteed financial payout to the publicly funded candidate the group opposes. Moreover, spending one dollar can result in the flow of dollars to multiple candidates the group disapproves of, dollars directly controlled by the publicly funded candidate or candidates.

In some ways, the burden the Arizona law imposes on independent expenditure groups is worse than the burden it imposes on privately financed candidates, and thus substantially worse than the burden we found constitutionally impermissible in *Davis*. If a candidate contemplating an electoral run in Arizona surveys the campaign landscape and decides that the burdens imposed by the matching funds regime make a privately funded campaign unattractive, he at least has the option of taking public financing. Independent expenditure groups, of course, do not.

Once the spending cap is reached, an independent expenditure group that wants to support a particular candidate—because of that candidate's stand on an issue of concern to the group—can only avoid triggering matching funds in one of two ways. The group can either opt to change its message from one addressing the merits of the candidates to one addressing the merits of an issue, or refrain from speaking altogether. Presenting independent expenditure groups with such a choice makes the matching funds provision particularly burdensome to those groups. And forcing that choice—trigger matching funds, change your message, or do not speak—certainly contravenes "the fundamental rule of protection under the First Amendment, that a speaker has the autonomy to choose the content of his own message." *Hurley v. Irish-American Gay, Lesbian and Bisexual Group of Boston, Inc.,* 515 U.S. 557, 573, 115 S.Ct. 2338, 132 L.Ed.2d 487 (1995).

2

Arizona, the Clean Elections Institute, and the United States offer several arguments attempting to explain away the existence or significance of any burden imposed by matching funds. None is persuasive.

Arizona contends that the matching funds provision is distinguishable from the law we invalidated in *Davis*. The State correctly points out that our decision in *Davis* focused on the asymmetrical contribution limits imposed by the Millionaire's Amendment. But that is not because—as the State asserts—the reach of that opinion is limited to asymmetrical contribution limits. It is because that was the particular burden on candidate speech we faced in *Davis*. And whatever the significance of the distinction in general, there can be no doubt that the burden on speech is significantly greater in this case than in *Davis*: That means that the law here—like the one in *Davis*—must be justified by a compelling state interest.

The State argues that the matching funds provision actually results in more speech by "increas[ing] debate about issues of public concern" in Arizona elections and "promot[ing] the free and open debate that the First Amendment was intended to foster." In the State's view, this promotion of First Amendment ideals offsets any burden the law might impose on some speakers.

Not so. Any increase in speech resulting from the Arizona law is of one kind and one kind only—that of publicly financed candidates. The burden imposed on privately financed candidates and independent expenditure groups reduces their speech; "restriction[s] on the amount of money a person or group can spend on political communication during a campaign necessarily reduces the quantity of expression." Thus, even if the matching funds provision did result in more speech by publicly financed candidates and more speech in general, it would do so at the expense of impermissibly burdening (and thus reducing) the speech of privately financed candidates and independent expenditure groups. This sort of "beggar thy neighbor" approach to free speech—"restrict[ing] the speech of some elements of our society in order to enhance the relative voice of others"—is "wholly foreign to the First Amendment."

We have rejected government efforts to increase the speech of some at the expense of others outside the campaign finance context. In *Miami Herald Publishing Co. v. Tornillo,* we held unconstitutional a Florida law that required any newspaper assailing a political candidate's character to allow that candidate to print a reply. We have explained that while the statute in that case " purported to advance free discussion, . . . its effect was to deter newspapers from speaking out in the first instance" because it "penalized the newspaper's own expression." *Pacific Gas & Elec. Co. v. Public Util. Comm'n of Cal.,* 475 U.S. 1, 10 (1986). Such a penalty, we concluded, could not survive First Amendment scrutiny. The Arizona law imposes a similar penalty: The State grants funds to publicly financed candidates as a direct result of the speech of privately financed candidates and independent expenditure groups. The argument that this sort of burden promotes free and robust discussion is no more persuasive here than it was in *Tornillo.*

Because the Arizona matching funds provision imposes a substantial burden on the speech of privately financed candidates and independent expenditure groups, "that provision cannot stand unless it is 'justified by a compelling state interest,' "

There is a debate between the parties in this case as to what state interest is served by the matching funds provision. The privately financed candidates and independent expenditure groups contend that the provision works to "level[ ] electoral opportunities" by equalizing candidate "resources and influence." The State and the Clean Elections Institute counter that the provision "furthers Arizona's interest in preventing corruption and the appearance of corruption."

1

There is ample support for the argument that the matching funds provision seeks to "level the playing field" in terms of candidate resources. The clearest evidence is of course the very operation of the provision: It ensures that campaign funding is equal, up to three times the initial public funding allotment. The text of the Citizens Clean Elections Act itself confirms this purpose. The statutory provision setting up the matching funds regime is titled "Equal funding of candidates.". The Act refers to the funds doled out after the Act's matching mechanism is triggered as "equalizing funds.". And the regulations implementing the matching funds provision refer to those funds as "equalizing funds" as well.

Other features of the Arizona law reinforce this understanding of the matching funds provision. If the Citizens Clean Election Commission cannot provide publicly financed candidates with the moneys that the matching funds provision envisions because of a shortage of funds, the statute allows a publicly financed candidate to "accept private contributions to bring the total monies received by the candidate" up to the matching funds amount. Limiting contributions, of course, is the primary means we have upheld to combat corruption. Indeed the State argues that one of the principal ways that the matching funds provision combats corruption is by eliminating the possibility of any *quid pro quo* between private interests and publicly funded candidates by eliminating contributions to those candidates altogether. See Brief for State Respondents 45–46. But when confronted with a choice between fighting corruption and equalizing speech, the drafters of the matching funds provision chose the latter. That significantly undermines any notion that the "Equal funding of candidates" provision is meant to serve some interest other than an interest in equalizing funds.

We have repeatedly rejected the argument that the government has a compelling state interest in "leveling the playing field" that can justify undue burdens on political speech. In *Davis,* we stated that discriminatory contribution limits meant to "level electoral opportunities for candidates of different personal wealth" did not serve "a legitimate government objective," let alone a compelling one. And in *Buckley,* we held that limits on overall campaign expenditures could not be justified by a purported government "interest in equalizing the financial resources of candidates." After all, equalizing campaign resources "might serve not to equalize the opportunities of all candidates, but to handicap a candidate who lacked substantial name recognition or exposure of his views before the start of the campaign."

"Leveling electoral opportunities means making and implementing judgments about which strengths should be permitted to contribute to the outcome of an election,"—a dangerous enterprise and one that cannot justify burdening protected speech. The dissent essentially dismisses this concern, but it needs to be taken seriously; we have, as noted, held that it is not legitimate for the government to attempt to equalize electoral opportunities in this manner. And such basic intrusion by the government into the debate over who should govern goes to the heart of First Amendment values.

The judgment of the Court of Appeals for the Ninth Circuit is reversed.

It is so ordered.

JUSTICE KAGAN, with whom JUSTICE GINSBURG, JUSTICE BREYER, and JUSTICE SOTOMAYOR join, dissenting.

Imagine two States, each plagued by a corrupt political system. In both States, candidates for public office accept large campaign contributions in exchange for the promise that, after assuming office, they will rank the donors' interests ahead of all others. As a result of these bargains, politicians ignore the public interest, sound public policy languishes, and the citizens lose confidence in their government.

Recognizing the cancerous effect of this corruption, voters of the first State, acting through referendum, enact several campaign finance measures previously approved by this Court. They cap campaign contributions; require disclosure of substantial donations; and create an optional public financing program that gives candidates a fixed public subsidy if they refrain from private fundraising. But these measures do not work. Individuals who "bundle" campaign contributions become indispensable to candidates in need of money. Simple disclosure fails to prevent shady dealing. And candidates choose not to participate in the public financing system because the sums provided do not make them competitive with their privately financed opponents. So the State remains afflicted with corruption.

Voters of the second State, having witnessed this failure, take an ever-so-slightly different tack to cleaning up their political system. They too enact contribution limits and disclosure requirements. But they believe that the greatest hope of eliminating corruption lies in creating an effective public financing program, which will break candidates' dependence on large donors and bundlers. These voters realize, based on the first State's experience, that such a program will not work unless candidates agree to participate in it. And candidates will participate only if they know that they will receive sufficient funding to run competitive races. So the voters enact a program that carefully adjusts the money given to would-be officeholders, through the use of a matching funds mechanism, in order to provide this assurance. The program does not discriminate against any candidate or point of view, and it does not restrict any person's ability to speak. In fact, by providing resources to many candidates, the program creates more speech and thereby broadens public debate. And just as the voters had hoped, the program accomplishes its mission of restoring integrity to the political system. The second State rids itself of corruption.

A person familiar with our country's core values—our devotion to democratic self-governance, as well as to "uninhibited, robust, and wide-open" debate, *New York Times Co. v. Sullivan,* 376 U.S. 254, 270, 84 S.Ct. 710, 11 L.Ed.2d 686 (1964)—might expect this Court to celebrate, or at least not to interfere with, the second State's success. But today, the majority holds that the second State's system—the system that produces honest government, working on behalf of all the people—clashes with our Constitution. The First Amendment, the majority insists, requires us all to rely on the measures employed in the first State, even when they have failed to break the stranglehold of special interests on elected officials.

I disagree. The First Amendment's core purpose is to foster a healthy, vibrant political system full of robust discussion and debate. Nothing in Arizona's anti-corruption statute, the Arizona Citizens Clean Elections Act, violates this constitutional protection. To the contrary, the Act promotes the values underlying both the First Amendment and our entire Constitution by enhancing the "opportunity for free political discussion to the end that government may be responsive to the will of the people."

FOR DISCUSSION

After this decision is there any way that public financing can be set up to address spending by rich opponents or independent groups? Do candidates have any advantage in opting for public financing, especially if it comes with limits on expenditures?

SHAUN MCCUTCHEON V. FEDERAL ELECTION COMMISSION

134 S.Ct. 1434, 188 L.Ed.2d 468 (2014)

In 1974 Congress passed amendments to the Federal Election Campaign Act that included among other provisions a limit on how much could be donated to individual federal candidates for office and a total aggregate cap on the total amount of money an individual may donate to federal candidates for office and Political Action Committees. After subsequently amended again by the 2002 Bipartisan Campaign Reform Act in the 2011–12 election cycle that cap was $123,200. Shaun McCutcheon had contributed to 16 different federal candidates and wanted to contribute to another 12 but could not because of the aggregate contribute limit. He challenged the aggregate limite before a three-judge District Court, asserting that they were unconstitutional under the First Amendment. The District Court denied their motion for a preliminary injunction and granted the Government's motion to dismiss. He appealed to the Supreme Court which reversed and remanded the district court decision.

Vote: 5–4

CHIEF JUSTICE delivered an opinion in which SCALIA, KENNEDY, and ALITO joined. THOMAS filed a concurring opinion, and BREYER wrote a dissent jointed by GINSBURG, SOTOMAYOR, and KAGAN.

There is no right more basic in our democracy than the right to participate in electing our political leaders. Citizens can exercise that right in a variety of ways: They can run for office themselves, vote, urge others to vote for a particular candidate, volunteer to work on a campaign, and contribute to a candidate's campaign. This case is about the last of those options.

The right to participate in democracy through political contributions is protected by the First Amendment, but that right is not absolute. Our cases have held that Congress may regulate campaign contributions to protect against corruption or the appearance of corruption. At the same time, we have made clear that Congress may not regulate contributions simply to reduce the amount of money in politics, or to restrict the political participation of some in order to enhance the relative influence of others.

Many people might find those latter objectives attractive: They would be delighted to see fewer television commercials touting a candidate's accomplishments or disparaging an opponent's character. Money in politics may at times seem repugnant to some, but so too does much of what the First Amendment vigorously protects.

If the First Amendment protects flag burning, funeral protests, and Nazi parades—despite the profound offense such spectacles cause—it surely protects political campaign speech despite popular opposition. Indeed, as we have emphasized, the First Amendment "has its fullest and most urgent application precisely to the conduct of campaigns for political office." *Monitor Patriot Co. v. Roy,* 401 U.S. 265, 272 (1971).

In a series of cases over the past 40 years, we have spelled out how to draw the constitutional line between the permissible goal of avoiding corruption in the political process and the impermissible desire simply to limit political speech. We have said that government regulation may not target the general gratitude a candidate may feel toward those who support him or his allies, or the political access such support may afford. "Ingratiation and access . . . are not corruption.". They embody a central feature of democracy—that constituents support candidates who share their beliefs and interests, and candidates who are elected can be expected to be responsive to those concerns.

Any regulation must instead target what we have called "*quid pro quo*" corruption or its appearance. That Latin phrase captures the notion of a direct exchange of an official act for money. "The hallmark of corruption is the financial *quid pro quo*: dollars for political favors." Campaign finance restrictions that pursue other objectives, we have explained, impermissibly inject the Government "into the debate over who should govern." And those who govern should be the *last* people to help decide who *should* govern.

The statute at issue in this case imposes two types of limits on campaign contributions. The first, called base limits, restricts how much money a donor may contribute to a particular candidate or committee. 2 U.S.C. § 441a(a)(1). The second, called aggregate limits, restricts how much money a donor may contribute in total to all candidates or committees. § 441a(a)(3).

This case does not involve any challenge to the base limits, which we have previously upheld as serving the permissible objective of combatting corruption. The Government contends that the aggregate limits also serve that objective, by preventing circumvention of the base limits. We conclude, however, that the aggregate limits do little, if anything, to address that concern, while seriously restricting participation in the democratic process. The aggregate limits are therefore invalid under the First Amendment.

II

A

Buckley v. Valeo, presented this Court with its first opportunity to evaluate the constitutionality of the original contribution and expenditure limits set forth in FECA. FECA imposed a $1,000 per election base limit on contributions from an individual to a federal candidate. It also imposed a $25,000 per year aggregate limit on all contributions from an individual to candidates or political committees. On the expenditures side, FECA imposed limits on both independent expenditures and candidates' overall campaign expenditures.

Buckley recognized that "contribution and expenditure limitations operate in an area of the most fundamental First Amendment activities." But it distinguished expenditure limits from contribution limits based on the degree to which each encroaches upon protected First Amendment interests. Expenditure limits, the Court explained, "necessarily reduce[] the quantity of expression by restricting the number of issues discussed, the depth of their exploration, and the size of the audience reached." The Court thus subjected expenditure limits to "the exacting scrutiny applicable to limitations on core First Amendment rights of political expression.". Under exacting scrutiny, the Government may regulate protected speech only if such regulation promotes a compelling interest and is the least restrictive means to further the articulated interest.

By contrast, the Court concluded that contribution limits impose a lesser restraint on political speech because they "permit[] the symbolic expression of support evidenced by a contribution but do[] not in any way infringe the contributor's freedom to discuss candidates and. As a result, the Court focused on the effect of the contribution limits on the freedom of political association and applied a lesser but still "rigorous standard of review." Under that standard, "[e]ven a ' "significant interference" with protected rights of political association' may be sustained if the State demonstrates a sufficiently important interest and employs means closely drawn to avoid unnecessary abridgement of associational freedoms."

The primary purpose of FECA was to limit *quid pro quo* corruption and its appearance; that purpose satisfied the requirement of a "sufficiently important" governmental interest. As for the "closely drawn" component, *Buckley* concluded that the $1,000 base limit "focuses precisely on the problem of large campaign contributions ... while leaving persons free to engage in independent political expression, to associate actively through volunteering their services, and to assist to a limited but nonetheless substantial extent in supporting candidates and committees with financial resources." The Court therefore upheld the $1,000 base limit under the "closely drawn" test.

The Court next separately considered an overbreadth challenge to the base limit. The challengers argued that the base limit was fatally overbroad because most large donors do not seek improper influence over legislators' actions. Although the Court accepted that premise, it nevertheless rejected the overbreadth challenge for two reasons: First, it was too "difficult to isolate suspect contributions" based on a contributor's subjective intent. Second, "Congress was justified in concluding that the interest in safeguarding against the appearance of impropriety requires that the opportunity for abuse inherent in the process of raising large monetary contributions be eliminated.

Finally, in one paragraph of its 139-page opinion, the Court turned to the $25,000 aggregate limit under FECA. As a preliminary matter, it noted that the constitutionality of the aggregate limit "ha[d] not been separately addressed at length by the parties." Then, in three sentences, the Court disposed of any constitutional objections to the aggregate limit that the challengers might have had:

> "The overall $25,000 ceiling does impose an ultimate restriction upon the number of candidates and committees with which an individual may associate himself by means of financial support. But this quite modest restraint upon protected political activity serves to prevent evasion of the $1,000 contribution limitation by a person who might otherwise contribute massive amounts of money to a particular candidate through the use of unearmarked contributions to political committees likely to contribute to that candidate, or huge contributions to the candidate's political party. The limited, additional restriction on associational freedom imposed by the overall ceiling is thus no more than a corollary of the basic individual contribution limitation that we have found to be constitutionally valid."

B

2

Buckley treated the constitutionality of the $25,000 aggregate limit as contingent upon that limit's ability to prevent circumvention of the $1,000 base limit, describing the aggregate limit as "no more than a corollary" of the base limit. The Court determined that circumvention could occur when an individual legally contributes "massive amounts of money to a particular candidate through the use of unearmarked contributions" to entities that are themselves likely to contribute to the candidate. *Ibid.* For that reason, the Court upheld the $25,000 aggregate limit.

Although *Buckley* provides some guidance, we think that its ultimate conclusion about the constitutionality of the aggregate limit in place under FECA does not control here. *Buckley* spent a total of three sentences analyzing that limit; in fact, the opinion pointed out that the constitutionality of the aggregate limit "ha[d] not been separately addressed at length by the parties." We are now asked to address appellants' direct challenge to the aggregate limits in place under BCRA. BCRA is a different statutory regime, and the aggregate limits it imposes operate against a distinct legal backdrop.

Most notably, statutory safeguards against circumvention have been considerably strengthened since *Buckley* was decided, through both statutory additions and the introduction of a comprehensive regulatory scheme. With more targeted anticircumvention measures in place today, the indiscriminate aggregate limits under BCRA appear particularly heavy-handed.

The intricate regulatory scheme that the Federal Election Commission has enacted since *Buckley* further limits the opportunities for circumvention of the base limits via "unearmarked contributions to political committees likely to contribute" to a particular candidate. Although the earmarking provision was in place when *Buckley* was decided, the FEC has since added regulations that define earmarking broadly. For example, the regulations construe earmarking to include any designation, "whether direct or indirect, express or implied, oral or written." The regulations specify that an individual who has contributed to a particular candidate may not also contribute to a single-candidate committee for that candidate. Nor may an individual who has contributed to a candidate also contribute to a political committee that has supported or anticipates supporting the same candidate, if the individual knows that "a substantial portion [of his contribution] will be contributed to, or expended on behalf of," that candidate.

In addition to accounting for statutory and regulatory changes in the campaign finance arena, appellants' challenge raises distinct legal arguments that *Buckley* did not consider. For example, presumably because of its cursory treatment of the $25,000 aggregate limit, *Buckley* did not separately address an overbreadth challenge with respect to that provision. The Court rejected such a challenge to the *base* limits because of the difficulty of isolating suspect contributions. The propriety of large contributions to individual candidates turned on the subjective intent of donors, and the Court concluded that there was no way to tell which donors sought improper influence over legislators' actions. The aggregate limit, on the other hand, was upheld as an anticircumvention measure, without considering whether it was possible to discern which donations might be used to circumvent the base limits. The Court never addressed overbreadth in the specific context of aggregate limits, where such an argument has far more force.

Given the foregoing, this case cannot be resolved merely by pointing to three sentences in *Buckley* that were written without the benefit of full briefing or argument on the issue.

III

The First Amendment "is designed and intended to remove governmental restraints from the arena of public discussion, putting the decision as to what views shall be voiced largely into the hands of each of us, . . . in the belief that no other approach would comport with the premise of individual dignity and choice upon which our political system rests." As relevant here, the First Amendment safeguards an individual's right to participate in the public debate through political expression and political association. When an individual contributes money to a candidate, he exercises both of those rights: The contribution "serves as a general expression of support for the candidate and his views" and "serves to affiliate a person with a candidate."

Those First Amendment rights are important regardless whether the individual is, on the one hand, a "lone pamphleteer[ ] or street corner orator[ ] in the Tom Paine mold," or is, on the other, someone who spends "substantial amounts of money in order to communicate [his] political ideas through sophisticated" means. Either way, he is participating in an electoral debate that we have recognized is "integral to the operation of the system of government established by our Constitution."

Buckley acknowledged that aggregate limits at least diminish an individual's right of political association. As the Court explained, the "overall $25,000 ceiling does impose an ultimate restriction upon the number of candidates and committees with which an individual may associate himself by means of financial support." But the Court characterized that restriction as a "quite modest restraint upon protected political activity." We cannot agree with that characterization. An aggregate limit on *how many* candidates and committees an individual may support through contributions is not a "modest restraint" at all. The Government may no more restrict how many candidates or causes a donor may support than it may tell a newspaper how many candidates it may endorse.

To put it in the simplest terms, the aggregate limits prohibit an individual from fully contributing to the primary and general election campaigns of ten or more candidates, even if all contributions fall within the base limits Congress views as adequate to protect against corruption. The individual may give up to $5,200 each to nine candidates, but the aggregate limits constitute an outright ban on further contributions to any other candidate (beyond the additional $1,800 that may be spent before reaching the $48,600 aggregate limit). At that point, the limits deny the individual all ability to exercise his expressive and associational rights by contributing to someone who will advocate for his policy preferences. A donor must limit the number of candidates he supports, and may have to choose which of several policy concerns he will advance—clear First Amendment harms that the dissent never acknowledges.

It is no answer to say that the individual can simply contribute less money to more people. To require one person to contribute at lower levels than others because he wants to support more candidates or causes is to impose a special burden on broader participation in the democratic process. And as we have recently admonished, the Government may not penalize an individual for "robustly exercis[ing]" his First Amendment rights.

The dissent faults this focus on "the individual's right to engage in political speech," saying that it fails to take into account "the public's interest" in "collective speech." (opinion of BREYER, J.). This "collective" interest is said to promote "a government where laws reflect the very thoughts, views, ideas, and sentiments, the expression of which the First Amendment protects."

But there are compelling reasons not to define the boundaries of the First Amendment by reference to such a generalized conception of the public good. First, the dissent's "collective speech" reflected in laws is of course the will of the majority, and plainly can include laws that restrict free speech. The whole point of the First Amendment is to afford individuals protection against such infringements. The First Amendment does not protect the government, even when the government purports to act through legislation reflecting "collective speech."

Second, the degree to which speech is protected cannot turn on a legislative or judicial determination that particular speech is useful to the democratic process. The First Amendment does not contemplate such "ad hoc balancing of relative social costs and benefits."

Third, our established First Amendment analysis already takes account of any "collective" interest that may justify restrictions on individual speech. Under that accepted analysis, such restrictions are measured against the asserted public interest (usually framed as an important or compelling governmental interest). As explained below, we do not doubt the compelling nature of the "collective" interest in preventing corruption in the electoral process. But we permit Congress to pursue that interest only so long as it does not unnecessarily infringe an individual's right to freedom of speech; we do not truncate this tailoring test at the outset.

IV

A

With the significant First Amendment costs for individual citizens in mind, we turn to the governmental interests asserted in this case. This Court has identified only one legitimate governmental interest for restricting campaign finances: preventing corruption or the appearance of corruption. We have consistently rejected attempts to suppress campaign speech based on other legislative objectives. No matter how desirable it may seem, it is not an acceptable governmental objective to "level the playing field," or to "level electoral opportunities," or to "equaliz[e] the financial resources of candidates." The First Amendment prohibits such legislative attempts to "fine-tun[e]" the electoral process, no matter how well intentioned.

As we framed the relevant principle in *Buckley,* "the concept that government may restrict the speech of some elements of our society in order to enhance the relative voice of others is wholly foreign to the First Amendment." The dissent's suggestion that *Buckley* supports the opposite proposition, simply ignores what *Buckley* actually said on the matter.

Moreover, while preventing corruption or its appearance is a legitimate objective, Congress may target only a specific type of corruption—"*quid pro quo*" corruption. As *Buckley* explained, Congress may permissibly seek to rein in "large contributions [that] are given to secure a political *quid pro quo* from current and potential office holders.". In addition to "actual *quid pro quo* arrangements," Congress may permissibly limit "the appearance of corruption stemming from public awareness of the opportunities for abuse inherent in a regime of large individual financial contributions" to particular candidates.

Spending large sums of money in connection with elections, but not in connection with an effort to control the exercise of an officeholder's official duties, does not give rise to such *quid pro quo* corruption. Nor does the possibility that an individual who spends large sums may garner "influence over or access to" elected officials or political parties. And because the Government's interest in preventing the appearance of corruption is equally confined to the appearance of *quid pro quo* corruption, the Government may not seek to limit the appearance of mere influence or access.

The dissent advocates a broader conception of corruption, and would apply the label to any individual contributions above limits deemed necessary to protect "collective speech." Thus, under the dissent's view, it is perfectly fine to contribute $5,200 to nine candidates but somehow corrupt to give the same amount to a tenth.

The line between *quid pro quo* corruption and general influence may seem vague at times, but the distinction must be respected in order to safeguard basic First Amendment rights. In addition, "[i]n drawing that line, the First Amendment requires us to err on the side of protecting political speech rather than suppressing it."

B

"When the Government restricts speech, the Government bears the burden of proving the constitutionality of its actions." Here, the Government seeks to carry that burden by arguing that the aggregate limits further the permissible objective of preventing *quid pro quo* corruption.

The difficulty is that once the aggregate limits kick in, they ban all contributions of *any* amount. But Congress's selection of a $5,200 base limit indicates its belief that contributions of that amount or less do not create a cognizable risk of corruption. If there is no corruption concern in giving nine candidates up to $5,200 each, it is difficult to understand how a tenth candidate can be regarded as corruptible if given $1,801, and all others corruptible if given a dime. And if there is no risk that additional candidates will be corrupted by donations of up to $5,200, then the Government must defend the aggregate limits by demonstrating that they prevent circumvention of the base limits.

As an initial matter, there is not the same risk of *quid pro quo* corruption or its appearance when money flows through independent actors to a candidate, as when a donor contributes to a candidate directly. When an individual contributes to a candidate, a party committee, or a PAC, the individual must by law cede control over the funds. The Government admits that if the funds are subsequently re-routed to a particular candidate, such action occurs at the initial recipient's discretion—not the donor's. As a consequence, the chain of attribution grows longer, and any credit must be shared among the various actors along the way. For those reasons, the risk of *quid pro quo* corruption is generally applicable only to "the narrow category of money gifts that are directed, in some manner, to a candidate or officeholder."

D

Finally, disclosure of contributions minimizes the potential for abuse of the campaign finance system. Disclosure requirements are in part "justified based on a governmental interest in 'provid[ing] the electorate with information' about the sources of election-related spending." They may also "deter actual corruption and avoid the appearance of corruption by exposing large contributions and expenditures to the light of publicity." Disclosure requirements burden speech, but—unlike the aggregate limits—they do not impose a ceiling on speech. For that reason, disclosure often represents a less restrictive alternative to flat bans on certain types or quantities of speech.

FOR DISCUSSION

What does the Roberts Court view as a form of quid pro quo corruption that would permit any type of campaign finance limits?

POLITICAL PATRONAGE AND ELECTION DAY REGULATIONS

The Jacksonian Era of the 1820s is often credited or blamed as ushering in the spoils system. Under spoils, victors in elections were awarded two prizes: first, the office they sought, and second, the opportunity to appoint their friends (usually members of the same political party) to government positions as a reward for supporting them. Such a system, while it encouraged loyalty, also proved inefficient (with significant turnover of government officials after incumbents lost) and corrupt. Spoils seemed often to place party loyalty above the public interest, or it encouraged officials to discriminate against some individuals because of their party membership, or it denied equality of opportunity to all seeking jobs with the government.

Beginning with the **Pendleton Act** in 1883, Congress began the process of creating a federal civil service to take some of the politics out of government hiring and service. At the same time that civil service reform occurred, efforts were also undertaken during the Progressive Era to clean up elections. Earlier it was noted how the Tillman Act, for example, sought to limit the role of corporate money in federal elections. However, other reforms were also undertaken to take the running of elections away from the political parties. Efforts were made, for example, to create secret ballots or to otherwise create more fair campaigns that did not intimidate voters or produce rigged elections.

One reform meant to limit political influence on elections was the passage of the Hatch Acts in the late 1930s. Congress, fearing that President Franklin Roosevelt had become too powerful, sought to limit the political activity of federal employees. The Acts limited the participation of federal workers in many aspects of campaigning and election. Both in *United Public Workers v. Mitchell* (330 U.S. 75, 1947) and then again in *United States Civil Service Commission v. National Association of Letter Carriers* (413 U.S. 548, 1973), the Court upheld the Hatch Acts.

Another issue began to surface in the 1970s. It examined the constitutionality of the spoils system. Specifically, it asked whether the use of party affiliation in government employment decisions violated the First Amendment. First in *Elrod v. Burns* (427 U.S. 347, 1976) and then in *Branti v. Finkel* (445 U.S. 507, 1979), the Court said that it did. Coming after these decisions, the Supreme Court again visited the issue of patronage in

Rutan v. Republican Party of Illinois (497 U.S. 62, 1990). Yet again, in this decision the Court struck down the use of party affiliation or partisanship in the content of public employment.

The ban on political campaigning near polling places is a common restriction put in place to prevent voter intimidation. It pits the competing First Amendment rights of voters against those of candidates and campaigners. Here the voters won in *Burson v. Freeman* (504 U.S. 191, 1992) where the Supreme Court upheld a ban on advertising within 100 feet of polling places.

The intent of the voter is a standard used in all states to determine how to count a vote. Is that standard enough? *Bush v. Gore* (531 U.S. 98, 2000) suggested not. The images of officials in different counties holding ballots up to the light to determine if a chad was punched, dimpled, or otherwise marked counted as a vote led some to think that this was the reason why the Court saw an equal protection problem here. What counted as a vote according to one official or county would not count the same to another. Thus, invoking *Reynolds v. Sims* (377 U.S. 533, 1964), the right to vote extended beyond the mere granting of franchise and went to the counting of votes. But should it also go to the mechanics of how elections are run, such as to the choice of what type of voting process or machine is used? After the 2000 election studies revealed that different types of voting systems have varying failure or malfunction rates. Is there not an equal protection issue here?

Bush v. Gore is still viewed as a highly partisan case. For Republicans, the case is about the Court protecting the integrity of elections. For Democrats, it is the ultimate political thicket that the Court thrust itself into—picking the president of the United States by halting a ballot recount and effectively awarding the presidency to Bush, even though Gore received more popular votes.

The cases offered in this section provide a summary of the many complex issues that come to play by seeking to understand how the Constitution regulates the American democracy. The question to ask is: Does the law regulate the politics, or vice versa?

RUTAN V. REPUBLICAN PARTY OF ILLINOIS

497 U.S. 62, 110 S.Ct. 2729, 111 L.Ed.2d 52 (1990)

The governor of Illinois, Jim Thompson, imposed a hiring and promotion freeze on the state, allowing hirings only with his permission. The freeze and the exception were challenged with claims that the governor was using both to hire members of a specific party. Specifically, Cynthia Rutan, who had worked for the state of Illinois since 1974, claimed that she had been passed over for promotions because she was not a member of the Republican Party and did not get its support when she sought a promotion in 1983. Ms. Rutan, along with four other plaintiffs, challenged the hiring freeze and the alleged use of partisanship by the governor in making personnel decisions. They challenged both as a violation of their First Amendment rights.

Vote: 5–4

JUSTICE BRENNAN delivered the opinion of the Court.

To the victor belong only those spoils that may be constitutionally obtained. *Elrod v. Burns*, 427 US 347 (1976), and *Branti v. Finkel*, 445 U.S. 507 (1980), decided that the First Amendment forbids government officials to discharge or threaten to discharge public employees solely for not being supporters of the political party in power, unless party affiliation is an appropriate requirement for the position involved. Today we are asked to decide the constitutionality of several related political patronage practices—whether promotion, transfer, recall, and hiring decisions involving low-level public employees may be constitutionally based on party affiliation and support. We hold that they may not.

I

The petition and cross-petition before us arise from a lawsuit protesting certain employment policies and practices instituted by Governor James Thompson of Illinois. On November 12, 1980, the Governor issued an executive order proclaiming a hiring freeze for every agency, bureau, board, or commission subject to his control. The order prohibits state officials from hiring any employee, filling any vacancy, creating any new position, or taking any similar action. It affects approximately 60,000 state positions. More than 5,000 of these become available each year as a result of resignations, retirements, deaths, expansion, and reorganizations. The order proclaims that "*no* exceptions" are permitted without the Governor's "express permission after submission of appropriate requests to [his] office." Governor's Executive Order No. 5 (Nov. 12, 1980).

Requests for the Governor's "express permission" have allegedly become routine. Permission has been granted or withheld through an agency expressly created for this purpose, the Governor's Office of Personnel (Governor's Office). Agencies have been screening applicants under Illinois' civil service system, making their personnel choices, and submitting them as requests to be approved or disapproved by the Governor's Office. Among the employment decisions for which approvals have been required are new hires, promotions, transfers, and recalls after layoffs.

By means of the freeze, according to petitioners, the Governor has been using the Governor's Office to operate a political patronage system to limit state employment and beneficial employment-related decisions to those who are supported by the Republican Party. In reviewing an agency's request that a particular applicant be approved for a particular position, the Governor's Office has looked at whether the applicant voted in Republican primaries in past election years, whether the applicant has provided financial or other support to the Republican Party and its candidates, whether the applicant has promised to join and work for the Republican Party in the future, and whether the applicant has the support of Republican Party officials at state or local levels.

Five people (including the three petitioners) brought suit against various Illinois and Republican Party officials in the United States District Court for the Central District of Illinois. They alleged that they had suffered discrimination with respect to state employment because they had not been supporters of the State's Republican Party and that this discrimination violates the First Amendment. Cynthia B. Rutan has been working for the State since 1974 as a rehabilitation counselor. She claims that, since 1981, she has been repeatedly denied promotions to supervisory positions for which she was qualified because she had not worked for or supported the Republican Party. Franklin Taylor, who operates road equipment for the Illinois Department of Transportation, claims that he was denied a promotion in 1983 because he did not have the support of the local Republican Party. Taylor also maintains that he was denied a transfer to an office nearer to his home because of opposition from the Republican Party chairmen in the counties in which he worked and to which he requested a transfer. James W. Moore claims that he has been repeatedly denied state employment as a prison guard because he did not have the support of Republican Party officials.

The two other plaintiffs, before the Court as cross-respondents, allege that they were not recalled after layoffs because they lacked Republican credentials. Ricky Standefer was a state garage worker who claims that he was not recalled, although his fellow employees were, because he had voted in a Democratic primary and did not have the support of the Republican Party. Dan O'Brien, formerly a dietary manager with the mental health department, contends that he was not recalled after a layoff because of his party affiliation, and that he later obtained a lower-paying position with the corrections department only after receiving support from the chairman of the local Republican Party.

II

A

In *Elrod,* we decided that a newly elected Democratic sheriff could not constitutionally engage in the patronage practice of replacing certain office staff with members of his own party "when the existing employees lack or fail to obtain requisite support from, or fail to affiliate with, that party." The plurality explained that conditioning public employment on the provision of support for the favored political party "unquestionably inhibits protected belief and association." It reasoned that conditioning employment on political activity pressures employees to pledge political allegiance to a party with which they prefer not to associate, to work for the election of political candidates they do not support, and to contribute money to be used to further policies with which they do not agree. The latter, the plurality noted, had been recognized by this Court as "tantamount to coerced belief." At the same time, employees are constrained from joining, working for or contributing to the political party and candidates of their own choice. "[P]olitical belief and association constitute the core of those activities protected by the First Amendment," the plurality emphasized. Both the plurality and the concurrence drew support from *Perry v. Sindermann*, 408 U.S. 593 (1972), in which this Court held that the State's refusal to renew a teacher's contract because he had been publicly critical of its policies imposed an unconstitutional condition on the receipt of a public benefit.

The Court then decided that the government interests generally asserted in support of patronage fail to justify this burden on First Amendment rights because patronage dismissals are not the least restrictive means for fostering those interests. The plurality acknowledged that a government has a significant interest in ensuring that it has effective and efficient employees. It expressed doubt, however, that "mere difference of political persuasion motivates poor performance," and concluded that, in any case, the government can ensure employee effectiveness and efficiency through the less drastic means of discharging staff members whose work is inadequate. The plurality also found that a government can meet its need for politically loyal employees to implement its policies by the less intrusive measure of dismissing, on political grounds, only those employees in policymaking positions. Finally, although the plurality recognized that preservation of the democratic process "may in some instances justify limitations on First Amendment freedoms," it concluded that the "process functions as well without the practice, perhaps even better." Patronage, it explained, "can result in the entrenchment of one or a few parties to the exclusion of others," and is a very effective impediment to the associational and speech freedoms which are essential to a meaningful system of democratic government.

Four years later, in *Branti*, we decided that the First Amendment prohibited a newly appointed public defender, who was a Democrat, from discharging assistant public defenders because they did not have the support of the Democratic Party. The Court rejected an attempt to distinguish the case from *Elrod,* deciding that it was immaterial whether the public defender had attempted to coerce employees to change political parties or had only dismissed them on the basis of their private political beliefs. We explained that conditioning continued public employment on an employee's having obtained support from a particular political party violates the First Amendment because of "the coercion of belief that necessarily flows from the knowledge that one must have a sponsor in the dominant party in order to retain one's job." "In sum," we said "there is no requirement that dismissed employees prove that they, or other employees, have been coerced into changing, either actually or ostensibly, their political allegiance." To prevail, we concluded, public employees need show only that they were discharged because they were not affiliated with or sponsored by the Democratic Party.

We find, however, that our conclusions in *Elrod* and *Branti* are equally applicable to the patronage practices at issue here. A government's interest in securing effective employees can be met by discharging, demoting or transferring staff members whose work is deficient. A government's interest in securing employees who will loyally implement its policies can be adequately served by choosing or dismissing certain high-level employees on the basis of their political views. Likewise, the "preservation of the democratic process" is no more furthered by the patronage promotions, transfers, and rehires at issue here than it is by patronage dismissals.

JUSTICE SCALIA, with whom CHIEF JUSTICE REHNQUIST and JUSTICE KENNEDY join, and with whom JUSTICE O'CONNOR joins as to Parts II and III, dissenting.

Today the Court establishes the constitutional principle that party membership is not a permissible factor in the dispensation of government jobs, except those jobs for the performance of which party affiliation is an "appropriate requirement." It is hard to say precisely (or even generally) what that exception means, but if there is any category of jobs for whose performance party affiliation is not an appropriate requirement, it is the job of being a judge, where partisanship is not only unneeded but positively undesirable. It is, however, rare that a federal administration of one party will appoint a judge from another party. And it has always been rare. Thus, the new principle that the Court today announces will be enforced by a corps of judges (the Members of this Court included) who overwhelmingly owe their office to its violation. Something must be wrong here, and I suggest it is the Court.

The choice between patronage and the merit principle—or, to be more realistic about it, the choice between the desirable mix of merit and patronage principles in widely varying federal, state, and local political contexts—is not so clear that I would be prepared, as an original matter, to chisel a single, inflexible prescription into the Constitution. Fourteen years ago, in *Elrod v. Burns,* Court did that. *Elrod* was limited however, as was the later decision of *Branti v. Finkel,* to patronage firings, leaving it to state and federal legislatures to determine when and where political affiliation could be taken into account in hirings and promotions. Today the Court makes its constitutional civil-service reform absolute, extending to all decisions regarding government employment. Because the First Amendment has never been thought to require this disposition, which may well have disastrous consequences for our political system, I dissent.

The whole point of my dissent is that the desirability of patronage is a policy question to be decided by the people's representatives; I do not mean, therefore, to endorse that system. But in order to demonstrate that a legislature could reasonably determine that its benefits outweigh its "coercive" effects, I must describe those benefits as the proponents of patronage see them: As Justice Powell discussed at length in his *Elrod* dissent, patronage stabilizes political parties and prevents excessive political fragmentation—both of which are results in which States have a strong governmental interest. Party strength requires the efforts of the rank-and-file, especially in "the dull periods between elections," to perform such tasks as organizing precincts, registering new voters, and providing constituent services. *Elrod,* 427 U.S. at 385 (dissenting opinion). Even the most enthusiastic supporter of a party's program will shrink before such drudgery, and it is folly to think that ideological conviction alone will motivate sufficient numbers to keep the party going through the off-years.

FOR DISCUSSION

Did the Court declare spoils and patronage to be unconstitutional as the dissent suggests? Are there any circumstances where you would think that party affiliation is a legitimate factor to consider for government employment?

As a result of *Rutan* and its other patronage decisions, the Court appears to have taken a stand against spoils and partisanship in the staffing of most government positions. Does this move make sense? Some critics, such as Justice Scalia, contend that the decision to use spoils or patronage is not a constitutional issue but a matter of policy and that efforts to outlaw spoils have hurt party discipline.

RELATED CASES

***Board of County Commissioners v. Umbehr:* 518 U.S. 668 (1996)**; and ***O'Hare Truck Service Inc. v. City of Northgate:* 518 U.S. 712 (1996).**

The Supreme Court again reaffirmed that the use of partisanship or party affiliation in the employment decisions, including even in the decision to hire independent contractors, violated the First Amendment.

BURSON V. FREEMAN

504 U.S. 191, 112 S.Ct. 1846, 119 L.Ed.2d 5 (1992)

The state of Tennessee prohibited political campaigning within 100 feet of polling places on election day. The law was challenged by Mary Freeman, who claimed that it violated her First Amendment free speech rights.

Vote: 5–3 (Justice Thomas did not participate)

JUSTICE BLACKMUN announced the judgment of the Court and delivered an opinion, in which CHIEF JUSTICE REHNQUIST, JUSTICE WHITE, and JUSTICE KENNEDY join.

Twenty six years ago, this Court, in a majority opinion written by Justice Hugo L. Black, struck down a state law that made it a crime for a newspaper editor to publish an editorial on election day urging readers to vote in a particular way. *Mills v. Alabama*, 384 U.S. 214 (1966). While the Court did not hesitate to denounce the statute as an "obvious and flagrant abridgment" of First Amendment rights, it was quick to point out that its holding "in no way involve[d] the extent of a State's power to regulate conduct in and around the polls in order to maintain peace, order and decorum there."

Today, we confront the issue carefully left open in *Mills*. The question presented is whether a provision of the Tennessee Code, which prohibits the solicitation of votes and the display or distribution of campaign materials within 100 feet of the entrance to a polling place, violates the First and Fourteenth Amendments.

The State of Tennessee has carved out an election day "campaign free zone" through § 2–7–111(b) of its election code. That section reads in pertinent part:

> Within the appropriate boundary as established in subsection (a) [100 feet from the entrances], and the building in which the polling place is located, the display of campaign posters, signs or other campaign materials, distribution of campaign materials, and solicitation of votes for or against any person or political party or position on a question are prohibited. Tenn. Code Ann. § 2–7–111(b) (Supp. 1991).

The Tennessee statute implicates three central concerns in our First Amendment jurisprudence: regulation of political speech, regulation of speech in a public forum, and regulation based on the content of the speech. The speech restricted by § 2–7–111(b) obviously is political speech. "Whatever differences may exist about interpretations of the First Amendment, there is practically universal agreement that a major purpose of that Amendment was to protect the free discussion of governmental affairs." *Mills v. Alabama*, 384 U.S., at 218. "For speech concerning public affairs is more than self expression; it is the essence of self government." *Garrison v. Louisiana*, 379 U.S. 64, 74–75 (1964). Accordingly, this Court has recognized that "the First Amendment 'has its fullest and most urgent application' to speech uttered during a campaign for political office."

The second important feature of § 2–7–111(b) is that it bars speech in quintessential public forums. These forums include those places "which by long tradition or by government fiat have been devoted to assembly and debate," such as parks, streets, and sidewalks. "Such use of the streets and public places has, from ancient times, been a part of the privileges, immunities, rights, and liberties of citizens." At the same time, however, expressive activity, even in a quintessential public forum, may interfere with other important activities for which the property is used. Accordingly, this Court has held that the government may regulate the time, place, and manner of the expressive activity, so long as such restrictions are content neutral, are narrowly tailored to serve a significant governmental interest, and leave open ample alternatives for communication.

The Tennessee restriction under consideration, however, is not a facially content neutral time, place, or manner restriction. Whether individuals may exercise their free speech rights near polling places depends entirely on whether their speech is related to a political campaign. The statute does not reach other categories of speech, such as commercial solicitation, distribution, and display. This Court has held that the First Amendment's hostility to content based regulation extends not only to a restriction on a particular viewpoint, but also to a prohibition of public discussion of an entire topic.

As a facially content-based restriction on political speech in a public forum, § 2–7–111(b) must be subjected to exacting scrutiny: The State must show that the "regulation is necessary to serve a compelling state interest and that it is narrowly drawn to achieve that end."

Despite the ritualistic ease with which we state this now familiar standard, its announcement does not allow us to avoid the truly difficult issues involving the First Amendment. Perhaps foremost among these serious issues are cases that force us to reconcile our commitment to free speech with our commitment to other constitutional rights embodied in government proceedings. This case presents us with a particularly difficult reconciliation: the accommodation of the right to engage in political discourse with the right to vote—a right at the heart of our democracy.

Tennessee asserts that its campaign free zone serves two compelling interests. First, the State argues that its regulation serves its compelling interest in protecting the right of its citizens to vote freely for the candidates of their choice. Second, Tennessee argues that its restriction protects the right to vote in an election conducted with integrity and reliability.

The interests advanced by Tennessee obviously are compelling ones. This Court has recognized that the "right to vote freely for the candidate of one's choice is of the essence of a democratic society." Indeed, No right is more precious in a free country than that of having a choice in the election of those who make the laws under which, as good citizens, they must live. Other rights, even the most basic, are illusory if the right to vote is undermined. *Wesberry* v. *Sanders*, 376 U.S. 1 (1964).

Accordingly, this Court has concluded that a State has a compelling interest in protecting voters from confusion and undue influence.

The Court also has recognized that a State "indisputably has a compelling interest in preserving the integrity of its election process." The Court thus has "upheld generally applicable and evenhanded restrictions that protect the integrity and reliability of the electoral process itself." In other words, it has recognized that a State has a compelling interest in ensuring that an individual's right to vote is not undermined by fraud in the election process.

To survive strict scrutiny, however, a State must do more than assert a compelling state interest—it must demonstrate that its law is necessary to serve the asserted interest. While we readily acknowledge that a law rarely survives such scrutiny, an examination of the evolution of election reform, both in this country and abroad, demonstrates the necessity of restricted areas in or around polling places.

During the colonial period, many government officials were elected by the *viva voce* method or by the showing of hands, as was the custom in most parts of Europe. That voting scheme was not a private affair, but an open, public decision, witnessed by all and improperly influenced by some. The opportunities that the *viva voce* system gave for bribery and intimidation gradually led to its repeal. Within 20 years of the formation of the Union, most States had incorporated the paper ballot into their electoral system. Initially, this paper ballot was a vast improvement. Individual voters made their own handwritten ballots, marked them in the privacy of their homes, and then brought them to the polls for counting. But the effort of making out such a ballot became increasingly more complex and cumbersome. Wishing to gain influence, political parties began to produce their own ballots for voters. These ballots were often printed with flamboyant colors, distinctive designs, and emblems so that they could be recognized at a distance. State attempts to standardize the ballots were easily thwarted—the vote buyer could simply place a ballot in the hands of the bribed voter and watch until he placed it in the polling box. Thus, the evils associated with the earlier *viva voce* system reinfected the election process; the failure of the law to secure secrecy opened the door to bribery and intimidation.

Approaching the polling place under this system was akin to entering an open auction place. As the elector started his journey to the polls, he was met by various party ticket peddlers "who were only too anxious to supply him with their party tickets." Often the competition became heated when several such peddlers found an uncommitted or wavering voter. Sham battles were frequently engaged in to keep away elderly and timid voters of the opposition. In short, these early elections "were not a very pleasant spectacle for those who believed in democratic government."

The problems with voter intimidation and election fraud that the United States was experiencing were not unique. Several other countries were attempting to work out satisfactory solutions to these same problems. Some Australian provinces adopted a series of reforms intended to secure the secrecy of an elector's vote. The most famous feature of the Australian system was its provision for an official ballot, encompassing all candidates of all parties on the same ticket. But this was not the only measure adopted to preserve the secrecy of the ballot. The Australian system also provided for the erection of polling booths (containing several voting compartments) open only to election officials, two "scrutinees" for each candidate, and electors about to vote. In sum, an examination of the history of election regulation in this country reveals a persistent battle against two evils: voter intimidation and election fraud. After an unsuccessful experiment with an unofficial ballot system, all 50 States, together with numerous other Western democracies, settled on the same solution: a secret ballot secured in part by a restricted zone around the voting compartments. We find that this wide spread and time tested consensus demonstrates that some restricted zone is necessary in order to serve the States' compelling interest in preventing voter intimidation and election fraud.

In conclusion, we reaffirm that it is the rare case in which we have held that a law survives strict scrutiny. This, however, is such a rare case. Here, the State, as recognized administrator of elections, has asserted that the exercise of free speech rights conflicts with another fundamental right, the right to cast a ballot in an election free from the taint of intimidation and fraud. A long history, a substantial consensus, and simple common sense show that some restricted zone around polling places is necessary to protect that fundamental right. Given the conflict between these two rights, we hold that requiring solicitors to stand 100 feet from the entrances to polling places does not constitute an unconstitutional compromise.

The judgment of the Tennessee Supreme Court is reversed and the case is remanded for further proceedings not inconsistent with this opinion.

FOR DISCUSSION

Bans on campaigning near the polls pit competing First Amendment rights of voters against those of candidates and campaigners. Here the voters won. Critics have argued that media reports on election returns before the polls close or reporting outcomes of polls adversely affect voter turnout. Given the clash between free press and voting rights, should restrictions on press coverage of election results be restricted? How about bans on election day campaigning overall?

Article II, Sec. 1, cl. 2:

Each State shall appoint, in such Manner as the Legislature thereof may direct, a Number of Electors, equal to the whole Number of Senators and Representatives to which the State may be entitled in the Congress: but no Senator or Representative, or Person holding an Office of Trust or Profit under the United States, shall be appointed an Elector.

BUSH V. GORE

531 U.S. 98, 121 S.Ct. 525, 148 L.Ed.2d 388 (2000)

The popular vote in 2000 for presidential candidates George Bush and Al Gore produced a margin of victory for the former of approximately 1,784 votes out of several million cast. The election was marred by allegations of bad ballot design, misvoting, voter intimidation, and a host of other issues. Under Florida law, Gore was able first to file a "protest," in which he asked for a recount of ballots in four counties, three of which used a punch card ballot design where a voter, using a stylus, punched a hole in a piece of paper to select a candidate. His claim was that many of the ballots that were not counted or invalidated actually had votes for him. Gore asked for more time to recount these votes. The Florida Supreme Court agreed, but its decision was vacated by the U.S. Supreme Court. Gore then filed a "contest" to the election, as provided for under state law, asking for a manual recount in two counties. The recount was challenged under a variety of state statutory and federal constitutional grounds. The Florida Supreme Court in a 4–3 decision permitted the recount. While the recount was occurring, the gap between Bush and Gore narrowed to a few hundred votes before the Supreme Court issued an injunction halting the recount. Florida's electoral votes thus went to Bush, who secured a narrow electoral college victory.

Vote: 5–4

PER CURIAM.

I

On December 8, 2000, the Supreme Court of Florida ordered that the Circuit Court of Leon County tabulate by hand 9,000 ballots in Miami-Dade County. It also ordered the inclusion in the certified vote totals of 215 votes identified in Palm Beach County and 168 votes identified in Miami-Dade County for Vice President Albert Gore, Jr., and Senator Joseph Lieberman, Democratic Candidates for President and Vice President. The Supreme Court noted that petitioner, Governor George W. Bush asserted that the net gain for Vice President Gore in Palm Beach County was 176 votes, and directed the Circuit Court to resolve that dispute on remand. The court further held that relief would require manual recounts in all Florida counties where so-called "undervotes" had not been subject to manual tabulation. The court ordered all manual recounts to begin at once. Governor Bush and Richard Cheney, Republican Candidates for the Presidency and Vice Presidency, filed an emergency application for a stay of this mandate. On December 9, we granted the application, treated the application as a petition for a writ of certiorari, and granted certiorari

The proceedings leading to the present controversy are discussed in some detail in our opinion in *Bush v. Palm Beach County Canvassing Bd.,* 531 U.S. 70 (2000) *(per curiam) (Bush I)*. On November 8, 2000, the day following the Presidential election, the Florida Division of Elections reported that petitioner, Governor Bush, had received 2,909,135 votes, and respondent, Vice President Gore, had received 2,907,351 votes, a margin of 1,784 for Governor Bush. Because Governor Bush's margin of victory was less than "one-half of a percent of the votes cast," an automatic machine recount was conducted under § 102.141(4) of the election code, the results of which showed Governor Bush still winning the race but by a diminished margin. Vice President Gore then sought manual recounts in Volusia, Palm Beach, Broward, and Miami-Dade Counties, pursuant to Florida's election protest provisions. A dispute arose concerning the deadline for local county canvassing boards to submit their returns to the Secretary of State (Secretary). The Secretary declined to waive the November 14 deadline imposed by statute. The Florida Supreme Court, however, set the deadline at November 26. We granted certiorari and vacated the Florida Supreme Court's decision, finding considerable uncertainty as to the grounds on which it was based.

On November 26, the Florida Elections Canvassing Commission certified the results of the election and declared Governor Bush the winner of Florida's 25 electoral votes. On November 27, Vice President Gore, pursuant to Florida's contest provisions, filed a complaint in Leon County Circuit Court contesting the certification. He sought relief pursuant to § 102.168(3)(c), which provides that "[r]eceipt of a number of illegal votes or rejection of a number of legal votes sufficient to change or place in doubt the result of the election" shall be grounds for a contest. The Circuit Court denied relief, stating that Vice President Gore failed to meet his burden of proof. He appealed to the First District Court of Appeal, which certified the matter to the Florida Supreme Court.

Accepting jurisdiction, the Florida Supreme Court affirmed in part and reversed in part. The court held that the Circuit Court had been correct to reject Vice President Gore's challenge to the results certified in Nassau County and his challenge to the Palm Beach County Canvassing Board's determination that 3,300 ballots cast in that county were not, in the statutory phrase, "legal votes."

The Supreme Court held that Vice President Gore had satisfied his burden of proof under § 102.168(3)(c) with respect to his challenge to Miami-Dade County's failure to tabulate, by manual count, 9,000 ballots on which the machines had failed to detect a vote for President ("undervotes"). Noting the closeness of the election, the Court explained that "[o]n this record, there can be no question that there are legal votes within the 9,000 uncounted votes sufficient to place the results of this election in doubt." A "legal vote," as determined by the Supreme Court, is "one in which there is a 'clear indication of the intent of the voter,' . . . " The court therefore ordered a hand recount of the 9,000 ballots in Miami-Dade County. Observing that the contest provisions vest broad discretion in the circuit judge to "provide any relief appropriate under such circumstances," the Supreme Court further held that the Circuit Court could order "the Supervisor of Elections and the Canvassing Boards, as well as the necessary public officials, in all counties that have not conducted a manual recount or tabulation of the undervotes . . . to do so forthwith, said tabulation to take place in the individual counties where the ballots are located."

The Supreme Court also determined that both Palm Beach County and Miami-Dade County, in their earlier manual recounts, had identified a net gain of 215 and 168 legal votes for Vice President Gore. Rejecting the Circuit Court's conclusion that Palm Beach County lacked the authority to include the 215 net votes submitted past the November 26 deadline, the Supreme Court explained that the deadline was not intended to exclude votes identified after that date through ongoing manual recounts. As to Miami-Dade County, the Court concluded that although the 168 votes identified were the result of a partial recount, they were "legal votes [that] could change the outcome of the election." The Supreme Court therefore directed the Circuit Court to include those totals in the certified results, subject to resolution of the actual vote total from the Miami-Dade partial recount.

The petition presents the following questions: whether the Florida Supreme Court established new standards for resolving Presidential election contests, thereby violating Art. II, § 1, cl. 2, of the United States Constitution and failing to comply with 3 U.S.C. § 5 and whether the use of standardless manual recounts violates the Equal Protection and Due Process Clauses. With respect to the equal protection question, we find a violation of the Equal Protection Clause.

B

The individual citizen has no federal constitutional right to vote for electors for the President of the United States unless and until the state legislature chooses a statewide election as the means to implement its power to appoint members of the Electoral College. U.S. Const., Art. II, § 1. This is the source for the statement in *McPherson* v. *Blacker*, 146 U.S. 1, 35 (1892), that the State legislature's power to select the manner for appointing electors is plenary; it may, if it so chooses, select the electors itself, which indeed was the manner used by State legislatures in several States for many years after the Framing of our Constitution. History has now favored the voter, and in each of the several States the citizens themselves vote for Presidential electors. When the state legislature vests the right to vote for President in its people, the right to vote as the legislature has prescribed is fundamental; and one source of its fundamental nature lies in the equal weight accorded to each vote and the equal dignity owed to each voter. The State, of course, after granting the franchise in the special context of Article II, can take back the power to appoint electors.

The right to vote is protected in more than the initial allocation of the franchise. Equal protection applies as well to the manner of its exercise. Having once granted the right to vote on equal terms, the State may not, by later arbitrary and disparate treatment, value one person's vote over that of another. It must be remembered that "the right of suffrage can be denied by a debasement or dilution of the weight of a citizen's vote just as effectively as by wholly prohibiting the free exercise of the franchise." *Reynolds v. Sims*, 377 U.S. 533 (1964).

There is no difference between the two sides of the present controversy on these basic propositions. Respondents say that the very purpose of vindicating the right to vote justifies the recount procedures now at issue. The question before us, however, is whether the recount procedures the Florida Supreme Court has adopted are consistent with its obligation to avoid arbitrary and disparate treatment of the members of its electorate.

Much of the controversy seems to revolve around ballot cards designed to be perforated by a stylus but which, either through error or deliberate omission, have not been perforated with sufficient precision for a machine to count them. In some cases a piece of the card—a chad—is hanging, say by two corners. In other cases there is no separation at all, just an indentation.

The Florida Supreme Court has ordered that the intent of the voter be discerned from such ballots. For purposes of resolving the equal protection challenge, it is not necessary to decide whether the Florida Supreme Court had the authority under the legislative scheme for resolving election disputes to define what a legal vote is and to mandate a manual recount implementing that definition. The recount mechanisms implemented in response to the decisions of the Florida Supreme Court do not satisfy the minimum requirement for non-arbitrary treatment of voters necessary to secure the fundamental right. Florida's basic command for the count of legally cast votes is to consider the "intent of the voter." This is unobjectionable as an abstract proposition and a starting principle. The problem inheres in the absence of specific standards to ensure its equal application. The formulation of uniform rules to determine intent based on these recurring circumstances is practicable and, we conclude, necessary.

The law does not refrain from searching for the intent of the actor in a multitude of circumstances; and in some cases the general command to ascertain intent is not susceptible to much further refinement. In this instance, however, the question is not whether to believe a witness but how to interpret the marks or holes or scratches on an inanimate object, a piece of cardboard or paper which, it is said, might not have registered as a vote during the machine count. The factfinder confronts a thing, not a person. The search for intent can be confined by specific rules designed to ensure uniform treatment.

The want of those rules here has led to unequal evaluation of ballots in various respects. As seems to have been acknowledged at oral argument, the standards for accepting or rejecting contested ballots might vary not only from county to county but indeed within a single county from one recount team to another.

An early case in our one person, one vote jurisprudence arose when a State accorded arbitrary and disparate treatment to voters in its different counties. *Gray* v. *Sanders*, 372 U.S. 368 (1963). The Court found a constitutional violation. We relied on these principles in the context of the Presidential selection process in *Moore* v. *Ogilvie*, 394 US 814 (1969), where we invalidated a county-based procedure that diluted the influence of citizens in larger counties in the nominating process. There we observed that "[t]he idea that one group can be granted greater voting strength than another is hostile to the one man, one vote basis of our representative government."

The State Supreme Court ratified this uneven treatment. It mandated that the recount totals from two counties, Miami-Dade and Palm Beach, be included in the certified total. The court also appeared to hold *sub silentio* that the recount totals from Broward County, which were not completed until after the original November 14 certification by the Secretary of State, were to be considered part of the new certified vote totals even though the county certification was not contested by Vice President Gore. Yet each of the counties used varying standards to determine what was a legal vote. Broward County used a more forgiving standard than Palm Beach County, and uncovered almost three times as many new votes, a result markedly disproportionate to the difference in population between the counties.

In addition, the recounts in these three counties were not limited to so-called undervotes but extended to all of the ballots. The distinction has real consequences. A manual recount of all ballots identifies not only those ballots which show no vote but also those which contain more than one, the so-called overvotes. Neither category will be counted by the machine. This is not a trivial concern. At oral argument, respondents estimated there are as many as 110,000 overvotes statewide. As a result, the citizen whose ballot was not read by a machine because he failed to vote for a candidate in a way readable by a machine may still have his vote counted in a manual recount; on the other hand, the citizen who marks two candidates in a way discernable by the machine will not have the same opportunity to have his vote count, even if a manual examination of the ballot would reveal the requisite indicia of intent. Furthermore, the citizen who marks two candidates, only one of which is discernable by the machine, will have his vote counted even though it should have been read as an invalid ballot. The State Supreme Court's inclusion of vote counts based on these variant standards exemplifies concerns with the remedial processes that were under way.

That brings the analysis to yet a further equal protection problem. The votes certified by the court included a partial total from one county, Miami-Dade. The Florida Supreme Court's decision thus gives no assurance that the recounts included in a final certification must be complete. Indeed, it is respondent's submission that it would be consistent with the rules of the recount procedures to include whatever partial counts are done by the time of final certification, and we interpret the Florida Supreme Court's decision to permit this. This accommodation no doubt results from the truncated contest period established by the Florida Supreme Court in *Bush I*, at respondents' own urging. The press of time does not diminish the constitutional concern. A desire for speed is not a general excuse for ignoring equal protection guarantees.

In addition to these difficulties the actual process by which the votes were to be counted under the Florida Supreme Court's decision raises further concerns. That order did not specify who would recount the ballots.

The county canvassing boards were forced to pull together ad hoc teams comprised of judges from various Circuits who had no previous training in handling and interpreting ballots. Furthermore, while others were permitted to observe, they were prohibited from objecting during the recount.

The recount process, in its features here described, is inconsistent with the minimum procedures necessary to protect the fundamental right of each voter in the special instance of a statewide recount under the authority of a single state judicial officer. Our consideration is limited to the present circumstances, for the problem of equal protection in election processes generally presents many complexities.

The question before the Court is not whether local entities, in the exercise of their expertise, may develop different systems for implementing elections. Instead, we are presented with a situation where a state court with the power to assure uniformity has ordered a statewide recount with minimal procedural safeguards. When a court orders a statewide remedy, there must be at least some assurance that the rudimentary requirements of equal treatment and fundamental fairness are satisfied.

Given the Court's assessment that the recount process underway was probably being conducted in an unconstitutional manner, the Court stayed the order directing the recount so it could hear this case and render an expedited decision. The contest provision, as it was mandated by the State Supreme Court, is not well calculated to sustain the confidence that all citizens must have in the outcome of elections. The State has not shown that its procedures include the necessary safeguards. The problem, for instance, of the estimated 110,000 overvotes has not been addressed, although Chief Justice Wells called attention to the concern in his dissenting opinion.

Upon due consideration of the difficulties identified to this point, it is obvious that the recount cannot be conducted in compliance with the requirements of equal protection and due process without substantial additional work. It would require not only the adoption (after opportunity for argument) of adequate statewide standards for determining what is a legal vote, and practicable procedures to implement them, but also orderly judicial review of any disputed matters that might arise. In addition, the Secretary of State has advised that the recount of only a portion of the ballots requires that the vote tabulation equipment be used to screen out undervotes, a function for which the machines were not designed. If a recount of overvotes were also required, perhaps even a second screening would be necessary. Use of the equipment for this purpose, and any new software developed for it, would have to be evaluated for accuracy by the Secretary of State, as required by Fla. Stat. § 101.015 (2000).

The Supreme Court of Florida has said that the legislature intended the State's electors to "participat[e] fully in the federal electoral process," as provided in 3 U.S.C. § 5. That statute, in turn, requires that any controversy or contest that is designed to lead to a conclusive selection of electors be completed by December 12. That date is upon us, and there is no recount procedure in place under the State Supreme Court's order that comports with minimal constitutional standards. Because it is evident that any recount seeking to meet the December 12 date will be unconstitutional for the reasons we have discussed, we reverse the judgment of the Supreme Court of Florida ordering a recount to proceed.

Seven Justices of the Court agree that there are constitutional problems with the recount ordered by the Florida Supreme Court that demand a remedy. The only disagreement is as to the remedy. Because the Florida Supreme Court has said that the Florida Legislature intended to obtain the safe-harbor benefits of 3 U.S.C. § 5 Justice Breyer's proposed remedy—remanding to the Florida Supreme Court for its ordering of a constitutionally proper contest until December 18—contemplates action in violation of the Florida election code, and hence could not be part of an "appropriate" order authorized by Fla. Stat. § 102.168(8) (2000).

The judgment of the Supreme Court of Florida is reversed, and the case is remanded for further proceedings not inconsistent with this opinion.

JUSTICE STEVENS, with whom JUSTICES GINSBURG and BREYER join, dissenting.

In the interest of finality, however, the majority effectively orders the disenfranchisement of an unknown number of voters whose ballots reveal their intent—and are therefore legal votes under state law—but were for some reason rejected by ballot-counting machines. It does so on the basis of the deadlines set forth in Title 3 of the United States Code. But, as I have already noted, those provisions merely provide rules of decision for Congress to follow when selecting among conflicting slates of electors. They do not prohibit a State from counting what the majority concedes to be legal votes until a bona fide winner is determined. Indeed, in 1960, Hawaii appointed two slates of electors and Congress chose to count the one appointed on January 4, 1961, well after the Title 3 deadlines.

Thus, nothing prevents the majority, even if it properly found an equal protection violation, from ordering relief appropriate to remedy that violation without depriving Florida voters of their right to have their votes counted. As the majority notes, "[a] desire for speed is not a general excuse for ignoring equal protection guarantees."

Finally, neither in this case, nor in its earlier opinion in *Palm Beach County Canvassing Bd.* v. *Harris,* 2000 WL 1725434 (Fla., Nov. 21, 2000), did the Florida Supreme Court make any substantive change in Florida electoral law. Its decisions were rooted in long-established precedent and were consistent with the relevant statutory provisions, taken as a whole. It did what courts do—it decided the case before it in light of the legislature's intent to leave no legally cast vote uncounted. In so doing, it relied on the sufficiency of the general "intent of the voter" standard articulated by the state legislature, coupled with a procedure for ultimate review by an impartial judge, to resolve the concern about disparate evaluations of contested ballots. If we assume—as I do—that the members of that court and the judges who would have carried out its mandate are impartial, its decision does not even raise a colorable federal question.

What must underlie petitioners' entire federal assault on the Florida election procedures is an unstated lack of confidence in the impartiality and capacity of the state judges who would make the critical decisions if the vote count were to proceed. Otherwise, their position is wholly without merit. The endorsement of that position by the majority of this Court can only lend credence to the most cynical appraisal of the work of judges throughout the land. It is confidence in the men and women who administer the judicial system that is the true backbone of the rule of law. Time will one day heal the wound to that confidence that will be inflicted by today's decision. One thing, however, is certain. Although we may never know with complete certainty the identity of the winner of this year's Presidential election, the identity of the loser is perfectly clear. It is the Nation's confidence in the judge as an impartial guardian of the rule of law.

I respectfully dissent.

FOR DISCUSSION

Was this a political decision, as many contend? Some see the majority Republican Court as having essentially decided the outcome of the 2000 presidential race. What did the Court say about the intent of the voter and ascertaining it in this case? Does applying different standards across different counties not raise an equal protection or perhaps a due process issue?

JUDICIAL SELECTION

Article II, section 2 of the Constitution invests in the president authority, subject to the advice and consent of the Senate, to nominate Justices for the Supreme Court and for the lower federal courts. Once confirmed, federal judges have lifetime appointments and do not face election or reconfirmation. But this type of judicial selection is not shared at the state level where elected judges are the norm.

Over time, states have displayed a variety of ways of selecting their judges. Until 1812, states used an appointment process to select their judges. In that year Georgia became the first state to use elections as a method of choosing at least some of its judges. Georgia was soon followed by Indiana and then Mississippi, and by the end of the Civil War the spirit of Jacksonian populism yielded 24 of the 34 states using elections to select judges. Every other state subsequently admitted to the union opted for judicial elections. By 1927, fears that judges were corrupted by party politics led 12 states to adopt non-partisan judicial races, and concern that judicial elections were not producing the most qualified judges ushered in the advent of merit selection systems. Merit plans, otherwise called or referred to as the Missouri Plan because it was the first state to adopt this method in 1940, involved the creation of a judicial commission that screens and then recommends qualified judicial candidates to the governor who then selects from that slate. Subsequently, after one or more years, there is a non-competitive retention election that lets the voters decide if they wish to keep that judge on the bench.

Fourteen states use the Missouri Plan to select judges. Four states—California, Maine, New Hampshire, and New Jersey—use gubernatorial appointment, while South Carolina and Virginia legislatures select their judges. Thirteen states, including Minnesota, Wisconsin, and Washington, used non-partisan elections, while eight states, including Texas, Pennsylvania, Ohio, and Illinois, allowed for partisan elections. Finally, eight states, including New York, employ hybrid or mixed methods to pick judges, often mixing elections with merit plan systems.

In addition to merit selection systems, many states adopted rules that placed limits on the activities of judicial candidates. Beginning in 1924, the American Bar Association issued a model code of judicial conduct that "should not announce in advance [their] conclusions of law on disputed issues of fact to secure class support." Subsequent ABA rules discouraged judicial candidates from affiliating with political parties and from personally soliciting campaign contributions. The great fear in allowing candidates to announce their positions, engage in partisan politics, or solicit contributions was that such activity would compromise the independence and impartiality of the judiciary. But the problem with such regulations, according to some critics, is that they violate the First Amendment, rendering it difficult to hold genuine elections if judicial candidates cannot address issues or campaign. Conversely, supporters of the restrictions assert that judicial elections are different than those for the legislature or Congress, for example, and therefore these limits preserve impartiality. Thus, there is a potential tension in the law—promoting judicial impartiality versus respecting the First Amendment rights surrounding electoral activity. These issues came to a head in *Republican Party of Minnesota v. White.*

Republican Party of Minnesota v. White. is actually two cases. There was the United States Supreme Court decision in 2002 (536 U.S. 765 (2002) "*White I*") and subsequently one by the 8th Circuit Court of Appeals (416 F.3d 738 (8th Cir. 2005) *White II*"). At issue in both was Canon 5 of the *Minnesota Code of Judicial Conduct.* The *Code* prohibited judicial candidates from announcing their views on disputed legal or political issues, affiliating themselves with political parties, or personally soliciting or accepting campaign contributions. In separate decisions, the Supreme Court and the 8th Circuit reviewed and struck down these three *Code* provisions regulating the speech and conduct of judicial candidates in Minnesota

The two *White* opinions declared most of Canon 5 unconstitutional. The reaction to opinions was significant. Many feared that the freeing up of judicial candidates to solicit money, announce their positions, and affiliate with parties would turn these elections into expensive, partisan, and special interest driven elections. The fear was that judicial elections across the country would look like races in states such as in Texas and Ohio which had become highly contentious and expensive.

In Minnesota there were attempts to redraft Canon 5 to address the concerns of the two *White* opinions. These efforts were unsuccessful. In *Wersel v. Sexton*, 613 F.3d. 821(8th Cir. 2010), the Eighth Circuit struck down on First Amendment grounds formerly Canon 5 (now Canon 4) of the Rules of Judicial Conduct which prevent judicial candidates from endorsing other candidates for office ("Endorsement"), or from personally soliciting campaign funds or soliciting for a political organization ("Solicitation"). The Court ruled that both clauses directly burden the political speech of judicial candidates. The Court conceded that although Minnesota had a compelling interest in maintaining judicial impartiality (defined as openmindedness or a lack of bias against parties), strict scrutiny of the Solicitation and Endorsement clauses indicate that the regulations are not narrowly tailored, not a least restrictive means, and fails over/underinclusiveness. In this case the Court issued an applied as opposed to a facial ruling, but examination of the opinion suggests little room to craft a valid rule. With this latest opinion, it looks as if all of the former Canon 5 restrictions are gone and judicial candidates are free to solicit, affiliation, and announce their positions similar to candidates for other political offices. Have the courts effectively stated that judicial elections are no different than those for other offices? Two other Supreme Court opinions offer mixed messages on this question.

Subsequent to the two *White* opinions, the Court in *New York State Board of Elections* v. *Lopez Torres*, 552 U.S. 196, 128 S.Ct. 791, 169 L.Ed.2d 665 (2008), the Supreme Court overturned a lower court decision that had declared unconstitutional the state's use of judicial conventions to select candidates for the position of New York Supreme Court Justice. In a 9–0 opinion the Court (again with Scalia writing the majority opinion) ruled that the First Amendment gives broad protection to political parties regarding how they select and endorse judicial candidates. *Lopez Torres*, while drawing some of its constitutional authority from the freedom of association political party cases, seemed to be another sign that the Court was sanctioning wide-open partisan selection for judges.

But then in In *Caperton v. Massey*, 556 U.S. 868, 129 S. Ct. 2252 (2009), the Supreme Court seemed to place limits on the two *White* decisions.

In *Caperton* a West Virginia jury found the A.T. Massey Coal Company and its affiliates liable for misrepresentation and tortious interference with a contract. The jury awarded Caperton, a competing group of coal interests, $50 million in compensatory and punitive damages. After the verdict but before the appeal, Massey's CEO/President Blankenship decided to support a candidate (Benjamin) challenging a sitting justice on the state supreme court of appeals. Blankenship gave $1,000 to Benjamin's campaign and $2.5 million to an organization supporting the candidate; he also expended $500,000 independently to support Benjamin. This $3 million was more than three times the total contributions from the rest of Benjamin's contributors. Benjamin won the election and Massey filed its appeal. Caperton requested Benjamin's recusal and he denied it. The court in a 3–2 vote, with Benjamin in the majority, reversed the lower court judgment. Caperton sought a rehearing and recusal of the three justices in majority, citing a close connection (one justice vacationing with Blankenship while the case was pending) and other reasons. Two of the justices (including the chief justice) recused themselves, but Benjamin stayed on as acting chief justice. Benjamin then selected two replacement justices to hear the case. The court again by a 3–2 vote sided with Massey. Caperton appealed to the United States Supreme Court, arguing that the failure to recuse violated the Due Process clause.

Writing for the Court in a 5–4 opinion, Justice Kennedy reversed, affirming that the Due Process clause incorporates a common law rule that a judge must recuse himself in cases where he has a personal interest or stake. Recusal is further required where the chance of actual bias is too high to be constitutionally tolerable. Here, because of Blankenship's role in getting Benjamin elected, the Court judged that the latter would feel a debt of gratitude to the former for his efforts. While the Court declined to argue that there was actual bias in the case, the combination of the dollar amount of the contributions and the timing of the contributions led to a risk of potential bias sufficiently high that it violated the Due Process clause.

According to Kennedy, although there is no allegation of a *quid pro quo* agreement, the fact remains that Blankenship's extraordinary contributions were made at a time when he had a vested stake in the outcome of the case. Just as "no man" (Kennedy's words) is allowed to be a judge in his own cause, similar fears of bias can arise when—without the consent of the other parties—a man chooses the judge in his own cause. And applying this principle to the judicial election process, here there was a serious, objective risk of actual bias that required Justice Benjamin's recusal. Justice Benjamin did undertake an extensive search for actual bias, but that is just one step in the judicial process; objective standards may also require recusal whether or not actual bias exists or can be proved. Due process "may sometimes bar trial by judges who have no actual bias and who would do their very best to weigh the scales of justice equally between contending parties."

Despite the *Massey* decision appearing to place some limits on *White*, many remain concerned about the impact the judicial elections can have upon judges. Former Supreme Court Justice O'Connor, for example, announced in 2010 that she was heading up a group working to eliminate elections and replace them with some type of merit selection. Yet others still believe that elections better promote accountability and open government and that the public has a right to select their judges. However, some of those fears were abated by the Supreme Court in *Williams-Yulee v. Florida Bar,* 135 S.Ct. 1656 (2015) Here the Supreme Court ruled in a 5–4 opinion upon a judicial conduct rule preventing a candidate for judicial official from personally solicited campaign funds. Contrary to the *White* opinions which suggested judicial candidates were no different than candidates for other offices, the Court say judges are different and with special needs of maintaining public confidence in the integrity of the judiciary. The Court also drew lines that distinguished the laws regulating judicial contributions from those given to other candidates for office. For now at least, the Court seemed to be saying that judges were different and could be subject to unique regulations.

REPUBLICAN PARTY OF MINNESOTA V. WHITE

536 U.S. 765, 122 S.Ct. 2528, 153 L.Ed.2d 694 (2002)

An individual running as a candidate for the Minnesota Supreme Court challenged on First Amendment free speech grounds rules prohibiting him from announcing positions his positions on legal and political issues that might come before the Court. He also challenged the rules preventing the candidate from soliciting funds and affiliating with a political party. District court and Court of Appeals ruled against him and the Supreme Court reversed, declaring that the rule preventing him from announcing his positons was unconstitutional.

Vote: 5–4

JUSTICE SCALIA delivered the opinion of the Court.

The question presented in this case is whether the First Amendment permits the Minnesota Supreme Court to prohibit candidates for judicial election in that State from announcing their views on disputed legal and political issues.

I

Since Minnesota's admission to the Union in 1858, the State's Constitution has provided for the selection of all state judges by popular election. Since 1912, those elections have been nonpartisan. Since 1974, they have been subject to a legal restriction which states that a "candidate for a judicial office, including an incumbent judge," shall not "announce his or her views on disputed legal or political issues." Minn.Code of Judicial Conduct, Canon 5(A)(3)(d)(i) (2000). This prohibition, promulgated by the Minnesota Supreme Court and based on Canon 7(B) of the 1972 American Bar Association (ABA) Model Code of Judicial Conduct, is known as the "announce clause." Incumbent judges who violate it are subject to discipline, including removal, censure, civil penalties, and suspension without pay. Lawyers who run for judicial office also must comply with the announce clause. Those who violate it are subject to, *inter alia,* disbarment, suspension, and probation.

In 1996, one of the petitioners, Gregory Wersal, ran for associate justice of the Minnesota Supreme Court. In the course of the campaign, he distributed literature criticizing several Minnesota Supreme Court decisions on issues such as crime, welfare, and abortion. A complaint against Wersal challenging, among other things, the propriety of this literature was filed with the Office of Lawyers Professional Responsibility, the agency which, under the direction of the Minnesota Lawyers Professional Responsibility Board, investigates and prosecutes ethical violations of lawyer candidates for judicial office. The Lawyers Board dismissed the complaint; with regard to the charges that his campaign materials violated the announce clause, it expressed doubt whether the clause could constitutionally be enforced. Nonetheless, fearing that further ethical complaints would jeopardize his ability to practice law, Wersal withdrew from the election. In 1998, Wersal ran again for the same office. Early in that race, he sought an advisory opinion from the Lawyers Board with regard to whether it planned to enforce the announce clause. The Lawyers Board responded equivocally, stating that, although it had significant doubts about the constitutionality of the provision, it was unable to answer his question because he had not submitted a list of the announcements he wished to make.

III

As the Court of Appeals recognized, the announce clause both prohibits speech on the basis of its content and burdens a category of speech that is "at the core of our First Amendment freedoms"—speech about the qualifications of candidates for public office. The Court of Appeals concluded that the proper test to be applied to determine the constitutionality of such a restriction is what our cases have called strict scrutiny; the parties do not dispute that this is correct. Under the strict-scrutiny test, respondents have the burden to prove that the announce clause is (1) narrowly tailored, to serve (2) a compelling state interest. In order for respondents to show that the announce clause is narrowly tailored, they must demonstrate that it does not "unnecessarily circumscrib[e] protected expression."

The Court of Appeals concluded that respondents had established two interests as sufficiently compelling to justify the announce clause: preserving the impartiality of the state judiciary and preserving the appearance of the impartiality of the state judiciary. Respondents reassert these two interests before us, arguing that the first is compelling because it protects the due process rights of litigants, and that the second is compelling because it preserves public confidence in the judiciary.* Respondents are rather vague, however, about what they mean by "impartiality." Indeed, although the term is used throughout the Eighth Circuit's opinion, the briefs, the Minnesota Code of Judicial Conduct, and the ABA Codes of Judicial Conduct, none of these sources bothers to define it. Clarity on this point is essential before we can decide whether impartiality is indeed a compelling state interest, and, if so, whether the announce clause is narrowly tailored to achieve it.

A

One meaning of "impartiality" in the judicial context—and of course its root meaning—is the lack of bias for or against either *party* to the proceeding. Impartiality in this sense assures equal application of the law. That is, it guarantees a party that the judge who hears his case will apply the law to him in the same way he applies it to any other party. This is the traditional sense in which the term is used. See Webster's New International Dictionary 1247 (2d ed.1950) (defining "impartial" as "[n]ot partial; esp., not favoring one more than another; treating all alike; unbiased; equitable; fair; just"). It is also the sense in which it is used in the cases cited by respondents and *amici* for the proposition that an impartial judge is essential to due process. *Tumey v. Ohio,* 273 U.S. 510, 523, 531–534, 47 S.Ct. 437, 71 L.Ed. 749 (1927) (judge violated due process by sitting in a case in which it would be in his financial interest to find against one of the parties); *Aetna Life Ins. Co. v. Lavoie,* 475 U.S. 813, 822–825, 106 S.Ct. 1580, 89 L.Ed.2d 823 (1986) (same); *Ward v. Monroeville,* 409 U.S. 57, 58–62, 93 S.Ct. 80,

* Although the Eighth Circuit also referred to the compelling interest in an "independent" judiciary, both it and respondents appear to use that term, as applied to the issues involved in this case, as interchangeable with "impartial."

34 L.Ed.2d 267 (1972) (same); *Johnson v. Mississippi,* 403 U.S. 212, 215–216, 91 S.Ct. 1778, 29 L.Ed.2d 423 (1971) *(per curiam)* (judge violated due process by sitting in a case in which one of the parties was a previously successful litigant against him); *Bracy v. Gramley,* 520 U.S. 899, 905, 117 S.Ct. 1793, 138 L.Ed.2d 97 (1997) (would violate due process if a judge was disposed to rule against defendants who did not bribe him in order to cover up the fact that he regularly ruled in favor of defendants who did bribe him); *In re Murchison,* 349 U.S. 133, 137–139, 75 S.Ct. 623, 99 L.Ed. 942 (1955) (judge violated due process by sitting in the criminal trial of defendant whom he had indicted).

We think it plain that the announce clause is not narrowly tailored to serve impartiality (or the appearance of impartiality) in this sense. Indeed, the clause is barely tailored to serve that interest *at all,* inasmuch as it does not restrict speech for or against particular *parties,* but rather speech for or against particular *issues.* To be sure, when a case arises that turns on a legal issue on which the judge (as a candidate) had taken a particular stand, the party taking the opposite stand is likely to lose. But not because of any bias against that party, or favoritism toward the other party. *Any* party taking that position is just as likely to lose. The judge is applying the law (as he sees it) evenhandedly.*

B

It is perhaps possible to use the term "impartiality" in the judicial context (though this is certainly not a common usage) to mean lack of preconception in favor of or against a particular *legal view.* This sort of impartiality would be concerned, not with guaranteeing litigants equal application of the law, but rather with guaranteeing them an equal chance to persuade the court on the legal points in their case. Impartiality in this sense may well be an interest served by the announce clause, but it is not a *compelling* state interest, as strict scrutiny requires. A judge's lack of predisposition regarding the relevant legal issues in a case has never been thought a necessary component of equal justice, and with good reason. For one thing, it is virtually impossible to find a judge who does not have preconceptions about the law. As then-Justice REHNQUIST observed of our own Court: "Since most Justices come to this bench no earlier than their middle years, it would be unusual if they had not by that time formulated at least some tentative notions that would influence them in their interpretation of the sweeping clauses of the Constitution and their interaction with one another. It would be not merely unusual, but extraordinary, if they had not at least given opinions as to constitutional issues in their previous legal careers." Indeed, even if it were possible to select judges who did not have preconceived views on legal issues, it would hardly be desirable to do so. "Proof that a Justice's mind at the time he joined the Court was a complete *tabula rasa* in the area of constitutional adjudication would be evidence of lack of qualification, not lack of bias." The Minnesota Constitution positively forbids the selection to courts of general jurisdiction of judges who are impartial in the sense of having no views on the law. Minn. Const., Art. VI, § 5 ("Judges of the supreme court, the court of appeals and the district court shall be learned in the law"). And since avoiding judicial preconceptions on legal issues is neither possible nor desirable, pretending otherwise by attempting to preserve the "appearance" of that type of impartiality can hardly be a compelling state interest either.

C

A third possible meaning of "impartiality" (again not a common one) might be described as open-mindedness. This quality in a judge demands, not that he have no preconceptions on legal issues, but that he be willing to consider views that oppose his preconceptions, and remain open to persuasion, when the issues arise

* Justice STEVENS asserts that the announce clause "serves the State's interest in maintaining both the appearance of this form of impartiality and its actuality." We do not disagree. Some of the speech prohibited by the announce clause may well exhibit a bias against parties—including Justice STEVENS' example of an election speech stressing the candidate's unbroken record of affirming convictions for rape, That is why we are careful to say that the announce clause is "*barely* tailored to serve that interest," The question under our strict scrutiny test, however, is not whether the announce clause serves this interest *at all,* but whether it is *narrowly tailored* to serve this interest. It is not.

in a pending case. This sort of impartiality seeks to guarantee each litigant, not an *equal* chance to win the legal points in the case, but at least *some* chance of doing so. It may well be that impartiality in this sense, and the appearance of it, are desirable in the judiciary, but we need not pursue that inquiry, since we do not believe the Minnesota Supreme Court adopted the announce clause for that purpose.

Respondents argue that the announce clause serves the interest in open- mindedness, or at least in the appearance of openmindedness, because it relieves a judge from pressure to rule a certain way in order to maintain consistency with statements the judge has previously made. The problem is, however, that statements in election campaigns are such an infinitesimal portion of the public commitments to legal positions that judges (or judges-to-be) undertake, that this object of the prohibition is implausible. Before they arrive on the bench (whether by election or otherwise) judges have often committed themselves on legal issues that they must later rule upon. Most frequently, of course, that prior expression will have occurred in ruling on an earlier case. But judges often state their views on disputed legal issues outside the context of adjudication—in classes that they conduct, and in books and speeches. Like the ABA Codes of Judicial Conduct, the Minnesota Code not only permits but encourages this. See Minn.Code of Judicial Conduct, Canon 4(B) (2002) ("A judge may write, lecture, teach, speak and participate in other extra-judicial activities concerning the law . . ."); Minn.Code of Judicial Conduct, Canon 4(B), Comment. (2002) ("To the extent that time permits, a judge is encouraged to do so . . ."). That is quite incompatible with the notion that the need for open-mindedness (or for the appearance of open-mindedness) lies behind the prohibition at issue here.

The short of the matter is this: In Minnesota, a candidate for judicial office may not say "I think it is constitutional for the legislature to prohibit same-sex marriages." He may say the very same thing, however, up until the very day before he declares himself a candidate, and may say it repeatedly (until litigation is pending) after he is elected. As a means of pursuing the objective of open-mindedness that respondents now articulate, the announce clause is so woefully underinclusive as to render belief in that purpose a challenge to the credulous.

Justice STEVENS asserts that statements made in an election campaign pose a special threat to open-mindedness because the candidate, when elected judge, will have a *particular* reluctance to contradict them. That might be plausible, perhaps, with regard to campaign *promises*. A candidate who says "If elected, I will vote to uphold the legislature's power to prohibit same-sex marriages" will positively be breaking his word if he does not do so (although one would be naïve not to recognize that campaign promises are—by long democratic tradition—the least binding form of human commitment). But, as noted earlier, the Minnesota Supreme Court has adopted a separate prohibition on campaign "pledges or promises," which is not challenged here. The proposition that judges feel significantly greater compulsion, or appear to feel significantly greater compulsion, to maintain consistency with *nonpromissory* statements made during a judicial campaign than with such statements made before or after the campaign is not self-evidently true. It seems to us quite likely, in fact, that in many cases the opposite is true. We doubt, for example, that a mere statement of position enunciated during the pendency of an election will be regarded by a judge as more binding—or as more likely to subject him to popular disfavor if reconsidered—than a carefully considered holding that the judge set forth in an earlier opinion denying some individual's claim to justice. In any event, it suffices to say that respondents have not carried the burden imposed by our strict- scrutiny test to establish this proposition (that campaign statements are uniquely destructive of open-mindedness) on which the validity of the announce clause rests.

Moreover, the notion that the special context of electioneering justifies an *abridgment* of the right to speak out on disputed issues sets our First Amendment jurisprudence on its head. "[D]ebate on the qualifications of candidates" is "at the core of our electoral process and of the First Amendment freedoms," not at the edges. *Eu,* 489 U.S., at 222–223, 109 S.Ct. 1013 (internal quotation marks omitted). "The role that elected officials play in our society makes it all the more imperative that they be allowed freely to express themselves on matters of current public importance." We have never allowed the government to prohibit candidates from communicating relevant information to voters during an election.

IV

There is an obvious tension between the article of Minnesota's popularly approved Constitution which provides that judges shall be elected, and the Minnesota Supreme Court's announce clause which places most subjects of interest to the voters off limits. (The candidate-speech restrictions of all the other States that have them are also the product of judicial fiat. The disparity is perhaps unsurprising, since the ABA, which originated the announce clause, has long been an opponent of judicial elections. See ABA Model Code of Judicial Conduct Canon 5(C)(2), Comment (2000) ("[M]erit selection of judges is a preferable manner in which to select the judiciary"); An Independent Judiciary: Report of the ABA Commission on Separation of Powers and Judicial Independence 96 (1997) ("The American Bar Association strongly endorses the merit selection of judges, as opposed to their election .... Five times between August 1972 and August 1984 the House of Delegates has approved recommendations stating the preference for merit selection and encouraging bar associations in jurisdictions where judges are elected ... to work for the adoption of merit selection and retention"). That opposition may be well taken (it certainly had the support of the Founders of the Federal Government), but the First Amendment does not permit it to achieve its goal by leaving the principle of elections in place while preventing candidates from discussing what the elections are about. "[T]he greater power to dispense with elections altogether does not include the lesser power to conduct elections under conditions of state-imposed voter ignorance. If the State chooses to tap the energy and the legitimizing power of the democratic process, it must accord the participants in that process ... the First Amendment rights that attach to their roles."

The Minnesota Supreme Court's canon of judicial conduct prohibiting candidates for judicial election from announcing their views on disputed legal and political issues violates the First Amendment. Accordingly, we reverse the grant of summary judgment to respondents and remand the case for proceedings consistent with this opinion.

It is so ordered.

JUSTICE STEVENS, with whom JUSTICE SOUTER, JUSTICE GINSBURG, and JUSTICE BREYER join, dissenting.

In her dissenting opinion, Justice GINSBURG has cogently explained why the Court's holding is unsound. I therefore join her opinion without reservation. I add these comments to emphasize the force of her arguments and to explain why I find the Court's reasoning even more troubling than its holding. The limits of the Court's holding are evident: Even if the Minnesota Lawyers Professional Responsibility Board (Board) may not sanction a judicial candidate for announcing his views on issues likely to come before him, it may surely advise the electorate that such announcements demonstrate the speaker's unfitness for judicial office. If the solution to harmful speech must be more speech, so be it. The Court's reasoning, however, will unfortunately endure beyond the next election cycle. By obscuring the fundamental distinction between campaigns for the judiciary and the political branches, and by failing to recognize the difference between statements made in articles or opinions and those made on the campaign trail, the Court defies any sensible notion of the judicial office and the importance of impartiality in that context.

The Court's disposition rests on two seriously flawed premises—an inaccurate appraisal of the importance of judicial independence and impartiality, and an assumption that judicial candidates should have the same freedom " 'to express themselves on matters of current public importance' " as do all other elected officials. Elected judges, no less than appointed judges, occupy an office of trust that is fundamentally different from that occupied by policymaking officials. Although the fact that they must stand for election makes their job more difficult than that of the tenured judge, that fact does not lessen their duty to respect essential attributes of the judicial office that have been embedded in Anglo-American law for centuries.

There is a critical difference between the work of the judge and the work of other public officials. In a democracy, issues of policy are properly decided by majority vote; it is the business of legislators and executives to be popular. But in litigation, issues of law or fact should not be determined by popular vote; it is the business of judges to be indifferent to unpopularity. Sir Matthew Hale pointedly described this essential attribute of the judicial office in words which have retained their integrity for centuries:

> " '11. That popular or court applause or distaste have no influence in anything I do, in point of distribution of justice.
>
> " '12. Not to be solicitous what men will say or think, so long as I keep myself exactly according to the rule of justice.'

Consistent with that fundamental attribute of the office, countless judges in countless cases routinely make rulings that are unpopular and surely disliked by at least 50 percent of the litigants who appear before them. It is equally common for them to enforce rules that they think unwise, or that are contrary to their personal predilections. For this reason, opinions that a lawyer may have expressed before becoming a judge, or a judicial candidate, do not disqualify anyone for judicial service because every good judge is fully aware of the distinction between the law and a personal point of view. It is equally clear, however, that such expressions after a lawyer has been nominated to judicial office shed little, if any, light on his capacity for judicial service. Indeed, to the extent that such statements seek to enhance the popularity of the candidate by indicating how he would rule in specific cases if elected, they evidence a lack of fitness for the office.

Of course, any judge who faces reelection may believe that he retains his office only so long as his decisions are popular. Nevertheless, the elected judge, like the lifetime appointee, does not serve a constituency while holding that office. He has a duty to uphold the law and to follow the dictates of the Constitution. If he is not a judge on the highest court in the State, he has an obligation to follow the precedent of that court, not his personal views or public opinion polls. He may make common law, but judged on the merits of individual cases, not as a mandate from the voters.

By recognizing a conflict between the demands of electoral politics and the distinct characteristics of the judiciary, we do not have to put States to an all or nothing choice of abandoning judicial elections or having elections in which anything goes. As a practical matter, we cannot know for sure whether an elected judge's decisions are based on his interpretation of the law or political expediency. In the absence of reliable evidence one way or the other, a State may reasonably presume that elected judges are motivated by the highest aspirations of their office. But we do know that a judicial candidate, who announces his views in the context of a campaign, is effectively telling the electorate: "Vote for me because I believe X, and I will judge cases accordingly." Once elected, he may feel free to disregard his campaign statements, *ante,* at 2537, but that does not change the fact that the judge announced his position on an issue likely to come before him *as a reason to vote for him.* Minnesota has a compelling interest in sanctioning such statements.

A candidate for judicial office who goes beyond the expression of "general observation about the law . . . in order to obtain favorable consideration" of his candidacy, *Laird v. Tatum,* 409 U.S. 824, 836, n. 5, 93 S.Ct. 7, 34 L.Ed.2d 50 (1972) (memorandum of REHNQUIST, J., on motion for recusal), demonstrates either a lack of impartiality or a lack of understanding of the importance of maintaining public confidence in the impartiality of the judiciary. It is only by failing to recognize the distinction, clearly stated by then-Justice REHNQUIST, between statements made during a campaign or confirmation hearing and those made before announcing one's candidacy, that the Court is able to conclude: "[S]ince avoiding judicial preconceptions on legal issues is neither possible nor desirable, pretending otherwise by attempting to preserve the 'appearance' of that type of impartiality can hardly be a compelling state interest either."

Even when "impartiality" is defined in its narrowest sense to embrace only "the lack of bias for or against either *party* to the proceeding," the announce clause serves that interest. Expressions that stress a candidate's unbroken record of affirming convictions for rape,* for example, imply a bias in favor of a particular litigant (the prosecutor) and against a class of litigants (defendants in rape cases). Contrary to the Court's reasoning in its first attempt to define impartiality, an interpretation of the announce clause that prohibits such statements serves the State's interest in maintaining both the appearance of this form of impartiality and its actuality.

When the Court evaluates the importance of impartiality in its broadest sense, which it describes as "the interest in openmindedness, or at least in the appearance of, open-mindedness" it concludes that the announce clause is "so woefully underinclusive as to render belief in that purpose a challenge to the credulous." It is underinclusive, in the Court's view, because campaign statements are an infinitesimal portion of the public commitments to legal positions that candidates make during their professional careers. It is not, however, the number of legal views that a candidate may have formed or discussed in his prior career that is significant. Rather, it is the ability both to reevaluate them in the light of an adversarial presentation, and to apply the governing rule of law even when inconsistent with those views, that characterize judicial open-mindedness.

The Court boldly asserts that respondents have failed to carry their burden of demonstrating "that campaign statements are uniquely destructive of open-mindedness,". But the very purpose of most statements prohibited by the announce clause is to convey the message that the candidate's mind is not open on a particular issue. The lawyer who writes an article advocating harsher penalties for polluters surely does not commit to that position to the same degree as the candidate who says "vote for me because I believe all polluters deserve harsher penalties." At the very least, such statements obscure the appearance of open-mindedness. More importantly, like the reasoning in the Court's opinion, they create the false impression that the standards for the election of political candidates apply equally to candidates for judicial office.**

The Court seems to have forgotten its prior evaluation of the importance of maintaining public confidence in the "disinterestedness" of the judiciary. Commenting on the danger that participation by judges in a political assignment might erode that public confidence, we wrote: "While the problem of individual bias is usually cured through recusal, no such mechanism can overcome the appearance of institutional partiality that may arise from judiciary involvement in the making of policy. The legitimacy of the Judicial Branch ultimately depends on its reputation for impartiality and nonpartisanship. That reputation may not be borrowed by the political Branches to cloak their work in the neutral colors of judicial action." *Mistretta v. United States,* 488 U.S. 361, 407, 109 S.Ct. 647, 102 L.Ed.2d 714 (1989).

Conversely, the judicial reputation for impartiality and open-mindedness is compromised by electioneering that emphasizes the candidate's personal predilections rather than his qualifications for judicial office. As an elected judge recently noted:

> "Informed criticism of court rulings, or of the professional or personal conduct of judges, should play an important role in maintaining judicial accountability. However, attacking courts and judges—not because they are wrong on the law or the facts of a case, but because the decision is considered

---

* See *Buckley v. Illinois Judicial Inquiry Board,* 997 F.2d 224, 226 (C.A.7 1993).

** Justice KENNEDY would go even further and hold that no content- based restriction of a judicial candidate's speech is permitted under the First Amendment. While he does not say so explicitly, this extreme position would preclude even Minnesota's prohibition against "pledges or promises" by a candidate for judicial office. A candidate could say "vote for me because I promise to never reverse a rape conviction," and the Board could do nothing to formally sanction that candidate. The unwisdom of this proposal illustrates why the same standards should not apply to speech in campaigns for judicial and legislative office.

wrong simply as a matter of political judgment—maligns one of the basic tenets of judicial independence—intellectual honesty and dedication to enforcement of the rule of law regardless of popular sentiment. Dedication to the rule of law requires judges to rise above the political moment in making judicial decisions. What is so troubling about criticism of court rulings and individual judges based solely on political disagreement with the outcome is that it evidences a fundamentally misguided belief that the judicial branch should operate and be treated just like another constituency-driven political arm of government. Judges should not have 'political constituencies.' Rather, a judge's fidelity must be to enforcement of the rule of law regardless of perceived popular will." De Muniz, Politicizing State Judicial Elections: A Threat to Judicial Independence, 38 Williamette L.Rev. 367, 387 (2002).

The disposition of this case on the flawed premise that the criteria for the election to judicial office should mirror the rules applicable to political elections is profoundly misguided. I therefore respectfully dissent.

FOR DISCUSSION

Historically judicial elections and voting for judges does not attract much attention, in part because voters know very little about the candidates. Scalia asserts that judicial candidates should be free to discuss issues so that voters could be better informed. Do you agree with Scalia?

REPUBLICAN PARTY OF MINNESOTA V. WHITE

416 F.3d 738 (8th Cir. 2005)

Same facts as the Supreme Court case, except the issue here is the rule preventing the candidate from affiliating with a party and soliciting funds. The Court declares this ban on both unconstitutional.

Vote: 12–3

BEAM, CIRCUIT JUDGE.

Judge Beam wrote for the majority.

This case is before us en banc upon remand from the United States Supreme Court. We briefly outline what has occurred in this matter since its inception, believing that it will be helpful in analyzing the issues presented

The Supreme Court's remand requires us to consider two issues in light of *White:* the constitutional viability of the partisan-activities and solicitation clauses of Canon 5.

I. BACKGROUND

Canon 5A(1) and 5B(1), the partisan-activities clause, and B(2), the solicitation clause, rein in the political speech and association of judicial candidates in Minnesota. The partisan-activities clause states, in relevant part:

Except as authorized in Section 5B(1), a judge or a candidate for election to judicial office shall not:

(a) identify themselves as members of a political organization, except as necessary to vote in an election;

. . . .

(d) attend political gatherings; or seek, accept or use endorsements from a political organization.

52 Minn.Stat. Ann., Code of Judicial Conduct, Canon 5, subd. A(1)(a), (d). Section 5B(1)(a) provides that "[a] judge or a candidate for election to judicial office may . . . speak to gatherings, *other than political organization gatherings,* on his or her own behalf."* *Id.* at subd. B(1)(a) (emphasis added). The solicitation clause states,

> A candidate shall not personally solicit or accept campaign contributions or personally solicit publicly stated support. A candidate may, however, establish committees to conduct campaigns for the candidate through media advertisements, brochures, mailings, candidate forums and other means not prohibited by law. Such committees may solicit and accept campaign contributions, manage the expenditure of funds for the candidate's campaign and obtain public statements of support for his or her candidacy. Such committees are not prohibited from soliciting and accepting campaign contributions and public support from lawyers, but shall not seek, accept or use political organization endorsements. Such committees shall not disclose to the candidate the identity of campaign contributors nor shall the committee disclose to the candidate the identity of those who were solicited for contribution or stated public support and refused such solicitation. A candidate shall not use or permit the use of campaign contributions for the private benefit of the candidate or others.

The facts of this case demonstrate the extent to which these provisions chill, even kill, political speech and associational rights. In his 1996 bid for a seat as an associate justice of the Minnesota Supreme Court, appellant Gregory Wersal (and others working on his behalf) identified himself as a member of the Republican Party of Minnesota, attended and spoke at the party's gatherings, sought the endorsement of the party, and personally solicited campaign contributions. In response to Wersal's appearance at and speech to a Republican Party gathering, a complaint was filed with the Minnesota Lawyers Professional Responsibility Board, alleging that Wersal's actions violated Canon 5A(1)(d). Although the Minnesota Office of Lawyers Professional Responsibility (OLPR) ultimately dismissed the complaint, the complaint accomplished its chilling effect. Wersal, fearful that other complaints might jeopardize his opportunity to practice law, withdrew from the race.

Wersal made a second bid for a seat on the Minnesota Supreme Court in 1998. In 1997 and 1998, Wersal asked the OLPR for advisory opinions regarding the solicitation and partisan-activities clauses. The OLPR's response was mixed, stating it would not issue an opinion regarding personal solicitation, in light of proposed amendments to the Canon and the fact that there were no judicial elections scheduled that particular year. It also stated that it would enforce the partisan-activities clause. Wersal then initiated this litigation. In the meantime, he was forced to write several letters to individuals who had indicated they would speak on his behalf at Republican Party conventions across the state, asking them not to do so in order to avoid violating Canon 5 and imploring them to "[p]lease be patient. I hope for a decision from the Federal Courts soon." He also had his campaign's legal counsel advise the chairman of the Republican Party of Minnesota that Canon 5 would prohibit Wersal from accepting or using any endorsement from the party. There is no question that Wersal sought to work within the confines of Canon 5 even as he sought to challenge it-confines that in the most direct of ways restricted his political speech and association, compelling him at one point to end a political campaign.

II. DISCUSSION

A. Judicial Selection in Minnesota

Minnesota has chosen to elect the judges of its courts. Minn. Const. art. 6, § 7. "The fundamental law of this state is, and always has been, that the selection of judges must be submitted to the electors . . . ." *State ex rel. La Jesse v. Meisinger,* 258 Minn. 297, 103 N.W.2d 864, 866 (1960). Some thirty-three states employ some form of contested election for their trial courts of general jurisdiction, their appellate courts, or both. American

* Canon 5 defines "political organization" as "an association of individuals under whose name a candidate files for partisan office"-a political party. Canon 5, subd. D.

Judicature Society, *Judicial Selection in the States: Appellate and General Jurisdiction Courts* (Jan.2004). As federal judges, we confess some bias in favor of a system for the appointment of judges. Indeed, there is much to be said for appointing judges instead of electing them, perhaps the chief reason being the avoidance of potential conflict between the selection process and core constitutional protections.

Yet, there is obvious merit in a state's deciding to elect its judges, especially those judges who serve on its appellate courts. It is a common notion that while the legislative and executive branches under our system of separated powers make and enforce public policy, it is the unique role of the judicial branch to *interpret,* and be quite apart from making that policy.

Without question, Minnesota may choose (and has repeatedly chosen) to elect its appellate judges. The very nature of its sovereignty within our federal system guarantees that. "[A] crucial axiom of our [federal form of] government [is that] the States have wide authority to set up their state and local governments as they wish." Indeed, "[t]hrough the structure of its government . . . a State defines itself as a sovereign Of course, that power of state self-determination is not boundless. "[It is an] axiom that, under our federal system, the States possess sovereignty concurrent with that of the Federal Government, subject ... to limitations imposed by the Supremacy Clause." The Supremacy Clause provides that the Constitution, and laws and treaties made pursuant to it, are the supreme law of the land. When a state engineers its governmental structure or processes in a way that curtails liberties guaranteed by the Constitution, that presumption of state self-determination is replaced, in this case, by a careful-even critical-judicial inquiry fashioned by the particular liberty at issue. If Minnesota sees fit to elect its judges, which it does, it must do so using a process that passes constitutional muster.

B. The First Amendment and Political Speech

Within this context, Minnesota has enacted Canon 5 in an effort to regulate judicial elections. In *White,* the Court held the announce clause of Canon 5, which prohibits judicial candidates from stating their views on disputed legal issues, unconstitutional. It falls to us now to determine whether the partisan-activities and solicitation clauses of Canon 5 are acceptable under the First Amendment.

The First Amendment commands that "Congress shall make no law . . . abridging the freedom of speech." U.S. Const. amend. I. Freedom of association is inherently a part of those liberties protected by the First Amendment. *See Buckley v. Valeo,* 424 U.S. 1, 15, 96 S.Ct. 612, 46 L.Ed.2d 659 (1976) ("The First Amendment protects political association as well as political expression."). If it were not so, many of the Amendment's guarantees would ring hollow.

An individual's freedom to speak, to worship, and to petition the government for the redress of grievances could not be vigorously protected from interference by the State unless a correlative freedom to engage in group effort toward those ends were not also guaranteed .... Consequently, we have long understood as implicit in the right to engage in activities protected by the First Amendment a corresponding right to associate with others in pursuit of a wide variety of political, social, economic, educational, religious, and cultural ends.

Roberts v. United States Jaycees, 468 U.S. 609, 622, 104 S.Ct. 3244, 82 L.Ed.2d 462 (1984) (citation omitted). The due process clause of the Fourteenth Amendment makes the First Amendment applicable to the states.

Protection of political speech is the very stuff of the First Amendment. " '[I]t can hardly be doubted that the constitutional guarantee [of the freedom of speech] has its fullest and most urgent application precisely to the conduct of campaigns for political office.' " *Buckley,* 424 U.S. at 15, 96 S.Ct. 612 (quoting *Monitor Patriot Co. v. Roy,* 401 U.S. 265, 272, 91 S.Ct. 621, 28 L.Ed.2d 35 (1971)). That is because our constitutional form of government not only was borne of the great struggle to secure such freedoms as political speech, but also because such freedom helps assure the continuance of that constitutional government. "In a republic where the people are sovereign, the ability of the citizenry to make informed choices among candidates for office is essential, for the identities of those who are elected will inevitably shape the course that we follow as a nation."

It cannot be disputed that Canon 5's restrictions on party identification, speech to political organizations, and solicitation of campaign funds directly limit judicial candidates' political speech. Its restrictions on attending political gatherings and seeking, accepting, or using a political organization's endorsement clearly limit a judicial candidate's right to associate with a group in the electorate that shares common political beliefs and aims.

C. The Strict Scrutiny Framework

Political speech-speech at the core of the First Amendment-is highly protected. Although not beyond restraint, strict scrutiny is applied to any regulation that would curtail it. The strict scrutiny test requires the state to show that the law that burdens the protected right advances a compelling state interest and is narrowly tailored to serve that interest. Strict scrutiny is an exacting inquiry, such that "it is the rare case in which . . . a law survives strict scrutiny." *Burson v. Freeman,* 504 U.S. 191, 211, 112 S.Ct. 1846, 119 L.Ed.2d 5 (1992).

D. Minnesota's Purported Compelling State Interest

In *Kelly,* Minnesota argued that Canon 5's restrictions on judicial candidate speech served a compelling state interest in maintaining the independence, and the impartiality, of the state's judiciary. Minnesota continues to argue that judicial independence, as applied to the issues in this case, springs from the need for impartial judges. Apparently, the idea is that a judge must be independent of and free from outside influences in order to remain impartial and to be so perceived. Thus, in *Kelly,* the panel majority understood the two notions, independence and impartiality, to be interchangeable,* as the Supreme Court promptly noted in *White,* 536 U.S. at 775 n. 6, 122 S.Ct. 2528. In *Kelly,* the panel majority analyzed the announce, partisan-activities, and solicitation clauses in light of impartiality as a compelling interest, but failed to define "impartiality." On appeal, the Supreme Court filled that void by fleshing out its meaning. Justice Scalia reasoned that impartiality in the judicial context has three potential meanings.

We note that Appellees fret over the kind of influence political parties have in not only elections, but also governmental decisions made thereafter. This case, however, is not about what happens after an election. And in whatever measure this concern is addressed to political parties, it must equally apply to interest groups. By way of illustration using the legislative context Appellees mention, it is likely that the AFL-CIO concerns itself just as much as do the political parties with who chairs the legislative committees dealing with labor matters. And Minnesota's bar associations and trial lawyer associations almost certainly express as much interest as do the political parties in who leads the judiciary committees. While the record does not discuss this point, it is an unavoidable political reality. The essential point is that treating political parties differently than interest groups lies at the heart of the underinclusiveness problem in this case. Such underinclusiveness bedevils any claim that "independence" is a compelling state interest because consorting with politically active interest groups-certainly a source of equally worrisome potential for influence or the appearance of influence-is not regulated at all, as we discuss in more detail. Thus, we proceed under Minnesota's original interchangeable use of "impartiality" and "independence."

The Minnesota Supreme Court's refusal to adopt the recommendations of its Advisory Committee discussed in footnote 3, seems to have prompted the dissent to advance yet another previously unrecognized

---

* In their supplemental brief to the en banc court, Appellees attempt to resurrect from earlier arguments to the court a notion of "independence," separate and distinct from "impartiality," that seeks to maintain real and apparent separation of the judiciary from political influences as a compelling state interest. The partisan-activities clause in particular, they argue, serves this interest by "ensur[ing] that the public views the judiciary as being independent of the strong political influences that pervade legislative and executive branch elections and continue to strongly influence legislative and executive branch decisions thereafter." Supplemental Br. on Remand of Defendants-Appellees at 10. This argument, however, falls prey to the same inherent underinclusiveness of Canon 5 that we discuss, with regard to its regulation of activities that concern only political parties.

and unprecedented definition of judicial independence-a separation of powers theory. The Minnesota Supreme Court said,

> [T]he separation of powers inherent in the creation of three distinct branches of government, one of which is the judicial branch, in article III, section 1 of the Minnesota Constitution provides the constitutional underpinning for the *independence* of the Minnesota judiciary. As the executive and legislative branches are inextricably intertwined with partisan politics, maintenance of an independent judicial branch is reliant on the freedom of its officials from the control of partisan politics.

In re Amendment of the Code of Judicial Conduct, No. C4–85–697, slip op. at 4 (Minn. Sept.14, 2004) (emphasis added).

Our opinion recognizes, citing *Gregory v. Ashcroft,* the right of a state to organize its government and to provide for separation of powers in its governmental structure. We also recognize the Supremacy Clause of the Constitution and the requirement that state action may not violate the Constitution-including the First Amendment.

There are, however, at least two other basic frailties to the dissent's arguments regarding Minnesota's interest in any separation of powers. First, neither the Supreme Court, nor any other court that we could find, has ever determined that a state's interest in maintaining a separation of powers is sufficiently compelling to abridge core First Amendment freedoms. While the dissent states that a separation of powers is a basic concept in Minnesota's constitution, the right to free political speech and association guaranteed by the First Amendment to the United States Constitution is no less basic a concept. Indeed, First Amendment rights are even more fundamental. The right to free and open elections undergirds the framework of government established by any constitution, state or federal. Second, nothing in our opinion or the remedies sought by Appellants serve to further blur any existing lines between the judicial, legislative and executive branches of Minnesota state government. Rather, it is the actions of the Minnesota Supreme Court in adopting Canon 5 that have, in fact, taken the courts into what the dissent describes as the "political branches" of government and compromised any separation of powers framework established by Minnesota's constitution.

Though the Minnesota constitution allows the legislature to provide for disciplining judges, and the state legislature has given the Minnesota Supreme Court the authority to censure or remove judges and to promulgate rules of *conduct for lawyers,* through Canon 5, and without apparent constitutional or statutory authority, the Minnesota Supreme Court has stepped into the legislative arena in an attempt to regulate the political climate of statewide elections, an authority seemingly granted only to the Minnesota legislature under its plenary powers. Indeed, without any stated or readily discernible authority whatsoever, the Canon writes political parties out of statewide judicial elections and allows other political interests to fully participate in a totally unregulated manner.

One possible meaning of "impartiality" is a "lack of preconception in favor of or against a particular *legal view*." Quickly discounting this uncommon use of the word, the Court said it could not be a compelling interest for a judge to "lack . . . predisposition regarding the relevant legal issues in a case" because such a requirement "has never been thought a necessary component of equal justice." The Court reasoned, first, that it is "virtually impossible" to find a judge who lacks any "preconceptions about the law," and second, that it would not be desirable to have such a judge on the bench. "Proof that a Justice's mind at the time he joined the Court was a complete *tabula rasa* in the area of constitutional adjudication would be evidence of lack of qualification, not lack of bias." We follow the Court's direction and likewise dismiss the idea that this meaning of impartiality could be a compelling state interest.

A second possible meaning is a "lack of bias for or against either *party* to [a] proceeding." Calling this the traditional understanding of "impartiality" and the meaning used by Minnesota and amici in their due process arguments, the Court explained that this notion "guarantees a party that the judge who hears his case will apply the law to him in the same way he applies it to any other party.". The Court implied, and we find it to be substantially evident, that *this* meaning of impartiality describes a state interest that is compelling. It can hardly be argued that seeking to uphold a constitutional protection, such as due process, is not per se a compelling state interest. And the rule laid down in *Tumey v. Ohio,* 273 U.S. 510, 47 S.Ct. 437, 71 L.Ed. 749 (1927), makes clear that the partiality of a judge as it relates to a party to a case violates due process protections: "[I]t certainly violates the Fourteenth Amendment, and deprives [a person] of due process of law, to subject his liberty or property to the judgment of a court the judge of which has a direct, personal, substantial, pecuniary interest in reaching a conclusion against him in his case." In *Bracy v. Gramley,* 520 U.S. 899, 117 S.Ct. 1793, 138 L.Ed.2d 97 (1997), the Court reiterated that "the floor established by the Due Process Clause clearly requires a fair trial in a fair tribunal, before a judge with no actual bias against the defendant or interest in the outcome of his particular case."

Being convinced that protecting litigants from biased judges is a compelling state interest, we turn to the "narrow tailoring" examination of the partisan-activities clause under this particular meaning of judicial impartiality. Because this meaning directs our attention to parties to the litigation rather than to ideas and issues, we analyze the regulation in this context before turning to other possible definitions of impartiality. We consider whether the partisan-activities clause actually addresses this compelling state interest and, if so, whether it is the least restrictive means of doing so.

In *White,* the Supreme Court found that the announce clause failed the narrow tailoring aspect of the strict scrutiny test, holding "[i]ndeed, the clause is barely tailored to serve that [lack of bias] interest *at all,* inasmuch as it does not restrict speech for or against particular *parties,* but rather speech for or against particular *issues.*" Thus, the Court found that clause was not narrowly tailored because it failed to advance a compelling interest. The same is true for the partisan-activities clause.

1. Unbiased Judges and the Narrow Tailoring of the Partisan-Activities Clause

In one sense, the underlying rationale for the partisan-activities clause-that *associating with a particular group* will destroy a judge's impartiality-differs only in form from that which purportedly supports the announce clause-that *expressing one's self on particular issues* will destroy a judge's impartiality. Canon 5, in relevant part, forbids a judicial candidate from identifying with a political organization, making speeches to a political organization, or accepting endorsements from or even attending meetings of a political organization, all of which are the quintessence of political associational activity. And beyond its importance in bringing about those rights textually protected by the First Amendment, association, as earlier noted, is itself an important form of speech, particularly in the political arena. Indeed, Minnesota argues that a party label is nothing more than shorthand for the views a judicial candidate holds. Inasmuch, then, as the partisan-activities clause seeks, at least in part, to keep judges from aligning with particular views on issues by keeping them from aligning with a particular political party, the clause is likewise "barely tailored" to affect any interest in impartiality toward parties. Thus, the Supreme Court's analysis of the announce clause under this meaning of "impartiality," to wit judicial bias, is squarely applicable to the partisan-activities clause.

To be sure, when a case arises that turns on a legal issue on which the judge (as a candidate) had taken a particular stand, [be that through *announcing* or *aligning with* particular views,] the party taking the opposite stand is likely to lose. But not because of any bias against that party, or favoritism toward the other party. *Any* party taking that position is just as likely to lose. The judge is applying the law (as he sees it) evenhandedly.

We recognize that the difference between the direct expression of views under the announce clause and expressing a viewpoint under the partisan-activities clause through association, is that the latter requires the aligning of one's self with other like-minded individuals-that is, the members of a political party.

Political parties are, of course, potential litigants, as they are in this case. Thus, in a case where a political party comes before a judge who has substantially associated himself or herself with that same party, a question could conceivably arise about the potential for bias in favor of that litigant. Yet even then, any credible claim of bias would have to flow from something more than the bare fact that the judge had associated with that political party. That is because the associational activities restricted by Canon 5 are, as we have pointed out, part-and-parcel of a candidate's speech for or against particular *issues* embraced by the political party. And such restrictions, we have also said, do not serve the due process rights of *parties*. In the case of a political party involved in a redistricting dispute, for example, the fact that the matter comes before a judge who is associated with the Republican or Democratic Party would not implicate concerns of bias for or against that party unless the judge were in some way involved in the case beyond simply having an "R" or "D," or "DFL" (denoting Minnesota's Democratic-Farmer-Labor Party) after his or her name. Thus, the partisan-activities clause does not advance an interest in impartiality toward litigants in a case where, without more, it is a like-minded political party which is one of the litigants.

And in those political cases where a judge is more personally involved, such as where the redistricting case is a dispute about how to draw that judge's district, and even in those cases discussed above that merely involve a political party as a litigant, recusal is the least restrictive means of accomplishing the state's interest in impartiality articulated as a lack of bias for or against parties to the case. Through recusal, the same concerns of bias or the appearance of bias that Minnesota seeks to alleviate through the partisan-activities clause are thoroughly addressed without "burn[ing] the house to roast the pig." Indeed, Canon 3 of the Minnesota Code of Judicial Conduct provides that a judge is to "disqualify himself or herself in a proceeding in which the judge's impartiality might reasonably be questioned."

Therefore, the partisan-activities clause is barely tailored at all to serve any interest in unbiased judges, and, at least, is not the least-restrictive means of doing so. Accordingly, it is not narrowly tailored to any such interest and fails under strict scrutiny.

2. Impartiality Understood as "Openmindedness," and the Partisan-Activities Clause

The third possible meaning of "impartiality" articulated by the Supreme Court in *White,* and the one around which its analysis of the announce clause revolved, was "described as openmindedness." The Court explained,

> This quality in a judge demands, not that he have no preconceptions on legal issues, but that he be willing to consider views that oppose his preconceptions, and remain open to persuasion, when the issues arise in a pending case. This sort of impartiality seeks to guarantee each litigant, not an *equal* chance to win the legal points in the case, but at least *some* chance of doing so.

The Court stopped short, however, of determining whether impartiality articulated as "openmindedness" was a compelling state interest because it found that, even if it were, the "woeful[ ] underinclusive[ness]" of the clause betrayed any intended purpose of upholding openmindedness.

We conclude that the partisan-activities clause is likewise "woefully underinclusive," calling into question its validity in at least two ways. First, it leads us to conclude, before even reaching a compelling interest inquiry, that like the announce clause, the partisan-activities clause was not adopted for the purpose of protecting judicial openmindedness. Second, under a compelling interest analysis, the clause's underinclusiveness causes us to doubt that the interest it purportedly serves is sufficiently compelling to abridge core First Amendment rights. We conclude that the underinclusiveness of the partisan-activities clause causes it to fail strict scrutiny.

a. Underinclusiveness Belies Purported Purpose

Underinclusiveness in a regulation may reveal that motives entirely inconsistent with the stated interest actually lie behind its enactment. In *White,* the Court found that, "as a means of pursuing the objective of openmindedness . . . the announce clause is so woefully underinclusive as to render belief in that purpose a challenge to the credulous." The underinclusiveness manifests itself in the inherently brief period of speech regulation during a political campaign relative to the many other instances in which a judicial candidate, especially an incumbent who is a candidate, has an opportunity to speak on disputed issues. The Court reasoned that if the purpose of the announce clause were truly to assure the openmindedness of judges, Minnesota would not try to address it through a regulation that restricted speech only during a campaign since candidates' views on contentious legal issues can be and are aired in the many speeches, class lectures, articles, books, or even court opinions given or authored before, during or after any campaign.

The same is true of the partisan-activities clause. The announce clause bars a judicial candidate from stating his views on disputed issues though "he may say the very same thing . . . up until the very day before he declares himself a candidate." The partisan-activities clause bars a judicial candidate from associative activities with a political party during a campaign, though he may have been a life-long, active member of a political party (even accepting partisan endorsements for nonjudicial offices) up until the day he begins his run for a judicial seat. A regulation requiring a candidate to sweep under the rug his overt association with a political party for a few months during a judicial campaign, after a lifetime of commitment to that party, is similarly underinclusive in the purported pursuit of an interest in judicial openmindedness. The few months a candidate is ostensibly purged of his association with a political party can hardly be expected to suddenly open the mind of a candidate who has engaged in years of prior political activity. And, history indicates it will be rare that a judicial candidate for a seat on the Minnesota Supreme Court will not have had some prior, substantive, political association. In sum, restricting association with a political party only during a judicial campaign, in supposed pursuit of judicial openmindedness, renders the partisan-activities clause "so woefully underinclusive as to render belief in that purpose a challenge to the credulous."

As for the appearance of impartiality, the partisan-activities clause seems even less tailored than the announce clause to an interest in openmindedness. While partisan activity may be an indirect indicator of potential views on issues, an affirmative enunciation of views during an election campaign more directly communicates a candidate's beliefs. If, as the Supreme Court has declared, a candidate may *speak* about her views on disputed issues, what appearance of "impartiality" is protected by keeping a candidate from simply *associating* with a party that espouses the same or similar positions on the subjects about which she has spoken? Moreover, even if there were some system in which it would make sense to allow one but not the other in pursuit of the same goal, cabining a candidate from a political party for the relatively short duration of a campaign would add nothing to an appearance of impartiality. Given this "woeful underinclusiveness" of the partisan-activities clause, it is apparent that advancing judicial openmindedness is not the purpose that "lies behind the prohibition at issue here."

b. Underinclusiveness Betrays "Compelling" Claim

While it is not necessary for us to reach the question of whether judicial openmindedness as defined in *White* is sufficiently compelling to abridge core First Amendment rights, we note that the underinclusiveness of Canon 5's partisan activities clause clearly establishes that the answer would be no. Whether Minnesota asserts a compelling state interest in judicial openmindedness is substantially informed by the fit between the partisan-activities clause and the purported interest at stake. A clear indicator of the compelling nature of an interest is whether the state has bothered to enact a regulation that guards the interest from all significant threats.

We are guided on remand by the law enunciated in *White,* and the Court's words bear repeating: "[A] law cannot be regarded as protecting an interest of the highest order, and thus as justifying a restriction upon truthful speech, when it leaves appreciable damage to that supposedly vital interest unprohibited." By its own terms, Canon 5's restrictions on association with "political organizations" apply only to "association[s] of individuals under whose name a candidate files for partisan office"-political parties. Yet, if mere association with an organization whose purpose is to advance political and social goals gives Minnesota sufficient grounds to restrict judicial candidates' activities, it makes little sense for the state to restrict such activity only with political parties. There are numerous other organizations whose purpose is to work at advancing any number of similar goals, often in a more determined way than a political party. Minnesota worries that a judicial candidate's consorting with a political party will damage that individual's impartiality or appearance of impartiality as a judge, apparently because she is seen as aligning herself with that party's policies or procedural goals. But that would be no less so when a judge as a judicial candidate aligns herself with the constitutional, legislative, public policy and procedural beliefs of organizations such as the National Rifle Association (NRA), the National Organization for Women (NOW), the Christian Coalition, the NAACP, the AFL-CIO, or any number of other political interest groups. While Minnesota expresses doubt that the influence an interest group can have over a candidate is comparable to that of a political party, the record in this case refutes the premise. Indeed, associating with an interest group, which by design is usually more narrowly focused on particular issues, conveys a much stronger message of alignment with particular political views and outcomes. A judicial candidate's stand, for example, on the importance of the right to keep and bear arms may not be obvious from her choice of political party. But, there can be little doubt about her views if she is a member of or endorsed by the NRA. Yet Canon 5 is completely devoid of any restriction on a judicial candidate attending or speaking to a gathering of an interest group; identifying herself as a member of an interest group; or seeking, accepting, or using an endorsement from an interest group. As a result, the partisan-activities clause unavoidably leaves appreciable damage to the supposedly vital interest of judicial openmindedness unprohibited, and thus Minnesota's argument that it protects an interest of the highest order fails.

c. Underinclusiveness Not Indicative of a Legitimate Policy Choice

The panel majority in *Kelly* did not find the underinclusiveness of the partisan-activities clause troublesome. It viewed it as a legitimate policy choice: "when underinclusiveness results from a choice to address a greater threat before a lesser, it does not run afoul of the First Amendment.". Association with political parties, goes the argument, is a greater threat to judicial openmindedness than association with interest groups because political parties have more power "to hold a candidate in thrall.". But to determine whether Minnesota has shown that association with political parties poses a greater menace to judicial openmindedness than association with other political interest groups, it is necessary to do at least some analysis of the two supposed threats. While the opinion in *Kelly* purports to examine the "threat" posed by political parties, it contains no discussion of any comparable danger advanced by association with special interest groups, despite ample record evidence that suggests the influence of these special groups is at least as great as any posed by political parties.

Minnesota has simply not met its heavy burden of showing that association with a political party is so much greater a threat than similar association with interest groups, at least with evidence sufficient for the drawing of a constitutionally valid line between them. As a result, cases granting some degree of deference to legislatures who seek to attack one form of a problem before addressing another form are not applicable here.

To the contrary "the notion that a regulation of speech may be impermissibly *underinclusive* is firmly grounded in basic First Amendment principles." *Ladue,* 512 U.S. at 51, 114 S.Ct. 2038. While the Court in *Erznoznik* stated in dictum that underinclusive classifications may be upheld, "on the sound theory that a legislature may deal with one part of a problem without addressing all of it," it was quick to add that "[t]his presumption of statutory validity, however, . . . has less force when a classification turns on the subject matter of expression." *Erznoznik,* 422 U.S. at 215, 95 S.Ct. 2268. Just as the Court did in *Erznoznik,* we reject the argument that the underinclusive regulation is valid. " '[A]bove all else, the First Amendment means that government has no power to restrict expression because of its message, its ideas, its subject matter, or its content.' As we have noted, political association is speech in and of itself. It allows a person to convey a message about some of his or her basic beliefs through such associations. Even if we were to believe that the partisan-activities clause regulates political parties and not interest groups because political parties somehow pose a greater "threat" by having a louder and more comprehensive voice, such a distinction would still turn, at least in part, on the content of the message each seeks to convey. Under such a rationale, it is the subject matter of the messages that is at stake-with political parties usually, but not always, emitting a variety of propositions and interest groups often advancing a more narrowly focused agenda. Such line-drawing based on the subject matter of expression is what the Court in *Erznoznik* considered suspect. *Erznoznik,* particularly, discredits any argument that the Minnesota Supreme Court is justified in dealing with one part of the perceived subject matter problem, and not all of it.

3. The Solicitation Clause

We now turn to an analysis of portions of the solicitation clause. The solicitation clause bars judicial candidates from personally soliciting individuals or even large gatherings for campaign contributions. "In effect, candidates are completely chilled from speaking to potential contributors and endorsers about their potential contributions and endorsements." And as the majority conceded in *Kelly,* such restriction depends wholly upon the subject matter of the speech for its invocation. Judicial candidates are not barred from personally requesting funds for any purpose other than when it is "related to a political campaign." Restricting speech based on its subject matter triggers the same strict scrutiny as does restricting core political speech

Moreover, the very nature of the speech that the solicitation clause affects invokes strict scrutiny. This is because the clause applies to requests for funds to be used in promoting a political message. It bears repeating that " '[i]t can hardly be doubted that the constitutional guarantee [of the freedom of speech] has its fullest and most urgent application precisely to the conduct of campaigns for political office.' " *Buckley,* 424 U.S. at 15, 96 S.Ct. 612 (quoting *Monitor Patriot Co. v. Roy,* 401 U.S. 265, 272, 91 S.Ct. 621, 28 L.Ed.2d 35 (1971)). And promoting a political message requires the expenditure of funds.

> [V]irtually every means of communicating ideas in today's mass society requires the expenditure of money. The distribution of the humblest handbill or leaflet entails printing, paper, and circulation costs. Speeches and rallies generally necessitate hiring a hall and publicizing the event. The electorate's increasing dependence on television, radio, and other mass media for news and information has made these expensive modes of communication indispensable instruments of effective political speech.

As Justice O'Connor stated in her *White* concurrence, "[u]nless the pool of judicial candidates is limited to those wealthy enough to independently fund their campaigns, a limitation unrelated to judicial skill, the cost of campaigning requires judicial candidates to engage in fundraising." 536 U.S. at 789–90, 122 S.Ct. 2528 (O'Connor, J., concurring). Insofar as the solicitation clause restricts the amount of funds a judicial candidate is able to expend on his or her political message, the regulation is of the same caliber as that struck down in *Buckley.*

Since strict scrutiny is clearly invoked, the solicitation clause must also be narrowly tailored to serve a compelling state interest. Minnesota asserts that keeping judicial candidates from personally soliciting campaign funds serves its interest in an impartial judiciary by preventing any undue influence flowing from financial support. We must determine whether the regulation actually advances an interest in non-biased or openminded judges. Appellants challenge only the fact that they cannot solicit contributions from large groups and cannot, through their campaign committees, transmit solicitation messages above their personal signatures. They do not challenge the campaign committee system that Canon 5 provides under which candidates may establish committees that may solicit campaign funds on behalf of the candidate. "Such committees shall not disclose to the candidate the identity of campaign contributors nor shall the committee disclose to the candidate the identity of those who were solicited for contribution or stated public support and refused such solicitation." 52 Minn.Stat. Ann., Code of Judicial Conduct, Canon 5, subd. B(2).

a. Unbiased Judges and the Narrow Tailoring of the Solicitation Clause

We first consider whether the solicitation clause serves an interest in impartiality articulated as a lack of bias for or against a party to a case. Keeping candidates, who may be elected judges, from directly soliciting money from individuals who may come before them certainly addresses a compelling state interest in impartiality as to parties to a particular case. It seems unlikely, however, that a judicial candidate, if elected, would be a "judge [who] has a direct, personal, substantial, pecuniary interest in reaching a conclusion [for or] against [a litigant in a case]," *Tumey,* 273 U.S. at 523, based on whether that litigant had contributed to the judge's campaign. That is because Canon 5 provides specifically that all contributions are to be made to the candidate's *committee,* and the committee "shall not" disclose to the candidate those who either contributed or rebuffed a solicitation. Thus, just as was true with the announce clause and its fit with an interest in unbiased judges, the contested portions of the solicitation clause are barely tailored at all to serve that end. An actual or mechanical reproduction of a candidate's signature on a contribution letter will not magically endow him or her with a power to divine, first, to whom that letter was sent, and second, whether that person contributed to the campaign or balked at the request. In the same vein, a candidate would be even less able to trace the source of funds contributed in response to a request transmitted to large assemblies of voters. So, the solicitation clause's proscriptions against a candidate personally signing a solicitation letter or making a blanket solicitation to a large group, does not advance any interest in impartiality articulated as a lack of bias for or against a party to a case.

b. Openminded Judges and the Narrow Tailoring of the Solicitation Clause

We next consider whether the solicitation clause as applied by Minnesota serves an interest in impartiality articulated as "openmindedness." Put another way, would allowing a judicial candidate to personally sign outgoing solicitation letters, or to ask a large audience to support particular views through their financial contributions, in some way damage that judge's "willing [ness] to consider views that oppose his preconceptions, and remain open to persuasion, when the issues arise in a pending case"? We think not. Given that Canon 5 prevents a candidate from knowing the identity of contributors or even non-contributors, to believe so would be a "challenge to the credulous." Thus, Minnesota's solicitation clause seems barely tailored to in any way affect the openmindedness of a judge. Accordingly, the solicitation clause, as applied by Minnesota, cannot pass strict scrutiny when applied to a state interest in impartiality articulated as openmindedness.

III. CONCLUSION

In *White,* the Supreme Court invalidated the announce clause and remanded the case to this court. Upon further consideration of the partisan-activities and solicitation clauses in light of *White,* we hold that they likewise do not survive strict scrutiny and thus violate the First Amendment. We therefore reverse the district court, and remand with instructions to enter summary judgment for Appellants.

JOHN R. GIBSON, CIRCUIT JUDGE, with whom MCMILLIAN and MURPHY, CIRCUIT JUDGES, join, dissenting.

The Court today strikes down the partisan activities clauses and the solicitation restriction as a matter of law, by summary judgment, ruling that the interests at stake are not compelling and that the clauses of Canon 5 are either too broad, or not broad enough, to justify their own existence. Preserving the integrity of a state's courts and those courts' reputation for integrity is an interest that lies at the very heart of a state's ability to provide an effective government for its people. The word "compelling" is hardly vivid enough to convey its importance. The questions of whether that interest is threatened by partisan judicial election campaigns and personal solicitation of campaign contributions, and whether the measures Minnesota has adopted were crafted to address only the most virulent threats to that interest, are in part factual questions, which we should not decide on summary judgment. Finally, the Court today adopts an approach to strict scrutiny that would deny the states the ability to defend their compelling interests, no matter how urgent the threat. For these reasons, I respectfully dissent.

I.

The partisan activities clauses and the solicitation restriction each serve an interest that is and has been recognized as compelling-protecting the judicial process from extraneous coercion.

B.

Corruption is a sufficiently serious threat to our institutions that the government may (1) seek to prevent it before it happens and (2) act against it in intermediate forms that are more subtle than bribery and explicit agreements. *See McConnell v. FEC,* 540 U.S. 93, 144, 150–54, 124 S.Ct. 619, 157 L.Ed.2d 491 (2003) (corruption and appearance of corruption extend beyond bribery to other arrangements which create "sense of obligation" in or "undue influence" over officeholders); *Shrink Missouri Gov't PAC,* 528 U.S. at 389, 120 S.Ct. 897 ("In speaking of 'improper influence' and 'opportunities for abuse' in addition to '*quid pro quo* arrangements,' we recognized a concern not confined to bribery of public officials, but extending to the broader threat from politicians too compliant with the wishes of large contributors. These were the obvious points behind our recognition that the Congress could constitutionally address the power of money to 'influence governmental action' in ways less 'blatant and specific' than bribery."); *Nat'l Right to Work Comm.,* 459 U.S. at 210, ("Nor will we second-guess a legislative determination as to the need for prophylactic measures where corruption is the evil feared.").

Admittedly, the concern with corruption in the campaign finance cases focuses on payment of money. While the solicitation clause also deals with money-raising, the partisan activities clauses do not, which distinguishes them from the campaign finance cases. Nevertheless, the Supreme Court's decision in *United States Civil Serv. Comm'n v. Nat'l Ass'n of Letter Carriers,* 413 U.S. 548, 93 S.Ct. 2880, 37 L.Ed.2d 796 (1973), demonstrates that the concern with corruption and undue influence is not limited to obligations resulting from payments of money. *Letter Carriers* recognized the danger partisan allegiances posed to neutral administration of justice. That case upheld restraints imposed by the Hatch Act on executive branch employees' political activities, in part because of the effect partisanship could have on the performance of their duties:

> It seems fundamental in the first place that employees in the Executive Branch of the Government, or those working for any of its agencies, should administer the law in accordance with the will of Congress, rather than in accordance with their own or the will of a political party. They are expected to enforce the law and execute the programs of the Government without bias or favoritism for or against any political party or group or the members thereof. A major thesis of the Hatch Act is that to serve this great end of Government-the impartial execution of the laws-it is essential that federal employees, for example, not take formal positions in political parties, not undertake to play substantial roles in partisan political campaigns, and not run for office on partisan political tickets. Forbidding activities like these will reduce the hazards to fair and effective government. 413 U.S. at 564–65, 93 S.Ct. 2880.
>
> *Letter Carriers* shows that what kind of obligations may be considered inconsistent with government office depends on the nature of the office in question. Where the office requires "impartial execution of the laws," partisan entanglements can be inconsistent with the demands of the office. *Letter Carriers* and the campaign finance cases are not separate lines of authority, but are closely connected, since the Supreme Court relied heavily on *Letter Carriers* in identifying and defining the anti-corruption interest in *Buckley v. Valeo.*

The Republican Party of Minnesota argues that the holding of *Letter Carriers* is irrelevant here because "the role of judges is closer to the role of legislators than [the] executive branch bureaucrats" affected by *Letter Carriers*. The Supreme Court in *White* specifically avoided equating the judicial office with the legislative: "[W]e neither assert nor imply that the First Amendment requires campaigns for judicial office to sound the same as those for legislative office."

The need for "neutrality" identified in *Letter Carriers* is even more important for the judicial branch than the executive. A long line of cases stresses the right of litigants to a neutral adjudicator. In *Marshall v. Jerrico, Inc.*, Justice Marshall wrote:

> The Due Process Clause entitles a person to an impartial and disinterested tribunal in both civil and criminal cases. This requirement of neutrality in adjudicative proceedings safeguards the two central concerns of procedural due process, the prevention of unjustified or mistaken deprivations and the promotion of participation and dialogue by affected individuals in the decisionmaking process. The neutrality requirement helps to guarantee that life, liberty, or property will not be taken on the basis of an erroneous or distorted conception of the facts or the law. At the same time, it preserves both the appearance and reality of fairness, "generating the feeling, so important to a popular government, that justice has been done," by ensuring that no person will be deprived of his interests in the absence of a proceeding in which he may present his case with assurance that the arbiter is not predisposed to find against him.
>
> (citations omitted).

The circumstances that can result in violation of the due process right to a neutral judge are not limited to situations in which a judge has a pecuniary interest at stake in the litigation. In *Ward v. Village of Monroeville*, 409 U.S. 57, 93 S.Ct. 80, 34 L.Ed.2d 267 (1972), due process was violated when the defendant was convicted by the mayor of a village that depended on fines collected in the mayor's court. The mayor himself did not share in the revenues, but the Supreme Court held:

> [T]he test is whether the mayor's situation is one "which would offer a possible temptation to the average man as a judge to forget the burden of proof required to convict the defendant, or which might lead him not to hold the balance nice, clear and true between the State and the accused . . . ." [quoting *Tumey v. Ohio*, 273 U.S. 510, 532, 47 S.Ct. 437, 71 L.Ed. 749 (1927).] Plainly that "possible temptation" may also exist when the mayor's executive responsibilities for village finances may make him partisan to maintain the high level of contribution from the mayor's court. This, too, is a "situation in which an official perforce occupies two practically and seriously inconsistent positions, one partisan and the other judicial," [and] necessarily involves a lack of due process of law in the trial of defendants charged with crimes before him.

Other cases in which a judge's neutrality was intolerably compromised by non-pecuniary considerations include *Johnson v. Mississippi*, 403 U.S. 212, 215–16, 91 S.Ct. 1778, 29 L.Ed.2d 423 (1971) (judge who had previously lost a civil rights suit to defendant could not try defendant for contempt); *In re Murchison*, 349 U.S. 133, 75 S.Ct. 623, 99 L.Ed. 942 (1955) (judge who acts as "one-man judge-grand jury" cannot then try indicted defendant); and *Offutt v. United States*, 348 U.S. 11, 17, 75 S.Ct. 11, 99 L.Ed. 11 (1954) (judge who had become "personally embroiled" with lawyer could not try the lawyer for contempt). There is no easily applied formula for deciding when a judge has an impermissible interest in litigation; "Circumstances and relationships must be considered." *Murchison*, 349 U.S. at 136, 75 S.Ct. 623. But even at a point where the judge cannot be said to be actually biased, "[O]ur system of law has always endeavored to prevent *even the probability* of unfairness." *Id.* (emphasis added).

We do not have to conclude that adjudication by judges who were selected without the protections of the partisan activities clauses violates the due process rights of the litigants. Indeed, we could not well do so, since, as the Supreme Court remarked in *White,* partisan judicial elections were common in the mid-nineteenth century, when the Fourteenth Amendment was adopted. Currently, some fifteen states maintain partisan judicial elections for at least some of their judges, and no one contends that the states may not choose this method of selection.

Nevertheless, the participation of judges who have been allowed or forced to make themselves dependent on party largesse for their continued tenure affects the state's ability to provide neutral judges and the public's perception of such neutrality. The state has a compelling interest in keeping its judges free from the odor of self-interest or partisanship. In *Cox v. Louisiana,* 379 U.S. 559, 85 S.Ct. 476, 13 L.Ed.2d 487 (1965), Cox was convicted of picketing near a courthouse "with the intent of influencing any judge, juror, witness, or court officer, in the discharge of his duty" after he demonstrated in protest against the arrest of students who would be tried by judges present at the courthouse during the demonstration. The law did not prohibit all picketing, but picketing done with the intent to influence the administration of justice. The Supreme Court stated that it was unlikely that the picketing would actually affect the judges' decisions in the students' cases. The Court did not suggest that if the state had allowed the picketing, it would have caused a due process violation for any particular litigant. However, the Court said, "A state may protect against the possibility of a conclusion by the public under these circumstances that the judge's action was in part a product of intimidation and did not flow only from the fair and orderly working of the judicial process." Thus, the state's interest in preserving the appearance of neutrality justified the restriction on expressive conduct. *Accord In re Chmura,* 461 Mich. 517, 608 N.W.2d 31, 40 (2000) ("state's interest . . . extends to preserving public confidence in the judiciary").

The New York Court of Appeals recently confirmed that a state has a compelling interest in presenting the appearance as well as the fact of due process:

> [L]itigants have a right guaranteed under the Due Process Clause to a fair and impartial magistrate and the State, as the steward of the judicial system, has the obligation to create such a forum and prevent corruption and the appearance of corruption, including political bias or favoritism.

In re Raab, 100 N.Y.2d 305, 763 N.Y.S.2d 213, 793 N.E.2d 1287, 1290–91 (2003) (per curiam).

In its September 2004 deliberations about whether to amend the partisan activities clauses of Canon 5, the Minnesota Supreme Court articulated just those concerns outlined above. The court stated:

> [T]he goal of an impartial judiciary is compelled by the due process rights of litigants. Due process requires decisionmakers who are fair, unbiased, and impartial, and importantly, decisionmakers who are perceived as such by the litigants who appear before them. Moreover, we cannot underestimate the importance of the public's perception that judges are fair, unbiased, and impartial to the continued respect for and legitimacy of the judicial branch. Without this perception, the public's confidence and support cannot be maintained and the very independence of the judicial branch mandated by the Constitution will be threatened.

In re Amendment of the Code of Judicial Conduct, No. C4–85–697, slip op. at 4–5 (Minn. Sept.14, 2004). These concerns fit within the concept of judicial open-mindedness, and they are a compelling state interest.

D.

The extent and severity of the threat to the state's interests are factual questions that must be proven empirically. In the proceedings in the district court, the Boards adduced sufficient evidence of that threat so that summary judgment for the plaintiffs would not have been appropriate. But recent events make it far less appropriate that our Court should enter judgment as a matter of law on questions of fact as to which there is no record before us.

The record below contained the affidavit of a former governor of Minnesota who stated that he had a lifetime of experience in understanding how Minnesota citizens "think and feel" and that partisan judicial campaigns would lessen Minnesotans' confidence "in the independence of the judiciary." A former Chief Justice of the Minnesota Supreme Court stated that partisan judicial campaigns would "put pressure on judges to decide cases in ways that would impress the judge's supporters favorably."

But far more important to our holding today is the fact that the Minnesota Supreme Court has recently reconsidered the provisions of Canon 5 at issue here, held hearings, and received public comment. It is a matter of interest that the parties in this case, in briefing and argument, made no mention of this development. As the canon was reconsidered, amended in part and reiterated in part while this case was pending on rehearing, failure to consider the effect of these developments may well cause this Court's opinion to be moot from its inception.

The Advisory Committee appointed by the Minnesota Supreme Court to study the issue concluded that there was a threat to the state's interest that required regulation of partisanship in judicial campaigns: "In considering the need for restrictions on the political activity of judicial election candidates, the Advisory Committee is also cognizant of the experience of actual or perceived corruption of the judiciary in states that permit partisan judicial elections." While we do not have access to the evidence before the Committee, widely available and publicized evidence substantiates the fear that the majority of the public believes that partisanship does influence the decisions of state courts. For instance, a poll conducted in 1999 showed that 81% of the respondents agreed that "politics influences court decisions." The Advisory Committee recommended deleting the party identification and the attend and speak clauses on narrow tailoring grounds. Advisory Committee Report at Comments-Canon 5. After receiving the Committee report and conducting a hearing and receiving public comment, the Minnesota Supreme Court decided to retain all three partisan activities clauses.

The Advisory Committee unanimously recommended against changing the ban on the judicial candidate's personal solicitation of campaign contributions. Advisory Committee Report at Canon 5B(2)-Personal Solicitation of Campaign Contributions. Again, widely available poll numbers support the Committee's conclusion that solicitation of campaign contributions carries with it a significant threat to the state's interest in freedom from external coercion of judges. For example, "a recent Wisconsin poll found that more than three-quarters of those surveyed believe that campaign contributions from lawyers and plaintiffs in high-profile cases influence the decisions of these judges in court," and a study in Texas "found that 83 percent of the public and 79 percent of lawyers believe that campaign contributions have a significant influence on a judge's decision." A summary of poll results compiled by the National Center for State Courts reported on fifteen recent polls, showing not only that the public believes campaign contributions affect judicial decisions, but also that lawyers and even judges agree. For instance, a poll from Texas showed that 48% of state appellate and trial judges surveyed believed that campaign contributions had a fairly significant or very significant degree of influence over judicial decisionmaking A Pennsylvania survey of registered voters showed that 95% of those surveyed believed that judges' decisions were influenced by large contributions to their election campaigns at least some of the time. *Id.* This is the kind of evidence that would substantiate the threat to judicial open-mindedness (and the appearance of it) from partisan obligations and from judicial campaign fund-raising.

The Court today errs grievously in issuing a ruling that strikes the provisions based on the 1997 factual record without considering the September 2004 record before the Minnesota Supreme Court. Since the holding is based on a factual record that antedates the most recent version of Canon 5, one must question whether the Court's holding today even applies to the current version of Canon 5, based as it is, on a 2004 factual determination which the Court does not take into account.

F.

Preserving judicial open-mindedness, and the appearance of it, should be recognized as the same compelling state interest in avoiding corruption interest that was identified in *Buckley v. Valeo* and the campaign finance cases. Though it is the same anti-corruption interest, the need to protect that interest is more urgent and vital in the context of the judiciary because in that context outside influences threaten litigants' due process interest in adjudication in accord with the law and the facts of their case. A further state interest in preserving the separation of powers between state branches of government should also be recognized as compelling. The Minnesota Supreme Court has recently re-examined Canon 5 and clarified that the Canon is meant to protect those state interests. Judicial integrity and separation of powers are interests of the highest importance in guaranteeing the proper functioning of state government and we have no warrant to deny their importance.

B.

The question at issue in our consideration of the partisan activities clauses, as in *Austin,* is whether there is a "crucial difference," in the threat posed by some entities that justified regulating them while leaving others unregulated. To rebut the inference of pretext, the government must show that the speech it has burdened poses a different, more serious threat to its asserted interest than the speech it chose not to regulate.

Recently, the Supreme Court has held that the differences between political parties and other interest groups could warrant differential regulation of the two kinds of groups. This distinction between political parties and other interest groups was at issue in *McConnell,* where the Court considered Title I of the Bipartisan Campaign Reform Act, which imposed restrictions on political parties' fund-raising activities that were not imposed on interest groups, such as the National Rifle Association, the American Civil Liberties Union or the Sierra Club. The plaintiffs contended that the distinction violated Equal Protection. The Court held the distinction was permissible, because

> Congress is fully entitled to consider the real-world differences between political parties and interest groups when crafting a system of campaign finance regulation. Interest groups do not select slates of candidates for elections. Interest groups do not determine who will serve on legislative committees, elect congressional leadership, or organize legislative caucuses. Political parties have influence and power in the legislature that vastly exceeds that of any interest group .... Congress' efforts at campaign finance regulation may account for these salient differences.
>
> 540 U.S. at 188, 124 S.Ct. 619.

Before the district court, the Boards contended that special restrictions on judicial candidates' reliance on political parties were necessary to protect Minnesota's tradition of non-partisan judicial elections, which dates from the enactment in 1912 of the statute making Minnesota judicial elections non-partisan.

The Minnesota Supreme Court greatly amplified that explanation when it decided to reject the Advisory Committee's proposed revisions to the partisan activities clauses in September 2004. The supreme court order stated, "We conclude that the restrictions on partisan political activity contained in our Code of Judicial Conduct are too important to undermine based on the possibility that they may be vulnerable to constitutional attack, particularly as we are convinced that there are sound bases for their constitutional validity."

The partisan activities clauses at issue here were adopted in 1997 as part of an effort to clarify and formalize Minnesota's tradition of non-partisan elections and to supplement the guidance given by the non-partisan election statute. The mere omission of party names from the ballot apparently does little to make campaigns non-partisan, as shown by the situations in Ohio and Michigan, where ostensibly non-partisan general elections are preceded by vigorous partisan campaigns.

The hearing the Minnesota Supreme Court held before the 1997 amendments to Canon 5 included consideration of whether partisan activities restrictions should be limited to political parties as defined in Canon 5 or whether they should apply to other advocacy groups. There was testimony on both sides of that issue. In addition to the testimony of Judge Meyer (which the Court quotes at slip op. 36–37 n. 13) and others against the definition adopted, DePaul Willette testified:

> Let's assume that the rule is not in place and two candidates in a race; one is endorsed by the republican party, one is endorsed by the democratic party. What do we have? We have a party race. It's not a nonpartisan contest. We have a party contest which will lead us, in my judgment, to the kind of fund-raising and the problems that Illinois and Texas are facing today with multi-million dollar budgets for people who want to retain or gain judicial positions.

Hearing before the Minnesota Supreme Court on Amendment to Canon 5 of the Code of Judicial Conduct, at 20–21 (Nov. 17, 1997).

Willette's testimony also refutes the idea that the Minnesota Supreme Court intentionally failed to address the threat from partisan activity by single-issue interest groups. Willette testified that one reason single-issue interest groups were not included in the partisan activities clauses is that single-issue groups would require a commitment that would have been banned under the announce clause at the time. Obviously, the announce clause can no longer play any role in the regulatory scheme; however, the Minnesota Supreme Court's expectation that the announce clause would serve to moderate a candidate's relation with interest groups was reasonable at the time and therefore tends to show that the partisan activities clauses were effective at the time adopted. Moreover, the invalidation of the announce clause has apparently had a profound effect on the pressures on judicial candidates in that it is apparently now common for organizations to send judicial candidates questionnaires asking them to state their positions on an array of disputed legal issues. In light of the invalidation of the announce clause, I believe a remand for further evidence on the issue of pretext would be more appropriate than for us to order summary judgment on a record with evidence supporting both sides of the question.

McConnell demonstrates that the distinction between political parties and other interest groups could be defended as a valid response to "salient differences" between the kind of threat each sort of organization poses to the state's interests. In addition to its institutional experience with non-partisan judicial elections since 1912, in 1997 the Minnesota Supreme Court had before it some evidence validating the distinction between political parties and other interest groups, and some challenging that distinction. It resolved that conflict, concluding that political parties posed the greater threat. The conclusion was reaffirmed in 2004 by a committee of lawyers and scholars charged with the task of scrutinizing Canon 5 for constitutional problems, and later by the Minnesota Supreme Court. Our Court errs in concluding as a matter of law that the distinction between political parties and other interest groups is pretextual. The evidence as to this distinction is best considered by the district court on remand.

Finally, this is a case in which the parameters of the evil addressed cannot be outlined with a high degree of precision. The difficulty is that the threat to the governmental interest is not from unambiguously evil conduct, but from behavior that forms part of a continuum with desired behavior-attempts of the citizenry to make their voices heard in their government. The critical and difficult question posed by this case is that the danger to judicial neutrality comes from that sometimes salutary behavior, at the point at which participation in the democratic process becomes undue influence over judicial decisionmaking, preventing a judge from acting as the law's representative, rather than as the representative of a political patron or donor. That point will vary from candidate to candidate, according to whether he or she is stubborn or persuadable, experienced or naive, young or old, poor or independently wealthy, ambitious or modest. No law can account for all these imponderables without restricting some candidate who would not have been swayed by temptation or leaving some candidate at liberty to compromise himself.

The Supreme Court acknowledged the same problem in the context of political contribution and expenditure restrictions. The use of money to influence elections and hence, government policy, is not simply either wholesome activism or influence-buying-the same action can partake of both, which is why someone has to decide when a contribution or expenditure goes from being civic activism to a bid for undue influence. For that reason, the Supreme Court has said that regulation of political contributions and expenditures can go beyond forbidding outright bribery to regulation of more subtle forms of conduct that pose the same kind of threat, but in a lesser degree or in a more ambiguous form. This was debated in *McConnell,* where the dissenters contended that bribery laws ought to be enough to protect the government's anti-corruption interest, but the Court's opinion held that the anti-corruption interest "extends beyond simple cash-for-votes corruption to curbing 'undue influence on an officeholder's judgment.' " When Congress grapples with such a protean concept as "undue influence on an officeholder," the Supreme Court applies strict scrutiny in such a way as to acknowledge that Congress' task requires exercise of some judgment. In contrast to the Supreme Court's approach, our Court today takes a bludgeon to a state's attempt to solve a delicate problem

FOR DISCUSSION

Do you see judges as running for office different from other candidates for office? Should the Constitution treat their free speech rights differently?

CAPERTON V. MASSEY COAL COMPANY

565 U.S. 868, 129 S.Ct. 2252, 173 L.Ed.2d 1208 (2009)

The facts are described in Justice Kennedy's opinion.

Vote: 5–4

JUSTICE KENNEDY delivered the opinion of the Court.

I

In August 2002 a West Virginia jury returned a verdict that found respondents A.T. Massey Coal Co. and its affiliates (hereinafter Massey) liable for fraudulent misrepresentation, concealment, and tortious interference with existing contractual relations. The jury awarded petitioners Hugh Caperton, Harman Development Corp., Harman Mining Corp., and Sovereign Coal Sales (hereinafter Caperton) the sum of $50 million in compensatory and punitive damages.

In June 2004 the state trial court denied Massey's post-trial motions challenging the verdict and the damages award, finding that Massey "intentionally acted in utter disregard of [Caperton's] rights and ultimately destroyed [Caperton's] businesses because, after conducting cost-benefit analyses, [Massey] concluded it was in its financial interest to do so." In March 2005 the trial court denied Massey's motion for judgment as a matter of law.

Don Blankenship is Massey's chairman, chief executive officer, and president. After the verdict but before the appeal, West Virginia held its 2004 judicial elections. Knowing the Supreme Court of Appeals of West Virginia would consider the appeal in the case, Blankenship decided to support an attorney who sought to replace Justice McGraw. Justice McGraw was a candidate for reelection to that court. The attorney who sought to replace him was Brent Benjamin.

In addition to contributing the $1,000 statutory maximum to Benjamin's campaign committee, Blankenship donated almost $2.5 million to "And For The Sake Of The Kids," a political organization formed under 26

U.S.C. § 527. The § 527 organization opposed McGraw and supported Benjamin. Blankenship's donations accounted for more than two-thirds of the total funds it raised. This was not all. Blankenship spent, in addition, just over $500,000 on independent expenditures—for direct mailings and letters soliciting donations as well as television and newspaper advertisements—" 'to support . . . Brent Benjamin.' "

To provide some perspective, Blankenship's $3 million in contributions were more than the total amount spent by all other Benjamin supporters and three times the amount spent by Benjamin's own committee. Caperton contends that Blankenship spent $1 million more than the total amount spent by the campaign committees of both candidates combined.

Benjamin won. He received 382,036 votes (53.3%), and McGraw received 334,301 votes (46.7%).

In October 2005, before Massey filed its petition for appeal in West Virginia's highest court, Caperton moved to disqualify now-Justice Benjamin under the Due Process Clause and the West Virginia Code of Judicial Conduct, based on the conflict caused by Blankenship's campaign involvement. Justice Benjamin denied the motion in April 2006. He indicated that he "carefully considered the bases and accompanying exhibits proffered by the movants." But he found "no objective information . . . to show that this Justice has a bias for or against any litigant, that this Justice has prejudged the matters which comprise this litigation, or that this Justice will be anything but fair and impartial." In December 2006 Massey filed its petition for appeal to challenge the adverse jury verdict. The West Virginia Supreme Court of Appeals granted review.

In November 2007 that court reversed the $50 million verdict against Massey. The majority opinion, authored by then-Chief Justice Davis and joined by Justices Benjamin and Maynard, found that "Massey's conduct warranted the type of judgment rendered in this case." It reversed, nevertheless, based on two independent grounds-first, that a forum-selection clause contained in a contract to which Massey was not a party barred the suit in West Virginia, and, second, that res judicata barred the suit due to an out-of-state judgment to which Massey was not a party. Justice Starcher dissented, stating that the "majority's opinion is morally and legally wrong." Justice Albright also dissented, accusing the majority of "misapplying the law and introducing sweeping 'new law' into our jurisprudence that may well come back to haunt us."

Caperton sought rehearing, and the parties moved for disqualification of three of the five justices who decided the appeal. Photos had surfaced of Justice Maynard vacationing with Blankenship in the French Riviera while the case was pending. Justice Maynard granted Caperton's recusal motion. On the other side Justice Starcher granted Massey's recusal motion, apparently based on his public criticism of Blankenship's role in the 2004 elections. In his recusal memorandum Justice Starcher urged Justice Benjamin to recuse himself as well. He noted that "Blankenship's bestowal of his personal wealth, political tactics, and 'friendship' have created a cancer in the affairs of this Court." Justice Benjamin declined Justice Starcher's suggestion and denied Caperton's recusal motion.

The court granted rehearing. Justice Benjamin, now in the capacity of acting chief justice, selected Judges Cookman and Fox to replace the recused justices. Caperton moved a third time for disqualification, arguing that Justice Benjamin had failed to apply the correct standard under West Virginia law-*i.e.,* whether "a reasonable and prudent person, knowing these objective facts, would harbor doubts about Justice Benjamin's ability to be fair and impartial." Caperton also included the results of a public opinion poll, which indicated that over 67% of West Virginians doubted Justice Benjamin would be fair and impartial. Justice Benjamin again refused to withdraw, noting that the "push poll" was "neither credible nor sufficiently reliable to serve as the basis for an elected judge's disqualification."

In April 2008 a divided court again reversed the jury verdict, and again it was a 3-to-2 decision. Justice Davis filed a modified version of his prior opinion, repeating the two earlier holdings. She was joined by Justice Benjamin and Judge Fox.

II

It is axiomatic that "[a] fair trial in a fair tribunal is a basic requirement of due process." Murchison, at 136, As the Court has recognized, however, "most matters relating to judicial disqualification [do] not rise to a constitutional level." *FTC v. Cement Institute,* 333 U.S. 683, 702 (1948). The early and leading case on the subject is *Tumey v. Ohio,* 273 U.S. 510 (1927). There, the Court stated that "matters of kinship, personal bias, state policy, remoteness of interest, would seem generally to be matters merely of legislative discretion."

The *Tumey* Court concluded that the Due Process Clause incorporated the common-law rule that a judge must recuse himself when he has "a direct, personal, substantial, pecuniary interest" in a case. This rule reflects the maxim that "[n]o man is allowed to be a judge in his own cause; because his interest would certainly bias his judgment, and, not improbably, corrupt his integrity." The Federalist No. 10, p. 59 (J. Cooke ed.1961) (J. Madison)

As new problems have emerged that were not discussed at common law, however, the Court has identified additional instances which, as an objective matter, require recusal. These are circumstances "in which experience teaches that the probability of actual bias on the part of the judge or decisionmaker is too high to be constitutionally tolerable." To place the present case in proper context, two instances where the Court has required recusal merit further discussion.

A

The first involved the emergence of local tribunals where a judge had a financial interest in the outcome of a case, although the interest was less than what would have been considered personal or direct at common law.

This was the problem addressed in *Tumey.* There, the mayor of a village had the authority to sit as a judge (with no jury) to try those accused of violating a state law prohibiting the possession of alcoholic beverages. Inherent in this structure were two potential conflicts. First, the mayor received a salary supplement for performing judicial duties, and the funds for that compensation derived from the fines assessed in a case. No fines were assessed upon acquittal. The mayor-judge thus received a salary supplement only if he convicted the defendant. Second, sums from the criminal fines were deposited to the village's general treasury fund for village improvements and repairs.

The Court held that the Due Process Clause required disqualification "both because of [the mayor-judge's] direct pecuniary interest in the outcome, and because of his official motive to convict and to graduate the fine to help the financial needs of the village." It so held despite observing that "[t]here are doubtless mayors who would not allow such a consideration as $12 costs in each case to affect their judgment in it."

The Court in *Lavoie* further clarified the reach of the Due Process Clause regarding a judge's financial interest in a case. There, a justice had cast the deciding vote on the Alabama Supreme Court to uphold a punitive damages award against an insurance company for bad-faith refusal to pay a claim. At the time of his vote, the justice was the lead plaintiff in a nearly identical lawsuit pending in Alabama's lower courts. His deciding vote, this Court surmised, "undoubtedly 'raised the stakes' " for the insurance defendant in the justice's suit.

B

The second instance requiring recusal that was not discussed at common law emerged in the criminal contempt context, where a judge had no pecuniary interest in the case but was challenged because of a conflict arising from his participation in an earlier proceeding. This Court characterized that first proceeding (perhaps pejoratively) as a " 'one-man grand jury.' "

In that first proceeding, and as provided by state law, a judge examined witnesses to determine whether criminal charges should be brought. The judge called the two petitioners before him. One petitioner answered questions, but the judge found him untruthful and charged him with perjury. The second declined to answer on the ground that he did not have counsel with him, as state law seemed to permit. The judge charged him with contempt. The judge proceeded to try and convict both petitioners.

This Court set aside the convictions on grounds that the judge had a conflict of interest at the trial stage because of his earlier participation followed by his decision to charge them. The Due Process Clause required disqualification. The Court recited the general rule that "no man can be a judge in his own case," adding that "no man is permitted to try cases where he has an interest in the outcome."

III

Based on the principles described in these cases we turn to the issue before us. This problem arises in the context of judicial elections, a framework not presented in the precedents we have reviewed and discussed.

Caperton contends that Blankenship's pivotal role in getting Justice Benjamin elected created a constitutionally intolerable probability of actual bias. Though not a bribe or criminal influence, Justice Benjamin would nevertheless feel a debt of gratitude to Blankenship for his extraordinary efforts to get him elected. That temptation, Caperton claims, is as strong and inherent in human nature as was the conflict the Court confronted in *Tumey* and *Monroeville* when a mayor-judge (or the city) benefited financially from a defendant's conviction, as well as the conflict identified in *Murchison* and *Mayberry* when a judge was the object of a defendant's contempt.

Justice Benjamin was careful to address the recusal motions and explain his reasons why, on his view of the controlling standard, disqualification was not in order. In four separate opinions issued during the course of the appeal, he explained why no actual bias had been established. He found no basis for recusal because Caperton failed to provide "objective evidence" or "objective information," but merely "subjective belief" of bias.

Following accepted principles of our legal tradition respecting the proper performance of judicial functions, judges often inquire into their subjective motives and purposes in the ordinary course of deciding a case. This does not mean the inquiry is a simple one.

The judge inquires into reasons that seem to be leading to a particular result. Precedent and *stare decisis* and the text and purpose of the law and the Constitution; logic and scholarship and experience and common sense; and fairness and disinterest and neutrality are among the factors at work. To bring coherence to the process, and to seek respect for the resulting judgment, judges often explain the reasons for their conclusions and rulings. There are instances when the introspection that often attends this process may reveal that what the judge had assumed to be a proper, controlling factor is not the real one at work. If the judge discovers that some personal bias or improper consideration seems to be the actuating cause of the decision or to be an influence so difficult to dispel that there is a real possibility of undermining neutrality, the judge may think it necessary to consider withdrawing from the case.

The difficulties of inquiring into actual bias, and the fact that the inquiry is often a private one, simply underscore the need for objective rules. Otherwise there may be no adequate protection against a judge who simply misreads or misapprehends the real motives at work in deciding the case. The judge's own inquiry into actual bias, then, is not one that the law can easily superintend or review, though actual bias, if disclosed, no doubt would be grounds for appropriate relief. In lieu of exclusive reliance on that personal inquiry, or on appellate review of the judge's determination respecting actual bias, the Due Process Clause has been implemented by objective standards that do not require proof of actual bias.

We turn to the influence at issue in this case. Not every campaign contribution by a litigant or attorney creates a probability of bias that requires a judge's recusal, but this is an exceptional case. We conclude that there is a serious risk of actual bias-based on objective and reasonable perceptions-when a person with a personal stake in a particular case had a significant and disproportionate influence in placing the judge on the case by raising funds or directing the judge's election campaign when the case was pending or imminent. The inquiry centers on the contribution's relative size in comparison to the total amount of money contributed to the campaign, the total amount spent in the election, and the apparent effect such contribution had on the outcome of the election.

Applying this principle, we conclude that Blankenship's campaign efforts had a significant and disproportionate influence in placing Justice Benjamin on the case. Blankenship contributed some $3 million to unseat the incumbent and replace him with Benjamin. His contributions eclipsed the total amount spent by all other Benjamin supporters and exceeded by 300% the amount spent by Benjamin's campaign committee. Caperton claims Blankenship spent $1 million more than the total amount spent by the campaign committees of both candidates combined.

Whether Blankenship's campaign contributions were a necessary and sufficient cause of Benjamin's victory is not the proper inquiry. Much like determining whether a judge is actually biased, proving what ultimately drives the electorate to choose a particular candidate is a difficult endeavor, not likely to lend itself to a certain conclusion. This is particularly true where, as here, there is no procedure for judicial factfinding and the sole trier of fact is the one accused of bias. Due process requires an objective inquiry into whether the contributor's influence on the election under all the circumstances "would offer a possible temptation to the average . . . judge to . . . lead him not to hold the balance nice, clear and true." In an election decided by fewer than 50,000 votes (382,036 to 334,301), Blankenship's campaign contributions-in comparison to the total amount contributed to the campaign, as well as the total amount spent in the election-had a significant and disproportionate influence on the electoral outcome.

The temporal relationship between the campaign contributions, the justice's election, and the pendency of the case is also critical. It was reasonably foreseeable, when the campaign contributions were made, that the pending case would be before the newly elected justice. The $50 million adverse jury verdict had been entered before the election, and the Supreme Court of Appeals was the next step once the state trial court dealt with post-trial motions. So it became at once apparent that, absent recusal, Justice Benjamin would review a judgment that cost his biggest donor's company $50 million. Although there is no allegation of a *quid pro quo* agreement, the fact remains that Blankenship's extraordinary contributions were made at a time when he had a vested stake in the outcome. Just as no man is allowed to be a judge in his own cause, similar fears of bias can arise when-without the consent of the other parties-a man chooses the judge in his own cause. And applying this principle to the judicial election process, there was here a serious, objective risk of actual bias that required Justice Benjamin's recusal.

Due process "may sometimes bar trial by judges who have no actual bias and who would do their very best to weigh the scales of justice equally between contending parties." *Murchison,* 349 U.S., at 136. The failure to consider objective standards requiring recusal is not consistent with the imperatives of due process. We find that Blankenship's significant and disproportionate influence-coupled with the temporal relationship between the election and the pending case " ' "offer a possible temptation to the average . . . judge to . . . lead him not to hold the balance nice, clear and true." ' " On these extreme facts the probability of actual bias rises to an unconstitutional level.

IV

Our decision today addresses an extraordinary situation where the Constitution requires recusal. Massey and its *amici* predict that various adverse consequences will follow from recognizing a constitutional violation here-ranging from a flood of recusal motions to unnecessary interference with judicial elections. We disagree. The facts now before us are extreme by any measure. The parties point to no other instance involving judicial campaign contributions that presents a potential for bias comparable to the circumstances in this case.

"The Due Process Clause demarks only the outer boundaries of judicial disqualifications. Congress and the states, of course, remain free to impose more rigorous standards for judicial disqualification than those we find mandated here today." Lavoie at 828. Because the codes of judicial conduct provide more protection than due process requires, most disputes over disqualification will be resolved without resort to the Constitution. Application of the constitutional standard implicated in this case will thus be confined to rare instances.

CHIEF JUSTICE ROBERTS, with whom JUSTICE SCALIA, JUSTICE THOMAS, and JUSTICE ALITO join, dissenting.

I, of course, share the majority's sincere concerns about the need to maintain a fair, independent, and impartial judiciary-and one that appears to be such. But I fear that the Court's decision will undermine rather than promote these values.

Until today, we have recognized exactly two situations in which the Federal Due Process Clause requires disqualification of a judge: when the judge has a financial interest in the outcome of the case, and when the judge is trying a defendant for certain criminal contempts. Vaguer notions of bias or the appearance of bias were never a basis for disqualification, either at common law or under our constitutional precedents. Those issues were instead addressed by legislation or court rules.

Today, however, the Court enlists the Due Process Clause to overturn a judge's failure to recuse because of a "probability of bias." Unlike the established grounds for disqualification, a "probability of bias" cannot be defined in any limited way. The Court's new "rule" provides no guidance to judges and litigants about when recusal will be constitutionally required. This will inevitably lead to an increase in allegations that judges are biased, however groundless those charges may be. The end result will do far more to erode public confidence in judicial impartiality than an isolated failure to recuse in a particular case.

II

In departing from this clear line between when recusal is constitutionally required and when it is not, the majority repeatedly emphasizes the need for an "objective" standard. The majority's analysis is "objective" in that it does not inquire into Justice Benjamin's motives or decisionmaking process. But the standard the majority articulates-"probability of bias"-fails to provide clear, workable guidance for future cases. At the most basic level, it is unclear whether the new probability of bias standard is somehow limited to financial support in judicial elections, or applies to judicial recusal questions more generally.

But there are other fundamental questions as well. With little help from the majority, courts will now have to determine:

1. How much money is too much money? What level of contribution or expenditure gives rise to a "probability of bias"?

2. How do we determine whether a given expenditure is "disproportionate"? Disproportionate *to what?*

3. Are independent, non-coordinated expenditures treated the same as direct contributions to a candidate's campaign? What about contributions to independent outside groups supporting a candidate?

4. Does it matter whether the litigant has contributed to other candidates or made large expenditures in connection with other elections?

5. Does the amount at issue in the case matter? What if this case were an employment dispute with only $10,000 at stake? What if the plaintiffs only sought non-monetary relief such as an injunction or declaratory judgment?

6. Does the analysis change depending on whether the judge whose disqualification is sought sits on a trial court, appeals court, or state supreme court?

7. How long does the probability of bias last? Does the probability of bias diminish over time as the election recedes? Does it matter whether the judge plans to run for reelection?

8. What if the "disproportionately" large expenditure is made by an industry association, trade union, physicians' group, or the plaintiffs' bar? Must the judge recuse in all cases that affect the association's interests? Must the judge recuse in all cases in which a party or lawyer is a member of that group? Does it matter how much the litigant contributed to the association?

9. What if the case involves a social or ideological issue rather than a financial one? Must a judge recuse from cases involving, say, abortion rights if he has received "disproportionate" support from individuals who feel strongly about either side of that issue? If the supporter wants to help elect judges who are "tough on crime," must the judge recuse in all criminal cases?

10. What if the candidate draws "disproportionate" support from a particular racial, religious, ethnic, or other group, and the case involves an issue of particular importance to that group?

11. What if the supporter is not a party to the pending or imminent case, but his interests will be affected by the decision? Does the Court's analysis apply if the supporter "chooses the judge" not in *his* case, but in someone else's?

12. What if the case implicates a regulatory issue that is of great importance to the party making the expenditures, even though he has no direct financial interest in the outcome (*e.g.*, a facial challenge to an agency rulemaking or a suit seeking to limit an agency's jurisdiction)?

13. Must the judge's vote be outcome determinative in order for his non-recusal to constitute a due process violation?

14. Does the due process analysis consider the underlying merits of the suit? Does it matter whether the decision is clearly right (or wrong) as a matter of state law?

15. What if a lower court decision in favor of the supporter is affirmed on the merits on appeal, by a panel with no "debt of gratitude" to the supporter? Does that "moot" the due process claim?

16. What if the judge voted against the supporter in many other cases?

17. What if the judge disagrees with the supporter's message or tactics? What if the judge expressly *disclaims* the support of this person?

18. Should we assume that elected judges feel a "debt of hostility" towards major *opponents* of their candidacies? Must the judge recuse in cases involving individuals or groups who spent large amounts of money trying unsuccessfully to defeat him?

19. If there is independent review of a judge's recusal decision, *e.g.*, by a panel of other judges, does this completely foreclose a due process claim?

20. Does a debt of gratitude for endorsements by newspapers, interest groups, politicians, or celebrities also give rise to a constitutionally unacceptable probability of bias? How would we measure whether such support is disproportionate?

21. Does close personal friendship between a judge and a party or lawyer now give rise to a probability of bias?

22. Does it matter whether the campaign expenditures come from a party or the party's attorney? If from a lawyer, must the judge recuse in every case involving that attorney?

23. Does what is unconstitutional vary from State to State? What if particular States have a history of expensive judicial elections?

24. Under the majority's "objective" test, do we analyze the due process issue through the lens of a reasonable person, a reasonable lawyer, or a reasonable judge?

25. What role does causation play in this analysis? The Court sends conflicting signals on this point. The majority asserts that "[w]hether Blankenship's campaign contributions were a necessary and sufficient cause of Benjamin's victory is not the proper inquiry." But elsewhere in the opinion, the majority considers "the apparent effect such contribution had on the outcome of the election," and whether the litigant has been able to "choos[e] the judge in his own cause." If causation is a pertinent factor, how do we know whether the contribution or expenditure had any effect on the outcome of the election? What if the judge won in a landslide? What if the judge won primarily because of his opponent's missteps?

26. Is the due process analysis less probing for incumbent judges-who typically have a great advantage in elections-than for challengers?

27. How final must the pending case be with respect to the contributor's interest? What if, for example, the only issue on appeal is whether the court should certify a class of plaintiffs? Is recusal required just as if the issue in the pending case were ultimate liability?

28. Which cases are implicated by this doctrine? Must the case be pending at the time of the election? Reasonably likely to be brought? What about an important but unanticipated case filed shortly after the election?

29. When do we impute a probability of bias from one party to another? Does a contribution from a corporation get imputed to its executives, and vice-versa? Does a contribution or expenditure by one family member get imputed to other family members?

30. What if the election is nonpartisan? What if the election is just a yes-or-no vote about whether to retain an incumbent?

31. What type of support is disqualifying? What if the supporter's expenditures are used to fund voter registration or get-out-the-vote efforts rather than television advertisements?

32. Are contributions or expenditures in connection with a primary aggregated with those in the general election? What if the contributor supported a different candidate in the primary? Does that dilute the debt of gratitude?

33. What procedures must be followed to challenge a state judge's failure to recuse? May *Caperton* claims only be raised on direct review? Or may such claims also be brought in federal district court under 42 U.S.C. § 1983, which allows a person deprived of a federal right by a state official to sue for damages? If § 1983 claims are available, who are the proper defendants? The judge? The whole court? The clerk of court?

34. What about state-court cases that are already closed? Can the losing parties in those cases now seek collateral relief in federal district court under § 1983? What statutes of limitation should be applied to such suits?

35. What is the proper remedy? After a successful *Caperton* motion, must the parties start from scratch before the lower courts? Is any part of the lower court judgment retained?

36. Does a litigant waive his due process claim if he waits until after decision to raise it? Or would the claim only be ripe after decision, when the judge's actions or vote suggest a probability of bias?

37. Are the parties entitled to discovery with respect to the judge's recusal decision?

38. If a judge erroneously fails to recuse, do we apply harmless-error review?

39. Does the *judge* get to respond to the allegation that he is probably biased, or is his reputation solely in the hands of the parties to the case?

40. What if the parties settle a *Caperton* claim as part of a broader settlement of the case? Does that leave the judge with no way to salvage his reputation?

These are only a few uncertainties that quickly come to mind. Judges and litigants will surely encounter others when they are forced to, or wish to, apply the majority's decision in different circumstances. Today's opinion requires state and federal judges simultaneously to act as political scientists (why did candidate X win the election?), economists (was the financial support disproportionate?), and psychologists (is there likely to be a debt of gratitude?).

FOR DISCUSSION

What is the exact constitutional violation that the majority identifies here that justified the overturning of the state court decision? Did the State Supreme Court justice actually do anything wrong?

WILLIAMS-YULEE V. FLORIDA BAR

135 S.Ct. 1656, 191 L.Ed.2d 570 (2015)

State candidate for judicial official personally solicited campaign funds contrary to judicial conduct rules. Florida Supreme Court publicly reprimanded her. She appealed the reprimand to the U.S. Supreme Court claiming the ban on solicitation violated her First Amendment Free Speech rights. The Supreme Court affirmed.

Vote: 5–4

CHIEF JUSTICE ROBERTS wrote for the Court joined by BREYER, SOTOMAYOR, and KAGAN. JUSTICE GINSBURG joined except as to Part II.

JUSTICE BREYER filed a concurring opinion.

JUSTICE GINSBURG filed an opinion concurring in part and concurring in the judgment, in which JUSTICE BREYER joined as to Part II.

JUSTICE SCALIA filed a dissenting opinion, in which JUSTICE THOMAS joined.

JUSTICE KENNEDY filed a dissenting opinion.

JUSTICE ALITO filed a dissenting opinion.

Our Founders vested authority to appoint federal judges in the President, with the advice and consent of the Senate, and entrusted those judges to hold their offices during good behavior. The Constitution permits States to make a different choice, and most of them have done so. In 39 States, voters elect trial or appellate judges at the polls. In an effort to preserve public confidence in the integrity of their judiciaries, many of those States prohibit judges and judicial candidates from personally soliciting funds for their campaigns. We must decide whether the First Amendment permits such restrictions on speech.

We hold that it does. Judges are not politicians, even when they come to the bench by way of the ballot. And a State's decision to elect its judiciary does not compel it to treat judicial candidates like campaigners for political office. A State may assure its people that judges will apply the law without fear or favor—and without having personally asked anyone for money. We affirm the judgment of the Florida Supreme Court.

I

A

In the early 1970s, four Florida Supreme Court justices resigned from office following corruption scandals. Florida voters responded by amending their Constitution again. Under the system now in place, appellate judges are appointed by the Governor from a list of candidates proposed by a nominating committee—a process known as "merit selection." Then, every six years, voters decide whether to retain incumbent appellate judges for another term. Trial judges are still elected by popular vote, unless the local jurisdiction opts instead for merit selection.

Amid the corruption scandals of the 1970s, the Florida Supreme Court adopted a new Code of Judicial Conduct. In its present form, the first sentence of Canon 1 reads, "An independent and honorable judiciary is indispensable to justice in our society.". Canon 1 instructs judges to observe "high standards of conduct" so that "the integrity and independence of the judiciary may be preserved." Canon 2 directs that a judge "shall act at all times in a manner that promotes public confidence in the integrity and impartiality of the judiciary." Other provisions prohibit judges from lending the prestige of their offices to private interests, engaging in certain business transactions, and personally participating in soliciting funds for nonprofit organizations.

Canon 7C(1) governs fundraising in judicial elections. The Canon, which is based on a provision in the American Bar Association's Model Code of Judicial Conduct, provides:

> "A candidate, including an incumbent judge, for a judicial office that is filled by public election between competing candidates shall not personally solicit campaign funds, or solicit attorneys for publicly stated support, but may establish committees of responsible persons to secure and manage the expenditure of funds for the candidate's campaign and to obtain public statements of support for his or her candidacy. Such committees are not prohibited from soliciting campaign contributions and public support from any person or corporation authorized by law."

Florida statutes impose additional restrictions on campaign fundraising in judicial elections. Contributors may not donate more than $1,000 per election to a trial court candidate or more than $3,000 per retention election to a Supreme Court justice. Fla. Stat. § 106.08(1)(a) (2014). Campaign committee treasurers must file periodic reports disclosing the names of contributors and the amount of each contribution.

Judicial candidates can seek guidance about campaign ethics rules from the Florida Judicial Ethics Advisory Committee. The Committee has interpreted Canon 7 to allow a judicial candidate to serve as treasurer of his own campaign committee, learn the identity of campaign contributors, and send thank you notes to donors.

Like Florida, most other States prohibit judicial candidates from soliciting campaign funds personally, but allow them to raise money through committees. According to the American Bar Association, 30 of the 39 States that elect trial or appellate judges have adopted restrictions similar to Canon 7C(1).

B

Lanell William-Yulee, who refers to herself as Yulee, has practiced law in Florida since 1991. In September 2009, she decided to run for a seat on the county court for Hillsborough County, a jurisdiction of about 1.3 million people that includes the city of Tampa. Shortly after filing paperwork to enter the race, Yulee drafted a letter announcing her candidacy. The letter described her experience and desire to "bring fresh ideas and positive solutions to the Judicial bench." The letter then stated:

> "An early contribution of $25, $50, $100, $250, or $500, made payable to 'Lanell Williams-Yulee Campaign for County Judge', will help raise the initial funds needed to launch the campaign and get our message out to the public. I ask for your support [i]n meeting the primary election fund raiser goals. Thank you in advance for your support."

Yulee signed the letter and mailed it to local voters. She also posted the letter on her campaign Web site.

Yulee's bid for the bench did not unfold as she had hoped. She lost the primary to the incumbent judge. Then the Florida Bar filed a complaint against her. As relevant here, the Bar charged her with violating Rule 4–8.2(b) of the Rules Regulating the Florida Bar. That Rule requires judicial candidates to comply with applicable provisions of Florida's Code of Judicial Conduct, including the ban on personal solicitation of campaign funds in Canon 7C(1).

Yulee admitted that she had signed and sent the fundraising letter. But she argued that the Bar could not discipline her for that conduct because the First Amendment protects a judicial candidate's right to solicit campaign funds in an election. The Florida Supreme Court appointed a referee, who held a hearing and recommended a finding of guilt. As a sanction, the referee recommended that Yulee be publicly reprimanded and ordered to pay the costs of the proceeding ($1,860).

The Florida Supreme Court adopted the referee's recommendations. The court explained that Canon 7C(1) "clearly restricts a judicial candidate's speech" and therefore must be "narrowly tailored to serve a compelling state interest." The court held that the Canon satisfies that demanding inquiry. First, the court reasoned, prohibiting judicial candidates from personally soliciting funds furthers Florida's compelling interest in "preserving the integrity of [its] judiciary and maintaining the public's confidence in an impartial judiciary." In the court's view, "personal solicitation of campaign funds, even by mass mailing, raises an appearance of impropriety and calls into question, in the public's mind, the judge's impartiality." Second, the court concluded that Canon 7C(1) is narrowly tailored to serve that compelling interest because it " 'insulate[s] judicial candidates from the solicitation and receipt of funds while leaving open, ample alternative means for candidates to raise the resources necessary to run their campaigns.' "

The Florida Supreme Court acknowledged that some Federal Courts of Appeals—"whose judges have lifetime appointments and thus do not have to engage in fundraising"—had invalidated restrictions similar to Canon 7C(1). 138 So.3d, at 386, n. 3. But the court found it persuasive that every State Supreme Court that had considered similar fundraising provisions—along with several Federal Courts of Appeals—had upheld the laws against First Amendment challenges. Florida's chief justice and one associate justice dissented. *Id.,* at 389. We granted certiorari.

II

The First Amendment provides that Congress "shall make no law . . . abridging the freedom of speech." The Fourteenth Amendment makes that prohibition applicable to the States. The parties agree that Canon 7C(1) restricts Yulee's speech on the basis of its content by prohibiting her from soliciting contributions to her election campaign. The parties disagree, however, about the level of scrutiny that should govern our review.

We have applied exacting scrutiny to laws restricting the solicitation of contributions to charity, upholding the speech limitations only if they are narrowly tailored to serve a compelling interest. As we have explained, noncommercial solicitation "is characteristically intertwined with informative and perhaps persuasive speech." Applying a lesser standard of scrutiny to such speech would threaten "the exercise of rights so vital to the maintenance of democratic institutions." *Schneider v. State (Town of Irvington),* 308 U.S. 147, 161, 60 S.Ct. 146, 84 L.Ed. 155 (1939).

The principles underlying these charitable solicitation cases apply with even greater force here. Before asking for money in her fundraising letter, Yulee explained her fitness for the bench and expressed her vision for the judiciary. Her stated purpose for the solicitation was to get her "message out to the public." As we have long recognized, speech about public issues and the qualifications of candidates for elected office commands the highest level of First Amendment protection. Indeed, in our only prior case concerning speech restrictions on a candidate for judicial office, this Court and both parties assumed that strict scrutiny applied. *Republican Party of Minn. v. White,* 536 U.S. 765, 774, 122 S.Ct. 2528, 153 L.Ed.2d 694 (2002). In sum, we hold today what we assumed in *White*: A State may restrict the speech of a judicial candidate only if the restriction is narrowly tailored to serve a compelling interest.

III

The Florida Bar faces a demanding task in defending Canon 7C(1) against Yulee's First Amendment challenge. We have emphasized that "it is the rare case" in which a State demonstrates that a speech restriction is narrowly tailored to serve a compelling interest. But those cases do arise. Here, Canon 7C(1) advances the State's compelling interest in preserving public confidence in the integrity of the judiciary, and it does so through means narrowly tailored to avoid unnecessarily abridging speech. This is therefore one of the rare cases in which a speech restriction withstands strict scrutiny.

A

The Florida Supreme Court adopted Canon 7C(1) to promote the State's interests in "protecting the integrity of the judiciary" and "maintaining the public's confidence in an impartial judiciary." The way the Canon advances those interests is intuitive: Judges, charged with exercising strict neutrality and independence, cannot supplicate campaign donors without diminishing public confidence in judicial integrity. This principle dates back at least eight centuries to Magna Carta, which proclaimed, "To no one will we sell, to no one will we refuse or delay, right or justice." Cl. 40 (1215), in W. McKechnie, Magna Carta, A Commentary on the Great Charter of King John 395 (2d ed. 1914). The same concept underlies the common law judicial oath, which binds a judge to "do right to all manner of people . . . without fear or favour, affection or ill-will," 10 Encyclopaedia of the Laws of England 105 (2d ed. 1908), and the oath that each of us took to "administer justice without respect to persons, and do equal right to the poor and to the rich," Simply put, Florida and most other States have concluded that the public may lack confidence in a judge's ability to administer justice without fear or favor if he comes to office by asking for favors.

The interest served by Canon 7C(1) has firm support in our precedents. We have recognized the "vital state interest" in safeguarding "public confidence in the fairness and integrity of the nation's elected judges." *Caperton v. A.T. Massey Coal Co.,* 556 U.S. 868, 889, 129 S.Ct. 2252, 173 L.Ed.2d 1208 (2009). The importance of public confidence in the integrity of judges stems from the place of the judiciary in the government. Unlike the executive or the legislature, the judiciary "has no influence over either the sword or the purse; . . . neither force nor will but merely judgment." The Federalist No. 78, p. 465 (C. Rossiter ed. 1961) (A. Hamilton) The judiciary's authority therefore depends in large measure on the public's willingness to respect and follow its decisions.

The parties devote considerable attention to our cases analyzing campaign finance restrictions in political elections. But a State's interest in preserving public confidence in the integrity of its judiciary extends beyond its interest in preventing the appearance of corruption in legislative and executive elections. As we explained in *White,* States may regulate judicial elections differently than they regulate political elections, because the role of judges differs from the role of politicians. 536 U.S., at 783, 122 S.Ct. 2528; *id.,* at 805, 122 S.Ct. 2528 (GINSBURG, J., dissenting). Politicians are expected to be appropriately responsive to the preferences of their supporters. Indeed, such "responsiveness is key to the very concept of self-governance through elected officials." *McCutcheon v. Federal Election Comm'n,* 572 U.S. ____, ____, 134 S.Ct. 1434, 1462, 188 L.Ed.2d 468 (2014) (plurality opinion). The same is not true of judges. In deciding cases, a judge is not to follow the preferences of his supporters, or provide any special consideration to his campaign donors. A judge instead must "observe the utmost fairness," striving to be "perfectly and completely independent, with nothing to influence or controul him but God and his conscience." Address of John Marshall, in Proceedings and Debates of the Virginia State Convention of 1829–1830, p. 616 (1830). As in *White,* therefore, our precedents applying the First Amendment to political elections have little bearing on the issues here.

The vast majority of elected judges in States that allow personal solicitation serve with fairness and honor. But "[e]ven if judges were able to refrain from favoring donors, the mere possibility that judges' decisions may be motivated by the desire to repay campaign contributions is likely to undermine the public's confidence in the judiciary." In the eyes of the public, a judge's personal solicitation could result (even unknowingly) in "a possible temptation . . . which might lead him not to hold the balance nice, clear and true." *Tumey v. Ohio,* 273 U.S. 510, 532, 47 S.Ct. 437, 71 L.Ed. 749 (1927). That risk is especially pronounced because most donors are lawyers and litigants who may appear before the judge they are supporting.

The concept of public confidence in judicial integrity does not easily reduce to precise definition, nor does it lend itself to proof by documentary record. But no one denies that it is genuine and compelling. In short, it is the regrettable but unavoidable appearance that judges who personally ask for money may diminish their integrity that prompted the Supreme Court of Florida and most other States to sever the direct link between judicial candidates and campaign contributors. As the Supreme Court of Oregon explained, "the spectacle of lawyers or potential litigants directly handing over money to judicial candidates should be avoided if the public is to have faith in the impartiality of its judiciary." *In re Fadeley,* 310 Ore. 548, 565, 802 P.2d 31, 41 (1990). Moreover, personal solicitation by a judicial candidate "inevitably places the solicited individuals in a position to fear retaliation if they fail to financially support that candidate.". Potential litigants then fear that "the integrity of the judicial system has been compromised, forcing them to search for an attorney in part based upon the criteria of which attorneys have made the obligatory contributions." A State's decision to elect its judges does not require it to tolerate these risks. The Florida Bar's interest is compelling.

B

Yulee acknowledges the State's compelling interest in judicial integrity. She argues, however, that the Canon's failure to restrict other speech equally damaging to judicial integrity and its appearance undercuts the Bar's position. In particular, she notes that Canon 7C(1) allows a judge's campaign committee to solicit money, which arguably reduces public confidence in the integrity of the judiciary just as much as a judge's personal solicitation. Yulee also points out that Florida permits judicial candidates to write thank you notes to campaign donors, which ensures that candidates know who contributes and who does not.

It is always somewhat counterintuitive to argue that a law violates the First Amendment by abridging *too little* speech. We have recognized, however, that underinclusiveness can raise "doubts about whether the government is in fact pursuing the interest it invokes, rather than disfavoring a particular speaker or viewpoint." In a textbook illustration of that principle, we invalidated a city's ban on ritual animal sacrifices because the city failed to regulate vast swaths of conduct that similarly diminished its asserted interests in public health and animal welfare. *Church of Lukumi Babalu Aye, Inc. v. Hialeah,* 508 U.S. 520, 543–547, 113 S.Ct. 2217, 124 L.Ed.2d 472 (1993).

Underinclusiveness can also reveal that a law does not actually advance a compelling interest. For example, a State's decision to prohibit newspapers, but not electronic media, from releasing the names of juvenile defendants suggested that the law did not advance its stated purpose of protecting youth privacy. *Smith v. Daily Mail Publishing Co.,* 443 U.S. 97, 104–105, 99 S.Ct. 2667, 61 L.Ed.2d 399 (1979).

Although a law's underinclusivity raises a red flag, the First Amendment imposes no freestanding "underinclusiveness limitation." *R.A.V. v. St. Paul,* 505 U.S. 377, 387, 112 S.Ct. 2538, 120 L.Ed.2d 305 (1992) (internal quotation marks omitted). A State need not address all aspects of a problem in one fell swoop; policymakers may focus on their most pressing concerns. We have accordingly upheld laws—even under strict scrutiny—that conceivably could have restricted even greater amounts of speech in service of their stated interests.

Viewed in light of these principles, Canon 7C(1) raises no fatal underinclusivity concerns. The solicitation ban aims squarely at the conduct most likely to undermine public confidence in the integrity of the judiciary: personal requests for money by judges and judicial candidates. The Canon applies evenhandedly to all judges and judicial candidates, regardless of their viewpoint or chosen means of solicitation. And unlike some laws that we have found impermissibly underinclusive, Canon 7C(1) is not riddled with exceptions. Indeed, the Canon contains zero exceptions to its ban on personal solicitation.

Yulee relies heavily on the provision of Canon 7C(1) that allows solicitation by a candidate's campaign committee. But Florida, along with most other States, has reasonably concluded that solicitation by the candidate personally creates a categorically different and more severe risk of undermining public confidence than does solicitation by a campaign committee. The identity of the solicitor matters, as anyone who has encountered a Girl Scout selling cookies outside a grocery store can attest. When the judicial candidate himself asks for money, the stakes are higher for all involved. The candidate has personally invested his time and effort in the fundraising appeal; he has placed his name and reputation behind the request. The solicited individual knows that, and also knows that the solicitor might be in a position to singlehandedly make decisions of great weight: The same person who signed the fundraising letter might one day sign the judgment. This dynamic inevitably creates pressure for the recipient to comply, and it does so in a way that solicitation by a third party does not. Just as inevitably, the personal involvement of the candidate in the solicitation creates the public appearance that the candidate will remember who says yes, and who says no.

In short, personal solicitation by judicial candidates implicates a different problem than solicitation by campaign committees. However similar the two solicitations may be in substance, a State may conclude that they present markedly different appearances to the public. Florida's choice to allow solicitation by campaign committees does not undermine its decision to ban solicitation by judges.

C

After arguing that Canon 7C(1) violates the First Amendment because it restricts too little speech, Yulee argues that the Canon violates the First Amendment because it restricts too much. In her view, the Canon is not narrowly tailored to advance the State's compelling interest through the least restrictive means.

By any measure, Canon 7C(1) restricts a narrow slice of speech. A reader of Justice KENNEDY's dissent could be forgiven for concluding that the Court has just upheld a latter-day version of the Alien and Sedition Acts, approving "state censorship" that "locks the First Amendment out," imposes a "gag" on candidates, and inflicts "dead weight" on a "silenced" public debate. But in reality, Canon 7C(1) leaves judicial candidates free to discuss any issue with any person at any time. Candidates can write letters, give speeches, and put up billboards. They can contact potential supporters in person, on the phone, or online. They can promote their campaigns on radio, television, or other media. They cannot say, "Please give me money." They can, however, direct their campaign committees to do so. Whatever else may be said of the Canon, it is surely not a "wildly disproportionate restriction upon speech."

Finally, Yulee contends that Florida can accomplish its compelling interest through the less restrictive means of recusal rules and campaign contribution limits. We disagree. A rule requiring judges to recuse themselves from every case in which a lawyer or litigant made a campaign contribution would disable many jurisdictions. And a flood of postelection recusal motions could "erode public confidence in judicial impartiality" and thereby exacerbate the very appearance problem the State is trying to solve. Moreover, the rule that Yulee envisions could create a perverse incentive for litigants to make campaign contributions to judges solely as a means to trigger their later recusal—a form of peremptory strike against a judge that would enable transparent forum shopping.

As for campaign contribution limits, Florida already applies them to judicial elections. Fla. Stat. § 106.08(1)(a). A State may decide that the threat to public confidence created by personal solicitation exists apart from the amount of money that a judge or judicial candidate seeks. Even if Florida decreased its contribution limit, the appearance that judges who personally solicit funds might improperly favor their campaign donors would remain. Although the Court has held that contribution limits advance the interest in preventing *quid pro quo* corruption and its appearance in political elections, we have never held that adopting contribution limits precludes a State from pursuing its compelling interests through additional means. And in any event, a State has compelling interests in regulating judicial elections that extend beyond its interests in regulating political elections, because judges are not politicians.

In sum, because Canon 7C(1) is narrowly tailored to serve a compelling government interest, the First Amendment poses no obstacle to its enforcement in this case. As a result of our decision, Florida may continue to prohibit judicial candidates from personally soliciting campaign funds, while allowing them to raise money through committees and to otherwise communicate their electoral messages in practically any way. The principal dissent faults us for not answering a slew of broader questions, such as whether Florida may cap a judicial candidate's spending or ban independent expenditures by corporations. Yulee has not asked these questions, and for good reason—they are far afield from the narrow regulation actually at issue in this case.

The judgment of the Florida Supreme Court is

Affirmed.

JUSTICE SCALIA, with whom JUSTICE THOMAS joins, dissenting.

An ethics canon adopted by the Florida Supreme Court bans a candidate in a judicial election from asking anyone, under any circumstances, for a contribution to his campaign. Faithful application of our precedents would have made short work of this wildly disproportionate restriction upon speech. Intent upon upholding the Canon, however, the Court flattens one settled First Amendment principle after another.

I

The first axiom of the First Amendment is this: As a general rule, the state has no power to ban speech on the basis of its content. One need not equate judges with politicians to see that this principle does not grow weaker merely because the censored speech is a judicial candidate's request for a campaign contribution. Our cases hold that speech enjoys the full protection of the First Amendment unless a widespread and longstanding tradition ratifies its regulation. No such tradition looms here. Georgia became the first State to elect its judges in 1812, and judicial elections had spread to a large majority of the States by the time of the Civil War. Yet there appears to have been no regulation of judicial candidates' speech throughout the 19th and early 20th centuries. The American Bar Association first proposed ethics rules concerning speech of judicial candidates in 1924, but these rules did not achieve widespread adoption until after the Second World War.

Because Canon 7C(1) restricts fully protected speech on the basis of content, it presumptively violates the First Amendment. We may uphold it only if the State meets its burden of showing that the Canon survives strict scrutiny—that is to say, only if it shows that the Canon is narrowly tailored to serve a compelling interest. I do not for a moment question the Court's conclusion that States have different compelling interests when regulating judicial elections than when regulating political ones. Unlike a legislator, a judge must be impartial—without bias for or against any party or attorney who comes before him. I accept for the sake of argument that States have a compelling interest in ensuring that its judges are *seen* to be impartial. I will likewise assume that a judicial candidate's request to a litigant or attorney presents a danger of coercion that a political candidate's request to a constituent does not. But Canon 7C(1) does not narrowly target concerns about impartiality or its appearance; it applies even when the person asked for a financial contribution has no chance of ever appearing in the candidate's court. And Florida does not invoke concerns about coercion, presumably because the Canon bans solicitations regardless of whether their object is a lawyer, litigant, or other person vulnerable to judicial pressure. So Canon 7C(1) fails exacting scrutiny and infringes the First Amendment. This case should have been just that straightforward.

FOR DISCUSSION

Does this decision signal that the Supreme Court is prepared to reverse its *Republican Party of Minnesota* decision? Has the Court now effectively said that judicial candidates and campaigns are different? How does the Court distinguish its ruling here from it campaign finance cases?

GLOSSARY

Associational Rights of the Party: First Amendment rights of political parties to conduct their affairs free of government regulation. Associational rights raise two questions: Who in the party is entitled to raise or invoke these rights? What associational rights do parties have?

Ballot Access: The right of candidates and parties to obtain access to either the primary or the general election ballot. Ballot access can refer to fees, deadlines, or signature or other requirements.

Blanket Primary: Political primary where voters do not have to be registered with any political party and they may vote for any candidate in a primary regardless of the latter's party affiliation.

Closed Primary: Political primary in which a voter has to be a registered member of a specific political party in order to vote for that party's candidate.

Decennial Census: Constitutionally mandated census that takes place every ten years at the start of a new decade. Following the census, state legislatures are required to reapportion their state legislative and congressional seats to conform with the one person, one vote requirement.

Facial Challenge: Challenging the constitutionality of a law by arguing that no matter how it is enforced or interpreted it is unconstitutional. Facial challenges are in contrast to **as applied challenges** that argue that a law is unconstitutional as enforced or interpreted in a particular circumstance.

Federal Election Campaign Act: Main federal law regulating federal elections and the financing of federal campaigns until the adoption of the Bipartisan Campaign Reform Act of 2002. Many of the 1974 amendments to FECA were declared unconstitutional in the 1976 *Buckley v. Valeo* decision.

Felon Disenfranchisement Laws: Laws that either temporarily or permanently take away the right to vote from individuals convicted of felony. These laws were upheld as constitutional in *Richardson v. Ramierez*.

Gerrymandering: Drawing of legislative or other district lines to favor or oppose a certain candidate or party for office. Gerrymandering, or the issue of redistricting, was once considered a political question the Court would not hear, but in *Baker v. Carr* they ruled it to be a justiciable issue.

Grandfather Clauses: One of several laws adopted after the Civil War to prevent freed slaves from voting. Grandfather laws prevented one from voting unless one's grandfather could have voted.

Majority-Minority Seats: Majority-minority seats are legislative seats composed of a majority of individuals of color. These seats are required to be constructed under the Voting Rights Act in order to enhance minority representation.

McCain-Feingold or the Bipartisan Campaign Reform Act of 2002: BCRA is a federal law placing limits on how candidates, political parties, and political organizations can raise and spend money to influence federal elections.

One Person, One Vote: Requirement that legislative and other district lines must contain the same number of individuals.

Open Primary: An open primary is one where a voter does not have to be a member of a specific political party to vote in its primary. However, once a voter decides to vote for one party candidate in a primary, the voter is restricted to only voting for that party in the primary. An open primary contrasts to a blanket primary, where voters can vote for any candidate in any primary race regardless of party.

Partisan Gerrymandering: The drawing of district lines to help or hurt a specific party. In *Davis v. Bandemer* the Supreme Court ruled that partisan gerrymanders are justiciable, but in subsequent cases it has divided over this question.

Pendleton Act: The Pendleton Act of 1883 created the federal civil service system, where individuals were supposed to be hired on merit and qualifications and not on party identification.

Poll Tax: Fee assessed on individuals when they vote. Originally poll taxes were viewed as a reform measure to extend the right to vote to those who did not own property. However, after the Civil War, poll taxes were used to prevent free slaves from voting. In *Harper v. Virginia Board of Elections*, poll taxes were declared unconstitutional. The Twenty-sixth Amendment also banned poll taxes.

Reapportionment: Redrawing of legislative or other district lines. Reapportionment is supposed to be based mainly on the basis of the one person, one vote requirement. However, the Supreme Court has ruled that deviation from this requirement is permitted in some cases to ensure that districts are compact or contiguous, or to ensure that they refrain from splitting up local governmental bodies such as towns.

Soft Money: Soft money refers to contributions given by individuals and groups to political parties. The 2002 BCRA banned soft money contributions to federal political parties and the ban was upheld in *McConnell v. FEC.*

Spoils System: The spoils or patronage system refers to practice by winning candidates of awarding government jobs to their supporters and friends, often in return for political support. The spoils system supposedly began at the federal level with President Andrew Jackson in the 1820s.

Tillman Act: The Tillman Act of 1908 made it illegal for corporations to expend money to affect a federal election. The Taft-Hartley Act of 1947 imposed a similar ban on labor unions.

Voting Rights Act: The Voting Rights Act was passed by Congress in 1965 in order to promote the voting rights of people of color. The Act has been amended and reauthorized several times, the last time being in 2006, at which time it was extended for another 25 years.

SELECTED BIBLIOGRAPHY

Bullock, Charles S III, Ronald Keith Gaddie, and Justin J. Wert. 1996. *The Rise and Fall of the Voting Rights Act.* Norman, OK: University of Oklahoma Press.

Canon, David T. 1999. *Race, Redistricting, and Representation: The Unintended Consequences of Black Majority Districts.* Chicago: University of Chicago Press.

Cronin, Thomas E. 1989. *Direct Democracy: The Politics of Initiative, Referendum, and recall.* Cambridge, MA: Harvard University Press.

Davidson, Chandler and Bernard Groffman. 1994. *Quiet Revolution in the South: The Impact of the Voting Rights Act, 1965–1990. Princeton: Princeton University Press.*

Ewald, Alec C. 2009. *The Way we Vote: The Local Dimension of American Suffrage*. Nashville, TN: Vanderbilt University Press.

Finkelman, Paul. 1992. *African Americans and the Right to Vote*. New York: Garland.

Fitrakis, Bob. 2006. *What Happened in Ohio: A Documentary Record of Theft and Fraud in the 2004 Election*. New York: New Press.

Freeman, Steve, and Joel Bleifuss. 2006. *Was The 2004 Presidential Election Stolen?: Exit Polls, Election Fraud, and the Official Count*. New York: Seven Stories Press.

Greene, Abner. 2001. *Understanding the 2000 Election: A Guide to the Legal Battles That Decided the Presidency*. New York: NYU Press.

Hall, Melinda Gann 2015. *Attacking Judges: How Campaign Advertising Influences State Supreme Court Elections*. Stanford, CA: Stanford University Press.

Hasen, Richard. 2003. *The Supreme Court and Election Law: Judging Equality from Baker v. Carr to Bush v. Gore*. New York: NYU Press.

Hull, Elizabeth A. 2006. *The Disenfranchisement of Ex-Felons*. Philadelphia: Temple University Press.

Keyssar, Alexander. 2000. *The Right to Vote: The Contested History of Democracy in the United States*. New York: Basic Books.

Lowenstein, Daniel Hayes, and Richard L. Hasen. 2008. *Election Law: Cases and Materials*. Durham, NC: Carolina Academic Press.

Lublin, David. 1997. *The Paradox of Representation: Racial Gerrymandering and Minority Interests in Congress*. Princeton, NJ: Princeton University Press.

Marshall, Thurgood. 1987. "Remarks of Thurgood Marshall at the Annual Seminar of the San Francisco Patent and Trademark Law Association in Maui, Hawaii." May 6.

Pinaire, Brian K. 2008. *The Constitution of Electoral Speech Law: The Supreme Court and Freedom of Expression in Campaigns and Elections*. Stanford, CA: Stanford University Press.

Ryden, David K. 1996. *Representation in Crisis: The Constitution, Interest Groups, and Political Parties*. Albany, NY: SUNY Press.

Scher, Richard K., et al. 1997. *Voting Rights and Democracy: The Law and Politics of Districting*. Chicago: Nelson-Hall Publishers.

Schultz, David. 2002. *Money, Politics, and Campaign Finance Reform Law in the States*. Durham, NC: Carolina Academic Press.

Schultz, David. 2007. "*Buckley v. Valeo, Randall v. Sorrell*, and the Future of Campaign Financing on the Roberts Court." *Nexus*, Vol. 12, p. 153–176.

Schultz, David. 2007. "The Party's Over: Partisan Gerrymandering and the First Amendment." *Capital Law Review*, Vol. 36, p. 153.

Schultz, David. 2008. "Lies, Damn Lies, and Voter IDs: The Fraud of Voter Fraud." Harvard Law & Policy Review Vol 1, p. 114.

Schultz, David. 2008. "Regulating the Political Thicket: Congress, the Courts, and State Reapportionment Commissions." Charleston Law Review, Vol. 3, p. 109–143.

Smith, Bradley A. 2001. *Unfree Speech: The Folly of Campaign Finance Reform*. Princeton, NJ: Princeton University Press.

Stephenson, Donald Grier, Jr. 2004. *The Right to Vote: Rights and Liberties Under the Law*. Santa Barbara, CA: ABC CLIO.

Urofsky, Melvin I. 2005. *Money & Free Speech: Campaign Finance Reform and the Courts*. Lawrence, KS: University Press of Kansas.

Zelden, Charles L. 2008. *Bush v. Gore: Exposing the Hidden Crisis in American Democracy*. Lawrence, KS: University Press of Kansas.

Appendix A

IN CONGRESS, JULY 4, 1776

The unanimous Declaration of the thirteen United States of America

When in the Course of human events it becomes necessary for one people to dissolve the political bands which have connected them with another and to assume among the powers of the earth, the separate and equal station to which the Laws of Nature and of Nature's God entitle them, a decent respect to the opinions of mankind requires that they should declare the causes which impel them to the separation.

We hold these truths to be self-evident, that all men are created equal, that they are endowed by their Creator with certain unalienable Rights, that among these are Life, Liberty and the pursuit of Happiness.—That to secure these rights, Governments are instituted among Men, deriving their just powers from the consent of the governed,—That whenever any Form of Government becomes destructive of these ends, it is the Right of the People to alter or to abolish it, and to institute new Government, laying its foundation on such principles and organizing its powers in such form, as to them shall seem most likely to effect their Safety and Happiness. Prudence, indeed, will dictate that Governments long established should not be changed for light and transient causes; and accordingly all experience hath shewn that mankind are more disposed to suffer, while evils are sufferable than to right themselves by abolishing the forms to which they are accustomed. But when a long train of abuses and usurpations, pursuing invariably the same Object evinces a design to reduce them under absolute Despotism, it is their right, it is their duty, to throw off such Government, and to provide new Guards for their future security.—Such has been the patient sufferance of these Colonies; and such is now the necessity which constrains them to alter their former Systems of Government. The history of the present King of Great Britain is a history of repeated injuries and usurpations, all having in direct object the establishment of an absolute Tyranny over these States. To prove this, let Facts be submitted to a candid world.

He has refused his Assent to Laws, the most wholesome and necessary for the public good.

He has forbidden his Governors to pass Laws of immediate and pressing importance, unless suspended in their operation till his Assent should be obtained; and when so suspended, he has utterly neglected to attend to them.

He has refused to pass other Laws for the accommodation of large districts of people, unless those people would relinquish the right of Representation in the Legislature, a right inestimable to them and formidable to tyrants only.

He has called together legislative bodies at places unusual, uncomfortable, and distant from the depository of their Public Records, for the sole purpose of fatiguing them into compliance with his measures.

He has dissolved Representative Houses repeatedly, for opposing with manly firmness his invasions on the rights of the people.

He has refused for a long time, after such dissolutions, to cause others to be elected, whereby the Legislative Powers, incapable of Annihilation, have returned to the People at large for their exercise; the State remaining in the mean time exposed to all the dangers of invasion from without, and convulsions within.

He has endeavoured to prevent the population of these States; for that purpose obstructing the Laws for Naturalization of Foreigners; refusing to pass others to encourage their migrations hither, and raising the conditions of new Appropriations of Lands.

He has obstructed the Administration of Justice by refusing his Assent to Laws for establishing Judiciary Powers.

He has made Judges dependent on his Will alone for the tenure of their offices, and the amount and payment of their salaries.

He has erected a multitude of New Offices, and sent hither swarms of Officers to harass our people and eat out their substance.

He has kept among us, in times of peace, Standing Armies without the Consent of our legislatures.

He has affected to render the Military independent of and superior to the Civil Power.

He has combined with others to subject us to a jurisdiction foreign to our constitution, and unacknowledged by our laws; giving his Assent to their Acts of pretended Legislation:

For quartering large bodies of armed troops among us:

For protecting them, by a mock Trial from punishment for any Murders which they should commit on the Inhabitants of these States:

For cutting off our Trade with all parts of the world:

For imposing Taxes on us without our Consent:

For depriving us in many cases, of the benefit of Trial by Jury:

For transporting us beyond Seas to be tried for pretended offences:

For abolishing the free System of English Laws in a neighbouring Province, establishing therein an Arbitrary government, and enlarging its Boundaries so as to render it at once an example and fit instrument for introducing the same absolute rule into these Colonies

For taking away our Charters, abolishing our most valuable Laws and altering fundamentally the Forms of our Governments:

For suspending our own Legislatures, and declaring themselves invested with power to legislate for us in all cases whatsoever.

He has abdicated Government here, by declaring us out of his Protection and waging War against us.

He has plundered our seas, ravaged our coasts, burnt our towns, and destroyed the lives of our people.

He is at this time transporting large Armies of foreign Mercenaries to compleat the works of death, desolation, and tyranny, already begun with circumstances of Cruelty & Perfidy scarcely paralleled in the most barbarous ages, and totally unworthy the Head of a civilized nation.

He has constrained our fellow Citizens taken Captive on the high Seas to bear Arms against their Country, to become the executioners of their friends and Brethren, or to fall themselves by their Hands.

He has excited domestic insurrections amongst us, and has endeavoured to bring on the inhabitants of our frontiers, the merciless Indian Savages whose known rule of warfare, is an undistinguished destruction of all ages, sexes and conditions.

In every stage of these Oppressions We have Petitioned for Redress in the most humble terms: Our repeated Petitions have been answered only by repeated injury. A Prince, whose character is thus marked by every act which may define a Tyrant, is unfit to be the ruler of a free people.

Nor have We been wanting in attentions to our British brethren. We have warned them from time to time of attempts by their legislature to extend an unwarrantable jurisdiction over us. We have reminded them of the circumstances of our emigration and settlement here. We have appealed to their native justice and magnanimity, and we have conjured them by the ties of our common kindred to disavow these usurpations, which would inevitably interrupt our connections and correspondence. They too have been deaf to the voice of justice and of consanguinity. We must, therefore, acquiesce in the necessity, which denounces our Separation, and hold them, as we hold the rest of mankind, Enemies in War, in Peace Friends.

We, therefore, the Representatives of the united States of America, in General Congress, Assembled, appealing to the Supreme Judge of the world for the rectitude of our intentions, do, in the Name, and by Authority of the good People of these Colonies, solemnly publish and declare, That these united Colonies are, and of Right ought to be Free and Independent States, that they are Absolved from all Allegiance to the British Crown, and that all political connection between them and the State of Great Britain, is and ought to be totally dissolved; and that as Free and Independent States, they have full Power to levy War, conclude Peace contract Alliances, establish Commerce, and to do all other Acts and Things which Independent States may of right do.—And for the support of this Declaration, with a firm reliance on the protection of Divine Providence, we mutually pledge to each other our Lives, our Fortunes and our sacred Honor.

—John Hancock

New Hampshire:

Josiah Bartlett, William Whipple, Matthew Thornton

Massachusetts:

John Hancock, Samuel Adams, John Adams, Robert Treat Paine, Elbridge Gerry

Rhode Island:

Stephen Hopkins, William Ellery

Connecticut:

Roger Sherman, Samuel Huntington, William Williams, Oliver Wolcott

New York:

William Floyd, Philip Livingston, Francis Lewis, Lewis Morris

New Jersey:

Richard Stockton, John Witherspoon, Francis Hopkinson, John Hart, Abraham Clark

Pennsylvania:

Robert Morris, Benjamin Rush, Benjamin Franklin, John Morton, George Clymer, James Smith, George Taylor, James Wilson, George Ross

Delaware:

Caesar Rodney, George Read, Thomas McKean

Maryland:

Samuel Chase, William Paca, Thomas Stone, Charles Carroll of Carrollton

Virginia:

George Wythe, Richard Henry Lee, Thomas Jefferson, Benjamin Harrison, Thomas Nelson, Jr., Francis Lightfoot Lee, Carter Braxton

North Carolina:

William Hooper, Joseph Hewes, John Penn

South Carolina:

Edward Rutledge, Thomas Heyward, Jr., Thomas Lynch, Jr., Arthur Middleton

Georgia:

Button Gwinnett, Lyman Hall, George Walton

Appendix B

THE FEDERALIST PAPERS

The Federalist Papers consist of 85 letters written by Alexander Hamilton, James Madison, and John Jay. They were published under the name of Publius in New York newspapers in 1787 and 1788, seeking to convince the state legislature to adopt the new proposed Constitution. Among the 85 letters, Federalist no. 10 and 51, attributed to James Madison, are considered one of the best descriptions on the needs for a new constitution and how it was supposed to work.

Federalist No. 10

To the People of the State of New York:

AMONG the numerous advantages promised by a wellconstructed Union, none deserves to be more accurately developed than its tendency to break and control the violence of faction. The friend of popular governments never finds himself so much alarmed for their character and fate, as when he contemplates their propensity to this dangerous vice. He will not fail, therefore, to set a due value on any plan which, without violating the principles to which he is attached, provides a proper cure for it. The instability, injustice, and confusion introduced into the public councils, have, in truth, been the mortal diseases under which popular governments have everywhere perished; as they continue to be the favorite and fruitful topics from which the adversaries to liberty derive their most specious declamations. The valuable improvements made by the American constitutions on the popular models, both ancient and modern, cannot certainly be too much admired; but it would be an unwarrantable partiality, to contend that they have as effectually obviated the danger on this side, as was wished and expected. Complaints are everywhere heard from our most considerate and virtuous citizens, equally the friends of public and private faith, and of public and personal liberty, that our governments are too unstable, that the public good is disregarded in the conflicts of rival parties, and that measures are too often decided, not according to the rules of justice and the rights of the minor party, but by the superior force of an interested and overbearing majority. However anxiously we may wish that these complaints had no foundation, the evidence, of known facts will not permit us to deny that they are in some degree true. It will be found, indeed, on a candid review of our situation, that some of the distresses under which we labor have been erroneously charged on the operation of our governments; but it will be found, at the same time, that other causes will not alone account for many of our heaviest misfortunes; and, particularly, for that prevailing and increasing distrust of public engagements, and alarm for private rights, which are echoed from one end of the continent to the other. These must be chiefly, if not wholly, effects of the unsteadiness and injustice with which a factious spirit has tainted our public administrations.

By a faction, I understand a number of citizens, whether amounting to a majority or a minority of the whole, who are united and actuated by some common impulse of passion, or of interest, adversed to the rights of other citizens, or to the permanent and aggregate interests of the community.

There are two methods of curing the mischiefs of faction: the one, by removing its causes; the other, by controlling its effects.

There are again two methods of removing the causes of faction: the one, by destroying the liberty which is essential to its existence; the other, by giving to every citizen the same opinions, the same passions, and the same interests.

It could never be more truly said than of the first remedy, that it was worse than the disease. Liberty is to faction what air is to fire, an aliment without which it instantly expires. But it could not be less folly to abolish liberty, which is essential to political life, because it nourishes faction, than it would be to wish the annihilation of air, which is essential to animal life, because it imparts to fire its destructive agency.

The second expedient is as impracticable as the first would be unwise. As long as the reason of man continues fallible, and he is at liberty to exercise it, different opinions will be formed. As long as the connection subsists between his reason and his self-love, his opinions and his passions will have a reciprocal influence on each other; and the former will be objects to which the latter will attach themselves. The diversity in the faculties of men, from which the rights of property originate, is not less an insuperable obstacle to a uniformity of interests. The protection of these faculties is the first object of government. From the protection of different and unequal faculties of acquiring property, the possession of different degrees and kinds of property immediately results; and from the influence of these on the sentiments and views of the respective proprietors, ensues a division of the society into different interests and parties.

The latent causes of faction are thus sown in the nature of man; and we see them everywhere brought into different degrees of activity, according to the different circumstances of civil society. A zeal for different opinions concerning religion, concerning government, and many other points, as well of speculation as of practice; an attachment to different leaders ambitiously contending for pre-eminence and power; or to persons of other descriptions whose fortunes have been interesting to the human passions, have, in turn, divided mankind into parties, inflamed them with mutual animosity, and rendered them much more disposed to vex and oppress each other than to co-operate for their common good. So strong is this propensity of mankind to fall into mutual animosities, that where no substantial occasion presents itself, the most frivolous and fanciful distinctions have been sufficient to kindle their unfriendly passions and excite their most violent conflicts. But the most common and durable source of factions has been the various and unequal distribution of property. Those who hold and those who are without property have ever formed distinct interests in society. Those who are creditors, and those who are debtors, fall under a like discrimination. A landed interest, a manufacturing interest, a mercantile interest, a moneyed interest, with many lesser interests, grow up of necessity in civilized nations, and divide them into different classes, actuated by different sentiments and views. The regulation of these various and interfering interests forms the principal task of modern legislation, and involves the spirit of party and faction in the necessary and ordinary operations of the government.

No man is allowed to be a judge in his own cause, because his interest would certainly bias his judgment, and, not improbably, corrupt his integrity. With equal, nay with greater reason, a body of men are unfit to be both judges and parties at the same time; yet what are many of the most important acts of legislation, but so many judicial determinations, not indeed concerning the rights of single persons, but concerning the rights of large bodies of citizens? And what are the different classes of legislators but advocates and parties to the causes which they determine? Is a law proposed concerning private debts? It is a question to which the creditors are parties on one side and the debtors on the other. Justice ought to hold the balance between them. Yet the parties are, and must be, themselves the judges; and the most numerous party, or, in other words, the most powerful faction must be expected to prevail. Shall domestic manufactures be encouraged, and in what degree, by restrictions on foreign manufactures? are questions which would be differently decided by the landed and the manufacturing classes, and probably by neither with a sole regard to justice and the public good. The apportionment of taxes on the various descriptions of property is an act which seems to require the most exact impartiality; yet there is, perhaps, no legislative act in which greater opportunity and temptation are given to a predominant party to trample on the rules of justice. Every shilling with which they overburden the inferior number, is a shilling saved to their own pockets.

It is in vain to say that enlightened statesmen will be able to adjust these clashing interests, and render them all subservient to the public good. Enlightened statesmen will not always be at the helm. Nor, in many cases, can such an adjustment be made at all without taking into view indirect and remote considerations, which will rarely prevail over the immediate interest which one party may find in disregarding the rights of another or the good of the whole.

The inference to which we are brought is, that the CAUSES of faction cannot be removed, and that relief is only to be sought in the means of controlling its EFFECTS.

If a faction consists of less than a majority, relief is supplied by the republican principle, which enables the majority to defeat its sinister views by regular vote. It may clog the administration, it may convulse the society; but it will be unable to execute and mask its violence under the forms of the Constitution. When a majority is included in a faction, the form of popular government, on the other hand, enables it to sacrifice to its ruling passion or interest both the public good and the rights of other citizens. To secure the public good and private rights against the danger of such a faction, and at the same time to preserve the spirit and the form of popular government, is then the great object to which our inquiries are directed. Let me add that it is the great desideratum by which this form of government can be rescued from the opprobrium under which it has so long labored, and be recommended to the esteem and adoption of mankind.

By what means is this object attainable? Evidently by one of two only. Either the existence of the same passion or interest in a majority at the same time must be prevented, or the majority, having such coexistent passion or interest, must be rendered, by their number and local situation, unable to concert and carry into effect schemes of oppression. If the impulse and the opportunity be suffered to coincide, we well know that neither moral nor religious motives can be relied on as an adequate control. They are not found to be such on the injustice and violence of individuals, and lose their efficacy in proportion to the number combined together, that is, in proportion as their efficacy becomes needful.

From this view of the subject it may be concluded that a pure democracy, by which I mean a society consisting of a small number of citizens, who assemble and administer the government in person, can admit of no cure for the mischiefs of faction. A common passion or interest will, in almost every case, be felt by a majority of the whole; a communication and concert result from the form of government itself; and there is nothing to check the inducements to sacrifice the weaker party or an obnoxious individual. Hence it is that such democracies have ever been spectacles of turbulence and contention; have ever been found incompatible with personal security or the rights of property; and have in general been as short in their lives as they have been violent in their deaths. Theoretic politicians, who have patronized this species of government, have erroneously supposed that by reducing mankind to a perfect equality in their political rights, they would, at the same time, be perfectly equalized and assimilated in their possessions, their opinions, and their passions.

A republic, by which I mean a government in which the scheme of representation takes place, opens a different prospect, and promises the cure for which we are seeking. Let us examine the points in which it varies from pure democracy, and we shall comprehend both the nature of the cure and the efficacy which it must derive from the Union.

The two great points of difference between a democracy and a republic are: first, the delegation of the government, in the latter, to a small number of citizens elected by the rest; secondly, the greater number of citizens, and greater sphere of country, over which the latter may be extended.

The effect of the first difference is, on the one hand, to refine and enlarge the public views, by passing them through the medium of a chosen body of citizens, whose wisdom may best discern the true interest of their country, and whose patriotism and love of justice will be least likely to sacrifice it to temporary or partial considerations. Under such a regulation, it may well happen that the public voice, pronounced by the representatives of the people, will be more consonant to the public good than if pronounced by the people themselves, convened for the purpose. On the other hand, the effect may be inverted. Men of factious tempers, of local prejudices, or of sinister designs, may, by intrigue, by corruption, or by other means, first obtain the suffrages, and then betray the interests, of the people. The question resulting is, whether small or extensive republics are more favorable to the election of proper guardians of the public weal; and it is clearly decided in favor of the latter by two obvious considerations:

In the first place, it is to be remarked that, however small the republic may be, the representatives must be raised to a certain number, in order to guard against the cabals of a few; and that, however large it may be, they must be limited to a certain number, in order to guard against the confusion of a multitude. Hence, the number of representatives in the two cases not being in proportion to that of the two constituents, and being proportionally greater in the small republic, it follows that, if the proportion of fit characters be not less in the large than in the small republic, the former will present a greater option, and consequently a greater probability of a fit choice.

In the next place, as each representative will be chosen by a greater number of citizens in the large than in the small republic, it will be more difficult for unworthy candidates to practice with success the vicious arts by which elections are too often carried; and the suffrages of the people being more free, will be more likely to centre in men who possess the most attractive merit and the most diffusive and established characters.

It must be confessed that in this, as in most other cases, there is a mean, on both sides of which inconveniences will be found to lie. By enlarging too much the number of electors, you render the representatives too little acquainted with all their local circumstances and lesser interests; as by reducing it too much, you render him unduly attached to these, and too little fit to comprehend and pursue great and national objects. The federal Constitution forms a happy combination in this respect; the great and aggregate interests being referred to the national, the local and particular to the State legislatures.

The other point of difference is, the greater number of citizens and extent of territory which may be brought within the compass of republican than of democratic government; and it is this circumstance principally which renders factious combinations less to be dreaded in the former than in the latter. The smaller the society, the fewer probably will be the distinct parties and interests composing it; the fewer the distinct parties and interests, the more frequently will a majority be found of the same party; and the smaller the number of individuals composing a majority, and the smaller the compass within which they are placed, the more easily will they concert and execute their plans of oppression. Extend the sphere, and you take in a greater variety of parties and interests; you make it less probable that a majority of the whole will have a common motive to invade the rights of other citizens; or if such a common motive exists, it will be more difficult for all who feel it to discover their own strength, and to act in unison with each other. Besides other impediments, it may be remarked that, where there is a consciousness of unjust or dishonorable purposes, communication is always checked by distrust in proportion to the number whose concurrence is necessary.

Hence, it clearly appears, that the same advantage which a republic has over a democracy, in controlling the effects of faction, is enjoyed by a large over a small republic,—is enjoyed by the Union over the States composing it. Does the advantage consist in the substitution of representatives whose enlightened views and virtuous sentiments render them superior to local prejudices and schemes of injustice? It will not be denied that the representation of the Union will be most likely to possess these requisite endowments. Does it consist in the greater security afforded by a greater variety of parties, against the event of any one party being able to outnumber and oppress the rest? In an equal degree does the increased variety of parties comprised within the Union, increase this security. Does it, in fine, consist in the greater obstacles opposed to the concert and accomplishment of the secret wishes of an unjust and interested majority? Here, again, the extent of the Union gives it the most palpable advantage.

The influence of factious leaders may kindle a flame within their particular States, but will be unable to spread a general conflagration through the other States. A religious sect may degenerate into a political faction in a part of the Confederacy; but the variety of sects dispersed over the entire face of it must secure the national councils against any danger from that source. A rage for paper money, for an abolition of debts, for an equal division of property, or for any other improper or wicked project, will be less apt to pervade the whole body of the Union than a particular member of it; in the same proportion as such a malady is more likely to taint a particular county or district, than an entire State.

In the extent and proper structure of the Union, therefore, we behold a republican remedy for the diseases most incident to republican government. And according to the degree of pleasure and pride we feel in being republicans, ought to be our zeal in cherishing the spirit and supporting the character of Federalists.

PUBLIUS.

Federalist No. 51

To the People of the State of New York:

TO WHAT expedient, then, shall we finally resort, for maintaining in practice the necessary partition of power among the several departments, as laid down in the Constitution? The only answer that can be given is, that as all these exterior provisions are found to be inadequate, the defect must be supplied, by so contriving the interior structure of the government as that its several constituent parts may, by their mutual relations, be the means of keeping each other in their proper places. Without presuming to undertake a full development of this important idea, I will hazard a few general observations, which may perhaps place it in a clearer light, and enable us to form a more correct judgment of the principles and structure of the government planned by the convention.

In order to lay a due foundation for that separate and distinct exercise of the different powers of government, which to a certain extent is admitted on all hands to be essential to the preservation of liberty, it is evident that each department should have a will of its own; and consequently should be so constituted that the members of each should have as little agency as possible in the appointment of the members of the others. Were this principle rigorously adhered to, it would require that all the appointments for the supreme executive, legislative, and judiciary magistracies should be drawn from the same fountain of authority, the people, through channels having no communication whatever with one another. Perhaps such a plan of constructing the several departments would be less difficult in practice than it may in contemplation appear. Some difficulties, however, and some additional expense would attend the execution of it. Some deviations, therefore, from the principle must be admitted. In the constitution of the judiciary department in particular, it might be inexpedient to insist rigorously on the principle: first, because peculiar qualifications being essential in the members, the primary consideration ought to be to select that mode of choice which best secures these qualifications; secondly, because the permanent tenure by which the appointments are held in that department, must soon destroy all sense of dependence on the authority conferring them.

It is equally evident, that the members of each department should be as little dependent as possible on those of the others, for the emoluments annexed to their offices. Were the executive magistrate, or the judges, not independent of the legislature in this particular, their independence in every other would be merely nominal.

But the great security against a gradual concentration of the several powers in the same department, consists in giving to those who administer each department the necessary constitutional means and personal motives to resist encroachments of the others. The provision for defense must in this, as in all other cases, be made commensurate to the danger of attack. Ambition must be made to counteract ambition. The interest of the man must be connected with the constitutional rights of the place. It may be a reflection on human nature, that such devices should be necessary to control the abuses of government. But what is government itself, but the greatest of all reflections on human nature? If men were angels, no government would be necessary. If angels were to govern men, neither external nor internal controls on government would be necessary. In framing a government which is to be administered by men over men, the great difficulty lies in this: you must first enable the government to control the governed; and in the next place oblige it to control itself. A dependence on the people is, no doubt, the primary control on the government; but experience has taught mankind the necessity of auxiliary precautions.

This policy of supplying, by opposite and rival interests, the defect of better motives, might be traced through the whole system of human affairs, private as well as public. We see it particularly displayed in all the subordinate distributions of power, where the constant aim is to divide and arrange the several offices in such a manner as that each may be a check on the other that the private interest of every individual may be a sentinel over the public rights. These inventions of prudence cannot be less requisite in the distribution of the supreme powers of the State.

But it is not possible to give to each department an equal power of self-defense. In republican government, the legislative authority necessarily predominates. The remedy for this inconveniency is to divide the legislature into different branches; and to render them, by different modes of election and different principles of action, as little connected with each other as the nature of their common functions and their common dependence on the society will admit. It may even be necessary to guard against dangerous encroachments by still further precautions. As the weight of the legislative authority requires that it should be thus divided, the weakness of the executive may require, on the other hand, that it should be fortified. An absolute negative on the legislature appears, at first view, to be the natural defense with which the executive magistrate should be armed. But perhaps it would be neither altogether safe nor alone sufficient. On ordinary occasions it might not be exerted with the requisite firmness, and on extraordinary occasions it might be perfidiously abused. May not this defect of an absolute negative be supplied by some qualified connection between this weaker department and the weaker branch of the stronger department, by which the latter may be led to support the constitutional rights of the former, without being too much detached from the rights of its own department?

If the principles on which these observations are founded be just, as I persuade myself they are, and they be applied as a criterion to the several State constitutions, and to the federal Constitution it will be found that if the latter does not perfectly correspond with them, the former are infinitely less able to bear such a test.

There are, moreover, two considerations particularly applicable to the federal system of America, which place that system in a very interesting point of view.

First. In a single republic, all the power surrendered by the people is submitted to the administration of a single government; and the usurpations are guarded against by a division of the government into distinct and separate departments. In the compound republic of America, the power surrendered by the people is first divided between two distinct governments, and then the portion allotted to each subdivided among distinct and separate departments. Hence a double security arises to the rights of the people. The different governments will control each other, at the same time that each will be controlled by itself.

Second. It is of great importance in a republic not only to guard the society against the oppression of its rulers, but to guard one part of the society against the injustice of the other part. Different interests necessarily exist in different classes of citizens. If a majority be united by a common interest, the rights of the minority will be insecure. There are but two methods of providing against this evil: the one by creating a will in the community independent of the majority that is, of the society itself; the other, by comprehending in the society so many separate descriptions of citizens as will render an unjust combination of a majority of the whole very improbable, if not impracticable. The first method prevails in all governments possessing an hereditary or self-appointed authority. This, at best, is but a precarious security; because a power independent of the society may as well espouse the unjust views of the major, as the rightful interests of the minor party, and may possibly be turned against both parties. The second method will be exemplified in the federal republic of the United States. Whilst all authority in it will be derived from and dependent on the society, the society itself will be broken into so many parts, interests, and classes of citizens, that the rights of individuals, or of the minority, will be in little danger from interested combinations of the majority. In a free government the security for civil rights must be the same as that for religious rights. It consists in the one case in the multiplicity of interests, and in the other in the multiplicity of sects. The degree of security in both cases will depend on the number of interests and sects; and this may be presumed to depend on the extent of country and number of people comprehended under the same government. This view of the subject must particularly recommend a proper federal system to all the sincere and considerate friends of republican government, since it shows that in exact proportion as the territory of the Union may be formed into more circumscribed Confederacies, or States oppressive combinations of a majority will be facilitated: the best security, under the republican forms, for the rights of every class of citizens, will be diminished: and consequently the stability and independence of some member of the government, the only other security, must be proportionately increased. Justice is the end of government. It is the end of civil society. It ever has been and ever will be pursued until it be obtained, or until liberty be lost in the pursuit. In a society under the forms of which the stronger faction can readily unite and oppress the weaker, anarchy may as truly be said to reign as in a state of nature, where the weaker individual is not secured against the violence of the stronger; and as, in the latter state, even the stronger individuals are prompted, by the uncertainty of their condition, to submit to a government which may protect the weak as well as themselves; so, in the former state, will the more powerful factions or parties be gradnally induced, by a like motive, to wish for a government which will protect all parties, the weaker as well as the more powerful. It can be little doubted that if the State of Rhode Island was separated from the Confederacy and left to itself, the insecurity of rights under the popular form of government within such narrow limits would be displayed by such reiterated oppressions of factious majorities that some power altogether independent of the people would soon be called for by the voice of the very factions whose misrule had proved the necessity of it. In the extended republic of the United States, and among the great variety of interests, parties, and sects which it embraces, a coalition of a majority of the whole society could seldom take place on any other principles than those of justice and the general good; whilst there being thus less danger to a minor from the will of a major party, there must be less pretext, also, to provide for the security of the former, by introducing into the government a will not dependent on the latter, or, in other words, a will independent of the society itself. It is no less certain than it is important, notwithstanding the contrary opinions which have been entertained, that the larger the society, provided it lie within a practical sphere, the more duly capable it will be of self-government. And happily for the REPUBLICAN CAUSE, the practicable sphere may be carried to a very great extent, by a judicious modification and mixture of the FEDERAL PRINCIPLE.

PUBLIUS.

The Federalist No. 78

The Judiciary Department
Alexander Hamilton

To the People of the State of New York:

WE PROCEED now to an examination of the judiciary department of the proposed government.

In unfolding the defects of the existing Confederation, the utility and necessity of a federal judicature have been clearly pointed out. It is the less necessary to recapitulate the considerations there urged, as the propriety of the institution in the abstract is not disputed; the only questions which have been raised being relative to the manner of constituting it, and to its extent. To these points, therefore, our observations shall be confined.

The manner of constituting it seems to embrace these several objects: 1st. The mode of appointing the judges. 2d. The tenure by which they are to hold their places. 3d. The partition of the judiciary authority between different courts, and their relations to each other.

First. As to the mode of appointing the judges; this is the same with that of appointing the officers of the Union in general, and has been so fully discussed in the two last numbers, that nothing can be said here which would not be useless repetition.

Second. As to the tenure by which the judges are to hold their places; this chiefly concerns their duration in office; the provisions for their support; the precautions for their responsibility.

According to the plan of the convention, all judges who may be appointed by the United States are to hold their offices *during good behavior*, which is conformable to the most approved of the State constitutions and among the rest, to that of this State. Its propriety having been drawn into question by the adversaries of that plan, is no light symptom of the rage for objection, which disorders their imaginations and judgments. The standard of good behavior for the continuance in office of the judicial magistracy, is certainly one of the most valuable of the modern improvements in the practice of government. In a monarchy it is an excellent barrier to the despotism of the prince; in a republic it is a no less excellent barrier to the encroachments and oppressions of the representative body. And it is the best expedient which can be devised in any government, to secure a steady, upright, and impartial administration of the laws.

Whoever attentively considers the different departments of power must perceive, that, in a government in which they are separated from each other, the judiciary, from the nature of its functions, will always be the least dangerous to the political rights of the Constitution; because it will be least in a capacity to annoy or injure them. The Executive not only dispenses the honors, but holds the sword of the community. The legislature not only commands the purse, but prescribes the rules by which the duties and rights of every citizen are to be regulated. The judiciary, on the contrary, has no influence over either the sword or the purse; no direction either of the strength or of the wealth of the society; and can take no active resolution whatever. It may truly be said to have neither FORCE nor WILL, but merely judgment; and must ultimately depend upon the aid of the executive arm even for the efficacy of its judgments.

This simple view of the matter suggests several important consequences. It proves incontestably, that the judiciary is beyond comparison the weakest of the three departments of power[4]; that it can never attack with success either of the other two; and that all possible care is requisite to enable it to defend itself against their attacks. It equally proves, that though individual oppression may now and then proceed from the courts of justice, the general liberty of the people can never be endangered from that quarter; I mean so long as the judiciary remains truly distinct from both the legislature and the Executive. For I agree, that "there is no liberty, if the power of judging be not separated from the legislative and executive powers."[5] And it proves, in the last place, that as liberty can have nothing to fear from the judiciary alone, but would have every thing to fear from its union with either of the other departments; that as all the effects of such a union must ensue from a dependence of the former on the latter, notwithstanding a nominal and apparent separation; that as, from the natural feebleness of the judiciary, it is in continual jeopardy of being overpowered, awed, or influenced by its

[4] The celebrated Montesquieu, speaking of them, says: "Of the three powers above mentioned, the judiciary is next to nothing."—*Spirit of Laws*. Vol. I, page 186.

[5] *Idem*, page 181.

co-ordinate branches; and that as nothing can contribute so much to its firmness and independence as permanency in office, this quality may therefore be justly regarded as an indispensable ingredient in its constitution, and, in a great measure, as the citadel of the public justice and the public security.

The complete independence of the courts of justice is peculiarly essential in a limited Constitution. By a limited Constitution, I understand one which contains certain specified exceptions to the legislative authority; such, for instance, as that it shall pass no bills of attainder, no *ex post facto* laws, and the like. Limitations of this kind can be preserved in practice no other way than through the medium of courts of justice, whose duty it must be to declare all acts contrary to the manifest tenor of the Constitution void. Without this, all the reservations of particular rights or privileges would amount to nothing.

Some perplexity respecting the rights of the courts to pronounce legislative acts void, because contrary to the Constitution, has arisen from an imagination that the doctrine would imply a superiority of the judiciary to the legislative power. It is urged that the authority which can declare the acts of another void, must necessarily be superior to the one whose acts may be declared void. As this doctrine is of great importance in all the American constitutions, a brief discussion of the ground on which it rests cannot be unacceptable.

There is no position which depends on clearer principles, than that every act of a delegated authority, contrary to the tenor of the commission under which it is exercised, is void. No legislative act, therefore, contrary to the Constitution, can be valid. To deny this, would be to affirm, that the deputy is greater than his principal; that the servant is above his master; that the representatives of the people are superior to the people themselves; that men acting by virtue of powers, may do not only what their powers do not authorize, but what they forbid.

If it be said that the legislative body are themselves the constitutional judges of their own powers, and that the construction they put upon them is conclusive upon the other departments, it may be answered, that this cannot be the natural presumption, where it is not to be collected from any particular provisions in the Constitution. It is not otherwise to be supposed, that the Constitution could intend to enable the representatives of the people to substitute their *will* to that of their constituents. It is far more rational to suppose, that the courts were designed to be an intermediate body between the people and the legislature, in order, among other things, to keep the latter within the limits assigned to their authority. The interpretation of the laws is the proper and peculiar province of the courts. A constitution is, in fact, and must be regarded by the judges, as a fundamental law. It therefore belongs to them to ascertain its meaning, as well as the meaning of any particular act proceeding from the legislative body. If there should happen to be an irreconcilable variance between the two, that which has the superior obligation and validity ought, of course, to be preferred; or, in other words, the Constitution ought to be preferred to the statute, the intention of the people to the intention of their agents.

Nor does this conclusion by any means suppose a superiority of the judicial to the legislative power. It only supposes that the power of the people is superior to both; and that where the will of the legislature, declared in its statutes, stands in opposition to that of the people, declared in the Constitution, the judges ought to be governed by the latter rather than the former. They ought to regulate their decisions by the fundamental laws, rather than by those which are not fundamental.

This exercise of judicial discretion, in determining between two contradictory laws, is exemplified in a familiar instance. It not uncommonly happens, that there are two statutes existing at one time, clashing in whole or in part with each other, and neither of them containing any repealing clause or expression. In such a case, it is the province of the courts to liquidate and fix their meaning and operation. So far as they can, by any fair construction, be reconciled to each other, reason and law conspire to dictate that this should be done; where this is impracticable, it becomes a matter of necessity to give effect to one, in exclusion of the other. The rule which has obtained in the courts for determining their relative validity is, that the last in order of time shall be preferred to the first. But this is a mere rule of construction, not derived from any positive law, but from the nature and reason of the thing. It is a rule not enjoined upon the courts by legislative provision, but adopted by themselves, as consonant to truth and propriety, for the direction of their conduct as interpreters of the law. They thought it reasonable, that between the interfering acts of an EQUAL authority, that which was the last indication of its will should have the preference.

But in regard to the interfering acts of a superior and subordinate authority, of an original and derivative power, the nature and reason of the thing indicate the converse of that rule as proper to be followed. They teach us that the prior act of a superior ought to be preferred to the subsequent act of an inferior and subordinate authority; and that accordingly, whenever a particular statute contravenes the Constitution, it will be the duty of the judicial tribunals to adhere to the latter and disregard the former.

It can be of no weight to say that the courts, on the pretense of a repugnancy, may substitute their own pleasure to the constitutional intentions of the legislature. This might as well happen in the case of two contradictory statutes; or it might as well happen in every adjudication upon any single statute. The courts must declare the sense of the law; and if they should be disposed to exercise WILL instead of JUDGMENT, the consequence would equally be the substitution of their pleasure to that of the legislative body. The observation, if it prove any thing, would prove that there ought to be no judges distinct from that body.

If, then, the courts of justice are to be considered as the bulwarks of a limited Constitution against legislative encroachments, this consideration will afford a strong argument for the permanent tenure of judicial offices, since nothing will contribute so much as this to that independent spirit in the judges which must be essential to the faithful performance of so arduous a duty.

This independence of the judges is equally requisite to guard the Constitution and the rights of individuals from the effects of those ill humors, which the arts of designing men, or the influence of particular conjunctures, sometimes disseminate among the people themselves, and which, though they speedily give place to better information, and more deliberate reflection, have a tendency, in the meantime, to occasion dangerous innovations in the government, and serious oppressions of the minor party in the community. Though I trust the friends of the proposed Constitution will never concur with its enemies,[6] in questioning that fundamental principle of republican government, which admits the right of the people to alter or abolish the established Constitution, whenever they find it inconsistent with their happiness, yet it is not to be inferred from this principle, that the representatives of the people, whenever a momentary inclination happens to lay hold of a majority of their constituents, incompatible with the provisions in the existing Constitution, would, on that account, be justifiable in a violation of those provisions; or that the courts would be under a greater obligation to connive at infractions in this shape, than when they had proceeded wholly from the cabals of the representative body. Until the people have, by some solemn and authoritative act, annulled or changed the established form, it is binding upon themselves collectively, as well as individually; and no presumption, or even knowledge, of their sentiments, can warrant their representatives in a departure from it, prior to such an act. But it is easy to see, that it would require an uncommon portion of fortitude in the judges to do their duty as faithful guardians of the Constitution, where legislative invasions of it had been instigated by the major voice of the community.

But it is not with a view to infractions of the Constitution only, that the independence of the judges may be an essential safeguard against the effects of occasional ill humors in the society. These sometimes extend no farther than to the injury of the private rights of particular classes of citizens, by unjust and partial laws. Here also the firmness of the judicial magistracy is of vast importance in mitigating the severity and confining the operation of such laws. It not only serves to moderate the immediate mischiefs of those which may have been passed, but it operates as a check upon the legislative body in passing them; who, perceiving that obstacles to the success of iniquitous intention are to be expected from the scruples of the courts, are in a manner compelled,

---

6 *Vide Protest of the Minority of the Convention of Pennsylvania*, Martin's Speech, etc.

by the very motives of the injustice they meditate, to qualify their attempts. This is a circumstance calculated to have more influence upon the character of our governments, than but few may be aware of. The benefits of the integrity and moderation of the judiciary have already been felt in more States than one; and though they may have displeased those whose sinister expectations they may have disappointed, they must have commanded the esteem and applause of all the virtuous and disinterested. Considerate men, of every description, ought to prize whatever will tend to beget or fortify that temper in the courts: as no man can be sure that he may not be to-morrow the victim of a spirit of injustice, by which he may be a gainer to-day. And every man must now feel, that the inevitable tendency of such a spirit is to sap the foundations of public and private confidence, and to introduce in its stead universal distrust and distress.

That inflexible and uniform adherence to the rights of the Constitution, and of individuals, which we perceive to be indispensable in the courts of justice, can certainly not be expected from judges who hold their offices by a temporary commission. Periodical appointments, however regulated, or by whomsoever made, would, in some way or other, be fatal to their necessary independence. If the power of making them was committed either to the Executive or legislature, there would be danger of an improper complaisance to the branch which possessed it; if to both, there would be an unwillingness to hazard the displeasure of either; if to the people, or to persons chosen by them for the special purpose, there would be too great a disposition to consult popularity, to justify a reliance that nothing would be consulted but the Constitution and the laws.

There is yet a further and a weightier reason for the permanency of the judicial offices, which is deducible from the nature of the qualifications they require. It has been frequently remarked, with great propriety, that a voluminous code of laws is one of the inconveniences necessarily connected with the advantages of a free government. To avoid an arbitrary discretion in the courts, it is indispensable that they should be bound down by strict rules and precedents, which serve to define and point out their duty in every particular case that comes before them; and it will readily be conceived from the variety of controversies which grow out of the folly and wickedness of mankind, that the records of those precedents must unavoidably swell to a very considerable bulk, and must demand long and laborious study to acquire a competent knowledge of them. Hence it is, that there can be but few men in the society who will have sufficient skill in the laws to qualify them for the stations of judges. And making the proper deductions for the ordinary depravity of human nature, the number must be still smaller of those who unite the requisite integrity with the requisite knowledge. These considerations apprise us, that the government can have no great option between fit character; and that a temporary duration in office, which would naturally discourage such characters from quitting a lucrative line of practice to accept a seat on the bench, would have a tendency to throw the administration of justice into hands less able, and less well qualified, to conduct it with utility and dignity. In the present circumstances of this country, and in those in which it is likely to be for a long time to come, the disadvantages on this score would be greater than they may at first sight appear; but it must be confessed, that they are far inferior to those which present themselves under the other aspects of the subject.

Upon the whole, there can be no room to doubt that the convention acted wisely in copying from the models of those constitutions which have established *good behavior* as the tenure of their judicial offices, in point of duration; and that so far from being blamable on this account, their plan would have been inexcusably defective, if it had wanted this important feature of good government. The experience of Great Britain affords an illustrious comment on the excellence of the institution.

PUBLIUS

Appendix C

Justices of the Supreme Court

Justice	Appointing President	Years of Service
1. John Jay*	Washington	1789–1795
2. John Rutledge*	Washington	1789–1791
3. William Cushing	Washington	1789–1810
4. James Wilson	Washington	1789–1798
5. John Blair, Jr.	Washington	1789–1796
6. James Iredell	Washington	1790–1799
7. Thomas Johnson	Washington	1791–1793
8. William Paterson	Washington	1793–1806
9. Samuel Chase	Washington	1796–1811
10. Oliver Ellsworth	Washington	1796–1800
11. Bushrod Washington	J. Adams	1798–1829
12. Alfred Moore	J. Adams	1799–1804
13. John Marshall*	J. Adams	1801–1835
14. William Johnson	Jefferson	1804–1834
15. Henry Brokholst Livingston	Jefferson	1806–1823
16. Thomas Todd	Jefferson	1807–1826
17. Gabriel Duvall	Madison	1811–1835
18. Joseph Story	Madison	1811–1845
19. Smith Thompson	Monroe	1823–1843

* Served as chief justice for part or all of their term.

20. Robert Trimble	J. Q. Adams	1826–1828
21. John McLean	Jackson	1829–1861
22. Henry Baldwin	Jackson	1830–1844
23. James Moore Wayne	Jackson	1835–1867
24. Roger Brooke Taney*	Jackson	1836–1864
25. Philip Pendleton Barbour	Jackson	1836–1841
26. John Catron	Jackson	1837–1865
27. John McKinley	Van Buren	1837–1852
28. Peter Vivian Daniel	Van Buren	1841–1860
29. Samuel Nelson	Tyler	1845–1872
30. Levi Woodbury	Polk	1846–1851
31. Robert Cooper Grier	Polk	1846–1870
32. Benjamin Robbins Curtis	Fillmore	1851–1857
33. John Archibald Campbell	Pierce	1853–1861
34. Nathan Clifford	Buchanan	1858–1881
35. Noah Haynes Swayne	Lincoln	1862–1881
36. Samuel Freeman Miller	Lincoln	1862–1890
37. David Davis	Lincoln	1862–1877
38. Stephan Johnson Field	Lincoln	1863–1897
39. Salmon Portland Chase*	Lincoln	1864–1873
40. William Strong	Grant	1870–1880
41. Joseph P. Bradley	Grant	1870–1892
42. Ward Hunt	Grant	1872–1882
43. Morrison Remick Waite*	Grant	1874–1888
44. John Marshall Harlan	Hayes	1877–1911
45. William Burnham Woods	Hayes	1880–1887
46. Stanley Matthews	Garfield	1881–1889
47. Horace Gray	Arthur	1881–1902
48. Samuel Blatchford	Arthur	1882–1893

49. Lucius Quintus Cincinnatus Lamar	Cleveland	1888–1893
50. Melville Weston Fuller*	Cleveland	1888–1910
51. David Josiah Brewer	Harrison	1889–1910
52. Henry Billings Brown	Harrison	1890–1906
53. George Shiras, Jr.	Harrison	1892–1903
54. Howell Edmunds Jackson	Harrison	1893–1895
55. Edward Douglas White*	Cleveland	1894–1910
56. Rufus Wheeler Peckham	Cleveland	1895–1909
57. Joseph McKenna	McKinley	1898–1925
58. Oliver Wendell Holmes, Jr.	T. Roosevelt	1902–1932
59. William Rufus Day	T. Roosevelt	1903–1922
60. William Henry Moody	T. Roosevelt	1906–1910
61. Horace Harmon Lurton	Taft	1909–1914
62. Charles Evens Hughes*	Taft	1910–1916
63. Willis Van Devanter	Taft	1910–1937
64. Joseph Rucker Lamar	Taft	1910–1916
65. Mahlon Pitney	Taft	1912–1922
66. James Clark McReynolds	Wilson	1914–1941
67. Louis Dembitz Brandeis	Wilson	1916–1939
68. John Hessin Clarke	Wilson	1916–1922
69. William Howard Taft*	Harding	1921–1930
70. George Sutherland	Harding	1922–1938
71. Pierce Butler	Harding	1922–1939
72. Edward Terry Sanford	Harding	1923–1930
73. Harlan Fiske Stone	Coolidge	1925–1941
74. Owen Josephus Roberts	Hoover	1930–1945
75. Benjamin Nathan Cardozo	Hoover	1932–1938
76. Hugo Lafayette Black	F. Roosevelt	1937–1971
77. Stanley Forman Reed	F. Roosevelt	1938–1957

78. Felix Frankfurter	F. Roosevelt	1939–1962
79. William Orville Douglas	F. Roosevelt	1939–1975
80. Francis Williams (Frank) Murphy	F. Roosevelt	1940–1949
81. Harlan Fiske Stone*	F. Roosevelt	1941–1946
82. James Francis Byrnes	F. Roosevelt	1941–1942
83. Robert Houghwout Jackson	F. Roosevelt	1941–1954
84. Wiley Blount Rutledge	F. Roosevelt	1943–1949
85. Harold Hitz Burton	Truman	1945–1958
86. Fred Moore Vinson*	Truman	1946–1953
87. Tom Campbell Clark	Truman	1949–1967
88. Sherman Minton	Truman	1949–1956
89. Earl Warren*	Eisenhower	1953–1969
90. John Marshall Harlan	Eisenhower	1955–1971
91. William Joseph Brennan, Jr.	Eisenhower	1956–1990
92. Charles Evans Whittaker	Eisenhower	1957–1962
93. Potter Stewart	Eisenhower	1958–1981
94. Byron Raymond White	Kennedy	1962–1993
95. Arthur Joseph Goldberg	Kennedy	1962–1965
96. Abe Fortas	Johnson	1965–1969
97. Thurgood Marshall	Johnson	1967–1991
98. Warren Earl Burger*	Nixon	1969–1986
99. Harry Andrew Blackmun	Nixon	1970–1994
100. Lewis Franklin Powell, Jr.	Nixon	1971–1987
101. William Hubbs Rehnquist*	Nixon	1971–2005
102. John Paul Stevens	Ford	1975–2010
103. Sandra Day O'Connor	Reagan	1981–2006
104. Antonin Scalia	Reagan	1986–2016
105. Anthony McLeod Kennedy	Reagan	1988–
106. David H. Souter	Bush	1990–2009
107. Clarence Thomas	Bush	1991–

108. Ruth Bader Ginsburg	Clinton	1993–
109. Stephen G. Breyer	Clinton	1994–
110. John Roberts.*	Bush	2005–
111. Samuel Alito	Bush	2006–
112. Sonya Sotomayor	Obama	2009–
113. Elena Kagan	Obama	2010–
114. Neil Gorsuch	Trump	2017–

Index